Fodor's

THAILAND

WELCOME TO THAILAND

Thailand conjures images of white sand beaches and cerulean waters, peaceful temples, and lush mountain jungles. In Bangkok, a 21st-century playground, the scent of spicy street food fills the air, and the Grand Palace recalls the country's traditions. Outside the capital, the wonders of the countryside enchant, whether you are elephant trekking in the northern hills, exploring Ayutthaya's splendid ruins, or diving in the waters of the idyllic southern coast. The unique spirit of the Thai people—this is the "land of smiles," after all—adds warmth to any visit.

TOP REASONS TO GO

★ **Beaches:** Pristine strands and hidden coves bring vacation daydreams alive.

★ **Food:** Rich curries, sour-spicy tom yum soup, and tasty pad thai are worth savoring.

★ **Architecture:** Resplendent stupas and pagodas evoke the glory of ancient kingdoms.

★ **Spas:** Luxurious retreats offer indulgences such as world-renowned Thai massage.

★ **Trekking:** On foot or by elephant, a trek to visit hill tribes is a memorable experience.

★ **Shopping:** Iconic night markets sell everything from hand-carved crafts to handbags.

Fodor's THAILAND

Publisher: Amanda D'Acierno, *Senior Vice President*

Editorial: Arabella Bowen, *Editor in Chief*; Linda Cabasin, *Editorial Director*

Design: Tina Malaney, *Associate Art Director*; Chie Ushio, *Senior Designer*; Erica Cuoco, *Production Designer*

Photography: Jennifer Arnow, *Senior Photo Editor*; Mary Robnett, *Photo Researcher*

Production: Linda Schmidt, *Managing Editor*; Evangelos Vasilakis, *Associate Managing Editor*; Angela L. McLean, *Senior Production Manager*

Maps: Rebecca Baer, *Senior Map Editor*; Henry Colomb and Mark Stroud, Moon Street Cartography; David Lindroth, *Cartographers*

Sales: Jacqueline Lebow, *Sales Director*

Marketing & Publicity: Heather Dalton, *Marketing Director*; Katherine Punia, *Publicity Director*

Business & Operations: Susan Livingston, *Vice President, Strategic Business Planning*; Sue Daulton, *Vice President, Operations*

Fodors.com: Megan Bell, *Executive Director, Revenue & Business Development*; Yasmin Marinaro, *Senior Director, Marketing & Partnerships*

Copyright © 2016 by Fodor's Travel, a division of Penguin Random House LLC

Writers: Karen Coates, Lara Dunston, Sophie Friedman, Dave Stamboulis, Simon Stewart, Adrian Vrettos

Editors: Róisín Cameron (lead project editor), Daniel Mangin

Production Editor: Jennifer DePrima

14th Edition

ISBN 978-1-101-87858-3

ISSN 1064–0993

All details in this book are based on information supplied to us at press time. Always confirm information when it matters, especially if you're making a detour to visit a specific place. Fodor's expressly disclaims any liability, loss, or risk, personal or otherwise, that is incurred as a consequence of the use of any of the contents of this book.

SPECIAL SALES

This book is available at special discounts for bulk purchases for sales promotions or premiums. For more information, e-mail specialmarkets@penguinrandomhouse.com.

PRINTED IN THE UNITED STATES OF AMERICA

10 9 8 7 6 5 4 3 2 1

CONTENTS

MAPS

ABOUT THIS GUIDE

Fodor's Recommendations

Everything in this guide is worth doing—we don't cover what isn't—but exceptional sights, hotels, and restaurants are recognized with additional accolades. **Fodor's Choice★** indicates our top recommendations. Care to nominate a new place? Visit Fodors.com/contact-us.

Trip Costs

We list prices wherever possible to help you budget well. Hotel and restaurant price categories from **$** to **$$$$** are noted alongside each recommendation. For hotels, we include the lowest cost of a standard double room in high season. For restaurants, we cite the average price of a main course at dinner or, if dinner isn't served, at lunch. For attractions, we always list adult admission fees; discounts are usually available for children, students, and senior citizens.

Hotels

Our local writers vet every hotel to recommend the best overnights in each price category, from budget to expensive. Unless otherwise specified, you can expect private bath, phone, and TV in your room. For expanded hotel reviews, facilities, and deals visit Fodors.com.

Top Picks

★ Fodor's Choice

Listings

✉ Address
📨 Branch address
☎ Telephone
📠 Fax
🌐 Website
📧 E-mail
🎟 Admission fee
🕘 Open/closed times
[M] Subway
✥ Directions or Map coordinates

Hotels & Restaurants

🏨 Hotel
🛏 Number of rooms
🍽 Meal plans
✕ Restaurant
✍ Reservations
👔 Dress code
💳 No credit cards
[$] Price

Other

⇨ See also
☞ Take note
⛳ Golf facilities

Restaurants

Unless we state otherwise, restaurants are open for lunch and dinner daily. We mention dress code only when there's a specific requirement and reservations only when they're essential or not accepted. To make restaurant reservations, visit Fodors.com.

Credit Cards

The hotels and restaurants in this guide typically accept credit cards. If not, we'll say so.

EUGENE FODOR

Hungarian-born Eugene Fodor (1905–91) began his travel career as an interpreter on a French cruise ship. The experience inspired him to write *On the Continent* (1936), the first guidebook to receive annual updates and discuss a country's way of life as well as its sights. Fodor later joined the U.S. Army and worked for the OSS in World War II. After the war, he kept up his intelligence work while expanding his guidebook series. During the Cold War, many guides were written by fellow agents who understood the value of insider information. Today's guides continue Fodor's legacy by providing travelers with timely coverage, insider tips, and cultural context.

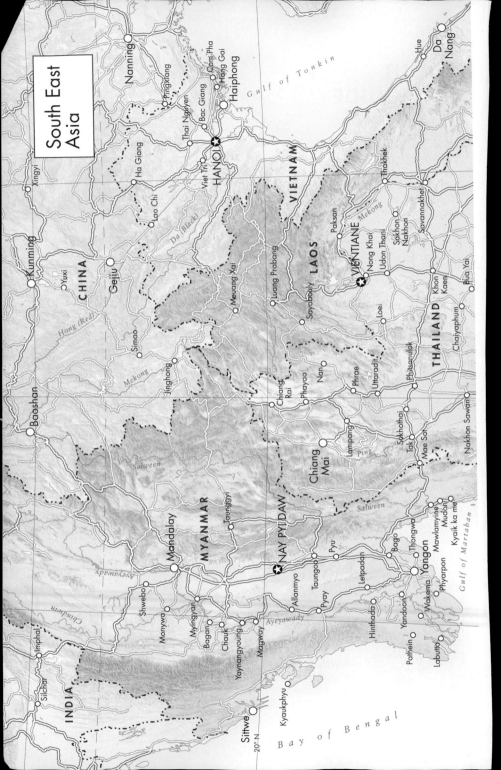

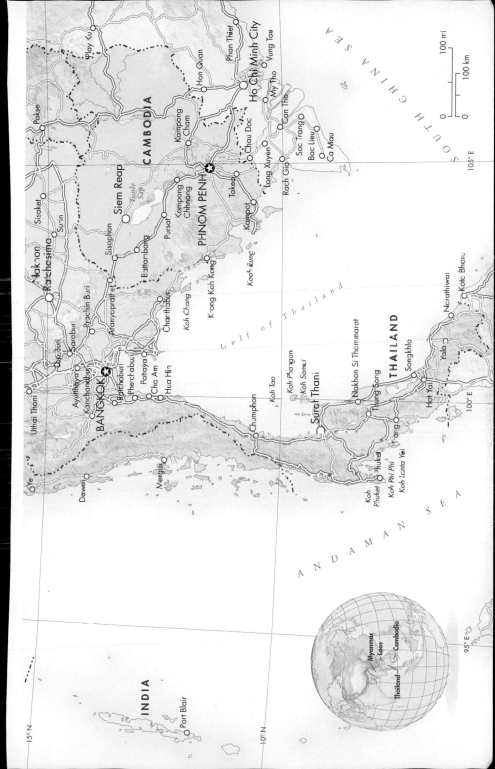

EXPERIENCE THAILAND

WHAT'S WHERE

The following numbers refer to chapters in the book.

2 Bangkok. In this boomtown of contrasts where old-world charm meets futuristic luxury, you can dine at street stalls or ritzy restaurants, visit the jaw-dropping Grand Palace, and shop at Chatuchak Weekend Market or Pathumwan's designer malls. At night there are hip mega-clubs and Patpong's famous red lights, as well as quieter romantic restaurants and wine bars.

3 Around Bangkok. Petchaburi has ancient temples and a royal retreat, while Thailand's oldest city, Nakhon Pathom, is home to Phra Pathom Chedi, the world's tallest Buddhist stupa.

4 The Gulf Coast Beaches. Thailand's two shores have alternating monsoon seasons, so there's great beach weather *somewhere* year-round. The Gulf has Pattaya's nightlife and the island trio of Koh Samui (good sailing), Koh Pha Ngan (full-moon revelry), and Koh Tao (diving). The coastal drive to Trat is a pleasant, winding trip through the countryside. And south to Pattani, adventurers will find infrequently visited regions off the primary tourist circuit.

5 Phuket and the Andaman Coast. Highlights of this spectacular coastal region include Phuket, Phang Nga Bay (with James Bond Island), and Krabi, which is a paradise for divers, rock climbers, and foodies.

6 Chiang Mai. This moat-encircled city is riddled with temples and markets, and deserves a lingering stop in any tour of the north. Wander the narrow alleys and brick roads of the old city, then dine in the university area alive with hip young crowds.

7 Northern Thailand. Chiang Rai is a chilled-out regional center and the gateway to the Golden Triangle, where Laos, Myanmar (Burma), and Thailand meet. Thailand's first capital, Sukhothai, has carefully restored ruins.

8 Cambodia. No Southeast Asia trip is complete without a visit to the temple ruins of Angkor. The capital, Phnom Penh, is a vibrant city with a thriving food scene. Cross the Tonle Sap (the great lake) to communities living in floating houses, or laze on Cambodia's spectacular coastline. There is also plenty to interest hikers, birders, and wildlife buffs.

9 Laos. Photogenic rivers, mountainous countryside, and the dreamy feeling of going back in time are major reasons to make the trip across the border. World Heritage sites Luang Prabang and Champasak both have beautiful temples and the Plain of Jars will wow any archaeology enthusiast.

10 Myanmar. Some say Bagan's temple ruins rival those of Siem Reap; in nearby Mandalay, the royal palace and Mandalay Hill offer a rich dose of history. The country's one-time capital, Yangon, is a chaotic, colorful feast for the eyes and the stomach; at quiet Inle Lake, villagers have made their homes on the water.

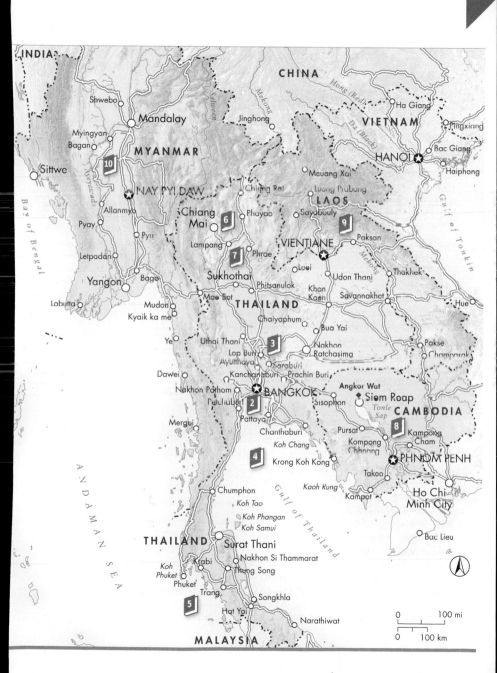

INDIA

CHINA

Shwebo

Mandalay

Jinghong

Hong (Red)

Ha Giang

VIETNAM

Pingxiang

Myingyan

Bagan

MYANMAR

Salween

Mekong

Da (Black)

HANOI

Bac Giang

Haiphong

Sittwe

10

NAY PYI DAW

Chiang Rai

Meuang Xai

Luang Prabang

LAOS

Allanmyo

Chiang Mai

6

Phayao

Sayaboury

9

Paksan

Gulf of Tonkin

Pyay

Pyu

Lampang

VIENTIANE

Phrae

Letpadan

7

Loei

Udon Thani

Thakhek

Bay of Bengal

Yangon

Bago

Sukhothai

Phitsanulok

Mekong

Mae Sot

THAILAND

Khon Kaen

Savannakhet

Hue

Labutta

Mudon

Kyaik ka me

Chaiyaphum

Bua Yai

Ye

Uthai Thani

3

Nakhon Ratchasima

Pakse

Champasak

Dawei

Lop Buri

Ayutthaya

Saraburi

Prachin Buri

Nakhon Pathom

BANGKOK

Petchaburi

2

Angkor Wat

Siem Reap

Sisophon

Tonle Sap

CAMBODIA

Mergui

Pattaya

Chanthaburi

Pursat

8

Kampong Cham

Koh Chang

4

Krong Koh Kong

Kompong Chhnang

Takeo

PHNOM PENH

A N D A M A N   S E A

Chumphon

Koh Tao

Kaoh Rung

Kampot

Ho Chi Minh City

Koh Phangan

Koh Samui

Gulf of Thailand

Bac Lieu

THAILAND

Surat Thani

Nakhon Si Thammarat

Koh Phuket

Krabi

Thung Song

Phuket

Trang

5

Songkhla

Hat Yai

Narathiwat

MALAYSIA

0   100 mi

0   100 km

NEED TO KNOW

THAILAND

Bangkok ★

Gulf of Thailand

AT A GLANCE

Capital: Bangkok

Population: 67,741,401

Currency: Thai Baht

Money: ATMs common in cities and tourist areas; cards accepted at some restaurants, shops, and hotels but cash is preferred.

Language: Thai

Country Code: 66

Emergencies: 999

Driving: On the left

Electricity: 220v/50 cycles; electrical plugs have two flat prongs (the same as in the U.S.).

Time: 11 hours ahead of New York during daylight savings time; 12 hours ahead in the winter.

Documents: Up to 30 days with a valid passport

Mobile Phones: GSM (900 and 1800 bands)

Major Mobile Companies: AIS, DTAC, Truemove-H

WEBSITES

Tourism Authority of Thailand: ⊕ www.tourismthailand.org

Thaizer: ⊕ www.thaizer.com

Go Thailand: ⊕ www.gothailand.com

GETTING AROUND

✈ **Air Travel:** Bangkok's two international airports are the country's busiest, followed by Phuket and Chiang Mai.

🚌 **Bus Travel:** Buses range from cheap and no-frills to air-conditioned, with nonstop service between major hubs.

🚗 **Car Travel:** Driving can be the easiest and most affordable way to tour rural areas (avoid cities), but traffic laws are routinely disregarded.

🚆 **Train Travel:** Though slower and pricier than buses, trains are more comfortable and safer. Trains go to (or close to) most major destinations, and many go through areas without major roads.

PLAN YOUR BUDGET

	HOTEL ROOM	MEAL	ATTRACTIONS
Low Budget	B400	B50	Wat Suthat admission, B20
Mid Budget	B1,500	B200	Jim Thompson House admission, B150
High Budget	B10,000	B600	Emerald Buddha Temple admission, B400

WAYS TO SAVE

Eat street food. Thai street food is usually hygienic, almost always delicious, and consistently inexpensive.

Stay in guesthouses. Thailand has numerous guesthouses catering to budget travelers, even in the bigger cities.

Travel by *songthaew*. A cheaper alternative to cabs, *songthaews* are pickup trucks converted into share taxis.

Visit lesser-known temples. While Thailand's big temples often charge hefty admission fees, some of the smaller ones are just as pretty and free to enter.

PLAN YOUR TIME

Hassle Factor	High. No matter where in North America you are departing from, expect to spend 18–24 hours in transit.
3 days	With three days, it's best to stick to Bangkok, with a day trip to Samut Prakan's Ancient City.
1 week	Presuming you are starting in Bangkok, you can either head north after a day or two in the city to Chiang Mai and either Chiang Rai or Pai, or head south to Phuket or one of the quieter islands.
2 weeks	Two weeks in Thailand is ample time to experience the cultural and natural marvels of the northern part of the country and the fun-and-sun vibe of the southern islands, with time left over to hang out in Bangkok.

WHEN TO GO

High Season: Thailand's high season runs from late November–February and is perfect for everything: the beaches in the south, trekking in the north, or exploring Bangkok. But accommodation rates sometimes double, and rooms can be scarce in hot spots like Phuket. The northern nights are chilly in winter, generally in the 50s, but as low as freezing.

Low Season: Thailand is at its hottest from March to May. Pollution in the north can reach dangerous levels toward the end of the dry season in March and April. By April you can find good hotel deals, if you can stand the heat, though some hotels in less touristy areas shut down for the hot season.

Value Season: Thailand's rainy season starts in June and continues through the first half of November. City sightseeing is okay during these months; downpours lower the temperature, and storms, though fierce, don't last all day. But flooding can make rural areas inaccessible, and it's not a reliable time to plan a trek.

BIG EVENTS

February: Buddhists give alms to monks and temples hold candlelight processions for Makha Bucha Day, a national holiday.

April: The Thai New Year is celebrated with the throwing of water during the Songkran festival.

November: Illuminated lanterns are launched into the air and floated on river during the Loi Krathong festival.

READ THIS

■ **The Beach,** Alex Garland. A backpacker searches for an island paradise.

■ **Thai Street Food,** David Thompson. A coffee-table book of recipes and colorful photos.

■ **A History of Thailand,** Chris Baker and Pasuk Phongpaichit. A concise history.

WATCH THIS

■ **Bridget Jones: The Edge of Reason.** The sequel takes Bridget to Thailand, where she spends a brief stint in jail.

■ **Bangkok Dangerous.** The American remake of a Thai thriller about a foreign hit man in Thailand.

■ **Brokedown Palace.** Two friends end up in a Thai prison after accidentally smuggling drugs.

EAT THIS

■ **Green papaya salad:** spicy, made from unripe papaya

■ **Pad thai:** noodles stir-fried with tamarind, shallots, eggs, and shrimp

■ **Mi krop:** crisp fried rice noodles in coconut broth

■ **Khao soi:** coconut egg-noodle soup

■ **Khao phat:** fried rice, with eggs and/or meat

■ **Mango and sticky rice:** served with sweet coconut cream

THAILAND TODAY

Political Strife. Business tycoon Thaksin Shinawatra, of the populist Thai Rak Thai party, was prime minister of Thailand between 2001 and 2006. Ever since, he has had devoted followers—and foes. Those political rifts have divided Thais for years, the last several of which have seen violent protests and crackdowns. In 2006, Thaksin was overthrown in a bloodless military coup while traveling overseas, and he went into exile. A general election in 2007 brought in the pro-Thaksin People's Power Party (PPP), run by Samak Sundaravej. Many considered him to be a puppet for Thaksin. He was dismissed in 2008 on a technicality: illegally hosting a cooking show while holding office. Meanwhile, political riots escalated in 2008, at times halting government operations and even temporarily shutting down the international airport. The worst riots in nearly two decades broke out in April and May 2010, when the anti-government "Red Shirts" staged protests across Bangkok. For weeks business and politics remained at a standstill until the military crushed the protests. Hundreds of people were injured and several killed as central Bangkok became a war zone. Nothing was resolved. Protesters went home but vowed to continue their fight against the government. In July 2011, Yingluck Shinawatra, the younger sister of Thaksin, led the Pheu Thai Party to victory and became prime minister. She oversaw a contentious political period through May 7, 2014, when she was removed from office for abuse of power. After yet more protests, on May 20, 2014, the military seized control, implemented martial law, repealed the constitution, ousted several former cabinet members, and put a tight rein on the country under the National Council for Peace and Order with General Prayuth Chan-ocha at the helm. On April 2, 2015, the government lifted martial law and replaced it with a controversial security order that gives the military junta widespread powers. And the political drama marches on.

Ethnic Diversity. Throughout its history, Thailand has absorbed countless cultural influences, and is home to groups with Chinese, Tibetan, Lao, Khmer, Malaysian, Burmese, and other origins. Migrating tribes from modern-day China, Cambodia, Myanmar, and the Malay Peninsula were the region's earliest inhabitants. Ancient trade routes meant constant contact with merchants traveling from India,

WHAT'S HOT IN THAILAND NOW

Thailand has always had a flair for art, creativity, and fun. You'll find that today in everything from fashion to interior design to the clever ads blaring across BTS stations as you wait for your train. Sophisticated Thai architects and designers create some of the world's most inviting spaces, using a mix of traditional materials (teak, silk, stone, clay) with modern elements and elegant styling. Visit a chic spa for a perfect example of this. This is a country oriented toward youth, and young Thais are as hip and connected as ever, wearing the trendiest clothes and obsessing with the latest digital devices (and if any of your Apple accoutrements break during your visit, you'll quickly find all necessary replacements). There's a small but growing contemporary

China, and other parts of Southeast Asia. Conflicts and treaties have continued to alter the country's borders—and ethnicity—into the 21st century. Contemporary Thailand's cultural richness comes from its ethnic diversity. Though Buddhism is the predominant religion, Hindu and animist influences abound, and there's a significant Muslim population in the south. Malay is spoken in the southern provinces; Lao and Khmer dialects of Thai are spoken in the northeast; and the hill tribes have their own dialects as well.

Mysticism. Many Thais believe in astrology and supernatural energy. The animist element of Thai spirituality dictates that everything, from buildings to trees, has a spirit. With so many spirits and forces out there, it's no surprise that appeasing them is a daily consideration. Thais often wear amulets blessed by monks to ward off evil, and they believe that tattoos, often of real or mythical animals or magic spells, bring strength and protect the wearer. Car license plates with lucky numbers (such as multiple nines) sell for thousands of baht; important events, such as weddings, house moves, and even births, are arranged, when possible, to fall on auspicious days, which are either divined by shamans or consist of lucky numbers. Newspapers solemnly report that politicians have consulted their favorite astrologers before making critical policy decisions. Businesses erect shrines to powerful deities outside their premises, sometimes positioned to repel the power of their rivals' shrines.

The importance of *Sanuk*. That's the word for Thai fun. Thais believe that every activity should be fun—work, play, even funerals. Of course, this isn't always practical, but it's a worthy aim. Thais enjoy being together in large parties, making lots of noise, and—as sanuk nearly always involves food—eating. They are also guided by a number of other behavior principles. Many, such as *jai yen* (cool heart) and *mai pen rai* (never mind), are rooted in the Buddhist philosophies of detachment, and result in a nonconfrontational demeanor and an easygoing attitude. Giving and sharing are important, since being generous is an act of merit making, a way of storing up points for protection in this life and in future lives.

art scene scattered across Bangkok (check out the Museum of Contemporary Art and the Bangkok Art and Culture Centre near the National Stadium BTS) and in the university area of Chiang Mai. Food in Thailand is always trendy, and city chefs are adept at mixing Thai flavors with other cuisines. Of course, cheap street eats never go out of style. Bangkok's drinking scene has evolved in recent years, too, to include an influx of wine bars and craft beer venues that cater to locals and foreigners alike. And perhaps no other metropolis on Earth has quite the collection of rooftop sky bars as Bangkok—don't miss a cocktail on an open-air patio 30 floors or more above the cacophony below.

TRANSPORTATION, THAI STYLE

With reasonably priced internal flights and reliable train and bus service, getting around Thailand can be efficient and straightforward. Taxis are often happy to travel distances of around 160 km (100 miles), and you can hire a car and driver for a fraction of what it would cost back home. But several quirkier modes of transport have true local color (though sometimes not much regard for safety).

Longtail Boat

The slim longtail boat gets its name from the huge V8 car engine that protrudes on an elongated pole from the back of the craft. Catch one of these brightly colored, 40-foot monsters to navigate the river in Bangkok for a bumpy, noisy, and exhilarating ride. When the going gets choppy, passengers huddle behind plastic sheeting. Garlands wrapped around the prow, dedicated to Mae Yanang, the goddess of travel, are also there for your protection.

Motorcycle

In cities there are so many motorcycles skittering between cars it seems every resident must own one. And no wonder: in the gridlocked traffic they're often the only way to get anywhere on time. Consequently, people frequently abandon taxis or cars and hop on motorcycle taxis (called "motorcy"), the drivers of which are notorious for two things: shady dealings and scary driving. Yet it's not uncommon to see entire families piled helmetless on a single vehicle. Women passengers usually ride sidesaddle, with both hands clasped between their knees to preserve modesty—a balancing act of high skill and great faith.

Samlor

The quaint *samlor* (literally meaning "three wheels") is a variation on a rickshaw: the driver pedals a three-wheeled bicycle, pulling an open carriage with room for two in back. It's a slow, quiet, and cheap way to travel short distances, and samlors are still common on the streets of provincial towns. Often, street vendors will attach the carriage to the front of the vehicle instead of the back and use it to display their wares.

Songthaew

Songthaews are converted pickup trucks with two benches in the back and a metal roof. Thais ride songthaews both within a town and between towns. They aren't cheaper than local buses, but they are more frequent and will sometimes drive slightly out of their way to drop you nearer your destination. Just stick out your hand as one passes, negotiate a price, and climb in back. Songthaews are often packed, and if all the seats are taken, Thais will just climb on the back and hang onto the railings. It's a bumpy ride on rural roads; for longer trips, you'll be more comfortable on the bus.

Tuk-Tuk

Although the *tuk-tuk* is practically Thailand's icon, it is in fact a Japanese import. This three-wheeled motorized taxi with open sides is a logical progression from the samlor. It's an atmospheric—that is, fume-filled, hot, and noisy—way to get around city streets, and a more pleasant ride on rural lanes, although you have to hunker down in the seat to actually see much, and you'll definitely feel every bump in the road. Tuk-tuks come in a variety of styles, including bullet-nosed models in Ayutthaya, elongated "hot rods" on the Eastern Gulf, and elevated versions nicknamed "Skylabs" in the northeast.

TOP EXPERIENCES

Beach and Dive Life

Thailand's beach culture is world-class. The famous Full Moon Parties on Koh Phangan heave with all-night raves; you may be happier lazing under coconut palms with a gentle massage between dips, or having a beach barbecue with fresh seafood on Koh Chang. For unforgettable underwater theater, head to one of Thailand's top dive sites, where facilities range from beginner courses of a few hours to live-aboard boats that stay out several days. Koh Tao, in the Gulf of Thailand, is popular, but the best locations are the Similan and Surin islands, where you meet nomadic island-hopping people known as Sea Gypsies and swim with whale sharks, clownfish, and leatherback turtles. That said, a simple snorkel will please those who prefer to stay closer to shore.

Mae Hong Son Loop

The 600-km (370-mile) route from Chiang Mai to Mae Hong Son and back is a stunningly picturesque drive through the country's hilliest regions, whether you take the northern route, via Pai, or the southern route via Mae Sariang. Give yourself at least four days, and stop frequently along the way. It's not as remote as it was in years past, but this will show you an entirely different Thailand, and the various tribal cultures that live among these mountains.

Kanchanaburi

It's well worth a short trip to this historic region to visit the Bridge over the River Kwai. Here, during World War II, forced laborers under Japanese control worked on the infamous "Death Railway" to Burma. Thousands died in the process. Kanchanaburi is just a couple of hours

by train from Bangkok and can be visited in a day- or overnight trip.

Spas

Treat yourself to a luxury spa retreat—anywhere in Thailand. This country is famous for its massage (ancient and other), and its spas are superb: relaxing and refreshing, amid beautiful scenery, at affordable rates. Looking for a cleanse? Thailand is a popular destination for these body overhauls, too.

Songkran Festival

Each April, during Thai New Year celebrations (Songkran), the country becomes a three-day street party of water fights. Participants go armed with cups, buckets, and water guns, and tourist centers like Khao San Road are packed with hordes of drenched merrymakers. Traditionalists complain that it's a far cry from the festival's origins—it began as a genteel bathing ritual to honor elders. For those seeking less raucous revelry, neighboring Cambodia and Laos also celebrate the holiday, in a slightly gentler manner. If you really want quiet, spend the new year in Phnom Penh, which empties as residents head to their home villages for the holiday. Cambodians, too, will sprinkle you with water—and then perhaps invite you home to eat a New Year's feast with the family.

Street Food

Rich and poor mingle over bowls of soups and curries at Thailand's street stalls. Many vendors are famous for a particular dish, whether pad thai; the spicy, sour shrimp soup *tom yum goong*; or duck with noodles. It's a wonderful journey of discovery, where you can chomp on seemingly anything, from deep-fried flowers to a mixed bag of insects.

THAILAND TOP ATTRACTIONS

Ancient Sukhothai

(A) Sukhothai is recognized as the first independent kingdom in what would eventually become Thailand. Its 13th-century ascendancy is referred to as the country's golden age: religion was codified; a writing system was introduced; and the arts flourished. The city's impressive ruins are preserved in Sukhothai Historical Park.

Chiang Mai

(B) Chiang Mai was the capital of the ancient kingdom of Lanna, which grew to prominence in the 13th century. Even after it became part of Siam, Lanna was largely independent until the early 20th century, due to its mountainous terrain, and it retains a distinct culture. Chiang Mai was located on historically important trade routes, and still has a varied ethnic population and significant old temples. It's the gateway for jungle and hill tribe treks.

The Grand Palace

(C) Bangkok's Grand Palace and the adjacent royal temple, Wat Phra Kaew, appear like a fairy-tale castle of golden domes and glittering spires within white fortified walls. They were the centerpieces of the new capital when it was built more than 200 years ago, and they still form Bangkok's most impressive architecture. Wat Phra Kaew contains the Emerald Buddha, Thailand's most revered religious image.

The Ruins of Ayutthaya

(D) Thailand's second capital, destroyed by the Burmese in 1767, Ayutthaya had 2,000 temples and a population greater than London in its heyday. The Ayutthaya Historical Park has many Thai- and Khmer-style ruins that evoke the city's lost grandeur.

Khao Sok National Park

(E) One of the most spectacular landscapes in Thailand, remote Khao Sok rewards the effort of the journey with lush greenery and towering mountain ranges. Although the chances of seeing a tiger are remote, there's plenty of other wildlife in Khao Sok National Park, and the chance to soak up this unique jungle atmosphere shouldn't be missed.

Koh Samui

(F) This small island in Thailand's Western Gulf is best appreciated by those who linger over its many charms. Explore the interior by car, indulge in some seriously luxurious spa treatments, and revel in the chilled-out nightlife that has made this an enduring favorite of those seeking the quintessential Thai beach vacation.

Wat Po

(G) Wat Po is Bangkok's oldest temple, and is sometimes called the country's first university. It has lessons in history and astrology inscribed on the walls, and people still come here to learn traditional medicine. Of the many buildings and images on-site, pride of place goes to the 147-foot-long Reclining Buddha, which shows the Buddha ascending into Nirvana after reaching enlightenment.

Ao Phang Nga

(H) One of the most arresting natural sights in Thailand is formed by the jungle-clad limestone karsts and islands that rise like towers around the waters of Ao Phang Nga, a marine national park close to Phuket. The most famous of the islands is Koh Khao Phing Kan, which was featured in the film *The Man With The Golden Gun,* and is hence better known as James Bond Island.

THAI MASSAGE

Thai massage, once only available at temples or tiny shophouses, has become much more popular in recent years. You'll find masseurs and masseuses at work all over the country—in bustling markets, at boutique spas, and in jungle hideaways.

Today massage is a pleasant and relaxing part of Thai culture, and you may see locals giving casual shoulder, back, and arm massages to their friends. But *nuad paen boran* (ancient massage) is also a branch of traditional Thai medicine. Originally it was taught and performed in Thai temples, which were historically places of physical—as well as spiritual—healing.

Traditional massage combines acupressure, reflexology, yoga, and meditation. Practitioners believe that 10 energy lines, called *sip sen,* link the body's meridian points. Blocked lines may lead to physical or spiritual ailments. Massage is thought to unblock the energy lines, clearing toxins and restoring balance to the body.

Where to Get Massage

Outdoors: At markets, on beaches, and at temple fairs, masseurs and masseuses set up shop alongside street vendors. On the beach you'll lie on a mat; at the market you'll probably be seated in a street-side plastic or lounge chair set up for foot massage. Prices vary—a one-hour foot massage might cost as little as B100 at a temple fair or B250 on a popular beach.

Resort and Hotel Spas: For five-star pampering, head to upscale hotels and resorts, whose luxurious, tranquil spas offer an extensive array of massages, including Swedish massage, plus other treatments like tai chi and new-age therapies. Expect to pay at least B2,500 or more for an hour-long massage at a top Bangkok hotel—a lot by Thai standards, but still less than what you'd pay back home.

Restrooms: In a few clubs and bars (both gay and straight), some visitors are alarmed when men's restroom attendants start massaging their shoulders as they stand at the urinal. If you don't like it, ask them to stop (*mai ow, kup*). Otherwise, a B10 tip is welcome.

Shophouses: These ubiquitous massage parlors offer no-frills service. Expect to share a room with other patrons (curtains separate the cots); if you're getting a foot massage, you may be seated in the shop window. There's often music, TV, or chatter in the background. A two-hour massage costs at least B400. Though many shophouses are legitimate businesses, some offer "extra" sexual services. To avoid embarrassing misunderstandings, steer clear of treatments with suggestive names, like "special" or "full body" massage. You can also ask the concierge at your hotel to recommend a reputable place.

Temples: Some temples still have massage facilities, and massages are often provided to the elderly at no charge. At Wat Po in Bangkok you can receive a massage in an open-air pavilion for B420 an hour.

Urban Spas: A growing phenomenon, urban spas are more upscale than shophouse parlors. They're often located in old Thai houses, with contemporary Asian-style private treatment rooms. You'll have more options here: simple Thai massage is still on the menu (for B1,000 and up per hour), along with body scrubs, facials, and various other treatments.

The Moves

Thai massage is an extremely rigorous, sometimes painful experience, and people with back, neck, or joint problems should not undergo it without seeking medical advice first. But it can also be very pleasurable. It's okay to ask if you want softer pressure (*bow bow, kup/ka*).

Massage artists primarily work with their hands, but they sometimes use elbows, knees, and feet to perform deep-tissue kneading. They occasionally apply balm to ease muscle aches, but they traditionally don't use oil. They may push and pull your body through a series of often contorted yogic stretching movements. There's normally a set sequence: you start lying on your back and the massage artist will work from your feet through your legs, arms, hands, and fingers. Then you turn over for legs, back, neck, head, and face. At the end the masseur will stretch your back across his or her upturned knees. Some people find that they have better flexibility after a massage, in addition to relief from muscular aches.

Massages are booked by the hour, and aficionados say two hours is best to get the full benefit. In most shophouse parlors the masseuse will first bathe your feet and then give you a pair of pajamas to wear. Spas have shower facilities. You can remove your underwear or not—whatever makes you comfortable.

The standard varies enormously. If you find a masseur or masseuse you like, take his or her name (sometimes they'll have an identifying number as well) and return to that person the next time.

Tipping

Tipping is customary. There aren't hard-and-fast rules about how much to tip, but B50 to B150 at a shophouse, and 10% to 20% in a spa, is about right.

Alternative Massage

Foot massage: This popular treatment is typically a half-hour or hour-long massage of the feet and lower legs, usually with oil or balm. Foot massage is based on

> ### BATHHOUSE
>
> Often classically ornate with names like Poseidon, barnlike bathhouses and saunas are fronts for prostitution. They offer the euphemistic "massage" for which Thailand has had a reputation since the Vietnam War. Luckily, they're fairly easy to avoid—masseuses are usually on display behind a glass partition, and the treatment menu will include options like "soapy massage."

the reflexology principle that manipulating pressure points in the feet can relieve disorders in other parts of the body.

Oil Massage: Most parlors and spas now offer oil massage, which is a gentler treatment based on Swedish massage and doesn't involve stretching. Masseurs will sometimes use oils with delicious aromas, such as lemongrass or jasmine.

Learn the Art of Massage

Bangkok's Wat Po is an acknowledged instruction center with an almost 200-year pedigree. A five-day, 30-hour course costs B9,500. You can get more information on their website, ⊕ *www.watpomassage. com*. The Thai Massage School in Chiang Mai (⊕ *www.tmcschool.com*) is also good. Many shophouse parlors in both cities now also offer courses (a one-hour session at a Khao San Road shophouse costs about B250).

IF YOU LIKE

Ancient Cities and Ruins

Prior to its current incarnation as a unified modern state, Thailand consisted of a series of smaller kingdoms. While some of these kingdoms were destroyed when neighboring armies invaded, others merely lost influence as they merged with other Siamese cities and remained beautifully intact.

Angkor Wat. This massive ancient Cambodian temple and its surrounding complex, built by a succession of Khmer kings between the 9th and 13th century, which has miraculously survived the ravages of time and the Khmer Rouge, is Southeast Asia's most spectacular architectural site. It's also the world's largest religious structure.

Ayutthaya. After a number of unsuccessful attempts, the Burmese sacked and brutally destroyed this city, which was the second Siamese capital, in 1767. The redbrick foundations of the Old City and its remaining stupas and wats are now beautiful ruins to explore.

Chiang Mai. The Old City of Chiang Mai has continued to develop so that today its streets include bars and minimarts. Regardless, a stroll through the back alleys, both inside and outside the old walls, reveals centuries-old masterpieces of Thai art and architecture.

Sukhothai. Thailand's first capital, Sukhothai was established in 1238 and saw more than 200 years of prosperity and artistic development known as Thailand's golden age. Sukhothai began to lose its regional influence in the 14th century, ultimately falling under Ayutthaya's control. Its Khmer- and Hindu-influenced sculpture and architecture are relatively unspoiled by the ages.

Beaches

Thailand's clear turquoise waters and soft, white, palm-fringed sands are stunning, and they offer plenty more to do than sunbathing and sunset strolls.

Koh Phi Phi. These six islands have some of the best diving and snorkeling in Thailand. Crowds flock to Maya Bay both for its spectacular scenery and because it's where the movie *The Beach* was filmed; Loh Samah Bay is more secluded.

Koh Samui. The beaches of Samui offer something to suit most travelers' moods: bustling Chaweng Beach, the fishermen's village of Bophut, the scented oils of spa retreats, and the briny aromas of beachfront shacks. Serious divers head for neighboring island Koh Tao.

Nang Cape/Railay Beach. These four connected beaches are only accessible by boat, but it's an easy 15-minute trip from Krabi Town on the mainland. Two of the beaches, Tonsai and East Railay, are rock-climbing centers; West Railay is known for its gorgeous sunsets; and beautiful Phra Nang has a cave with phallic offerings left for a fabled princess.

Phang Nga Bay. This national marine park is an eerily beautiful landscape dotted with limestone islands and karsts that rise like vertical sculptures from the sea. Many people come to kayak, to visit James Bond Island, or explore sea caves with prehistoric rock art.

Similan Islands. These nine islands in the Andaman Sea, part of the Mu Koh Similan National Marine Park, are considered Thailand's best dive sites. Visibility is exceptional, and encounters with whale sharks are not uncommon. The isolation heightens the appeal.

Shopping

The first time you set foot in one of Thailand's ubiquitous markets you'll be absolutely mesmerized by the variety of goods, from hand-carved figurines to polo shirts with the alligator slightly askew. In larger cities, malls sell international brands at prices significantly lower than in Singapore or Hong Kong.

Bangkok's Chinatown. In Bangkok, if you ask where you can buy something, the answer is usually, "Try Chinatown." Anything goes in this labyrinthine quarter, equally flush with gold shops and grubby souvenir stalls.

Bangkok's Shopping Streets. Bangkok's glitziest megamalls are located on a section of Thanon Rama I and Thanon Ploenchit. A skywalk links the malls, including upscale Siam Paragon, Siam Center, and Central World, allowing you to bypass the heat and congestion of the busy streets below. There's a lot more than clothing here, too—great bookshops, fabrics, electronics, Ferraris, iPads. Siam Paragon mall even has an aquarium where you can scuba dive.

Chatuchak Weekend Market. Also called "JJ," this is one of the world's largest markets. Every weekend, thousands of locals and tourists flock to northern Bangkok to navigate the mazes of stalls shopping for pets, clothing, souvenirs, and almost anything else imaginable.

Night Markets. Put on your best bargaining face and hit the streets of Silom, Patpong, Sukhumvit, and Khao San for the best night-market shopping in Bangkok. Most towns, including Chiang Mai, Pattaya, and Hua Hin, have great souvenirs available after dark.

Trekking

Thailand's mountain forests would be good for trekking for their rugged beauty alone, but this terrain is also home to hill tribes—Karen, Hmong, Yao, and others—that maintain many of their traditional languages and cultures. The more remote the village, the more likely this is so (and the more challenging the trek). Do some research on tour operators to make an informed choice.

Chiang Mai. The city is one of two northern centers for both easygoing and adventurous tours to hill tribe villages, some of which accommodate overnight visitors. Elephant rides and bamboo rafting are often included. From here it's easy to get to departure points in Pai and Mae Hong Son.

Chiang Rai. Another northern gem for soft-adventure enthusiasts, Chiang Rai has many tour operators and individual guides. Lahu, Akha, and Lisu villages are all easily accessible from here. There's a growing number of eco-conscious initiatives, and it pays to shop around, both here and in Chiang Mai. Guesthouses can often recommend guides.

Kanchanaburi. Though Kanchanaburi itself is a touristy town, the surrounding area offers some of the most untouched landscape in the country. Parts of Sai Yok National Park, with its Kitti's Hog-nosed Bats (the world's smallest mammal), are easy to reach from Kanchanaburi, as is Erawan Waterfall.

Luang Prabang region. Treks in northern Laos transport you back in time—somewhat. These days, even some of the most remote hill country villages have cell phones, solar panels, and micro hydropower systems that generate enough power to run a TV.

WHERE TO STAY BEACHSIDE

Thailand's beaches are so inviting you might be tempted to sleep under the stars. And you can do that if you like, but there are tons of other surf-side lodging choices. So even if you're on a budget, there's no need to camp out—or move inland.

Budget Bungalows

Warm weather and beautiful palm-fringed beaches mean you can spend just a few dollars on a room and still be in paradise. **Somewhere Else** on Koh Lanta has funky huts and friendly staff; **Smile Bungalows** on Koh Phangan has great ocean views. At the cheapest places you'll share a bathroom, have cold showers, and sleep to the whirring of a rickety fan (unless the power's out).

Private Houses

Rental houses are much less pricey than resort villas and come in all sorts of styles. A few websites to check are ⊕ *www.thailandretreats.com*, ⊕ *www.worldvacationrentals.net* and ⊕ *raileibeachclub.com*. Newspapers like the *Bangkok Post* and the *Pattaya Mail* often list rentals and agents.

Rangers Huts

Many national parks, including the Surin Islands and Similan Islands, have accommodation in rangers' huts, bookable through the national park authorities (⊕ *www.dnp.go.th/parkreserve*) or Thai Forest Booking (⊕ *www.thaiforestbooking.com*). Prices start at around B300 per person in a very basic hut that sleeps up to 10 people, sometimes more.

Resorts

Eco: At earth-friendly resorts, the emphasis is on using natural materials and preserving resources and land. **Chumphon Cabana Beach Resort** (⊕ *www.cabana.co.th*) uses bacteria to clean wastewater and produce organic fertilizer.

Luxury Living: There's no shortage of exclusive beach resorts, and though these getaways have traditionally been part of large chains, smaller players—some of them independent—are becoming more common. A number of resorts, such as **Pimalai Resort** on Koh Lanta (⊕ *www.pimalai.com*) and **Amanpuri Resort** on Phuket (⊕ *www.amanpuri.com*), are offering villa-type accommodations for those who want resort amenities but more privacy than hotel rooms afford. Spas like **Chiva-Som** in Hua Hin (⊕ *www.chivasom.com*) are luring pop stars and models through their doors.

Thai Style: In Thailand, the term *resort* is often used for any accommodation that's not in an urban area—it doesn't necessarily mean there are extra facilities. That said, some of these lower-key Thai-style resorts are worth checking out. Though they're not as sumptuous as luxury resorts, they're often tastefully executed and come with a moderate price tag. At friendly **Sarikantang** on Koh Pha Ngan (⊕ *www.sarikantang.com*), the priciest bungalows are around $190 in high season; **Black Tip Dive Resort and Watersport Center** on Koh Tao (⊕ *www.blacktipdiving.com*) runs a great diving school.

Stilt Houses

Bungalows and houses built on stilts above the water make romantic, exotic accommodations. Some are custom built for tourist luxury; others are rustic but still breathtaking.

GREAT ITINERARIES

HIGHLIGHTS OF THAILAND: BANGKOK, BEACHES, AND THE NORTH

10 days

To get the most out of your Thailand vacation, decide what you'd particularly like to do—party in the big city, lie on the beach, go trekking, and so on—and arrange your trip around the region best suited for that activity. Every region has so much to offer, you'll barely scratch the surface in two weeks. However, if you don't know where to start, the following itinerary will allow you see three very different areas of the country without requiring too many marathon travel days.

Almost every trip to Thailand begins in **Bangkok,** which is a good place to linger for a day or two, because some of the country's most astounding sights can be found in and around the **Old City.** You'll probably be exhausted by the pace in a few days, so head down to the beach, where you can swim in clear seas and sip cocktails on white sands. After relaxing for a few days, you'll be ready for more adventures, so head to Thailand's second city, **Chiang Mai.** The surrounding countryside is beautiful, and even a short stay will give you a chance to visit centuries-old architecture and the **Elephant Conservation Center.**

Days 1 and 2: Bangkok

Experience the Old Thailand hiding within this modern megalopolis by beginning your first day with a tour of **Bangkok's Old City,** with visits to the stunning **Grand Palace** and **Wat Po's Reclining Buddha.** Later in the day, hire a longtail boat and spend a couple of hours exploring the canals. On the river you'll catch a glimpse

of how countless city people lived until not long ago, in wooden stilt houses along the water's edge. For a casual evening, head to the backpacker hangout of **Khao San Road** for a cheap dinner, fun shopping, and bar-hopping. For something fancy, take a ferry to the **Mandarin Oriental Hotel** for riverside cocktails and dinner at Le Normandie.

Start Day 2 with the sights and smells of **Chinatown,** sampling some of the delicious food along the way. Then head north to silk mogul **Jim Thompson's House,** a fine example of a traditional teak abode, with antiques displayed inside. If you're up for more shopping, the malls near **Siam Square** are great browsing territory for local and international fashion, jewelry, and accessories. The malls also have a couple of movie theaters and a bowling alley—Siam Paragon even has an aquarium with sharks. CentralWorld, touted as "the largest lifestyle shopping destination,"

TIPS

Temples and royal buildings, such as Bangkok's Grand Palace, require modest dress (no shorts or tank tops).

Take a taxi to the Grand Palace or an express boat to nearby Tha Chang Pier. Wat Po is a 10-minute walk south. Hire a longtail boat to get to the canals and back at Tha Chang Pier. Khao San Road is a short taxi ride from the pier.

Bangkok Airways owns the airport at Koh Samui, and flights there are relatively expensive due to taxes, but if you book online directly from Bangkok Airways, you might get reduced airfare. Nok Air and AirAsia also offer cheap flights to nearby Surat Thani or Nakhon Si Thammarat, from which you can take a ferry to the island.

Late November through April is the best time to explore the Andaman Coast. For the Gulf Coast there's good weather from late November until August.

Hotels in the south are frequently packed during high season and Thai holidays, so book in advance.

includes some 500 shops, 50 restaurants, 21 movie theaters, an office tower, hotel and more. Later, grab a meal at **Ban Khun Mae,** then if you've any energy left, head over to **Lumphini Stadium** for a Thai boxing match.

Days 3 to 5: The Beaches

Most island destinations are within a few hours flying time from Bangkok. It's roughly an hour to Samui or Trat (jumping-off point for Koh Chang); an hour 20 minutes to Phuket and Krabi. Hua Hin is roughly a 5- to 5½-hour bus or railway journey from Bangkok.

Get an early start and head down to the beach regions. Your choices are too numerous to list here, but **Koh Samui, Phuket,** and **Krabi** are all good bets if time is short because of the direct daily flights that connect them with Bangkok. Peaceful **Khao Lak** is only a two-hour drive from the bustle of Phuket, and **Koh Chang** is just a couple of hours by ferry from Trat Airport. Closer to Bangkok, **Koh Samet** and **Hua Hin** are three hours away by road. But if you have at least three days to spare, you can go almost anywhere that piques your interest—just make sure the time spent traveling doesn't overshadow the time spent relaxing.

Samui, Phuket, and Krabi are also good choices because of the variety of activities each offers. Though **Samui** has traditionally been backpacker terrain, there are now a number of spa retreats on the island. You can also hike to a waterfall, careen down a treetop zip line, or take a side trip to **Angthong National Marine Park. Phuket** is the country's main diving center, offering trips to many nearby reefs. There's great sailing around Phuket, too. On **Krabi** you can enjoy a relaxing afternoon and cheap beachside massage at gorgeous **Phra Nang Beach**; go rock climbing on limestone cliffs; kayak from bay to bay; and watch the glorious sunset from nearby **Railay Beach.**

Day 6: Chiang Mai

Chiang Mai is 1 hour by air, about 10 hours by bus or 12–15 hours by train from Bangkok.

Though it shouldn't be a terribly taxing day, getting to **Chiang Mai** requires some travel time, so you should get an early start. Wherever you are, you'll most likely have to make a connecting flight in Bangkok; if you're pinching pennies, this actually works in your favor, because it's cheaper to book two separate flights on a low-cost airline than to book one ticket from a more expensive airline "directly" from one of the beach airports to Chiang Mai—you'll have to stop in Bangkok anyway. If you play your cards right, you should be in Chiang Mai in time to check into your hotel and grab a late lunch. Afterward, stroll around the **Old City**, and in the evening go shopping at the famous night market.

Day 7: Chiang Mai
If traveling by saengthaew, allow one hour from downtown Chiang Mai to Doi Suthep; if traveling by motorcycle or private car, allow ½ hour each way.

Spend the day exploring the city and visiting the dazzling hilltop wat of **Doi Suthep**. Ring the dozens of bells surrounding the main building for good luck. On the way back to Chiang Mai, drop in at the seven-spired temple called **Wat Chedi Yot** or check out the pandas at the zoo. Chiang Mai is famous for its massage and cooking schools, so if you're interested in trying a class in either—or just getting a massage—this is the place to do it.

Day 8: Lampang
Lampang is 60 miles outside of Chiang Mai, and the elephant center is midway between. Allow a full day.

An easy side trip from Chiang Mai, **Lampang** has some beautiful wooden-house architecture and a sedate way of getting around, in pony-drawn carriages.

A short ride out of town is one of northern Thailand's most revered temples, **Wat Phra That Lampang Luang,** which contains the country's oldest wooden building. It's an excellent example of classic Lanna architecture. At the **Elephant Conservation Center,** between Chiang Mai and Lampang, you can take elephant rides, watch

the pachyderms bathing in the river, and hear them playing in an orchestra. Proceeds go to promoting elephant welfare.

Day 9: Around Chiang Mai
30 minutes to 1 hour from central Chiang Mai, depending on traffic.

Your last day in the region can be spent in a variety of ways. Shoppers can take taxis to the nearby **Hang Dong** district with furniture and art shops as well as handicrafts villages such as **Baan Tawai**; or to **Lamphun**, which has some pre-Thai-era temple architecture from the 7th century. Active types can head to **Doi Inthanon National Park,** where there are great views across the mountains toward Myanmar, plus bird-watching, hiking to waterfalls, and wildlife that includes Asiatic black bears.

Day 10: Bangkok
Head back to Bangkok. If you're not flying home the moment you step off the plane from Chiang Mai, spend your final day in the city doing some last-minute shopping at the city's numerous markets, such as **Pratunam, Phahurat,** and the weekend-only **Chatuchak.** Or just relax in **Lumphini Park.**

FOUR-COUNTRY TOUR

14 Days
It's just about possible to see all four countries in two weeks, if you concentrate on a few highlights. Do you want to focus on cultural sites and cities? Do you need a few relaxing days at the beach? Determine your priorities first, then set your itinerary. Here is one possible route that will hit a bit of everything—Bangkok buzz, ancient temples, quiet beaches, and more.

Days 1–2 Bangkok
Follow Days 1 and 2 of the Essential Thailand itinerary.

Day 3 Chiang Mai

Chiang Mai is roughly 1 hour from Bangkok. Take a morning flight.

Your first stop should be Chiang Mai's Old City for a quick but tasty street-side lunch and a tour of the city's famous ancient temples including Wat Phra Singh. In the afternoon, hire a car or catch a sangthaew up to Doi Suthep, the mountain temple overlooking the city. If the weather is clear, it's a great spot to experience sunset. Eat dinner at one of the restaurants along the base of the mountain, or on the ever-popular Nimmanhaemin Road for a taste of the local college crowd. Overnight at Bussaba Bed and Breakfast for local flavor.

Day 4: Yangon

1 hour 20 minutes from Chiang Mai.

When you touch down in Yangon, plan on first seeing the Shwedagon Pagoda—and expect at least a half-hour's travel time from the city center. After the Shwedagon, head to the swarming 19th Street (known as Beer Street) for cheap outdoor eating and drinking, local style. Or, for an upscale evening, visit the Strand Hotel for cocktails and dinner. The city is changing fast. (*The Irrawaddy* and *Myanmar Times* are good sources of local information on the latest hipster cafés.) If your schedule allows, visit the Sule Pagoda in the heart of the city. Afterward, wander the crowded streets and sidewalk vendors to get the pulse of Yangon. Overnight at the Sule Shangri-La, formerly the iconic Trader's Hotel.

Days 5–6: Bagan

1 hour 15 minute flight from Yangon.

There are several morning flights to Bagan on various local airlines (Myanmar, Yangon, Air Bagan, Mann Yadanarponn Airways—but check schedules online, as these may change frequently). When you arrive in Bagan, you'll have plenty to explore throughout this sprawling ancient capital site of more than 2,000 ruins over two days. It's a bit like wandering through the Angkor complex in Cambodia. On Day 5 hire a private taxi for the day. The following day, bicycles (available for rent) remain a pleasant way to explore the ruins on your own (though dress accordingly; this can be a long, hot day). Typically, accommodations are divided among three places: Nyaung-U, which caters more toward budget travelers; New Bagan, which offers midrange options; and Old Bagan, with upscale lodging.

Day 7: Bagan—Yangon—Bangkok—Koh Samet

1 hour 15 minute flight between Bagan and Yangon; 1 hour 20 minutes between Yangon and Bangkok; 3½ hours between Bangkok and Koh Samet.

This will be a long travel day, so start early and schedule time between your flights with ample room for delays, as you will need to transfer in Yangon. From Bangkok airport, arrange shuttle transportation to Koh Samet, three hours by road and 30 minutes by ferry from Bangkok. Enjoy the beautiful beaches and the many seafood shacks that set up along the shore every afternoon. Treat yourself to a stay at the Paradee resort and relax after your long travel day.

Day 8: Koh Samet—Bangkok—Siem Reap

Siem Reap is 1 hour 5 minutes by direct flight from Bangkok.

Rise early and head to beautiful Ao Kieu beach on the south of the island to spend the morning lounging on the beach. In the afternoon, return to Bangkok airport for your evening flight to Siem Reap. Check into the luxurious Amansara or the boutique Heritage Suites Hotel and relax—you'll need energy for the following two days of temple tours.

Days 9–10: Siem Reap

You'll want to arrange a tour of the Angkor Archaeological Park as soon as you arrive. (Any hotel can help you; one of the best ways to see the temples is to hire a tuk tuk driver so you can experience the scenes in open-air style.) Many visitors choose to spend at least one sunrise at Angkor Wat and one sunset on the hilltop Phnom Bakheng. The temple complex is vast, so talk to your guide, pick up one of the many freely available printed temple pamphlets, and design the itinerary that best suits your interests. If you have time after the second day at Angkor Wat, wander the old city and shop at the Psa Chas market. On your last night in Siem Reap, savor a modern Cambodian meal at Cuisine Wat Damnak.

Days 11–13: Luang Prabang

Luang Prabang is a 2-hour direct flight from Siem Reap.

Spend the morning touring Siem Reap's Angkor National Museum, then catch an afternoon direct flight to Luang Prabang in time for a sunset drink on the Mekong. The entire UNESCO World Heritage City is accessible by foot, so wear sturdy shoes and plan full days of walking. Rise early on Day 12 (just before sunrise) to catch the parade of Buddhist monks out for their morning alms. Afterward, you'll find enough temples, shops, and restaurants to keep you busy in the historical district. Spend Day 13 taking in the views from Phu Si Hill, getting a massage at one of the town's many spas and perhaps trying your hand at a Lao cooking class. You can take a ferryboat across the Mekong and explore some of the old temple ruins directly across from the Luang Prabang peninsula. Another option is to hire a boat upriver to the Pak Ou Caves, filled with Buddha statues. Plan on a full afternoon. After a riverside dinner, wander through the handicrafts market that sets up along Sisavangvong Road. Stay in the 3 Nagas Boutique hotel, in a UNESCO-heritage protected mansion, or splash out on the Amantaka resort for your final night.

Day 14: Luang Prabang—Bangkok—home

Bangkok is a 1 hour 50 minute flight from Luang Prabang.

Catch a flight to Bangkok to connect to your flight home.

ECOTOURISM IN THAILAND

Though the tourism boom has been great for Thailand's economy, it has had many negative effects on Thai culture and natural resources. These problems, which range from water pollution to sex tourism to the transformation of hill tribe villages into virtual theme parks, are difficult to rein in. The good news is that a growing number of tour operators and hotel proprietors are addressing these issues, and are therefore worthy of your support.

Planning Your Trip

Though the worldwide eco trend is catching on in Thailand, truly eco-friendly companies are still thin on the ground. Many businesses describe themselves as "eco," so ask some tough questions about what the company does to preserve the environment and help local communities before you book. And as always, don't be afraid to shop around. Your critical eye will help raise standards. Here are a few questions you might ask.

Accommodations: Ask whether the hotel or resort is energy efficient. Does it use alternative power sources? What steps does it take to conserve water and reduce waste? If it's a beach hotel, how does it handle sewage? Does it recycle? Is the building made with any natural or recycled materials? Does it employ members of the local community? Does it contribute any percentage of profits to health, education, or wildlife preservation initiatives?

Elephant Treks: It's important to find out how tour operators treat their elephants. You might ask how many hours a day the elephants work, and whether you'll be riding in the afternoon heat, or resting until it's cooler.

Hill Tribe Tours and Other Expeditions: How much the operator knows about the village or wilderness area you'll be visiting is often telling, so ask for details. Also, does the operator work with any NGOs or other interest groups to protect the culture and/or the environment?

Resources

The umbrella group **Thailand Community Based Tourism Institute** (⊕ *www.cbt-i.org*) is a good place to start. It provides information about tour agencies and community programs that promote culturally sensitive tourism.

"Voluntourism"—travel that includes an effort to give back to local communities—is a growing trend in Thailand, and a number of organizations are now offering educational travel programs that incorporate some volunteer work. Lots of businesses are offering eco-minded tours. Here are a few reputable resources that will get you started.

The **Educational Travel Center** (⊕ *www.etc.co.th*) organizes cultural exchanges and ecotours, as well as volunteer programs at a variety of destinations.

The Himmapaan Foundation (⊕ *himmapaan.com*) is a reforestation initiative near Chiang Mai. Participants work alongside tribespeople and forestry experts to promote biodiversity.

Lost Horizons (⊕ *www.losthorizonsasia.com*) runs several thematic ecotourism trips in Thailand, including jungle treks, kayaking, beach retreats, and animal conservation.

Wild Asia (⊕ *www.wildasia.org*) is a regional nonprofit group that works on responsible travel. The website has useful information.

Animal Rights

Though preserving wildlife habitats is a priority in Thailand's national parks, illegal poaching is still rampant. There's such high demand for tiger products (not only skins, but also teeth, bones, and penises, which are used as charms or in traditional medicines) that tigers are now virtually extinct in Thailand.

Elephants are revered in Thailand, where they have a long history as laborers. But mechanization has made elephants' traditional timber-hauling jobs obsolete, and elephant handlers (*mahouts*) now rely on elephant shows, treks, and other tourism-related business for their livelihood. Unfortunately, these endeavors often lead to mistreatment. Yet if there's no work, handlers can't afford the 550 pounds of food and 60 gallons of water an elephant consumes each day; malnutrition is another problem for Thai elephants. Organizations like **PeunPa** focus on broader issues, including educating village communities on the importance of wildlife conservation and how to combat problems like illegal trafficking of endangered species.

What You Can Do

Whatever kind of trip you're planning, there are a few simple things you can do to ensure that you're part of the solution, not part of the problem

Don't litter. Sadly, garbage is a common sight on Thailand's once-pristine beaches. Litter is hazardous to marine life. You can help by disposing of your rubbish properly; you can also pay a little extra for biodegradable glass water bottles. If you plan to travel regularly in the developing world, consider buying a hand-pump water purifier, available at many sporting-goods stores for $20 and up. You can make your own clean water wherever you go, instead of generating a trail of disposable water bottles.

ECOTOURISM VERSUS SUSTAINABLE TOURISM

Ecotourism is travel to natural areas to observe and learn about wildlife; tourism that refrains from damaging the environment; or tourism that strengthens conservation and improves the lives of local people.

Sustainable tourism has a wider scope that encompasses the definition of ecotourism but also includes increased ecological responsibility throughout the entire travel industry, in everything from city hotels to cruise shops. Not all ecotourism is sustainable tourism.

Don't disturb animal and plant life. Whether you're trekking or snorkeling, be as unobtrusive as possible. Don't remove plants or coral for souvenirs, and don't feed fish or other animals, even if your guide says it's okay.

Respect local customs. Though it may seem like a matter of etiquette, demonstrating respect for a culture is part of ecotourism. Thais tend to be exceedingly tolerant of western behavior, but tourists who are ignorant about basic customs have a negative effect on the communities they encounter. Take a little time to learn about major cultural mores (especially those related to Buddhism). Thais will appreciate your efforts.

BUDDHISM IN THAILAND

Almost 95% of Thailand's population is Buddhist (4% is Muslim, and the remaining 1% is Taoist, Confucianist, Hindu, Christian, and Sikh). Buddhism is considered one of the foundations of Thai nationhood, represented on the flag by two white bars between red bars for the people and a central blue bar for the monarchy. Thai kings are required to be Buddhist: King Rama IV spent 27 years as a forest monk before ascending the throne in 1851. The country has 400,000 monks and novices, many of whom take alms bowls into the street each day to receive food from laypeople.

Origins

Buddhism first showed up in Thailand in the Dvaravati Mon kingdom between the 6th and 9th centuries. The Dvaravati capital of Nakhon Pathom, 55 km (34 miles) west of Bangkok, was the region's first Buddhist center. In the 14th century, Buddhism became the official religion of Sukhothai, the first Thai kingdom. In 1997 it was written into the constitution as the state religion of modern Thailand. There are two main branches of Buddhism in Asia: Theravada, found today in Thailand, Myanmar, Cambodia, Laos, and Sri Lanka; and Mahayana, which spread north from India to China, Korea, Vietnam, and Japan. The Mahayana movement emerged from Theravada, the original teachings of the Buddha, in the 1st century. It's a less austere doctrine than Theravada, which stresses devotion to study and meditation. *(For more on Buddhism, see The Buddha in Thailand.)*

Practice and Rituals

Thai children learn Buddhist teachings (*dharma*) in school, and most males will at some time ordain as a *bhikkhu* (monk). Some only do this for a few days, but many join the monkhood each July for the three-month Rains Retreat (sometimes referred to as Buddhist Lent, when monks are required to remain in their wats for the duration of the rainy season) in July, which is marked by major festivals, such as the Candle Parade, in Nakhon Ratchasima. Joining the monkhood, even for a short time, is such an important event that employers grant time off for the purpose. Women wanting to devote their lives to Buddhism may become white-robed nuns, known as *mae chi*. However, women aren't allowed to be officially ordained in Thailand, though a growing feminist lobby questions their lower status and is pushing for ordination. Although most Thais don't visit temples regularly, wats are the center of community life and sometimes serve as schools, meeting halls, and hospitals. Alongside spiritual guidance and funeral rites, monks provide ceremonies in houses and businesses to bring good fortune, and will even bless vehicles to keep drivers safe from accidents or cell phones to keep them ringing with business. They are also traditional healers, and created many of the herbal remedies that now form the basis for spa treatments.

Modern Concerns

Many commentators fear that modernization is eroding Thailand's traditional Buddhist values, and that material rewards will overshadow the Buddha's teachings. It's true that greater personal wealth has brought consumerism to the middle classes, and young Thais are exposed to western culture through foreign education, TV, and the Internet. However, Buddhism continues to be a dominant influence on the national psyche.

COUPS & THE KING
THAILAND'S TURBULENT HISTORY
by Karen Coates

Thais share a reverence for their king, Bhumibol Adulyadej, who has been the nation's moral leader and a unifying figure since 1946. Thais are also united by a deep pride in their country, a constitutional monarchy and the only Southeast Asian nation never colonized by Europeans. But this hasn't stopped political turmoil from roiling beneath the surface and erupting.

Though northeastern Thailand has been inhabited for about 2,500 years, it wasn't until 1238 that Thai princes drove the Cambodian Khmers out of central Thailand and established Sukhothai, the first centralized Thai state. There was conflict again in the late 14th century, when the rival state of Ayutthaya conquered Sukhothai. After over 400 years of power, Ayutthaya in turn was defeated by the Burmese in the late 18th century, and the Thais established a new capital in Bangkok.

As European influence in Southeast Asia grew, Thailand alternated between periods of isolation and openness to foreign trade and ideas. Western-style democracy was one idea that took hold in the early 20th century. But since then a pattern has emerged in Thai politics: a prime minister is elected, allegations of corruption surface, the public protests, and the leader is ousted.

King Rama V
(1853–1910)
and family

TIMELINE
4,000–2,000 BC Rice first cultivated in Thailand

1238
Sukhothai kingdom
founded

1350
Ayutthaya kingdom
founded

4000 BC   1200   1300   1400

(top) Pottery found at Ban Chianq; (left) stone face at Bayon in Angkor Thom, Cambodia; (bottom) Khmer elephant-shaped box.

4000–2000 BC

Bronze & Rice

Scientists think that northeastern Thailand was a hotbed for agricultural innovation. In fact, the Mon people from modern-day Myanmar who settled in Ban Chiang may have been Asia's first farmers. Archaeologists have found ancient pottery, bronze rings, spearheads, bracelets, and axes.

500–1400

Great Migrations

Historians believe the Thais' ancestors were the ethnic Tai people of southern China. The Tai migrated south into modern-day Thailand in waves, but the biggest southern push came after the Mongols invaded their kingdom in the 13th century. The fleeing Tai settled in the Mekong River Valley, inventing elaborate agricultural systems to farm rice. Around this time, the Khmers of what is today called Cambodia were extending the Angkor empire west into Thailand.

1238–1438

Sukhothai & the Golden Age

In 1238 chieftains established the first Thai kingdom at Sukhothai in central Thailand, kicking out the Khmer overlords. The Sukhothai kingdom united many Thai settlements and marked the beginning of a prosperous era when, legend has it, the rivers were full of fish, and the paddies were lush with rice. In the late 13th century, King Ramkhamhaeng created a writing system that is the basis of the modern Thai alphabet.

1511
Portuguese arrive

1782
Capital moves to Bangkok

1767
Ayutthaya falls to Burmese invaders

(left) Interior of Wat Po, Bangkok; (top) Royal jewelry from Ayutthaya; (bottom) Buddha statue from Ayutthaya.

Ayutthaya Kingdom

1350–1767

King Ramathibodi founded the kingdom of Ayutthaya, 45 miles up the Chao Phraya River from Bangkok, in 1350 and took over Sukhothai 25 years later. The king made Theravada Buddhism the kingdom's official religion and established the Dharmashastra, a legal code with roots in Hindu Indian texts. Ayutthaya, a city of canals and golden temples, became wealthy and prominent.

European Influence

1511–1800s

The Portuguese were the first Europeans to arrive in Thailand establishing an embassy in Ayutthaya in 1511. But they brought more than ambassadors: The Portuguese also brought the first chilies to the country, making a huge contribution to Thai cuisine.

Over the following centuries of European trade and relations, Thailand's kings charted a sometimes tenuous course of autonomy as their neighbors were colonized by the Portuguese, Dutch, English, and French.

Burmese Invasion & New Beginnings

1767–1809

In 1767 the Burmese sacked Ayutthaya, destroying palaces, temples, artwork, and written records. But within two years, General Phraya Taksin ran out the Burmese and established a new capital at Thonburi, which is today a part of Bangkok. Taksin became king but was forced from power and executed in 1782. After this coup, Buddha Yodfa Chulaloke the Great (known as Rama I) took control. He moved the capital across the river, where he built the Grand Palace in the image of past Thai kingdoms.

1893–1907
Territory ceded
to French

| 1850 | 1875 | 1900 |

(left) King Mongkut
with queen;
(top) *The King and I*;
(bottom) 19th-century
tin coin.

The King and I & Beyond

1851–1931

In 1862, Anna Leonowens, an English schoolteacher, traveled to Bangkok with her son to serve as royal governess to King Mongkut's wives and children. Leonowens's memoirs inspired Margaret Landon's controversial novel *Anna and the King of Siam*, which in turn was the basis for the well-known Broadway musical *The King and I* and the subsequent film.

Thais were deeply offended by the film, which portrays the king as foolish and barbaric; *The King and I* was consequently banned in Thailand. A 1999 remake, *Anna and the King*, followed Leonowens's version of the story more closely, but Thais, who are extremely devoted to their royal family, still found this version culturally insensitive.

Mongkut (or Rama IV) earned the nickname "Father of Science and Technology" for his efforts to modernize the country. He signed a trade treaty with Great Britain, warding off other colonial powers while opening Thailand to foreign innovation.

After Rama IV's death in 1868, his son Chulalongkorn became king. Also called "Rama the Great," Chulalongkorn is credited with preserving Thailand's independence and abolishing slavery.

Constitutional Era

1932–41

Thailand moved toward Western-style democracy when young intellectuals staged a bloodless coup against King Prajadhipok (Rama VII) in 1931. Thailand's first constitution was signed that year and parliamentary elections were held the next. In the new system—a constitutional monarchy similar to England's—the king is still head of state, but he doesn't have much legal power.

In 1939 the government changed the country's name from Siam to Thailand. The new name refers to the Tai people; Tai also means "free" in Thai.

1939 Siam renamed Thailand	1942 Alliance formed with Japan	
	1944 Phibun ousted	
1932 First elections held	1946 Rama IX crowned	1959–75 Vietnam War
1925	**1950**	**1975**

1

(left) Bridge over the River Kwai; (top) U.S. pilot in Vietnam; (bottom) Postage stamp c. 1950 featuring king Bhumibol Adulyadej.

World War II

1941–46

In 1941, Japan helped Thailand win a territorial conflict with France over parts of French Indochina (modern-day Cambodia, Laos, and Vietnam.) Later that year, the Japanese demanded free passage through Thailand so that they could attack Malaya and Burma. In 1942, under the leadership of Phibun, a military general elected prime minister in 1938, Thailand formed an alliance with Japan.

The Japanese conquered Burma and began to construct the Thailand–Burma "Death Railway," so named because over 100,000 Asian forced-laborers and Allied POWs died while working on it. Meanwhile, an underground resistance called Seri Thai gathered strength as Thais turned against the Phibun regime and the Japanese occupation. Phibun was ousted in 1944 and replaced by a government friendly to the Allies.

In 1946 King Rama VIII was murdered. He was succeeded by his brother, the beloved Bhumibol Adulyadej (Rama IX), who is currently the world's longest-serving head of state.

The Vietnam War

1961–75

While publicly staying neutral, the Thai government let the U.S. Air Force use bases throughout Thailand to bomb Laos and Cambodia between 1961 and 1975. Meanwhile, Bangkok and Thailand's beaches became playgrounds to thousands of soldiers on leave. The Westernization of Thai popular culture has roots in the Vietnam era, when restaurants and bars catered to beer- and Coke-drinking Americans.

TIMELINE
1973–81 Violence against students and activists

1997
Asian Financial Crisis

2001
Thaksin
Shinawatra
elected

2006
Thaksin
outsted

1975   1985   1995   2005

(left) Protesters occupying the Government House garden. Bangkok, September 3rd 2008; (top) Banner demanding that ousted P.M. Thaksin Shinawatra and his wife return to Thailand to stand trial; (bottom) Samak Sundaravej.

1973–PRESENT

Unrest

A new democracy movement gained force in 1973, when protesters charged the streets of Bangkok after students were arrested on antigovernment charges. On October 14, protests erupted into bloody street battles, killing dozens. More violent outbreaks occurred on October 6th, 1976, and again in "Black May" of 1992, when a military crackdown resulted in more than 50 deaths.

In 2001, billionaire Thaksin Shinawatra was elected prime minister on a platform of economic growth and rural development. The year after he was elected, he dissolved the liaison between the

Muslim southern provinces and the largely Buddhist administration in Bangkok, rekindling bloody unrest after years of quiet. The situation escalated until insurgents attacked a Thai army arsenal in early 2004; at this writing, over 3,500 people have been killed in frequent outbursts of violence in southern Thailand.

Meanwhile, Thaksin and his family were railed with corruption and tax-evasion charges. In September 2006 he was ousted by a junta, which controlled the country until voters approved a new constitution and elected Samak Sundaravej prime minister. Samak took office in early 2008, but in September, after months of protests, the Constitutional Court

demanded his resignation because he had accepted money for hosting a televised cooking show (it's illegal for a prime minister to have other income). Parliament quickly elected Somchai Wongsawat, Thaksin's brother-in-law, to replace Samak.

The protests did not end there. In late 2008 Somchai was forced to step down, and Parliament voted in Abhisit Vejjajiva, leader of the opposition party. Since 2011, anti-government protests have increased, and 2014 saw a coup d'etat and the establishment of a military junta. Thailand's long voyage toward democracy is ongoing.

BANGKOK

WELCOME TO BANGKOK

TOP REASONS TO GO

★ **The Canals:** They don't call it "Venice of the East" for nothing. Sure, boat tours are touristy, but the sights, from Khmer wats to bizarre riverside dwellings, are rare and wonderful.

★ **Street Food:** Bangkok may have the best street food in the world. Don't be afraid to sample the more exotic offerings. They're often fresher and better than the food you'd get at a hotel restaurant.

★ **Amazing Shopping:** Some of Asia's most high-tech malls sell high-end designer goods in amazing settings.

★ **Sky-High Sipping:** "Bar with a view" is taken to the extreme when you sip martinis in open-air spaces atop lofty towers.

★ **Temple-Gazing:** From the venerable Wat Po to the little wats that don't make it into guidebooks, Bangkok's collection of temples is hard to top.

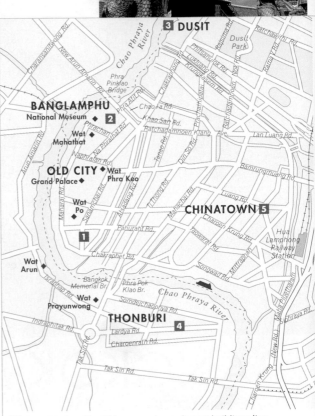

1 The Old City. The Old City is the historic heart of Bangkok, and home to opulent temples like Wat Po.

2 Banglamphu. North of the Old City, Banglamphu is mostly residential; it's known for the famous backpacker street Khao San Road, but it has much more to offer than just touristy kicks with fellow foreigners.

3 Dusit. North of Banglamphu is this royal district, where elegant buildings line wide avenues. Dusit Park is one of the city's most appealing green spaces.

4 Thonburi. Across the river from the Old City is Thonburi, a mostly residential neighborhood, whose most notable attraction is Wat Arun.

5 Chinatown. East of the Old City in labyrinthine Chinatown are shops selling Buddhas and spices; the open-air fruit and vegetable

GETTING ORIENTED

Bangkok's endless maze of streets is part of its fascination and its complexity—getting around a labyrinth is never easy. Although the S-curve of the Chao Phraya River can throw you off base, it's actually a good landmark. Most of the popular sights are close to the river, and you can use it to get swiftly from one place to another. Also look at the Skytrain and subway to help you navigate and get around quickly.

markets here are among Bangkok's most vibrant.

6 Pathumwan. This area, which can be considered Bangkok's "downtown," is home to the city's greatest collection of shopping malls as well as the popular Pratunam clothing market.

7 Silom and Bang Rak. In this busy area you'll find Lumphini Park, Bangkok's largest park and a pleasantly green space to escape from the harried pace of the city. With many bars and restaurants, the Silom area also includes the infamous red-light district of Patpong. At the east end of Bang Rak lies the Chao Phraya River, and many opulent hotels.

8 Sukhumvit. Sukhumvit Road is a bustling district filled with high-end restaurants, hotels, and shops, as well as the red-light areas of Nana and Soi Cowboy.

9 Northern Bangkok. This area includes the Victory Monument and all points north, such as the famous Chatuchak Weekend Market, the northern bus station of Mo Chit, and the budget air terminal at Don Mueang.

Updated
by Dave
Stamboulis

Bangkok, also known as the City of Angels and Venice of the East, will hit you like a ton of bricks. Hot, polluted, and chaotic, it thrills with energy, and the sightseeing, shopping, and eating possibilities are so vast that you'll have little time to rest. When you do find a moment, though, you can pamper yourself at spas, skyline-view bars, luxurious hotels, and excellent restaurants.

The city is a mesmerizing blend of old and new, East and West, and dizzying contradictions. Temples and red-light districts, languid canals and permanent gridlock, street-side vendors and chic upscale eateries, all exist side by side. Bangkok rarely fails to make an impression, and yes, you might need to spend a few days on the beach to recover from it all.

Bangkok is not known for jaw-dropping tourist attractions, but it does have an endless supply of worthwhile pilgrimages. The Grand Palace, Wat Phra Kaew, and the Emerald Buddha are tops on most visitors' itineraries, and lesser-known temples, such as Wat Benjamabophit, the golden stupa of Wat Sakhet, and Wat Suthat all merit a look. Besides temples, there are plenty of niche touring possibilities. Take in a venom-extraction and python-feeding show at the Queen Saowapha Snake Farm, or go to the nearby Jim Thompson House to learn all about the famed Thai silk industry. If architecture appeals to you, there is the Suan Pakkard Palace with its antique-teak-house collection. Even more astounding is Vimanmek Mansion, the world's largest golden teak building.

The Old City is a major destination for travelers, as it's home to opulent temples like Wat Po and Wat Phra Kaew. Across the river is Thonburi, a mostly residential neighborhood, where you can find Wat Arun. At the northern tip of the Old City is Banglamphu, one of Bangkok's older residential neighborhoods. It's best known now for Khao San Road, a backpacker hangout, though the neighborhood has much more to offer, especially when it comes to street food. North of Banglamphu is Dusit, the royal district since the days of Rama V.

East of the Old City is Chinatown, a labyrinth of streets with restaurants, shops, and warehouses. Chinatown deserves at least a day on every travel itinerary—be sure to check out the sprawling Flower Market and the nearby Thieves market. Farther down the Chao Phraya River is bustling Silom Road, a major commercial district. Patpong, the most famous of several red-light districts, is also here. Bang Rak is home to some of the city's leading hotels: the Mandarin Oriental, the Peninsula, the Royal Orchid Sheraton, and the Shangri-La. To the north of Rama IV Road is Bangkok's largest green area, Lumphini Park.

Continue north and you reach Sukhumvit Road, once a residential area. More recently, Thong Lor, farther east along Sukhumvit, has become an "in" neighborhood. The Nana and Asok areas of Sukhumvit are now home to even busier red-light entertainment districts (Nana and Soi Cowboy) than Patpong.

In all these neighborhoods you will find cuisine unrivaled for spice, taste, and variation. From multicourse meals to small bites from street vendors, the one constant here is food that's fresh and delicious at every level. You can lunch on superlative roast duck or wonton noodles on a street corner, and dine that evening on the sophisticated creations of world-class chefs. Your choices aren't limited to spicy Thai, either. A recent foodie revolution has resulted in the introduction of excellent French, Italian, and other restaurants—you'd need a few months to survey all the options available.

PLANNING

WHEN TO GO
From late October to late February, when Bangkok is at its coolest (85°F) and driest, is the best time to visit. By April the humidity and heat create a sticky stew that lasts until the rains begin in late June.

PLANNING YOUR TIME
For a city its size, Bangkok is short on sights, though hardly lacking them, and the heat, traffic, and chaos can be overwhelming. No wonder, then, that many visitors to Thailand quickly repair south to the islands. That said, two full days are the minimum for getting a quick fix of the country's dynamic capital, and three would be better. You just need to pace yourself. The Skytrain, subway, and river ferries will help you dodge some of the traffic, but the heat and urban sprawl can exhaust you. Don't try to pack too much into one day and you'll have more fun. Plan on half a day to take in the Grand Palace and Wat Po and another half to visit one or two other nearby sights. Later, enjoy a meal along the riverside and have a drink at a skyscraper's rooftop bar. Another day could be well spent exploring Chinatown in the morning and the Jim Thompson House or Snake Farm in the afternoon, followed by a dinner cruise on the river. Food lovers can take an extra day to explore the markets and hole-in-wall restaurants. If in town on the weekend, be sure to visit Chatuchak Market.

GETTING HERE AND AROUND

Bangkok has two main airports, multiple bus terminals, and a centrally located main railway station. Planes, buses, and trains connect Bangkok to all of Thailand's major cities and towns. Bangkok is large, so once here remember to pace yourself and to take a break to escape the midday heat. The traffic is unbearable, so do yourself a favor and skip driving in the city.

AIR TRAVEL

Bangkok's Suvarnabhumi International Airport (pronounced "Su-wan-na-poom") is about 30 km (18 miles) southeast of the city. About 25 km (16 miles) north of the city is the former international airport, Don Mueang, which now receives many domestic flights and has become the terminal for budget airlines. A free shuttle service connects the two airports.

Airports Don Mueang International Airport. ⊠ *222 Vipavadee Rangsit Rd., North Bangkok* ☎ *02/535–1111* ⊕ *www.donmueangairportthai.com* Ⓜ *Subway: Chatuchak Park; Skytrain: Mo Chit, then taxi.* **Suvarnabhumi International Airport.** ⊠ *999 Bang Na-Trat Rd., Bang Phlii, Samutprakarn* ☎ *02/132888* ⊕ *www.suvarnabhumiairport.com* Ⓜ *Airport Link: Suvarnabhumi.*

AIRPORT TRANSFERS

Inexpensive and available around the clock, taxis are the most convenient way to get between downtown and the airport. ■**TIP**➜ Make sure to have some baht on hand to pay for your taxi. Get a taxi by heading to one of the taxi counters on Level 1, near Entrances 3, 4, 7, and 8. State your destination to the dispatcher at the counter, who will lead you to your taxi. Allow 30 to 90 minutes to get downtown, depending on traffic. A trip downtown will cost between B250 and B300, plus any expressway tolls. ■**TIP**➜ Avoid drivers who insist on a fixed price or refuse to turn on their meters.

The Airport Rail Link system is your best option during rush hour. The express train (B150) takes 15 minutes to reach Makkasan Terminal, next to the Phetchaburi MRT subway stop. A local train (B65) that takes 23 minutes stops at the Phaya Thai BTS Station, convenient for those staying on the Skytrain line. The entrance to the system is on the airport's lower level.

Buses and minivans headed for Bangkok depart from the Airport Bus Station, which is reached in 10 minutes via a free shuttle bus you can catch front of the airport.

Contacts Airport Rail Link. ⊠ *Makkasan Station, New Petchaburi Rd.* ☎ *02/308–5600* ⊕ *www.srtet.co.th* Ⓜ *Subway: Petchaburi; Skytrain: Phaya Thai.*

Suvarnabhumi Airport Bus Station. ⊠ *999, Moo 1, Suvarnabhumi Airport, Nang Prue, Samutprakarn* ☎ *02/134–4099* ⊕ *www.bangkokairportonline.com/node/56.*

BUS TRAVEL

Getting Here: Bangkok has three major terminals for buses headed from other parts of the country. Buses to and from Hua Hin, Koh Samui, Phuket, and points south and west arrive at the Southern Bus Terminal, in Thonburi. The Eastern Bus Terminal, called Ekkamai, is for buses headed to and from Pattaya, Rayong, and Trat provinces. Buses to and from Chiang Mai and points north arrive at the Northern Bus Terminal. Minivans to nearby destinations like Hua Hin, Cha-am, Pattaya, Kanchanaburi, and elsewhere depart from Victory Monument.

Bus companies generally sell tickets on a first-come, first-served basis. This is seldom a problem because service is frequent. The most comfortable buses are those of Nakhon Chai Air, which has its own terminal near Mo Chit. Nakhon Chai connects Bangkok with many destinations within Thailand.

Getting Around: Bangkok Mass Transit Authority provides bus service in the city. For a fare of B8 on non-air-conditioned buses and B12 to B25 on air-conditioned ones, you can travel virtually anywhere in Bangkok. Air-conditioned microbuses charge B25. Most buses operate from 5 am to around 11 pm, but a few routes operate around the clock. You can pick up a route map at most bookstalls for B35, or just to ask locals which bus is headed to your destination.

Contacts Bangkok Mass Transit Authority. ⊠ 131 Thiemruam-mitre Rd., Huay Khwang, Huai Khwang ☎ 02/246-0339, 02/1348 hotline ⊕ www.bmta.co.th. **Bangkok Southern Bus Station (Sai Tai Mai).** ⊠ Borommaratchachonnani Rd., Bangkok Noi ☎ 02/894-6122, 02/435-1190 ⊕ www.transitbangkok.com. **Mo Chit Northern Bus Station.** ⊠ Kamphaeng Phet 2 Rd., Chatuchak ☎ 02/936-2852, 02/936-2842 ⊕ www.transitbangkok.com **Nakhon Chai Air Bus Station.** ⊠ 27 Vipavadi-Rangsit Rd., Soi 19, Chatuchak ☎ 02/1624 booking number, 02/0009 ⊕ www.nca.co.th Ⓜ Subway. Chatuchak Park; Skytrain: Mo Chit.

BOAT TRAVEL

The Chao Phraya River is a great way to bypass the traffic that clogs most of the city. The vessels of Chao Phraya Express Boat (fares from B10 to B32, depending on distance) can get crowded, especially at peak times, but they're still far more pleasant than sitting in a taxi as it navigates bumper-to-bumper traffic. The company also operates a tourist boat that serves eight piers near sightseeing attractions. A one-day pass (B150) for this boat can also be used to board express boats.

Contacts Chao Phraya Express Boat. ⊠ Saphan Taksin Pier, Bang Rak ☎ 02/449-3000, 02/445-8888 hotline ⊕ www.chaophrayaexpressboat.com Ⓜ Skytrain: Saphan Taksin.

SKYTRAIN AND SUBWAY TRAVEL

Although the BTS Skytrain covers just a fraction of the capital (it bypasses the Old City and Dusit, for example), it is surprisingly convenient for visitors, with routes above Sukhumvit, Silom, and Phaholyothin roads. ■TIP→ If you are traveling between two points along the route, the Skytrain is by far the best way to go. Rates run between B15 and B40. Like the Skytrain, the MRT subway covers only a small section of the city, but it's a great way to get from the city center out to the train stations. The subway runs daily from 6 am until midnight. Fares are from B15 to B40. Although the Skytrain and subway are separate entities and use different fare and ticketing systems, the two connect at three points: Sala Daeng Station and Silom Station, Asok Station and Sukhumvit Station, and Mo Chit Station and Chatuchak Station.

Contacts **BTS Skytrain.** ✉ *1000 Phahonyothin Rd., Chatuchak* ☎ *02/617–7300, 02/617–7341 tourist information* ⊕ *www.bts.co.th.* **MRT Bangkok Metro.** ✉ *189 Rama IX Rd., Huay Khwang* ☎ *02/354–2000* ⊕ *www.bangkokmetro.co.th.*

TAXI TRAVEL

Taxis can be an economical way to get around, provided you don't hit gridlock. Most taxis have meters, so avoid drivers whose cabs lack one or who claim that it is broken. The rate for the first 1 km (½ mile) is B35, with an additional baht for every 55 yards after that; a 5-km (3-mile) journey costs about B60. ∎**TIP→ Ask your concierge to write the name of your destination and its cross streets in Thai.**

TRAIN TRAVEL

The central train station in Bangkok is Hualamphong, located near Chinatown and accessible by subway. Trains here connect Bangkok and many destinations with Thailand.

Contacts **Hualamphong Station.** ✉ *Phra Ram IV Rd., Chinatown* ☎ *02/222–0175, 02/220–1690* ⊕ *www.railway.co.th* Ⓜ *Subway: Hualamphong.*

HEALTH AND SAFETY

For a city of its size, Bangkok is relatively safe; however, you still need to practice common sense. Don't accept food or drinks from strangers, as there have been reports of people being drugged and robbed. If you plan to enjoy a massage in your hotel room, put your valuables in the safe. Bangkok is no more dangerous for women than any other major city, but it's still best to avoid walking alone at night (take a taxi if you're out late).

∎**TIP→ Beware of hustlers who claim that your hotel is overbooked.** They'll try to convince you to switch to one that pays them a commission. Also avoid anyone trying to sell you on an overpriced taxi or limo. Proceed to the taxi stand; these taxis will use a meter.

Contact the Tourist Police first in an emergency. For medical attention, Bumrungrad Hospital and Bangkok Nursing Hospital are considered the best.

Emergency Services **Ambulance.** ✉ *Bangkok* ☎ *1669.* **Fire.** ✉ *Bangkok* ☎ *199.* **Police.** ✉ *Bangkok* ☎ *191.* **Tourist Police.** ✉ *Bangkok* ☎ *1155.*

Hospitals **Bangkok Nursing Home Hospital.** ✉ *9/1 Convent Rd., Silom (Bang Rak)* ☎ *02/686–2700* ⊕ *www.bnhhospital.com* Ⓜ *Subway: Silom; Skytrain: Sala Daeng.* **Bumrungrad Hospital.** ✉ *33 Sukhumvit, Soi 3, Sukhumvit* ☎ *02/667–1000* ⊕ *www.bumrungrad.com* Ⓜ *Skytrain: Ploenchit.*

MONEY MATTERS

Major banks all exchange foreign currency, and most have easily accessible ATMs that accept foreign bank cards. Currency-exchange offices are common, but don't wait until the last minute. It's distressing to try to find one when you're out of baht.

VISITOR INFORMATION

Tourist Authority of Thailand. The Tourist Authority of Thailand, open daily from 8:30 to 4:30, is heavier on colorful brochures than hard information, but it can supply materials about national parks and out-of-the-way destinations. A 24-hour hotline provides information about

TWO DAYS IN BANGKOK

Start your first day with the most famous of all Bangkok sights, the Grand Palace. In the same complex is the gorgeously ornate Wat Phra Kaew. Not far south of the Grand Palace is Bangkok's oldest and largest temple, Wat Po, famous for its enormous Reclining Buddha and for being a great place for a traditional Thai massage. Later, take the ferry up to Banglamphu (get off at the Phra Athit pier), where you can enjoy a river walk at Santichaiprakarn Park and the Phra Sumen Fort before checking out the hip restaurants and bars that front Phra Athit Road, which parallels the river. From here, lively Khao San

Road and all of its shopping are just a short stroll away.

The next day, start out in Chinatown, where you can spend hours browsing the food and spice markets, peeking into temples and shops, and just absorbing the atmosphere. Next, work your way to the Chao Phraya River, ferry down to the Saphan Taksin Pier, and take a *klong* (canal) tour, which will give you a glimpse of the fascinating canal life in Bangkok. If it's a weekend, head to Kukrit Pramoj Heritage House; if it's a weekday, visit the Jim Thompson House. Take the Skytrain in the evening either to Silom or Sukhumvit Road, where great restaurants and bars await.

attractions, festivals, and the arts. You can use the hotline to register complaints or request assistance from the Tourist Police. ✉ *1600 New Phetchaburi Rd., Ratchathewi* ☎ *02/250–5500, 1672 tourist hotline* ⊕ *www.tourismthailand.org* Ⓜ *Subway: Phetchaburi.*

EXPLORING

THE OLD CITY

TOP ATTRACTIONS

Grand Palace and Wat Phra Kaew. *See highlighted "The Grand Palace" feature in this chapter.* ✉ *Sanam Chai and Na Phra Lan Rd. A few hundred meters east of Tha Chang ferry pier, Sana Chai Rd., Bangkok* ☎ *102623–5500* ⊕ *www.palaces.thai.net* ⬜ *B500, includes admission to Wat Phra Kaew and Vimanmek Mansion* ⊘ *Daily 8:30–4:30.*

Queen Sirikit Museum of Textiles. Within the Grand Palace complex, in the old Ministry of Finance building, this interesting little museum tells the story of Thai silk through a lovely display of the current queen's most celebrated outfits. There are daily silk-making demonstrations, and a particularly good gift shop. ✉ *Ratsadakorn-bhibhathana building, Old City* ⊹ *Just inside main visitors' gate, Grand Palace* ⊕ *www.qsmtthailand.org* ⬜ *Included in Grand Palace ticket, or B150 for museum alone* ⊘ *Daily 9–3:30.*

Wat Po (*Temple of the Reclining Buddha*). The city's largest wat has what is perhaps the most unusual representation of the Buddha in Bangkok. The 150-foot sculpture, covered with gold, is so large it fills an entire viharn. Especially noteworthy are the mammoth statue's 10-foot feet, with the 108 auspicious signs of the Buddha inlaid in mother-of-pearl. Many people ring the bells surrounding the image for good luck.

Behind the viharn holding the Reclining Buddha is Bangkok's oldest open university. A century before Bangkok was established as the capital, a monastery was founded here to teach traditional medicine. Around the walls are marble plaques inscribed with formulas for herbal cures, and stone sculptures squat in various postures demonstrating techniques for relieving pain. The monks still practice ancient cures, and the **massage school** is now famous. A Thai massage (which can actually be painful, though therapeutic) lasts one hour and costs less than B200 (you should also tip from B50 to B100). Appointments aren't necessary—you usually won't have to wait long if you just show up. Massage courses of up to 10 days are also available.

At the northeastern quarter of the compound there's a pleasant three-tier temple containing 394 seated Buddhas. Usually a monk sits cross-legged at one side of the altar, making himself available to answer questions (in Thai). On the walls, bas-relief plaques salvaged from Ayutthaya depict stories from the *Ramakien*, a traditional tale of the human incarnation of Vishnu. Around the temple area are four tall chedis decorated with brightly colored porcelain. Each chedi represents one of the first four kings of the Chakri Dynasty. Don't be perturbed by the statues that guard the compound's entrance and poke good-natured fun at *farang* (foreigners). These towering figures, some of whom wear farcical top hats, are supposed to scare away evil spirits—they were modeled after the Europeans who plundered China during the Opium Wars. ⊠ *Chetuphon Rd., Old City* ☎ *02/225–9595* ⊕ *www.watpho. com* ⊠ *B100* ⊙ *Daily 8:30–5.*

NEED A BREAK?

Taking in all the sights can be exhausting, especially on a hot and muggy day. Fortunately, two parks by the Grand Palace provide some respite from the heat. **Sanam Luang** is north of the palace and Wat Phra Kaew. Trees offer shade and benches a place to sit with a cold drink and a snack from one of the vendors. You can also buy bread if you want to feed the numerous pigeons. **Suan Saranrom**, across from the southeast corner of the palace and the northeast corner of Wat Po, is smaller but just as pleasant. It's surrounded by well-kept government buildings. In the late afternoon you can join the free community aerobics sessions.

Wat Saket. A well-known landmark, the towering gold chedi of Wat Saket, also known as the Golden Mount, was once the highest point in the city. King Rama III began construction of this temple, but it wasn't completed until the reign of Rama V. On a clear day the view from the top is magnificent. Every November, at the time of the Loi Krathong festival, the temple hosts a popular fair with food stalls and performances. ■TIP→ To reach the gilded chedi you must ascend an exhausting 318 steps, so don't attempt the climb on a hot afternoon. ⊠ *Chakkaphatdi Phong Rd., Old City* ☎ *02/621–0576* ⊠ *B20* ⊙ *Daily 8–5.*

WORTH NOTING

Democracy Monument. One of Bangkok's biggest and best-known landmarks, the monument anchors a large traffic circle three blocks from the eastern end of Khao San Road. Not frequented much by tourists, it commemorates the establishment of a constitutional monarchy in Thailand in 1932. ⊠ *Ratchadamnoen Rd., at Dinso Rd., Old City* ⊒ *Free.*

National Gallery. Although it doesn't get nearly as much attention as the National Museum, the gallery has a permanent collection of modern and traditional Thai art that is worth seeking out. There are also frequent temporary shows from around the country and abroad. To get to the gallery, walk down Na Phra That Road, past the National Theater and toward the river. Go under the bridge, then turn right and walk about 200 meters (650 feet); the gallery is on your left. The building used to house the royal mint. ⊠ *4 Chao Fa Rd., Phra Nakhon* ☎ *02/281-2224* ⊒ *B100* ☉ *Wed.–Sun. 9–4.*

National Museum. There's no better place to acquaint yourself with Thai history than the National Museum, which also holds one of the world's best collections of Southeast Asian art. The exhibitions of Thai artworks and artifacts begin with the ceramic utensils and bronze ware of the Ban Chiang people (4000–3000 BC). Most of the masterpieces from the northern provinces are displayed here, not in museums there. ■TIP→ **Free guided tours in English take place on Wednesday and Thursday, usually at 9:30 am.** ⊠ *4 Na Phra That Rd., Phra Nakhon* ☎ *02/224-1333* ⊒ *B200* ☉ *Wed.–Sun. 9–4* Ⓜ *Skytrain: Hua Lamphong.*

October 14 Memorial. The memorial honors Thais killed during a student-led uprising against military rule. That revolt began on October 14, 1973, and tributes to people killed in October 1976 and May 1992 in similar protests have also been incorporated. Although most of the inscriptions are written in Thai, the memorial is a sobering sight, especially being so close to the Democracy Monument, which acknowledges the establishment of the constitutional monarchy. Traffic is always whizzing about, the gate is often closed, and there seem to be no regular hours, though there are painting exhibitions at times. ⊠ *Ratchadamnoen and Tanao Rds., Banglamphu* ✛ *2½ blocks west of Democracy Monument* ⊒ *Free.*

BANGLAMPHU

In the northern part of the Old City, Banglamphu offers pleasant strolls, interesting markets, and Khao San Road, one of the world's best-known backpacker hubs. Visitors from dozens of countries

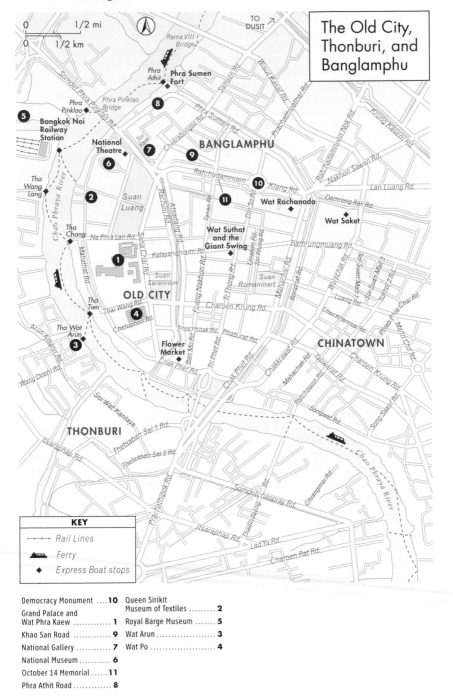

The Old City, Thonburi, and Banglamphu

KEY

⊢——→ Rail Lines

🚢 Ferry

◆ Express Boat stops

TUK-TUKS

Though colorful three-wheeled tuk-tuks are somewhat of a symbol of Bangkok, they're really only a good option when traffic is light—otherwise you can end up sitting in gridlock, sweating, and sucking in car fumes. They're also unmetered, their drivers prone to overcharging; unless you are good at bargaining, you may well end up paying more for a tuk-tuk than for a metered taxi. Some tuk-tuk drivers drive like madmen, and an accident in a tuk tuk can be scary. Expats are loath to enter a tuk-tuk, but for many tourists, a trip to Bangkok isn't complete without a ride.

■**TIP**→ Watch out for unscrupulous tuk-tuk drivers who offer cut-rate tours, then take you directly to jewelry and clothing shops that pay them a commission. If a trip to Bangkok does not seem complete without a tuk-tuk adventure, pay half of what the driver suggests, insist on being taken to your destination, and hold on for dear life.

populate the scene year-round, served by an equally diverse selection of restaurants and street vendors. During high season 10,000 people a day call the area home.

Khao San Road. This thoroughfare, whose name means "Shining Rice," has been the heart of the international backpacking scene for decades. In the past few years, stabs at trendiness have been made, with new outdoor bars, a glut of negligible western restaurants, and some reasonably nice hotels sharing the space with the ubiquitous low-budget guesthouses, some of which aren't actually budget anymore. The road has become popular as well with Thais, who frequent the bars and watch the farang.

Sunset marks the start of a busy street market. Khao San is closed to traffic at night, making early evening the best time to stroll or sit back and people-watch. The frenetic activity can, depending on your perspective, be infectious or overwhelming. During Songkran, the Thai New Year, in mid-April, Khao San turns into one huge wet-and-wild water fight. Join in the fun only if you don't mind being soaked to the bone. ⊠ *Khao San Rd., Banglamphu* ✣ *Between Chakrapong and Tanao Rds.; head southeast from Phra Athit ferry pier.*

Phra Athit Road. Chao Phraya breezes cool the short path that leads from the Phra Athit ferry pier to Santichaiprakarn Park, a tree-lined spot at the northern end of Phra Athit Road. The park, a delightful place to sit and watch the river, contains **Phra Sumen Fort,** one of the two remaining forts of the original 14 built under King Rama I. Some of the buildings along Phra Athit Road itself date back more than 100 years. At night the street, a favorite of university students, comes alive with little bars and restaurants hosting live music. ⊠ *Phra Athit Rd., Banglamphu* ✣ *Take taxi, or Chao Phraya ferry to Phra Athit pier.*

DUSIT

More than any other neighborhood in the city, this area north of Banglamphu seems calm and orderly. Its tree-shaded boulevards and elegant buildings befit the district that holds Chitlada Palace, the official residence of the king and queen. The neighborhood's layout was the work of King Rama V, the first of the country's monarchs to visit Europe. He returned with a grand plan to remake his capital after the great cities he had visited. Dusit is a sprawling area, but luckily the major attractions—the Dusit Zoo and the numerous museums on the grounds of Vimanmek Mansion—are close together.

Chitlada Palace. The king used to reside at this palace across from Dusit Park. Although it's closed to the public, the outside walls are a lovely sight, especially when lighted to celebrate the king's birthday, December 5. The extensive grounds shelter a herd of royal white elephants, though it's difficult to see them. ⊠ *Ratchawithi Rd. and Rama V Rd., Dusit* Ⓜ *Skytrain: Victory Monument (take a taxi from the station).*

FAMILY **Dusit Zoo.** Komodo dragons and other rarely seen creatures, among them the Sumatran rhinoceros, are on display at this charming little zoo. Also on hand are the usual suspects, including giraffes and hippos. While adults sip coffee at the cafés, children can ride elephants. ⊠ *Ratchawithi Rd. and Rama V Rd., Dusit* ☎ *02/281–2000* ⊕ *www. dusitzoo.org* 💷 *B150, children B70* ☉ *Daily 8–6* Ⓜ *Skytrain: Victory Monument (take a taxi from station).*

Vimanmek Mansion. The spacious grounds within Dusit Park include 20 buildings you can visit, but the mansion, considered the largest golden-teak structure in the world, is the highlight. The mansion's original foundation remains on Koh Si Chang, south of Bangkok in the Gulf of Thailand. King Rama V had the mansion dismantled and moved to its present location, using it as his residence from 1901 to 1906 while the Grand Palace was being renovated. The building itself is extensive, with more than 80 rooms.

The other 19 buildings include the **Royal Family Museum,** with portraits of the royal family, and the **Royal Carriage Museum,** with carriages and other vehicles used by the country's monarchs through the ages. There are several small air-conditioned restaurants offering a limited menu of Thai food. Admission includes everything on the grounds and the classical Thai dancing shows that take place mid-morning and mid-afternoon (usually 10:30 am and 2 pm). English-language tours are available every half hour starting at 9:15. Proper attire is required (no shorts, tank tops, or sandals). ⊠ *Ratchawithi Rd., near Dusit Zoo, Dusit* ☎ *02/628–6300* ⊕ *www.vimanmek.com* 💷 *B100, free with ticket from Grand Palace* ☉ *Daily 9:30–4 (last entry at 3:15)* Ⓜ *Skytrain: Victory Monument (take a taxi from station).*

Wat Benjamabophit (*Marble Temple*). Built in 1899, this wat is a favorite with photographers because of its open spaces and bright, shining marble. Statues of the Buddha line the courtyard, the magnificent interior has crossbeams of lacquer and gold, and an exquisite bronze seated Buddha is the focal point of the ordination hall's main altar. But Wat Benjamabophit is more than a glorious structure. The monastery here is a seat

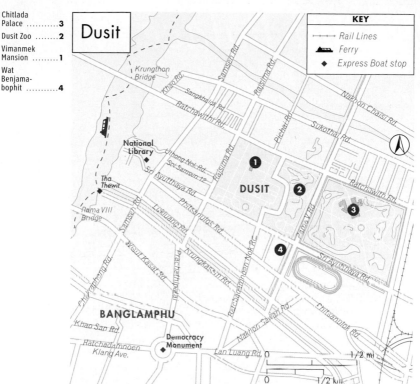

Dusit

KEY

⊢───┤ Rail Lines

🚌 Ferry

◆ Express Boat stop

of learning that appeals to Buddhist monks with intellectual yearnings. ✉ *Nakhon Pathom Rd., Dusit* ☎ 02/280–2273 ⬛ *B20* ☺ *Daily 8–5:30* Ⓜ *Skytrain: Victory Monument (take a taxi from station).*

THONBURI

Largely residential, Thonburi is where travelers go to take a ride along the city's ancient waterways. Most of Thonburi beyond the riverbank is of little interest to visitors. Many locals claim it retains more "Thai-ness" than the rest of Bangkok, but you'd have to live here, or visit for a long time, to appreciate that.

Royal Barge Museum. Splendid ceremonial barges are berthed on the Thonburi side of the Chao Phraya River. The boats, carved in the early part of the 19th century, take the form of mythical creatures in the *Ramakien.* The most impressive is the red-and-gold royal vessel called *Suphannahongse* (Golden Swan), used by the king on special occasions. Carved from a single piece of teak, it measures about 150 feet and weighs more than 15 tons. Fifty oarsmen propel it along the river, accompanied by flag wavers, two coxswains, and a rhythm-keeper. The museum is extremely difficult to find, so you may want to join a

Continued on page 64

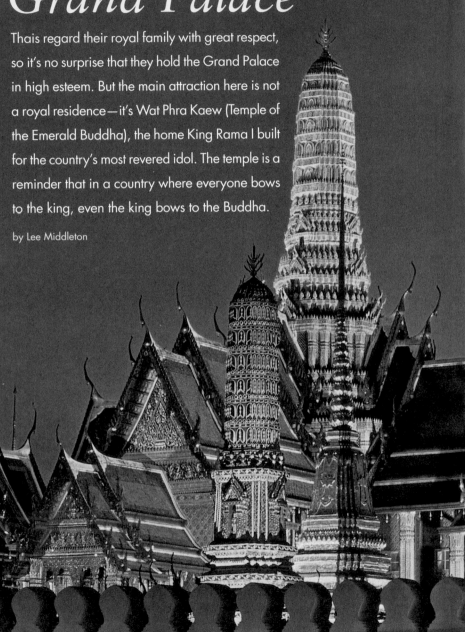

the Grand Palace

Thais regard their royal family with great respect, so it's no surprise that they hold the Grand Palace in high esteem. But the main attraction here is not a royal residence—it's Wat Phra Kaew (Temple of the Emerald Buddha), the home King Rama I built for the country's most revered idol. The temple is a reminder that in a country where everyone bows to the king, even the king bows to the Buddha.

by Lee Middleton

When Rama I was crowned in 1782, he wanted to celebrate the kingdom's renewed power. He moved the capital to Bangkok and set out to exceed the grandeur of Ayutthaya, once one of Asia's finest cities. The result was the dazzling Grand Palace compound, protected by a high white wall over a mile long. Rama I both ruled from and lived in the palace. Indeed, the royal family resided here until 1946, and each king who came to power added to the compound, leaving a mark of his rule and the era. Today, the Grand Palace compound's official use is for state occasions and ceremonies like coronations. The current monarch, King Bhumibol (Rama IX), lives in Chitralada Palace which is closed to the public and is in Bangkok's Dusit District, northeast of the palace.

GRAND PALACE COMPOUND

The palace grounds and Wat Phra Kaew are open to visitors, but many of the buildings in the complex are not. If you arrive by boat, you will land at Chiang Pier (tha Chang). Make your way to the main entrance on Na Phra Lan Road. **Wat Phra Kaew** is the best place to begin your tour. Other highlights are **Phra Thinang Amarin Winichai Mahaisun** (Amarinda Winichai Throne Hall), **Chakri Maha Prasat** (Grand Palace Hall), **Dusit Maha Prasat** (Audience Hall), **Phra Thinang Borom Phiman** (Borom Phiman Mansion), and the **Wat Phra Kaew Museum.**

Mural at the Grand Palace.

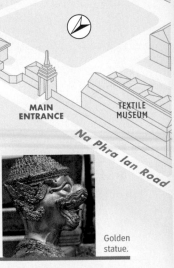

Phra Thinang Borom Phiman
5

1
Wat Phra Kaew

PRASAT PHRA DHEPBIDORN

HOR PHRA MONTHIAN DHARMA

PHRA MONDOP

Shop

PHRA WIHARN YOD

PHRA SIRATANA CHEDI

HOR PHRA NAGA

SALA SAHADAYA

MAIN ENTRANCE

TEXTILE MUSEUM

Na Phra lan Road

1 Wat Phra Kaew. King Rama I built Wat Phra Kaew—now regarded as Thailand's most sacred temple—in 1785. The main building, called *ubosoth*, houses the Emerald Buddha. The ubosoth has three doors; only the king and queen are allowed to enter through the central door.

2 Phra Thinang Amarin Winichai Mahaisun. The only part of Rama I's original residence that's open to visitors is used today for royal events such as the king's birthday celebration. Inside this audience hall are an antique boat-shaped throne from Rama I's reign that's now used to hold Buddha images during ceremonies, and a second throne with a nine-tiered white canopy where the king sits. At the entrance, you'll see gold-topped red poles once used by royal guests to tether their elephants.

Wat Phra Kaew.

Golden statue.

3 Chakri Maha Prasat.
Rama V's residence, built in 1882, is the largest of the palace buildings. The hybrid Thai–European style was a compromise between Rama V, who wanted a neoclassical palace with a domed roof, and his advisors, who thought such a blatantly European design was inappropriate. Rama V agreed to a Thai-style roof; Thais nicknamed the building farang sai chada or "the westerner wearing a Thai hat."

4 Dusit Maha Prasat. Built in 1784, the Audience Hall contains Rama I's original teak and mother-of-pearl throne. Today the hall is where Thais view royal remains, which are placed here temporarily in a golden urn.

5 Phra Thinang Borom Phiman. King Rama V built this French-style palace for his son (the future Rama VI) in 1903. Though later kings did not use the palace much, today visiting dignitaries stay here.

6 Wat Phra Kaew Museum. Stop by after touring the compound to learn about the restoration of the palace and to see the seasonal robes of the Emerald Buddha. Labels are in Thai, but free English tours occur regularly

PHRA THINANG BUDDHA RATANA STARN

PHRA THINANG SRIDHALA PIROMYA

2 Phra Thinang Amarin Winichai Mahaisun

PHRA THINANG MOONSTARN BAROMART

Inner Palace Area (Closed To Public)

PHRA THINANG SOMUT DEVARAJ UBBAT

PHRA THINANG PHIMAN RATAYA

Ticket PHIMANCHAISRI GATE

3 Chakri Maha Prasat

4 Dusit Maha Prasat

APHONPIMOK PHASAT PAVILION

Wat Phra Kaew Museum

SALA LUKHUM

6

CHANG PIER

Elephants, or chang, symbolize independence, power, and luck in Thai culture. Kings once rode them into battle, and the palace even included a department to care for royal elephants. This pier is named for the kings' beasts, which were bathed here. Many elephant statues also grace the complex grounds. Notice how smooth the tops of their heads are—Thais rub the heads of elephants for luck.

Chang Pier

TOURING TIPS

■ Free guided tours of the compound are available in English at 10:00, 10:30, 1:30, and 2:00 daily; personal audio guides are available for B100 plus a passport or credit card as a deposit.

■ The best way to get here is to take the Skytrain to Taksin Station and then board the Chao Phraya River Express boat to Chang Pier. It's a short walk from the pier to the palace entrance. You can also take a taxi to the Grand Palace but you may end up wasting time in traffic or getting ripped off.

■ Admission includes a free (though unimpressive) guidebook and admission to the Vimanmek Palace in Dusit, as long as you go within a week of visiting the compound.

✉ Sana Chai Rd., Old City

☎ 02/224–1833

🎫 B500, admission includes entrance to Wat Phra Kaew, Vimanemek Teak Mansion, and Museum of Textiles.

🕑 Daily 8:30–3:30.

■ Don't listen to men loitering outside the grounds who claim that the compound is closed for a Buddhist holiday or for cleaning, or who offer to show you the "Lucky Buddha" or take you on a special tour. These phony guides will ultimately lead you to a gift shop where they receive a commission.

■ Allow half a day to tour the complex. You'll probably want to spend three hours in Wat Phra Kaew and the other buildings, and another half-hour in the museums.

■ Wat Phra Kaew is actually worth two visits: one on a weekday (when crowds are thinner and you can explore at a leisurely pace) and another on a Sunday or public holiday, when the smell of flowers and incense and the murmur of prayer evoke the spirituality of the place.

The Grand Palace.

WAT PHRA KAEW

As you enter the temple compound, you'll see 20-foot-tall statues of fearsome creatures in battle attire. These are *yakshas*—guardians who protect the Emerald Buddha from evil spirits. Turn right to see the murals depicting the *Ramakien* epic. Inside the main chapel, which is quiet and heavy with the scent of incense, you'll find the Emerald Buddha.

Yaksha.

THE RAMAKIEN

The *Ramakien* is the 2,000-year-old Thai adaptation of the famous Indian epic the *Ramayana*, which dates from around 400 BC. Beginning at the temple's north gate (across from Phra Wihan Yot [the Spired Hall]) and continuing clockwise around the cloister, 178 mural panels illustrate the story, which, like most epics, is about the struggle between good and evil. It begins with the founding of Ayutthaya (City of the Gods) and Lanka (City of the Demons) and focuses on the trials and tribulations of Ayutthaya's Prince Rama: his expulsion from his own kingdom; the abduction of his wife, Sita; and his eventual triumph over the demon Tosakan.

Sita's Abduction

Section of *Ramakien*.

Rama's wife Sita is abducted by the evil demon king, Tosakan, ruler of Lanka. Disguising himself as a deer, Tosakan lures Sita to his palace. A battle ensues, forming a large part of the long and detailed epic, which concludes when Rama rescues Sita.

THE APSONSI

The beautiful gilded figures on the upper terraces of Wat Phra Kaew are *apsonsi*—mythical half-angel, half-lion creatures who guard the temple. According to Thai mythology, apsonsi inhabit the Himavant Forest, which is the realm between earth and the heavens.

Ramakien battle scene.

Apsonsi.

THE EMERALD BUDDHA

Thailand's most sacred Buddha image is made of a single piece of jade and is only 31 inches tall. The statue, which historians believe was sculpted in Thailand in the 14th or 15th century, was at one point covered in plaster; in 1434 it was discovered in Chiang Rai as the plaster began to flake.

When the king of nearby Chiang Mai heard about the jade Buddha, he demanded it be brought to him. According to legend, the statue was sent to the king three times, but each time the elephant transporting it veered off to Lampang, 60 miles southeast of Chiang Mai. Finally the king came to the Buddha, building a temple at that spot.

The Buddha was kept at various temples in northern Thailand until Laotian invaders stole it in 1552. It stayed in Laos until the 18th century, when King Rama I captured Vientiane, the capital, reclaimed the statue, and brought it to Bangkok.

Perched in a gilded box high above the altar, the diminutive statue is difficult to see. This doesn't deter Thai Buddhists, who believe that praying before the Emerald Buddha will earn them spiritual merit, helping to ensure a better rebirth in the next life.

The king is the only person allowed to touch the Emerald Buddha. Three times a year, he changes the Buddha's robes in a ceremony to bring good fortune for the coming season. The Buddha's hot season attire includes a gold crown and jewels; in the rainy season, it wears a headdress of gold, enamel, and sapphires; and, in the

Emerald Buddha in hot season outfit.

cool season, it's adorned in a mesh robe of gold beads.

Most Thais make an offering to the Buddha when they visit the temple. Inexpensive offerings, for sale outside the temple, generally include three joss sticks, a candle, and a thin piece of gold leaf stuck on a sheet of paper. At some wats, Thais stick gold leaves on the Buddha, but since that's not possible here, keep it as a souvenir or attach it to another sacred image (some elephant statues have gold leaves on their heads.) Light the candle from others that are already burning on the front alter, then light the incense with your candle.

WHAT'S A WAT?

A *wat* is a Buddhist temple or monastery, typically made up of a collection of shrines and structures in an enclosed courtyard, rather than a single building. Traditionally, monks reside in wats, but Wat Phra Kaew is a ceremonial temple, not a place of Buddhist study, so monks don't live here.

HONORING THE EMERALD BUDDHA

Thais usually follow an offering with three prostrations, or bows, to the Buddha. To prostrate, sit facing the Buddha with your legs folded or your feet tucked under you—then follow the sequence below. After prostrating you can sit in front of the Buddha in prayer or meditation for as long as you like.

1) Hold your hands together in a *wai* (palms together, fingers pointing up) at your heart.

2) Bring the wai up to touch your forehead,

3) Place your palms on the ground and bow your forehead until it's touching the ground between them.

4) Sit up, bring your hands back into a wai in front of your heart, and repeat.

TEMPLE ETIQUETTE

Even if you don't want to make an offering, pray, or prostrate, it's OK to linger in the temple or sit down. Here are a few other things to keep in mind:

■ Appropriate dress—long-sleeved shirts and long pants or skirts—is required. Open-toed shoes must be "closed" by wearing socks. If you've come scantily clad, you can rent a sarong at the palace.

■ Never point with your hands or your feet—at the Emerald Buddha, other sacred objects, or even another person. If you sit down in the temple, make sure not to accidentally point your feet in the Buddha's direction.

■ When walking around religious monuments, try to move in a clockwise direction. Thais believe that the right side of the body is superior to the left, so it's more respectful to keep your right side closer to sacred objects.

■ Keep your head below the Buddha and anything else sacred. Thais will often bend their knees and lower their heads when walking past a group of older people or monks; it's a gesture of respect even if their heads aren't technically below the monks'.

Offerings.

tour or take a taxi whose driver knows the area. ■TIP➔ Steer clear of scam artists offering tours or claiming that the museum is closed. ⊠ *Khlong Bangkok Noi, 80/1 Th Arun Amarin, Thonburi* ☎ *02/424–0004* 🎟 *B100* ⊙ *Daily 9–5.*

Fodor's Choice **Wat Arun** (*Temple of Dawn*). If this riverside spot is inspiring at sunrise,
★ it's even more marvelous toward dusk, when the setting sun throws amber tones over the entire area. The temple's design is symmetrical, with a square courtyard containing five Khmer-style prangs. The central prang, which reaches 282 feet, is surrounded by four attendant prangs at each of the corners. All five are covered in mosaics made from broken pieces of Chinese porcelain. Energetic visitors can climb the steep steps to the top of the lower level for the view over the Chao Phraya; the less ambitious can linger in the small park by the river, a peaceful spot to gaze across at the city. ⊠ *Arun Amarin Rd., Thonburi* ☎ *02/466–3167* 🎟 *B50* ⊙ *Daily 7:30–5:30* Ⓜ *Subway: Hualamphong (then river ferry).*

CHINATOWN

Almost as soon as Bangkok was founded, Chinatown started to form; it's the city's oldest residential neighborhood. Today it's an integral part of the city, bustling with little markets (and a few big ones), teahouses, and restaurants. Like much of the Old City, Chinatown is a great place to explore on foot. Meandering through the maze of alleys, ducking into herb shops and temples along the way, can be a great way to pass an afternoon, though the constant crowd, especially on hot days, does wear on some people.

Yaowarat Road, crowded with gold shops and excellent restaurants, is the main thoroughfare. Pahurat Road, Bangkok's "Little India," is full of textile shops, some quite literally underground. Many of the Indian merchant families on this street have been here for generations.

■TIP➔ Getting to Chinatown is easiest by boat, but you can also start at the Hua Lamphong subway station and head west to the river. The amount of traffic in this area cannot be overemphasized: avoid taking a taxi into the neighborhood if you can help it.

Fodor's Choice **Flower Market** (*Pak Khlong Talat*). This street lined with flower shops
★ is busy around the clock, but it's most interesting at night when more deliveries are heading in and out. This is where individuals and buyers for restaurants, hotels, and other businesses purchase their flowers. Just stroll into the warehouse areas and watch the action. Many vendors only sell flowers in bulk, but others sell small bundles or even individual flowers. As everywhere else where Thais do business, there are plenty of street stalls selling food. This very photogenic area that sees few tourists is well worth a visit. ⊠ *Chakraphet Rd., between Pripatt and Yod Fa Rds., Chinatown* Ⓜ *Subway: Hua Lamphong.*

Thieves Market (*Nakorn Kasem*). Once known for reasonable prices for antiques, this market now more closely resembles a flea market. It's not worth a visit on its own, but if you're strolling through Chinatown, pop into this warren of little shops. Mostly electronic goods are sold, and it really starts slowing down about 5 in the afternoon. For shopping,

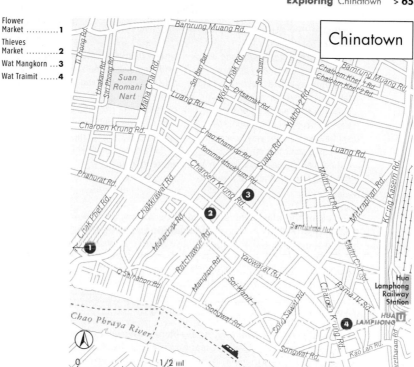

Chinatown

2

the Chatuchak Weekend Market is much better. ⊠ *Yaowarat Rd. and Chakraphet Rd., Chinatown* Ⓜ *Subway: Hua Lamphong.*

Wat Mangkorn (*Neng Noi Yee*). Unlike most Bangkok temples, this one has a glazed ceramic roof topped with fearsome dragons. Neng Noi Yee is a Buddhist shrine, but its statues and paintings also incorporate Confucian and Taoist elements. The wat is especially appealing during Chinese New Year, when thousands of Thais visit the temple to burn incense and make merit. ⊠ *Pom Prap Sattru Phai, Chinatown* ☎ *02/222–3975* ⊙ *Daily 6–6* Ⓜ *Subway: Hua Lamphong.*

Fodor's Choice   **Wat Traimit** (*Temple of the Golden Buddha*). The temple has little archi-
★   tectural merit, but off to its side is a small chapel containing the world's largest solid-gold Buddha, cast about nine centuries ago in the Sukhothai style. Weighing 5½ tons and standing 10 feet high, the statue is a symbol of strength and power that can inspire even the most jaded person. It's believed that the statue was brought first to Ayutthaya. When the Burmese were about to sack the city, it was covered in plaster. Two centuries later, still in plaster, it was thought to be worth very little; when it was being moved to a new Bangkok temple in the 1950s it slipped from a crane and was left in the mud by the workmen. In the morning, a temple monk who had dreamed that the statue was divinely inspired went to see the Buddha image. Through

SOI BOYS

At many *sois* (side streets) you will find clusters of motorcycle taxis. Their drivers, called "soi boys," will take you anywhere in Bangkok, although they are best for short trips within a neighborhood. Many soi boys know their way around the city better than taxi drivers. Fares are not negotiable—the drivers have set rates to nearby points, usually a bit less than a taxi. Motorcycles can be dangerous; helmets, when available, are often nothing more than a thin piece of plastic without a chinstrap. The risks and discomforts limit their desirability, but motorcycles can be one of the best ways to get around Bangkok, especially if you're in a hurry.

a crack in the plaster he saw a glint of yellow, and soon discovered that the statue was pure gold. In addition to the Buddha, Wat Traimit's museum devoted to Tha Chinese history is worth checking out. ✉ *Tri Mit Rd., Chinatown* ☎ *02/225-9775, 089/002-2700* ⊕ *www. wattraimitr-withayaram.com* ✉ *B40 for statue, B100 for museum* ⊙ *Daily 8–4:30* Ⓜ *Subway: Hua Lamphong.*

PATHUMWAN

Bangkok has many downtowns that blend into each other, but Pathumwan, which encompasses two major shopping areas, Siam Square and the Rajaprasong Junction, along with important attractions such as Erawan Shrine and the intriguing Jim Thompson House, is the closest thing to a "downtown" in Central Bangkok. Gaysorn Shopping Centre (for luxury goods) and the gigantic Central World mall are at Rajaprasong Junction, the intersection of Ratchadamri and Ploenchit roads. Among the numerous markets bearing Pathumwan addresses are the ones in Pantip Plaza—Thailand's biggest computer center and, with five floors of computer stores, an overwhelming shopping experience—and the Pratunam Market garment district. *See Shopping, below, for more about these malls and markets.*

TOP ATTRACTIONS

Erawan Shrine (*San Phra Phrom*). Completed in 1956, this is not a particularly old shrine by Bangkok standards, but it's one of the more active ones, with many people stopping by on their way home to pray to Brahma. Thai dancers and a small traditional orchestra perform for a fee to increase the likelihood that your wish will be granted. The shrine's location at one of Bangkok's most congested intersections, next to the Grand Hyatt Erawan and near the Chitlom Skytrain station, detracts a bit from the experience. Even with a traffic jam right outside the gates, though, the mix of burning incense, dancers in traditional dress, and many people praying is a memorable sight. Entry is free, but many people leave a small donation. A crazed man smashed the main statue in early 2006 and then was beaten to death by people outside the shrine. More recently, the shrine was the scene of a bomb attack in mid-2015, in which 22 people, including tourists, were killed, and

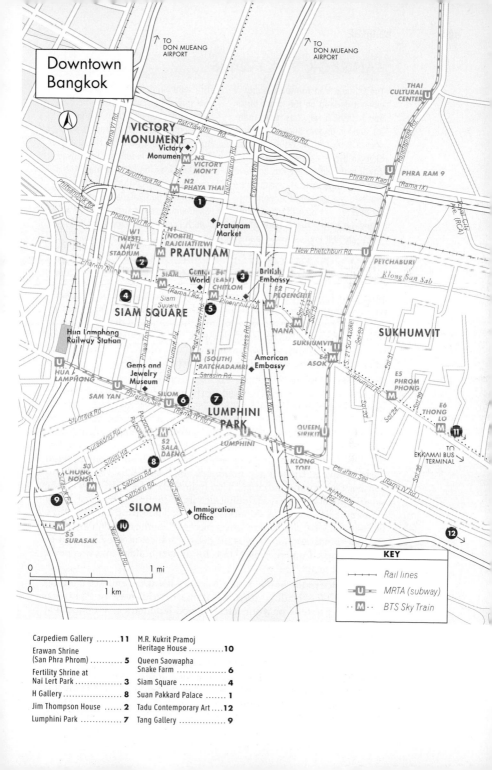

Downtown Bangkok

TO DON MUEANG AIRPORT

TO DON MUEANG AIRPORT

THAI CULTURAL CENTER

PHRA RAM 9

VICTORY MONUMENT
Victory Monument

N3 VICTORY MON'T

N2 PHAYA THAI

Pratunam Market

PRATUNAM

British Embassy

W1 (WEST) NAT'L STADIUM

N1 (NORTH) RAJCHATHEWI

SIAM

Center World

CHITLOM

PLOENCHIT

PETCHABURI

Klong San Sab

SUKHUMVIT

SIAM SQUARE

Hua Lamphong Railway Station

NANA

SUKHUMVIT

ASOK

PHROM PHONG

THONG LO

HUA LAMPHONG

Gems and Jewelry Museum

SILOM

SAM YAN

S1 (SOUTH) RATCHADAMRI

American Embassy

LUMPHINI PARK

QUEEN SIRIKIT

EKKAMAI BUS TERMINAL

SALA DAENG

LUMPHINI

CHONG NONSI

KLONG TOEI

SILOM

Immigration Office

SURASAK

0 _____ 1 mi

0 _____ 1 km

KEY

⊢—⊢—⊢ Rail lines

–U– MRTA (subway)

··M·· BTS Sky Train

BANGKOK'S SKYWAYS

The Skytrain transformed the city when it opened on the king's birthday in 1999. It now has more than 30 stations on two lines that intersect at Siam Square. Although the Skytrain bypasses many parts of the city, it is the speediest way to travel when its route coincides with yours. The fare is B15 to B52, depending on how far you plan to travel, and trains run from 5 am to midnight. Trains are still impressively clean and efficient, although they can get tremendously crowded at rush hour.

The sights in downtown Bangkok are spread out, but most are near Skytrain stations. Stations are generally about three minutes apart, so a trip from Chong Nonsi to National Stadium, which is four stations away, will take less than 12 minutes. At three stations—Chatuchak Park, Sukhumvit, and Saladaeng—the Skytrain intersects with the subway, which is convenient for some intercity travel.

more than 125 were injured. After both incidences, the shrine has been repaired and is as popular as ever. For those who are a bit spooked by its past, there are fantastic views of both the shrine and the worshipping going on from the Rajaprasong Skywalk up above, from where many visitors take pictures. ⊠ *Ratchadamri and Ploenchit Rds., Pathumwan* ⌖ *Free (small donation customary)* Ⓜ *Skytrain: Chitlom.*

Fodor's Choice   **Jim Thompson House.** Formerly an architect in New York City, Jim
★ Thompson ended up in Thailand at the end of World War II after a stint as an officer in the Office of Strategic Services, the predecessor to the CIA. After embarking on a couple of other business ventures, he moved into silk and is credited with revitalizing Thailand's silk industry. The success of this project alone would have made him a legend, but the house he left behind is also a national treasure. Thompson imported parts of several up-country buildings, some as old as 150 years, to construct his compound of six Thai houses. Three are still exactly the same as their originals, including details of the interior layout. With true appreciation and a connoisseur's eye, Thompson furnished the homes with what are now priceless pieces of Southeast Asian art. Adding to Thompson's notoriety is his disappearance: in 1967 he went to the Malaysian Cameron Highlands for a quiet holiday and was never heard from again.

The entrance to the house is easy to miss—it's at the end of an unprepossessing lane, leading north off Rama I Road, west of Phayathai Road (the house is on your left). A good landmark is the National Stadium Skytrain station—the house is north of the station, just down the street from it. An informative 30-minute guided tour starts every 15 minutes and is included in the admission fee. ■TIP➔ **The grounds also include a silk and souvenir shop and a restaurant that's great for a coffee or cold-drink break.** ⊠ *Soi Kasemsong 2, Rama I Rd., Pathumwan* ☎ *02/216–7368* ⊕ *www.jimthompsonhouse.com* ⌖ *B150* ◷ *Daily 9–5* Ⓜ *Skytrain: National Stadium.*

Suan Pakkard Palace. Eight antique teak houses built high on columns sit amid the undulating lawns and shimmering lotus pools of this engaging complex. The houses, which exhibit porcelain, stone heads, traditional paintings, and Buddha statues, were dismantled at their original sites and reassembled here. At the back of the garden is the serene Lacquer Pavilion, worth a look for its gold-covered paneling with scenes from the life of the Buddha. Academics and historians debate how old the murals are—whether they're from the reign of King Narai (1656–88) or from the first reign of the current Chakri Dynasty, founded by King Rama I (1782–1809). ⊠ *352–354 Sri Ayutthaya Rd., Phaya Thai* ☎ *02/245–4934* ⊕ *www.suanpakkad.com* 🏷 *B100* ☉ *Daily 9:30–4* Ⓜ *Skytrain: Phaya Thai (10-min walk east of station).*

WORTH NOTING

Fertility Shrine at Nai Lert Park. Hundreds of phalluses, from small wooden carvings to big stone sculptures decorated with ribbons, place this shrine honoring the female fertility spirit Chao Mae Tuptim in a category all its own. Women visit the shrine when trying to conceive, leaving offerings of lotus and jasmine. If Bangkok gossip is correct, the shrine has a good success rate. To get here, go to the Swissotel Nai Lert Park and walk to the end of the ground-level garage; the shrine will be on your right. Though open all the time, it's best visited before dusk. ⊠ *Swissotel Nai Lert Park, 2 Wittayu (Wireless Rd.), Pathumwan* 🏷 *Free* ☉ *Daily 24 hrs* Ⓜ *Skytrain: Chitlom.*

Siam Square. Fashion, education, and diverse shopping converge in glitzy Siam Square. Thailand's most prestigious college, Chulalongkorn University, is here, along with neon-splashed designer and other malls. At night along the sidewalk, a bohemian and latest-fashions outdoor market scene unfolds. ⊠ *Thanon Rama I, Pathumwan* Ⓜ *Skytrain: Siam.*

SILOM AND BANG RAK

The Silom area, with a mix of tall buildings, residential streets, and entertainment areas, is Bangkok's busiest business district. Some of the city's finest hotels and restaurants are in this neighborhood, which retains some charm despite being so developed and layered in concrete. Although the entire neighborhood across the Chao Phraya River falls under the post code name and number of Bang Rak, locals are more likely to term places that are on Silom Road as Silom, on Sathorn Road as Sathorn, and call the area around the riverside Bang Rak.

H Gallery. The gallery presents solo exhibitions by renowned Asian artists, many of them Thai. ⊠ *201 Sathorn Rd., Soi 12, Sathorn* ☎ *085/021–5508* ⊕ *www.hgallerybkk.com* ☉ *Closed Tues.* Ⓜ *Skytrain: Surasak.*

Lumphini Park. Two lakes enhance this popular park, one of the biggest in the center of the city. You can watch children feed bread to the turtles or teenagers rowing a boat to more secluded shores. During the dry season (from November to February), keep an eye and an ear out for Music in the Park, which starts around 5 pm each Sunday on the Singha stage; different bands each week play classical music or Thai oldies. There are many embassies in the immediate vicinity. The Royal Bangkok Sports

CLOSE UP

Roaming the Waterways

Bangkok used to be known as the "Venice of the East," but many of the *klongs* (canals) that once distinguished this area have been paved over. Traveling along the few remaining waterways, however, is one of the city's delights. You'll see houses on stilts, women washing clothes, and kids going for a swim. Traditional wooden canal boats are a fun (although not entirely practical) way to get around town.

Klong Saen Saeb, just north of Petchaburi Road, is the main boat route. The fare is B25, and during rush hour boats pull up to piers at one-minute intervals. Klong boats provide easy access to the Jim Thompson House and are a handy alternative way to get to Khao San Road during rush hour. The last stop is Pan Pha, which is about a 15-minute walk from the eastern end of Khao San Road.

Ferries (sometimes called river buses) ply the Chao Phraya River. The fare for these express boats is based on how far you travel; the price ranges from B13 to B32. The river can be an efficient way to get around as well as a sightseeing opportunity. Under the Saphan Taksin Skytrain stop, there is a ferry pier where passengers can cross the river to Thonburi for B3. Many hotels run their own boats from the pier at Saphan Taksin. From here you can get to the Grand Palace in about 10 minutes and the other side of Krungthon Bridge in about 15 minutes. Local line boats travel specific routes from 6 am to 6 pm.

These boats stop at every pier and will take you all the way to Nonthaburi, where you'll find quaint, car-free Koh Kret. A pleasant afternoon trip when the city gets too hot, the island has a Mon community and specializes in pottery.

A Chao Phraya Tourist Boat day pass provides a fun introduction to the river, and at B150 for the day it's a bargain. One advantage of the tourist boat is that while traveling from place to place there's a running commentary in English about the historic sights along the river. The tourist boat starts at the pier under the Saphan Taksin Skytrain station, but you can pick it up at any of the piers where it stops, and you can get on and off as often as you like.

Longtail boats, so called for the extra-long propeller shaft that extends behind the stern, operate like taxis. Boatmen will take you anywhere you want to go for B300 to B500 per hour. This is a great way to see the canals. The best place to hire these boats is at the Central Pier at Sathorn Bridge. A private longtail trip up the old klongs to the Royal Barge Museum and the Khoo Wiang Floating Market starts at the Chang Pier near the Grand Palace. Longtails often quit running at 6 pm.

Club is just west of the park. ⊠ *Rama IV Rd., Pathumwan* Ⓜ *Subway: Silom and Lumphini stations; Skytrain: Sala Daeng.*

M.R. Kukrit Pramoj Heritage House. Former Prime Minister Kukrit Pramoj's house reflects his long, influential life. After Thailand became a constitutional monarchy in 1932, he formed the country's first political party and was prime minister in 1974 and 1975. (Perhaps he practiced for that role 12 years earlier, when he appeared with Marlon Brando as a Southeast Asian prime minister in *The Ugly American.*) He died in 1995, and much of his living quarters—five interconnected teak houses—has been preserved. Throughout his life, Kukrit was dedicated to preserving Thai culture, and his house and grounds are monuments to a bygone era; the place is full of Thai and Khmer art and furniture from different periods. The landscaped garden with its Khmer stone-work is also a highlight. It took Pramoj 30 years to build the house, so it's no wonder that you can spend the better part of a day wandering around. ⊠ *S. Sathorn Rd. 19, Soi Phra Pinit, Sathorn* ☎ *02/286–8185* ⊕ *www.kukritshousefund.com* 🖃 *B50* ☉ *Daily 10–4* Ⓜ *Skytrain: Chong Nonsi (10-min walk from station).*

FAMILY
Fodor's Choice
★

Queen Saowapha Snake Farm. The Thai Red Cross established this unusual and fascinating snake farm and toxicology research institute in 1923, and it is well worth a visit. Venom from cobras, pit vipers, and some of the other 56 types of deadly snakes found in Thailand is collected and used to make antidotes for snakebite victims. Venom extraction takes place on weekday mornings at 11. The snake handling show and photo op is at 2:30 on weekdays and 11 on weekends and holidays. A few displays can be viewed any time, but photo op is the big draw. ⊠ *1871 Rama IV Rd., Pathumwan* ☎ *02/252–0161, 02/252–0167* ⊕ *www.saovabha.com/en/snakefarm_service.asp* 🖃 *B200* ☉ *Weekdays 8:30–3, weekends 9:30–1* Ⓜ *Subway: Silom; Skytrain: Sala Daeng.*

Tang Gallery. This gallery features works by Chinese artists, including con-temporary oil and watercolor paintings and ceramic sculptures. ⊠ *The Silom Galleria, 919/3 Silom Rd., Soi 19, 5th fl., Silom* ☎ *02/630–1114* ⊕ *www.tangcontemporary.com* ☉ *Daily 11–7* Ⓜ *Skytrain: Sala Daeng.*

SUKHUMVIT

Carpediem Gallery. A vivacious, charismatic Singaporean woman owns this gallery that often exhibits oversize artworks. Though based in Sukhumvit, her gallery displays works south of Silom in the Zanotti wine restaurant. ⊠ *Baan Sukhumvit, 119/1–2 Sukhumvit, Soi 36, Napasap Sup, Soi 5, Sukhumvit (Klong Toey)* ☎ *089/115–4014, 02/661–4323* ⊕ *rama9art.org/gallery/carpediem* Ⓜ *Skytrain: Thong Lo.*

Tadu Contemporary Art. This gallery shows works in many media by dynamic contemporary artists. ⊠ *Thaiyarnyon Building, 2225 Sukhum-vit, Soi 87, 2nd fl., Phra Khanong* ☎ *02/311–4951, 02/331–8848, 086/609–2671* Ⓜ *Skytrain: Bang Chak.*

WHERE TO EAT

Thais are passionate about food, and love discovering out-of-the-way shops that prepare unexpectedly tasty dishes. Nowhere is this truer—or more feasible—than in Bangkok. The city's residents always seem to be eating, so the tastes and smells of Thailand's cuisine surround you day and night. That said, Bangkok's restaurant scene is also a minefield, largely because the relationship between price and quality at times seems almost inverse. For every hole-in-the-wall gem serving the best sticky rice, *larb* (meat salad), and *som tam* (the hot-and-sour green-papaya salad that is the ultimate Thai staple) you've ever had, there's an overpriced hotel restaurant serving touristy, toned-down fare. In general, the best Thai food is found at the most bare-bones, even run-down restaurants, not at famous, upscale places.

If you want a break from Thai food, many other world cuisines are represented. Best among them is Chinese, although there's decent Japanese and Korean food as well. The city's ubiquitous noodle shops have their roots in China, as do roast-meat purveyors, whose historical inspiration was Cantonese. Western fare tends to suffer from the distance, although in the past few years many upscale and trendy western eateries have opened, some of them quite excellent.

As with anything in Bangkok, travel time is a major consideration when choosing a restaurant. If you're short on time or patience, choose a place that's an easy walk from a Skytrain or subway station. ■**TIP→ The easiest way to reach a riverside eatery is often on a Chao Phraya River express boat.**

Prices in the reviews are the average cost of a main course at dinner or, if dinner is not served, at lunch. Use the coordinate (✣ B2) at the end of each listing to locate a site on the Where to Eat in Bangkok map.

WHAT IT COSTS IN BAHT

	$	$$	$$$	$$$$
RESTAURANTS	under B200	B201–B300	B301–B400	over B400

Restaurant prices are for a main course, excluding tax and tip.

DINNER CRUISES

Though they're definitely touristy, dinner cruises on the Chao Phraya River are worth considering. They're a great way to see the city at night, although the food is often subpar. You might even want to skip the dinner, just have drinks, and dine at a real Thai restaurant afterward. Two-hour cruises on modern boats or refurbished rice barges include a buffet or set-menu dinner, and often feature live music and sometimes a traditional dance show. Many companies also offer a less expensive lunch cruise, though the heat can make these a little unpleasant. In general, it's wise to reserve a few days in advance, and reservations are a must for some of the more popular dinner cruises.

$$$$ THAI 🍴 **Horizon.** The buffet dinner cruise aboard the *Horizon* departs each evening at 7:30 pm. [$] *Average main: B2,300* ✉ *Shangri-La Hotel, 89 Soi Wat Suan Plu, Charoen Krung (New Rd.), Bang Rak* ☎ *02/236–7777* 🌐 *www.shangri-la.com/bangkok/shangrila/dining* 💳 *No credit cards* 🕓 *No lunch* [M] *Skytrain: Saphan Taksin.*

$$$$ THAI 🍴 **Manohra Song.** The most beautiful dining boat on the river, the *Manohra Song* departs on both lunch and dinner cruises. The vessel is smaller than most of its peers, with less space to walk around. You can order mediocre meals two ways off set menus: the gold one, with 12 dishes, costs B2,500 per person; the silver one, with eight dishes, costs B1,750. [$] *Average main: B1,750* ✉ *Anantara Bangkok Riverside Hotel, 257/1–3 Charoen Nakhorn, Thonburi* ☎ *02/476–0022* 🌐 *www.*

manohracruises.com ▭ *No credit cards* Ⓜ *Skytrain: Saphan Taksin, then hotel boat.*

$ ✕ **Yok Yor.** Departing each evening at 8 pm, the *Yok Yor* is a little like a
THAI floating restaurant. The boat ride costs B160, and the food is ordered
à la carte—which in this case is a plus. Ⓢ *Average main: B200* ✉ *885
Somdet Chao Phraya 17, Klong San* ☎ *02/863–0565* ⊕ *www.yokyor.
co.th* ▭ *No credit cards* ⊗ *No lunch.*

COOKING CLASSES

A Thai cooking class can be a great way to spend a half day—or longer.
You won't become an expert, but you can learn a few fundamentals and
some of the history of Thai cuisine. You can also find specialty classes
that focus on things like fruit carving (where the first lesson learned is
that it's more difficult than it looks) or hot-and-spicy soups. All cooking schools concentrate on practical dishes that students will be able
to make at home, usually with spices that are internationally available,
and all revolve around the fun of eating something you cooked (at least
partly) yourself. ■TIP➜ Book cooking classes ahead of time, as they
fill up fast. Most classes are small enough to allow individual attention
and time for questions. Prices vary from B2,000 to more than B10,000.

Blue Elephant Cooking School. Long a favorite, and connected with the
same-named restaurant, this school has a very friendly staff. The Thai
dishes taught here are heavily westernized. ✉ *233 S. Sathorn Rd., Ket
Sathorn* ☎ *02/673–9353* ⊕ *www.blueelephant.com* 🍽 *From B2,800 per
half day* Ⓜ *Skytrain: Surasak.*

Oriental Cooking School. The cooking school at the Mandarin Oriental
hotel is Bangkok's most established and expensive one, but the classes
are fun and informative, and the dishes tend to be more interesting and
authentic than those at other schools. Classes are taught in a beautiful
century-old house across the river from the hotel. ✉ *Mandarin Oriental,
48 Oriental Ave., Bang Rak* ☎ *02/659–9000* ⊕ *www.mandarinoriental.
com/bangkok* 🍽 *From B34,000 for a half day* Ⓜ *Skytrain: Saphan Taksin then hotel boat.*

THE OLD CITY

The Old City has every type of restaurant, including many holes-in-the-
wall serving excellent food.

$$$ ✕ **Raan Jay Fai.** "Cult following" would be putting it mildly: it is said
THAI that some people come to Thailand just for a serving of the *pad khee
mao* (drunken noodles) at this small open-air eatery with cafeteria-style
tables, green bare lightbulbs, and a culinary wizard presiding over a
charcoal-fired wok. The dish, which nearly everyone orders, is a rice-
noodle preparation with seafood including basil, crabmeat, giant shrimp,
and hearts of palm. At around B400, this is a major splurge by Bangkok
noodle standards. Some diners find it wildly overpriced, though many
foodies swear by it. The lump crabmeat fried with curry powder, though
not as popular, is also recommended. For a real splurge, try the fresh
abalone. Ⓢ *Average main: B400* ✉ *327 Mahachai Rd., Phra Nakhon*
☎ *02/223–9384* ▭ *No credit cards* ⊗ *Closed Sat. No lunch* ✛ *C3.*

BANGLAMPHU

Touristy Khao San Road is north of the Old City, though the tame Thai food available in this backpacker mecca is nothing to go out of your way for. Don't be afraid to sample the street food in the alleyways away from Khao San Road—it often makes for a memorable meal.

> **WORD OF MOUTH**
>
> "Maybe I've gotten more daring, but I enjoy going where I see Thai people eat—street markets and smaller local restaurants. The neighborhood between City Hall and the Grand Palace has some great local restaurants." –JohnH

$ INDIAN 🍴 **Roti-Mataba.** In a century-old building across from Santichaiprakarn Park on the Chao Phraya, this little restaurant serves decent, if not innovative, Indian cuisine. Few things on the menu cost more than B100. You can hear the roti—unleavened, whole wheat flatbread—sizzling near the door. The bread is filled with your choice of vegetables, chicken, beef, fish, or seafood, or just sweetened with thick condensed milk. Many curries, including *massaman,* a Muslim variation with a strong peanut flavor, are served at a steam table. Avoid the narrow downstairs dining area, which is unpleasantly hot and usually crowded. There's a more comfortable air-conditioned room upstairs, though the most atmospheric tables are out on the street in front. [$] *Average main: B60* ✉ *136 Phra Athit Rd., Banglamphu* ☎ *02/282–2119* 🌐 *www.roti-mataba.net* 💳 *No credit cards* 🕒 *Closed Mon.* ✥ *B2.*

DUSIT AND NORTHERN BANGKOK

Northern Bangkok is worth dining in only if you happen to be in the neighborhood for sightseeing, or if you really want to get to a part of the river that's off the beaten track.

$ THAI 🍴 **Aw Taw Kaw Market.** Bangkok's best food bargains are found at this legendary spot in the Chatuchak market. It's noisy, and you'll be inundated with sights and smells in the rows of food stalls; walk around and let your senses take over. The seafood, including raw crab, curried crab, and steamed whole fish with garlic and chili, is especially tasty. Items are dished out in plastic baggies; finding a seat and utensils can be a challenge. The trick is to buy something small at one of the few cafélike establishments that have seats, plates, and cutlery—then open your bags and feast. [$] *Average main: B100* ✉ *Phaholyothin Rd., North Bangkok (Chatuchak)* 💳 *No credit cards* [M] *Subway: Chatuchak Park; Skytrain: Mo Chit* ✥ *D1.*

$$$$ CHINESE 🍴 **Dynasty.** This restaurant has long been a favorite among government ministers and corporate executives, both for its outstanding Cantonese cuisine and its 11 private areas, perfect for business lunches or romantic dinners. The main dining room is elegant, with crimson carpeting, carved screens, lacquer furniture, and porcelain objets d'art. The Peking duck is among the draws (as are the jellyfish salad and drunken chicken), and the seasonal specialties include everything from hairy crabs (October and November) to Taiwanese eels (March). The service is efficient and friendly without being obtrusive. The restaurant

is near Chatuchak Park, in northern Bangkok. [$] *Average main: B750* ✉ *Centara Grand at Central Plaza Lad Phrao, 1695 Phaholyothin Rd., Chatuchak* ☎ *02/541–1234* 🌐 *www.centarahotelsresorts.com* ✍ *Reservations essential* [M] *Subway: Phahon Yothin* ✣ *E1.*

$$ THAI 🍴 **Kaloang Home Kitchen.** An alley near the National Library leads to this off-the-beaten-track restaurant on the Chao Phraya. Kaloang might not look like much, with its plastic chairs and simple tables on a ramshackle pier, but it's a local favorite, as much for the riverside location as the reasonably good seafood. Breezes coming off the water keep things comfortably cool most evenings. The generous grilled seafood platter is a bargain; so is the plate of grilled giant river prawns. Try the *yam pla duk foo*, a spicy grilled-fish salad that goes great with a cold beer. Also notable is the *larb goong*, a spicy ground-shrimp salad with banana blossoms. [$] *Average main: B200* ✉ *2 Sri Ayutthaya Rd., Dusit* ☎ *02/281–9228, 02/282–7581* 🌐 *www.kaloanghome.com* ✣ *C2.*

THONBURI

Thonburi has restaurants boasting unparalleled river views, along with dinner cruises.

$$$$ STEAKHOUSE 🍴 **Prime.** Bangkok's best steak house is a winner in multiple categories: design, views, and cocktails, but most of all cuisine. It all begins with the groundbreaking interior architecture, which skillfully incorporates the sweeping river and city views and the restaurant's open kitchen while still managing to feel intimate—an almost alchemical feat. Start with one of the signature martinis before moving on to the Caesar salad, prepared table-side, and perhaps a magnificent shellfish platter with fresh, briny oysters and lobster tails. Then there is the meat: whether it's Wagyu beef flown in from Australia or USDA Prime, no expense is spared in the kitchen (or on the bill). The grilling is done over an extremely hot open flame. The wine list is one of the best in the city, but everything is very expensive. [$] *Average main: B1,800* ✉ *Hilton Millennium, 123 Charoen Nakorn Rd., Klong San* ☎ *02/442–2000* 🌐 *www.3.hilton.com* ⏲ *No lunch* [M] *Skytrain: Saphan Taksin, then hotel boat* ✣ *C5.*

$$$$ THAI 🍴 **Sala Rim Naam.** The main reason to come here is to soak up the atmosphere, which includes a classical Thai dancing show. As the evening darkens and cools down, the twinkling lights of passing boats set a romantic mood at the outdoor tables overlooking the river. The restaurant itself is touristy, with westernized renditions of Thai food. There are set dinners and buffet lunches with plenty of choices. ■ **TIP→ To get here, take the complimentary shuttle boat across the Chao Phraya River from the Oriental Hotel.** [$] *Average main: B500* ✉ *Mandarin Oriental, 48 Oriental Ave., Bang Rak* ☎ *02/659–9000* 🌐 *www.mandarinoriental.com/bangkok* ✍ *Reservations essential* [M] *Skytrain: Saphan Taksin, then hotel boat* ✣ *C6.*

$$$ THAI 🍴 **Supatra River House.** Its Chao Phraya River location across from the Grand Palace makes this restaurant worth a visit. A free ferry from Maharaj Pier shuttles diners back and forth. In the former home of Khunying Supatra, founder of the city's express boat business, the restaurant has a small museum dedicated to the art she collected. The set

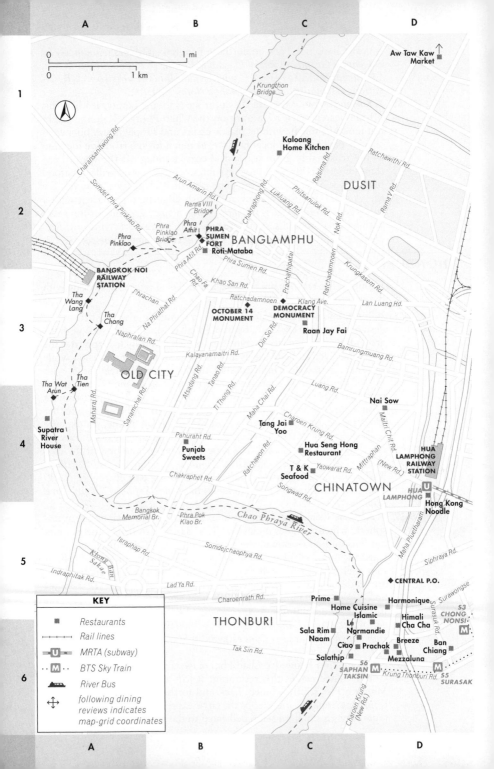

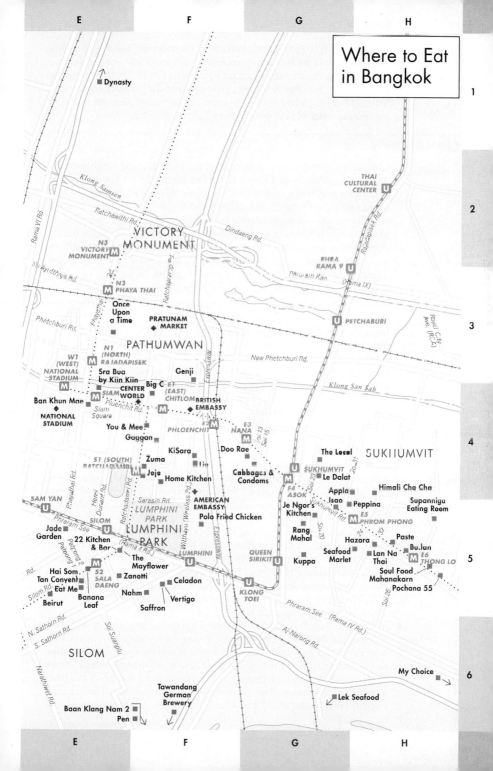

Where to Eat in Bangkok

Dynasty

THAI CULTURAL CENTER U

VICTORY MONUMENT

N3 VICTORY MONUMENT M

PHRA RAMA 9 U (Rama IX)

N2 PHAYA THAI M

PETCHABURI U

Once Upon a Time

PRATUNAM MARKET

PATHUMWAN

New Phetchburi Rd.

Klong San Sab

W1 (WEST) NATIONAL STADIUM

N1 (NORTH) RAJADAPISEK M

Sra Bua by Kiin Kiin

Genji

Big C

E1 (EAST) CHITLOM M

BRITISH EMBASSY

SUKHUMVIT

CENTER WORLD

Ban Khun Mae

SIAM M

Siam Square

NATIONAL STADIUM

You & Mee

Gaggan

PHLOENCHIT M

E2 PHLOENCHIT

E3 NANA

Doo Rae

The Local

KiSara

Zuma

Jojo

Home Kitchen

Lim

Cabbages & Condoms

SUKHUMVIT U

Le Dalat

E4 ASOK M

Appla

Isao

Je Ngor's Kitchen

Peppina

Himali Cha Cha

Supanniga Eating Room

S1 (SOUTH) RATCHADAMRI M

Sarasin Rd.

LUMPHINI PARK

AMERICAN EMBASSY

Polo Fried Chicken

E5 PHROM PHONG M

Rang Mahal

Hazara

Paste

Bo.lan

SAM YAN U

Jade Garden

22 Kitchen & Bar

SILOM U

LUMPHINI PARK

LUMPHINI U

Seafood Market

Lan Na Thai

E6 THONG LO M

The Mayflower

Kuppa

Soul Food Mahanakorn

Pochana 55

Hai Som Tan Convent

52 SALA DAENG M

Zanotti

Celadon

QUEEN SIRIKIT U

Eat Me

Banana Leaf

Nahm

Vertigo

Beirut

Saffron

KLONG TOEI

Phraram See (Rama IV Rd.)

SILOM

N. Sathorn Rd.

S. Sathorn Rd.

Ai-Narong Rd.

My Choice

Tawandang German Brewery

Lek Seafood

Baan Klang Nam 2

Pen

menus, from B750 to B1,200, make for easy ordering, but à la carte you can also sample dishes such as steamed sea bass in soy or spicy lemon. Thai dancing shows take place on Saturday at 7:30. [$] *Average main: B330* ✉ *266 Soi Wat Rakhang, Arunamarin Rd., Thonburi (Siriraj)* ☎ *02/411–0305, 02/411–0874* 🌐 *www.supatrariverhouse.net* ✍ *Reservations essential* [M] *Skytrain: Saphan Taksin, then river ferry* ✣ *A4.*

CHINATOWN

Chinatown is impressive in large part for its food. The neighborhood draws huge crowds of Thais who spend big bucks on specialties like shark's fin and bird's nest, which you'll see advertised on nearly every restaurant's storefront. Most of the food is Cantonese; many of these restaurants are indistinguishable from what you'd find in Hong Kong. In the middle of Chinatown, just off Yaowarat, there's a massive Indian cloth market known as Phahurat, and many Indian restaurants do business nearby. Don't overlook Chinatown's street food, the noodle and dumpling shops, and the fruit and spice markets.

$ CHINESE 🍴 **Hong Kong Noodle.** This famous noodle shop would be at home in Tokyo or Hong Kong, with its three narrow floors, the top one a no-shoes-allowed tearoom with sofas and floor seating. The second floor has regular table seating and a counter with benches along the window that offer great people-watching on the street below. It's a little more chic than your average noodle stand, but still quite cheap, and the location near the Hua Lamphong subway station makes it a good place to refuel before exploring the neighborhood or while waiting for your train. Plenty of noodle dishes are served, but the rice dishes are equally good. [$] *Average main: B99* ✉ *513–514 Rong Muang Rd., at Rama IV, Chinatown* ☎ *02/613–8977* 💳 *No credit cards* [M] *Subway: Hua Lamphong* ✣ *D4.*

$$$ CHINESE 🍴 **Hua Seng Hong Restaurant.** This expensive but worthwhile Chinatown classic takes you straight to Hong Kong with its excellent Cantonese roast meats—try the sinfully fatty duck—and soft, tasty goose foot–and–abalone stew. Don't pass up the fried pancake with eggs and plump oysters; the dim sum is also impressive. The restaurant is crowded and bustling, and service is authentically brusque. Like many of the neighboring Chinatown restaurants, the place hawks the inexplicably prized shark's fin and bird's nest dishes, but here as elsewhere, they're not worth the sky-high prices—both taste essentially like slightly more resilient glass noodles. Hua Seng Hong has other Bangkok locations, but this is the original and most lively spot. [$] *Average main: B350* ✉ *371–373 Yaowarat Rd., Chinatown (Samphanthawong)* ☎ *02/222–0635* 🌐 *www.huasenghong.co.th* ✣ *C4.*

$ ASIAN 🍴 **Nai Sow.** Regulars say this Chinese-Thai restaurant next to Wat Plaplachai has the city's best *tom yum goong* (spicy shrimp soup). Chefs may come and go, but the owner somehow manages to keep the recipe to this signature dish a secret. The food here is consistently excellent; try the *naw mai thalay* (sea asparagus in oyster sauce), the *phad kra prao kai moo goong* (spicy chicken, pork, and shrimp with basil leaves), the curried beef, or the sweet-and-sour mushrooms. Simpler options, like

Continued on page 83

BANGKOK STREET FOOD

by Robin Goldstein & Alexis Herschkowitsch

In Thailand a good rule of thumb is, the less you pay for food, the better it is. And the food offered by street vendors is very cheap and very good. At any hour, day or night, Thais crowd around sidewalk carts and stalls, slurping noodles or devouring fiery *som tam* (green papaya salad) all for just pennies.

The cooks at street stalls are Thailand's true culinary giants.

If you only eat at upscale restaurants geared to foreigners, you'll miss out on the chili, fish sauce, and bright herbal flavors that define Thai cuisine. Even if you're picky, consider trying simple noodle dishes and skewered meats.

A typical meal costs between B20 and B50 (you pay when you get your food), and most stalls have a few tables and chairs where you can eat.

Street food in Bangkok.

Vendors don't adhere to meal times, nor are different foods served for breakfast, lunch, or dinner, as Thais often eat multiple snacks throughout the day rather than full meals. It's OK to combine foods from more than one cart; vendors won't mind, especially if they're selling something like a curried stew that comes in a plastic bag with no utensils. Find a different stall that offers plates and cutlery, order rice, and add your curry to the mix. Enjoy!

SOM TAM

Thai chefs use contrasting flavors to create balance in their cuisine. The popular green papaya salad is a good example, with dried shrimp, tart lime, salty fish sauce, crunchy peanuts, and long thin slices of green papaya. Pair it with sticky rice for a refreshing treat on a hot day.

SOUR Lime adds a welcome tartness to salads and other dishes, counteracting sweetness.

SPICY Thais like it hot, sometimes using more than 10 fiery chili peppers per dish.

SALTY Instead of salt, Thais often use fish sauce and fermented shrimp paste, which have more nuanced flavors.

BITTER Roasted peanuts add a pleasant bitterness and crunch.

SWEET Palm sugar, a dark brown, natural, aromatic sweetener—will make you wonder why you've been using refined sugar all your life.

STAYING HEALTHY

Sanitary standards in Thailand are far higher than those in many developing countries. By taking a few precautions, you can safely enjoy this wonderful cuisine.

Fruit from Chatusak Market, Bangkok.

■ Avoid tap water. It's the bacteria in the water supply that causes most problems. The water on the table at stalls and restaurants is almost always purified, but stick with bottled water to play it safe.

■ Lots of flies are never a good sign. Enough said.

■ Know your stomach. Freshly cooked, hot food is least likely to contain bacteria. Steer clear of raw foods and fruits that cannot be peeled if you know you're sensitive.

■ Use common sense when selecting a street vendor or a restaurant. Crowds mean high turnover, which translates into fresher food.

WHAT SHOULD I ORDER?

Locals will probably be eating the cart's specialty, so if you're not sure what to order, don't be afraid to point. The following are a few common and delicious dishes you'll find in Bangkok.

LARB Another refreshing and flavorful shredded salad, larb (pronounced lahb) consists of ground meat or fish, lime, fish sauce, and a generous helping of aromatic kaffir lime leaves.

Larb.

PAD Noodles come in many varieties at street carts, and vendors add their own twists. Noodle soups with meat or innards, though traditionally Chinese or Vietnamese, are common in Bangkok, as are *pad khee mao* (drunken noodles) with vegetables, shellfish, or meat, wok-singed and served without broth. Another popular dish is *pad khee mao*—decadently big rice noodles with river prawns and basil.

Pad Thai.

TOM YUM This delicious and aromatic water-based soup—flavored with fish sauce, lemongrass, kaffir lime leaves, and vegetables—is a local favorite. *Tom yum goong,* with shrimp, is a popular variation.

YANG Thais love these marinated meat sticks, grilled over charcoal. Pork is usually the tastiest.

Tom yum.

WILL IT BE TOO SPICY?

Because most Thai cooks tone things down for foreigners, the biggest battle can sometimes be getting enough heat in your food. To be sure that your dish is spicy, ask for it *phet phet* (spicy); if you want it mild, request *mai phet* (less spicy). If you get a bite that's too spicy, water won't help—eat a bite of rice or something sweet to counteract the heat.

Food on sale at Damnoen Saduak floating market.

WHAT ARE ALL THE CONDIMENTS FOR?

At some street stalls, particularly soup and noodle shops, you'll be offered an array of seasonings and herbs to add to your dish: chilies marinated in salty fish sauce or soaking in oil; fresh herbs like mint, cilantro, and Thai basil; crunchy bits of toasted rice, peanuts, or fried onions; and lime wedges. Although it's a good idea to taste things you don't recognize so you don't over-flavor your meal, our advice is to pile it on!

Though it has a bad rap, the flavor enhancer MSG is sometimes used at street stalls and restaurants in Thailand. You can ask for food without it *(mai sai phong chu rat)* if it doesn't agree with you. You may also see MSG, a crystal that looks like white sugar, in a little jar on your table, along with sugar, chili paste, and fish sauce.

Two varieties of Thai basil.

YOU WANT ME TO EAT WHAT?

Pan-fried, seasoned insects such as ants, grasshoppers, and cockroaches, are popular snacks in Thailand. A plastic bag full of these crunchy delicacies will cost you about B20 or 50¢. To try your hand at insect-eating, start small. Little guys like ants are the most palatable, since they really just taste like whatever they've been flavored with (lime or chili, for example). Cockroaches have a higher squeamish factor: You have to pull the legs and the wings off the larger ones. And stay away from the silkworm cocoons, which do not taste any better than they sound.

At fruit stalls in Bangkok you may find the durian, a husk-covered fruit famous for its unpleasant smell. In fact the scent, which is a bit like spicy body odor, is so overpowering that some Thai hotels don't let you keep durians in your room. But don't judge the durian by its smell alone: Many love the fruit's pudding-like texture and intense tropical flavor, which is similar to passion fruit. Buy one at a fruit stand, ask the seller to cut it open, and taste its yellow flesh for yourself.

(above) Deep fried bugs (actual size).
(below) Durian.

fried rice, are also very good. The fried taro is an unusual and appealing dessert. $ *Average main: B150* ✉ *3/1 Maitrichit Rd., Chinatown (Pom Prap Sattru Phai)* ☎ *02/222–1539* ⚐ *Reservations not accepted* Ⓜ *Subway: Hua Lamphong* ✛ *D4.*

$

INDIAN ✕ **Punjab Sweets.** This vegetarian south Indian restaurant is always jam-packed with members of the local Indian community enjoying delicately crispy *pani poori* (crispy shells filled with potato and onion) or earthy samosas. The lighting is low, and the place is a bit drab, but the food is first-rate. There's an adjacent restaurant under the same management that serves meat, too. $ *Average main: B60* ✉ *11/1 Chakraphet Rd., Chinatown* ☎ *02/222–6541, 081/869–3815* ⊕ *www.punjabsweets. webs.com* Ⓜ *Subway: Hua Lamphong* ✛ *B4.*

$$

THAI ✕ **T & K Seafood.** Proudly displaying the freshest catches on ice out front, this enormous and popular seafood restaurant with outdoor tables outside its bustling corner location opens daily at 4:30 pm and serves until as late as 1:30 am. Whole fish is always a good option, and generally cheaper than the crustaceans, which are also tasty. The place offers both shark's fin and bird's nest soup, but if you've had either of these once, that's probably enough. Stick with such Thai options as the *pla kapong neung manao* (steamed sea bass), and you can't go wrong. $ *Average main: B300* ✉ *49–51 Phadungdao Rd., Chinatown (Samphanthawong)* ☎ *02/223-1519* ☽ *No lunch* Ⓜ *Subway: Hua Lamphong* ✛ *C4.*

$$

CHINESE ✕ **Tang Jai Yoo.** An open-air ground-floor seafood restaurant, full of festive round tables, Tang Jai Yoo is a great find. Whole crabs, lobsters, or sea leech come live from tanks inside the restaurant; stewed turtle soup is a fun departure from mainstream Thai cuisine. Roasted pigskin is one of the best terrestrial options. Ordering off the set menus is the best way to sample a variety of dishes. $ *Average main: B250* ✉ *85-89 Yaowapanit Rd., Chinatown (Samphanthawong)* ☎ *02/224–2167* Ⓜ *Subway: Hua Lamphong* ✛ *C4.*

PATHUMWAN

Unimaginably busy Pathumwan, which includes Siam Square, has a little bit of everything, from humble lunch stops to power-dining extravaganzas.

$

THAI ✕ **Ban Khun Mae.** Casually upmarket and aimed at tourists, this Siam Square restaurant serves authentic Thai cuisine in an atmosphere a few notches above that of the simple family restaurants. The dining area, filled with big round tables, is subdued, comfortable, and inviting. Start with the sensational *sai oua* northern sausages, and definitely order the steamed pancakes filled with minced pork. Finish with the *tum tim krob* (water-chestnut dumpling in coconut syrup with tapioca), and you'll likely leave both happy and satisfied. $ *Average main: B150* ✉ *458/6–9 Siam Sq., Soi 8, Rama I Rd., Pratunam* ☎ *02/250–1952 up to 13* ⊕ *www.bankhunmae.com* Ⓜ *Skytrain: Siam* ✛ *E4.*

$

THAI ✕ **Big C.** The food court on the fifth floor of the Big C shopping mall offers a staggering selection of authentic Thai (and a few Chinese) dishes at rock-bottom prices, with virtually nothing exceeding B80. Service is cafeteria style: you choose, point, and then bring your tray to one of the tables in the middle of the bustling mall. Before you order, you'll prepay at the cashier station and receive a debit card; your selections are deducted from the balance. B200 should be plenty for two, and you can get a refund on any unspent baht after you're done. Highlights include very spicy chicken with ginger, Cantonese-style honey-roasted pork with crackly skin, and excellent sweetened Thai iced tea with milk. [$] *Average main: B60* ✉ *Big C Supercenter, 97/11 Ratchadamri Rd., opposite Central World Plaza, Pratunam* ☎ *02/250–4888* 🌐 *www.bigc.co.th* 💳 *No credit cards* [M] *Skytrain: Chitlom* ✣ *F4.*

$$$$ INDIAN Fodor's Choice ★ 🍴 **Gaggan.** Named Asia's best restaurant in 2015, Gaggan is an absolute must for serious food lovers. Chef Gaggan Anand worked under the renowned Ferran Adrià at el Bulli restaurant, in Catalonia, Spain, and he's taken his mentor's teachings about molecular gastronomy to heart. The chicken tikka here comes with chutney foam, and the mutton *bhuna gosh* is vacuum-packed and bathed in water for a day. It works best to try one of the tasting menus; they range in price from B1,800 to B4,000. Some call Gaggan's cuisine molecular masala, though the chef describes it as "progressive Indian cooking." Whatever it is, it's provocative, tasty, and certainly not cheap. [$] *Average main: B500* ✉ *68/1 Soi Langsuan, near Ploenchit Rd., Pathumwan* ☎ *02/652–1700* 🌐 *www.eatatgaggan.com* 🕒 *No lunch* ✍ *Reservations essential* [M] *Skytrain: Ploenchit* ✣ *F4.*

$$$$ JAPANESE 🍴 **Genji.** It's not uncommon for newcomers to find the atmosphere chilly at Bangkok's many fine Japanese restaurants, but Genji is the happy exception. The staff here is uniformly pleasant. There's an excellent sushi bar and several small private rooms where you can enjoy succulent grilled eel or a Kobe beef roll with asparagus and fried bean curd. The well-conceived set menus for lunch and dinner provide a nice change from typical Thai fare. Lunch seats fill up quickly, and dinner sometimes requires a wait. [$] *Average main: B750* ✉ *Swissotel Nai Lert Park, 2 Wittayu (Wireless Rd.), Pathumwan* ☎ *02/253–0123* 🌐 *www.swissotel.com/bangkok* [M] *Skytrain: Ploenchit* ✣ *F4.*

$ THAI 🍴 **Home Kitchen** (*Khrua Nai Baan*). A true hole-in-the-wall where friends gather to celebrate the simple act of enjoying meals together, this restaurant turns out well-made local cuisine. Thai classics everyone should try at least once on a Bangkok trip excel here, among them tom yum goong (hot-and-sour soup with giant river prawns), redolent of lemongrass, Kaffir lime leaves, and galangal; the delicately crispy oyster omelet; the crispy catfish salad with green mango; and the fried whole fish in chili-and-lime sauce. A larger air-conditioned section of the restaurant operates just down the street. [$] *Average main: B150* ✉ *94 Langsuan Rd., Soi 7, just north of Lumphini Park, Pathumwan* ☎ *02/253–1888* 🌐 *www.khruanaibaan.com* 🕒 *No lunch* [M] *Subway: Lumphini* ✣ *F4.*

$$$$ ITALIAN 🍴 **Jojo.** A romantic, candlelit outdoor patio and a sleekly contemporary indoor dining space set a stylish tone that's echoed in the equally refined Italian cuisine served here. Begin with an antipasto plate starring burrata cheese, followed by the signature dish of squid-ink tagliolini in Boston lobster sauce. For dessert there's a tiramisu martini. The peerless wine list and the prices befit the luxe surroundings. [$] *Average main: B900* ✉ *The St. Regis Bangkok, 159 Rajadamri Rd., Pathumwan* ☎ *02/207–7815*

www.stregis.com/bangkok ▭ *No credit cards* ⚶ *Reservations essential* Ⓜ *Skytrain: Rajadamri* ✛ *F4.*

$$$$
JAPANESE

✕ **KiSara.** Upscale KiSara serves superb sushi, and the sake selection will please almost everyone. The service is almost uncomfortably deferential, but never pompous. Not surprisingly, the tea is delicious, and the sushi rice is expertly vinegared; you might find yourself ordering it as a side and eating it plain. The prized Matsuzaka beef dish is tasty, with an almost overwhelming surfeit of fat marbled throughout the meat. The prices at dinner are sky-high, but the set lunches are less expensive. $ *Average main: B800* ⊠ *Conrad Bangkok, 87 Wittayu (Wireless Rd.), Pathumwan* ☎ *02/690–9233* ⊕ *www.conradhotels.com/bangkok* Ⓜ *Skytrain: Ploenchit* ✛ *F4.*

$$$$
CHINESE

✕ **Liu.** You'll want to be spotted at this Chinese restaurant whose concept and design come from the creator of the equally snazzy Green T. House in Beijing. Light color wood dominates the interior, and the overall effect is soothing—and that's before the superior service you'll receive here. The cuisine, described as "neoclassic Chinese," is a fusion of different regional styles; the chefs are especially proud of the fried frogs' legs. Reserve well ahead, especially for the always overbooked dim sum lunches. $ *Average main: B450* ⊠ *Conrad Bangkok, 87 Wittayu (Wireless Rd.), Pathumwan* ☎ *02/690–9250, 02/690–9255* ⊕ *www.conradhotels.com/bangkok* ⚶ *Reservations essential* Ⓜ *Skytrain: Ploenchit* ✛ *F4.*

$$
THAI

✕ **Once Upon a Time.** Period photos of the royal family, movie stars, and beauty queens cover the pink walls of this restaurant that occupies two old teak houses. Antiques fill the dining rooms, and tables are set up in the garden between the houses. *Mieng kan,* a traditional snack of dried shrimp, dried coconut, peanuts, pineapple, chili pepper, and sweet tamarind sauce rolled together in a green leaf, makes an excellent appetizer. Afterward, move on to the chopped pork with chili sauce, beef fillet with pickled garlic, or whole grouper, served steamed or fried. The restaurant is down Soi 17 a ways, across the street from Pantip Plaza, the giant electronics market. $ *Average main: B250* ⊠ *32 Phetchaburi, Soi 17, Ratchathewi* ☎ *02/252–8629, 02/653–7857* ⊕ *www.onceuponatimeinthailand.com* Ⓜ *Skytrain: Ratchathewi* ✛ *E3.*

$
THAI

✕ **Polo Fried Chicken.** Though not everyone agrees that the fried chicken served here is Bangkok's best, this place is legendary, always packed with Thais and foreigners sampling chicken flavored with black pepper and plenty of golden-brown garlic. The best way to enjoy it is with sticky rice and a plate of som tam papaya salad, all for under B300. The restaurant is a bit hard to find—as you enter Soi Polo (Soi Sanam Khli), it's about 50 yards in on your left. At lunchtime, get here before noon to score a table before the office workers descend. If you're reasonably close to Lumphini Park, Polo will deliver to your hotel for B30. $ *Average main: B150* ⊠ *137/1–2 Soi Polo (Soi Sanam Khli), off Wittayu (Wireless Rd.), Pathumwan* ☎ *02/251–2772, 02/252–0856* ▭ *No credit cards* ⚶ *Reservations not accepted* Ⓜ *Skytrain: Ploenchit* ✛ *F5.*

$$$$ THAI **Fodor's Choice** ★

🍴 **Sra Bua by Kiin Kiin.** Luxurious and utterly unique, this restaurant upends the conventional wisdom about Thai cuisine and technique. Having dinner in this amazing place based on Copenhagen's highly praised Kiin Kiin restaurant is akin to attending a culinary magic show. Chef Henrik Yde-Andersen's tasting menus represent a veritable catalog of Thai flavors and dishes, though you may not recognize many of them through his foams, emulsions, and powders, with plenty of smoky liquid nitrogen hissing off the plates to heighten the effect. It's not just all show, though: the food is divine. You can order à la carte, but to experience the true range of Yde-Andersen's talents, consider splurging on the B2,700 menu. [$] *Average main: B900* ✉ *Siam Kempinski, 991/9 Rama I Rd., Pathumwan* ☎ *02/162–9000* 🌐 *www.kempinski.com/en/bangkok* ✍ *Reservations essential* ✥ *E4.*

$$ THAI

🍴 **You & Mee.** Hotel restaurants in Bangkok often disappoint, but this casual spot surprises with high-quality food at reasonable prices. Come for the good selection of noodles or the *khao tom* (rice soup) and congee buffets. ■ **TIP→ There's a khao tom buffet at lunch and dinner for B450 and B550 respectively.** [$] *Average main: B250* ✉ *Grand Hyatt Erawan, 494 Ratchadamri Rd., Pathumwan* ☎ *02/254–1234* 🌐 *bangkok.grand.hyatt.com* [M] *Skytrain: Chitlom* ✥ *F4.*

$$$$ JAPANESE FUSION **Fodor's Choice** ★

🍴 **Zuma.** A posh eatery with branches from Dubai to Miami, Zuma serves innovative Japanese fare. Working in an open kitchen, the chefs prepare signature dishes like the dragon maki made with prawn tempura, freshwater eel, avocado, and spicy tempura flakes, and the *buta bara yuzu miso* pork belly skewers with yuzu and miso mustard. The cocktails are equally exotic: the Rhubabu, for instance, is made with rhubarb-infused vodka, sake, and crushed passion fruit, and the Mandarin Fizz combines Japanese shochu infused with jasmine, gin, apple juice, mandarin purée, and sorbet. The restaurant, which comes off like an ultrasophisticated *izikaya* (a sake bar that serves food), is inside the St. Regis but not part of the hotel. [$] *Average main: B700* ✉ *The St. Regis Bangkok, 159 Ratchadamri Rd., Pathumwan* ☎ *02/252–4707* 🌐 *www.zumarestaurant.com* [M] *Skytrain: Rajadamri* ✥ *F4.*

SILOM

Silom has Bangkok's widest selection of restaurants, many in hotels, on the upper floors of skyscrapers, or around Patpong. You'll find everything from authentic, humble northern Thai food to elaborate, wallet-busting international cuisine.

$$$$ SEAFOOD **Fodor's Choice** ★

🍴 **22 Kitchen & Bar.** Stylish and vibrant, this recently launched rooftop restaurant and bar seems poised for major success. The young chef, part Hawaiian and part Mexican, showcases the best of the Pacific Rim in both entrées and tapa-size plates designed for sharing. Creative combinations such as oysters with kimchi puree, scallop carpaccio with avocado salsa, and Peruvian ceviche with spiced milk will leave your taste buds in awe, with the views of Lumphini Park and the Bangkok cityscape from the 22nd-floor perch—not to mention the well-crafted cocktails—only enhancing the delight. [$] *Average main: B800* ✉ *Dusit Thani Bangkok, 946 Rama IV Rd., 22nd fl., Silom* ☎ *02/200–9000*

⊕ *www.dusit.com/dusitthani/bangkok* ⊙ *No lunch* Ⓜ *Subway: Silom; Skytrain: Sala Daeng* ⊹ *E5.*

$$$ ✕ **Baan Klang Nam 2.** If you cruise the Chao Phraya River at night, you'll probably end up gazing upon the clapboard house this restaurant occupies, wishing you were among the crowd dining at this most romantic spot. The place is less touristy than others of its type, most of which are inside big hotels. Spicy fried crab with black pepper, steamed fish with soy sauce, river prawns with glass noodles, and stir-fried crab with curry powder are excellent choices from the seafood-centric menu. There's another branch, also on Rama III Road, at 288 Soi 14, but this one has more atmosphere. Ⓢ *Average main: B390* ⊠ *762/7 Bangkok Sq., Rama III Rd., Yannawa* ⊹ *Just south of Silom* ☎ *02/682–7180* ⊕ *www.baanklangnam.net* Ⓜ *Skytrain: Chong Nonsi, then taxi* ⊹ *F6.*

THAI

$ ✕ **Ban Chiang.** This old wooden house is an oasis in the concrete city; the decor is turn-of-the-20th-century Bangkok, with antique prints and old photographs adorning the walls. Ban Chiang is popular with the farang set, so your food won't come spicy unless you request it that way. Try the salted prawns or deep-fried grouper with garlic and white pepper, or dried whitefish with mango dip. Finish with banana fritters accompanied by coconut ice cream. Ⓢ *Average main: B175* ⊠ *14 Soi Srivieng, Surasak Rd., just north of Sathorn Rd., Bang Rak* ☎ *02/236– 7045, 02/266–6994* ⊕ *www.banchiangthairestaurant.com* Ⓜ *Skytrain: Surasak* ⊹ *D6.*

THAI

$ ✕ **Banana Leaf.** If you need to recuperate from Silom Road shopping, stop here for wonderful cheap eats. Try the baked crab with glass noodles, grilled black band fish, deep-fried fish with garlic and pepper, or grilled pork with coconut-milk dip. The menu also includes equally enticing vegetarian selections. There's a B400 minimum to pay by credit card. Ⓢ *Average main: B150* ⊠ *Silom Complex, 191 Silom Rd., 4th fl., Silom* ⊹ *Near Skytrain station's south exit* ☎ *02/231–3124* ⊕ *www. bananaleafthailand.com* Ⓜ *Skytrain: Sala Daeng* ⊹ *E5.*

THAI

$$ ✕ **Beirut Restaurant.** A stone's throw from the hustle and bustle of Patpong, this relaxed neighborhood joint is a good place to enjoy an authentic Lebanese meal. Crispy falafel, grilled and stewed lamb dishes, hummus, tabbouleh, and other Middle Eastern favorites are all on the menu. The restaurant also has branches in Thong Lor and Sukhumvit. Ⓢ *Average main: B250* ⊠ *Silom Building, 64 Silom Rd., Silom* ☎ *02/632–7448* ⊕ *www.beirut-restaurant.com* ▭ *No credit cards* Ⓜ *Subway: Silom; Skytrain: Sala Daeng* ⊹ *E5.*

LEBANESE

$$$$ ✕ **Breeze.** Practically in the clouds at the State Tower, home of some of the city's priciest restaurants, this ultrahip eatery is where you'll spot international jet-setters and Bangkok's moneyed set. The startlingly futuristic design may leave you feeling transported to 2060, an effect that's most pronounced at night when the dining room glows with purple neon. The chefs show their proficiency with seafood in such dishes as wasabi prawns and wok-fried Maine lobster with champagne. There's a tasting menu—for a jaw-dropping B4,300—but you can also order à la carte. Open footwear, shorts, and singlets are not permitted. Ⓢ *Average main: B1,500* ⊠ *State Tower, 1055 Silom Rd., 52nd fl., Bang*

MODERN ASIAN

Rak ☎ *02/624–9555* ⊕ *www.lebua.com/breeze* ⊘ *No lunch* ⚠ *Reservations essential* Ⓜ *Skytrain: Saphan Taksin* ✛ *D6.*

$$$$ ✕ **Celadon.** Lotus ponds reflect the city's beautiful evening lights at this
THAI   romantic restaurant. The upmarket Thai food is good, with elegant
touches that cater to locals as well as foreigners. The extensive menu
includes preparations of enormous river prawns, excellent red duck
curry, stir-fried morning glory, and a good version of banana-blossom
salad. Some of the seafood dishes can be prepared in different styles, but
the best choice is usually with chili and basil. Ask for your dishes spicy
if you want the more authentic Thai balance of flavors—sometimes the
dishes are a bit too sweet. Ⓢ *Average main: B500* ✉ *Sukhothai Hotel,
13/3 S. Sathorn Rd., Sathorn* ☎ *02/344–8888* ⊕ *www.sukhothai.com*
⊘ *No lunch* Ⓜ *Subway: Lumphini* ✛ *F5.*

$$$$ ✕ **Ciao.** A riverside location with pleasant breezes and great views pro-
ITALIAN   vides a relaxed setting for Ciao's classical Italian fare. From bruschetta
to focaccia, everything on the menu is made with fine and fresh ingredients, meats and cheeses imported from Italy, and plenty of attention
to detail. Entrées include eggplant ravioli and saffron risotto; for more
adventurous eaters, there's pigeon breast with coffee sauce. Top-notch
wines complement the elegant food and surroundings. Ⓢ *Average main:
$800* ✉ *Mandarin Oriental, 48 Oriental Ave., Bang Rak* ☎ *02/659–
9000* ⊕ *www.mandarinoriental.com* ⊘ *Closed Wed. No lunch* Ⓜ *Skytrain: Saphan Taksin, then hotel shuttle boat* ✛ *D6.*

$$$$ ✕ **Eat Me.** This Aussie establishment is both a high-end eatery and a
INTERNATIONAL swank art gallery where temporary exhibits provide just the right atmosphere. Some think that the works of art on the walls and on the plates
are less of a draw than the young and hip crowd. Dishes like Japanese
cod in spicy coconut cream and the scallop ceviche with honeydew
and yuzu are just a few of the eclectic offerings that lean heavily on
seafood. If you're in the neighborhood to people-watch, Eat Me won't
disappoint. Ⓢ *Average main: B800* ✉ *Soi Pipat 2, Silom* ☎ *02/238–0931*
⊕ *www.eatmerestaurant.com* ⊘ *No lunch* Ⓜ *Subway: Silom; Skytrain:
Sala Daeng* ✛ *E5.*

$ ✕ **Hai Som Tam Convent.** A good sign of quality, this restaurant is packed
THAI with Thais sharing tables filled with northeastern favorites like grilled
chicken, spicy papaya salad, and savory minced pork. The open-air dining area can be hot, and it's often crowded and noisy, but that's part of
the fun. The staff doesn't speak much English, so the best way to order
is to point to things that look good on neighboring tables. Ⓢ *Average
main: B80* ✉ *2/4–5 Soi Convent, off Silom Rd., Silom* ☎ *02/631–0216*
▭ *No credit cards* ⊘ *Closed Sun.* Ⓜ *Subway: Silom; Skytrain: Sala
Daeng* ✛ *E5.*

$$ ✕ **Harmonique.** Choose between tables on the terrace or in the dining
THAI   rooms of this small house near the river. Inside, Thai antiques, chests
scattered with bric-a-brac, and bouquets that seem to tumble out of
their vases create relaxing clutter, as though you're dining at a rela-
tive's house. The staff is very good at helping indecisive diners choose
from the brief menu. The massaman (peanut sauce–based curry) pork
spareribs, the mild crab curry, and the deep-fried fish with lemongrass
are all excellent. *Chu-chee* (coconut-curry) prawns or *larb moo* (spicy

The view is spectacular from Bangkok's famous Sky Bar, in one of the city's tallest buildings.

pork salad) are slightly more interesting dishes, as is the *hoa mouk*—fish curry in a banana leaf. Over the years the crowd has become more touristy, but there are still Thais who eat here regularly. [$] *Average main: B250* ✉ *22 Charoen Krung (New Rd.), Soi 34, Bang Rak* ☎ *02/237–8175, 02/630–6270* ⏲ *Closed Sun.* [M] *Skytrain: Saphan Taksin* ✣ *D5.*

$$ INDIAN

🍴 **Himali Cha Cha.** Cha Cha, who cooked for Indian Prime Minister Jawaharlal Nehru, died in 1996, but his recipes live on and are prepared with equal ability by his son Kovit. The tandoori chicken is locally famous, but the daily specials, precisely explained by the staff, are often too intriguing to pass up. The breads and the mango *lassi* (yogurt drinks) are delicious. The northern Indian cuisine includes garlic naan and cheese naan, served with various dishes—the mutton tandoori is particularly good. The typical Indian-themed decor sets the mood at this oldie but goodie. A branch on Convent Soi in Silom serves similar food in a more spacious dining area, and there is a location at Sukhumvit Soi 31. [$] *Average main: B300* ✉ *1229/11 Charoen Krung (New Rd.), Bang Rak* ☎ *02/235–1569, 02/630–6358* 🌐 *www.himalichacha.com* [M] *Skytrain: Saphan Taksin* ✣ *D5.*

$ INDIAN

🍴 **Home Cuisine Islamic Restaurant.** Finding really good *khao mok gai* (chicken biryani) can be a challenge in Bangkok, but the rendition at this gem of a restaurant shines. Home Cuisine specializes in biryani, and its mutton just might be even better than its chicken. Both are served with pickled eggplant and a side dish of sweet yogurt sauce. There are plenty of Thai dishes on the menu, but stick with the biryani. The restaurant is a 15-minute walk from the Saphan Taksin Skytrain station. If arriving by taxi, tell the driver to come in via Soi 40. [$] *Average main: B120* ✉ *185*

Charoen Krung, Soi 36, near French Embassy, Bang Rak ☎ *02/234–7911* ▭ *No credit cards* ⊙ *No lunch Sun.* Ⓜ *Skytrain: Saphan Taksin* ✛ *D5.*

$$$$
CHINESE
✕ **Jade Garden.** You won't find a better dim sum brunch in Bangkok than the one at Jade Garden. The decor is more understated than at many expensive Chinese restaurants, with a remarkable wood-beam ceiling and softly lighted screens. Private dining rooms are available with notice. Two good dinner specials are fried Hong Kong noodles and pressed duck with tea leaves. Look for the monthly "special promotion" dish starring seasonal ingredients. Ⓢ *Average main: B500* ⊠ *Montien Hotel, 54 Surawong Rd., Silom* ☎ *02/233–7060* ⊕ *www.montien.com/ bangkok* Ⓜ *Subway: Silom; Skytrain: Sala Daeng* ✛ *E5.*

$$$$
FRENCH
✕ **Le Normandie.** Atop the Mandarin Oriental, this legendary restaurant commands an impressive view of the Chao Phraya. France's most highly esteemed chefs periodically take over the kitchen, often importing ingredients from the old country to use in their creations. Even when no superstar is on the scene, the food is remarkable. The pricey menu—it's hard to spend less than B5,000 at dinner— often includes classic dishes like slow-cooked shoulder of lamb. The best bet is the prix-fixe discovery menu for B4,700. A jacket is required for men at dinner. Ⓢ *Average main: B2,100* ⊠ *Mandarin Oriental, 48 Oriental Ave., Bang Rak* ☎ *02/659–9000* ⊕ *www.mandarinoriental.com* ⊙ *No lunch Sun.* ⌖ *Reservations essential* 🏛 *Jacket required* Ⓜ *Skytrain: Saphan Taksin, then hotel shuttle boat* ✛ *C6.*

$$
THAI
Fodor's Choice
★
✕ **Lek Seafood.** This unassuming storefront beneath an overpass is the sort of establishment that brings international foodies flocking to Bangkok. They come for the spicy crab salad with lemongrass, the catfish with toasted rice salad, and the fried grouper topped with chili sauce— all expertly cooked and perfectly balanced with the five flavors. The interior here is nothing special, with poor lighting and bluish walls, but the lively buzz makes up for it. Locals in the know head to Lek because it's less expensive than many other seafood places. Ⓢ *Average main: B300* ⊠ *156 Narathiwat Ratchanakharin Rd., Soi 3, below Skytrain station, Bang Rak* ☎ *02/636–6460* ⊙ *No lunch* Ⓜ *Skytrain: Chong Nonsi* ✛ *G6.*

$$$$
CHINESE
Fodor's Choice
★
✕ **The Mayflower.** Regulars at this top Cantonese restaurant include members of the Thai royal family, heads of state, and business tycoons. These VIPs favor the six opulent private rooms (one-day notice required), but the main dining room is equally stylish, with carved wood screens, porcelain vases, and an air of refinement that befits the outstanding food. Peking duck skin is served without a shred of meat, with roti-like pancakes, plum sauce, and fresh onions. Dim sum options are also stellar, especially the fried taro and pork rolls and the green-tea steam rolls. Razor clams, when in season, are always a big hit. The wines poured here are excellent, if pricey. Ⓢ *Average main: B620* ⊠ *Dusit Thani Bangkok, 946 Rama IV Rd., Silom* ☎ *02/200–9000* ⊕ *www. dusit.com/dusitthani/bangkok/dining/the-mayflower* ⌖ *Reservations essential* Ⓜ *Subway: Silom; Skytrain: Sala Daeng* ✛ *E5.*

$$$$ MODERN EUROPEAN 🍴 **Mezzaluna.** This blockbuster restaurant soars above the rest of Bangkok in the massive State Tower. A string quartet serenades you and the city's nouveau riche while you dine on innovative European-influenced preparations of caviar, foie gras, lobster, and so on. The food is good, if not great, but more importantly the view is peerless. Don't come, though, unless you're ready to spend: this might be the most expensive restaurant in Bangkok. Four-course tasting menus start at B4,900, and seven-course ones go for B5,900 and up. [$] *Average main: B4,900* ✉ *State Tower, 1055 Silom Rd., 65th fl., Bang Rak* ☎ *02/624–9555* 🌐 *www.lebua.com* ⏲ *Closed Mon. No lunch* ✍ *Reservations essential* [M] *Skytrain: Saphan Taksin* ✥ *D6.*

$$$$ THAI Fodor'sChoice ★ 🍴 **Nahm.** Master chef David Thompson won accolades for his Thai eatery in London, and his outpost in Bangkok has been hailed as one of the world's finest restaurants. Nahm may be run by a foreigner, but the Thai preparations here are the city's best, with all the food bursting with flavor and not softened for foreign palates. Diners' favorites include the blue swimmer crab with coconut and turmeric curry, frog with chilies and cumin leaves, and grilled southern mussels. You can sample Nahm's hits by choosing the set menu for B1,700. Carefully selected wines from around the globe pair well with the fantastic food. [$] *Average main: B600* ✉ *Metropolitan Hotel, 27 S. Sathorn Rd., Sathorn* ☎ *02/625–3333* 🌐 *www.comohotels.com/metropolitanbangkok/dining/nahm* ⏲ *No lunch weekends* ✍ *Reservations essential* [M] *Subway: Lumphini* ✥ *F5.*

$$$$ THAI Fodor'sChoice ★ 🍴 **Pen.** This spacious restaurant has little in the way of atmosphere, but seafood aficionados come here to splurge. Expensive by Thai restaurant standards, it's still a bargain compared to most hotel restaurants. Many dishes are nearly impossible to find outside Thailand: enormous charcoal-grilled river prawns, Chinese-style mantis prawns, delectable mud crabs, sliced green mango in tamarind sauce, and deep-fried parrot fish with shallots. Even though this seafood temple is a little out of the way in Yannawa, it's not to be missed. [$] *Average main: B420* ✉ *2068/4 Chan Rd., Chong Nonsi, Yannawa* ✥ *Just south of Silom* ☎ *02/287–2907, 02/286–7061* [M] *Skytrain: Chong Nonsi, then taxi* ✥ *F6.*

$ CHINESE 🍴 **Prachak.** This little place with bare walls and tile floor serves superb *pet* (roast duck) and *moo daeng* (red pork), making it a favorite of many locals. The restaurant is famous for its wonton noodle soup. It's been in business for more than a century, and wealthy Thai families often send their maids here to bring dinner home. You may want to follow their lead, as the dining room can get crowded. Whether you eat in or take out, get here early—by 6 pm there's often little duck left, and by 8:30 pm the doors are shut tight. Finding Prachak is challenging, because it doesn't have an English sign. It's on busy Charoen Krung, near the Shangri-La Hotel, across the street from the big Robinson shopping center. [$] *Average main: B80* ✉ *Bang Rak Market, 1415 Charoen Krung (New Rd.), Bang Rak* ☎ *02/234–3755* 🌐 *www.prachakrestaurant.com* 💳 *No credit cards* [M] *Skytrain: Saphan Taksin* ✥ *D6.*

$$$$ THAI 🍴 **Saffron.** The creative modern Thai menu at Saffron is even more exciting than the stunning views from the 52nd floor of the Banyan Tree Bangkok. Try the signature *khong wang ruam,* Thai appetizers

for two, whose delicacies include grilled satay chicken, banana blossom salad, and crispy rice noodles wrapped in prawns. The giant prawns in yellow curry with saffron are also superb. Make sure to have a pre-dinner drink at the adjoining bar out on the balcony—the views are just dazzling. $ *Average main: B550* ⊠ *Banyan Tree Bangkok, 21/100 S. Sathorn Rd., Sathorn* ☎ *02/679–1200* ⊕ *www.banyantree.com/en/ bangkok* ☾ *No lunch* Ⓜ *Subway: Lumphini* ✛ *F5.*

$$$$
THAI
✕ **Salathip.** On a veranda facing the Chao Phraya River, this restaurant has a setting that practically guarantees a romantic evening. Be sure to reserve an outside table so you can enjoy the breeze. Although the food may not have as many chilies as some would like, the Thai standards are represented on the menu. Phuket lobster dishes and curried river prawns are among the ones to consider trying. The set menus include seven or eight Thai favorites and are worth the splurge of B1,600 (or more). The live traditional music makes everything taste even better. $ *Average main: B425* ⊠ *Shangri-La Hotel, 89 Soi Wat Suan Plu, Charoen Krung (New Rd.), Bang Rak* ☎ *02/236–7777* ⊕ *www.shangri-la.com/bangkok* ☾ *No lunch* ⚇ *Reservations essential* Ⓜ *Skytrain: Saphan Taksin* ✛ *C6.*

$$$
ECLECTIC THAI
✕ **Tawandang German Brewery.** You can't miss Tawandang—it resembles a big barrel. Food may be an afterthought to the 40,000 liters of lager and other beers brewed here each month, but the kitchen turns out decent Thai food, with some German and Chinese fare thrown in for good measure. The taproom, which is really why you should come, is especially boisterous when Bruce Gaston's Fong Nam Band performs its Thai-western fusion music. On nights the band's not playing, local singers warble Thai and western favorites. ■**TIP→ Tell taxi drivers the restaurant's full name, or you might be taken to a nightclub also called Tawandang.** $ *Average main: B350* ⊠ *462/61 Rama III Rd., Yannawa* ☎ *02/678–1114* ⊕ *www.tawandang.co.th* ☾ *No lunch* Ⓜ *Skytrain: Chong Nonsi, then taxi* ✛ *F6.*

$$$$
SEAFOOD
✕ **Vertigo.** You'll feel on top of the world at this classy 61st-floor space, one of the loftiest open-air restaurants anywhere. Tables are set near roof's edge for maximum effect. The international menu focuses on grilled seafood prepared with flair, and the service is friendly, but as with most of Bangkok's rooftop restaurants, you're paying for the sky-high ambience, not the food. Set menus here start at B2,900 for three courses, rising to B7,900 for seven. Because Vertigo is outdoors and so high up, it frequently closes when there are high winds, so you should have a backup plan. Food service doesn't start until 6:30, but it's nice to come for a sunset drink and enjoy the stupendous views. $ *Average main: B1,250* ⊠ *Banyan Tree Bangkok, 21/100 S. Sathorn Rd., 61st fl., Sathorn* ☎ *02/679–1200* ⊕ *www.banyantree.com/en/bangkok* ☾ *No lunch* ⚇ *Reservations essential* Ⓜ *Subway: Lumphini; Skytrain: Sala Daeng* ✛ *F5.*

$$$$
ITALIAN
Fodor's Choice
★
✕ **Zanotti.** Everything about Zanotti is top drawer, from the attentive service to the extensive menu focusing on the regional cuisines of Piedmont and Tuscany. You can order anything from pizza and pasta to fish and steak, but the traditional osso buco served with gremolata and saffron risotto is recommended. There's an unusually broad Italian wine list with selections by the bottle, glass, or carafe. The prix-fixe lunches

are a bargain. The low ceilings and closely grouped tables lend the place some intimacy, but the vibe is more lively than romantic, especially during the lunch and dinner rushes. [$] *Average main: B600* ⊠ *Saladaeng Colonnade Condominium, 21/2 Saladaeng Rd., Silom* ☎ *02/636–0002, 02/636–0266* ⊕ *www.zanotti-ristorante.com* ⚒ *Reservations essential* [M] *Skytrain: Sala Daeng* ✛ *E5.*

SUKHUMVIT

Sukhumvit is Bangkok's hippest area for dining and going out. Consequently, many of the restaurants here have more style than substance, but there's good food to be had, and the area of Thong Lor has evolved into a food-lover's paradise.

$$$
ITALIAN
Fodor's Choice
★
✕ **Appia.** A food critic turned restaurateur and the son of a Roman butcher teamed up to create this homey trattoria. Jarrett Wrisley, best known for the Bangkok street-food parlor Soul Food Mahanakorn, and his business partner, Paolo Vitaletti, a five-star chef whose dad toiled in a storied Roman meat market, run this small place for which reservations are highly advisable. Menu standouts include fresh-off-the-rotisserie porchetta; organic pork rolled with fennel, rosemary, and garlic; oxtail stew with herb gremolata; and divine Caprese in Puglia made with burrata cheese. Marvelous Italian wines have been chosen to enhance diners' appreciation of this masterful cuisine. [$] *Average main: B400* ⊠ *20/4 Sukhumvit, Soi 31, Sukhumvit* ☎ *02/261–2056* ⊕ *www. appia-bangkok.com* ⊗ *Closed Mon. No lunch Tues.–Sat.* ⚒ *Reservations essential* ▤ *No credit cards* [M] *Skytrain: Phrom Phong* ✛ *H4.*

$$$$
THAI
Fodor's Choice
★
✕ **Bo.lan.** Named after its two owners, a Thai-western couple, Bo.lan consistently appears on lists of Thailand and Asia's best restaurants. Relocated in 2014 to a renovated old house just off Sukhumvit, the restaurant is striving to have a zero carbon footprint within a few years—the owners grow their own vegetables, recycle organic waste, and purify their groundwater. In the here and now, their menu tantalizes taste buds with fresh and seasonal dishes like stir-fried soft pork bone with Thai rum and northern curry chicken with betel, fern, and indigenous spices. With its classy interpretations of traditional Thai cuisine, this place represents the best of what gourmet Bangkok is up to these days. Several tasting menus are offered for dinner from about B2,300 (B1,000 for lunch). [$] *Average main: B2,280* ⊠ *24 Sukhumvit, Soi 53, Sukhumvit* ☎ *02/260–2961* ⊕ *www.bolan.co.th* ⊗ *Closed Mon.* ⚒ *Reservations essential* [M] *Skytrain: Thong Lor* ✛ *H5.*

$$$
THAI
✕ **Cabbages & Condoms.** Don't be put off by the restaurant's odd name and the array of contraceptives for sale. This popular place raises funds for Thailand's main family-planning program. The food, geared to foreign tastes, is competently prepared; the dishes of note include the deep-fried chicken wrapped in pandanus leaves, the fried fish with mango sauce, and the crispy duck salad. C&C is comfortable and funky, with fairy lights giving it a warm, inviting glow. [$] *Average main: B300* ⊠ *10 Sukhumvit, Soi 12, Sukhumvit* ☎ *02/229–4610* ⊕ *www.cabbagesandcondoms.com* [M] *Subway: Sukhumvit; Skytrain: Asok* ✛ *G4.*

$$ ✕ **Doo Rae.** Many authentic Korean restaurants do business in Sukhum-
KOREAN vit Plaza, but this unpretentious spot is one of the best. Even with three
stories of tables, there's often a wait day or night. Barbecue featuring
bulgogi (thin slices of beef in a tasty marinade) is a good way to go—you
cook the meat yourself over a grill at your table—as are the substantial
kimchi and tofu stews. Drinks include sake and *soju*, a rice-based drink
similar to vodka but with a lower alcohol content. $ *Average main:
B300* ✉ *212/15 Sukhumvit Plaza, Soi 12, Sukhumvit* ☎ *02/653–3815*
Ⓜ *Subway: Sukhumvit; Skytrain: Asok* ✛ *G4.*

$$$$ ✕ **Hazara.** After a long day of sightseeing, the chic atmosphere at this
INDIAN upscale Indian eatery instantly alters one's mood. Plush couches and
beautiful drapes create a cozy feel, and there's a great drink list. Some
patrons feel the food doesn't hold a candle to the cheap Indian street
food you can find elsewhere in the city. Though the menu isn't overly
creative, there are some interesting options, including lentil soup and
tandoori chicken. Many vegetarian dishes and different types of naan
are also prepared. $ *Average main: B450* ✉ *29 Sukhumvit Rd., Soi
38, Phra Khanong* ☎ *02/713–6048* ⊕ *www.facebars.com* ☾ *No lunch*
Ⓜ *Skytrain: Thong Lor* ✛ *H5.*

$$$ ✕ **Isao.** Bangkok has hundreds of Japanese restaurants, but only Isao has
SUSHI a line out the door 365 nights a year. The reason is simple: this humble
Fodor's Choice little eatery serves up the most creative sushi rolls west of California.
★ The owner studied under the chef at the revered Green Tea in Chicago,
and the repeat clientele attests to the enthusiasm for his culinary flights
of fancy. Try the Jackie, a caterpillar-shape sushi roll with shrimp and
tempura, or the Volcano, a baked scallop in cream sauce fashioned to
resemble molten lava. The spicy tuna and salmon rolls are transcen-
dent, and the prices, compared to just about any other Japanese joint,
are very reasonable. Reservations are not accepted. Just show up, give
your name, and join the happy masses. $ *Average main: B350* ✉ *5
Sukhumvit, Soi 31, Sukhumvit* ☎ *02/258–0645* ⊕ *www.isaotaste.com*
🍽 *Reservations not accepted* Ⓜ *Skytrain: Phrom Phong* ✛ *G5.*

$$ ✕ **Je Ngor's Kitchen.** Locals adore this eatery for dishes like the glorious
THAI steamed Chinese cabbage with scallop sauce, the stir-fried crab in red
curry, and deep-fried rock lobster. The decor is homey but attractive,
with warm colors. The set menus for lunch are reasonably priced. Other
branches dot Bangkok, but the Sukhumvit location is the biggest. $ *Av-
erage main: B250* ✉ *68/2 Sukhumvit, Soi 20, Sukhumvit* ☎ *02/258–
8008* ⊕ *www.jengor-seafoods.com* Ⓜ *Skytrain: Phrom Phong* ✛ *G5.*

$$$ ✕ **Kuppa.** This light and airy space maintains the aura of its former life
CAFÉ as a warehouse, but it's certainly more chic than shabby these days, with
polished metal and blond wood adding a hip counterpoint to the cement
floors. An advantage to such a broad space is that, unlike at many
downtown eateries, each table has plenty of room around it. Kuppa
serves traditional Thai fare as well as many international dishes, and it
has attracted a dedicated following for its coffee, roasted on the premises, and impressive desserts. The one drawback is that the portions are
somewhat small for the price. $ *Average main: B350* ✉ *39 Sukhumvit
Rd., Soi 16, Sukhumvit (Klong Toey)* ☎ *02/663–0450, 02/258–0194*
⊕ *www.kuppa.co.th* Ⓜ *Subway: Sukhumvit; Skytrain: Asok* ✛ *G5.*

$$$$ THAI

🍴 **Lan Na Thai.** This hangout attracts a cool, mainly international clientele. The reasonably authentic Thai lineup includes the ubiquitous green papaya salad, steamed freshwater prawns, and duck with Kaffir lime leaf. More exciting are dishes such as the sea bass wrapped in a banana leaf and the pork belly made with Chiang Mai–style curry paste. The decor—plush comfortable seating, large tapestries—and toned-down dishes are geared to foreigners, but sometimes that's just the ticket after a long day of exploring. [$] *Average main: B500* ✉ *29 Sukhumvit Rd., Soi 38, Phra Khanong* ☎ *02/713–6048* 🌐 *www.facebars.com* 🕒 *No lunch* [M] *Skytrain: Thong Lo* ✣ *H5.*

2

$$ VIETNAMESE

🍴 **Le Dalat.** Classy Le Dalat, a favorite with Bangkok residents, consists of several intimate dining rooms in what was once a private home. Don't pass up the *naem neuang,* a garlicky grilled meatball you garnish with bits of garlic, ginger, hot chili, star apple, and mango before wrapping it in a lettuce leaf and popping it in your mouth. Seafood dishes—which are among the pricier options—include *cha ca thang long,* Hanoi-style fried fish with dill. [$] *Average main: B250* ✉ *57 Soi Prasarnmitr, Sukhumvit, Soi 23, Sukhumvit* ☎ *02/259–9593* 🌐 *www.ledalatbkk.com* ✍ *Reservations essential* [M] *Subway: Sukhumvit; Skytrain: Asok* ✣ *G4.*

$$$ THAI Fodor's Choice ★

🍴 **The Local.** This emphasis at this restaurant in a century-old house is on fresh traditional fare and hard-to-find regional specialties. Two worth investigating are *pla ta pien,* a local river fish stewed for 30 hours with sugarcane and ginger, and the lemongrass salad with wild betel leaves. Also of note are the southern-style pork underbelly stewed for four hours and served with quail and duck eggs, the homemade ice cream, and creative cocktails like tom yum martinis and dragonfruit mojitos. The Local, whose owner's family has run restaurants for many decades, receives high praise for its outdoor terrace, wood floors, and antiques and old photos. Along with the regular menu, make sure you're handed the smaller one with his recent additions. [$] *Average main: B320* ✉ *32 Sukhumvit, Soi 23, Sukhumvit* ☎ *02/664–0664* 🌐 *www.thelocalthaicuisine.com* [M] *Subway: Sukhumvit; Skytrain: Asok* ✣ *G4.*

$$ THAI

🍴 **My Choice.** Thais with a taste for their grandmothers' traditional recipes have flocked to this restaurant off Sukhumvit Road since the mid-'80s. The *ped aob* (whole roasted duck) is particularly popular. The interior is plain, so when the weather is cool most people prefer to sit outside. [$] *Average main: B250* ✉ *5 Sukhumvit, Soi 36, Sukhumvit (Klong Toey)* ☎ *02/258–6174, 02/259–9470* [M] *Skytrain: Thong Lo* ✣ *H6.*

$$$$ THAI Fodor's Choice ★

🍴 **Paste Restaurant.** An upscale, intimate eatery run by an experienced Australian-Thai husband-and-wife team, Paste elevates traditional Thai food and flavors to a whole new level. The duo's small menu includes a master-stock poached organic pork neck with red grapefruit and toasted sticky rice, an ensemble that melts pleasingly in your mouth, and steamed sea bass with white turmeric, fennel, and lemongrass. Paste has opened a second branch upstairs in the Gaysorn Shopping Centre, more convenient if you're staying downtown, but this original location is cozier. [$] *Average main: B480* ✉ *120/6 Soi Song Phi Nong, Sukhumvit, Soi 49, Sukhumvit* ✣ *Opposite Samitivej Sukhumvit*

Hospital ☎ *02/392–4313* ⊕ *pastebangkok.com* ⊗ *Closed Mon. No lunch* ⌂ *Reservations essential* Ⓜ *Skytrain: Thong Lor* ✛ *H5.*

$$$
PIZZA
Fodor's Choice
★

✕ **Peppina.** Hands down Bangkok's best pizzeria, warmly industrial-looking Peppina is booked solid on most nights. Chef Paolo Vitaletti of Appia trattoria fame is behind this restaurant whose experienced Neapolitan pizza chef works his magic in a beehivelike oven sculpted by Italian artisans. The attention to detail is evident in the special dough that's left to rise overnight and in the fresh buffalo mozzarella and other ingredients flown in from Italy. A good bet is the pie stuffed with aged sheep's cheese. Start the evening with an appetizer like the heavenly bruschetta with asparagus, ham, and stracciatella cheese. Exquisite soups, salads, and pastas are also on the menu. Beverages include craft beers, a few signature cocktails, and smartly selected wines. Ⓢ *Average main: B390* ⊠ *27/1 Sukhumvit, Soi 31, Sukhumvit* ☎ *02/119–7677* ⊕ *www.peppinabkk.com* ⌂ *Reservations essential* ✛ *H5.*

$
THAI

✕ **Pochana 55.** You wouldn't expect much by looking at this nondescript restaurant from the outside, but locals have been packing it night after night for years. The place, which started out as a late night *khao tom* rice soup eatery, has expanded to having one of the most extensive and tastiest Thai-Chinese menus in town. Just about any dish is a winner, but you will notice that many diners order a plate of *aw suan* (oyster and egg soufflé), some tom yum (hot-and-sour) soup, and a sizzling beef or fish platter. If you are in town during the rainy season, try the *dok krajon* (literally translated as "little flower") salad made with local vegetables, pork, and spices. Ⓢ *Average main: B150* ⊠ *1087–1093 Sukhumvit Rd., Thong Lor* ✛ *100 meters (110 yds) east of the corner of Sukhumvit 55* ☎ *02/391–2021* ▭ *No credit cards* ⊗ *No lunch* ✛ *H5.*

$$$
INDIAN

✕ **Rang Mahal.** Savory food in a pleasant setting with 26th-floor city views results in steady repeat business at this upscale Indian restaurant. The *bindi do piaza* (stir-fried onion and okra) is interesting, the *rogunjosh kashmiri* (mutton curry) is a hit, and the homemade naan breads are flavorful. The main dining room has Indian music, which can be loud to some ears, but there are smaller rooms for a quieter meal. Bring a jacket—the air-conditioning can be overpowering—and request a window seat for those great views. Ⓢ *Average main: B400* ⊠ *Rembrandt Hotel, 19 Sukhumvit, Soi 18, Sukhumvit (Klong Toey)* ☎ *02/261–7100* ⊕ *www.rembrandtbkk.com* ⊗ *No lunch Mon.–Sat.* ⌂ *Reservations essential* Ⓜ *Subway: Sukhumvit; Skytrain: Asok* ✛ *G5.*

$$$$
SEAFOOD THAI

✕ **Seafood Market.** The market is miles from the ocean, but the fish here is so fresh that it seems as though the boats must be nearby. As in a supermarket, you take a small cart and choose from an array of seafood—crabs, prawns, lobsters, clams, oysters, and fish. Keep in mind that most customers' eyes are bigger than their stomachs, and order with restraint. The waiter takes your selections to the chef, who cooks it however you prefer. The seafood at this 1,500-seat, garishly fluorescent-lit establishment is way overpriced (plus you pay a charge for the cooking), and the atmosphere is extremely touristy, but the place is always packed and it makes for a fun night out. Ⓢ *Average main: B450* ⊠ *89 Sukhumvit, Soi 24, Sukhumvit (Klong Toey)* ✛ *Closer to Rama IV Rd.;*

take taxi down Sukhumvit 24 ☎ *02/261–2071* ⊕ *www.seafood.co.th* ⌲ *Reservations essential* Ⓜ *Skytrain: Phrom Phong ✛ H5.*

$$ ✕ **Soul Food Mahanakorn.** Launched by food critic Jarrett Wrisley, this
THAI gem of a restaurant and bar is in a converted Chinese shophouse in
Fodor'sChoice trendy Thong Lor and is usually packed to the rafters. It's no surprise,
★ as the place serves some of the city's best Thai food, from *heng lay* (a
curry popular in the north) to *larb pet* (roast duck salad) and an array of
fresh vegetables served with several spicy chili sauces. The double-pour
drinks here are every bit as good as the food, with concoctions like a
Lycheegrass Collins or Lo-So Mojito using local ingredients. $ *Average
main: B250* ✉ *56/10 Sukhumvit, Soi 55, Thong Lor* ☎ *02/714–7708*
⊕ *www.soulfoodmahanakorn.com* ⊘ *No lunch* ⌲ *Reservations essen-
tial* Ⓜ *Skytrain: Thong Lor ✛ H5.*

$$ ✕ **Supanniga Eating Room.** Thanaruek Laoraowirodge, a successful res-
THAI taurateur in New York City and Bangkok, has earned high praise for
Fodor'sChoice this cozy shophouse venue that specializes in regional dishes based on
★ the recipes of one of his grandmothers. The *kalum tod nam pla* (fried
Chinese cabbage) and the *moo chamuang* (pork stew made with Thai
herbs and cha muang leaves) are just two of the dazzlers on the eclectic
menu. The au courant cocktails go well with the food. $ *Average main:
B210* ✉ *160/11 Soi Sukhumvit 55, Thong Lor ✛ Between Thong Lor
Soi 6 and 8* ☎ *02/714–7608* ⊕ *www.supannigaeatingroom.com* Ⓜ *Skytrain: Thong Lor ✛ H4.*

WHERE TO STAY

Bangkok offers a staggering range of lodging choices, and even some
of the best rooms are affordable to travelers on a budget. The city has
nearly 500 hotels and guesthouses, and the number is growing. In fact,
competition has brought the prices down at many hotels; unfortunately,
the service has suffered at some as a result of cutting corners to lower
prices. Still, you'll feel more pampered here than in many other cities.

For first-class lodging, few cities in the world rival Bangkok. In recent
years the Mandarin Oriental, Peninsula, Shangri-La, and a handful of
others have been repeatedly rated among the best in the world, with
newer players like the Sofitel So and St. Regis receiving major accolades.
If there were a similar comparison of the world's boutique hotels, Bangkok's would be near the top, too. These high-end hotels are surprisingly
affordable, with rates comparable to standard hotels in New York or
London. Business hotels also have fine service, excellent restaurants,
and amenities like health clubs and spas.

Wherever you stay, remember that prices fluctuate enormously, and that
huge discounts are the order of the day. Internet discounts are widely
available, and booking online can often save you up to several thousand
baht. ■TIP➔ **Always ask for a better price, even when you are checking
in.** Deals may be more difficult to come by during the high season from
November through February, but during low season they're plentiful.

*Use the coordinate (✛ B2) at the end of each listing to locate a site on
the Where to Stay in Bangkok map.*

Hotels are concentrated in four areas: in Silom and Bang Rak (home to many of riverfront hotels); around Siam Square and along Phetchaburi Road in Pathumwan; along Sukhumvit Road, which has the greatest number of hotels and an abundance of restaurants and nightlife; and in the Chinatown and the Old City neighborhoods, which have a smaller number of properties, most of which are affordable. Backpackers often head to Khao San Road, also home to some newer, more upmarket guesthouses.

Visit Fodors.com for expanded hotel reviews.

WHAT IT COSTS IN BAHT			
$	$$	$$$	$$$$
HOTELS	under B2,000	B2,001–B4,000	B4,001–B6,000	over B6,000

Hotel prices are for a standard double in high season, excluding service charge and tax.

THE OLD CITY

$$$
B&B/INN
Fodor's Choice
★

Chakrabongse Villas. On the banks of the Chao Phraya River in an old part of the city, these traditional Thai houses were originally built up-country and then transported to the grounds of the Chakrabongse House, which was built in 1908. **Pros:** unique hotel experience; beautiful surroundings; large discounts during low season. **Cons:** fills up quickly; feels isolated; extremely expensive. $ *Rooms from: B5,000* ⊠ *396 Maharaj Rd., Tatien* ☎ *02/222–1290, 02/622–1900* ⊕ *www. thaivillas.com* ⇨ *4 rooms, 3 bed-and-breakfast rooms* ⦿ *Breakfast* Ⓜ *Skytrain: Saphan Taksin, then river ferry* ✛ *A4.*

$$
HOTEL

Phranakorn Nornlen. Ideal for travelers seeking an artsy, off-the-beaten-track experience, this cute boutique guesthouse is in the old Phra Nakhon district. **Pros:** artsy setting; friendly and helpful staff; in a real Bangkok neighborhood well off the tourist track. **Cons:** far from Skytrain and subway; difficult to find; lacks pool, gym, and other hotel amenities. $ *Rooms from: 2200* ⊠ *46 Thewet, Soi 1, Phranakorn, Bangkhunprom, Krungkasem, Phra Nakhon* ☎ *02/628–8188* ⊕ *www. phranakorn-nornlen.com* ⇨ *20 rooms* ⦿ *Breakfast* ✛ *C2.*

$$$
HOTEL

Royal Princess Larn Luang. This hotel with three restaurants of its own is perfectly situated for exploring Dusit, the Old City, and Chinatown, and it's a short taxi ride away from riverside eateries. **Pros:** beautiful pool area; fair number of creature comforts; quiet neighborhood. **Cons:** restaurants not outstanding; isolated location; smallish bathrooms. $ *Rooms from: B4,600* ⊠ *269 Larn Luang Rd., Old City* ☎ *02/281–3088* ⊕ *www. royalprincesslarnluang.com* ⇨ *167 rooms* ⦿ *Breakfast* ✛ *D3.*

$$$$
RESORT
Fodor's Choice
★

The Siam Hotel. Old Hollywood meets art deco at this family-owned property on the Chao Phraya River in the regal Dusit neighborhood. **Pros:** everything right on the property; great location; exclusive and private; truly classy. **Cons:** very pricey; a long way from public transportation; far from nightlife. $ *Rooms from: B17,970* ⊠ *3/2 Thanon Khao, Vachirapayaabal, Dusit* ☎ *02/206–6999* ⊕ *www.thesiamhotel. com* ⇨ *28 suites, 10 villas, 1 cottage* ⦿ *Breakfast* Ⓜ *Skytrain: Saphan Taksin, then hotel's private boat* ✛ *C1.*

WHERE SHOULD I STAY?

	Neighborhood Vibe	Pros	Cons
North Bangkok	This relatively quiet business and residential neighborhood has plenty of local culture but few tourist attractions.	This is the closest neighborhood to Don Mueang, the domestic and low-budget carrier airport—helpful if you have an early flight.	It's a ways from downtown, which means you'll spend a lot on taxis getting to the city center. Public transportation options are limited.
The Old City, Banglamphu, and Dusit	These central neighborhoods are the historic heart of the city. Today they're full of places to stay in all price ranges.	Tons of dining and lodging options here to match any budget; you'll be near many major attractions, like the Grand Palace and Wat Benjamabophit.	May feel chaotic to some, too touristy to others. Not easily accessible by subway or Skytrain. Not the cheapest part of town.
Chinatown	The utter chaos of Chinatown is not for everybody. You'll be inundated by the sights and sounds—expect a lot of neon.	There are some good hotel deals here, the neighborhood is one of a kind, the food scene is great, and the street markets are fascinating.	Hectic and not the most tourist-friendly part of town. Limited hotel selection, terrible traffic, and public transportation options are not convenient.
Thonburi	You'll rub elbows with the locals in this mostly residential neighborhood across the river from the Old City.	Tucked away in peaceful seclusion from the noise and chaos of Bangkok; stellar river views.	Everything else is on the other side of the Chao Phraya, so expect to take the ferry a lot and spend more on taxis.
Pathumwan	The neighborhood that makes up Bangkok's "downtown," this sprawling area is full of markets and mega-malls and has several tourist attractions.	A shopper's paradise, and relatively convenient to subway and Skytrain. Many super-posh hotels; this is the place to stay if you're traveling in style.	Horrible traffic—you'll run up in a taxi tab sitting in gridlock. Most options are pricey, and may be noisy because there's lots of nightlife nearby.
Silom and Bang Rak	Another part of the central area, this neighborhood is the city's biggest business hub and also has the greatest concentration of restaurants. Nightlife is fun, too.	Popular area with travelers, so lots of comfortable restaurants and bars. Convenient subway–Skytrain connection here.	Can be clogged with traffic. Not the most authentic Thai experience, and because it's partially a business district, there's a lot of less-than-charming concrete.
Sukhumvit	This central tourist- and expat-heavy neighborhood is the nightlife area in Bangkok, and you'll find everything from Irish pubs to hostess bars. There's also a good restaurant scene here.	If you want to party, this is the place to be. A wide range of hotels here, from dirt cheap to über-ritzy, and public transit is convenient.	Fast-paced; some areas are noisy well into the night, and you may run into some shady dealings, though there are plenty of classier establishments here as well.

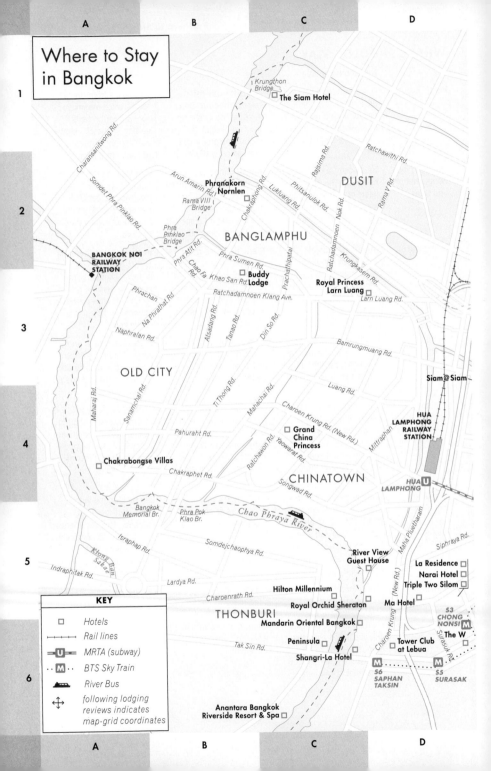

Where to Stay in Bangkok

KEY

☐ Hotels

┼ Rail lines

🚇 U MRTA (subway)

⋯⋯ M BTS Sky Train

🚌 River Bus

↔ following lodging
reviews indicates
map-grid coordinates

Krungthon Bridge
The Siam Hotel

Charansanitwong Rd.
Somdet Phra Pinklao Rd.
Arun Amarin Rd.
Rama VIII Bridge
Phra Pinklao Bridge

Phranakorn Nornlen

Chakraphong Rd.
Lukluang Rd.
Rajsima Rd.
Phitsanulok Rd.
Nok Rd.
Ratchawithi Rd.
Rama V Rd.

DUSIT

BANGLAMPHU

Phra Atit Rd.
Chao Fa Rd.
Khao San Rd.
Phra Sumen Rd.
Prachathipatai
Ratchadamnoen Nok Rd.
Krungkasem Rd.

BANGKOK NOI RAILWAY STATION

Buddy Lodge

Royal Princess Larn Luang
Larn Luang Rd.

Phrachan
Na Phrathat Rd.
Ratchadamnoen Klang Ave.

Naphralan Rd.
Atsadang Rd.
Tanao Rd.
Din So Rd.
Bamrungmuang Rd.

OLD CITY

Maharaj Rd.
Sanamchai Rd.
Ti Thong Rd.
Mahachai Rd.
Luang Rd.

Siam@Siam

Pahuraht Rd.
Charoen Krung Rd. (New Rd.)
Mittraphan

HUA LAMPHONG RAILWAY STATION

Chakrabongse Villas

Grand China Princess

Ratchawon Rd.
Yaowarat Rd.
Chakraphet Rd.
Songwad Rd.

CHINATOWN

HUA LAMPHONG U

Bangkok Memorial Br.
Phra Pok Klao Br.

Chao Phraya River

Israphap Rd.
Somdejchaophya Rd.

Klong Ban Sakae
Indraphitak Rd.
Lardya Rd.

Mahla Phueth.aram
Siphraya Rd.

River View Guest House

La Residence ☐
Narai Hotel ☐
Triple Two Silom ☐

Charoenrath Rd.
Hilton Millennium
Royal Orchid Sheraton

Ma Hotel

Charoen Krung (New Rd.)
Surasak Rd.

53 CHONG NONSI M

THONBURI

Mandarin Oriental Bangkok

The W

Peninsula

Tak Sin Rd.
Shangri-La Hotel

Tower Club at Lebua

M S6 SAPHAN TAKSIN

M S5 SURASAK

Anantara Bangkok Riverside Resort & Spa

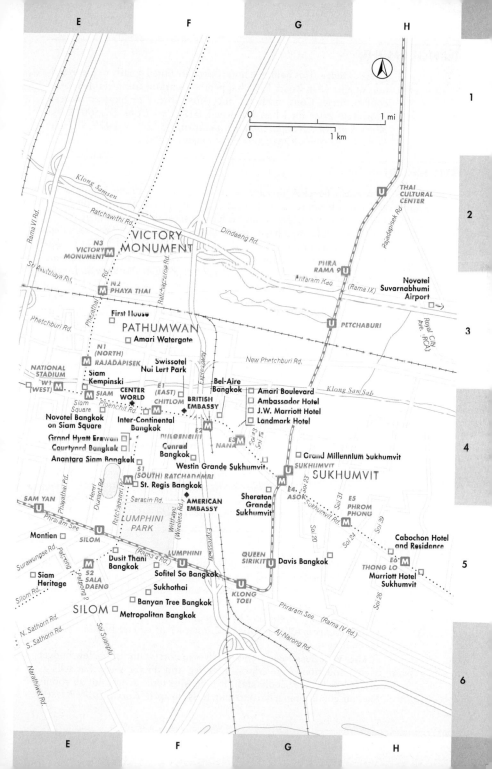

BANGLAMPHU

$ HOTEL **🏨 Buddy Lodge.** This boutique hotel has contributed greatly to the trendiness of Khao San Road. **Pros:** happening location; comfortable rooms; cool clientele. **Cons:** nothing fancy; no subway or Skytrain access; exorbitant price for Khao San Road. [$] *Rooms from: B1,500* ✉ *265 Khao San Rd., Banglamphu (Pranakorn)* ☎ *02/629–4477* 🌐 *www.buddylodge.com* 🛏 *76 rooms* 🍴 *No meals* ✣ *B3.*

THONBURI

$$$$ RESORT **🏨 Anantara Bangkok Riverside Resort & Spa.** Getting to the Anantara is a pleasant adventure in itself—free boats shuttle guests across the Chao Phraya River from the Taksin Bridge. **Pros:** resort feel; lots of activities; great service. **Cons:** a hassle to get into the city; may feel too secluded; not all rooms have views. [$] *Rooms from: B6,500* ✉ *257/1–3 Charoennakorn Rd., Thonburi* ☎ *02/476–0022* 🌐 *www.bangkok-riverside.anantara.com* 🛏 *408 rooms* 🍴 *Breakfast* [M] *Skytrain: Saphan Taksin, then hotel boat* ✣ *C6.*

$$$ HOTEL Fodor's Choice ★ **🏨 Hilton Millennium.** Lording over the Chao Phraya River in postmillennial splendor, this flagship Hilton designed with cutting-edge flair competes successfully with Bangkok's other hotel giants but has far lower rates. **Pros:** snazzy amenities; cool pool area; reasonable prices. **Cons:** rooms somewhat small; across the river from downtown pursuits. [$] *Rooms from: B4,700* ✉ *123 Charoennakorn Rd., Klong San* ☎ *02/442–2000* 🌐 *www3.hilton.com* 🛏 *543 rooms* 🍴 *No meals* [M] *Skytrain: Saphan Taksin* ✣ *C5.*

$$$$ HOTEL Fodor's Choice ★ **🏨 Peninsula.** The rooms at the Peninsula have plenty of high-tech gadgets, among them bathrooms with hands-free phones and mist-free TV screens, and bedside controls that dim the lights, turn on the sound system, and close the curtains. **Pros:** beautiful pool; exceptional service; awesome views. **Cons:** most attractions are across the river; on-site dining not very good; outrageously expensive for Bangkok. [$] *Rooms from: B17,000* ✉ *333 Charoen Krung (New Rd.), Thonburi (Klong San)* ☎ *02/861–2888* 🌐 *bangkok.peninsula.com* 🛏 *370 rooms, 65 suites* 🍴 *Breakfast* [M] *Skytrain: Saphan Taksin* ✣ *C6.*

CHINATOWN

$$$ HOTEL **🏨 Grand China Princess.** One good reason for staying in Chinatown is the chance to experience the sights and sounds of the city's oldest neighborhood. **Pros:** great city and river views; much Chinese food nearby. **Cons:** popular with big groups; neighborhood not overly tourist-friendly. [$] *Rooms from: B4,400* ✉ *215 Yaowarat Rd.* ☎ *02/224–9977* 🌐 *www.grandchina.com* 🛏 *155 rooms, 22 suites* 🍴 *Breakfast* [M] *Subway: Hua Lamphong* ✣ *C4.*

$ HOTEL **🏨 River View Guest House.** This family-run hotel is one of the few budget accommodations to overlook the river, and it's the view that sells it. **Pros:** river view; friendly staff; inexpensive rates. **Cons:** not all rooms have air-conditioning; hard to find; feels cheap. [$] *Rooms from: B1,800*

✉ *768 Soi Panurangsri, Songwat Rd., Chinatown (Samphanthawong)* ☎ *02/234–5429* ⊕ *www.riverviewbkk.com* ⇨ *45 rooms* ⦿ *No meals* Ⓜ *Skytrain: Saphan Taksin* ✛ *D5.*

PATHUMWAN

$$$ ▭ **Amari Watergate.** The spacious
HOTEL and comfortable rooms at the
Amari chain's Bangkok flagship
are swathed in silks and other
rich fabrics. **Pros:** many amenities;
executive floor; massive pool. **Cons:**
huge; impersonal feel. $ *Rooms from: $4,700* ✉ *847 Phetchburi Rd., Pathumwan* ☎ *02/653–9000* ⊕ *www.amari.com* ⇨ *569 rooms, 26 suites* ⦿ *Breakfast* Ⓜ *Skytrain: Chitlom* ✛ *E3.*

$$$$ ▭ **Anantara Siam Bangkok.** One of
HOTEL Bangkok's more elegant hotels,
until early 2015 a Four Seasons property, the Anantara Siam still attracts local society for morning coffee and afternoon tea in the formal lobby, where a string quartet often plays. **Pros:** accessible location; great pool; magnificent tearoom. **Cons:** decor verges on stuffy; not all rooms have nice views; extremely pricey in season. $ *Rooms from: B13,550* ✉ *155 Ratchadamri Rd., Pathumwan* ☎ *02/126–8866* ⊕ *siam-bangkok.anantara.com* ⇨ *354 rooms, 19 suites* ⦿ *No meals* Ⓜ *Skytrain: Rajadamri* ✛ *F4.*

$$$$ ▭ **Conrad Bangkok.** Though this hotel is one of the largest in Bangkok, the
HOTEL service doesn't suffer—the staff is attentive, and the beautifully designed
Fodor'sChoice rooms are perfect down to the smallest detail. **Pros:** two destination res-
★ taurants; fun nightlife; sprawling pool area; attentive staff. **Cons:** huge; not on the river. $ *Rooms from: B6,400* ✉ *87 Wittayu (Wireless Rd.), Pathumwan* ☎ *02/690–9999* ⊕ *www.conradhotels.com/bangkok* ⇨ *391 rooms, 20 suites* ⦿ *No meals* Ⓜ *Skytrain: Ploenchit* ✛ *F4.*

$$ ▭ **Courtyard Bangkok.** Although it lacks the luxury of Bangkok's high-
HOTEL end lodgings, this reasonably priced Marriott property has a young, hip vibe. **Pros:** good value; family-friendly. **Cons:** unremarkable room decor; not as luxurious as other Marriotts. $ *Rooms from: B3,500* ✉ *155/1 Soi Mahadlekluang 1, Rachadamri Rd., Pathumwan* ☎ *02/690–1888* ⊕ *www.marriott.com* ⇨ *316 rooms* ⦿ *No meals* Ⓜ *Skytrain: Rajadamri* ✛ *F4.*

$$ ▭ **First House.** Tucked behind the Pratunam Market, this lodging in the
HOTEL bustling garment district is an excellent value. **Pros:** reasonably priced; attractive rooms; comfortable furniture. **Cons:** not much natural light in rooms; neighborhood on the noisy side. $ *Rooms from: B2,100* ✉ *14/20–29 New Phetchburi Rd., Soi 19, Ratchathewi* ☎ *02/254–0300* ⊕ *www.firsthousebkk.com* ⇨ *100 rooms* ⦿ *Breakfast* Ⓜ *Airport Link: Ratchaprarop* ✛ *E3.*

$$$$ ▭ **Grand Hyatt Erawan.** This stylish hotel hovers over the auspicious
HOTEL Erawan Shrine. **Pros:** easy access to many points in the city; world-class

---

WORD OF MOUTH

"Staying along the river is lovely. You can watch the endlessly fascinating river traffic, and being on the river means it is slightly cooler than in the canyons of downtown—and the air is a cleaner as well. Also, many of the major wats are located near the river so you can take the water taxis to get there." —Kathie

spa; 10 restaurants. **Cons:** not on the river; expensive rates; room rate doesn't include breakfast. $ *Rooms from: B12,500* ✉ *494 Ratchadamri Rd., Pathumwan* ☎ *02/254–1234* ⊕ *www.bangkok.grand.hyatt. com* ↩ *380 rooms, 44 suites* ⏐○⏐ *No meals* Ⓜ *Skytrain: Chitlom* ✛ *F4.*

$$$
HOTEL
⊞ **Inter-Continental Bangkok.** In one of the city's prime business districts, this fine hotel caters well to its corporate clientele. **Pros:** good location; handy fitness room; executive floor. **Cons:** small pool; many business travelers; expensive in-season rates. $ *Rooms from: B5,600* ✉ *973 Ploenchit Rd., Pathumwan* ☎ *02/656–0444* ⊕ *www.icbangkok.com* ↩ *381 rooms, 39 suites* ⏐○⏐ *No meals* Ⓜ *Skytrain: Chitlom* ✛ *F4.*

$$$
HOTEL
⊞ **Novotel Bangkok on Siam Square.** Convenient to shopping, dining, and entertainment, this sprawling hotel is a short walk from the Skytrain central station, which puts much of the city within reach. **Pros:** good service; convenient location; cozy rooms. **Cons:** not many in-room amenities; pricey. $ *Rooms from: B5,050* ✉ *392/44 Siam Sq., Soi 6, Pathumwan* ☎ *02/209–8888* ⊕ *www.novotelbkk.com* ↩ *423 rooms* ⏐○⏐ *Breakfast* Ⓜ *Skytrain: Siam* ✛ *E4.*

$$$$
HOTEL
Fodor'sChoice
★
⊞ **The St. Regis Bangkok.** The first hotel in Thailand to offer guests around-the-clock personal butler service, the St. Regis has always been all about pampering. **Pros:** centrally located; elegant rooms; personal butler service. **Cons:** expensive rates; can be a bit stuffy. $ *Rooms from: B9,500* ✉ *159 Rajadamri, Pathumwan* ☎ *02/207–7777* ⊕ *www.stregis. com/bangkok* ↩ *227 rooms* ⏐○⏐ *No meals* Ⓜ *Skytrain: Rajadamri* ✛ *F4.*

$$$$
HOTEL
Fodor'sChoice
★
⊞ **Siam Kempinski.** The palatial Siam Kempinski combines sheer elegance with the feel of an escapist resort in the middle of the city. **Pros:** central location; some rooms have direct pool access; notable restaurants; eminently splurge-worthy. **Cons:** super pricey; must walk through mall to enter hotel if on foot; standard room rate doesn't include breakfast. $ *Rooms from: B11,000* ✉ *991/9 Rama I Rd., Pathumwan* ☎ *02/162–9000* ⊕ *www.kempinski.com/bangkok* ↩ *303 rooms* ⏐○⏐ *No meals* Ⓜ *Skytrain: Siam* ✛ *E4.*

$$$
HOTEL
⊞ **Siam@Siam.** This boutique lodging is definitely where the cool kids stay, but that doesn't mean you won't feel welcome if you're traveling with children. **Pros:** great location; superhip crowd; creative rooms. **Cons:** can be noisy; some rooms have little natural light. $ *Rooms from: B5,500* ✉ *865 Rama I Rd., Wang Mai, Pathumwan* ☎ *02/217–3000* ⊕ *www. siamatsiam.com* ↩ *203 rooms* ⏐○⏐ *Breakfast* Ⓜ *Skytrain: Siam* ✛ *E3.*

$$$
HOTEL
⊞ **Swissotel Nai Lert Park.** The best thing about this upscale hotel is the delightful garden, so be sure to ask for a room that looks out on the swaying palm trees surrounding the free-form swimming pool. **Pros:** tropical vegetation; beautiful pool; executive floor. **Cons:** sometimes overrun with groups; not on river. $ *Rooms from: B4,500* ✉ *2 Wittayu (Wireless Rd.), Pathumwan* ☎ *02/253–0123* ⊕ *www.swissotel. com/bangkok* ↩ *299 rooms, 38 suites* ⏐○⏐ *No meals* Ⓜ *Skytrain: Ploenchit* ✛ *F4.*

SILOM

$$$$
HOTEL
⊞ **Banyan Tree Bangkok.** After checking in on the ground floor, you soar up to your room at this 60-story hotel—the light-filled suites in the impossibly slender tower all have sweeping views of the city. **Pros:**

wonderful views; cozy rooms; feel on top of the world. **Cons:** not near public transportation; expensive rates. $ *Rooms from: B6,100* ✉ *21/100 S. Sathorn Rd., Sathorn* ☎ *02/679–1200* ⊕ *www.banyantree. com/bangkok* ⤳ *327 rooms* ⦿*No meals* Ⓜ *Subway: Lumphini* ✛ *F5.*

$$$ 🏨 **Dusit Thani Bangkok.** The distinctive pyramidal shape of this high-rise
HOTEL hotel across from Lumphini Park, Bangkok's best public park, makes it immediately identifiable, and its proximity to the Skytrain and subway stations makes it a convenient base for exploring the city. **Pros:** relaxing retreat; noteworthy restaurants; near subway and Skytrain stations. **Cons:** small pool; busy with conference goers and functions. $ *Rooms from: B5,500* ✉ *946 Rama IV Rd., Silom* ☎ *02/200–9000* ⊕ *www.dusit.com/dusitthani/bangkok* ⤳ *517 rooms, 30 suites* ⦿*No meals* Ⓜ *Subway: Silom; Skytrain: Sala Daeng* ✛ *F5.*

$ 🏨 **La Residence.** You'd expect to find this charming little hotel on Paris's
HOTEL Left Bank—the rooms are small but comfortable, and each is individually decorated with an unerring eye for detail. **Pros:** cozy, elegant atmosphere; quiet surroundings; plenty of charm. **Cons:** not as cheap as it once was; rooms a bit small. $ *Rooms from: B1,800* ✉ *173/8–9 Surawong Rd., Bang Rak* ☎ *02/233–3301* ⊕ *www.laresidencebangkok com* ⤳ *19 rooms, 4 suites* ⦿*No meals* Ⓜ *Skytrain: Chong Nonsi* ✛ *D5.*

$$ 🏨 **Ma Hotel.** The expansive marble lobby is your first clue that this hotel
HOTEL is head and shoulders above others in its price range. **Pros:** good value; friendly staff; short walk from river. **Cons:** pool is indoors; popular with tour groups. $ *Rooms from: B2,500* ✉ *412 Surawong Rd., Si Phraya, Bang Rak* ☎ *02/234–5070* ⊕ *www.mahotelbangkok.com* ⤳ *243 rooms* ⦿*Breakfast* Ⓜ *Skytrain: Surasak* ✛ *D5.*

$$$$ 🏨 **Mandarin Oriental Bangkok.** With a rich history dating back to 1879,
HOTEL the Mandarin is one of Bangkok's most prestigious hotels. **Pros:** excel-
Fodor's Choice lent staff; butler service in all rooms; outstanding pool. **Cons:** popular
★ for private functions; can be very crowded; charge for Wi-Fi. $ *Rooms from: B15,150* ✉ *48 Oriental Ave., Bang Rak* ☎ *02/659–9000* ⊕ *www. mandarinoriental.com/bangkok* ⤳ *358 rooms, 35 suites* ⦿*Breakfast; No meals* Ⓜ *Oriental* ✛ *C6.*

$$$$ 🏨 **Metropolitan Bangkok.** A modern aesthetic, a pop-star clientele, and
HOTEL a sexy staff make this one of the city's hippest hotels. **Pros:** very hip; nice city views; free yoga classes. **Cons:** has declined in popularity; not on river; high prices. $ *Rooms from: B6,500* ✉ *27 S. Sathorn, Sathorn* ☎ *02/625–3333* ⊕ *www.comohotels.com/metropolitanbangkok* ⤳ *160 rooms, 9 suites* ⦿*Breakfast* Ⓜ *Subway: Lumphini; Skytrain: Sala Daeng or Chong Nonsi* ✛ *E5.*

$$ 🏨 **Montien.** This hotel within stumbling distance of Patpong has been
HOTEL remarkably well maintained since it was built in 1970. **Pros:** regal decor; lots of space; fun and happening neighborhood. **Cons:** not the most modern hotel; popular with tour groups. $ *Rooms from: B3,200* ✉ *54 Surawong Rd., Silom* ☎ *02/233–7060* ⊕ *www.montien.com/bangkok* ⤳ *475 rooms* ⦿*Breakfast* Ⓜ *Subway: Silom; Skytrain: Sala Daeng* ✛ *E5.*

$$ 🏨 **Narai Hotel.** Dating back to 1969, this is one of Bangkok's older
HOTEL hotels, but it's well kept up and conveniently located by the business district on Silom Road. **Pros:** fun neighborhood; short walk to river. **Cons:** unexciting pool and decor; long walk to Skytrain. $ *Rooms from:*

B3,200 ⊠ 222 Silom Rd., Silom ☎ 02/237–0100 ⊕ www.naraihotel. co.th ⤴ 475 rooms ❍❘ Breakfast Ⓜ Skytrain: Chong Nonsi ✛ D5.

$$$ **⛾ Royal Orchid Sheraton.** Of the luxury hotels along the riverfront, this
HOTEL 28-story palace is most popular with tour groups. **Pros:** nice river
views; comfortable beds; good prices for a river hotel. **Cons:** often
busy with groups; tired decor; far from public transportation unless
you use boat shuttle. $ *Rooms from: B6,000 ⊠ 2 Charoen Krung
Rd., Soi 30 (Captain Bush La.), Bang Rak ☎ 02/266–0123 ⊕ www.
royalorchidsheraton.com ⤴ 726 rooms, 26 suites ❍❘ No meals Ⓜ Sky-
train: Saphan Taksin ✛ D5.*

$$$$ **⛾ Shangri-La Hotel.** One of Bangkok's most prestigious riverfront prop-
HOTEL erties, the Shangri-La rivals even the more famous Mandarin Oriental.
Fodor's Choice **Pros:** breathtaking lobby; gorgeous pool and terrace; private balconies
★ available. **Cons:** older wing not as nice as newer area; slightly imper-
sonal feel; buffet breakfast costs extra. $ *Rooms from: B7,900 ⊠ 89 Soi
Wat Suan Plu, Charoen Krung (New Rd.), Bang Rak ☎ 02/236–7777
⊕ www.shangri-la.com/bangkok ⤴ 802 rooms, 66 suites ❍❘ No meals
Ⓜ Skytrain: Saphan Taksin ✛ C6.*

$$ **⛾ Siam Heritage.** The family that runs the Siam Heritage has created
HOTEL a classy boutique hotel with a purpose—to preserve and promote
Thai heritage. **Pros:** reasonably priced; family run; cool Thai decor.
Cons: not on river; rooms and pool a bit small. $ *Rooms from:
B2,500 ⊠ 115/1 Surawong Rd., Bang Rak ☎ 02/353–6166 ⊕ www.
thesiamheritage.com ⤴ 73 rooms ❍❘ Breakfast Ⓜ Subway: Silom; Sky-
train: Sala Daeng ✛ E5.*

$$$$ **⛾ Sofitel So Bangkok.** An architectural gem, this elegant hotel is designed
HOTEL around the five elements of water, earth, wood, metal, and fire: the
Fodor's Choice "earth" rooms, for example, resemble blue caves, and "water" rooms
★ come with bathtubs overlooking the Bangkok skyline. **Pros:** fantastic location; superior service; free computers for in-room use; knockout breakfast buffet. **Cons:** not all rooms have park views; expensive;
can get very busy. $ *Rooms from: B6,741 ⊠ 2 N. Sathorn Rd., Sath-
orn ☎ 02/624–0000 ⊕ www.sofitel-so-bangkok.com ⤴ 238 rooms
❍❘ Breakfast Ⓜ Subway: Lumphini ✛ F5.*

$$$$ **⛾ Sukhothai.** On 6 landscaped acres near Sathorn Road, the Sukhothai
HOTEL has numerous courtyards that make the hustle and bustle of Bangkok
seem worlds away. **Pros:** beautiful decor in suites; spacious grounds;
great restaurant. **Cons:** expensive rates; standard rooms not be worth
the price. $ *Rooms from: B12,700 ⊠ 13/3 S. Sathorn Rd., Sathorn
☎ 02/344–8888 ⊕ www.sukhothai.com ⤴ 210 rooms ❍❘ No meals
Ⓜ Subway: Lumphini ✛ F5.*

$$$$ **⛾ Tower Club at Lebua.** With a beautiful rooftop bar, great restaurants,
HOTEL and more than a bit of flair, the ultraluxurious Tower Club section of
Fodor's Choice the Lebua at State Tower hotel has spacious rooms with stunning upper-
★ floor views and prices to match. **Pros:** stunning panorama; use of Tower
Lounge; spacious rooms. **Cons:** sky-high rates; popular with see-and-be-
seen crowd; long wait for the elevators. $ *Rooms from: B7,500 ⊠ 1055
Silom Rd., Silom ☎ 02/624–9999 ⊕ www.lebua.com/tower-club ⤴ 221
rooms ❍❘ Breakfast Ⓜ Skytrain: Saphan Taksin ✛ D6.*

$$ ⬚ **Triple Two Silom.** The trendy sister property of the adjacent Narai
HOTEL Hotel has spacious rooms with wood floors and modern fittings in the
standard hip colors these days: deep brown, cream, black, and red.
Pros: tasteful decor; friendly and helpful staff. **Cons:** some rooms can
be noisy; not a great option for kids. $ *Rooms from: B3,800* ✉ *222
Silom Rd., Silom* ☎ *02/627–2222* ⊕ *www.tripletwosilom.com* ⬧ *75
rooms* ⦿ *Breakfast* Ⓜ *Skytrain: Chong Nonsi* ✛ *D5.*

$$$$ ⬚ **The W.** From the 800 tuk-tuk lights illuminating the ground floor to
HOTEL the sixth-floor terrace's whale-shape swimming pool, complete with
Siamese cat statues, the high-flying W is loaded with snazzy art and
design touches. **Pros:** great central location; 24-hour pool and fitness
center; nice mix of modern and traditional. **Cons:** no views; check-in
area can get busy; often occupied with events. $ *Rooms from: B9,000*
✉ *106 N. Sathorn Rd., Silom* ☎ *02/344–4000* ⊕ *www.whotels.com/
bangkok* ⬧ *403 rooms* ⦿ *No meals* ✛ *D6.*

SUKHUMVIT

$$ ⬚ **Amari Boulevard.** In a dashing pyramid-shape tower just off Sukhumvit
HOTEL Road, the Amari is convenient to shops, restaurants, and the Skytrain.
Pros: interesting architecture; close to Skytrain. **Cons:** uninspired restaurant; slack service; street can get noisy at night. $ *Rooms from: B3,200*
✉ *2 Sukhumvit, Soi 5, Sukhumvit* ☎ *02/255 2930* ⊕ *www.amari.com/
boulevard* ⬧ *309 rooms* ⦿ *Breakfast* Ⓜ *Skytrain: Nana* ✛ *G4.*

$$ ⬚ **Ambassador Hotel.** With a dozen restaurants, a shopping center with
HOTEL scores of stores, and even a bird sanctuary, the Ambassador doesn't
lack for diversions and facilities. **Pros:** in the heart of central Sukhum-
vit; relatively inexpensive. **Cons:** impersonal, generic; noise from the
main drag; staff not the most helpful. $ *Rooms from: $2,200* ✉ *171
Sukhumvit, Soi 11, Sukhumvit* ☎ *02/254–0444* ⊕ *www.amtel.co.th*
⬧ *760 rooms* ⦿ *Breakfast* Ⓜ *Skytrain: Nana* ✛ *G4.*

$$ ⬚ **Bel-Aire Bangkok.** This well-managed hotel is steps from clamorous
HOTEL Sukhumvit Road—thankfully, it's on the quiet end of a bustling street,
away from the bars. **Pros:** quieter than most in neighborhood; sleek
lobby; swimming pool. **Cons:** feels expensive for what it is; often busy
with tour groups; mediocre restaurant. $ *Rooms from: B2,500* ✉ *16
Sukhumvit, Soi 5, Sukhumvit* ☎ *02/253–4300* ⊕ *www.belairebangkok.
com* ⬧ *152 rooms* ⦿ *No meals* Ⓜ *Skytrain: Nana* ✛ *F4.*

$$$ ⬚ **Cabochon Hotel and Residence.** A colonial-style boutique hotel with
HOTEL small and large suites and a few multibedroom residences, the Cabochon
Fodor's Choice is a period piece out of 1920s Shanghai. **Pros:** colonial-style property
★ with period decor; antiques-filled rooms; rooftop pool. **Cons:** restau-
rant food is not special; expensive. $ *Rooms from: B5,800* ✉ *14/29
Sukhumvit, Soi 45, Sukhumvit* ☎ *02/259–2871, 02/259–2872* ⊕ *cabo-
chonhotel.com* ⬧ *8 rooms* ⦿ *Breakfast* ▭ *No credit cards* Ⓜ *Skytrain:
Phrom Phong and Thong Lor* ✛ *H5.*

$$ ⬚ **Davis Bangkok.** Two hotels in one, the Davis has a main building
HOTEL and another one two doors down with a separate lobby and reception
area. **Pros:** individually decorated rooms; beautiful pool area. **Cons:**
not close to public transit; uninteresting view from rooms. $ *Rooms
from: B2,700* ✉ *80 Sukhumvit, Soi 24, Sukhumvit* ☎ *02/260–8000*

🌐 *www.davisbangkok.net* 🛏 *247 rooms, 2 villas* 🍴 *Breakfast* [M] *Skytrain: Phrom Phong* ✥ *G5.*

$$$$ HOTEL 🏨 **Grand Millennium Sukhumvit.** A futuristic facade of soaring glass and odd angles sets the tone at this upscale lodging whose sleek rooms and suites come equipped with cutting-edge technology. **Pros:** beautiful modern decor; interesting exterior architecture; crisp service. **Cons:** many business travelers; bathrooms lack privacy. [$] *Rooms from: B7,400* ✉ *30 Sukhumvit, Soi 21, Sukhumvit* ☎ *02/204–4000* 🌐 *www.millenniumhotels.com/grandmillenniumsukhumvitbangkok* 🛏 *325 rooms* 🍴 *No meals* [M] *Subway: Sukhumvit; Skytrain: Asok* ✥ *G4.*

$$$ HOTEL 🏨 **J. W. Marriott Hotel.** The Marriott's convenience to restaurants, businesses, and one of the city's biggest red-light districts will turn some travelers off and others on. **Pros:** very friendly staff; nice gym; many dining options. **Cons:** not as nice as the Marriott in Thonburi; close to red-light district. [$] *Rooms from: B5,460* ✉ *4 Sukhumvit, Soi 2, Sukhumvit* ☎ *02/656–7700* 🌐 *www.marriott.com* 🛏 *441 rooms, 39 suites* 🍴 *No meals* [M] *Skytrain: Nana* ✥ *G4.*

$$$ HOTEL 🏨 **Landmark Hotel.** The generous use of polished wood in the reception area may suggest a grand European hotel, but the Landmark prides itself on being thoroughly modern. **Pros:** modern amenities; discount packages frequently available; good for business travelers. **Cons:** may be too formal for families; some rooms noisy. [$] *Rooms from: B4,700* ✉ *138 Sukhumvit Rd., Sukhumvit* ☎ *02/254–0404* 🌐 *www.landmarkbangkok.com* 🛏 *399 rooms, 42 suites* [M] *Skytrain: Nana* ✥ *G4.*

$$$ HOTEL 🏨 **Marriott Hotel Sukhumvit.** This snazzy urban-design property brings five-star luxury to the Thong Lor area. **Pros:** tall building with great views; nice outdoor pool; close to trendy Thong Lor restaurants and bars; ultramodern rooms. **Cons:** not in the heart of the city; away from tourist areas; horrible rush-hour traffic. [$] *Rooms from: B5,200* ✉ *2 Sukhumvit, Soi 57, Thong Lor* ☎ *02/797–0000* 🌐 *www.marriott.com* 🛏 *295 rooms and suites* 🍴 *Breakfast* [M] *Skytrain: Thong Lor* ✥ *H5.*

$$$$ HOTEL 🏨 **Sheraton Grande Sukhumvit.** The Sheraton soars 33 floors above the noisy city streets, and the suites on the upper floors get tons of natural light. **Pros:** close to fun nightlife; near public transportation; impressive views from most rooms. **Cons:** somewhat impersonal due to size; pricey. [$] *Rooms from: B9,000* ✉ *250 Sukhumvit Rd., Sukhumvit (Klong Toey)* ☎ *02/649–8888* 🌐 *www.sheratongrandesukhumvit.com* 🛏 *420 rooms, 36 suites* 🍴 *No meals* [M] *Subway: Sukhumvit; Skytrain: Asok* ✥ *G4.*

$$$$ HOTEL 🏨 **Westin Grande Sukhumvit.** All fancy with sleek surfaces and neon lighting, the Westin is very convenient to Sukhumvit nightlife—it's just out the front door. **Pros:** near Skytrain and subway; nightlife just out the front door; comfortable beds. **Cons:** on-site restaurants not great; overpriced compared to nearby options. [$] *Rooms from: B7,300* ✉ *259 Sukhumvit Rd., Sukhumvit* ☎ *02/207–8000* 🌐 *www.westingrandesukhumvit.com* 🛏 *362 rooms, 31 suites* 🍴 *No meals* [M] *Subway: Sukhumvit; Skytrain: Asok* ✥ *G4.*

SUVARNABHUMI AIRPORT

$$$$ HOTEL **Novotel Suvarnabhumi Airport.** This stunning hotel near Bangkok's main airport rents rooms in four-hour blocks, a boon during lengthy layovers. **Pros:** no set check-in time; five minutes from airport via free shuttle service; restaurants, spa, gym, and pool. **Cons:** far from town; big and impersonal; plane noise. [$] *Rooms from: B8,000* ✉ *Moo 1 Nongprue Bang Phli, Samutprakarn* ☎ *02/131–1111* 🌐 *www.novotel.com* 🛏 *612 rooms* 🍴 *No meals* ✥ *H3.*

2

NIGHTLIFE AND PERFORMING ARTS

English-language newspapers the *Bangkok Post* and the *Nation* have the latest information on current festivals, exhibitions, and nightlife. Better yet, try picking up a copy of *BK Magazine* for the most recent listings for arts and entertainment. *Bangkok 101* is a monthly magazine with extensive listings and reviews of new hot spots.

NIGHTLIFE

The city that was once notorious for its raunchy sex trade is now entertaining a burgeoning class of professionals hungry for thumping discos, trendy cocktail lounges, and swanky rooftop bars. There are also stricter rules that limit the sale of alcohol (11 pm from stores). Most bars and clubs close around 2 am, though nighthawks can probably find a place or two open until 5 or 6.

There are a few notable nightlife sections: the area off Sukhumvit Soi 55 (also called Soi Thonglor) is full of bars and nightclubs; Sukhumvit Soi 11 has evolved into a hot-and-heavy bar and club hangout, and trendy and happening new places are springing up around Sathorn Road and the adjoining Suan Phlu.

LADYBOYS

One of the most surprising aspects of Thai culture to first-time visitors is the "ladyboy." These men act, dress, and make themselves up to look—often convincingly—like women. Many are found in districts catering to salacious foreign visitors, but this doesn't mean they are sex workers or gay. In fact, many Thais refer to them as a "third sex," Thai men with feminine characteristics and mannerisms, more so than most women. You may hear them referred to as "katoey," but that is a derogatory term—they prefer to be called "ladyboy."

If you want to take a walk on the wild side, Bangkok still has three thriving red-light districts: Patpong, Nana Plaza, and Soi Cowboy. Patpong, the largest and most touristy, includes three streets that run between Surawong and Silom roads. Nana Plaza, at Sukhumvit Soi 4, is packed with three floors of hostess bars, go-go clubs, and ladyboy clubs. Soi Cowboy, off Sukhumvit Road at Soi 21 (the Asok intersection), is where many expats go, finding it slightly more relaxed and less of a tourist trap than Patpong or Nana.

Even though it may not seem like it, live sex shows are officially banned and prostitution is illegal. The government doesn't always turn a blind eye, so exercise caution and common sense.

NORTHERN BANGKOK

There aren't too many pubs frequented by foreigners around here, but the area around Victory Monument does have the long-running Saxophone, along with an excellent smattering of bars and pubs along the nearby Soi Rangnam.

BARS AND PUBS

Saxophone. Popular with locals and expats, Saxophone hosts rhythm and blues, jazz, blues, rock, reggae, and sometimes ska bands. ⊠ *3/8 Phayathai Rd., Victory Monument* ☎ *02/246–5472* ⊕ *www.saxophonepub. com* Ⓜ *Skytrain: Victory Monument.*

BANGLAMPHU

Brown Sugar, one of Bangkok's longest-running jazz haunts, tops the list of bars in Banglamphu.

JAZZ BARS

Brown Sugar. A good place to carouse over live jazz and occasionally blues, smoky Brown Sugar has been in business for three decades. ⊠ *469 Wanchat Junction, Phrasumen Rd., Banglamphu* ☎ *02/282–0396, 089/499–1378* ⊕ *www.brownsugarbangkok.com* ⊘ *Closed Mon.*

THONBURI

The best reason to visit Thonburi is to take in the river views at some of the fancier hotel bars.

BARS AND PUBS

Longtail Bar. Though not particularly authentic, this bar distinguishes itself with a tropical feel that is elusive in Bangkok—it will make you crave a mai tai by the breezy river. You'll have to sail about 30 minutes downriver from the Saphan Taksin Skytrain stop on one of the Anantara resort's dedicated boats, which can be pleasant on a nice night. ⊠ *Anantara Bangkok Riverside, 257 Charoennakorn Rd., Samrae Thonburi, Thonburi* ☎ *02/476–0022* ⊕ *www.bangkokriverdining.com.*

PATHUMWAN

The heart of Bangkok has fewer pubs than you'd imagine, but places like the St. Regis have great views, and Siam Square is home to dance spots like Concept CM2.

BARS AND PUBS

Bacchus Wine Bar. You'll find four laid-back floors and a long list of worthy wines here. ⊠ *20/6–7 Ruam Rudee, Pathumwan* ☎ *02/650–8986* Ⓜ *Skytrain: Ploenchit.*

Concept CM2. This flashy, energetic club hosts live pop bands every night. Be prepared to pay a steep B550 entrance fee on weekends (B250 on weekdays), which does include a free drink; the price goes up B100 after 11. ⊠ *Novotel Siam Square, 392/44 Rama I, Siam Sq., Soi 6, Pathumwan* ☎ *02/209–8888* ⊕ *www.novotelbkk.com/cm2-live-jam* Ⓜ *Skytrain: Siam.*

Diplomat Bar. Come here for smooth music, a sophisticated crowd, and a splendid selection of Scotch and cigars. Cigar makers are sometimes

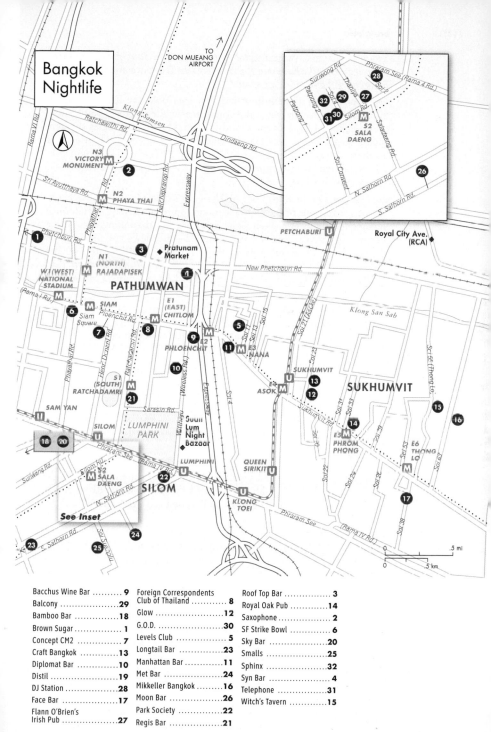

Bangkok Nightlife

brought in from Cuba just to roll here. ⊠ *Conrad Bangkok, 87 Wittayu (Wireless Rd.), Pathumwan* ☎ *02/690–9999* ⊕ *www.conradhotels.com/ bangkok* Ⓜ *Skytrain: Ploenchit.*

Regis Bar. From this 12th-floor bar that overlooks the Royal Bangkok Sports Club, you can watch the horse races while sipping a Siam Mary, the Bangkok version of the Bloody Mary. The bar continues the age-old St. Regis tradition of champagne sabering (opening a bottle using a saber), displayed nightly just after sunset. ⊠ *The St. Regis Bangkok, 159 Rajadamri Rd., Pathumwan* ☎ *02/207–7777* ⊕ *www.stregis.com/ bangkok* Ⓜ *Skytrain: Rajadamri.*

Roof Top Bar. On the 83rd floor of Thailand's tallest building, this glass-enclosed bar is one of the highest drinking spots in the city. With lounge singers and neon Heineken signs, it's kitschier than competitors like Vertigo and Skybar, but not to be missed—the views are amazing—is the revolving **Observatory Point** (B400 after 6, B300 before), on the floor above the bar. ⊠ *Baiyoke Sky Hotel, 222 Ratchaprarop Rd., Pathumwan* ☎ *02/656–3000* ⊕ *baiyokesky.baiyokehotel.com* Ⓜ *Skytrain: Chitlom.*

SF Strike Bowl. One of the city's hottest nightspots, this futuristic bowling alley, lounge, and bar has a sleek style that rivals most nightclubs. A DJ spins house music heard above the clatter of falling pins. ⊠ *MBK Center, 444 Phayathai Rd., 7th fl., Pathumwan* ☎ *02/611–7171* Ⓜ *Skytrain: National Stadium.*

JAZZ BARS

Foreign Correspondents Club of Thailand. The club hosts live jazz on Friday night—films, lectures, and art openings on other nights—and has a pretty nice bar. Nonmembers are welcome. ⊠ *Maneeya Center, 518/5 Ploenchit Rd., Pathumwan* ☎ *02/652–0580* ⊕ *www.fccthai.com* Ⓜ *Skytrain: Chitlom.*

SILOM AND BANG RAK

Many of the best rooftop bars and upscale lounges are in Silom's high-rise towers and in fashionable spots along the Chao Phraya River. Here's where you'll also find the notorious Patpong red-light district and the Silom Soi 4 gay bars.

BARS AND PUBS

Distil. Thai A-listers have made Distil, on the 64th floor of one of Bangkok's tallest buildings, their stomping ground. It's done up in chic black, coffee, and slate tones. A full-time sommelier is on hand to take care of your wine desires, and you can order a Hangovertini, created one floor down at the Sky Bar for the Hollywood film *Hangover II.* ⊠ *Lebua at State Tower, 1055 Silom Rd., 64th fl., Bang Rak* ☎ *02/624–9555* ⊕ *www.lebua.com/distil* Ⓜ *Skytrain: Saphan Taksin.*

Flann O'Brien's Irish Pub. A convenient location near the gateway to Patpong means that this place is always jumping. If you're a Beatles fan, check out the Betters on Friday night; the band plays starting at 9 pm. ⊠ *62/1–4 Silom Rd., Bang Rak* ☎ *02/632–7515* ⊕ *flann-obriens.com* Ⓜ *Subway: Silom; Skytrain: Sala Daeng.*

2

Ku Dé Ta. The views are fabulous at this dining, drinking, and dancing complex that's the talk of the town. Elevators whisk jet-setting patrons up the Sathorn Square Building to the 39th and 40th floors, which contain several high-end sushi, grill, and Asian-fusion restaurants, along with a huge nightclub, complete with DJs and dancers. At an adjacent Japanese-style lounge, some of Bangkok's best mixologists whip up dazzling cocktails. Legal and other issues will likely lead to a name change, perhaps to Cé La Vi (the name of sister clubs in Singapore and Hong Kong), though the party will continue on just the same. ⊠ *Sathorn Square Building, 98 N. Sathorn Rd., 39th and 40th fls., Sathorn* ☎ *02/108–2000* ⊕ *celavi.com* Ⓜ *Skytrain: Chong Nonsi.*

Met Bar. Decked out in red and black, this place is filled with people chilling out on comfortable couches. It used to be *the* place to go out in Bangkok, but those glory days seem to be over. Still, the decor is fun. ⊠ *27 S. Sathorn Rd., Sathorn* ☎ *02/625–3333* ⊕ *www.comohotels. com/metropolitanbangkok* Ⓜ *Subway: Lumphini; Skytrain: Sala Daeng.*

Fodor'sChoice ★ **Moon Bar.** The views are staggering at the Banyan Tree Bangkok's 61st-floor alfresco bar. The cocktails cost an equally staggering B550, but for the vistas alone they're worth every baht. Come a bit before sunset—the bar opens at 5—to get the best view from the low-slung seating, and don't forget your camera. If the weather is clear, you can stargaze using the bar's telescope. If the weather's bad at all, the place will be closed. ⊠ *Banyan Tree Bangkok, 21/100 S. Sathorn Rd., Sathorn* ☎ *02/679–1200* ⊕ *www.banyantree.com/bangkok* Ⓜ *Subway: Lumphini.*

Park Society. The sophisticated rooftop bar adjoining the same-named restaurant has marvelous skyline views and the finest perspective on vast Lumphini Park. Watch the sunset colors while downing a raspberry martini or glass of wine from the globe-trotting selection. If you're in a romantic mood, inquire about the private cabanas, complete with butlers, upstairs in the Hi So section. ⊠ *Sofitel So Bangkok, 2 N. Sathorn Rd., Sathorn* ☎ *02/624–0000* ⊕ *www.sofitel-so-bangkok.com* Ⓜ *Subway: Lumphini.*

Fodor'sChoice ★ **Sky Bar.** There's nothing else quite like this bar on the 63rd floor of one of Bangkok's tallest buildings. Head toward the pyramidlike structure emitting eerie blue light at the far end of the restaurant and check out the head-spinning views. The place's most famous concoction, the Hangovertini, was made famous by the Hollywood film *(Hangover II)* shot here. ⊠ *Lebua at State Tower, 1055 Silom Rd., 63rd fl., Bang Rak* ☎ *02/624–9555* ⊕ *www.lebua.com/sky-bar* Ⓜ *Skytrain: Saphan Taksin.*

GAY BARS

Silom Soi 2 and Silom Soi 4 are the center of Bangkok's gay scene, with every establishment from restaurants to bars to clubs all catering to a gay clientele.

Balcony. Sometimes the party spills out onto the street at this bar that overlooks the crowds along Soi 4. Balcony has a friendly staff and one of the best happy hours on the soi. ⊠ *86–88 Silom, Soi 4, Bang Rak* ☎ *02/235–5891* ⊕ *www.balconypub.com* Ⓜ *Subway: Silom; Skytrain: Sala Daeng.*

CLOSE UP

Thai Puppetry

For hundreds of years Thailand's puppeteers have entertained both royal courts and village crowds with shadow puppets and marionettes. Historically, the *Ramakien,* Thailand's version of the ancient Indian *Ramayana* epic, provided puppeteers with their subject matter. Today performances are more varied: many stick to the *Ramakien* or other Thai folklore and moral fables; some are contemporary twists on the classic material; and some depart from it entirely. It's an art form that exemplifies Thailand's lively blend of tradition and innovation.

SHADOW PUPPETS

Shadow puppets—carved animal hide stretched between poles—showed up in Thailand during the mid-13th century. Historians believe the art form originated in India more than 1,000 years ago and traveled to Thailand via Indonesia and Malaysia. By the 14th century, shadow puppetry had become a leading form of entertaining in Ayutthaya, where it acquired the name *nang yai* or "big skin," which is also what large shadow puppets are called.

Today nang yai troupes perform at village festivals, temple fairs, marriages, and royal ceremonies, as well as in theaters. Puppeteers maneuver colorful, intricately carved leather puppets behind a transparent backlighted screen. A narrator and musicians help tell the story. A classical music ensemble called a *piphat* adds to the charged dramatic atmosphere with rapid-paced *ranat* (xylophone-like instrument), drums, and haunting oboe.

Nang yai are used to form the set at shadow-puppet performances, while smaller puppets called *nang thalung* are the characters. There are some macabre traditions about how shadow puppets should be made, though it's unclear how often, if ever, these customs are followed today. Nang yai are supposed to be made from the hide of a cow or buffalo that has died a violent and accidental death, while nang thalung should be made with the skin from the soles of a dead puppet-master's feet, so that the puppets are literally walking in the footsteps of the former artist. Clown characters' lips should be formed from a small piece of skin from the penis of a deceased puppeteer.

Wherever the animal skin comes from these days, it must be carefully prepared. The hide is cured and stretched, then carved (puppet makers use stencils to outline the intricate, lacy designs) and painted. Puppet makers then mount the leather on sticks. You won't see shadow puppets for sale much, though some markets sell greeting cards with paper cut to resemble shadow puppets. You may find authentic shadow puppets at antiques markets.

Though today shadow puppetry is much more common in Thailand's south, the largest shadow-puppet troupe in Thailand, **Nang Yai Wat Khanon Troupe** (*T. Soifah, Amphur Photharam, Rachburi 03/223–3386*), performs in Damnoen Saduak, at Wat Khanon, next to the floating market. Performances, which are on Saturday at 10 am and cost B200, are hour-long versions of *Ramakien* stories performed in Thai.

MARIONETTES

Marionettes, born from a blend of shadow puppets and *khon,* a

2

traditional form of Thai dance, entered the scene at the beginning of the 20th century when Krae Saptawanit, a renowned khon performer, began to make them. Krae's first 2-foot-tall puppet was a miniature version of his own stage persona, with an elaborate costume, a golden mask, and long, curling finger extensions. Soon after, Krae formed a touring troupe of khon puppet performers.

Marionette choreography is highly stylized and symbolic. It takes three experienced puppeteers to manipulate each doll into a series of gymnastic twists and graceful dance moves. Puppeteers dance alongside and behind the puppets, but they remain in shadow; the dramatically lighted and costumed dolls take center stage. As in nang yai, classical Thai music adds to the intense atmosphere and indicates the mood of the story.

The art of puppet making—or *hadtasin*—requires great attention to detail. Marionettes consist of a frame covered with papier-mâché. Most of the frame is made of wood. Parts that must be able to move independently— like the head, neck, and hands—are made of aluminum and wire, which are more malleable. The hand joints require the most attention, since they must be capable of intricate khon movements. Puppet makers must also attach the sticks the puppeteers will use to make the puppets move.

Once the frame is constructed, the puppet maker adds layers of papier-mâché and then paints the top layer, paying particular attention to the face. The puppets wear ornate costumes of silk and gold leaf. According to tradition, the puppet maker must clap three times to create the completed marionette's soul.

At the **Baan Tookkatoon Hookrabok Thai Puppet Museum** (*Soi Vibavhadi 60, Laksi 02/579-8101 www. tookkatoon.com Weekdays 9-5*), you can watch marionette makers at work and purchase puppets. There's also a substantial private collection in the museum, which is a beautiful wooden house. You may even catch an impromptu show. Admission is free, but advance booking is required.

OTHER SHOWS

Chiang Mai is a hot spot for contemporary puppet troupes. **Hobby Hut** (⊕ *www.cmaipuppet. com*) and **Wandering Moon** (⊕ *www. wanderingmoontheatre.com*) are both based here.

In the southern province of Nakhon Si Thammarat, about three hours by bus from Krabi or Surat Thani, national artist and puppeteer Suchart Sapsin's house has been turned into the **Shadow Puppet Museum** (*10/18 Si Thammarat Rd., Soi 3, Nakhon Si Thammarat 07/534-6394*), with regular 20-minute performances (B100) in a small theater; a workshop; and a gallery.

Keep an eye out for performances at fringe festivals and temple fairs throughout the country. For information about upcoming shows, check the website of the Tourism Authority of Thailand (⊕ *www. tourismthailand.org*).

DJ Station. A young crowd packs this snappy-looking bar to bask in the "fun, lust, and joy" (or so the website says). The B200 cover charge includes a drink. ⊠ *8/6–8 Silom, Soi 2, Silom* ☎ *02/266–4029* ⊕ *www. dj-station.com* Ⓜ *Subway: Silom; Skytrain: Sala Daeng.*

G.O.D. This place, whose name is short for Guys on Display, is famous for its drag show every night at midnight and its balcony where you can watch the dance floor. Most of the action doesn't get going until the wee hours. The cover charge is B300. ⊠ *60/18–21 Silom Rd., Soi 2/1, Silom* ☎ *02/632–8033* Ⓜ *Subway: Silom; Skytrain: Sala Daeng.*

Sphinx. Subtle Egyptian motifs lend an exotic atmosphere to Sphinx, which has a sleek decor and a sophisticated dinner menu. ⊠ *100 Silom, Soi 4, Bang Rak* ☎ *02/234–7249* ⊕ *www.sphinxbangkok.com* Ⓜ *Subway: Silom, Skytrain: Sala Daeng.*

Telephone. Bangkok's most venerable gay bar, the pub-style Telephone is hopping every night of the week. The telephones are on the table so you can chat up your neighbors. The staff is friendly and knowledgeable about the neighborhood. ⊠ *114/1 Silom, Soi 4, Bang Rak* ☎ *02/234–3279* ⊕ *www.telephonepub.com* Ⓜ *Subway: Silom; Skytrain: Sala Daeng.*

JAZZ BARS

Bamboo Bar. This legendary watering hole hosts international musicians playing easy-on-the-ears jazz. ⊠ *Mandarin Oriental, 48 Oriental Ave., Bang Rak* ☎ *02/659–9000* ⊕ *www.mandarinoriental.com* Ⓜ *Skytrain: Saphan Taksin.*

Fodor'sChoice
★   **Smalls.** The impresario behind the late Q Bar opened this Parisian-style space that feels more Berlin or New York—or Paris—than Bangkok. There's an open-air rooftop hangout and the second floor is sceney, but downstairs is the place to be, if only to check out the French antiques and the traditional absinthe spigot. Jazz performances take place on the ground floor on Wednesday night; on Sunday there's Vietnamese pho, and on Monday the drinks are two for the price of one for hospitality-industry members. ⊠ *186/3 Suan Phlu, Soi 1, Sathorn* ✛ *Down Suan Phlu from Sathorn intersection, on right* ☎ *095/585–1398* Ⓜ *Subway: Lumphini.*

SUKHUMVIT

There's an incredible mix of bars and clubs around Sukhumvit. Lower Sukhumvit (Asok and Nana) is where you'll find the Nana Plaza and Soi Cowboy red-light districts. Farther east, the neighborhoods of Thong Lor and Ekkamai are *the* places for wealthy young Thais to party. Expect tables full of whiskey-drinking revelers listening to live music. There are also plenty of expat pubs in this area, many of which are also popular with Thais.

BARS AND PUBS

Craft Bangkok. Boutique beer lovers flock to this hip outdoor spot where all the brews are 100% craft. Bottles include U.S. craft favorites like Rogue, Anderson Valley, and Deschutes, but there are Czech, Scandinavian, and Japanese entries as well. The central location just off of Sukhumvit is a plus, and there's a second branch at 981 Silom Road. ⊠ *16 Sukhumvit, Soi 23, Sukhumvit* ✛ *About 200 meters (655 feet) up*

Soi 23 on right ☎ *02/661–3220* ⊕ *www.craftbangkok.com* Ⓜ *Subway: Sukhumvit; Skytrain: Asok.*

Face Bar. A strong South Asian theme—the bar shares the space with an Indian restaurant called Hazara—makes this a comfortable spot to enjoy a couple of drinks. Seating is on cushy pillows in semiprivate areas. ⊠ *29 Sukhumvit, Soi 38, Phra Khanong* ☎ *02/713–6048* ⊕ *www. facebars.com/en/bangkok/restaurant/bar* Ⓜ *Skytrain: Thong Lor.*

Levels Club. With its open dance floor, set under a giant colored chandelier, Bangkok's happening club of the moment packs in the young and restless. International DJs spin music and many special events take place. On Thursday night, ladies get their first three drinks before midnight free. ⊠ *Aloft Hotel, 39–45 Sukhumvit, Soi 11, Sukhumvit* ☎ *082/308–3246* ⊕ *www.levelsclub.com* Ⓜ *Skytrain: Nana.*

Manhattan Bar. Sexy and stylish, this lounge is adorned with velvet chairs, low tables, and black-and-white photos of New York City. This is the place to enjoy fine martinis, along with crab cakes, fresh oysters, and other tapas-style dishes. An elegant choice in the Sukhumvit neighborhood, this place never fails to impress. ⊠ *J. W. Marriott Hotel, 4 Sukhumvit Rd., Soi 2, Sukhumvit* ☎ *02/656–7700* ⊕ *www.marriott. com* Ⓜ *Skytrain: Nana.*

Mikkeller Bangkok. The craft-beer gypsy brewers from Denmark opened up shop in Bangkok at this hideaway in a residential garden home. More than 30 brews are on tap, many of them experimental and avant garde specimens found only at the world's few Mikkeller branches. Try a hoppy IPA or a Vanilla Shake Imperial Stout, which tastes more like a fine coffee than a beer. The garden is a fine spot to relax in, and there is a bottle shop on the premises. ⊠ *26 Ekkamai, Soi 10, Yaek 2, Watthana* ✢ *Hidden off Soi 10 (call or check website map)* ☎ *02/381–9891* ⊕ *www.mikkellerbangkok.com* Ⓜ *Skytrain: Ekkamai.*

Royal Oak Pub. With many different brews on tap and in bottles, this very British pub is a place for serious beer drinkers. Activities to keep you entertained include a quiz on Wednesday and a disco night on the last Friday of the month. ⊠ *595/10–11 Sukhumvit, Soi 33, Sukhumvit* ☎ *02/662–1652* ⊕ *www.royaloakthailand.com* Ⓜ *Skytrain: Phrom Phong.*

Syn Bar. Creative design elements at this bar decorated in cool grays and reds include floating seating. DJs start spinning on most nights at 9 pm for a crowd that loves the pretty cocktails served here. ⊠ *Swissotel Nai Lert Park, 2 Wittayu (Wireless Rd.), Sukhumvit* ☎ *02/253–0123* ⊕ *www.swissotel.com/bangkok* Ⓜ *Skytrain: Ploenchit.*

DANCE CLUBS

Glow. An underground dance club with cutting-edge electronic music, Glow lights up Sukhumvit with an eternally trendy, beautiful crowd. The sound system is out of this world, and the club has the biggest vodka selection in the city. ⊠ *96/4–5 Sukhumvit, Soi 23, Sukhumvit* ☎ *02/261–3007* Ⓜ *Subway: Sukhumvit; Skytrain: Asok.*

JAZZ BARS

Witch's Tavern. This place serves up live music on Friday and weekends, and good drinks and hearty English fare all week long. With ladies' drinks free from 5 pm to 9 pm on Wednesday, it shouldn't surprise that the tavern is one of the top draws in town that evening. ⊠ *306/1 Sukhumvit 55, Thong Lor* ☎ *02/391–9791* ⊕ *www.witch-tavern.com/ New_site* Ⓜ *Skytrain: Thong Lo.*

PERFORMING ARTS

A contemporary arts scene is relatively new to Thailand, but the last decade has seen great changes in the fine arts: artists are branching out into all kinds of media, and modern sculpture and artworks can be found in office buildings, parks, and public spaces. Music options range from piano concertos and symphonies to rock concerts and blues-and-jazz festivals.

Bangkok offers a variety of theater and dance performances, among them traditional puppet shows and masked dance dramas known as khon. For Thais, classical dance is more than graceful movements. The dances depict tales from the religious epic *Ramakien*. Performances are accompanied by a woodwind called the piphat, which sounds like an oboe, as well as a range of percussion instruments. In addition to conventional theaters, many restaurants present classical dance.

OLD CITY

THEATER AND DANCE

National Theatre. Classical dance and drama can usually be seen at the theater on the last Friday of the month. ⊠ *Na Phra That Rd., Old City* ☎ *02/224–1342.*

Sala Chalerm Krung Royal Theatre. A former student at the Ecole des Beaux-Arts in Paris designed this theater in a style that might best be described as Thai Deco. The venue hosts traditional khon, a masked dance-drama based on tales from the *Ramakien*. ⊠ *66 Charoen Krung (New Rd.), Old City* ☎ *02/222–0434* ⊕ *www.salachalermkrung.com* Ⓜ *Skytrain: Saphan Taksin.*

SILOM

THEATER AND DANCE

Sala Rim Naam. Across from the Mandarin Oriental, Sala Rim Naam stages a beautiful dance show nightly at 8:15, accompanied by a touristy dinner. ⊠ *Mandarin Oriental, 48 Oriental Ave.* ☎ *02/659–9000* ⊕ *www.mandarinoriental.com/bangkok* Ⓜ *Skytrain: Saphan Taksin.*

Silom Village. This place appeals mostly to foreigners, but it also draws Thais. The block-size complex, open daily from 10 to 10, presents classical dance performances and has a restaurant that serves all the Thai favorites. ⊠ *286 Silom Rd., Silom* ☎ *02/234–4448* ⊕ *www.silomvillage. co.th* Ⓜ *Subway: Silom; Skytrain: Sala Daeng.*

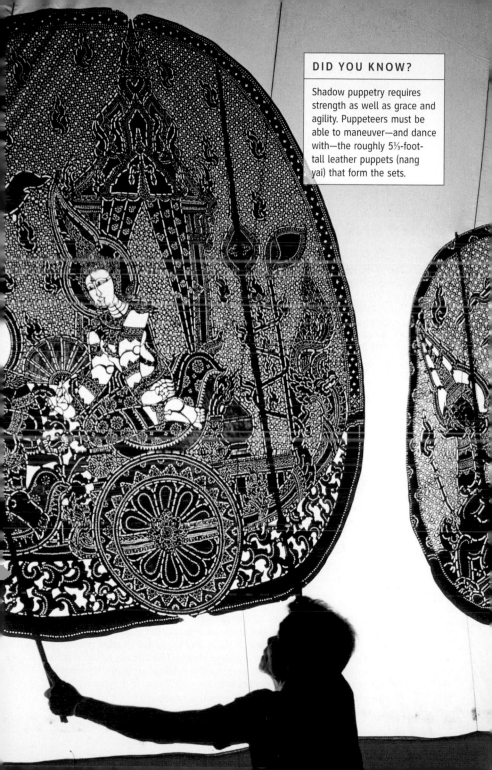

NORTHERN BANGKOK
THEATER AND DANCE

Siam Niramit. This 2,000-seat theater presents *Journey to the Enchanted Kingdom of Siam*, a history of Thailand told in words and music. The 80-minute performance begins at 8 pm nightly. ⊠ *19 Tiamruammit Rd., Huai Khwang* ☎ *02/649–9222* ⊕ *www.siamniramit.com* ☒ *B1,500; with dinner B1,850* Ⓜ *Subway: Thailand Cultural Center.*

Thailand Cultural Center. The center hosts local and international groups, including opera companies, symphony orchestras, and modern dance and ballet troupes. ⊠ *Ratchadaphisek Rd., Huai Khwang* ☎ *02/247–0028* Ⓜ *Subway: Thai Cultural Center.*

SPORTS AND THE OUTDOORS

Thailand has an abundance of outdoor activities, but it's often difficult to find any within Bangkok. Due to elevated temperatures, Bangkok residents generally head to the malls on weekends to cool off. Soccer is immensely popular, and the Thai Premier League has matches at several stadiums around town during the season. Bangkok offers visitors one of the most intense spectator sports in the world, *muay thai* (Thai kickboxing). This is the national sport. Seeing a match is a quintessential Bangkok experience.

MUAY THAI

Lumpinee Boxing Stadium. The stadium, which debuted in 2014 after moving north of the city from Lumphini Park, hosts muay thai matches on Tuesday, Friday, and Saturday, starting at around 6:30 pm. Most hotels can book tickets that include transportation to and from the stadium. ⊠ *6 Ramintra Rd., Anusawaree, Bang Khen* ⌖ *About 10 km (6½ miles) south of Don Mueang airport* ☎ *02/522–6843 stadium, 02/282–3141 office* ⊕ *www.muaythailumpinee.net* ☒ *B1,000–B2,000* Ⓜ *Subway: Chatuchak Park, then taxi from either; Skytrain: Mo Chit.*

Ratchadamnoen Stadium. The sprawling Ratchadamnoen Stadium presents muay thai bouts on Monday, Wednesday, Thursday, and Sunday from 6:30 pm to 10 pm. Ringside seats for most matches cost about B2,000. ⊠ *1 Ratchadamnoen Nok Rd., Pom Prap Sattru Phai, Banglamphu* ☎ *02/281–4205* ☒ *B1,000–B2,000.*

SHOPPING

Many tourists are drawn to Bangkok for its relatively cheap silk, gems, and tailor-made clothes. But there are many other goods worth seeking out: quality silverware, fine porcelain, and handmade leather goods—all at prices well below those in western shops. The already reduced prices can often be haggled down even further—haggling is mainly reserved for markets, but shopkeepers will let you know if they're willing to discount, especially if you start walking away.

CLOSE UP

Muay Thai, the Sport of Kings

2

Thais are every bit as passionate about their national sport as Americans are about baseball. Though it's often dismissed as a blood sport, muay thai is one of the world's oldest martial arts, and it was put to noble purposes long before it became a spectator sport.

Muay thai is believed to be more than 2,000 years old. It's been practiced by kings and was used to defend the country. It's so important to Thai culture that until the 1920s muay thai instruction was part of the country's public school curriculum.

Admittedly, some of the sport's brutal reputation is well deserved. There were very few regulations until the 1930s. Before then, there were no rest periods between rounds. Protective gear was unheard of—the exception was a groin protector, an essential item when kicks to the groin were still legal. Boxing gloves were introduced to the sport in the late 1920s. Hand wraps did exist, but some fighters actually dipped their wrapped hands in resin and finely ground glass to inflict more damage on their opponents.

Techniques: Developed with the battlefield in mind, muay thai moves mimic the weapons of ancient combat. Punching combinations, similar to modern-day boxing, turn the fists into spears that jab relentlessly at an opponent. The roundhouse kick—delivered to the thigh, ribs, or head—turns the shinbone into a devastating striking surface. Elbow strikes to the face and strong knees to the abdomen mimic the motion of a battle-ax. Finally, strong front kicks, using the ball of the foot to jab at the abdomen, thigh, or face, mimic an array of weapons.

Rules: Professional bouts have five three-minute rounds, with a two-minute rest period between rounds. Fights are judged using a point system, with judges awarding rounds to each fighter, but not all rounds are given equal weight—the later rounds are more important, as judges view fights as "marathons," with the winner being the fighter who's fared best throughout the entire match. The winner is determined by majority decision. Of course, a fight can also end decisively with a knockout or a technical knockout (wherein a fighter is conscious, but too injured to continue).

Rituals: The "dance" you see before each match is called the *ram muay* or *wai kru* (these terms are often used interchangeably, though the wai kru really refers to the homage paid to the *kru* or trainer). The ram muay serves to honor the fighter's supporters and his god, as well as to help him warm up, relax, and focus. Both fighters walk around the ring with one arm on the top rope to seal out bad spirits, pausing at each corner to say a short prayer. They then kneel in the center of the ring facing the direction of their birthplace and go through a set of specific movements, often incorporating aspects of the *Ramakien*. Fighters wear several good-luck charms, including armbands (*kruang rang*) and a headpiece (*mongkron*). The music you hear during each bout is live. Though it may sound like the tune doesn't change, the musicians actually pay close attention to the fight and they will speed up to match its pace—or to encourage the fighters to match theirs.

Don't be fooled by a tuk-tuk driver offering to take you to a shop. Shop owners pay drivers a commission to lure in unsuspecting tourists. ■TIP➔ Patronizing reputable dealers will help you avoid getting scammed on big-ticket items like jewelry.

Thai antiques and old images of the Buddha require a special export license; check out the Thai Board of Investment's Web site at ⊕ *www. boi.go.th/english* for rules on exporting and applications to do so.

The city's most popular shopping areas are along **Silom Road and Surawong Road,** where you can find quality silk; **Sukhumvit Road,** which is rich in leather goods; **Yaowarat Road in Chinatown,** where gold trinkets abound; and along **Oriental Lane and Charoen Krung (New Road),** where there are many antiques shops. The shops around **Siam Square** and at the **World Trade Center** attract both Thais and foreigners. **Peninsula Plaza,** across from the Anantara Siam Bangkok hotel in the embassy district, has upscale shops. If you're knowledgeable about fabric, you can find bargains at the textile merchants who compete along Pahuraht Road in Chinatown and **Pratunam Road off Phetchaburi Road.** You can even take the raw material to a tailor and have something made.

OLD CITY

JEWELRY

Thailand is known for its sparkling gems, so it's no surprise that the country exports more colored stones than anywhere in the world. You'll find things you wouldn't find at home, and prices are far lower than in the United States. There are countless jewelry stores on Silom and Surawong roads. Scams are common, so it's best to stick with established businesses. ■TIP➔ Deals that seem too good to be true probably are.

Johny's Gems. If you call first, this long-established firm will send a car—a common practice of the city's better stores—to take you to the shop near Wat Phra Kaew. The selection is massive, and you can order custom-design pieces. ⊠ *199 Fuengnakorn Rd., Phra Nakhon* ☏ *02/224–4065* ⊕ *www.johnysgems.com* ⊙ *Closed Sun.*

Lin Jewelers. The jewelry sold at this highly respected shop is more expensive than average, but so is the quality. ⊠ *9 Charoen Krung (New Rd.), Soi 38, Bang Rak* ☏ *02/234–2819* ⊕ *www.linjewelers.com* Ⓜ *Skytrain: Saphan Taksin.*

BANGLAMPHU

MARKETS

Khao San Road. Backpacker central in Banglamphu, this street has some of Bangkok's most enjoyable street shopping. If the hip clothes, cheesy souvenirs, used books, and B10 pad thai don't make the trip here worth it, the people-watching will. ⊠ *Khao San Rd., Banglamphu* ✛ *Between Chakrapong and Tanao Rds.; head southeast from Phra Athit ferry pier.*

Bargaining in Bangkok

Even if you've honed your bargaining skills in other countries, you might still come up empty-handed in Thailand. The aggressive techniques that work well in say, Delhi, won't get you very far in Bangkok. One of the highest compliments you can pay for any activity in the Land of Smiles is calling it *sanuk* (fun), and haggling is no exception. Thais love to joke and tease, so approach each bargaining situation playfully. However, be aware that Thais are also sensitive to "losing face," so make sure you remain pleasant and respectful throughout the transaction.

As you enter a market stall, smile and acknowledge the proprietor. When something catches your eye, inquire politely about the price, but don't immediately counter. Keep your voice low—you're more likely to get a deal

if it's not announced to the whole shop—then ask for a price just slightly below what you want. Don't get too cavalier with your counteroffer—Thai sellers generally price their wares in a range they view as fair, so asking to cut the initial price in half will most likely be seen as an insult and might end the discussion abruptly. In most cases, the best you can hope for is 20% to 30% discount.

If the price the shopkeeper offers in return is still high, turn your smile up another watt and say something like, "Can you discount more?" If the answer is no, your last recourse is to say thank you and walk away. If you are called back, the price is still negotiable; if you aren't, maybe the last price quoted wasn't such a bad one after all.

—Molly Petersen

CHINATOWN

MARKETS

Asiatique the Riverfront. In a prime spot along the Chao Phraya River, this complex of eateries, bars, and shops occupies 10 old warehouses with retro and industrial themes. You can get here via a free shuttle boat from the Saphan Taksin Pier next to the Skytrain station of the same name. ⊠ *2194 Charoenkrung Rd., Bangkor Laem* ☎ *02/108–4488* ⊕ *www.thaiasiatique.com* Ⓜ *Skytrain: Saphan Taksin, then free shuttle boat from nearby pier.*

Phahurat Market. This Indian market near Chinatown is known for its bargain textiles. A man with a microphone announces when items at a particular stall will be sold at half price, and shoppers surge over to bid. It's best to come in the evening, when it's cooler and many street vendors are selling snacks. ⊠ *Phahurat Rd., Phra Nakhon* ✛ *Near intersection of Chakraphet Rd., after Yaowarat* Ⓜ *Subway: Hua Lamphong.*

Sampeng Lane Market. Bangkok's best-known and oldest textile center—lots of fabrics here—is located in the heart of Chinatown. ⊠ *Soi Sampeng (Soi Wanit 1), off Yaowarat Rd., Sanpanthawong* Ⓜ *Subway: Hua Lamphong.*

PATHUMWAN

CLOTHING AND FABRICS

Thai silk gained its reputation only after World War II, when technical innovations made it less expensive. Two fabrics are worth seeking out: mudmee silk, produced in the northeastern part of the country, and Thai cotton, which is soft, durable, and easier on the wallet than silk. Many people who visit Bangkok brag about a custom-made suit that was completed in just a day or two, but the finished product often looks like the rush job that it was. If you want an excellent cut, give the tailor the time he needs, which could be up to a week at a reputable place.

Greyhound. This shop sells casual yet chic street wear. ⊠ *Siam Paragon, 991/1 Rama 1 Rd., 1st fl., Pathumwan* ☎ *02/129–4358* ⊕ *www. greyhound.co.th* Ⓜ *Skytrain: Siam.*

Issue. Impeccably tailored Indian-influenced designs are the specialty here. ⊠ *226/10 Siam Sq., Soi 3, Pathumwan* ☎ *02/658–4416* Ⓜ *Skytrain: Siam.*

Marco Tailor. One of the best custom tailor shops in Bangkok, Marco Tailor sews a suit equal to those on London's Savile Row. It's not cheap, but it's cheaper than what you'd pay in London. ⊠ *430/33 Siam Sq., Soi 7, Pathumwan* ☎ *02/252–0689* Ⓜ *Skytrain: Siam.*

Prayer Textile Gallery. Napajaree Suanduenchai studied fashion design in Germany, and more than two decades ago opened this business in her mother's former dress shop. She makes stunning items in naturally dyed silks and cottons and in antique fabrics from the farthest reaches of Thailand, Laos, and Cambodia. ⊠ *197 Phayathai Rd., near Siam Sq., Pathumwan* ☎ *02/251-7549* ⊕ *www.prayertextilegallery.com* Ⓜ *Skytrain: Siam.*

Sretsis. Three Thai sisters, darlings of the local design scene, created Sretsis, a feminine design label that has fashionistas around the world raving. ⊠ *Central Embassy, 1031 Ploenchit Rd., 2nd fl., Pathumwan* ☎ *02/160-5874* ⊕ *www.sretsis.com* Ⓜ *Skytrain: Chitlom.*

MARKETS

Pratunam Market. Hundreds of vendors selling inexpensive clothing jam the sidewalk each day here. The market is a popular destination for Indians, who drop by in the evening to sample the dozens of surrounding Indian, Nepali, and Pakistani restaurants. ⊠ *Phetchaburi and Ratchaprarop Rds., Pathumwan* Ⓜ *Skytrain: Chitlom.*

SHOPPING CENTERS

Central Chitlom. The flagship location of Thailand's largest department store chain has a good selection of jewelry, clothing, and fabrics, including a Jim Thompson silk shop. ⊠ *1027 Ploenchit Rd., Pathumwan* ⊕ *www.central.co.th* Ⓜ *Skytrain: Chitlom.*

Central World. At more than 1 million square meters (nearly 11 million square feet), this monster claims to be Southeast Asia's biggest mall. It's packed with local and international retailers, as well as a multiplex cinema, a hotel, and many dining options. ⊠ *999/9 Rama I Rd., Pathumwan* ⊕ *www.centralworld.co.th* Ⓜ *Skytrain: Chitlom.*

2

Gaysorn Shopping Centre. This upscale shopping center may outshine all the others with its white marble and chrome fixtures. You'll find all the requisite European labels as well as local designers such as Fly Now, Senada, and Sretsis. ⊠ *999 Ploenchit Rd., at Ratchadamri Rd., Pathumwan* ⊕ *www.gaysorn.com* Ⓜ *Skytrain: Chitlom.*

MBK Center. An impressive seven stories high, this is one of the busiest malls in the city. It's not as stylish as Siam Centre—the main attractions are stores selling cheap clothes and electronics—but there are many other shops, as well as an IMAX movie theater and a bowling alley. ⊠ *444 Phayathai Rd., at Rama I Rd., Pathumwan* ⊕ *www.mbk-center. co.th* Ⓜ *Skytrain: Siam, Ratchathewi.*

Pantip Plaza. This mall exists for the computer nerd in everyone. It houses an enormous number of shops selling computer hardware and software (some legal, most not). Shopping here can be overwhelming, but if you know what you're looking for, the bargains are worth it. ■ TIP→ Not all electronics will be compatible with what you have back home, so do your research. ⊠ *604/3 Phetchaburi Rd., Pathumwan* ⊕ *www.pantipplaza.com* Ⓜ *Subway: Phetchaburi; Skytrain: Chitlom.*

Siam Centre. Bangkok's young hipsters come here for the latest fashions. With one-of-a-kind handmade clothing, shoes, and accessories, this place oozes style, but be forewarned that the clothes are all made to Thai proportions, so they often run small. ⊠ *Siam Tower, Rama I and Phayathai Rds., Pathumwan* ☎ *02/658–1000* ⊕ *www.siamcenter.co.th* Ⓜ *Skytrain: Siam.*

Siam Discovery. Full of shops selling international labels, this mall has the added bonus of the most grandiose movie theater in all of Thailand, the Grand EGV. ⊠ *989 Rama I Rd., at Phayathai Rd., Pathumwan* ⊕ *www. siamdiscovery.co.th* Ⓜ *Skytrain: Siam.*

Siam Paragon. With 250 stores, including all the big international brands from Porsche to Chanel, this mall also has a multiplex cinema and tons of restaurants. Oh yes, and an underwater marine park where you can swim with sharks. ⊠ *991/1 Rama 1 Rd., Pathumwan* ☎ *02/610–8000* ⊕ *www.siamparagon.co.th* Ⓜ *Skytrain: Siam.*

SILOM

CLOTHING AND FABRICS

Jim Thompson Thai Silk Company. The shops of the pioneering company are prime places to buy silk by the yard and as ready-made clothes. The prices are high, but the staff members are knowledgeable. In addition to this Bang Rak shop there are numerous other locations throughout the city, including at the Mandarin Oriental, the Peninsula, and the Central Chitlom shopping center. ⊠ *9 Surawong Rd., Bang Rak* ☎ *02/632–8100* ⊕ *www.jimthompson.com* Ⓜ *Subway: Silom; Skytrain: Sala Daeng.*

LEATHER

Chaophraya Bootery. You can get custom-made cowboy boots for around $200 here. The shop also stocks a large inventory of ready-made leather shoes, boots, and accessories. ⊠ *141 Sukhumvit, Soi 11, Sukhumvit* ☎ *02/253–5400* Ⓜ *Skytrain: Nana.*

Siam Leather Goods. This shop is a good stop for shoes and jackets, along with pants, skirts, and purses, belts, and other accessories. ⊠ *River City Shopping Complex, 23 Charoen Krung (New Rd.), Bang Rak* ☎ *02/237–0077* ⊕ *www.siamleathergoods.com* Ⓜ *Skytrain: Saphan Taksin.*

MARKETS

Patpong. Asking a taxi driver to take you to Patpong may prompt a smirk, but for fake Rolex watches, imposter Louis Vuitton handbags, and western-size clothing, there's no better place than this notorious red-light-district street. Be wary of pickpockets, though. It gets very crowded and tightly packed here. ⊠ *Silom Rd. at Soi 2, Silom* Ⓜ *Subway: Silom; Skytrain: Sala Daeng.*

PORCELAIN, CERAMICS, AND CELADON

Benjarong. This massive ceramics shop has a huge inventory and will make to order dining sets, bowls, and vases. ⊠ *River City Shopping Complex, 23 Charoen Krung (New Rd.), 3rd fl., Bang Rak* ☎ *02/237–0077* ⊕ *www.thaibenjarong.com* Ⓜ *Skytrain: Saphan Taksin.*

PRECIOUS METALS

Lin Silvercraft. Among all the knickknacks stacked from floor to ceiling, this shop has some of the most finely crafted silver cutlery in town. ⊠ *3 Charoen Krung (New Rd.), Soi 38, Bang Rak* ☎ *02/235–2108, 02/234–2391* ⊕ *www.linjewelers.com* Ⓜ *Skytrain: Saphan Taksin.*

Siam Bronze Factory. For quality works in bronze, try this showroom near the Mandarin Oriental. ⊠ *1250 Charoen Krung (New Rd.), Bang Rak* ☎ *02/234–9436* ⊕ *siambronze.com* ⊗ *Weekdays 9–5:30, Sat. 9–5* Ⓜ *Skytrain: Saphan Taksin.*

SUKHUMVIT

CLOTHING AND FABRICS

Naj Collection. This store stocks some of the best silk products you will find, from accessories to home decor. It shares space in a traditional Thai house with Naj Exquisite Thai Cuisine, which serves very tasty traditional food. ⊠ *42 Convent Rd., off N. Sathorn Rd., Silom* ⊕ *Opposite Bangkok Nursing Hospital* ☎ *02/664–0664* ⊕ *www.najcollection.com* ⊗ *Daily 10–10* Ⓜ *Subway: Silom; Skytrain: Sala Daeng.*

2

Raja Fashions. Photographs here show former heads of state proudly modeling their new suits made by Raja Fashions. Raja has a reputation for tailoring some of the finest men's and women's fashions in Bangkok. ✉ *160/1 Sukhumvit, between Soi 6 and 8, Sukhumvit* ☎ *02/253–8379* ⊕ *www.rajasfashions.com* ⊗ *Weekdays and Sat. 10:30–8* Ⓜ *Subway: Sukhumvit; Skytrain: Nana.*

JEWELRY

Uthai's Gems. With top-quality gems, reliable service, and hordes of repeat clients, it's no wonder you need an appointment to peruse the huge inventory at Uthai's Gems. ✉ *28/7 Soi Ruam Rudi, Pathumwan* ☎ *02/253–8582* ⊗ *Daily 10–6* Ⓜ *Skytrain: Ploenchit.*

SHOPPING CENTERS

Emporium. One of the first malls in Bangkok, this glitzy place has a little sales area on the sixth floor full of beautiful silks, incense, and glassware, all reasonably priced. The mall has recently been renovated and expanded to include Em Quartier, with exclusive high-end shops and fine dining on both sides of Sukhumvit. ✉ *622 Sukhumvit Rd., between Sois 24 and 26, Sukhumvit* ☎ *02/269–1000* ⊕ *www.theemdistrict.com* ⊗ *Daily 10–10* Ⓜ *Skytrain: Phrom Phong.*

Terminal 21. The levels at this upscale mall represent different parts of the world. There's a San Francisco section, for instance, complete with cable cars and a miniature Golden Gate Bridge, plus a London floor, an Istanbul, and many others. The food court on the top floor, is one of Bangkok's best, there is a multiplex cinema, and many shops and restaurants to hang out in. ✉ *2,88 Sukhumvit, Soi 19, at Asok Montri Rd., Sukhumvit* ☎ *02/108–0888* ⊕ *www.terminal21.co.th* ⊗ *Daily 10–10* Ⓜ *Subway: Sukhumvit, Skytrain: Asok.*

NORTHERN BANGKOK

DUTY-FREE SHOPPING

King Power International Group. If you want the convenience of duty-free shopping, try King Power. You pay for the items at the shop, then pick them up at Suvarnabhumi Airport when you depart Thailand (or simply take them with you). You need your passport and an airline ticket, and you need to make your purchase at least eight hours before leaving the country. The airport branch is open 24 hours. ✉ *King Power Complex, 8/2 Rangnam Rd., Phayathai, Ratchathewi* ☎ *02/205–8888* ⊕ *www.kingpower.com* Ⓜ *Skytrain: Victory Monument.*

MARKETS

Fodor's Choice ★ **Chatuchak Weekend Market.** You can purchase virtually anything at the city's largest market, including silk items in a mudmee (tie-dyed before weaving) design that would sell for five times the price in the United States. Despite its name the market is open from Wednesday through Sunday, though only the plant section is open on Wednesday and Thursday. It's best to come on Friday or the weekend—in the morning before the place gets too crowded and hot.

An afternoon at JJ, as it is known by locals ("ch" is pronounced "jha" in Thai, so phonetically Chatuchak is Jatujak), is not for the faint of heart: up to 200,000 people visit each day, and there are more than 15,000 vendors. But what's a little discomfort when there are such fantastic bargains to be had? Go prepared with bottles of water, comfortable shoes, and make sure to print out a copy of the map of the market from the website. Strategically placed food vendors mean you don't have to stop shopping to grab a bite.

Easy to reach, Chatuchak is across the street from the northern terminus of the Skytrain and near the Northern Bus Terminal. Just follow the crowd. Once inside, even with a map, it's easy to get turned around in the mind-boggling array of goods, but this is also part of the joy that Chatuchak has to offer—wandering through the maze of vendors and suddenly stumbling upon a beautiful teak table, handmade skirt, or colorful paper lamp.

The borders between the market's many sections can be a bit hazy— the stalls with animals, for example, spill into the silverware area—but you can keep your bearings by remembering that the outer ring has mainly new clothing and shoes, with some plants, garden supplies, and home decor. The next ring is primarily used (and some new) clothing and shoes plus accessories like jewelry, belts, and bags. Farther in are pottery, antiques, furniture, dried goods, and live animals. ⊠ *Phaholyothin Rd., Chatuchak* ⊕ *www.chatuchak.org* ⊗ *Wed.–Sun. 6–6 (Wed. and Thurs. plant section only)* Ⓜ *Subway: Chatuchak Park; Skytrain: Mo Chit.*

SPAS

Venues offering traditional massage are common in Bangkok—you can even pamper yourself while sightseeing at Wat Po. The staff at your hotel can recommend reputable therapists. If you have the time, pull out all the stops with a two-hour massage. ■**TIP**➜ **Spa treatments at top hotels tend to fill up at least a day in advance, so plan ahead.**

PATHUMWAN

Anantara Spa. A relaxing massage with warm oils is among the many treatments available at the Anantara Siam Bangkok. You can even arrange for a poolside massage. ⊠ *155 Ratchadamri Rd., Pathumwan* ☎ *02/126–8866* ⊕ *http://siam-bangkok.anantara.com* Ⓜ *Skytrain: Ratchadamri.*

COMO Shambhala. The ultimate urban escape, this spa relaxes you upon arrival with a cup of ginger-lemongrass tea. There's a wide range of treatments. The Metropolitan Bath treatment starts with an invigorating salt scrub, followed by a luxurious soak and a relaxing massage. ⊠ *Metropolitan Hotel, 27 S. Sathorn Rd., Sathorn* ☎ *02/625–3355* ⊕ *www.comoshambhala.com* Ⓜ *Subway: Lumphini; Skytrain: Sala Daeng.*

I. Sawan Spa. This spa's facilities are among the city's most cutting-edge, relaxing, and beautiful. The "residential spa cottages," suites clustered around a courtyard adjacent to the spa, have their own treatment spaces. Reasonably priced spa packages are available. ✉ *Grand Hyatt Erawan, 494 Ratchadamri Rd., Pathumwan* ☎ *02/254–1234* ⊕ *www. bangkok.grand.hyatt.com* Ⓜ *Skytrain: Ratchadamri.*

Seasons Spa. The seventh-floor spa at the Conrad Bangkok offers a full lineup of massages and other detox and stress-relieving treatments— some as brief as 30 minutes—along with facials, manicures, and other beauty regimens. The signature treatments all involve a bathing ritual. The 11 treatment rooms have fine city views. ✉ *Conrad Bangkok, 87 Wittayu (Wireless Rd.), Pathumwan* ☎ *02/690–9355* ⊕ *www. conradhotels.com/bangkok* Ⓜ *Skytrain: Ploenchit.*

SILOM

Mandarin Oriental Spa. A gentle massage in genteel surroundings is what you'll get at the Mandarin's spa. Amid the wood-panel sophistication you can treat yourself to facials, wraps, and massage. The signature treatments run 90 minutes and will leave you feeling exquisitely pampered. ✉ *Mandarin Oriental, 48 Oriental Ave., Bang Rak* ☎ *02/659–9000* ⊕ *www.mandarinoriental.com/bangkok* Ⓜ *Skytrain: Saphan Taksin.*

Ruen Nuad. An inexpensive but excellent option for traditional Thai massage is Ruen Nuad. A 90-minute Thai massage costs B500, an oil massage B700. ✉ *42 Thanon Convent, 2nd fl., Bang Rak* ☎ *02/632– 2662* Ⓜ *Subway: Silom; Skytrain: Sala Daeng.*

SUKHUMVIT

Oasis Spa. The treatments at Oasis Spa take place in a Thai-style house. Among the inventive treatments are a coffee-bean body scrub and detoxifying algae and green-tea body wraps. A second branch is at Sukhumvit, Soi 31. ✉ *88 Sukhumvit, Soi 51, Sukhumvit* ☎ *02/662– 6171* ⊕ *www.oasisspa.net* Ⓜ *Skytrain: Thong Lo.*

Yunomori Onsen Spa. Bangkok's first Japanese hot spring, this traditional bathhouse has first-class spa treatments. There's even real spring water, thousands of gallons of it, trucked up from the famed Raksawarin Hot Springs in Ranong. Choose from among several pools, from a toasty hot tub down to a cold plunge pool. There are also a steam room and a sauna. ✉ *A-Square 120/5, Sukhumvit, Soi 26, Sukhumvit* ✛ *Take a taxi down Sukhumvit, Soi 26 to A-Square* ☎ *02/259–5778* ⊕ *www. yunomorionsen.com* Ⓜ *Skytrain: Phrom Phong.*

AROUND
BANGKOK

WELCOME TO AROUND BANGKOK

TOP REASONS TO GO

★ **Heading into the Wild:** A huge expanse of untouched jungle surrounds Kanchanaburi, a launchpad for trekking, elephant riding, and river rafting.

★ **Floating Markets:** This area has more floating markets than anywhere else in Thailand. The most famous is at Damnoen Saduak, the region's sole market that still operates daily.

★ **Seeing Old Siam:** History awaits outside Bangkok at a Neolithic site, the remains of a Khmer temple (Muang Singh Historical Park in Kanchanaburi), and in Nakhon Pathom, Thailand's oldest seat of Buddhist learning.

★ **Bridge on the River Kwai:** For a glimpse of more recent history, visit the remnants of the "Death Railway" in Kanchanaburi and walk across the bridge made famous by the movie *The Bridge on the River Kwai*.

★ **River Views in Ayutthaya:** This city, an easy day trip from Bangkok, combines great river views with an island full of fascinating wats.

1 Day Trips from Bangkok. When people head south, it's usually to visit Thailand's famous beaches, but along the way are the floating market at Damnoen Saduak and Muang Boran, a huge park with replicas of the country's landmarks. To the west of Bangkok is Nakhon Pathom, keeper of Thailand's biggest stupa.

2 Phetchaburi. Phetchaburi has many interesting temples and a few royal summer palaces. Three hours south of Bangkok, it makes for a long day trip. Hire a car and driver to make the trip easier or visit as part of a one- or two-day trip to the coastal resort of Hua Hin.

3 Kanchanaburi and Nearby. Kanchanaburi, two hours west of Bangkok, is best known as the site of the famous Bridge on the River Kwai. If you're not in a hurry to get back to Bangkok, you can continue your exploration of stunning Kanchanaburi Province, with day trips to 13th-century Khmer ruins and two national parks containing waterfalls.

4 Sangklaburi. Kanchanaburi Province's farthest attraction is Sangklaburi. This city on Myanmar's doorstep supports Thai,

Mon, Karen, and Bangladeshi communities, and boats here travel to a village submerged in a reservoir.

5 Ayutthaya and Nearby. Within easy reach of Bangkok, Ayutthaya is a historically significant ruin, and once one of the country's most important cities. Nearby Bang Pa-In, with its famous Royal Palace, and Lopburi, with its monkey-infested temples, are a bit farther off the beaten track.

GETTING ORIENTED

3

If you need respite from the heat, noise, and pollution of Bangkok, the surrounding countryside offers many possibilities. There are several sights directly outside the city, easily reached in a few hours by bus, train, or taxi. Kanchanaburi Province can become a mini-vacation all on its own, with Kanchanaburi city being a gateway to Thailand's wilderness.

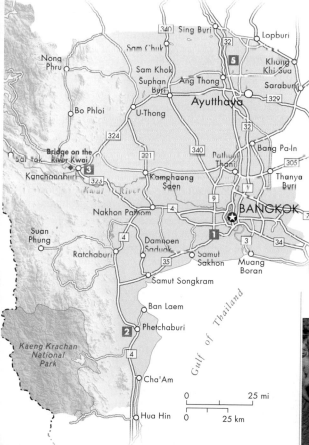

Sing Buri, Lopburi, Sam Chuk, Nong Phru, Khong Khi Sua, Sam Khok, Saraburi, Suphan Buri, Ang Thong, Ayutthaya, Bo Phloi, U-Thong, 324, Bang Pa-In, Bridge on the River Kwai, 301, 340, Pathum Thani, Sai Yok, Kanchanaburi, 323, Kwai River, Kamphaeng Saen, Thanya Buri, Nakhon Pathom, BANGKOK, Suan Phung, Damnoen Saduak, Ratchaburi, Samut Sakhon, Muang Boran, Samut Songkram, Ban Laem, Phetchaburi, Kaeng Krachan National Park, Cha'Am, Gulf of Thailand, Hua Hin

0 25 mi
0 25 km

Updated by
Simon Stewart

Escaping the congestion and chaos of Bangkok is quite simple, and a must for anyone who wants a truly memorable Thailand experience. The surrounding provinces and cities make for a comfortably paced day trip, or an easy getaway for a few days. However you spend your time, you're sure to encounter amazing scenery, interesting culture, and unforgettable adventure.

Only 50 km (31 miles) west of Bangkok is a small haven for those seeking enlightenment. The province of Nakhon Pathom has the tallest Buddha monument in the world, Phra Pathom Chedi.

Travel a little farther west and you'll be in Kanchanaburi, with its mixture of tranquil scenery, war museums, and temples. Kanchanaburi is most known for the Bridge on the River Kwai, but there's plenty to keep you occupied. If you're an explorer at heart, this is a great starting-off point for visiting national parks, rafting, hiking, and riding elephants.

If you're interested in seeing a more traditional aspect of Thailand, head down to Damnoen Saduak. Here you'll be surrounded by the colors and smells of a market while drifting along in a small, wooden boat. The floating market primarily caters to tourists, so most of the vendors sell souvenirs and produce.

History buffs and Buddhists should travel a bit farther south to the seaport town of Phetchaburi for its wats and palaces. Don't be frightened of the monkeys that roam the streets here.

Don't have time to travel the entire country? The peaceful grounds of Muang Boran, an outdoor park-museum, is shaped roughly like Thailand and displays replicas of important monuments from all parts of the country.

For seafood served Thai style, head to Samut Songkram, where you'll be able to eat your fill of clams and other fruit of the sea along the Gulf of Thailand.

If you have more time, check out Sangklaburi. Thai, Mon, Karen, and Bangladeshi communities flourish in this city near the Myanmar border. Many people who venture to Sangklaburi go on trekking tours and visit the Thai border town of Three Pagodas Pass.

PLANNING

WHEN TO GO

On weekends and national holidays, particularly during the mid-April Buddhist New Year water festival, Kanchanaburi and the restaurants at Samut Songkram are packed with Thais. In high season (from November to March) the floating market in Damnoen Saduak has more tourists than vendors. The waterfalls of Kanchanaburi Province are at their best during or just after the rainy season (from June to November). The fossil shells in Don Hoi Lod in Samut Songkram are best seen in dry season or at low tide in rainy season. See the fireflies in Ampawa between May and October.

PLANNING YOUR TIME

You can take in all the highlights north and west of Bangkok in about a week. Three or four days are enough to experience the top Kanchanaburi Province sights, starting with the serene River Kwai and the town of Kanchanaburi. From there you can take day trips to explore the waterfalls and other natural wonders. Historic Ayutthaya, a drive of little more than an hour from downtown Bangkok, is an easy day trip, as are Lopburi and the floating market at Damnoen Saduak.

GETTING HERE AND AROUND

BUS TRAVEL

Most buses depart from Bangkok's Southern Bus Terminal; tickets are sold on a first-come, first-served basis, but service is so frequent that it's seldom a problem finding an empty seat.

CAR TRAVEL

Distances from Bangkok are short enough to drive, though it's more relaxing to hire a car and driver.

TAXI AND SONGTHAEW TRAVEL

Taking one of Bangkok's air-conditioned taxis is a good way to access sights, particularly those in Nakhon Pathom, Samut Songkram, and Muang Boran. Estimate around B500 per hour, with the final amount dependent upon your bargaining skills. Standard rates for trips outside of Bangkok, implemented by the Ministry of Transport, are displayed in many, though not all, taxis and if available should be used as a starting point for any negotiations.

Outside Bangkok, *songthaews* (pickups with wooden benches in the truck bed) are often the closest thing to taxis.

HEALTH AND SAFETY

The region is generally safe, and the towns mentioned *in this chapter* have hospitals. Take normal precautions and keep valuables on your person at all times when traveling by bus or train. Too-good-to-be-true deals—particularly involving gems—are *always* a rip-off. On a more amusing note, the monkeys of Phetchaburi are cute but cunning, and may relieve you of your possessions, especially food.

MONEY MATTERS

Generally speaking, finding banks and ATMs isn't difficult, especially in towns. Most main bank branches close at 4 pm, with many smaller branches, often located in shopping malls and department stores, remaining open into the evening and on weekends. Remember that the farther out from civilization you travel, the fewer ATMs you'll find. Don't expect to withdraw money outside a national park or in a tribal village. It's probably best if before leaving Bangkok you exchange the money you think you'll require.

RESTAURANTS

The areas around Bangkok allow you to sample both regional and non-Thai ethnic foods. Kanchanaburi and Sangklaburi have Mon, Karen, Bangladeshi, and Burmese communities serving their own specialties. A must-try is *laphae to*, a Burmese salad of nuts and fermented tea leaves. In Nakhon Pathom try the excellent rice-based dessert *khao larm*. Phetchaburi is famous for its desserts and for *khao chae*, chilled rice soaked in herb-infused water.

HOTELS

An overnight stay is essential in Sangklaburi and highly recommended in Kanchanaburi and Phetchaburi. Stay in Damnoen Saduak the night before you visit the floating market to avoid an early-morning bus ride.

Luxury accommodations are more common in most provincial towns, but be prepared to stay at a resort on the outskirts if you want to sample the very best. It's best to book ahead on weekends and national holidays in Kanchanaburi.

WHAT IT COSTS IN BAHT				
	$	$$	$$$	$$$$
RESTAURANTS	under B200	B200–B300	B301–B400	over B400
HOTELS	under B2,000	B2,000–B4,000	B4,001–B6,000	over B6,000

Restaurant prices are for a main course, excluding tax and tip. Hotel prices are for a standard double in high season, excluding service charge and tax.

TOURS

Asian Trails. It's easy to travel in the areas around Bangkok on your own, but this company organizes trips to the floating markets, as well as trekking trips, homestays, and bicycle tours. ⊠ *Bangkok* ☎ *02/626–2000* ⊕ *www.asiantrails.travel* ✉ *From B2,600.*

Diethelm Travel. Ayutthaya, Kanchanaburi, and the Damnoen Saduak floating market are among the stops on this outfit's four-day, three-night Central Highlights Journey, led by an English-speaking guide. The all-inclusive fee covers lodging, meals, and entrance and boat fees. One-day excursions to the floating market and other attractions are also available. ☎ *02/660–7000* ⊕ *www.diethelmtravel.com/Thailand* ✉ *B19,200 for Highlights tour; call for shorter trips' pricing.*

DAY TRIPS FROM BANGKOK

MUANG BORAN

20 km (12 miles) southeast of Bangkok.

An easy and popular day trip from Bangkok, Muang Boran provides a captivating introduction to Thailand's architectural and cultural highlights via replicas and reconstructions.

GETTING HERE AND AROUND

BUS TRAVEL The best bus choice from Bangkok to Muang Boran (two hours; B30) is the air-conditioned Bus 511, which leaves every half hour from Bangkok's Southern Bus Terminal; take it to the end of the line at Pak Nam. You can also catch this bus on Sukhumvit Road. Transfer to Songthaew 36 (B10), which goes to the entrance of Muang Boran.

CAR TRAVEL Driving to Muang Boran requires engaging Bangkok's heavy and unpredictable traffic. Take the Samrong–Samut Prakan expressway and turn left at the Samut Prakan intersection onto Old Sukhumvit Road. Muang Boran is well signposted on the left at Km 33. The trip should take less than two hours.

EXPLORING

Muang Boran (*Ancient City*). An outdoor museum with more than 100 replicas and reconstructions of Thailand's most important architectural sites, monuments, and palaces, this park is shaped like the country, and the attractions are placed roughly in their correct geographical position. A "traditional Thai village" on the grounds sells crafts, but the experience is surprisingly untouristy. The park stretches over 320 acres, and takes about four hours to cover by car. Or you can rent a bicycle at the entrance for B50. Small outdoor cafés throughout the grounds serve decent Thai food. ⊠ *296/1 Sukhumvit Rd., Bangpoo, Samut Prakan* 🏠 *02/709–1648* ⊕ *www.ancientcitygroup.net/ancientsiam/en* 🔁 *B700* 🕙 *Daily 9–7.*

DAMNOEN SADUAK

109 km (68 miles) southwest of Bangkok.

The image of this frenetic market of floating vendors selling all sorts of raw and prepared food is so evocative that it has become an ad agency favorite. Though the market can feel touristy, a visit here is a memorable way to experience a Thai tradition.

GETTING HERE AND AROUND

Getting to Damnoen Saduak can be tricky. It's probably best to join one of the tours offered at most hotels and guesthouses.

Canary Travel Thailand. Kanchanaburi and the floating market at Damnoen Saduak are among the destinations on sightseeing and package tours booked by this agency that specializes in western Thailand. Canary Travel does online and phone bookings, will arrange a pick up from your hotel in Bangkok, and offers several multiday stay packages. ⊠ *10*

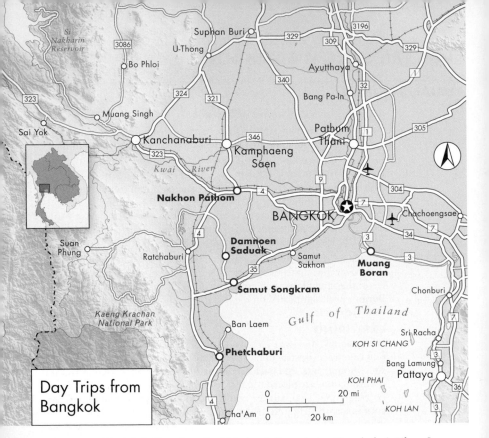

Day Trips from Bangkok

Tani Rd., Banglamphu,Taladyod, Pranakorn, Bangkok ✢ Khao San Rd. ☎ 026/291687 ⊕ www.canarytravelthailand.com ✉ From B800.

BUS TRAVEL Buses to Damnoen Saduak (from two to three hours; B73) leave Bangkok's Southern Bus Terminal every 20 minutes starting at 5 am. From the station in Damnoen Saduak, walk or take a songthaew along the canal for 1½ km (1 mile) to the floating market. Buses also run from Nakhon Pathom and Samut Songkram.

CAR TRAVEL Take Route 4 (Phetkasem Road) and turn left at Km 80. Continue for 25 km (16 miles) along the Bang Phae–Damnoen Saduak Road. The drive from Samut Songkram to Damnoen Saduak, along Route 325, is pleasant, particularly if you go via Ampawa. The entire trip takes two hours.

EXPLORING

Damnoen Saduak floating market. A colorful market of produce and other foods sold by vendors on small boats, Damnoen Saduak is an icon of Thai tourism. Often overrun with visitors, the market comes off a bit like a Disney World exhibit and bears only passing resemblance to the authentic commercial life of this canal-strewn corner of Thailand. On the other hand, even though it feels like a theatrical production, this is one of the few opportunities to witness a fading Thai tradition, and some of the food—including noodle soup, seafood dishes, grilled meats, mango ice cream, coconut pancakes, and fried bananas—is quite tasty. The best way to enjoy the market is to hire a boat and come early. The area only becomes more crowded as the day progresses and ever more tour groups arrive. ⊠ *Off Rte. 325, 109 km (68 miles) southwest of Bangkok.*

WHERE TO EAT AND STAY

You'll find plenty of food stalls and small street restaurants, as well as fruits and vegetables, along the main road.

$

RESORT

🍴 **Baan Sukchoke Country Resort.** The small wooden bungalows surrounding a pond are a bit rickety, but they're clean and comfortable. **Pros:** countryside atmosphere; helpful staff. **Cons:** aging facilities; a bit out of town. $ *Rooms from: B450* ⊠ *103 Moo 5 T. Thanat* ☎ *032/254301* ▭ *No credit cards* ➴ *40 rooms* 🍴 *No meals.*

$

HOTEL

🍴 **Little Bird Hotel.** Convenience is the top selling point of this hotel a 10-minute walk from the boats for the floating market and close to banks, stores, and cafés. **Pros:** most convenient hotel to the floating market; arranges market tours. **Cons:** no hot water; basic rooms, $ *Rooms from: B400* ⊠ *Moo 1/8 Amphur Damnernsaduak* ☎ *0320/254382, 03/225–4382* ⊕ *www.noknoihotel.com* ▭ *No credit cards* ➴ *30 rooms* 🍴 *No meals,*

SAMUT SONGKRAM

72 km (45 miles) south of Bangkok.

The provincial town of Samut Songkram has little to recommend it, but the many nearby attractions make this an enjoyable day trip from Bangkok. There are terrific seafood restaurants along the waterfront at Don Hoi Lod; the area is also a good base for exploring some of the surrounding villages on the canal network, such as Ampawa, with its small floating market.

GETTING HERE AND AROUND

BUS TRAVEL Buses depart from Bangkok's Southern Bus Terminal for Samut Songkram (1½ hours; B50) every hour from 3 am to 6:30 pm. Bus 996 can drop you off at Ampawa.

CAR TRAVEL Route 35, the main road south to Samut Songkram (one hour), is mainly a two-lane highway that can be slow going if there's heavy traffic. Add an extra half hour to all trip times for possible delays.

SONGTHAEW
TRAVEL In town there are frequent songthaews to Don Hoi Lod and Ampawa (10 minutes; B20). Drivers stop taking passengers at 5 pm.

SAFETY AND PRECAUTIONS

Ampawa can be crowded, especially during holidays. Keep a careful eye on your possessions. Make sure you keep an eye on the time if you are taking a songthaew from Don Hoi Lod to Ampawa.

ESSENTIALS

Emergencies Mae Khlong Song Hospital. ⊠ *198/1 Ratrasit Rd.* ☎ *034/715001* ⊕ *www.maeklonghospital.com.*

EXPLORING

FAMILY **Ampawa.** The charming village of Ampawa, 10 km (7 miles) by songthaew from Samuk Songkram, has a **floating market** similar to, but smaller than, the one in Damnoen Saduak. The market opens on Friday, Saturday, and Sunday evening from 5 to 9. The food market in the street adjacent to the canal starts at around 1 pm. Featured in a Thai movie, popular **fireflies tours** allow you to enjoy both the market and the beautiful insect-lighted trees. The bugs are best seen from May to October and in the waning moon. The hour-long tours usually run every half hour from 6:30 to 9 pm. You can arrange a tour directly at the pier (B650 for a boat) or through your hotel (around B70 per person). Unless you have private transportation, you'll have to spend the night in Ampawa, as the last bus back to Bangkok is in the early evening. ✉ *Samut Songkram* 🎟 *Free.*

FAMILY **Don Hoi Lod.** On weekends Thai families flock to the village of Don Hoi Lod, about 3 km (2 miles) south of Samut Songkram, to eat the clams (try them with garlic and pepper) and other seafood dishes at the tree-shaded restaurants at the mouth of the Mae Khlong River. The village is named after a local clam with a tubular shell, the fossilized remains of which are found on the riverbanks. The best times to view the fossils are March and April, when the water is low. The rest of the year you can also see the fossils in the early morning and in the evening at low tide. ✉ *Off Rte. 35.*

WHERE TO EAT AND STAY

There are many homestay options in Ampawa for every budget. The TAT office in Kanchanaburi *(see Kanchanaburi, below)* has details.

$ SEAFOOD FAMILY 🍴 **Kunpao.** Among the last in a long row of seafood places in Don Hoi Lod, this restaurant on wooden stilts is usually packed with Thai families who come to enjoy the gentle breeze and the fried sea perch, horseshoe-egg spicy salad, and grilled prawns. The atmosphere is both busy and relaxed. Try to get one of the few sit-on-the-floor tables directly above the water. There's a playground for kids. Avoid weekends and holidays if you are looking for quiet. [$] *Average main: B120* ✉ *1/3 Moo 4, Bangyakang* ☎ *034/723703* ✍ *Reservations not accepted.*

$ RESORT 🏨 **Thanicha Healthy Resort.** In an old wooden house close to the market, this boutique hotel by the main canal is a perfect weekend escape from Bangkok. **Pros:** nice café and restaurant in front; free Wi-Fi in hotel. **Cons:** busier and more expensive on weekends. [$] *Rooms from: B1,590* ✉ *261 T. Ampawa A., Ampawa* ☎ *034/725511* 🌐 *www.thanicha.com* 💳 *No credit cards* 🛏 *25 rooms* 🍽 *No meals.*

NAKHON PATHOM

56 km (35 miles) west of Bangkok.

Reputed to be Thailand's oldest city (it's thought to date from 150 BC), Nakhon Pathom was once the center of the Dvaravati kingdom, an affiliation of Mon city-states between the 6th and the 11th centuries. The region's first center of Buddhist learning, established about a millennium ago, it's home to the Buddhist monument Phra Pathom Chedi.

Continued on page 146

THAI MARKETS
by Hana Borrowman

For an authentic Thai shopping experience, forget air-conditioned malls and head to the traditional markets, or *talaats*. Take a deep breath and prepare for an intoxicating medley of colors, sounds, smells, and tastes.

Entrepreneurs set up shop wherever there's an open space—roadsides, footbridges, and bustling waterways. You'll find all sorts of intriguing items: caramelized crickets and still-wriggling eels; "potency" potions made from pigs' feet; fierce-looking hand weapons like elegant samurai swords and knife-edged brass knuckles; temple offerings; plastic toys; and clothing.

Markets are an integral part of Thai life. Locals stop by for a meal from their favorite food vendor or to sit at a coffee stall, gossiping or discussing politics. Whole families take part: You might see an old woman bargaining with a customer at a hardware stall while her grandchild sleeps in a makeshift hammock strung up beneath the table.

Damnoen Saduak's floating market.

GREAT FINDS

Low prices make impulse buys almost irresistible. Here are a few things to keep your eyes out for while you shop.

Housewares. You'll find metal "monks' bowls" like those used for alms-collection, cushions, wicker baskets, carved tables, and ornate daybeds. Polished coconut-shell spoons and wooden salad servers are more practical if you're not up for shipping home your wares. Small wooden bowls and utensils start at around B150.

Memorabilia. Toy *tuk-tuks* (three-wheeled cabs) made from old tin cans, sequined elephants sewn onto cushion covers, satin Muay Thai boxer shorts, wooden frogs that croak—all make great and inexpensive souvenirs, and most Thai markets have them in droves.

Jewelry. Throughout the country, hill-tribe women sell beautiful silver and beaded jewelry. Silver bangles start at B250 and chunky silver rings with semiprecious stones like opal and mother-of-pearl are B350 and up. You'll also find "precious" gemstones and crystals, but you're better off making serious purchases at reputable shops in Bangkok.

Silk. Thailand is famous for its bright, beautiful silks. Raw Thai silk has a relatively coarse texture and a matte finish; it's good value, and wonderful for curtains and upholstery. You'll also find bolts of less expensive shimmering satins, and ready-made items like pajamas, purses, and scarves.

Prices vary enormously—depending on quality and weight—from B100 to upwards of B700 a meter. To test for authenticity, hold the fabric up to the light: If it's pure silk, the color changes, but fake silk shines a uniformly whitish tone. You can also ask for a swatch to burn—pure fibers crumble to ash, while synthetics curl or melt.

Clothes. Markets have tons of clothing: the ubiquitous Thai fisherman pants; factory seconds from The Gap; knockoff designer jeans; and, invariably, frilly underwear. But some of Thailand's edgiest designers are touting more modern apparel at markets as well. It's hard to say whether these up-and-comers are following catwalk trends or vice-versa. Bangkok fashion houses like **Sretsis** (feminine dresses; ⊕ www.sretsis.com) and **Greyhound** (casual, unisex urbanwear; ⊕ www.greyhound.co.th) are good places to scope out styles beforehand. Prices vary greatly—a cheaply made suit could cost as little as B1,000, while an expertly tailored, high-quality version might be B20,000 or more. But it's difficult to determine quality unless you're experienced.

FLOATING MARKETS

Sunday morning at Damnoen Saduak.

Floating markets date from Bangkok's "Venice of the East" era in the 19th century, when canal-side residents didn't have to go to market—the market came to them. Many waterways have been filled in to create roads, so there are only a handful of floating markets left. These survivors have a nostalgic appeal, with vendors in straw hats peddling produce, flowers, snacks, and crafts against a backdrop of stilt houses and riverbanks.

Thailand's original floating market in Damnoen Saduak (↪ *above*) is very famous, but it's also crowded and overpriced. Still, you can get a taste of the old river life here, in addition to lots of touristy souvenirs. If you visit, try to stay nearby so that you can arrive near dawn; the market is open from 6 AM till noon, but by 9 it's usually swarming with sightseers.

The Amphawa Floating market near Samut Songkram, set on a leafy waterway dotted with temples and traditional Thai homes, is less crowded and more authentic.

LOGISTICS

Many hotels and guesthouses can arrange a longtail boat and an oarsman for you. You can also just head to the pier, though it's a good idea to ask your hotel what going rates are first. Private boats start at around B500 an hour, but oarsmen may try to charge much more. Haggle hard, and don't get in a boat before you've agreed on price and duration. If you join a group of locals in a boat, you'll often pay a set rate per person.

Longtail boat.

SHOPPING KNOW-HOW

Most markets begin to stir around dawn, and morning is the best time to visit—it's not too hot, and most Thais do their marketing early in the day, so you'll get to watch all the local action. Avoid rainy days: The scene loses a lot of its allure when everything's covered in plastic sheets.

Flower market in Bangkok.

SHOPPING TIPS

■ Check prices at less touristy spots—Chinatown, Pratunam Market, and MBK in Bangkok—to get a sense of cost.

■ Keep money and valuables like cell phones tucked away.

■ Avoid tuk-tuk drivers who offer you a shopping tour. They'll pressure you to drop a lot of cash at their friends' stalls.

■ Look for the One Tambon One Product (OTOP) government stamp on market goods. A tambon is a subdistrict—there are over 7,000 in the country, and one handmade, locally sourced product is selected from each.

■ Steer clear of exotic animal products, such as lizard skins, ivory, tortoiseshell, and anything made of tiger. These products may come from endangered animals; if so, it's illegal to leave Thailand with them or bring them into the U.S. If not illegal, they may be counterfeit.

■ Only buy antiques at reputable shops; real Thai antiques cannot be exported without a license, which good shops provide. Most so-called antiques at markets are knockoffs.

■ Thai markets are full of counterfeits—DVDs, computer software, and designer clothes and accessories. In addition to being illegal, these items vary in quality, so examine the products and your conscience carefully before you buy.

Straw hats for sale.

HOW TO BARGAIN

Thais love theatrical bargaining, and it's customary to haggle over nearly everything. Here are some tips for getting a fair price. The most important thing is to have fun!

DO

- Decide about how much you're willing to pay before you start bargaining.

- Let the vendor set the opening price. This is the standard etiquette; vendors who make you go first may be trying to take you for a ride. Vendors who don't speak English may type their price into a calculator, and you can respond in kind.

- Come equipped with a few Thai phrases, such as "How much is this?" "A discount?" and "Expensive!"

- Bargain quietly, and if possible, when the vendor is alone. Vendors are unlikely to give big discounts in front of an audience.

- Be polite, no matter what. Confidence and charming persistence are winning tactics in Thailand—not hostility.

- Honor your lowest bid if it's accepted.

DON'T

- Don't lose your temper or raise your voice. These are big no-no's in the land of smiles.

- Don't hesitate to aim low. Your opening counteroffer should be around 50% or 60% of the vendor's price, and you can expect to settle for 10% to 30% off the initial price. If you're buying more than one item, shoot for a bigger discount.

- Don't be afraid to walk away. Often the vendor will call you back with a lower price.

- Don't get too caught up in negotiating. It's OK to back down if you really want something.

- Don't bargain for food—prices are fixed.

Woman displaying Thai silk.

GETTING HERE AND AROUND

BUS TRAVEL   Buses depart from Bangkok's Southern Bus Terminal for Nakhon Pathom (one hour; B46) every hour from 5:30 am to 8 pm.

CAR TRAVEL   Driving west from Bangkok, allow an hour to get to Nakhon Pathom on Route 4.

TRAIN TRAVEL   From Bangkok, 10 trains a day run at regular intervals to Nakhon Pathom (1½ hours; from B14 to B20). Some of the Nakhon Pathom trains continue on to Phetchaburi (four hours; from B94 to B114) and points farther south. Trains to Kanchanaburi also stop in Nakhon Pathom.

EXPLORING

Phra Pathom Chedi. The tallest Buddhist monument in the world, Phra Pathom Chedi tops out at 417 feet, just higher—but less ornate—than the chedi at Shwe Dagon in Myanmar. Erected in the 6th century, the site's first chedi was destroyed in a Burmese attack in 1057. Surrounding the chedi is one of Thailand's most important temples, which contains the ashes of King Rama VI.

The terraces around the temple complex are full of fascinating statuary, including Chinese figures, a large reclining Buddha, and an unusual Buddha seated in a chair. By walking around the inner circle surrounding the chedi, you can see novice monks in their classrooms through arched stone doorways. Traditional dances are sometimes performed in front of the temple, and during Loi Krathong, a festival in November that celebrates the end of the rainy season, a fair is set up in the adjacent park. ⊠ *Khwa T. Phrapathom Chedi Rd., off Phetkasem Rd.* 🚃 *B50* ⏱ *Daily 5 am–6 pm.*

Phra Pathom Chedi National Museum. Next to Phra Pathom Chedi is the Phra Pathom Chedi National Museum, which contains Dvaravati artifacts such as images of the Buddha, stone carvings, and stuccos from the 6th to the 11th century. ⊠ *Khwa T. Phrapathom Chedi Rd., Samut Songkram* 🚃 *B30* ⏱ *Wed.–Sun. 9–noon and 1–4.*

FAMILY   **Sampran Riverside.** Roses are just a part of this complex where herbs, bananas, and various flowers, including orchids, flourish. Within the complex are traditional houses and a performance stage, where shows include dancing, Thai boxing, sword fighting, and even wedding ceremonies (daily at 2:45 pm). The park, popular with Thai families, has restaurants and a nice hotel with rooms starting at B2,600. ⊠ *Km 32, Pet Kasem Rd., Samut Songkram* ☎ *034/322544* ⊕ *www. sampranriverside.com* 🚃 *B20, B550 with lunch and show* ⏱ *Daily 6–6.*

Sanam Chandra Palace. While still a prince, the future King Rama VI commissioned this palace, completed in 1911, that's notable architecturally for its French and British flourishes. The surrounding park, which includes ponds, broad lawns, and several other buildings, is a lovely place to relax. Paying the admission fee grants you access to the grounds and all the buildings, where English signs and translations provide information and guidance. Photography is prohibited in some areas. ⊠ *Samut Songkram* ✦ *Follow Petchkasem Rd. 2½ km (1½ miles) west from Phra Pathom Chedi* 🚃 *B50* ⏱ *Tues.–Sun. 9–4.*

WHERE TO EAT

The road from Nakhon Pathom train station has several cafés, and a market where food stalls sell one-plate Thai meals. Similar dining options are at the entrance of the chedi. Keep an eye out for Nakhon Pathom specialties such as *khao larm* (sticky rice, palm sugar, and black beans grilled in hollowed-out bamboo sections) and sweet, pink-flesh pomelo (a large citrus fruit).

PHETCHABURI

132 km (82 miles) south of Bangkok.

This small seaport town with many wats once linked the old Thai capitals of Sukhothai and Ayutthaya with trade routes on the South China Sea and Indian Ocean. Phetchaburi is famous for *khao chae,* a chilled rice dish with sweetmeats once favored by royals that has become a summer tradition in posh Bangkok hotels. You can find it around the day market on Phanit Charoen Road—look for people eating at stalls from small silver bowls—along with *khanom jeen thotman* (noodles with curried fish cake). The city was also a royal retreat during the reigns of Rama IV and Rama V (1851–1910) and has two palaces open to the public. Phetchaburi's wats are within, or easily accessible on foot from, the town center, particularly along Matayawong, Pongsuriya, and Phrasong roads. ■TIP→ Steer clear of the gangs of monkeys on the streets and around Khao Wang, especially with food in your hands.

GETTING HERE AND AROUND

BIKE TRAVEL A bike or a motorbike rented at Rabieng Guesthouse (B120 per day for a bike, B200 per day for a motorbike) is a good way to get around town.

BUS TRAVEL Phetchaburi-bound buses depart Bangkok's Southern Bus Terminal (two hours; B126) every 30 minutes from 5 am to 9 pm. The Phetchaburi Bus Station is north of town, near the night market, but the bus lets you off at the side of the road, which can be a little intimidating. Don't worry; there is a motorcycle taxi stand there with a few drivers who will be happy to help you. This area doesn't have many English speakers, so be patient.

CAR TRAVEL If you're driving, take Route 35, the main road south from Bangkok, then continue on Route 4 to Phetchaburi Province. The trip takes 90 minutes. On the way back to Bangkok, there are two alternatives. Follow signs to Samut Songkram for the shorter trip along Route 35.

TRAIN TRAVEL All trains to southern Thailand stop at Phetchaburi (three hours; from B94 to B114). The train station is north of Phetchaburi on Rot Fai Road. You can hire motorbikes taxis or tuk-tuks from the train or bus station to get to sights or downtown.

EXPLORING

TOP ATTRACTIONS

Khao Luang Cave. Studded with stalactites, this cave overflows with images of the Buddha, among them a 10-meter-long reclining one. Most were put in place by kings Rama IV and Rama V. For a donation of B20

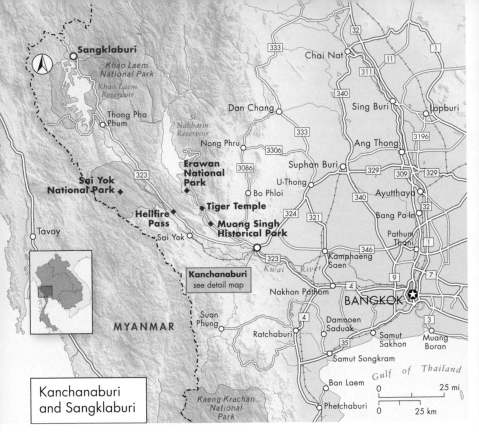

Kanchanaburi
see detail map

Kanchanaburi
and Sangklaburi

or so to pay for the electricity, a nun will light up the rear of the cave for you. A two-minute walk from the parking lot—including some steep stairs—gains you access to the cave. Watch out for the monkeys along the way. **Wat Tham Klaep,** a large monastery at the bottom of the hill below the cave, is open to the public. ■TIP➜ **The cave is best appreciated on a clear morning, between 9 and 10, when the sun shines in and reflects off the brass iconography.** ⊠ *Phetchaburi* ✛ *Off Rot Fai Rd., 5 km (3 miles) north of Phra Nakhon* ▨ *Free* ◷ *Daily 9–4.*

Phra Nakhon Khiri Historical Park (*Khao Wang*). On a forested hillside at the edge of Phetchaburi, the park includes one of King Rama IV's palaces and a series of temples and shrines. Many of these are set high on the hilltop and have good views. Monkeys are a major shoplifting hazard around the gift shops at the foot of the hill. There's a hillside tram (B50) for those not up for the strenuous walk. ⊠ *Phetchaburi* ✛ *Off Phetkasem Rd. east of Rte. 4* ☎ *032/401006, 032/425600* ▨ *B150* ◷ *Daily 9–4.*

Wat Mahathat Worawihan. This 800-year-old Khmer-influenced structure on the western side of the Phetchaburi River is a royal temple. Besides the magnificent architecture, an interesting feature of this wat is a subtle political joke. Look around the base of the Buddha statue outside the main temple. A ring of monkeylike Atlases supports the large Buddha image, but one of the monkeys is not like the others. See if you can find him! ✉ *Bandai-it and Damnoen Kasem Rds.* 🎫 *Free* ⏲ *Daily 6–6.*

WORTH NOTING

Phra Ram Ratchaniwet. Intended as a rainy-season retreat by King Rama V and started in 1910, the palace was eventually completed by King Rama VI in 1916, Phra Ram Ratchaniwet was modeled on a palace of Germany's Kaiser Wilhelm, and consequently has a grand European-style design with art-nouveau flourishes. The dining room has ornate ceramic tiles. ✉ *Ratchadamnoen Rd.* ☎ *032/428083* 🎫 *B50* ⏲ *Daily 9–4.*

3

Wat Yai Suwannaram. Built during the Ayutthaya period, this wat has a 300-year-old painting in its main hall, a small library on stilts above a fishpond (to deter termites), and an ax mark above one of the temple doors that was supposedly left by a Burmese invader. ✉ *Phongsunyia Rd., less than 1 km (½ mile) after crossing river* ⏲ *Daily 5 am–6 pm.*

WHERE TO EAT AND STAY

$ THAI 🍴 **Rabieng Restaurant.** In a small wooden house by the river, this family-run restaurant serves many classic Thai dishes and a few western ones. American music plays in the background. Attached to Rabieng Guesthouse, this is among the few places open past sunset. Try the spicy banana-blossom salad or the stuffed chicken with pandanus leaves. [$] *Average main: B100* ✉ *1 Shesrain Rd.* ☎ *032/425707* 💳 *No credit cards.*

$ B&B/INN 🏨 **Rabieng Guesthouse.** In a cluster of dark-wood plank buildings, these basic rooms are just big enough for beds. **Pros:** restaurant overlooking the river; walking distance to bus terminal. **Cons:** thin walls next to noisy road; shared bathrooms. [$] *Rooms from: B240* ✉ *1 Shesrain Rd.* ☎ *032/425707* 💳 *No credit cards* 🛏 *10 rooms with shared bath* 🍽 *No meals.*

$ HOTEL 🏨 **Royal Diamond Hotel.** About 3 km (2 miles) northwest of town, the Royal Diamond is one of Phetchaburi's few choices for those seeking a hotel instead of a guesthouse. **Pros:** close to Phra Nakhon Khiri Historical Park. **Cons:** out of town. [$] *Rooms from: B1,000* ✉ *555 Moo 1, Phetkasem Rd., Tambon Rai-Som* ☎ *032/411061 up to 70* 🌐 *www.royaldiamondhotel.com* 🛏 *58 rooms* 🍽 *Breakfast.*

KANCHANABURI PROVINCE

The city of Kanchanaburi is home to interesting and sometimes moving World War II historic sites, among them the Bridge on the River Kwai. In and around the city are museums, cave temples, tribal villages, and waterfalls. Hiking, rafting and elephant trekking are among the main activities. Kanchanaburi is the main access point to the large national parks of western Thailand, including Erawan, Muang Singh, and Sai Yok.

KANCHANABURI

140 km (87 miles) west of Bangkok.

Kanchanaburi is laid out along the Mae Khlong and Kwai Yai rivers. Several museums and war cemeteries document the building of the

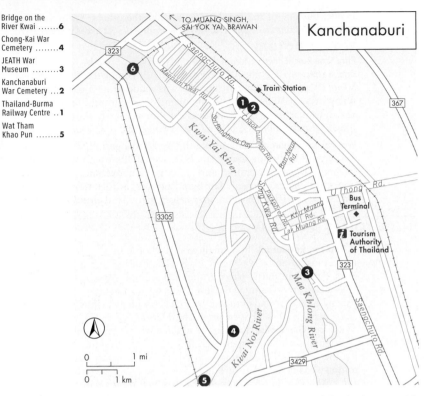

Thailand-Burma Railway during World War II and the high cost paid
in death and suffering. A visit to some of these attractions will put into
context the city's top one, the Bridge on the River Kwai.

GETTING HERE AND AROUND

BUS TRAVEL Air-conditioned buses headed to Kanchanaburi leave from Bangkok's
Southern Bus Terminal (two hours; B85) every 20 minutes from 5 am
to 10:30 pm. Buses also leave eight times a day from Bangkok's Mo
Chit Northern Bus Terminal (three hours; B115).

CAR TRAVEL Allow two hours to reach Kanchanaburi along Route 4. The first half
is on a busy truck route that continues to southern Thailand, but the
second half is more pleasant, through agricultural land. The road to
Kanchanaburi passes through Nakhon Pathom.

**TAXI AND
SONGTHAEW
TRAVEL** In town, options for getting around include pedicabs and motorcycles
with sidecars. Songthaews are better for longer forays out of town and
can be flagged down. The few tuk-tuks and taxis are harder to find.
Drivers are notorious for hiking up prices for tourists, so bring your
best bargaining face.

TRAIN TRAVEL Two Kanchanaburi-bound trains (three hours; B100) leave every day
from Bangkok Noi Railway Station, on the Thonburi side of the Chao
Phraya River.

3

ESSENTIALS

Visitor and Tour Information Tourism Authority of Thailand (*TAT*). ✉ *325 Saengchuto Rd.* ☎ *034/623691* ⊕ *www.tourismthailand.org.*

EXPLORING

TOP ATTRACTIONS

Bridge on the River Kwai. Kanchanaburi is most famous as the location of this bridge, a section of the Thailand-Burma Railway immortalized in director David Lean's epic 1957 film *The Bridge on the River Kwai*. During World War II, the Japanese, with whom Thailand sided, forced about 16,000 prisoners of war and from 50,000 to 100,000 civilian slave laborers from neighboring countries to construct the railway, a supply route through the jungles of Thailand and Burma. Sure-footed visitors can walk across the bridge, whose arched portions are original. In December, a big fair takes place with a sound-and-light show depicting the Allied bombing of the structure late in the war. Next to the bridge is a plaza with restaurants and souvenir shops. ✉ *Maenamkwai and New Zealand Rds.* 🎫 *Free.*

JEATH War Museum. The letters in the first part of its name an acronym for Japan, England, America, Australia, Thailand, and Holland, this museum sits a little more than 2 km (1 mile) downriver from the Bridge on the River Kwai. The museum, founded in 1977 by a monk from the adjoining Wat Chaichumpol, is housed in a replica of the bamboo huts that were used to hold prisoners of war. On display are railway spikes, aerial photographs, newspaper clippings, and original sketches by ex-prisoners depicting their living conditions. ✉ *Wat Chaichumpol, Bantai* ☎ *034/515263* 🎫 *B40* ⊙ *Daily 8–4:30.*

Thailand-Burma Railway Centre. A walk through the center's nine chronologically arranged galleries provides a good overview of the railway's history. Though small, the center is well designed and packed with informative displays. The second-floor coffee shop at the end of the exhibits has a view of the adjacent Kanchanaburi War Cemetery. ✉ *73 Jaokannun Rd.* ☎ *034/512721* ⊕ *www.tbrconline.com* 🎫 *B120* ⊙ *Daily 9–5.*

WORTH NOTING

Chong-Kai War Cemetery. The serene and simple resting place of many of the soldiers forced to work on the Thailand-Burma Railway has neatly organized rows of grave markers. On the grounds of a former hospital for prisoners of war, the cemetery is a little out of the way, and therefore rarely visited. To get here, hire a tuk-tuk or moto-taxi for about B60. ✉ *Kanchanaburi* ✛ *West side of river, 3 km (2 miles) from town* 🎫 *Free.*

Kanchanaburi War Cemetery. Next to noisy Saengchuto Road, this cemetery has row upon row of neatly laid-out graves: 6,982 Australian, British, and Dutch prisoners of war are laid to rest here. The remains of the American POWs were returned to the United States during the Eisenhower administration. A remembrance ceremony is held every April 25th, Australia and New Zealand Army Corps Day. ✉ *Saengchuto Rd., across from train station* 🎫 *Free.*

Wat Tham Khao Pun. One of the Kanchanaburi area's best cave-temples, the wat displays Buddhist and Hindu statues and figurines amid stalagmites and stalactites. During World War II the Japanese used the cave complex as storerooms. A local may appear at the small shrine outside the cave and offer to direct you, but you can walk through the cave by yourself. Paying a donation to enter the cave is voluntary. ✉ *Kanchanaburi* ✣ *Rte. 3228, west side of river, 1½ km (1 mile) southwest of Chong-Kai War Cemetery* 🎫 *Free* ⏲ *Daily 9–4.*

WORD OF MOUTH

"I defy anyone not to have a tear in your eye when reading the inscriptions on the graves at the War Cemetery." —Fiona

WHERE TO EAT

$ THAI ✕ **Apple's Restaurant.** This quiet garden restaurant is decked out in wood with lots of local flourishes. The massaman curry is popular with backpackers. Made with heaps of palm sugar, it's a good balm for stomachs struggling with chili overdose. More authentic (hotter) dishes are available on request. A good choice among these is the whole fish with lemongrass, lime juice, and crushed chili. [$] *Average main: B120* ✉ *153/4 Moo 4, Thamakhan Muang* ☎ *034/512017, 081/948–4646* 🌐 *www.applenoi-kanchanaburi.com.*

$ THAI ✕ **Keeree Tara.** With a great view of the River Kwai Bridge from its terraces, this floating restaurant has a sophisticated look. It caters mostly to Thais, so the food can be quite spicy—if you can't handle it, ask the waiter to tone the heat down (say "*mai phet*"). The place serves a range of local dishes, but the fish soups and curries are the best choices. [$] *Average main: B150* ✉ *43/1 River Kwai Rd.* ☎ *034/624093* 🌐 *www.keereetara.com.*

$ THAI ✕ **Mae Nam Restaurant.** The busiest of the floating restaurants at the southern end of the River Kwai Yai where it merges with the Kwai Noi, Mae Nam serves Thai seafood standards, including grilled prawns and red curry with snakehead fish, a freshwater relative of the catfish. A singer performs each night. The riverfront serenity is disrupted periodically by the loud music of the disco and karaoke boats that meander past. The restaurant has no English sign, but you'll find it next to the Café de Paradiso. [$] *Average main: B120* ✉ *5/7 Song Kwai Rd.* ☎ *034/512811* 🌐 *www.maenamraft.com.*

$ SEAFOOD ✕ **River Kwai Floating Restaurant.** Follow the crowds to this open-air restaurant in the shadow of the railway bridge. Fish dishes, fried with pungent spices or lightly grilled, dominate the menu, and there are many soups and curries. The local specialty is *yeesok,* a fish caught fresh from the Kwai Yai and Kwai Noi rivers. Another tasty choice is the *tom yum goong,* hot-and-sour shrimp soup. The chefs tone down the food for foreigners, so if you want yours spicy, say so. [$] *Average main: B130* ✉ *Kanchanaburi* ✣ *Beside River Kwai Bridge* ☎ *034/512595* 💳 *No credit cards.*

WHERE TO STAY

$ RESORT FAMILY 🏨 **Apple Retreat and Guesthouse.** At this longtime favorite, choose between guesthouse rooms set around a central courtyard and simple, comfortable rooms in a two-story building on the opposite side of the river. **Pros:** good restaurant; knowledgeable owners; unique tours. **Cons:** can fill quickly in high season; simple decor. [$] *Rooms from: B1,200*

✉ 153/4 Moo 4, Thamakhan Muang ☎ 034/512017, 081/948–4646 🌐 www.applenoi-kanchanaburi.com 🛏 16 rooms 🍴 No meals.

$$ RESORT 🏨 **Felix River Kwai Resort.** Kanchanaburi's first luxury hotel has faded somewhat, but it's still a good value. **Pros:** right by the famous bridge; wonderful tropical garden. **Cons:** taxi required for trips to city center. *[$] Rooms from: B3,450 ✉ 9/1 Moo 3, Tambon Thamakham ☎ 034/551000, 02/634–4111 in Bangkok 🌐 www.felixriverkwai.co.th 🛏 255 rooms 🍴 Breakfast.*

$ RESORT FAMILY 🏨 **Kasem Island Resort.** On an island in the middle of the Mae Khlong River, this resort has one of the area's most enviable locations. **Pros:** nice view; unique location. **Cons:** isolated. *[$] Rooms from: B1,000 ✉ 44–48 Chaichumpol Rd. ☎ 081/499–4941, 02/255–3603 in Bangkok 🌐 www.kasemisland.com 💳 No credit cards 🛏 18 bungalows, 15 raft houses 🍴 Breakfast.*

$$ RESORT 🏨 **Pavilion Rim Kwai Resort Kanchanaburi.** Wealthy Bangkok residents who want to retreat into the country without giving up creature comforts head to this resort near the Eruwan Waterfall. **Pros:** some rooms have great views; huge pool; pretty garden. **Cons:** far from town; a bit outdated. *[$] Rooms from: B1,300 ✉ 79/2 Moo 4, Km 9, Ladya-Frawan Rd., Tambon Wangdong ☎ 034/513800 🌐 www.pavilionhotels.com 🛏 191 rooms 🍴 Breakfast.*

$$ RESORT 🏨 **River Kwai Village.** Most of the simple rooms in this jungle hideaway in the River Kwai Valley are in single-story log cabins, but more adventurous types can opt for "raftels"—rooms on rafts floating in the river. **Pros:** jungle location; river views. **Cons:** very far from town; no nighttime entertainment. *[$] Rooms from: B3,450 ✉ 72/12 Moo 4, Tambon Thasaso ☎ 02/674–5555, 02/251–7828 in Bangkok 🌐 www.riverkwaivillage.com 🛏 191 rooms, 24 raftels 🍴 No meals.*

$ RESORT 🏨 **Sam's House.** A popular launching pad for treks, Sam's House has a trio of air-conditioned floating rooms that are nice, if a little cramped, as well as less expensive rooms set away from the river. **Pros:** some rooms have nice river views; can arrange tours. **Cons:** more expensive than other budget options. *[$] Rooms from: B800 ✉ 14/2 River Kwai Rd. ☎ 034/515956 🌐 www.samsguesthouse.com 💳 No credit cards 🛏 38 rooms 🍴 No meals.*

SPORTS AND THE OUTDOORS

RAFTING

Daylong rafting trips on the Kwai Yai or Mae Khlong rivers allow you venture far into the jungle. The mammoth rafts, which resemble houseboats, are often divided into separate sections for eating, sleeping, and sunbathing. **■ TIP→ Be careful when taking a dip—the currents can sometimes suck a swimmer down.** Rates start at about B450. Longer trips are also available.

TREKKING

Jungle treks of one to four days are possible all over the region. They typically include bamboo rafting, elephant riding, visits to Karen villages, sampling local food, and sometimes a cultural performance. Stick to tour companies with Tourism Authority of Thailand licenses, which will be prominently displayed on the premises.

Good Times Travel. A reputable agency with a good track record, Good Times offers all the usual highlights, including national parks, rafting, caves, and Karen village stays. The agency's day trips and multiday excursions depart from Kanchanaburi or Bangkok; the price per person depends on the size of your group. ⊠ *63/1 River Kwai Rd.* ☎ *034/624441* ⊕ *www.good-times-travel.com* ✉ *From B2,550 per person (2 participants).*

RSP Jumbo Travel. You can book everything here from day trips to waterfalls to weeklong itineraries that include rafting, elephant riding, and off-road adventures. Some tours include stays at upmarket hotels, so you don't have to give up creature comforts. ⊠ *3/13 Chao Kun Nen Rd.* ☎ *034/514906* ⊕ *www.jumboriverkwai.com* ✉ *From B750 for half-day excursion.*

SHOPPING
Blue sapphires from the Bo Phloi mines, 45 km (28 miles) north of Kanchanaburi town, are for sale at many shops and stalls in the plaza near the bridge. The price is determined by the size and color of the stone, and, as usual, your bargaining skills. You'll do best when there are few tourists around and business is slow. Stick to stalls with licenses.

AROUND KANCHANABURI PROVINCE

The third-largest province in Thailand, Kanchanaburi has scenic jungles, rivers, waterfalls, and mountains, especially near Sangklaburi, as you approach the Myanmar border. For centuries it was a favorite invasion route into Siam for the Burmese. Today it is home to Karen and Mon communities, whose villages can be visited.

GETTING HERE AND AROUND
The region is easily accessible by car. Roads 323 and 3199 take you to the main sights. It's also quite easy to travel around by public transportation, although package tours can be helpful if you have limited time. Reaching less-popular sights, such as Muang Singh Historical Park, is complicated if you don't have private transportation. Consider hiring a songthaew (around B750 for half a day). Public buses from Kanchanaburi leave the bus station, or from Saengchuto Road, close to the guesthouse area on River Kwai Road. There's also a private minibus office near the main bus station; minibuses go to many places in the province, but are more expensive than public buses and fill up quickly. Sai Yok Noi National Park is accessible by train.

MUANG SINGH HISTORICAL PARK
45 km (28 miles) northwest of Kanchanaburi.

Ban Khao Museum. This two-room exhibition of 4,000-year-old Neolithic remains is 8 km (5 miles) from Muang Singh Historical Park. Cars and motorcycles are your only options for getting here. ⊠ *323 Ban Khao, Kanchanaburi* ☎ *034/654058* ✉ *B50* ☉ *Wed.–Sun. 9–4.*

Muang Singh Historical Park. King Chulalongkorn reportedly discovered this 13th- to 14th-century Khmer settlement while traveling along the Kwai Noi River. The restored remains of the city range from mere foundations to a largely intact, well-preserved monument and building complex. There are also examples of Khmer statues and pottery and a prehistoric burial site. You can navigate the expansive grounds with the aid of taped commentary in English, Thai, or French, available at the park's entrance. Bicycle rentals cost around B20 per hour. If you don't want to make the 45-minute drive from Kanchanaburi, take the train to Tha Kilen Station (one hour; B15); the park is a 1-km (½-mile) walk west. There are lodgings and a small café on the grounds. ⊠ *Tha Kilen* ☎ *034/591122, 034/591334* 🎫 *B50* ☺ *Daily 9–6.*

TIGER TEMPLE
25 km (15 miles) northwest of Kanchanaburi.

Tiger Temple. Also known as Wat Pa Luanta Bua Yannasampanno, the Tiger Temple is a forest monastery that houses several kinds of animals on its grounds, most notably tigers. Every day at 3, the 30 or so tigers are brought into a canyon for a photo op that lasts no more than a minute. The rest of the day you can see some of the tigers in their cages, as well as wild boars and water buffaloes.

Controversy surrounds this site. Some locals are concerned about safety (though no injuries have been reported), and many suspect that the tigers have been drugged to make them docile around visitors. Many tour operators claim they'd rather not promote Tiger Temple, but can't afford to lose customers. ⊠ *Km 21, Rte. 323, Kanchanaburi* ☎ *083/777–8006* 🎫 *B600* ☺ *Daily 9–4.*

ERAWAN NATIONAL PARK
65 km (40 miles) northwest of Kanchanaburi.

Fodor's Choice ★ **Erawan National Park.** Some of Kanchanaburi Province's most spectacular scenery can be found in this park. The main attraction, **Erawan Waterfall**, has seven tiers; the topmost supposedly resembles the mythical three-headed elephant (Erawan) belonging to the Hindu god Indra. Getting to the top requires a steep 2-km (1-mile) hike. Comfortable footwear is essential for the two-hour trek, and don't forget to bring water. You can swim at each level of the waterfall (levels two through five are the most popular). The first tier has a small café, and there are several others near the visitor center. There are also eight-person bungalows costing from B800 to B2,400—the ones nearest the waterfall are quieter.

The park is massive; the waterfall is near the main entrance—so, too, are the visitor center and accommodations. Five caves are among the park's other highlights. One of the caves, **Ta Duang,** has wall paintings, and another, **Ruea,** has prehistoric coffins. The caves are much farther away and are accessed via a different road. About 2 km (1 mile) from the park is Erawan Village; songthaews (B500–B600) leave from its market and travel to the park entrance and the caves. Erawan-bound Bus 8170 leaves Kanchanaburi's bus station every 50 minutes; the trip takes 90 minutes. ⊠ *Erawan National Park, Kanchanaburi* ☎ *034/574222, 034/574234* ⊕ *www.dnp.go.th* 🎫 *B300* ☺ *Daily 8–4:30.*

HELLFIRE PASS

70 km (43 miles) northwest of Kanchanaburi.

Fodor'sChoice   **Hellfire Pass.** The museum at Hellfire Pass is a moving memorial to
★   the Allied prisoners of war who built the River Kwai railway, 12,399
of whom died in the process. Along with a film and exhibits, there's
a 4½-km (3-mile) walk along a section of the railway, including the
notorious Hellfire Pass, one of the most grueling sections to build. The
pass got its name from the fire lanterns that flickered on the mountain
walls as the men worked through the night. Many people do the walk
in the early morning, before the museum opens and before it gets too
hot. Allow 2½ hours round-trip for the walk. Take plenty of water and
snacks; there's a small shack near the museum that sells drinks, but
not much food. The pass can be busy on weekends (when an average
of 500 people a day visit). Bus 8203 (two hours) makes the trip to the
museum. The last bus back to Kanchanaburi is at 4 pm. The drive by car
takes about an hour. ⊠ *Rte. 323, Km 66, Kanchanaburi* ☎ *034/531347*
⊕ *www.dva.gov.au* ⊠ *Free* ☉ *Daily 9–4.*

SAI YOK NATIONAL PARK

97 km (60 miles) northwest of Kanchanaburi.

Sai Yok National Park. The national park's main attraction is **Sai Yok Yai
waterfall,** which flows into the Kwai Noi River. The waterfall, an easy
walk from the visitor center, is single tier and not nearly as spectacular as Erawan's. More unique are the **bat caves,** 2 km (1 mile) past the
waterfall. They are the only place you can see the thumb-size Kitti's
hog-nosed bat, the world's smallest mammal. Rent flashlights at the
visitor center. Other caves worth visiting include Tham Wang Badan
and Lawa Cave.

This part of the park has several options for accommodations, all without electricity. The private raft houses on the Kwai Noi River are the
more scenic choices. The accommodations near the waterfall have inexpensive restaurants that are more pleasant than the food stalls near the
visitor center.

Driving here from Bangkok or Kanchanaburi you'll pass **Sai Yok Noi
waterfall,** also within the park's boundaries. Despite being taller than
Sai Yok Yai, Sai Yok Noi has less water, but there's enough to swim
in from June to November, when the area is often packed with Thai
families on weekends.

Buses to Sai Yok Yai leave Kanchanaburi every 30 minutes from 6 am
to 6:30 pm; buses to Sai Yok Noi depart from Kanchanaburi every 30
minutes from 6 am to 5 pm. Either trip takes about two hours. Sai Yok
Noi is 2 km (1 mile) from Nam Tok Station, the terminus of the Death
Railway. Trains leave Kanchanaburi each day at 5:52 am and 10:20
am. If you're driving to either waterfall from Bangkok or Kanchanaburi, take Route 323. ⊠ *Park headquarters, Rte. 323, Km 97, Sai Yok*
☎ *034/686024* ⊕ *www.dnp.go.th* ⊠ *B300* ☉ *Daily 7–6.*

SANGKLABURI

203 km (126 miles) northwest of Kanchanaburi.

This sleepy town sits on a large lake created by the Khao Laem Dam. There was once a Mon village here, but when the dam was built in 1983 it was almost completely covered by water. (Some parts, including a temple, are still visible beneath the surface.) The Mon people were relocated to a village on the shore opposite Sangklaburi.

Due to its proximity to Myanmar's border, Sangklaburi is also home to Karen and Bangladeshi communities, whose residents you'll spot in the town's small night market. Jungle trekking and visits to Karen villages are popular activities for visitors. You can also cross into Myanmar at Three Pagodas Pass with a passport photo and $10 (U.S. currency only—there's an exchange facility at the border), but you can't go any farther than the Myanmar border town of Phayathonzu.

GETTING HERE AND AROUND

BUS TRAVEL Air-conditioned buses from Bangkok's Northern Bus Terminal leave for Sangklaburi four times a day (6½ hours; B330). The last direct Bangkok-bound bus leaves Sangklaburi early in the afternoon. Air-conditioned buses from Kanchanaburi (three hours) leave hourly between 7:30 am and 4:30 pm. Guesthouses are accessible by motorcycle taxi (B10) or songthaew (B60) from the station.

CAR TRAVEL The 2½- to 3-hour drive from Kanchanaburi, on well-paved Route 323, passes fields of pomelo, corn, and banana palms. Myanmar's mist-shrouded mountains are in the distance.

MOTORCYCLE TAXI TRAVEL Motorcycle taxis (B10–B20) are the favored way to get around this sprawling provincial town. For longer trips, ask your hotel to arrange car transport.

EXPLORING

Mon village. To make way for Khao Laem Dam, a village settled a half century ago by Mon people from Myanmar was relocated to the shore opposite Sangklaburi. The village has a temple with Indian and Burmese influences and a bronze-color pyramid chedi that's beautifully illuminated at night. A dry-goods market in the village sells Chinese and Burmese clothes and trinkets, with Mon dishes available at nearby food stalls. Get here by car or boat, or walk across Thailand's longest wooden bridge.

WHERE TO EAT AND STAY

$ ✕ **Burmese Inn Restaurant.** This terrace restaurant with a view of the
THAI wooden bridge across the lake serves local fish dishes and other Thai and Burmese specialties like *laphae to,* a salad of nuts, beans, and fermented tea leaves. It also serves salads and sandwiches, as well as western-style breakfasts. The service is quite laid-back. $ *Average main: B70* ✉ *Burmese Inn, 52/3 Moo 3, Tambon Nongloo* ☎ *034/595146* ▬ *No credit cards.*

$　**🏠 Burmese Inn.** These homey bungalows, run by an Austrian and his
B&B/INN　Thai wife, sit on a flower-filled hillside above the lake. **Pros:** lots of
information on the region; good restaurant. **Cons:** cheapest rooms are
tiny, dark, and far from clean. $ *Rooms from: B475* ⊠ *52/3 Moo 3,
Tambon Nongloo* ☎ *034/595146, 086/168–1801* ⊕ *www.en.burmese-
inn.com* ▭ *No credit cards* ⮌ *19 rooms* ⏐◯⏐ *No meals.*

$　**🏠 P Guest House.** The stone bungalows here sit in a stepped garden lead-
B&B/INN　ing down to the lake. **Pros:** wooden deck for sunbathing and swimming;
all rooms are very clean. **Cons:** no air-conditioning in most rooms.
$ *Rooms from: B900* ⊠ *81/2 Moo 1, Tambon Nongloo* ☎ *034/595061*
⊕ *www.p-guesthouse.com* ▭ *No credit cards* ⮌ *34 rooms* ⏐◯⏐ *No meals.*

$　**🏠 Pornphailin Riverside.** These bungalows sit on the water's edge, but
B&B/INN　the guesthouse itself is a long walk from town. **Pros:** stunning view of
the lake; clean rooms. **Cons:** away from town. $ *Rooms from: B900*
⊠ *60/3 Moo 1, Soi Tonpeung* ☎ *034/595322* ⊕ *www.riverside.ppailin.
com* ⮌ *53 rooms* ⏐◯⏐ *No meals.*

AYUTTHAYA, BANG PA-IN, AND LOPBURI

Ayutthaya and its environs encompass an important historical journey that traces Thailand's cultural developments from Buddhist art
and architecture to modern government and language. Ayutthaya gets
the most attention, drawing day-trippers from Bangkok, but a visit to
Lopburi, with its Khmer temples and French-influenced Phra Narai
Ratchaniwet, lends additional historical context to the museums and
ransacked ruins found at Ayutthaya's historical park and the 18th-
century Royal Palace in nearby Bang Pa-In.

AYUTTHAYA

72 km (45 miles) north of Bangkok.

Fodor's Choice　A UNESCO World Heritage Site, carefully preserved Ayutthaya pro-
★　vides a fascinating snapshot of ancient Siam. Scattered ruins testify to
the kingdom's brutal demise at the hands of the Burmese in 1767, while
broad thoroughfares preserve a sense of its former greatness. Although
the modern town is on the eastern bank of the Pa Sak, most of the temples are on an island. An exception is Wat Yai Chai Mongkol, a short
tuk-tuk ride away. Ayutthaya is best appreciated in a historical context,
and a visit to the Historical Study Center is a must for first-time visitors.

Certain sites are guaranteed to take your breath away—Wat Phra Si
Sanphet, Wat Yai Chai Mongkol, Wat Phra Mahathat, and Wat Ratchaburana, to name a few. Aside from the temples, Ayutthaya's friendly
guesthouses, welcoming people, and floating restaurants make for a
refreshing change from Bangkok.

Ayutthaya was named by King Ramatibodi after a mythical kingdom
of the gods portrayed in the pages of the Ramayana legend. The city
was completed in 1350 and became both a powerhouse of Southeast
Asia and reputedly one of the region's most beautiful royal capitals. It
was originally chosen as a capital for its eminently defensible position,
lying on an island formed by a bend of the Chao Phraya River, where it

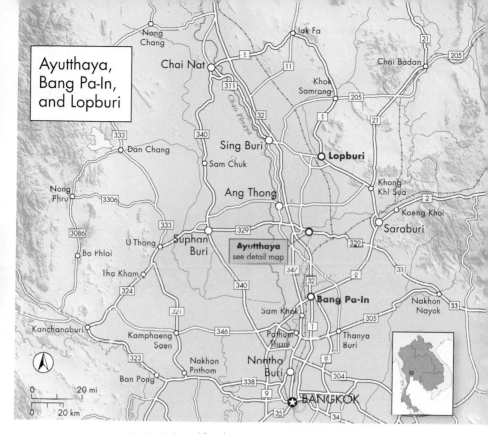

Ayutthaya, Bang Pa-In, and Lopburi

meets the Pa Sak and Lopburi rivers. Early residents created the island by digging a curving canal along the northern perimeter, linking the Chao Phraya to the Lopburi River.

Ayutthaya quickly changed from being essentially a military base to an important center for the arts, medicine, and technology. Trade routes opened up following Siam's first treaty with a western nation (Portugal, in 1516), and soon afterward the Dutch, English, Japanese and, most influentially, the French, accelerated Ayutthaya's rise to importance in international relations under King Narai the Great. After Narai's death in 1688 the kingdom plunged into internal conflict and was laid waste by Burmese invading forces in 1767.

GETTING HERE AND AROUND

BOAT TRAVEL **River King Cruise.** This outfit runs day trips from Bangkok to Ayutthaya that include lunch. Pickups, from most Bangkok hotels, which will help you book these tours, take place at around 6:30 am. You'll take a bus to Ayutthaya, stopping at Bang Pa-In Palace along the way, and return by boat to Bangkok at 4 pm. ⊠ *180 Soi 14, Charoen Nakhon Rd., Bangkok* ☎ *02/673–0966* 💲 *B1,700.*

BUS TRAVEL Hourly buses to Ayutthaya (1½ hours) leave Bangkok's Mo Chit Northern Bus Terminal between 6 am and 7 pm. Tickets cost B50 for the 1½-hour trip.

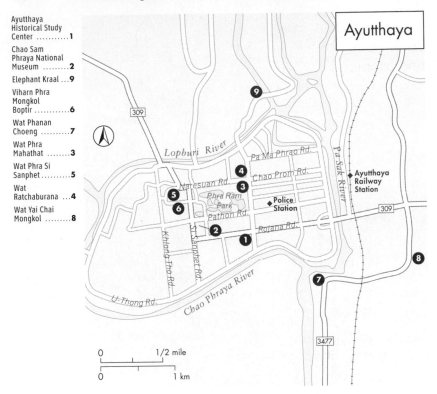

CAR TRAVEL
Driving to Ayutthaya from Bangkok is an easy day trip once you're beyond the congestion of the big city. Kanchanaphisek Road, Bangkok's outer ring road, is the best route, costing around B130 in tolls. Following this road will bring you to Bang Pa-In—a good opportunity to visit the Royal Palace before continuing to Ayutthaya.

TAXI AND TUK-
TUK TRAVEL
All forms of local transport are available from samlors to songthaews, but the brightly colored tuk-tuks are most popular. Tuk-tuks can be hired for an hour for about B300 or the day for about B800 to B1,000, and make easier work of Ayutthaya's historical sites. Though the island site of the Old City is quite compact, don't be tempted to tour it on foot; hire a tuk-tuk (about B600 for an afternoon) or a three-wheel bicycle cab (about B500).

TRAIN TRAVEL
The Northeastern Line, which heads all the way up to Isan, has frequent service from Bangkok to Ayutthaya. Beginning at 4:30 am, trains depart about every 40 minutes from Bangkok's Hua Lamphong Station, arriving in Ayutthaya 80 minutes later.

ESSENTIALS

Visitor and Tour Information Tourist Authority of Thailand (TAT). ⊠ *Si Sanphet Rd.* ☎ *035/246076* ⊕ *www.tourismthailand.org.*

EXPLORING

TOP ATTRACTIONS

Viharn Phra Mongkol Bopitr. When this temple's roof collapsed in 1767, one of Thailand's biggest and most revered bronze Buddha images was revealed. It lay here uncovered for almost 200 years before a huge modern viharn was built in 1951. Historians have dated the image back to 1538. ⌧ *Off Naresuan Rd.* 🎫 *Free* ☉ *Weekdays 8–4:30, weekends 8–5:30.*

Wat Phanan Choeng. This bustling temple complex on the banks of the Lopburi River is an interesting diversion from the dormant ruins that dominate Ayutthaya. A short B3 ferry ride across the river sets the scene for its dramatic origins. The temple was built in 1324 (26 years before Ayutthaya's rise to power) by a U-Thong king in atonement for the death of his fiancée. Instead of bringing his bride, a Chinese princess, into the city himself, the king arranged an escort for her. Distraught at what she interpreted to be a lackluster welcome, the princess threw herself into the river (at the site of the current temple) and drowned. ⌧ *Ayutthaya ✛ East of the Old City* 🎫 *Free* ☉ *Daily 8–5.*

Wat Phra Si Sanphet. The royal family worshipped at this wat, Ayutthaya's largest temple. The 14th-century structure lost its 50-foot Buddha in 1767, when the invading Burmese melted it down for its 374 pounds of gold. The trio of chedis survived, and are the best existing examples of Ayutthaya architecture; enshrining the ashes of several kings, they stand as eternal memories of a golden age. If the design looks familiar, it's because Wat Phra Si Sanphet was the model for Wat Phra Keo at the Grand Palace in Bangkok. Beyond the monuments you can find a grassy field where the Royal Palace once stood. The foundation is all that remains of the palace that was home to 33 kings. ⌧ *Naresuan Rd.* 🎫 *B50* ☉ *Daily 7–6:30.*

WORTH NOTING

Ayutthaya Historical Study Center. Financed by the Japanese government, this educational center houses fascinating audiovisual displays about Ayutthaya. Models of the city as a rural village, as a port city, as an administrative center, and as a royal capital detail the site's history. ⌧ *Rotchana Rd., between Si San Phet and Chikun Rds.* 🕾 *035/245124* 🎫 *B100* ☉ *Weekdays 9–4:30, weekends 9–5.*

Chao Sam Phraya National Museum. This museum on spacious grounds in the center of the Old City was opened by the king and queen of Thailand in 1961. Its many exhibits include Buddhist sculpture from the Dvaravati, Lopburi, Ayutthayan, and U-Thong periods. Also on display is a jewel-encrusted sword with which one Ayutthayan prince killed his brother in an elephant-back duel. ⌧ *Rotchana Rd., at Si San Phet Rd.* 🕾 *035/241587* 🎫 *B150* ☉ *Wed.–Sun. 9–4.*

Elephant Kraal. Thailand's only intact royal kraal was built to hold and train elephants for martial service; it was last used during King Chulalongkorn's reign in 1903. The restored teak stockade is a gateway to the Royal Elephant Kraal Village, which cares for about 100 elephants. Though it looks like a working village, it's primarily a business—rehabilitating and parenting elephants for work on tours around Ayutthaya and for TV and film productions. Warning: never get too close to an elephant, and always be aware of your surroundings. ⊠ *Rte. 3060, 5 km (3 miles) north of Ayutthaya* ☎ *035/321982* 🖾 *Free to view elephants; B200 to ride on one* ☉ *Daily 8–5.*

Wat Phra Mahathat. Building began on this royal monastery in 1374 and was completed during the reign of King Ramesuan (1388–95). The tree-shaded, parklike grounds, a pleasant place to linger, contain what's left of the monastery's 140-foot prang. The brick Khmer-style prang, which collapsed twice between 1610 and 1628, and again in the early 20th century, barely reflects its former glory. Partially in ruins, the prang is said to contain relics of the Lord Buddha. It and the beheaded Buddhas that remain in Wat Phra Mahathat are a result of the Burmese sacking of the temple in 1767. ⊠ *Sois Naresuan and Chikun* 🖾 *B50* ☉ *Daily 8–6:30.*

Wat Ratchaburana. Across from Wat Phra Mahathat stands Wat Ratchaburana, whose Khmer-style prang dominates the skyline. King Borommaracha II (Chao Sam Phraya) built this temple in 1424 to commemorate the death of his two older brothers, whose duel for the throne ironically left him as king. Their relics, including their swords, were buried in a crypt under the prang's base, which was looted in 1957. Arrests were made, however, and the retrieved treasures can now be seen in the Chao Sam Phraya National Museum. ⊠ *Sois Naresuan and Chikun* 🖾 *B50* ☉ *Daily 8:30–4:30.*

Wat Yai Chai Mongkol. King Naresuan constructed the enormous chedi at Wat Yai Chai Mongkol, the largest in Ayutthaya, after defeating the Burmese crown prince during a battle atop elephants in 1593. A recent painting of the battle is one of the temple's highlights. The chedi now leans a significant bit, as later enlargements are weighing down the foundation. The complex, parts of which date to 1357, was totally restored in 1982. Linger a while to pay your respects to the huge reclining Buddha, or climb to the top for a spectacular view. The site closes at 5 pm, but you can enter after that if the gates are left open, as they often are. The view at sunset is beautiful, and you'll completely escape the crowds. ⊠ *Ayutthaya* ✢ *Off Rte. 3477, 1 km (½ mile) south of Rte. 309* 🖾 *B20* ☉ *Daily 8–5.*

WHERE TO EAT

$

THAI

✗ **Bann KunPra.** Handsome locally fired floor tiles are among the original features of the century-old teak home this atmospheric old restaurant occupies. Step onto the riverside terrace and you could be in Venice—the waterway throbs with life, with tiny tugs pulling impossibly large barges loaded with rice. The restaurant has its own small jetty, where an excursion boat calls every evening for guests awaiting a dinner cruise. The 10 guest rooms above the restaurant all have great river views.

$ *Average main: B150* ⊠ *48 Moo 3, Huarattanachai U-Thong Rd.*
☎ *035/241978* ⊕ *www.bannkunpra.com.*

$ ✗ **Pae Krung Kao.** An appealing mélange of local flora and traditional
THAI Thai decor greets patrons as they enter this charming bar and restaurant
on the bank of the Pa Sak River. The visual delights continue in the low-
ceilinged dining areas, which are packed with every kind of collectible
imaginable, from old bottles to timepieces. Half the restaurant sits on a
pontoon floating on the water. The excellent food is uncompromisingly
Thai, but you'll have to get a somewhat early start if you don't want
to be rushed—the restaurant closes at 9:30 pm. $ *Average main: B150*
⊠ *4 Moo 2, U-Thong Rd.* ☎ *035/241555.*

WHERE TO STAY

A stay in Ayutthaya allows you to wander among the ruins at night, a
romantic experience indeed. Most tourists leave Ayutthaya by 4 pm,
but those who remain are treated to a less hectic and more genuine version of Thai hospitality. This is particularly the case at the small-scale
guesthouses along the waterfront, some in historic, beautifully restored
timber-built homes. These lodgings often provide far better value than
Ayutthaya's older, more established hotels, which look impressive from
afar but often have rooms of questionable or no taste and lack a personal touch.

$$ ⛉ **Classic Kameo Hotel.** This hotel's grandiose lobby borders on gaudy,
HOTEL but the clean, tasteful rooms with firm beds and modern bathrooms
make up for it. **Pros:** close to tourist sights; clean. **Cons:** overdone
lobby. $ *Rooms from: B2,400* ⊠ *210–211, 148 Moo 5 Rojana Rd.*
☎ *035/212535* ⊕ *www.kameocollection.com* ⬌ *77 rooms, 131 suites*
⦿ *Breakfast.*

$$ ⛉ **Krungsri River Hotel.** A refreshingly cool and spacious marble-floor
HOTEL lobby distinguishes this luxury hotel. **Pros:** near the train station; river
views. **Cons:** dated decor in some rooms. $ *Rooms from: B2,100*
⊠ *27/2 Moo 11, Rojana Rd.* ☎ *035/244333* ⊕ *www.krungsririver.com*
⬌ *200 rooms* ⦿ *Breakfast.*

$ ⛉ **Luang Chumni Village.** This warren of six snug teak rooms is one of
HOTEL the most popular lodgings in town, so booking well ahead is essential.
Pros: serene atmosphere; lots of polished teak; tropical gardens. **Cons:**
some guests may miss an en suite bathroom. $ *Rooms from: B1,200*
⊠ *2/4 Rojana Rd.* ☎ *035/322990* ⊕ *www.luangchumnivillage.com* ⬌ *6*
rooms ⦿ *Breakfast.*

BANG PA-IN

20 km (12 miles) south of Ayutthaya.

This village, a popular stopping point between Bangkok and Ayutthaya,
has a few architectural sites of note: a Thai palace, a European-style
temple, and a Chinese pagoda, all grouped around a lake and open
fields with bushes trimmed in the shapes of various animals. Most visitors spend about two hours at the palaces and topiary gardens before
heading for Ayutthaya, though if the weather's not too hot you might
be tempted to linger longer on the banks of Bang Pa-In's calm lake.

GETTING HERE AND AROUND

BUS TRAVEL   Buses regularly leave from Bangkok's Northern Bus Terminal to Bang Pa-In Bus Station, less than half a mile from the palace. Fares are about B50 for an air-conditioned bus. From Ayutthaya, buses leave from the station on Naresuan Road (☎ *035/335304*).

CAR TRAVEL   Once you get out of Bangkok's labyrinthine roads, it's also easy to get to Bang Pa-In by car. Get on Route 1 (Phahonyothin Road) to Route 32. It's a 30-minute drive here from Ayutthaya along Route 32.

SONGTHAEW TRAVEL   Songthaews travel regularly between the bus stations in Bang Pa-In and Ayutthaya.

TAXI TRAVEL   One-way taxi fares from Bangkok to Bang Pa-In should be about B800 (depending on your starting point), but be sure that the driver agrees to a fare before departing, or you may be charged more upon arrival.

TRAIN TRAVEL   Trains from Bangkok's Hua Lamphong Station take an hour to get to Bang Pa-In Station, where you can catch a tuk-tuk or songthaew to the palace. The train fares, which are generally less than B70, vary by class of travel.

EXPLORING

Royal Palace. Bang Pa-In's extravagant Royal Palace sits amid well-tended gardens. The original structure, built by King Prasat on the banks of the Pa Sak River, was used by the Ayutthaya kings until the Burmese invasion of 1767. After being neglected for 80 years, it was rebuilt during the reign of Rama IV and became the favored summer palace of King Rama V until tragedy struck. When the king was delayed in Bangkok, he sent his wife ahead on a boat that capsized. Although she could easily have been rescued, people stood by helplessly because a royal could not be touched by a commoner on pain of death. The king built a pavilion in her memory; be sure to read the touching inscription engraved on the memorial.

King Rama V was interested in the architecture of Europe, and many Western influences are evident here. The most beautiful building, however, is the **Aisawan Thippaya,** a Thai pavilion that seems to float on a small lake. A series of staggered roofs leads to a central spire. The structure is sometimes dismantled and taken to represent the country at worldwide expositions. China also fascinated the two rulers, and **Phra Thinang Warophat Phiman,** nicknamed the Peking Palace, is a replica of a Chinese imperial court palace. It was built from materials custom-made in China—a gift from Chinese Thais eager to win the king's favor. It contains a collection of exquisite jade and Ming porcelain.

The site's most striking structure, though, is a Buddhist temple built in best British neo-Gothic style, **Wat Nivet Thamaprawat,** which even has a fine steeple, buttresses, a belfry, and stained-glass windows. ⌂ *Bang Pa-In* ☎ *035/261548* ☑ *B100* ☉ *Tues.–Thurs. and weekends 8–4.*

SHOPPING

Bang Sai Folk Arts and Craft Centre. The center was set up by Queen Sirikit in 1982 to train farming families to make traditional crafts for extra income. Workers regularly demonstrate their technique, and a small souvenir shop provides the chance to buy the fruits of their labors. The center holds an annual fair at the end of January. ⊠ *Bang Pa-In* ✛ *Off Rte. 3442, 24 km (14½ miles) south of Bang Pa-In* ☏ *035/366252* 🎫 *B100* 🕑 *Weekdays 9–5, weekends 9–6.*

LOPBURI

75 km (47 miles) north of Ayutthaya, 150 km (94 miles) north of Bangkok.

Lopburi is off the beaten track for most tourists, and those who do come here are generally outnumbered by the city's monkey population. Some foreigners show up on their way to or from Ayutthaya, but few stay overnight. The rarity of foreigners may explain why locals are so friendly and eager to show you their town—and to practice their English. Samlors are available, but most of Lopburi's attractions are within easy walking distance of downtown and the train station.

MONKEY BUSINESS

Lopburi has an unusually large monkey population. The monkeys cluster around the monuments, particularly Phra Prang Sam Yot. Each November the Lopburi Inn organizes a monkey banquet, in which a grand buffet is laid out for the monkeys and much of the town's population comes out to watch them feast.

One of Thailand's oldest cities, Lopburi has been inhabited since the 4th century. After the 6th century its influence grew under the Dvaravati rulers, who dominated northern Thailand until the Khmers swept in from the east. From the beginning of the 10th century until the middle of the 13th, when the new Thai kingdom drove them out, the Khmers used Lopburi as their provincial capital. During the Sukhothai and early Ayutthaya periods, the city's importance declined until, in 1664, King Narai made it his second capital to escape the heat and humidity of Ayutthaya. He employed French architects to build his palace; consequently, Lopburi is a strange mixture of Khmer, Thai, and western architecture. Lopburi is a day trip from Bangkok or Ayutthaya. Its sights can be covered in a few hours. There are few comfortable overnight accommodations.

GETTING HERE AND AROUND

BUS TRAVEL   Buses to Lopburi leave Bangkok's Mo Chit Northern Bus Terminal (Mo Chit) about every 20 minutes between 6 am and 7 pm. Tickets for the three-hour journey start at around B120 for air-conditioned buses. Lopburi is an hour and a half from Ayutthaya on the green Bus 607 from Ayutthaya's bus terminal. Lopburi's bus station is about 6 km (3½ miles) from town, making it necessary to take a tuk-tuk or songthaew into town.

CAR TRAVEL   If you're driving from Bangkok, take Route 1 (Phahonyothin) north via Salaburi. The trip will take up to two hours.

TRAIN TRAVEL   The Northeastern train line has frequent service from Bangkok. Three morning and two afternoon trains depart for the three-hour trip from Bangkok's Hua Lamphong Station. Trains back to Bangkok run in the early and late afternoon. Advance tickets aren't necessary. Fares for air-conditioned cars on the express train cost about B350. Lopburi's station is downtown near the historic sites and lodgings on Na Phra Kan Road.

ESSENTIALS

Visitor and Tour Information Tourist Authority of Thailand (TAT). ✉ *Ropwat-prathat Rd.* ☎ *036/424089* 🌐 *www.tourismthailand.org.*

EXPLORING

Phra Narai Ratchaniwet. This palace's well-preserved buildings, completed between 1665 and 1677, have been converted into museums. Surrounding the buildings are castellated walls and triumphal archways grand enough to admit an entourage mounted on elephants. The most elaborate structure is the Dusit Mahaprasat Hall, built by King Narai to receive foreign ambassadors. The roof is gone, but you can spot the mixture of architectural styles: the square doors are Thai and the domed arches are western. North of Phra Narai Ratchaniwet is the restored Wat Sao Thong Thong. ✉ *Ratchadamneon Rd.* ☎ *036/411458* 🎫 *B150* 🕓 *Daily 8:30–4:30.*

Phra Prang Sam Yot. Lopburi's most famous landmark is this Khmer shrine whose three prangs symbolize the sacred triad of Brahma, Vishnu, and Shiva. King Narai converted the shrine into a Buddhist temple, and a stucco image of the Buddha sits serenely before the central prang. The most memorable aspect of the monument is its hundreds of resident monkeys, including mothers and nursing babies, wizened old males, and aggressive youngsters. Hold tight to your possessions, as the monkeys steal everything from city maps to digital cameras. Most tourists wind up having a blast with the monkeys, though. Approach them and stand still for a minute, and you'll soon have monkeys all over your head, shoulders, and just about everywhere else—a perfect photo op. ✉ *Vichayen Rd.*

Vichayen House. Built for the French King Louis XIV's personal representative, De Chaumont, Vichayen House was later occupied by King Narai's infamous Greek minister, Constantine Phaulkon, whose political schemes eventually resulted in the ouster of all westerners from Thailand. When King Narai was dying in 1668, his army commander, Phra Phetracha, seized power and beheaded Phaulkon. ✉ *Vichayen Rd.* 🎫 *B30* 🕓 *Wed.–Sun. 9–noon and 1–4.*

Wat Phra Si Rattana Mahathat. Built by the Khmers, this wat underwent so many restorations during the Sukhothai and Ayutthaya periods that it's difficult to discern the three original Khmer prangs—only the central one is intact. Several Sukhothai- and Ayutthaya-style chedis sit within the compound. ✉ *Na Phra Karn Rd.* 🎫 *B40* 🕓 *Daily 6–6.*

WHERE TO EAT AND STAY

$ THAI 🍴 **Bualuang Restaurant.** This is the sort of local restaurant that you shouldn't miss on your travels, a place for trying true regional specialties, including spicy salted soft-shell crab, steamed blue crabs, mussels in a hot pot, and charcoal-grilled cottonfish and snakehead fish. There are also multicourse Chinese-style set meals for six or more people. [$] *Average main: B100* ✉ *46/1 Moo 3* ☎ *036/413009, 036/422669.*

$ ✕ **White House.** Right next to the night market and a popular haunt for
THAI travelers, the White House serves standard Thai and seafood dishes,
including a good crab in yellow curry. There's an English-language
menu, so it's easy to know what you're ordering. The second-floor
terrace is lively yet romantic, as is the tree-shaded garden below. The
owner, Mr. Piak, is a good source of information about the area. Make
sure to flip through his interesting guest book. $ *Average main: B80*
✉ *18 Phraya Kumjud Rd.* ☎ *036/413085.*

$$ ⚇ **Lopburi Inn Resort.** This monkey-theme retreat is the best value in
RESORT Lopburi, with stylish rooms decorated in a modern Thai style, a gener-
ous buffet breakfast, and a good range of facilities including a pleas-
ant pool. **Pros:** pool; Wi-Fi access; gym. **Cons:** far from main sights.
$ *Rooms from: B1,200* ✉ *17/1–2 Ratchadamnoen Rd.* ☎ *036/614790,
036/420777* ⊕ *www.lopburiinnresort.com* ⇨ *100 rooms* ❚❙ *Breakfast.*

$ ⚇ **Noom Guesthouse.** The seven rooms at this comfortable city-center
B&B/INN guesthouse are basically furnished but are more than adequate, and
the bathrooms are well-appointed. **Pros:** central location. **Cons:** street
noise can be heard in rooms; on-street parking. $ *Rooms from: B300*
✉ *15/17 Phayakamjad Rd., City Center* ☎ *036/427693, 089/104–1811*
⊕ *www.noomguesthouse.com* ⇨ *7 rooms* ❚❙ *No meals.*

THE GULF COAST BEACHES

WELCOME TO
THE GULF COAST BEACHES

TOP REASONS
TO GO

★ **Sunset at Hua Hin:** Take a stroll down the wide beaches at Hua Hin for unbeatable views of the setting sun—the same ones the king and queen of Thailand have enjoyed from their nearby palace.

★ **Relaxing Quick Getaway:** Bangkok weekenders flock to Cha-am to enjoy the sun, surf, seafood, and inexpensive accommodations. Off all the beaches a quick hop from Bangkok, this is by far the most laid-back.

★ **Island Diving:** A divers' heaven, the small island of Koh Tao has escaped the worst excesses of tourist development. Divers also flock to even tinier Koh Nang Yuan.

★ **Midnight Revelry:** Thirteen times a year as many as 10,000 locals and visitors descend on the island of Koh Phangan for a late-night, full-moon beachfront bacchanal.

★ **Dramatic Koh Samui:** A drive around the dramatic rocky coastline of Thailand's third-largest island takes you from one eye-popping view to another.

GETTING ORIENTED

4

The Gulf Coast region southeast and southwest of Bangkok contains something for nearly everyone, from secluded spots in the marine national parks to flashy resort towns whose bar scenes are bigger draws than their beaches. These destinations bordering the Gulf of Thailand, sometimes called the Gulf of Siam, include high-profile Pattaya, Koh Chang, and Koh Samui.

1 **The Eastern Gulf.**
Several resort areas on the Gulf of Thailand's eastern shores are close enough to Bangkok to be easy weekend trips. Pattaya can be wild and crazy, though a few of its resorts are secluded and sedate. Farther east lie some splendid islands, among them Koh Samet, a longtime favorite of Bangkok residents. Koh Chang, farther east, has experienced considerable expansion in recent years.

2 **The Western Gulf.**
The gulf areas west and southwest of Bangkok share a sliver of a peninsula with neighboring Myanmar. Cha-am and Hua Hin teem with Bangkok escapees on weekends and holidays. As you continue south along the peninsula the beaches, all reachable from Surat Thani, get better and better.

3 **Koh Samui.** Though very developed, the most popular Western Gulf destination isn't too frenzied. The island's beaches are gorgeous, and the weather's often perfect.

Updated by
Simon Stewart

With its white sandy beaches, crystal-blue water, and laid-back lifestyle, the Gulf Coast captures the imaginations of travelers worldwide. East of Bangkok lie high-profile Pattaya, along with the islands of Koh Samet and Koh Chang, two longtime escape-from-Bangkok favorites. Popular spots near the capital to the west include Cha-am and Hua Hin, both near the top of a peninsula that stretches south to Malaysia. The very developed island of Koh Samui is about halfway down this strip. On both sides of the gulf, the beaches only get prettier the farther south you go.

You don't have to travel far from Bangkok to find exhilarating beaches. The Eastern Gulf offers several close enough for a weekend getaway. Gaudy Pattaya is a full-on, often salacious party place, though many resorts are secluded from the risqué main town, and families will find suitable situations as well. Farther southeast along the coastline, which extends to Thailand's border with Cambodia, are some swell beach resorts and even better islands. Two islands worth considering, as many Bangkok residents do, are tiny Koh Samet and Thailand's second-largest island, Koh Chang. The latter has seen considerable growth this decade, with classy resorts now dominating the modest budget bungalows of days past.

A bit south of Bangkok along the Western Gulf's narrow peninsula, which Thailand shares with Myanmar, lie Cha-am and Hua Hin. Cha-am has bigger resorts and more stand-alone ones; Hua Hin has both world-class resorts and less fancy accommodations. As with their close-to-Bangkok counterparts on the gulf's eastern side, these two cities can fill up with escapees from the capital on weekends, but they're less busy during the week. Scores of beaches worth exploring can be found farther south. You can reach them all from Surat Thani, which is a one-hour flight or an 11-hour train ride from Bangkok. Northeast of

Surat Thani is the very developed island of Koh Samui, popular in part because daily flights from Bangkok make it so easy to access.

PLANNING

WHEN TO GO
The best time to visit the Gulf Coast is between December and March, when the seas are mostly calm and the skies generally clear. On the Eastern Gulf, Pattaya and Koh Samet are year-round destinations. Many places in Koh Chang and nearby islands used to close down during the rainy season, but no more. The big car ferries continue to run on a limited schedule during the rainy season, and most resorts and hotels stay open, offering cheaper rates. On the Western Gulf, Cha-am and Hua Hin are busy year-round. Flying to Koh Samui is still convenient in low season, and the island and its neighbors are beautiful even with cloudiness and rain.

PLANNING YOUR TIME
Disparate and geographically far apart, the many beaches along the Gulf of Thailand would take nearly a month just to survey. With Bangkok serving as the urban divider, most travelers choose either the gulf's east or west coast to explore, and then concentrate on one or at most a few places. Except for divers and hikers, this region is largely about relaxing and taking your time. Where you end up and how long you stay depend on what you're looking for. It only takes a day, for instance, to figure out what wild Pattaya is all about, but if this is your thing you could spend a fun week or two here. Ditto for genteel Koh Samet or developed, but not too hyper, Koh Chang. As with their east-coast counterparts, the west-coast beaches would take about two weeks to explore even superficially. Both Cha-am and Hua Hin, the closest of the major west-coast beaches to Bangkok, become very crowded on weekends and holidays; if you can arrange to visit at other times, you'll have a mellower experience. The farther south you go from Hua Hin, the less you need to worry about when you visit, except during major holidays or, in the case of Koh Phangan, the Full Moon Party that takes place every four weeks.

GETTING HERE AND AROUND
AIR TRAVEL
Relatively inexpensive flights depart daily from Bangkok for all the major beach destinations: Surat Thani, Trat, Koh Samui, and Pattaya. It's generally cheaper to fly to Surat Thani, mostly because the government owns the airport. There are some flights from Chiang Mai to the beaches. Thai Airways and Bangkok Airways have regular flights, as do the budget carriers Air Asia and Nok Air. All the airports in this region are small and much easier to deal with than Bangkok's Suvarnabhumi.

BOAT AND FERRY TRAVEL
Boats depart from the mainland to the islands from Chumphon and Surat Thani. High-speed catamarans, regular passenger ferries, and "slow boats," which are car ferries, make these trips. The main boat operators are Lomprayah, Seatran, Songserm, and Raja.

■TIP➔ Don't take the chance of traveling on rickety or overcrowded boats. Because of lax safety standards, dangerously crowded boats are all too common. Ensure that life jackets are available and that the crew takes safety seriously. Responsible companies—and there are many—keep safety concerns front and center.

Contacts Lomprayah. ☎ 02/629–2569, 02/629–2570 in Bangkok, 077/427765 in Samui, 077/456176 on Koh Tao ⊕ www.lomprayah.com. **Raja Ferry.** ☎ 077/471151 in Surat Thani, 077/377452 in Koh Phangan ⊕ www.rajaferryport. com. **Seatran Ferry & Express.** ☎ 02/240–2582 in Bangkok, 077/275060 in Surat Thani, 077/426000 in Koh Samui, 077/238679 in Koh Phangan ⊕ www. seatranferry.com. **Songserm.** ☎ 02/280–8073 in Bangkok, 077/377704 in Surat Thani, 077/420157 in Koh Samui ⊕ www.songserm-expressboat.com.

BUS TRAVEL

Buses travel regularly between Bangkok and all major destinations in southern Thailand. Bus service within the south is also good. ■TIP➔ Public buses have a better reputation than private bus companies, on which travelers often report thefts from luggage compartments and other annoyances.

CAR TRAVEL

Eastern Gulf resorts are fairly close to Bangkok, so driving is a possibility. The worst part is getting out of Bangkok. On the Western Gulf, it's a long, exhausting drive farther south to Chumphon, Surat Thani, or Krabi. It may be cheaper, safer, and more convenient to hire a car and driver. This is best done while in Bangkok; your hotel can make arrangements.

MOTORCYCLE TRAVEL

Scooters may seem like a fun way to explore the islands and beaches, but think twice before renting one. Every year hundreds of foreigners are killed or injured in accidents along the Gulf Coast. The consequences of even a minor wreck can be dire if you're only wearing shorts and flip-flops. If you've never driven a motorcycle before, this is not the time to learn.

SONGTHAEW, TAXI, AND TUK-TUK TRAVEL

Most areas of the south have everything from samlors to tuk-tuks to songthaews. "Metered" taxis can be found in the larger towns and on Samui. Drivers don't actually run the meters, however, and are unscrupulous bargainers.

TRAIN TRAVEL

One daily train departs Bangkok's Hua Lamphong Station for Sri Racha and Pattaya; there's more frequent service to Hua Hin, Chumphon, and Surat Thani. In general, bus travel is a better way to go in southern Thailand.

HEALTH AND SAFETY

Malaria is very rare but not unheard of in Thailand's southeast. Health authorities have done a great job controlling mosquitoes in and around the southern resorts, but you'll still need a good supply of repellent.

Be careful at the beach, as the sun is stronger than you think. Wear a hat and plenty of sunscreen. Protective clothing while diving or snorkeling is a good idea, as accidentally brushing against or stepping on coral can be painful. Keep an eye out for sea urchins and even more dangerous creatures like jellyfish, especially during the monsoon season. If you are stung, seek medical attention immediately.

Strong undertows often develop during monsoon season, especially along the west coast. Pay attention to posted warnings and listen if locals tell you not to swim.

Condoms are available in southern Thailand; not all brands are equally reliable, so it may be simpler to bring any you'll need.

Take the same safety precautions you would in any other location. When traveling to isolated spots, let someone know where you are going and how long you expect to be away, and be aware of strangers you encounter along the way. Though rare, serious incidents involving tourists have taken place on the southern gulf islands, including two murders and the suspicious deaths of several others.

MONEY MATTERS

Banks and ATMs are numerous, but it's always a good idea to carry some extra cash. Places on remote islands often don't accept credit cards. Some add a small service charge, typically 3%, when you pay with a credit card.

RESTAURANTS

Dining options in the beach regions vary from exclusive and expensive resort restaurants to wooden shacks that seem moments from toppling over. On Koh Chang and Koh Samet "dining rooms" are set up each night on the beach. Pattaya, Hua Hin, and Samui have the widest range of restaurants, from fast-food chains to five-star restaurants.

Prices in the reviews are the average cost of a main course at dinner or, if dinner is not served, at lunch.

HOTELS

There's something for everyone in this region, from luxurious retreats to simple thatch huts on the beach. Many places combine the two experiences by offering fancy bungalows. Rates fluctuate widely: in holiday periods they can more than double. Always double-check your rate when you book. In general, prices are lower than what you'd pay in Bangkok, but higher than in other parts of the country.

WHAT IT COSTS IN BAHT			
	$	$$	$$$	$$$$
Restaurants	under B200	B201–B300	B301–B400	over B400
Hotels	under B2,000	B2,001–B4,000	B4,001–B6,000	over B6,000

Restaurant prices are for a main course, excluding tax and tip. Hotel prices are for a standard double in high season, excluding service charge and tax.

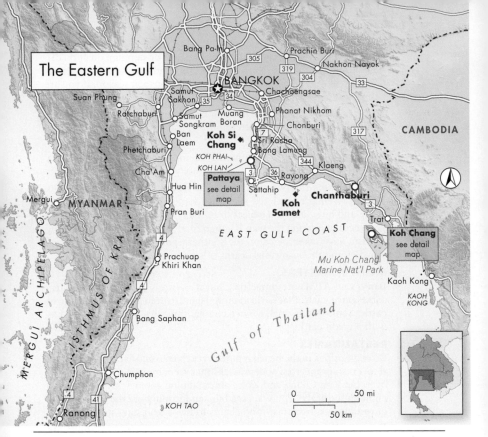

THE EASTERN GULF

The Eastern Gulf has long been a favorite escape from the heat and humidity of Bangkok. Its proximity to the capital means that weekend trips are possible, which in turn means that the area is overrun with sunseekers during long or holiday weekends. As the capital becomes more and more congested and its residents more affluent, the region is growing rapidly. Some of the closer beaches have become so crowded that people now continue down the coast to quieter shores.

Many people go no farther than the coastal city of Pattaya, a notorious commercial sex hub and a popular weekend beach retreat for Bangkok residents. Pattaya is the most highly developed area in the Eastern Gulf, so much so that high government officials often point to the area as an example of the evils of unchecked expansion. For years the city has worked to clean up its beaches and its act, but it remains an eyesore. If you're looking for raucous entertainment, though, this is the spot. If you're not, numerous secluded resorts in and around the city provide some isolation and a shield from Pattaya's seedier sections.

PATTAYA

147 km (88 miles) southeast of Bangkok.

Pattaya's proponents boast that their city has finally emerged as a legitimate upscale beach destination. This is partly true: recent years have seen the opening of chic restaurants and more family-friendly attractions. Still, Pattaya remains a city as divided as ever between sand and sex—and the emphasis still falls clearly on the latter. ■TIP➔ If you're averse to encountering live sex shows and smut shops at every turn, avoid Pattaya. Commercial sex is not just a reality here: it is the lifeblood of the city.

Pattaya was not always like this. Until the end of the 1950s it was a fishing village with an unspoiled natural harbor. Even after affluent Bangkok residents discovered the area, it remained small and tranquil. Then came the Vietnam War, with thousands of American soldiers stationed at nearby air and naval bases. They piled into Pattaya, and the resort grew with the unrestrained fervor of any boomtown. But the boom eventually went bust. Pattaya was nearly abandoned, but its proximity to Bangkok and the beauty of the natural harbor ensured that it didn't crumble completely.

In the late 1990s, after much talk and government planning, Pattaya started regaining popularity. Two expressways were finished, making the trip from Bangkok even easier. Now that Bangkok's international airport is located on the southeast side of the capital, it is even more convenient to visit Pattaya.

Curving Beach Road, with palm trees on the beach side and modern resort hotels on the other, traces the arc of Pattaya Bay in the heart of the city. Bars, clubs, and open-air cafés proliferate on the pedestrian streets by the old pier. South of here lies Jomtien, an agreeable, if somewhat overdeveloped, beach. The bay's northern part is Pattaya's quietest, most easygoing section. Pattaya's big water-sports industry caters to jet-skiers, paragliders, and even water-skiers.

GETTING HERE AND AROUND

Buses to Pattaya leave from Bangkok's Eastern Bus Terminal on Sukhumvit at least every hour daily. The journey takes about an hour and a half, and fares are cheap—usually around B120. You can also drive from Bangkok, and many rental companies vie for your business. One of the cheapest available is Thai Rent a Car. A number of taxi and limousine services are available, including Pattaya4leisure.

Contacts Pattaya4leisure. ⊕ *www.pattaya4leisure.com.* **Thai Rent A Car.** ☎ *02/737–8888* ⊕ *www.thairentacar.com.*

SAFETY AND PRECAUTIONS

Pattaya is a city built on prostitution, and it has all the trappings that go with the seedy atmosphere generated by the sex trade. Street thefts do happen, and thefts from hotels are not unheard of. Take sensible precautions with valuables, always use hotel safes, and avoid late-night strolls down dark streets. Tourist police are on duty, and in recent years they've been joined by tourist police volunteers—expat residents acting as liaisons with the regular police units.

Visitor and Tour Information Tourism Authority of Thailand. ✉ *382/1 Moo 10, Chaihat Rd.* ☎ *038/427667, 038/428750* ⊕ *www.tourismthailand.org.*

EXPLORING

FAMILY **Nong Nooch Village.** If you want to see elephants and monkeys in one trip, head to the small zoo at Nong Nooch Village. Despite its touristy nature—the elephants do silly tricks like driving scooters—this is a pleasant place, particularly if you're traveling with children. Two restaurants serve refreshments you can enjoy beneath a coconut tree. Hotels arrange transportation for morning and afternoon visits to the zoo, which is 15 km (9 miles) south of Pattaya. ✉ *163 Sukhumvit Rd., Bang Saray* ☎ *038/709358* ⊕ *www.nongnoochgardenpattaya.com/performances* ✑ *B400* ⊙ *Daily 9–5:30; shows at 9:45, 10:30, 3, and 3:30.*

FAMILY **Pattaya Elephant Village.** This elephant sanctuary's few dozen pachyderms display their skills in a two-hour show. Demonstrations include bathing, the elephants' roles in ceremonial rites, and their usefulness in construction. Everything is staged, but it's amusing to see the animals at work and play. Unlike other places with elephant shows, this one has a reputation for treating its animals with respect. Tickets are available from most hotels and travel agents in town. Between 8 and 5, you can take a one-hour elephant ride for an extra B1,200. ✉ *48/120, Moo 7, Tambol Nong Prue* ☎ *038/249818, 038/249853* ⊕ *www.elephant-village-pattaya.com* ✑ *B650* ⊙ *Daily 10:30–4; shows at 2:30 pm.*

FAMILY **Ripley's Believe It or Not.** Curiosities from all over are on display at this centrally located attraction that's a worldwide tourist-area staple. The authentic items and novelties run the gamut from shrunken heads to optical illusions. ✉ *218 Garden Park Royal Shopping Center, Moo 10, Beach Rd.* ☎ *038/710294* ⊕ *www.ripleysthailand.com* ✑ *B500* ⊙ *Daily 10–10.*

Sanctuary of Truth. A wealthy businessman started building this massive teak structure in 1981, and it's still not finished. The aim of the sanctuary, whose intricate carvings blend modern and traditional styles, is to make a statement about the balance of different cultures. The waterfront setting north of Pattaya is pleasant. ✉ *206/2 Moo 5, Naklua Rd., Banglamung* ☎ *038/367229, 038/367230* ⊕ *www.sanctuaryoftruth.com* ✑ *B500* ⊙ *Daily 8–6.*

BEACHES

Jomtien Beach. Pattaya Beach's quieter neighbor to the south, Jomtien Beach is less gaudy, less crowded, and a bit less expensive. The white sand, cleaner water, and cordoned-off swimming areas are also draws. Shaded areas with deck chairs cover large sections of the beach, and vendors sell food and drink at inflated prices. Water sports play a dominant role here; you can rent Jet Skis, paragliders, and speedboats up and down the beach. Jomtien is home to a few windsurfing schools. **Amenities:** food and drink. **Best for:** swimming; windsurfing. ✉ *Moo 12.*

Koh Lan. From Pattaya Bay, speedboats take just 15 minutes to reach the island of Koh Lan. The beaches have white sand, and the water is cleaner than at Pattaya Beach. Koh Lan gets busy by midday, so arrive early if you want peace and quiet. The waters are crowded with speedboats and other motorized craft—some speedboat operators are reckless, so be cautious when swimming. Food and drink vendors wander among the shaded deck chairs, although the prices are steep. Ferries leave South Pattaya Pier daily from 10 am to 6:30 pm; a ride costs B50. Speedboats can be hired for B2,200. **Amenities:** food and drink. **Best for:** partiers; swimming. ✉ *Koh Lan.*

Pattaya Beach. The city's namesake beach is slightly murky, but its sand is golden and fine, and safe swimming areas have been added in recent years. You can rent shaded deck chairs by the hour, and food vendors and trinket merchants wander up and down the beach. The bay is usually crowded with small boats, Jet Skis, and other diversions. Parallel to the shore, Pattaya Beach Road has a landscaped walkway that separates the beach from the restaurants, shopping malls, and resorts on the opposite side. **Amenities:** food and drink. **Best for:** walking. ✉ *Pattaya Beach Rd.*

WHERE TO EAT

$$$ ITALIAN
🍴 **The Bay.** Giuseppe Zanotti's flashy restaurant represents the hip, modern side of Pattaya. Here you can dine at sleek modern tables overlooking the Dusit resort's expansive pool and shimmering Pattaya Bay. The menu is not only luxe—as in a rack of venison with porcini mushrooms and juniper berries—but it's also authentic. The *gnochetti sardi,* Sardinian gnocchi, is as tasty as it is in the old country. [$] *Average main: B400* ✉ *Dusit Thani Pattaya, 240/2 Pattaya Beach Rd.* ☎ *038/425611* 🌐 *www.dusit.com* 🕓 *Closed Sun.*

$$$ SWISS
🍴 **Bruno's.** This restaurant and wine bar has built a good reputation among the expat community. The set B450 lunch menu is a bargain, and the à la carte dinner menu includes interesting options such as black ink noodles with lobster ragout. The international cuisine slants European, but you can also find grilled steak and other American staples. The wine selection is extensive enough to necessitate a walk-in cellar. [$] *Average main: B400* ✉ *306/63 Chateau Dale Plaza, Thappraya Rd.* ☎ *038/364600, 038/364601* 🌐 *www.brunos-pattaya.com.*

$$$$ ECLECTIC
🍴 **Flare.** The vibe at this discreet, sophisticated spot is intimate and romantic. The mainly modern Thai food includes classics such as an amazing *massaman* beef and red curry dish, but the chefs also prepare grilled meats and seafood and baked fish. For the quality of service, the caliber of the cooking, and the superb wine collection, this restaurant is one of Pattaya's best. [$] *Average main: B500* ✉ *Pattaya Hilton Hotel, Soi 9, Pattaya Beach Rd.* ☎ *038/253000* 🌐 *www1.hilton.com* 🕓 *No lunch* ✍ *Reservations essential.*

$$$$ INTERNATIONAL
🍴 **Mantra.** This enormous ultramodern restaurant is one of the most talked-about eateries in Pattaya. With dishes from Japan to Italy and countries in both directions in between, Mantra tries to cover too much territory, but some items are finely realized: brick-oven pizza with arugula and four cheeses, for instance, or Wagyu beef sizzled on a lava stone. Curiously enough, just about the only cuisine you won't find here is Thai. [$] *Average main: B600* ✉ *Amari Ocean Pattaya, Pattaya Beach Rd.* ☎ *038/429591* 🌐 *www.mantra-pattaya.com* 🕓 *No lunch Mon.–Sat.* ✍ *Reservations essential.*

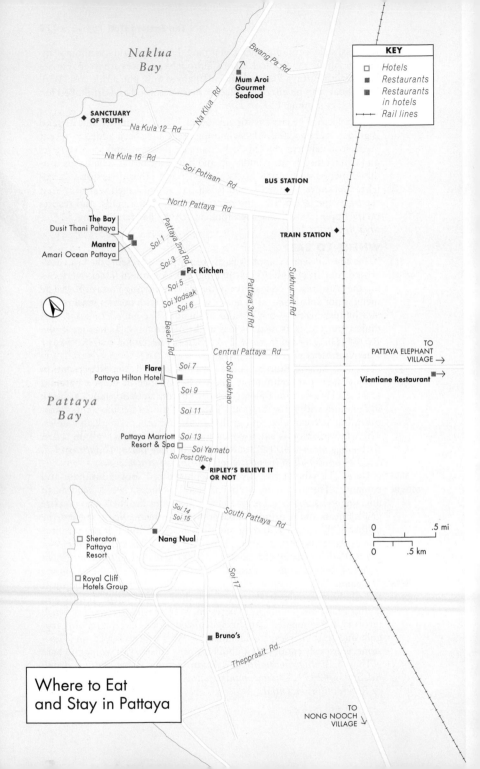

Naklua
Bay

Bwang Pa Rd

**Mum Aroi
Gourmet
Seafood**

Na Klua Rd

KEY

☐ *Hotels*
■ *Restaurants*
■ *Restaurants
in hotels*
┼┼┼ *Rail lines*

◆ **SANCTUARY
OF TRUTH**

Na Kula 12 Rd

Na Kula 16 Rd

Soi Potisan Rd

BUS STATION ◆

North Pattaya Rd

TRAIN STATION ◆

The Bay
Dusit Thani Pattaya

Mantra
Amari Ocean Pattaya

Soi 1

Soi 3

Pattaya 2nd Rd

■ **Pic Kitchen**

Soi 5

Soi Yodsak
Soi 6

Pattaya 3rd Rd

Sukhumvit Rd

Beach Rd

Central Pattaya Rd

TO
PATTAYA ELEPHANT
VILLAGE →

Vientiane Restaurant ■ →

Flare
Pattaya Hilton Hotel ■

Soi 7

Soi Buakhao

Soi 9

Soi 11

Pattaya
Bay

Pattaya Marriott
Resort & Spa ☐

Soi 13

Soi Yamato

Soi Post Office

◆ **RIPLEY'S BELIEVE IT
OR NOT**

Soi 14
Soi 15

South Pattaya Rd

☐ Sheraton
Pattaya
Resort

■ **Nang Nual**

☐ Royal Cliff
Hotels Group

Soi 17

0 ━━━━ .5 mi
0 ━━━━ .5 km

■ **Bruno's**

Thepprasit Rd.

TO
NONG NOOCH
VILLAGE ↓

**Where to Eat
and Stay in Pattaya**

$$ ✕**Mum Aroi Gourmet Seafood.** For a different side of Pattaya, head north
SEAFOOD of the city to this beautiful, romantic seafood restaurant that sits right
on the waterfront. The almost exclusively Thai clientele chooses lob-
sters, giant tiger prawns, crabs, oysters, and fish from a series of huge
tanks, and enjoys them amid shimmering pools, palm trees, and sweep-
ing bay views. There is no English-language menu, so you'll have to
point to what you want. Prices are reasonable, especially given the
upmarket feel of the place. $ *Average main: B200* ✉ *83/4 Na Klua Rd.,
near Ananya Beachfront Condominium* ☎ *038/223252.*

$$ ✕**Nang Nual.** At the southern end of Pattaya Beach Road is one of the
SEAFOOD city's best places for seafood. A huge array of freshly caught fish is laid
out on blocks of ice at the entrance; point to what you want, explain
how you'd like it cooked (most people prefer grilled), and ask for some
fried rice on the side. A menu filled with photographs of the dishes helps
you bridge the language gap, and the staff will understand the cooking
method as long as you don't make it too complicated. For meat lovers, the huge steaks are a treat. There's a dining room upstairs, but ask
for a table on the terrace overlooking the ocean. A newer branch sits
across from Jomtien Beach, near the Sigma Resort. $ *Average main:
B200* ✉ *214–10 S. Pattaya Beach Rd.* ☎ *038/428177.*

$$ ✕**Pic Kitchen.** At this upscale series of classic teak pavilions, you can
THAI dine inside or outside and choose from table seating, floor seating, or
sofas in the jazz pit. The Thai cuisine is consistently good, especially the
deep-fried crab claws, the spicy eggplant salad, and the ubiquitous *som
tam* (green papaya salad). All dishes can be prepared mild or spicy; if
you're not into chilies, try the mild ginger-scented white snapper. $ *Av-
erage main: B200* ✉ *255 Soi 5, Pattaya 2 Rd.* ☎ *038/428374* ⊕ *www.
pic-kitchen.com.*

$$ ✕**Vientiane Restaurant.** Named after the capital of Laos, this eatery serves
ASIAN satisfying Lao cuisine, as well as Thai, Chinese, and western dishes.
Those from Thailand's northeastern province of Isan include what is
arguably the best green papaya salad in Pattaya. For something with
less heat, try the *gai yang* (roast chicken) with sticky rice. Dishes are
usually very spicy, so be sure to specify if you prefer gentler use of chilies. The dining room is air-conditioned, but if the evening's pleasant
ask for a terrace table. $ *Average main: B200* ✉ *68 Moo 10 South
Pattaya, Banglamung* ☎ *038/411298* ⊕ *www.sites.google.com/site/
restaurantvientiane/home.*

WHERE TO STAY

$$ ⊡**Amari Ocean Pattaya.** Step into the modern, open-air lobby here, and
HOTEL you'll immediately be transported to a tropical paradise worlds away
Fodor'sChoice from Pattaya's hectic streets. **Pros:** luxurious tower rooms; superb
★ service. **Cons:** not all rooms have great views; building looks impos-
ing. $ *Rooms from: B3,100* ✉ *240 Pattaya Beach Rd.* ☎ *038/418418*
⊕ *www.amari.com/ocean-pattaya* ⇆ *513 rooms, 14 suites* ⊚ *Breakfast.*

$$$ ⊡**Dusit Thani Pattaya.** At the northern end of Pattaya Beach, this sprawl-
RESORT ing hotel has superb bay views. **Pros:** calm amid the Pattaya frenzy;
many rooms have private balconies with great views. **Cons:** rudimentary
service; can feel large and impersonal. $ *Rooms from: B6,000* ✉ *240/2*

Pattaya Beach Rd. ☎ *038/425611, 02/636–3333 in Bangkok* 🌐 *www.dusit.com/dtpa* 🛏 *442 rooms, 15 suites* 🍴 *Breakfast.*

$$$ HOTEL 🏨 **Pattaya Hilton Hotel.** In the middle of the beach yet convenient to much of Pattaya, especially the shopping mall the hotel looms over—the Hilton serves up business-class luxury. **Pros:** central location; outstanding restaurants. **Cons:** unimaginative room decor. [$] *Rooms from: B5,700* ✉ *333/101 Moo 9, Nong Prue, Banglamung, Pattaya Beach Rd.* ☎ *038/253000* 🌐 *www3.hilton.com* 🛏 *302 rooms, 19 suites* 🍴 *No meals.*

$$ HOTEL 🏨 **Pattaya Marriott Resort & Spa.** This traditional-style hotel is all about its location, a block from the beach and in the heart of the entertainment area. **Pros:** convenient to in-town activity; beautiful garden area; high level of service. **Cons:** few parking spaces available; pricey for what it delivers. [$] *Rooms from: B3,500* ✉ *218 Beach Rd.* ☎ *038/412120, 02/477–0767 in Bangkok* 🌐 *www.marriotthotels.com* 🛏 *287 rooms, 8 suites* 🍴 *No meals.*

$$$ RESORT 🏨 **Royal Cliff Hotels Group.** High on a bluff about 1½ km (1 mile) south of town, this four-hotel ensemble, a Thai institution, is known far and wide for its gulf views, setting, and staggering size. **Pros:** attractive Thai decor; beautiful views. **Cons:** tricky to get to beach; so-so dining; out-of-town location. [$] *Rooms from: B4,600* ✉ *Jomtien Beach, 353 Phra Tamnak Rd.* ☎ *038/250421, 02/2820999 in Bangkok* 🌐 *www.royalcliff.com* 🛏 *966 rooms, 162 suites* 🍴 *No meals.*

$$$ HOTEL Fodor's Choice ★ 🏨 **Sheraton Pattaya Resort.** This spectacular resort established a new standard not only for Pattaya, but also the entire Eastern Gulf. **Pros:** unbeatable setting; luxurious spa. **Cons:** rooms small for price. [$] *Rooms from: B5,800* ✉ *437 Phra Tamnak Rd., 1½ km (1 mile) south of town* ☎ *038/259888* 🌐 *www.sheraton.com/pattaya* 🛏 *114 rooms, 40 cabanas, 2 villas* 🍴 *Breakfast.*

NIGHTLIFE

Nightlife in Pattaya centers on the sex trade. Scattered throughout town (though mostly concentrated on Sai Song) are hundreds of beer bars—low-key places whose hostesses merely want to keep customers buying drinks. Raunchier go-go bars are mostly found on the southern end of town. Pattaya's, and perhaps Thailand's, most shockingly in-your-face red-light district is on Soi 6, about a block in from the beach. Whether you find it intriguing or beyond the pale, the street is a sight to behold, with hundreds of prostitutes lined up shoulder-to-shoulder at all hours, spilling out of bars and storefronts and catcalling to every male passerby. Gay bars are in the sois between Pattaya Beach Road and Pattaya 2 Road called Pattayaland.

■ TIP→ Generally, the only bars in town that are somewhat removed from the commercial sex trade are in pricey hotels.

Below we've listed a few alternatives to the red-light district scene.

Latitude. At this hotel bar you'll get a great view of the sunset over the Gulf of Thailand—through plate-glass windows or, better yet, alfresco—while sipping wines or well-crafted cocktails, perhaps accompanied by tapas. There's a small library adjacent to the wine bar. ✉ *Sheraton Pattaya Resort, 437 Phra Tamnak Rd.* ☎ *038/259888* 🌐 *www.sheraton.com/pattaya.*

Mantra. The see-and-be-seen spot for business executives and visiting jet-setters, Mantra is as popular for drinks as it is for food. Don't miss the secluded table surrounded by ornate curtains. ⊠ *Amari Ocean Pattaya, Pattaya Beach Rd.* ☎ *038/428–1611* ⊕ *www.amari.com/ocean-pattaya.*

Mulligan's Pub and Restaurant. Antique Irish liquor posters adorn the walls of this pub that's as authentically Irish as it gets in Pattaya. Sports play a central role, with large flat-screen TVs showing all manner of events. The staff is friendly and well trained. ⊠ *Central Festival Pattaya Beach, 333/99 Moo 9 Beach Rd.* ☎ *038/043388.*

Tiffany. For a taste of Pattaya's spicier side, check out this cabaret extravaganza (B550) that's famous all over Thailand. All the beautiful dancers are really young men, but you'd never know it. ⊠ *464 Moo 9, Pattaya 2 Rd.* ☎ *038/421711* ⊕ *www.tiffany-show.co.th.*

Tony's. In the heart of the nightlife district, this place presents live music. Grab a beer and head to the outdoor terrace. ⊠ *Walking Street Rd.* ☎ *038/425795.*

SPORTS AND THE OUTDOORS

Pattaya Beach is the spot for water sports. Waterskiing starts at B1,500 for 30 minutes, jet-skiing costs B1,000 for 30 minutes, and parasailing runs B500 for 15 minutes. Big inflatable bananas, yet another thing to dodge when you're in the water, hold five people and are towed behind a speedboat. They go for B1,000 or more for 30 minutes. For windsurfing, head to Jomtien Beach. ■ TIP→ Beware of a common scam among shady Jet Ski vendors who try to charge for preexisting damage. Before heading out, inspect the equipment and take pictures of any dings, dents, or scratches.

KOH SAMET

30 minutes by passenger ferry from Ban Phe, which is 223 km (139 miles) southeast of Bangkok.

Koh Samet's beautiful beaches are a hit with Thais and Bangkok expats, especially on weekends. Although newer resort areas beckon, Koh Samet remains popular with laid-back travelers who just want to sunbathe and read on the beach. There are no high-rises, and just one rutted road for songthaews.

GETTING HERE AND AROUND

Koh Samet is a 30-minute passenger ferry ride—costing between B100 and B200 depending on destination—from one of three piers in the small village of Ban Phe, a 90-minute minibus ride east of Pattaya. Ferries to Koh Samet dock at Na Duan on the north shore and An Vong Duan on the eastern shore. The islands' beaches are an easy walk from either village.

EXPLORING

Koh Samet National Park. The entire island of Koh Samet is a national marine park. Koh Samet's other name is Koh Kaeo Phitsadan (Island with Sand Like Crushed Crystal), so it isn't surprising that its fine sand is in great demand by glassmakers. The smooth water is another

Continued on page 190

Thailand's Beaches

Thailand is a beach-lover's paradise, with nearly 2,000 miles of coastline divided between two stunning shores. Whether you're looking for an exclusive resort, a tranquil beach town, an island with great rock-climbing, or a secluded cove, you can find the right atmosphere on the Andaman or the Gulf coast.

by Martin Young

With so many beaches to choose from, deciding where to go can be overwhelming. What time of year you're traveling helps narrow things down, since the two coasts have different monsoon seasons. In general, the Andaman Coast has bigger waves and better water clarity, although the Gulf Coast has some great snorkeling and diving spots too, particularly around the islands. On both coasts there are windy spots ideal for wind- and kitesurfing, and peaceful bays that beckon swimmers and sunbathers.

Sea temperature averages near a luxurious 80 degrees on both coasts, and almost all beaches are sandy; Andaman beaches tend to have more powdery sand, while Gulf sand is a bit grainier. Developed beaches on both coasts offer tons of activities like sailing, fishing, and rock climbing.

Ao Nang beach, Krabi.

Southern Beaches

Kanchanaburi

Kamphaeng Saen

BANGKOK

Nakhon Nayok

305

319

304

33

317

Suan Phung

Samut Sakhon

34

Muang Boran

Chachoengsae

Ratchaburi

35

Samut Songkram

Chonburi

Sri Racha

7

Phanat Nikhom

Ban Laem

Phetchaburi

Bang Lamung

Pattaya

344

Klaeng

Kaeng Krachan Nat'l Park

Cha'Am

KOH PHAI

3

36

Rayong

Chantaburi

Hua Hin

Hua Hin

Sattahip

KOH SAMET

2

3

Pran Buri

Khao Takiab

Haad Sai Kaew

1

Trat

4

3

EAST GULF COAST

KOH CHANG

Haad Sai Khao

Prachuap Khiri Khan

Mu Koh Chang Marine Nat'l Park

Gulf of Thailand

BURMA (MYANMAR)

Mergui

MERGUI ARCHIPELAGO

ISTHMUS OF KRA

Bang Saphan

4

4

Tung Wa Laen

Chumphon

5

KOH TAO

Sairee

WEST GULF COAST

41

Ranong

Angthong Marine Nat'l Park

12

KOH PHANGAN

Haad Thong Nai Pan

Haad Rin

13

KOH SAMUI

Chaweng

Mae Nam

SURIN ISLANDS

Surat Thani

4

Ban Ta Khun

401

Don Sak

Sichon

SIMILAN ISLANDS

Koh Miang

7

44

41

Tha Sala

Phang Nga

Nakhon Si Thammarat

Pak Phanang

402

Khao Lak

KOH PHUKET

Nai Yang

9

KOH YAO YAI

10

Ao Nang

Krabi

Thung Song

408

4

Koh Poda

Railay Beach

8

Karon
Kata

Phuket

11

41

Phatthalung

0   50 mi

0   50 km

KOH PHI PHI

14

6

Klong Dao

KOH LANTA

Trang

Maya Bay
Loh Samah Bay

KOH TA LIBONG

Songkhla

ANDAMAN COAST

KOH TARUTAO

Hat Yai

Pattani

KOH RAWI

Satun

Andaman Sea

LANGKAWI

MALAYSIA

Narathiwat

TOP SPOTS

(left) Kata beach, Phuket (right) Maya Bay, famous from the Hollywood film *The Beach*.

4

1 On mountainous **Koh Chang**, hillside meets powdery white sand and calm, clear water at **Haad Sai Khao**. 🤿 🏃 🛶

2 **Koh Samet** is famous for its sugary beaches and crystal-clear water; there's room for everyone on **Haad Sai Kaew**, the island's longest beach. 🤿 🏃

3 Water sports enthusiasts like **Hua Hin**'s wide, sandy beach. Just south, **Khao Takiab**'s longer, wider beach is more popular with locals, but gets busy on weekends and holidays. 🎣 🏃 🏄 ⛵

4 Kitesurfers love long, quiet **Tung Wa Laen** beach for its winds and shallow water. 🏄 🛶

5 **Koh Tao**'s most developed beach, **Sairee**, is *the* place to learn to dive and has gorgeous sunsets. 🤿 🛶

6 Laid-back **Klong Dao** on **Koh Lanta** has long expanses of palm-fringed white sand and azure water. 🤿 🛶

7 The clear water around the nine **Similan Islands** is Thailand's best underwater playground. **Koh Miang** has some basic bungalows and tranquil white-sand beaches. 🤿 🛶

8 On **Phuket**, neighboring beaches **Karon** and **Kata** have killer sunsets, great waves, and plenty of daytime and nighttime activities. 🏄 🛶

9 **Nai Yang**, a tranquil, curving beach on northern **Phuket**, is a pretty place to relax. 🤿 🏄

10 **Ao Nang** has a nice strip of shops and restaurants and stunning views of the islands in Phanga Bay from its beach. Boats to **Koh Poda**—a small island with white coral sand, hidden coves, and jaw-dropping views—leave from here. 🤿 🏃 🛶

11 **Railay Beach** peninsula has limestone cliffs, knockout views, and crystal-clear water. 🤿 🏃

12 Backpackers flock to **Haad Rin** for **Koh Phangan**'s famous full moon parties. To get away from the crowds, head north to **Haad Thong Nai Pan**, a beautiful horseshoe bay on **Phangan**'s more remote east coast. 🎣 🏃 🛶

13 **Chaweng**, **Koh Samui**'s busiest beach, has gently sloping white sand, clear water, and vibrant nightlife. On the north coast, less developed **Mae Nam** beach is a natural beauty. 🎣 🏃 🛶

14 On **Koh Phi Phi**, breathtaking **Maya Bay**, where the movie *The Beach* was shot, gets very crowded; small but beautiful **Loh Samah Bay** on the other side of the island is less hectic. 🎣 🏃 🛶 ⛵

KEY	
🛶	Diving
🎣	Fishing
🛶	Kayaking
🏃	Land Sports
⛵	Sailing
🤿	Snorkeling
🏄	Surfing

BEACH FINDER

Key: ▫ = Available ■ = Exceptional

BEACH	NATURAL BEAUTY	DESERTED	PARTY SCENE	THAI CULTURE	RESORTS	BUNGALOWS	GOLF	SNORKELING/DIVING	SURFING	KITEBOARDING/WINDSURFING	ACCESSIBILITY
EASTERN GULF											
Pattaya	▫		■		▫	▫		▫	▫	■	■
Koh Samet	■	■		▫		▫					▫
Koh Chang	▫		▫		▫	■		■			▫
Koh Si Chang	▫	▫		▫		▫					▫
WESTERN GULF											
Cha-am	▫	▫		■	▫	▫					■
Hua Hin	■		■	▫	▫	▫	▫			▫	■
Takiab Beach	▫	▫			▫	▫		■		■	■
Koh Samui	■	▫	▫	▫	■	▫	▫	▫		▫	■
Koh Phangan	■	▫	▫	▫	▫	■		▫		▫	▫
Koh Tao	■	▫	▫	▫	▫	■		■			▫
KOH PHUKET											
Mai Khao Beach	▫	■			▫	■		▫			■
Nai Yang Beach	▫	■			▫	■		▫			■
Nai Thon & Layan Beaches	▫	■			▫	■		▫			
Bang Thao Beach	▫	■	▫		▫	■	▫	▫		■	
Pansea, Surin & Laem Beaches	▫	▫			▫	▫		▫			
Kamala Beach	■	▫	▫	▫	▫	▫		▫			■
Patong	■		■	▫	■	■	▫	▫		▫	■
Karon Beach	■	▫	▫	▫	■	■		▫			▫
Kata Beach	▫	▫	■	▫	■	▫		▫	■		▫
Nai Harn	▫	■		■	▫	▫		▫			▫
Chalong		■		■			▫				▫
ANDAMAN COAST											
Phang Nga Bay	■		■					■			
Koh Yao	▫	■			▫	▫		■			
Khao Lak	■		▫		▫	▫	▫	■			▫
Similan Islands	■	▫		▫		▫		■			
Surin Islands	■	▫		▫		▫		■			
Ao Nang	▫		■	▫	■	■		■	▫		▫
Nang Cape/Railay Beach	■	▫	■	▫	■	■		■			
Koh Phi Phi	■	▫	■	▫		■	■	■			
Koh Lanta	▫	▫	▫			■	■	▫	■		▫

KEY: ▫ = Available   ■ = Exceptional

GOOD TO KNOW

WHAT SHOULD I WEAR?

On most beaches, bikinis, Speedos, and other swimwear are all perfectly OK. But wear *something*—going topless or nude is generally not acceptable. Women should exercise some caution on remote beaches where skimpy attire might attract unwanted attention from locals.

Once you leave the beach, throw on a cover up or a sarong. Unbuttoned shirts are fine, but sitting at a restaurant or walking through town in only your bathing suit is tacky, though you'll see other travelers doing it. Some areas have a Muslim majority, and too much exposed skin is frowned upon.

WHAT TO WATCH OUT FOR

■ **The tropical sun.** Wear strong sunscreen. Drink lots of water. Enough said.

■ **Undertows** are a danger, and most beaches lack lifeguards.

■ **Jellyfish** are a problem at certain times of year, usually before the rainy season. If you are stung, apply vinegar to the sting—beachside restaurants will probably have some. ("Jellyfish sting" in Thai is *maeng ga-proon fai*, but the locals will probably understand your sign language.)

■ **Nefarious characters,** including prostitutes and drug dealers, may approach you, particularly in Patong and Pattaya. As with hawkers, a firm "No, thank you" should send them on their way.

Beachside dining on Khao Lak.

WHAT TO EXPECT

Eating & Drinking: most popular beaches have a number of bars and restaurants.

Restrooms: few beaches have public facilities, so buy a drink at a restaurant and use theirs.

Rentals & Guides: You can arrange rentals and guides once you arrive. A dive trip costs B2,000 to B3,000 per person; snorkeling gear starts at about B300 a day; a surfboard or a board and kite is B1,000 to B1,500 a day; and a jet-ski rental runs around B500 for 15 minutes.

Hawkers: Vendors selling fruit, drinks, sarongs, and souvenirs can become a nuisance, but a firm "No, thank you" and a smile is the only required response.

Beach chairs: The chairs you'll see at many beaches are for rent; if you plop down in one, someone will usually appear to collect your baht.

BEACH VOCABULARY

Here are a few words help you decipher Thai beach names.
Ao means "bay."
Haad means "beach."
Koh means "island."
Talay means "sea."

4

IN FOCUS THAILAND'S BEACHES

attraction. The beaches are the shorelines of a series of little bays—more than 10 along the island's east side alone. The beaches are busier on the northern tip near Na Duan and become less so as you travel south, with the exception of An Vong Duan, the second ferry stop. The government has been unable, or unwilling, to control development on some parts of Koh Samet, but it is still serene and beautiful in many places. Development is greatest in the village and northern beaches. Other irritants involve Jet Skis, which despite being prohibited in national parks can be heard roaring away in some places. Trash is also an increasingly vexing issue. All the beaches have licensed ladies offering one- and two-hour Thai massages, which generally cost B100 an hour not including tip. ✈ *30-minute ferry ride from Ban Phe* 🚢 *B200.*

BEACHES

Ao Kiu. On the southern end of Koh Samet, this beautiful and secluded beach has crystal-blue waters and fine white sand that lend the strand a picture-postcard feel. If you're looking to relax, Ao Kiu is an ideal choice. **Amenities:** food and drink. **Best for:** solitude. ⊠ *Koh Samet.*

Ao Vong Duan. This beautiful shoreline of a half-moon bay is packed with resorts and restaurants, so food and drink are never far away. Ao Vong Duan is the epicenter of water sports on Koh Samet, with Jet Skis and speedboats operating from the beach. The white sands and crystal-blue waters make the beach worth a visit, and the beaches of Ao Cho to the north and Ao Thian to the south are an enjoyable five-minute stroll away. **Amenities:** food and drink; water sports. **Best for:** sunrise; walking. ⊠ *Koh Samet.*

Haad Sai Kaew. This beach on Koh Samet's northeastern edge is the island's longest and busiest one. The sand is white and the water is clear, though in the rainy season the sea does get a little rough. A few boats operate from the beach, but Haad Sai Kaew is a better place to relax than the crowded beaches of Pattaya. All manner of food and drink is available from the nearby resorts and restaurants. **Amenities:** food and drink; water sports. **Best for:** partiers. ⊠ *Beach Rd.*

Nanai Beach. One of the few sandy stretches on Koh Samet's southern shore, this is among the island's quieter options. The beach is beautiful, and its views include the mainland. **Amenities:** none. **Best for:** solitude; walking. ⊠ *Koh Samet.*

WHERE TO STAY

The island has many bungalows and cottages, with and, less frequently these days, without electricity. *Although the resorts below have good restaurants, you'll have a more memorable experience at one of the delicious seafood joints that set up along the beach each afternoon.*

$$$$
RESORT
Paradee Resort. For serious luxury away from the fray, head to this resort on Ao Kiew Beach. **Pros:** beautiful grounds; secluded. **Cons:** very pricey; may feel isolated; not good for families. 💲 *Rooms from: B11,800* ⊠ *76 Moo 4, Rayong* ☎ *038/644283 up to 88* ⊕ *www.kohsametparadee.com* 📞 *40 bungalows* ﹖️⊙﹗*No meals.*

$$
RESORT
Samed Cliff Resort. The resort's bungalows are simply furnished, but they're clean and comfortable and have the requisite amenities, including hot water and air-conditioning. **Pros:** beachside dining; on

scenic stretch of beach. **Cons:** rooms look dated; few creature comforts. [$] *Rooms from: B2,300* ✉ *Noi Na Beach* ☎ *016/457115, 02/635–0800 in Bangkok* 🌐 *www.samedcliff.com* 🛏 *38 bungalows* 🍴 *No meals.*

$ RESORT 🏨 **Vong Deuan Resort.** This resort has the best bungalows on Ao Vong Duan Beach, and is near much of the island's activity. **Pros:** well located; fun atmosphere. **Cons:** not all bungalows have air-conditioning; could use sprucing up. [$] *Rooms from: B1800* ✉ *Ao Vong Duan Beach* ☎ *01/446–1944, 038/651777 in Ban Phe* 🌐 *www.vongdeuan.com* 🛏 *45 bungalows* 🍴 *No meals.*

CHANTHABURI

4

100 km (62 miles) east of Rayong, 180 km (108 miles) east of Pattaya.

Chanthaburi has played a big role in Thai history. It was here that the man who would become King Taksin gathered and prepared his troops to retake Ayutthaya from the Burmese after they sacked the capital of Siam in 1767. The King Taksin Shrine, shaped like a house-size helmet from that era, is on the north end of town. The French occupied the city from 1893 to 1905, and you can spot some architecture from that era along the river. Gems and jewelry form an important part of the town's modern economy, and you will see plenty of evidence of the gem trade in and around town. Most visitors stop here on the way to Koh Chang, attracted by either gem shopping or the fruit season in May and June.

GETTING HERE AND AROUND

Buses make the 90-minute journey from Rayong and Ban Phe. There's also a bus from Bangkok's Eastern Bus Terminal that takes from four to five hours.

EXPLORING

Cathedral of Immaculate Conception. Chanthaburi's French influence is evident in its dual-spired Catholic cathedral, across the river from the center of town. Christian Vietnamese who migrated to the area erected the first church on this site in 1711, and the cathedral has been rebuilt four times since. The present Gothic-inspired structure was completed in the early 1900s when the city was under French control. The best time to visit is during the morning market, when local foods, fruits, and desserts are sold on the grounds. ✉ *At junction of Chanthanumint and Santisuk Rds.* ✥ *Past eastern end of Sichan Rd., take footbridge across Chanthaburi River* 🎟 *Free.*

Gem Market. Chanthaburi's gem mines are mostly closed, but the Gem Market, in the center of town, still attracts traders. You can often see them sorting through rubies and sapphires and making deals worth hundreds of thousands of baht. The market, an assortment of tables and stalls, takes place on Friday and Saturday along Sichan Road and various alleys off and near it. ✉ *Sichan Rd.* 🎟 *Free.*

KOH CHANG

1 hour by ferry from Laem Ngop, which is 15 km (9 miles) southwest of Trat; Trat is 400 km (250 miles) southeast of Bangkok.

Koh Chang, or Elephant Island, is the largest and most developed of the 52-island archipelago that became Mu Koh Chang National Park in 1982. Most of the 30-km-long (18-mile-long) island is mountainous—there are only a few small beaches and only nine villages, some accessible only by boat. Beautiful, albeit somewhat inaccessible, rain forest covers a large portion of this little paradise, making it ideal for those wanting more than just sun and sand. But the island is also a good bet for seaside relaxation: the beaches are picturesque and lack the overheated party scene of Pattaya. As the tourism industry grows on Koh Chang, mid-level resorts are becoming more common than expensive upscale establishments. Resorts are also being built on some of the other islands in the national park, including Koh Mak. ■TIP➜ **Every beach on Koh Chang has something being built or renovated. Before you book your hotel, make sure there is no major construction project going on nearby.**

GETTING HERE AND AROUND

To get to Koh Chang you must first get to Trat, 96 km (60 miles) southeast of Chanthaburi. The easiest way is to take one of Bangkok Airways' daily flights. There are also air-conditioned buses from Bangkok's Eastern and Northern bus terminals; the trip takes a bit more than five hours and costs about B270.

BOAT TRAVEL   Take a ferry from one of three piers in Trat (Laem Ngop, Center Point, or Ao Thammachat) to one of two piers on Koh Chang. The trip takes a little more than half an hour, and the fare is roughly B140 round-trip.

SONGTHAEW   Once you're on the island, songthaews are the easiest way to get around.
TRAVEL   They cost between B30 and B50 per ride, or more if you venture toward the eastern part of the island.

VISITOR AND TOUR INFORMATION

Tourism Authority of Thailand. ⊠ *100 Moo 1, near Laem Ngop pier, Trat* ☎ *039/597255, 039/597259.*

EXPLORING

Mu Koh Chang National Park. All of Koh Chang is part of this 52-island marine national park. Koh Chang is mostly mountainous, and there are only a few beaches, the best of them along the western shore. Haad Sai Khao (White Sand Beach) is the farthest north and the most developed. A few miles south is the more serene Haad Khlong Phrao, a long, curving stretch of pale golden sand. Nearby Haad Kai Bae is a mix of sand and pebbles. Still farther south is Haad Ta Nam (Lonely Beach), which is perhaps the most picturesque of all. But it's also the smallest one and therefore more crowded. In the southwest corner of the island is the fishing village Bang Bao, with restaurants, dive shops, and cheap bungalows. The east coast is beautiful, but it's mostly rugged rain forest, and beaches are in short supply. ⊠ *Koh Chang* ✢ *Take Koh Chang Ferry (30 mins) from Trat.*

BEACHES

Haad Kai Bae. Its mix of pebbles and sand makes Kai Bae less popular than nearby strands, but this beach provides the best, and safest, swimming on Koh Chang. Quiet and relaxed, still enjoying a sleepy feel, Kai Bae has only a few restaurants and resorts. **Amenities:** food and drink. **Best for:** solitude; swimming. ⊠ *Haad Kai Bae.*

Haad Khlong Phrao. A quieter option than Sai Kaew's main beach, Khlong Phrao is an arc of golden sand leading down to placid waters. Scattered around the beach are a few high-end resorts and restaurants. The shallow waters discourage boaters, but also don't invite much swimming. **Amenities:** food and drink. **Best for:** walking. ⊠ *Haad Khlong Phrao.*

Haad Sai Khao. With numerous resorts and some great restaurants, Koh Chang's busiest beach is ideal for those seeking a bustling atmosphere. The beach remains free from deck chair vendors, but a few hawkers wander through during the day. Especially during the rainy season, between June and October, severe riptides can occur, and swimming can be unsafe for extended periods. **Amenities:** food and drink. **Best for:** parties. ⊠ *Haad Sai Khao.*

Haad Ta Nam (*Lonely Beach*). Koh Chang's hangout for the backpacker set has murky, sometimes rough water that's not ideal for swimming, but the vibe is cool. Though the beach itself is strewn with rocks, the hammock-lined bars draw patrons seeking a bit of spiritual enlightenment, cheap drinks, or both. Despite its name, beautiful Lonely Beach can get crowded. **Amenities:** food and drink. **Best for:** parties. ⊠ *Haad Ta Nam.*

WHERE TO EAT

$$ ╳ **Buffalo Bill Steak House.** Off the sand but still close, this restaurant
AMERICAN at White Sands Beach serves generally good, if pricey, cuisine. Steaks, burgers, fish, pastas, and salads are all on the menu. Burnt orange walls, a stone floor, and plenty of cowhide, finished leather, and dark-stained wood lend the place a playful Wild West–meets-the-outback feel, as do the mechanical bull, the horned cow-skull lamps, and the array of cowboy hats $ *Average main: B200* ⊠ *9/6 Moo 4, White Sand Beach* ✛ *Opposite Mac Hotel, next to C&W* ☎ *39/551451* ⊕ *www.buffalobill-kohchang.com* ▭ *No credit cards.*

$ ╳ **Cookies.** The best feature of Cookies Hotel is its delightful beachfront
ECLECTIC restaurant, where the Thai food is consistently good and inexpensive. The *tom yum talay* (hot-and-sour seafood soup) could be hotter, but it's definitely a standout. The banana shakes and banana pancakes alone are worth a visit. The concrete bungalows are basic and somewhat careworn, but they're close to the beach and the rates are reasonable, even during high season. $ *Average main: B150* ⊠ *Cookies Hotel, 7/2 Moo 4, Haad Sai Khao* ☎ *039/551107* ⊕ *www.cookieskohchang.com.*

$ ╳ **Magic Resort Restaurant.** A refreshing breeze cools the open-air din-
SEAFOOD ing area of this low-key resort that has good views of the coastline and the surrounding high hills. Sitting over the water, the restaurant is in a rather worn wooden structure, but the trade-off is the very good seafood—try the crab if you want something spicy. There's also a

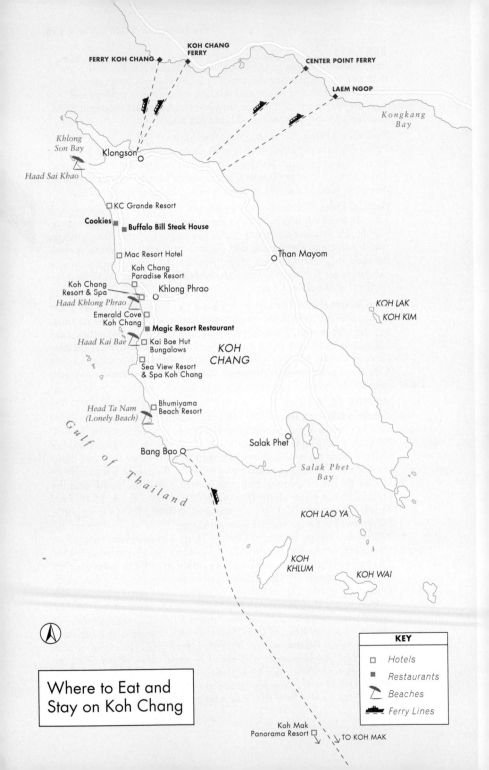

FERRY KOH CHANG

KOH CHANG
FERRY

CENTER POINT FERRY

LAEM NGOP

*Kongkang
Bay*

*Khlong
Son Bay*

Klongson

Haad Sai Khao

☐ KC Grande Resort

Cookies ■

■ **Buffalo Bill Steak House**

☐ Mac Resort Hotel

Than Mayom

Koh Chang
Paradise Resort

Koh Chang
Resort & Spa

Khlong Phrao

Haad Khlong Phrao

KOH LAK

KOH KIM

Emerald Cove
Koh Chang ☐

■ **Magic Resort Restaurant**

Haad Kai Bae ☐ Kai Bae Hut
Bungalows

*KOH
CHANG*

Sea View Resort
& Spa Koh Chang

*Head Ta Nam
(Lonely Beach)*

Bhumiyama
Beach Resort

Salak Phet

G u l f   o f   T h a i l a n d

Bang Bao

*Salak Phet
Bay*

KOH LAO YA

*KOH
KHLUM*

KOH WAI

KEY

☐	*Hotels*
■	*Restaurants*
⏝	*Beaches*
🚢	*Ferry Lines*

Where to Eat and
Stay on Koh Chang

Koh Mak
Panorama Resort ☐ → TO KOH MAK

reasonably priced western menu. Breakfast is served all day. $ *Average main: B150* ✉ *34 Moo 4, Haad Khlong Phrao* ☎ *039/557074.*

WHERE TO STAY

$$
RESORT
Bhumiyama Beach Resort. These two-story bungalows set in a tropical garden have a modern look and a luxurious feel, with white walls and much polished wood. **Pros:** good deal; interesting decor; next to Lonely Beach. **Cons:** slightly claustrophobic feel; some rooms lack sea views. $ *Rooms from: B2,900* ✉ *99/1 Moo 4, Lonely Beach* ☎ *039/558067 up to 69, 02/266–4388 in Bangkok* ⊕ *www.bhumiyama.com* 📶 *43 rooms* ⋈ *Breakfast.*

$$
RESORT
Fodor's Choice
★
Emerald Cove Koh Chang. Koh Chang's top hotel lives up to its five-star reputation with spacious and tastefully decorated rooms with hardwood floors and private balconies. **Pros:** fancy feeling; high level of service. **Cons:** expensive rates; unexciting dining; a little isolated. $ *Rooms from: B3,500* ✉ *88/8 Moo 4 Tambol, Haad Khlong Phrao* ☎ *039/552000, 02/255–3960 in Bangkok* ⊕ *www.emeraldcovekohchang.com* 📶 *165 rooms* ⋈ *Breakfast.*

$
RESORT
Kai Bae Hut Bungalows. There are many strings of bungalows on Kai Bae Beach, but this property is the most established and reliable. **Pros:** fun people; central location. **Cons:** some rooms far from beach; some bungalows could use upgrading. $ *Rooms from: B1,500* ✉ *10/3 Moo 4, Kai Bae Beach* ☎ *09/936–1149, 039/557128* ⊕ *www.kaibaehut.com* ⊟ *No credit cards* 📶 *24 bungalows, 30 hotel rooms* ⋈ *No meals.*

$$
RESORT
KC Grande Resort. The bungalows here range from fan-cooled huts to spacious, amenities-laden suites, and some of the best accommodations are right on the beach. **Pros:** beautiful location; bungalows feel very private. **Cons:** atmosphere may feel stuffy; least expensive rooms not so desirable. $ *Rooms from: B3,200* ✉ *1/1 Moo 4, White Sand Beach* ☎ *039/551199, 02/539–5424 in Bangkok* ⊕ *www.kckohchang.com* ⊟ *No credit cards* 📶 *61 bungalows* ⋈ *No meals.*

$
RESORT
Koh Chang Paradise Resort. With all the amenities of a big-city hotel, these bungalows are spacious and have private porches for enjoying the breeze. **Pros:** cool beachside pool; lovely location. **Cons:** not luxurious; subpar food. $ *Rooms from: B1,500* ✉ *39/4 Moo 4, Haad Khlong Phrao* ☎ *039/551100, 039/551101* ⊕ *www.kohchangparadise.com* 📶 *69 bungalows* ⋈ *Breakfast.*

$$
RESORT
Koh Chang Resort & Spa. On the edge of the bay, this self-contained complex was one of the first major lodgings built on Koh Chang. **Pros:** good for couples; nice spa. **Cons:** rooms small and tired; disappointing food. $ *Rooms from: B2,700* ✉ *Klong Prao Beach* ☎ *039/551082, 02/692–0094 in Bangkok* ⊕ *www.kohchangresortandspa.com* 📶 *145 rooms* ⋈ *Breakfast.*

$
RESORT
Mac Resort Hotel. An ocean-view room with a hot tub and private balcony—or if not that a poolside beachfront bungalow—is the way to go at the Mac. This is a friendly place, and there's a nightly barbecue on the beach. **Pros:** reasonable rates; generally cool guests; wide range of accommodations. **Cons:** not fancy; noise from nearby nightclub heard in some rooms. $ *Rooms from: B1,500* ✉ *7/3 Moo 4, Sai Khao Beach* ☎ *039/551124, 01/864–6463* 📶 *25 rooms* ⋈ *Breakfast.*

4

$$
RESORT   ⊡ **Sea View Resort & Spa Koh Chang.** At the far end of the beach, this resort is quieter than most at Kai Bae. Choose between bungalows a stone's throw from the surf or rooms in a building looming over the strand. **Pros:** nice beach; beautiful grounds. **Cons:** removed from action; limited food options. $ *Rooms from: B3,600* ⊠ *10/2 Moo 4, Haad Kai Bae* ☎ *039/529022* ⊕ *www.seaviewkohchang.com* ⇱ *74 rooms, 2 suites* ⊙ *Breakfast.*

SPORTS AND THE OUTDOORS
HIKING AND TREKKING
Hiking trips, particularly to some of the island's waterfalls, are popular. It's a good idea to hire a guide if you plan to venture farther than one of the well-traveled routes, as good maps of the mostly jungle terrain are hard to come by.

Ban Kwan Chang. On the northern end of the island, this outfit conducts elephant treks endorsed by the Asian Elephant Foundation, so you can trust that the animals are treated humanely. Half-day tours (from 8:30 to noon; B900 per person) include a bathing and feeding session and a 90-minute journey into the jungle, as well as transportation from your hotel. There are also shorter treks. Most hotels can arrange trips for you. ⊠ *Koh Chang* ☎ *08/9247–3161.*

Jungle Way. The entertaining and stoic Lek runs full- and half-day treks that provide insight into the local environment and way of life. Jungle Way, which also offers elephant rides and fishing and has bungalow huts for overnight stays, is based in the northern village of Klongson. ⊠ *Klongsan* ☎ *09/223–4795.*

SCUBA DIVING AND SNORKELING
Scuba diving, including PADI-certified courses, is readily available. Divers report that the fish are smaller than in other parts of Thailand, but the coral is better. Prices run from B3,500 for an introductory dive to more than B20,000 for dive-master certification. Snorkeling off a boat costs as little as B900 a day. Snorkelers usually just tag along on dive boats, but boat snorkeling excursions also take place.

OK Diving. This company conducts day dives and snorkeling excursions and offers scuba courses. ⊠ *Haad Klong Phrao* ☎ *09/936–7080.*

Ploy Scuba Diving. One of the big names in the business, Ploy offers scuba courses and dives for everyone from beginners to dive masters. The main office is on Bang Bao Pier on the south of the island, and there are satellite offices on other beaches. ☎ *039/558033* ⊕ *www. ploytalaygroup.com/ployscubadiving.htm.*

Thai Fun. This outfit's 10-hour, 15-island tour of the marine park includes a buffet lunch, excursions to two or more islands, and two snorkeling stops. The cost is around B1,400. ☎ *06/141–7498.*

Water World Diving. Day dives, certification courses, and snorkeling excursions are among this company's activities. ⊠ *Koh Chang Plaza, Haad Khlong Phrao* ☎ *09/224–1031.*

Koh Mak, an island just south of Koh Chang, is known for its spectacular sunsets.

KOH SI CHANG

40 minutes by ferry from Sri Racha, which is 100 km (62 miles) south-east of Bangkok.

For centuries Koh Si Chang was considered a gateway to Thailand, the spot where huge sailing ships docked and smaller barges loaded goods bound for Bangkok and Ayutthaya. This is still a hardworking port, which means rubbish from the shipping and fishing industries creates a bit of an eyesore. But it's a clean island otherwise. Koh Si Chang isn't known for its beaches—most of the coast is rocky—but it's off the main tourist routes, so it has an easygoing pace that makes it a real escape. It's relatively close to Bangkok, so Thais flood the island on weekends, in particular for the spectacular seafood available in Koh Si Chang's simple eateries. During the week, however, it's peaceful. All the sights are within easy walking distance, and there aren't many cars around. Weekend lodging should be booked in advance.

GETTING HERE AND AROUND

To get here, first take a B100 bus to Sri Racha, less than three hours by bus from Bangkok's Eastern Terminal. In Sri Racha, catch an hourly ferry to Koh Si Chang. The ride is less than an hour, and it's B50 each way. Transportation around the island is limited to motorcycle taxis, which will take you to most places for B20, and the island's unique "stretch tuk-tuks," which cost about B50 to most spots.

EXPLORING

Chudhadhuj Palace. King Rama V built this summer palace and named it after his son, Prince Chudhadhuj, who was born on the island on July 5, 1893. Earlier in the 19th century, King Rama V's father, King Rama IV, had learned that the island's residents lived longer than anywhere else in Thailand and had concluded that Koh Si Chang's climate was responsible. The palace was abandoned in 1894 when France blockaded the Gulf of Thailand during a political crisis. Few buildings remain today, but the palace gardens are great for a stroll. King Rama V also commissioned another residence here, Vimanmek Mansion, which in 1901 he had moved to Bangkok. All that remains is the mansion's beachside foundation. Nearby, an old wooden pier has been restored to its former glory. ✉ *Koh Si Chang* ✣ *2 km (1 mile) south of town.*

Khao Yai Temple. Hordes of weekend visitors from Bangkok descend on this temple on the north side of town. Khao Yai is a hodgepodge of shrines and stupas lining a 400-step walkway up a steep hillside. It's an arduous climb to the main temple building, but the view of the northern half of the island, the mainland, and rows of barges and ships is worth the effort. Koh Si Chang has no natural water sources. From this perch, you can see that nearly every roof on the island has a big jar for collecting water. ✉ *Koh Si Chang* ✣ *North of town.*

Wat Yai Prik. It's easy to spot this temple west of town as you near the island by boat—atop a hill, it has eight enormous reservoirs. The wat often donates drinking water to villagers when they need it. But Yai Prik is as dedicated to the spiritual as it is to the practical. Meditation courses are taught, and signs throughout explain Buddhist principles. Simplicity rules here: though donations are accepted, the monks don't collect money to build ornate temples. ✉ *Koh Si Chang* ✣ *West of town.*

WHERE TO EAT

$ SEAFOOD 🍴 **Lek Noi.** This place doesn't look like much—it's little more than a shack with plastic chairs and simple wooden tables—but many locals say this the best place for seafood on the island. Lek Noi is a little more than a kilometer (½ mile) out of town on the way to Chudhadhuj Palace. [$] *Average main: B80* ✉ *Mekhaamthaew Rd.* 💳 *No credit cards.*

$ ECLECTIC 🍴 **Pan & David.** The owners are a Thai-American couple, so it's not surprising that their eatery serves a mix of their native dishes. The best ones, among them spaghetti with a spicy seafood sauce, inventively combine the two influences. Ocean breezes cool the open-air dining area. [$] *Average main: B120* ✉ *167 Moo 3, Mekhaamthaew Rd.* ☎ *038/216629.*

WHERE TO STAY

$ RESORT 🏨 **Rim Talay Resort.** If you want to be lulled to asleep by the sound of the surf, stay in one of this trio of boats that have been converted into bungalows. **Pros:** unique concept; cheap rates. **Cons:** rooms could be more comfortable. [$] *Rooms from: B1,000* ✉ *130 Moo 3, Mekhaamthaew Rd.* ☎ *038/216116* 💳 *No credit cards* 🛏 *20 bungalows* 🍽 *No meals.*

$ HOTEL **Sichang Palace Hotel.** The island's biggest hotel is comfortable enough and has a central location. **Pros:** well located; reliable option. **Cons:** can feel empty on weekdays; few amenities. [$] *Rooms from: B1,500* ✉ *81 Atsadang Rd.* ☎ *038/216276 up to 78* 🌐 *www.sichangpalace.com* 💳 *No credit cards* 🛏 *56 rooms* 🍴 *No meals.*

THE WESTERN GULF

South of Bangkok lies the Western Gulf coast, hundreds of miles of shoreline where resort towns are the exception rather than the rule. Most towns along the gulf are either small fishing villages or culturally and historically significant towns like Surat Thani. Some touristy areas have grown up around the smaller villages, but they are considerably less developed than some of their counterparts in the other coastal areas. Thus, the allure of the Western Gulf is its charming towns, spectacular beaches, and not-yet-overgrown tourist destinations.

About three hours south of Bangkok are the laid-back beaches of Cha-am and Hua Hin. Bangkok residents have traveled to Hua Hin since the 1920s, when King Rama VII built a palace here. Where royalty goes, high society inevitably follows, but despite the attention the city received, Hua Hin was spared the pitfalls of rapid development.

Another 483 km (300 miles) south is Surat Thani, the former capital of an ancient Siamese kingdom. As the center of its civilization, Surat Thani developed its own artistic and architectural style. In modern times it has remained an important commercial and historic Thai city, and the province is home to one of the most pristine tropical forests in Thailand, Khao Sok National Park. However, most travelers know Surat Thani only as a departure point for the islands off its coast, primarily Koh Samui.

CHA-AM

163 km (101 miles) south of Bangkok, 40 km (25 miles) from Petchaburi.

It may not be the most picturesque seaside town, but Cha-am does offer an authentic Thai-style beach experience. The pier at the north end of Cha-am Beach is the center of this small quiet town. Its main street, Ruamchit Beach Road, passes by a tree-lined strip of beach on one side and restaurants, bars, guesthouses, and hotels on the other. Fresh seafood is available at small cafés along this road, where there are also stalls selling trays of deep-fried squid, shrimp, and tiny crab for around B25. Cha-am retains its sleepy charm, and those searching for peace and quiet may find their niche here.

GETTING HERE AND AROUND

Buses leave Bangkok's Southern Bus Terminal every 30 minutes between 6:30 am and 7 pm; the 2½-hour trip costs around B150. Once you're here, tuk-tuks are the best way to get around.

4

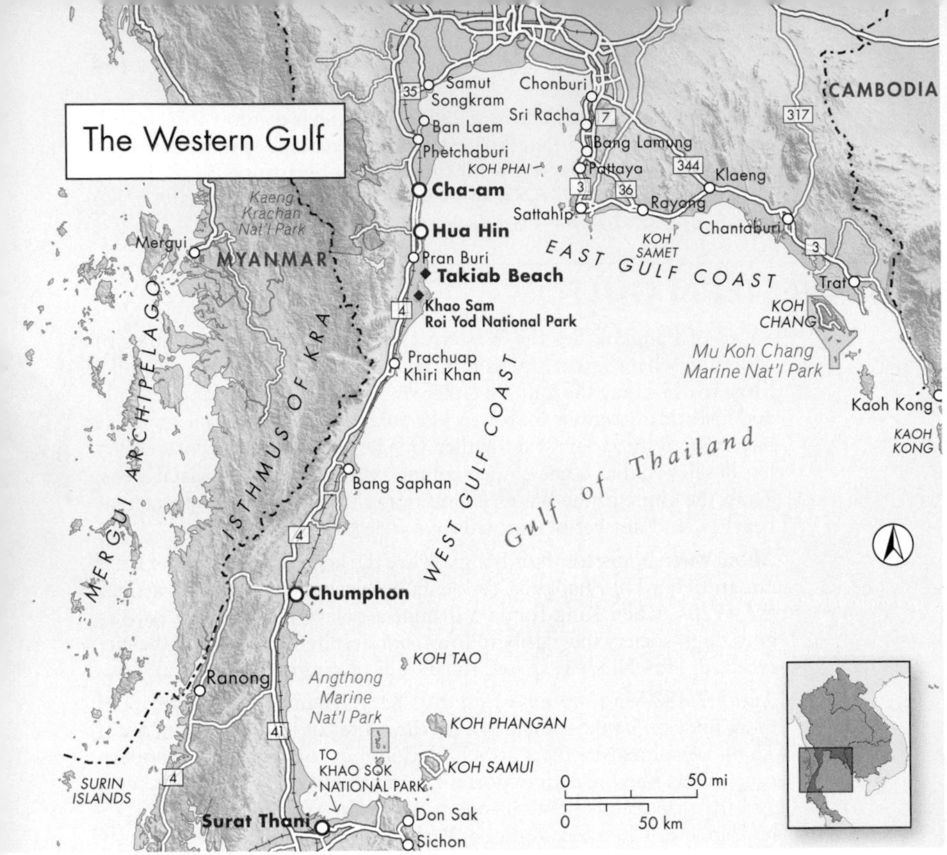

VISITOR AND TOUR INFORMATION

Tourism Authority of Thailand. ✉ *Petchkasem Rd.* ☎ *032/471005, 032/471502* 🌐 *www.tourismthailand.org.*

BEACHES

Cha-am Beach. At Cha-am's broad town beach you can often see Bangkok families gathered at umbrella-covered tables for all-day meals, stocking up on fresh fruit and seafood and cold beer from wandering vendors. The beach's sand, though, is fairly dark and dirty. Most visitors head to one of the all-inclusive resorts farther away, where the sand is prettier and the water better for swimming. **Amenities:** food and drink; parking; toilets. **Best for:** walking. ✉ *Ruamchit Beach Rd.*

WHERE TO EAT AND STAY

$ SEAFOOD 🍴 **Poom Restaurant.** The steady stream of locals is one clue that the seafood here ranks among the town's best. Try the charcoal-grilled whole fish, large prawns, crab, and squid—all fresh and accompanied by a delicious chili sauce. The metal-table-and-plastic-chair decor is nothing special, but there's outside seating under the trees. If you can't take the heat, head to the restaurant next door. Owned by the same people, it has an air-conditioned dining area. [$] *Average main: B120* ✉ *274/1 Ruamchit Rd.* ☎ *032/471036.*

$$ **Regent Beach Cha-am.** Taking a swim couldn't be easier than at this
RESORT resort with a quartet of pools amid the dozens of bungalows facing the
beach. **Pros:** pretty layout; fun nightlife. **Cons:** unpredictable availability. *§Rooms from: B2,000* ⊠ *849/21 Cha-am Beach* ☎ *032/451240,
02/251–0305 in Bangkok* ⊕ *www.regent-chaam.com* ⌁ *630 rooms,
30 suites* ⓘ *Breakfast.*

$$ **Sabaya Jungle Resort.** Whether relaxing in your room or chilling out
RESORT in the common area, you'll feel at home at this attractive resort. **Pros:**
nice spa; cool rooms; breathtaking location. **Cons:** not on the beach;
unexciting pool. *§Rooms from: B2,000* ⊠ *304/7 Nong Chaeng Rd.*
☎ *032/470716, 032/470717* ⊕ *www.sabaya.co.th* ⌁ *16 bungalows*
ⓘ *No meals.*

HUA HIN

66 km (41 miles) from Cha-am, 189 km (118 miles) south of Bangkok.

The golden sands near the small seaside city of Hua Hin have long
attracted Bangkok's rich and famous. The most renowned visitors are
the king and queen of Thailand, who now use the Klai Kangwol Palace
north of Hua Hin town as their primary residence. The palace was completed in 1928 by King Rama VII, who gave it the name Klai Kangwol,
which means "Far From Worries."

Hua Hin is a year-round destination. Weekends and Thai public holidays are times to avoid, when the Bangkok set floods the city—prices
rise and the streets become noticeably busier.

GETTING HERE AND AROUND

The bus is the most convenient way to get here from Bangkok. Buses
depart hourly from the Southern Bus Terminal; the trip takes three hours
and costs about B200. Minivans (B280) head here from Bangkok's
Khao San Road or Victory Monument and are generally faster than
buses, though some operators try to squeeze in too many passengers.

Bus Contact Hua Hin. ⊠ *Dechanuchit St.*

EXPLORING

Chatchai Street Market. This long-established market is a favorite with
locals and tourists. Residents come during the day to purchase meats,
seafood, and produce; after 5 pm you'll find everything from jewelry
and clothing to toys and artworks. The evening market also has interesting eats, including Thai *kanom* (sweets), exotic fruits, barbecue meats,
and traditional Thai dishes. ⊠ *Dechanuchit St.*

OFF THE
BEATEN
PATH
Khao Sam Roi Yod National Park. You'll pass rice fields, sugar palms, pineapple plantations, and crab farms as you make your way to this park
south of Hua Hin, the gloriously named "300 Peaks." The park has
two main trails and is a great place to spot wildlife, especially monitor
lizards and barking deer. With a little luck you can spot the adorable
dusky langur, a type of monkey also known as the spectacled langur
because of the white circles around its eyes. About a kilometer (½ mile)
from the park's headquarters is Khao Daeng Hill, which is worth a hike
up to the viewpoint, especially at sunrise. Another 16 km (10 miles)
from the headquarters is Haad Laem Sala, a white-sand beach. Near the

beach is Phraya Nakhon Cave, once visited by King Rama V. The cave has an opening in its roof where sunlight shines through for a beautiful effect. If you don't have a car or haven't hired one, you'll have to take a bus to the Pranburi District in Prachuab Kiri Khan Province. From here you take a songthaew to the park. ✉ *Hua Hin* ✥ *About 63 km (39 miles) south of Hua Hin* ☎ *032/619078* 🌐 *www.dnp.go.th* 🎫 *B300.*

BEACHES

Hua Hin Beach. Hua Hin's namesake beach is the nicest of those along this part of the coast, but it's also the most popular. Though not as stunning as other Thai beaches, it's a wide, 7-km-long (4½-mile-long) boulevard of golden sand. Vendors hawk food and drink nonstop, but you can escape this parade by booking a relaxing beach massage or by taking a horseback ride to less populated sections. Water sports can be arranged at various points. The water can get rough and the sea isn't clear, but you definitely can swim here. Shaded deck-chair areas make for easy relaxing, though these have been curtailed somewhat following 2014 corruption allegations. **Amenities:** food and drink; water sports. **Best for:** walking. ✉ *Hua Hin* ✥ *Off Petchkasem Rd.*

WHERE TO EAT

$$ SEAFOOD

🍴 **Buffalo Bill's at Fisherman's Wharf.** This surf-and-turf restaurant takes pride in using the best of the region's produce and seafood. Try the beer-batter fish-and-chips served in traditional newspaper wrapping. You can start your day with the best eggs Benedict in town or wrap it up with an afternoon beer or cocktails. The Sunday roast provides you a chance to mingle with the expat community. [$] *Average main: B250* ✉ *8 Chomsin Rd.* ☎ *08/07274710* 🌐 *www.buffalobillshuahin.com.*

$ SEAFOOD

🍴 **Koti.** A longtime local favorite for Thai-style seafood, Koti has a no-nonsense decor and a packed dining room that attests to the flavor of dishes like *hor mok talay* (steamed seafood curry). The large menu includes such crowd-pleasers as fried fish with garlic and pepper. [$] *Average main: B120* ✉ *61/1 Petchkasem Rd.* ☎ *032/511252* 💳 *No credit cards* 🕒 *No lunch.*

$$ FRENCH FUSION

🍴 **Orchids Restaurant.** The chefs at this Thai-French restaurant acknowledge its Asian influences while relying mainly on French technique. The results are often fantastic. Prawns might come, for instance, Thai-style in a curry with fresh coriander in coconut milk, or with echoes of France in vermouth sauce. Seafood and steaks figure prominently on the menu, but there are also salads and lighter fare. The understated decor favors traditional Thai wooden finishes. [$] *Average main: B250* ✉ *Fulay Hotel, 110/1 Naresdamri Rd.* ☎ *032/513670* 🌐 *www.fulayhuahin.com* 💳 *No credit cards.*

$ SEAFOOD

🍴 **Sang Thai.** Ignore this open-air restaurant's ramshackle setting and concentrate on its eclectic seafood dishes. Popular with Thais (always a good sign) Sang Thai serves everything from grilled prawns with bean noodles to fried grouper with chili and tamarind juice. Don't miss the *kang* (huge prawns). [$] *Average main: B150* ✉ *Naresdamri Rd., down by the wharf* ☎ *032/512144.*

WHERE TO STAY

$$$
RESORT

🎬 **Anantara.** Surrounded by a 10-foot-tall terra-cotta wall, this beach resort calls to mind an ancient Thai village. **Pros:** lots of elephants; inspiring setting; many activities. **Cons:** verges on stuffy; expensive rates. $ *Rooms from: B5,000* ✉ *43/1 Phetkasem Beach Rd.* ☎ *032/520250* ⊕ *www.anantara.com* ⤴ *187 rooms* ◎ *Breakfast.*

$$$
HOTEL
Fodor's Choice
★

🎬 **Centara Grand Beach Resort and Villas.** Even if you don't stay at this local landmark, its old-world charm makes it worth a visit. **Pros:** pretty grounds; cool atmosphere. **Cons:** pricey; not a party destination. $ *Rooms from: B5,300* ✉ *1 Damnernkasem Rd.* ☎ *032/512021 up to 38, 02/541–1125 in Bangkok* ⊕ *www.centarahotelsresorts.com* ⤴ *207 rooms, 30 suites* ◎ *No meals.*

$$$$
HOTEL
Fodor's Choice
★

🎬 **Chiva-Som.** One of the best spa resorts in the region—and possibly the world—Chiva Som has tasteful and comfortable rooms accented with natural woods. **Pros:** unique spa program; high level of service; great variety of activities and services. **Cons:** not for partiers; expensive. $ *Rooms from: B18,000* ✉ *73/4 Petchkasem Rd.* ☎ *032/536536* ⊕ *www.chivasom.com* ⤴ *57 rooms* ◎ *No meals.*

$$$
RESORT
Fodor's Choice
★

🎬 **Dusit Thani Hua Hin Hotel.** The spacious lobby at this hotel between Hua Hin and Cha-am serves as a lounge for afternoon tea and evening cocktails, sipped to the soft melodies of traditional Thai music. **Pros:** beachfront setting; traditional architecture; lots of amenities. **Cons:** need a car (or taxi) to get around; some rooms need freshening up. $ *Rooms from: B4,600* ✉ *1349 Petchkasem Rd., Cha-am* ☎ *032/520009, 02/6363333 in Bangkok* ⊕ *www.dusit.com/dusitthani/huahin* ⤴ *291 rooms, 9 suites* ◎ *Breakfast.*

$$
RESORT

🎬 **Evason Hideaway and Evason Hua Hin Resort.** These neighboring properties are set on a quiet beach in Pranburi, about 20 minutes south of Hua Hin. The newer Hideaway resort has villas and suites, all of which have private plunge pools and outdoor tubs, along with lounging areas with umbrella-shaded daybeds. **Pros:** super-comfortable accommodations; access to double the amenities. **Cons:** out of the way; too quiet for some; not-so-great beach. $ *Rooms from: B3,700* ✉ *9/22 Moo 5 Paknampran, Pranburi* ☎ *032/618200 Hideaway, 032/632111 resort* ⊕ *www.sixsenses.com/Evason-Hua-Hin* ⤴ *Hideaway: 17 suites, 38 villas; resort: 185 rooms, 40 villas* ◎ *Breakfast.*

$
B&B/INN

🎬 **Fulay Guesthouse.** On a pier that juts out over the water, this guesthouse is unlike any other in Hua Hin. The Cape Cod–blue planks of the pier match the color of the trim around the whitewashed walls. **Pros:** hard to beat the price; cool location. **Cons:** questionable decor; some rooms lack air-conditioning. $ *Rooms from: B500* ✉ *110/1 Naresdamri Rd.* ☎ *032/513145, 032/513670* ⊕ *www.fulayhuahin.net* ▬ *No credit cards* ⤴ *14 rooms* ◎ *No meals.*

$$$$
HOTEL

🎬 **Hilton Hua Hin Resort and Spa.** In the liveliest part of town, the Hilton is perfect for fun-and-sun enthusiasts who want to be close to the action. **Pros:** central location; rooms with great views; high-tech touches. **Cons:** narrow road leading to the hotel. $ *Rooms from: B6,500* ✉ *33 Naresdamri Rd.* ☎ *032/512888* ⊕ *www.hua-hin.hilton.com* ⤴ *255 rooms, 41 suites* ◎ *Breakfast.*

$ HOTEL **Jed Pee Nong Hotel.** On one of the main streets leading to the public entrance to Hua Hin Beach, Jed Pee Nong has bungalows clustered around a swimming pool and standard rooms in a high-rise building. **Pros:** reasonable rates; prime location. **Cons:** nothing fancy; lots of nearby foot traffic; lacking in amenities. [$] *Rooms from: B1,500* ✉ *17 Damnernkasem Rd.* ☎ *032/512381* 🌐 *www.jedpeenonghotel-huahin.com* 🛏 *40 rooms* 🍴 *No meals.*

$ HOTEL **Sirin Hotel.** About a block from the beach, this hotel has huge, comfortable rooms with extra-large beds and plenty of light streaming in through the wide windows. **Pros:** large rooms; central location. **Cons:** rooms need some renovation. [$] *Rooms from: B1,500* ✉ *6/3 Damnernkasem Rd.* ☎ *032/511150, 032/512045* 🌐 *www.sirinhuahin.com* 🛏 *25 rooms* 🍴 *Breakfast.*

$ B&B/INN **Victor Guesthouse.** A successor to the Pattana Guesthouse—remodeled, renamed, and rebranded by the same owners—these two teakwood houses are hidden down a small alley in the heart of Hua Hin. After the much-needed makeover, the rooms, some of which share a bathroom, now feel bright and airy. **Pros:** ideal for budget travelers; cute for what it is. **Cons:** no adjacent beach; sounds from adjacent rooms easily heard. [$] *Rooms from: B400* ✉ *60 Naresdamri Rd.* ☎ *032/511564* 💳 *No credit cards* 🛏 *13 rooms* 🍴 *No meals.*

SPORTS AND THE OUTDOORS

GOLF

Hua Hin Golf Tours. This company can arrange play at any of the area's 10 or so courses, and no surcharge is added to the greens fee. You can rent clubs, and free transportation is provided. Packages that include accommodations are available. ✉ *Hua Hin* ☎ *032/530119* 🌐 *www.huahingolf.com.*

Royal Hua Hin Golf Course. This course, the area's oldest, sits across the tracks from the quaint wooden Hua Hin Railway Station. Though it shows its age in some spots, Royal Hua Hin has a great layout, and the setting is incomparable. There's a lounge for refreshments. ✉ *Hua Hin* ✥ *Off Prapokklao Rd.* ☎ *032/512475* 🎟 *B2,500, includes caddie* ⛳ *18 holes, 6678 yards, par 72.*

NIGHTLIFE

Hua Hin Brewing Company. Local bands energetically perform Thai and western pop-rock music here nightly. Although this isn't a true brewpub (the beers are made in Bangkok), the selection is good, and you can try a sampler of three tasty beers. The outdoor patio offers a full multicultural dining menu and is a prime spot to people-watch. ✉ *Hilton Hua Hin Resort and Spa, 33 Naresdamri Rd.* ☎ *032/512888.*

TAKIAB BEACH

4 km (2½ miles) south of Hua Hin.

Directly to the south of Hua Hin, Khao Takiab is a good alternative for people who wish to avoid Hua Hin's busier scene. Takiab is favored by well-off Thais who prefer Takiab's exclusivity to Hua Hin's touristy atmosphere, and you can find many upscale condos and small luxury hotels here. The beach itself is wide and long, but the water is murky and shallow and not very suitable for swimming.

GETTING HERE AND AROUND

To get to Takiab, flag down a songthaew (B20) on Petchkasem Road in Hua Hin. You can also hire a horse and trot down the coast.

BEACHES

Khao Takiab Beach. Sunbathing is the ideal activity at Khoa Tokiab, especially during low tide, when the golden, sandy strand is flat and dry. Jet-skiing, banana boating, and other water-sports activities are available here, all the more enjoyable than in Hua Hin because the beach and water are less crowded. A granite headland also named Khao Takiab separates the beach's northern and southern sections. On the headland's northern side, there's a tall standing image of the Buddha. You can hike to the top of the hill, where you'll find a small Buddhist monastery and several restaurants with excellent views. **Amenities:** food and drink; water sports. **Best for:** walking. ✉ *Takiab Beach* ✣ *South of Hua Hin Beach.*

4

WHERE TO EAT AND STAY

$$ THAI 🍴 **Supatra-by-the-Sea.** On the northern side of the Khao Takiab headland, this restaurant has outdoor seating with views of the nearby standing Buddha. The dining room is exquisitely designed in Lanna style and has water-lily ponds beside several tables. Entrées are mainly seafood, such as prawn soup with a deep-fried green omelet, although other Thai dishes and vegetarian options are also on the extensive menu. The full bar serves inventive cocktails, which may be enjoyed beside the beach. [$] *Average main: B150* ✉ *122/63 Takiab Rd.* ☎ *032/536561* 🌐 *www.supatra-bythesea.com.*

$$ HOTEL FAMILY 🏨 **Chom View Hotel.** This serene hotel is on the beach but with easy access to the rest of Hua Hin. The accommodations range from clean and simple standard rooms to expansive seaview duplexes. **Pros:** family-friendly; two pools; modern decor. **Cons:** can feel isolated. [$] *Rooms from: B2,900* ✉ *93 Soi Huatanon 23, Nongkae, Hua Hin* ✣ *Off Petkasem Rd.* ☎ *032/655–2925* 🌐 *www.chomviewhotel.com* 🛏 *134 rooms* 🍽 *Breakfast* 💳 *No credit cards.*

$$ HOTEL 🏨 **Kaban Tamor Resort.** The rooms at this resort are tucked inside two-story structures that were designed to resemble seashells, but actually look more like mushrooms. **Pros:** easy beach access; cute rooms. **Cons:** tacky exterior; very oriented to Thai customers. [$] *Rooms from: B2,200* ✉ *122/43–57 Takiab Beach* ☎ *032/655041* 🌐 *www.kabantamor.com* 🛏 *23 rooms* 🍽 *No meals.*

CHUMPHON

400 km (240 miles) south of Bangkok, 211 km (131 miles) south of Hua Hin.

Chumphon is regarded as the gateway to the south, because trains and buses connect to Bangkok to the north, to Surat Thani and Phuket to the south, and to Ranong to the southwest. Ferries to Koh Tao dock at Pak

Nam at the mouth of the Chumphon River, 11 km (7 miles) southeast of town. Most of the city's boat services run a free shuttle to the docks.

GETTING HERE AND AROUND

Buses leave regularly from Bangkok's Southern Terminal. The journey takes between six and nine hours; most buses leave at night, so you'll arrive early in the morning, and tickets are between B300 and B600. Though buses are cheaper and more reliable, the *Southern Line* train from Bangkok's Hualamphong Station stops here. In Chumphon proper, tuk-tuks are a ubiquitous and easy way to get around.

BEACHES

Thung Wua Laen Beach. Small islands that make up one of the world's strangest bird sanctuaries dot the horizon of this excellent 3-km (2-mile) stretch of curving white-yellow sand. Vast flocks of swifts breed on the islands, and their nests are harvested, not without controversy, for the bird's-nest soup served in Chinese restaurants throughout Southeast Asia. It's such a lucrative business that the concessionaires patrol their properties with armed guards. But all is calm and serene on the beach, which is just north of Chumphon. To get here, catch a songthaew on the street across from the bus station. **Amenities:** food and drink. **Best for:** solitude. ✉ *Chumphon.*

WHERE TO STAY

$ HOTEL 🏨 **Chumphon Cabana Beach Resort.** This resort at the southern end of Thung Wua Laen Beach is a great place to stay if you plan to make brief visits to Koh Samui and other nearby islands. **Pros:** convenient for island-hopping; eco-friendly vibe. **Cons:** you won't be fawned over; rooms nothing special. [$] *Rooms from: B1,650* ✉ *69 Moo 8 Thung Wua Laen Beach* ☎ *077/560245* 🌐 *www.cabana.co.th* 🛏 *73 rooms* 🍴 *No meals.*

$ HOTEL 🏨 **Marokot Hotel.** Lodging options are few in Chumphon, but this centrally located hotel has comfortable rooms and provides a reasonable level of service. **Pros:** inexpensive; centrally located. **Cons:** some rooms lack air-conditioning; few amenities. [$] *Rooms from: B990* ✉ *102–112 Taweesinka Rd.* ☎ *077/503628 up to 32* 🌐 *www.morakothotel.com* 💳 *No credit cards* 🛏 *60 rooms* 🍴 *No meals.*

SURAT THANI

193 km (120 miles) south of Chumphon, 685 km (425 miles) south of Bangkok.

Surat Thani is where you board the boats bound for Koh Samui. Though not particularly attractive, Surat Thani has a few culturally interesting sights that make it a good destination for those easily bored by the beach, and the mountains and greenery of Khao Sok National Park are a few hours away by bus. There are also some good restaurants and a handsome hotel.

GETTING HERE AND AROUND

You can get here from Bangkok by bus or train, but flying is the most efficient way to arrive. Thai Air Asia often has low fares. Bus trips from Bangkok's Southern Bus Terminal take about 10 hours and cost from

B400 to B800. There's also an overnight train here from Bangkok's Hua Lamphong Station.

VISITOR AND TOUR INFORMATION

Tourism Authority of Thailand. ⊠ *5 Talat Mai Rd.* ☎ *077/281828* ⊕ *www. tourismthailand.org.*

EXPLORING

San Chao Night Market. Every night the sleepy downtown turns into an electrifying street fair centered around the San Chao Night Market, which is illuminated by the lights of numerous food stalls and shop carts. The market is popular with tourists and locals, especially for the tasty seafood meals on offer. ⊠ *Surat Thani* ✛ *Alley off Na Muang Rd.*

OFF THE BEATEN PATH

Khao Sok National Park. A landscape of tall mountains, lush greenery, and small streams, this 161,000-acre park contains the most beautiful forest in Thailand. The diverse and rare wildlife that thrives here includes gaurs, bantengs, sambar deer, bears, Malayan tapirs, macaques, gibbons, mouse deer, and porcupines. Khao Sok is one of the few places to see a rafflesia, the world's largest flower, and rare bird species such as hornbills live here. Hiking, boat rides, and night safaris are some of the activities that take place in the park.

Rain is inevitable in Khao Sok, as the weather is influenced by monsoon winds from both the northeast and west—the best and driest time to visit is between December and April. Both the national park and some private resorts offer various types of lodging, but don't expect too much. Only very basic accommodations can be found in the park. There is additional private accommodation outside the park, most notably an oddly shaped tree-house accommodation 1 km (½ mile) before the park's entrance. The bus ride (B80) from the station in Surat Thani to the park takes about 2½ hours. The TAT office in Surat Thani has information about the park. ⊠ *Moo 6 Phanom* ✛ *190 km west of Surat Thani* ☎ *077/395154* ⊕ *www.dnp.go.th* ⌧ *300B.*

WHERE TO STAY

$ **Wang Tai Hotel.** This modern high-rise offers everything you need for
HOTEL a Surat Thani stopover as you prepare for your onward journey. **Pros:** tasty food; handy location; great views. **Cons:** the rooms are tatty; doesn't feel particularly Thai. $ *Rooms from: B1,000* ⊠ *1 Talad Mai Rd.* ☎ *077/283020, 02/253-7947 in Bangkok* ⊕ *www.wangtaisurat. net* ⌁ *230 rooms* ◉| *Breakfast.*

KOH SAMUI

20 km (12 miles) by boat east of Don Sak.

Fodor's Choice Koh Samui is the most popular tourist destination on the Western Gulf
★ coast, which isn't surprising, considering the island's gorgeous beaches, perfect weather, and sparkling blue, almost turquoise, water. Koh Samui has seen rapid development since the 1990s, and you'll encounter hotels in all price ranges.

Koh Samui is half the size of Phuket, so you could easily drive around it in a day. But Koh Samui is best appreciated by those who take a slower, more casual approach. Most people come for the sun and sea, so they head straight to their hotel and rarely venture beyond its beach. But it's worth exploring beyond your lodging. Every beach has its own character, and you might find the perfect one for you.

One beach many visitors find to their liking is Chawaeng. On Koh Samui's east coast, this stretch of glistening white sand is divided into two main sections—Chawaeng Yai (yai means "big") and Chawaeng Noi (noi means "little"). You'll find the greatest variety of hotels, restaurants, and bars here. Despite the crowds, Chawaeng is no Pattaya or Patong—the mood is very laid-back. A rocky headland separates Chawaeng Lamai Beach, whose clear water and long stretch of sand were the first place on the island to attract developers. More budget accommodations are available here than in Chawaeng, and there are some happening nightclubs.

On the west coast of Koh Samui, Na Thon is the island's primary port and the spot where ferries arrive from the mainland. It's home to the island's governmental offices, including the Tourism Authority of Thailand, and there are banks, foreign-exchange booths, travel agents, shops, restaurants, and cafés by the ferry pier. A few places rent rooms, but there's really no reason to stay here—nicer accommodations can be found a short songthaew ride away.

To the north and east of Na Thon lie a few beaches worthy of exploration. Laem Yai, 5 km (3 miles) north, has great seafood. East of here, a small headland separates two low-key communities on the northern shore, Mae Nam and Bophut Beach. Mae Nam is also the departure point for boats bound for Koh Phangan and Koh Tao *(see Side Trips from Koh Samui, below).* Just south of the Samui's northeastern tip you'll find sandy Choengmon Beach, a good area for swimming that's not overdeveloped.

GETTING HERE AND AROUND

AIR TRAVEL Bangkok Airways offers multiple daily flights from Bangkok, and Thai Airways has a morning and an evening flight. At around $200, the hour-long flight is a bit pricier than other flights within Thailand, mainly because the airport is owned by Bangkok Airways and not, as in most cases in Thailand, by the government.

BOAT TRAVEL From Surat Thani's Donsak Pier, ferries leave every couple of hours for Koh Samui's Na Thon Pier on the west coast; the trip takes roughly two hours. Tour operators in Surat Thani and Koh Samui have information on the ferry schedules, or you can also just head to the pier. Expect to pay around B250 for the trip.

CAR AND TAXI TRAVEL Koh Samui is a delight to explore, and it's one of the few destinations where having a car can come in really handy. A drive along the coastal road will provide one beautiful view after another; the interior of the island isn't as scenic. Budget and Hertz have counters at the Koh Samui airport, and National has its counter in downtown Koh Samui. Thai Rent a Car has a counter near the airport, and the company will deliver your car to you when you land. TA Car Rental is a reputable local company based on Samui.

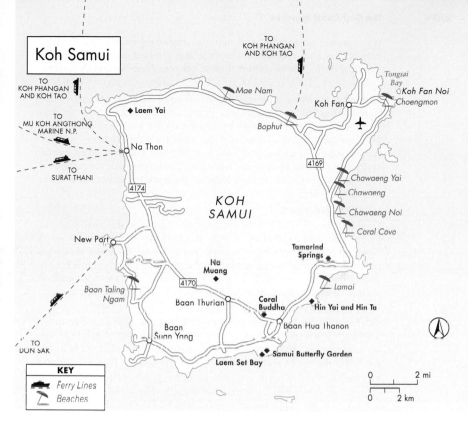

Koh Samui

TO
KOH PHANGAN
AND KOH TAO

TO
KOH PHANGAN
AND KOH TAO

TO
MU KOH ANGTHONG
MARINE N.P.

TO
SURAT THANI

◆ Laem Yai

Na Thon

4174

TO
DON SAK

New Port

Baan Taling
Ngam

4170

Baan Thurian

Baan
Suan Yang

Laem Set Bay

Na
Muang

Mae Nam

Bophut

4169

**KOH
SAMUI**

Coral
Buddha

Baan Hua Thanon

Samui Butterfly Garden

Koh Fan

Tongsai
Bay

◊ *Koh Fan Noi*

Choengmon

Chawaeng Yai

Chawaeng

Chawaeng Noi

Coral Cove

Tamarind
Springs

Lamai

Hin Yai and Hin Ta

KEY

 Ferry Lines

Beaches

0 — 2 mi

0 — 2 km

Taxis don't always meet incoming flights at the airport in Koh Samui, but they can easily be called.

Car4You Samui. This low-cost outfit rents a range of vehicles, from economy to specialty and luxury cars. ⊠ *42/15 Moo 4 Bophut* ☏ *086/4768031* ⊕ *www.samui4ucarrent.com.*

VISITOR INFORMATION

Contacts Tourism Authority of Thailand. ⊠ *Na Thon* ☏ *077/421281* ⊕ www.tourismthailand.org.

EXPLORING

TOP ATTRACTIONS

OFF THE
BEATEN
PATH

Mu Koh Angthong National Marine Park. This archipelago of 42 islands covers some 102 square km (40 square miles) and lies 35 km (22 miles) northwest of Koh Samui. The seven main islands are Wua Talap Island (which houses the national park's headquarters), Phaluai Island, Mae Koh Island, Sam Sao Island, Hin Dap Island, Nai Phut Island, and Phai Luak Island. The islands contain limestone mountains, strangely shaped caves, emerald-green lakes and ponds. Most tourists visit on a one-day trip, which can be arranged from Koh Samui. Prices vary depending on the tour (some offer kayaking around several islands, and others take you out on small speedboats for snorkeling or cave tours). The park is open year-round, although the seas can be rough and the water less clear during the monsoon season, between October and December. ✉ *Koh Samui* ☎ *077/286025, 077/420225* ⊕ *www.dnp.go.th* 💲 *B200.*

Na Muang. On the inland road to Na Thon lies the village of Baan Thurian, famous for its durian trees. A track to the right climbs up into jungle-clad hills to the island's best waterfall, Na Muang. The 105-foot falls are spectacular—especially just after the rainy season—as they tumble from a limestone cliff into a small pool. You are cooled by the spray and warmed by the sun. For a thrill, swim through the curtain of falling water; you can sit on a ledge at the back to catch your breath. ✉ *Baan Thurian.*

WORTH NOTING

Coral Buddha. About 4 km (2½ miles) from Lamai, at the small Chinese fishing village of Baan Hua Thanon, the road that forks inland toward Na Thon leads to the Coral Buddha, a small temple complex built on a natural rock formation carved by years of erosion. One of Samui's most serene and least touristy spots, the Coral Buddha provides a glimpse of a more fundamental, traditional world of Buddhism less apparent at brasher, more high-profile destinations. ✉ *Baan Hua Thanon.*

Koh Fan. Off the northeastern tip of Koh Samui is Koh Fan (not to be confused with Koh Fan Noi), a little island with a huge Buddha image covered in moss. The island is best visited at sunset, when the light off the water shows the statue at its best. ✉ *Koh Samui.*

Koh Fan Noi. Just offshore at Choengmon Beach is Koh Fan Noi, a little island with a narrow strip of sandy beach. The waters are shallow enough to wade to the island. Despite the hectic pace of development on Samui, the beautiful beach here remains nearly deserted. ✉ *Choengmon Beach.*

Samui Butterfly Garden. Kaleidoscopic clouds of butterflies flutter throughout the garden's 2 netted acres of meandering walkways. ✉ *Laem Set Bay* ☎ *077/424020* ⊕ *Apr.–Oct., daily 10–4; Nov.–Mar., daily 9–5* 💲 *B150.*

BEACHES

Bophut Beach. Quaint and romantic Bophut has a devoted following of return visitors who enjoy its quiet vibe. This north-shore beach is narrow, but more than wide enough for sunbathing. The water is like glass, making it good for swimming, though it's deep enough to be unsuitable for young children. Bophut has a bit of nightlife. Central Bophut, known to everyone as Fisherman's Village, has a beachside strip of old houses that have been converted into restaurants, bars, and boutiques. **Amenities:** food and drink. **Best for:** swimming. ✉ *Bophut.*

Chawaeng Noi Beach. The smaller and less developed of the east-coast beaches adjoining Chawaeng town, Chawaeng Noi lacks the charms and spectacular golden curve of its bigger brother, Chawaeng Yai. It's quieter and more relaxed, though, and there are nearby resorts where you can grab a snack. **Amenities:** food and drink; water sports. **Best for:** solitude. ⊠ *Chawaeng.*

Chawaeng Yai Beach. Travelers in search of sun and fun flock here, especially during high season. The northern half of this beautiful east-coast beach is a hit with backpackers because it's lined with budget lodgings. The southern half, more popular with the package tourists, is lined with high-end resorts. Chawaeng Yai is a great swimming beach. The fine sand is brilliant white, and the waters are clear and usually calm. During the day, tourists pack in and the water buzzes with Jet Skis and banana boats. At night the streets come alive as shops, bars, and restaurants vie for your vacation allowance. **Amenities:** food and drink; water sports. **Best for:** swimming. ⊠ *Chawaeng.*

Choengmon Beach. A mellow spot on Samui's northeastern coast, this beach is blessed with crystal clear water. Choengmon was once pitched as the island's next big thing. There's hardly a boom, but a few guest-houses, a handful of luxury resorts, and some restaurants are scattered along the wide shore. The sand is firm and strewn with pebbles and shells, but the beach is adequate for sunbathing, and there's an interesting rock formation at one end. A few of the eating options are right on the beach. **Amenities:** food and drink; water sports. **Best for:** swimming. ⊠ *Choengmon.*

Lamai Beach. Popular Lamai lacks the glistening white sand of Chawaeng Beach, but its water is clear and the beach is ideal for swimming. The steeply shelved shoreline might be too much for kids, though. Numerous bars and restaurants line the beach, emphasizing that Lamai is mostly for young people looking to party. Almost every visitor to Koh Samui makes a pilgrimage to the point marking the southern end of Lamai Beach to see two rocks, named Hin Yai (Grandmother Rock) and Hin Ta (Grandfather Rock). Erosion has shaped the rocks to resemble weathered and wrinkled private parts. It's nature at its most whimsical. Laem Set Bay, small rocky cape on the southeastern tip of the island, is just south of Lamai. It's a good 3 km (2 miles) off the main road, so it's hard to reach without your own car. Head here to escape the hustle and bustle of Samui. **Amenities:** food and drink; water sports. **Best for:** partiers; swimming. ⊠ *Lamai.*

Mae Nam Beach. The long, curving beach at Mae Nam has coarse, golden sand shaded by tall coconut trees. It's one of the island's more unspoiled beaches—inexpensive guesthouses and a few luxurious resorts share the 5-km (3-mile) strand. Quiet both day and night, this north shore beach has little nightlife and only a scattering of restaurants. The shallow waters are suitable for swimming, and several water-sports companies operate in the area. **Amenities:** food and drink; water sports. **Best for:** swimming. ⊠ *Mae Nam.*

WHERE TO EAT

CHAWAENG

$$
SEAFOOD
✕**Captain Kirk.** One of Chawaeng's more touristy options, this place scores with attractive decor and rooftop views. About half the menu is Thai food, and this is the half that should keep your attention. Prawns

Koh Samui's accessibility and beautiful beaches make it a popular destination year-round.

with garlic and pepper rarely disappoint, whereas the French fare—well, what were you expecting? $ *Average main: B250* ⊠ *167/42 Moo 2, 2nd fl., Chawaeng* ☎ *081/270–5376* ▭ *No credit cards.*

$$ ✕ **Eat Sense.** Despite its manicured grounds, this is not a resort, just
SEAFOOD   a restaurant that serves great Thai food. The dining area has several small fountains and towering palms from which hang giant paper lanterns—you can dine on the patio beside the beach or on couches beneath white umbrellas. The exotic creations include Phuket lobster with eggplant and Kaffir lime leaves in a green curry paste. The locally caught fish, always a treat, is served in all kinds of exotic sauces and styles. Before dinner enjoy creative cocktails, some of them served in coconut shells, watermelons, or other natural containers. Reservations are recommended, particularly during high season. $ *Average main: B300* ⊠ *Chawaeng Beach Rd., Chawaeng* ✛ *Near Central Samui Resort* ☎ *077/414242* ⊕ *www.eatsensesamui.com.*

$ ✕ **Ninja.** This no-frills dining room serving authentic Thai cuisine is
THAI   popular with locals and foreigners. Curries such as massaman (peanut-based) or *panaeng* (red chili paste and coconut milk) are solid choices, but you really can't go wrong here. Save room for *khao niew mamuang* (mango and sticky rice) and other classic desserts. Ninja's expansive menu includes large color photographs of every dish on the menu, along with phonetic Thai and English captions. $ *Average main: B100* ⊠ *Samui Ring Rd., Chawaeng Beach* ▭ *No credit cards.*

$$$$ ✕ **The Page.** Stick to the fun and interesting cocktails here, not the so-so
THAI   wine list, and after a few sips you'll feel as hip as the surroundings. The menu is Thai, with all the favorites like prawns with garlic and

pepper, and sea bass with chili and basil. The setting, overlooking the beach, feels way cooler than most of Chawaeng's hectic scene. And it's always nice to unwind amid smart design elements such as the lounging figurines that dot the property. $ *Average main: B500* ✉ *14/1 Moo 2, Chawaeng Beach* ☎ *077/422767* ⊕ *www.thelibrary.co.th.*

$$
SEAFOOD
✕ **Tarua Samui Seafood.** The view is definitely what you come here for— high up on a mountain, the restaurant juts out above a rocky beach and turquoise waters. But the food is also memorable. Raw shrimp have an silky texture, and the massive grilled prawns with garlic or curry are delicious. Check the seafood tank as you walk in; you might spy something you can't resist. $ *Average main: B250* ✉ *210/9 Moo 4, Chawaeng* ☎ *077/960635* ▭ *No credit cards.*

$$$$
BRAZILIAN
✕ **Zico's.** That disc on your table isn't a coaster—flip it over to signal that you need a break from the never-ending parade of food the staff courteously delivers. Hungry again? Flip it back to sample more of the all you can-eat barbecue consisting of 15 different skewers of beef, fish, lamb, and shrimp. There's an ample salad bar as well. Brazilian samba musicians set an upbeat tone, but authentic Brazilian dancers steal the show, shaking up the room in skimpy outfits and posing for photos with awestruck diners. $ *Average main: B900* ✉ *38/2 Samui Ring Rd., Chawaeng Beach* ☎ *077/231560* ⊕ *www.zicossamui.com* ⚭ *Reservations essential.*

LAMAI

$$$$
MEDITERRANEAN
✕ **The Cliff.** Halfway along the road from Chawaeng to Lamai, the Cliff perches on a big boulder overlooking the sea. You can have lunch or dinner either inside the spartan dining room or out on the scenic terrace. The lunch menu includes sandwiches and hamburgers; among the dinner highlights are steaks and Mediterranean specialties. The prices are a bit high for the small servings, and the service isn't great, but the Cliff is a nice place to enjoy a drink and check out the view. In the evening, cooler than thou staff serve cocktails in the enclosed, air conditioned club. $ *Average main: B500* ✉ *124/2 Samui Ring Rd., Lamai Beach* ☎ *077/448508* ⊕ *www.thecliffsamui.com* ⚭ *Reservations essential.*

$
SEAFOOD
✕ **Mr. Pown Seafood Restaurant.** Though hardly fancy, this place serves reliable Thai seafood, as well as some German and English fare. Try the red curry in young coconut—a moderately spicy, not quite "red" curry with cauliflower and string beans served inside a coconut—or the catch of the day. The staff is courteous, if perhaps a little jaded from interacting with the tourist clientele. There are better restaurants in Lamai Beach, but not at this price and in this location. $ *Average main: B100* ✉ *Central Lamai Beach* ▭ *No credit cards.*

BAAN TALING NGAM

$$$$
SEAFOOD
✕ **The Virgin Coast.** Thai fusion cuisine and a relaxing tropical ambience await guests at this reincarnation of the popular Five Islands restaurant. Now in a slightly different location and renamed the Virgin Coast, the restaurant offers the same laid-back charm, superlative service, and high-quality cooking. Western influences elevate the traditional and contemporary Thai dishes on the menu. The emphasis is on seafood, but vegetarian and meat dishes are prepared, too. $ *Average main: B500* ✉ *Baan Taling Ngam* ☎ *089/499–6334* ⊕ *www.thevirgincoastsamui. com* ▭ *No credit cards.*

4

MAE NAM

$ CAFÉ 🍴 **Angela's Bakery & Café.** On the main road running through Mae Nam, Angela's serves salads and sandwiches, both traditional and inventive. Among the latter, the "Hot Bandana" is a tasty vegetarian sandwich baked inside a bread bowl and wrapped in a bandana. Entrées represent Samui's British influence: bangers and mash, fish-and-chips, and the like. Angela's also sells more than 40 desserts, 20 types of bread, several flavors of muffins, and various imported meats and cheeses—everything you might need for a picnic on the beach. [$] *Average main: B100* ✉ *64/29 Samui Ring Rd., Mae Nam Beach* ☎ *077/427396* 💳 *No credit cards.*

$ SEAFOOD 🍴 **Bang Po Seafood.** Mere feet from lapping waves, this shack serves up the freshest seafood at the best of prices. The jarringly purple baby octopus soup and the sour curry with whole fish are two great options. Price-conscious sushi fans may well fall in love with the sea-urchin salad; $3 gets you more *uni* than one person can possibly eat. [$] *Average main: B100* ✉ *56/4 Moo 6, Mae Nam Beach* ☎ *077/420010* 💳 *No credit cards.*

$ SEAFOOD 🍴 **Kohseng.** This two-story seafood restaurant has been feeding Mae Nam residents for decades. The interior is simple, with lots of dark wood. The menus are in both Thai and English, though the staff's English is a bit rough around the edges. The most famous dish, stir-fried crab with black pepper, is highly recommended. Prices are low, even by Koh Samui standards. [$] *Average main: B80* ✉ *95 Soi Kohseng, Mae Nam Beach* ☎ *077/425365* 💳 *No credit cards.*

$ THAI 🍴 **Twin Restaurant.** The friendly twin sisters who run this nine-table, open-air restaurant serve Thai and western food for breakfast, lunch, and dinner. You can peek into the clean kitchen, where the two prepare tasty, inexpensive dishes like curry soup, along with steaks and other more upmarket fare. Right on the main road, Twin is very easy to find. [$] *Average main: B100* ✉ *237 Samui Ring Rd., Mae Nam Beach* ☎ *077/247037* 💳 *No credit cards.*

$ SEAFOOD 🍴 **Whan Tok.** Perched on the water, this family-owned joint is filled with locals who come for the seafood—the massive prawns are great, and the seafood soups have wonderfully flavorful broths. Finding the place is half the fun; the sign out front has no writing in English, so if you're coming by cab, ask someone at your hotel to write out the name in Thai. The delicious, inexpensive food is worth the extra effort. [$] *Average main: B80* ✉ *37/1 Moo 5, Mae Nam Beach* ☎ *081/597–3171* 💳 *No credit cards.*

BOPHUT

$$ FRENCH 🍴 **La Sirene.** For elegant French cooking, try this small bistro on the waterfront whose owner moved here from Nice. The three-course tasting menu might include such delicacies as a shark with pineapple entrée, along with a salad and a dessert. À la carte offerings include shrimp in cognac sauce and mussels in a white-wine cream sauce, and various Thai dishes are also prepared. A few tables are in the dining room, but the real delight here is to sit on the deck overlooking the boats moored a few yards offshore. [$] *Average main: B240* ✉ *65/1 Bophut Beach, Bophut* ☎ *077/425301, 081/797–3499.*

$$$$ SEAFOOD 🍴 **Ocean 11.** This restaurant's unapologetically western menu attracts Americans and Europeans. Soft-shell crab on arugula and white snapper baked in a banana leaf provide a refreshing change of pace from Thai-centric fare. It's all about the atmosphere here: warm, inviting, and right on the beach. If you're feeling homesick, drop in for rack of lamb, duck confit, or penne with prawns. [$] *Average main: B660* ✉ *23 Moo 4, Bophut* ☎ *077/245134* 🌐 *www.o11s.com* 🕒 *Closed Mon.*

$ SEAFOOD 🍴 **Starfish and Coffee.** You won't find any starfish on the menu, but a great deal more than coffee is served here. Fish, crab, squid, prawns, and mussels are cooked in garlic and pepper, chili and basil, and several other primarily Thai styles. The interior represents a funky fusion of Thai and Chinese style, and there's always cool music playing. Seating is outdoors by the sea or indoors on rattan chairs or floor pillows. [$] *Average main: B120* ✉ *51/7 Moo 1, Bophut* ☎ *077/427201.*

$$ ECLECTIC 🍴 **Villa Daudet.** The menu hops the continents at this restaurant that serves French, Thai, and Italian cuisine. *Moules marinières* (mussels in white wine and garlic) are a good option. Villa Daudet also doubles as a bar, adding to the Bophut nightlife scene, which still has nothing on nearby Chawaeng. A cozy interior of warm oranges and walls adorned with locally tinged design flourishes lends the place a slightly more upscale feel than its neighbors. [$] *Average main: B240* ✉ *33/1 Moo 1, Bophut* ☎ *083/643–6656* 🕒 *Closed Mon.*

CHOENGMON

$$$ INTERNATIONAL 🍴 **Dining on the Rocks.** Arranged on several terraces, the tables here all have panoramic sea views—arrive before sunset to get the full effect. In addition to entrées, there are small plates, among them the iced *tom yum* gazpacho with oysters, that blend western and Thai flavors. To get a sense of the chef's ambition and range, though, choose the set menu. There's often live music in the evenings. [$] *Average main: B100* ✉ *Six Senses Samui, 9/10 Moo 5, Baan Plai Laem, Bophut* ☎ *077/245678* 🌐 *www.sixsenses.com/resorts/samui/destination.*

WHERE TO STAY

CHAWAENG

$ B&B/INN Fodor's Choice ★ 🏨 **AKWA Guesthouse.** Rooms at Australian proprietor Timothy Schwan's guesthouse have giant pop-art paintings on the walls, chairs in the shape of giant hands, and kitschy lamps. **Pros:** hip feel; fun crowd; stunning design. **Cons:** can be noisy; not ideal for families. [$] *Rooms from: B750* ✉ *28/12 Moo 3 S. Chawaeng Beach Rd., Chawaeng Beach* ☎ *04/660–0551* 🌐 *www.akwaguesthouse.com* 💳 *No credit cards* 🛏 *5 rooms* 🍽 *No meals.*

$$ RESORT 🏨 **Al's Resort.** The newer deluxe villas at this resort are fashionably Thai, with Thai art on the walls, outdoor showers, and wooden bed frames, trims, and desks. **Pros:** trendy place; hip crowd. **Cons:** older rooms not as nice; not ideal for families. [$] *Rooms from: B2,600* ✉ *200 Moo 2, Chawaeng Beach* ☎ *077/422154* 🌐 *www.alsresortsamui.com* 🛏 *26 rooms, 17 villas* 🍽 *Breakfast.*

$$$ RESORT 🏨 **Amari Koh Samui.** This luxurious resort faces a beach where the water's too shallow for swimming—which can be an advantage, as

it keeps the crowds away. **Pros:** local touches to the rooms; lovely views; on the beach. **Cons:** some rooms are across the road from the beach. [$] *Rooms from: B4,400* ✉ *Samui Ring Rd., Chawaeng Beach* ☎ *077/422015, 02/255–4588 in Bangkok* 🌐 *www.amari.com* 🛏 *179 rooms, 8 suites* 🍴 *Breakfast.*

$$ RESORT 🏨 **Baan Talay Resort.** Bungalows huddled around a shimmering pool are the focal point at Baan Talay, but the real reasons to stay here are the few huts just a stone's throw from the beach. **Pros:** close to beach. **Cons:** outdated decor. [$] *Rooms from: B3,900* ✉ *17/36 Moo 3 Chawaeng Beach Rd., Chawaeng Beach* ☎ *077/413555* 🌐 *www.baantalay.com* 🛏 *54 rooms* 🍴 *Breakfast.*

$$$ RESORT 🏨 **The Briza.** Rather than attempt yet another iteration of Thai design, this resort opted for what can best be described as a fusion of Indian and Chinese styles for its villas. **Pros:** unique style; luxurious, secluded, and exclusive. **Cons:** very expensive; not the life of the party. [$] *Rooms from: B5,500* ✉ *173/22 Moo 2, Chawaeng Beach* ☎ *077/231997, 02/251–3118 up to 21 in Bangkok* 🌐 *www.thebriza.com* 🛏 *57 villas* 🍴 *Breakfast.*

$$$ RESORT 🏨 **Buri Rasa.** One of many hotels along a happening stretch of Chawaeng Beach, Buri Rasa blends in well with the party scene yet manages to retain a semblance of a relaxing getaway feel. **Pros:** chill vibe; fun pool; great design. **Cons:** on party stretch of beach; some foot traffic. [$] *Rooms from: B5,600* ✉ *11/2 Moo 2, Chawaeng Beach* ☎ *077/230222* 🌐 *www.burirasa.com* 🛏 *32 rooms* 🍴 *Breakfast.*

$$$$ RESORT 🏨 **Centara Grand Beach Resort.** This spacious resort has more amenities than any other resort on Chawaeng Beach. **Pros:** plenty of activities; good for families. **Cons:** may feel big and impersonal; you pay a lot for what you get. [$] *Rooms from: B8200* ✉ *38/2 Samui Ring Rd., South Chawaeng Beach* ☎ *077/230500* 🌐 *www.centarahotelsresorts.com* 🛏 *199 rooms, 9 suites* 🍴 *Breakfast.*

$$ RESORT 🏨 **Iyara Beach Hotel and Plaza.** A getaway for young urbanites who don't want to give up the luxuries of home, this complex includes a maze of boutiques, including Lacoste and Bossini. **Pros:** good deal; close to many activities; luxurious rooms. **Cons:** feels a bit hectic; many rooms lack views. [$] *Rooms from: B2,500* ✉ *90/13–16 Chawaeng Beach, Chawaeng Beach* ☎ *077/231629* 🌐 *www.iyarabeachhotelandplaza.com* 🛏 *76 rooms, 2 suites* 🍴 *No meals; Breakfast.*

$$$$ RESORT 🏨 **The Library.** This place is so fun that it's worth a visit for its amusingly hip decor—check out the white figures reading books on the lawn, inviting you to lounge as well. **Pros:** very stylish; cool, young crowd. **Cons:** pricey; not ideal if you're looking for quiet; not suited to families. [$] *Rooms from: B12,500* ✉ *14/1 Moo 2 Chawaeng Beach, Chawaeng Beach* ☎ *077/422767* 🌐 *www.thelibrary.co.th* 🛏 *26 rooms and suites* 🍴 *Breakfast.*

$$$ RESORT 🏨 **Montien House.** Two rows of charming bungalows line the path leading to the beach at this comfortable little resort. **Pros:** cute rooms; attentive staff and management. **Cons:** not much pizzazz; lacks creature comforts. [$] *Rooms from: B6,800* ✉ *5 Moo 2, Chawaeng Beach* ☎ *077/422169* 🌐 *www.montienhouse.com* 🛏 *57 rooms, 3 suites* 🍴 *Breakfast.*

$$$ ☷ **Muang Kulaypan Hotel.** This hotel emphasizes design more than some
RESORT of its neighbors—expect simple lines, minimal furnishings, and sharp
contrasts. **Pros:** interesting decor; sea views from many rooms. **Cons:**
expensive rates; can be noisy; standard rooms lack sea views. $ *Rooms
from: B4,300* ⊠ *100 Samui Ring Rd., Chawaeng Beach* ☎ *077/230849,
077/230850* ⊕ *www.kulaypan.com* ⤶ *41 rooms, 1 suite* ⓘ○ *Breakfast.*

$$$$ ☷ **Muang Samui Spa Resort.** At this tranquil resort, a meandering garden
RESORT path with small bridges and stepping-stones crosses a flowing, fish-filled
stream. **Pros:** different style; well-kept grounds. **Cons:** feels sprawling;
expensive. $ *Rooms from: B15,000* ⊠ *13/1 Moo 2, Chawaeng Beach*
☎ *077/429700, 02/553–1008 in Bangkok* ⊕ *www.muangsamui.com*
⤶ *53 suites* ⓘ○ *Breakfast.*

$$$ ☷ **Nora Beach Resort and Spa.** A big plus of this hotel is that about two
RESORT dozen rooms have sea views and many overlook the pool, so you're
almost guaranteed an aquatic perspective. **Pros:** comfortable surroundings; spacious bathrooms. **Cons:** unexciting furnishings; not cheap.
$ *Rooms from: B5,000* ⊠ *222 Moo 2 Chawaeng Beach, North Cha-
waeng Beach* ☎ *077/413999, 077/429400* ⊕ *www.norabeachresort.
com* ⤶ *90 rooms, 23 suites* ⓘ○ *Breakfast.*

$$$$ ☷ **Poppies.** Dozens of cheerful employees are on hand to attend to your
RESORT every need at this romantic beachfront resort on the quiet southern end
Fodor'sChoice of Chawaeng Beach. **Pros:** snappy service; immediate area not too crazy.
★ **Cons:** a little staid; not cheap. $ *Rooms from: B8,500* ⊠ *Samui Ring
Rd., South Chawaeng Beach* ☎ *077/422419* ⊕ *www.poppiessamui.com*
⤶ *24 cottages* ⓘ○ *No meals.*

$$$$ ☷ **Sheraton Samui Resort.** A landscaped terrace leads down to a private
RESORT beach at this resort on the less crowded southern end of Chawaeng Noi.
If you want to do more than catch rays, this is the place for you—the
Sheraton offers every kind of beach activity imaginable. **Pros:** great
views from pool terrace; good beachside restaurant; lots of beach activities. **Cons:** may be too quiet for some people. $ *Rooms from: B6,600*
⊠ *86 Moo 3 Chawaeng Noi Beach, Chawaeng* ☎ *077/422020* ⊕ *www.
sheratonsamui.com* ⤶ *117 rooms, 24 suites* ⓘ○ *Breakfast; No meals.*

LAMAI

$$ ☷ **Aloha Resort.** All the rooms at this oceanfront resort have private ter-
RESORT races or balconies that face in the general direction of the beach. **Pros:** ideal
for families; reasonable price. **Cons:** some rooms not so nice. $ *Rooms
from: B2,550* ⊠ *128 Moo 3 Lamai Beach, Lamai* ☎ *077/424014* ⊕ *www.
alohasamui.com* ⤶ *74 rooms, suites, and bungalows* ⓘ○ *No meals.*

$$ ☷ **Lamai-Wanta.** These incredibly spartan rooms are kept immaculately
RESORT clean—perhaps not surprising, given that the owners are a nurse and
doctor couple. **Pros:** cool pool; beautiful beach. **Cons:** blah decor; lacks
spunk. $ *Rooms from: B2,600* ⊠ *124/264 Moo 3 T. Maret Lamai
Beach, Lamai* ☎ *077/424550* ⊕ *www.lamaiwanta.com* ⤶ *40 rooms,
10 bungalows* ⓘ○ *Breakfast.*

$$$$ ☷ **Pavilion.** This amiable place offers a little respite from the down-
RESORT town hustle and bustle. **Pros:** quiet; hot tubs in some rooms. **Cons:**
some rooms pricey; not the most modern hotel. $ *Rooms from: B6,400*
⊠ *124/24 Lamai Beach, Lamai* ☎ *077/424030* ⊕ *www.pavilionsamui.
com* ⤶ *70 rooms* ⓘ○ *Breakfast.*

4

$$$ RESORT **Renaissance Koh Samui Resort & Spa.** At the far northern end of Lamai, the Renaissance sits on its own secluded, private beach—two small beaches to be exact. **Pros:** sprawling grounds; high-end feel. **Cons:** isolated location; pricey. [$] *Rooms from: B4,700* ✉ *208/1 Moo 4 T. Maret, Lamai Beach* ☎ *077/429300* 🌐 *www.renaissancehotels.com/usmbr* 🛏 *45 rooms, 33 suites* 🍴 *No meals.*

BAAN TALING NGAM

$$$$ RESORT **InterContinental Samui Baan Taling Ngam Resort.** The name means "home on a beautiful bank," but that doesn't come close to summing up the stunning location of this luxurious hotel. **Pros:** beautiful views; plenty of activities. **Cons:** can't lounge on beach; somewhat isolated. [$] *Rooms from: B8,000* ✉ *295 Moo 3 Taling Ngam Beach, Baan Taling Ngam* ☎ *077/429100, 02/653–2201 in Bangkok* 🌐 *www.samui.intercontinental.com* 🛏 *40 rooms, 30 villas* 🍴 *No meals.*

MAE NAM AND LAEM YAI

$$$$ RESORT **Belmond Napasai.** The word *napasai* means "clear sky," and if you book a beachfront room you can enjoy the view of both the sky *and* the sea from your outdoor terrace, from inside your room, or even from your bathtub. **Pros:** great views; super staff. **Cons:** pricey; some rooms not as nice as others. [$] *Rooms from: B10,500* ✉ *65/10 Baan Tai, Mae Nam* ☎ *077/429200* 🌐 *www.napasai.com* 🛏 *69 rooms* 🍴 *Breakfast.*

$ RESORT **The Florist Resort.** This guesthouse is tiny, but in a cute and cozy way. **Pros:** good bang for your buck; easy beach access. **Cons:** not as comfortable as some mega-chains; staff not so attentive. [$] *Rooms from: B1,300* ✉ *190 Moo 1 Tambon Maenam, Mae Nam Beach* ☎ *077/425671* 🌐 *www.floristresort.com* 🛏 *32 rooms* 🍴 *Breakfast.*

$$$$ RESORT Fodor's Choice ★ **Four Seasons Koh Samui.** This is easily one of the most spectacular hotels in the world. **Pros:** ultimate luxury and relaxation; cool room design. **Cons:** might break the bank; golf carts necessary to get around. [$] *Rooms from: B28,900* ✉ *219 Moo 5 Angthong, Laem Yai* ☎ *077/243000* 🌐 *www.fourseasons.com/kohsamui* 🛏 *74 villas* 🍴 *No meals.*

$$$$ RESORT Fodor's Choice ★ **Santiburi Resort and Spa.** The villas of this beachfront estate have the feel of a billionaire's holiday hideaway; accordingly, this is one of the most expensive lodgings on the island. **Pros:** on a private beach; elegant rooms; good restaurants. **Cons:** not ideal for families. [$] *Rooms from: B19,000* ✉ *12/12 Samui Ring Rd., Mae Nam Beach* ☎ *077/425031, 02/636–3333 in Bangkok, 800/223–5652 in U.S.* 🌐 *www.santiburi.com* 🛏 *71 villas and suites* 🍴 *No meals.*

BOPHUT

$$$ RESORT **Absolute Sanctuary.** If you're on vacation to detox, this is the spot—and if you aren't, well, it probably isn't. **Pros:** prime yoga facilities; unique concept. **Cons:** no fun if you're not detoxing. [$] *Rooms from: B4,300* ✉ *88 Moo 5 Tambol, Bophut* ☎ *077/601190* 🌐 *www.absolutesanctuary.com* 🛏 *38 rooms* 🍴 *Breakfast.*

$$$$ RESORT **Anantara Bophut Resort and Spa.** Anantara captures the essence of Samui: coconut trees dot the grounds, monkey statues and sculptures decorate the interior, and, of course, there's a beautiful beach. **Pros:** decent dining; pretty place. **Cons:** feels quite big; not for young party crowd. [$] *Rooms*

from: B10,000 ✉ *101/3 Samui Ring Rd., Bophut Beach* ☎ *077/428300* 🌐 *www.anantara.com* 🛏 *82 room, 24 suites* 🍴 *Breakfast.*

$$ RESORT 🏨 **Bandara Resort and Spa.** Bandara gets high marks for its location on the nicest stretch of Bophut Beach. **Pros:** ideal location; attentive staff. **Cons:** pool not inviting; unexciting room decor. [$] *Rooms from: B3,200* ✉ *178/2 Moo 1 Tambol, Bophut* ☎ *077/245795* 🌐 *www.bandarasamui.com* 🛏 *151 rooms* 🍴 *No meals.*

$$$$ RESORT 🏨 **Bo Phut Resort and Spa.** Not every beach hotel that claims to be a "resort and spa" measures up, which is why the massages, scrubs, and herbal steam therapies here are such a pleasant surprise. **Pros:** spectacular spa; nice restaurant. **Cons:** a bit overpriced; not the most happening location. [$] *Rooms from: B8,100* ✉ *12/12 Moo 1, Bophut* ☎ *077/245777* 🌐 *www.bophutresort.com* 🛏 *61 rooms* 🍴 *Breakfast.*

$$$ RESORT 🏨 **Punnpreeda.** Although it doesn't quite achieve the effortless cool it's striving for, Punnpreeda is still a fine place to stay. **Pros:** fun atmosphere; convenient shuttle. **Cons:** not ideal for families; not on Koh Samui's hip strip. [$] *Rooms from: B3,800* ✉ *199 Moo 1, Bang Rak Beach, Bophut* ☎ *077/246333* 🌐 *www.punnpreedapoolvilla.com* 🛏 *25 rooms* 🍴 *Breakfast.*

$$$$ RESORT 🏨 **Zazen.** A minimalist Japanese style makes this hotel a refreshing change of pace, especially if you've been in Thailand for a while. **Pros:** on a nice stretch of beach; great atmosphere. **Cons:** expensive; not a party destination. [$] *Rooms from: B7,000* ✉ *177 Moo 1, Bophut* ☎ *077/425085* 🌐 *www.samuizazen.com* 🛏 *35 rooms* 🍴 *No meals.*

CHOENGMON

$$$ RESORT 🏨 **Imperial Boathouse.** A fleet of 34 converted rice barges provides the most fanciful accommodations at this extraordinary resort. **Pros:** extraordinary setting, fanciful accommodations. **Cons:** some standard rooms lack sea views. [$] *Rooms from: B4,100* ✉ *83 Choeng Mon Beach, Choengmon* ☎ *077/425460, 02/2540023 in Bangkok* 🌐 *www.imperialhotels.com/boathouse* 🛏 *168 rooms, 8 suites, 34 boat suites* 🍴 *Some meals.*

$$ RESORT 🏨 **Kandaburi Resort and Spa.** Vaguely Balinese in design, this classy boutique hotel makes use of dark woods—often as a stunning contrast against stark white or shimmering gold. **Pros:** aesthetically pleasing; pretty beach. **Cons:** most rooms lack beach views; service is indifferent. [$] *Rooms from: B3,800* ✉ *20 Moo 2, Choengmon* ☎ *077/428888, 077/414424* 🌐 *www.kandaburi.com* 🛏 *175 rooms, 8 suites* 🍴 *Breakfast.*

$$$$ RESORT 🏨 **Q Signature Samui.** Formerly known as the Samudra Retreat, this hotel has an all-inclusive feel, and some rooms are part of a timeshare program. **Pros:** private beach; nearly incomparable views. **Cons:** iffy service; dated room decor; isolated. [$] *Rooms from: B6,500* ✉ *24/73 Moo 5, Choengmon Beach* ☎ *077/428100* 🌐 *www.qsignaturekohsamui.com* 🛏 *123 rooms* 🍴 *Some meals.*

$$$$ RESORT 🏨 **Sala Samui.** Bright, nearly all-white rooms open onto private courtyards on one side and curtain-enclosed bathrooms on the other. **Pros:** lots of privacy; good dining options. **Cons:** costly; beach views could be better. [$] *Rooms from: B11,000* ✉ *10/9 Moo 5 Baan Plai Laem, Bophut* ☎ *077/245888* 🌐 *www.salasamui.com* 🛏 *69 rooms* 🍴 *Breakfast.*

$$ **Samui Honey Cottages.** The cottages at this small resort on one of the
RESORT island's quieter beaches have glass sliding doors and peaked roofs, and
bathrooms have showers with glass ceilings. **Pros:** well located; welcoming staff. **Cons:** not that special; no real nightlife. $ *Rooms from:
B3,000* ⊠ *24/34 Moo 5, Choengmon Beach* ☎ *077/245032, 077/279093*
⊕ *www.samuihoney.com* ⌘ *19 bungalows, 1 suite* ⦿ *Breakfast.*

$$$$ **Six Senses Samui.** From the moment that you're introduced to your pri-
RESORT vate butler, you'll realize that this is not just another high-end resort—
Fodor's Choice you're about to embark on an amazing experience. **Pros:** butler service;
★ excellent restaurant; every whim catered to. **Cons:** expensive; sprawling
property difficult to navigate. $ *Rooms from: B13,200* ⊠ *9/10 Moo 5,
Baan Plai Laem, Bophut* ☎ *077/245678* ⊕ *www.sixsenses.com/resorts/
samui/destination* ⌘ *66 villas* ⦿ *Breakfast.*

$$$$ **Tongsai Bay.** The owners of this splendid all-suites resort managed to
RESORT build it without sacrificing even one of the tropical trees that give the
place a refreshing and natural sense of utter seclusion. **Pros:** beautiful
exterior and interior; luxurious bungalows; romantic setting. **Cons:**
beach so-so for lounging; staff could be more attentive. $ *Rooms from:
B10,750* ⊠ *84 Tongsai Bay, Choengmon* ☎ *077/245480, 077/245544*
⊕ *www.tongsaibay.co.th* ⌘ *83 suites* ⦿ *Breakfast.*

$$ **White House Beach Resort and Spa.** Step back in time as you pass under
RESORT the Khmer-style stone facade and enter the classic lobby, which is filled
with giant Chinese vases, Persian carpets, and classic Lanna art. **Pros:**
quiet location on beach. **Cons:** some rooms need updating. $ *Rooms
from: B3,000* ⊠ *59/3 Moo 5, Choengmon Beach* ☎ *077/247921 up to
23* ⊕ *www.samuithewhitehouse.com* ⌘ *32 rooms, 8 junior suites, 3
Thai suites* ⦿ *Breakfast.*

NIGHTLIFE

You'll find the most nighttime action in central Lamai and on Chawaeng's Soi Green Mango—a looping street chockablock with beer bars and nightclubs of all sizes.

Ark Bar. One of Samui's original nightlife venues on the beach, the Ark throws a free barbecue every Wednesday around sunset. ⊠ *159/75 Moo 2, Chawaeng Beach* ☎ *077/422047, 077/413798* ⊕ *www.ark-bar.com.*

Islander Pub & Restaurant. The many large-screen TVs at this popular place broadcast Thai, Australian, and Malaysian programs—lots of sports—and there are pool competitions and quiz nights. ⊠ *166/79 Chawaeng Beach Rd., Central Chawaeng* ☎ *077/230836.*

POD. The most popular and stylish of several nightclubs clustered together on Soi Green Mango, the huge POD bar and disco gets pumping after midnight. The staff is friendly and the drinks are relatively cheap. ⊠ *Soi Green Mango, Chawaeng* ☎ *083/692-7911.*

Q Bar Samui. Sexy bartenders pour premium spirits and international DJs spin music at this upscale nightclub with same-named siblings in Bangkok and Singapore. Q Bar sits high on a hillside north of Chawaeng Lake—take a taxi to get here and back. ⊠ *47/57 Moo 2, Bophut* ☎ *081/956-2742* ⊕ *www.qbarsamui.com.*

Reggae Pub. A must if you're a reggae fan, this longtime favorite with several bars and dance floors has a nonstop party atmosphere. ⊠ *Chawaeng Lakeside Rd., Chawaeng* ☎ *077/422331.*

Swing Bar. In the center of Lamai, the Swing Bar offers . . . swings. The concept is simple: you sit on swings while sipping very reasonably priced drinks and eating good Thai food. The experience is not as precarious as it sounds. ⊠ *109/12 Moo 3 Maret, Lamai Beach* ☎ *077/424208* ⊕ *www. richresortsamui.com.*

SPORTS AND THE OUTDOORS

Canopy Adventures. For a bird's-eye view of the jungle, zip-line through the air on 330 yards of wire strung between six tree houses. This outfit also arranges fun expeditions to waterfalls. ⊠ *Koh Samui* ☎ *077/414150* ⊕ *www.canopyadventuresthailand.com* ⊠ *B2,200.*

Namuang Travel and Tour. This company conducts elephant treks around a delightful safari park. You'll pass a couple of waterfalls and see other animals, but the elephants are the stars of the show. The photo ops are limitless. ⊠ *Koh Samui* ☎ *077/418680* ⊕ *www.namuangsafarisamui. com* ⊠ *From B700.*

Santiburi Samui Country Club. The Santiburi Resort has a driving range and a beautiful 18-hole course that incorporates the natural terrain of the Samui mountains to create a challenging multilevel golfing experience. You can play 9 holes for half the full-course greens fee. ⊠ *Koh Samui* ☎ *077/421700, 02/664–4270* ⊕ *www.santiburi-hotel.com* ⊠ *Greens fee B3,000 for resort guests, B4,000 for nonguests, plus B750 for mandatory cart and B300 for caddy (exclusive of tip)* ⚑ *18 holes, 6930 yards, par 72.*

SPAS

Tamarind Springs Forest Spa. Koh Samui has a few top-end spas, as well as several in the luxury hotels, but the island's ultimate spa experience is at Tamarind Springs. Many different treatments are available, from hot-oil massages to herbal rubs to the Over the Top massage package, which lasts 2½ hours. The spa employs the latest treatment methods, including the use of Tibetan singing bowls. The plunge pools, hot tubs, and tearoom are built harmoniously into Tamarind's boulder-strewn hillside. ⊠ *205/7 Thong Takian, Lamai Beach* ☎ *077/424221* ⊕ *www. tamarindsprings.com.*

SIDE TRIPS FROM KOH SAMUI

KOH PHANGAN

12 km (7 miles) by boat north of Koh Samui.

As Koh Samui developed into an international hot spot, travelers looking for a more laid-back scene headed for Koh Phangan. Decades ago, the few wanderers who arrived here stayed in fishermen's houses or slung hammocks on the beach. Investors bought up beach property with plans for sprawling resorts, but before commercial development marred too much of the island, the allure of Koh Tao's crystalline waters starting drawing away a lot of the attention.

Haad Rin Town has many good restaurants, shops, and bars. It's densely built up, and not very quiet, but full of fun. The town is sandwiched between the beaches of Haad Rin West and Haad Rin East.

While Haad Rin boomed as a result of its world-famous Full Moon Party, most of Koh Phangan's smaller beaches continued to develop, but at a much slower pace. For now, most of Koh Phangan remains a destination for backpackers looking for beautiful beaches with budget accommodations, and hippies (old-school and nouveau) searching for chilled-out beaches and alternative retreats.

Boats from the mainland drop passengers off at the main pier in Thong Sala. It's an uninteresting town, but there are taxis that can shuttle you around the island.

If you want to find the beach that most appeals to you, take a long-tail boat (a simple motorized vessel named for its shape) around the island—the trip takes a full day and stops in many places along the way, including Haad Rin. Close to Haad Rin are Haad Sarikantang, Haad Yuan, and Haad Thien: good choices for those interested in going to the Full Moon Party, but who want to stay on a nicer, more relaxing beach.

If you aren't here for the Full Moon Party, head up the east coast to quieter Haad Thong Nai Pan, or even farther afield. One of the island's most remote beaches—and the most beautiful—is Haad Kuat, which has gorgeous white sand and simple accommodations. Haad Salad and Haad Yao, on the northwest coast, are similarly remote beaches for those looking for relaxation.

GETTING HERE AND AROUND
The best way to get here is by ferry from Koh Samui, or from Surat Thani via Koh Samui. Boats depart hourly from Surat Thani's Donsak Pier for Na Thon Pier on Koh Samui; the price includes the hour-long bus ride from Surat Thani's airport to the pier. After the 2½-hour voyage to Samui, passengers must disembark and catch a second boat to Koh Phangan's Thong Sala Pier, a 30-minute journey. Seatran boats depart from Koh Samui for Koh Phangan daily at 8 am and 1:30 pm. Return travel from Koh Phangan to Koh Samui is at 10:30 am and 4:30 pm.

If you take a Songserm ferry instead, you won't have to switch boats on Samui; however, Songserm makes the Surat Thani–Koh Samui–Koh Phangan run only once a day, leaving Surat Thani at 8 am and returning from Koh Phangan at 12:30 pm.

There are a number of ways to travel between Koh Phangan and either Koh Samui or Koh Tao—Lomphrayah and Seatran boats are the best options. Boats to and from Koh Tao take from 2 to 2½ hours.

Even though most beaches are accessible via songthaew pickup trucks, the island's twisting roads make it easier and safer to beach-hop via boat. It is unwise to travel around Koh Phangan on a motorcycle: the roads are not safe, and accidents involving motorcycles are a far too regular occurrence.

SAFETY AND PRECAUTIONS

Koh Phangan has become famous for its full-moon parties and for numerous other parties associated with the moon's waxing and waning. These events attract as many as 10,000 revelers, and the criminal element knows this. Break-ins are a problem. Thieves assume you're out partying, so don't leave valuables in your room.

The biggest problem is drugs, which are treated very seriously by Thai authorities. There are all-too-frequent stories of travelers who have been arrested, either for purchasing or consuming, so expect harsh treatment if you're caught.

TIMING

The Full Moon Party, probably the biggest draw to the island, happens 13 times a year on Haad Rin East. If you want some peace and quiet, consult your lunar calendar. At other times the island is a tranquil place.

BEACHES

Haad Kuat (*Bottle Beach*). With a quarter mile of fine white sand, this isolated beach on the island's north coast is a sunbather's paradise. The vibe is decidedly young and funky, and there are several places to grab a decent meal. Get here by songthaew from Thong Sala Pier, or by longtail boat from nearby Thong Nai Pan. Haad Kuat might be more difficult to reach than other beaches, but it's one of Koh Phangan's best and definitely worth the effort. **Amenities:** food and drink; water sports. **Best for:** partiers. ⊠ *Haad Kuat.*

Haad Rin. If you are looking for the party, then head to Haad Rin. The beach is divided into two parts, Haad Rin West and Haad Rin East, each with its own personality. Haad Rin West has swimmable water, but you needn't settle for this beach when Haad Rin East is only a short walk away. Beautiful Haad Rin East is lined with bungalows and bars, although the water isn't nearly as pristine as at the more remote beaches. Every four weeks, Haad Rin East gets seriously crowded when throngs of young people gather on the beach for an all-night Full Moon Party. **Amenities:** food and drink. **Best for:** partiers; swimming. ⊠ *Haad Rin.*

Haad Sarikantang. Just south of Haad Rin, this smaller strand is close to the party yet relatively peaceful. Also known as Leela Beach, Haad Sarikantang has picturesque palms, fine white sand, and clear blue water. Resorts and restaurants surround the beach. **Amenities:** food and drink. **Best for:** swimming. ⊠ *Haad Sarikantang.*

Haad Thien. A small strip north of the party beaches at Haad Rin, this is an ideal choice for those seeking relaxation and smaller crowds. The sand is a fine yellow and the waters are shallow and clear. A few resort hotels and several good restaurants do business on the waterfront or near the beach. **Amenities:** food and drink; water sports. **Best for:** swimming. ⊠ *Haad Thien.*

Haad Thong Nai Pan. On a horseshoe bay at the island's northern end, Haad Thong Nai Pan is split into two. The northern part is the most beautiful, with stunning golden sands set around crystal-blue waters.

Koh Phangan's beaches are popular with travelers looking for a tranquil getaway.

The seas are usually calm, but swimming can be rough when the monsoon rains sweep in. Guesthouses and midrange resorts surround the beach. Food and drink are available from the nearby restaurants. **Amenities:** food and drink; water sports. **Best for:** swimming. ✉ *Haad Thong Nai Pan.*

Haad Yuan. A 10-minute boat ride from Haad Rin, small beautiful Haad Yuan is worlds away. Extremely quiet most of the time, the beach is wide and clean, with fine sand and crystal-blue waters. The rocky outcrop at one end makes a fine photo backdrop. The swimming is good here, but the water occasionally gets rough. **Amenities:** food and drink. **Best for:** swimming. ✉ *Haad Yuan.*

WHERE TO EAT

Haad Rin has the most restaurants, but you'll find plenty of simple seafood restaurants on other beaches as well.

$ SEAFOOD 🍴 **Lucky Crab Restaurant.** As if striving to please every last one of the island's international visitors, this fun restaurant serves entrées from around the world. The specialty, though, is grilled seafood, prepared with one of 12 sauces. Select your fish, select your sauce, and then enjoy the breeze from the ceiling fans while you await your food. The sizzling seafood in a hot pan is also worth trying. [$] *Average main: B150* ✉ *94/18 Haad Rin W, Haad Rin* ☎ *077/375125, 077/375498* 💳 *No credit cards.*

$ CAFÉ 🍴 **Nira's Home Bakery.** The alluring scent of fresh baked goods immediately delights all who enter this funky place. The owner, who picked up his baking skills while living and working in Germany, opened Nira's in the mid-1980s, before the island even had electricity. Traditional homemade lasagna, fresh fruit juices, and gourmet sandwiches are a few of the specialties here. [$] *Average main: B80* ✉ *74/10 Moo 1 Thong Sala, Haad Rin* 💳 *No credit cards.*

WHERE TO STAY

HAAD RIN

$ RESORT 🏨 **Buri Beach Resort.** What you get at this Haad Rin West property is an international-standard hotel room, complete with modern amenities, but pretty much lacking the Thai island vibe. **Pros:** feels new; nice views. **Cons:** a bit generic; room decor could be nicer. [$] *Rooms from: B1,400* ✉ *120/1 Moo 6 Haad Rin, Haad Rin Nai Beach* ☎ *077/375481* 🌐 *buribeach.com* 🛏 *106 rooms* 🍴 *Breakfast.*

$$ RESORT 🏨 **Cocohut Resort.** This resort is on mellow Haad Sarikantang, a five-minute walk from Haad Rin West. **Pros:** good deal; cute quarters. **Cons:** not so scenic; not the best swimming beach; staff can seem brusque. [$] *Rooms from: B3,000* ✉ *130/20 Leela Beach, Haad Sarikantang* ☎ *077/375368* 🌐 *www.cocohut.com* 🛏 *76 bungalows, 24 rooms* 🍴 *Breakfast.*

$$ RESORT 🏨 **Phangan Bayshore Resort.** On Haad Rin East near the action but away from the crowds, this was one of the island's original resorts. **Pros:** close to the party; good value; spacious layout. **Cons:** some rooms need renovation. [$] *Rooms from: B2,300* ✉ *141 Moo 6 Haad Rin, Haad Rin* ☎ *077/375227* 🌐 *www.phanganbayshore.com* 🛏 *71 rooms* 🍴 *No meals.*

$$ RESORT 🏨 **Sarikantang.** On Haad Sarikantang, this small resort is a short walk from the festive atmosphere at Haad Rin. The nicer accommodations have outdoor showers and baths, hot water, air-conditioning, and hammocks, while some of the wooden bungalows have only the most basic amenities. **Pros:** lots of ocean views; friendly staff. **Cons:** could be more central; least expensive rooms not comfortable. [$] *Rooms from: B2,100* ✉ *129/3 Leela Beach, Haad Sarikantang* ☎ *077/375055, 077/375056* 🌐 *www.sarikantang.com* 🛏 *47 rooms* 🍴 *Breakfast.*

$ RESORT 🏨 **Sea View Haad Rin Resort.** These simple wooden huts directly on the beach at the "quieter" northern end of Haad Rin East are the best deal in the area—for the best location. **Pros:** good deal; extremely low-key vibe. **Cons:** not near the action; some rooms lack air-conditioning. [$] *Rooms from: B700* ✉ *134 Moo 6 Haad Rin East, Haad Rin* ☎ *077/375160* 🌐 *www.seaviewsunrise.com* 💳 *No credit cards* 🛏 *40 rooms* 🍴 *No meals.*

HAAD YUAN

$ RESORT 🏨 **Barcelona Resort.** For very few baht you get a private cottage on Haad Yuan with doors on two walls that unfold to reveal a wraparound deck. **Pros:** low price; fun experience. **Cons:** no air-conditioning; few amenities. [$] *Rooms from: B400* ✉ *Haad Yuan* ☎ *077/375113* 🌐 *www.imagealchemy.org/sites/barcelona* 💳 *No credit cards* 🛏 *35 rooms* 🍴 *No meals.*

HAAD THONG NAI PAN

$ RESORT 🏨 **Dolphin Bungalows.** These are the perfect beach bungalows, built entirely of wood with shuttered windows and hammocks slung on the decks. **Pros:** lush grounds; cool crowd. **Cons:** not beachfront; few creature comforts. [$] *Rooms from: B600* ✉ *61 Moo 5, Haad Tong Nai Pan* ☎ *077/445135* 💳 *No credit cards* 🛏 *20 rooms* 🍴 *No meals.*

$ RESORT 🏨 **Longtail Beach Resort.** The bungalows and restaurant at this well-landscaped resort in northern Koh Phangan are built of wood, thatch, and bamboo in traditional southern Thai style. **Pros:** close to the beach; inexpensive; local touches to the rooms and resort. **Cons:** no pool. [$] *Rooms from: B1,250* ✉ *2/5 Moo 5 Thong Nai Pan Yai Beach, Haad Thong Nai Pan* ☎ *77/445018* 🌐 *www.longtailbeachresort.com* 🛏 *22 bungalows* 🍴 *No meals.*

$$$ RESORT 🏨 **Panviman Resort.** The big attractions at this cheerful resort on Koh Phangan's northern coast are its two restaurants: one is a circular dining area that's open to the ocean breezes; the other is a seaside terrace. **Pros:** good for families; shuttle service. **Cons:** high rates; not near interesting nightlife. [$] *Rooms from: B5,200* ✉ *22/1 Moo 5 Thong Nai Pan Noi Bay, Haad Thong Nai Pan* ☎ *077/445101, 077/445220* 🌐 *www.panviman.com/kohphangan* 🛏 *72 rooms, 32 cottages* 🍴 *Breakfast.*

HAAD KUAT

$ RESORT 🏨 **Smile Bungalows.** Of the guesthouses on northern Koh Phangan's Haad Kuat, this one on the beach's western end is the best. **Pros:** cool views; fun staff. **Cons:** no air-conditioning; lacks amenities. [$] *Rooms from: B550* ✉ *74/9 Moo 7 Haad Kuat, Haad Kuat* ☎ *085/429–4995* 🌐 *www.smilebungalows.com* 💳 *No credit cards* 🛏 *25 rooms* 🍴 *No meals.*

NIGHTLIFE

Haad Rin East is lined with bars and clubs—music pumps and drinks pour from dusk until dawn, seven days a week, 365 days a year. All this culminates in a huge beach party with tens of thousands of revelers every full moon (or the night after, if the full moon lands on a major Buddhist holiday). Check out 🌐 *www.fullmoonparty-thailand.com* for details.

KOH TAO

47 km (29 miles) by boat north of Koh Phangan.

In just a few decades, the tiny island of Koh Tao has evolved from a sleepy backwater to a sought-after diving getaway, with lodgings that range from basic bungalows to luxurious resorts. The peace and quiet may have disappeared from the main beaches, with a strong, backpacker-oriented, party scene in the island's two main areas. Along with cheap drinks, the bars, pubs, and clubs in each offer all manner of pub crawls and late-night shenanigans. This said, the primary reason to come here remains the underwater world. Koh Tao is an excellent place to get your scuba certification. Many operators don't have pools, so the initial dives must be done in the shallow, crystal clear ocean water. Advanced divers will appreciate the great visibility, decent amount of coral, and exotic and plentiful marine life.

GETTING HERE AND AROUND

Getting to Koh Tao is easy—it's on the scheduled ferry routes out of Koh Phangan and Koh Samui, and several boats a day make the trip from Chumphon on the mainland. Catamarans take 1½ hours, high-speed Seatran vessels take two hours, and regular ferry service takes six.

Lomprayah Catamaran has 1¾-hour trips between Koh Samui and Koh Tao for B500 twice daily, at 7 am and 5 pm. In addition, speedboats leave at 8:30 am from Bophut Pier on the north side of Koh Samui, taking snorkelers on day trips to the island and its neighbor, Koh Nang Yuan.

Contacts Lomprayah High Speed Catamaran. ⊠ *Koh Phangan* ⊕ *www. lomprayah.com.*

SAFETY AND PRECAUTIONS

Koh Tao is generally safe, but the 2014 murders of two backpackers and reports of suspicious deaths have heightened concerns about safety. The vibe on Koh Tao is relaxed, but you still need to take the same general precautions you would for any tourist destination.

EXPLORING

4

Koh Nang Yuan. The three small islands of Koh Nang Yuan lie close to Koh Tao. At high tide the islands, separated by shallow, translucent water, look like the endpoints of an obtuse triangle. At low tide the receding water exposes two narrow sandbars that connect the outer islands, which contain bungalows for overnight stays, to the central island, which has a lodge, a restaurant and beach bar, and a coffee shop. The islands are privately owned by the Nangyuan Island Dive Resort, and all visitors who wish to set foot on Koh Nang Yuan must shell out a B100 fee. Although many visitors opt to pay, others simply dock off-shore to snorkel and dive the gorgeous waters surrounding the islands. To get here from Koh Tao, you can kayak from Sairee Beach or hire a longtail boat (B200 round-trip from Sairee) to ferry you here. The trip takes about 15 minutes—it works best to arrange your return with the same operator. While you are visiting, be sure to slip up to the viewpoint on the southern island to snap photos guaranteed to make your friends back home jealous. ■ TIP→ The islands are busy throughout the day; it's best to visit early in the morning or late in the afternoon. ⊠ *Koh Tao* ✚ *15-min longtail ride from Koh Tao* ⊕ *www.nangyuan.com* 💰 *B100.*

BEACHES

Chalok Baan Kao Beach. A peaceful strand on Koh Tao's southern shore, Chalok Baan Kao has a relaxed, friendly vibe. The beach itself lacks the crystal-blue water and golden sands of other beaches in the region, but it's reasonably good for swimming. Budget accommodations surround the beach. **Amenities:** food and drink. **Best for:** solitude; swimming. ⊠ *Koh Tao.*

Sairee Beach. Palm trees at crescent-shape Sairee, Koh Tao's most popular beach, arch over the aquamarine water as if yearning to sip from the sea. Along the thin sliver of golden sand sit rustic, traditional wooden beach huts with bohemian youths lounging in hammocks; novice divers practicing in seaside pools; and European students sampling cocktails at basic beach bars. On the far northern end of the beach, a few resorts nestle amid manicured landscapes. Sairee faces west, making it great for watching the sunset and for kayaking to Koh Nang Yuan. **Amenities:** food and drink; water sports. **Best for:** partiers. ⊠ *Koh Tao.*

Divers travel between Koh Tao's islands by longtail boats.

WHERE TO EAT

$$
THAI

✕ **The Gallery.** Combining fine dining and photography, this restaurant-gallery serves delicate interpretations of southern Thai classics—fish dishes, curries, grilled seafood, and the like. The service is first-rate, the ambience relaxed and romantic. $ *Average main: B300* ✉ *10/29 Moo 1 Sairee Village* ☎ *77/456547* ⊕ *www.thegallerykohtao.com* ▭ *No credit cards.*

$$
INTERNATIONAL

✕ **Taste of Home.** At first glance, this simple open-air eatery seems nothing special, but pleasant surprises await those who sample its eclectic international fare. The portions are generous—order the Wiener schnitzel, and you'll be amazed it even fits on the plate—and the welcome even more so. The prices here are quite reasonable, too. $ *Average main: B200* ✉ *Sairee Beach* ⊹ *East Sairee, opposite the Yellow Hotel* ☎ *086/0120727* ▭ *No credit cards.*

WHERE TO STAY

$
RESORT

⊡ **Black Tip Dive Resort and Watersport Center.** On Tanote Bay, on Koh Tao's eastern shore, this resort makes a perfect base for snorkeling because of the colorful coral, the interesting fish, and even the small black-tip reef sharks that cruise around at sunset. **Pros:** great for divers; transportation around island easily arranged. **Cons:** far from action; some rooms lack hot water or private bathrooms. $ *Rooms from: B800* ✉ *40/6 Tanote Bay* ☎ *077/456867* ⊕ *www.blacktipdiving.com* ⇆ *25 bungalows* ❍ *No meals.*

Diving and Snorkeling Responsibly

Decades of visitors scuba diving on Thailand's islands and reefs have had far greater negative effects on marine life than any tsunami. All divers needs to be aware of, and consequently minimize, their impact on the environment.

Touch nothing, stand only on sand: As fascinating as something you see may be, resist the urge to handle it, and never stand on anything that isn't sand. Coral is extremely fragile, urchins are as painful as they look, and although sharks may be no threat to divers, you can appreciate the foolishness of grabbing one's tail. Other dangers to both you and the environment are less obvious: eels live within holes in rocks and reef; turtles are reptiles that require air to breathe, and even some dive instructors are guilty of "hitching a ride" on them, causing the turtles to expend precious air. Furthermore, don't feed fish human food—feeding them bread, peas, or even M&Ms may be entertaining, but it rewards aggressive fish to the detriment of species diversity.

Secure diving equipment, maintain level buoyancy: Divers should make sure equipment is securely fastened or stored, so that no items are lost or scrape against coral. Divers should also maintain level buoyancy to prevent inadvertent brushes with coral,

as well as to save air. Snorkelers who need to remove their masks should pull them down around their necks rather than up on their foreheads. Masks can fall off and quickly sink, and a mask on the forehead is considered a symbol of distress.

Check your pockets, no butts: Minimize underwater pollution when snorkeling by checking your pockets before jumping into the water. Conscientious divers can clip a stuff sack to their BCDs to pocket random trash they encounter. Lastly, if you smoke, don't flick cigarette butts into the water.

Protect yourself and nature: Sunscreen is a must anytime you are exposed to Thailand's tropical sun. Snorkeling unprotected is a guaranteed skin disaster (and painful obstacle to the rest of your holiday); however, sunblock, when dissolving into the water from hundreds of visitors each day, is bound to take its toll on the marine environment. You can limit the amount of sunscreen you must slather on by covering your back with a lycra rash guard or a short- or long-sleeve shirt while snorkeling.

Follow the credo, "Leave only footprints, take only memories." Try to minimize your impact on this ecosystem in which you are only a visitor.

4

$ **⛱ Charmchuree Villa.** Whether you opt to stay in one of the uniquely
RESORT designed tropical villas, a deluxe room, or a (very) basic bungalow,
Fodor's Choice you'll enjoy a tiny corner of heaven on the private beach at Jansom
★ Bay. Rooms and thatch-roof villas are built into the landscape, constructed on or around massive boulders and trees, and situated to maximize exposure to the magnificent views of Sairee Beach. **Pros:** private beach; sweeping views. **Cons:** isolated; feels spread out; staff is very lax.

$ Rooms from: B1,200 ⊠ 30/1 Moo 2, Jansom Bay ☎ 077/456393, 077/456394 ⊕ www.charmchureevilla.com ⇨ 40 rooms ⧌ Breakfast.

$$
RESORT
⌨ **Chintakiri Resort.** Set against a mountain backdrop and surrounded by a lush garden, this resort close to Sairee Beach has 19 wooden bungalows with spectacular views of the turquoise ocean. **Pros:** spectacular views; eco-friendly. **Cons:** long uphill access to the resort; breakfast is processed food. $ Rooms from: B2,900 ⊠ 19/59–77 Moo 3, Chalok Baan Kao ☎ 77/456391 ⊕ www.chintakiriresort.com ⇨ 19 bungalows ⧌ Breakfast ⊟ No credit cards.

$$$
RESORT
⌨ **Koh Tao Cabana.** On the far northern end of Sairee Beach, this is one of Koh Tao's few boutique resorts. **Pros:** attractive decor; stylish resort. **Cons:** so-so food; some rooms lack easy beach access. $ Rooms from: B4,500 ⊠ 16 Moo 1 Baan Haad Sai Ree, Sairee Beach ☎ 077/456504 ⊕ www.kohtaocabana.com ⇨ 33 villas and cottages ⧌ Breakfast.

$$$
RESORT
⌨ **Koh Tao Coral Grand Resort.** On the quieter northern end of Sairee Beach, this resort is a good place to get your scuba certification. **Pros:** feels peaceful; lots of amenities. **Cons:** can be noisy; some foot traffic. $ Rooms from: B3,300 ⊠ 15/4 Moo 1, Sairee Beach ☎ 077/456431 ⊕ www.kohtaocoral.com ⇨ 42 rooms ⧌ Breakfast.

$$$$
RESORT
Fodor's Choice
★
⌨ **The Place Luxury Boutique Villas.** A place of total escape that provides serious pampering, this resort nestles on the hillside above Sairee Beach. **Pros:** private infinity pools with each villa; isolation; stunning views out to sea. **Cons:** a bit of a hike up to the highest villas. $ Rooms from: B9,000 ⊠ 15/4 Moo 2 Sairee Beach, Kah Tao ☎ 87/887–5066 ⊕ www.theplacekohtao.com ⇨ 9 villas ⧌ No meals ⊟ No credit cards.

PHUKET AND THE ANDAMAN COAST

WELCOME TO PHUKET AND THE ANDAMAN COAST

TOP REASONS TO GO

★ **Sunsets at Railay Beach:** The sunsets here are unbeatable, however you choose to view them—floating in a kayak, strolling along the sand, or lounging in a beachfront bungalow.

★ **Kayaking Phang Nga Bay:** Phang Nga Bay's maze of islands is ideal for gliding alongside towering cliffs.

★ **Discovering Koh Lanta:** Second in size after Phuket, but far less chaotic, this has become an artsy, laid-back destination for travelers in the know, with long sandy beaches studded with tiny bars, and glorious sunsets.

★ **Camping at Koh Similan:** This gorgeous national park has a handful of tents for rent. Hire a longtail boat to do some snorkeling while you're here.

★ **Exploring Koh Phi Phi:** The jewel of Phang Nga Bay cannot be truly appreciated from one beach. Make day trips aboard a longtail boat: Maya Bay is a must-see and quieter Loh Samah Bay is magical.

MYANMAR

Ranong

SURIN ISLANDS

ISTHMUS OF KRA

Surat Thani

SIMILAN ISLANDS

Phang Nga

Khao Lak

Thung Song

KOH YAO YAI

Krabi

KOH PHUKET

1 Phuket

KOH PHI PHI

3

2

ANDAMAN COAST

Andaman Sea

KOH LANTA

Trang

KOH TA LIBONG

0   50 mi

0   50 km

1 **Phuket.** Phuket is the hub of the western coast, with daily flights from Bangkok landing in its airport and ferries to Koh Phi Phi, Krabi, and the Similan and Surin islands departing from its docks. Though it's got its share of overdevelopment issues, Phuket has many beautiful beaches.

2 **The Andaman Coast.** Krabi has beautiful limestone cliffs shooting straight up out of the water that have become popular with rock climbers.

3 **Koh Phi Phi.** This area suffered severe damage from the 2004 tsunami, but it has by now resumed its status as a prime destination for snorkeling and diving.

GETTING ORIENTED

Thailand's western shore fronts the Andaman Sea, home to the islands of Phuket, Koh Phi Phi, Koh Lanta, and various marine parks. The Andaman Coast thrives during dry season, when tourists are drawn here from around the globe to enjoy stunning beaches, dramatic limestone cliffs that rise from the sea, and lush tropical landscapes. The area is also celebrated for restaurants that increasingly push the boundaries of Thai cuisine, multifaceted nightlife and shopping, and a huge range of trendy boutique resorts with high end spa facilities.

5

EATING AND DRINKING WELL IN SOUTHERN THAILAND

Get ready for the south's distinctive flavors. Turmeric, peanuts, and coconut milk are a few ingredients that play larger roles here than they do in the north. And, of course, there's no shortage of delectable fresh seafood.

The freshness of the seafood here cannot be overstated. Spicy seafood salad (pictured above).

Southern Thailand has a larger Muslim population than the rest of the country, and you'll find this halal diversity in southern cuisine, along with Malaysian, Lao, and even Indian influences along the coast. Spiciness is a defining characteristic of southern food, though as in other regions, restaurants that cater to tourists sometimes tone down the chilies (beware: if you ask for something to be very spicy, locals will be glad to challenge you). A meal in the south is all about the experience. Though you'll run into some tourist traps in areas like Phuket, in general you're likely to find the real deal—authentic cuisine at decent prices. It's hard to beat a frosty Chang beer and fresh crab married with a complex curry paste and coconut cream, just steps from the edge of the turquoise Andaman Sea.

SEAFOOD

In the Andaman Coast it's all about abundant seafood varieties. Beachside shacks serve all sorts of aquatic treats, from octopus to crab—and foodies will absolutely love the prices. Imagine a heaping plate of fresh, grilled sea bass for just a few dollars; that same dish stateside would have a couple more zeros attached to it.

GAENG MASSAMAN

A Muslim dish by origin (its name is derived from Musulman, an older version of the word "Muslim"), massaman curry has a distinct flavor that's somewhat reminiscent of Indian cuisine. It's not usually a spicy dish, but peanuts add a big burst of flavor and an even bigger crunch. Coconut milk softens everything, and the result is a soupy and comforting curry. It's made with a variety of meats but rarely fish.

GAENG SOM

Known as sour curry, this dish is usually spicy as well as tart. It's made with fish sauce instead of coconut milk, and the flavor can take some getting used to. It's typically made with fish (*gaeng som pla*) and green vegetables, such as cabbage and beans. Sour curry is runnier than coconut-milk curries—more like a sauce—and tends to acquire a greenish hue from all the vegetables it contains.

KHAO MOK KAI

This simple but delicious chicken-and-rice dish is a Thai version of Indian chicken *biryani*, which means "fried" or "roasted." Chicken—which is usually on the bone—lies under a fragrant mound of rice, which owes its bright yellow color to a liberal amount of turmeric. Though turmeric often shows up in Indian cuisine, this is one of its few cameos in southern Thailand food.

Deep-fried shallots add another element of textural complexity.

BOO PAHT PONG KAREE

Curry-powder crab is not a traditional, soupy curry: whole crab is fried in a mixture of curry powder and other spices. The piquant curry is a perfect counterpoint to the sweet crabmeat. Coconut milk is often used to moisten the mix and moderate the spiciness. You'll find other kinds of seafood prepared this way in the south, but crab is particularly tasty.

PLA

Whole fish such as *garoupa* (grouper) is often on the menu in the south, and is so much more flavorful than fillets. Garlic and chilies are common seasonings, and the skin is usually cooked until it's deliciously crispy. It may be spicy, but whole fish is definitely a treat you don't get too often stateside. You can also find steamed versions and less spicy seasonings like ginger.

Updated by
Simon Stewart
For its amazing setting, variety, and charm, Phuket has consistently been voted as one of the world's favorite tourist destinations, both for budget travelers and those seeking sumptuous luxury. Though it has its share of overdevelopment issues, the island has many beautiful beaches and a dazzling variety in restaurants, hotels, activities, and nightlife. Once you leave Phuket and head for the Andaman Coast, though, the attractions become even more spectacular. The coastline delivers spectacular limestones karsts, secluded islands with crystal waters, and miles of unspoiled beaches.

Phuket is the busy hub of the western coast, with daily flights from Bangkok landing in its airport and ferries to scenic but often packed Ko Phi Phi, Krabi, and the dreamy Similan and Surin islands departing daily from its docks. Beyond Phuket, the secrets of this magical coastline begin to reveal itself. Krabi has powdery white sand and magnificent limestone cliffs shooting straight up out of emerald waters that have become popular with all levels of rock-climbing enthusiasts. Railay Beach is especially popular among adventurers who enjoy acrobatics, climbing, and alternative ideologies. Nearby the Phang Nga National Marine Park attracts nature lovers because of its world-renowned post-card-perfect locations, such as Koh Phing Kan, known as James Bond Island. Post-tsunami Ko Phi Phi is a prime destination for snorkeling and diving (you may actually see more divers than fish in some waters as it gets incredibly busy in high season), along with being a mainstay of the easygoing backpacker tourist circuit. Koh Lanta has developed its own scene and attracts visitors who like fewer crowds and more offbeat individuality—as reflected in some of its quirky shops and restaurants; it combines lovely beaches with colorful villages where you will meet interesting locals and expats who differ from those in other parts of the Andaman coast. Ao Nang has become very popular over the years, and numerous resorts have sprung up near its popular beaches and shops to cater to all tastes and budgets.

A note of caution: don't take the chance of getting on rickety or overcrowded boats. Speedboats can often be hired to travel the ferry routes. Ensure that life jackets are available and that the crew takes safety seriously.

PHUKET AND THE ANDAMAN COAST PLANNER

WHEN TO GO
The peak season on the Andaman Coast is November through April. The monsoon season is May through October, during which high seas can make beaches unsafe for swimming (a number of tourist deaths are registered each year in the treacherous monsoon waters) though hotel prices are considerably lower.

PLANNING YOUR TIME
Visitors to Phuket and the Andaman Coast can find a new activity every day; you could spend weeks in this region and still not do the same thing twice. It has a great tourism infrastructure. Children and families will find plenty to do and see, as will singles and couples.

GETTING HERE AND AROUND
AIR TRAVEL
There are daily, relatively inexpensive flights from Bangkok to all of the major beach destinations: Surat Thani, Phuket, and Krabi. It is generally less expensive to fly to Phuket and Surat Thani than to other southern airports. There are also some flights from Chiang Mai to the beaches. Thai Airways, Bangkok Airways, and Phuket Air have regular flights, as do the budget carriers Air Asia and Nok Air. If you're flexible with your dates, you can find some ridiculously cheap fares. Keep in mind that planes fill up fast during the high season, and the lowest fares are mostly available if booked weeks or months in advance. *(See Air Travel in Travel Smart Thailand).* All the airports in this region are small and much easier to deal with than Bangkok's Suvarnabhumi.

BUS TRAVEL
Buses travel regularly between Bangkok and all major destinations in the Andaman coast. There's also good bus service within the south. Many Bangkok travel agents charge three times the price for bus tickets, and organize a long, exhausting, and convoluted trip with various stops to the main bus stations. It's best to visit a Tourism Authority of Thailand office to purchase your tickets, and then get to the bus station under your own steam; you will save both time and money. Buses leave from Bangkok's Southern Bus Terminal, generally in the late afternoon and evening. The trip to Phuket takes from 12 to 14 hours, depending on the bus and road conditions. You'll need to go to either a travel agent or to the bus station to check exact times and purchase tickets in advance, especially for VIP buses. Costs run from B550 for a large 32-seat air-conditioned bus to B1,300 for a 24-seat air-conditioned

VIP bus. Most long-haul VIP buses travel overnight, but day trips are recommended, as Thailand's highways grow even more dangerous at night. There are buses from Phuket to almost every major destination in southern Thailand. This includes, but is not limited to: Surat Thani, Krabi, Trang, Hat Yai, Satun, Phang Nga, and the ferry crossing to Koh Samui. You can check departure times at your hotel or the centrally located bus station just east of Montri Road, two blocks north of Phang Nga Road in Phuket Town. ■ TIP➔ Private buses are less reputable than public buses.

CAR TRAVEL

You can take Highway 4 from Thonburi in Bangkok all the way to the causeway at the north end of Phuket Island, where it turns into Highway 402. It's a long, exhausting, and not particularly recommended, drive, but once you're out of the capital all you have to do is follow the compass due south. Follow Highway 4 to Chumphon, where it jogs west and south and follows the Andaman Sea coast to Phuket Island. Phuket Town is 862 km (517 miles) from Bangkok; bus companies make the trip in 13 to 15 hours. *(See Car Travel in Travel Smart Thailand.)*

MOTORCYCLE TRAVEL

Cheap and readily available, scooters are probably the easiest hassle-free (park anywhere) way to get around and discover all sites and beaches, but think twice before renting one. Accidents are not uncommon on Phuket, Lanta, or Ao Nang, as the Thais tend to speed, some tourists drink and drive, and proper safety equipment is often shunned. If you've never driven a motorcycle before, this is not the time or place to learn. A somewhat safer option could be to hire a tuk-tuk.

SONGTHAEW, TAXI, AND TUK-TUK TRAVEL

Most areas of the south have a variety of motorized taxi services from samlors to tuk-tuks to songthaews. Some "metered" taxis can be found in most of the region now, but they usually don't run their meters, preferring to set a price at the start of the trip. So if you do take one of these make sure to ask for the meter to be on, as it will often be much cheaper.

TRAIN TRAVEL

Bangkok is connected to Sri Racha and Pattaya via one daily train; there are more frequent trains to Hua Hin, Chumphon, and Surat Thani. There are regular express trains to Surat Thani, the closest station to Phuket, which leave Bangkok's Hua Lamphong Station. From Surat Thani you can take a bus to Phuket. Express trains from Bangkok's Hua Lamphong railway station stop at Surat Thani on their way south. The journey takes 12 hours or so; if you leave Bangkok at 3 pm, you'll arrive at a dark train station in Surat Thani at around 3 am. *(See Train Travel in Travel Smart Thailand.)* Bus services or flights, though, are generally considered to be a far better way to get to the Andaman coast.

HEALTH AND SAFETY

Malaria and dengue fever are rare but not unheard of in Thailand's southeast. Health authorities have done a great job controlling mosquitoes around the southern resorts, but you'll still need a good supply of repellent. Wear long-sleeve shirts and long pants at dusk to reduce the chances of dengue.

As with any developed resort locations, the dangers and annoyances usually involve petty theft. Phuket has its fair share of crime, usually thefts from hotel rooms or pickpockets operating in the entertainment areas. Ensure that your valuables are secured at all times. Brawls caused by too much liquor and sun can also be a problem. There are many bars and pubs here, and some tend to overindulge. The police do patrol the area, but violence does occasionally break out.

Be careful at the beach, as the sun is stronger than you think. Wear a hat and plenty of sunscreen. Protective clothing while diving or snorkeling is a good idea, as accidentally brushing against or stepping on coral can be painful. Keep an eye out for dangerous creatures like jellyfish, especially during the monsoon season, and sea urchins. If you are stung, seek medical attention immediately.

Strong undertows often develop during monsoon season, especially along the west coast. Pay attention to posted warnings and listen if locals tell you not to swim.

MONEY MATTERS

Banks and ATMs are everywhere, and can always be found outside the numerous 7-Eleven stores, but it's still always a good idea to carry some extra cash. Remote islands do not widely accept credit cards, but have many eager currency exchangers. Some places add a small service charge, typically 3%, when you pay with a credit card, much to the chagrin of the major credit card companies who have tried, and failed, to stamp out the practice.

RESTAURANTS

Restaurants of all sorts are available in the beach regions, from exclusive (and usually expensive) resort eateries to wooden shacks that seem like they're about to fall over. Lanta food stalls pop up just before dusk on the beaches, where in the daytime there's only sand and sunbathers. Phuket has a wide range of restaurants, from the fast-food giants of America (with some Thai adaptations on their menus) to beach huts to five-star western-style restaurants, but Ao Nang and Koh Lanta now also have a great many dining spots to choose from.

Prices in the reviews are the average cost of a main course at dinner or, if dinner is not served, at lunch.

HOTELS

Hotel prices in beach areas are generally lower than what you'd pay in Bangkok (Phuket excluded) but higher than in other parts of the country. There are budget bungalows and guesthouses everywhere, though if you haven't booked ahead in high season you may end up in a questionable room with just a humble fan. At the other end of the spectrum are upscale resorts that run more than $1,000-plus a night—though they are some of the most luxurious resorts in the world.

Many places combine the two experiences by offering pricey luxury bungalows. Rates fluctuate widely—in holiday periods they can more than double. Always double-check your rate when you book.

Prices in the reviews are the lowest cost of a standard double room in high season.

WHAT IT COSTS IN BAHT			
$	$$	$$$	$$$$
Restaurants	under B200	B201–B300	B301–B400	over B400
Hotels	under B2,000	B2,001–B4,000	B4,001–B6,000	over B6,000

Restaurant prices are for a main course, excluding tax and tip. Hotel prices are for a standard double in high season, excluding service charge and tax.

PHUKET

Phuket (or "Koh" Phuket—Koh is "island" in Thai, but this is rarely used because Phuket is so large) is one of the region's economic powerhouses—millions of tourists visit the island every year, enjoying the many delights that are offered in this established resort island. Phuket is a modern, vibrant island with more than 6 million annual visitors, a number that is only increasing year to year. If you've never been to Phuket, you will likely love it; returning visitors will find a new island that eagerly greets its next wave of tourism.

Phuket is linked to the mainland by a causeway, and the rest of the world by an international airport. Its indented coastline and hilly interior make the island seem larger than its 48-km (30-mile) length and 21-km (13-mile) breadth. Before tourism, Phuket was already making fortunes out of tin mining and rubber plantations. After backpackers discovered Phuket in the early 1970s, word quickly spread about its white, sandy beaches and cliff-sheltered coves, its plunging waterfalls and impressive mountains, its cloudless days and fiery sunsets.

Unfortunately, tourism has brought serious problems. Entrepreneurs built massive resorts, first in Patong, then spreading out around the island. Phuket remains plagued by horrendous traffic and overdevelopment, which can take visitors by surprise, but there are also places where you can isolate yourself from the rest of the island. In recent years, the authorities have tried hard to rein in some of the worst excesses of overdevelopment and have, to a certain extent, succeeded in quieter places. However, development still continues apace in Patong and Phuket town.

Even though it may seem like every other business here is a tour operator or dive shop or tailor or jeep rental or pub, there's a lot to love about the island. The beaches are still beautiful, and this remains a top destination for snorkeling and diving (with more than 180 registered dive shops). The island offers some of the most exclusive resorts and spas in the world, yet the food, drink, and accommodations are cheap compared to most visitors' home countries (though Phuket is quite expensive by Thai standards). And direct flights to the island make this a convenient getaway.

■ TIP➜ When planning your trip, keep in mind that the monsoon season runs from May to October, and swimming on the west side of the coast is not advisable during this time, as the current can be dangerous.

This section starts with Phuket Town, the hub of the island, and is organized counterclockwise from there. It's best to pick one or two choice spots and stick with them. The frazzling travel between destinations can undo any relaxation you enjoyed the previous day.

GETTING HERE AND AROUND

AIR TRAVEL Phuket's airport is at the northern end of the island. All hotels are to the south. Check to see whether yours offers a free shuttle. Taxis meet all incoming flights. Fares are higher than in Bangkok; expect to pay B850 to Patong, Kata, or Karon, or B550 to Phuket Town. On your way back to the airport, you have to book a taxi for a minimum of B600. Many hotels charge B400 to B500 per person for the journey.

There are also frequent minibus and van services to Phuket Town, Patong, Kata, and Karon that cost between B150 and B200. However, it might be worth springing for a cab, as not all van drivers are reputable, and some might try to take you on an extended detour to a friend's shop or restaurant.

CAR TRAVEL Though roads on Phuket are badly congested and poorly marked, It can be handy to have a car on the island. All hotels can arrange for car rentals. Look for Avis, Budget, and Hertz at the airport. In town you can find rental cars at various private shops near the Pearl and Metropole hotels, as well as at shops along all the major beaches. Prices will be a little lower than those at the airport, but not by a lot. If you're driving, make sure you have a GPS, or pick up at least two or three tourist maps (available at the airport, travel agencies, and most any tourism-related office), as they differ in details.

TAXI, TUK-TUK, AND SONGTH-AEW TRAVEL Taxis are starting to become common on Phuket. Recently there have been a number of metered taxis added to the island's fleet of passenger vehicles. However, these taxis are few in number, and it's often difficult to get the drivers to switch on their meters (as opposed to charging inflated set prices). Tuk-tuks are registered, insured, and plentiful; drivers will be happy to take you to your destination for an absurd price. Be ready to bargain hard or simply walk away. Fares within any one town shouldn't be much more than B50 per trip, but drivers will often demand a flat B100. Keep in mind that you can catch a minivan from the airport to Phuket Town for B1800, a distance of 30 km (19 miles). Taxi prices from town to town are pretty standard, and are controlled by a local cartel, something that the authorities have tried, and failed, to break in recent years.

Motorcycle taxis—you ride on the back, behind the driver—are cheaper than tuk-tuks and taxis, but much more dangerous.

The best and cheapest way of getting between beaches on the island is by songthaew. You catch songthaews in front of the market on Ranong Road or at the bus stops in the beach towns. These are marked on most maps, and locals can help you find them. Prices run from B30 to B50 per trip. They run every half hour from 7 am to 5 pm. If you miss that last songthaew, you may end up spending B400 on a tuk-tuk. ■TIP➜ You can sometimes arrange a cut-rate ride on the sly with a hotel taxi driver who's heading your way. If he drives alone, he makes no money. If he takes you for, say, half the normal hotel fare, he gets to keep that, which will probably pay for his dinner.

■TIP→ Some hotels and resorts provide shuttle service to other beaches—check before you shell out your own money for transportation.

PHUKET TOWN

862 km (539 miles) south of Bangkok.

Though few tourists linger here, Phuket Town, the provincial capital, is one of the more culturally interesting places on the island to spend half a day. About one-third of the island's population lives here, and the town is an intriguing mix of old Sino-Portuguese architecture and the influences of the Chinese, Muslims, and Thais that inhabit it. The old Chinese quarter along Talang Street is especially good for a stroll, as its history has not yet been replaced by modern concrete and tile. And this same area has a variety of antiques shops, art studios, and trendy cafés. Besides Talang, the major thoroughfares are Ratsada, Phuket, and Ranong roads. Ratsada connects Phuket Road (where you'll find the Tourism Authority of Thailand office) to Ranong Road, where there's an aromatic local market filled with fruits, vegetables, spices, and meats.

GETTING HERE AND AROUND

Phuket Town is in the center of the island. Taxis, tuk-tuks, motorcycles, and local buses will take you from here to the surrounding beaches and to the airport. Expect to pay approximately B550 to travel from the town to the airport or Patong via taxi—a little more to most other southern beaches and a little less to more northern beaches. The price will depend on your negotiation techniques. The best place to pick up transport is at the bus station in the center of town. Ranong Road also has a songthaew terminal, where minibuses depart for the most popular beaches every half hour. The fare is B30 to B100.

VISITOR INFORMATION AND TOURS

As the saying goes, you can't throw a stone in Phuket without hitting a tour operator. Nearly all of them are selling the same package tours and renting the same cars and motorcycles, so feel free to comparison shop and haggle over prices. Common half-day sightseeing tours include visits to Wat Chalong, Rawai Beach, Phromthep Cape, and Khao Rang.

In general, be wary of what tour operators tell you; they are in business to sell you a trip to the beach, not to tell you how to get there on your own. If you feel you have been ripped off, note the offender's name and other info and report him to the local Tourism Authority of Thailand (TAT) office. Also let the manager at your hotel know, so he or she can steer other tourists clear.

Dive Asia. On Kata Beach but with branches right across southern Thailand, Dive Asia is a PADI-certified instructor and operator that's been in business for more than 20 years. They do a multitude of day trips to different dive sites and snorkeling spots. ☎ *076/330598* ⊕ *www.diveasia.com* ✉ *From B3,400.*

John Gray's Sea Canoe. This company is known internationally for ecotourism trips, including awesome canoeing through Phang Nga Bay. Look for their flyers at travel agencies. Various tours are offered, from day trips to longer overnight stays. ☎ *076/254505 up to 7* ⊕ *www.seacanoejohngray. com* ✉ *From B3,950.*

Thailand Divers. Day trips by boat, snorkeling, and a broad range of diving courses are offered by this well-organized, friendly, and highly professional agency. ✉ *198/12, Rat-U-Thit Rd., Patong Beach, Patong* ☎ *076/292052* ⊕ *www.thailand divers.com* ✉ *From B4,200.*

Tourism Authority of Thailand The efficient Tourism Authority of Thailand in Phuket Town provides up-to-date maps, CDs, and brochures, as well as thorough infor-

> ### ELEPHANT SHOWS
>
> On Phuket there are many opportunities to ride elephants or see them at work. Many were former logging elephants, whose jobs are now to "entertain" tourists. Before forking over your money, examine how the animals are kept and treated, and whether they show signs of abuse, such as sores on their legs from chains. Even well-respected businesses have been accused of mistreating elephants. If you believe chaining an elephant to a concrete slab in a park or putting him on stage in a show is wrong, then don't pay to see or ride him. Better yet, write a letter to the establishment and the Tourism Authority of Thailand.

mation about local excursions. ✉ *73-75 Phuket Rd., Amphoe Muang* ☎ *076/212213* ⊕ *www.tourismthailand.org.*

EXPLORING
TOP ATTRACTIONS

Big Buddha. The Big Buddha is one of the island's most revered landmarks. The huge, white-marble Buddha image sits on top of Nakkerd Hills between Chalong and Kata. It is 45 meters high, and the site offers the best 360-degree views of the island. Take the road from Phuket's main artery—it's a must-visit island destination. ✉ *Phuket Town.*

Khao Rang. If you want to get your bearings, there's a fine view of Phuket Town, the island's interior, and even the 45-meter-high Big Buddha from atop Khao Rang, a hill northwest of town. It can be a tricky drive—you'll need to watch carefully for street signs, as many aren't marked or are covered by foliage, but it's worth it if you want to get a fresh perspective. From the town's center, take either Ranong or Thalang Road west and turn north on Kho Sim Bi Road. Follow the winding, ascending, forested road. There are a few restaurants and a picnic area once you reach the top, where you can relax and soak in the views. ✉ *Northwest.*

FAMILY **Phuket Thai Village & Orchid Garden.** About 5 km (3 miles) north of Phuket Town is the Phuket Thai Village and Orchid Garden, offering gardens and cultural shows. A 500-seat amphitheater presents various aspects of southern culture. Here you can see classical dance, shadow puppet shows, Thai boxing exhibitions, sword fighting, and an "elephants-at-work" show. It is the best place to be introduced to the more traditional aspects of Thai living, which is not so apparent to most who travel to the region nowadays. ✉ *Thepkasati Rd.* ☎ *076/214860, 076/214861* 🌐 *www.phuketthaivillage.com* 🎟 *B400 entry, B600 for show and lunch or dinner* ⏲ *Shows at 11–noon and 5:30–6:30* ⏲ *Restaurant closes at 10 pm.*

Thalong National Museum. The National Museum, opposite the Heroine's Monument, has an engaging exhibition of the island's culture and history, including its encounter with the Burmese and their defeat by the island's two heroines. The building itself gives a glimpse into local culture, with its attractive architecture and design. The halls each show a different period of local and wider Thai history. ✉ *12 km (7 miles) north of Phuket Town, Srisoonthorn* ☎ *076/311426* 🎟 *B100* ⏲ *Daily 9–4 except holidays.*

WORTH NOTING

Heroines Monument. Several miles north of Phuket Town, dominating a major crossroads, is the Heroines Monument, a tribute to a pair of women who rallied the locals and repelled Burmese invaders in 1785. At the time, Phuket was without a leader after the governor's death and the Burmese tried to capitalize on this moment of weakness. The governor's wife and her sister persuaded all the town women to dress as men and pretend to bear arms against the Burmese. They didn't really fight, but the Burmese believed them to be a powerful army, so they retreated. The people of Phuket hold these two women in great esteem. Some stories, however, differ, having the two women actually fighting. ✉ *12 km (7 miles) north of Phuket Town.*

WHERE TO EAT

$ CAFÉ 🍴 **Chino Café Gallery.** Coffee lovers will immediately yearn for a cup upon entering, as the air carries the smell of freshly ground espresso. The loveliest aspect of this café is its natural wood decor, which gives it a new-age trendy aesthetic. The café-gallery also sells nice souvenirs, notebooks, and postcards made with natural materials. [$] *Average main: B115* ✉ *4 Talang Rd., Taladyai Muang* ☎ *081/979–6190* 💳 *No credit cards.*

$$ INDIAN 🍴 **Khanasutra, A Taste of India.** This restaurant's name is not making false promises—the Sikh owner and Indian chef turn out flavorful, authentic Indian cuisine. The fish tikka is recommended. Part of the unique decor is a bedouin-style tent, where you can enjoy a few cocktails after dinner. The staff, or more accurately the owner, makes the dining experience a memorable one. [$] *Average main: B270* ✉ *18-20 Takua Pa Rd., Tambol Thalad Nuea* ☎ *081/894–0794, 076/256192* 💳 *No credit cards* ⏲ *Closed Tues. No lunch Sun.*

$ CAFÉ 🍴 **Kopi de Phuket.** For a good cup of coffee, try this artsy store, which sells funky designer souvenirs and serves traditional Thai food and international snacks, sandwiches, desserts, and shakes. It's across from the Honda Shop/Nai Yao Restaurant. It opens daily at 9:30 am. [$] *Average main: B143* ✉ *Phuket Rd.* ☎ *076/212225* 🌐 *www.kopidephuket.com* 💳 *No credit cards.*

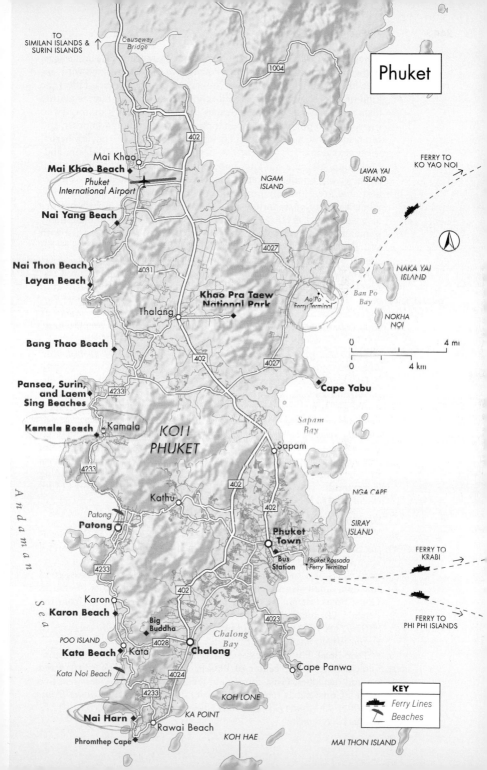

TO
SIMILAN ISLANDS &
SURIN ISLANDS

*Causeway
Bridge*

1004

Phuket

Mai Khao
Mai Khao Beach
*Phuket
International Airport*

FERRY TO
KO YAO NOI

*LAWA YAI
ISLAND*

*NGAM
ISLAND*

402

Nai Yang Beach

Nai Thon Beach
Layan Beach

4031

*NAKA YAI
ISLAND*

4027

**Khao Pra Taew
National Park**

*Ao Po
Ferry Terminal*

*Ban Po
Bay*

*NOKHA
NOI*

Thalang

0   4 mi

0   4 km

402

4027

Bang Thao Beach

**Pansea, Surin,
and Laem
Sing Beaches**

4233

Cape Yabu

Kamala Beach Kamala

*KOH
PHUKET*

*Sapam
Bay*

Sapam

4233

NGA CAPE

Kathu

402

*SIRAY
ISLAND*

402

Patong
Patong

**Phuket
Town**

*A
n
d
a
m
a
n*

4233

Bus
Station

*Phuket Rossada
Ferry Terminal*

FERRY TO
KRABI

402

Karon
Karon Beach

Big
Buddha

4023

*Chalong
Bay*

FERRY TO
PHI PHI ISLANDS

*S
e
a*

POO ISLAND

4028

Kata Beach Kata

Chalong

Kata Noi Beach

4024

Cape Panwa

KOH LONE

KEY

4233

Nai Harn
Phromthep Cape

Rawai Beach

KA POINT

KOH HAE

MAI THON ISLAND

Ferry Lines
Beaches

$ THAI Fodor's Choice ★ 🍴 **Kopitiam by Wilai.** The walls of this unique restaurant-café in the heart of the architecturally quaint Sino-Portuguese district are lined with vintage black-and-white images of Phuket, which pretty much reflect the kind of food served up here—old-school Thai-Chinese fare. Signature dishes are inspired by secret recipes of owner Wiwan's mother (who owns the also popular Wilai restaurant nearby) and grandmother, and often include Chinese medicinal ingredients from her uncle's herbal shop next door. Try *bak kut teh*, a pungent shiitake-mushroom-and-pork soup, and *mee sua pad*, noodles with seafood and spices, as well as the crispy noodle and egg salad. Ice teas like Butterfly Pea Flower and lime are especially good for cooling your insides on a hot day, while a variety of smoothies and good coffee made in a cloth bag are also worth a try. ■ **TIP→ For a delicious snack, buy some of the creamy homemade pepper cookies or crunchy caramel peanuts to take with you.** [$] *Average main: B145* ✉ *18 Thalang Rd.* ☎ *083/6069776* 💳 *No credit cards* 🕒 *Closed Sun.*

$ THAI Fodor's Choice ★ 🍴 **Raya Restaurant.** In the heart of Phuket Old Town, this beloved restaurant is in a historical Sino-Thai mansion, built in the early 20th century. The charming decor is traditional Thai, with a nod to its Portuguese past, and the atmosphere is as much part of the experience as the outstanding food. Authentic Phuket dishes are the specialty here; try the yellow crab curry with rice noodles or the whole red snapper with roasted garlic. [$] *Average main: B150* ✉ *48/1 New Debuk Rd., Muang* ☎ *076/218155* 💳 *No credit cards.*

$ THAI 🍴 **Tunk-ka Cafe.** A favorite haunt of local businessfolk and dating couples, Tunk-ka Cafe is nestled in a jungle setting atop of the biggest hill of Phuket Town. Serving up proper Thai food made from the freshest local ingredients, it is surprising that this restaurant attracts few foreign visitors, although for some that may be a plus. The views are marvelous, especially at sunset, and more than justify the tuk-tuk drive up. The Ruby Red dessert (red water chestnut in coconut cream with lashes of young coconut and jack fruit) will satisfy even the most demanding sweet tooth. [$] *Average main: B180* ✉ *Top of Rang hill* ☎ *076/211500, 082/412–2131* 💳 *No credit cards.*

WHERE TO STAY

$$ B&B/INN 🏨 **Casa Blanca.** The best among a string of boutique B&Bs in the charming Sino-Portuguese district, Casa Blanca is comprised of 17 tasteful rooms with cream walls and wooden floors, and either garden courtyard views or a small balcony looking out onto the street. **Pros:** good location; small swimming pool; historic building with lots of charm. **Cons:** breakfast not included; hot water access erratic; far from the beach. [$] *Rooms from: B2000* ✉ *26 Phuket Rd., Talat Yai, Muang* ☎ *076/219019* 🌐 *www.casablancaphuket.com* 💳 *No credit cards* 🛏 *17 rooms* 🍽 *No meals.*

$ HOTEL 🏨 **Pearl Hotel.** For a less expensive option, this is a comfortable, convenient hotel in the center of Phuket Town, though it's a little tired around the edges. **Pros:** convenient location; shuttle service; great live music. **Cons:** needs renovation; basic; can be noisy. [$] *Rooms from: B1300* ✉ *42 Montri Rd.* ☎ *076/211044* 🌐 *www.pearlhotel.co.th* 🛏 *212 rooms* 🍽 *No meals.*

$$ 🏨 **Royal Phuket City Hotel.** This is arguably Phuket Town's best address,
HOTEL with rooms that are spacious and contemporary. **Pros:** large rooms;
good gym; conference center. **Cons:** some rooms lack views; in-room
Wi-Fi is extra; a little short on personality. $ *Rooms from: B2300*
✉ *154 Phang Nga Rd., Phuket* ☎ *076/233333* ⊕ *www.royalphuketcity.*
com 🛏 *251 rooms.*

$ 🏨 **Sino House.** This much-needed recent addition to Phuket Town pro-
HOTEL vides a pleasant option from the larger, often less charming hotels in
the area. **Pros:** central; 50% discount for the spa for all guests; basic
kitchenette. **Cons:** poor English; noisy a/c; dull views. $ *Rooms from:*
B2000 ✉ *1 Montree Rd., Talad –Yai, Muang* ☎ *076/232494 up to 5*
⊕ *www.sinohousephuket.com* 🚫 *No credit cards* 🛏 *57 rooms.*

KHAO PRA TAEW NATIONAL PARK

19 km (12 miles) north of Phuket Town.

Located in the north of the island, Khao Pra Taew is the last virgin rain
forest in Phuket. You can take a hike through the park (8 km) or just
take a walk up to the beautiful Tonsai waterfall. The Gibbon Project
is one of the major draws to the park, but the park itself is worth a
visit for those who want to wander through a real tropical rain forest.

GETTING HERE AND AROUND

You can take a taxi, tuk-tuk, or motorcycle here from any of the island's
beaches or from Phuket Town. The cost depends on distance—a taxi
from Phuket Town would be about B400, a tuk-tuk a little more. If
you're driving, take Highway 4027, watch the signs, and turn west
toward Bang Pae Waterfall and the Gibbon Rehabilitation Center.

EXPLORING KHAO PRA TAEW NATIONAL PARK

Thailand's islands have several national parks, and this one is home
to Phuket's last remaining virgin forest and populations of endangered
animals. The park has two easily accessible waterfalls. The Gibbon
Center, which works to protect the primates and educate visitors about
them, is part of the park.

You'll have to pay the standard foreigner's fee to enter the park: B200
(Thais pay B40). To access **Tonsai Waterfall** on the other side of the
park, follow the signs and turn east off Highway 402. Here you can
find two trails (600 meters and 2 km [1 mile]), through rich, tropical,
evergreen forest. Expect buckets of rain in the monsoon season. Gib-
bons, civets, macaques, mouse deer, wild boar, lemurs, and loris live in
the park, but spotting one would be a rare and impressive feat.

The park advertises the good deeds of the Gibbon Center, and indeed
it's a worthy cause. (What they don't tell you is that the center, which
sits near the parking lot at Bang Pae, receives none of your entrance
fee.) After visiting the center, follow the paved trail along the water-
fall. It's a relatively easy hike, quite lush in the rainy season. Both park
entrances have bathrooms, parking lots, and food stalls. If you plan to
visit both waterfalls, make sure you get entrance tickets at your first
stop—they're good for both sites.

CLOSE UP

The Gibbon Rehabilitation Project

Just inside Khao Pra Taew National Park, between a hillside jungle and a gurgling stream, dozens of gibbons swing from branch to branch, filling the forest with boisterous hooting.

It seems like a happy sign of jungle life, but something is wrong with this picture. These animals are not roaming around free; instead, they live in cages near the park entrance as part of the Gibbon Rehabilitation Project. Most of these small apes were poached from jungles around Thailand and kept as pets or zoo and bar amusements. They were forced to perform shows, do tricks, drink beer, or get their pictures taken with tourists before they were rescued by this project. As a branch of the Wild Animal Rescue Foundation of Thailand, the center aims to rehabilitate the gibbons in their natural habitat, with the intention of releasing the animals into the wild (though some animals that were abused will never be able to live freely again).

The center holds more than 60 gibbons. They're kept in large cages, away from visitors. The idea is to purge them of their familiarity with people, although visitors can hear them in the distance and glimpse their playful leaps through the trees. All gibbons are named, and their life stories are posted at the center for tourists to read: Lamut and Pai Mei were working as tourist attractions at Patong Beach before their rescue. A baby, called Bam-Bam, was found in a cardboard box at a roadside. Saul, a young blond male, is missing a patch of fur, which researchers think could be the result of bullets that grazed him when his mother was shot.

When new gibbons arrive at the center they get a complete medical checkup, including tests for HIV, hepatitis, and tuberculosis. It costs $700 a year to treat, feed, and house each animal, and although the center sits within the national park, it receives none of the $5 entrance fee. In fact, the center receives no funding from the Thai government— it survives on donations alone. For B1,500, the price of a good night out in Patong, visitors can "adopt" a gibbon for a year. If you're unable to make it out to the center, the website of the Gibbon Rehabilitation Project (⊕ *www.gibbonproject.org*) has information on how to adopt a gibbon or make a donation.

—Karen Coates

MAI KHAO BEACH

37 km (23 miles) northwest of Phuket Town.

On the northwest coast of Phuket, this 11-km-long beach is still undeveloped by Phuket standards, as it is part of the Sirinat National Park. The only significant constructions along it are a smattering of resorts and Phuket International Airport near Nai Yang Beach. The sand here is possibly the coarsest of any on Phuket, but it is practically deserted most of the time

EXPLORING

Mai Khao Beach. This is Phuket's northernmost beach, still a haven for leatherback turtles that lay their eggs here between November and February. It is a rare event, but it does happen sometimes. You can pop into the Marriott Resort for a bite at their beach club, or visit the next-door Sirinath Marine National Park (established to protect the turtles) here. Mai Khao connects with Nai Yang Beach to form Phuket's longest stretch of sand, and is ideal for long walks or a jog. It's dangerous to swim during the monsoons. **Amenities:** food and drink. **Best for:** solitude; sunset; walking. ✉ *Phuket.*

> **WORD OF MOUTH**
>
> "The J. W. Marriott is a beautiful property. Great pools, very lush landscaping, and lots to do. With dozens of torches lit up at night, it is very impressive. Yet, it is isolated and may be best enjoyed with kids. If you are traveling during a school vacation the hotel will be packed with younguns. Most spots are 15+ minutes away. We took taxis for dinner most every night. We had some very good meals and prices were much less then eating at the hotel. Yet, in truth, we much prefer being closer to stores and restaurants."
>
> —tengohambre

WHERE TO STAY

$$$ RESORT Fodor's Choice ★ 🏨 **J. W. Marriott Resort & Spa.** Wow; this secluded resort offers the longest stretch of sand on the island and has spotlessly clean, luxurious rooms with impeccable classic Thai design. **Pros:** long and quiet beach; Thai-style rooms; a wide range of amenities. **Cons:** may be too isolated for some; surf sometimes too rough for swimming. [$] *Rooms from: B4400* ✉ *231 Moo 3, Mai Khao, Phuket* ☎ *076/338000* 🌐 *www.marriott.com/HKTJW* 🛏 *265 rooms* 🍴 *Breakfast.*

NAI YANG BEACH

34 km (20 miles) northwest of Phuket Town.

Smaller than its northerly neighbor, and one of the most relaxed beaches on Phuket, Nai Yang attracts a local and expat crowd. Parts of the beach are inside Sirinath National Park, which helps to preserve the beach from the worst excesses of Phuket development. There is a good selection of places to stay, and folks head here if they want isolation and a calm ambience.

GETTING HERE AND AROUND

Nai Yang Beach is accessible from Highway 4027, the main road running through the island. Taxis, tuk-tuks, and motorcycles will take you to and from other parts of the island. ■ **TIP→ Transport is often difficult to find on the road through Nai Yang Beach.** Your hotel may be able to help arrange transportation.

BEACHES

Nai Yang Beach. Nai Yang Beach is really a continuation south of Mai Khao, making a long stretch of sand good for a jog or swimming in the dry season. Casuarina trees line the gently curving shore offering shade. It's a far quieter beach than most, with a strip of trees and a small string of beachside restaurants and bars, tour guides, tailors, and shops. Fishing boats anchor nearby, making for picture-perfect sunrises and sunsets. **Amenities:** food and drink. **Best for:** snorkeling; swimming; sunsets; sunrises. ✉ *Nai Yang Beach Rd., near airport, Phuket.*

WHERE TO STAY

You can find tasty, fresh seafood at Nai Yang's beachside restaurants.

$$$ HOTEL FAMILY Fodor's Choice ★ 🏨 **Indigo Pearl.** Phuket's tin-mining history is the inspiration for the Indigo Pearl, and the resort features interesting collectibles from the Na-Rarong family mines, with a design-conscious decor that blends funky postindustrial (concrete features strongly) with a hint of Thai rustic luxury. **Pros:** great breakfast; unique decor; good spa. **Cons:** some rooms affected by noise from nearby beach bar; lots of mosquitoes. [$] *Rooms from: B4300* ✉ *Nai Yang Beach and National Park, Phuket Town* ☎ *076/327006, 076/327015* 🌐 *www.indigo-pearl.com* 💳 *No credit cards* 🛏 *177 rooms.*

NAI THON AND LAYAN BEACHES

30 km (18½ miles) northwest of Phuket Town.

It's one of the smallest beaches on the island, and the tropical rain forest that acts as a natural barrier keeps many visitors away, but this beach exudes a calm and relaxed vibe. There are a few resorts on the beach, but they are unobtrusive and you can easily feel alone when wandering along the wide, sandy expanse.

GETTING HERE AND AROUND

Nai Thon and Layan beaches are easily accessible from all parts of Phuket Island. Taxis, tuk-tuks, and motorcycles will gladly ferry you to and from these quiet beaches.

BEACHES

Nai Thon and Layan Beaches. A few miles north of Bang Thao Bay, follow a smaller highway off the main routes (4030 and 4031) along a scenic coastline reminiscent of California's Pacific Coast Highway. These beaches are good for swimming and snorkeling in the dry season. Layan is a wildlife hot spot, as the lake behind the beach attracts lots of wildfowl. Nai Thon is 1-km long and still has few accommodations. **Amenities:** food and drink. **Best for:** snorkeling; swimming; walking. ✉ *Phuket Town.*

WHERE TO STAY

$$$$ RESORT 🏨 **The Pavilions.** Many resorts claim that they're set up so that you never have to leave your villa, but the Pavilions really means it. **Pros:** fabulous views from the bar; great amenities; real sense of privacy. **Cons:** a bit isolated; no children under 14. [$] *Rooms from: B9000* ✉ *31/1 Moo 6, Cherngtalay, Thalang* ☎ *076/317600, 091/621–4841 in Bangkok* 🌐 *www.pavilions-resorts.com* 🛏 *30 villas.*

$$$$ RESORT 🏨 **Trisara.** Opulence is the standard at the Trisara resort; rooms feature a variety of Thai wooden art pieces, silk throw pillows on the divans, and 32-inch plasma TVs hidden in the walls. **Pros:** beautiful Thai decor; golf course; subtle and professional service. **Cons:** often fully

booked; pricey. [$] *Rooms from: B21000* ✉ *60/1 Moo 6, Srisoonthorn Rd., Cherngtalay, Phuket Town* ☎ *076/310100, 076/310355* 🌐 *www.trisara.com* 🛏 *42 rooms.*

BANG THAO BEACH

22 km (14 miles) northwest of Phuket Town.

Dotted with resorts and villas along its 4-mile stretch, Bang Thao beach is a favorite of those seeking a more refined pace than that of the more popular and developed Phuket beaches. The waters here are shallow and there is a good depth of beach to wander along.

Once the site of a tin mine, Bang Thao Beach (a resort area collectively called Laguna Phuket) now glistens with the more precious metals worn by its affluent visitors. Due to the ingenuity of Ho Kwon Ping and his family, this area was built nearly 20 years ago in a spot so damaged from mining that most thought it beyond repair. Now it's recovered enough to support an array of accommodations, eateries, and golf courses set around the lagoons.

The Laguna Beach Resort has been instrumental in showcasing this part of Phuket and has picked up an enviable international reputation. It holds a famous international triathlon each year, and also hosts many other events throughout the year. However, as anywhere on the island, some of the older resorts are showing signs of age and tropical weather damage, despite frequent renovations.

GETTING HERE AND AROUND

Bang Thao Beach is accessible from Highway 4027. Taxis, tuk-tuks, and motorcycles can all take you to and from the beach. Getting away from the beach is sometimes a little difficult, but if you wait on the beach road a taxi or another form of transport will materialize eventually. If you get stuck, ask for help at one of the resorts. There's a free shuttle service between the resorts along the shore.

BEACHES

Bang Thao Beach. The beach itself is a long stretch (4 miles) of white sand, with vendors offering a variety of sports equipment rental, inexpensive seafood, beach massages, and cocktails. The beach is good for swimming in the hot season, the lagoon for kayaking anytime. The atmosphere is relaxed, making this a beach well suited to young families. **Amenities:** food and drink; showers; toilets; water sports. **Best for:** sunset; swimming; walking. ✉ *Bang Thao, Soi Ao Bangtao, Cherng Talay.*

WHERE TO EAT

$ INTERNATIONAL 🍴 **Am & Lee's Restaurant.** The British and Thai owners both influence the menu here, with traditional Thai foods being just as tasty as the British-pub-food-inspired pies, jacket potatoes, stews, and sandwiches. The restaurant, which is part of the Baan Puri complex, is especially popular for its friendly service and hearty breakfasts. [$] *Average main: B120* ✉ *69/34 Moo 3, Bang Thao Beach* ☎ *081/787–9767* 💳 *No credit cards.*

$ SEAFOOD THAI 🍴 **Seafood.** The friendly ladies at this popular street-side shanty serve made-to-order seafood, noodles, and stir-fry. Every meal comes with a bowl of aromatic cardamom soup, which can be a great tonic. During the day there are beach deliveries available if you find you don't want to move from your particular spot in the sun. It's safe for foreign bellies, but if you're wary of street food or spicy food, you probably won't be comfortable here. $ *Average main: B100* ⊠ *Phuket Town* ✛ *About 5 km (3 miles) east of resort. Look for small sign on left side of road that reads "Seafood." If you reach mosque, you've gone too far* ▬ *No credit cards.*

WHERE TO STAY

$

RESORT

▦ **Allamanda Laguna Phuket.** Unlike the other four resorts in the area, this property sits on the lagoon instead of the beach, and therefore offers lower rates; you definitely get more bang for your buck here. **Pros:** good choice of rooms with different amenities; shuttle boat service; relaxing ambience. **Cons:** away from the beach; not ideal for families; can get busy. $ *Rooms from: B1600* ⊠ *29 Moo 4, Srisoonthorn Rd., Cherngtalay, Phuket Town* ☎ *076/362700* ⊕ *www.allamandaphuket. com* ⤳ *131 suites* ⦿❘ *Breakfast.*

$

RESORT

FAMILY

▦ **Andaman Bangtao Bay Resort.** Don't expect opulence, but this small, friendly, and beautifully situated resort offers clean, comfortable rooms only 20 meters from the beach, with nice en suite bathrooms, a/c, and satellite TV, details of traditional Thai decor, and beachfront patios. **Pros:** nice location; friendly service; good restaurant. **Cons:** beach is not that great; pool very small; a little pricey for what you get. $ *Rooms from: B1900* ⊠ *82/9 Moo 3 Cherngtalay, Bang Thao Beach* ☎ *076/270246, 081/599–7889* ⊕ *www.andamanbangtaobayresort.com* ▬ *No credit cards* ⤳ *8 rooms* ⦿❘ *Breakfast.*

$$$$

RESORT

FAMILY

Fodor'sChoice

★

▦ **Banyan Tree Phuket.** Of the quintet of resorts on Laguna Beach, this is the most exclusive—and expensive. **Pros:** peaceful setting; great spa; children's programs. **Cons:** pricey; resort is huge. $ *Rooms from: B12000* ⊠ *33 Moo 4, Srisoonthorn Rd., Cherngtalay, Amphur Talang, Phuket* ☎ *076/372400* ⊕ *www.banyantree.com* ⤳ *123 villas* ⦿❘ *Breakfast.*

$$

RESORT

FAMILY

▦ **Sunwing Resort and Spa.** Families keep coming back to this resort, as it really has it all for kids of every age, keeping them busy with numerous facilities and well-organized daily activities, babysitting services, discos, and shows. **Pros:** safe, fun environment for kids; two restaurants have varied, interesting menus; resort shop sells all the essentials. **Cons:** somewhat remote from shops or restaurants; poolside can be chaotic. $ *Rooms from: B3500* ⊠ *22 Moo #2 Chueng Thalay, Phuket* ☎ *076/314263 up to 5* ⊕ *www.sunwingphuket.com* ▬ *No credit cards* ⤳ *283 rooms* ⦿❘ *Breakfast.*

PANSEA, SURIN, AND LAEM SING BEACHES

21 km (12 miles) northwest of Phuket Town.

If you want luxury accommodation, then look no further than these picturesque beaches on Phuket's west coast. Many of the island's rich set have houses here, sprinkled among high-end resorts. The sand is white and the waters are crystal clear, but the scene here has remained pretty quiet.

GETTING HERE AND AROUND

The beaches are accessible from Highway 4027. Taxis, tuk-tuks, and motorcycles can all take you to and from the beach. A taxi to or from Phuket Town should cost approximately B550 to B700; expect to pay a little more for a tuk-tuk.

BEACHES

Laem Sing Beach. Laem Sing is a lovely little beach off the beaten path but well worth the 10-minute trek down a rocky track. This minor inconvenience means that in contrast to the majority of Phuket's beaches, this is quiet and uncluttered. It's just off the winding coastal road between Kamala and Surin. Luckily there are a couple of food stalls, so you don't need to haul refreshments down with you. **Amenities:** food and drink; toilets; parking (B30). **Best for:** solitude; swimming. ⊠ *Laem Sing Beach, just off road from Kamala-Surin.*

Surin Beach. This is a peaceful, long stretch of sandy beach that gets busy on the weekends as it is popular with local Thais and expatriates. There are grassy areas shaded by pine trees that make good spots to take refuge from the midday sun. Best avoided during the rainy season as the seas can get rough and there are some strong, dangerous currents. Tasty treats can be bought from local vendors working the beach. **Amenities:** food and drink; toilets. **Best for:** swimming; walking; snorkeling. ⊠ *Surin Beach* ✛ *Go through Kamala and continue past Laem Singh Beach. Take sharp left turn down to beach when you reach the three way junction. It's a 25-min drive north from Patong.*

WHERE TO EAT AND STAY

There are many little restaurants with cheap and tasty Thai and western food along the shore, and just sitting on the beach will bring many offers of beachside food delivery. Menus will be thrust on you and orders delivered to your beach towel in just minutes.

$$$$
RESORT
Fodor's Choice
★

⛱ **Amanpuri Resort.** You'd be hard pressed to find a more sparklingly dignified hotel in Thailand—not one quite as expensive (the nightly rate for the largest of the villas is more than $8,000!). **Pros:** private beach; great sunsets; multiaward winning. **Cons:** too isolated for some; service can be apathetic at times. $ *Rooms from: B21000* ⊠ *Pansea Beach, Phuket, Phuket Town* ☎ *076/324333* ⊕ *www.amanpuri.com* ⇆ *40 pavilions, 31 villas* ⑩ *Breakfast.*

$
B&B/INN

⛱ **Surin Bay Inn.** For reasonably priced accommodations near Surin Beach (only a few minutes' walk away), try this small hotel. **Pros:** nice restaurant; great rooms for moderate price; particularly helpful staff. **Cons:** not on beach; no elevator; only top-floor rooms have good views. $ *Rooms from: B1100* ⊠ *106/11 Surin Beach, Surin Beach* ☎ *076/271601* ⊕ *www.surinbayinn.com* ⇆ *12 rooms* ⑩ *Breakfast.*

$$$$
RESORT

⛱ **The Surin Phuket.** Almost completely concealed by a grove of coconut palms, this resort has more than 100 thatch-roof cottages overlooking a quiet beach. **Pros:** great location; private beach. **Cons:** layout a little confusing; long walk (uphill) from the beach to top villas; isolated. $ *Rooms from: B6200* ⊠ *118 Moo 3, Cherngtalay, Phuket, Phuket* ☎ *076/621580 up to 82* ⊕ *www.thesurinphuket.com* ⇆ *103 chalets* ⑩ *Breakfast.*

KAMALA BEACH

18 km (11 miles) west of Phuket Town.

Unlike the more upscale enclaves to the north, Kamala Beach has some reasonably priced accommodations that attract longer-stay visitors, and is a good launchpad for the rest of the island, as it retains its calm and quiet. The area, a curving strip of coral sand embraced by coconut palms south of Bang Thao, suffered some of the worst destruction on Phuket during the 2004 tsunami.

GETTING HERE AND AROUND

A taxi from Phuket Town or Patong Beach will cost about B500.

EXPLORING

Kamala Beach is quieter and less touristy than neighboring Patong, and attracts a more laid-back crowd. The beach is quite small, but has a distinct feel to it, with mangrove trees and blue water.

Kamala Beach. Kamala beach is unremarkable but endearing, particularly to pensioners who return here year after year for the beach's more reserved ambience. Kamala can get cramped during the day and offers numerous accommodation and dining options, but if you're staying, don't expect a lively nightlife. **Amenities:** food and drink. **Best for:** swimming; water sports. ✉ *Phuket.*

WHERE TO STAY

$ RESORT 🏨 **Baan Chaba.** If you're looking for a bungalow or hotel on the beach, you'll find several options at the north end of Kamala (none of which have views of the beach, and some of which are absurdly priced). **Pros:** spacious bungalows; reasonable rates. **Cons:** not beachfront; lacks amenities. [$] *Rooms from: B1000* ✉ *95/3 Moo 3, Kamala Beach, Kathu, Phuket, Phuket* ☎ *076/279158* 🌐 *www.baanchaba.com* 💳 *No credit cards* 🛏 *8 bungalows* 🍴 *No meals.*

$ B&B/INN 🏨 **PapaCrab Boutique Guesthouse.** This small, friendly, family-run boutique guesthouse is in a quiet spot near the town. **Pros:** excellent price for what is offered; good service; just off the beach. **Cons:** not great views; patchy Wi-Fi; no landline in rooms. [$] *Rooms from: B950* ✉ *93/5 Moo 3, Kamala Beach, Kamala Beach* ☎ *084/744–0482* 🌐 *phuketpapacrab.com* 💳 *No credit cards* 🛏 *10 rooms* 🍴 *No meals.*

PATONG

13 km (8 miles) west of Phuket Town.

You'd hardly believe it today, but Patong was once the island's most remote beach, completely cut off by the surrounding mountains and only accessible by boat. Today it's a thriving, thronged, beach-resort community frequented by both Bangkokians, down for a weekend of fun in the sun, and international visitors. Patong is a great place for new visitors to Thailand looking for a nice beach with characteristic Thai experiences, like muay thai (Thai boxing), street shopping, and authentic Thai food, as well as familiar facilities, like Starbucks, sushi bars, and chain hotels.

The beachfront has long been a congested mishmash of high-end hotels and restaurants, patrolled by hawkers and beach vendors. The sidewalk is clearer since the Thai army intervened to try and force out the overabundance of illegal businesses; however, things are still not perfect. You can stroll along several miles of boutiques, western restaurants and bars, ice-cream parlors, and upscale nightlife venues, interspersed with traditional Thai market stalls selling food, cheap T-shirts, and knockoff goods. The lively nightlife scene remains a big draw for many tourists, but the sheer variety of restaurants, hotels, and entertainment on offer ensures Patong's popularity with a wide variety of visitors.

PATONG'S SULLIED REPUTATION

Patong has, on occasion, been portrayed as a sleazy environment crawling with prostitutes, but this is something of an exaggeration. It is a far cry from Pattaya or Patpong in Bangkok, and most visitors are not directly affected by anything untoward, spending the majority of their days playing on the beach, and their evenings at the busy bars and restaurants along Thaweewong Road. The sex trade certainly does exist here, and girly bars abound, as do clubs starring "ladyboys," and some may feel that it is not an ideal destination for families.

GETTING HERE AND AROUND

Every street, hotel, and shop in Patong seems to have a ready team of taxis, tuk-tuks, and motorcycles whose drivers are all more than happy to ferry you around. Just pick your vehicle of choice and bargain hard. Tuk-tuks to Phuket Town should cost approximately B500; to Karon will be B400; and to Kamala is around B300. It can be a little frustrating to get to the beach during morning rush hour, because the road from Phuket Town is often congested.

EXPLORING

Patong Beach. Once cluttered with beach umbrellas, Patong Beach now has some room for both sunbathing and playing soccer or Frisbee on the beach. Every conceivable beach activity from wakeboarding to jet skiing to parasailing is available. Patong became so popular because of its picture-perfect paradisical nature, and now its popularity has caused some degradation of the environment, particularly noticeable when the monsoon rains wash the grime off the street and onto the beach. **Amenities:** food and drink; showers; toilets. **Best for:** water sports; partiers; walking; swimming; sunsets. ⊠ *Patong Beach, Thaweewong Rd., Phuket.*

WHERE TO EAT

$$$$ ✗ **Baan Rim Pa.** On a large terrace that clings to a cliff at the north end of
THAI   Patong Beach, this restaurant has some tables set back from the edge, but you'll then miss the gorgeous ocean views. The food is among the best Phuket has to offer. Well-thought-out set menus make ordering simpler for those unfamiliar with Thai food. They tend to turn down the heat on many favorite dishes, so you may be disappointed if you like spicier fare. The restaurant has a piano bar open Tuesday through Sunday.

$ *Average main: B1450* ⊠ *223 Prabaramee Rd., Kalim Beach, Patong* ☎ *076/340789* ⊕ *www.baanrimpa.com* ⚑ *Reservations essential.*

$$$$ ✗ **Da Maurizio.** An Italian bar-ristorante is the last in the trio of Patong's
ITALIAN cliff restaurants. Dining is just above a secluded beach. Try pizza, fettuccine, ravioli, and other Italian traditions, or opt for fresh seafood baked in a wood-burning oven. The restaurant prides itself on its use of exclusively organic ingredients. $ *Average main: B1000* ⊠ *223/2 Kalim Rd., Patong* ☎ *076/344079* ⊕ *www.baanrimpa.com/italian-restaurant/* ⚑ *Reservations essential.*

$$$$ ✗ **Le Versace.** With the best views in Patong, Le Versace delivers with a
FRENCH stunning decor, which, if we are being honest, may be a bit too kitsch for some tastes, but will be the perfect dining experience for others. This is a formidable fine dining experience in Patong and offers a sumptuous menu. The flavor is unapologetically French, with modern twists on classic French cuisine. Arrive at sunset for the best views, but the backdrop offers a special experience at all times. $ *Average main: B900* ⊠ *206/5-6 Prabaramee Rd. Patong Beach, Phuket* ☎ *76/346005* ⊕ *www.leversace.com* ⊟ *No credit cards.*

$ ✗ **Sam's Steaks & Grill.** In the Holiday Inn Resort, this stylish restau-
STEAKHOUSE rant serves prime cuts of imported beef prepared with notable French flair. The lively, popular restaurant serves elegantly presented, delectable meals in a calming ambience, away from the madding crowds on Patong's busy streets. $ *Average main: B950* ⊠ *52 Thaweewong Rd.* ☎ *076/370200* ⊟ *No credit cards.*

WHERE TO STAY

$ 🏨 **FunDee Boutique Hotel.** In the heart of Patong and close to all the
HOTEL action, the boutique FunDee is a good budget option for this bustling locale. **Pros:** central but quiet location; Wi-Fi; good service. **Cons:** bit of a trek to the beach (10 minutes); only one elevator; no views. $ *Rooms from: B600* ⊠ *232/3-4 PhungMuang Sai Gor Rd., Patong Kathu* ☎ *076/366780* ⊕ *www.fundee.co.th* ⊟ *No credit cards* ⌁ *36 rooms* ⊙*No meals.*

$$ 🏨 **Holiday Inn.** This is no ordinary Holiday Inn: this stylish, modern hotel
RESORT exudes the kind of sophistication that most people would never imagine
FAMILY possible from a Holiday Inn or from Patong in general. **Pros:** central location; children's programs; next to beach. **Cons:** family atmosphere not ideal for everyone; large complex. $ *Rooms from: B3400* ⊠ *52 Thaweewong Rd., Patong Beach* ☎ *076/349991 up to 2, 076/370200* ⊕ *www.phuket.holiday-inn.com* ⌁ *405 rooms* ⊙*Breakfast.*

$$ 🏨 **Impiana Resort Patong.** This hotel's chief attraction is its unbeat-
RESORT able location, right in the middle of the city yet facing the beach. **Pros:** beachfront spa; good restaurant and bar; best location in Patong. **Cons:** busy beach road traffic; check for rooms with a view; beach fills up. $ *Rooms from: B3500* ⊠ *41 Taweewong Rd.* ☎ *076/340138* ⊕ *phukethotels. impiana.com.my* ⌁ *68 rooms* ⊙*No meals.*

$ 🏨 **Red Planet Phuket Hotel.** This convenient, practical hotel is new to the
HOTEL scene and has a great location. **Pros:** immaculate; cheap; great modern amenities. **Cons:** no pool. $ *Rooms from: B700* ⊠ *56 Raj, Uthit 200 Pee Rd., Karon Beach* ⚐ *Opposite Patong Post Office* ☎ *26/135888* ⊕ *www. redplanethotels.com* ⌁ *60 rooms* ⊙*No meals* ⊟ *No credit cards.*

NIGHTLIFE

The vast majority of tourists only venture as far as Bang La Road, a walking street that is more like a carnival than something disturbingly sleazy. Children pose for photos with flamboyant and friendly transvestites; honeymooning couples people-watch from numerous beer bars along the traffic-free promenade; and everyone else simply strolls the strip, some stopping to dance or play Connect Four, Jenga, or a curiously popular nail-hammering game with friendly Thai hostesses.

There are also regularly scheduled muay thai fights at the arena on the corner of Bang La and Rat-U-Thit Songroipee roads.

The Boat Bar Disco & Cabaret. With numerous male staff, two dance performances every night, and live DJ sessions, this gay-friendly bar attracts huge crowds for fun, late-night parties. ⊠ *125/20 Rath-U-Thit Rd., Paradise Complex* ☎ *076/342206* ⊕ *www.boatbar.com.*

Simon Cabaret. With the varied nightlife in Patong, it's no surprise to find a sensational drag show here. The famous Simon Cabaret treats you to a beautifully costumed and choreographed show. There are two shows daily, at 7:30 and 9:30. ⊠ *8 Sirirach Rd.* ☎ *076/342011.*

Thaweewong Road. Patong has a reputation for its happening nightlife, and the seedy side of it is easily avoidable. Some of the more tasteful nightlife venues are on **Thaweewong Road**, including **Saxophone**, a relative of the legendary same-named Bangkok jazz and blues bar, and the neighboring **Rock City**, which plays hard rock, metallica, and other rock genres. Both bars host live music events every night. ⊠ *Thaweewong Rd.*

Whitebox Restaurant & Bar. Let's face it, in Patong it can be difficult to come by a sophisticated spot to enjoy a drink. Whitebox, designed in a white, contemporary, minimalist style, is a restaurant serving fusion Thai-European food that generally looks better than it tastes, but its rooftop bar, offering creative cocktails and tapas paired with open sea views, hits the bill. The rooftop bar opens from August to May. ⊠ *245/7 Prabaramee Rd.* ☎ *076/346271* ⊕ *www.whitebox.co.th.*

KARON BEACH

20 km (12 miles) southwest of Phuket Town.

Just south of Patong lie Karon Beach and its smaller northern counterpart, Karon Noi. Bunches of hotels, restaurants, tailors, dive operators, and gift shops line the main beach strip to serve the influx of tourists, though Karon is also home to a small community of local artists, who live and work in a cluster of huts and galleries.

GETTING HERE AND AROUND

Taxis, tuk-tuks, and motorcycles take you to and from Karon Beach. A taxi costs about B400 for the 5-km (3-mile) ride to Patong; a tuk-tuk is about B300.

EXPLORING

Getting your bearings is easy in Karon. There's a small village just off the traffic circle to your left as you enter town from Patong. For the glut of resorts, continue your journey down the beach road. You can also find quality restaurants, bars, and cheerful shops, as well as the beautiful long beach.

FAMILY **Dino Park Mini Golf.** The Flintstones-style buildings along the road in central Karon village belong to Dino Park Mini Golf. Street-side are a dinosaur-theme bar and restaurant, but the real fun is inside: 18 holes of miniature golf, featuring a swamp, a lava cave, and a real live Tyrannosaurus Rex (well, the kids will think so!). Afterward, grab a bite at the restaurant and get your orders taken by Fred and Wilma. ✉ *Karon Beach* ☎ *076/330625* 🌐 *www.dinopark.com* 🎟 *B240* 🕒 *Daily 10 am–midnight.*

Karon Beach. It's impossible not to be tempted by this long stretch of white sand and good dry-season swimming (it's great for running year-round). You will find that the beach is more open than most in Phuket—there are no trees covering the beach and precious little shade. The beach is also strewn with a few rocks; however, on the whole, it is a beautiful, clean, and open space that will appeal to those looking to get away from the more frantic pace of Patong. **Amenities:** food and drink; water sports; showers. **Best for:** snorkeling; sunset; swimming; walking. ✉ *Karon Beach.*

WHERE TO EAT

$$$$ BRAZILIAN 🍴 **El Gaucho.** Churrasco (Brazilian grilled meat) is the specialty at the Mövenpick resort's restaurant, with sunset views that make dining here a genuinely delightful experience. There's a soothing orange-and-red theme running through El Gaucho that the setting sun only serves to magnify. This is a big restaurant, with room for 100 diners, but it manages to be atmospheric, with discreet background music and friendly staff. The terrace overlooks Karon Beach, and diners can enjoy lovely views of the Andaman Sea. [$] *Average main: B900* ✉ *Karon Beach Square Movenpick Resort, Karon Beach, Karon Beach* 🌐 *www.moevenpick-hotels.com/en/asia/thailand/phuket/resort-phuket-karon-beach/restaurants/restaurants/el-gaucho/* 💳 *No credit cards.*

$$$ ECLECTIC Fodor's Choice ★ 🍴 **On the Rock.** Built, you guessed it, on a rock overlooking Karon Beach, this restaurant has great views of the water. Seafood is the specialty, but well-made Italian and traditional Thai dishes are also on the menu. It's part of the Marina Cottage hotel. Book a couple of days in advance to ensure you get a beachside table. [$] *Average main: B350* ✉ *47 Karon Rd., south end of Karon Beach* ☎ *076/330625, 076/330493 up to 5* 🌐 *www.marinaphuket.com/restaurants.html* ✍ *Reservations essential.*

WHERE TO STAY

$$$ B&B/INN 🏨 **Fantasy Hill Bungalows.** Standing on a hill between the two beach areas of Kata and Karon, these well-situated accommodations are great value. **Pros:** garden courtyard; balconies; good location. **Cons:** few amenities; not all rooms have a/c; breakfast is extra. [$] *Rooms from: B400* ✉ *8/1 Karon Rd., Karon Beach* ☎ *076/330106* ✉ *fantasyhill@hotmail.com* 💳 *No credit cards* 🛏 *18 rooms, 6 bungalows* 🍽 *No meals.*

CLOSE UP

A Festival for Health and Purity

Phuket's most important festival is its annual Vegetarian Festival, held in late September or early October. Though no one knows the precise details of the event's origins, the most common story is that it started in 1825, when a traveling Chinese opera group fell ill. The Taoist group feared that their illnesses were the result of their failure to pay proper respects to the nine Emperor Gods. After sticking to a strict vegetarian diet to honor these gods, they quickly recovered. This made quite an impression on the local villagers, and the island has celebrated a nine-day festival for good health ever since. Devotees, who wear white, abstain from eating meat, drinking alcohol, and having sex. Along with detoxing the body, the festival is meant to renew the soul—not killing animals for food is supposed to calm and purify the spirit.

The festival involves numerous temple ceremonies, parades, and fireworks.

But what most fascinates visitors are the grisly body-piercing rituals. Some devotees become mediums for warrior spirits, going into trances and mutilating their bodies to ward off demons and bring the whole community good luck. These mediums pierce their bodies (tongues and cheeks are popular choices) with all sorts of things from spears to sharpened branches to florescent light bulbs. Supposedly, the presence of the spirits within them keeps them from feeling any pain.

The events are centered on the island's five Chinese temples. Processions are held daily from morning until mid-afternoon. The Tourism Authority of Thailand office in Phuket Town can provide a list of all activities and their locations. Note that you might want to invest in earplugs—it's believed that the louder the fireworks, the more evil spirits they'll scare away.

$

HOTEL

🏨 **In On the Beach.** This place way at the north end of Karon is literally on the beach, with great sea views from many of the rooms, which are decorated in a modern, functional style. **Pros:** beach location; quiet; nice swimming pool. **Cons:** slightly removed from center of town; ground-floor rooms lack some privacy; noisy a/c. $ *Rooms from: B1750* ✉ *Moo 1, Patak Rd.* ☎ *076/398220 up to 4* ⊕ *www.karon-inonthebeach.com* ↩ *30 rooms* ❍ *Breakfast.*

$$

RESORT
FAMILY

🏨 **Le Meridien.** Between Patong and Karon Beach, this sprawling resort has more bars, cafés, and restaurants than in many small towns, while the range of outdoor diversions—everything from tennis to waterski-ing—means you never have to leave the property. **Pros:** large swimming pool; excellent activities; private beach. **Cons:** too big for some; not all rooms have a view. $ *Rooms from: B3750* ✉ *29 Soi Karon Nui, Karon, Muang, Phuket* ☎ *076/370100* ⊕ *www.lemeridienphuketbeachresort. com* ↩ *470 rooms* ❍ *Breakfast.*

$$$$

RESORT

🏨 **Marina Phuket Resort.** This surprisingly quiet option has luxury cot-tages that stretch over the lush hillside that separates Karon from Kata Beach—those higher on the hill are the quietest. **Pros:** good location; private beach and nice pool; free airport shuttle. **Cons:** difference in amenities between rooms; pool closes after sunset; no hotel loungers on beach. $\boxed{\$}$ *Rooms from: B7500* ✉ *47 Karon Rd.* ☎ *076/330493 to 5, 076/330625* ⊕ *www.marinaphuket.com* ↩ *89 rooms* ¶◯¶ *Breakfast.*

$$$
RESORT
FAMILY

📺 **Moevenpick Resort and Spa.** This resort takes great pride in its service levels, with polite, knowledgeable and informative staff;live Thai music greets you as you enter an expansive lobby lavishly decorated with Thai art. **Pros:** beachfront location; amazing facilities; close to Karon Town. **Cons:** slight package-tour feel; old structure; large complex. $\boxed{\$}$ *Rooms from: B4500* ✉ *509 Patak Rd., Karon Beach* ☎ *076/396139* ⊕ *www.moevenpick-hotels.com* ↩ *175 rooms 159 suites* ¶◯¶ *Breakfast.*

$
RESORT
FAMILY

📺 **Phuket Orchid Resort.** This resort is slightly inland, but the beach is a short walk away, and the lack of a beachfront brings the rates down considerably (which makes it very popular). **Pros:** interesting design influences including Khmer and Chinese; great pool; budget. **Cons:** not on beach; only partly renovated. $\boxed{\$}$ *Rooms from: B1500* ✉ *34 Luang Pohchuan Rd., Karon Muang, Phuket* ☎ *076/396519* ⊕ *www.katagroup.com* ↩ *525 rooms* ¶◯¶ *Breakfast.*

KATA BEACH

22 km (13 miles) southwest of Phuket Town.

Popular for its stunning white-sand beach with turquoise waters, and especially appealing to families for its serene ambience, Kata Beach is made up of its southern part, where numerous resorts are located, and its central part, which is a stone's throw from Karon to the north. There's plenty to see and do besides relaxing and taking in the beautiful landscape. Surfing is one of the main draws to Kata, from May to October, which brings with it a lively nightlife scene and a thriving restaurant base. This is a family destination as well, mainly because Kata lacks the in-your-face bar scene of Patong, and has a greater variety of restaurants and shopping than its neighbor, Karon, to the north.

GETTING HERE AND AROUND

Taxis, tuk-tuks, and motorcycles all vie for your attention to take you to and from Kata Beach. Expect to pay B500 into Phuket Town or B400 into Patong by taxi, and about B50 more for a tuk-tuk.

BEACHES

Walking around Kata is easy—just follow the beach road from north to south. Kata Yai is the main beach and located near the main shopping street of Thai Na. To the south, Kata Noi is almost exclusively taken up with the long and expensive Kata Thani Phuket Beach Resort. This is a public beach (as all beaches in Thailand are), so be sure to exercise your beach rights and soak up some sun on delightfully quiet Kata Noi if you're in the area.

Kata Beach. Of the three most popular beaches on the west coast of Phuket, this is the calmest of the lot. A shady sidewalk runs the length of the beach. Club Med dominates a large hunk of the beachfront, keeping the development frenzy to the southern end. There's also a committed group of regulars here who surf the small local breaks. This is one of the calmer beach scenes in Phuket, and so is especially good for families. **Amenities:** food and drink; water sports. **Best for:** sunset;

surfing; swimming; windsurfing. ✉ *Pakbang Rd., Laem Sai.*

WHERE TO STAY

$$$ RESORT **Boathouse by Montara.** Mom Tri's Boathouse is still a classic address on the beach at the south end of Kata, even if it's no longer its snazziest. **Pros:** excellent restaurant; cooking class available; good wine selection. **Cons:** swimming pool area a bit on the small side. [$] *Rooms from: B4900* ✉ *Kata Beach, Phuket, Karon Beach* ☎ *076/330015* 🌐 *www.boathousephuket.com* 🛏 *33 rooms, 6 villas* 🍴 *Breakfast.*

WORD OF MOUTH

"Kata Beach on Phuket is my idea of an idyllic beach and you will find plenty of nice little boutique hotels within your price range [in October]. For a big night out, Karon and Patong beaches are a quick taxi ride away and offer plenty of wild and crazy options. Kata itself is nice and relaxed by day and has plenty of little bars and restaurants." —shanek

$ B&B/INN **Kata Noi Bay Inn.** If you want to enjoy the serenity of Kata Noi without draining your wallet, here's the spot. **Pros:** quiet location; good value; small balconies. **Cons:** poor views; rooms lack amenities. [$] *Rooms from: B600* ✉ *4/16 Moo 2, Patak Rd., Kata Noi Beach, Phuket, Karon Beach* ☎ *076/333308 up to 09* 🛏 *22 rooms* 🍴 *No meals.*

$$ RESORT FAMILY **Katathani Phuket Beach Resort.** This long, sprawling lodge fronts most of the Kata Noi beach. **Pros:** peaceful beach location; six swimming pools and another four for children; spacious, well-kept grounds. **Cons:** large and rather impersonal touch; the food is average; in-room Wi-Fi extra charge. [$] *Rooms from: B3400* ✉ *14 Kata Noi Rd., Karon, Muang, Phuket, Karon Beach* ☎ *076/330124 up to 6* 🌐 *www.katathani.com* 🛏 *479 rooms* 🍴 *No meals.*

$$$ RESORT **Sawasdee Village.** A few minutes' walk from Kata beach, this resort comprises a spacious garden with four large swimming pools, lush greenery, beautiful stone-carved fountains, and a complex of villas and rooms designed and decorated in a Thai -Moroccan style. **Pros:** attentive staff; good dining. **Cons:** 10 minutes from Kata Beach; rooms on the small side; mosquitoes. [$] *Rooms from: B4000* ✉ *38 Katekwan Rd.* ☎ *076/330870 up to 1* 🌐 *www.phuketsawasdee.com* 💳 *No credit cards* 🛏 *40 rooms* 🍴 *Some meals.*

$ HOTEL **Villareal Heights.** Owners Phil and Jo have transformed Villareal Heights from a good boutique hotel into an exceptional one, mainly because of the enthusiastic service. **Pros:** great management; top activity advice; nice views from higher floors. **Cons:** pool shared with hotel next door; location a little out of the way; no elevator. [$] *Rooms from: B1000* ✉ *214/14 Patak Rd., Suksan Pl., Tambon Karon* ☎ *086/0320263* 🌐 *www.villareal-heights.com* 💳 *No credit cards* 🛏 *19 rooms.*

NAI HARN

18 km (11 miles) southwest of Phuket Town.

Less busy than other nearby beaches and more popular among locals, Nai Harn offers a small but interesting choice of accommodations and nearby attractions, such as Nai Harn lake and viewpoints such as the Phromthem Cape, as well as simple but authentic restaurants.

GETTING HERE AND AROUND

This is the southernmost beach on Phuket. You can get here from Phuket Town or along the coastal road through Kata, Karon, and Patong. Taxis, tuk-tuks, and motorcycles will all take you to and from Nai Harn; a taxi to or from Phuket Town should be about B550, and it costs B800 to get to the airport.

EXPLORING

Nai Harn. South of Kata Beach the road cuts inland across the hills before it drops into yet another beautiful bay, Nai Harn. On the north side of the bay is the gleaming-white Royal Meridien Phuket Yacht Club. On the south side is a nice little beach, removed for now from the tailors and cheap restaurants that have sprung up at the entrance to the Royal Meridien. ⊠ *Nai Harn.*

Phromthep Cape. From the top of the cliff at Phromthep Cape, the southernmost point on Koh Phuket, you're treated to a fantastic, panoramic view of Nai Harn Bay, the coastline, and a few outlying islands. At sunset you can share the view with swarms of others who pour forth from tour buses to view the same sight. If you're driving, arrive early if you want a parking spot. There's a lighthouse atop the point. ⊠ *Nai Harn.*

WHERE TO EAT AND STAY

$
THAI
✕ Phromthep Cape Restaurant. Although it doesn't look like much from the Phromthep Cape parking lot, views from the tables out back are hard to beat. Just slightly down the hill from the lighthouse, this place enjoys unobstructed perspectives of the cape and coastline. Plus, you get lower prices and better views than at most other places on the island that play up their panoramas. The restaurant serves Thai food, specializing in fresh seafood, and some western fare. $ *Average main: B180* ⊠ *94/6 Moo 6, Rawai Beach* ☎ *076/288656, 076/288084* ⊕ *www.phuketdir.com/phromthepcaperest.*

$$$$
HOTEL
⌂ Tha Nai Harn Hotel. This place used to be home to the annual King's Cup Regatta—now the only yachts here exist as decorative carvings on the walls, but the place is still every inch a luxury destination. **Pros:** modern Thai furnishings; great views; on a lovely beach. **Cons:** isolated location; needs some modernizing. $ *Rooms from: B7000* ⊠ *Nai Harn Beach, Phuket 23/3 Moo 1, Vises Rd.* ☎ *076/380200* ▭ *No credit cards* ⌁ *64 rooms, 25 suites* ⦿ *No meals.*

CAPE YAMU

21km (13 miles) east of Phuket Town

The headland at Yamu is an isolated part of Phuket and, because of the isolation, is particularly quiet and exclusive. There is no beach here, but the rocky point hosts some of Phuket's most exclusive properties. Boats at the jetty whisk travelers off to beach spots on Phuket and nearby islands. There are a few local villages and several high-end gated communities.

GETTING HERE AND AROUND

This is an isolated cape on Phuket's eastern side. You can get here from Phuket Town or along the main arterial roads from Phuket Airport or any of Phuket's main destinations. Taxis are the best choice to get here, but minivans serve the destination from the airport; a taxi to or from Phuket Town should be about B700; from Patong it will cost about B800, and it costs B800 to get to the airport.

WHERE TO EAT AND STAY

$$$$ INTERNATIONAL Fodor's Choice ★ 🍴 **Breeze.** Situated on top of the cape, overlooking the isolated bay, Breeze is a strong contender for the finest restaurant in this part of Phuket. The sea breeze (hence the name) blows gently through the open dining area, giving it a romantic and natural ambience. The views over the bay further enhance the dining experience. The menu is limited to a few specialties, taken from a diverse international selection, including braised pork shoulder, duck breast, and salmon, but all the food produced is of a high standard. The roasted scallops are particularly worth sampling. *[$] Average main: B750 ✉ Luem Yamu, Phuket ✈ Atop the farthest part of the cape, just outside the Point Yamu hotel ☎ 81/271–2320 🌐 www.breezecapeyamu.com 💳 No credit cards.*

$$$$ HOTEL FAMILY Fodor's Choice ★ 🏨 **Point Yamu by COMO.** From the moment you enter the vast, open lobby, the care that has gone into the intricate design of this stunningly situated hotel is apparent. **Pros:** playful minimalist design; luxury rooms, most with plunge pools; service levels are extraordinary. **Cons:** isolated. *[$] Rooms from: B16000 ✉ 225 Moo 7, Paklok, Talang, Thalang ☎ 76/360100 🌐 www.comohotels.com 🛏 106 rooms 🍽 Breakfast.*

$$$ HOTEL Fodor's Choice ★ 🏨 **Thanyapura Sports Hotel and Mind Center.** Unusual in its concept and style, Thanyapura is a paradise for sporty people of all ages and levels as well as professional athletes (including Olympic gold medalists), who regularly come here from around the world to train in a pristine, relaxing environment with pacifying mountain views. **Pros:** highly professional staff; unbeatable sports facilities; excellent spa. **Cons:** remote location; quiet from 10 pm; a bit of a mishmash between hotel and sports resort. *[$] Rooms from: B3250 ✉ 120/1 Moo 7 Thepkasattri Rd., Thepkasattri, Thalang ☎ 076/336000 🌐 www.thanyapura.com 💳 No credit cards 🛏 77 rooms at sports hotel, 38 rooms at retreat 🍽 Breakfast.*

CHALONG

11 km (7 miles) south of Phuket Town.

The waters in horseshoe-shape Chalong Bay are usually calm, as the entrance is guarded by Koh Lone and Koh Hae. It's not a scenic stop in itself—it's more of a working port than a beach. The reason to come is to see Wat Chalong. From the jetty you can charter boats or book one-day or half-day trips to Koh Hae, Koh Lone, and other nearby islands for snorkeling, diving, parasailing, and other activities (B750–B1,600).

Ao Chalong is a wide-open bay that is most frequently used as a jumping-off point for surrounding islands. Head for the pier where you can catch ferries to nearby islands. One road takes you from the northern end to the southern end of the bay.

GETTING HERE AND AROUND

Chalong Bay is an easy 11-km (7-mile) ride from Phuket Town. Taxis, tuk-tuks, and motorcycles will all take you here.

EXPLORING

Wat Chalong. Not far from Chalong Bay you can find Wat Chalong, the largest and most famous of Phuket's Buddhist temples. It enshrines gilt statues of two revered monks who helped quell an 1876 Chinese rebellion. They're wrapped in brilliant saffron robes. Wats are generally open during daylight hours, and you can show up at 5 pm to see the resident monks pray. ✉ *Chalong.*

WHERE TO EAT

$$ SEAFOOD 🍴 **Kan Eang at Pier.** Grab a palm-shaded table next to the seawall and order some delicious grilled fish. Be sure that your waiter understands whether you want yours served *phet* (spicy hot) or *mai phet* (not spicy). Succulent and sweet crabs should be a part of any meal here. It's right on the waterfront to the south of the pier. [$] *Average main: B200* ✉ *44/1 Viset Rd.* ☎ *076/381212.*

$ CAFÉ 🍴 **Sentai Coffee and Restaurant.** With a cozy living-room feel, decor including vintage items such as an antique gramophone and a sewing machine, and good freshly ground coffee and delicious desserts, Sentai is the ideal place for an afternoon stopover to recharge your batteries. If you want more than sugar and caffeine, order a traditional Thai dish or a recipe closer to home from their food menu. [$] *Average main: B100* ✉ *36/9 Moo 9 Choafa Rd.* ☎ *081/797–8327* 💳 *No credit cards.*

$$$ ECLECTIC 🍴 **Vset.** For fine dining, look no further: award-winning chef Ronnie Macuja has created a menu based on simplicity and exquisite style, serving picture-perfect and flavorsome western-fusion food. The decor is contemporary and welcoming, and the location pleasant. The cognac-flamed lobster bisque with micro greens is a great way to start your feast, followed by an interesting rendition of the catch of the day or the equally popular steak with mushroom cappuccino. [$] *Average main: B400* ✉ *By Chalong Pier* ☎ *076/381159* 💳 *No credit cards.*

WHERE TO STAY

$$$$ RESORT Fodor's Choice ★ 🏨 **Sri panwa.** Perfectly situated on a lush headland, this beautifully designed resort has a cool, contemporary vibe that makes it popular with visiting celebrities seeking luxurious seclusion. **Pros:** stunning, 360-degree ocean views; truly exceptional service from young, friendly staff; one of the world's best rooftop bars. **Cons:** gradient might be tricky for those with mobility problems. [$] *Rooms from: B28,000* ✉ *88 Moo 8, Sakdidej Rd., Vichit, Muang* ☎ *76/371000* 🌐 *www.sripanwa.com* 🛏 *52 villas* 🍽 *No meals.*

THE ANDAMAN COAST

The Andaman Coast stretches from Ranong Province, bordering Myanmar (Burma) to the north, to Satun Province, flanking Malaysia to the south. Along this shore are hundreds of islands and thousands of beaches. Because of their proximity to Phuket, Phang Nga and Krabi provinces are the two most appealing destinations on the Andaman Coast.

Phang Nga Bay National Park is Phang Nga's most heralded attraction, drawing thousands of day-trippers from Phuket. There are dozens of little islands to explore, as well as offshore caves and startling karst formations rising out of the sea. Most visitors make an obligatory stop at Phing Kan Island, made famous by the James Bond movie *The Man with the Golden Gun.*

The Similan and Surin islands national parks are well known to scuba divers for their crystalline waters and abundant marine life. You can camp or stay in a national park bungalow on either of the islands; no commercial lodging is available in either park. Many divers opt to stay on live-aboard ships departing from Phuket or Khao Lak.

Khao Lak Lamru National Park attracts nature lovers, while the beaches along this coast draw beachgoers who want a vibe more tranquil than Phuket has to offer. Travelers looking for even greater seclusion head to the Koh Yao Islands, which have cultural tours and homestays that provide insight into southern Thai lifestyles.

Krabi Province lies to the east of Phuket. Its capital, Krabi Town, sits on the northeastern shore of Phuket Bay. Once a favorite harbor for smugglers bringing in alcohol and tobacco from Malaysia, the town has been transformed into a gateway to the nearby islands. Ao Nang, a short distance from Krabi Town, has evolved into a quaint beach town. Ao Nang and nearby Noppharat Thara exist simply to cater to tourists, with restaurants and shopping for every taste. Ao Nang is a more convenient base of operations than Krabi Town for exploring nearby islands and beaches. Longtail boats and ferries depart from Ao Nang for Koh Phi Phi, Koh Lanta, Nang Cape, and the multitude of smaller islands in eastern Phang Nga Bay.

The islands of Koh Phi Phi were once idyllic retreats, with secret silver-sand coves, unspoiled stretches of shoreline, and limestone cliffs dropping precipitously into the sea. After it was portrayed in the film *The Beach* (2000), Phi Phi became a hot (overcrowded) property. The beaches on Phi Phi are still stunning and are some of the most accessible in Thailand. Luxury resorts have spread themselves across the sands here and a multitude of restaurants, bars, and smaller guesthouses fill the demand for lodging. Many of the budget accommodations that dominated the island for years have upgraded their facilities (and their prices) in a hit-and-miss process of development—some have achieved grandeur, or class, others are tacky and overpriced for what they offer. It appears that unchecked development is the norm. The buildings are creeping higher each year, and the resorts have generally become more high-end; but beware, the terms "resort" and "deluxe" are used liberally, so do not rely too much on impressions created by artful photographs in websites.

Farther south, more adventurous travelers are discovering the relative serenity of Krabi's "hidden" gem, Koh Lanta. It's one of the largest islands in Thailand, with beautiful beaches, accommodations for budget travelers, and a few activities such as elephant-trekking in the jungle.

PHANG NGA BAY NATIONAL MARINE PARK

100 km (62 miles) north of Phuket, 93 km (56 miles) northwest of Krabi.

The looming limestone karsts are the most spectacular feature of Phang Nga Bay, made famous in movies and a thousand picture postcards.

GETTING HERE AND AROUND

Many travel agencies in Phuket offer half-day tours of the area, and this is the way most travelers see the park. Another option is to take a bus heading north from Phuket Town (B120) to one of two inlets near the town of Phang Nga, where you can hire a longtail boat and explore at your own pace, but unless you speak Thai or are intrepid, this is likely to be more of a hassle than it's worth. At the western inlet, you can rent a boat for about B1,800 for two hours. The second inlet sees fewer foreign tourists, so the prices are better—about B1,200 for three hours. The bay can also be explored via tour boat, speedboat, or sea canoe. Most tourists don't arrive from Phuket until 11 am, so if you get into the bay earlier, you can explore it in solitude. To get an early start, you may want to stay overnight in the area. Be sure to take time to appreciate the sunsets, which are particularly beautiful on the island of **Koh Mak**.

EXPLORING

From stunning monoliths that rise from the sea to the secluded, crystal clear bays, Phang Nga Bay is a must-see for any nature lover. The only way to visit is by boat. Tours (B1,000 to B3,000) can be arranged through your hotel or resort if you're staying in the area.

There are several key sights around Phang Nga Bay. The island of **Koh Panyi** has a Muslim fishing village consisting of houses built on stilts. Restaurants are no bargain, tripling their prices for tourists. **Koh Phing Kan,** now known locally as James Bond Island, is a popular tour destination. The island of **Koh Tapu** resembles a nail driven into the sea. **Kao Kien** has overhanging cliffs covered with primitive paintings of elephants, fish, and crabs. Many are thought to be at least 3,500 years old.

James Bond Island. Named for tourist purposes after the 1974 Bond film *The Man With The Golden Gun* starring Roger Moore as 007, and traditionally known as Koh Phing Kan, this natural attraction has unfortunately fallen victim to greedy tour operators and merchants, losing the beauty that made it famous. Visiting this island (with a stopover often not longer than half an hour) usually involves a day trip that involves stops to the equally jaded Koh Panyee island, known for its charming Muslim gypsy fishing village, a lunch break, and other stops such as to the Monkey Caves. The water in this zone is visibly polluted, the landscape can easily be beat by a multitude of other stunning landscapes around Thailand's south, and the throng of other tourists can be as buzzy for some as unbearable for others. ⊠ *Phang Nga Bay.*

Koh Panyee. The island of Koh Panyee has a Muslim fishing village with houses built on stilts. The whole village backs onto a looming limestone cliff, giving it some protection from Mother Nature. The village is an interesting study in marine sustainability, but it does have the feel of a

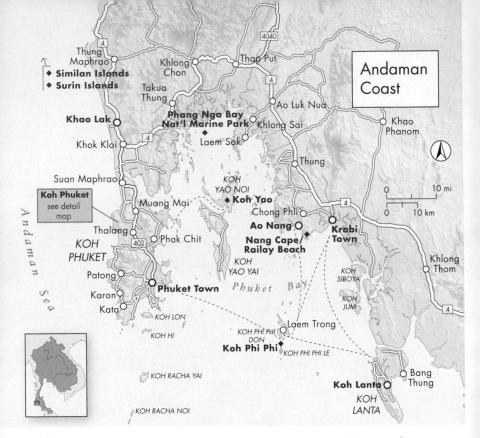

Andaman Coast

Thung Maphrao

◆ **Similan Islands**
◆ **Surin Islands**

Khao Lak

Khok Kloi

Suan Maphrao

Koh Phuket
see detail map

Thalang

KOH PHUKET

Patong

Karon

Kata

KOH LON

KOH HI

Khlong Chon

Takua Thung

Phang Nga Bay Nat'l Marine Park

Muang Mai

402

Phak Chit

Thap Put

4040

Ao Luk Nua

Khlong Sai

Khao Phanom

◆ Laem Sak

Thung

KOH YAO NOI

◆ **Koh Yao**

Chong Phli

Ao Nang

Nang Cape/ Railay Beach

Krabi Town

KOH YAO YAI

Phuket Bay

KOH SIBOYA

Khlong Thom

KOH JUM

Laem Trong

KOH PHI PHI DON

Koh Phi Phi

KOH PHI PHI LE

KOH RACHA YAI

Phuket Town

Andaman Sea

Koh Lanta

Bang Thung

KOH LANTA

KOH RACHA NOI

0   10 mi

0   10 km

tourist trap. Restaurants are no bargain, tripling their prices for tourists. ⊠ *Phang Nga Bay.*

Tham Lot Cave. Tham Lot is a large, limestone, stalactite-studded cave that has an opening large enough for boats to pass through. It can be explored by canoe or an inflatable boat, floating along seawater to enjoy the sight of impressive stalactites and stalagmites, some as long as 100 meters. No guide required. ⊠ *Tarnboke Koranee National Park, Ao Luk District, Phang Nga Bay.*

Fodor's Choice
★

Wat Tham Cave. The Buddha Cave, or fully named in Thai as Wat Tham Suwan Khuha, is a large, impressive cavern with a temple gate, filled with a broad and beautiful variety of Buddha statues placed in various spots, inspiring tourists to stop and relax wherever feels right to them. It's mostly known for its giant gold statue of a reclining Buddha, before which a stage is set where faithful visitors can light incense and pray under his gaze. Before or after your uphill walk through the cave, you may get to meet the many gray monkeys jumping down from the top of the hill and ropy trees to be fed, so have some peanuts, bananas, or coconut handy if you want to interact with them. There are several tourist stalls around selling snacks and other items such as jewelry and souvenirs. ⊠ *6 miles outside Phang Nga, Phang Nga Bay.*

WHERE TO STAY

$$$$ RESORT Fodor's Choice ★ 🏨 **Aleenta Resort and Spa Phan-Nga.** Stylish design, a romantic atmosphere, and a beautiful beach contribute to the Aleenta experience. **Pros:** great sunset views from some suites; quiet, relaxing location. **Cons:** fills up early in high season; not all rooms have sea views. [$] *Rooms from: B6300* ✉ *33 Moo 5, Khokkloy, Phang Nga, Phang Nga Bay* ☎ *066/25148112* 🌐 *www.aleenta.com* 🛏 *15 suites and villas* 🍴 *Breakfast.*

$ RESORT FAMILY 🏨 **Andaman Princess Resort and Spa.** The centerpiece here is an enormous pool with a long bridge over it, surrounded by endless manicured lawns. **Pros:** leisurely atmosphere; nice restaurant; prime location. **Cons:** needs renovation; a bit pricey for what you get. [$] *Rooms from: B1600* ✉ *Phang Nga Bay* ☎ *076/592222 up to 9* 🌐 *www.andamanprincessresort.com* 💳 *No credit cards* 🛏 *82 rooms* 🍴 *Breakfast.*

$ B&B/INN 🏨 **Ao Phang Nga National Park.** In addition to the camping grounds (where you can rent tents), the park has a few well-built bungalows within its grounds. **Pros:** excellent location; good base for exploring the area; decent service. **Cons:** some rooms are basic; lack of amenities; often booked up. [$] *Rooms from: B100* ✉ *80 Ban Tha Dan, Koh Panyi, Phang Nga Bay* ☎ *025/620760 for reservations* 💳 *No credit cards* 🛏 *15 bungalows.*

$$$$ RESORT FAMILY 🏨 **Golden Buddha Beach Resort.** This eco-resort has its own stunning 10-km (6-mile) beach where the endangered giant leatherback turtle nests, beautiful beachfront and beach-adjacent homes, a spa offering a relaxing range of treatments, yoga classes (it's a prime yoga retreat destination), and a desert-island feel. **Pros:** wonderful beach; helpful, friendly staff; ideal for nature lovers. **Cons:** no kitchen in-house; remote; no a/c. [$] *Rooms from: B9800* ✉ *131 Moo 2, Ko Phra Thong* ☎ *081/919–5228* 🌐 *www.goldenbuddharesort.com* 💳 *No credit cards* 🛏 *25 homes* 🍴 *No meals.*

KOH YAO

30 mins by boat from Bangrong Pier, Phuket, or 45 mins by boat from Chaofa Pier, Krabi.

Koh Yao Noi is the most developed of this pair of islands, Noi (little) and Yai (large), but it is stills worlds away from the development on Phuket and other parts of the Andaman. The focus of the island is nature, and activities such as eco-projects, kayaking, snorkeling, and diving are the primary focus of travelers who venture to the shores.

GETTING HERE AND AROUND

Public ferry is the easiest, most scenic, and cheapest way to get to and from Koh Yao Noi. Most of the tourist developments can be found on Koh Yao Noi. Ferries from Bangrong Pier to the north of Phuket leave regularly throughout the day and cost B150 per person. You can also travel from Chaofa Pier in Krabi for B160.

EXPLORING

Koh Yao Yai and Koh Yao Noi are the two large islands in the center of Phang Nga Bay. Both are quiet, peaceful places, fringed with sandy beaches and clear water.

A visit to Koh Yao will allow you to experience the local culture and customs while exploring the beauty of the islands (kayaks and mountain bikes are popular transportation options). The Ecotourism Club provides homestays if you really want the full experience of the islands; otherwise, most resorts provide day tours or information for self-guided exploration.

Koh Yao Noi Ecotourism Club. Most inhabitants of the islands still make their living by traditional means such as fishing, rubber tapping, and batik painting. Considering their size and proximity to Phuket and Krabi, it's surprising how little development these islands have seen. During the 1990s many tourists began to discover the islands and the impact was negative. To reduce the impact on the land and their culture, the villagers residing on Koh Yao organized the "Koh Yao Noi Ecotourism Club" to regulate growth on the islands. They've certainly been successful—they even picked up an award for tourism development sponsored by Conservation International. ✉ *Phuket.*

WHERE TO STAY

$$$ B&B/INN 🏨 **Koh Yao Homestay.** Organized by a community of Koh Yao residents who invite tourists to experience their way of life, the community provides visitors with lodging in their own homes, meals (consisting primarily of fish caught by village fishermen), and knowledge about local customs. **Pros:** up-close cultural experience; ecotourism at its best; well organized. **Cons:** homestay accommodations don't suit everyone; usually very basic. [$] *Rooms from: B6500* ✉ *Baan Laem Sai, Koh Yao Noi, Phang Nga* ☎ *089/9703384* 🌐 *www.kohyaohomestay.com* 💳 *No credit cards* 🛏 *10 rooms* 🍴 *All meals.*

$$$$ RESORT Fodor's Choice ★ 🏨 **Koyao Island Resort.** Koyao Island Resort has one of the best views among beach resorts in Thailand; from east-facing Haad Pa Sai you can take in a panoramic vista of a string of magnificent islands. **Pros:** captivating views of nearby islands; attentive service; many activities. **Cons:** not family oriented; open air can make you more mosquito accessible; beach itself could be better. [$] *Rooms from: B6500* ✉ *24/2 Koh Yao Noi, Phang Nga* ☎ *076/597474 up to 76* 🌐 *www.koyao.com* 🛏 *15 villas* 🍴 *Breakfast.*

KHAO LAK

80 km (50 miles) north of Phuket.

Khao Lak is a place to go to if you want a relaxed, low-key holiday. It just cuts the right side of developed to offer all the amenities you might want, without the overdevelopment characteristic of much of the Andaman coastline.

GETTING HERE AND AROUND

VIP and first-class buses leave for Khao Lak from Bangkok's Southern Bus Terminal each evening around 6 or 7 pm. The journey takes at least 12 hours. There's also regular bus service here from other beach areas. The journey to Phuket takes about two hours and costs around B200 (by taxi expect to pay anywhere between B1,600 and B2,000). There's no direct bus from Phuket to Khao Lak, but you can take a local bus bound for Ranong, Surat Thani, or Kuraburi and ask to get dropped off in Khao Lak.

The usual array of motorcycles, songthaews, and taxis will shuttle you around the area.

EXPLORING

Khao Lak Beach. Khao Lak Beach proper lies to the south of the national park, and most resorts and dive operators purporting to hail from Khao Lak actually line the coasts of Nang Thong, Bang Niang, Khuk Khak, and Bang Sak beaches to the north. As a result of Khao Lak's booming popularity, many properties stay open during the low season; however, Khao Lak is best visited near or during the high and dry season (November to May) when you can be sure that all businesses are in full operation. **Amenities:** food and drink; showers; toilets; water sports. **Best for:** sunset; swimming; walking; surfing. ✉ *Thanon Phet Kasem.*

Khao Lak Lamru National Marine Park. Khao Lak Lamru National Marine Park's rolling green hills and abundant wildlife are a primary attraction. The park grounds cover more than 325 square km (125 square miles) from the sea to the mountains, including a secluded sandy beach and several waterfalls. The park preserves some pristine tropical evergreen forest that is often supplanted in the south by fruit and rubber trees. Wildlife includes wild pigs, barking deer, macaques, and reticulated pythons. Walking trails lead to waterfalls with swimmable pools. Three rudimentary cabins are available for overnight stays, as are tent rentals for visitors who do not have their own. The park headquarters, on the road from Khao Lak Beach to Khao Lak town, provides information about exploring or staying in the park. ☎ *025/794842, 025/578–0529 National Park Division in Bangkok* 🌐 *www.dnp.go.th.*

WHERE TO EAT

$ THAI 🍴 **Hill Tribes Restaurant.** Allow your taste buds to celebrate this loving tribute to northern Thai cuisine. The chefs here specialize in seafood and fish dishes made according to traditional recipes from the northern hill tribes folk, which provide a pleasant change from southern fare. Try the tempura of banana flowers, the sizzling seafood hot plate, or the prawns fried with herbs in a red-whisky sauce, and don't miss out on the mouthwatering sticky rice with coconut cream and ripe mango for dessert. [$] *Average main: B145* ✉ *Bangniang, Phetchkasem Rd. 13/22* ☎ *086/283–0933* 🌐 *www.hilltribe-restaurant.com* 💳 *No credit cards.*

$ THAI 🍴 **Namwa Restaurant.** Unassuming and earthy, Namwa delivers on all fronts: sumptuous food with generous portions, great service, and a bill that will keep you smiling all night. Namwa is easy to miss, and there is nothing fancy to see, but the food is cooked with care and love, and definitely delivers flavor. The traditional Thai favorites are all here, but added are great seafood dishes, served from fresh catch. [$] *Average main: B150* ✉ *Khao Lak* ☎ *81/0790191* 💳 *No credit cards.*

$ THAI FAMILY 🍴 **Smile.** Showing a special awareness to diners with food allergies and diabetes and offering a menu especially designed for vegetarians and vegans, this successful restaurant serves delicious Thai curries, a wonderful choice of appetizers, and salads and stir-fries made with an interesting French twist. $ *Average main: B200* ⊠ *29/31 Phetkasem Rd., Phangnga* ☎ *083/391–2600* ▬ *No credit cards.*

$ ✕ **Smoh Ruer Restaurant.** A few minutes' tuk-tuk ride north from the busy
THAI part of town, Smoh Ruer is a high-end (in food, not price) local eatery occasionally chanced upon by a few lucky travelers. There's nothing chancy about the food, however. Prepared in the local Khao Lak style, dishes include a mightily spicy wild-boar red curry, perfectly cooked prawns fried in sesame oil on a bed of rice noodles and celery, and the mellow egg-fried morning glory in oyster sauce. $ *Average main: B160* ⊠ *12/2 M.6 T.Khukkak* ☎ *089/288–9889, 089/875–9018* ▬ *No credit cards.*

WHERE TO STAY

$ 🏨 **Baan Krating.** Occupying a wonderful spot on a cliff above a beach,
RESORT this boutique resort boasts a beautiful view and a path down to the shore that travels within Khao Lak Lamru National Marine Park. **Pros:** relaxed atmosphere; captivating views; clean rooms. **Cons:** spartan accommodations; slightly worn; a bit of a trek to beach. $ *Rooms from: B1100* ⊠ *28 Khao Lak, Takuapa, Phang Nga* ☎ *076/485188 up to 9* ⊕ *www.baankrating.com* ⤻ *24 cottages* ⦿ *No meals.*

$ 🏨 **Centara Seaview Resort and Spa.** The octagonal villas with high ceilings,
RESORT four-poster beds, and whirlpool tubs epitomize the luxury available to
FAMILY guests. **Pros:** tiered pool; luxurious feel; friendly staff. **Cons:** not the best views; somewhat costly; beach not ideal. $ *Rooms from: B1700* ⊠ *18/1 Moo 7, Petchkasem Rd., Khuk Khak* ☎ *076/429800* ⊕ *www. centarahotelsresorts.com* ▬ *No credit cards* ⤻ *197 rooms* ⦿ *Breakfast.*

$ 🏨 **Green Beach Resort.** Standard clapboard bungalows have wooden
RESORT floors, rattan walls, and bamboo furniture. **Pros:** inexpensive; beachfront. **Cons:** slightly tacky exterior; bland feeling. $ *Rooms from: B1600* ⊠ *13/51 Moo 7, Haad Nangtong, Khuk Khak* ☎ *076/420046* ⊕ *www.khaolakgreenbeachresort.com* ⊙ *Closed May–Nov.* ⤻ *40 bungalows* ⦿ *No meals.*

$$$ 🏨 **La Flora.** This is a lovely, service-oriented boutique resort where rooms
RESORT are fashionably decorated in a modern Asian aesthetic, and most have
Fodor'sChoice balconies or daybeds. **Pros:** tasteful, spacious rooms; stunning villas;
★ lovely beach with deep waters. **Cons:** families may find it a little isolated; dining is not outstanding; rooftop bar understaffed. $ *Rooms from: B4400* ⊠ *59/1 Moo 5, Khuk Khak, Phang Nga* ☎ *076/428000, 026/798828* ⊕ *www.lafloraresort.com* ⤻ *125 rooms, 13 villas* ⦿ *Breakfast.*

$$ 🏨 **Mukdara Beach Resort.** This sumptuous resort has been designed in
RESORT classical Thai style, with a great deal of emphasis on wood and traditional craftsmanship. **Pros:** villas on beach; tasteful Thai furnishings; luxurious. **Cons:** large resort, so not intimate; layout of some rooms is odd. $ *Rooms from: B2800* ⊠ *26/14 Moo 7, Thanon Khuk Khak, Takuapa, Phang Nga* ☎ *076/429999* ⊕ *www.mukdarabeach.com* ⤻ *70 rooms, 64 villas, 7 suites* ⦿ *Breakfast.*

$ 🏨 **Nang Thong Bay Resort.** The majority of rooms here are surprisingly
RESORT inexpensive cottages that face the beach and are surrounded by well-maintained gardens. **Pros:** good value; well located; new pool. **Cons:** disappointing restaurant; service a little amiss. $ *Rooms from: B1000*

✉ *Khao Lak, Takuapa, Phang Nga* ☎ *076/485088 up to 89* 🌐 *www.nangthong.com* 🛏 *82 rooms* 🍴 *No meals.*

$$$$ RESORT FAMILY 🏨 **Pullman Khao Lak Beach & Spa Resort.** The Pullman is on an isolated 12-km (7-mile) stretch of beach to the north of Khao Lak town. **Pros:** fun for kids; nice spa facilities; luxurious elegance. **Cons:** service is slack; not for romantic getaways; slightly commercial feel. [$] *Rooms from: B8000* ✉ *9/9 Moo 1, Tambol Kuk Kak, Amphur Takua Pa, Phang Nga* ☎ *076/427500* 🌐 *www.pullmankhoalak.com* 🛏 *243 rooms* 🍴 *No meals.*

$$$$ RESORT 🏨 **The Sarojin.** This exquisite boutique resort's smaller size makes it more intimate and exclusive than nearby megaresorts. **Pros:** intimate and exclusive; cooking classes; unique aesthetics. **Cons:** price a bit higher than at comparable resorts. [$] *Rooms from: B7150* ✉ *60 Moo 2, Khuk Khak, Takuapa, Phang Nga* ☎ *076/427900 up to 07* 🌐 *www.sarojin.com* 🛏 *56 rooms* 🍴 *No meals.*

SIMILAN ISLANDS

70 km (45 miles) or 1½ hours by boat from Thaplamu Pier.

Fodor's Choice ★ The Similan Islands are synonymous with two things: beautiful, unspoiled beaches and diving in crystal-blue waters. There are nine islands in this archipelago, each with its own number and name. Huge boulders adorn the white, sandy beaches and beneath the waters lies some of the world's best diving.

GETTING HERE AND AROUND

BOAT TRAVEL Speedboats to Similan National Park leave from Thap Lamu Pier in the Tai Muang District just south of Khao Lak beach at 8:30 am when the park is open to the public (November to May). Once you reach Koh Similan, motorboats will take you to other islands for between B250 and B600, depending on distance.

You can also take a private tour boat from Thap Lamu Pier for around B2,000 per person. The tour boat departs from Thap Lamu at 8 am daily and returns at 2 pm. Direct tickets, booked through the national parks, cost B2,000; however, private tours are a better value.

EXPLORING

Jack's Similan. Tour groups, such as Jack's Similan, have their own smaller tents set up in this area and rent them out for the same fee charged by the national park. There are also overnight packages, which include tours of the islands, camping, and food. ✉ *79/36 Moo 5 Tablamu* ☎ *076/443205* 🌐 *www.jacksimilan.com.*

Koh Miang. Koh Miang, where the park headquarters is located, has bungalows with 24-hour electricity and even some with air-conditioning; some bungalows have ocean views as well. Beachside camping is also available on Koh Miang (the park rents out roomy tents, large enough to stand in, which have two camping cots). Koh Similan has no bungalows, but has the same large tents for rent, as well as an area for visitors to set up their own tents. If you choose to visit the island to stay at the park, expect to pay B2,500 to B3,000 for a round-trip boat transfer. Once on the island, you can hire a longtail boat to explore the other islands. ■ **TIP→ The park is extremely popular with Thais, so**

5

book well in advance if you're planning a visit during a Thai holiday. The islands are more enjoyable, and more explorable, if visited mid-week. The park entrance fee is B500 per visit. Note that the islands are normally closed to visitors from mid-May until early November. ☎ 076/595045 *for campsite reservations,* 02/562–0760 *for bungalow reservations* ⊕ *www.dnp.go.th.*

Mu Koh Similan. The Mu (group) Koh Similan National Marine Park consists of the nine Similan Islands, as well as Koh Tachai and Koh Bon, which are farther north. The diving around the Similan Islands is world-class, with visibility of up to 120 feet; abundant blue, green, and purple coral; and rare marine life, such as the whale shark, the world's largest fish. In addition to sparkling, crystal clear water, the Similan Islands also have ultrafine, powdery white-sand beaches and lush tropical forests. The National Park Service allows visitors to stay on the beaches of Koh Miang (Island 4) and Koh Similan (Island 8). ■ TIP➜ If you plan to dive, contact a dive operator in Phuket or Khao Lak; there are no dive shops on the islands, though snorkeling gear is available for rent from the ranger stations. .

SURIN ISLANDS

60 km (37 miles) or 2 hours by boat from Kuraburi Pier.

Sixty kilometers (37 miles) off the west coast of Phang Nga, the five Surin Islands are special for their diving and fishing. The national park status has stopped all development here and this is a strong draw for tourists to come and see an unspoiled part of Thailand. There is a community of "sea gypsies" living here, who have become a slight tourist attraction in themselves.

GETTING HERE AND AROUND

Khuraburi Pier, north of Khao Lak beach, is the departure point for boats to the Surin Islands, and can be reached by any bus going to or from Ranong (about B200 from Phuket or Krabi). Songthaews will take you to the pier, approximately 9 km (5½ miles) out of town. Expect to pay B1,000 and up for boat trips to the various islands. Negotiating prices is not really an option here. An easier option is to book a trip through your resort. They will arrange your transportation to Khuraburi and your boat ticket.

EXPLORING

On the Surin islands the visibility and diversity of marine life is spectacular, and this is arguably the most unspoiled Thai island retreat, owing to its remote location and low number of visitors. Note that the park is normally closed during the rainy season (June to November).

Surin Islands. Mu Koh Surin National Marine Park is a remote island paradise practically unknown to anyone other than adventurous scuba divers and Thais. Five islands make up the national park, each with sea turtles, varieties of sharks, and plentiful coral. If you get tired of sun and sea, there are several hiking trails that lead to waterfalls and a sea gypsy village. ⊠ *Phang Nga Bay.*

Tropical forest meets powdery white sand on the Similan Islands.

WHERE TO STAY

$ RENTAL 🏨 **Koh Surin Nua.** There are 10 recently built, comfortable, fan-cooled, wooden huts on Koh Surin Nua (B2,000), and tent camping is allowed at a site that has decent facilities, including toilets and showers. [$] *Rooms from:* ☎ *02/562–0760 inquiries and bungalow reservations, 076/491378* 🌐 *www.dnp.go.th* 💳 *No credit cards* 🛏 *10 bungalows* 🍴 *No meals.*

KRABI

814 km (506 miles) south of Bangkok, 180 km (117 miles) southeast of Phuket, 43 km (27 miles) by boat east of Koh Phi Phi.

Krabi is a major travel hub in southern Thailand. Travelers often breeze through without stopping to enjoy the atmosphere, which is a shame, because Krabi is a friendly town with great food and charming people. Locals are determined to keep Phuket-style development at bay, and so far they are succeeding. There are a few good restaurants in town, and there's excellent seafood at the night market (try the fish cakes with sweet chili sauce), which also sells clothes, accessories, and souvenirs.

GETTING HERE AND AROUND

AIR TRAVEL Flying is the easiest way to get here from Bangkok. Thai Airways, Bangkok Airways, and Air Asia all have daily flights to Krabi International Airport. One-way prices from Bangkok range from B1,000 to B3,500; the flight takes about an hour.

The airport is a 20-minute ride from Krabi Town, and there are taxis (B400) and minibuses (B150) waiting outside the airport. These vehicles can also take you to other nearby (and not-so-nearby) beach areas. Minivans don't leave until they're full, which can happen quickly or after a long wait. Your best bet is to check in with the minivans first to make sure you get a seat if one is about to depart—if not, you can opt for a taxi. Another, more recent transport addition, is the regular bus service to and from Krabi Town. The bus departs hourly (B100) from 6 am and runs throughout the day until 10 pm.

BUS AND SONGTHAEW TRAVEL Buses from Bangkok to Krabi leave from Bangkok's Southern Bus Terminal and take at least 12 hours. VIP and first-class buses leave once every evening around 6 or 7 pm. Public buses leave Krabi for Bangkok at 8 am and 4 and 5:30 pm. First-class buses travel between Phuket and Krabi (a three-hour journey) every hour. Getting around town or to Ao Nang is best done by songthaew. You can find songthaews at the corner of Maharat Soi 4 and Pruksa Uthit Road.

Bus and boat combination tickets are available from Krabi to Koh Samui and Koh Phangan.

There are a few bus terminals in Krabi, but if you don't arrive at the pier, songthaews can take you there; if you've purchased a combination ticket, this transfer is included.

CAR TRAVEL The airport has Avis, National, and Budget rental counters. Prices start at about B1,500 per day; for a little more, you can also rent a four-wheel-drive jeep in town.

SAFETY AND PRECAUTIONS

Krabi is a sleepy, laid-back town with little crime and few annoyances, but taking routine precautions with your valuables is always a good idea. People drive annoyingly fast, so take care when crossing the road, especially at the major junctions.

VISITOR INFORMATION

Krabi has its own small Tourism Authority of Thailand (TAT) offices, where you can pick up maps and brochures, as well as information about local excursions. Tour operators and your hotel's tour desk are also good sources of information.

Contacts Krabi Tourist Information Center. ✉ *Uttarakit Rd.* ☎ *075/622163.*

EXPLORING

Wat Tham Sua. Just 3 km (2 miles, or 10 minutes' drive) from Krabi Town is Wat Tham Sua, with its giant Buddha statue and scenic surrounding landscapes. Built in 1976 as a monastery and meditation retreat, Wat Tham Sua is both respected by the local population and popular with tourists. Locals come to participate in Buddhist rituals, while most tourists to climb the 1,277 steps to panoramic views of the cliffs, Krabi Town, Krabi River, and the Panom Benja mountain range. There's also a cave with many chambers, which can be fun to explore, though it's not terribly attractive. A really large tree grows outside the entrance. The wat is between Krabi Town and the airport. ✉ *Tambon Muang Chum, 4 km (2½ miles) after Wachiralongkorn Dam.*

OFF THE BEATEN PATH

Than Bokkharani National Park. Between Krabi and Phang Nga is this forested park, which has several emerald-green ponds surrounded by tropical foliage, including wild gardenia and apocynaceae. The pools are filled with refreshing cool water, fed by a mountain spring 4 km (2½ miles) away. The largest pond is 130 feet by 100 feet, deep and suitable for swimming. The pools are best visited in the dry season, as they get quite murky when it rains. ⊠ *From Krabi: take Hwy. 4 to Ao Luek, then turn onto Rte. 4039* ☎ *075/681071* ⊠ *B400.*

WHERE TO EAT

$$
INTERNATIONAL

✕ **Carnivore Steak and Grill.** As the name suggests, meat lovers can find high-quality imported cuts served with delicious sauces and sides at this well-known restaurant. Fish lovers can also be satisfied here, with fresh lobster bisque, perfectly grilled tuna steak, or white snapper in butter-and-garlic-cream sauce. The efficient service adds to the lively atmosphere. ⑨ *Average main: B230* ⊠ *127 Moo 3* ☎ *075/661061* ⊕ *www. carnivore-thailand.com* ▭ *No credit cards* ⚜ *Reservations essential.*

$
THAI

✕ **Chao Fa Pier Street Food Stalls.** Looking for local quality food at a low price? This strip of street-side food stalls serves everything from simple fried rice and papaya salad to more sophisticated southern delicacies such as *kanom jeen* (rice noodles topped with whatever sauces and vegetables you want). Open from nightfall until midnight, these stalls provide an excellent opportunity to discover some exotic and enjoyable Thai foods. Walk along the street and enjoy the carnival atmosphere—the local stall holders are more than happy to let you try the assorted delicacies before deciding what to buy. This is one of the highlights of Krabi Town, and the street enjoys a nationwide reputation. ⑨ *Average main: B60* ⊠ *Chao Fa Pier, Khong Kha Rd.* ▭ *No credit cards.*

$$
SEAFOOD

✕ **Frog and Catfish.** At the Frog and Catfish you can try some regional specialties that are not that easy to come across. Located in the small village of Din Daeang Noi, the restaurant serves great seafood (try the fresh crab spring rolls) as well as delicious curries. The owner is always happy to share his knowledge about the region to travelers hungry for new perspectives. ⑨ *Average main: B175* ⊠ *76 Moo 6, Din Daeng Noi* ☎ *084/773–0301* ⊕ *www.frogandcatfishkrabi.com* ▭ *No credit cards.*

$$
SEAFOOD
Fodor's Choice
★

✕ **Marina Villa.** Opened in 2011, this restaurant sits on the banks of Krabi River on a picturesque marina and specializes in thoughtfully presented Thai seafood dishes. It's a favorite for well-to-do Krabi locals. The attentive staff wear different-colored uniforms each day, influenced by flowery Hawaiian fashion. The space itself is modern and dimly lighted with blues and greens, but weather permitting, tables by the river are the way to go. Signature dishes include the spicy green curry with crab, grilled white snapper stuffed with lemongrass and pandan leaves, and the large, juicy mussels with garlic and chili. Most meals are accompanied by whisky or beer on the rocks, Thai style. ⑨ *Average main: B300* ⊠ *Next to yacht club, Krabi Marina* ☎ *075/611635, 086/276–8556* ▭ *No credit cards* ⚜ *Reservations essential.*

$
CAFÉ

✕ **Relax Coffee and Restaurant.** The menu at this street-side café includes more than 10 different breakfast platters; a number of sandwiches, such as chicken satay, served on homemade freshly baked brown bread, baguette, or ciabatta; many Thai dishes, including 10 different barracuda plates; and, not surprisingly, a huge variety of coffee drinks, like raspberry latte frappés. It's in the heart of the hotel district and caters mainly to foreigners. [$] *Average main: B100* ✉ *7/4 Chaofa Rd.* ☎ *075/611570* 💳 *No credit cards* ⏲ *Closed 2nd and 4th Fri. of each month.*

$ SEAFOOD 🍴 **Ruen Pae.** This massive floating restaurant aboard a large, flat barge serves Thai standards, with an emphasis on seafood dishes. It's at the Chao Fa Pier beside the night market. The restaurant is popular with locals and tourists alike, so get there early on Friday and Saturday evenings. [$] *Average main: B100* ✉ *Ut-tarkit Rd.* ☎ *076/611956, 075/611148* 💳 *No credit cards* ⏲ *Closed Mon.*

WHERE TO STAY

$ HOTEL 🏨 **Hometel.** A solid budget choice, this little family-run hotel is a great base for those using Krabi as a stepping-stone to the tropical islands beyond. **Pros:** central; speedy, free Wi-Fi; good restaurant. **Cons:** book well in advance; not enough natural light in the rooms; some rooms are small. [$] *Rooms from: B500* ✉ *7 Soi 10 Maharaj Rd., Pak Nam* ☎ *075/622301* 💳 *No credit cards* 🛏 *10 rooms* 🍽 *No meals.*

$ RESORT 🏨 **Krabi Maritime Park and Spa Resort.** Featuring a mangrove forest, a sprawling lagoon, a large swimming pool, and views of Krabi's signature limestone cliffs, this resort extends over 25 acres. **Pros:** impressive views over the mangroves and forest; decorative touches in the rooms and lobby; lovely gardens. **Cons:** staff inattentive at times; needs a makeover; free Wi-Fi only in lobby. [$] *Rooms from: B1400* ✉ *1 Thungfa Rd.* ☎ *075/620028 up to 35* 🌐 *www.maritimeparkandspa.com* 🛏 *221 rooms.*

$ HOTEL 🏨 **Krabi River Hotel.** Not to everyone's taste because it's so basic, the Krabi River Hotel is at the marina (earmarked for major development), and is a good budget option for Krabi. **Pros:** pleasant riverside location; some rooms have lovely views; free Wi-Fi. **Cons:** off the main drag; rooms at the back are small and have no views; breakfast not included. [$] *Rooms from: B600* ✉ *73/1 Kongkha Rd.* ☎ *075/612321* 💳 *No credit cards* 🛏 *20 rooms* 🍽 *No meals.*

NIGHTLIFE

The Rooftop Bar. On the top of Hello KR Mansion, this alfresco bar offers drinks, live DJ sessions, occasional fire shows, and beautiful views, especially at sunset. ✉ *52/1 Chao Fa Rd.* ☎ *084/385-2316.*

EN ROUTE

Shell Cemetery is a pleasant beach park between Ao Nang and Krabi Town. It has a small information center explaining how snails from tens of millions of years ago were preserved for us to wonder about today. The fossils are probably not that interesting to most people, but the beach here is pleasant for a dip (although sunbathing in skimpy suits would be inappropriate, as many Thai families picnic on the hill above). Also, the view from the hill is quite nice, and if you're cruising on a motorbike, this is a fine place to get some shade in between destinations.

AO NANG

20 km (12 miles) from Krabi Town. In the daytime, Ao Nang is busy with visitors flowing to and from beaches. In the evening, storefronts light up the sidewalk and open-air restaurants provide excellent places to kick back with a beer and watch the crowd go by. For a more romantic atmosphere, head to the half-dozen seafood restaurants atop a pier extending from the bend in Liab Chai Haad Road in between Ao Nang and Noppharat Thara beaches. During the day, longtail boats depart from Ao Nang for the more spectacular beaches and waters of Hong, Poda, Gai, Lanta, and the Phi Phi islands, as well as nearby Railay Beach. Less adventurous types can find nicer sand and better water for swimming on the far eastern end of the beach or at Noppharat Thara Beach National Park to the west.

> **WORD OF MOUTH**
>
> "I would second the vote for Krabi—specifically Ao Nang or Railay. In terms of scenic beauty right on your doorstep, it's hard to beat. There are also quite a few interesting things to see and do away from the beaches, including hot springs, mangrove forests, and elephant treks." —MichaelBKK

GETTING HERE AND AROUND

Buses from Bangkok headed to Krabi stop here. If you fly into Krabi, it takes about 45 minutes to Ao Nang in a taxi. Songthaews travel between Ao Nang and Krabi Town regularly. The fare shouldn't be more than B80; you can find them on the main road, displaying Krabi–Ao Nang signs. A taxi from the airport will cost you considerably more usually the minimum fare is B650.

EXPLORING

Klong Muang Farther north are the beaches of Klong Muang and **Tubkaak**, isolated, beautiful stretches of sand with amazing views of the limestone karst islands on the horizon. The beaches are largely occupied by upmarket resorts such as the Sheraton and The Tubkaak, and none of the amenities come free. **Amenities:** water sports; food and drink; toilet. **Best for:** solitude; sunset; walking. ⊠ *Krabi.*

Laem Son Beach. A narrow river pier delineates the western edge of Noppharat Thara National Park. Here you can catch boats departing from the pier to Railay, Phi Phi, and Lanta, or simply cross to the other side and enjoy the unspoiled natural beauty of Laem Son Beach. There are a few cheap beachside bungalows to stay at. **Amenities:** none. **Best for:** solitude; sunset; walking; swimming. ⊠ *Krabi.*

Noppharat Thara Beach. Noppharat Thara Beach is a 15-minute walk from central Ao Nang. Since the renovated walking path was extended from Ao Nang in 2004, a mishmash of development followed (even though it's supposedly part of the national park). The beach is still pleasant but many of the trees have been uprooted to make way for resorts. **Amenities:** food and drink. **Best for:** swimming; walking. ⊠ *96 Moo 3, Nopphara Thara, Krabi.*

WHERE TO EAT

$ ✕ **Ao Nang Cuisine.** The tender chicken satay (curry chicken skewers),
THAI   an otherwise ordinary dish, is skillfully prepared at this traditional restaurant, with a side of spicy peanut sauce. More elaborate Thai dishes
are available for tourists who are tired of street-side barbecue seafood.
Excellent value for both quantity and quality. $ *Average main: B100*
⊠ *245/4 Liab Chai Haad Rd., Krabi* ☎ *075/695399.*

$ ✕ **Krua Thara.** There are two positive signs at this restaurant before you
SEAFOOD   even try the food—locals hanging out, and the fish and seafood that
will end up on your plate are on display in tanks in all their variety.
You'll find every kind of fresh catch prepared using lots of local herbs
and spices at this friendly, colorful place. $ *Average main: B115* ⊠ *82
Moo 5, Nopparat Thara Rd., Krabi* ☎ *075/637361* ⊟ *No credit cards.*

$ ✕ **Lae Lay Grill.** The seafood here is perfectly cooked and artfully pre-
SEAFOOD   sented, but what makes Lae Lay Grill special is its location. The restaurant is on a terrace on a hill overlooking Ao Nang and the sea, which
makes it a highly romantic spot from sunset on, but also lovely during
the day. Staff will pick you up from your hotel and bring you here by
van. $ *Average main: B200* ⊠ *89 Moo 3, Ao Nang* ☎ *075/661588*
⊕ *www.laelaygrill.com* ⊟ *No credit cards.*

WHERE TO STAY

$ ⊞ **Alis Hotel and Spa.** Whitewashed walls and red, ceramic-tile floors
HOTEL   contribute to the Moroccan design at Alis Hotel. **Pros:** polite, helpful
staff; good facilities for the price. **Cons:** whitewash needs to be reap-
plied; staff can be apathetic. $ *Rooms from: B1750* ⊠ *125 Moo 3,
Ao Nang, Krabi* ☎ *075/638000, 02/801–0760 in Bangkok* ⊕ *www.
alisthailand.com* ⤳ *34 rooms* ⑲ *Breakfast.*

$ ⊞ **Anyavee Ao Nang Resort & Spa.** The resort is a cluster of four-story
RESORT   buildings in Thai design, including northern-style peaked roofs. **Pros:**
good selection of facilities; great location for nature lovers. **Cons:** a bit
removed from beach; exterior needs some renovation. $ *Rooms from:
B1900* ⊠ *31/3 Liab Chai Haad Rd., Ao Nang, Krabi* ☎ *075/695051 up
to 54* ⊕ *www.anyavee.com* ⤳ *71 rooms* ⑲ *Breakfast.*

$ ⊞ **The Cliff.** You can get a great view of the cliff that inspired the hotel's
RESORT   name as soon as you step into the lobby. **Pros:** atmospheric design;
stunning location; good Wi-Fi connection. **Cons:** not on beach; some
rooms are very stuffy. $ *Rooms from: B1750* ⊠ *85/2 Liab Chai Haad
Rd., Ao Nang, Krabi* ☎ *075/638117 up to 18* ⊕ *www.thecliffkrabi.com*
⤳ *20 rooms, 1 suite* ⑲ *Breakfast.*

$$$ ⊞ **Dusit Thani Krabi Beach Resort.** The resort is built around an expansive
RESORT   mangrove forest, and there's a wide, sandy beach on the premises. **Pros:**
FAMILY   beachfront location; great amenities; stylish. **Cons:** location may disap-
point beach purists—water isn't crystal clear; Wi-Fi connection only in
reception area; a little worn in places. $ *Rooms from: B5000* ⊠ *155
Klong Muang Beach, Nongtalay, Krabi* ☎ *075/628000* ⤳ *246 rooms,
6 suites* ⑲ *Some meals.*

$ ⊞ **Emerald Bungalow.** On isolated Laem Son Beach, this family-run resort
B&B/INN   offers genuine Thai hospitality. **Pros:** close to national park; relaxed
atmosphere; decent restaurant. **Cons:** a bit pricey for basic lodgings; too
remote for some. $ *Rooms from: B1400* ⊠ *Noppharat Thara Beach,*

Krabi ☎ *081/892–1072, 081/956–2566* 🌐 *www.the-emerald-bungalow-resortkrabi.com* 💳 *No credit cards* 🛏 *36 rooms* 🍴 *No meals.*

$ HOTEL 🏨 **J Mansion.** Top-floor rooms peek out over surrounding buildings for a nice view of the sea. **Pros:** large rooms; good views from top floor; friendly staff. **Cons:** slow Internet connection; very basic. [$] *Rooms from: B1000* ✉ *23/3 Moo 2, Ao Nang Beach, Krabi* ☎ *075/637878* 🌐 *www.jmansionaonang.com/accommodation.htm* 🛏 *21 rooms* 🍴 *No meals.*

$$ RESORT 🏨 **Krabi Resort.** The only beachfront bungalows in Ao Nang town, the best swimming is here as well as a seaside park with plenty of benches positioned for gazing at the sea. **Pros:** great location; lots of facilities for the price. **Cons:** breakfast buffet can be a little stale and bland. [$] *Rooms from: B2400* ✉ *232 Liab Chai Haad Rd., Ao Nang, Krabi* ☎ *075/637030 up to 35, 02/208–9165 in Bangkok* 🌐 *www.krabiresort.net* 🛏 *130 rooms, 2 suites* 🍴 *Breakfast.*

$ B&B/INN 🏨 **Phra Nang Inn.** The resort has a wonderfully kooky vibe—you might find headboards decorated with bright paintings of seashells and fish in the Coconut Wing and a few pieces of furniture might look like they're made from tree branches in the Betel-nut Wing. **Pros:** airport shuttle available; central location. **Cons:** decor not for everyone. [$] *Rooms from: B1400* ✉ *119 Liab Chai Haad Rd., Ao Nang, Krabi* ☎ *075/637130* 🌐 *www.vacationvillage.co.th/phrananginn* 🛏 *74 rooms* 🍴 *Breakfast.*

$ HOTEL 🏨 **The Small, Krabi.** This sleek boutique hotel stands quietly in one of the busier parts of Ao Nang, offering proximity to shopping, dining, drinking, and swimming at the Noppharatthara and Ao Nang beaches on either side. **Pros:** cleanliness and attention to detail; great location; short walk to beach. **Cons:** no big pool; having a TV in the bathroom is not to everyone's taste. [$] *Rooms from: B2000* ✉ *167 MOO 3 Tambon Aonang Amphur Muang, Krabi* ☎ *075/661590* 🌐 *www.thesmallhotelgroup.com/krabi/* 💳 *No credit cards* 🛏 *38 rooms* 🍴 *No meals.*

$ HOTEL FAMILY 🏨 **Srisuksant Resort.** On the eastern end of Noppharat Thara, Srisuksant is a short walk from Ao Nang's shops and directly across from the beach. **Pros:** nice pools; well set up for kids and families; friendly staff. **Cons:** a little overwhelming for couples without kids. [$] *Rooms from: B2000* ✉ *145 Noppharat Thara Beach, Krabi* ☎ *075/638002 up to 04* 🌐 *www.srisuksantresort.com* 🛏 *66 rooms* 🍴 *Breakfast.*

$$$$ RESORT 🏨 **The Tubkaak Boutique Resort.** Each of the elegant wooden buildings here resembles a *kor lae*, a traditional southern Thai fishing boat. **Pros:** relaxed environment; beach location; great pool area. **Cons:** disappointing restaurant; rooms are small. [$] *Rooms from: B7500* ✉ *123 Taab Kaak Beach, Nongtalay, Krabi* ☎ *075/628400* 🌐 *www.tubkaakresort.com* 🛏 *44 rooms, 2 suites* 🍴 *No meals.*

NIGHTLIFE

Encore Café. Encore Café has live music five to seven nights a week from prominent local and expat musicians who play rock, reggae, blues, jazz, funk, folk, and fusion western-Thai tunes. Hidden back behind the main road in central Ao Nang, this is one of the few places to hear quality music while knocking back some beers and eating Thai and western pub grub. ✉ *245/23 Liab Chai Haad Rd., Nang Beach, Ao Nang, Krabi* ☎ *075/637107.*

5

Friends Suki. A great bar that invites you to wind down after a long day, by sipping a refreshing cocktail or two in the company of expats who can offer insider tips on the town and surrounding areas. ✉ *Moo 2, 4203 Rd., Krabi* ☎ *075/695751.*

The Last Fisherman's. The last—and most scenic—social spot on the end of Ao Nang beach is where you should have your frosty drink just before sunset, although it's open for lunch as well. If you're peckish in the early afternoon or at night, a plain surf and turf, barbecue buffet, salads, and gooey desserts are on the menu. ✉ *266 Moo 2, Krabi* ☎ *075/637968.*

NANG CAPE/RAILAY BEACH

15 mins by longtail boat east of Ao Nang.

Be careful not to strain your neck admiring the skyscraping cliffs as your longtail boat delivers you to Nang Cape. Here four interconnected beaches are collectively referred to as Railay Beach; the isolated beaches of Tonsai, Phra Nang, East Railay, and West Railay, only accessible by boat, are sandy oases surrounded by impressive verdant, vertical cliffs. The sand on these beaches is talcum-powder white and soft, the water is crystalline, and the crowd is an offbeat blend of bohemian travelers and fitness enthusiasts.

GETTING HERE AND AROUND

Longtails will ferry you here from Ao Nang. Prices vary depending on time of day and which beach you're headed to, but expect to pay around B100 or B120 each way. Prices can rise dramatically in the evening, so leave early to save money.

EXPLORING

Nang Cape/Railay Beach. The four beaches that make up Railay Beach are connected by walking paths, and each has its own attractions. Tonsai Beach, with a pebble-strewn shore and shallow, rocky water, caters to budget travelers and rock climbers. West Railay has powdery white sand, shallow but swimmable water, gorgeous sunset views, and many kayaks for hire. East Railay, a mangrove-lined shore unsuitable for beach or water activities, draws rock-climbing enthusiasts, as well as younger travelers looking for late-night drinks and loud music. Phra Nang Beach, one of the nicest beaches in all Krabi, is ideal for swimming, sunbathing, and rock-climbing. **Amenities:** food and drink; bathrooms; water sports. **Best for:** sunset; swimming; snorkeling. ✉ *Nang Cape.*

WHERE TO EAT

There are plenty of bars and restaurants along the beaches. Most restaurants serve standard Thai and western fare—no gourmet renditions *yet.* As you move away from the beach, you'll find less expensive and more atmospheric places, including some climber hangouts where trainings and socializing with fellow climbers take place.

$ INDIAN

🍴 **Utopia International Delights.** Utopia offers a change of culinary style at Railay, serving tasty Indian food like butter chicken or chicken tikka masala, crispy samosas, and refreshing yogurt lassies, in a friendly, outdoor setting. The owners are sensitive to people with nut allergies and make sure what you order matches your spice tolerance. [$] *Average main: B150* ✉ *Nang Cape* 💳 *No credit cards.*

WHERE TO STAY

$$$
RESORT
⊞ **Bhu Nga Thani Resort and Spa.** Located on the quieter Railay East Beach, the lovely infinity pool and a popular spa make this a good option for those staying at Railay, though East Beach faces out onto a mangrove swamp, and there is better swimming to be had at Tonsai or West beach. **Pros:** most rooms have ocean views; bars and restaurants nearby; resort arranges excursions. **Cons:** 10-minute walk from boat drop; not on a swimming beach; food can be hit or miss. $ *Rooms from: B4000* ⊠ *Railay East Beach, 479 Moo 2 Ao Nang, Nang Cape* ☎ *075/819451-4* ⊕ *www.bhungathani.com* ▭ *No credit cards* ⇆ *60 rooms* ⦿*No meals.*

$$$
B&B/INN
⊞ **Koh Jum Lodge.** On the island of Koh Jum, in Phang Nga Bay between Krabi, Phi Phi, and Koh Lanta, Koh Jum Lodge has rooms in 20 wooden cottages designed in traditional Thai architectural style. **Pros:** traditional Thai design; helpful management and staff; stunning sunset over the Phi Phi Islands. **Cons:** a bit isolated from resort towns; difficult to access in off peak season; food and drinks pricey. $ *Rooms from: B4500* ⊠ *286 Moo 3, Koh Siboya, Nua Klong, Krabi, Nang Cape* ☎ *075/618275, 089/921–1621* ⊕ *www.kohjumlodge.com* ⇆ *20 bungalows* ⦿*Breakfast.*

$$
RESORT
⊞ **Railay Bay Resort and Spa.** Great Thai food ($$) and a beachside patio and bar from which you can watch the sunset are a few good reasons to visit Railay Bay Resort and Spa. Basic cottages and rooms in a row of modern two-story buildings are suitable reasons to lodge here, also. **Pros:** alluring views; central location; decent food. **Cons:** staff may not speak great English; pricey spa; patchy Wi-Fi. $ *Rooms from: B3500* ⊠ *145 Moo 2, Railay West Beach, Krabi, Nang Cape* ☎ *075/622998 up to 9* ⊕ *www.railaybayresort.com* ⇆ *140 rooms, 10 suites* ⦿*Breakfast.*

$
B&B/INN
⊞ **Railay Garden View.** Among the best of the less expensive options on Railay, this place offers clean bungalows in a garden setting, and a great location near the beach. **Pros:** complimentary breakfast; good restaurant; free Wi-Fi. **Cons:** keep an eye on your belongings; no sea view; noise from longtail boats can get tiring. $ *Rooms from: B750* ⊠ *147 M. 5, Saithai district* ☎ *085/888–5143, 084/295–1112* ⊕ *www. railaygardenview.com/en/* ▭ *No credit cards* ⇆ *10 rooms* ⦿*Breakfast.*

$
RESORT
⊞ **Railay Phutawan Resort.** From practically everywhere you stand in this resort, you can enjoy overwhelming vistas of the bay and climber-covered limestone cliffs. **Pros:** inexpensive; stunning views; good food. **Cons:** no advance booking; lacking facilities; an uphill trek to get there. $ *Rooms from: B2000* ⊠ *Moo 1, Railay East Beach, Krabi, Nang Cape* ☎ *075/621731* ⊕ *www.railayphutawan.com* ▭ *No credit cards* ⇆ *20 bungalows* ⦿*Breakfast.*

$
HOTEL
⊞ **Railay Princess Resort and Spa.** Thai-style lamps and silk throw pillows on the beds and sofas are colorful touches at this quiet retreat midway between East and West Railay beaches. **Pros:** quiet location; good value; tasteful details. **Cons:** not on beach; furniture looks cheap. $ *Rooms from: B1900* ⊠ *145/1 Moo 2, Railay Beach, Ao Nang, Nang Cape* ☎ *075/819401 up to 03, 075/819407 up to 09* ⊕ *www.krabi-railayprincess.com* ⇆ *59 rooms* ⦿*No meals.*

5

$ RENTAL FAMILY Fodor's Choice ★ **Railei Beach Club.** Each of the 24 privately owned homes here is individually named and designed, giving each its own unique character. **Pros:** great choice of accommodation and prices; good location; sunsets. **Cons:** fills up early in high season; some staff can be aloof; bring your own beach towels. [$] *Rooms from: B2000* ✉ *Railay West Beach, 200 Moo 2, Railay* ☎ *075/622582, 086/685–9359* 🌐 *www.raileibeachclub.com* 🛏 *24 houses* 🍴 *No meals.*

$$$$ RESORT **Rayavadee Resort.** Scattered across 26 landscaped acres, this magnificent resort is set in coconut groves with white-sand beaches on three sides. **Pros:** great dining variety; intricate room design; plenty of facilities. **Cons:** notably nonecological use of wood; beach very busy during the day; during low tide boat access is challenging. [$] *Rooms from: B12000* ✉ *214 Moo 2, Tambol Ao Nang, Amphur Muang* ☎ *075/620740 up to 3* 🌐 *www.rayavadee.com* 🛏 *98 rooms, 5 suites* 🍴 *Breakfast.*

SPORTS AND THE OUTDOORS

ROCK CLIMBING

Climbers discovered the cliffs around Nang Cape in the late 1980s. The mostly vertical cliffs rising up out of the sea were, and certainly are, a dream come true for hard-core climbers. Today anyone daring enough can learn to scale the face of a rock (and to jump off it) in one of the most beautiful destinations in the world. There are 500 to 600 established climbing routes. Notable feats include the Tonsai Beach overhang and Thaiwand Wall, where climbers must use lanterns to pass through a cave and then rappel down from the top. Beginners can learn some skills through half-day or full-day courses for fixed rates of B1,200 or B2,000, respectively. Most climbing organizations are found on East Railay. Slightly less adventurous, or more spendthrift, types can try the free climb to "the lagoon." The lagoon itself isn't all that impressive, but the view from the top is spectacular. The trailhead for the fairly arduous climb up the occasionally near-vertical mud, rock, vine, and fixed-rope ascent is along the path to Phra Nang Beach, immediately across from the gazebo. Watch out for monkeys!

Cliffs Man. This is one of the more reputable rock-climbing schools. ✉ *East Railey, Nang Cape* ☎ *075/621768, 012/304619.*

King Climbers. All the guides here are accredited by the ACGA and have a minimum of five years' climbing experience. ✉ *East Railey, Nang Cape* ☎ *075/637125* 🌐 *www.railay.com.*

Tex Rock Climbing. Half-day to three-day climbing courses can be arranged here. ✉ *East Railey, Nang Cape* ☎ *075/631509.*

KOH LANTA

70 km (42 miles) south of Krabi Town.

Long beaches, crystal clear water, and a laid-back natural environment are Koh Lanta's main attractions. Although "discovered" by international travelers in the early 2000s, Koh Lanta remains fairly quiet. Early development resulted in the construction of hundreds of budget bungalows and several swanky resorts along the west coast of Lanta

The 2004 Tsunami

Both of Thailand's coasts had been experiencing a tourism boom for years—with many places facing the consequences of overdevelopment—when the tsunami hit the Andaman Coast on December 26, 2004. Several beaches on Phuket, the beach area of Khao Lak, and much of Koh Phi Phi were devastated by the waves, and although many areas on the Andaman Coast were unaffected by the tsunami, tourism on that shore came to a near standstill in the months following the disaster.

More than 12 years later, the situation is considerably different. Phuket's affected beaches have been completely redeveloped, including much improved beachfront sidewalks, street lighting, restaurants, bars, and cafés on par with western beach destinations. Phi Phi Island was rebuilt a bit more slowly, but now development has surpassed pre-tsunami levels. Most development along Tonsai and Loh Dalam initially focused on upgrading salvageable budget accommodations to nicer, midrange standards to fill the void left as the largest resorts planned their reconstruction. The middle and high-end resorts have now reentered

the market, and Phi Phi is once again booming, with plenty of bars and restaurants. Khao Lak also has more hotels, restaurants, and activities than it did before 2004. These days the tsunami's lasting effects are not visible to the naked eye, but many Andaman Coast locals lost friends and family, and their lives have been irrevocably altered.

Overdevelopment is an issue, as it was before the disaster. Once adventurous travelers find a new, secluded, undeveloped beach and start talking about it, rapid development follows at a frightening pace. In many spots this development hasn't been regulated or monitored properly, and the country is now pulling in the tourist dollars at the expense of the environment. It's a cycle that's hard to stop. Redevelopment in the tsunami areas began quite slowly, while developers and local businesses awaited government regulations. In some instances, the planning paid off (Phi Phi now has much-needed wastewater treatment facilities), but as most areas waited for regulations that never arrived, no-holds-barred development quickly followed.

Yai (Lanta Noi's coast is less suitable for development); however, as one of the largest islands in Thailand, Lanta was able to absorb the "boom" and therefore remains relatively uncluttered. In addition, Lanta is approximately 70 km (44 miles) south of Krabi Town, far enough outside established tourist circuits that visitor arrivals have increased a little more slowly than at other Krabi and Phang Nga beaches and islands.

Most smaller resorts are closed during the low season (May through October). However, some do open in late October and remain open until mid-May—during these (slightly) off times, the weather is still generally good, and you can find that the rates are much lower and the beaches much less crowded.

GETTING HERE AND AROUND

Krabi's airport is about two hours from Koh Lanta by taxi (B2,300–B3,000) or minibus (B350). Minibuses depart from Krabi Town and Ao Nang, not the airport. There's no direct bus service from Bangkok to Koh Lanta; you'll have to take the bus to Trang or Krabi and then continue on in a minivan (songthaews will take you from the bus station to the minivans bound for Koh Lanta). There are two short (15 minutes) Ro-Ro ferries crossings between the mainland and Lanta catering specifically to those coming by car or bus. There's one direct passenger ferry every morning from Krabi at 11:30 am; it costs B400.

One main road runs along the island that will take you to all major resorts. Pickup trucks masquerading as taxis and motorcycles with side-cars will take you wherever you want to go. Negotiate hard for good fares; prices start at about B60 for a short ride of 1 km (½ mile).

SAFETY AND PRECAUTIONS

Lanta is one of Thailand's quieter islands, not because it lacks a tourism infrastructure but because the traditional way of life is strong here. The majority of inhabitants are Muslim, and this guides much of the island's development. The girly bars, the loud late-night discos, and the hectic frenzy of a drinking culture are largely absent. This means that there's a low crime rate, even for Thailand, though precautions should still be taken.

BEACHES

Klong Dao Beach and Phra Ae Beach, both on Lanta Yai's west coast, are the most developed. If you head south, you'll reach calmer Klong Nin Beach and southern Lanta's quiet, scenic coves. Southern Lanta beaches consist of several widely dispersed small coves and beaches ending at Klong Chak National Park. Immediately south of Klong Nin the road suddenly becomes well paved (much smoother than the road from Long Beach to Klong Nin), making the southern beaches accessible by road as well as by taxi boat. The nicest of the southern beaches is Bakantiang Beach, a beautiful one to visit on the way to the national park.

Bakantiang (Kantiang) Beach. The last beach before the national park on the southern tip of Koh Lanta, the crescent-shape Kantiang beach is small but truly stunning. The fine white sands are favored by travelers in the know, or expat residents who want to get away from the busier beaches. The village that backs the beach is the friendliest on the island and there are a few food stalls and roadside cafés that serve up some of the tastiest food on Koh Lanta. **Amenities:** food and drink; toilets; showers. **Best for:** sunset; swimming; snorkeling. ✉ *Last stop on main road heading south, before national park.*

FAMILY   **Klong Dao Beach.** Klong Dao Beach is a 2-km-long (1-mile-long) beach on the northern coast of Lanta Yai, the larger of the two islands that comprise Koh Lanta. Most resorts along Klong Dao are larger facilities catering to families and couples looking for a quiet environment. The water is shallow but swimmable, and at low tide the firm, exposed sand is ideal for long jogs on the beach. **Amenities:** food and drink; toilets.

Best for: sunset; swimming; walking. ⊠ *To right of Lanta's main road, first beach after port town Saladan.*

Klong Nin Beach. Klong Nin Beach, approximately 30 minutes south of Long Beach by car or boat, is one of the larger, nicer beaches toward the southern end of Lanta Yai. Klong Nin is less developed and more tranquil than Long Beach. A typical day on Klong Nin can be a long walk on the silky soft sand interrupted by occasional dips in the sea, a spectacular sunset, a seaside massage, and a candlelight barbecue beneath a canopy of stars. Central Klong Nin, near Otto bar, is the best for swimming, as rocks punctuate the rest of the shoreline. Kayaks are available from some resorts, and longtail boat taxis are for hire along the sea. Most resorts here rent motorbikes as well, as the road to the south is much smoother than the road from Long Beach. **Amenities:** food and drink; toilets. **Best for:** sunset; swimming; walking; solitude. ⊠ *To right of Lanta's main road from Saladan, after intersection for Old Town and Southern Lanta.*

Phra Ae Beach. Long and wide, Phra Ae Beach (aka Long Beach) is Lanta Yai's main tourist destination. The sand is soft and fine, perfect for both sunbathing and long walks. The water is less shallow than at other Lanta beaches, and therefore more suitable for diving in and having a swim. However, kayaks, catamarans, and other water activities, while available, are not as ubiquitous as on other islands. Although most lodging consists of simple budget resorts, the beachfront does have several three- and four-star accommodations. Along the beach and on the main road are many restaurants, bars, Internet cafés, and dive operators. **Amenities:** food and drink; showers; toilets; water sports. **Best for:** sunset; swimming; walking. ⊠ *Second beach to right of Lanta's main road from port town Saladan.*

SPORTS AND THE OUTDOORS

Diving, snorkeling, hiking, and elephant trekking are a few activities available on Koh Lanta and the nearby islands.

Diving Koh Lanta. Diving and snorkeling activities are available on Koh Lanta and the nearby islands. Trips can be arranged through dive and tour operators, though most people choose to book through their own resort. Popular nearby dive sites are **Koh Ha** and **Koh Rok,** off Koh Lanta. ⊠ *Koh Lanta.*

Elephant Trekking. If you would like to enjoy Koh Lanta from another viewpoint, elephant trekking is available near Phra Ae (Long) Beach. Long treks or short treks are available, plus a detailed presentation about elephant welfare and local projects. ⊠ *Koh Lanta.*

Emerald Cave. A boat trip to the famous **Emerald Cave** on Koh Muk is a worthwhile experience. Swim and snorkel through a dark water cave to an idyllic lagoon. ⊠ *Koh Lanta.*

WHERE TO EAT

KLONG DAO

$ ✕ **Fat Monkey (Ling Uan).** Two kitchens, and two cuisines—Thai and
EUROPEAN western. Fat Monkey serves an extensive range of Thai dishes but is best known and loved for its large, juicy burgers. In a refreshing, pretty

garden, this popular venue is great for kicking back after a long day of adventure tours and enjoying a tasty meal and an ice-cream cocktail in a fun and friendly atmosphere. $ *Average main: B200* ✉ *Center of Klong Dao beach, Klong Dao Rd., Saladan* ☎ *087/886–5017* ⊟ *No credit cards* ⊘ *Closed Mon.*

$
THAI

✕ **Picasso Restaurant.** This quirky beachfront restaurant at the Chaba Guesthouse serves traditional Thai fare, well cooked and featuring some less commonly found traditional dishes, such as pumpkin soup with pineapple, as well as friendly service. Proprietor and artist Khun Toi creates pastel-color oil paintings and surreal sculptures incorporating shells and driftwood from Klong Dao Beach. The guesthouse offers clean, comfortable bungalows. $ *Average main: B100* ✉ *Klong Dao Beach, Lanta Yai* ☎ *075/684118, 099/738–7710* ⊟ *No credit cards.*

$
THAI
Fodor's Choice
★

✕ **Time for Lime.** Time for Lime is a large, open-air kitchen-restaurant right off the beach, where you can learn to cook fresh, seasonal, and creative Thai food (with Chinese, Malaysian, and Indian twists), under fun, expert instruction. Their excellent classes include a valuable theoretical introduction to Thai food and a five-hour option, during which you will prepare, and learn to beautifully present, your own feast. Each night the restaurant serves a different three-course set menu, and reclining chairs are placed on the recessed sandbar while music plays and wonderful cocktails (try the chili margarita) are served. Time For Lime also offers basic yet comfortable bungalows. ■TIP→ All proceeds from Time For Lime go to the owner Junie's extremely worthy cause: the Lanta Animal Welfare, which has already offered much-needed help to the many strays on the island. Take time to visit and volunteer! Find out more: www.lantaanimalwelfare.com. $ *Average main: B200* ✉ *72/2 Klong Dao Beach, Lanta Yai, Saladan* ☎ *075/684590, 089/967–5017* ⊕ *www.timeforlime.net* ⊟ *No credit cards* ⊘ *Restaurant closed Nov.–Apr. Classes: May–mid-Oct., closed Sun.–Fri.; mid-Oct.–Apr., closed Mon.*

OLD TOWN

$
THAI

✕ **Caoutchouc.** At the end of a small dirt road, and barely above sea level, is Caoutchouc, run by its French owner and his chef partner. The café-restaurant is in a wooden, traditional house with high ceilings from which colorful Chinese lanterns hang, swaying in the sea breeze. You can sit inside or choose to relax on the scenic wraparound terrace at the water's edge, taking in beautiful views of the horizon. The chef is a Thai sea gypsy whose highly sophisticated culinary vision and style differs in subtle but also pronounced ways from the standard southern fare. He has a love of fresh products, particularly fish, and lovingly cooks what is in season or accessible that day, so don't expect a menu. ■TIP→ As it is off the beaten track and less busy in the evenings, the restaurant only stays open if it receives reservations. $ *Average main: B145* ✉ *Moo 1, Old Town* ☎ *075/697060, 084/629–0704* ⊟ *No credit cards.*

$
FRENCH

✕ **Shanti Shanti.** This large beach hut stands on the sand looking out to the ocean, and serves crepes with homemade French jam, cocktails, ice cream, and coffees to accompany the lovely view, as well as having a small shop selling clothes and accessories. Owner Fafa is a young French artist (his works decorate the café, and are on sale) who traveled broadly in India before settling in Koh Lanta, where he creates decorative pieces made from things he finds in his natural environment. He also makes edible art in the form of his fantastic ice cream. Cross your fingers that the day you visit he will have made his by now well-known and loved chai, sweet basil, Provence lavender, or Kerala cinnamon-flavored ice cream, or Indonesian chocolate sherbet. $ *Average main: B150* ⊠ *Klong Nin, Old Town* ☎ *083/748–9527* ▭ *No credit cards* ☽ *Closed Tues.*

PHRA AE

$

THAI

Fodor's Choice

★

✕ **Cook Kai.** From the outside, this place appears to be a standard, wooden Thai beach restaurant, but the creative cooking elevates it out of the ordinary. Sizzling "hotpan" dishes of seafood in coconut cream, stir-fried morning glory, and sweet-and-sour shrimp are succulent. Specials, such as duck curry served in a hollowed-out pineapple, change daily and augment the already extensive menu. $ *Average main: B115* ⊠ *Moo 6, Klong Nin Beach* ☎ *081/606–3015* ⊕ *www.cook-kai.com* ▭ *No credit cards.*

$

THAI

✕ **Lap Royot.** Thai street food is a class of its own, and you will find it absolutely everywhere you turn, though some eateries are definitely more refined than others. This extremely casual roadside restaurant serves 100% authentic, basic, and cheap food that locals seem to relish. Try the Isaan (northeastern) catfish *larb*, the zingy *som tam* (spicy papaya salad) or the fat noodles cooked in a thick pork broth, and sticky barbecue chicken. $ *Average main: B50* ⊠ *Toward northern end of Klong Dao Beach, Klong Dao Rd.* ☎ *No phone* ▭ *No credit cards.*

$$

THAI

✕ **The Red Snapper.** Serving Thai and European fusion food in an atmospheric garden setting, with a compact menu that creative chef Ed Qarré renews every six weeks, Red Snapper, unsurprisingly, has become one of the island's most happening restaurants. If you're hungry order one of their large platters, or opt for a wonderful selection of tapas dishes if your palate is yearning for adventure; the eponymous red snapper is always succulent and fresh. Cocktails, too, are innovative; try the Thaipiroska for a locally inspired alcoholic kick. $ *Average main: B250* ⊠ *176 Moo 2, Koh Lanta* ☎ *078/856965* ⊕ *www.redsnapper-lanta.com* ▭ *No credit cards* ♨ *Reservations essential.*

$$

THAI

✕ **Tides.** This high-profile restaurant in Layana Resort and Spa welcomes outside visitors for a romantic and sophisticated dinner. Set on a polished seafront terrace, Tides serves specials of the day such as grilled giant prawns, as well as more traditional Thai dishes like green curry, and a selection of international classics with a sophisticated spin. Their sommelier has extensive knowledge of the restaurant's wine list and will take time to find the perfect combination for your meal. Start out your night at sunset, by sinking into one of the resort's giant beanbags set on the beach right in front of the restaurant, and order a Coco Loco cocktail and Kaffir-lime toasted peanuts, before moving to the dining area for an elegant meal. $ *Average main: B250* ⊠ *272 Moo 3 Saladan, Phra Ae Beach* ☎ *075/607100* ⊕ *www.layanaresort.com* ▭ *No credit cards.*

5

KLONG NIN

$ 🍴 **Otto Bar & Grill.** This is one of the most popular old-time bars in Koh Lanta, mostly owing to its vibrant owner, Otto, a been-there, done-that, mature rocker-hippie whose joie de vivre remains charmingly intact. The bar and grill stands right on the beach and is open all day, serving delicious cocktails made with exotic fruits, and a variety of barbecue meats (burgers have a following) and salads, made by its British chef. Otto also has few basic bungalows backed away from the beach. [$] *Average main: B130* ✉ *Klong Nin Beach* 🌐 *ottolanta.com* 💳 *No credit cards.*

INTERNATIONAL
Fodor's Choice ★

SOUTHERN LANTA

$ 🍴 **Drunken Sailors Coffeeshop.** Drunken Sailors is a friendly, laid-back meeting point for tech-savvy travelers (free Wi-Fi), young families, trendy locals, and expats. The Thai-American owners effortlessly create a sense of ease; beanbags and hammocks that are occupied throughout the day attest to this. Playful and homey dishes inspired by the United States, Thailand, and India make up the menu; try the tuna wasabi sub, or the DK veggie samosas in puff pastry, or go for one of their burgers. ■ **TIP→ Round the back, Drunken Sailors has a shop selling original Thai-chic clothes, accessories, and funky jewelry made by a young local artist.** [$] *Average main: B100* ✉ *116 Moo 5, Koh Lanta Yai, Kantiang Bay* ☎ *075/665076* 💳 *No credit cards.*

AMERICAN THAI
FAMILY

$ 🍴 **Phad Thai Rock n' Roll.** Everything is in the name at this tiny roadside eatery, where you can try fresh, authentic, and delicious pad thai made with shrimp, chicken, vegetables, or all of the above, by the talented rock musician-owner. Meet musicians, sip a delicious, healthy, and creative smoothie and watch the world go by. ■ **TIP→ Ask the owner when his next gig is. His band, Why Not, attracts huge crowds of locals, expats, and tourists alike and guarantees a rocking night out.** [$] *Average main: B70* ✉ *92 Moo 5, Kantiang Bay* ☎ *080/784–8729* 💳 *No credit cards.*

THAI

WHERE TO STAY

KLONG DAO

$$$ 🏨 **Costa Lanta.** The coolest thing about Costa Lanta is the room design; each room at this trendy boutique resort is a convertible box, so if you're too hot you can open up the "walls" and allow the breeze to blow through. **Pros:** quiet, green location; art deco design; innovative housing. **Cons:** not great value; not on best beach. [$] *Rooms from: B4250* ✉ *212 Klong Dao Beach, Lanta Yai* ☎ *075/618092, 075/668186* 🌐 *www.costalanta.com* 🛏 *22 rooms* 🍽 *Breakfast.*

RESORT

$ 🏨 **Southern Lanta.** With a fun slide plunging into a big pool and several two-bedroom villas (each with large multibed rooms), Southern Lanta is understandably popular with families. **Pros:** family-friendly; good location; pleasant restaurant. **Cons:** needs redecoration; pool crowds easily; limited views. [$] *Rooms from: B1000* ✉ *105 Klong Dao Beach, Lanta Yai* ☎ *075/684175 up to 77* 🌐 *www.southernlanta.com* 🛏 *100 bungalows* 🍽 *Breakfast.*

RESORT
FAMILY

$$$ 🏨 **Twin Lotus Resort and Spa.** This resort is as much an architectural and interior-design exhibition as it is a sophisticated and tranquil retreat. **Pros:** quality dining; appealing in-room facilities; stunning location. **Cons:** may be too quiet for families; service can be slack.

RESORT

$ *Rooms from: B4200* ✉ *199 Moo 1, Klong Dao Beach, Koh Lanta Yai* ☎ *075/560–7000, 02/361–1946 up to 49 in Bangkok* 🌐 *www.twinlotusresort.com* 🛏 *81 rooms* 🍴 *No meals.*

PHRA AE

$ B&B/INN 🏨 **Best House.** The Best House lobby, an inviting high-ceilinged room with comfortable chairs, white tile floors, and wooden beams, offers a good sense of what you can expect from the accommodations. **Pros:** inexpensive; near the beach; friendly service. **Cons:** rooms are basic; no pool; no in-room amenities. $ *Rooms from: B1000* ✉ *5/1 Moo 3, Phra Ae Beach, Lanta Yai* ☎ *075/684560, 084/464–1500* 🌐 *www.besthouselantaguesthouse.com* 💳 *No credit cards* 🕒 *Closed Apr.–Oct.* 🛏 *30 rooms* 🍴 *No meals.*

$$ RESORT 🏨 **Lanta Nakara.** If you're staying in a resort on a beautiful, white-sand beach with crystal clear, blue water, you should treat yourself to a room with a view. **Pros:** friendly staff; great views. **Cons:** bland design; free Wi-Fi only in lobby. $ *Rooms from: B3700* ✉ *172 Moo 3, Phra Ae Beach, Saladan* ☎ *075/684198* 🌐 *www.lantalongbeach.com* 🛏 *41 cottages* 🍴 *Breakfast.*

$ RESORT 🏨 **Lanta Sand Resort and Spa.** Large ponds with water lilies and spraying fountains cover the grounds of Lanta Sand Resort and Spa. Aged-brick paths meander from villa to pool to spa, where aromatic candles burn, illuminating Thai silk tapestries. **Pros:** spacious rooms; romantic; near beach. **Cons:** far from any town; noisy a/c in some rooms; prices too high for what's on offer. $ *Rooms from: B1750* ✉ *279 Moo 3, Phra Ae Beach, Lanta Yai* ☎ *075/684633, 089/724–2682* 🌐 *www.lantasand.com* 🛏 *78 rooms* 🍴 *No meals.*

$$$$ RESORT Fodor's Choice ★ 🏨 **Layana Resort and Spa.** Guests repeatedly return to the Layana for a real sense of pampering, understated luxury, and a relaxed, peaceful environment. **Pros:** varied breakfast buffet includes healthy juice bar; many activities organized in-house; lovely beach. **Cons:** strictly no children; some bungalows lack sea views; not for party animals. $ *Rooms from: B7500* ✉ *272 Moo 3, Saladan, Phra Ae Beach, Koh Lanta* ☎ *075/607100, 02/713–2313 in Bangkok* 🌐 *www.layanaresort.com* 🛏 *50 rooms* 🍴 *Breakfast.*

$ B&B/INN FAMILY 🏨 **Somewhere Else.** If you like your huts to be of progressive design, go Somewhere Else—the six octagonal rooms in the front of the clearing are particularly cool, with fold-down windows, wooden floors, and loose-pebble bathroom floors. **Pros:** very friendly and helpful staff; wonderful beach location; nice restaurant. **Cons:** no hot water; no TV. $ *Rooms from: B900* ✉ *253 Moo 3, Phra Ae Beach, Lanta Yai* ☎ *091/536–0858, 089/731–1312* 💳 *No credit cards* 🕒 *Closed June–Sept.* 🛏 *16 rooms* 🍴 *No meals.*

KLONG NIN

$$ B&B/INN 🏨 **Lanta Miami Resort.** The affordable, beachside bungalows at the Lanta Miami are clean, spacious, and with big beds, and have nicely sized, tiled bathrooms. **Pros:** great location; comfortable; nice pool. **Cons:** some rooms lack hot water; staff can be unaccommodating; rooms without sea views are a bit stuffy. $ *Rooms from: B1000* ✉ *13 Moo 6, Klong Nin Beach, Lanta Yai* ☎ *075/662559* 💳 *No credit cards* 🕒 *Closed June–Sept.* 🛏 *26 rooms* 🍴 *Breakfast.*

$ RESORT **Lanta Paradise Beach Resort.** It's a short walk along the beach to the best swimming spot, but the sand gets so hot you'll be glad to have the pool outside your room. **Pros:** prime location; impressive western food at restaurant; nice views. **Cons:** not the best value; very basic rooms; lack of amenities. [$] *Rooms from: B1100* ✉ *67 Moo 6, Klong Nin Beach, Lanta Yai* ☎ *075/662569, 089/473–3279* 🌐 *www.lantaparadisebeachresort.com* 💳 *No credit cards* 🕒 *Closed June–Sept.* 🛏 *34 rooms* 🍴 *Breakfast.*

$$$ RESORT FAMILY **Rawi Warin Resort and Spa.** This enormous, lively resort with luxuriously outfitted rooms and high-tech amenities, stretches gracefully across an entire hillside along the road from Klong Khong Beach to Klong Nin. The resort features, among many other things, a 24-seat minitheater, a music room, a video game room, a dive shop, and a beautiful private beach. **Pros:** many amenities; helpful staff; family-friendly. **Cons:** not great value; beach is rocky; activities are limited. [$] *Rooms from: B4000* ✉ *139 Moo 8, Lanta Yai Island, Krabi* ☎ *026/643490 up to 48, 02/434–5526 in Bangkok* 🌐 *www.rawiwarin.com* 🛏 *185 rooms* 🍴 *Breakfast.*

SOUTHERN LANTA

$$ HOTEL **Mango House.** In the laid-back and increasingly trendy Old Town, or Sri Raya, Mango House is a home away from home, with three seafront suites and three villas, all in Chinese-style wooden houses that stand on stilts over the water. **Pros:** welcoming atmosphere; comfortable rooms; a great base for exploring the Old Town. **Cons:** private property next to rooms is shabby; no a/c. [$] *Rooms from: B2500* ✉ *45 Sriraya Rd., Moo 2, Old Town* ☎ *089/948–6836* 🌐 *www.mangohouses.com* 💳 *No credit cards* 🛏 *6 rooms.*

$ B&B/INN **Narima Resort.** With almost all of its bungalows overlooking a refreshing view of Koh Ha, and with relaxing balconies where you can sway in a hammock or kick back in a palm-straw rocking chair, Narima definitely generates a sense of calm. **Pros:** spanning views; pleasant hosts; professional dive school. **Cons:** rocky beach; bathrooms are rough around the edges; restaurant could be better. [$] *Rooms from: $120* ✉ *98 M. 5 Klong Nin Beach, Lanta Yai* ☎ *075/662668, 075/662670* 🌐 *www.narima-lanta.com* 🛏 *32 rooms.*

$$$$ RESORT Fodor's Choice ★ **Pimalai Resort and Spa.** Pimalai's mantra is "peace, serenity and solitude," explaining why royalty and celebrities regularly favor the elegant resort, which offers seductive yet unpretentious luxury in a place where the rain forest meets the sea, fronting a stunning beach. **Pros:** gorgeous Andaman beach with crystal clear water; beautiful location and architecture; friendly, helpful management and staff; uniquely luxurious ambience. **Cons:** prices also exclusive; fills up fast. [$] *Rooms from: B7000* ✉ *99 Moo 5, Bakantiang Beach, Lanta Yai* ☎ *075/607999* 🌐 *www.pimalai.com* 🛏 *72 rooms, 7 suites, 40 private villas* 🍴 *No meals.*

NIGHTLIFE

Bob Bar. A living tribute to reggae, colorful owner Bob welcomes his adoring clientele with a big smile, cold beer, and friendly banter in this laid-back, popular bar. ✉ *Klong Dao, Ban Koh Lanta.*

The Frog Wine Cellar and Restaurant. In Saladan port town near the pier, this wine bar with an atmospheric garden setting offers a nice change of scene for those interested in sampling wines and accompanying appetizers. They have labels from 12 countries. ⊠ *295/19 Moo 3, Klong Dao Beach* ⊕ *www.thefroglanta.com.*

Funky Monkey. Designed to look like the inside of a jungle, this roadside bar-club is the venue for live gigs that get locals, expats, and tourists dancing together until the late hours. Outside, benches offer respite from blaring music and a place to snack from nearby street food stalls. Not as fun on nights when there isn't a live performance. ⊠ *Klong Dao Rd., Koh Lanta.*

KOH PHI PHI

48 km (30 miles) or 90 mins by boat southeast of Phuket Town, 42 km (26 miles) or 2 hours by boat southwest of Krabi.

The Phi Phi Islands consist of six islands. The largest, Phi Phi Don, is shaped like a butterfly: the "wings," covered by limestone mountains, are connected by a flat 2-km (1-mile) narrow body featuring two opposing sandy beaches. Phi Phi Don is the only inhabited island.

Nowadays, the island looks remarkably developed when contrasted with its humble roots some 30 years ago. The tsunami of 2004 has not had any lasting impact and, if you were unaware that such a catastrophe had taken place, you would think it was a beautiful island under a lot of development, rather than one that was destroyed and has been rebuilt. There's quite a bit of construction these days as resorts as well as budget accommodations update and renovate their facilities. The popularity of the Phi Phi Islands stems from the outstanding scuba diving; leopard sharks, turtles, and sea horses are some species still frequenting popular reefs.

As Phi Phi becomes more developed, people have been forced away from the center of Ao Dalerm beach. Other beaches have been discovered and now bear the brunt of growing tourist numbers on the island. Long Beach has become popular, but still retains its charm.

GETTING HERE AND AROUND

Ferries depart from Ratsada Pier on Phuket five times daily and reach Phi Phi Don two hours later. PP Cruiser also takes two hours to reach Phi Phi Don, but departs from Phuket's Makham Pier. A one-way ticket is B650, and a round trip ticket is B1000. Ferries traveling to Phuket from Ao Nang or Koh Lanta stop at Koh Phi Phi in the high season (November to April) as well. From Krabi, boats depart four times each day and cost B650. A few years ago local authorities implemented a B20 "clean-up" tax collected upon arrival at the dock. It's not clear, however, how this money is being used, as there have been no immediately apparent improvements to the island's environment.

BEACHES

Laem Tong Beach. Accessible by boat only, Laem Tong Beach is more secluded than some of the other Phi Phi beaches. The turquoise waters are warm and the beach is bordered by jungle. All this gives Laem Tong more of a tropical-island-paradise feel than other busier Phi Phi beaches. Perfect for couples who want an intimate and romantic location. ■TIP➔ Local fishermen can bring you here and take you to other nearby destinations on their longtail boats for less money than organized trips. **Amenities:** food and drink; toilets. **Best for:** swimming; sunrise; snorkeling. ⊠ *Northern Phi Phi.*

Loh Dalum Beach. On the other side of the Phi Phi Don Island from Tonsai Village, Loh Dalum has all the hallmarks of a tropical paradise: clear emerald waters, views onto the beautiful bay, white sandy beach. However, it is touristy, busy, and noisy—an unfortunate symptom of Phi Phi's popularity. Beach bars put on spectacular fire shows at night and the partying lasts well into the early hours. Swimming is best at high tide. **Amenities:** food and drink; showers; toilets; water sports **Best for:** partiers; swimming. ⊠ *Koh Phi Phi Don.*

Long Beach. Long Beach, a few minutes' longtail boat ride from Tonsai, affords visitors a calmer and more relaxing experience away from the madding crowds. The white sands are almost silky underfoot and there are gorgeous views of Phi Phi Leh. Day-trippers often only stay for a dip and lunch, so the rest of the time it's pretty peaceful. **Amenities:** food and drink; toilets. **Best for:** snorkeling; swimming. ⊠ *Long Beach, Koh Phi Phi.*

Tonsai Beach. This is not a place for the fainthearted; it is crowded, noisy, and not the cleanest. The best time to visit is in the early morning when most of the young revelers are sleeping off the excesses of the previous night. **Amenities:** toilets; showers; water sports. **Best for:** partiers. ⊠ *Ton Sai, Koh Phi Phi.*

OFF THE BEATEN PATH

Phi Phi Lae. A popular day trip from Phi Phi Don is a visit to nearby Phi Phi Lae via longtail or speedboat. The first stop is Viking Cave, a vast cavern of limestone pillars covered with crude drawings. Most boats continue on for an afternoon in **Maya Bay**, aka "The Beach." If you don't mind thronging crowds (the snorkelers practically outnumber the fish), Maya Bay is a spectacular site. If you get a really early jump on everyone, cruise into a bay and leave first tracks along the powdery sand beach; otherwise, head to **Loh Samah Bay**, on the opposite side of the island. Loh Samah Bay may, in fact, be the better option. Though smaller, it is as beautiful as Maya Bay but receives less attention. ⊠ *Koh Phi Phi.*

OFF THE BEATEN PATH

Bamboo Island. Alternatively, you can take a 45-minute trip by longtail boat to circular Bamboo Island, with a superb beach around it. The underwater colors of the fish and the coral are brilliant. The island is uninhabited, but you can spend a night under the stars if you're adventuresome. ⊠ *Koh Phi Phi.*

CLOSE UP

Tsunami Memorials

On the eastern end of Loh Dalam Beach is the Phi Phi Tsunami Memorial Park, a tiny garden with a small plaque listing some of the names of those who lost their lives in the 2004 tsunami. Several benches have been dedicated to the memory of others lost in the disaster. The memorial is a little sad, because it seems so small in relation to the devastation that claimed 5,395 lives. Regardless, it is a nice little park, and looking out across the beach and sea, one cannot help but be moved.

Another memorial, this one underwater, is 66 feet deep, off the coast of Monkey Beach. The granite memorial consists of three pyramid-shape plaques arranged in the shape of an equilateral triangle; the plaques are the exact number of centimeters apart as the number of victims taken by the sea. The bases of the pyramids contain philosophical quotations, and the three markers symbolize the elements of land, water, and air in which humans must learn to live in balance. In the center of the triangle rests a single granite stand that describes the tsunami's occurrence. In addition, 2,874 (the number of missing persons) centimeters from the memorial is a traditional Thai sala made from tsunami debris. It is the first underwater memorial monument on earth.

WHERE TO EAT

$$
SEAFOOD

✕ **Chao Koh Restaurant.** As you stroll Tonsai's walking path, you'll surely notice the catch of the day on display in front of Chao Koh Restaurant (opposite the Chao Koh Resort). Kingfish, swordfish, and barracuda, grilled with garlic and butter, white wine, or marsala sauce, and served with rice or a baked potato, is a mere B250. Clams, crabs, shrimp, Phuket lobster, and live rock lobsters are priced by weight. Chao Koh also serves a variety of Thai salads, appetizers, noodles, and curry dishes, but seafood is their specialty. This restaurant is popular with day-trippers, and often fills up with boatloads of people herded in by their guides. $ *Average main: B230* ⊠ *Tongsai Bay* ☎ *075/620800* 🚫 *No credit cards.*

$
ITALIAN

✕ **Ciao Bella.** It's hardly a local haunt in Napoli or Rome, but for Phi Phi, this offers a tasty rendition of basic Italian cuisine to be enjoyed in a candle-lighted seaside ambience under the moon. Their pizza and focaccia comes from a wood-fired oven, and inventive pasta dishes and classic appetizers such as bruschetta, caprese salad, and prosciutto di Parma round out the menu. $ *Average main: B145* ⊠ *9 Koh Phi Phi Muu* ☎ *081/894–1246* 🚫 *No credit cards.*

$
MIDDLE EASTERN

✕ **Hippies Restaurant and Bar.** On the eastern end of Tonsai Beach, Hippies serves a mixture of international food, from burgers and steaks to pasta and pizza. The staff at both the restaurant and seaside bar are friendly. Once the sun sets, this is the most happening beach bar in Tonsai, with people dancing on the sand, a large projector screening music concerts, and regular fire shows. $ *Average main: B200* ⊠ *Tonsai Beach* 🚫 *No credit cards.*

$ CAFÉ 🍴 **Phi Phi Bakery.** Craving fresh-baked doughnuts, Danish, croissants, mouthwatering eggs Benedict, porridge, or real coffee rather than the vile instant stuff? Check out the family-run Phi Phi Bakery, which serves American, continental, and Thai breakfast and brunch specials and freshly baked pastries (the cinnamon buns are especially good). They also serve Thai and western standards for lunch and dinner. [$] *Average main: B150* ✉ *97 Moo 7, Tonsai Village* ☎ *075/601017* 💳 *No credit cards.*

WHERE TO STAY

$$ RESORT 🏨 **Arayaburi Resort.** The rooms here are modern and clean, and all have tile floors, which keeps the resort looking fresh. **Pros:** private beach; quiet away from the noise of Tonsai; great views out to sea. **Cons:** sometimes slippy access when it rains. [$] *Rooms from: B2200* ✉ *69 Laem Hin Beach* ☎ *076/281360* 🌐 *www.arayaburiphiphi.com* 🛏 *38 rooms* 🍽 *No meals.*

$$ RESORT 🏨 **Bay View Resort.** Every bungalow here has a large deck with a great view of both Phi Phi Lae and Tonsai Bay. The rooms are old with hardwood floors. **Pros:** quiet location; great views; breakfast included. **Cons:** removed from main village; not on best beach. [$] *Rooms from: B2200* ✉ *69 Laem Hin Beach* ☎ *076/281360 up to 64* 🌐 *www.phiphibayview.com* 🛏 *109 bungalows* 🍽 *Breakfast.*

$ B&B/INN 🏨 **Chao Koh Phi Phi Lodge.** Chao Koh Phi Phi Lodge is a collection of unfortunately lime green, basic but comfortable bungalows near Tonsai Bay. There's a great swimming pool, and the resort features family-size suites. **Pros:** budget accommodation; short walk from the beach; nice pool. **Cons:** bungalows have gaudy exteriors; very basic standards; somewhat pricey for what you get. [$] *Rooms from: B1760* ✉ *Tonsai Bay* ☎ *075/620800* 🌐 *www.chaokohresort.com* 🛏 *44 bungalows* 🍽 *Breakfast.*

$$ RESORT Fodor's Choice ★ 🏨 **Holiday Inn Resort.** The Holiday Inn couldn't have a better location—it's on more than 50 acres of tropical gardens along a beach with only three other resorts, which has gorgeous blue water with a sandy sea floor, where you can swim and snorkel year-round. **Pros:** secluded, private beach; attentive staff. **Cons:** set away from the main part of Koh Phi Phi. [$] *Rooms from: B3600* ✉ *Laem Tong Beach* ☎ *075/627300* 🌐 *www.phiphi.holidayinn.com* 🛏 *130 bungalows* 🍽 *Some meals.*

$ RESORT 🏨 **Paradise Resort.** Despite having undergone renovations and pushing up its prices, this place continues to offer great value for money. **Pros:** budget rooms in idyllic location; clean rooms; great beach massage service. **Cons:** some rooms lack air-conditioning; Wi-Fi at extra charge; may be too quiet for some. [$] *Rooms from: B1700* ✉ *Long Beach* ☎ *091/968–3982 up to 89* 🌐 *www.paradiseresort.co.th* 💳 *No credit cards* 🛏 *25 rooms* 🍽 *No meals.*

$$ RESORT 🏨 **Phi Phi Erawan Palm Resort.** Erawan Palm is a small, comfortable resort in the middle of Laem Tong Beach, next to the sea gypsy village. **Pros:** relaxed resort feel; interesting museum; nice location. **Cons:** boat ride away from main village; decor shows some age. [$] *Rooms from: B3100* ✉ *Moo 8, Laem Tong Beach* ☎ *075/627500* 🌐 *www.pperawanpalms.com* 🛏 *18 cottages* 🍽 *No meals.*

$$$
RESORT
FAMILY

⚎ **Phi Phi Island Village Beach Resort.** At this resort you'll find breezily spacious, thatch-roofed bungalows with sharp, bright, contemporary interiors. **Pros:** stunning location; luxurious pool area; isolation and peace. **Cons:** a little remote; how you get there depends on the tide; staff can be a little lax. $ *Rooms from: B5000 ⊠ 49 Moo 8 Loh Bagao Bay ☎ 075/628900 ⊕ www.phiphiislandvillage.com ⊟ No credit cards ⇪ 144 bungalows, 12 villas ❑Breakfast.*

$$
RESORT

⚎ **Phi Phi Natural Resort.** Beautiful sunrise views from the seaside bungalows are this resort's biggest draw. **Pros:** daily boat service to Phuket and Krabi; lovely views at moderate prices. **Cons:** lacks amenities compared to other resorts in price range; remote; can get too busy. $ *Rooms from: B2200 ⊠ 53 Moo 8, Laem Tong Beach ☎ 075/613000 ⊕ www. phiphinatural.com ⇪ 70 rooms ❑Breakfast.*

$
RESORT

⚎ **Phi Phi Viewpoint Resort.** On the western hillside overlooking Loh Dalam Bay, Phi Phi Viewpoint Resort was the sole survivor of the 2004 tsunami that devastated the resorts on this beautiful beach. **Pros:** good location overlooking bay. **Cons:** some huts are basic for the price. $ *Rooms from: B1900 ⊠ 107 Loh Dalam Bay ☎ 075/618111 ⊕ www. phiphiviewpoint.com ⇪ 54 huts, 1 suite.*

$$
RESORT

⚎ **Phi Phi Villa Resort.** Large thatch-covered huts in a natural setting give Phi Phi Villa a relaxing island feeling quite different from bustling Tonsai Bay, a short walk away. **Pros:** budget prices; close to the action; yoga. **Cons:** noise from nearby bars; rocky beach not great for swimming. $ *Rooms from: B2200 ⊠ Tonsai Bay ☎ 075/601100 ⊕ www. phiphivillaresort.com ⇪ 55 bungalows ❑Breakfast.*

$$$$
RESORT
Fodor's Choice
★

⚎ **Zeavola.** This resort takes its name from a flower, the name of which translates in Thai to "love of the sea," which certainly is fitting, as the water off the powdery white-sand Laem Tong Beach is simply stunning. **Pros:** stunning beach location; tasteful design; private. **Cons:** doubled service charge on food. $ *Rooms from: B8600 ⊠ 11 Moo 8, Laem Tong, Koh Phi Phi ☎ 075/627000 ⊕ www.zeavola.com ⇪ 52 villas ❑Breakfast.*

NIGHTLIFE

Many people come to Phi Phi for two reasons only: to go to Maya Bay during the day, and to party in Tonsai Bay at night. Once you head down the side streets away from the beach there are mazes of bars and clubs competing in stereo wars, filled with young travelers eager to drink and dance the night away. If you like Khao San Road in Bangkok, you will love Tonsai Bay at night. The most popular of these bars, located near the 7-Eleven in the center of "town," are **Tiger Bar** and **Reggae Bar.** Along the path running parallel to the sea there are several popular bars, notably **Apache Bar,** which has an impressive "katoey" (drag cabaret) show, and farther to the east are fire shows at the popular beach spots **Hippies Bar** and **Carpe Diem.**

Reggae Bar. The boxing ring in the center of the bar draws crowds, eager for some muay thai action. There are five bars dotted around the complex, keen staff, and a wild atmosphere. The fun gets started when the audience is invited to fight one another in the ring. ⊠ *Tonsai Bay.*

Slinky Beach Bar. If you're young, restless, and like to party all night, Slinky is for you. It gathers the wild crowd and regularly hosts theme parties and fire shows. It doesn't get more rowdy and crowded than this on Koh Phi Phi. ⊠ *Loh Dalum Bay.*

Sunflower Bar. More remote beaches around the island have more subdued nightlife, primarily centered on resort restaurants and bars. One of the best of these is Sunflower Bar, which is on the eastern end of Loh Dalam Beach, next to the Tsunami Memorial Park. Constructed almost entirely of driftwood or old wooden bungalows, this laid-back beach bar is a great place to enjoy scenic sea views and listen to local reggae bands jamming beneath the stars. ⊠ *Loh Dalum Bay.*

Tiger Bar. Tiger Bar is the heart and soul of nightlife on Phi Phi, with live music, DJs, and a dance floor that doesn't get going until late. This is the place to drink away the small hours. There is a chill-out area complete with relaxing sofas and a cocktail menu, which will wilt even the strongest liver. ⊠ *Tonsai Bay ✛ Next to Papaya Restaurant.*

5

6

CHIANG MAI

WELCOME TO CHIANG MAI

TOP REASONS TO GO

★ **History:** Two excellent museums chronicle Chiang Mai's history, which is vividly on display in the architecture of the Old City.

★ **Temples and Monastery Gardens:** The Old City alone has more than 30 ancient temples, where monks are happy to sit with visitors and explain the principles of Buddhism and their cloistered life.

★ **Local Eating:** Chiang Mai's restaurants serve the full range of northern Thai cuisine from menus that usually stretch to more than 100 individual dishes, often costing no more than two dollars.

★ **Views for Miles:** Chiang Mai allows easy access to spectacular mountain scenery, crisscrossed by trekking trails that lead to remote hill tribe villages where visitors are welcome guests. The mountainous region north of the city also offers dazzling leisure activities, from elephant trekking to white-water rafting and rock climbing.

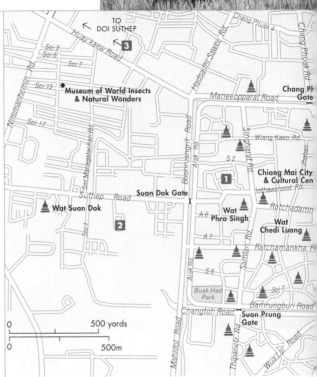

1 The Old City. An 800-year-old moat surrounds the Old City. Much of the wall that once encircled the city has been restored, and the most important of its five original gates, called Thapae, fronts a broad square where markets and festivals are constantly in full swing. Most of Chiang Mai's principal attractions, including its oldest temples, lie within this square mile and are easily accessible on foot.

2 Beyond the Old City. The shortage of available land in the Old City means that most of Chiang Mai's hotels, guesthouses, restaurants, and commercial premises are located in the areas beyond the moat. Some of the city's liveliest nightspots are beyond the walls, and deserve some attention.

GETTING ORIENTED

Modern Chiang Mai is expanding on all sides, but the Old City is relatively compact. First-time visitors would do well to find accommodations within this square mile of busy roads and quiet lanes containing reminders of the eight centuries Chiang Mai served as a citadel and bulwark against invasion from Burma. A stroll through the backstreets and lanes—known as *sois*—is one of the top pleasures of a visit. Two ring roads with underpasses keep traffic flowing around the city center.

6

3 Greater Chiang Mai. Two ring roads and a "Super Highway" allow easy access to the rapidly growing residential suburbs and to the mountains that rise east, west, and north of the city. Day trips to the mountains, including Thailand's highest peak, Doi Inthanon, or the city's "guardian mountain," Doi Suthep, can include an action-packed program of elephant riding, white-water rafting, and brief jungle hikes and still leave time for a leisurely evening back in Chiang Mai.

Updated by
Lara Dunston

Cosmopolitan Chiang Mai, Thailand's second city, is regarded by many as its rightful, historic capital. It's a fascinating and successful mix of old and new, where 1,000-year-old temples and quiet pagoda gardens exist side by side with glittering new hotels and shopping malls. Simple restaurants serving local fare rub shoulders with sophisticated restaurants that would merit notice in any western metropolis.

The city is enjoying boom times and expanding at a giddy rate as it continues to develop beyond its role as a provincial city to become a gateway to Myanmar, Laos, and western China. Since the late 1990s, luxury hotels have been shooting up, attracting more business and leisure travelers. The country's main highway, Highway 1, bypasses Chiang Mai as it runs between Bangkok and Chiang Rai, but the city is at the center of a spider's web of highways reaching out in all four directions of the compass, with no major city or town more than a day's drive away. As one local magazine put it, "Chiang Mai is on the fast track to the future"—quite literally, since plans have been approved to build a high-speed rail link with Bangkok, reducing the current 696-km (430-mile), 12-hour journey to less than four hours.

First impressions of modern Chiang Mai can be disappointing. The immaculately maintained railroad station and the chaotic bus terminal are in so-so areas, and the drive into the city center is not all that scenic. First-time visitors ask why they can't see the mountains that figure so prominently in the travel brochures. But once you cross the Ping River, Chiang Mai begins to take shape. Enter the Old City, and Chiang Mai's brooding mountain, Doi Suthep, is now in view—except when shrouded in the month of March, when heavy air pollution is caused by farmers burning their fields for the planting season.

Whenever you visit, there's bound to be a festival in progress, and with guesthouses and restaurants in the Old City vying with each other for the most florid decoration, it feels like a party year-round. In the heart of the Old City, buildings more than three stories high have been banned, and many of the streets and sois have been paved with flat, red cobblestones. Strolling these narrow lanes, lingering in the quiet cloisters of a temple, sipping hill tribe coffee at a wayside stall, and fingering local fabrics in one of the many boutiques are among the chief pleasures of a visit to Chiang Mai.

PLANNING

WHEN TO GO

The best time to visit is during the dry season between November and February, when days are pleasantly sunny and evenings refreshingly cool. From March to June the weather can be uncomfortably hot, and pollution is heavy in March and April. From July to October the monsoon rains drench the city. ■TIP→ Pollution has become so bad that travelers with breathing problems are advised to avoid the city in March and April, the hottest months of the year, and should check pollution levels before coming in other months.

PLANNING YOUR TIME

Most visitors come to Chiang Mai for only a few days—hardly time enough to take in all its attractions and enjoy all the city has to offer. At least a week's stay is recommended; Chiang Mai's temples alone demand a couple of days' attention, and the surrounding upland countryside is packed with attractions worthy of a day trip.

FESTIVALS AND ANNUAL EVENTS

April sees the city's main holiday, Songkran, or the "water festival," which can offer a refreshing opportunity to cool off in the scorching heat. Book accommodation months in advance for Songkran and expect to pay high-season rates. Songkran is the hedonistic celebration of the Thai New Year, but Loy Kratong in November, a combination of thanksgiving and prayers for future prosperity, is a quieter occasion. Small boatlike receptacles called *kratong* are launched into the Ping River, surrounding lakes, and even ponds. The simultaneous release of thousands of hot-air lanterns into the night sky above Chiang Mai as part of the celebration, usually around the middle of November, is an awesome sight. Awesome, too, is the annual flower festival in February, at which you will likely encounter exotic shrubs and flowers you've never seen before, many of them decorating the huge floats that wend their way through the city in one of its most spectacular processions.

GETTING HERE AND AROUND
AIR TRAVEL

Thai Airways operates several daily flights to Chiang Mai from Bangkok (1 hour 10 minutes) and two direct flights daily from Phuket (1 hour 50 minutes). Bangkok Airways has six flights daily from Bangkok to Chiang Mai. In peak season flights are heavily booked. Thai Air Asia and Nok Air, two airlines based at Bangkok's Don Mueang airport, offer budget flights.

Chiang Mai International Airport is about 5 km (3 miles) south of the Old City. A taxi ride to the Old City costs B150, a trip in a songthaew about B60.

Airports and Transfers Bangkok Airways. ☎ 053/281519 ⊕ www. bangkokair.com. **Chiang Mai International Airport.** ☎ 053/270222 ⊕ www. chiangmaiairportthai.com. **Thai Airways.** ☎ 053/920999, 053/920920 ⊕ www.thaiairways.com.

BUS TRAVEL

VIP buses travel between Bangkok's Northern Bus Terminal and Chiang Mai, stopping at Lampang on the way. For B300 to B850 you get a comfortable 10- to 12-hour ride in a modern bus with reclining seats, blankets and pillows, TV, onboard refreshments, and lunch or dinner at a motorway stop. You can take cheaper buses, but the faster service is well worth the few extra baht.

Chiang Mai's Arcade Bus Terminal serves Bangkok, Chiang Rai, Mae Hong Son, and destinations within Chiang Rai Province. Chang Phuak Bus Terminal serves Lamphun, Chiang Dao, Tha Ton, and destinations within Chiang Mai Province.

CAR TRAVEL

The well-paved roads around Chiang Mai are no problem for most drivers—even the mountainous Mae Sa route north of Chiang Mai is perfectly drivable. However, Thai drivers are notoriously reckless and accidents are frequent. Two major car-rental agencies in Chiang Mai are Avis and Hertz; Budget has a good range of four-wheel-drive vehicles. Many hotels have motorcycle rentals.

Avoid driving in the city during rush hours, which start as early as 7 in the morning and 3 in the afternoon, and pay attention to no-parking restrictions (usually from 9 am to noon and 3 pm to 6 pm). Parking is prohibited on many streets on alternate days, but the explanatory signs are mostly in Thai. Your best bet is to note on which side of the street vehicles are parking. Chiang Mai's traffic police clamp and tow away vehicles parked illegally. Parking lots are numerous and charge as little as B20 for all-day parking.

Hiring a driver with a car is the most convenient way to visit the hard-to-find temples outside the city. This option is expensive, though, and can start at B1,500 ($50) for a half day to B3,000 ($100) for a day trip. It is more affordable to drive yourself. Car-rental agencies also handle car-and-driver hires.

TAXI, TUK-TUK, AND SONGTHAEW TRAVEL

Metered taxis, which can be flagged down on the street, are being introduced gradually in Chiang Mai, replacing the noisier, dirtier song-thaews. The basic taxi charge is B30; you'll pay about B100 for a ride across the Old City. Tuk-tuks are generally cheaper than taxis, but you are expected to bargain—offer B20 or so less than the driver demands. The songthaews that trundle around the city on fixed routes are the cheapest form of transportation—from B25 per person if traveling with other people, but more if you hire the whole vehicle. If he has to make a detour, you'll be charged an extra B20 or so. Settle on the fare before

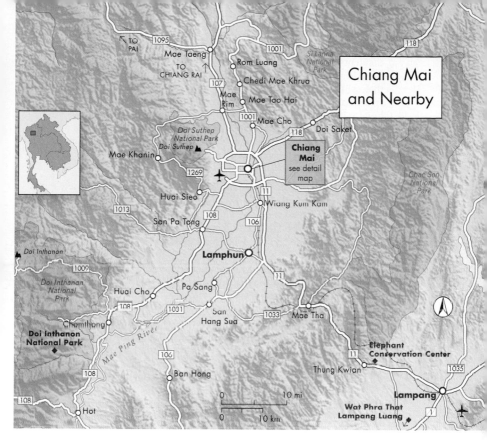

you get in. If your Thai is limited, just hold up the relevant number of fingers. If you hold up three and your gesture evokes the same response from the driver, you'll be paying B30.

TRAIN TRAVEL

The State Railway links Chiang Mai to Bangkok and points south. As the uninteresting trip from Bangkok takes about 13 hours, overnight sleepers are the best choice. The overnight trains are invariably well maintained, with clean sheets on rows of two-tier bunks. ■TIP→ Spending a few extra baht for a first-class compartment is strongly recommended. In second class you may be kept awake by partying passengers. Trains for the north depart from Bangkok's Hualamphong Railway Station and arrive in the Chiang Mai Railway Station. First class fares from Bangkok to Chiang Mai range from B1,450 for a sleeper to B600 or B800 for a day train *(See Train Travel in Travel Smart Thailand)*.

SAFETY AND PRECAUTIONS

Motorcycle accidents are a daily occurrence. Though rentals are easily available, riding a motorbike or scooter is inadvisable unless you are an experienced rider. If you do ride, cover your skin and wear a good helmet.

Incidents of street crime involving foreign visitors are rare, and when they do occur they are energetically investigated by the police. Nevertheless, the usual precautions should be taken when walking the city streets, and particularly the sois, at night. Leave your valuables in your hotel (either in a room safe or with the proprietor). If you leave your passport in the hotel, make sure to carry a copy—it's an offense not to carry some form of identification. Women are advised to carry handbags on the side of the sidewalk that's farthest from the street.

TOURS AND CLASSES

Every other storefront in Chiang Mai seems to be a tour agency, but professionally run. Pick up a list of agencies approved by the Tourism Authority of Thailand before choosing one; the Chiang Mai branch is in a small building on the eastern bank of the Mae Ping River, opposite the New Bridge, open daily from 8:30 to 4:30.

Prices vary quite a bit, so shop around, and carefully examine the offerings. Each hotel also has its own travel desk with ties to a tour operator. The prices are often higher, as the hotel adds its own surcharge. If spending time in monasteries makes you wonder about the lives of the monks, or if you find yourself so enthralled by delicious dishes that you want to learn how to prepare them, you're in luck. Chiang Mai has hundreds of schools offering classes in anything from aromatherapy to Zen Buddhism. The city also has dozens of cooking classes—some in the kitchens of guesthouses, others fully accredited schools—teaching the basics of Thai cuisine. Courses cost from B800 to B1,000 a day. *Cooking courses are listed in this chapter under Shopping.* Alternative medicine, cooking, and massage are the other most popular courses, but by no means the most exotic. In three weeks at the Thailand's Elephant Conservation Center near Lampang, you can train to become a fully qualified mahout.

CLASSES

American University Alumni. The alumni group has been offering Thai language courses for more than two decades. Charges vary according to the duration of the course and the number of pupils. ⊠ *24 Ratchadamnoen Rd.* ☎ *053/278407, 053/277951* ⊕ *www.learnthaiinchiangmai.com.*

TOUR OPERATORS

Best Tuk Tuk Tours. A Thailand-born American named Paul Collins designs custom tours based on guests' schedules and interests. Fluent in Thai, Paul is a knowledgeable guide to the sights in and around Chiang Mai. ⊠ *Chiang Mai* ☎ *084/948–3315* ⊕ *besttuktuktours.wix. com/besttuktuktours* ⊡ *Prices vary based on sights and length of tour.*

Nathlada Boonthueng. A TAT-registered English-speaking guide with a deep knowledge of the region, Nathlada "Timmy" Boonthueng is one of the best local independent operators. She conducts half-day, full-day, and multiday tours for groups and individuals. ⊠ *Chiang Mai* ☎ *081/531–6884* ⊕ *www.chiangmaidestination.com* ⊡ *From B500 for ½-day group tours.*

SpiceRoads Cycle Tours. Themed cycling tours and holidays of varying durations are the specialty of this very professional Asian-based company. ✉ *1 Moon Muang Rd., Soi 7, Old City* ☎ *053/215837* ⊕ *www. spiceroads.com* ✍ *From B1,000 for ½-day tour.*

Top North. This outfit arranges various one-day mountain tours and multiday trekking tours to hill tribe villages. ✉ *41 Moon Muang Rd.* ☎ *053/279–6235* ⊕ *www.topnorthtourchiangmai.com.*

TRAVEL AGENCIES
Pu-Chlee Travel. Puwana Mekara (Tony for short) and Thanchanok Wongkhajorn (also known as Ann) run this travel service in the heart of the Old City. Both are fluent in English and highly qualified. ✉ *Old City* ☎ *083/764–6644.*

World Travel Service. From its central office in Bangkok, Thailand's oldest travel agency organizes tours of Chiang Mai and northern Thailand lasting from one to seven days. ✉ *100/16 Huay Kaew Rd.* ☎ *053/217850, 02/233 5900 up to 9* ⊕ *www.worldtravelservice.co.th*

VISITOR INFORMATION
Contacts Tourist Authority of Thailand (Chiang Mai). ✉ *105/1 Chiang Mai–Lamphun Rd.* ☎ *053/248604, 053/241466* ⊕ *www.tourismthailand.org/Chiang-Mai.*

EXPLORING

The compact Old City can be explored easily on foot or by bicycle. The system of one-way streets can be confusing, but the plan keeps traffic moving quite effectively around the moat, which is crossed by bridges at regular intervals. The moated "one square mile" of the Old City contains 38 of Chiang Mai's temples, including its oldest and most historic ones. The so-called Lanna style of architecture—stepped eaves, dark teak, and gleaming white stucco construction—has been adopted by the owners of boutique hotels in the Old City, where high-rise buildings are banned.

THE OLD CITY

Covering roughly 2½ square km (1 square mile) and crisscrossed by winding lanes Chiang Mai's Old City is bounded by remains of the original city wall and a wide, water-filled moat.

TOP ATTRACTIONS
Fodor's Choice ★ **Wat Chedi Luang.** In 1411 King Saen Muang Ma ordered his workers to build a chedi "as high as a dove could fly." He died before the structure was finished, as did the next king. During the reign of the following king, an earthquake knocked down about a third of the 282-foot spire, and it's now a superb ruin. The parklike grounds contain assembly halls, chapels, a 30-foot-long reclining Buddha, and the ancient pillar. The

> ### WORD OF MOUTH
>
> "I like Chiang Mai because it's a great-looking city. Except for a few spots, Bangkok is a fundamentally ugly city with relatively nondescript architecture. Chiang Mai, on the other hand, has many more treats for the eye."   –rizzuto

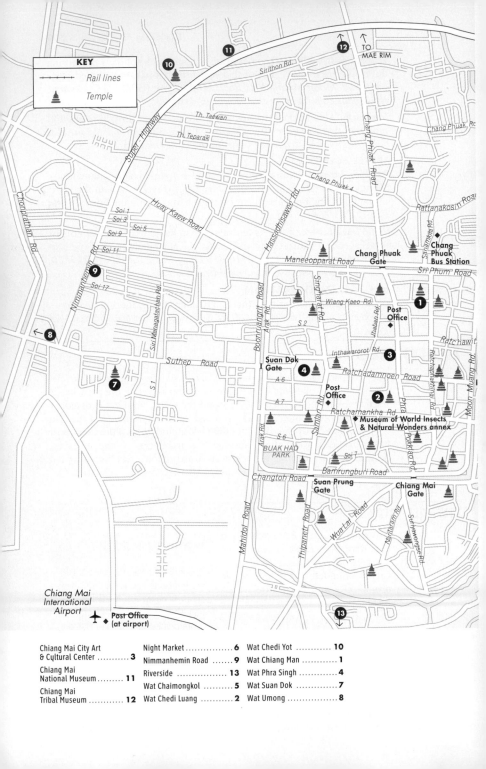

KEY

Rail lines

Temple

Th. Taewan

Th. Teparak

Super Highway

Sirithon Rd.

TO MAE RIM

Chang Phuak Rd.

Rattanakos'n Road

Chang Phuak 4

Chang Phuak Road

Huay Kaew Road

Soi 1
Soi 3
Soi 9
Soi 5
Soi 11
Soi 17

Nimmanhemin Rd.

Sri Managalasthan Rd.

Hassadhisawee Rd.

Maneeopparat Road

Chang Phuak Gate

Chang Phuak Bus Station

Sanammin Rd.

Sri Phum Road

Wiang Kaeo Rd.

Post Office

1

Boonruangrit Road

Arak Rd.

Singharat Rd.

Uhaban Rd.

S 2

Inthawararot Rd.

3

Ratchawit

Suthep Road

S 1

Suan Dok Gate

4

A 6

A 7

Samlan Rd.

Ratchadamnoen Road

Post Office

2

Ratchamankha Rd.

Ratchaphakhinai Rd.

Phra

Moon Muang Rd.

Museum of World Insects & Natural Wonders annex

S 6

BUAK HAD PARK

Arak Rd.

Soi 7

Bamrungburi Road

Pokklao Rd.

Changtoh Road

Suan Prung Gate

Chiang Mai Gate

Mathidol Road

Thipanetr Road

Wua Lai Road

Nohtaam Rd.

Suriwongse Rd.

Chiang Mai International Airport

Post Office (at airport)

13

Chonprathan Rd.

9

8

7

10

11

12

Chiang Mai City Art & Cultural Center 3
Chiang Mai National Museum 11
Chiang Mai Tribal Museum 12
Night Market 6
Nimmanhemin Road 9
Riverside 13
Wat Chaimongkol 5
Wat Chedi Luang 2
Wat Chedi Yot 10
Wat Chiang Man 1
Wat Phra Singh 4
Wat Suan Dok 7
Wat Umong 8

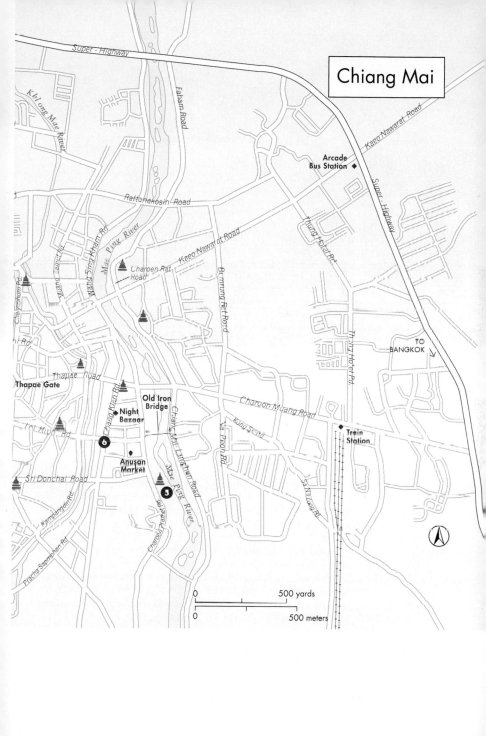

Chiang Mai

Super - Highway

Khlong Mae River

Faham Road

Kaeo Nawarat Road

Super - Highway

Arcade
Bus Station ◆

Rattanakosin Road

Thung Hotel Rd.

Mae Ping River

Kaeo Nawarat Road

Charoen Rat
Road

Bumrung Pet Road

Thung Hotel Rd.

TO
BANGKOK

Thapae Road

Thapae Gate

Old Iron
Bridge

Charoen Muang Road

Chiang Mai Lamphun Road

Kulng Sund

Wa Phon Rd.

Train
Station

Night
Bazaar

⑥

Anusan
Market

Mae Ping River

⑤

Sri Donchai Road

Wampangdin Rd.

Charoen Prathet Road

Pracha Sampharn Rd.

| 0 | | 500 yards |
| 0 | | 500 meters |

Elephants flank the ruined chedi at Wat Chedi Luang.

main assembly hall, a vast, pillared building guarded by two *nagas*, mythical snakes believed to control the irrigation waters in rice fields, was restored in 2008. ⊠ *103 Phrapokklao Rd., between Ratchamankha and Ratchadamnoen Rds., Old City.*

Wat Chiang Man. Chiang Mai's oldest monastery, dating from 1296, is typical of northern Thai architecture. It has massive teak pillars inside the bot, and two important images of the Buddha sit in the small building to the right of the main viharn. The Buddha images are supposedly on view only on Sunday, but sometimes the door is unlocked. ⊠ *Ratchaphakhinai Rd., Old City.*

Fodor'sChoice
★

Wat Phra Singh. Chiang Mai's principal monastery was extensively renovated in 2006. In the western section of the Old City, the beautifully decorated wat contains the Phra Singh Buddha, with a serene and benevolent expression that is enhanced by the light filtering in through the tall windows. Also of note are the temple's facades of splendidly carved wood, the elegant teak beams and posts, and the masonry. Don't be surprised if a student monk approaches you to practice his English. ⊠ *Phra Singh Rd. and Singharat Rd., Old City.*

WORTH NOTING
Chiang Mai City Arts & Cultural Center. The handsome city museum is housed in a colonnaded palace that was the official administrative headquarters of the last local ruler, Chao (Prince) Inthawichayanon. Around its quiet central courtyard are 15 rooms with exhibits documenting the history of Chiang Mai. In another small, shaded courtyard is a delightful café. The palace was built in 1924 in the exact center of the city, the site of the ancient city pillar that now stands in the compound

Old City Tour

A good place to start a tour of the Old City is at the Thapae Gate, near the oldest part of Chiang Mai. Heading west on Ratchadamnoen Road and turning north on Ratchaphakhinai Road brings you to Wat Chiang Man, the oldest temple in Chiang Mai. Backtracking down Ratchaphakhinai Road and heading west on Ratchadamnoen Road brings you to Wat Chedi Luang and Wat Phra Singh. Several other worthwhile temples are outside the city walls. To the east is the serene Wat Chaimongkol. It's an easy walk from the Thapae Gate if the sun isn't too strong. You'll want to take a tuk-tuk to Wat Suan Dok, one of the largest temples in the region. A bit farther away are the verdant grounds of Wat Umong.

of nearby Wat Chedi Luang. In front of the museum sit statues of the three kings who founded Chiang Mai. ⊠ *Phrapokklao Rd., Old City* 📞 *053/217793, 053/219833* 💰 *B90* ⏰ *Tues.–Sun. 8:30–5.*

BEYOND THE OLD CITY

Outside the borders of the Old City, Chiang Mai expands into urban sprawl; although there are several worthy sights and a handful of identifiable areas, which have preserved or developed some individual style. Shopaholics have to venture outside the enclosing moat and make for the famous Night Market or Nimmanhemin Road, the preserve of Chiang Mai's "Hi-So" (High Society) both a 10-minute tuk-tuk ride away from the city center. Chiang Mai's best and liveliest nighttime scene is to be found on the other side of the city in the Riverside quarter bordering the Ping River.

TOP ATTRACTIONS

Chiang Mai Tribal Museum. The varied collection at this museum, more than 1,000 pieces of traditional crafts from the hill tribes living in the region, is one of the finest in the country and includes farming implements, hunting traps, weapons, colorful embroidery, and musical instruments. The museum is off the road to Mae Rim, about 1 km (½ mile) from the National Museum. ⊠ *Ratchangkla Park, Chotana Rd.* 📞 *053/210872* 💰 *Free* ⏰ *Daily 9–4.*

Night Market. Sandwiched between the Old City and the riverside, this market opens for business around 6 pm. It's also, and confusingly, known as the Night Bazaar, though the evening portion technically goes by the name Night Market. Labels aside, more than 200 stalls—selling fake brands, knickknacks, and some goods worth checking out—line a half-mile section of Chang Klan Road. Some visitors find the scene tacky, commercial, or too much of a zoo, but others visitors find a trip here engaging, if only for the many food purveyors. The area is also a major nighttime entertainment zone. Loi Kroh Road, which bisects the market, is filled with bars where girls-for-hire outnumber customers. ⊠ *Chang Klan Rd., between Thapae and Sri Donchai Rds.* 💰 *Free* ⏰ *Daily from 6 pm.*

Wat Chaimongkol. Although rarely visited, this small temple is well worth the journey. Its little chedi contains holy relics, but its real beauty lies in the serenity of the grounds. Outside the Old City near the Mae Ping River, it has only 18 monks in residence. ⊠ *Charoen Prathet Rd.*

Wat Chedi Yot. Wat Photharam Maha Viharn is more commonly known as Wat Chedi Yot, or Seven-Spired Monastery. Built in 1455, it's a copy of the Mahabodhi temple in Bodh Gaya, India, where the Buddha is said to have achieved enlightenment. The seven intricately carved spires represent the seven weeks that he subsequently spent there. The sides of the chedi have striking bas-relief sculptures of celestial figures, most of them in poor repair but one bearing a face of hauntingly contemporary beauty. The temple is just off the highway that circles Chiang Mai, but its green lawns and shady corners are strangely still and peaceful. ⊠ *Super Hwy., between Huay Kaew and Chang Phuak Rds.*

> **TEMPLE KNOW-HOW**
>
> Most temple complexes open around 6 am and don't close until 6 or 8 pm, although the hours can be irregular and the doors may be locked for no apparent reason. If that's the case, approach any monk and explain that you'd like to visit. He'll normally open up the temple. There's no admission charge, except at Wat Phra That Doi Suthep (B40) and the viharn (assembly hall) of Wat Phra Singh (B20), but leave some change in one of the collection boxes. By making a donation you're also "making merit" and easing your journey to the hereafter.

Wat Suan Dok. One of Chiang Mai's largest temples, Wat Suan Dok is said to have been built on the site where bones of Lord Buddha were found. Some of these relics are believed to be inside the chedi; others were transported to Wat Phra That Doi Suthep. At the back of the viharn is the bot housing Phra Chao Kao, a superb bronze Buddha figure cast in 1504. Chiang Mai aristocrats are buried in stupas in the graveyard. ⊠ *Suthep Rd., west of the Old City.*

Wat Umong. The most unusual temple in Chiang Mai is Wat Umong, dating from 1296. According to local lore, a monk named Jam liked to go wandering in the forest. This irritated King Ku Na, who often wanted to consult with the sage. So he could seek advice at any time, the king built this wat for the monk in 1380. Along with the temple, tunnels were constructed and decorated with paintings, fragments of which may still be seen. Beyond the chedi is a pond filled with hungry carp. Throughout the grounds the trees are hung with snippets of wisdom such as "Time unused is the longest time." ⊠ *Off Suthep Rd., past Wat Suan Dok.*

WORTH NOTING

Chiang Mai National Museum. This northern Thai–style building contains many statues of Lord Buddha, including a bust that measures 10 feet high. There's also a huge Buddha footprint of wood with mother-of-pearl inlay. The exhibits have been skillfully arranged into topics such as the early history of the Lanna region, the founding of Chiang Mai,

King Saen Muang Ma designed Wat Chedi Luang to house his father's ashes.

and the development of city's distinctive art forms. The centerpiece of one display is a regal bed covered with mosquito netting that was used by an early prince of Chiang Mai. ⊠ *Super Hwy. (Chiang Mai–Lampang Rd.)* ☎ *053/221308* 🖃 *B30* ☺ *Wed.–Sun. 9–4.*

Nimmanhemin Road. Chiang Mai's version of Bangkok's hip Sukhumvit area is a mile-long strip west of the Old City. Cafés, pubs, bars, restaurants, discos (Warm Up is the most famous), art galleries, and chic boutiques line this street that's usually packed with students from the nearby Chiang Mai University. Spend time exploring the jumble of side streets off the main drag, where more restaurants, party places, and boutiques jostle for space. ⊠ *Nimmanhemin Rd., between Huay Kaew and Suthep Rds.* ✤ *Also accessible via Super Hwy.*

Riverside. Chinese traders originally settled this area 1½ km (1 mile) south of the Old City, and some of their well-preserved homes and commercial premises now house smart restaurants, attractive guesthouses, galleries, boutiques, and antiques shops. This stretch of the Ping River has given its name to its most well-known restaurant and music bar, The Riverside. Its popularity has spawned a row of upbeat restaurants offering live music and fine river views enjoyed by a predominantly young, enthusiastic Thai clientele. This is where to venture to see Thais at play. ⊠ *Charoen Rat Rd.*

CLOSE UP

Monk Chat

If you're like most people, a visit to Chiang Mai's numerous temples is likely to leave you full of unanswered questions. Head to Wat Suan Dok or Wat Chedi Luang, where help is at hand. The monks and novice monks who reside in the two temples eagerly welcome foreign visitors for chats about the history of their temples, the Buddhist faith, and Thai history and culture. Their enthusiasm isn't totally altruistic—they're keen to practice their English.

The talkative monks at Wat Suan Dok are all students of a religious university attached to the temple. Their "monk chat" takes place 5:30 to 7:30 pm on Monday, Wednesday, and Friday. Their counterparts at Wat Chedi Luang can be approached Monday to Saturday, noon to 6:30, as they relax under the trees of their parklike compound. They urge foreign visitors to converse with them about Lanna culture, life in a monastery, or, as one monk put it, "anything at all."

GREATER CHIANG MAI

Beyond the highway that surrounds Chiang Mai you will find plenty to hold your attention. The most famous sight is Wat Phra That Doi Suthep, the mountaintop temple that overlooks the city. The mountain road that skirts Doi Suthep, winding through the thickly forested Mae Sa Valley, is lined with tourist attractions for much of the way, from bungee-jumping towers to orchid farms. Several operators have created a network of zip lines through the forest, enabling more adventurous visitors to swing Tarzan-style for more than a mile at tree-top level.

TOP ATTRACTIONS

Bhubing Palace. The summer residence of the royal family is a serene mansion that shares an exquisitely landscaped park with the more modest mountain retreats of the crown prince and princess. The palace itself cannot be visited, but the gardens are open to the public. Flower enthusiasts swoon at the sight of the roses—among the blooms is a variety created by the king himself. A rough, unpaved road to the left of the palace brings you after 4 km (2½ mile) to a village called Doi Pui Meo, where many of the Hmong women are busy creating finely worked textiles (the songthaew return fare there is B300). On the mountainside above the village are two tiny museums documenting hill tribe life and the opium trade. ⊠ *Off Huay Kaew Rd., 6 km (4 miles) past Wat Phra That Doi Suthep* ⊕ *bhubingpalace.org* ⊠ *Gardens B50* ⊗ *Gardens daily 8:30–4:30, except when royal family in residence (usually Jan.).*

FAMILY **Chiang Mai Night Safari.** Modeled on Singapore's famous game park, the Chiang Mai Night Safari realized a long-held dream of Thaksin Shinnawatra, Thailand's prime minister until he was deposed in a 2006 coup. The 800-acre reserve on the edge of Doi Suthep-Pui National Park, 10 km (6 miles) from downtown Chiang Mai, has more than 100 species of wild animals, including tigers, leopards, jaguars, and elephants. For a thrill, board one of the special trams and

Most boys are ordained as monks at least temporarily, often for the three-month Rains Retreat.

tour the grounds after dark. ⊠ *Km 10, Chiang Mai–Hod Rd.* ⊕ *www. chiangmainightsafari.com* ⊒ *B800* ☉ *Daily 11–10.*

Fodor's Choice
★

Wat Phra That Doi Suthep. As in so many chapters of Thai history, an elephant is closely involved in the legend surrounding the foundation of the late-14th-century Wat Phra That, northern Thailand's most revered temple and one of only a few enjoying royal patronage. The elephant was dispatched from Chiang Mai carrying religious relics from Wat Suan Dok. Instead of ambling off into the open countryside, it stubbornly climbed up Doi Suthep. When the elephant came to rest at the 3,542-foot summit, the decision was made to establish a temple to contain the relics at that site. Over the centuries the temple compound grew into the glittering assembly of chedis, bots, viharns, and frescoed cloisters you see today. The vast terrace, usually smothered with flowers, commands a breathtaking view of Chiang Mai. Constructing the temple was quite a feat—until 1935 there was no paved road to the temple. Workers and pilgrims alike had to slog through thick jungle. The road was the result of a large-scale community project: individual villages throughout the Chiang Mai region contributed the labor, each laying 1,300-foot sections.

Getting here and around: In Chiang Mai, you can find songthaews at Chang Phuak Gate, the Central Department Store (Huay Kaew Road), and outside Wat Phra Singh to take you on the 30-minute drive to this temple. When you arrive, you are faced with an arduous but exhilarating climb up a broad, 304-step staircase. Flanking it are 16th-century tiled balustrades that take the customary form of nagas, the mythical snakes believed to control irrigation waters. A funicular railway provides a

The History of Chiang Mai

Chiang Mai's rich history stretches back 700 years to the time when several small tribes, under King Mengrai, banded together to form a new nation called Anachak Lanna Thai. Their first capital was Chiang Rai, but after three decades they moved it to the fertile plains near the Mae Ping River to a site they called Napphaburi Sri Nakornping Chiang Mai.

The Lanna Thai eventually lost their independence to Ayutthaya and, later, to expansionist Burma. Not until 1774—when the Burmese were finally driven out—did the region revert to the Thai kingdom. After that, the region developed independently of southern Thailand. Even the language is different, marked by a more relaxed tempo. In the last 50 years the city has grown well beyond its original moated city walls, expanding far into the neighboring countryside.

much easier way to the top, but the true pilgrim's path is up the majestic steps. ⊠ *Huay Kaew Rd.* 🚌 *B70 (includes funicular)* ⊙ *Daily 6–6.*

WORTH NOTING

FAMILY **Chiang Mai Zoo.** The cages and enclosures of this zoo on the lower slopes of Doi Suthep are spaced out along paths that wind leisurely through shaded woodlands. If the walk seems too strenuous, you can hop on an electric trolley or a monorail car that stops at all the sights. The monorail system runs through a "twilight" zone of the zoo, where you're assured of seeing the animals emerge for their evening prowls to their watering holes. The most popular animals are two giant pandas, Lin Hui and Chuang Chuang and their female offspring, Lin Bing—the only ones in captivity in Southeast Asia. Koala bears from Australia are also a big attraction—kids are invited to cuddle them. ⊠ *100 Huay Kaew Rd.* 🕾 *053/221179* ⊕ *www.chiangmaizoo.com* 🚌 *B150; pandas B100 additional; B150 monorail* ⊙ *Daily 8–4:30.*

FAMILY **Chiang Mai Zoo Aquarium.** A walk-through underwater tunnel more than 146 meters (160 yards) long provides dramatic views of the thousands of aquatic creatures that live here. Several varieties of sharks, including the Great White, swim around visitors as they make their way through the viewing tunnel. More daring guests can don mask and snorkel and join the big fish in the water (B1,000). There's also a daily water ballet performance by a stunning mermaid. The aquarium is next to the city's zoo. ⊠ *Chiang Mai Zoo, 100 Huay Kaew Rd.* 🕾 *053/893111* ⊕ *www. chiangmaiaquarium.com* 🚌 *B520* ⊙ *Weekdays 10–4, weekends 9–4:30.*

Darapirom Palace. This Lanna-style mansion was the last home of Jao Dararasamee, daughter of a late-19th-century ruler of Chiang Mai and the favorite wife of King Chulalongkorn. The low-eaved and galleried building has been restored and furnished with many of the princess's antiques, including clothes she designed herself. It's a living museum of 19th-century Lanna culture and design, well worth the 12-km (8-mile) journey from Chiang Mai. ⊠ *Chiang Mai–Mae Rim Rd.* 🚌 *B20* ⊙ *Tues.–Sun. 9–5.*

FAMILY **Doi Suthep National Park.** You don't have to head to the distant mountains to go trekking during your stay in Chiang Mai. Doi Suthep, the 3,542-foot peak that broods over the city, lends its name to a national park with plenty of hiking trails to explore. One of these, a path taken by pilgrims over the centuries preceding the construction of a road, leads up to the gold-spired **Wat Phra That Doi Suthep.** It's a half-day hike from the edge of the city to the temple compound. Set off early to avoid the heat of the midday sun. If it's not a public holiday, you'll probably be alone on the mountain. The trail begins at the entrance of the national park, reached by a five-minute ride in one of the songthaews that wait for passengers at the end of Huay Kaew Road, near the entrance to Chiang Mai Zoo.

> ## THE MAE SA VALLEY
>
> This beautiful upland valley winds behind Chiang Mai's Doi Suthep and Doi Pui mountain ranges. A well-paved 100-km (60-mile) loop that begins and ends in Chiang Mai is lined by resorts, country restaurants, tribal villages, an elephant center, a tiger reserve, a snake farm, a monkey colony, orchid hothouses, and the Queen Sirikit Botanical Gardens. The route follows Highway 1001 north from Chiang Mai, turning left at Mae Rim onto Highway 1096 and then 1269, returning to Chiang Mai from the south on Highway 108.

An easy hike lasting about 45 minutes brings you to one of Chiang Mai's least known but most charming temples, **Wat Pha Lat.** This modest ensemble of buildings is virtually lost in the forest. Make sure to explore the compound, which has a weathered chedi and a grotto filled with images of the Buddha. After you leave Wat Pha Lat, the path becomes steeper. After another 45 minutes you emerge onto the mountain road, where you can flag down a songthaew if you can't take another step. Otherwise, follow the road for about 200 yards; a break in the forest marks the uphill trail to **Wat Phra That.** Keep a sharp lookout for snakes; they thrive on the mountain, and some of them are highly venomous. ⊠ *Huay Kaew Rd.* ☎ *053/210244* ☜ *B200* ⊙ *Daily 6–6.*

Elephant Nature Park. There are several elephant reserves north of Chiang Mai, but for a truly authentic up-close experience this one is hard to beat. More than 30 elephants, including four youngsters, roam freely in the natural enclosure formed by a narrow mountain valley an hour's drive away. Visitors can stroll among the elephants, feeding and bathing them in the river that runs through the park. There are no elephant rides or circuslike shows; Sangduen ("Lek") Chailert, a Ford Foundation laureate who runs the reserve, insists that the animals in her care live as close to nature as possible. Visits, which last a full day, can be arranged online or at the park's Old City office; the rate includes pickup at your Chiang Mai hotel and your return. ⊠ *Old City office, 1 Ratchamankha Rd., Phra Singh* ☎ *053/272855, 053/208246 up to 7* ⊕ *www.elephantnaturepark.org* ☜ *B2500.*

FAMILY **Elephant Training Center.** The pachyderms here are treated well and seem to enjoy showing off their skills. They certainly like the dip they take in the river before demonstrating log-rolling routines and giving rides. ⊠ *Mai Sa Valley road between Mae Rim and Samoeng* ☎ *053/206247* ⊕ *www.maesaelephantcamp.com* ⊠ *B150; B800 for ½-hr elephant ride* ⊙ *Shows daily at 8, 9:40, noon, and 1:30.*

NEED A BREAK? ╳ **Mae Sa Valley Garden Resort.** If you're visiting the Elephant Training Center, stop for lunch at this place whose thatched cottages sit amid beautifully tended gardens. The owner's honey-cooked chicken with chili is particularly good. ⊠ *Mae Rim–Samoeng Rd.* ☎ *053/290051 and 2* ⊕ *www. maesavalleyresort.com.*

Sankamphaeng Hot Springs. Among northern Thailand's most spectacular hot springs, these ones include two geysers that shoot water high into the air. The spa complex, set among beautiful flowers, includes an open-air pool and several bathhouses of various sizes. There's a rustic restaurant with a view over the gardens, and small chalets with hot tubs are rented either by the hour (B200) or for the night (B800). Tents and sleeping bags can also be rented for B80. The spa is 56 km (35 miles) north of Chiang Mai, beyond the village of San Kamphaeng. Songthaews bound for the spa leave from the riverside flower market in Chiang Mai. ⊠ *Moo 7, Tambon Ban Sahakorn, Mae-On* ☎ *053/929077, 053/929099* ⊠ *B20* ⊙ *Daily 8–6.*

Wiang Kum Kam. When King Mengrai decided to build his capital on the Ping River, he chose a site a few miles south of present-day Chiang Mai. He selected a low-lying stretch of land, but soon realized the folly of his choice when the river flooded during the rainy seasons. Eight years after establishing Wiang Kum Kam, he moved to higher ground and began work on Chiang Mai. Wiang Kum Kam is now being excavated, and archaeologists have been amazed to uncover a cluster of buildings almost as large as Chiang Mai's Old City.

Wiang Kum Kam Tours. You can travel to Wiang Kum Kam as the locals did for centuries—by boat. Wiang Kum Kam Tours will pick you up at your hotel for the 20-minute river cruise to the site's nearest jetty, where a horse-drawn carriage awaits to complete the journey. There are four cruises a day. Reservations are essential. ⊠ *Chiang Mai ✛ 4 km (2½ miles) south of Chiang Mai on old Chiang Mai–Lamphun Rd.* ☎ *053/252873, 081/885–0663* ⊠ *Free.*

WHERE TO EAT

All the city's top hotels serve reasonably good food, but for the best Thai cuisine go to the restaurants in town. The greatest variety—from traditional Thai to Italian—are to be found within the Old City, and Nimmanhemin Road, about 2 km (1 mile) northwest of downtown, is a star-studded restaurant row. The best fish restaurants, many of them Chinese-run, are found at the Anusan Market, near the Night Bazaar. Chiang Mai also has northern Thailand's best European-cuisine restaurants.

	WHAT IT COSTS IN BAHT			
	$	$$	$$$	$$$$
Restaurants	under B200	B201–B300	B301–B400	over B400

Restaurant prices are for an average main course, excluding tax and tip.

Use the coordinate (✣ B2) at the end of each listing to locate a site on the Where to Eat and Stay in Chiang Mai map.

THE OLD CITY

$ THAI Fodor's Choice ★ 🍴 **Dash Teak House.** In a beautiful, traditional, two-story teak house with a balcony overlooking a garden, Dash is arguably the Old Town's best restaurant and the most professionally run. Guests receive a warm welcome from the Thai mother-son team who returned to Thailand to open the restaurant after living many years in the United States. Expect generous servings of classic Thai food from across the country. The *khao soi* (chicken curry noodle soup), *gaeng hang lay* (pork curry), and other Lanna specialties stand out. [$] *Average main: B150* ✉ *38/2 Moon Muang Rd., Soi 2, Old City* ☎ *053/279230* 🌐 *dashteakhouse.com* *Reservations essential* 💳 *No credit cards* ✣ *F4.*

$$ ECLECTIC 🍴 **Ginger & Kafe.** The former House restaurant transferred its kitchen and dining room to the adjacent Ginger & Kafe, which is part of the same property, overlooking the city moat. The formal, fine-dining experience has become much more relaxed, with guests invited to make themselves comfortable on plump, plush armchairs and sofas and even on large cushions scattered over the polished teak floor. The cuisine remains distinctly eclectic, however, with old favorites such as the many tapas and innovative salads still on the menu. [$] *Average main: B300* ✉ *199 Moon Muang Rd., Old City* ☎ *053/419011* 🌐 *www.thehousethailand.com* 💳 *No credit cards* ✣ *F3.*

$ ITALIAN 🍴 **Graph Table.** The young Thai couple behind the superb Graph Café have followed it up with this stylish yet casual trattoria nearby. The chef, who learned to cook Italian from a Sicilian-born friend, crafts authentic, fresh, handmade pastas and pizzas made to order. The produce used is local and organic as much as possible. The fantastic breakfasts include the Monet, eggs with mashed avocado and salad. The coffee is excellent. [$] *Average main: B120* ✉ *Moon Muang Rd., Soi 6, Old City* ☎ *086/567–3330* 💳 *No credit cards* ✣ *E3.*

$ THAI Fodor's Choice ★ 🍴 **Huen Phen.** The small rooms in this restaurant, once a private home, brim with bric-a-brac typical of the region. Select a table in any of the dining rooms or out in the plant-filled garden. The house and garden are open only in the evening; lunch is served in a street-front extension packed daily with hungry Thais. A specialty here at the Old City's best Lanna restaurant is gaeng hang lay with *kao nio* (sticky rice). The *larb nua* (spicy ground beef fried with herbs) and the deep-fried pork ribs are two more dishes not to be missed. [$] *Average main: B150* ✉ *112 Ratchamankha Rd., Old City* ☎ *053/814548* 💳 *No credit cards* ✣ *D4.*

$ CAFÉ 🍴 **Overstand.** Owned by an Australian barista and his Chiang Mai–born wife, this cool little café in the Thapae Gate area serves excellent

6

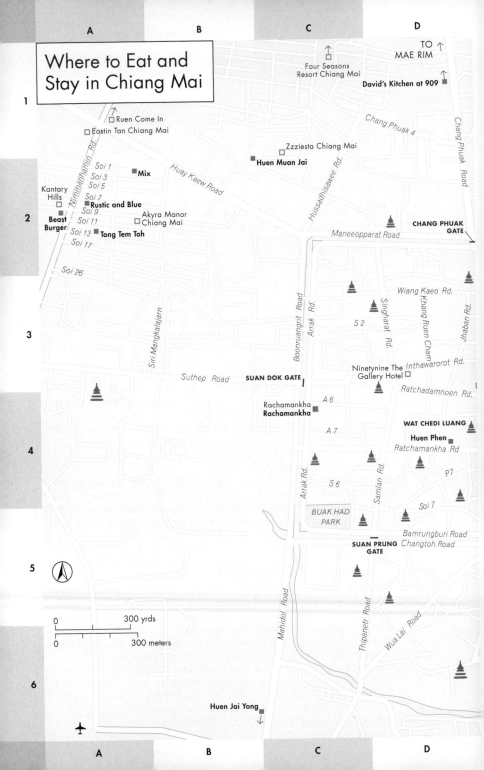

Where to Eat and Stay in Chiang Mai

A · B · C · D

1

TO MAE RIM

Four Seasons Resort Chiang Mai

David's Kitchen at 909

Chang Phuak 4

Chang Phuak Road

Ruen Come In

Eastin Tan Chiang Mai

Zzziesta Chiang Mai

Huen Muan Jai

Nimmanhamin Rd.

Soi 1
Soi 3
Soi 5
Soi 7
Soi 9
Soi 11
Soi 13
Soi 17

Soi 26

Mix

Huay Kaew Road

Hussadhisawee Rd.

2

Kantary Hills

Rustic and Blue

Beast Burger

Akyra Manor Chiang Mai

Tong Tem Toh

Maneeopparat Road

CHANG PHUAK GATE

Boonruangrit Road

Arrak Rd.

Wiang Kaeo Rd.

Singharat Rd.

Khang Ruen Cham

Jhaban Rd.

3

Siri Mangkalajarn

Suthep Road

SUAN DOK GATE

S 2

Ninetynine The Gallery Hotel

Inthawarorot Rd.

Ratchadamnoen Rd.

Rachamankha
Rachamankha

A 6

A 7

WAT CHEDI LUANG

Huen Phen

Ratchamankha Rd

4

Arrak Rd.

S 6

Samlan Rd.

Soi 7

P 7

BUAK HAD PARK

Bamrungburi Road
Changtoh Road

SUAN PRUNG GATE

5

300 yrds

300 meters

Mahidol Road

Thipanetr Road

Wua Lai Road

6

Huen Jai Yong

A · B · C · D

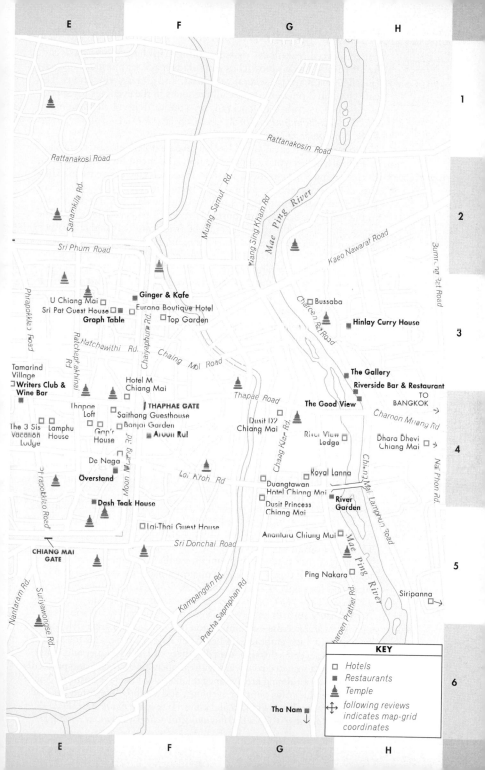

coffee sourced from local roasters, along with hearty breakfasts and healthy Aussie-style sandwiches and salads made with organic ingredients. There are always several vegetarian and gluten-free options. The café closes at 2 pm but occasionally reopens in the evenings for special events such as craft-beer, cocktail, or wine tastings. [$] *Average main: B120* ✉ *Ratchamankha, Soi 2, Old City* ☎ *095/323–7360* ⏲ *Closed Tues. No dinner* 💳 *No credit cards* ✥ *E4.*

$$$$ THAI Fodor's Choice ★ 🍴 **Rachamankha.** A meal at the Rachamankha hotel's elegant restaurant is a must whether you're a guest or not. The menu focuses on Lanna, Burmese, and Shan cuisine, a sensible approach given the entwined history of these northern neighbors. The formal dining room inside, decorated with tasteful antiques, is best during the day, but reserve a table in the softly lit, brick-lined courtyard if you'll be here after dark. The servers are discreetly attentive, and the prices are reasonable for such impeccably prepared food. [$] *Average main: B700* ✉ *6 Ratchamankha, Soi 9, Old City* ☎ *053/904111* 🌐 *www.rachamankha.com* ✍ *Reservations essential* 💳 *No credit cards* ✥ *C4.*

$ ECLECTIC 🍴 **Writers Club & Wine Bar.** You don't have to be a journalist to dine at Chiang Mai's unofficial press club—the regulars include not only media types but also anyone from hard-up artists and eccentric local characters to successful entrepreneurs. Expect the usual classic Thai dishes, including salads, stir-fries, and curries. The house wines are decent and sensibly priced. Reservations are essential on Friday and Sunday. [$] *Average main: B150* ✉ *141/3 Ratchadamnoen Rd., Old City* ☎ *053/814187* 💳 *No credit cards* ⏲ *Closed Sat.* ✍ *Reservations essential* ✥ *E4.*

BEYOND THE OLD CITY

$ THAI 🍴 **Aroon Rai.** This simple, open-sided restaurant has prepared such traditional northern dishes as frogs' legs fried with ginger for more than 30 years. Try the *tabong* (boiled bamboo shoots fried in batter) and *sai ua* (pork sausage with herbs). There is take-out service. [$] *Average main: B100* ✉ *45 Kotchasarn Rd.* ☎ *053/276947* 💳 *No credit cards* ✍ *Reservations not accepted* ✥ *F4.*

$ BURGER FAMILY 🍴 **Beast Burger.** If you find yourself craving western fast food, skip the global franchises and make a beeline for this brilliant gourmet food truck. Run by two young Thai siblings and open in the evenings until 11 or sold out, it's parked permanently outside the Thanachart Bank. The burgers are made with premium-quality ingredients and are perfectly cooked. If they don't have you going back for seconds, the onion rings and fries will. [$] *Average main: B150* ✉ *Nimmanhemin Rd., Soi 11* ☎ *080/124–1414* ⏲ *No lunch* 💳 *No credit cards* ✥ *A2.*

$ ECLECTIC 🍴 **The Gallery.** Awards have been heaped on this attractive riverside restaurant for its architecture—a combination of Chinese and Lanna styles—and its cuisine, which embraces dishes from Asia, Europe, and the United States. Guests enter through a small gallery of local antiques and handicrafts, cross a secluded courtyard with an open-air barbecue, and proceed into a teak-floor dining area with eggplant-color linens. A northern Thai string ensemble plays on most evenings, and a subtly integrated bar-café presents accomplished live jazz and blues. [$] *Average main: B200* ✉ *25–29 Charoen Rat Rd.* ☎ *053/248601* 🌐 *www.thegallery-restaurant.com* ✥ *H3.*

$$ ECLECTIC 🍴 **The Good View.** The name of this waterfront restaurant is a nod to its sweeping Ping River view, which along with the food and live music attracts a big nightly crowd. It's no place for a quiet evening—partying Thais tend to occupy the maze of tables. Stick to the excellent Thai menu and pass on the indifferent western cuisine. The pad thai and grilled perch are particularly good. [$] *Average main: B200* ✉ *13 Charoen Rat Rd., at river* ☎ *053/241866* ✥ *H4.*

$ ASIAN 🍴 **Hinlay Curry House.** Tucked away in a corner of a former businessman's mansion, this small, open-sided Asian restaurant specializes in inexpensive curry dishes from India, Burma, and Thailand. Daily specials, accompanied by two varieties of rice or a selection of Indian breads, are written on a blackboard. The tiny terrace overlooks the grounds of the mansion, whose present owners run the restaurant. [$] *Average main: B120* ✉ *8/1 Na Watket Rd., Soi 1, Wat Ket* ☎ *053/242621* 💳 *No credit cards* ✥ *H3.*

$ THAI 🍴 **Huen Muan Jai.** On a backstreet in an increasingly cool local neighborhood dotted with cafés and small eateries, this restaurant in a traditional teak house serves authentic Lanna cuisine. Try the *nam prik ong* (tomato minced-pork dip) served with crispy vegetables, the *larb moo* (a rich minced-pork salad) the locally revered gaeng hang lay. Don't be surprised if you find yourself returning for a another meal. Most patrons do. Before you leave, check out the framed wall photos of the owner-chef's appearance on *Iron Chef Thailand.* [$] *Average main: B100* ✉ *24 Ratchpruek Rd.* ☎ *053/404998* 🌐 *www.huenmuanjai.com* 🕒 *Closed Wed.* 💳 *No credit cards* ✥ *B2.*

$$ THAI 🍴 **Mix Restaurant and Bar.** Thai foodies extol this glamorous restaurant for its unique form of Thai-global fusion cuisine and the awesome molecular cocktails. The selection of beers and wines from around the world also impresses. With 200-plus options, the menu is way too long. Some dishes can be hit or miss, but when the chefs get things right the results are divine. Skip the international and European menus and go for classic Thai with a twist. The tacky photo menu is actually helpful—the unusual flavor combinations might put you off if not for the photos of pretty plates. [$] *Average main: B240* ✉ *36 Nimmanhemin Rd., Soi 1* ☎ *053/216878* 🌐 *www.mixrestaurantandbar.com* 💳 *No credit cards* ✥ *A2.*

$$$ ECLECTIC 🍴 **River Garden.** This handsome Lanna-style restaurant complex sits next to Chiang Mai's historic "Iron Bridge," and its spacious outside terrace commands views of the bridge and the Ping River. The chefs prepare the full range of authentic, if pricey, Thai dishes, along with steaks, succulent spare ribs, and other western food. There's also an extensive sushi bar. [$] *Average main: B310* ✉ *33/12 Charoen Prathet Rd.* ☎ *053/234493* 💳 *No credit cards* ✍ *Reservations essential* ✥ *F4.*

$$ INTERNATIONAL 🍴 **Riverside Bar & Restaurant.** The ever-popular Riverside has an informal waterfront location and a modern and elegant dining room across the road. The boisterous atmosphere of the riverside venue is replaced at the latter by a more sophisticated dining experience, although there's nightly live music here, too. A candlelight dinner in the romantic central courtyard on a warm evening is especially recommended. [$] *Average main: B250* ✉ *9/11 Charoen Rat Rd.* ☎ *053/243239* 🌐 *www.theriversidechiangmai.com* ✍ *Reservations essential* ✥ *H4.*

$
INTERNATIONAL

X **Rustic and Blue.** Part tearoom, part casual eatery, this rustic place whose furnishings include tables made of recycled wood focuses on food crafted from fresh organic ingredients sourced from local farmers and artisanal producers. The all-day breakfasts are hugely popular—try the brioche French toast brûlée with fresh fruit—but the pizzas and salads, among them a fine one with heirloom tomatoes, have many fans, too. You can order craft beers and cocktails, but the soothing aromatic herbal teas are often just the ticket after a long day traipsing around temples. $ *Average main: B110* ⊠ *Nimmanhemin Rd., Soi 7* ☎ *086/654–7178* ▭ *No credit cards* ✥ *A2.*

$
THAI

X **Tha Nam.** The crumbling old building that once housed this pictur-esque restaurant was demolished and a brand-new Tha Nam opened for business a few hundred yards along the river. Formal tables and chairs replaced the antique furniture that matched the historic setting of the old establishment, but the menu is basically the same (try the gaeng hang lay or chicken in pandan leaves), and the riverside location is per-haps more attractive than before. There is occasionally live music. $ *Av-erage main: B150* ⊠ *7168 Moo 3 Pa Dad Rd.* ☎ *052/001111* ⊕ *www. thanuhm.com* ✥ *G6.*

$
THAI

X **Tong Tem Toh.** Follow your nose to the street-side barbecue of this cool Lanna restaurant on a busy alley off Nimmanhemin Road. The casual place is popular with young Thais, who love the great, affordable cui-sine and the beer-garden atmosphere. Start with the northern Thai hors d'oeuvre platter that includes fermented pork sausages, pork crackling, spicy relishes, and raw vegetables. Also delicious is the ant-egg and glass-noodle soup. Get here on time—the kitchen closes sharply at 9 pm. $ *Average main: B100* ⊠ *11 Nimmanhemin Rd., Soi 13* ☎ *053/854701* ▭ *No credit cards* ✥ *A2.*

GREATER CHIANG MAI

$$$$
EUROPEAN
Fodor's Choice
★

X **David's Kitchen at 909.** Dress up for this award-winning restaurant owned by a warm and welcoming British-Thai husband-wife front-of-house team and an excellent Thai chef. The three pride themselves on their old-fashioned hospitality, so don't be surprised if one of them greets you at the door and walks you out at the end of the night. The modern Euro-pean cuisine, also endearingly old-school, makes for a wonderful change from Thai if you've been traveling in the country for a while. The braised lamb shank with red-wine sauce and mashed potatoes is superb washed down with a big red, but save room for the sticky-toffee pudding. The set menus, B499 for a two-course lunch and B999 for a three-course dinner, are a fantastic value. $ *Average main: B700* ⊠ *90/9 Moo 3 Sanpisuur Rd., north off Hwy. 3029* ☎ *053/110732* ⊕ *www.davidskitchenat909. com* ⌣ *Reservations essential* ▭ *No credit cards* ✥ *D1.*

$
THAI

X **Huen Jai Yong.** Ask a Thai chef where to find Chiang Mai's finest and most authentic Lanna food, and you'll likely be directed to this rustic restaurant a 30-minute drive south of the Old City. The place occupies an old timber house and several air-conditioned rooms in a contempo-rary building that wraps around the back garden. Start with the *nam prik num* (roasted green-chili relish) and *kap moo* (pork crackling), and don't miss the rich, aromatic gaeng hang lay. Few staff members speak

English, and you're unlikely to see any foreigners, but there is an English menu (you might have to ask for it). Prices are exceedingly reasonable for the quality. The only issue is transportation. If you're carless, the best strategy is to take a taxi and pay the driver to wait. $ *Average main: B60* ⊠ *65 Moo 4 San Kamphaeng Rd., Tambon Buak Khang, off Hwy. 1317* ☎ *086/671–8710* ⊟ *No credit cards* ✛ *B6.*

WHERE TO STAY

Soaring tourist numbers—particularly young Chinese visitors with newly acquired wealth and the urge and freedom to travel—have fueled an unprecedented hotel building boom in recent years. Most of the new properties are in the traditional so-called Lanna style, and the most luxurious of them rival hotels in Bangkok. One, the Dhara Dhevi, justly claims to be among Asia's finest. Except for the high season, from December to February, prices are far lower than in the capital. Charming, modestly priced guesthouses and small hotels abound, and some are right on the water. ■ **TIP→** Watch out for guesthouses that advertise cheap room rates and then tell you the accommodation is only available if you book an expensive tour. Always ask if there's a tour requirement with your room rate. All hotels and most guesthouses accept dollars, but if you are paying in greenbacks check the offered exchange rate carefully; it can be as much as 10% less than what is obtainable in banks and at exchange booths.

WHAT IT COSTS IN BAHT			
$	**$$**	**$$$**	**$$$$**
Hotels under B2,000	B2,001–B4,000	B4,001–B6,000	over B6,000

Hotel prices are for a standard double in high season, excluding service charge and tax.

For expanded hotel reviews, visit Fodors.com.

Use the coordinate (✛ B2) at the end of each listing to locate a site on the Where to Eat and Stay in Chiang Mai map.

THE OLD CITY

$
B&B/INN
The 3 Sis Vacation Lodge. A sacred Bhodi tree stands sentinel outside this attractive hotel that looks out directly onto Wat Chedi Luang, one of Chiang Mai's most historic temples. **Pros:** famous Sunday market is right outside; three leading temples within walking distance; 24-hour convenience store next door. **Cons:** temple dogs can be noisy; busy main-road location; limited parking. $ *Rooms from: B1,500* ⊠ *150 Phrapokklao Rd., Old City* ☎ *053/273243* ⊕ *www.the3sis.com* ⏎ *39 rooms* ⊘ *No meals* ✛ *E4.*

$
B&B/INN
Fodor'sChoice
★
Banjai Garden. A French restaurateur and his Thai wife renovated this sturdy old Chiang Mai residence into a clean and comfortable guesthouse. **Pros:** easy access to bars and restaurants; shaded garden; delightful owners; clean Lanna-style rooms; good value. **Cons:** books up far

ahead in high season; some rooms share a bath. $ *Rooms from: B1,100* ✉ *43 Phrapokklao Rd., Soi 3, Old City* ☎ *085/716–1635* ⊕ *www. banjai-garden.com* ▭ *No credit cards* ➦ *7 rooms* ❄️ *No meals* ✚ *F4.*

$$ 🔲 **De Naga.** This Lanna-style boutique hotel is ideally located, with
HOTEL   many bars and restaurants nearby. **Pros:** excellent service by English-speaking staff; good restaurant; shady terrace with comfortable garden furniture. **Cons:** nighttime noise from neighboring bars; small pool; unreliable Internet. $ *Rooms from: B3,000* ✉ *21/2 Moon Muang Rd., Old City* ☎ *053/209030* ⊕ *www.denaga.com* ➦ *55 rooms* ❄️ *Breakfast* ✚ *E4.*

$$ 🔲 **Eurana Boutique Hotel.** One of Chiang Mai's most attractive boutique
HOTEL   properties, the Eurana is a haven of peace and understated luxury on a quiet lane near busy Sompet Market. **Pros:** secluded Old City location; cool and leafy garden; nearby market. **Cons:** noisy dogs; rowdy neighborhood bars; insects. $ *Rooms from: B3,500* ✉ *Moon Muang Rd., Soi 7, Old City* ☎ *053/219402* ⊕ *www.euranaboutiquehotel.com* ➦ *72 rooms* ❄️ *Breakfast* ✚ *F3.*

$ 🔲 **Gap's House.** This inn is both well placed for exploring the Old City
B&B/INN   and removed from the hustle and bustle, sunk dreamily in a backstreet tropical oasis. **Pros:** total seclusion; reliable tours; luxuriant garden. **Cons:** moody owner; noisy plumbing; no parking; does not take reservations. $ *Rooms from: B470* ✉ *3 Ratchadamnoen Rd., Soi 4, Old City* ☎ *053/278140* ⊕ *www.gaps-house.com* ▭ *No credit cards* ➦ *19 rooms* ❄️ *Breakfast* ✚ *E4.*

$$ 🔲 **Hotel M Chiang Mai.** Adjacent to the Thapae Gate and bordering
HOTEL   the moat, this refurbished old favorite has a terrace that hums with activity on the weekend. **Pros:** central location; cozy rooms; bright ground-floor café. **Cons:** no pool; some traffic noise in rooms facing moat; limited parking. $ *Rooms from: B2,400* ✉ *2–6 Ratchadamnoen Rd.* ☎ *053/211069* ⊕ *www.hotelmchiangmai.com* ➦ *75 rooms* ❄️ *Breakfast* ✚ *F4.*

$ 🔲 **Lamphu House.** An excellent choice for first-time visitors, this Old
HOTEL   City budget boutique hotel is a short stroll from Wat Chedi Luang and several other star attractions. **Pros:** near star attractions; balconies; stunning swimming pool. **Cons:** compact rooms; few amenities; reception staff speaks little English. $ *Rooms from: B790* ✉ *1 Phrapokklao Rd., Soi 9, Old City* ☎ *053/274966* ⊕ *www.lamphuhousechiangmai.com* ➦ *41 rooms* ❄️ *No meals; Breakfast* ▭ *No credit cards* ✚ *E4.*

$ 🔲 **Ninety Nine The Gallery Hotel.** Elegant for the price, this midrange
HOTEL   hotel with a fantastic location near the Sunday-night market and other attractions has rooms to suit most budgets. **Pros:** saltwater swimming pool; elegant for the price; fantastic location. **Cons:** many rooms are small; staff doesn't speak much English. $ *Rooms from: B1,200* ✉ *99 Intrawarorot Rd., Old City* ☎ *053/326338* ⊕ *99thegalleryhotel.com* ➦ *53 rooms and suites* ❄️ *Breakfast* ▭ *No credit cards* ✚ *D3.*

$$$$ 🔲 **Rachamankha.** The luxurious rooms at this small hotel on a quiet
HOTEL   lane near Wat Phra Singh straddle a series of hushed brick courtyards
Fodor's Choice   enclosed by triple-eave Lanna-style buildings. **Pros:** peaceful setting;
★   helpful staff; pool; free parking. **Cons:** so-so neighborhood; noisy temple dogs; rooms too spartan for some; children under age 12 not permitted.

$ | Rooms from: B8,000 ⊠ 6 Ratchamankha Rd., Soi 9 ☎ 053/904111 ⊕ www.rachamankha.com ⊃ 24 rooms, 1 suite ⦿ Breakfast ✛ C4.

$
HOTEL
⌂ **The Saithong Guesthouse.** The friendly little Saithong has 10 air-conditioned and richly colored, well-furnished rooms in Lanna style. **Pros:** central location; short walk to moat and Sunday market; helpful travel desk. **Cons:** no parking; noisy neighborhood music bars; patchy Internet. $ Rooms from: B900 ⊠ Ratchadamnoen Rd., Soi 3, Old City ☎ 053/418672 ⊕ www.saithongguesthouse.com ⊃ 10 rooms ⦿ No meals ✛ E4.

$$
HOTEL
⌂ **Sri Pat Guest House.** Family-run, spotlessly clean, and stylishly furnished, this little hotel on a cobbled lane a short walk from the moat is one of the best deals in the Old City. **Pros:** friendly, helpful Thai owner; lively village street scene; proximity to Sompet Market. **Cons:** noisy neighborhood dogs; no double beds; no parking. $ Rooms from: B3,500 ⊠ 16 Moon Muang Rd., Soi 7, Old City ☎ 053/218716 ⊕ www.sri-patguesthouse.com ⊃ 24 rooms ⦿ No meals ✛ E3.

$$$$
HOTEL
⌂ **Tamarind Village.** A canopy of towering, interlaced bamboo leads to the main entrance of this stylish village-style hotel in the center of the Old City. **Pros:** quiet, secluded location; short walk to center of Old City; good restaurant. **Cons:** relatively small rooms; pricey. $ Rooms from: B6,700 ⊠ 50/1 Ratchadamnoen Rd. ☎ 053/418896 up to 9 ⊕ www.tamarindvillage.com ⊃ 42 rooms, 3 suites ⦿ Breakfast ✛ E4.

$
HOTEL
⌂ **Thapae Loft.** The industrial-chic design of this midrange boutique hotel is refreshing, as are the air-conditioned rooms. **Pros:** stylish; spacious rooms; well located for Old City exploring. **Cons:** tiny swimming pool; disappointing breakfast. $ Rooms from: B1,800 ⊠ 142 Ratchaphakhinai Rd., Old City ☎ 053/280700 ⊕ www.thapaeloft.com ⊃ 29 rooms and suites ⦿ Breakfast ▬ No credit cards ✛ E4.

$
B&B/INN
⌂ **Top Garden Boutique Guest House.** Small and intimate, this guesthouse has the feel of a boutique hotel. **Pros:** secluded; close to the bar and restaurant scene; helpful owners. **Cons:** no pool; no parking; traffic noise. $ Rooms from: B360 ⊠ 13 Chaiyapoom Rd., Old City ☎ 053/232538 ⊕ www.topgarden-chiangmai.com ▬ No credit cards ⊃ 10 rooms ⦿ Breakfast ✛ F3.

$$$
HOTEL
⌂ **U Chiang Mai.** A Lanna-style boutique hotel in the exact center of the Old City, the U Chiang Mai was constructed around a century-old teak house, the home of a former governor. **Pros:** 24-hour room rate, so if you arrive at 10 pm, you don't have to leave until 10 pm the next day; spa and massage; helpful tour desk. **Cons:** exposed pool that's open to view from most rooms; no parking; high bar and restaurant prices. $ Rooms from: B4,200 ⊠ 70 Ratchadamnoen Rd., Old City ☎ 053/327000 ⊕ www.uhotelsresorts.com/uchiangmai ⊃ 79 rooms ⦿ No meals ✛ E3.

BEYOND THE OLD CITY

$$$
HOTEL
⌂ **Akyra Manor Chiang Mai.** With enormous rooms and luxurious extras that include high-thread-count Egyptian cotton sheets and state-of-the-art technology, this five-star suites-only boutique property on a happening Nimmanhemin side street could hold its own in Bangkok. **Pros:** spacious suites; attention to detail; excellent restaurant; abundant

amenities. **Cons:** small rooftop; limited public spaces. [$] *Rooms from: B5,200* ✉ *22/2 Nimmanhemin Rd., Soi 9* ☎ *053/2162197* 🌐 *theakyra.com/chiang-mai* 🛏 *30 suites* 🍴 *Breakfast* 💳 *No credit cards* ✥ *A2.*

$$$$ HOTEL Fodor's Choice ★ 🏨 **Anantara Chiang Mai Resort & Spa.** The former grounds of the British Consulate now house this waterfront oasis whose rooms and suites have private terraces overlooking either the Mae Ping River or the verdant gardens. **Pros:** historic setting but contemporary feel; private terraces; faultless service; riverside location; renowned restaurant; immense pool; complimentary minibar. **Cons:** some find the metallic, rust-color facade off-putting; water features could be better lighted at night. [$] *Rooms from: B9,200* ✉ *123 Charoen Prathet Rd.* ☎ *053/253333* 🌐 *www.chiang-mai.anantara.com* 🛏 *52 rooms, 32 suites* 🍴 *No meals; Breakfast* ✥ *H5.*

$ B&B/INN 🏨 **Bussaba.** A former 19th-century Chinese trader's home has been beautifully converted into a bed-and-breakfast inn at the heart of a riverside road lined by similar reminders of a bygone era. **Pros:** near main market and riverside bars and restaurants; home-away-from-home atmosphere; friendly, helpful owners. **Cons:** on busy street; front-facing upper rooms suffer from traffic noise; limited parking; no restaurant. [$] *Rooms from: B1,100* ✉ *124–128 Charoen Rat Rd., T. Wat Ket, City Center* ☎ *053/244067, 081/999–2504* 🌐 *www.bussababedchiangmai.com* 💳 *No credit cards* 🛏 *8 rooms* 🍴 *Breakfast* ✥ *G3.*

$$$ HOTEL 🏨 **Duangtawan Hotel Chiang Mai.** With its modern exterior and 24 stories, the Duangtawan dominates the city center and the busy Night Bazaar. **Pros:** Night Bazaar is on the doorstep; underground parking; well-equipped fitness center. **Cons:** noisy tour groups; sometimes delays checking in and out; anonymous chain-hotel atmosphere. [$] *Rooms from: B5,750* ✉ *132 Loi Kroh Rd., City Center* ☎ *053/905000* 🌐 *www.duangtawanhotelchiangmai.com* 🛏 *507 rooms* 🍴 *Breakfast* ✥ *G4.*

$$$ HOTEL 🏨 **Dusit D2 Chiang Mai.** This contemporary hotel makes a complete break from the traditional Lanna style so prevalent in Chiang Mai. Clean lines, brushed-steel-and-glass surfaces, and cubist upholstery set the tone in the interiors, from the airy lobby to the beautifully lighted rooms, where a wealth of cushions compensates for the somewhat minimalist look. **Pros:** in the thick of the shopping scene; short stroll to Night Bazaar; excellent buffet lunch deals. **Cons:** small pool; rooms aren't spacious; modern style might not appeal to those seeking traditional Thai charm. [$] *Rooms from: B4,500* ✉ *100 Chang Klan Rd., T. Chang Klan, A. Muang* ☎ *053/999999* 🌐 *dusitd2chiangmai.dusit.com* 🛏 *131 rooms* 🍴 *Breakfast* ✥ *G4.*

$$ HOTEL 🏨 **Dusit Princess Chiang Mai.** This centrally located hotel is ideal if you'd like to step out of the lobby right into the tumult of downtown Chiang Mai. The bustling Night Market is at the front door, and the Night Bazaar is barely a block away. **Pros:** central location; close to Night Bazaar; helpful travel desk. **Cons:** noisy street scene; package-tour clientele; service can be patchy. [$] *Rooms from: B3,000* ✉ *112 Chang Klan Rd.* ☎ *053/253900* 🌐 *www.dusit.com/dusitprincess/chiangmai* 🛏 *182 rooms, 16 suites* 🍴 *No meals* ✥ *G4.*

$$ HOTEL 🏨 **Eastin Tan Hotel Chiang Mai.** The expansive rooms and apartment-suites in this chic boutique hotel, the tallest building on hip Nimmanhemin

Road, have views of Suthep mountain on one side of the property and funky Think Park and glam Maya Mall on the other. **Pros:** in the heart of the action; spacious rooms; stunning views. **Cons:** slow check-in; the bar-restaurant is quiet. $ *Rooms from: B2,100* ⊠ *165 Huay Kaew Rd.* ☏ *052/001999* ⊕ *www.eastintanchiangmai.com* ☎ *98 rooms and 30 suites* �‖ *Breakfast* ⊟ *No credit cards* ✛ *A1.*

$$
HOTEL
⊞ **Kantary Hills.** A showpiece of the Thailand-based Cape & Kantary Hotels collection, this large and stylish complex dominates the glitzy Nimmanhemin Road district. **Pros:** free coffee, tea, and snacks in the reading room; live music in the restaurant; boutiques. **Cons:** noisy neighborhood; discos and bars; heavy road traffic; gridlock at night. $ *Rooms from: B4,000* ⊠ *44 Nimmanhemin Rd., Soi 12* ☏ *053/222111* ⊕ *www. kantarycollection.com* ☎ *100 rooms, 70 suites* �‖ *Breakfast* ✛ *A2.*

$
HOTEL
⊞ **Lai-Thai Guest House.** This rambling guesthouse on a busy thoroughfare just outside the moat is a budget travelers' favorite, so book far ahead. **Pros:** good value; courtyard pool; open-air café and restaurant; efficient travel service. **Cons:** rooms have thin walls; some night noise from partying backpackers; drab neighborhood. $ *Rooms from: B1,000* ⊠ *111/4–5 Kotchasarn Rd.* ☏ *053/271725* ⊕ *www.laithai.com* ☎ *110 rooms* �‖ *No meals* ✛ *F5.*

$$$$
HOTEL
⊞ **Ping Nakara Hotel.** It's hard to believe that this stunning riverside property was built in 2009; a masterpiece of colonial-style architecture, it's furnished throughout with exquisite antiques. **Pros:** quiet corners; peaceful ambience; garden teatime service; big rooms. **Cons:** drab, main-road neighborhood; some rooms get road noise; so-so restaurant. $ *Rooms from: B6,200* ⊠ *135/9 Charoen Prathet Rd., A. Muang, City Center* ☏ *053/252999* ⊕ *www.pingnakara.com* ⊟ *No credit cards* ☎ *19 rooms* �‖ *Breakfast* ✛ *H5.*

$
HOTEL
⊞ **River View Lodge.** Facing a grassy lawn that runs down to the Mae Ping River, this lodge lets you forget the noise of the city. **Pros:** riverside location; breezy poolside gazebo; river views. **Cons:** small pool; small parking lot with narrow access; service can be less than attentive. $ *Rooms from: B1,800* ⊠ *25 Charoen Prathet Rd., Soi 4* ☏ *053/271109* ⊕ *www. riverviewlodge.com* ☎ *35 rooms* �‖ *Breakfast* ✛ *H4.*

$
HOTEL
⊞ **Royal Lanna.** Truly regal in its proportions, the Royal Lanna rises high over the downtown Night Market scene. **Pros:** near Night Market; close to bars and restaurants; large car park. **Cons:** soulless atmosphere in public areas; favored by tour groups; service can be slow and unhelpful. $ *Rooms from: B1,200* ⊠ *119 Loi Kroh Rd.* ☏ *053/818773* ⊕ *www.royallannahotelchiangmai.com* ⊟ *No credit cards* ☎ *274 rooms* �‖ *No meals* ✛ *G4.*

$$
B&B/INN
⊞ **Ruen Come In.** An extremely hospitable Thai couple runs this two-story teak-timbered hotel whose main building was the family home before the children left the nest. **Pros:** massive rooms; superb food; swimming pool; owners speak English. **Cons:** few facilities; Old City not within walking distance. $ *Rooms from: B2,500* ⊠ *79/3 Sirithorn Rd.* ☏ *053/212516* ⊕ *www.ruencomein.com* ☎ *10 rooms, 3 suites* �‖ *Breakfast* ⊟ *No credit cards* ✛ *A1.*

$$$$
HOTEL
⊞ **Siripanna Villa Resort and Spa.** On Chiang Mai's southern edge, this attractive ensemble of detached villas nestles within tropical gardens on

6

a large site near the celebrated Gymkhana Club, the city's oldest sports club. **Pros:** stylish restaurants; attentive service; Gymkhana sports facilities (including golf course) available to visitors; sizable online discounts, even for high season, if booked well in advance. **Cons:** isolated location; unreliable transportation to town; insects. $ *Rooms from: B6,500 ⊠ 36 Rat Uthit Rd.* ☏ *053/371999* ⊕ *www.siripanna.com* ⤳ *74 rooms and villas* ⦿ *Breakfast* ⊹ *H5.*

$$　⌗ **Zzziesta Chiang Mai.** A cute-as-a-button three-story boutique property,
B&B/INN　the Zzziesta scores points with travelers for its inventive contemporary design, quiet location near Nimmanhemin Road, and eager-to-please owner and staff. **Pros:** inventive design; feels clean and new; less than a mile from Old City; free bicycles for guest use; convenient to Nimmanhemin Road restaurants, bars, and shops. **Cons:** books up very quickly, especially in high season; no elevator; front desk not staffed between 10 pm and 8 am; limited parking. $ *Rooms from: B2,100 ⊠ Sermsuk Rd., 22/1 Soi Mengrairassamee* ☏ *098/808–9406* ⤳ *10 rooms* ⦿ *Breakfast* ⊟ *No credit cards* ⊹ *C2.*

GREATER CHIANG MAI

$$$$　⌗ **Dhara Dhevi Chiang Mai.** A Thai billionaire turned 60 acres of farm-
RESORT　land on the eastern outskirts of Chiang Mai into one of Asia's most
Fodor'sChoice　extraordinary hotels, re-creating a walled Lanna city surrounded by a
★　moat. **Pros:** total seclusion; beautiful grounds; spa treatments. **Cons:** run-down neighborhood; navigating the complex can be difficult; little nightlife. $ *Rooms from: B15,120 ⊠ 51/4 Chiang Mai–San Kamphaeng Rd., Moo 1, Tambon Tasala* ☏ *053/888888* ⊕ *www.dharadhevi.com* ⤳ *54 suites, 69 residences* ⦿ *Breakfast* ⊹ *H4.*

$$$$　⌗ **Four Seasons Resort Chiang Mai.** One of the finest hotels in South-
RESORT　east Asia, the magnificent Four Seasons commands 20 acres of tropical
Fodor'sChoice　countryside above the lush Mae Rim Valley. **Pros:** peaceful moun-
★　tain setting; idyllic pool; impeccable, attentive service. **Cons:** limited access for those with mobility problems; 40-minute drive from town; little nightlife. $ *Rooms from: B21,000 ⊠ Mae Rim–Samoeng Old Rd.* ☏ *053/298181, 800/545–4000 in U.S.* ⊕ *www.fourseasons.com/ chiangmai* ⤳ *98 suites and villas* ⦿ *Breakfast* ⊹ *C1.*

NIGHTLIFE

Chiang Mai has dozens of places where you can grab a beer or a cocktail, listen to live music, or both. Two centers of action are the Riverside area, where restaurants like the Good View double as bars later in the evening, and Nimmanhemin Road heading south from Huay Kaew Road. As with elsewhere in Thailand, many Bangkok-style hostess bars are easy to find, most notably at the western end of Loi Kroh Road, the southern end of Moon Muang Road, and the Bar Beer Center next to the Top North Hotel on Moon Muang Road.

BARS

Doqaholic Cafe. A mostly young crowd heads to this fun open-air space to sip craft beers, top-shelf liquor, and premium cocktails and enjoy the rock and other bands or solo performers. ✉ *Think Park, Nimmanhemin and Huay Kaew Rds.* ☎ *083/003–0406, 089/434–5646.*

Maya Lifestyle Shopping Center rooftop bars. The several rooftop bars on the sixth floor of the high-end Maya mall hardly rival their skyscraping counterparts in Bangkok, but they do offer smart cocktails with a splendid city view. On the floor below are a cineplex, a high-tech karaoke bar, and an arcade with new and classic games. ✉ *55 Moo 5 Huay Kaew Rd., at Nimmanhemin Rd.* ☎ *052/081555* ⊕ *www.mayashoppingcenter.com.*

Mixology. The look at this bar on the western edge of the Old City is part industrial, part bric-a-brac shop, but the well-mixed cocktails are au courant, and the crowd is upbeat. The place serves burgers, including pork ones, and other comfort food. A signature libation, the High Flyer, involves bourbon, dark rum, amaretto, vanilla syrup, and bitters. ✉ *61/6 Arak Rd. 4 A, near Ratchamankha Rd., Old City* ☎ *088/261–3057* ☞ *Closed Mon.*

Wine Connection. In reality a retail shop, this well-stocked spot has outside bistro tables where customers can sample wines until late. Wine buffs, still a newish breed here, crowd the tables on most evenings. Food can be ordered from a neighboring bistro. ✉ *Nim City Daily Plaza, 197 Mahidol Rd.* ☎ *053/808688* ⊕ *www.wineconnection.co.th.*

Writers Club & Wine Bar. Chiang Mai's unofficial press club is open to anyone who enjoys networking in good company. The decor is "eclectic colonial." ✉ *141/3 Ratchadamnoen Rd.* ☎ *053/814187.*

DANCE CLUBS

Monkey Club. Packed on most nights with young Thais, this club has an indoor music stage and a bar. There's also a large garden. ✉ *Nimmanhemin Rd., Soi 9.*

Warm Up. The local Hi-So (High Society) crowd hits the discos and music bars of the Nimmanhemin Road area, a major nightlife scene. Visiting ravers under 40 won't feel out of place in haunts like Warm Up. ✉ *9 Nimmanhemin Rd.* ☎ *053/226–9978.*

KHANTOKE

Khantoke (or *kantoke*) originally described a revolving wooden tray on which food is served, but it has now come to mean an evening's entertainment combining a seemingly endless menu of northern cuisine and presentations of traditional music and dancing. With sticky rice, which you mold into balls with your fingers, you sample delicacies like kap moo (pork crackling), *nam prik naw* (a spicy dip made with onions, cucumber, and chili), and *kang kai* (a chicken-and-vegetable curry).

Kantoke Palace. At the ever-popular Kantoke Palace, a series of dances that might involve umbrellas, swords, or other props is followed by an audience-participation circle dance. The food is not what you're coming for, though the specialty cocktails aren't bad. ⊠ *288/19 Chang Klan Rd.* ☎ *053/272757* ⊕ *www.kantokepalace.com.*

Khum Khantoke. The costumes at the templelike Khum Khantoke are as sumptuous as the surroundings. The welcoming parade sets things in motion. ⊠ *Chiang Mai Business Park, 139 Moo 4 Nong Pakrung* ☎ *053/304121 up to 3* ⊕ *khumkhantoke.com.*

Old Chiang Mai Cultural Center. This fine ensemble of old-style teak-built houses offers a multicourse dinner accompanied by traditional music and dancing. Grab a seat on the floor to experience the show up close. ⊠ *185/3 Wualai Rd.* ☎ *053/202–9935* ⊕ *www.oldchiangmai.com.*

MUSIC

Chiang Mai's lively music scene caters to just about every taste. Jazz aficionados call the city Thailand's New Orleans, and some say it offers better quality music at lower prices than Bangkok does. Most music bars are found on Nimmanhemin Road, in the Old City, or along the Mae Ping River.

Brasserie. Noteworthy local bands play at this venue just east of the Old City. ⊠ *94/1–2 Chaiyapoom Rd., Soi 1* ☎ *053/241665.*

Gallery. The café-bar adjacent to the same-named restaurant presents some of the city's best jazz. ⊠ *31–35 Charoen Rat Rd.* ☎ *053/248601* ⊕ *www.thegallery-restaurant.com* ☾ *Closed Tues.*

The Good View. The east bank of the Ping River between Nawarat Bridge and Nakorn Ping Bridge resounds after dark with live rock, jazz, and Motown oldies. Most of the decibels come from the Good View, which hosts bands nightly. ⊠ *13 Charoen Rat Rd.* ☎ *053/241866.*

Fodor's Choice ★ **North Gate Jazz Co-Op.** This is the city's most popular bar for jazz music. Tuesdays are jam-session nights, but the place, on the northern edge of the Old City, is packed every night of the week. ⊠ *91/1-2 Sriphum Rd., opposite Chang Phuak Gate, Old City.*

Zoe in Yellow. An alleyway just east of Ratchaphakhinai Road in the Old City is a magnet for backpackers and rasta-Thais who nightly pack the cluster of open-air or open-sided music bars, including Zoe in Yellow. Babylon Cafe, Heaven Beach, and Roots, Rock, Reggae are also worth checking out. ⊠ *40/12 Ratchawithi Rd., east of Ratchaphakhinai Rd., Old City* ☎ *084/222–9388* ⊕ *zoeinyellowchiangmai.com.*

SPORTS AND THE OUTDOORS

BOATING

Book ahead for boat tours via phone if possible.

Mae Ping River Cruise. Various Mae Ping River cruises, including lunch and dinner sailings, depart daily from the landing at Wat Chai Mongkol, just downriver from the Iron Bridge. ⊠ *133 Charoen Prathet Rd.* ☎ *053/274822, 01/885–0663* ⊕ *www.maepingrivercruise.com.*

Scorpion-Tailed River Cruise. For a taste of how the locals used to travel along the Mae Ping, board a scorpion-tail boat, so called because of the large rudder at the stern of this sturdy Siamese craft. Services run from the east bank of the river, between Nawarat Bridge and Rattanakosin Bridge. Scorpion-Tailed River Cruise operates several 90-minute trips daily between 9 and 4:30. English-speaking guides provide commentary. ⊠ *Charoen Rat Rd.* ☎ *081/960–9398* ⊕ *www. scorpiontailedrivercruise.com.*

DANCE

Thai Dance Institute. Surprise your friends by learning the ancient and graceful art of Thai dancing at one of the institute's two-hour classes. ⊠ *53 Kohklong Rd., Nonghoy* ☎ *053/801375* ⊕ *www. thaidanceinstitute.com* 🍴 *B1,500.*

GOLF

Chiang Mai is ringed by championship golf courses that challenge players of all levels.

Alpine Golf Resort Chiangmai. This luxurious golf resort offers family weekends where nonplayers can enjoy spa treatments or stroll in the subtropical grounds. The top-rated course, redesigned in 2008 by Ron Garl, winds through a beautiful valley. ⊠ *San Kamphaeng* ☎ *053/880888* ⊕ *www.alpinegolfresort.com* 🍴 *B4,000; B300 caddie; B1,000 club rental* 🏌 *18 holes, 7541 yards, par 72.*

Chiangmai Highlands Golf and Spa Resort. This comfortable golf resort offers "stay and play" golfing packages with varied accommodation options and extras that include foot massages. The course, designed by Schmidt Curley, opened in 2005. Its 18th hole, par 5, provides a famously challenging conclusion to a round played here. ⊠ *167 Moo 2 Onuar, Mae On* ☎ *053/261354* ⊕ *www.chiangmaihighlands.com* 🍴 *B3,500; B300 caddie; B1,500 club rental* 🏌 *18 holes, 7062 yards, par 72.*

Chiengmai Gymkhana Club. The city's oldest sports club, founded in 1898 by the son of the author of *Anna and the King of Siam* and others, has a 9-hole course just 2 km (1 mile) from the city center. ⊠ *349 Chiang Mai–Lamphun Rd., Nong Hoi* ☎ *053/241035* ⊕ *www. chiengmaigymkhana.com* 🍴 *B300 for 9 holes, B600 for 18 holes; caddie B100 per 9 holes; club rental B300* 🏌 *9 holes, 2909 yards, par 36.*

Golfasian. Several specialist agencies offer tours of the best golf courses around Chiang Mai. The most comprehensive is Golfasian, established in Bangkok in 1997. Some packages include accommodations, transfers, and various extras. ⊠ *29 Bangkok Business Center, Soi Ekamai-Sukhumvit 63, Unit 1105* ☎ *02/714–8470* ⊕ *www.golfasian.com.*

HORSEBACK RIDING

J & T Happy Riding. This outfit sponsors trail rides through the beautiful Mae Sa Valley. Beginners are welcome. The stables are opposite the Mae Sa Orchid Farm. ⊠ *Mae Rim–Samoeng Rd.* ☎ *081/5957–1137.*

6

Travel Shoppe. The Shoppe arranges morning horseback tours along trails north of Chiang Mai. The fee is B2,500 for one person, B2,200 per person for two, and includes hotel pickup and return. ✉ *2/2 Chaiyapoom Rd., near Thapae Gate* ☎ *053/874091* ⊕ *www.travel-shoppe.com.*

ROCK CLIMBING

The Peak Adventure Tour Company. This company takes groups, including beginners, on tours to rock faces in the mountains around Chiang Mai. One-day tours cost B1,800, and three-day intensive training sessions, including accommodations, can be booked for B6,500. Peak Adventure also offers other adventure activities, from white-water rafting to quad biking. ✉ *302/4 Chiang Mai–Lamphun Rd.* ☎ *053/800567* ⊕ *www. thepeakadventure.com.*

THAI BOXING

There are several places where you can see muay thai boxing and—if you dare (not advisable)—even participate. Locals consider the Friday-night matches at Kawila Boxing to be more authentic than the Thursday-evening ones at Thapae Boxing Stadium, which is more convenient for most tourists. For a more amateur scene, check out the fights on Saturday night at the Loi Kroh Entertainment Complex, on Loi Kroh Road near the Night Market.

Kawila Boxing Stadium. Friday night is fight night at this popular muay thai boxing venue whose grittier location attracts a less touristy crowd than the one at Thapae stadium. The most expensive seats are about B600, so it doesn't cost a fortune to get thrillingly close to the action, which generally but not always starts at 9 pm. Inquire at your hotel or guesthouse how best to get here; the stadium is away from where most tourists stay. ✉ *Kong Sai Rd., near San Pa Koy Market* ☎ *053/296048.*

Thapae Boxing Stadium. Professional muay thai boxing contestants square off every Thursday night at this stadium just outside the Old City's Thapae Gate. Matches start at 8 pm. Tickets cost from B400 to B600. ✉ *Beer Bar Center , Moon Muang Rd., beside Top North Hotel* ⊕ *www. thapaestadium.com.*

YOGA

Weena Yoga Studio. You can drop in on group classes at this modest yoga center for B300, with discounts for multiple classes. Private classes start at B800 per hour. ✉ *The Ring, Nimmanhemin Rd., Soi 17* ☎ *085/353–8108* ⊕ *www.weenayoga.com.*

The Yoga Tree. Classes are offered here in everything from hatha yoga to meditation, but the main focus is a children's program called Kids Yoga Now. Call for prices. ✉ *65/1 Arak Rd.* ☎ *604/730–1026* ⊕ *www. theyogatree.com.*

ZIP LINING

Flight of the Gibbon. Flying Tarzan-style through the jungle of northern Thailand is the ultimate adventure trip for many visitors. Several operators maintain zip-lines in stretches of thick forest north of Chiang Mai. Flight of the Gibbon has been established the longest and is reputedly the most reliable. It has more than 7 km (4½ miles) of lines. As you glide along on them you probably won't see a gibbon, but you'll certainly feel like one. ⊠ *Mae Sa Valley Rd.* ☎ *053/010660 up to 64* ⊕ *www. treetopasia.com* ✉ *B3,599.*

SHOPPING

The delightful surprise about shopping in Chiang Mai is that you don't have to part with much of your hard-earned money—even the most elaborately crafted silver, for instance, costs a fraction of what you'd expect to pay at home. Fine jewelry priced at just above the current market value, as well as pewter, leather, and silk, are on display all around the city. The most popular buys are vibrant hill tribe textiles and products made from textiles, such as handbags and shoes; handicrafts, from handmade paper to pretty parasols; hippy clothes; knockoff bags; and accessories and jewelry.

ANTIQUES

Shopping for antiques should present few problems if you follow certain commonsense rules. Examine each item very carefully for signs of counterfeiting—new paint or varnish, tooled damage marks—and ask for certificates of provenance and written guarantees that the goods can be returned if proved counterfeit. ■ TIP→ Reputable stores will always provide certificates of provenance, aware that penalties for dishonest trading are severe. If you're in doubt about a deal, contact the Tourist Police. The Night Bazaar has two floors packed with "antiques," many of which were manufactured yesterday (and hence come with no guarantee of authenticity).

The road south to Hang Dong (take the signposted turn before the airport) is lined with antiques shops. Just outside Hang Dong you'll reach the craft village of Ban Tawai. You could spend an entire morning or afternoon rummaging through its antiques shops and storerooms.

Lanna Antique Shop. This shop on the second floor of Night Bazaar sells genuine antiques and supplies proof. ⊠ *Night Bazaar, Chang Klan Rd.*

ART

Chiang Mai has a vibrant artists' scene. Small galleries can be found all over.

The Gallery. Beautiful traditional Thai paintings, carvings, sculptures, and other artworks are displayed and sold at the fine gallery attached to The Gallery restaurant. ⊠ *25–29 Charoen Rat Rd.* ☎ *053/248601* ⊕ *www.thegallery-restaurant.com.*

H Gallery and Wine Bar. An important contemporary-art showcase, H Gallery exhibits the works of emerging and established Asian artists. The original space is in Bangkok. ✉ *141/3 Ratchadamnoen Rd.* ✛ *Mae Rim, near Four Seasons resort* ☎ *085/0215508* ⊕ *www.hgallerybkk.com.*

Suvannabhumi Art Gallery. Mon art from Myanmar is on permanent display at this gallery run by a charming and knowledgeable Mon art lover named Mar Mar. She mounts regular exhibitions of work by leading artists. ✉ *116–11 Charoen Rat Rd.* ☎ *081/031–5309* ⊕ *www.suvannabhumiartgallery.com.*

Wattana Art Gallery. The celebrated Thai artist Wattana Wattanapun runs this gallery whose eclectic artworks represent the full range of Thailand's artistic expression. ✉ *100/1 Soi Wat Umong* ☎ *053/278747, 089/4291883* ⊕ *www.wwattanapun-art.com.*

> **FIVE-STAR PRODUCTS**
>
> To encourage each tambon (community) to make the best use of its special skills, the Thai government set up a program called OTOP, which stands for "One Tambon, One Product." It's been a great success. Some 27,000 community-based artisans and manufacturers have joined the program, and nearly 600 products have been given five-star ratings. About half are food or beverage items, but there are also clothes, housewares and decorations, handicrafts, and souvenirs. You can buy the products everywhere; look for the OTOP symbol. ⊕ *www.otop5star.com*

COOKING CLASSES

Baan Thai Cookery School. The classes at this cooking school are among Chiang Mai's best. A one-day course costs B1,000, including transportation, snacks, and a cookbook to take home. ✉ *11 Ratchadamnoen Rd., Soi 5, Old City* ☎ *053/357339* ⊕ *www.cookinthai.com* ⚎ *Reservations essential.*

Chiang Mai Thai Cookery School. Sompon Nabnian, an internationally recognized TV chef, runs this school. A one-day beginner's course costs B1,450. The five-day master class costs B6,700. ✉ *47/2 Moon Muang Rd., Old City* ☎ *053/206388* ⊕ *www.thaicookeryschool.com.*

Thai Farm Cooking School. The one-day classes at this popular school run by a genial husband-and-wife team take place at its working farm. Participants visit a food market before heading to the farm, where dishes are prepared and then enjoyed. The B1,300 fee includes transportation to and from lodgings or other points in or near the Old City. ✉ *Office, Moon Muang Rd., Soi 9, Old City* ☎ *081/288–5989, 087/174–9285* ⊕ *www.thaifarmcooking.com.*

HANDICRAFTS

For two of Chiang Mai's specialties, lacquerware and exquisite paper products, take a taxi or songthaew to any of the outlets along San Kamphaeng Road (also known as the Golden Mile). Large emporiums that line the 10-km (6-mile) stretch sell a wide variety of items. Whole communities here devote themselves to their traditional trades. One community rears silkworms, for instance, providing the raw product for the looms humming in workshops.

Outside the city center, the highways running south and east of Chiang Mai—those leading to Hang Dong and San Kamphaeng—are lined for several miles with workshops stocked with handicrafts of every description. They're a favorite destination for tuk-tuk drivers, who receive a commission on goods bought by their passengers. ■TIP➔ Be very specific with tuk-tuk drivers about what you're looking for before setting out—otherwise you might find yourself ferried to an expensive silverware outlet when all you want to buy is an inexpensive souvenir.

For local handicrafts, head to Thapae Road and Loi Kroh Road. Across the Nawarat Bridge, Charoen Rat Road is home to a row of refurbished old teak houses with a handful of boutiques selling interesting crafts such as incense candles and carved curios. Farther afield, along Nimmanhemin Road, a whole neighborhood of crafts shops has developed. The first lane on the left, Soi 1, has some of the most rewarding ones.

Baan Tawai Village. Four kilometers (2½ miles) beyond Baan Tawai lies a community of shops dealing in antiques and handicrafts. At workshops you can see teak, mango, rattan, and water hyacinth being worked into attractive and unusual items. If you end up buying a heavy piece of teak furniture, the dealer will arrange for its shipping. ☒ *90 Moo 2, Tambon Baan Tawai, near Hang Dong* ☎ *081/882–4882* ⊕ *www. ban-tawai.com.*

Hilltribe Products Promotion Center. At this government-supported crafts store west of the Old City you can learn about and purchase handicrafts made by Akha, Hmong, Karen, Lahu, Lisu, and Yao people in their native villages. The money you pay for a woven mat or carved mask goes directly to the local communities. ☒ *21/17 Suthep Rd.* ☎ *053/277743.*

Northern Village. Chiang Mai's largest handicrafts retail outlet has an astounding selection of ceramics, jewelry carvings, and silks and other textiles. ☒ *CentralPlaza Airport Chiangmai, 2 Mahidol Rd.* ☎ *053/999199.*

Thai Tribal Crafts. Operated by the Baptist Christian Service Foundation, Thai Tribal Crafts has more than 25 years' experience in retailing the products of northern Thailand's hill tribe people. The organization prides itself on its "fair trade" policy and the authenticity of its products. In addition to the main store on Bamrungrat Road, there are locations at the Northern Village section of the CentralPlaza Airport Chiangmai mall and at 25/9 Moon Muang Road near the Thapae Gate. ☒ *208 Bamrungrat Rd., near Kaeo Nawarat Rd.* ☎ *053/241043* ⊕ *www.ttcrafts.co.th.*

Umbrella Making Center. Among the crafts you can find at this large sales outlet in the village of Bo Sang, 10 miles east of Chiang Mai, are hand-painted umbrellas made from lacquered paper and tree bark. Hundreds of these are displayed at the center. The artists here will paint traditional designs on anything from a T-shirt to a suitcase—travelers have discovered that this is a handy way of helping identify their luggage on an airport carousel. ⊠ *11/2 Moo 3 Tambon Bo Sang ⚓ On Hwy. 1014 just northeast of Hwy. 1006* ☎ *053/338324.*

Vaniche. The factory showroom of Vaniche sells the company's cute, creative, handmade soft toys, dolls, accessories, and gifts aimed mainly at children and teens. ⊠ *133 Ban Rasksa Moo* ☎ *053/262786* ⊕ *www. vaniche.com.*

JEWELRY

Chiang Mai is renowned for its gems and semiprecious stones. If gold is your passion, make your way to the Chinese district. All the shops that jostle for space at the eastern end of Chang Moi Road are reliable, invariably issuing certificates of authenticity. The city's silver district, Wualai Road, is lined for several hundred yards with shops where you can sometimes see silversmiths at work. ■**TIP→** Avoid the unscrupulous dealers at the Night Market.

Nova. This stunning jewelry shop has an attached studio where striking contemporary pieces are created in gold, silver, platinum, and stainless steel. Some pieces incorporate common materials, such as stone and rosewood, into their designs. At the Nova Artlab school you can take jewelry-making workshops lasting from one to five days. ⊠ *179 Thapae Rd.* ☎ *053/273058* ⊕ *www. nova-collection.com.*

> ### SHOPPING SECRETS
>
> Before setting off on a shopping expedition, buy a copy of *Shopping Secrets of Chiang Mai*, a comprehensive 280-page visitors' guide containing in-depth information on virtually everything the city has to offer. It's available in most bookstores. Or page through the local English-language monthlies *Guidelines* and *Art & Culture Lanna*, available free of charge in most hotels. Both are packed with information and feature local crafts by trustworthy dealers.

Orchid Jade Factory. The factory claims to be the world's largest retailer of jadeite. The hard-sell tactics here can be irksome, but the showrooms display fabulous jade jewelry and ornaments, and visitors are invited to watch the craftspeople at work. ⊠ *7/7 Srivichai Rd., opposite entrance to Doi Suthep Mountain* ☎ *053/295021 up to 23* ⊕ *www.orchidjade.com.*

Shiraz. This small, specialized shop has an unchallenged reputation for reliability, expertise, and good value. If the owner, Mr. Nasser, is behind the counter or at work in his office workroom, you're in luck—you won't find a more knowledgeable gems expert in Chiang Mai. ⊠ *170 Thapae Rd.* ☎ *053/252382* ⊕ *www.shirazjewelrychiangmai.com.*

Siam Royal Orchid Shop. A Chiang Mai jewelry specialty features orchid blooms, rose petals, other flowers, leaves, and seeds set in gold. Not to everyone's taste, but certainly unique. The Siam Royal Orchid booth at Northern Village has a spectacular selection. ⊠ *CentralPlaza Airport Chiangmai, Mahidol 2 Alley, Mueang Chiang Mai District, 1st. fl.* ☎ *053/245598, 053/249803* ⊕ *www.royalorchidcollection.com.*

PAPER

The groves of mulberry trees grown in northern Thailand aren't only used to feed the silkworms—their bark, called *saa*, produces a distinctive, fibrous paper that is fashioned into every conceivable form: writing paper and envelopes, boxes, book covers, and picture frames.

HQ PaperMaker. This is the biggest and best paper outlet in Chiang Mai. On its first floor is a gallery whose works include paintings done by elephants at the Elephant Conservation Center near Lampang. ✉ *3/31 Samlan Rd.* ☎ *053/814717* ⊕ *www.hqpapermaker.com.*

Siam Promprathan. All sorts of mulberry papers, some of them richly colored, are carried here. ✉ *95/3 Moo 4, Ratchawithi Rd., San Kamphaeng* ☎ *053/331768, 053/392214.*

STREET MARKETS

Kalare Night Bazaar. A permanent bazaar, this is in a big entertainment complex on the eastern side of the Night Market on Chang Klan Road (clearly marked). It's packed with boutiques, stalls, and cheap restaurants, and there's a beer garden where nightly performances of traditional Thai dances take place. ✉ *Chang Klan Rd.*

Fodor'sChoice
★ **Night Bazaar.** The justifiably famous Night Bazaar, on Chang Klan Road, is a kind of open-air department store filled with stalls selling everything from inexpensive souvenirs to pricey antiques. In the afternoon and evening traders set up tented stalls, confusingly known as the Night Market, along Chang Klan Road and the adjoining streets. You're expected to bargain, so don't be shy. Do, however, remain polite. Many vendors believe the first and last customers of the day bring good luck, so if you're after a real bargain (up to 50% off) start your shopping early in the day. ✉ *Chang Klan Rd.*

Walking Streets. Chiang Mai has two so-called walking streets, closed off to traffic to make way for weekly markets. One is held on **Wualai Road** (the "silver street") on Saturday evening. The other, much larger one, takes up the whole of **Ratchadamnoen Road** and surrounding streets on Sunday. The goods at both of these markets are cheaper and more authentic than most of what you'll find at the Night Bazaar and Night Market. ✉ *Chiang Mai.*

TEXTILES

Chiang Mai and silk are nearly synonymous, and here you can buy the product *and* see it being manufactured. Several companies along San Kamphaeng Road open their workrooms to visitors and explain the process of making fine silk, from the silkworm to the loom. ■**TIP→** These shops are favorite destinations of package tours, so prices tend to be higher than in other parts of town or at the Night Market.

Shinawatra Thai Silk. Silk and other local textiles can be reliably bought at this company's shops, where you can also purchase made-do-order clothing and home-decor items. This is a good place to learn about how silk is made and how the industry has evolved in Thailand. ✉ *18 Huay*

Continued on page 346

SILK-MAKING IN THAILAND

by Dave Stamboulis

According to legend, the Chinese empress His-Ling discovered silk nearly 5,000 years ago when a cocoon fell into her teacup, and she watched it unwind into a fine filament. As China realized the value of these threads, the silk trade was born, spreading through Asia, along what became known as the Silk Road.

For centuries, the Chinese protected the secret of silk production, beheading anyone who tried to take silk-worm eggs out of the country. But, eventually, smuggled worms, along with silk-making knowledge, made it to other parts of Asia. As the demand for silk grew, Chinese traders searched for the best climates in which to cultivate worms; historians believe that these traders brought sericulture, or silk-making, to Thailand about 2,000 years ago. Archaeologists have found silk remnants in the ruins of Baan Chiang near Udon Thani.

Though silkworms thrived, the silk business did not take on a large scale in Thailand, because Buddhist Thais were reluctant to kill the silkworms—an unavoidable part of the process. But a few families in Isan did continue to produce silk, using native plants like Palmyra Palm and jackfruit to make natural bleaches and dyes. After World War II, American businessman Jim Thompson discovered Thailand's cottage industry and helped expand it, founding the Thai Silk Company in 1951. Queen Sirikit, King Bhumibol's wife, has also been a long-term supporter of sericulture through her SUPPORT organization, which teaches traditional crafts to rural Thais.

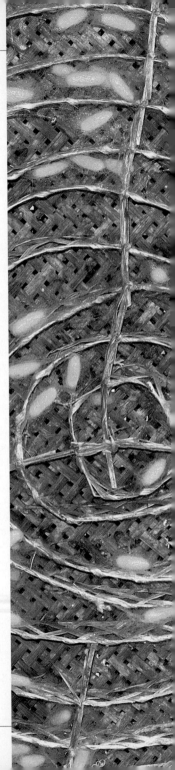

Silk cocoons in the final stage of incubation, Surin.

HOW SILK IS MADE

20mm

Adult female bombyx mari.

Female moth laying eggs.

Larvae eating mulberry leaves.

Silkworms are really the caterpillars of bombyx mari, the silk moth. The process begins when a mature female moth lays eggs—about 300 at once. When the eggs hatch 10 days later, the larvae are placed on trays of mulberry leaves, which they devour. After this mulberry binge, when the worms are approximately 7 cm (2.75 in) long, they begin to spin their cocoons. After 36 hours the cocoons are complete.

Before the worms emerge as moths—destroying the cocoons in the process—silk makers boil the cocoons so they can unravel the intact silk filament. The raw silk, which ranges in color from gold to light green, is dried, washed, bleached, and then dyed before being stretched and twisted into strands strong enough for weaving. The course, knotty texture of Thai silk is ideal for hand-weaving on traditional looms—the final step to creating a finished piece of fabric.

Silk cocoons.

Boiling cocoons to remove silk.

DID YOU KNOW?

Thai silk moths reproduce 10 or more times per year—they're much more productive than their Japanese and Korean counterparts, which lay eggs only once annually.

A worm can eat 25,000 times its original weight over a 30-day period, before encasing itself in a single strand of raw silk up to 900 m (3,000 ft) long.

Woman sifting through cocoons.

CHECK IT OUT

In Bangkok, the Naj Collection has an excellent reputation and top quality products, and the Jim Thompson outlets are quite good, as are Shinawatra's.

Naj Collection
✉ *42 Convent Rd. (Opposite BNH Hospital), Silom, Bangkok* ☎ *662/632–1004-6* ⊕ *www.najcollection. com.*

Jim Thompson Outlet
✉ *9 Surawong Rd., Suriyawong, Bangrak, Bangkok* ☎ *02/632–8100, 02/234–4900* ⊕ *www.jimthompson. com.*

Shinawatra Thai Silk
✉ *94 Sukhumvit Soi 23, North Klong Toei, Wattana, Bangkok* ☎ *02/258-0295-9* ⊕ *www.shinawatrathaisilk. com*

Man works a traditional loom.

VARIETIES OF THAI SILK
Most Thai silk is a blend of two different colors, one for the warp (threads that run lengthwise in a loom) and the other for the weft (strands that are woven across the warp.) Smoother silk, made with finer threads, is used for clothing, while rougher fabric is more appropriate for curtains. To make "striped" silk, weavers alternate coarse and smooth threads. Isan's famous mudmee silk, which is used mainly for clothing, consists of threads that are tie-dyed before they are woven into cloth.

Mudmee silk

SHOPPING TIPS

Appraising silk quality is an art in itself. But there are a few simple ways to be sure you're buying pure, handmade fabric.

■ Examine the weave. Hand-woven, authentic silk has small bumps and blemishes—no part of the fabric will look exactly like any other part. Imitation silk has a smooth, flawless surface.

■ Hold it up to the light. Imitation silk shines white at any angle, while the color of real silk appears to change.

■ Burn a thread. When held to a flame, natural fibers disintegrate into fine ash, while synthetic fabrics melt, smoke, and smell terrible.

■ Though this isn't a foolproof method, consider the price. Genuine silk costs five to 10 times more than an imitation or blended fabric. You should expect to pay between B250 and B350 a meter for high-quality, clothing-weight silk. Men's shirts start at B800 but could be more than B2,000; women's scarves run from B350 to B1,500. At Bangkok shops that cater to westerners, you'll pay considerably more, though shops frequented by Thais have comparable prices throughout the country.

Fine Thai silk on bobbins.

Kaew Rd. ☎ *053/221076, 053/888535* ⊕ *www.shinawatrathaissilk. com* ✉ *Dhara Dhevi Chiang Mai, 51/4 Chiang Mai–San Kamphaeng Rd., Tambon Tasala* ☎ *053/888535.*

Studio Naenna. A renowned authority on local textiles founded this gallery and weaving studio on a heavily forested slope of Doi Suthep Mountain. There's a city branch on Nimmanhemin Road. ✉ *138 Huay Kaew Rd., Soi 8* ☎ *053/226042* ⊕ *www.studio-naenna.com.*

SPAS

Chiang Mai has no shortage of massage parlors (the respectable kind), where the aches of a day's strenuous sightseeing can be kneaded away with a traditional massage. Your hotel can usually organize either an in-house massage or recommend one of the city's numerous centers. Chiang Mai also has dozens of spas specializing in Thai massage and various treatments involving traditional herbs and oils.

There are also several options if you wish to learn the art of Thai massage yourself.

Ban Sabai Village Resort and Spa. At this spa you can get your massage in a wooden Thai-style house or a riverside sala. For one treatment of note, the steamed herb massage, soothing herbs are placed on the body. The various fruit-based body masks, among them ones containing honey-tamarind and pineapple, are also very popular. ✉ *219 Moo 9 San Pee Sua* ☎ *053/854778 and 9, 082/7628310* ⊕ *www.bansabaivillage.com.*

Oasis Spa. Oasis has two first-class establishments in Chiang Mai. Both offer a full range of massage styles, from Swedish to traditional Thai. The mouthwatering body scrubs include Thai coffee, honey and yogurt, and orange, almond, and honey. ✉ *102 Sirimungklajan Rd.* ☎ *053/980111* ⊕ *www.oasisspa.net/destination/chiangmai* ✉ *Oasis Spa Lanna, 4 Samlan Rd.*

Rada Massage and Spa. Good massages with or without accompanying herbal treatments are given at Rada, also known as Dara. A one-hour full-body massage costs B300. ✉ *2/2 Nimmanhemin Rd., Soi 3* ☎ *089/9556–1103* ⊕ *radaspachiangmai.com.*

Thai Massage School. The school, one of Thailand's oldest such establishments, is authorized by the Thai Ministry of Education. A 30-hour, five-day, Level 1 introductory course costs B7,500. ✉ *Old Medicine Hospital, 238/1 Wualai Rd.* ☎ *053/201663* ⊕ *www.tmcschool.com.*

SIDE TRIPS FROM CHIANG MAI

DOI INTHANON NATIONAL PARK

90 km (54 miles) southwest of Chiang Mai.

GETTING HERE AND AROUND

Although there are minibus services from the nearest village, Chom Tong, to the summit of Doi Inthanon, there is no direct bus route from Chiang Mai. The most convenient way to access the park is either to book a tour with a Chiang Mai operator or hire a car and driver in Chiang Mai for around B3,000. If you're driving a rental car (about B2,000 per day), take Highway 108 south (the road to Hot), and after 36 km (22 miles) turn right at Chom Thong onto Road 1099, a sinuous 48-km (30-mile) stretch winding to the mountain's summit. ■ TIP→ The ashes of Chiang Mai's last monarch, King Inthawichayanon, are contained on Road 1099 in a secluded stupa that draws hundreds of thousands of pilgrims annually.

SAFETY AND PRECAUTIONS

The regular flow of visitors to the mountain ensures that it's a perfectly safe destination, although you should stick to marked paths and forest trails. A guide (obtainable at the national park headquarters) is recommended if you plan a long hike on the thickly forested mountain slopes.

TIMING

Doi Inthanon is a full day's outing from Chiang Mai. Chalets near the national park headquarters are available if you plan to stay overnight. Dawn on the mountain is an unforgettable experience, with the tropical sun slowly penetrating the upland mist against a background of chattering monkeys, barking deer, and birdsong.

EXPLORING

FAMILY

Fodor's Choice

★

Doi Inthanon National Park. Doi Inthanon, Thailand's highest mountain (8,464 feet), rises majestically over a national park of staggering beauty. Many have compared the landscape—thick forests of pines, oaks, and laurels—with that of Canada. Only the tropical vegetation on its lower slopes, and the 30 villages that are home to 3,000 Karen and Hmong people, remind you that this is indeed Asia. The reserve is of great interest to nature lovers, especially birders who come to see the 362 species that nest here. Red-and-white rhododendrons run riot, as do plants found nowhere else in Thailand.

Hiking trails penetrate deep into the park, which has some of Thailand's highest and most beautiful waterfalls. The Mae Klang Falls, just past the turnoff to the park, are easily accessible on foot or by vehicle, but the most spectacular are more remote and involve a trek of 4 to 5 km (2½ to 3 miles). The Mae Ya Falls are the country's highest falls, but even more spectacular are the Siribhum Falls, which plunge in two parallel cataracts from a 1,650-foot-high cliff above the Inthanon Royal Research Station. The station's vast nurseries are a gardener's dream, filled with countless varieties of tropical and temperate plants. Rainbow trout—unknown in the warm waters of Southeast Asia—are raised here in tanks fed by cold streams plunging from the mountain's heights, then served at the station's restaurant. The national park office provides maps and guides for trekkers and bird-watchers. Accommodations are available: B1,000 for a two-person chalet, B6,500 for a villa for up to eight people. The park admission fee is collected at a tollbooth at the start of the road to the summit. ⊠ *Amphur Chomthong* ☎ *053/286728, 053/286730* ⊕ *www.dnp.go.th/parkreserve* ⚞ *B200 per person, plus B30 per car* ☾ *Daily 9–6.*

LAMPHUN

26 km (16 miles) south of Chiang Mai.

Lamphun claims to be the oldest existing city in Thailand (but so does Nakhon Pathom). Originally called Nakhon Hariphunchai, it was founded in AD 660. Its first ruler was a queen, Chamthewi, who has a special place in Thailand's pantheon of powerful female leaders. There are two striking statues of her in the sleepy little town, and one of its wats bears her name. Queen Chamthewi founded the eponymous dynasty, which ruled the region until 1932. Today the compact little city is the capital of Thailand's smallest province, and also a textile and silk production center.

Lamphun has two of northern Thailand's most important monasteries, dating back more than 1,000 years. The smallest of them, Wat Chamthewi, holds the remains of the city's fabled 8th-century ruler, Queen Chamthewi. The other, Wat Phra That Hariphunchai, is a walled treasure house of ancient chapels, chedis, and gilded Buddhas.

Several Chiang Mai travel agencies offer day trips to Lamphun, including Cattleya Tour and Travel Service. Once you're here, the Tourism Authority of Thailand office, opposite the main entrance to Wat Hariphunchai, has irregular hours but is generally open on weekdays from 9 to 5.

GETTING HERE AND AROUND

BUS TRAVEL The provincial buses from Chiang Mai to Lampang stop at Lamphun, a 40-minute drive south on Highway 106, a busy but beautiful road shaded by 100-foot-tall rubber trees. The buses leave half-hourly from Chiang Mai's city bus station and from a stop next to the TAT office on the road to Lamphun. Minibus songthaews also operate a service to Lamphun. They leave from in front of the TAT office. Fares for all services to Lamphun are about B120. Lamphun has no bus station; buses stop at various points around town, including at the TAT office and outside Wat Hariphunchai.

TRAIN TRAVEL One slow daily Bangkok–Chiang Mai train stops at Lamphun, where a samlor (pedicab) can take you the 3 km (2 miles) into town for about B30, but the bus is more practical.

TUK-TUK AND SONGTHAEW TRAVEL Lamphun is a compact city, easy to tour on foot, although Wat Chamthewi is on the outskirts and best visited by tuk-tuk or songthaew.

SAFETY AND PRECAUTIONS

Lamphun knows little street crime, although the usual precautions are recommended if walking the city streets at night—leave valuables in your hotel safe or with the management. Women visitors are advised to carry handbags on the side away from the street.

TIMING

One day is sufficient for Lamphun, which is less than an hour from Chiang Mai. The tiny provincial capital has very little nightlife (though that's part of its charm), few restaurants, and only one hotel up to international standards.

EXPLORING

Ku Chang. Lamphun has one of the region's most unusual cemeteries, an elephant's graveyard called Ku Chang. The rounded chedi is said to contain the remains of Queen Chamthewi's favorite war elephant. ⊠ *Ku Chang Rd.*

National Museum. Just outside Wat Phra That Hariphunchai, the National Museum has a fine selection of Dvaravati-style stuccowork. The collection of Lanna antiques is also impressive. ⊠ *Inthayongyot Rd.* ☎ *053/511186* 💰 *B30* ⊙ *Wed.–Sun. 8:30–4.*

Fodor's Choice **Wat Chamthewi.** About 2 km (1 mile)
★ west of Lamphun's center is Wat Chamthewi, often called the "topless chedi" because the gold that once covered the spire was pillaged sometime during its history. Work began on the monastery in AD 755, and despite a modern viharn added to the side of the complex, it retains an ancient, weathered look. Suwan Chang Kot, to the right of the entrance, is the most famous of the two chedis, built by King Mahantayot to hold the remains of his mother, the legendary Queen Chamthewi. The five-tier sandstone chedi is square; on each tier are Buddha images that get progressively smaller. All are in the 9th-century Dvaravati style, though many have obviously been restored. The other chedi was probably built in the 10th century, though most of what you see today is the doings of King Phaya Sapphasit, who reigned during the 12th century. You'll probably want to take a samlor down the narrow residential street to the complex. This is not an area where samlors generally cruise, so ask the driver to wait for you. ⊠ *Lamphun–San Pa Tong Rd.*

Fodor's Choice **Wat Phra That Hariphunchai.** The temple complex of the 11th-century
★ Wat Phra That Hariphunchai is dazzling. Through gates guarded by ornamental lions lies a three-tier, sloping-roof viharn, a replica of the original that burned down in 1915. Inside, note the large Chiang Saen–style bronze image of the Buddha and the carved *thammas* (Buddhism's universal principals) to the left of the altar. As you leave the viharn, you pass what is reputedly the largest bronze gong in the world, cast in 1860. The 165-foot Suwana chedi, covered in copper and topped by a golden spire, dates from 847. A century later King Athitayarat, the 32nd ruler of Hariphunchai, added a nine-tier umbrella, gilded with 14 pounds of gold. At the back of the compound—where you can find a shortcut to the center of town—there's another viharn with a standing Buddha, a sala housing four Buddha footprints, and the old museum. ⊠ *Inthayongyot Rd.* 💰 *B40* ⊙ *Daily 6 am–8 pm.*

LAMPHUN'S NATIVE FRUIT

The countryside surrounding Lamphun is blanketed with orchards of *lamyai*, a sweet cherry-size fruit with a thin, buff-color shell. The annual lamyai festival brings the town to a halt in the first week of August with parades, exhibitions, a beauty contest, and copious quantities of lamyai wine. The lamyai-flower honey is reputed to have exceptional healing and aphrodisiacal powers. You can buy lamyai at the market stalls along the 100-yard covered wooden bridge opposite Wat Phra That Hariphunchai.

6

WHERE TO EAT

$ ✕ **Add Up Coffee Bar.** An attractive riverside haunt next to the visitor
THAI   information center, Add Up is more than just a coffee shop. The usual
Thai dishes are served, but it's the western specialties that are full of
surprises, among them the ice cream, made under American license
and very delicious. The same people run Spa Food, a vegetarian-only
annex next door. $ *Average main: B120* ✉ *22 Lobmuangnai Rd.*
☎ *053/561466.*

$ ✕ **Lamphun Ice Restaurant.** The odd name of this restaurant seems to
ASIAN   derive from its origins as an ice-cream parlor. The interior has cozy
booths that give the place the feel of a vintage soda fountain. The
Chinese, Thai, and Indian food served here is the real thing—try the
sensational Indian-style crab curry. $ *Average main: B115* ✉ *Chaimon-
gkol Rd.* ✛ *Opposite southern gate of Wat Phra That Hariphunchai*
☎ *053/511452.*

$ ✕ **Ton Fai.** This restaurant, named for the colorful flame tree, occupies an
THAI   ancient house and its shady backyard. Inside, you can climb the stairs
to a teak-floor dining room with tables set beneath the original rafters.
The river breeze wafting in through the shuttered windows cools the
room. Though simple, the menu includes many northern Thai delights.
$ *Average main: B120* ✉ *183 Chaimongkol Rd., Tambon Nai Muang*
☎ *053/530060* ▭ *No credit cards.*

WHERE TO STAY

$ 🏠 **Lamphun Will.** Most people visit Lamphun only as a day trip, but
HOTEL   if you're going to stay, this is the town's top hotel, and it wouldn't
look out of place in central Chiang Mai. The modern, boxy facade is
typical of the almost minimalist style throughout. **Pros:** great views of
Wat Chamthewi from café-terrace; cozy rooms. **Cons:** remote edge-
of-town location. $ *Rooms from: B1,700* ✉ *204/10 Charmmathewi
Rd., Tambon Naimuang, Amphur Muang* ☎ *053/534865* ⊕ *www.
lamphunwillhotel.com* ⬎ *79 rooms* ¶○¶ *Breakfast.*

SHOPPING

Lamphun's silk and other fine textiles make a visit to this charming city
worthwhile. It has its own version of Venice's Rialto Bridge, a 91-meter-
long (100-yard-long) covered wooden bridge lined on both sides with
stands whose vendors mostly sell silk, textiles, and local handicrafts.
The bridge is opposite the main entrance to Wat Phra That Hariphunchai, Inthayongyot Road. The market is open daily from 9 to 6.

Lampoon Thai Silk. Eight kilometers (5 miles) from Lamphun on the main
Lampang highway is one of the area's largest silk businesses, where you
can watch women weave at wooden looms. ✉ *8/2 Panangjitawong Rd.,
Changkong* ☎ *053/510329.*

LAMPANG

*65 km (40 miles) southeast of Lamphun, 91 km (57 miles) southeast
of Chiang Mai.*

At the end of the 19th century, when Lampang was a thriving center of
the teak trade, the well-to-do city elders gave the city a genteel look by

buying a fleet of English-built carriages and a stable of nimble ponies to pull them through the streets. Until then, elephants had been a favored means of transportation—a century ago the number of elephants, employed in the nearby teak forests, nearly matched the city's population. The carriages arrived on the first trains to steam into Lampang's fine railroad station, which still looks much the same as it did back then. More than a century later, the odd sight of horse-drawn carriages still greets visitors to Lampang. The brightly painted, flower-bedecked carriages, driven by hardened types in Stetson hats and cowboy boots, look touristy, but the locals also use them to get around the city, albeit for considerably less than the B150 visitors are usually charged for a short city tour.

Apart from some noteworthy temples and a smattering of fine teak shophouses and private homes, not much else remains of Lampang's prosperous heyday. An ever-dwindling number of sturdy 19th-century teak houses can be found among the maze of concrete. Running parallel to the south bank of the Wang River is a narrow street of ancient shops and homes that once belonged to the Chinese merchants who catered to Lampang's prosperous populace. ■TIP➜ The riverfront promenade is a pleasant place for a stroll; some of the cafés and restaurants along it have terraces overlooking the water.

Lampang's tourist office is on Thakhraonoi Road near the clock tower. It keeps irregular hours; officially it's open daily from 9 to 5, but as in Lamphun, you might find the office closed on weekends and even on some afternoons.

GETTING HERE AND AROUND

AIR TRAVEL Lampang Airport, which handles domestic flights, is just west of downtown. Songthaews run to the city center for around B50. Bangkok Airways and Nok Air have several flights a day from Bangkok's Don Mueang Airport.

BUS TRAVEL Buses from Chiang Mai to Lampang, with a stop at the Elephant Conservation Center, leave every half hour from near the Tourism Authority of Thailand office on the road to Lamphun. Lampang's bus station is 2 km (1 mile) south of the city, just off the main highway to Bangkok. Faster VIP buses from Bangkok to Chiang Mai—operated by various companies—stop at Lampang; they leave Chiang Mai's Arcade Bus Station about every hour throughout the day. Fares from Chiang Mai range from about B40 to B150.

SONGTHAEW AND CAR- RIAGE TRAVEL Within Lampang, songthaews are the cheapest way of getting around, though traveling via the city's horse-drawn carriages is much more thrilling. Carriages are at various city stands, with the largest contingent of carriages outside the Wiengthong Hotel.

TRAIN TRAVEL All Bangkok–Chiang Mai trains stop at Lampang, where a samlor can take you the 3 km (2 miles) into town for about B40. By train, Lampang is about 2½ hours from Chiang Mai and 11 hours from Bangkok. First-class fares from Bangkok range from B1,300 for a sleeper to B600 or B800 for a day train.

Elephants embrace at the Lampang Elephant Conservation Center.

ESSENTIALS

TOURS **Lampang Holiday Tours.** This travel agency arranges tours of the temples and Lampang's old quarter. ✉ *260/22 Chatchai Rd.* ☎ *054/310403.*

SAFETY AND PRECAUTIONS Lampang is a famously friendly city, with a sizable expat population, mostly teachers and retirees. There are few cases of street crime or theft involving foreigners. The usual precautions are nevertheless advised, particularly if walking on less busy streets at night—leave valuables in your hotel room safe or with the management.

TIMING Lampang is worth at least one overnight stay. It has a large selection of comfortable hotels and a few restaurants (notably the Riverside) where a pleasant evening can be spent.

EXPLORING

FAMILY
Fodor'sChoice
★

Elephant Conservation Center. On the main highway between Lampang and Chiang Mai is the internationally known Elephant Conservation Center. So-called training camps are scattered throughout the region, but many of them are little more than overpriced sideshows. This is the real thing: a government-supported research station. Here you can find the special stables that house the 10 white elephants owned by the king, although only those who are taking the center's mahout (keeper) training course are allowed to see them. The 36 "commoner" elephants (the most venerable are more than 80 years old) get individual care from more than 40 mahouts. The younger ones evidently enjoy the routines they perform for the tourists—not only the usual log-rolling, but painting pictures (a New York auction of their work raised thousands of dollars for the center). There's even an elephant band—its trumpeter is truly a star. The elephants are bathed every day at 9:30 and 1:15, and perform at 10, 11, and 1:30. You can even take an elephant ride through the center's extensive grounds, and if you fancy becoming a mahout you can take a residential course in elephant management. The center's hospital, largely financed by a Swiss benefactor, is a heart-rending place, treating elephants injured by mines sown along the Burmese border. Its latest mine victim won international renown in 2008 by becoming the first elephant in the world to be fitted successfully with an artificial leg. ✉ *Baan Tung Kwian* ✛ *Km 28–29 Lampang-Chiang Mai Hwy., Hang Chat* ☎ *054/829333* ⊕ *www.thailandelephant.org* 💳 *B200* ☉ *Daily 8–4.*

Wat Phra Kaew Don Tao. Near the banks of the Wang River, this temple is dominated by its tall chedi, built on a rectangular base and topped with a rounded spire. More interesting, however, are the Burmese-style shrine and adjacent Thai-style sala. The 18th-century shrine has a multitier roof. The interior walls are carved and inlaid with colored stones; the ornately engraved ceiling is painted with enamel. The sala, with the traditional three-tier roof and carved-wood pediments, houses a Sukhothai-style reclining Buddha. Legend has it that the sala was once home to the Emerald Buddha, which now resides in Bangkok. In 1436, when King Sam Fang Kaem was transporting the statue from Chiang Rai to Chiang Mai, his elephant reached Lampang and refused to go farther. The Emerald Buddha is said to have remained here for the next 32 years, until the succeeding king managed to get it to Chiang Mai. ✉ *Phra Kaew Rd.*

Fodor's Choice ★ **Wat Phra That Lampang Luang.** One of the most venerated temples in the north, Wat Phra That Lampang Luang is also one of the most striking. Surrounded by stout laterite defense walls, the temple, near the village of Ko Khang, has the appearance of a fortress, exactly what it was when the legendary Queen Chamthewi founded her capital here in the 8th century. The Burmese captured it two-and-a-half centuries ago but were ejected by the forces of a Lampang prince—a bullet hole marks the spot where he killed the Burmese commander. The sandy temple compound has much to hold your interest, including a tiny chapel with a hole in the door that creates an amazing, inverted photographic image of the wat's central, gold-covered chedi. The temple's ancient viharn has a beautifully carved wooden facade; note the intricate decorations around the porticoes. A museum has excellent wood carvings, but its treasure is a small emerald Buddha, which some claim was carved from the same stone as its counterpart in Bangkok. ✉ *Lampang* ✛ *15 km (9 miles) south of Lampang in Koh Kha district* ☉ *Tues.–Sun. 9–4.*

Wat Sri Chum. Workers from Myanmar were employed in the region's rapidly expanding logging business, and these immigrants left their mark on the city's architecture. Especially well preserved is Wat Sri Chum, a 19th-century Burmese temple. Pay particular attention to the viharn, as the eaves are covered with beautiful carvings. Inside you can find gold-and-black lacquered pillars supporting a carved-wood ceiling. To the right is a bronze Buddha cast in the Burmese style. Red-and-gold panels on the walls depict temple scenes. ✉ *Sri Chum Rd.*

6

WHERE TO EAT

$ THAI 🍴 **Rim Wang.** This simple Thai restaurant sits on the banks of the Wang River, 2 km (1 mile) down the main 1034 highway in the village of Ko Kha. Fresh fish is a daily specialty, but try the plump fish cakes or a crispy version of *larb,* a popular minced-pork dish. [$] *Average main: B100* ✉ *Hwy. 1034, Ko Kha* ☎ *054/281104* 💳 *No credit cards.*

$ ECLECTIC 🍴 **The Riverside.** A random assortment of wooden rooms and terraces gives this place an easygoing charm—perched above the sluggish Wang River, it's a great place for a casual meal. The moderately priced Thai and European fare is generally excellent, and on weekends the chef serves up a credible pizza. On most nights a band performs, but there are so many quiet corners that you can easily escape the music. The quietest corner of all is the Riverside's own guesthouse, a cozy ensemble of teak rooms a short walk from the restaurant. [$] *Average main: B150* ✉ *328 Tipchang Rd.* ☎ *054/221861.*

WHERE TO STAY

For expanded hotel reviews, visit Fodors.com.

$ HOTEL 🏨 **Asia Lampang.** Although this hotel sits on a bustling street, most of the rooms are quiet enough to ensure a good night's sleep. **Pros:** central location; open-sided restaurant with view of busy street scene. **Cons:** unexciting lobby; some rooms need refurbishing. [$] *Rooms from: B550* ✉ *229 Boonyawat Rd.* ☎ *054/227844, 02/642–5497 Bangkok reservations* 🌐 *www.asialampanghotel.com* 🛏 *71 rooms.*

$$ RESORT 🏨 **Lampang River Lodge.** Nature lovers are well catered to at this remote lodge, a simple riverside resort isolated in woodland and a 15-minute drive south of Lampang's bright lights. **Pros:** beautifully landscaped grounds; magical riverside bar; ample parking. **Cons:** far from city center; shuttle bus to Lampang infrequent; patchy restaurant service. [$] *Rooms from: B2,800* ✉ *330 Moo 11 Tambon Champoo, off Chiang Mai–Lampang Hwy. 11* ☎ *054/336640* 🌐 *www.lampangriverlodge.com* 🛏 *60 rooms.*

$ HOTEL 🏨 **Lampang Wiengthong.** One of the city's best hotels, this modern high-rise has some luxuriously appointed rooms and suites. **Pros:** central location; bathrooms with tubs; horse-carriage stand in front of hotel. **Cons:** chain-hotel atmosphere; package-tour groups. [$] *Rooms from: B1,750* ✉ *138/109 Phaholyothin Rd.* ☎ *054/225801* 🌐 *www.lampangwiengthong.co.th* 🛏 *235 rooms.*

$ B&B/INN Fodor's Choice ★ 🏨 **Riverside Guest House.** Under the same management as the nearby Riverside restaurant, this utterly enchanting place has the same rustic coziness. **Pros:** homey atmosphere; garden hammocks; river views. **Cons:** noisy neighborhood dogs; no restaurant on-site; some rooms share baths. [$] *Rooms from: B400* ✉ *286 Talad Kao Rd.* ☎ *054/227005* 🌐 *www.theriverside-lampang.com* 🛏 *19 rooms* 🍽 *No meals.*

CLOSE UP

Thailand's Elephants

The United States has its eagle. Britain acquired the lion. Thailand's symbolic animal is the elephant, which has played an enormous role in the country's history through the ages. It even appeared on the national flag when Thailand was Siam. It's a truly regal beast—white elephants enjoy royal patronage, and several are stabled at the National Elephant Institute's conservation center near Lampang.

But the elephant is also an animal of the people, domesticated some 2,000 years ago to help with the heavy work and logging in the teak forests of northern Thailand. Elephants were in big demand by the European trading companies, which scrambled for rich harvests of teak in the late 19th century and early 20th century. At one time there were nearly as many elephants in Lampang as people.

Early on, warrior rulers recognized their usefulness in battle, and "Elephants served as the armored tanks of pre-modern Southeast Asian armies," according to the late American historian David K. Wyatt. The director of the mahout training program at the Lampang conservation center believes he is a reincarnation of one of the foot soldiers who ran beside elephants in campaigns against Burmese invaders.

INCREASING THREATS

Though many elephants enjoy royal status, the gentle giant is under threat. Ivory poaching, cross-border trade in live elephants, and urban encroachment have reduced Thailand's elephant population from about 100,000 a century ago to just 2,500 today. Despite conservation efforts, even these 2,500 face an uncertain future as mechanization and a 1988 government ban on private logging threw virtually all elephants and their mahouts out of work. Hundreds of mahouts took their elephants to Bangkok and other big cities to beg for money and food. The sight of an elephant begging for bananas curbside in Bangkok makes for an exotic snapshot, but the photo hides a grim reality. The elephants are kept in miserable urban conditions, usually penned in the tiny backyards of city tenements. It's been estimated that the poor living conditions, unsuitable diet, and city pollution combine to reduce their life expectancy by at least five years.

HUMANE ALTERNATIVES

A nationwide action to rescue the urban elephants and resettle them in the country—mostly in northern Thailand—is gathering pace. The National Elephant Institute near Lampang is a leader in this field, thanks largely to the efforts of an American expert, Richard Lair, and two young British volunteers. The 40 or so elephants that have found refuge at the center actually pay for their keep by working at various tasks, from entertaining visitors with shows of their logging skills to providing the raw material (dung) for a papermaking plant. The center has a school of elephant artists, trained by two New York artists, and an elephant orchestra. The art they make sells for $1,000 and more on the Internet, and the orchestra has produced two CDs. Several similar enterprises are dotted around northern Thailand. All are humanely run, and represent a far better alternative to a life on the streets of Bangkok or in a Pattaya cabaret show.

6

SHOPPING

Lampang is known for its blue, white, and orange pottery, much of it incorporating the image of a cockerel, the city's emblem. The city has a Saturday evening street market, on Talad Kao Road, where vendors sell pottery, fabrics, and handicrafts. ■TIP➔ You can find the best bargains at markets a few miles south of the city on the highway to Bangkok, or north of the city on the road to Chiang Mai.

Indra Ceramic. Lampang's biggest pottery outlet is west of the city center on the road to Phrae. You can see the ceramics being made and even paint your own designs. The extensive showrooms feature a ceramic model city. ⊠ *382 Vajiravudh Damnoen Rd., Lampang–Phrae Hwy., 2 km (1 mile) west of city center* ☎ *054/315591* ⊕ *www.indraceramic.com.*

Srisawat Ceramics. In Lampang proper, Phaholyothin Road has several small showrooms. The best place in central Lampang for pottery is Srisawat Ceramics. ⊠ *316 Phaholyothin Rd.* ☎ *054/218139* ⊕ *www.tcie.com.*

NORTHERN
THAILAND

WELCOME TO NORTHERN THAILAND

TOP REASONS TO GO

★ **Natural Wonders:** Northern Thailand is mountain country. Beyond Chiang Mai, the peaks rise to the borders of Myanmar and Laos, crisscrossed by deep valleys and fast-flowing rivers. National parks welcome hikers and campers to wild areas of outstanding natural beauty and hill tribe villages lost in time. At the southern edge of the region lie the ruins of Sukhothai, a cradle of Siamese civilization.

★ **Shopping:** The region is world famous for its silks, and the night markets of Mae Hong Son and Chiang Rai have an astonishing range of handicrafts, many of them from hill tribe villages.

★ **Eating:** Northern Thai cuisine is considered the country's tastiest. Chiang Rai and Pai have excellent restaurants, but even the simplest food stall can serve up delicious surprises.

★ **Temples:** The golden spires of thousands of temples dot the region. Each can tell you volumes about Buddhist faith and culture—particularly the haunted ruins of Sukhothai.

MYANMAR (BURMA)

Fang
Doi Ang Khang
Wiang Haeng
107
1322
1095
Pai
Chiang Dao
Phra
Mae Hong Son
Tapai
1001
Doi Mae Ya
Mae Taeng
Mae Rim
118
Khun Yuam
Doi Suthep
Chiang Mai
1263
Hang Dong
2
Doi Inthanon
108
Lamphun
Mae Chaem
108
Pa Sang
11
Doi Inthanon National Park
Ban Hong
Mae Sariang
108
Hot
106
1103
Mae Pok
105
1099
Salween River
0   30 mi
0   30 km
106
Mae Ping Nat'l Park
Thoen
Mae Phrik
Pang A
Mae Rawan
Ban Tak
Tak

1 Nan and Nearby. Northern Thailand's most remote provincial capital is a fascinating destination. Nan is reached by a long but worthwhile drive from either Chiang Mai or Chiang Rai along empty highways lined by fruit orchards, paddy fields, and jungle-clad uplands. The city's Pumin temple and its unique frescoes are reason enough to tackle the journey.

2 The Mae Hong Son Loop. Set two or three days aside for traveling Thailand's famous tourist trail, which begins and ends in Chiang Mai, winding through spectacular mountain scenery for much of the way. Although the route is named after its principal town, Mae Hong Son, the quiet village of Pai has become a major destination.

Tachilek
Mae Sai
Golden Triangle
Chiang Saen
Chiang Khong
Houay Say (Houayxay)
Doi Mae Salong
Mae Chan
1089
3
1
Chiang Rai
LAOS
Mekong River
1020
Wiang Chai
Thoeng
Mae Suai
Phan
18
1
Wang Nua
Phayao
Song Khwae
Chae Son National Park
Tha Wang Pha
1120
Ngao
Nan
1
1035
101
Wiang Sa
1
103
Lampang
101
Phrae
11
Wiang Kosai National Park
11
101
Uttaradit
Si Satchanalai Historical Park
Si Satchanalai
Phae
Thung Salaem
Ban Dara
Sawankhalok
11
101
Nong Makhang
4
New Sukhothai
Sukhothai Historical Park
Wang Thong
Phitsanulok
Buddha Statue Temple

GETTING ORIENTED

A journey through northern Thailand feels like venturing into a different country from the region centered around far-off Bangkok: the landscape, the language, the architecture, the food, and even the people up north are quite distinct. Chiang Mai is the area's natural capital, but Chiang Rai is developing rapidly. Both cities are not smaller versions of Bangkok, but rather bustling regional centers in their own right. Just beyond each of them rises the mountain range that forms the eastern buttress of the Himalayas. The region's northernmost section borders Myanmar and Laos, and improved land crossings into Laos from here have made forays into that country a popular side trip.

7

worthy side trip. Beyond its fascinating past, the area has much to recommend it: mountain scenery, boat trips on the Mekong River, and a few luxurious resorts.

4 Sukhothai and Nearby. To history buffs, the soul of the country is to be found in the cities of Sukhothai and Si Satchanalai. These strongholds of architecture and culture evoke Thailand's ancient civilizations, while Sukhothai's well-developed tourist industry makes it the natural hub for exploring the region.

3 Chiang Rai and the Golden Triangle. The northernmost region of Thailand is known mostly for its former role as the center of the opium trade; a museum in Ban Sop Ruak devoted to the subject is a

EATING AND DRINKING WELL IN NORTHERN THAILAND

To most food lovers, Thailand's northern reaches are a culinary hot spot, literally and figuratively. The distinctive Laotian and Burmese influences, as seen in the spicy salads, grilled river fish, and other delicacies prepared here likely resemble no Thai food you've tasted back home. Through rice paddies, across plains, and along the majestic Mekong, a healthy peasant's diet of fresh river fish, sticky rice, sausage, and spicy salads replaces the richer shellfish and coconut curries of Thailand's center and south.

Westerners may not like the frogs, lizards, and even rice-paddy rats that are often added to spicy curry. Snakehead fish with mango salad (above).

Thailand's expansive north encompasses various ethnicities and immigrant groups, making it hard to pigeonhole the food. Universal, however, are searingly sour curries centering on sharp herbs and spices rather than coconut milk; salt-rubbed river fish grilled over open coals; and salads integrating lime, fermented shrimp, and dried chili.

CLEVER COOKING IN NORTHERN THAILAND

The food of the far north is distinctly different from that of the rest of Thailand. In this poorer region of the country, cooks are sometimes inspired by whatever's on hand. Take salted eggs, for example. They're soaked in salt and then pickled, preserving a fragile food in the hot environment and adding another tasty salty and briny element to dishes.

PLA DUK YANG

You'll find grilled river fish through-out the north, and snakehead fish is one of the region's most special treats. As opposed to the south, where fish is sometimes deep-fried or curried, here it is usually stuffed with big, long lemon-grass skewers and grilled over an open fire, searing the skin. Add the spicy, sour curry that's served atop the fish—and throw in *som tam* salad and sticky rice for good measure—and you've got a quintessential northern meal.

SOM TAM

Som tam, a ragingly hot green papaya salad prepared with a mortar and pestle, originated from the northeastern Isaan region, but is also found in the north. Tease out the differences between three versions: *som tam poo*, also found in Myanmar, integrating black crab shells (a challenging texture, to say the least); *som tam pla*, an Isaan version with salt fish and long bean; and the traditional Thai *som tam*, ground with peanuts and tiny dried and fermented shrimp.

KHAO LAM

On highways, meandering rural roads, and at most markets you'll find women selling tubes of bamboo filled with sticky rice and coconut. The rice is grilled over smoky coals, which adds a woodiness to the rice's rich, sweet, salty flavor. (Slowly peel off the bamboo to eat it.) The rice can be black or white, and sometimes is

cooked with minuscule purplish beans. In mango season, *khao neaw ma muang* (mango with sticky rice) is the ultimate salty-sweet dessert.

KHAO SOI

This comforting noodle dish, believed to have Chinese Muslim origins, is ubiquitous in the north. Egg noodles and chicken pieces (generally a leg per serving) swim in a hearty stock fortified by coconut milk, flavored with turmeric and ginger and topped with deep-fried noodles. Add your own chili paste and lime to taste. Cheap and hearty, it's a street stall favorite in Chiang Mai.

GAENG HANG LAY

Another northern favorite, most probably of Burmese origin, is a rich and complex slow-cooked pork curry (usually pork belly and ribs). It owes its unique flavor to the Indian-influenced use of dried spices such as coriander and cumin seeds, cardamom pods, star anise, and ground nuts (peanuts). It's best served with a side dish of sticky rice that is used to mop up the sauce.

Updated by
Lara Dunston

Northern Thailand begins where the flat rice-growing countryside above Bangkok rises north toward the mountains bordering Myanmar and Laos. The vast region is strikingly different, both culturally and geographically, from the south. The north has its own language ("Kham Muang"), cuisine, traditional beliefs and rituals (many of them animist), and a sturdy architectural style these days called Lann a ("a million rice fields"). The north's distinguishing physical feature, the mountains, contributed to the development of distinctive cultures and subcultures by isolating the mostly rural residents. Even today the daunting terrain is protecting them from too rapid an advance of outside influences.

Although Chiang Mai is the natural capital of northern Thailand it's not the only city in the region deserving inclusion in a Thailand itinerary. Chiang Rai, Chiang Saen, Mae Hong Son, Phrae, and Nan have enough attractions, particularly historic temples, to make at least overnight visits worthwhile. The ancient city of Sukhothai, with its stunning ensemble of temple ruins, is a stand-alone destination in its own right but can be easily integrated into a tour of the north. The mountains and forested uplands that separate these fascinating cities are studded with simple national park lodges and luxury resorts, hot-water spas, elephant camps—the list is endless.

Chiang Rai is a particularly suitable base for exploring the region further—either on treks to the hill tribe villages that dot the mountainsides or on shorter jaunts by elephant. The fast-flowing mountain rivers provide ideal conditions for white-water rafting and canoeing. The truly adventurous may want to head for one of the national parks, which offer overnight accommodations and the services of guides.

GREAT ITINERARIES

To really get a feel for northern Thailand, plan on spending at least a week here.

If You Have 2 Days. Spend your first day exploring the streets of Chiang Mai. On the second day rise early and drive up to Wat Phra That Doi Suthep. In the afternoon, visit Chiang Rai and its mountainous surroundings.

If You Have 5 Days. Begin your stay in the north in Chiang Mai, flying from there to Mae Hong Son, and take a tour of a nearby Karen village. Set out the next day by hired car or bus for Chiang Rai, stopping over for one night at Pai. On the third day, en route for Chiang Rai, you might consider overnighting in Tha Ton or Chiang Dao. On the fourth and fifth days make a circular tour to Chiang Saen to see its excavated ruins and meet the Mekong River, then to Ban Sop Ruak to visit the magnificent Hall of Opium museum. Finally, head to Mae Sai for a look at Burmese crafts in the busy local markets.

If You Have 7 Days. If you're lucky enough to have a week or more in northern Thailand, you'll have plenty of time to stay a night with a hill tribe family. Treks to these mountain villages, often done on elephants, can be arranged from Chiang Mai, Chiang Rai, Mae Hong Son, and other communities. Sukhothai, a must-see destination, is a day's journey to the south, so the best way to include it in your itinerary is to return to Chiang Mai and catch a long-distance VIP bus to Sukhothai, where a tour of the well-preserved ruins of ancient Siam's most advanced and most civilized kingdom will take up one day. From Sukhothai, another six-hour bus ride returns you to Bangkok.

From Chiang Rai, circular routes run through the city's upland surroundings and deep into more remote mountains, where descendants of Chinese soldiers who fled after the Communist takeover of their country grow coffee and tea. Nan is tucked away in the mountainous corner bordering Laos, and Myanmar lies just over the nearest range from Mae Hong Son and Mae Sariang. The so-called Mae Hong Son Loop, a spectacular road starting and ending in Chiang Mai, runs through a small market town, Pai, that has developed over the years into a major tourist destination. First discovered by backpackers doing the "Loop," the town's simple guesthouses are now making way for smart resorts designed for Bangkok businesspeople seeking a quiet weekend in the north.

PLANNING

WHEN TO GO

Northern Thailand has three seasons. The region is hottest and driest from February to May. The rainy season is from June to October, with the wettest weather in September. Unpaved roads are often impassable at this time of year. The best time to visit is between November and March, when the days are warm, sunny, and generally cloudless, and the nights are pleasantly cool. (At higher altitudes, it can be quite cold in the evening.) Book hotel accommodations a month or two ahead of the Christmas and New Year holiday periods and the Songkran New Year's celebration, in mid-April.

GETTING HERE AND AROUND

Northern Thailand appears to be a very remote area of Asia, around 700 km (420 miles) from the country's capital, Bangkok, and far from other major centers. In fact, this region—bounded on the north, east, and west by Myanmar and Laos—is easily accessible. Chiang Mai and Chiang Rai are northern Thailand's major centers.

AIR TRAVEL

Main cities and towns are linked to Bangkok by frequent and reliable air service. There are dozens of flights a day from Bangkok to Chiang Mai and Chiang Rai, and regular flights from the capital to Mae Hong Son and Nan. Flight schedules to these two towns change with frustrating regularity, so check with your airline or travel agent for the latest information.

BUS TRAVEL

An excellent regional bus service links towns and remote villages via a network of highways. The main north–south artery, Highway 1, connects Bangkok with Chiang Rai and the Golden Triangle. Highway 11 branches off for Chiang Mai at Lampang, itself a major transport hub with a long-distance bus terminal, a railroad station, and an airport. From Chiang Mai you can reach the entire region on well-paved roads, with travel times not exceeding eight hours or so. The journey on serpentine mountain roads to Mae Hong Son, however, can be very tiring, requiring a stopover in either the popular resort town of Pai or quieter Mae Sariang. Chiang Rai is a convenient stopover on the road north to the Golden Triangle.

CAR TRAVEL

Driving in Thailand is not for the faint of heart; hiring a car and driver is usually a better option (⇨ *Car Travel in Travel Smart Thailand*). ■TIP→ Between Christmas and New Year's Day the highway between Chiang Mai, Chiang Rai, Pai, and Mae Hong Son may be packed with bumper-to-bumper traffic.

MOTORCYCLE TRAVEL

Motorcycles are a cheap and popular option for getting around cities and towns. Rental agencies are numerous, and most small hotels have their own. Do not rent a motorcycle unless you are an experienced rider. Tourists are involved in motorcycle accidents on a daily basis.

ESSENTIALS
SAFETY AND PRECAUTIONS

Malaria and other mosquito-borne diseases are rare in northern cities, but if you're traveling in the jungle during the rainy season (from June to October), consider taking antimalarials. If you're trekking in the mountains or staying at hill tribe villages, pack mosquito repellent. Spray your room about a half hour before turning in, even if windows have screens and beds have mosquito nets.

Chiang Rai and other communities in northern Thailand are generally safe. However, it's a good idea to leave your passport, expensive jewelry, and large amounts of cash in your hotel safe. Keep a copy of your passport with you at all times, as police can demand proof of identification and levy a fine if you don't produce it. Always walk holding bags on the side of you facing away from the street. In a medical emergency, head to Chiang Rai or Chiang Mai. The police hotline is 191.

MONEY MATTERS

ATMs are everywhere in Chiang Rai and Pai, and most towns and larger villages have at least one machine. Every bank has at least one ATM, but if there are no convenient banks, head for a branch of the ubiquitous convenience-store chain 7-Eleven, where an ATM is invariably to be found next to the entrance. Banks are open on weekdays from 9:30 to 3:30, closing on weekends and public holidays. All banks have an exchange counter; money can also be exchanged at some outlets in central Chiang Rai. Most businesses and restaurants accept credit cards (usually preferring MasterCard or Visa). Simpler Thai restaurants accept only cash.

RESTAURANTS

Northern cuisine differs significantly from cuisine in the rest of Thailand, although most restaurants serve both. You'll have no problem finding plain *khao suay* (steamed rice) or fragrant jasmine rice, for example, though locals prefer the glutinous *khao niao* (sticky rice). A truly northern and very popular Muslim specialty is *khao soi*, a delicious pork or chicken curry with crispy and soft noodles, served with pickled cabbage and onions; lively debates take place at Chiang Mai dinner tables about the best restaurants to find it.

Another northern specialty is *gaeng hang lay*, a pork curry redolent of its many dried spices. Chiang Mai's famous sausages are found throughout the north try *sai ua* (crispy pork sausage) and *mu yo* (spicy sausage). Noodles of nearly every variety can be bought for a few baht from food stalls everywhere, and some fried-noodle dishes, particularly pad thai, have found their way onto many menus. Other northern dishes to try include *nam pik ong* (pork, chilies, and tomatoes), *gaeng ke gai* (chicken curry with chili leaves and baby eggplant), and *kap moo* (crispy pork served with *nam pik num*, a mashed chili dip). Western food is served at all larger hotels and at all international restaurants, although the local version of a western breakfast may not measure up to its counterpart back home.

HOTELS

Northern Thailand has the full range of accommodations, from simple guesthouses to five-star resorts. Mostly in Chiang Mai and Chiang Rai but also studding the region's mountains are classy resorts and spas, many of them with all the luxury and facilities of Chiang Mai's top hotels. Chiang Rai, Sukhothai, and Pai contain many boutique hotels—small, comfortable, and well-appointed establishments of no more than 40 or so rooms. Most of these are built in "Lanna" style, reminiscent of this region's earlier architecture, with the accent on dark teak and white stucco. Some of the top hotels are internationally known for embracing a "contemporary Asian" look, combining sleek lines with decorative Oriental features.

WHAT IT COSTS IN BAHT				
	$	$$	$$$	$$$$
Restaurants	under B200	B201–B300	B301–B400	over B400
Hotels	under B2,000	B2,001–B4,000	B4,001–B6,000	over B6,000

Restaurant prices are for a main course, excluding tax and tip. Hotel prices are for a standard double in high season, excluding service charge and tax.

VISITOR INFORMATION

Tours of northern Thailand are offered by Bangkok travel agencies, but it's best to book with one of the many reliable companies in Chiang Mai or Chiang Rai, which are likely to have a deeper local knowledge of the region. Mountain tours of one or two days, which pack in elephant riding, white-water rafting, jungle trekking, and visits or overnights in hill tribe villages, are popular. They are invariably led by guides with close knowledge of their region who speak acceptable English. If you're touring alone or as a couple, you can draw up your own itinerary (omitting, for instance, visits to "Long Neck" villages, a controversial issue in Thailand), but it's far more fun to join a group—and, of course, it's cheaper, starting at B1,000 a day. Tours are also arranged by the Tourism Authority of Thailand (or TAT; ⊕ *www.tourismthailand.org*), which has offices in Chiang Mai, Chiang Rai, Mae Hong Son, and Nan.

NAN AND NEARBY

Visitors looking for off-the-beaten-track territory usually head north from Chiang Mai and Chiang Rai to the Golden Triangle or west to Mae Hong Son. Relatively few venture east, toward Laos, but if time permits it's a region well worth exploring. At its center, some 70 km (42 miles) from the Laotian border, is Nan, the provincial capital and ancient royal residence. The city is very remote; roads to the border end in mountain trails, and there are no frontier crossings, although there are ambitious, long-term plans to run a highway through the mountains to Luang Prabang in Laos.

Two roads link Nan with the west and the cities of Chiang Mai, Chiang Rai, and Lampang—they are both modern highways that sweep through some of Thailand's most spectacular scenery, following river valleys, penetrating forests of bamboo and teak, and skirting upland terraces of rice and maize. Hill tribe villages sit on the heights of the surrounding Doi Phu Chi (Phu Chi Mountains), where dozens of waterfalls, mountain river rapids, and revered caves beckon travelers with time on their hands. Here you can find Hmong and Lahu villages untouched by commercialism, and jungle trails where you, your elephant, and mahout beat virgin paths through the thick undergrowth.

The southern route from Chiang Mai to Nan passes through the ancient town of Phrae, the center of Thailand's richest teak-growing region and

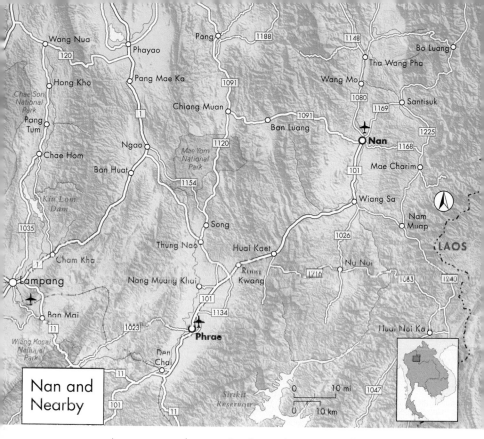

Nan and
Nearby

a pleasant overnight stop. An alternative route to Chiang Mai passes through the town of Phayao, beautifully located on a shallow, shimmering lake with a waterside promenade where restaurants feature freshly caught fish on their daily menu specialties. The region has three wild, mountainous national parks: Doi Phak Long, 20 km (12 miles) west of Phrae on Highway 1023; Doi Luang, south of Chiang Rai; and Doi Phukku, on the slopes of the mountain range that separates Thailand and Laos, some 80 km (48 miles) northeast of Nan.

NAN

318 km (198 miles) southeast of Chiang Mai, 270 km (168 miles) southeast of Chiang Rai, 668 km (415 miles) northeast of Bangkok.

Near the border of Laos lies the city of Nan, a provincial capital founded in 1272. According to local legend, Lord Buddha, passing through the Nan Valley, spotted an auspicious site for a temple to be built. By the late 13th century Nan was brought into Sukhothai's fold, but, largely because of its remoteness, it maintained a fairly independent status until the last few decades.

Nan is rich in teak plantations and fertile valleys that produce rice and superb oranges. The town of Nan itself is small; everything is within walking distance. Daily life centers on the morning and evening markets. The Nan River, which flows past the eastern edge of town, draws visitors at the end of Buddhist Lent, in late October or early November, when traditional boat races are held. Each longtail boat is carved out of a single tree trunk, and at least one capsizes every year, to the delight of the locals. In mid-December Nan honors its famous fruit crop with a special Golden Orange and Red Cross Fair—there's even a Miss Golden Orange contest. It's advisable to book hotels well ahead of time for these events.

Tourist information about Nan Province, Nan itself, and Phrae is handled by the Tourism Authority of Thailand's regional office in Chiang Rai.

GETTING HERE AND AROUND

AIR TRAVEL Kan Air flies on Thursday and Sunday between Chiang Mai and Nan. The flight takes 45 minutes. Nok Air runs at least a couple of 95-minute flights daily from Bangkok to Nan. Schedules and fares for both airlines vary with the season. Songthaews meet incoming flights. It costs about B50 for the 3-km (2-mile) drive south into central Nan.

BUS TRAVEL Several air-conditioned buses leave Bangkok and Chiang Mai daily for Nan, stopping en route at Phrae. The 11-hour journey from Bangkok to Nan costs from B400 to B600; the journey from Chiang Mai to Nan takes six hours and costs between B300 and B400. Air-conditioned buses also make the five-hour journey from Lampang to Nan. There's local bus service between Nan and Phrae.

CAR TRAVEL Hiring a car and driver is the easiest way to get to Nan from Lampang or Chiang Mai. It costs about B1,500 per day.

TAXI AND TUK-TUK TRAVEL City transport in Nan is provided by tuk-tuks, songthaews, and samlors. All are cheap, and trips within the city should seldom exceed B30.

TRAIN TRAVEL Nan is not on the railroad route, but a relatively comfortable way of reaching the city from Bangkok is to take the Chiang Mai–bound train and change at Den Chai to a local bus for the remaining 146 km (87 miles) to Nan. The bus stops en route at Phrae.

ESSENTIALS

SAFETY AND PRECAUTIONS The mountainous border between Thailand and Laos is just an hour's drive from Nan, and until recently was a haven for smugglers, keeping local police busy. Foreign visitors rarely encounter reminders of this picaresque past, and street crime is rare. But elementary precautions such as leaving valuables in the hotel safe or with the hotel management are advised.

TIMING Nan is worth visiting for the Wat Pumin frescoes, but otherwise it has little to keep a visitor for more than a day or two. The surrounding countryside and the nearby mountains have a wild beauty, and a day tour is recommended.

TOURS Trips range from city tours of Nan and short cycling tours of the region to jungle trekking, elephant riding, and white-water rafting. Nan is the ideal center from which to embark on treks through the nearby mountains, as well as raft and kayak trips along the rivers that cut through them. Khun Chompupach Sirsappuris has run Nan's leading tourist agency, Fhu Travel and Information, for more than 25 years. She speaks fluent English and knows the region like her own backyard.

Contacts **Fhu Travel.** ✉ *453/4 Sumondhevaraj Rd.* ☎ *054/710636* ⊕ *www. fhutravel.com.* **River Raft.** ✉ *50/6 Norkam Rd.* ☎ *054/710940* ⊕ *www. nanriverraft.com.*

EXPLORING

TOP ATTRACTIONS

Wat Ming Muang. With its all-white exterior Wat Ming Muang strikes a dramatic pose offset slightly by the exterior's surfeit of intricate carvings. (Photo ops galore.) The wat contains a stone pillar erected at the founding of Nan, some 800 years ago. Don't miss the interior murals, some of which depict life here in days gone by. ✉ *Suriyaphong Rd.*

Wat Phra That Chae Hang. Its golden central stupa a signature Nan image, this 14th-century wat draws worshippers from all over Thailand born in the astrological year of the rabbit. The serenely posed main Buddha and a reclining Buddha are among the visual highlights inside. ✉ *Nan ⌖ 1 km (3 miles) southeast of central Nan off Hwy. 1168.*

Fodor'sChoice **Wat Pumin.** Nan has one of the region's most unusual and beautiful
  ★   temples, Wat Pumin, whose murals alone make a visit to this part of northern Thailand worthwhile. It's an economically constructed temple, combining the main shrine hall and viharn, and qualifies as one of northern Thailand's best examples of folk architecture. To enter, you climb a short flight of steps flanked by two superb *nagas* (mythological snakes), their heads guarding the north entrance and their tails the south. The 16th-century temple was extensively renovated in 1865 and 1873, and at the end of the 19th century murals picturing everyday life were added to the inner walls. Some have a unique historical context—like the French colonial soldiers disembarking at a Mekong River port with their wives in crinolines. A fully rigged merchant ship and a primitive steamboat are portrayed as backdrops to scenes showing colonial soldiers leering at the pretty local girls corralled in a palace courtyard. Even the conventional Buddhist images have a lively originality, ranging from the traumas of hell to the joys of courtly life. The bot's central images are also quite unusual—four Sukhothai Buddhas locked in conflict with the evil Mara. ✉ *Phalong Rd.* ⊙ *Daily 8–6.*

WORTH NOTING

National Museum. To get a sense of the region's art, visit the National Museum, which occupies a mansion built in 1923 for the prince who ruled Nan, Chao Suriyapong Pharittadit. The house itself is a work of art, a synthesis of overlapping red roofs, forest green doors and shutters, and brilliant white walls. There's a fine array of wood and bronze Buddha statues, musical instruments, ceramics, and other works of Lanna art. The revered "black elephant tusk" is also an attraction. The tusk, about a meter (3 feet) long, weighs 18 kg (40 pounds). It's actually dark brown in color, but that doesn't detract at all from its special role as a local good-luck charm. ✉ *Phalong Rd.* ☎ *054/710561* 🎟 *B100* ⊙ *Wed.–Sun. 9–4.*

Wat Chang Kham. This wat has one of only seven surviving solid-gold Buddha images from the Sukhothai period. Its large chedi is supported by elephant-shape buttresses. ✉ *Suriyaphong Rd.*

Wat Hua Wiang Tai. Gaudy Wat Hua Wiang Tai has a naga running along the top of the wall and lively murals painted on the viharn's exterior. ✉ *Sumonthewarat Rd.*

Wat Suan Tan. A 15th-century bronze Buddha image is the centerpiece of this wat that's the scene of all-night fireworks during the annual Songkran festival in April. ✉ *Tambon Nai Wiang.*

WHERE TO EAT

$$ THAI 🍴 **Ruen Kaew.** Its name means Crystal House, and this riverside restaurant, open seven days a week, really is a gem. Guests step in through a profusion of bougainvillea onto a wooden deck directly overlooking the Nan River. A Thai band and singers perform nightly. The Thai menu has some original touches—the chicken in a honey sauce, for instance, is a rare delight. [$] *Average main: B240* ✉ *1/1 Sumondhevaraj Rd.* ☎ *054/710631, 089/558–2508.*

$$ THAI 🍴 **Suriya Garden.** This substantial restaurant on the banks of the Nan River is a larger version of the nearby Ruen Kaew, with a wooden deck overlooking the water. Like its neighbor, it has added some interesting specialties, among them Chinese-style white bass or pig's trotters, to the conventional Thai menu. A band and solo vocalists perform nightly. [$] *Average main: B220* ✉ *9 Sumondhevaraj Rd.* ☎ *054/710687.*

WHERE TO STAY

$ HOTEL 🏨 **Dhevaraj Hotel.** Built around an attractive interior courtyard, which is lighted for evening dining, the Dhevaraj is a full-service operation. **Pros:** interior courtyard; central location; large rooms. **Cons:** so-so breakfast; patchy service; street noise; dated decor. [$] *Rooms from: B1,200* ✉ *466 Sumondhevaraj Rd.* ☎ *054/751577* 🌐 *www.dhevarajhotel.com* 🛏 *160 rooms* 🍽 *Breakfast.*

$ HOTEL 🏨 **Nan Boutique Hotel.** So-called boutique hotels are rare in rural Thailand, but this accommodation fully lives up to its name. **Pros:** free bicycles; busy restaurant with international menu; friendly service. **Cons:** no pool; long walk to town center; rooms with double beds not always available. [$] *Rooms from: B1,850* ✉ *1/11 Kha Luang Rd., city* ☎ *054/775532* 🌐 *tazshotels.com* 🛏 *32 rooms* 🍽 *Breakfast.*

$ HOTEL 🏨 **Nan Keereethara Hotel.** A ranch-style complex of buildings on the outskirts of the city, this hotel sits amid 12 acres of gardens. **Pros:** pool; shaded gardens; friendly service. **Cons:** away from town center; some rooms lack privacy. [$] *Rooms from: B850* ✉ *99 Yantarakitkosol Rd., Dutai, Muang Nan* ☎ *054/741343* 🌐 *www.nankeereethara.com* 🛏 *125 rooms, 4 suites* 🍽 *No meals* 💳 *No credit cards.*

PHRAE

110 km (68 miles) southeast of Lampang, 118 km (73 miles) southwest of Nan.

A market town in a narrow valley well off the beaten path, Phrae is renowned in northern Thailand for its fine teak houses. It's a useful stopover on the 230-km (143-mile) journey from Lampang to Nan, but has little to offer the visitor apart from ruined city walls, some attractive and historic temples, and the sturdy teak buildings that attest to its former importance as a center of the logging industry.

GETTING HERE AND AROUND

The domestic airline Nok Air flies daily between Bangkok and Phrae. The flight takes about 90 minutes. Daily air-conditioned buses from Bangkok and Chiang Mai headed for Nan stop at Phrae. It's a 10-hour journey from Bangkok and a five-hour one from Chiang Mai. Air-conditioned buses travel between Lampang and Phrae (three hours) daily. There's local bus service between Phrae and Nan, an uncomfortable but cheap journey of two to three hours between each center. Hiring a car and driver in Lampang or Chiang Mai is the easiest way to get here, but doing this costs about B3,000 per day.

ESSENTIALS

SAFETY AND PRECAUTIONS Phrae is a friendly place, where everybody knows everybody and where the police rarely have more to do than ticket wrongly parked motorists. You're perfectly safe to walk the streets at night, although you might like to leave valuables in the hotel safe or with the management. You needn't carry much cash—there's not much to spend it on here.

TIMING Phrae has little to keep the visitor apart from a comfortable room as a stopover on the road to Nan.

EXPLORING

Ban Prathap Chai. There are many teak houses to admire all over Phrae, but none match this large one near the city's southern edge. Like many such houses, it's actually a reconstruction of several older houses—in this case nine of them supported on 130 huge centuries-old teak posts. The result is remarkably harmonious. A tour of the rooms open to public view provides a glimpse of bourgeois life in the region. The space between the teak poles on the ground floor of the building is taken up by stalls selling handicrafts, including carved teak ⊠ *Tambon Pa Maet* ✚ *Hwy. 1022, 10 km (6 miles) east of Phrae* 🖼 *B10* 🕙 *Daily 8–5.*

Wat Chom Sawan. A Burmese architect designed this beautiful monastery built during the reign of King Rama V (1868–1910). The bot and viharn combine to make one giant sweeping structure. ⊠ *Yantarakitkosol Rd., on northeastern edge of town.*

Wat Luang. Phrae's oldest structure lies within the Old City walls. Although the wat was founded in the 12th century, renovations and expansions completely obscure so much of the original design that the only section visible from that time is a Lanna chedi with primitive elephant statues. A small museum on the grounds contains sacred Buddha images, swords, and texts. ⊠ *Kham Lue Rd.*

Fodor'sChoice ★ **Wat Phra That Cho Hae.** On a hilltop in Tambon Pa Daeng, this late-12th-century temple is distinguished by its 33-meter-tall (108-foot-tall) golden chedi and breathtaking interior. The chedi is linked to a viharn, a later construction that contains a series of murals depicting scenes from the Buddha's life. The revered Buddha image is said to increase a woman's fertility. Cho Hae is the name given to the cloth woven by the local people, and in the fourth lunar month (June) the chedi is wrapped in this fabric during the annual fair. A fairly steep multitier staircase leads up to the temple. ⊠ *Hwy. 1022, 8 km (5 miles) east of Phrae.*

Wat Phra That Chom Chang. In a woodland setting about 2 km (1 mile) east of the more famous Wat Phra That Cho Hae, this smaller wat has a chedi said to contain a strand of Lord Buddha's hair. A large standing Buddha stands watch over the gate, and the grounds contain an enormous reclining Buddha. ✉ *Hwy. 1022, 10 km (6 miles) east of Phrae.*

WHERE TO EAT

For a quick bite, there's a night market at Pratuchai Gate with numerous stalls offering cheap, tasty food.

$ THAI 🍴 **Pan Jai.** For authentic Lanna cuisine, you can't do better than this simple but superb restaurant. You're automatically served *kanom jin* (Chinese noodles) in basketwork dishes, with a spicy meat sauce, raw and pickled cabbage, and various condiments. If that's not to your taste, then order the *satay moo,* thin slices of lean pork on wooden skewers, served with a peanut-sauce dip. In the evening every table has its own steam pot and barbecue for preparing the popular northern specialty *moo kata,* a kind of pork stew. The open-sided, teak-floor dining area is shaded by ancient acacia trees, making it a cool retreat on warm evenings. [$] *Average main: B100* ✉ *Chatawan Rd. 3* 💳 *No credit cards.*

WHERE TO STAY

$ HOTEL 🏨 **Maeyom Palace Hotel.** Despite its name, this hotel is far from palatial, but it does have comfortable rooms. **Pros:** mountain views from some rooms; pleasant pool. **Cons:** impersonal, chain-hotel atmosphere; traffic noise; some rooms need refurbishing; dated feel over all. [$] *Rooms from: B1,225* ✉ *181/6 Yantarakitkosol Rd.* ☎ *054/521028 up to 35* ✎ *wccphrae@hotmail.com* 🛏 *104 rooms* 🍽 *Breakfast.*

$ HOTEL 🏨 **Nakorn Phrae Tower.** A curious but effective combination of a conventional high-rise and a Lanna-style aesthetic distinguishes this comfortable central Phrae hotel. **Pros:** friendly service; large rooms. **Cons:** favored by tour groups; traffic noise; no pool; dated decor. [$] *Rooms from: B1,200* ✉ *3 Muanghit Rd.* ☎ *054/521321* 🛏 *139 rooms* 🍽 *Breakfast.*

THE MAE HONG SON LOOP

Remote Mae Hong Son is reached along a mountainous stretch of road known to travelers as "the Loop." The route runs from Chiang Mai to Mae Hong Son via Pai if you take the northern route, and via Mae Sariang if you take the southern one. Many visitors find the northern route through Pai (six hours) the more attractive trip, but the southern route through Mae Sariang (eight hours) easier to drive. The entire Loop is about 600 km (360 miles) long. **■ TIP→ Allow at least four days to cover the Loop, longer if you want to leave the road occasionally and visit the hot springs, waterfalls, and grottos along the way.**

PAI

160 km (99 miles) northwest of Chiang Mai, 110 km (68 miles) east of Mae Hong Son.

Although Pai lies in a flat valley, a 10-minute drive in any direction brings you to a rugged upland terrain with stands of wild teak, groves of towering bamboo, and clusters of palm and banana trees hiding out-of-the-way resorts catering to visitors who seek peace and quiet. At night the surrounding fields and forest seem to enfold the town in a black embrace. As you enter Pai from the direction of Chiang Mai, you'll pass by the so-called World War II Memorial Bridge, which was stolen from Chiang Mai during the Japanese advance through northern Thailand and rebuilt here to carry heavy armor over the Pai River. When the Japanese left, they neglected to return the bridge to Chiang Mai. Residents of that city are perfectly happy, as they eventually built a much more handsome river crossing.

Exhausted backpackers looking for a stopover along the serpentine road between Chiang Mai and Mae Hong Son discovered Pai in the late 1980s. In 1991 it had seven modest guesthouses and three restaurants; now its frontier-style streets are lined with restaurants and bars of every description, cheap guesthouses and smart hotels, art galleries, and chic coffeehouses, while every class of resort, from back-to-nature to luxury,

nestles in the surrounding hills. Thus far, Pai has managed to retain its slightly off-the-beaten-path appeal, but that may change as Bangkok property investors pour money into its infrastructure.

Disastrous floods and mudslides in the surrounding mountains devastated this popular tourist haunt in 2005, but the town rapidly recovered, and now the only reminders of the catastrophe are high-water marks on the walls of a few buildings and empty swaths of riverside land. The former market town hosts thousands of visitors in high season, when they outnumber the locals.

GETTING HERE AND AROUND

AIR TRAVEL Kan Air flies on Friday and weekends between Chiang Mai and Pai and daily during the Christmas and New Year holiday period. The flight takes less than a half hour in a 12-seater Cessna aircraft, an excellent alternative to the long, torturous drive.

BUS TRAVEL Buses traveling between Mae Hong Son and Chiang Mai stop in Pai. They take four hours for the 120-km (75-mile) journey from Chiang Mai and an additional five hours to cover the 130 km (81 miles) from Pai to Mae Hong Son. Fares for each stretch vary from about B100 to B200. Buses stop in the center of Pai.

CAR TRAVEL A hired car does the trip from Chiang Mai to Pai one hour faster than the buses, and cuts the journey time from Pai to Mae Hong Son by about the same margin. Cars and four-wheel-drive vehicles can be hired from many companies in Chiang Mai from B1,000 and upward a day. A driver costs about B3,000 per day.

ESSENTIALS

SAFETY AND PRECAUTIONS Pai had a crime problem, but it was caused by drug-taking young foreign visitors, not the locals. A police crackdown appears to have cleaned up the town, but keep your wits about you when visiting the local bars.

TIMING Some foreign visitors come to Pai intending to stay a few days and never leave. It's that kind of place. There's not much to do in Pai besides exploring the surrounding countryside by day and partying by night, so if trekking, bike tours, river rafting, and late nights are not your thing, you'll want to get going again after one or two days.

TOURS **Thai Adventure Rafting.** This outfit organizes wild-water rafting on the Pai River, as well as sightseeing, elephant riding, mountain biking, and bamboo rafting tours. ✉ *39 Moo 3 Chaisongkram Rd. Vieng Tai, Mae Hong Son* ☎ *053/699111* 🌐 *www.thairafting.com* ☞ *From B1,150 per person for 2 people for ½-day cycling tour.*

EXPLORING

Pai Canyon. It's a short if occasionally hair-raising walk from the canyon's parking area to a beautiful view of the valley below. ■ **TIP→ Wear sturdy shoes on this walk as the footing is unstable in places.** ✉ *Pai* ✣ *8 km (5 miles) south of Pai on Hwy. 1095.*

WHERE TO EAT

$ CAFÉ 🍴 **All About Coffee.** One of Pai's historic merchant houses has been converted into a coffee shop that could grace any fashionable city street in the world. More than 20 different kinds of java are on the menu, which also lists the many delicacies from the café's own bakery. [$] *Average* *main: B100 ✉ 100 Moo 1 Chaisongkram Rd. ☎ 053/699429 ▭ No credit cards ⏲ Closes at 6 pm.*

$ MEXICAN 🍴 **Cafecito.** This cool little café is a wonderful choice if you need a change from Thai or just want fantastic food. In an increasingly hip neighborhood on the edge of town, Cafecito serves authentic Mexican food and excellent coffee from beans roasted on the premises. The chef makes his own corn tortillas and salsas. He also whips up tasty chilaquiles and enormous breakfast burritos. [$] *Average main: B150 ✉ 258 Moo 8 Vieng Tai ☎ ⏲ Closes at 6 pm. Closed July and Aug. ✍ Reservations not accepted ▭ No credit cards.*

$ ECLECTIC 🍴 **Edible Jazz.** The international menu at this friendly café, which includes pad thai, pizzas, pastas, burgers (meat and vegetarian), and good burritos, matches the diversity of the live jazz music performed here. [$] *Average main: B150 ✉ 24/1 Chaisongkram Rd. Vieng Tai ☎ 087/177–7455 ▭ No credit cards.*

$ BURGER 🍴 **Maya Burger Queen.** After 10 years in Britain, a Pai entrepreneur named Ping returned to her home town and opened this highly successful burger restaurant. Her burgers are packed with the best local beef and are served with hand-cut choice potatoes. The modest establishment is also the place to share tips with the travelers who gather here nightly. [$] *Average main: B150 ✉ Tedsaban Rd. ☎ 081/381–9141 ▭ No credit cards.*

$ ECLECTIC 🍴 **Om Garden Cafe.** Fragrant with incense, this hippie-chic café is set in an idyllic, shaded courtyard garden. Furnished with mismatched rattan and bamboo sofas and wooden tables, it's decorated with colorful cushions, filmy curtains, and Buddha statues. The food is healthy, hearty, and wholesome. Follow a big fresh organic salad and fruit shake with a slice of house-baked cake. [$] *Average main: B175 ✉ 4 Wiang Tai ☎ 082/451–5930 ▭ No credit cards.*

$$ MEDITERRANEAN Fodor's Choice ★ 🍴 **Silhouette.** Pai's best restaurant serves outstanding Thai-inspired European cuisine, made from fresh, mostly organic, local produce. There are generous sharing plates if you're with friends, or smaller tapas and charcuterie and cheese boards if you only want to graze while listening to the nightly live jazz. Panoramic mountain views and the quirky house sense of style only add to the pleasure of having a meal here. [$] *Average main: B250 ✉ Reverie Siam Resort, 476 Moo 8 Vieng Tai ☎ 053/699870 🌐 reveriesiam.com ✍ Reservations essential ▭ No credit cards.*

PAI: DEMURE HAMLET OR PARTY TOWN?

Pai has a sizable Muslim population, which is why some of the guesthouses post notices asking foreign visitors to refrain from public displays of affection. Immodest clothing is frowned on, so bikini tops and other revealing garb are definitely out. The music bars close early, meaning that by 1 am the town slumbers beneath the tropical sky. Nevertheless, quiet partying continues behind the shutters of the teak cabins that make up much of the tourist lodgings. This is, after all, backpacker territory.

WHERE TO STAY

$ B&B/INN **Brook View.** The brook babbles right outside your cabin window if you ask for a room with a view at this little resort. **Pros:** near town, but still "away from it all"; ample parking; pretty breakfast gazebo. **Cons:** some cabins are small, with no river view; staff keeps a low profile; uninteresting neighborhood. [$] *Rooms from: B1,500* ✉ *132 Moo 1 Vieng Tai* ☎ *053/699366* 🌐 *www.paibrookview.com* 💳 *No credit cards* 🛏 *18 rooms and villas* 🍴 *No meals.*

> **WORD OF MOUTH**
>
> "We stayed in Pai when driving the Loop from Chiang Mai and loved it. There were a few hippie types about, but it was nothing like Khao San Road [in Bangkok]. There are quite a few backpackers' hostels in the center but we stayed just outside of town, and it was very peaceful. A great place to stay for a few days. In fact I preferred it to Mae Hong Son."
>
> –crellston

$ B&B/INN **Cave Lodge.** The chatter of gibbons wakes you up at this remote mountain lodge between Pai and Mae Hong Son. The cave after which it is named, just a short walk from the lodge, is one of the region's most spectacular caverns, with wall paintings and prehistoric coffins. **Pros:** bread and pastries from the wood-fired oven, nature. **Cons:** snakes on the grounds; Pai 42 km (26 miles) away; Mae Hong Son is 64 km (40 miles) away. [$] *Rooms from: B600* ✉ *15 Moo 1, Pang Mapha* ☎ *053/617203* 🌐 *www.cavelodge.com* 💳 *No credit cards* 🛏 *17 rooms* 🍴 *Breakfast.*

$$ RESORT **Pai Tree House Resort.** The rooms with the best views at this riverside lodging outside Pai are only for the most adventurous travelers—they're in the upper branches of an enormous rain tree. **Pros:** terrace bar-restaurant; fine river views; peaceful location. **Cons:** 20-minute drive from town; popular for seminars; can get crowded. [$] *Rooms from: B2,300* ✉ *90 Moo 2, Tambon Maehee* ☎ *081/911–3640* 🌐 *www.paitreehouse.com* 🛏 *19 rooms* 🍴 *No meals.*

$$ HOTEL **Paivimaan Resort.** *Vimaan* means "heaven," and this fine resort commands a heavenly spot on the banks of the Pai River. **Pros:** friendly family welcome; close to town center. **Cons:** villa rooms are small; noise from riverside developments; insects. [$] *Rooms from: B4,000* ✉ *73 Moo 3 Tedsaban Rd.* ☎ *053/699403* 🌐 *www.paivimaan.com* 🛏 *12 rooms, 5 villas* 🍴 *Breakfast.*

$$$ RESORT Fodor's Choice ★ **Reverie Siam Resort.** This boutique resort has beautiful rooms decorated with antiques and vintage pieces, and there are two stunning swimming pools. **Pros:** loads of style; hospitable on-site owners; superb staff; fantastic low-season rates. **Cons:** pricey in high season; on the edge of town. [$] *Rooms from: B5,000* ✉ *476 Moo 8 Vieng Tai* ☎ *053/699870* 🌐 *reveriesiam.com* 🛏 *20 rooms* 🍴 *Breakfast* 💳 *No credit cards.*

NIGHTLIFE

Bepop. In high season Pai is packed with backpackers looking for a place to party. Pai's top music bar is Bepop, which throbs nightly to the sounds of visiting bands. ✉ *Moo 8, 188 Rangsiyannon Rd. Vieng Tai* ☎ *053/699128.*

Ting Tong Bar. A good place to chill out in the early evening is the aptly named Ting Tong ("crazy") Bar. On warm rainless evenings you can lie on cushions and count the stars. ✉ *55 Moo 4 Vieng Tai* ☎ *048/073781.*

MAE HONG SON

245 km (152 miles) northwest of Chiang Mai via Pai, 368 km (229 miles) via Mae Sariang.

Stressed-out residents of Bangkok and other cities have transformed this remote, mountain-ringed market town into one of northern Thailand's major resort areas. Some handsome hotels now grace the landscape here. Overseas travelers love the town because of its easy access to beautiful countryside.

For a small town, Mae Hong Son has a surprising number of noteworthy temples, many erected by the Burmese. Two of the temples, Wat Chong Kham and Wat Kham Klang, sit on the shore of a placid lake in the center of town, forming a breathtaking ensemble of golden spires. Within a short drive are dozens of villages inhabited by the Karen, the so-called "longneck" people. Fine handicrafts are produced in these hamlets, whose inhabitants trek daily to Mae Hong Son to sell their wares at the lively morning market and along the lakeside promenade.

Although Mae Hong Son offers a welcome cool retreat during the sometimes unbearably hot months of March and April, the mountains can be obscured during that part of the year by the fires farmers set to clear their fields. One of the local names for Mae Hong Son translates as "City of the Three Mists." The other two are the clouds that creep through the valleys in the depths of winter and the gray monsoons of the rainy season.

GETTING HERE AND AROUND

AIR TRAVEL One domestic carrier, Kan Air, flies several times daily between Chiang Mai and Mae Hong Son. The Mae Hong Son Airport is at the town's northern edge. Songthaews run to the city center for around B50. In March and April, smoke from slash-and-burn fires often causes flight cancellations.

BUS TRAVEL Chiang Mai's Arcade Bus Terminal serves Mae Hong Son. Several buses depart daily on an eight-hour journey that follows the northern section of the Loop, via Pai. Buses stop in the center of town.

CAR TRAVEL The most comfortable way to travel the route and enjoy the breathtaking mountain scenery is to let somebody else do the driving. The Loop road brings you here from either direction: the northern route through Pai (six hours) is a more attractive trip; the southern route through Mae Sariang (eight hours) is easier driving.

If you choose to rent a car, you'll probably do it in Chiang Mai, but if needed Avis has an office at Mae Hong Son Airport.

TOURS A tourist info kiosk with erratic hours stands on the corner of Khunlum Prapas and Chamnansathit roads. An efficient travel agency, Amazing Mae Hong Son, has an office at the airport. In the center of town, Discover Mae Hong Son books day tours of local hill tribe villages.

Travel Agencies Amazing Mae Hong Son. ✉ Mae Hong Son 📠 053/620650. Discover Mae Hong Son. ✉ Mae Hong Son ☎ 053/611537.

ESSENTIALS

SAFETY AND PRECAUTIONS Mae Hong Son, lying close to the often disputed Myanmar border, has a lawless history, and around 50 years ago was a place of internal exile for political dissidents. But those days lie long in the past, and today Mae Hong Son is a quiet backwater with little street crime. You can safely walk even its unlit lanes at night.

TIMING It's possible to spend a restful week or so in Mae Hong Son, but most visitors overnight here while traveling the Loop, a popular route that also takes in Pai and Mae Sariang. The Burmese temples can occupy a morning or afternoon of sightseeing, but the town has little else to offer. It is, however, a good base from which to visit the hill tribe villages of the region.

EXPLORING

TOP ATTRACTIONS

Wat Chong Klang. This 19th-century temple is worth visiting to see a collection of figurines brought from Burma more than a hundred years ago. The teakwood carvings depict an astonishing range of Burmese individuals, from peasants to nobles. ✉ *Chamnansathit Rd.*

Wat Hua Wiang. Mae Hong Son's most celebrated Buddha image, one of the most revered in northern Thailand, is inside this 19th-century temple. Its origins are clear: note the Burmese-style long earlobes, a symbol of the Buddha's omniscience. ⊠ *Panishwatana Rd.*

Wat Phra That Doi Kong Mu. On the top of Doi Kong Mu, this temple has a remarkable view, especially at sunset, of the surrounding mountains. The temple's two chedis contain the ashes of 19th-century monks. ⊠ *Mae Hong Son ✛ 2km (1 mile) west of Mae Hong Son.*

> **SUNSET VIEWS**
>
> For a giddy view of Mae Hong Son and the surrounding mountains, take a deep breath and trudge up Doi Kong Mu, a hill on the western edge of town. It's well worth the effort. From here you can see the mountains on the border of Myanmar. The view is particularly lovely at sunset. There's another shade of gold to admire, a flame-surrounded white-marble Buddha in a hilltop temple called Wat Phra That Doi Kong Mu.

WORTH NOTING

FAMILY **Thampla-Phasua Waterfall National Park.** About 28 km (17 miles) north of Mae Hong Son on the Pai road, this park has one of the region's strangest sights—a grotto with a dark, cisternlike pool overflowing with fat mountain carp. The pool is fed by a mountain stream that is also full of thrashing fish fighting to get into the cave. Why? Nobody knows. It's a secret that draws thousands of Thai visitors a year. Some see a mystical meaning in the strange sight. The cave is a pleasant 10-minute stroll from the park's headquarters. ⊠ *70 Moo 1 Huay Pa* ☎ *053/619036.*

Wat Chong Kham. A wonderfully self-satisfied Burmese-style Buddha, the cares of the world far from his arched brow, watches over this 19th-century temple, which has a fine pulpit carved with incredible precision. ⊠ *Chamnansathit Rd.*

WHERE TO EAT

$ ✕ **Bai Fern.** Mae Hong Son's main thoroughfare, Khunlum Prapas Road, THAI is lined with inexpensive restaurants serving local cuisine, and this is among the best. In the spacious dining room you eat in typical Thai style, amid solid teak columns and beneath whirling fans. Among the many Thai dishes, the pork ribs with pineapple or roast chicken in pandanus leaves stand out as highly individual and tasty creations. An adjoining coffee corner offers free Wi-Fi. $ *Average main: B150* ⊠ *87 Khunlum Prapas Rd.* ☎ *053/611374.*

$$ ✕ **La Tasca.** Mae Hong Son's only Italian restaurant serves excellent pas-ITALIAN tas, pizzas, and a much-acclaimed calzone. La Tasca also has an extensive Thai menu, and the wine list is impressive. On cool evenings, take a table on the small terrace overlooking Mae Hong Son's main street. $ *Average main: B250* ⊠ *88/4 Khunlum Prapas Rd.* ☎ *053/611344.*

WHERE TO STAY

$$ 🏨 **Fern Resort.** The room rate at Fern is relatively expensive, but it buys RESORT unexpected luxury amid beautiful countryside outside Mae Hong Son. Thirty bungalows in steep-eaved Shan style are scattered over a valley of former rice paddies. **Pros:** regular barbecue nights; fine mountain views; friendly owners. **Cons:** 15-minute drive from town, though there's a

shuttle bus; mosquitoes; small bathrooms. $ *Rooms from: B3,000* ✉ *10 Ban Hua Nam Mae Sakut, Tambon Pha Bong* ☎ *053/686110, 053/686111* ⊕ *www.fernresort.info* ⤳ *30 rooms* ❑ *Breakfast.*

$$
HOTEL

Imperial Mae Hong Son Resort. Set among mature teak trees, this fine hotel was designed to blend in with the surroundings—bungalows in landscaped gardens have both front and back porches, giving the teak-floored and bamboo-furnished rooms a light and airy feel. **Pros:** pleasant walks in the grounds; large rooms; satellite TV. **Cons:** some rooms need refurbishing; long walk from town, though there is shuttle service; insects. $ *Rooms from: B2,550* ✉ *149 Moo 8 Tambon Pang Moo* ☎ *053/611473, 02/261–9000 in Bangkok* ⊕ *www.imperialhotels.com/imperialmaehongson* ⤳ *104 rooms* ❑ *Breakfast.*

$
HOTEL

Panorama Hotel. This centrally located hotel lives up to its name with upper-floor rooms that have views of the mountains surrounding the city. **Pros:** central location; helpful tour desk; good restaurant. **Cons:** some rooms showing their age; traffic noise. $ *Rooms from: B1,000* ✉ *51 Khunlum Prapas Rd.* ☎ *053/611757 up to 62* ⊕ *www.panorama.8m.com* ⤳ *60 rooms* ❑ *Breakfast.*

$
RESORT

Rim Nam Klang Doi. This retreat about 7 km (4 miles) outside Mae Hong Son is an especially good value. **Pros:** helpful tour service; fine local walks; good restaurant. **Cons:** shuttle service to town is erratic; small bathrooms; unreliable plumbing. $ *Rooms from: B1,020* ✉ *108 Ban Huay Dua* ☎ *053/612142* ⤳ *39 rooms* ❑ *No meals.*

KHUN YUAM

64 km (40 miles) south of Mae Hong Son, 100 km (62 km) north of Mae Sariang.

In the mountain village of Khun Yuam, along the southern route of the Loop between Mae Hong Son and Mae Sariang, you can find one of the region's most unusual and, for many, most poignant museums, the Thai–Japan Friendship Memorial Hall.

GETTING HERE AND AROUND

Most visitors to Khun Yuam stop here on their southern Loop travels by bus or car along winding mountain roads (so the going can be slow). The village is small and can be covered easily on foot.

ESSENTIALS

TIMING It only takes an hour or so to tour the town's main attraction, the Thai–Japan Friendship Memorial Hall.

EXPLORING

Thai–Japan Friendship Memorial Hall (*aka World War II Memorial Museum*). This museum that goes by two names commemorates the hundreds of Japanese soldiers who died here on their chaotic retreat from the Allied armies in Burma. Locals took in the dejected and defeated men. A local historian later gathered the belongings they left behind: rifles, uniforms, cooking utensils, personal photographs, and documents; they provide a fascinating glimpse into a little-known chapter of World War II. Outside is a graveyard of old military vehicles, including an Allied truck presumably commandeered by the Japanese on their retreat east. ✉ *Mae Hong Son Rd., Khun Yuam* ☎ *B40* ⊙ *Daily 8–4.*

WHERE TO EAT AND STAY

$ B&B/INN **Ban Farang Guesthouse.** If you're visiting the Thailand–Japanese Friendship Memorial or just needing an overnight stop on the Mae Hong Son Loop, this modest guesthouse offers clean rooms and a simple restaurant. **Pros:** clean rooms; pleasant countryside walks. **Cons:** plumbing can be unreliable; no nightlife. [$] *Rooms from: B815* ✉ *499 Moo 1, Khun Yuam* ☎ *051/622086* 🌐 *www.banfarang-guesthouse.com* ▭ *No credit cards* 🛏 *20 rooms* 🍴 *Breakfast; No meals.*

MAE SARIANG

175 km (109 miles) southwest of Chiang Mai, 140 km (87 miles) south of Mae Hong Son.

The southern route of the Loop runs through Mae Sariang, a neat little market town that sits beside the Yuam River. With comfortable hotels and a handful of good restaurants, the town makes a good base for trekking in the nearby Salawin National Park or for boat trips on the Salawin River, which borders Myanmar.

GETTING HERE AND AROUND

Buses from Chiang Mai's Chang Phuak bus station take about four hours to reach Mae Sariang. Fares range from B200 to B300. A few songthaews ply the few streets of Mae Sariang, but the town is small and compact, and can be covered easily on foot.

Tours of the border region around Mae Sariang are offered by travel agencies in Mae Hong Son. Two of the leading ones are Amazing Mae Hong Son and Discover Mae Hong Son.

ESSENTIALS

SAFETY AND PRECAUTIONS Despite its proximity to the sometimes disputed Myanmar border, Mae Sariang is perfectly safe for visitors. There is little crime, although elementary precautions are advised—leave valuables and large amounts of cash in your hotel safe or with the management.

TIMING Mae Sariang is a beautiful, laid-back little town. If you're looking for relaxation, a stay of two or three days provides a welcome break on the long Mae Hong Son Loop route.

EXPLORING

Mae Sariang and Nearby. Near Mae Sariang the road winds through some of Thailand's most spectacular mountain scenery, with seemingly endless panoramas opening up through gaps in the thick teak forests that line the route. You'll pass hill tribe villages where time seems to have stood still, and Karen women go to market proudly in their traditional dress. Salawin National Park is west of Mae Sariang on Highway 1194, though the road doesn't proceed very far into this beautiful wilderness area that has hiking and biking trails. ✉ *Hwy. 108.*

WHERE TO EAT

$$ THAI Fodor's Choice ★ **✕ Coriander in Redwood.** An early-20th-century English log-trader's home has been carefully restored into an attractive restaurant. The structure is completely constructed of redwood, which reflected in the lamplight lends the dining room and bar a warm, soothing glow. Tables are also arranged under the trees of a leafy garden. Coriander attracts a regular

clientele, who come from far afield for its Thai cuisine and western-style dishes such as steaks of locally reared beef. $ *Average main: B300* ⊠ *12 Moo 2 Langpanich Rd.* ☏ *053/683309* ⊕ *www.riverhousehotelgroup. com/coriander-in-redwood* ⟡ *Reservations essential.*

WHERE TO STAY

$$ ⛉ **Riverhouse Hotel.** Cooling breezes from the Yuam River waft through
HOTEL the open-plan reception area, lounge, and dining room of this attractive hotel, built so completely of teak that even the snug bathrooms are timber-walled. **Pros:** cozy; timber-walled bathrooms; homey public lounge area; river views. **Cons:** limited restaurant menu; no nightlife; traffic noise. $ *Rooms from: B2,300* ⊠ *77 Langpanich Rd.* ☏ *053/621201* ⊕ *www.riverhousehotelgroup.com/hotel* ▬ *No credit cards* ⇦ *12 rooms* ⦿ *No meals.*

$$ ⛉ **Riverhouse Resort.** The pink facade of this modern hotel might appear
HOTEL to be an incongruous intrusion in this neat little border town, but it hides a smart and comfortable interior. **Pros:** riverside garden; fine views; ample parking. **Cons:** disappointing breakfast; long walk to town center; insects. $ *Rooms from: B2,700* ⊠ *6/1 2m Langpanich Rd.* ☏ *053/683066* ⊕ *www.riverhousehotelgroup.com/resort* ▬ *No credit cards* ⇦ *14 rooms* ⦿ *Breakfast.*

CHIANG RAI AND THE GOLDEN TRIANGLE

7

This fabled area is a beautiful stretch of rolling uplands that conceal remote hill tribe villages and drop down to the broad Mekong, which is backed on its far side by the mountains of Laos. Although some 60 km (37 miles) to the south, Chiang Rai is its natural capital and a city equipped with the infrastructure for touring the entire region.

The area's involvement in the lucrative opium trade began in the late 19th century, when migrating hill tribes introduced poppy cultivation. For more than 100 years the opium produced from poppy fields was the main source of income here. Even today, despite vigorous official suppression and a royal project to wean farmers away from the opium trade, the mountains of the Golden Triangle conceal isolated poppy plantations.

Despite its associations with the opium trade, the Golden Triangle is still the term used to refer to the geographical region, varying in size and interpretation from the few square yards where the borders of Thailand, Myanmar, and Laos actually meet to a 40,000-square-km (15,440-square-mile) area where the opium-yielding poppies are still cultivated. That region includes much of Thailand's Chiang Rai Province, where strenuous and sometimes controversial police raids have severely curbed opium production and trade. The royal program to encourage farmers to plant alternative crops is also paying dividends.

The Golden Triangle's apex is the riverside village of Ban Sop Ruak, once a bustling center of the opium trade. An archway on the Mekong riverbank at Ban Sop Ruak invites visitors to step symbolically into the Golden Triangle, and a large golden Buddha watches impassively over the river scene. In a nearby valley where poppies once grew stands a

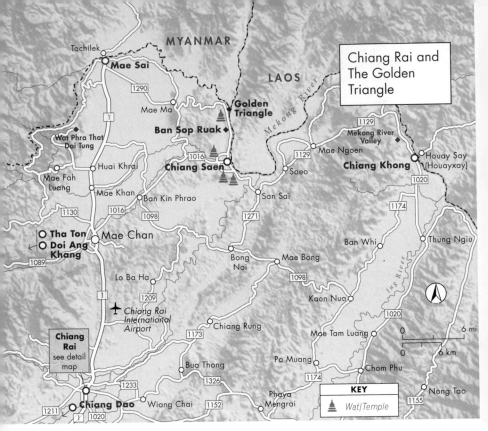

huge museum, the Hall of Opium, which describes the history of the worldwide trade in narcotics.

Winding your way from Chiang Mai to Chiang Rai will take you past Chiang Dao, best known for its astonishing cave complex; Tha Ton, a pretty riverside town on the Myanmar border, which has many outdoor activities; and Doi Ang Khang, a small, remote settlement—with one fancy resort.

CHIANG DAO

72 km (40 miles) north of Chiang Mai.

The dusty, rather dilapidated village of Chiang Dao has two claims to fame: Thailand's third-highest mountain, 7,500-foot Doi Chiang Dao, which leaps up almost vertically from the valley floor; and the country's most spectacular caves, which penetrate more than 10 km (6 miles) into the massif. If you want to explore more of the mountain, hire a guide.

GETTING HERE AND AROUND

Buses bound for Chiang Dao depart regularly from Chiang Mai's Chang Phuak Bus Terminal. The fare is between B100 and B200, depending on the type of service (express, air-conditioned, etc.). Buses stop on the main road in town.

If you need information about Chiang Dao, the best source is Khun Wicha of the Chiang Dao Nest. The innkeeper knows the town and its attractions so well that she has produced a charming map for visitors.

ESSENTIALS

TIMING Chiang Dao's famous caves can be explored in a couple of hours, but many visitors are so captivated by the mountain scenery that they stay for a few days. The hike to the top of Chiang Dao mountain takes at least six hours, and most trekkers bivouac overnight at the top.

TOURS **Contact Khun Wihalaya, Chiang Dao Nest** ✉ *Chiang Dao* ☎ *053/456242* 🌐 *www.chiangdao.com/nest.*

EXPLORING

Chiang Dao Caves. Caves have a mystic hold over Buddhist Thais, so foreign visitors to Chiang Dao's famous caverns find themselves vastly outnumbered by the locals. If you're at all claustrophobic, join a group of Thais to explore the caves, which are thought to penetrate more than 10 km (6 miles) into the small town's guardian mountain, Doi Chiang Dao. The sights in the lighted portion, only a few hundred yards, include spectacular stalagmites and stalactites, along with hundreds of Buddha statues and other votive items placed there by devout Buddhists. If you want to explore past the lighted areas, you can hire a local guide with a lantern for about B100. The mountain itself can be scaled without difficulty in a day, but even just an hour or two of tough walking can bring you to viewpoints with amazing panoramas. ✉ *Chiang Dao* ✛ *About 3 km (2 miles) west of town* ☎ *053/248604* 💲 *B20* 🕐 *Daily 7–5.*

WHERE TO STAY

$ **Chiang Dao Nest.** Describing itself as a mini-resort, the Nest consists
RESORT of two groups of chalets, a mile apart from each other, nestling at the
Fodor'sChoice foot of Chiang Dao mountain. **Pros:** total seclusion; great food; bicycles
★ available. **Cons:** dim lighting makes bedtime reading difficult; insects; unheated pool water can be cold in winter. 💲 *Rooms from: B1,045* ✉ *144/4 Moo 5* ☎ *053/456242* 🌐 *www.chiangdao.com/nest* 🚫 *No credit cards* 🍴 *23 chalets* 🍽 *No meals.*

$ **Rim Doi Resort.** Rim Doi means "on the edge of the mountain," so
RESORT it's fitting that two extraordinary peaks loom over this peaceful little resort near Chiang Dao. After a day exploring the nearby caves or venturing into the mountains, it's just the place to relax and prepare for the journey farther north. **Pros:** pleasant walks on the grounds; well-stocked lake for perch fishing; open-air restaurant. **Cons:** staff has limited English-language skills; insects; chalet accommodation is very

---

NAMING THE GOLDEN TRIANGLE

U.S. Assistant Secretary of State Marshall Green coined the term "Golden Triangle" in 1971 during a preview of the historic visit by President Richard Nixon to China. The Nixon Administration was concerned about the rise of heroin addiction in the United States and wanted to stem the flow of opium from China, Thailand, Myanmar, and Laos. The greatest source of opium was the wild territory where the Mekong and Ruak rivers formed porous borders between Thailand, Myanmar, and Laos—the "golden triangle" drawn by Green on the world map.

7

basic. $ *Rooms from: B850* ✉ *46 Moo 4 Muang Ghay* ☎ *053/375028* ⊕ *www.rimdoiresort.com* ⌦ *18 rooms, 22 chalets* ❢⊘❘ *No meals.*

DOI ANG KHANG

60 km (36 miles) north of Chiang Dao.

Ang means "bowl," and that sums up the mountaintop location of this remote corner of Thailand. A tiny, two-street settlement shares the small valley with the orchards and gardens of a royal agricultural project, which grows temperate fruits and vegetables found nowhere else in Thailand.

GETTING HERE AND AROUND

From Chiang Dao take Highways 1178 and 1340 north to Doi Ang Khang. Local bus services connect the two towns, stopping in the center of Doi Ang Khang.

ESSENTIALS

TIMING Doi Ang Khang is for nature lovers, who tend to relax for a few days amid its orchards and gardens. It's a long drive from either Chiang Mai or Chiang Rai, so at least an overnight stay is recommended. There's no nightlife, however, and after 9 the small community is wrapped in slumber.

TOURS The Tony Smile Travel agency organizes day trips to Doi Ang Khang.

Travel Agency Tony Smile Travel. ☎ *053/744762, 081/998–5719.*

EXPLORING

Royal Agricultural Station Angkhang (*Doi Ang Khang*). A project of the royal family, this mountainside facility, average elevation 1,400 meters (4,600 feet), has both agricultural and political objectives. Developing new and more efficient farming practices is one goal; fruit-tree, tea, and coffee research is another; and a third is to wean northern farmers off opium production. Remote and fascinating, the station is beloved by bird-watchers for its numerous rare species, and there are many flower gardens. The orchards, gardens, and hothouses here are open to the public, and at various times of the year you can buy pears, apples, plums, and peaches harvested directly from the trees. ✉ *Off Hwy. 1249* ✛ *From Chiang Dao, north on Hwy. 1178, east and then north on Hwy. 1340, and north on Hwy. 1249* ☎ *053/969489* ⊕ *www. angkhangstation.com* ☞ *B50* ☉ *Daily 6–6.*

WHERE TO EAT AND STAY

$$ ⛺ **Ang Khang Nature Resort.** This stylish country resort in the mountains

RESORT near Doi Ang Khang is now part of the Mosaic Collection. **Pros:** pretty gardens; first-rate cuisine at Camellia restaurant; open log fire in the lobby in cool season. **Cons:** 2 km (1 mile) from the village center; no nightlife; insects. $ *Rooms from: B2,200* ✉ *1/1 Moo 5 Baan Koom, Tambon Mae Ngon* ☎ *053/450110* ⊕ *www.mosaic-collection.com/ angkhang* ⌦ *72 rooms, 2 suites* ❢⊘❘ *No meals; Breakfast.*

Northern Thailand Then and Now

As late as 1939, northern Thailand was a semiautonomous region of Siam, with a history rich in tales of kings, queens, and princes locked in dynastic struggles and wars. The diversity of cultures you find here today is hardly surprising, because the ancestors of today's northern Thai people came from China, and the point where they first crossed the mighty Mekong River, Chiang Saen, became a citadel-kingdom of its own as early as 773. Nearly half a millennium passed before the arrival of a king who was able to unite the citizens of the new realm of Lanna.

That fabled ruler, King Mengrai (1259–1317), established a dynasty that lasted two centuries. Mengrai's first capital was Chiang Rai, but at the end of the 13th century he moved his court south and in 1296 founded a new dynastic city, Chiang Mai. Two friendly rulers, King Ngarm Muang of Phayao and King Rama Kampeng of Sukhothai, helped him in the huge enterprise, and the trio sealed their alliance in blood, drinking from a chalice filled from their slit wrists. A monument outside the city museum in the center of Chiang Mai's Old City commemorates the event. Nearby, another monument marks the spot where King Mengrai died, in 1317, after being struck by lightning in one of the fierce storms that regularly roll down from the nearby mountains.

Lanna power was weakened by waves of attacks by Burmese and Lao invaders, and for two centuries—from 1556 to the late 1700s—Lanna was virtually a vassal Burmese state. The capital was moved south to Lampang, where Burmese power was finally broken and a new Lanna dynasty, the Chakri, was established under King Rama I.

Chiang Mai, nearby Lamphun (also at the center of Lanna-Burmese struggles), and Lampang are full of reminders of this rich history. Lampang's fortified Wat Lampang Luang commemorates with an ancient bullet hole the spot where the commander of besieging Burmese forces was killed.

To the north is Chiang Rai, a regal capital 30 years before Chiang Mai was built. This quieter, less-developed town is evolving into a base for exploring the country's northernmost reaches. In the far north Chiang Saen, site of the region's first true kingdom, is being excavated, its 1,000-year-old walls slowly taking shape again. Chiang Saen is on the edge of the fabled Golden Triangle. This mountainous region, bordered by Myanmar to the west and Laos to the east, was once ruled by the opium warlord Khun Sa, whose hometown, Ban Sop Ruak, has a magnificent museum that traces the story of the spread of narcotics.

Chiang Mai and Chiang Rai are ideal bases for exploring the hill tribe villages, where people live as they have for centuries. The communities closest to the two cities have been overrun by tourists, but if you strike out on your own with a good map you may still find some that haven't become theme parks. Most of the villages are bustling crafts centers, where the colorful fabrics you see displayed in Bangkok shop windows take shape before your eyes. The elaborately costumed villagers sell their wares in the night markets of Chiang Mai and Chiang Rai.

7

THA TON

90 km (56 miles) north of Chiang Dao.

North of Chiang Dao lies the pretty resort town of Tha Ton, which sits on the River Kok right across the border from Myanmar. The local temple, Wat Tha Ton, is built on a cliff overlooking the town. From the bridge below boats set off for trips on the River Kok, some of them headed for Chiang Rai, 130 km (81 miles) away.

Tha Ton is a pleasant base for touring this mountainous region. The 1089 and 1130 highways that run north, close to the Myanmar border, pass through villages that are more Chinese than Thai. The largest of these, Mae Salong, is on Highway 1234. Most of the Chinese in the area are descendants of the Nationalist forces who fled their homeland after the Communists' 1949 victory in the civil war that gave birth to the People's Republic of China. Based at first mostly in Burma, the Nationalists arrived in Chiang Rai Province in large numbers in the early 1960s. Many of these families have prospered cultivating tea, coffee, and fruit.

GETTING HERE AND AROUND

Six buses a day leave Chiang Mai's Chang Phuak station for the four-hour journey to Tha Ton. Fares range from B150 to B250. Boats leave Chiang Rai for the four-hour upstream journey to Tha Ton. The single fare is B350.

ESSENTIALS

TIMING Travelers on the northern route from Chiang Dao to Chiang Rai find it convenient to overnight in Tha Ton, but the town has little to justify a longer stay.

TOURS AND ACTIVITIES **Maekok River Village Resort.** For information about Tha Ton and its beautiful surroundings, inquire at this resort, where proprietors Bryan and Rosie Massingham are knowledgeable and helpful hosts. Their travel desk can arrange everything from on-site classes and activities lasting an hour or two to multiday off-site treks for guests and nonguests. ✉ *Tha Ton–Chiang Rai Rd.* ☎ *053/053628, 053/801257* 🌐 *www.maekok-river-village-resort.com.*

WHERE TO STAY

$ RESORT 🏨 **Mae Salong Flower Hills Resort.** The border hills of Myanmar lie just beyond the grounds of this resort hotel whose timber-built chalets have fine views of tea plantations and the surrounding mountains. **Pros:** authentic Chinese restaurant; ceremonial teatime on the resort terrace; tropical gardens. **Cons:** erratic bathroom plumbing; long walk to village center; no nightlife. [$] *Rooms from: B1,100* ✉ *779 Moo 1, Doi Mae Salong, Mae Salong* ☎ *053/765495* 🌐 *www.maesalongflowerhills.com* 💳 *No credit cards* 🛏 *45 chalets* 🍴 *Breakfast.*

$$ RESORT FAMILY Fodor's Choice ★ 🏨 **Maekok River Village Resort.** This remarkable resort, a combination of hotel and outdoor education center, is in a beautiful location on the Kok River, with sweeping views of the winding waterway, rice paddies, maize fields and orchards, and the mountains beyond. **Pros:** friendly and knowledgeable British management; fine open-sided restaurant; snug bar with open fireplace for winter evenings. **Cons:** kids at the education

center can be noisy; some rooms are cramped; tour buses call regularly. $ *Rooms from: B3,300* ✉ *1 km (½ mile) from Tha Ton on road to Chiang Rai* ☎ *053/053628* ⊕ *www.maekok-river-village-resort.com* ▤ *No credit cards* ⇄ *36 rooms* ⦿ *Breakfast.*

CHIANG RAI

180 km (112 miles) northeast of Chiang Mai, 780 km (485 miles) north of Bangkok.

Chiang Rai attracts more and more visitors each year, and it's easy to see why. Six hill tribes—the Akha, Yao, Meo, Lisu, Lahu, and Karen—all live within Chiang Rai Province. Each has different dialects, customs, handicrafts, and costumes, and all still venerate animist spirits despite their increasing acquaintance with the outside world. You can learn about their cultures and lives at a museum in town, and as in Chiang Mai, they make daily journeys to the markets of Chiang Rai, where you can meet them and enjoy their handiwork. The best of the markets is a night bazaar, just off Phaholyothin Road, which has a cluster of small restaurants and food vendors.

Despite having luxury hotels and sufficient restaurants and bars to keep night owls happy, Chiang Rai comes off as quieter and less flashy than Chiang Mai, and therein many find its charm. It's also a city with far more greenery, a pleasant contrast to Chiang Mai. ■TIP➔ **Climbing to the top of Doi Tong, a modest hill on the northeastern edge of Chiang Rai, is a great way to learn the lay of the land. From the grounds of the 13th-century Wat Doi Tong, you'll have a fine view of the Mae Kok River and the mountains beyond.**

GETTING HERE AND AROUND

AIR TRAVEL   Thai Airways has several daily flights from Bangkok to Chiang Rai. Chiang Rai International Airport is 6 km (4 miles) northeast of the city. Incoming flights are met by songthaews and tuk-tuks, whose drivers charge about B50 for the journey to central Chiang Rai.

BOAT AND   Longtail boats and rafts set off daily from Tha Ton for the 130-km
FERRY TRAVEL   (81-mile) trip downstream to Chiang Rai.

BUS TRAVEL   Chiang Rai is served by buses that leave regularly from Chiang Mai's two terminals. The trip takes from three to four hours and costs between B80 and B200. Buses to Chiang Rai also leave regularly between 8 am and 7:15 pm from Bangkok's Northern Bus Terminal (12 hours; from B600 to B700). Express buses (B180) leave hourly from Chiang Mai's Arcade Terminal.

CAR TRAVEL   Roads are well paved throughout the Golden Triangle, presenting no problem for drivers. The area is bisected by the main north–south road, Highway 110, and crisscrossed by good country roads. In Chiang Rai the most prominent car-rental companies are Avis, National, and Budget.

TAXI AND TUK-   Tuk-tuks are the common way of getting around Chiang Rai. A trip
TUK TRAVEL   across town costs from B40 to B50. Songthaews can also be hailed on the street and hired for trips to outlying areas. The fare inside the city is B15. To go anywhere farther afield is a matter of negotiation.

7

CLOSE UP

Chiang Rai's Origins

With Chiang Rai, an elephant once again played a central role in the foundation of an important Thai city. Legend has it that a royal elephant ran away from its patron, the 13th-century king Mengrai, founder of the Lanna kingdom. The beast stopped to rest on the banks of the Mae Kok River. The king regarded this as an auspicious sign, and in 1256 built his capital, Chiang Rai, on the site. But little is left from those heady days: the Emerald Buddha that used to reside in Wat Phra Keo is now in Bangkok's Grand Palace, and a precious Buddha image in the 15th-century Wat Phra Singh has long since disappeared.

Travel desks are found in all Chiang Rai hotels and they are generally efficient and reasonably priced.

ESSENTIALS

SAFETY AND PRECAUTIONS Take the usual urban precautions when visiting Chiang Rai: leave valuables either in your room safe or with the hotel management. Carry only a copy of your passport. The small, ill-lighted lanes around the central market can seem a bit threatening at night, but there's actually little crime.

TIMING Chiang Rai has few sights of note, so a leisurely walk around town will take at most a few hours. The city makes an ideal base for exploring the surrounding upland countryside and mountains, though, so a stay of at least two or three days is recommended.

TOURS Chiang Rai is an excellent base from which to set out trekking through the nearby mountains or canoeing and rafting on the region's rivers.

Golden Triangle Tours. The major hotels in Chiang Rai and the Golden Triangle Resort in Chiang Saen organize minibus tours of the region, and the hotels' travel desks will arrange treks to the hill tribe villages. ⊠ 590 Phaholyothin Rd. ☎ 053/713918, 053/740478 ⊕ www. goldenchiangrai.com ✉ Check website or call for prices, which vary depending on group size.

Track of the Tiger. This company is a pioneer of soft-adventure tourism from rock climbing and biking to cooking and golf. ⊠ Maekok River Village Resort, Box 3, Mae Ai ☎ 053/053628, 053/801257 ⊕ www. maekok-river-village-resort.com ✉ Check website or call for prices, which vary depending on group size.

VISITOR INFORMATION **Tourist Authority of Thailand (Chiang Rai).** ⊠ 448/16 Singhaklai Rd. ☎ 053/744674, 053/717434 ⊕ www.tourismthailand.org/chiang-rai.

EXPLORING

TOP ATTRACTIONS

Hilltribe Museum & Education Center. The cultures, ways of life, and crafts of the many hill tribe people that populate the Chiang Rai region are displayed and explained at this exemplary museum in the city center. The museum also supports its own travel service, PDA Tour, which organizes visits to hill tribe villages under the motto "We don't

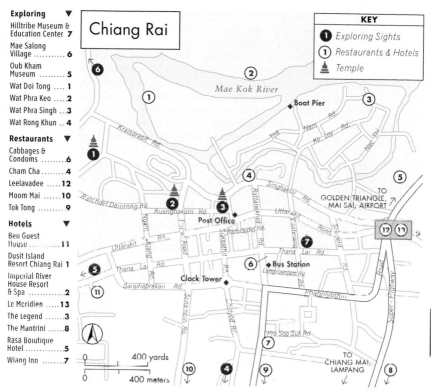

Chiang Rai

KEY

❶ *Exploring Sights*

① *Restaurants & Hotels*

▲ *Temple*

support human zoos!" ✉ *PDA Bldg., 620/25 Thanalai Rd., 3rd fl.* ☎ *053/740088* ⊕ *www.pdacr.org.*

OFF THE BEATEN PATH

Mae Salong Village (*Santikhiri*). Visit this remote mountain village northwest of Chiang Rai, and you could be excused for believing you'd strayed over a couple of borders and into China. The one-street hamlet—the mountainside leaves no room for further expansion—is the home of the descendants of Chinese Nationalist troops who arrived here in the 1960s after spending a dozen or so years in Burma following the Communists' ascension to power in China. The settlers established orchards and tea and coffee plantations that now drape the mountainsides; in December and January, visitors crowd the slopes to admire the cherry blossoms and swaths of sunflowers. Call at any of the numerous tea shops for a pot of refreshing oolong. A local bus service runs from Chiang Rai to Mae Salong (the village's official, Thai, name is Santikhiri), and most Chiang Rai travel agents offer day tours for about B3,000. ✉ *Mae Salong ✛ 61 km (38 miles) from Chiang Rai, Hwy. 1 north to Hwys. 107 and 1089 west.*

Oub Kham Museum. Lanna history and culture are vividly chronicled at this jewel of a facility on the outskirts of Chiang Rai. The museum, in an attractive complex of historic buildings, displays several centuries' worth of local artifacts, including the throne and coronation robes of a 16th-century Lanna ruler. ✉ *81/1 Rai Mai Luang Rd.* ☎ *B300* ⊙ *Daily 8–6.*

Wat Rong Khun. One of Thailand's most astonishing temples, Wat Rong Khun stands like a glistening, icing sugar–coated wedding cake beside the A-1 Chiang Rai–Bangkok motorway south of Chiang Rai. Popularly called the White Temple because of its lustrous snow-white exterior, the extraordinary structure is being built by internationally renowned Thai artist Chalermchai Kositpipat, assisted by a team of more than 40 young artists, craftsmen, and construction workers, as a Buddhist act of winning merit. They have been working on the massive project for 10 years, and Chalermchai doesn't expect it to be finished in his lifetime. The glistening effect comes from thousands of reflective glass mosaics set into the white stucco. Even the fish in the temple's ornamental pool are white Chinese carp. A songthaew ride to the temple from Chiang Rai costs about B50. ✉ *13 km (8 miles) south of Chiang Rai on A-1 Chiang Rai–Bangkok motorway* 🎟 *Free* ⏲ *Daily 8–6.*

WORTH NOTING

Wat Doi Tong. Near the summit of Doi Tong, this temple overlooks the Mae Kok River. The ancient pillar that stands here once symbolized the center of the universe for devout Buddhists. The sunset view is worth the trip. ✉ *Winitchaikul Rd.*

Wat Phra Keo. The Emerald Buddha, which now sits in Thailand's holiest temple, Wat Phra Keo in Bangkok, is said to have been discovered when lightning split the chedi housing it at this similarly named temple at the foot of the Doi Tong in Chiang Rai. A Chinese millionaire financed a jade replica in 1991, and though it's not the real thing, the statuette is still strikingly beautiful. ✉ *Trairat Rd.*

Wat Phra Singh. This 14th-century temple is worth visiting for its viharn, distinguished by some remarkably delicate wood carving and for colorful frescoes depicting the life of Lord Buddha. A sacred Indian Bhoti tree stands in the peaceful temple grounds. ✉ *Singhaklai Rd.*

WHERE TO EAT

$$ THAI 🍴 **Cabbages & Condoms.** Most of the modest price of your meal at this quirkily named restaurant, one of three in Thailand, goes toward the country's leading nongovernmental organization that specializes in HIV/AIDS education. The cuisine is Thai, geared somewhat to western tastes. A band plays at lunchtime and in the evenings. [$] *Average main: B220* ✉ *Thanalai Rd. 620/1, City Center* ☎ *053/740657.*

$ THAI 🍴 **Cham Cha.** Climb the stairs at this busy restaurant to avoid the lunchtime crowds and take an upstairs table overlooking a garden dominated by the handsome cham cha tree that gives the place its name. Ignore the western dishes on the menu and go for traditional northern Thai specialties such as *tom djuet,* a delicious soup laced with tofu and tiny pork dumplings. Find the restaurant next to the Chiang Rai tourist office. [$] *Average main: B150* ✉ *447/17 Singhaklai Rd.* ☎ *053/744191* 💳 *No credit cards* ⏲ *Closed Sun. No dinner.*

$ THAI 🍴 **Leelavadee.** The name of this attractive open-sided restaurant signifies the strongly perfumed frangipani trees that frame its riverside setting. The gargantuan menu embraces Chinese, Thai, and Japanese cuisine, but the specialty is northern Thai food, including fresh fish from the Kok and Mae Kong rivers. If you're in an adventurous mood, try the frogs' legs. $ *Average main: B200* ✉ *58 Moo 19 Kaew Wai Rd.* ☎ *053/600–0000, 089/999–8444* ⊕ *leelawadeechiangrai.com* ▭ *No credit cards.*

$ ✕ **Moom Mai.** A garden panorama of ceramic dolls and other tiny figures
THAI greets you at this enchanting restaurant, where the tables are distributed among the shrubs and ornamental trees. Many of the dining areas are half-hidden thatched bowers. The locals love the place for its informality, its nightly live folk music, and its excellent lineup of northern Thai specialties and Chinese-influenced dishes such as deep-fried chopped prawns in dumplings. $ *Average main: B150* ✉ *64 Sankhongluang Rd. Moo 16, Tambon Robwiang* ☎ *053/716416* ▭ *No credit cards.*

$ ✕ **Tok Tong.** Chinese and northern Thai dishes dominate the extensive
THAI menu at this timber-built traditional restaurant in a garden setting on Chiang Rai's main street. The curries can be spicy, so make sure the person taking your order is aware of your tastes. A Thai traditional ensemble plays nightly. $ *Average main: B150* ✉ *45/12 Phaholyothin Rd.* ☎ *053/756369* ▭ *No credit cards.*

WHERE TO STAY

$ 🛏 **Ben Guest House.** This family-run inn has comfortable, reasonably
B&B/INN priced accommodations. **Pros:** friendly staff with deep knowledge of the region, lively evening scene; pool. **Cons:** cheaper rooms are very basic; thin walls; young clientele can be noisy; 10- to 15-minute walk to town center. $ *Rooms from: B700* ✉ *351/10 San Khong Noi Rd., Soi 4* ☎ *053/716775* ⊕ *www.benguesthousechiangrai.com* ▭ *No credit cards* ⇆ *30 rooms* ⏹ *No meals.*

$$ 🛏 **Dusit Island Resort Chiang Rai.** This gleaming white high-rise com-
RESORT plex on a Mae Kok River island has tons of amenities, including a large outdoor pool. **Pros:** great breakfast; bathrooms with tubs; river views. **Cons:** some guests say the property is showing its age; far from town; insects. $ *Rooms from: B3,900* ✉ *1129 Kraisorasit Rd.* ☎ *053/607999, 02/009000 in Bangkok* ⊕ *www.dusit.com/dusitthani/ islandresortchiangrai* ⇆ *270 rooms* ⏹ *Breakfast.*

$$$ 🛏 **Imperial River House Resort and Spa.** Now part of the Imperial hotel
RESORT group, this stylish, formerly privately owned riverside hotel has retained its individual character while avoiding chain-hotel characteristics. **Pros:** views; massage; tropical gardens; good off-season rates online. **Cons:** far from town; insects; popular with golfers, who are often noisy in the bar. $ *Rooms from: B4,200* ✉ *482 Moo 4 Mae Kok Rd., Muang* ☎ *053/750830 up to 34* ⊕ *www.imperialriverhouse.com* ▭ *No credit cards* ⇆ *36 rooms* ⏹ *No meals.*

$$$ 🛏 **Le Meridien.** Large and luxurious, this hotel commands a stretch of the
RESORT Mae Kok River and views of the northern mountain range. **Pros:** shuttle bus service until 10 pm; library; helpful tour desk. **Cons:** shabby neighborhood; slow room service; insects. $ *Rooms from: B5,780* ✉ *221/2 Moo 20 Kwaewai Rd.* ☎ *053/603333* ⊕ *lemeridienchiangrai.com* ▭ *No credit cards* ⇆ *159 rooms* ⏹ *No meals.*

$$$ 🛏 **The Legend.** Large, tastefully furnished rooms, vast bathrooms,
RESORT secluded terraces, an open-air gourmet restaurant, and unrestricted
Fodor'sChoice views of the distant mountains make it easy for the Legend to live up
★ to its name. **Pros:** elegant and peaceful; impeccably designed; reliable

Continued on page 401

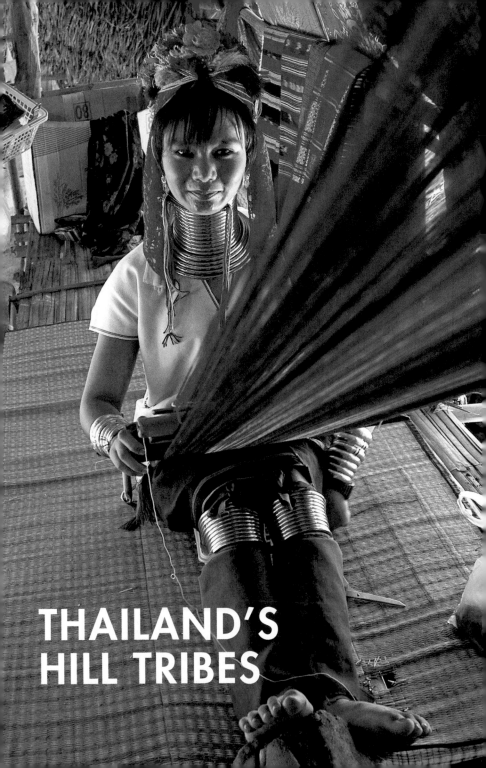

THAILAND'S
HILL TRIBES

Thailand's hill tribes populate the remote, mountainous regions in the north. They welcome visitors, and their villages have become major attractions—some are even dependent on tourist dollars. But other villages, especially those that are harder to reach, have retained an authentic feel; a knowledgeable guide can take you to them.

Hill tribes are descendants of migratory peoples from Myanmar (Burma), Tibet, and China. There are at least 10 tribes living in northern Thailand, and they number a little over half a million, a mere 1% of Thailand's population. The tribes follow forms of ancestral worship and are animists; that is, they believe in a world of spirits that inhabit everything—rivers, forests, homes, and gardens. Historically, some tribes made a living by cultivating poppies for opium, but this practice has mostly died out.

Many tribespeople claim to be victims of official discrimination, and it is indeed often difficult for them to gain full citizenship. Although the Thai government has a program to progressively grant them citizenship, the lack of reliable documentation and the slow workings of the Bangkok bureaucracy are formidable obstacles. However, Thais normally treat hill tribe people with respect; in the Thai language they aren't called "tribes" but Chao Khao, which means "Owners of the Mountains."

Visiting the Chao Khao is a matter of debate. Some of the more accessible villages have become Disneyland-like, with tribespeople, clad in colorful costumes, who are eager to pose in a picture with you—and then collect your baht. In general, the farther afield you go, the more authentic the experience.

Even if you don't visit a village, you'll likely encounter tribespeople selling their crafts at markets in Chiang Mai, Chiang Rai, and Mae Hong Son.

The four tribes you're likely to encounter in northern Thailand are the Karen, Hmong, Akha, and Lisu.

(left) Long neck woman, Chiang Mai; (top) Akha girls wearing ornate headdresses.

KAREN

ORIGINS: Myanmar

POPULATION: 400,000

DID YOU KNOW? The famous "long necks" are actually the Paduang tribe, a subdivision of the Karen.

CRAFTS THEY'RE KNOWN FOR: weaving, beaded jewelry, handmade drums.

The majority of Thailand's hill tribe population is Karen, and there are an estimated 7 million of them living in Myanmar as well. The Karen are the most settled of the tribes, living in permanent villages of well-constructed houses and farming plots of land that leave as much of the forest as possible undisturbed. Though Karen traditionally hold Buddhist and animist beliefs, many communities follow Christianity, which missionaries introduced in colonial Burma.

(top) Karen woman weaving; (bottom) Paduang girls.

LONG NECKS

Traditionally, Paduang women have created the illusion of elongated necks—considered beautiful in their culture—by wrapping brass coils around them. The process begins when a girl is about 5 years old; she will add rings each year. The bands, which can weigh up to 12 lbs, push down on the collarbone, making the neck appear long.

Some human rights groups call the Paduang villages "human zoos" and say that you should not visit because tourism perpetuates the practice of wearing neck coils, which can be harmful. But, most of Thailand's Paduang are refugees who have fled worse conditions in Myanmar, and Thailand's three Paduang villages depend on tourism. Some Paduang women object not to tourism but to the fact that they earn as little as $50 a month from tour operators who profit handsomely. If you go, try to find an operator who treats the Paduang equitably.

HMONG

ORIGINS: China

POPULATION: 80,000

DID YOU KNOW? The Hmong wear elaborate silver lockets to keep their souls firmly locked into their bodies.

CRAFTS THEY'RE KNOWN FOR: needlework, batik, decorative clothing and headdresses.

At the night markets of Chiang Mai and Chiang Rai, you'll recognize Hmong women by their colorful costumes and heavy silver jewelry. There are two divisions of Hmong, White and Blue; White Hmong women wear baggy black pants and blue sashes, while Blue Hmong women wear knee-length pleated skirts. But the divisions "white" and "blue" don't refer to traditional Hmong costumes. "Blue" is a translation of the Hmong word "ntsuab," which also means "dark," a description given to a branch of Hmong whose members once practiced cannibalism. Hmong communities that rejected cannibalism were described as "dlawb," which means "innocent" or "white."

(right) Hmong children.

AKHA

ORIGINS: Tibet

POPULATION: 33,000

DID YOU KNOW? Akha villages are defined by a set of wooden gates, often decorated with charms meant to ward off evil spirits.

CRAFTS THEY'RE KNOWN FOR: silver belt buckles and bracelets, decorative hats and clothing, *saw oo* (fiddles).

The Akha once thrived on opium production, shielded from outside interference by the relative inaccessibility of the remote mountaintop sites they chose for their settlements. Today, all but the most remote communities grow alternative crops, such as rice, beans, and corn. They're a gentle, hospitable people whose women wear elaborate headdresses decorated with silver, beads, and feathers. Akha men wear hollow bracelets containing a silver bead, which they believe keeps them in touch with ancestral spirits.

Akha women wearing traditional headdresses.

7

IN FOCUS THAILAND HILL TRIBES

LISU

ORIGINS: Tibet

POPULATION: 25,000

DID YOU KNOW? The Lisu pass their history from generation to generation in the form of a song.

CRAFTS THEY'RE KNOWN FOR: silver belt buckles, saw oo, large beaded hats.

Though they're not the most numerous, the business-like Lisu are the tribe you're most likely to meet on day trips out of Chiang Mai and Chiang Rai. More than any other hill tribe, the Lisu have recognized the earning power of tourism. As tourist buses draw up, women scramble to change from their everyday clothes into the famous multicolored costumes they normally wear only on high days and holidays.

Lisu women.

THE SHAN

Though sometimes referred to as a hill tribe, the Shan, who live predominantly in Myanmar, are actually a large minority (there are an estimated 6 million) who have been fighting for their own state for decades. They have lived in the area for 1,000 years and are believed to be descendents of the Tai people, the original inhabitants of the region. The Shan who reside in Thailand have fled persecution in Myanmar. Unlike the hill tribes, the Shan are predominantly Buddhist. Shan craftspeople make some of the silver jewelry and ornaments you'll find at markets.

Shan women wearing traditional bamboo hats.

VISITING HILL TRIBE COMMUNITIES

(top) Akha woman with children;
(bottom) Karen woman.

ETIQUETTE

Hill-tribe people tend to be conservative, so do follow a few simple guidelines on your visit.

- Dress modestly.
- Keep a respectful distance from religious ceremonies or symbols, and don't touch any talismans without asking first.
- Avoid loud or aggressive behavior and public displays of affection.
- Always ask permission before taking a person's picture.

TREKKING

Meeting and staying with tribespeople is one of the main attractions of trekking in northern Thailand. Some day trips include brief stops at villages, which are often little more than theme parks. But if you book a trek of three days or more you're sure to encounter authentic hill tribes living as they have for centuries.

Chao Khao are hospitable to westerners, often organizing spontaneous parties at which home-brewed rice whiskey flows copiously. If you stay overnight, you'll be invited to share the community's simple food and sleep on the floor in one of their basic huts.

Virtually all travel operators offer tours and treks to hill tribe villages. The **Mirror Foundation** (⊠ 106 Moo 1, Ban Huay Khom, T. Mae Yao, Chiang Rai, ☎ 053/ 737412 ⊕ www.themirrorfoundation.org), an NGO that works to improve the lives of hill tribes near Chiang Rai, can arrange culturally respectful tours. The foundation's current projects include bringing volunteer teachers to tribal villages and preventing the exploitation of hill tribe women and children.

■ TIP→ To avoid being taken to a tourist trap instead of an authentic village, ask the operator to identify the tribes you'll visit and to describe their culture and traditions. It's a good sign if the operator can answer your questions knowledgeably; the information will also add greatly to the pleasure of your trip.

DAY TRIPS

You can also take daytrips to see hill tribes from Chiang Mai, Chiang Rai, or Mae Hong Son. The villages appear on few maps, so it's not advisable to set out on your own; a guide or driver who knows the region well is a better bet. You can easily hire one for about B1,000 per day; ask the TAT in Chiang Mai or Chiang Rai for recommendations.

Several Chiang Mai operators offer "three country" one-day tours of the Golden Triangle: a boat trip to a Laotian island in the Mekong River; a brief shopping trip to the tax-free Myanmar border town of Tachilek; and a stop at a Thai hill tribe village on the way home. The fare of B800 to B1,000 includes lunch. These tours are likely to feel fairly touristy.

SHOPPING FOR HILL TRIBE CRAFTS

Embroidered textiles at a market near Chiang Mai.

Over the past few decades, the Thai royal family has worked with the government to wean hill tribe farmers off cultivating opium poppies. One initiative has been financing workshops for manufacturing traditional handicrafts, such as basketry, weaving, and woodworking. Some of these royal projects, located near hill tribe villages, offer both employment and on-site training. The workshops also prevent the crafts from dying out and create a market for products that were originally only distributed within the tribal communities.

WORKSHOPS

The Doi Tung mountain, 40 km (25 mile) north of Chiang Rai, is home to 26 hill tribe villages as well as the **Doi Tung Development Project** (☎ *053/767001* ⊕ *www.doitung.org*), a royal project based at the late Queen Mother's former summer palace. The tribes living in the mountain villages produce handicrafts; the project workshops also employ hill tribe craftsmen and women. Both the villages and the project welcome visitors. Daily tours of the project grounds are available for B100; tribespeople sell crafts at a shop and at stalls on the grounds.

Though it's not for the faint of heart, a very curvy 16-km (10-mile) road leads to the top of Doi Tung from the village of Huai Krai, 20 km (12 mile) south of Mae Sai via Highway 101. Local buses and songthaews from Huai Krai will take you here; you can also hire a driver or a guide.

MARKETS & STORES

Although hill tribe crafts are abundant at the night markets in Chiang Mai, Chiang Rai, and Mae Hong Son, serious collectors prefer government-run stores whose products come with certificates of authenticity. Prices are fixed at these stores but are comparable to what you'll pay at markets (upscale hotel boutiques, however, inflate prices substantially). Expect to pay at least B500 for a silver ring or belt buckle and as much as B2,500 for a bracelet or necklace; around B300 for a meter of woven cloth; and B300 to 400 for a simple wooden instrument like a bamboo flute.

airport pickup; riverside location and views. **Cons:** standard rooms have no bathtubs; city center is a 10-minute drive away; confusing signposting can make it difficult to find your room at night. [$] *Rooms from: B4,410* ✉ *124/15 Kohloy Rd., Amphoe Muang* ☎ *053/910400, 053/719649, 02/642–5497 in Bangkok* 🌐 *www.thelegend-chiangrai.com* 🛏 *79 rooms* 🍴 *No meals.*

$$ HOTEL 🏨 **The Mantrini.** Only the tropical vegetation hints that this highly stylish hotel is in Thailand and not a boutique establishment in central Milan or Munich. **Pros:** beautifully designed; shady pool area; friendly staff. **Cons:** drab neighborhood; noisy bars nearby; 15-minute drive to city center. [$] *Rooms from: B2,400* ✉ *292/13 Moo 13, Robwiang, A. Muang* ☎ *053/601555 up to 9* 🌐 *www.mantrini.com* 🛏 *63 rooms* 🍴 *Breakfast.*

$$ HOTEL 🏨 **Rasa Boutique Hotel.** Rich hues, warm lighting, and grand Moroccan architectural flourishes set a distinctly exotic tone at this boutique hotel well away from the city center. **Pros:** secluded swimming pool; good restaurant; romantic setting. **Cons:** shabby neighborhood; far from city center. [$] *Rooms from: B3,000* ✉ *789/7 Phaholyothin Rd.* ☎ *053/717454* 🌐 *www.rasaboutiquehotelchiangrai.com* 🛏 *30 rooms* 🍴 *No meals.*

$$ HOTEL 🏨 **Wiang Inn.** In the heart of downtown, this sleek, modern hotel is among the best in central Chiang Rai. Spacious rooms are decked out in dark woods and fine fabrics. **Pros:** best facilities of in-city hotels; good restaurant; central location. **Cons:** standard rooms have only single beds; impersonal chain-hotel atmosphere; karaoke room noise can be disturbing. [$] *Rooms from: B2,800* ✉ *893 Phaholyothin Rd.* ☎ *053/711533* 🌐 *www.wianginn.com* 🛏 *260 rooms* 🍴 *No meals.*

SPORTS AND THE OUTDOORS

BOATING

For something adventurous, catch a bus to the border town of Tha Ton and board a high-powered longtail boat there and ride the rapids 130 km (81 miles) to Chiang Rai. Boats leave from a pier near the town bridge at noon and take about three to four hours to negotiate the bends and rapids of the river, which passes through thick jungle and past remote hill tribe villages. The single fare is B350. For a more leisurely ride to Chiang Rai, board a raft, which takes two days and nights to reach the city, overnighting in hill tribe villages. Fares start at B1,000. ■ **TIP→ Take bottled water and (most important) a hat or umbrella to shade you from the sun.** The best time to make the trip is during October and November, when the water is still high but the rainy season has passed.

GOLF

Santiburi Country Club. Chiang Rai has one of northern Thailand's finest golf courses, the Santiburi Country Club, laid out by the celebrated Robert Trent Jones Jr. The course is set among rolling hills 10 km (6 miles) outside Chiang Rai. The ranch-style clubhouse has an excellent restaurant and coffee shop, and the facilities include a sauna. Visitors are welcome, and clubs, carts, and shoes can be rented. Reservations are required. ✉ *12 Moo 3 Huadoi-Sobpao Rd.* ☎ *053/662821*

7

up to 26, 053/717377 ⊕ *www.santiburi.com/chiangrai* 🖃 *Weekdays B1,580, weekends B2,150* ⚘ *18 holes, 6982 yards, par 72.*

PARK

Phu Sang. Some 90 km (56 miles) due east of Chiang Rai is perhaps the region's most beautiful national park, Phu Sang, which has one of Thailand's rarest natural wonders, cascades of hot water. The temperature of the water that tumbles over the 85-foot-high falls never drops below 33°C (91°F), and a nearby pool is even warmer. The park has some spectacular caves, and is crisscrossed by nature trails teeming with bird life. One hour's drive north lies the mountainous border with Laos, straddled by 5,730-foot-high Phu Chee Fah, a favorite destination for trekkers and climbers. You reach Phu Sang National Park via Thoeng, 70 km (43 miles) east of Chiang Rai on Highway 1020. The park rents cabins for B500 a night. Entrance to the park costs B200, and B30 for a vehicle. Call or make contact through the website for reservations. ⊠ *Chiang Rai* ☎ *054/401099* ⊕ *www.dnp.go.th.*

SHOPPING

Chiang Rai has a **night market,** on Robviang Nongbua Road, and although it's much smaller than Chiang Mai's, there many handicrafts and textiles on offer. A central section of Thanalai Road is closed to traffic on Saturday nights for a "walking street" market, and San Khon Noi Road is made a pedestrian-only area for a Sunday market.

T.S. Jewelry & Antiques. This place has a very large selection of jewelry and antiques from northern Thailand, Myanmar, and Laos. ⊠ *877–879 Phaholyothin Rd.* ☎ *053/711050.*

EN ROUTE

Doi Tung. If you're traveling north from Chiang Rai on Highway 110, watch for the left-hand turn at Km 32 to Doi Tung. The road winds 42 km (26 miles) to the summit, where an astonishing view opens out over the surrounding countryside. The temple here, Wat Phra That Doi Tung, founded more than a millennium ago, is said to be the repository of some important relics of Lord Buddha, including a collarbone. The shrine attracts pilgrims from as far away as India and China, for whom its huge Chinese Buddha figure is an important symbol of good fortune. On the mountain slopes below the temple is the summer home built for the king's late mother. The fine mansion is closed to the public, but the gardens, an explosion of color in all seasons, are open unless particularly important guests are staying. ⊠ *Chiang Rai.*

CHIANG SAEN

59 km (37 miles) north of Chiang Rai, 239 km (149 miles) northeast of Chiang Mai, 935 km (581 miles) north of Bangkok.

A one-road town on the banks of the Mekong River, Chiang Saen was home to the future King Mengrai, who built a citadel here in the 12th century. Two ancient chedis are all that remain standing to remind the visitor of Chiang Saen's ancient glory, but government-financed excavation is gradually uncovering evidence of the citadel. The ancient flooring and walls that have been exposed are providing tantalizing clues about one of the region's first royal palaces. Little of the citadel survived the incursion by the Burmese in 1588, and the remaining fragments were ravaged by fire when the last of the Burmese were ousted in 1786.

The embarkation point for river trips to Myanmar, Laos, and China, Chiang Saen is being developed as a major Mekong River port.

GETTING HERE AND AROUND

Two buses daily run between Chiang Mai's Chang Phuak bus station and Chiang Saen, taking 4½ hours. The fare is about B150; buses stop in the center of town and at the boat piers. Songthaews provide the local transportation. Rides cost B20.

ESSENTIALS

SAFETY AND PRECAUTIONS Chiang Saen is a river port and something of a smugglers' haven, which keeps the local police busy. Foreign visitors are left alone, though the usual precautions are advised when walking the riverside promenade at night. Leave valuables in your hotel safe or with the hotel or guesthouse management.

TIMING Chiang Saen is an ideal base from which to explore the Golden Triangle, so plan on staying two or three days—longer if the town's ancient ruins and museum attract your interest.

EXPLORING

National Museum. Next door to Wat Phra That Luang, the National Museum exhibits artifacts from the Lanna period, as well as some Neolithic discoveries. The museum also has a good collection of carvings and traditional handicrafts from the hill tribes. ✉ *Rd. to Chiang Rai, 1 km (½ mile) from town center* ☎ *053/777102* 🎟 *B40* 🕒 *Wed.–Sun. 9–4.*

Wat Pa Sak. The name of this wat, Chiang Saen's oldest chedi, refers to the 300 *ton sak* (teak trees) planted in the surrounding area. The stepped temple, which narrows to a spire, is said to enshrine holy relics brought here when the city was founded. ✉ *Chiang Saen.*

Wat Phra That Luang. Some scholars attribute this imposing octagonal wat inside the city walls to Chiang Saen's namesake, King Saen Phu (1325–34), though others speculate that it predates him. ✉ *Chiang Saen.*

WHERE TO STAY

$ HOTEL 🏨 **De River Boutique Resort.** Most rooms at this small, Lanna-style hotel 1 km (½ mile) east of the National Museum directly overlook the Mekong, with sweeping views across its swirling waters to the hills of Laos on the opposite bank. **Pros:** sunrise from one's private balcony; riverside walks; wonderful views. **Cons:** staff has poor English skills; Ban Sop Ruak a 15-minute drive away; no transportation. [$] *Rooms from: B1,400* ✉ *455 Moo 1 Tambon Wiang* ☎ *053/784488* 🌐 *www.deriverresort.com* 🛏 *18 rooms* 🍴 *Breakfast.*

$ B&B/INN 🏨 **Golden Home.** The Mekong River is just across the road from this small resortlike guesthouse. **Pros:** central location; pleasant garden; good restaurants and shopping nearby. **Cons:** small, basic rooms; staff lacks English skills; traffic noise. [$] *Rooms from: B700* ✉ *41 Moo 1 Wiang* ☎ *053/784205* 🌐 *www.goldenhome46.com* 🛏 *7 cabins* 🍴 *Breakfast.*

7

BAN SOP RUAK

8 km (5 miles) north of Chiang Saen.

Ban Sop Ruak, a village in the heart of the Golden Triangle, was once the domain of the opium warlord Khun Sa. Thai and Burmese troops hounded him out in 1996 and he spent the remaining years until his death in 2007 under house arrest in Yangon, where he lived comfortably in the company of a personal seraglio of four young Shan women. His picaresque reputation still draws those eager to see evidence of the man who once held the region under his thumb.

This simple riverside town has one main street, 1 km (½ mile) in length, that winds along the southern bank of the Mekong River. It's lined with stalls selling souvenirs and textiles from Laos. Waterfront restaurants serve up fresh catfish and provide vantage points for watching the evening sun dip over the mountains to the west.

GETTING HERE AND AROUND

Songthaews (about B50) are the only transport service from Chiang Saen to Ban Sop Ruak. A taxi service is operated by Golden Shan Travel (⊠ *587 Ban Sop Ruak High St. 57150*☎ *053/784198*), which also offers tours of the Golden Triangle, Mae Salong, Doi Tung, and hill tribe villages for B3,000 and B3,500.

ESSENTIALS

SAFETY AND PRECAUTIONS Although Ban Sop Ruak was once the center of the Golden Triangle illegal narcotics trade, it's a law-abiding little town now, and the one main street is perfectly safe, even late at night. Nevertheless, it's advisable to leave valuables in your hotel safe or with the hotel or guesthouse management.

TIMING Ban Sop Ruak is the Golden Triangle, with enough points of interest to warrant a stay of at least two or three days. The Hall of Opium alone is extensive enough to take up a whole day, and boat trips to Burma and Laos beckon.

EXPLORING

Fodor's Choice
★

Hall of Opium. The magnificent Hall of Opium is a white stucco, glass, marble, and aluminum building nestling in a valley above the Mekong. The site of the museum is so close to former poppy fields that a plan is still being considered to extend the complex to encompass an "open-air" exhibit of a functioning opium plantation. The museum traces the history of the entire drug trade, including a look at how mild stimulants like coffee and tea took hold in the West. It even attempts to give visitors a taste of the "opium experience" by leading them through a long tunnel where atmospheric music wafts between walls bearing phantasmagoric bas-relief scenes. The synthetic smell of opium was originally pumped into the tunnel but the innovation was dropped after official complaints.

The entrance tunnel emerges into a gallery where the nature of the opium-producing poppy is described on an information panel. It's an arresting introduction to an imaginatively designed and assembled exhibition, which reaches back into the murky history of the opium trade and takes a long look into a potentially darker future. ⊠ *Main street* ☎ *053/784444* ⊕ *www.maefahluang.org* 🎫 *B300* ⊙ *Tues.–Sun. 10–3:30.*

Imperial Golden Triangle Resort. Even if you don't stay overnight, pay a visit to this sumptuous resort that has the best views over the confluence of the Mae Sai, Ruak, and Mekong rivers. ✉ *222 Ban Sop Ruak* 🌐 *www.imperialhotels.com.*

Longtail excursion boats. Longtail excursion boats captained by experienced river men tie up at the Ban Sop Ruak jetty, and the B500 fee covers a 90-minute cruise into the waters of Myanmar and Laos and a stop at a Laotian market. You can take a short trip into Myanmar by visiting the Golden Triangle Paradise Resort, which sits in isolated splendor on the Burmese bank of the Mekong, about 1 km (½ mile) upstream from the Golden Triangle. The Thai immigration office at the Ban Sop Ruak jetty makes a photocopy of your passport for the Burmese authorities for B200. ✉ *Ban Sop Ruak.*

Opium Museum. Opium is so linked to the history of Ban Sop Ruak that the small town now has two museums devoted to the subject. This smaller one is in the center of town. A commentary in English details the growing, harvesting, and smoking of opium. Many of the exhibits, such as carved teak opium boxes and jade and silver pipes, are fascinating. ✉ *Main street* 🎟 *B30* ⏲ *Daily 7–6.*

WHERE TO STAY

$$$$ RESORT Fodor's Choice ★

🏨 **Anantara Golden Triangle Elephant Camp & Resort.** The Anantara is one of the Golden Triangle's top addresses, a true symphony of styles created by Thailand's leading interior designer and architect, Bill Bensley. **Pros:** stunning place to stay; great restaurant; particularly fine views from the rooms; huge bathrooms. **Cons:** access to some rooms involves much stair climbing; isolated position far from village center; steep bar prices. [$] *Rooms from: B32,000* ✉ *229 Moo 1* ☎ *053/784084, 02/476 0022 in Bangkok* 🌐 *goldentriangle.anantara.com* 🛏 *106 rooms, 4 suites* 🍴 *Breakfast.*

$$$$ RESORT Fodor's Choice ★

🏨 **Four Seasons Tented Camp Golden Triangle.** Elephant lovers, beware—you may never want to leave this pachyderm haven. **Pros:** unique, up-close elephant experiences; beautiful setting; interesting regional activities; luxury with a touch of adventure. **Cons:** location might be too remote for some (requires car and boat rides); some tents are far from the main buildings and up steep paths, so may not be suitable for all guests; insects. [$] *Rooms from: B75,000* ✉ *499 Moo 1 Tambon Wiang, Chiang Saen* ☎ *053/910200* 🌐 *www.fourseasons.com/goldentriangle* 🛏 *15 tents* 🍴 *All-inclusive.*

$$ HOTEL

🏨 **Imperial Golden Triangle Resort.** From the superior rooms in this high-eaved, Lanna-style hotel you are treated to magnificent views of three rivers rushing together. **Pros:** spectacular sunsets over the Mekong; excellent travel service; pleasant restaurant terrace. **Cons:** many rooms involve flights of stairs; service staff can be offhand; poor language skills. [$] *Rooms from: B3,000* ✉ *222 Ban Sop Ruak* ☎ *053/784001 up to 5, 02/261–9000 reservations* 🌐 *www.imperialhotels.com/imperialgoldentriangle* 🛏 *73 rooms* 🍴 *Breakfast.*

CHIANG KHONG

64 km (40 miles) east of Ban Sop Ruak, 53 km (33 miles) northeast of Chiang Rai.

This small Mekong River town is gearing up to become a main way station on the planned Asian Highway, and a bridge is being built across the river to the Laotian harbor town of Houay Say (Houayxay). Small skiffs carry people across the Mekong between Chiang Khong and Houay Say, from whose pier daily boats set off for the two-day trip to the World Heritage town of Luang Prabang in Laos. Chiang Khong is a convenient overnight stop before embarking on this excursion.

Chiang Khong has little to attract the visitor apart from the magnificent vistas from the riverside towpath to the hills of Laos across the Mekong. The town's one 300-year-old temple has an interesting Chiang Saen–style chedi but is in need of repair. Textiles from China and Laos can be bought cheaply in Chiang Khong's market.

GETTING HERE AND AROUND

The paved road east out of Chiang Saen parallels the Mekong River for much of the way en route to Chiang Khong and a halfway point commands a magnificent view of the wide river valley far below. A refreshment stall and tables cater to thirsty travelers. Songthaews ply the route for about B100, but you can also hire a speedboat (B500) to go down the river, a thrilling three hours of slipping between the rocks and rapids. Not too many tourists make the journey, especially to villages inhabited by the local Hmong and Yao tribes. The rugged scenery along the Mekong River is actually more dramatic than that of the Golden Triangle.

ESSENTIALS

SAFETY AND PRECAUTIONS Despite its location on the Laotian border and the occasional arrest of a smuggler or two, Chiang Khong is safe for foreign visitors. Nevertheless, caution is advised when walking the riverside promenade at night—leave valuables and excess cash in your hotel safe or with the management.

TIMING Chiang Khong is the official border crossing to Laos, and few visitors linger longer than one night, waiting for the Mekong River ferry.

TOURS Chiang Khong is the embarkation point for the Laotian pier where boats for Luang Prabang are moored. Most Chiang Khong guesthouses have travel desks where tickets for the river cruise to the Laotian World Heritage site can be bought.

Ann Tours. This outfit headquartered in Vietnam conducts multiday tours in northeastern Thailand. Ann Tours has other offerings in Thailand, Laos, Vietnam, and Cambodia, and creates custom itineraries. ✉ *166 Moo 8 Saiklang Rd.* ☎ *053/655198* ⊕ *www.anntours.com* ✉ *Prices vary depending on group size.*

EXPLORING

The Hub Pub. It's backpacker and world-traveler heaven at this hub of three enterprises—a pub, a cycling museum, and a hostel (the Funky Box)—owned by Alan Bate, holder of the Guinness World Record for fastest bicycling trip around the world. His voyage took place in 2010.

A block from the river and the same from the Nam Khong River Side hotel, the Hub Pub is a great place to hang with the ultraconvivial host, share stories with him and other travelers, check out memorabilia from his title-winning 106-day journey, and sip a drink appropriate to the hour. It'll make your day or night, or maybe even both. ⊠ *Soi 2* ☎ *082/765–1839* ⊕ *www.worldcyclingrecord.com* ⊙ *Daily 9 am–midnight.*

WHERE TO EAT AND STAY

$
HOTEL
🍴 **Nam Khong River Side.** This hotel edges the south bank of the Mekong River, with most of its rooms, including the rooftop **Fai Nguen Restaurant,** commanding unobstructed views to the hills of Laos on the other side. **Pros:** free Wi-Fi throughout; helpful travel desk can organize boat trips to Luang Prabang in Laos; fine views from the terrace. **Cons:** small bathrooms; drab neighborhood; traffic noise. 💲 *Rooms from: B1,700* ⊠ *174–176 Moo 8 Tambon Wiang* ☎ *053/791796, 053/791801* ⊕ *www.namkhongriverside.com* ☞ *40 rooms* 🍴 *Breakfast.*

MAE SAI

25 km (16 miles) west of Ban Sop Ruak, 60 km (37 miles) north of Chiang Rai.

From Ban Sop Ruak you can travel west on a dusty road to Mae Sai, a Thai-Burmese border town that straddles the Mae Sai River. The market that nestles next to the border bridge is packed with jewelry stalls, where the careful buyer can find some bargains, including rubies and jade from Myanmar. The cross-border trip is the town's main tourist attraction, though.

GETTING HERE AND AROUND

Buses leave six times daily from Chiang Mai's Chang Phuak bus station for the five-hour journey to Mae Sai. The fare is about B150. Regular bus service also runs between Chiang Rai and Mae Sai (one hour; B50). Around town songthaews are the only means of getting around other than on an organized tour, for which the travel agency Mae Khong Travel is recommended.

ESSENTIALS

SAFETY AND
PRECAUTIONS
There are occasional bomb attacks by Burmese anti-regime activists in Tachileik, the Burmese town separated from Mae Sai by only a bridge. Hostilities between Burmese and Thai troops sometimes break out, closing the border. Mae Sai itself is safe for foreign visitors, although it's advisable to leave valuables, excess cash, and passports in your hotel safe or with the management.

TIMING
Mae Sai is essentially a day-trip destination. Many visitors travel from Chiang Mai or Chiang Rai just to shop at the markets in Tachileik.

TOURS
EXPLORING

Kengtung. For $30 you can get a three-night visa that lets you travel 63 km (39 miles) north to Kengtung, a quaint Burmese town with colonial-era structures built by the British alongside old Buddhist temples. ⊠ *Mae Sai.*

Tachileik. Foreigners may cross the river to visit Tachileik on a one-day visa ($10) obtainable at the Burmese immigration office at the bridge. The town is a smaller version of Mae Sai, but with a vast tax-free emporium, a busy market, and three casinos packed with Thai gamblers. ✉ *Mae Sai.*

Wat Phra That Doi Wao. For the best view across the river into Myanmar, climb up to Wat Phra That Doi Wao—the 207-step staircase starts behind the Top North Hotel. ✉ *Mae Sai.*

WHERE TO EAT

$ THAI 🍴 **Rabiang Kaew.** Set back from the main road by a wooden bridge, this restaurant built in the northern style has an unmistakable charm. Antiques adorning the dining room add to its rustic style. The Thai fare is tasty and expertly prepared. [$] *Average main: B120* ✉ *356/1 Phaholyothin Rd.* ☎ *053/731172.*

WHERE TO STAY

$ HOTEL 🏨 **Piyaporn Pavilion.** This modern hotel lacks any Thai character, offering instead standard western-style rooms and furnishings. **Pros:** pleasant riverside walks; helpful travel desk; large bathrooms with tubs. **Cons:** no restaurant; chain-hotel atmosphere; street noise. [$] *Rooms from: B625* ✉ *925/36 Moo 1 Wiang Pang Kham* ☎ *053/734511 up to 13, 053/642113 up to 15* 🛏 *80 rooms* 🍽 *Breakfast.*

$ HOTEL 🏨 **Top North Hotel.** This centrally located hotel is comfortable and simply appointed, and locals praise its restaurant's northern Thai cuisine. **Pros:** authentic northern Thai food; central location; Wi-Fi throughout. **Cons:** not much Thai character; service staff could be friendlier; street-side rooms can be noisy. [$] *Rooms from: B615* ✉ *306 Phaholyothin Rd.* ☎ *053/731955* 🛏 *24 rooms* 🍽 *No meals.*

$ HOTEL 🏨 **Wang Thong.** This riverside high-rise hotel was originally intended to cater to business executives trading across the nearby Thai-Burmese border, but now the guests are mostly travelers. **Pros:** pleasant riverside walks; panoramic views from the restaurant; large pool. **Cons:** noisy tour groups tend to take over the public rooms and outside terrace; chain-hotel feel; staffers lack English-language skills; poor upkeep. [$] *Rooms from: B1,215* ✉ *299 Phaholyothin Rd.* ☎ *053/733388* 🛏 *150 rooms* 🍽 *No meals.*

SHOPPING

Thais take household goods and consumer products across the river, where Myanmar residents trade them for sandalwood, jade, and rubies. Though you may want to see Myanmar, the prices and quality of the goods will not be better than in Mae Sai.

■ **TIP→ Rubies aren't the only red gems here. Mae Sai is also justifiably proud of its sweet strawberries, which ripen in December or January, found at local markets and as far away as Chiang Rai and Chiang Mai.**

Mengrai Antique. Near the bridge, this place has a good reputation. ✉ *Phaholyothin Rd.* ☎ *053/731423, 081/949–1493.*

SUKHOTHAI AND NEARBY

In the valley of the Yom River, protected by a rugged mountain range in the north and richly forested mountains in the south, lies Sukhothai. The many ruins here mark the birthplace of the Thai nation and its emergence as a center for Theravada Buddhism. North of Sukhothai 80 km (50 miles) is quieter Si Satchanalai, whose historical park contains the remnants of more temples and monuments. Southeast of Sukhothai 60 km (37 miles) is Phitsanulok. Despite having fewer reminders of its brief turn centuries ago as the kingdom's capital, this modern provincial administrative seat can make a good base for exploring the area.

PHITSANULOK

377 km (234 miles) north of Bangkok, 60 km (37 miles) southeast of Sukhothai.

For a brief span in the 14th century, after the decline of Sukhothai and before the rise of Ayutthaya, Phitsanulok was the kingdom's capital. Farther back in history, it was a Khmer outpost called Song Kwae, though only an ancient monastery remains of that incarnation. This onetime military stronghold has grown away from its roots, leaving only a few reminders like Wat Phra Si Rattana Mahathat and the revered Phra Buddha Chinnarat image. The wat is on Naresuan Road, a major thoroughfare named for the city's most illustrious son, Naresuan the Great, who ruled as King of Ayutthaya from 1590 to 1605.

The current city of Phitsanulok, 5 km (3 miles) from the old site, is a hub of commerce, transportation, and communication with few architectural blessings. It does have two outstanding sights to see, however, Wat Phra Si Rattana Mahathat and the Sgt. Maj. Thawee Folk Museum, an engaging collection of quotidian artifacts. In the evening, tempting food stalls line the promenade along the Nan River. Phitsanulok's mix of attractions and access to outward-bound excursions make it an enjoyable diversion, and its modern hotels make it a comfortable place to spend a night or two while touring Sukhothai region.

GETTING HERE AND AROUND

AIR TRAVEL Nok Air, Thai Air Asia, and Kan Air fly from Bangkok to Phitsanulok, whose airport is 8 km (5 miles) south of town. The flight takes 50 minutes.

Phitsanulok Airport. ⊠ *Phitsanulok ✈ 8 km (5 miles) south of Phitsanulok, off Hwy. 1064* ☎ *055/301010.*

BUS TRAVEL Buses to Phitsanulok regularly leave Bangkok's Northern Terminal. Fares on an air-conditioned "VIP" bus start at around B260 for the six-hour trip. The terminal also has buses for travel to and from Chiang Mai via Lampang or via Phrae and Phayao, and to Mae Sot via Tak. Phitsanulok's terminal is downtown, just 1 km (½ mile) from Wat Phra Si Mahatat (known locally as Wat Yai). Inexpensive buses depart Sukhothai for Phitsanulok roughly every hour; the trip takes about 1½ hours.

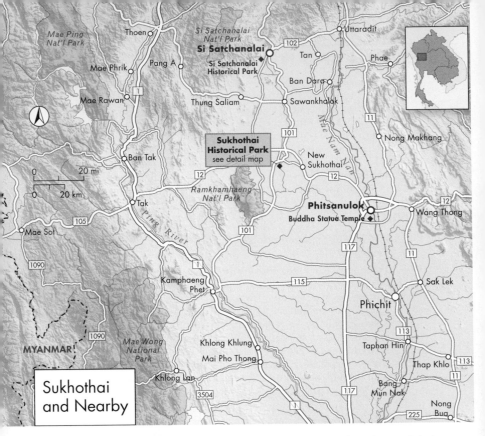

Sukhothai
and Nearby

There's a cheap, cramped, tin-can bus service within Phitsanulok, but you're best off using the open-sided (often cooler and less stuffy) songthaews, motorized samlors, or eco-friendly pedal-powered samlors.

Bus Contacts Phitsanulok Bus Station. ✉ *834/44–45 Mittaparp Rd.* ☎ *055/242430, 055/242030.*

CAR TRAVEL A car is a good way to get around the region. Highway 12 from Sukhothai is a long, straight, and reasonably comfortable 59-km (37-mile), one-hour drive. To get to Phitsanulok from Bangkok, take the four-lane Highway 117; the drive from Bangkok takes about 4½ hours. Both Avis and Budget have car-rental desks at the Phitsanulok airport. Economy cars rent for about B1,500 a day; SUVs cost B3,500. Add B1,000 a day for a driver. ■**TIP➜ Make sure to request an English-speaking driver.** Bigger hotels in Phitsanulok offer chauffeur services at similar prices, but are more tour-oriented and generally offer no more than a one-day trip.

SAMLOR AND Most of the sights in Phitsanulok are within walking distance, but sam-
TAXI TRAVEL lors are easily available. Bargain hard—most trips should cost about B30. Taxis are available for longer trips; you can find a few loitering around the train station.

ESSENTIALS

MONEY
MATTERS
There are plenty of ATMs and exchange kiosks in town; Naresuan Road has most of Phitsanulok's banks.

SAFETY AND
PRECAUTIONS
Take elementary precautions when visiting Phitsanulok. Leave valuables, unneeded cash, and your passport either in the room safe or with the management.

TIMING
With its historic temples, interesting museums, riverside promenade, and waterfront restaurants, Phitsanulok merits at least an overnight stay.

TOURS AND
INFORMATION
The local office of the Tourism Authority of Thailand, TAT, recommends several local travel agents, including Rang Thong Tour.

Travel Agency Rang Thong Tour. ✉ *55/37 Surasi Commercial Center* ☎ *055/259973.*

Visitor Information Tourist Authority of Thailand (TAT). ✉ *209/7–8 Buromtrailokanat Rd., Surasi Trade Center* ☎ *055/252743* ⊕ *www.tourismthailand.org/phitsanulok.*

EXPLORING

Sgt. Maj. Thawee Folk Museum. This fascinating museum of traditional tools, cooking utensils, animal traps, and handicrafts alone would justify a visit to Phitsanulok. In the early 1980s, Sergeant-Major Khun Thawee traveled to small villages, collecting rapidly disappearing objects of everyday life. He crammed them into a traditional house and barn, and for a decade nothing was properly documented. Visitors stumbled around tiger traps and cooking pots, with little to help them decipher what they were looking at. But Khun Thawee's daughter came to the rescue, and now the marvelous artifacts are systematically laid out, all 10,000 of them. You can now understand the use of everything on display, from the simple wood pipes hunters played to lure their prey, to elaborate rat guillotines. Thawee was honored with two university doctorates for his work in preserving such rare items. He also took over a historic foundry, which casts brass Buddhas and temple bells. The museum is a 15 minute walk south of the railway station, on the east side of the tracks, and the foundry is directly opposite. ✉ *Wisut Kasat Rd.* ☎ *055/212749 museum, 055/258715 foundry (phone ahead before visiting)* 💰*B100* 🕑 *Tues. Sun. 8:30 4:30.*

Wat Phra Si Rattana Mahathat. Commonly known as Wat Yai (the Great Temple), this temple established in the mid-14th century developed into a large monastery with typical ornamentation. Particularly noteworthy are the viharn's wooden doors, inlaid with mother-of-pearl in 1756 at the behest of King Boromkot. Behind the viharn is a 100-foot corn-cob-style prang with a vault containing Buddha relics. The many religious souvenir stands make it hard to gain a good view of the complex, but the *bot,* or chapel, is a fine example of the traditional three-tier roof with low sweeping eaves, designed to diminish the size of the walls, accentuate the nave, and emphasize the image of the Buddha.

Within the viharn is what many consider the world's most beautiful image of the Buddha, Phra Buddha Chinnarat. It was probably cast in the 14th century, during the late Sukhothai period. Its mesmerizing beauty and the mystical powers ascribed to it draw streams of pilgrims—among the most notable of them was the Sukhothai's King Eka Thossarot, who journeyed here in 1631. According to folklore, the king applied with his own hands the gold leaf that covers the Buddha. Many copies of the image have been made, the best-known one residing in Bangkok's Marble Temple. ✉ *Phitsanulok* ✣ *Off Akathodsarod Rd., just north of Hwy. 12 and east of Nan River* ⏲ *Daily 8–6.*

WHERE TO EAT

Phitsanulok has a good range of dining options, from its popular pontoon and riverside restaurants to daytime canteen-style restaurants near the central clock tower on Phayalithai Road. The Muslim restaurants on Pra Ong Dam Road, opposite the town's mosque, are great for curry and roti breakfasts. The night-bazaar promenade along the Nan River contains some basic early-evening places to enjoy the sunset, including the infamous "flying vegetable restaurants," where you can sample the province's famed *pak bung fire dang* (stir-fried morning glory). And the veggies do fly here—when the cooks fling the morning glory to waiters, who deftly catch the food on their plates. Akathodsarod Road near the Topland Hotel is a good bet for late-night noodles.

$ SEAFOOD 🍴 **Boo Bpen Seafood.** Although not on the river, this seafood restaurant has the edge on the competition because of its spacious bench seating and garden atmosphere. House specialties include *gai khua kem* (roasted chicken with salt) and *boo nim tort gratium* (crab fried in garlic), and are worth a nibble, but for something more substantial, the barbecue prawns are a must, sampled with the chili, lime, and fish-sauce dip. Bands play on a small central stage. [$] *Average main: B150* ✉ *Sanambin Rd.* ☎ *055/211110* 💳 *No credit cards.*

$$ SEAFOOD 🍴 **Phraefahthai.** An extensive menu in English makes this teak pontoon eatery on the Nan the most comfortable riverside experience. The emphasis is on fresh seafood—the *pla taptim* (St. Peter's fish, a delicious freshwater variety found everywhere in Thailand), served steamed with a spicy lemon-and-lime sauce, is a good choice. Phraefahthai draws many tourists, as well as local businesspeople and their families. Strikingly lighted up at night, it's impossible to miss from anywhere on the river. [$] *Average main: B210* ✉ *100/49 Phutabucha Rd.* ☎ *055/242743.*

WHERE TO STAY

$$ HOTEL 🏨 **Grand Riverside Hotel.** The name is no misnomer—this impressive hotel is very grand indeed. **Pros:** plentiful free parking; shopping mall; nearby market. **Cons:** unreliable Wi-Fi; some rooms beginning to show their age; staff lacks English-language skills. [$] *Rooms from: B2,100* ✉ *59 Praroung Rd.* ☎ *055/248333* 🌐 *www.tgrhotel.com* 🛏 *79 rooms* 🍽 *Breakfast.*

$ HOTEL 🏨 **Pailyn Hotel.** The rooms at this white high-rise are quite large, with picture windows adding plenty of light—rooms on the higher floors have the best view of the river. **Pros:** convenient location; friendly service; tour desk. **Cons:** tour groups delay attention at reception desk; noisy disco; dated decor and fixtures. [$] *Rooms from: B1,500* ✉ *38 Boromatrailokart Rd.* ☎ *055/252411, 02/215–7110 in Bangkok* 🛏 *247 rooms* 🍽 *Breakfast.*

$$ RESORT **Pattara Resort & Spa.** This luxury hotel is an attractive group of Sukhothai-style chalets built around a palm-fringed tropical lagoon. **Pros:** central yet peaceful location; shady pool area; massage. **Cons:** slow room service; small bathrooms; mosquitoes. [$] *Rooms from: B3,100* ✉ *349/40 Chaiyanupap Rd.* ☎ *055/282966* 🌐 *www.pattararesort.com* 🛏 *64 rooms* 🍴 *No meals; Breakfast.*

SUKHOTHAI

56 km (35 miles) northwest of Phitsanulok, 427 km (265 miles) north of Bangkok, 1 hour by bus from Phitsanulok.

Fodor's Choice ★ Sukhothai, which means "the dawn of happiness," holds a unique place in Thailand's history. Until the 13th century most of Thailand consisted of small vassal states under the thumb of the Khmer Empire based in Angkor Wat. But the Khmers had overextended their reach, allowing the princes of two Thai states to combine forces. In 1238 one of the two princes, Phor Khun Bang Klang Thao, marched on Sukhothai, defeating the Khmer garrison commander in an elephant duel. Installed as the new king of the region, he took the name Sri Indraditya and founded a dynasty that ruled Sukhothai for nearly 150 years. His youngest son became the third king of Sukhothai, Ramkhamhaeng, who ruled from 1279 to 1299. Through military and diplomatic victories he expanded the kingdom to include most of present-day Thailand and the Malay Peninsula.

By the mid-14th century Sukhothai's power and influence had waned, and Ayutthaya, once its vassal state, became the capital of the Thai kingdom. Sukhothai was gradually abandoned to the jungle, and a new town grew up about 14 km (9 miles) away. A decade-long restoration project costing more than $10 million created 70-square-km (27-square-mile) Sukhothai Historical Park, which contains 193 historic monuments. Sukhothai is busiest during the Loi Krathong festival, which is celebrated in the Historical Park each year on the full moon in November. Its well-orchestrated, three-day light-and-sound show is the highlight. At this time the town's hotels and guesthouses are booked weeks in advance.

New Sukhothai, where all intercity buses arrive, is a quiet town where most inhabitants are in bed by 11 pm. Its many guesthouses are a magnet for tourists coming to see the ruins, and you'll see quite a few *farang* (foreigners), especially young British, German, and American couples, wandering around, drinking at the bars, or browsing the sidewalk food stalls. New Sukhothai's night market is sleepy by the region's standards—don't expect much of an urban cultural experience here. If you've come specifically to visit the Historical Park, seek accommodation at one of the guesthouses or hotels that ring the Old City, rather than making the uncomfortable B50 songthaew or samlor journey there every day from the newer part of town.

GETTING HERE AND AROUND

AIR TRAVEL Bangkok Airways flies daily from Bangkok to Sukhothai Airport, which is north of town. The airline owns and operates the airport and is its exclusive occupant. You can also fly into Phitsanulok Airport

Sukhothai declined in power in the 15th century, but its temples and palaces were left intact.

(see above). Served by Nok Air, Thai, Asian, and Kan Air, that airport is 72 km (45 miles) southeast of Sukhothai.

Contacts Sukhothai Airport. ⊠ *Sawankhalok ✈ 31 km (19 miles) north of Sukhothai, off Hwy. 1195* ☎ *02/134–3960 Bangkok Airways.*

BICYCLE TRAVEL Because the sights are so spread out, the best way to explore the Historical Park is by bicycle; you can rent one for about B40 a day from outlets opposite the entrance.

BUS TRAVEL Buses to Sukhothai depart from Bangkok's Northern Bus Terminal (Mo Chit) daily from 7 am to 11 pm, leaving roughly every 20 minutes. There are five main companies to choose from, but all charge about the same, most with prices under B300. One company, Win Tours, operates "super VIP" buses that offer comfort and service comparable to business-class air travel. The journey takes about seven hours. Buses from Sukhothai's new bus terminal on the bypass road depart at the same times and for the same prices.

Contacts Sukhothai Bus Station. ⊠ *Bypass Rd., off Hwy. 101* ☎ *055/614529.*

CAR TRAVEL Highway 12 from Phitsanulok leads to Sukhothai and is a long, straight, and reasonably comfortable 59-km (37-mile), one-hour drive. Car rentals are available at Sukhothai airport. The drive from Bangkok, along the four-lane Highway 117, is about 440 km (273 miles), or roughly seven hours. From Chiang Mai, take the M1 and head to the town of Tak, where Highway 12 branches east to Sukhothai.

SAMLOR AND
SONGTHAEW
TRAVEL

Sukhothai does not have local buses, and most of the population gets around in souped-up samlors or songthaews.

ESSENTIALS

SAFETY AND
PRECAUTIONS

When touring the Historical Park, bring a bottle of water with you—the day will get hotter than you think.

TIMING

At least two days are needed to tour the magnificent Sukhothai Historical Park, and even a glancing survey of the Ramkhamhaeng National Museum's holdings requires an additional morning or afternoon. Depending on your means of transportation, touring the rest of the city could take a few hours or the better part of a day. It's best to tour Sukhothai in the late afternoon to avoid the midday sun and enjoy the late evening's pink-and-orange hues.

If you use Sukhothai as a base for exploring the ruins of Si Satchanalai and the potteries and museum of Sawankhalok, at least an additional two days are mandatory.

TOURS AND
INFORMATION

In the Old City the main travel agency is run by the Vitoon guesthouse, whose owner, Kuhn Michael, is a knowledgeable guide who speaks English well. The guesthouse has fleets of bicycles and motorbikes and runs a taxi service.

Travel Agency Vitoon Guesthouse. ⊠ *49 Moo 3 Jarodvithithong Rd., Old City* ☎ *055/697045.*

Visitor Information Tourism Authority of Thailand Sukhothai Office. ⊠ *130 Jarodvithithong* ☎ *055/616228* ⊕ *www.tourismthailand.org/sukhothai.*

EXPLORING
TOP ATTRACTIONS

Ramkhamhaeng National Museum. The region's most significant artifacts are in Bangkok's National Museum, but the many pieces on display at this fine facility demonstrate the gentle beauty of the Sukhothai era. One of several impressive exhibits reveals how refinements in the use of bronze enabled artisans to create the graceful walking Buddhas. ⊠ *Jarodvithithong Rd., just before Historical Park entrance, Old City* ☎ *B40* ⊗ *Daily 9:30–4.*

Wat Mahathat. Sitting amid a tranquil lotus pond, Wat Mahathat is the largest and most beautiful monastery in Sukhothai. Enclosed in the compound are some 200 tightly packed chedis, each containing the funeral ashes of a member of the Sukhothai nobility. Towering above them is a large central chedi, notable for its bulbous, lotus-bud prang. Wrapping around the chedi is a frieze of 111 monks, their hands raised in adoration. Probably built by Sukhothai's first king, Wat Mahathat owes its present form to King Lö Thai, who in 1345 erected the lotus-bud chedi to house two important relics brought back from Sri Lanka by the monk Sisatta. This Sri Lankan–style chedi became the symbol of Sukhothai and classical Sukhothai style. Copies of it were made in the principal cities of its vassal states, signifying a magic circle emanating from Sukhothai, the spiritual and temporal center of the empire. ⊠ *Old City* ☎ *B150 (includes all Historical Park sites)* ⊗ *Daily 8:30–4:30.*

Continued on page 424

THE BUDDHA IN THAILAND

Buddhism plays a profound role in day-to-day Thai life. Statues of the Buddha are everywhere: in the country's 30,000 *wats* (temples), in sacred forest caves, in home shrines, and in cafés and bars. Each statue is regarded as a direct link to the Buddha himself and imparts its own message—if you know what to look for.

by Howard Richardson

The origins of Buddhism lie in the life of the Indian prince Siddhartha Gautama (563 BC– 483 BC), who became the Buddha (which simply means "awakened"). Statues of the Buddha follow ancient aesthetic rules. The Buddha must be wearing a monastic robe, either covering both shoulders or leaving the right shoulder bare. His body must display sacred marks, or *laksanas*, such as slender toes and fingers, a full, lion-like chest, and long eyelashes. Many statues also have elongated earlobes, a reminder of the Buddha's original life as a prince, when he wore heavy earrings. Buddha statues are in one of four positions: sitting, standing, walking, or reclining.

Detail of Reclining Buddha's head.

Statues of the Buddha have their hands arranged in a *mudra* or hand position. The mudras, which represent the Buddha's teachings or incidents in his life, were created by his disciples, who used them to enhance their meditation. There are about 100 mudras, but most are variations on six basic forms.

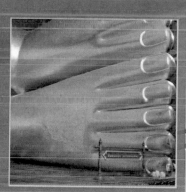

Detail of top of Reclining Buddha's foot.

Reclining Buddha,
Wat Po, Bangkok.

Detail of bottom of Reclining Buddha's foot.

WHAT THE BUDDHA TAUGHT

Gautama taught that there are three aspects to existence: *dukkha* (suffering), *anicca* (impermanence), and *anatta* (the absence of self). He believed that unfulfilled desire for status, self-worth, and material possessions creates dukkha, but that such desire is pointless because anicca dictates that everything is impermanent and cannot be possessed. Therefore, if we can learn to curb desire and cultivate detachment, we will cease to be unhappy.

The ultimate goal of Buddhism is to reach enlightenment or nirvana, which is basically the cessation of struggle—this happens when you have successfully let go of all desire (and by definition, all suffering). This signals the end to *samsara*, the cycle of reincarnation that Buddhists believe in. Buddhists also believe in karma, a law of cause and effect that suggests that your fate in this life and future lives is determined by your actions. Among the ways to improve your karma—and move toward nirvana—are devoting yourself to spirituality by becoming a monk or a nun, meditating, and *tham boon*, or merit making. Making offerings to the Buddha is one form of tham boon.

Thai painting of monks listening to the Buddha speak at a temple.

THE MIDDLE WAY

Gautama's prescription for ending dukkha is an attitude of moderation towards the material world based on wisdom, morality, and concentration. He broke this threefold approach down further into eight principles, called the Noble Eightfold Path or the Middle Way.

Wisdom:
Right Understanding: to understand dukkha and its causes.

Right Thought: to resist angry or unkind thoughts and acts.

Morality:
Right Speech: to avoid lying, speaking unkindly, or engaging in idle chatter.

Right Action: to refrain from harming or killing others, stealing, and engaging in sexual misconduct.

Right Livelihood: to earn a living peacefully and honestly.

Concentration:
Right Effort: to work towards discipline and kindness, abandoning old, counterproductive habits.

Right Mindfulness: to be aware of your thoughts, words, and actions; to see things as they really are.

Right Concentration: to focus on wholesome thoughts and actions (often while meditating.)

DID YOU KNOW?

Burmese invaders damaged many Buddha statues when they sacked Ayutthaya in 1767. The head of one statue became lodged in the roots of a tree at Wat Phra Mahathat, where it remains today.

THE BUDDHA'S POSITIONS

Standing Buddha in saffron robes, Bangkok.

STANDING

The Buddha stands either with his feet together or with one slightly in front of the other. The standing posture is often accompanied by certain hand positions to signify driving away fear or appealing to reason.

 Wat Phra Mahathat, Sukhothai; Wat Benjamabophit, Bangkok.

RECLINING

Many scholars believe that reclining sculptures depict the Buddha dying and simultaneously reaching nirvana. According to another story, the Buddha is showing a proud giant who has refused to bow to him that he can lie down and still make himself appear larger than the giant. The Buddha then took the giant to the heavens and showed him angels that made the Buddha himself appear small, teaching the giant that there are truths beyond the realm of our own experience.

⇨ Wat Po, Bangkok.

Reclining Buddha ornament.

SITTING

Seated Buddhas are the most common. The Buddha can sit in three different postures: adamantine or lotus, with legs crossed and feet resting on opposite thighs; heroic, a half-lotus position with one leg folded over the other; or western, with legs hanging straight down, as if sitting in a chair.

⇨ Wat Suthat, Bangkok (heroic style).

THE LAUGHING BUDDHA

The Laughing Buddha, whose large belly and jolly demeanor make him easy to recognize, is a folkloric character based on a 9th century Chinese monk known for his kindness. The Laughing Buddha does not figure into Thai Buddhism but you may see him at temples in Bangkok's Chinatown. And because he represents good fortune and abundance, some Thai shops sell Laughing Buddhas as lucky charms. Laughing Buddha statues often carry sacks full of sweets to give to children.

Seated Buddha, Wat Suthat, Bangkok.

WALKING

Walking statues represent the Buddha going into the community to spread his teachings. Traditionally, walking Buddhas were constructed in relief. The first walking Buddha statues were created in Sukhothai, and you can still see a few in the city's ruins.

⇨ Wat Sra Sri, Sukhothai and Wat Phra Phai Luang, Sukhothai.

Walking Buddhas, Wat Phra Mahathat, Sukhothai.

WHAT DO THE BUDDHA'S HANDS MEAN?

MEDITATION

The Buddha's hands are in his lap, palms pointing upwards. This position represents a disciplined mind.

⇨ National Museum, Bangkok;
Phra Pathom Chedi, Nakhon Pathom.

SETTING THE WHEEL IN MOTION

In this mudra, the Buddha's thumbs and forefingers join to make a circle, representing the Wheel of Dharma, a symbol for Buddhist law.

⇨ Cloisters of Wat Benjamabophit, Bangkok;
Phra Pathom Chedi, Nakhon Pathom.

REASONING

This posture, which signifies the Buddha's preference for reason and peace rather than hasty or thoughtless action, is similar to the absence of fear mudra, but the Buddha's thumb and forefinger are touching to form a circle.

⇨ Cloisters of Wat Benjamabophit, Bangkok;
Sukhothai Historical Park.

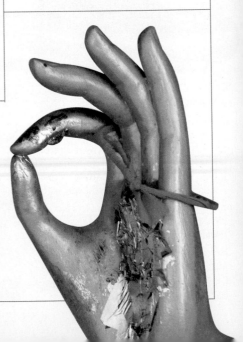

SUBDUING MARA

Mara is a demon who tempted the Buddha with visions of beautiful women. In this posture, the Buddha is renouncing these worldly desires. He sits with his right hand is on his right thigh, fingers pointing down, and his left hand palm-up in his lap.

⇨ Wat Suthat, Bangkok; Wat Mahathat, Sukhothai; Phra Pathom Chedi, Nakhon Pathom.

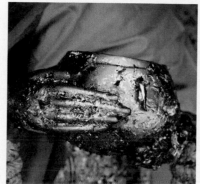

Hand and alms bowl detail; Nakhon Pathom Chedi, Nakon Pathom.

CHARITY

Buddhas using this mudra are usually standing, with their right arm pointing down, palm facing out, to give or receive offerings. In some modern variations, the Buddha is actually holding an alms bowl.

⇨ National Museum, Bangkok.

ABSENCE OF FEAR

One or both of the Buddha's arms are bent at the elbow, palms facing out and fingers pointing up (like the international gesture for "Stop!") In this attitude the Buddha is either displaying his own fearlessness or encouraging his followers to be courageous.

⇨ Cloisters of Wat Benjamabophit, Bangkok.

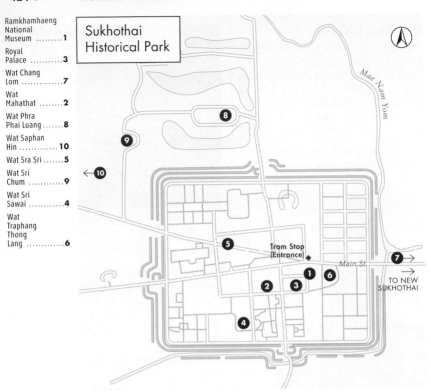

Sukhothai
Historical Park

Wat Sri Chum. Like many other sanctuaries, Wat Si Chum was originally surrounded by a moat. The main structure is dominated by a statue of the Buddha in a seated position. The huge but elegant stucco image is one of the largest in Thailand, measuring 11¼ meters (37 feet) from knee to knee. Enter the *mondop*, a ceremonial structure, through the passage inside the left inner wall. Keep your eyes on the ceiling: more than 50 engraved slabs illustrate scenes from the *Jataka*, which are stories about the previous lives of Lord Buddha. ☒ *Old City* ✛ *Northwest of Old City walls* 🖃 *B150 (includes all Historical Park sites).*

WORTH NOTING

Royal Palace. Thais imagine Sukhothai's government as a monarchy that served the people, stressing social needs and justice. Slavery was abolished, and people were free to believe in their local religions, Hinduism and Buddhism (often simultaneously), and to pursue their trades without hindrance. In the 19th century a famous stone inscription of King Ramkhamhaeng was found among the ruins of the palace across from Wat Mahathat. Now in the National Museum in Bangkok, it is sometimes referred to as Thailand's Declaration of Independence. The inscription's best-known quote reads: "This city Sukhothai is good. In the water there are fish, in the field there is rice. The ruler does not levy tax on the people who travel along the road together, leading their oxen on the way to trade and riding their horses on the way to sell. Whoever wants to trade in elephants, so trades. Whoever wants to trade in horses, so trades." ✉ *Old City* 🖃 *B150 (includes all Historical Park sites)* ⊙ *Daily 8–4:30.*

Wat Chang Lom. Due east of the park is one of Sukhothai's oldest monasteries. Its bell-shape pagoda, thought to have been built in the latter part of the 14th century, is of Sri Lankan influence. The pagoda is perched on a three-tier square base atop damaged elephant buttresses. In front of the chedi are a viharn and solitary pillars; the remains of nine other chedis have been found within this complex. ✉ *Old City* ✛ *2 km (1 mile) east of park entrance, behind Legendha Sukhothai Resort (west of resort, turn north on small lane, cross bridge, and make first right).*

THE TRACES OF A NATION

The optimism that accompanied the birth of the nation at Sukhothai is reflected in the art and architecture of the period. Strongly influenced by Sri Lankan Buddhism, the monuments left behind by the architects, artisans, and craftsmen of those innovative times had a light, often playful touch. Statues of the Buddha show him as smiling, serene, and confidently walking toward a better future. The iconic image of the walking Buddha originated in Sukhothai. Note also the impossibly graceful elephants portrayed in supporting pillars.

Wat Phra Phai Luang. This former Khmer structure, once a Hindu shrine, was converted to a Buddhist temple. Surrounded by a moat, the sanctuary is encircled by three laterite prangs, similar to those at Wat Sri Sawai—the only one that remains intact is decorated with stucco figures. In front of the prangs are the remains of the viharn and a crumbling chedi with a seated Buddha on its pedestal. Facing these structures is the mondop, a square structure with a stepped pyramid roof, built to house religious relics. ✉ *Donko Rd., Old City* ✛ *North of Old City walls, opposite Tourist Information Center* 🖃 *B150 (includes all Historical Park sites)* ⊙ *Daily 8:30–4:30.*

Wat Saphan Hin. This pretty wat is reached by following a slate pathway and climbing a 200-meter (656-foot) hill. An amazing standing Buddha, nearly 12 meters (40 feet) tall, gazes down on the mere mortals who complete the climb. ✉ *West of Old City walls, Old City* 🖃 *Free.*

Wat Sra Sri. This peaceful temple sits on two connected islands within a lotus-filled lake that supplied the monks with water and served as a boundary for the sacred area. A Sri Lankan–style chedi dominates six smaller chedis, and a large stucco seated Buddha looks down a row of columns, past the chedis, and over the lake to the horizon.

Especially wondrous is the walking Buddha beside the Sri Lankan–style chedi. The walking Buddha is a Sukhothai innovation, and the most ethereal of Thailand's artistic styles. The depiction of the Buddha is often a reflection of political authority, and is modeled after the ruler. Under the Khmers, authority was hierarchical, but the kings of Sukhothai represented the ideals of serenity, happiness, and justice. The walking Buddha is the epitome of Sukhothai's art; he appears to be floating on air, neither rooted on Earth nor placed on a pedestal above the reach of the common people. ✉ *Old City* 🎟 *B150 (includes all Historical Park sites)* ⏲ *Daily 8:30–4:30.*

Wat Sri Sawai. Sukhothai's oldest structure may be this Khmer-style one with three prangs—similar to those found in Lopburi—surrounded by a laterite wall. The many stucco Hindu images and scenes suggest that Sri Sawai was probably first a Hindu temple, later converted to a Buddhist monastery. ✉ *Old City* 🎟 *B150 (includes all Historical Park sites)* ⏲ *Daily 8:30–4:30.*

Wat Traphang Thong Lang. The square mondop of Wat Traphang Thong Lang is the main sanctuary, the outer walls of which contain beautiful stucco figures in niches—some of Sukhothai's finest art. The north side depicts the Buddha returning to preach to his wife. On the west side he preaches to his father and relatives. Note the figures on the south wall, where the story of the Buddha is accompanied by an angel descending from heaven. ✉ *Sukhothai* ✥ *East of park entrance opposite Ramkhamhaeng museum* ⏲ *Daily 8:30–4:30.*

WHERE TO EAT

Some of the best food in town can be found at the local food stalls that line the main street before and after the bridge. If you're in the mood for something sweet, look for the stand selling delicious Thai crepes filled with condensed milk, right at the bridge on the city-center side. But it's hard to go wrong almost anywhere in or near the night market or along that street.

$$ THAI 🍴 **Celadon.** The open-air Celadon, overlooking gardens and rice paddies, is one of Sukhothai's most stylish restaurants. Copies of works from Sukhothai's ancient celadon factories are on display, and the menu is full of equally historic dishes—*yam tua pool,* for instance, a spicy salad of shrimp and tiny beans. [$] *Average main: B300* ✉ *Ananda Museum Gallery Hotel, 10 Moo 4 Jarodvithithong Rd. , Banlum Muang* ☎ *055/622428 up to 30* 🌐 *www.ananda-hotel.com.*

$ THAI 🍴 **Dream Café.** While waiting for your meal, feast your eyes on the extraordinary antiques that fill this restaurant whose gnarled doors first opened more than 20 years ago. The rustic tile floor, the glowing teak tables and chairs, and the nooks and crannies packed with fascinating odds and ends—everything from old lamps to fine ceramics—combine in perfect harmony. The modified Thai food plays things safe; be sure to ask for things spicier if that's your preference. Behind the restaurant are four rustic but romantic rooms to let ($), aptly named Cocoon House, set in a fairy-tale garden. [$] *Average main: B150* ✉ *86/1 Singhawat Rd.* ☎ *055/612081.*

WHERE TO STAY

$$$ HOTEL 🏨 **Ananda Museum Gallery Hotel.** The Ananda has redefined the concept of luxury lodging in Sukhothai; as you might expect from a hotel that is also an art gallery, the rooms are well composed, their design informed by a deep sense of minimalism along with a healthy dose of feng shui. **Pros:** aesthetic surroundings; fine furnishings; elegant Celadon restaurant a destination itself. **Cons:** on a busy highway; taxi fare to town is expensive; some guests may find museumlike stillness unsettling at

CLOSE UP

The Festival of Loi Krathong

On the full moon of the 12th lunar month, when the tides are at their highest and the moon at its brightest, the Thais head to the waterways to celebrate Loi Krathong, one of Thailand's most anticipated and enchanting festivals.

INDIAN INFLUENCES

Loi Krathong was influenced by Diwali, the Indian lantern festival that paid tribute to three Brahman gods. Thai farmers adapted the ceremony to offer tribute to Mae Khlong Kha, the goddess of the water, to thank her for blessing the land with water.

Ancient Sukhothai is where the festival's popular history began, with a story written by King Rama IV in 1863. The story concerns Naang Noppamart, the daughter of a Brahman priest who served in the court of King Li-Thai, grandson of King Ramkhamhaeng the Great. She was a woman of exceptional charm and beauty who soon became his queen. She secretly fashioned a *krathong* (a small float used as an offering), setting it alight by candle in accordance with her Brahmanist rites. The king, upon seeing this curious, glimmering offering, embraced its beauty, adapting it for Theravada Buddhism and thus creating the festival of Loi Krathong.

Krathong were traditionally formed by simply cupping banana leaves. Offerings such as dried rice and betel nut were placed at the center along with three incense sticks representing the Brahman gods. Today krathong are more commonly constructed by pinning folded banana leaves to a buoyant base made of a banana tree stem; they're decorated with scented flowers, orange candles (said to represent the Buddhist monkhood),

and three incense sticks, whose meaning was changed under Li-Thai to represent the three forms of Buddhist existence.

MODERN MEANINGS

Contemporary young Thai couples "loi" their "krathong" to bind their love in an act almost like that of a marriage proposal, while others use the ceremony more as a way to purge any bad luck or resentments they may be harboring. Loi Krathong also commonly represents the pursuit of material gain, with silent wishes placed for a winning lottery number or two. The festival remains Thailand's most romantic vision of tradition, with millions of Thais sending their hopes floating down the nearest waterway.

Although it's celebrated nationwide, with events centered around cities such as Bangkok, Ayutthaya, Chiang Mai, and Tak, the festival's birthplace of Sukhothai remains the focal point. The Historical Park serves as a kind of Hollywood back lot, with hundreds of costumed students and light, sound, and pyrotechnic engineers preparing for the fanfare of the annual show, which generally happens twice during the evening. With the Historical Park lighted and Wat Mahathat as its stage, the show reenacts the story of Sukhothai and the legend of Loi Krathong. Following this, governors, dignitaries, and other celebrity visitors take part in a spectacular finale that includes sending off the krathong representing the king and queen, and fireworks.

7

night. $ *Rooms from: B2,600* ✉ *10 Moo 4 Jarodvithithong Rd., Ban-lum Muang* ☎ *055/622428 up to 31* ⊕ *www.ananda-hotel.com* 🛏 *32 rooms, 2 suites* 🍴 *Breakfast.*

$$
HOTEL
Fodor'sChoice
★

📷 **The Legendha Sukhothai Resort.** This attractive Sukhothai-style resort hotel blends so well with the outskirts of the Historical Park that it could easily pass for a creation of the aesthetic King Ramkhamhaeng himself. **Pros:** welcome fruit basket; friendly, helpful staff; chlorine-free pool. **Cons:** inconvenient location between Historical Park entrance and the new city center; expensive hotel transportation; insects. $ *Rooms from: B3,600* ✉ *214 Moo 3, Tambon Muangkao, Old City* ☎ *055/697249* ⊕ *www.legendhasukhothai.com* 🛏 *62 rooms* 🍴 *Breakfast.*

$
RESORT

📷 **Lotus Village.** French owner Michel Hermann has expanded his modest guesthouse into one of Sukhothai's finest resort hotels, adding a spa with massage rooms and a sauna. **Pros:** helpful owners; lovely grounds; nearby market and ethnic restaurants; massage. **Cons:** shabby neighborhood; long walk (at night through dark streets) to town; ugly flood-protection walls block river views. $ *Rooms from: B615* ✉ *170 Ratchathanee Rd.* ☎ *055/621484* ⊕ *www.lotus-village.com* ▬ *No credit cards* 🛏 *10 rooms* 🍴 *Breakfast.*

$
HOTEL

📷 **Pailyn Sukhothai Hotel.** King Bhumibol Adulyadej is among the past guests at this hotel noteworthy for its subtly contemporary Thai look. **Pros:** tasteful modern decor; atrium lounge; pool. **Cons:** unattractive neighborhood; expensive taxi ride to town or Historical Park; tour groups can be noisy. $ *Rooms from: B1,225* ✉ *10/2 Moo 1 Jarodvithithong Rd.* ☎ *055/633335 up to 9, 02/215–5640 in Bangkok* 🛏 *230 rooms* 🍴 *Breakfast.*

$$
RESORT
FAMILY
Fodor'sChoice
★

📷 **Sukhothai Heritage Resort.** Swank is the word for this luxury resort at just about the midpoint between the historical parks in Sukhothai and Si Satchanalai. **Pros:** gracious service; elegant design; superlative breakfast; countryside setting; large pool. **Cons:** location near Sukhothai airport may be too remote for some guests; not convenient to historical parks. $ *Rooms from: B3,300* ✉ *999 Moo 2 Tambon Klongkrajong, 40 km (25 miles) north of Sukhothai, Sawankhalok* ☎ *055/647567, 02/250–4527 in Bangkok* ⊕ *www.sukhothaiheritage.com* 🛏 *61 rooms, 7 suites* 🍴 *Breakfast.*

SI SATCHANALAI

80 km (50 miles) north of Sukhothai.

Si Satchanalai, a sister city to Sukhothai, was governed by a son of Sukhothai's reigning monarch. Despite its secondary position, the city grew to impressive proportions, and the remains of about 200 of its temples and monuments survive, most of them in a ruined state, but many well worth seeing.

With its expanse of neatly mowed lawns, Sukhothai is sometimes criticized for being too well groomed. But Si Satchanalai, spread out on 228 acres on the banks of the Mae Yom River, remains a quiet place with a more ancient, undisturbed atmosphere. It isn't difficult to find the ruins of a temple where you won't be disturbed for hours. Accommodations near the park are limited, so most visitors stay in Sukhothai, but

Si Satchanalai Historical Park has plenty of casual dining spots where you can get lunch.

GETTING HERE AND AROUND

Most visitors to Si Satchanalai reach it as part of a tour from Sukhothai (most hotels can set you up with a guide). If you want to go on your own, hop on a bus bound for the town of Sawankhalok. The ride from Sukhothai takes 1½ hours and costs around B40. Take a taxi from Sawankhalok to the Historical Park, asking the driver to wait while you visit the various temples. You can also tour the site by bicycle or on top of an elephant. The Vitoon Guesthouse in Sukhothai also offers day trips to Si Satchanalai and Sawankhalok; it's opposite the entrance to the Sukhothai Historical Park.

> ### HISTORIC POTTERY
>
> Around Sukhothai and Si Satchanalai you can find reproductions of the pottery made in this region when Sukhothai was the capital of the country.

SAFETY AND PRECAUTIONS

Although you might find yourself alone in the Si Satchanalai ruins, the area is perfectly safe.

TIMING

Si Satchanalai Historical Park is a day's outing from Sukhothai.

ESSENTIALS

Tour Information Vitoon Guesthouse. ⊠ *49 Moo 3 Jarodvittiong Rd., Old City* ☏ *055/697045.*

EXPLORING
TOP ATTRACTIONS

Sawankhaworaranayok National Museum. Sukhothai grew wealthy on the fine ceramics it produced from the rich earth around the neighboring town of Sawankhalok. The ceramics were so prized that they were offered as gifts from Sukhothai rulers to the imperial courts of China, and they found their way as far as Japan. Fine examples of 1,000-year-old Sawankhalok wares are on display at this museum. The exhibits include pieces retrieved from the wrecks of centuries-old vessels that were headed to China and Japan but sank in typhoons and storms. Sukhothai Historical Park contains the ruins of many kilns used to fire the types of pottery on view here. ⊠ *Off Hwy. 1201, 17 km (10½ miles) south of Si Satchanalai, Sawankhalok* ⚐ *About 2 km (1 mile) from Sawankhalok town center* ☏ *B40* ⊙ *Daily 8:30–2.*

Wat Chang Lom. Near the entrance, Wat Chang Lom shows strong Sri Lankan influences. The 39 elephant buttresses are in much better condition than their counterparts at the same-named temple in Sukhothai. The main chedi was completed by 1291. As you climb the stairs that run up the side, you'll come across seated images of the Buddha. ⊠ *Si Satchanalai* ☏ *Free.*

Wat Chedi Jet Thaew. This complex to the south of Wat Chang Lom has seven rows of ruined chedis, some with lotus-bud tops that are reminiscent of the larger ones at Sukhothai. The chedis contain the ashes of members of Si Satchanalai's ruling family. ⊠ *Si Satchanalai* ☏ *Free.*

WORTH NOTING

Wat Nang Phya. To the southeast of Wat Chedi Jet Thaew, this temple has well-preserved floral reliefs on its balustrade and stucco reliefs on the viharn wall. ⊠ *Si Satchanalai* 🎫 *Free.*

Wat Suam Utayan. As you leave the park, stop at this wat to see a Si Satchanalai image of Lord Buddha, one of the few still remaining. ⊠ *Si Satchanalai* 🎫 *Free.*

CAMBODIA

WELCOME TO CAMBODIA

TOP REASONS TO GO

★ **Angkor Temple Complex:** Hands-down Southeast Asia's most magnificent archaeological treasure, Angkor has hundreds of ruins, many still hidden deep in the jungle.

★ **Education and enlightenment:** You'll learn a heap about history, warfare and human tragedy, science, and archaeology.

★ **Off-the-beaten-path beaches:** Along the Gulf of Thailand lie a few of Southeast Asia's most unspoiled beaches and (generally) unpolluted waters. You'll eat some delicious seafood here.

★ **Philanthropy:** Work with street kids, give blood, buy a cookie to support the arts—if you're looking to do good while you travel, you'll find plenty of exciting and meaningful opportunities here.

★ **Southeast Asia's rising star:** Gradually earning worldwide attention, Siem Reap is developing into one of the hippest cities in Southeast Asia.

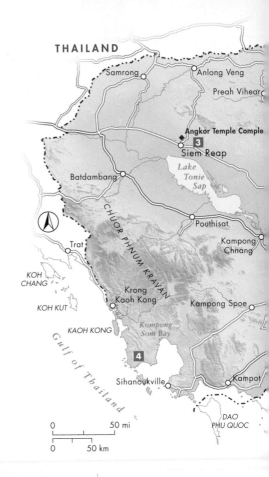

1 Phnom Penh and Nearby. In the capital, you'll find a great deal to see and do: a palace and war monuments, great food and fine wine, and ample opportunities for people-watching along the breezy riverfront. It's an eye-opening place—a city that's come a long way in postwar recovery. And the stories its residents have to tell are both tragic and optimistic.

LAOS

Stoeng Treng

Kong River

Srepok River

Lumphat

Mekong River

Kampong Thum

Kratie

Senmonorom

2

Kampong Cham

1 PHNOM
PENH

VIETNAM

Svay
Rieng

Tay Ninh

Takev

GETTING ORIENTED

Cambodia is one of Southeast Asia's smallest countries—about the size of the state of Washington. The country is bordered by Thailand to the west and northwest, Laos to the northeast, and Vietnam to the east and southeast. In the south, Cambodia faces the Gulf of Thailand, which provides access to the Indian and Pacific oceans. The coastline here is small and isolated by a low mountain range, but is developing rapidly. Much of the country is a low-lying plain dominated by the region's largest lake, Tonle Sap, and a network of waterways forming the start of the Mekong Delta. Its northern border with Thailand is a remarkable escarpment, rising from the plains to heights of up to 549 meters (1,800 feet)—a natural defensive border and the site of many ancient fortresses.

8

2 North of Phnom Penh. As you travel north, you'll see some of Asia's last remaining, but ever-decreasing jungles, where wildlife populations are actually increasing. Get a glimpse of the rare Irrawaddy dolphin at Kratie. There are still seven ethnic hill tribes in the far north in Ratanakkiri Province.

3 Siem Reap and Angkor Temple Complex. Angkor Wat is the largest religious structure ever built, and it's but one temple in a complex of hundreds. Siem Reap, a rapidly growing city, is the gateway to Angkor and other adventurous excursions.

4 Southern Cambodia. The once-sleepy coast has perked up. Whether you stay at a high-end resort, in a hillside bungalow, or in an island hut, it remains a treat to enjoy the laid-back beach ambience. Sihanoukville is now a bustling party-coastal resort while Kep is reemerging as a stylish getaway.

NEED TO KNOW

CAMBODIA

Phnom Penh ⭐

AT A GLANCE

Capital: Phnom Penh

Population: 15,135,200

Currency: Riel

Money: ATMs in cities; U.S. dollars widely accepted (even preferred), credit cards only in tourist places.

Language: Khmer

Country Code: 855

Emergencies: Call local police.

Driving: On the right

Electricity: 230v/50 cycle; plugs are either U.S. standard two-prong, European standard with two round prongs, or U.K. standard three-prong. Power adapter needed.

Time: 11 hours ahead of New York during daylight savings; 12 hours otherwise

Documents: 30 days or more with valid passport; visa on arrival

Mobile Phones: GSM (900 and 1800 bands)

Major Mobile Companies: Metfone, Smart, Cellcard, qb

WEBSITES

Ministry of Tourism: ⊕ www.tourismcambodia.org

Tourism Cambodia: ⊕ www.tourismcambodia.com

GETTING AROUND

✈ **Air Travel:** Siem Reap International Airport is the largest, followed by Phnom Penh International Airport.

🚌 **Bus Travel:** The bus network is comprehensive, and bus travel is cheap. It's also the safest cross-country transportation, aside from flying.

🚗 **Car Travel:** Visitors are strongly advised against driving. Foreign licenses are not valid, rules of the road aren't observed, and driving is dangerous.

PLAN YOUR BUDGET

	HOTEL ROOM	MEAL	ATTRACTIONS
Low Budget	$40	$5	Temple of the Emerald Buddha, $3
Mid Budget	$80	$10	Angkor National Museum, $12
High Budget	$150	$20	3-day pass to Angkor Temples, $40

WAYS TO SAVE

Dine at night markets. Try amazing local cuisine and eclectic delights, all at cheap prices.

Hire a driver Instead of taking multiple taxis, a hired car with a driver costs about $50 a day. Agree on the price beforehand and go anywhere you want.

Take local transport. Within cities and for shorter journeys, *motos* (motorcycle taxis), and *tuk-tuks* (three-wheeled cabs) are the best and cheapest ways of getting around.

Hire a freelance tour guide. Get referrals of English-speaking freelance guides from your hotel, for a lower price than a tour company would charge.

PLAN YOUR TIME

Hassle Factor	High. There are no direct flights from the U.S. to Cambodia, but flights to nearby Asian hubs are frequent.
3 days	Fly into Siem Reap. Explore the many temples of Angkor. By night visit Siem Reap's night markets and downtown.
1 week	You have time to explore the temples of Angkor in more depth (there are some 300 but only the largest have been excavated). Then head to Phnom Penh and take a river cruise down the Mekong. If time permits, hit the beaches of Sihanoukville.
2 weeks	Explore Angkor and Siem Reap in depth, followed by a trip to Battambang, Cambodia's second-largest city. Then head to Phnom Penh, and a day trip up the Mekong to Koh Dach. Relax at the beaches of Sihanoukville then check out Kep and Kampot.

WHEN TO GO

High Season: The northeastern monsoon blowing toward the coast ushers in the cool, dry season in November, which lasts through February with temperatures between 65°F and 80°F. December and January are the coolest months. Book well in advance for mid-April's New Year celebrations and for the Water Festival in November.

Low Season: By April the southwestern monsoon blows inland from the Gulf of Thailand bringing downpours that last an hour or more most days (more in July–September). This rainy, humid season runs through October, with temperatures ranging from 80°F to 95°F.

Value Season: March and October are buffer months between Cambodia's wet and dry seasons. Expect fewer crowds, decent weather, and discounted room rates.

BIG EVENTS

February: On the full moon in February, Meak Bochea commemorates the Buddha's first sermon to 1,250 of his disciples.

April: Khmer New Year is a new-moon festival spread over the three days following the winter rice harvest.

May: The Royal Ploughing Ceremony is a celebration of the start of the summer planting season held in front of the Royal Palace in Phnom Penh.

November: The Water Festival, or Bonn Om Touk, ushers in the fishing season, and marks the "miraculous" reversal of the Tonle Sap waters.

READ THIS

■ **The Rent Collector,** Camron Wright. Hope and survival in the slums of Cambodia.

■ **Never Fall Down,** Patricia McCormick. Biography of Arn Chorn-Pond, survivor of the Cambodian genocide.

■ **The Map of Lost Memories,** Kim Fay. Female treasure hunter searches for a lost temple in early-20th-century Cambodia.

WATCH THIS

■ **Lara Croft: Tomb Raider.** Angkor Wat has a starring role in this Angelina Jolie blockbuster.

■ **The Killing Fields.** American journalists and their Cambodian interpreter get caught up in the horrors of war.

■ **Two Brothers.** A tale of the bond between a set of twin tiger cubs.

EAT THIS

■ **Fish amok:** A fish-and-coconut concoction that takes two days to make

■ **Bai sach chrouk:** Pork and rice

■ **Kdam chaa:** Fried local Kep crab in Kampot peppercorns

■ **Banh chiao:** Fried pancake stuffed with pork, shrimp, and bean sprouts

■ **Prahok:** A fermented fish paste

■ **Kuyteav:** Beef noodle soup

Updated by
Adrian Vrettos

It's not by chance that Cambodia has become highly popular among eclectic travelers of all sensibilities, whether they're seeking lush jungles spotted with dusty temple ruins, idyllic beaches with an air of luxury, artsy boutique hotels, exciting nouvelle cuisine, or ethical shopping, among numerous other vibrant options. Its rich—some may say loaded—history has peeled away to reveal the admirably dynamic, positive, and creative ability of its people to pull through and launch into new beginnings, bringing Cambodia to the world stage as a destination that stands on its unique cultural identity.

Phnom Penh is the bustling capital, where visitors can dip into the darkest corners of the country's traumatized past by walking through the Killing Fields one day, and the next exploring the hip, edgy, new design boom exemplified by the city's hotels, restaurants, bars, and shops. Siem Reap is still a leading draw because it's the base for visiting the country's architectural crown jewel, the stunning Angkor Wat, which continues to epitomize the merging of spirituality and symbolism. Then there's the South, where once-sleepy coastlines are being transformed, sometimes into tasteless seaside party zones, but in other cases into enchanting havens of stylish beach chic.

An interesting trend with which tourists are met when exploring Cambodia is the staunch support given to local communities by NGOs, the creation of which blossomed in the early 1990s. In the aftermath of Cambodia's grueling civil war, foreign aid groups and governments have poured billions of dollars into the country, but not without coming under scrutiny. Around half of them have faced criticism for lack of structure, profiteering, and the commercialization of humanitarian efforts. Nonprofit organizations—in most cases working toward a better Cambodia—address a wide range of humanitarian, cultural, and environmental issues. Today there are about 3,500 registered NGOs in Cambodia, which has the second-highest number of NGOs per capita in the world, after Rwanda. Many nonprofits now run accommodations, restaurants, and travel agencies that provide the visitor with more than they expect to receive on vacation—the chance to help, and an education. But it's worth checking out the legitimacy of an organization before parting with your money. Do-good travel options are noted in this chapter's listings.

PLANNING

WHEN TO GO

Cambodia has two seasons, both affected by the monsoon winds. The northeastern monsoon blowing toward the coast ushers in the cool, dry season in November, which lasts through February, with temperatures between 65°F (18°C) and 80°F (27°C). December and January are the coolest months. It heats up to around 95°F (35°C) and higher in March and April, when the southwestern monsoon blows inland from the Gulf of Thailand, bringing downpours that last an hour or more most days. This rainy, humid season runs through October, with temperatures ranging from 80°F (27°C) to 95°F (35°C). The climate in Phnom Penh is always very humid. Thanks to climate change, Cambodia now experiences rainstorms in the dry season, cool temperatures in the hot season, and a lot of unpredictability. Bring your umbrella, although higher end resorts usually offer one along with your bathrobe and slippers.

It's important to book in advance if you plan on visiting during mid-April's New Year celebrations, or for the Water Festival in Phnom Penh in November. Strangely, the New Year is one of the best times to see the capital—at least in terms of lower rates and crowds—because the majority of Phnom Penh residents come from somewhere else and they all go home for the holidays.

GETTING HERE AND AROUND

AIR TRAVEL

After many years of "semi aviation isolation" Phnom Penh is opening up to the rest of the world, with Qatar Airways being one of the first international carriers to fly here, although still not directly.

There are half a dozen flights from Vietnam's Ho Chi Minh City each day to Phnom Penh (prices start at $120 one way) and the travel time is about 45 minutes. Carriers who fly direct include Vietnam Airlines, Qatar Airways, and Cambodia Angkor Air. You can also fly to Siem Reap from Ho Chi Minh City. The flight takes about an hour and costs from $150 one way. There are five flights a day from Hanoi to Siem Reap; these take one hour 40 minutes, and fares start at $150 one way. Vietnam Airlines is the only carrier offering regular direct flights to Siem Reap from both Ho Chi Minh City and Hanoi.

Regular air service links Phnom Penh and Siem Reap to Bangkok and Vientiane. Domestic flights run between Phnom Penh and Siem Reap. Air Asia, Bangkok Airways, Lao Airlines, Royal Khmer Airlines, Siem

Reap Airways, and Thai Airways have flights to Cambodia *(Air Travel in Travel Smart Thailand)*.

Contacts Cambodia Angkor Air. ✉ *17D Omkhun St., Siem Reap* ☎ *063/969–2681, 063/636–3666* ⊕ *www.cambodiaangkorair.com.* **Qatar Airways.** ✉ *Phnom Penh* ☎ *023/963800* ⊕ *www.qatarairways.com.* **Vietnam Airlines.** ✉ *No. 41, St. 214, Samdech Pan, Phnom Penh* ☎ *023/990840, 023/215998 reservation and ticketing* ⊕ *www.vietnamairlines.com.*

BOAT TRAVEL

Boats do travel from Ho Chi Minh City to Phnom Penh, but they take three days and are a sightseeing option rather than quick A-to-B travel. From Phnom Penh, ferries called "bullet boats" travel along the Tonle Sap to reach Siem Reap and Angkor; they no longer ply waters between Sihanoukville and Koh Kong, however, so the only way to go is by road. You can buy tickets from a tour operator, your hotel's concierge, or at the port in Phnom Penh. ■**TIP→ Bullet boats, though fast, can be dangerous.** Smaller (but noisy) ferries travel daily between Siem Reap's port and Battambang, on the Sangker River. Ask about water levels before booking a ticket; in dry season the water can get so low the boat may get stuck for hours at a time. For those who like to sit atop in the fresh air, take lots of suntan lotion.

BUS TRAVEL

Cambodia has a comprehensive bus network, and bus travel is cheap and generally of a good standard. It's also usually the safest cross-country transportation, aside from flying. Travel from neighboring countries is easy, reliable, and cheap. Buses from Thailand and Vietnam operate daily.

Bus Contacts Giant Ibis. ✉ *3E0 St. 106, Khan Doun Penh* ☎ *023/987808, 023/999333* ⊕ *www.giantibis.com.* **GST Express Bus.** ✉ *13 St. 142, Phnom Penh* ☎ *023/218114, 012/895550.* **Hua Lian.** ✉ *St. 182 and Monireth Blvd., west of Buddha Pagoda, near Olympic Stadium, Phnom Penh* ☎ *012/376807.* **Mekong Express.** ✉ *103 Eo, Sisowath Quay, Phnom Penh* ☎ *012/787839 Head Office, 070/833399 Riverside branch* ⊕ *catmekongexpress.com.* **Neak Krorhorm Travel.** ✉ *4 St. 108, next to old market, Phnom Penh* ☎ *098/219496, 012/495249.*

CAR TRAVEL

If you want to get to a destination quickly, hiring a driver with a car is probably the most effective way, but it can be a hair-raising ride. A hired car with a driver costs about $50 a day, but agree on the price beforehand. ■**TIP→ We strongly advise against driving yourself.** Foreign drivers licenses are not valid here, rules of the road aren't observed, most drivers drive dangerously, and most of the main roads are in terrible condition.

MOTO AND TUK-TUK TRAVEL

Within cities and for shorter journeys, *motos* (motorcycle taxis) and *tuk-tuks* (three-wheeled cabs) are the best and cheapest ways of getting around. Tuk-tuk drivers will greet (or hassle) you at every street corner, providing you with the opportunity of learning to haggle.

BORDER CROSSINGS

Border crossing have become more regulated over the past few years and the corruption and minor bribery that used to be commonplace has diminished dramatically. There are five main border crossings between Vietnam and Cambodia, the busiest and most popular being Moc Bai–Bavet, with a regular bus service between Ho Chi Minh City and Phnom Penh; this is the recommended way to go. When getting on the bus to return to Vietnam from Phnom Penh, the driver's assistant will ask you for your passport, which will be kept until you reach the border. This may appear strange, but it's the standard procedure, so don't worry. Other crossings include Ving Xuong–Kaam Samnor, on the river, if you're traveling by boat; Tinh Bien–Phnom Den, if you are traveling to or from Kep; and O Yadao–Le Thanh, if you want to cross into the north of the country.

PASSPORTS AND VISAS

One-month single-entry tourist visas, which cost $30, are available at all border crossings *listed above* and at the airports. You may need a passport photo—if you don't have one with you, it's an added $5 to have it made there (no added wait; sometimes you might not even be asked for a photo). When crossing on the bus from Vietnam, bus operators will ask for a fee of $5 for helping "fix" your visa. This is not compulsory and you can arrange your own visa at the border, but it does make the crossing slightly less of a hassle. Don't forget that you must have your visa for Vietnam in advance, and the dates must be relevant. If you are over or under the specified dates on your visa you will be charged on average $10 per day.

MONEY MATTERS

The Cambodian currency is the riel, but the U.S. dollar is accepted everywhere, with many high-end businesses actually requiring payment in dollars. Don't be surprised to get change in riel when you pay in dollars. *All prices are given in dollars in this chapter.* Thai baht are usually accepted in bordering provinces.

The official exchange rate is approximately 4,000 riel to one U.S. dollar or 20,000 Vietnamese Dong. It's possible to change dollars to riel just about anywhere. Banks and businesses usually charge 2% to cash traveler's checks.

ATMs are available in Phnom Penh, Siem Reap, and Sihanoukville, mostly at ANZ and Canadia banks, although there are numerous other banks starting to install them. Using an ATM will cost you $5 per withdrawal. Credit cards are accepted at major hotels, restaurants, and at some boutiques. Cambodian banking hours are shorter than in many western countries, generally from 8 am until 3 or 4 pm. ATMs are available 24 hours.

WHAT IT COSTS IN U.S. DOLLARS			
	$	$$	$$$	$$$$
RESTAURANTS	Under $8	$8–$12	$13–$16	over $16
HOTELS	Under $50	$50–$100	$101–$150	over $150

Restaurant prices in the reviews are the average cost of a main course at dinner or, if dinner isn't served, at lunch. Hotel prices in the reviews are the lowest cost of a standard double room in high season. For expanded reviews, facilities, and current deals, visit Fodors.com.

HEALTH AND SAFETY

If a real health emergency arises, evacuation to Bangkok is the best option.

Cambodia is far safer than many people realize, but you still need to exercise common sense. Most violence occurs against Cambodians. A decade ago, tourists were often mugged and sometimes even killed in Phnom Penh and on the beaches of Sihanoukville. Keep most of your cash, valuables, and your passport in a hotel safe, and avoid walking on side streets after dark—and it's best to avoid abrupt or confrontational behavior overall. Siem Reap has less crime than the capital, but that's starting to change. ■TIP➔ Avoid motos late at night. Moto theft is one of Cambodia's most widespread crimes.

Land mines laid during the civil war have been removed from most major tourist destinations. Unexploded ordnance is a concern, however, around off-the-beaten-track temples, where you should only travel with a knowledgeable guide. As a general rule, never walk in uncharted territory in Cambodia, unless you know it's safe.

Cambodia has one of Asia's most atrocious road records. Accidents are common in the chaotic traffic of Phnom Penh and on the highways, where people drive like maniacs, and will not hesitate to make speedy U-turns on a busy two-way street. The better the road, the scarier the driving. Unfortunately, chauffeurs are some of the worst offenders. Wear a seat belt if they're available, and if you rent a moto, wear a helmet. If you are in a tuk-tuk, just hold on tight.

TOURS AND PACKAGES

5oceans Travel. This company, run by two dynamic women, has been at the forefront of tourism in Cambodia for more than a decade and is the official representative for most of the carriers flying to Cambodia. 5oceans arranges trips ranging from comprehensive day-long tours of Phnom Penh to bespoke one-month adventures around the country. ⊠ 147 St. 51 (Pasteur), Khan Daun Penh ☎ 023/986920, 023/221869 ⊕ www.5oceanscambodiatours.com ☜ From $30.

FAMILY
Fodor's Choice
★

Beyond Unique Escapes. Expert and ethical, this tour operator for the Siem Reap Area offers the usual Angkor Temple tours, but also some more unusual temple adventures, where you can experience sunrise or sunset at a remote ruin far from the crowds. Other highly rated options include trips to villages to participate in village activities, which vary depending on the season. ⊠ Sivatha Blvd. and Pub St. (St. 8), Old

Market ☎ *077/562565, 063/969269* ⊕ *www.beyonduniqueescapes.com* ▣ *From $20.*

Hanuman Travel. If it's adrenaline thrills you're after, a cultural experience, or an exploration filled with adventure, this tour operator will tailor your trip to suit your needs. They can also recommend and book your accommodations. ✉ *12 St. 310, Sangkat Tonle Bassac* ☎ *023/218396* ⊕ *www.hanuman. travel* ▣ *From $85.*

Fodor's Choice **oSmoSe Conservation Ecotourism Education.** An agent of positive change
★ in the area, oSmoSe, a nonprofit organization, has been fighting to conserve the unique biosphere of Tonle Sap and Prek Toal by reeducating local villagers from poachers to protectors of the environment that sustains them. They also lobby against big commercial interests that have been involved in short-term exploitation of the ecosystem, and have successfully helped to reharmonize many aspects of human coexistence with nature. On their exceptional tours you get to visit a bird sanctuary with an expert guide and also experience floating villages in a fascinating and respectful way. ✉ *St. 27, Wat Bo* ☎ *012/832812, 063/765506* ⊕ *www.osmosetonlesap.net* ▣ *From $105.*

BEGGARS

Beggars will sometimes approach you in Cambodia. Many NGO workers who work with the homeless advise against giving handouts on the street. Instead, you should acknowledge the people who greet you, politely decline, and make a donation to an organization that operates larger-scale programs to aid beggars and street kids.

VISITOR INFORMATION

Once you arrive, pick up a visitor's guide (separate editions for Phnom Penh, Siem Reap, and Sihanoukville), as well as any of the various pocket guides, the best of these being Cambodia Pocket Guide (www.cambodiapocketguide.com), widely available free at airports, hotels, and restaurants.

Andy Brouwer (⊕ *www.andybrouwer.blogspot.com* or ⊕ *www.andy brouwer.co.uk*), a longtime traveler to Cambodia, has dedicated a good part of his life to informing people about the country where he lives. **Tales of Asia** (⊕ *www.talesofasia.com*) is an excellent source of information, with travelers' stories, road reports, and up-to-date travel information.

The **Ministry of Tourism** (⊕ *www.tourismcambodia.org*) has some information on its website. **Tourism Cambodia** (⊕ *www.tourismcambodia.com*) has more detailed descriptions of top attractions. You can also visit the Tourist Information Center in Phnom Penh at 262 Monivong Boulevard, Khan Daun Penh.

PHNOM PENH AND NEARBY

Cambodia's capital is also the country's commercial and political hub, a busy city undergoing rapid change. Over the past few years the number of international hotels, large restaurants, sidewalk cafés, art galleries, boutiques, Internet cafés, and sophisticated nightclubs has

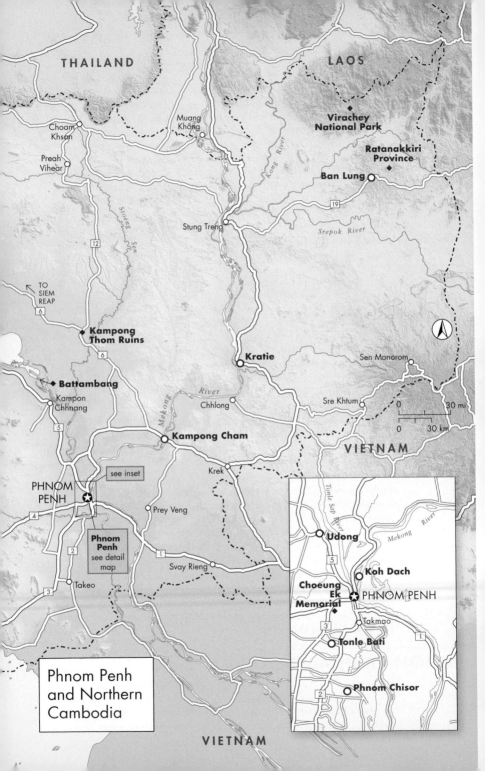

THAILAND

LAOS

Choam
Khsan

Muang
Khong

Virachey
National Park

Preah
Vihear

Ratanakkiri
Province

Ban Lung

12

19

Stung Treng

Srepok River

Kong River

Stung Sen

TO
SIEM
REAP

6

Kampong
Thom Ruins

6

Kratie

Sen Monorom

Battambang

Kampon
Chhnang

River

Chhlong

Sre Khtum

5

Mekong

Kampong Cham

0   30 mi

0   30 km

Krek

VIETNAM

PHNOM
PENH

see inset

4

Prey Veng

Phnom
Penh
see detail
map

1

2

Svay Rieng

3

Takeo

Phnom Penh
and Northern
Cambodia

VIETNAM

Tonle Sap River

Mekong River

Udong

5

Koh Dach

Choeung
Ek
Memorial

PHNOM PENH

3

Takmao

1

Tonle Bati

2

Phnom Chisor

increased dramatically. So has the city traffic: motorbikes and fight for space with cars and SUVs.

Phnom Penh is the natural gateway to anywhere in Cambodia: a slew of the north's accessible towns, far-off Ratanakkiri Province in the northeast, the beaches of Sihanoukville and Kep, and Kampot nearby in the south. Cambodia's roads have come a long way in the past few years, but many in rural areas remain potholed and difficult in the rainy season (particularly in the vicinity of the Thai border). Roads heading out of the capital lead to day-trip destinations like the beaches of Tonle Bati, a small lake with a couple of temples nearby, the lovely temple at Phnom Chisor to the south, and the pagoda-topped hill of Udong and the Mekong island of Koh Dach in the north.

PHNOM PENH

The capital of Cambodia, Phnom Penh is strategically positioned at the confluence of the Mekong, Tonle Sap, and Bassac rivers. The city dates back to 1372, when a wealthy woman named Penh, who lived at the eastern side of a small hill near the Tonle Sap, is said to have found four Buddha statues hidden in a large tree drifting down the river. With the help of her neighbors, she built a hill (a *phnom*) with a temple on top, and invited Buddhist monks to settle on its western slope. In 1434 King Ponhea Yat established his capital on the same spot and constructed a brick pagoda on top of the hill. The capital was later moved twice, first to Lovek and later to Udong. In 1866, during the reign of King Norodom, the capital was moved back to Phnom Penh.

It was approximately during this time that France colonized Cambodia, and the French influence in the city is palpable—the legacy of a 90-year period that saw the construction of many colonial buildings, including the grandiose post office and train station (both still standing, though the latter is threatened by potential development plans). Some of the era's art-deco architecture remains, in varying degrees of disrepair. Much of Phnom Penh's era of modern development took place after independence in 1953, with the addition of tree-lined boulevards, large stretches of gardens, and the Independence Monument, built in 1958.

Today Phnom Penh has a population of about 2 million people. But during the Pol Pot regime's forced emigration of people from the cities, Phnom Penh had fewer than 1,000 residents. Buildings and roads deteriorated, and most side streets are still a mess. The main routes are now well paved, however, and the city's wats (temples) have fresh coats of paint, as do many homes. This is a city on the rebound, and its vibrancy is in part due to the abundance of young people, many of whom were born after the war years. Its wide streets are filled with motorcycles, which weave about in a complex ballet, making it a thrilling achievement merely to cross the street. You can try screwing up your courage and stepping straight into the flow, which should part for you as if by magic, but if you're not quite that brave—and people have been hit doing this—a good tip is to wait for locals to cross and tag along with them.

8

There are several wats and museums worth visiting, and the Old City has some attractive colonial buildings scattered about, though many disappear as time goes on. The wide park that lines the waterfront between the Royal Palace and Wat Phnom is a great place for a sunset stroll, particularly on weekend evenings when it fills with Khmer families, as do the other parks around town: Hun Sen Park, the Vietnamese monument area, and the promenade near the monstrous new Naga Casino. On a breezy evening you'll find hundreds of Khmers out flying kites.

GETTING HERE AND AROUND

AIR TRAVEL Vietnam Airlines flies direct to Phnom Penh from Ho Chi Minh City, four times a day. Flights take 45 minutes and prices start $150. Qatar Air flies once every day, and is slightly cheaper, with prices from $120.

Phnom Penh's modern Pochentong Airport is 10 km (6 miles) west of downtown. The international departure tax is $25, and the charge for domestic departures is $5 to $15. A taxi from the airport to downtown Phnom Penh costs $15. ■TIP➜ Motorcycles and tuk-tuks are cheaper than taxis (around $5), but it's a long, dusty ride.

Cambodia Angkor Air. ✉ *House 206A, Preah Norodom Blvd.* ☎ *023/666–6786, 023/666–6788, 023/212564* ⊕ *www.cambodiaangkorair.com.*

Vietnam Airlines. ✉ *Phnom Penh* ☎ *024/3832–0320* ⊕ *www. vietnamairlines.com.*

BUS TRAVEL Phnom Penh has a half dozen or more private bus companies with regular service from all major Cambodian cities. Major bus stations include the Central Market, Sisowath Quay near the ferry port, and the Hua Lian Station near the Olympic Stadium. Mekong Express charges a little more than other bus companies, but routes are direct and buses are clean and comfortable, with onboard tour guides and a bathroom (bring your own paper, which is a golden rule anywhere public in Cambodia). Most long-distance bus tickets cost $3 to $18, depending on the destination and distance. Newcomer bus company Giant Ibis also provides free Wi-Fi. Tickets can be purchased at the bus companies' offices or through most hotels and guesthouses.

Even though there are regular buses from Ho Chi Minh City to Phnom Penh, and the reverse, it's advisable to book ahead. The trip takes six to seven hours and is pretty straightforward. There are a couple of stops en route as well as the lengthier layover at the border crossing; prices range from $10–$20.

TAXI, MOTO, AND CYCLO TRAVEL The most common forms of transportation are the moto (motorcycle taxi) and tuk-tuk. They cruise the streets in abundance, and gather outside hotels and restaurants—wherever you walk, you'll attract them. The standard fare for a short trip on a moto is $1 to $2; tuk-tuks run a little higher, up to $4, but with a little haggling you can quickly reach an agreed amount. Taxis don't cruise the streets, but there are usually a couple parked outside large hotels, and the receptionist can call one. Almost all drivers speak varying degrees of English, some fluently.

VISITOR AND TOUR INFORMATION

Guides can also be hired right at the Royal Palace and National Museum.

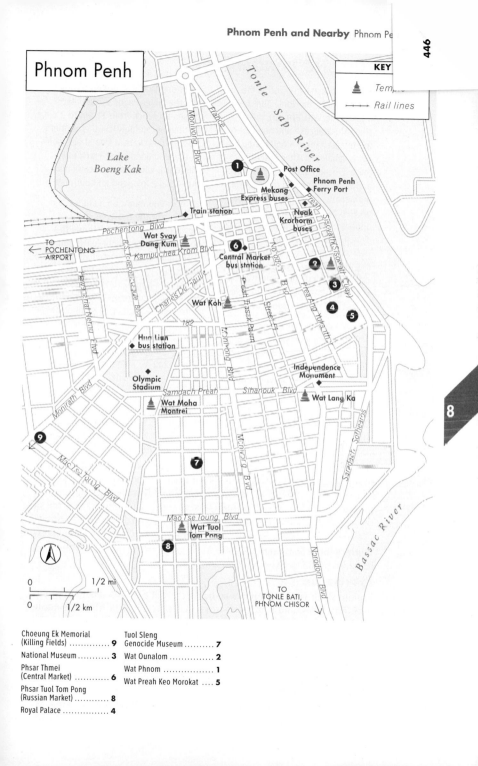

Phnom Penh

Tonle Sap River

Lake Boeng Kak

Post Office

Phnom Penh Ferry Port

Mekong Express buses

Neak Krorhorm buses

Train station

Pochentong Blvd

Wat Svay Dang Kum

TO ← POCHENTONG AIRPORT

Kampuchea Krom Blvd

Central Market bus station

Charles De Gaulle

Wat Koh

182

Hun Lian bus station

Olympic Stadium

Samdach Preah

Sihanouk Blvd

Wat Lang Ka

Independence Monument

Wat Moha Montrei

Mao Tse Toung Blvd

Mao Tse Toung Blvd

Wat Tuol Tom Pong

TO TONLE BATI, PHNOM CHISOR

Bassac River

0 ——— 1/2 mi
0 ——— 1/2 km

8

TOURING PHNOM PENH

Start your tour early, just as the sun rises over the Tonle Sap. Take a tuk-tuk to **Wat Phnom**, then climb the staircase and head for the temple, where King Ponhea Yat is venerated. After descending the hill, head east to the Tonle Sap and walk south along the riverfront promenade. Across the street you are greeted by a plethora of breakfast options; pick the restaurant of your choice. After eating, return to the riverfront, where you have a fine view of the Chroy Changvar Peninsula. The cobbled riverside path leads you to **Wat Ounalom,** one of Phnom Penh's largest and oldest pagodas.

After visiting the wat, continue south on Sisowath Quay, past a busy strip of bars and restaurants, and on to a huge lawn in front of the cheerful yellow **Royal Palace.** On the grounds of the palace is the must-see **Wat Preah Keo Morokat,** aka the Silver Pagoda. The palace closes for lunch from 11 am to 2 pm, so plan accordingly. On the northern side of the palace a side street leads to the traditional-style **National Museum,** which is a peaceful and quiet place to spend an hour or two.

By now you might be hungry again. As you exit the museum, head north on Street 13 to **Friends the Restaurant** for a light lunch and tasty drink. From there, if you think you can hack it, catch a tuk-tuk to the **Tuol Sleng Genocide Museum,** which will require an hour or more with a clear head. It's a somber, sobering experience, and most locals wouldn't dream of visiting. Afterward, head to the trendy Street 240 for some good food and interesting shopping.

Diethelm Travel. River cruises, bird-watching, biking adventures, and culinary experiences are some of the great packages on offer. ✉ *65 St. 240* ☏ *023/219151* ⊕ *www.diethelmtravel.com/cambodia* ✈ *From $25.*

Exo Travel. Formerly know as Exotissimo, this company specializes in tours around Southeast Asia. Most of the tours are packages, but even so many shine a light on unique aspects local Khmer culture, past and present. Temple tours, cooking classes, and cycling trips are some of the experiences on offer. ✉ *SSN Center, 66 Norodom Blvd., 6th fl.* ☏ *023/218948* ⊕ *www.exotravel.com* ✈ *From $160.*

Tourist Information Center. ✉ *262 Monivong Blvd., Khan Daun Penh* ☏ *023/218585* ⊕ *www.tourismcambodia.com.*

EXPLORING

Phnom Penh is an easy place to navigate and explore. There are markets, museums, and historical sites to visit. You will be able to explore the highlights of the city's tourist attractions in three to four days. All hotels will be able to arrange a range of transportation options for your tours around the city.

TOP ATTRACTIONS

Choeung Ek Memorial (*Killing Fields*). In the mid- to late 1970s thousands of Khmer Rouge prisoners who had been tortured at the infamous Tuol Sleng prison were taken to the Choeung Ek extermination camp for execution. Today the camp, 14 km (9 miles) southwest of downtown

Phnom Penh, is a memorial, and the site consists of a monumer stupa built in 1989 and filled with 8,000 skulls, which were from mass graves nearby. It's an extremely disturbing sight: many of the skulls, which are grouped according to age and sex, bear the holes and slices from the blows that killed them. The site is at the end of a rough and dusty road, and can be reached in 30 minutes by motorbike, tuk-tuk ($12 is a reasonable price), or car. ■TIP→ The audio tour, available in English, is excellent and well worth the small additional fee. ✉ *Sangkat Cheung Ek* ☎⊕ *www.phnompenh.gov.kh* ✉ *$2, $5 with audio tour* ☉ *Daily 8–5.*

Fodor's Choice
★

National Museum. Within this splendid, Khmer-style rust-red landmark, next to the Royal Palace, lie many archaeological treasures. This is one of Cambodia's two main museums, and houses impressive relics that have survived war, genocide, and widespread plundering. Exhibits chronicle the various stages of Khmer cultural development, from the pre-Angkor periods of Fu Nan and Zhen La (5th–8th century) to the Indravarman period (9th century), the classical Angkor period (10th–13th century), and post-Angkor period. Among the more than 5,000 artifacts and works of art are 19th-century dance costumes, royal barges, and palanquins. A palm-shaded central courtyard with lotus ponds houses the museum's showpiece: a sandstone statue of the Hindu god Yama, the Leper King, housed in a pavilion. ■TIP→ Guides, who are usually waiting just inside the entrance, can add a lot to a visit here. ✉ *Sts. 13 and 178* ☎ *023/217647/8* ⊕ *cambodiamuseum.info* ✉ *$3* ☉ *Daily 8–5.*

Phsar Tuol Tom Ponug (*Russian Market*). This popular covered market earned its nickname in the 1980s, when the wives and daughters of Russian diplomats would often cruise the stalls on the lookout for curios and antiques. Today the market has a good selection of Cambodian handicrafts. Wood carvings and furniture abound, as do "spirit houses" used for offerings of food, flowers, and incense. Colorful straw mats and hats, as well as baskets, are in high demand. The market is the city's best source for art objects, including statues of the Buddha and Hindu gods; you can also buy valuable old Indochinese coins and paper money printed during different periods of Cambodia's turbulent modern history. A jumble of stalls concentrated at the market's south side sells CDs, videos, and electronics. It's also a great place to buy overstock clothes from Cambodia's numerous garment factories at a fraction of their official retail price. ✉ *South of Mao Tse Tung Blvd., between Sts. 155 and 163* ☉ *Daily 7–5:30.*

Royal Palace. A walled complex that covers several blocks near the river, the official residence of current King Preah Norodom Sihamoni and former residence of the late King Sihanouk and Queen Monineath Sihanouk, is a 1913 reconstruction of the timber palace built in 1866 by King Norodom. The residential areas of the palace are closed to the public, but within the pagoda-style compound are a number of structures worth visiting. These include Wat Preah Keo Morokat; the Throne Hall, with a tiered roof topped by a 200-foot-tall tower; and a pavilion donated by the Emperor Napoléon III and shipped here from France. Guides can be hired at the entrance for $8. ✉ *Sothearos*

8

The Royal Palace's Throne Hall is used today for ceremonies like coronations and royal weddings.

between Sts. 184 and 240 ✉ *$3, plus $2 for a camera, $5 for a video camera* ⊙ *Daily 7:30–11, 2–5.*

Tuol Sleng Genocide Museum. This museum is a horrific reminder of the cruelty of which humans are capable. Once a neighborhood school, the building was seized by Pol Pot's Khmer Rouge and turned into a prison and interrogation center, the dreaded S-21. During the prison's four years of operation, some 14,000 Cambodians were tortured here; most were then taken to the infamous Killing Fields for execution. The four school buildings that made up S-21 have been left largely as they were when the Khmer Rouge left in January 1979. The prison kept extensive records and photos of the victims, and many of the documents are on display. Particularly chilling are the representations of torture scenes painted by S-21 survivor Vann Nath. Locals generally reveal they have never set foot here. ✉ *St. 113 (Boeng Keng Kang) and St. 350* ✉ *$3* ⊙ *Daily 8–5.*

Fodor's Choice ★ **Wat Preah Keo Morokat** (*The Silver Pagoda*). Within the Royal Palace grounds is Phnom Penh's greatest attraction: the Temple of the Emerald Buddha, built 1892 to 1902 and renovated in 1962. The temple is often referred to as the **Silver Pagoda** because of the 5,329 silver tiles—more than 5 tons of pure silver—that make up the floor in the main *vihear* (temple hall). At the back of the vihear is the venerated **Preah Keo Morokat** (Emerald Buddha)—some say it's carved from jade, whereas others maintain that it's Baccarat crystal. In front of the altar is a 200-pound solid-gold Buddha studded with 2,086 diamonds. Displayed in a glass case are the golden offerings donated by Queen Kossomak Nearyreath (King Norodom Sihamoni's grandmother) in

1969; gifts received by the royal family over the years are st
other glass cases. The gallery walls surrounding the temple com
which serves as the royal graveyard, are covered with murals depicting
scenes from the Indian epic, the *Ramayana*. Pride of place is given to
a bronze statue of King Norodom on horseback, completed in Paris in
1875 and brought here in 1892. There's a nearby shrine dedicated to the
sacred bull Nandi. ⊠ *Samdech Sothearos Blvd., between Sts. 240 and
184* ▭ *Included in admission to Royal Palace* ☉ *Daily 7:30–11, 2–5.*

WORTH NOTING

Phsar Thmei (*Central Market*). An inescapable sightseeing destination
in Phnom Penh is the colonial-era Central Market, built in the late
1930s on land that was once a watery swamp. This wonderfully ornate
building with a large dome retains some of the city's art-deco style.
The market's Khmer name, Phsar Thmei, translates as "new" market
to distinguish it from Phnom Penh's original market, Phsar Chas, near
the Tonle Sap River; it's popularly known as Central Market, however.
Entry into the market is through one of four grand doors that face the
directions of the compass. The main entrance, facing east, is lined with
souvenir and textile merchants hawking everything from cheap T-shirts
and postcards to expensive silks, handicrafts, and silverware. Other
stalls sell electronic goods, cell phones, watches, jewelry, household
items, shoes, secondhand clothing, flowers, and just about anything
else you can imagine. Money changers mingle with beggars and war
veterans with disabilities asking for a few hundred riel. ⊠ *Kampouchea
Krom Blvd. and St. 130* ☉ *Daily 5–5.*

Wat Ounalom. On the riverfront, a little way north of the National
Museum, the 15th-century Wat Ounalom is now the center of Cambodian Buddhism. Until 1999 it housed the Institute Buddhique, which
originally contained a large religious library destroyed by the Khmer
Rouge in the 1970s. Wat Ounalom's main vihear, built in 1952 and
still intact, has three floors; the top floor holds paintings illustrating
the lives of the Buddha. The central feature of the complex is the large
stupa, **Chetdai**, which dates to Angkorian times and is said to contain
hair from one of the Buddha's eyebrows. Four niche rooms here hold
priceless bronze sculptures of the Buddha. The sanctuary is dedicated to
the Angkorian king Jayavarman VII (circa 1120–1215). In much more
recent times the wat served as a temporary sanctuary for monks fleeing
the police and soldiers in post-election political riots. ⊠ *Sisowath Blvd.*
☏ *012/773361* ▭ *Free* ☉ *Daily 6–6.*

Wat Phnom. According to legend, a wealthy woman named Penh found
four statues of the Buddha hidden in a tree floating down the river, and
in 1372 she built this hill and commissioned this sanctuary to house
them. It is this 90-foot knoll for which the city was named: Phnom
Penh means "Hill of Penh." Sixty years later, King Ponhea Yat had a
huge stupa built here to house his ashes after his death. You approach
the temple by a flight of steps flanked by bronze friezes of chariots in
battle and heavenly *apsara* (traditional Khmer dancing figures). Inside
the temple hall, the vihear, are some fine wall paintings depicting scenes
from the Buddha's lives, and on the north side is a charming Chinese
shrine. The bottom of the hill swarms with vendors selling devotional

8

CAMBODIAN CUISINE

Cambodian cuisine is distinct from that of neighbors Thailand, Laos, and Vietnam, although some dishes are common throughout the region. Fish and rice are the mainstays, and some of the world's tastiest fish dishes are to be had in Cambodia. The country has the benefit of a complex river system that feeds Southeast Asia's largest freshwater lake, plus a coastline famous for its shrimp and crab. Beyond all that, Cambodia's rice paddies grow some of the most succulent fish around. (Besides fish, Cambodians also eat a lot of pork, more so than beef, which tends to be tough.)

Be sure to try *prahok*, the Cambodian lifeblood—a stinky-cheeselike fermented fish paste that nourishes the nation. *Amok*, too, is a sure delight. Done the old-fashioned way, it takes two days to make this fish-and-coconut concoction, which is steamed in a banana leaf.

Down south, Kampot Province grows world-renowned aromatic pepper. If you're coming from a northern climate, try a seafood dish with whole green peppercorns on the stalk. You won't find it (not fresh, anyway) in your home country.

Generally, the food in Cambodia is far tamer and less flavorsome that of Thailand or Laos, but seasoned heavily with fresh herbs. Curried dishes, known as *kari*, show the ties between Indian and Cambodian cuisine. As in Thailand, it is usual in Cambodian food to use fish sauce in soups, stir-fry, and as a dipping sauce. There are many variations of rice noodles, which give the cuisine a Chinese flavor. Beef noodle soup, known simply as *kuyteav*, is a popular dish brought to Cambodia by Chinese settlers. Also, *banh chiao*, a crepe-like pancake stuffed with pork, shrimp, and bean sprouts and then fried, is the Khmer version of the Vietnamese *bánh xèo*. Cambodian cuisine uses many vegetables. Mushrooms, cabbage, baby corn, bamboo shoots, fresh ginger, Chinese broccoli, snow peas, and bok choy are all found in Cambodian dishes from stir-fry to soup.

Usually, meals in Cambodia consist of three or four different dishes, reflecting the tastes of sweet, sour, salty, and bitter. The dishes are set out and you take from which dish you want and mix with your rice. Eating is usually a communal experience, and it is appropriate to share your food with others.

candles and flowers, food stands (one with a monkey protecting a couple of dogs) with rather unappetizing food, and beggars. ✉ *Norodom Blvd. and St. 94* 🎫 *$1* 🕐 *Daily 7–6:30.*

WHERE TO EAT

Phnom Penh is quickly becoming one of the top culinary cities in Asia. With delectable Khmer food at all levels, from street stands to five-star establishments, plus an influx of international restaurants, you'll eat well in Phnom Penh. The country's colonial history means you'll find many French-inspired restaurants, too.

$ ✕ **The Corn.** The focus here is on delicately spiced Khmer-inspired vegan
CAMBODIAN dishes. Try the rich, creamy sweet potato, pumpkin, and coconut curry, with subtle texture and flavors that continue to emerge with every

Where to Stay and Eat in Phnom Penh

0   1/2 mi
0   1/2 km

Tonle Sap River

Lake Boeng Kak

Tepui

France
Monivong Blvd

WAT PHNOM
Hotel Raffles Le Royal
Sunway Hotel
Van's
MEKONG EXPRESS BUSES
NEAK KRORHORM BUSES
Sher-e-Punjab
TRAIN STATION
Preah Sisowath

(—10) AIRPORT
Pochentong Blvd

PHSAR THMEI (CENTRAL MARKET)
California 2
Veiyo Tonle
WAT SVAY DANG KUM
CENTRAL MARKET BUS STATION

Kampuchea Krom Blvd

R.S. Teracos ovaqule Blvd

Lebiz Hotel and Library

Charles De Gaulle

Karma
Amanjaya
WAT OUNALOM
Lux Riverside
Friends the Restaurant
FCC FCC
Frangipani Palace
Khmer Borane
The Plantation Hotel
Nordom Blvd

WAT KOH

182
Preah Tresak Paem
Street 51
Monivong Blvd

HUA LIAN BUS STATION

The Pavilion
Preah Ang Yukanthor

OLYMPIC STATIUM
White Mansion
INDEPENDENCE MONUMENT
K'nyay

ST63
Monirath Blvd
Hawahariat Nerhu Blvd

Samdach Preah
Sihanouk Blvd
The Corn
Shiva Shakti
Romdeng
WAT LANG KA
Malis

WAT MOHA MONTREI

Digby's
Deco

Hotel InterContinental

Mao Tse Toung Blvd

TOUL SLENG GENOCIDE MUSEUM

Samdach Sethearos

Topaz

WAT TUOL TOM PONG

Mao Tse Toung Blvd

Bassac River

PHSAR TUOL TOM PONG (RUSSIAN MARKET)

Norodom Blvd

8

KEY

☐ Hotels
■ Restaurants
┼─ Rail lines
▲ Temple

mouthful, or a clean, crisp green mango, carrot, and herb salad with smoked tofu. The refreshingly tangy homemade ginger beer is a real winner on a hot, sultry Phnom Penh evening. A limited number of Thai curry-style meat and fish dishes is also available. *Average main: $5* ⊠ *25K Suramarit Blvd.* ☎ *017/773757* ⊟ *No credit cards.*

$$$

EUROPEAN

✕ **Deco.** With its two-tone color scheme, the art-deco (as the name suggests) dining area is the ideal place to enjoy a top-notch lunch or dinner. Deco reflects the changing face of Phnom Penh. Seasonal produce sourced locally, coupled with top-grade produce from around the world, is transformed by executive chef Casper von Hofmannsthal into modern European dishes infused with tastes of Asia. As for the cocktails, it's worth coming here just to sample the classic Negroni or the popular Deco Bramble (a mix of Bombay Sapphire and homemade blackberry syrup, finished with a dash of lemon). *Average main: $13* ⊠ *Corner of Sts. 57 and 352* ☎ *017/577327* ⊕ *www.decophnompenh. com* ⊘ *No lunch Sun.* ⚲ *Reservations essential.*

$$

AMERICAN

✕ **Digby's.** A restaurant, coffee shop, butcher shop, and deli all rolled into one—if it's meat you're after, this is the place. Their locally sourced meat is all certified (a rarity in Cambodia) and all the gourmet sausages and cold cuts are prepared, cured, and smoked on the premises. Whether you pop in for a quick sandwich or a full meal this is a great place to satiate any carnivorous cravings, in an up-and-coming part of town. *Average main: $10* ⊠ *No 34A, 306 St., Boeung Keng Kang 1* ☎ *023/226677* ⊕ *www.digbysbutchery.com.*

$$

INTERNATIONAL

✕ **FCC.** It's not really a Foreign Correspondents Club, and you don't have to be a journalist to join the lively international crowd that gathers here every day, but it is one of the favored hangouts of the local expat community. People drop in as much for the atmosphere of the French colonial building and its open river views as for the tasty food, which is as eclectic as the diners. The beer is always cold, the cocktails icy, and you can grab a reliable burger or pizza if you're in need of a change from Khmer fare (having said that, the beef Lok Lak is one of the best in town). *Average main: $8* ⊠ *363 Sisowath Quay* ☎ *023/724014* ⊕ *www.fcccambodia.com.*

$

SPANISH TAPAS

Fodor's Choice

★

✕ **Friends the Restaurant.** Before Romdeng, there was Friends the Restaurant. This extremely popular nonprofit eatery near the National Museum serves a huge range of small tapas, fruit juices, salads, and international dishes. Admire the colorful artwork, then visit the Friends store next door, filled with souvenirs and trinkets, whose proceeds help the NGO continue provide much-needed assistance training and helping underprivileged youths. Best to book ahead as it is usually packed and people are prepared to stand in line—for good reason: the food is great. *Average main: $5* ⊠ *215 St. 13* ☎ *012/802072* ⊕ *www.tree-alliance. org* ⊟ *No credit cards* ⚲ *Reservations essential.*

$

CAMBODIAN

✕ **Karma.** Located on the riverfront, Karma offers tasty Khmer and western fare in well-sized portions that are great value for money. Karma is one of the better restaurants to ease your way into the local cuisine (the Fish Amok and Pork Loc Lak are recommended), if you happen to start your Cambodian adventure in Phnom Penh. *Average main: $5* ⊠ *273c Sisowath Quay* ☎ *089/788841.*

$ 🍴 **Khmer Borane.** This casual, breezy riverfront café on the bottom floor of an old colonial-era building attracts a steady crowd. Try something from the extensive list of classic Khmer dishes; the pomelo salad and fish soup with lemon and herbs are both good choices. If those don't please your palate, Khmer Borane also offers a wide variety of western dishes at reasonable prices. [$] *Average main: $5* ✉ *389 Sisowath Quay* ☎ *012/290092* 💳 *No credit cards.*

CAMBODIAN

LOCAL EATS

For a local treat, try the afternoon **noodle shops** on Street 178 near the National Museum. These street-side eateries pack in the Khmer crowds, serving quick fried noodles and rice-flour-and-onion cakes. They're popular among locals, and cheap (less than a dollar per serving). You won't find the cleanest of restaurants here, but everything is well cooked and you'll get a tasty snack with an eye for what it's like to eat Khmer-style. Don't get here before 4 pm

$ 🍴 **K'nyay.** Khmer cuisine doesn't get much better than at K'nyay. This elegantly designed restaurant, finding its feet again after moving to this new location, serves modern, simple, but tasty dishes, offering a great range of vegetarian and vegan choices. Not surprisingly, it has become a favorite of the local expat community, who also come to enjoy the breezy terrace. It's also open for breakfast on weekends. [$] *Average main: $4* ✉ *The Terrace on 95, 43 St. 95, corner of St. 348* ☎ *093/665225* 🕒 *Closed Mon.*

VEGETARIAN

$$$ 🍴 **Malis.** The Phnom Penh elite frequent this upscale, traditional Khmer restaurant in a peaceful garden, as its chef Luu Meng is a Cambodian celebrity who has worked on TV with the likes of Gordon Ramsay. The long menu features a great variety of fresh fish and seafood, soups, complex curries, and grilled meats. The prices are a little high by Cambodian standards, but it makes for an enjoyable change if you're looking for something out of the ordinary, and you certainly get what you pay for. [$] *Average main: $13* ✉ *136 St. 11 (Preah Norodom)* ☎ *023/221022* 🌐 *www.malis-restaurant.com* ✍ *Reservations essential.*

CAMBODIAN

$ 🍴 **Romdeng.** Some of the country's tastiest provincial Khmer dishes are served at this gorgeously redesigned house in a residential area. The adventurous can try the three flavors of *prahok,* Cambodia's signature fermented fish paste, or even fried spiders. If those don't suit your tastes, Romdeng (which means "galangal" in Khmer) offers plenty of piquant soups, curries, salads, and meat dishes. Have a glass of palm wine to sip with the meal, and enjoy the paintings on the walls—artwork by former street kids. The restaurant is part of the Mith Samlanh (Friends) group, so your dollars will help the former street kids who are trained to work here. [$] *Average main: $5* ✉ *74 St. 174* ☎ *092/219565* 🌐 *www.tree-alliance.org* 💳 *No credit cards.*

CAMBODIAN

$ 🍴 **Sher-e-Punjab.** Follow the aroma of pungent spices into this restaurant and prepare for a hearty curry and all the essential sides at the capital's best Indian restaurant. The accommodating staff and exotically spiced fare more than compensate for the modest appearance of this much raved-about restaurant. Complimentary *poppadoms,* dips, and chutney satiate the hunger pangs as you mull over the varied menu. Try the melt-in-your-mouth tandoori chicken and don't miss out on the freshly

INDIAN

baked naan. Like at all good curry houses, the vegetarian options are packed full of flavor. $ *Average main: $6* ✉ *16 St. 130* ☎ *023/216360, 092/992901* ⊕ *sherepunjabcambodia.com.*

$$ ✕ **Shiva Shakti.** Succulent samosas, vegetable *pakoras* (fritters), spicy lamb masala, butter chicken, and prawn *biryani* (with rice and vegetables) are among the favorites served at this small Indian restaurant. In the pleasant dining room a statue of the elephant-headed Hindu god Ganesha stands by the door, and reproductions of Mogul art line the walls. There are also a few tables on the sidewalk next to their little bar. It's just east of the Independence Monument. $ *Average main: $9* ✉ *17 St. 63, Khan Chamkarmon* ☎ *012/813817, 023/213062* ☾ *Closed Mon.*

INDIAN

$ ✕ **ST 63.** One of the best restaurants in town, ST 63 is run by a young Cambodian couple who aim to make international cuisine accessible and affordable for a local crowd, and at the same time showcase the best of Cambodian cuisine for foreign crowds. All the delicious dishes are well presented and amazingly well priced. The Cha Kdao Sach Maon (spicy hot chicken with basil) is one of the finest to be had. They also whisk up creamy smoothies and refreshing cocktails, keeping the place buzzing with a cool mix of locals, expats, and tourists. $ *Average main: $5* ✉ *179 St. 63, Boeung Keng Kang 1 (BKK1), Chamkamon District* ☎ *015/647062.*

CAMBODIAN
Fodor's Choice
★

$$$$ ✕ **Tepui.** Built in 1903, Chinese House (home to Tepui) is among the few colonial houses in Phnom Penh that remains in its original state, a mix of Chinese and French colonial architecture. But don't let the location's name mislead you—the food is combination of South American and Asian tastes, with specialties such as corn empanadas filled with beef picadillo and goat cheese cream, or red tuna tartare with wasabi emulsion. An impressive painting of a Chinese girl with ruby-red lips is the centerpiece in this sophisticated restaurant. There is a lively bar on the ground floor. ■**TIP→** Have your tuk-tuk wait for you outside to avoid any delays after dinner. $ *Average main: $17* ✉ *Chinese House, 45 Sisowath Quay, cross St. 84, in front of Phnom Penh Port* ☎ *023/991514, 017/873101* ⊕ *www.chinesehouse.asia* ☾ *Closed Sun. No lunch* ⚓ *Reservations essential.*

SOUTH
AMERICAN
Fodor's Choice
★

$$$$ ✕ **Topaz.** The first-class French specialties and extensive wine list at this fine restaurant make it a longtime Phnom Penh favorite. Imported cuts of beef from Cape Grim in Tasmania and other highest-quality ingredients cooked to perfection mean that Topaz remains one of the most feted places to dine in the city, even with its growing restaurant scene. It's a great choice for an intimate, candlelight meal. Note that Topaz is open for lunch early, around 11 am, but closes again at 2 pm; dinner starts at 6 pm. $ *Average main: $25* ✉ *182 Norodom Blvd.* ☎ *089/211888, 023/221622* ⊕ *www.topaz-restaurant.com.*

FRENCH

$$$$ ✕ **Van's.** In the elegant setting of the beautifully restored 1880's Indochina Bank Building, next to the post office, you can dine on exquisite French cuisine. Walk past the old vaults, and up to the colonnaded dining area on the first floor. Dishes such as duck confit paupiette with duck liver, or fillet of grouper with a matelote sauce are popular. ■**TIP→** There are business-lunch specials for a reasonable $20 for a three-course meal. Van's also has a swanky cocktail bar-lounge on the

FRENCH

roof terrace above the restaurant. $ *Average main: $25* ⊠ *5 St. 102* ☎ *023/722067* ⊕ *vans-restaurant. com* ♿ *Reservations essential.*

$ **✕ Veiyo Tonle.** This Khmer-owned and -operated nonprofit restaurant on the riverfront serves excellent traditional Khmer dishes, pizzas (39 varieties!), pastas, and more. Proceeds go toward an orphanage established by the owner. The children put on an Apsara dance show on the weekends at the restaurant. $ *Average main: $7* ⊠ *237 Sisowath Quay* ☎ *012/847419, 011/737670* ▤ *No credit cards.*

CAMBODIAN

> ### STOCKING THE FRIDGE
>
> **Veggy's.** If your room or suite has a kitchenette or an ample mini-refrigerator, check out Veggy's, which features fine wines, cheeses, and meats from around the world. It also supplies imported dry goods and fresh veggies, as the name indicates. ⊠ *23 St. 240* ☎ *023/211534* ⊙ *Daily 8 am–10 pm.*

WHERE TO STAY

These days the capital offers a plethora of accommodations for all budgets. Phnom Penh has several international-standard hotels, including the Cambodiana Hotel refurbishment of a 1960s building, a creation by the architect Lu Ban Hap, at the behest of the late King Sihanouk. Clean and comfortable boutique hotels and trendy guesthouses have sprung up across the city, particularly in the Boeung Kak area. Most charge less than $50 a night. If you haven't found what you're looking for, wander the riverfront and its side streets. You're bound to discover something to your liking among the dozens upon dozens of options. ■ TIP→ When booking a hotel, check for special offers and promotions—many establishments offer deals. If you're doing business in Cambodia, be sure to say so, as additional discounts may apply.

8

$$$ **⊞ Amanjaya Pancam Hotel.** With chic rosewood furnishings and Khmer silk textiles in the rooms and soapstone-finished bathrooms, Amanjaya is the classiest hotel on the banks of the Tonle Sap River. **Pros:** glorious riverside location; great restaurant and bar; breakfast included. **Cons:** noisy traffic all day; no pool; patchy Wi-Fi. $ *Rooms from: $135* ⊠ *1 St. 154, Sisowath Quay* ☎ *023/219579* ⊕ *www.amanjaya-pancam-hotel. com* ⊅ *21 suites* ❑ *Breakfast.*

HOTEL

$ **⊞ California 2.** Clean, cheerful, and good value, the bar that doubles as the reception somewhat sets the tone of this easygoing, friendly guesthouse just east of Wat Phnom. **Pros:** close to bus stops; bar draws in a good crowd; friendly staff. **Cons:** rooms a little on small side; no elevator. $ *Rooms from: $27* ⊠ *79 Sisowath Quay* ☎ *077/503144* ⊕ *www. cafecaliforniaphnompenh.com* ⊅ *10 rooms* ❑ *Breakfast.*

B&B/INN

$$ **⊞ FCC.** Ideally located on the riverfront, cooled by the river breezes, and across from the National Museum, the FCC is well known as a hub for expats and visitors who hang out at its lively restaurant-bar on the second and third floors. **Pros:** charm of old-style correspondents' digs; lively restaurant-bar; excellent location. **Cons:** a little ragged around the edges; street noise; patchy hot water. $ *Rooms from: $60* ⊠ *363 Sisowath Quay* ☎ *023/991641, 023/210142* ⊕ *www.fcccambodia.com* ⊅ *9 rooms* ❑ *Breakfast.*

HOTEL

$$ HOTEL
🏨 **Frangipani Palace Hotel.** The fifth in a local chain, the Frangipani Palace Hotel is currently the only hotel in Phnom Penh with a rooftop pool, from where you can enjoy lovely panoramic views of the capital, especially at sunset. **Pros:** scenic rooftop pool and bar; good spa; high-end restaurant; central location. **Cons:** not all rooms have a view; piped music throughout; only one elevator for eight floors. [$] *Rooms from: $75* ✉ *27 St. 178, Sangkat Cheychumneas, Khan Daun Penh* ☎ *023/223320, 023/223340* 🌐 *www.frangipanipalacehotel.com* 🛏 *72 rooms* 🍴 *Breakfast.*

$$$ HOTEL
🏨 **Hotel InterContinental.** One of Phnom Penh's finest hotels is on the far edge of town, where it's long been a favorite of business travelers and tycoons requiring VIP treatment. **Pros:** many amenities and services (including a concierge and executive floor); good selection of bars and restaurants; dramatic views. **Cons:** location in business district; far from city's main attractions; Internet charge. [$] *Rooms from: $140* ✉ *296 Blvd. Mao Tse Tung* ☎ *023/424888, 008/0031–221211 worldwide booking* 🌐 *www.intercontinental.com* 🛏 *346 rooms, 28 suites* 🍴 *Breakfast.*

$$$$ HOTEL
🏨 **Hotel Raffles Le Royal.** Phnom Penh's ritziest hotel, first opened in 1929, was practically destroyed during the Khmer Rouge years, and was meticulously restored by the Raffles group in 1996. **Pros:** great location; old-world luxury. **Cons:** style may not be to everyone's tastes; service has become quite lackadaisical. [$] *Rooms from: $240* ✉ *92 Rukhak Vithei Daun Penh* ☎ *023/981888, 800/768–9009 in U.S., 800/1–723–3537 international access* 🌐 *www.raffles.com* 🛏 *133 rooms, 37 suites* 🍴 *Breakfast; Some meals.*

$$ HOTEL
🏨 **Lebiz Hotel and Library.** This boutique hotel's futuristic urban-chic style is geared mainly to hip professionals; large glaringly white rooms are activated by splashes of bright colors and decked out with techie facilities such as DVD player, LCD screen, and iPod dock. **Pros:** affordable designer comfort; cool minimalist style; friendly staff. **Cons:** breakfast somewhat lacking; location central but requires a good walk; interior design too clinical for some. [$] *Rooms from: $55* ✉ *79F St. 128* ☎ *023/998608* 🌐 *www.lebizhotel.com* 🛏 *27 rooms* 🍴 *No meals.*

$$ HOTEL
🏨 **Lux Riverside Hotel.** The rooms here are immaculate, spacious, and surprisingly pleasant for a budget property. **Pros:** river views; nice rooms; parking. **Cons:** noisy locale; no windows in back rooms; dodgy Wi-Fi reception in some rooms. [$] *Rooms from: $50* ✉ *2 St. 136, Sangkat Phsar Kandal, Khan Daun Penh* ☎ *023/722828, 023/722318* 🌐 *www.luxriversidehotels.com* 🛏 *100 rooms, 2 apartments* 🍴 *Breakfast.*

$$ HOTEL Fodor's Choice ★
🏨 **The Pavilion.** A discreet green oasis in the heart of bustling Phnom Penh, the Pavilion is in a lovingly restored building of the raging 1920s, with a swimming pool surrounded by palm, banana, and jackfruit trees. **Pros:** free massage for new arrivals, to work out those travel aches; limo pickup service; good spa; great location. **Cons:** rooms and bathrooms are a little small; no children under 16 allowed; fills quickly. [$] *Rooms from: $80* ✉ *227 St. 19, Khan Daun Penh* ☎ *023/222280* 🌐 *www.thepavilion.asia* 🛏 *27 rooms, 3 suites, 1 studio* 🍴 *Breakfast.*

$$ HOTEL Fodor's Choice ★ **The Plantation.** Your dollar travels far at this large boutique hotel built around a grand 1930s villa in the heart of the city. **Pros:** super restaurant; the larger of the two pools is only for guests; good location. **Cons:** only one shower at the main pool; slight overcharging for outsourced activities and transportation booked through reception. [$] *Rooms from: $65* ✉ *28 St. 184* ☎ *023/215151* 🌐 *theplantation.asia* 🛏 *69 rooms, 1 suite* 🍴 *Breakfast.*

$$ HOTEL **Sunway Hotel.** Near Wat Phnom and the U.S. Embassy, this is a primary choice among business travelers. **Pros:** in the heart of the business district; excellent lounge bar; no-smoking in all rooms. **Cons:** slightly dated architecture; only the suites have balconies. [$] *Rooms from: $99* ✉ *1 St. 92* ☎ *023/430333* 🌐 *phnompenh.sunwayhotels.com* 🛏 *138 rooms* 🍴 *Breakfast.*

$$$ HOTEL FAMILY **White Mansion Hotel.** This glossy boutique hotel on the hip, upscale 240 Street has suites on the top floors with balconies overlooking great vistas of the city, while rooms on the ground floor have terraces that lead directly to the pool. **Pros:** spacious rooms; child-friendly; nice monochrome design. **Cons:** open showers can be messy; elevator only goes up to third floor. [$] *Rooms from: $100* ✉ *26 St. 240* ☎ *023/555–0955* 🌐 *www.hotelphnompenh-whitemansion.com* 🛏 *30 rooms* 🍴 *Breakfast.*

NIGHTLIFE AND PERFORMING ARTS

NIGHTLIFE

What makes the nightlife here enjoyable is how easy it is to get from place to place in this compact city. Most of the dusk-to-dawn nightspots are near the Tonle Sap riverside, along streets 240 and 51. A useful website for upcoming events and venue information is www.lengpleng.com, which is updated every Thursday or Friday. **■ TIP→ Keep your wits about you after dark in Phnom Penh—robberies are common, and although foreigners aren't specifically targeted, they are certainly not exempt from the rise in crime.**

8

BARS AND PUBS

Katty Perry Pizza. Though not a bar, this food cart has to have a mention as a popular feature of Phnom Penh nightlife. It's a pizza oven that is attached to a moped and carted around to all the best bars in town. Even though most bars serve food, they don't seem to mind much that their clientele dart out to order a toasty pizza from Katty Perry's, which is then delivered straight to their table. ✉ *Phnom Penh.*

Le Moon Terrace Bar. This is an ideal spot to visit with a bunch of friends for a night of cocktails accompanied by sparkling views of the Tonle Sap and Mekong rivers, as well as Wat Ounalom. On the rooftop of the Amanjaya Pancam Hotel, the bar also serves finger food. ✉ *1 St. 154, Sisowath Quay* ☎ *023/214747* 🌐 *www.amanjaya-pancam-hotel.com.*

Score Sports Bar & Grill. Open until 2 am every morning, this sports haunt is a favorite of expats, locals, and tourists who want to catch a game live on one of many LCD screens, while enjoying a tipple among a chatty, enthusiastic crowd. The food isn't the best in town, but most people don't come only to eat. ✉ *Wat Lanka, 5 St. 282, between Sts. 51 and 57* ☎ *023/221357.*

DANCE CLUBS

Blue Chilli. Phnom Penh is a gay-friendly city, and Blue Chilli, behind the National Museum, is one of the most popular and oldest bars for

CLOSE UP

Cambodia's Festivals

Like many Southeast Asian nations, Cambodia celebrates a lot of important festivals. Quite a few of them are closely tied to Buddhism, the country's predominant religion.

Meak Bochea: On the day of the full moon in February, this festival commemorates the Buddha's first sermon to 1,250 of his disciples. In the evening, Buddhists parade three times around their respective pagodas.

Khmer New Year: Celebrated at the same time as the Thai and Lao lunar new year (mid-April), it's a new-moon festival spread over the three days following the winter rice harvest. People celebrate by cleaning and decorating their houses, making offerings at their home altars, going to Buddhist temples, and splashing lots and lots of water on each other. Be forewarned: foreigners are fair game.

Visakha Bochea: This Buddhist festival on the day of the full moon in May celebrates the Buddha's birth, enlightenment, and death.

Chrat Preah Nongkol: The Royal Plowing Ceremony, a celebration of the start of the summer planting season, is held in front of the Royal Palace in Phnom Penh in May. The impressive ceremony includes soothsaying rites meant to predict the outcomes for the year's rice harvest.

Pchum Ben (All Souls' Day): In mid-October the spirits of deceased ancestors are honored according to Khmer tradition. People make special offerings at Buddhist temples to appease these spirits.

Bonn Om Touk: The Water Festival ushers in the fishing season, and marks the "miraculous" reversal of the Tonle Sap waters. It's celebrated in November throughout the country: longboat river races are held, and an illuminated flotilla of *naga,* or dragon boats, adds to the festive atmosphere. The biggest races are held in Phnom Penh in front of the Royal Palace, and the king traditionally presides.

locals, expats, and tourists. The lively, friendly bar hosts entertaining drag shows and other performances throughout the week, as well as DJ sets that will keep you dancing until the early hours. ⊠ *36Eo St. 178* ☎ *012/566353* ⊕ *www.bluechillicambodia.com.*

Epic. As the name might suggest, this place, which opened in 2014, is for big nights out—a high-tech dance club, near the Russian Embassy, that caters to the high fliers of the capital, including jet-setters, A-list celebrities, and serious ravers. The daily party goes on until 5 am. Check the website for details of upcoming events. ⊠ *122B Sangkat Tonle Bassac, Chamkamon District* ☎ *023/210454, 010/600608* ⊕ *www.epic.com.kh.*

GATHERING PLACES **Pontoon Club and Lounge.** The first club in the Cambodian capital that brings top DJs from around the world for happening live sets draws an accidental as well as a dedicated music-loving crowd. ⊠ *80 St. 172* ☎ *016/779966, 010/300400* ⊕ *www.pontoonclub.com.*

Fodor's Choice ★ **Samai.** Difficult to find but well worth the effort, this microdistillery-bar, near the Aen Mall, is one of the trendiest joints in Phnom Phen's flourishing bar scene. Excellent Samai brand rum is distilled on-site in 200-year-old copper stills and makes a great base for the Moorish-Asian-inspired cocktails. The downside: it's only open on Thursday nights—for now. ⊠ *9b St. 830, off Sothearos Blvd.* ☎ *023/224143.*

Show Box. Very near Tuol Sleng, but quite a distance from the main "happening" spots in town, Show Box has a clever strategy to draw in custom—it gives out free beer every day from 6:30–7 pm. Once there, many end up staying all night for the laid-back vibe and the company of a youthful, artsy crowd. ⊠ *11 St. 330, Chamkamon District* ☎ *017/275824.*

MUSIC CLUBS **Equinox Bar.** If it's live music you're after, this is the place to come. The best local bands play here, along with touring groups and artists. Check out the website to see if anything tickles your fancy when you're in town. ⊠ *3A St. 278* ☎ *023/676–7593* ⊕ *equinox-cambodia.com.*

WINE BARS **The Alley Bar.** This place, on an alleyway between Streets 240 and 244, attracts a hip clientele with its sophisticated bites, good selection of wines, and classy cocktails. The modern lounge setting, tucked away in an alley near the trendy Street 240, occasionally hosts events and live music. ⊠ *82 St. 244* ☎ *095/222405* ⊕ *thealleybar2405.com* ☾ *Closed Sun.*

Bouchon Wine Bar. A novel addition to the Phnom Penh nightlife scene, Bouchon serves a dapper selection of more than 40 French wines and accompanying light meals (well, light by French standards) or finger food, in a buzzily sophisticated, industrial, nouveau-pub atmosphere that attracts an eclectic international crowd. Wine labels are also stamped on the wooden tables, and you can sample different varieties by the bottle or by the glass. ⊠ *3 St. 246* ☎ *077/881103.*

PERFORMING ARTS

Various Phnom Penh theaters and restaurants offer programs of traditional music and dancing, many organized by nonprofit groups that help Cambodian orphans, disadvantaged kids, and individuals with a disability. Siem Reap perhaps has more venues, but most there are run by for-profit companies in the tourism industry.

Chaktomuk Hall. This architectural landmark, built in 1960 by Vann Molyvann, hosts performances of traditional music and dance organized by the Ministry of Culture, and is also a venue for business events such as conferences. Dates and times of the occasional shows are listed in the English-language newspaper, *Cambodia Daily*, and the *Phnom Penh Post.* ⊠ *Sisowath Quay, north of St. 240* ☎ *023/725119.*

FAMILY **Plae Pakaa.** Established to create work opportunities for talented local artists, Plae Pakaa puts on three shows, each performed twice a week at 7 pm (no show on Sunday). They are organized by the Marion Institute with Cambodian Living Arts and take place in the National Museum gardens. The beautifully staged performances showcase the rich diversity of Cambodian culture, from Apsara dances to traditional ceremonies, theater, music, and contemporary dance. If you're only in town for two or three days you can catch a different performance each night. ⊠ *National Museum, St. 3, corner of St. 178* ☎ *017/998570* ⊕ *www.cambodianlivingarts.org* ☞ *$15.*

Women parade near the Royal Palace in celebration of Bonn Om Touk, Cambodia's water festival.

Sovanna Phum Khmer Art Association. The privately run association organizes educational workshops for young Cambodians in dance, music, and theater, and hosts performances featuring shadow puppets, folk dances, and traditional music every Friday and Saturday at its theater. ✉ *166 St. 99, corner of St. 484, Chamkamon District* ☎ *012/846020, 012/837056* ⊕ *sovannaphumtheatre.com.*

SHOPPING

The city has many shops and a few markets selling everything from fake antiques to fine jewelry, while several polished boutiques sell items made with local materials and offer sustenance to socially disadvantaged individuals. Prices are generally set at shops, so save your bargaining skills for the markets. The best shops are to be found on Streets 178 and 240.

ANTIQUES AND FINE ART

Couleurs d'Asie. As well as presenting regular exhibitions of contemporary and classic-style Khmer art, Couleurs d'Asie sells beautifully crafted accessories and home style items made by local artists in sumptuous silks and other locally sourced materials. The store closes at 3 pm on Sunday. ✉ *33 St. 240* ☎ *023/221075* ⊕ *www.couleursdasie.net.*

Le Lezard Bleu. Like its newer twin in Siem Reap, Le Lezard Bleu is a boutique-gallery-shop featuring housewares creations inspired by Cambodian culture and made by local artisans, as well as a collection of antique objets d'art. It mainly stocks posters, sculptures, prints, and silks. ✉ *61 St. 240* ☎ *023/986978* ⊕ *lelezardbleu.com.*

X-EM Design. It's more of a showroom than a shop, where Em Riem showcases his own works as well as inviting other fresh Cambodian artists to exhibit here—a must for design and art lovers and collectors. ⊠ *13 St. 178, west of Norodom Blvd.* ☎ *023/722252.*

BOOKS AND NEWSPAPERS

Monument Books. The specialty at this bookstore, to the north of the Independence Monument, is titles covering Cambodia and Southeast Asia as a whole, but you can also find all the latest best sellers, cookbooks, daily worldwide press, and more. They also have a store at the airport. ⊠ *111 Norodom Blvd.* ☎ *023/217617* ⊕ *www.monument-books.com.*

CLOTHING

Ambre. After studying at Paris School of Fine Arts and the Esmod School of Fashion Design, Romyda Keth made her name for herself abroad. Since returning to her native Cambodia she opened her own fashion shop in an old colonial villa and showcases her creations there. Her designs are a big hit locally and internationally. ⊠ *No. 37, 178 St.* ☎ *023/217935* ⊕ *www.romydaketh.net.*

CRAFTS

Daughters of Cambodia Boutique. Within Phnom Penh's red-light district and offering employment opportunities to sex-trafficking victims, this boutique sells men's and women's clothing and accessories, children's toys, and home style items. There is also a lovely café and a spa on the premises. ⊠ *65 St. 178* ☎ *077/657678* ⊕ *daughtersofcambodia.org.*

Friends 'n' Stuff. Trendy, playful, and eco-friendly accessories can be found here, next to the ultrapopular Friends restaurant and just north of the National Museum. Check out the locally crafted laptop cases made from recycled bicycle tires, handbags made from food packets, glossy hardback books about Cambodia, and other fun stuff—and all for the worthy cause of helping street children achieve a quality of life. ⊠ *215 St. 13, Khan Daun Penh* ☎ *023/220596* ⊕ *www.mithsamlanh.org.*

Rajana. Interesting, locally handcrafted jewelry, silks, home style items, stationery, and clothing are sold at this shop next to the Russian Market, and the proceeds go toward the Rajana Association, which trains local artisans. ■ **TIP→** Check out the old war-scrap necklaces and recycled spark-plug figurines. The store has other locations in Sihanoukville and Siem Reap. ⊠ *Psar Tuol Tom Poung (Russian Market), 170 St. 450* ☎ *023/993642* ⊕ *www.rajanacrafts.org.*

Watthan Artisans Cambodia. This is an organization worth supporting, producing attractive women's accessories, decorative objects, and knickknacks in silk, cotton, wood, and clay—all made on-site by people with physical disabilities. Watthan Artisans products can also be found at the great Colours of Life store behind the FCC. ⊠ *Wat Than Pagoda, 180 Norodom Blvd.* ☎ *023/216–321* ⊕ *www.wac.khmerproducts.com.*

MARKETS

Psar Reatrey Night Market. This lively riverfront market attracts locals and tourists alike for basic clothing, traditional handmade souvenirs, accessories, and gift shopping until midnight. Several stands sell freshly made local dishes as well as drinks like sugarcane and bean juices, and there is a large sitting area covered in rattan mats. ⊠ *Sisowath Quay, between St. 106 and St. 108.*

Cambodia Then and Now

Internationally, Cambodia is best known for two contrasting chapters of its long history. The first is the Khmer Empire, which in its heyday covered most of modern-day Southeast Asia. Today the ruins of Angkor attest to the nation's immutable cultural heritage. The second chapter is the country's recent history and legacy of Khmer Rouge brutality, which left at least 1.7 million Cambodians dead. In 1993 the United Nations sponsored democratic elections that failed to honor the people's vote. Civil war continued until 1998, when another round of elections was held, and violent riots ensued in the aftermath. Cambodia's long-standing political turmoil—both on the battlefield and in much more subtle displays—continues to shape the nation's day-to-day workings. Through decades of war, a genocide, continued widespread government corruption, high rates of violence and mental illness, the provision of billions of dollars in international aid, and the disappearance of much of that money, Cambodia has suffered its demons. Yet Cambodians are a forward-thinking, sharp-minded, and friendly people, whose warm smiles are not yet jaded by tourism and do not belie the inordinate suffering their nation has so recently endured. Though practically destroyed by the regional conflict and homegrown repression of the 1970s, individual Cambodians have risen from those disasters, and a new, hard-working, and young middle class has blossomed.

ECOLOGY

More than half of Cambodia was once blanketed in forests, but the landscape has changed in recent decades as a result of ruthless and mercenary deforestation. The country is blessed with powerful waters: the Mekong and Tonle Sap rivers, and Tonle Sap lake, which feeds 70% of the nation. The surrounding mountain ranges, protecting Cambodia's long river valleys, are home to hill tribes and some of the region's rarest wildlife species.

The three ranges of low mountains—the northern Dangkrek, the exotically named Elephant Mountains in the south, and the country's highest range, the Cardamoms, in the southwest—formed natural barriers against invasion and were used as fortresses during the war years. Among these ranges is a depression in the northwest of Cambodia connecting the country with the lowlands in Thailand; by allowing communication between the two countries, this geographic feature played an important part in the history of the Khmer nation. In eastern Cambodia the land rises to a forested plateau that continues into the Annamite Cordillera, the backbone of neighboring Vietnam.

COLONIZATION, WAR, AND INVASION

As the seat of the Khmer Empire from the 9th to the 13th century, Cambodia developed a complex society based first on Hinduism and then on Buddhism. After the decline of the Khmers and the ascendancy of the Siamese, Cambodia was colonized by the French, who ruled from the mid-1860s until 1953.

Shortly after the end of World War II, during which the Japanese had occupied Cambodia, independence became the rallying cry for all of Indochina. Cambodia became a sovereign power with a monarchy ruled by King Norodom Sihanouk, who abdicated in favor of his father in 1955 and entered the public stage as a mercurial politician.

In the early 1970s the destabilizing consequences of the Vietnam War sparked a horrible chain of events. The U.S. government secretly bombed Cambodia, arranged a coup to oust the king, and invaded parts of the country in an attempt to rout the Vietcong. Civil war ensued, and in 1975 the Khmer Rouge, led by French-educated Pol Pot, emerged as the victors. A regime of terror followed. Under a program of Mao Tse-tung–inspired reeducation centered on forced agricultural collectives, the cities were emptied and hundreds of thousands of civilians were tortured and executed. Hundreds of thousands more succumbed to starvation and disease. During the four years of Khmer Rouge rule, somewhere between 1 and 2 million Cambodians—almost one-third of the population—were killed.

By 1979 the country lay in ruins. Vietnam, unified under the Hanoi government, invaded the country in response to a series of cross-border attacks and massacres in the Mekong Delta by the Khmer Rouge. The invasion forced the Khmer Rouge into the hills bordering Thailand, where they remained entrenched and fighting for years. United Nations–brokered peace accords were signed in 1991. International mediation allowed the return of Norodom Sihanouk as king and the formation of a coalition government that included Khmer Rouge elements after parliamentary elections in 1993. But civil war continued.

RECONCILIATION AND RECOVERY?

In 1997 Second Prime Minister Hun Sen toppled First Prime Minister Norodom Ranariddh in a coup. During the following year's national elections, Hun Sen won a plurality and formed a new government, despite charges of election rigging. Pol Pot died in his mountain stronghold in April 1998, and the remaining Khmer Rouge elements lost any influence they still had.

It has taken years for the United Nations and the Cambodian government to establish a tribunal that will bring to justice the few surviving key leaders of the Khmer Rouge regime. Proceedings began in 2007, but only one former Khmer Rouge leader (Duch, the infamous head of Tuol Sleng) is in jail; Ta Mok, the so-called Butcher, was the only other Khmer Rouge leader to be imprisoned, but he died in 2006. The others remain free; many have blended with ease into current society, and some remain in the folds of the Cambodian government.

Foreign investment and the development of tourism have been very strong in recent years, but it remains to be seen whether domestic problems can truly be solved by Prime Minister Hun Sen (a former Khmer Rouge commander) and his hard-line rule.

Psar Thmei. The largest market in Phnom Penh, popularly known as the Central Market, is an art-deco-style structure in the center of the city that sells foodstuffs, household goods, fake antiques, and some silver and gold jewelry. You're expected to bargain—start off by offering half the named price and you'll probably end up paying about 70%. Take your time to find what you want as the vendors can be pushy. It's busiest in the morning. ⊠ *Blvd. 128 (Kampuchea Krom), at St. 76 and Neayok Souk St.*

Psar Tuol Tom Pong. A popular location for discovering some of the best bargains in town, the Psar Tuol Tom Pong, or Russian Market, next to Wat Tuol Tom Pong, sells a great variety of Cambodian handicrafts, traditional Krama scarves, Khmer wood carvings, baskets, knockoff electronics, and much more. ⊠ *Sts. 155 and 440.*

SILK

Kravanh House. This shop has one of the city's best selections of raw silk and silk products. Land-mine victims and their families work closely with this outlet. ⊠ *13 St. 178* ☎ *012/731770, 023/990195.*

Sayon Silkworks. Offering employment to impoverished women from remote regions, Sayon Silkworks has a fine collection of silk accessories, quilts, and other home elements, such as cushions and bolsters, in exquisite colors and patterns. ⊠ *40 St. 178* ☎ *023/990219* ⊕ *www. sayonsilkworks.com.*

Silk & Pepper. Choose from made-to-order clothing, jewelry, gifts, and home accessories from this interesting fair-trade establishment in the heart of Phnom Penh. They are serious about their silks, and source only the best materials, crafted with the age-old ikat Cambodian weaving technique. ⊠ *33 St. 178* ☎ *012/851234, 023/222692* ⊕ *www. silkandpepper.com.*

TONLE BATI

33 km (20 miles) south of Phnom Penh.

On weekends Phnom Penh residents head for this small lake a half-hour drive south on Highway 2. It has a beach with refreshment stalls and souvenir stands. Note that you'll encounter many beggars and children clamoring for attention here. The nearby, but more remote **Ta Phrom**, a 12th-century temple built around the time of Siem Reap's Angkor Thom and Bayon, is less chaotic. The five-chambered laterite temple has several well-preserved Hindu and Buddhist bas-reliefs. Nearby is an attractive, smaller temple, **Yeah Peau.** Both temples are free and open to the public at all times. Phnom Tamao, Cambodia's leading zoo, is about 11 km (7 miles) farther south, but it's not worth a detour.

GETTING HERE AND AROUND

Hiring a car and driver in Phnom Penh is perhaps the easiest way to visit Tonle Bati, and if you do this, you can easily combine the trip with Phnom Chisor. The drive takes about 30 minutes. Nearly hourly GST and Neak Krorhorm buses head to Tonle Bati. Buses drop you within walking distance of the lake, but there are also moto-taxis available.

Diethelm Travel *(Essentials in Phnom Penh)* arranges tours to Tonle Bati.

PHNOM CHISOR

55 km (34 miles) south of Phnom Penh.

A trip to Phnom Chisor is worth the drive just for the view from the top of the hill of the same name. There's a road to the summit, but most visitors prefer the 20-minute walk to the top, where stunning vistas of the Cambodian countryside unfold. At the summit the 11th-century temple, which is free and open to the public, is a Khmer masterpiece of laterite, brick, and sandstone.

GETTING HERE AND AROUND

Though the (decent) bus ride is cheap, you can combine Tonle Bati and Phnom Chisor in one trip if you hire a car and driver (about $50 per day), perhaps the easiest way to visit Phnom Chisor. The drive takes about 20 minutes from Tonle Bati or 40 minutes from Phnom Penh. Takeo-bound GST and Neak Krorhorm buses (departing from Phnom Penh every hour) stop at Prasat Neang Khmau; from there you can hire a moto to take you up the hill. The whole trip should take no more than an hour.

Diethelm Travel *(See Essentials in Phnom Penh)* and Hanuman Travel *(See Cambodia Planner)* arrange tours to Phnom Chisor.

KOH DACH

30 km (19 miles) north of Phnom Penh.

This Mekong River island's main attractions are its beach and its handicrafts community of silk weavers, wood carvers, potters, painters, and jewelry makers. The beach isn't spectacular by Southeast Asian standards, but it is convenient for Phnom Penh getaways. In all, the trip over to the island is quick; most people spend about half a day on this excursion, but you can dwell longer if you want a relaxing beach day.

GETTING HERE AND AROUND

Any tuk-tuk or moto driver can take you to Koh Dach from Phnom Penh. Alternatively, you can hire a car and driver for the day (about $50 per day). The trip takes approximately two hours each way, and involves a ferry trip to the island.

Diethelm Travel *(See Essentials in Phnom Penh)* and Hanuman Travel *(See Cambodia Planner)* arrange tours to Koh Dach.

UDONG

45 km (28 miles) north of Phnom Penh.

This small town served as the Khmer capital from the early 1600s until 1866, when King Norodom moved the capital south to Phnom Penh. Today it's an important pilgrimage destination for Cambodians paying homage to their former kings. You can join them on the climb to the pagoda-studded hilltop, site of the revered Vihear Prah Ath Roes assembly hall, which still bears the scars of local conflicts from the Khmer Rouge era.

GETTING HERE AND AROUND

Udong is best reached by catching a GST or Neak Krorhorm bus to Kampong Chhnang from the Central Bus Station and getting off at the junction at the Km 37 mark. Motos and tuk-tuks will then take you to the temples. The bus costs around $1.

You can also take a boat from Phnom Penh; this can be arranged through your hotel or any travel agent.

Diethelm Travel, Exotissimo *(Essentials in Phnom Penh)*, and Hanuman Travel *(Cambodia Planner)* arrange tours to Udong.

NORTH OF PHNOM PENH

If you're looking to go even farther afield, you can visit the ancient ruins of Kampong Thom or Kampong Cham; see highly endangered freshwater Irrawaddy dolphins at Kratie; or head to the remote and largely undeveloped provinces of Ratanakkiri or Mondulkiri, both of which offer trekking opportunities among hill tribes. The city of Battambang (Cambodia's second largest) may be closer to Siem Reap on the map, but Phnom Penh is the logical jumping-off point for a visit there. Note that many of these destinations are quite removed from one another or accessed via different routes, and thus can't be combined in one tour. ■TIP→ During rainy season the road to Ratanakkiri can be tricky to navigate.

KAMPONG CHAM

125 km (78 miles) northeast of Phnom Penh.

Cambodia's third-largest city was also an ancient Khmer center of culture and power on the Mekong River, and it has a pre-Angkorian temple, **Wat Nokor.** (Sadly, the temple itself is in a state of disrepair and the $2 entry fee unmerited.) Just outside town are the twin temple-topped hills, Phnom Pros and Phnom Srei (included in the price). Ask a local guide to explain the interesting legend surrounding their creation. In the ecotourism village of Cheungkok, about 5 km (3 miles) south of town, you can see silk making, carving, and other traditional crafts in progress and also buy the wares directly from villagers. All profits are reinvested in the village.

Kampong Cham can be visited in a few hours, but with Cheungkok it is an all-day trip.

GETTING HERE AND AROUND

You can get to Kampong Cham from Phnom Penh by taxi or bus; the trip takes about three hours. Any guesthouse or hotel can arrange for a taxi. Expect to pay $6 for a single bus ticket and $50 for a taxi from Phnom Penh. The buses (GST, Hua Lian Mekong Express, and Neak Krorhorm) leave hourly from the bus station at the Central Market.

WHERE TO EAT AND STAY

Kampong Cham has the usual local food stalls and shophouses, but few restaurants of note.

$ CAMBODIAN 🍴 **Smile.** Buddhism for Social Development Action runs this experiential training restaurant. Even so, the dining experience (Khmer and western, leaning heavily towards Italian, food served) on the whole is better than many professional setups. The dining area is spacious, lime green and white, and cooled by overhead fans. Meals can also be enjoyed outside in front of the restaurant with open views onto the Mekong River. [$] *Average main: $3* ✉ *6 Mort Tunle St. (aka Riverside St.)* ☎ *017/997709* 🌐 *www.bsda-cambodia.org.*

$ HOTEL 🏨 **Monorom VIP Hotel.** The heavy, sculpted wooden furniture and ruffled curtains of the large rooms may be too much for some, but it's apparent that the owners of this hotel have made a real effort to create a pleasant and polished environment. **Pros:** central, riverside location; comfortable beds; nice views. **Cons:** bored, inattentive staff; no breakfast; not all rooms have views. [$] *Rooms from: $20* ✉ *Mort Tunle St. (aka Riverside St.)* ☎ *097/733–2526, 092/777102* 🌐 *www.monoromviphotel.com* 🛏 *50 rooms, 1 suite* 🍽 *Breakfast.*

$ B&B/INN FAMILY 🏨 **Rana.** Rana offers a one-of-a-kind, well-organized experiential homestay for adults or families in the Cambodian countryside. **Pros:** unique window into local life; culturally educational; friendly owners. **Cons:** doesn't accept lone travelers; two-night minimum stay; a certain level of fitness is required for the activities; no electricity or running water. [$] *Rooms from: $25* ✉ *Srey Siam* ☎ *012/686240* 🌐 *rana-ruralhomestay-cambodia.webs.com* 💳 *No credit cards* 🛏 *2 rooms* 🍽 *Some meals.*

KOMPONG THOM RUINS

160 km (99 miles) north of Phnom Penh.

These ruins, exactly halfway between Phnom Penh and Siem Reap, are even older than those at Angkor. They are all that remain of the 7th-century Sambor Prei Kuk, the capital of Zhen La, a loose federation of city-states. The ruins, which are free and open to the public at all times, are near the Stung Sen River, 35 km (22 miles) northeast of the provincial town of Kampong.

GETTING HERE AND AROUND

The ruins are a day trip by taxi from Siem Reap (two hours; $50) or Phnom Penh (three hours; also $50, or $10 per person, shared). The journey can be dusty and hot in the dry season and muddy and wet in the rainy season. You can catch a bus to the town of Kompong Thom from Siem Reap ($5) or Phnom Penh ($5), and arrange local transportation via tuk-tuk or moto (about $25 for the full tour of the ruins).

KRATIE

340 km (217 miles) northeast of Phnom Penh.

Kratie is famous for the colony of freshwater Irrawaddy dolphins that inhabits the Mekong River some 15 km (9 miles) north of town. ■ **TIP→ The dolphins are most active in the early morning and late afternoon.** Taxis and hired cars with driver from Kratie charge about $10 for the journey to the stretch of river where the dolphins can be observed. You will likely have to hire a local boatman to take you to where the dolphins are, as they move up and down the river.

GETTING HERE AND AROUND

Several bus companies from Phnom Penh's Central Bus Station offer regular service to Kratie (six to seven hours; $10). Expect delays in the wet season. You can also get a shared taxi or hire your own driver, but as always buses are a far safer option.

Diethelm Travel *(Essentials in Phnom Penh)* arranges tours to Kratie.

WHERE TO EAT AND STAY

Kratie has an abundance of local food shops. Most guesthouses have simple menus, and there is a lively food-stall scene in town.

$ ✕ **Tokae Restaurant.** Next to Kratie's busy marketplace, this is one of the
CAMBODIAN   better places to eat in town. The kitchen provides decent and inexpensive traditional Khmer fare, catering to a mostly tourist clientele, and the staff is cheerful and efficient. $ *Average main: $3* ⊠ *10 St.*

$$ 🖼 **Rajabori Villas Resort.** After the long bus or taxi trip to Kratie, it is
RESORT   another 20 minutes by boat and tuk-tuk to get to Rajabori Villas Resort, so getting here is not for the fainthearted, but those who do make the extra effort will enjoy a stay in a traditional Khmer bungalow on the isolated island of Koh Trong. **Pros:** cheap bike rentals for exploring the island; peaceful location (no cars); nature all around. **Cons:** food and drinks on the expensive side; getting to and from the resort can be challenging. $ *Rooms from: $50* ⊠ *Koh Trong* ☎ *012/770150, 012/959115* ⊕ *www.rajabori-kratie.com* ⇱ *15 bungalows* ⏵◯⏴ *Breakfast.*

RATANAKKIRI PROVINCE

Ban Lung is 635 km (395 miles) northeast of Phnom Penh.

Both Ratanakkiri and neighboring Mondulkiri provinces are mountainous and once covered with dense jungle, which is rapidly giving way to mainly rubber plantations, and together they are home to 12 different Khmer Loeu ethnic-minority groups. The government has developed four community-based projects in the region. The eventual aim is to reinvent large sections of the area as ecotourism destinations, making them self-sufficient and helping the communities reduce the impact on the natural resources.

GETTING HERE AND AROUND

From Phnom Penh there's daily bus service to Ban Lung (12-plus hours; $10) on GST bus lines. The journey is much improved from a few years ago with the opening of the resurfaced road, but construction is still ongoing. Minibuses are faster and only a little more expensive ($13). There are no scheduled flights available, but charter companies do the trip regularly; visit any travel agent for details. Share-taxis are always an option, but not the most attractive one—it's an arduous drive.

Diethelm Travel *(Essentials in Phnom Penh)* arranges tours to Ratanakkiri.

In Ban Lung you can hire a jeep with a driver-guide or, if you're very adventurous, rent a motorcycle, to visit the fascinating destinations an hour or two away.

CLOSE UP

Religion in Cambodia

As in neighboring Thailand, Laos, and Vietnam, Buddhism is the predominant religion in Cambodia. But animism and superstition continue to play strong roles in Khmer culture and society. Many people believe in powerful *neak ta,* or territorial guardian spirits. Spirit shrines are common in Khmer houses as well as on temple grounds and along roadsides. The Khmer Loeu hill tribes, who live in the remote mountain areas of Ratanakkiri and Mondulkiri provinces, and some tribes of the Cardamom Mountains are pure animists, believing in spirits living in trees, rocks, and water.

The main layer of Cambodian religion is a mix of Hinduism and Buddhism. These two religions reached the country from India about 2,000 years ago and played a pivotal role in the social and ideological life of the earliest kingdoms. Buddhism flourished in Cambodia in the 12th to 13th century, when King Jayavarman VII embraced Mahayana Buddhism. By the 15th century, influenced by Buddhist monks from Siam and Sri Lanka, most Cambodians practiced Theravada Buddhism.

Cambodian religious literature and royal classical dance draw on Hindu models, such as the *Reamker,* an ancient epic about an Indian prince searching for his abducted wife and fighting an evil king. Brahman priests still play an important role at court rituals.

Cambodia's Muslim Chams, who number a few hundred thousand, are the descendants of the Champa Kingdom that was based in what is today Vietnam. They have had a presence in this area since the 15th century, when they were forced from the original kingdom. The country's 60,000 Roman Catholics are mainly ethnic Vietnamese. A small Chinese minority follows Taoism.

8

EXPLORING

Ratanakkiri Province is remote, but it is slowly building a reputation as an ecotourism destination, and the government is trying hard to promote tourism to this part of Cambodia. Intrepid travelers will find natural and cultural attractions, including waterfalls, jungle treks, lakes, and villages.

Ban Lung. The provincial capital is a small, sleepy town that holds a certain romance as a far-flung capital, away from the influence of Phnom Penh, but otherwise offers little more than slow-paced local life and clouds of red dust in the dry season—or mud in the wet season. Arrive with everything you need, as western goods are sometimes difficult to obtain. Most of the decent hotels are located around Kan Seng lake.

Bokeo. A visit to the gem mines of the Bokeo area, 30 km (20 miles) east of Ban Lung, can be arranged through your hotel, or any moto driver in Ban Lung can take you there. Some of the mines are increasingly deep, claustrophobic, man-sized potholes, and mining is for semiprecious stones such as zircon. As you drive through the villages in the area, the villagers line up to sell you their finds. *Bokeo* literally means "gem mine."

Virachey National Park. This lush and scenic jungle, 35 km (22 miles) northeast of Ban Lung, is home to the two-tiered Bu Sra Waterfall and lots of wildlife. Tuk-tuks and motos will take you there from Ban Lung ($15), but all treks and eco-activities should be prearranged in Ban Lung at the park's visitor information center. The best way to discover the area and possibly spot some of the ever dwindling rare species found there is through one of the local tour operators, who can arrange two- to seven-day trips. A tour is best arranged through your hotel. ✉ *Banlung* 🎫 *$5.*

FAMILY Fodor's Choice ★ **Yeak Laom Lake.** Lodged in a volcanic crater 5 km (3 miles) east of Ban Lung, this mystical lake, bordered by jungle, is sacred to many of the Khmer Loeu hill tribes. It's a half mile in diameter and 154 feet deep, and there are three wooden jetties from which to launch yourself into the cool waters. Swing from a hammock in one of the wooden huts lining the shore—these cost $3 to rent for the day, but if you order food it's free. The local specialty is *prung,* bamboo stuffed with vegetables, meat, and local herbs and spices which is cooked over an open fire. Stalls at the entrance sell jungle honey, as well as the usual kramas and other craftwork cloths. Take a tuk-tuk ($3) or moto from Ban Lung. ✉ *Banlung* 🎫 *$1.50* 🕑 *7–6.*

WHERE TO EAT AND STAY

$ INTERNATIONAL 🍴 **Gecko House Restaurant.** Asian dishes such as curries, sweet-and sour chicken and salads, and western fare such as burgers and sandwiches are decent, if not outstanding. The quirkily contemporary restaurant (check out the gravel floor) turns into a fun bar serving refreshing ice-cold beers most nights of the week, and there is free, speedy Wi-Fi. [$] *Average main: $4* ✉ *Banlung* ☎ *012/422228* 💳 *No credit cards.*

$$ HOTEL 🏨 **Terres Rouge Lodge and Restaurant.** The former residence of the governor of Ratanakiri Province has been transformed into a scenic resort with a beautifully landscaped tropical garden. **Pros:** spacious rooms, some with lake views; beautiful, colonial building; good restaurant and bar. **Cons:** sporadic service; some rooms are showing a little wear and tear; noise from nearby construction sites. [$] *Rooms from: $75* ✉ *Boeung Kan Siang Lake, Banlung* ☎ *012/770650* 🌐 *www.ratanakiri-lodge.com* 🛏 *22 rooms, 7 suites* 🍽 *Breakfast.*

$ B&B/INN 🏨 **Yaklom Hill Lodge.** This popular lodge has an eco-friendly philosophy and offers clean, well-maintained wooden cottages and a traditional hill tribe house in a jungle setting about 5 km (3 miles) outside the city. **Pros:** lush natural location; friendly staff; ecological (off the grid); some lodging options good for families or groups of up to eight people. **Cons:** no hot water most of the day; basic facilities only; definitely off the beaten track. [$] *Rooms from: $15* ✉ *Rd. 78, Banlung* ☎ *011/790510* 🌐 *yaklom.blogspot.com* 💳 *No credit cards* 🛏 *15 cottages, 1 house* 🍽 *Breakfast.*

BATTAMBANG

290 km (180 miles) northwest of Phnom Penh.

Cambodia's second-largest city straddles the Sanker River in the center of the country's rice bowl. Dusty Battambang is bypassed by most visitors to Cambodia, but it's an interesting city to explore. ■**TIP➔ The French left their mark here with some fine old buildings, more than you'll find in most Cambodian cities these days.**

GETTING HERE AND AROUND

All the major bus companies depart daily from Phnom Penh's Central Market to Battambang (five hours; $5–$9), and in some cases, on to Poipet. For the more adventurous, lovely but lengthy boat trips are a good option. The ride to Siem Reap can take anywhere between 5 and 10 hours ($20). A hired car with a driver costs about $50 a day, but settle on the price before setting off.

TOURS

Capitol Tours. Covering most of Cambodia, this company offers interesting tour packages, including temple excursions, river rides, and bird-watching. ⊠ *739 La Ae St., near Boeung Chhouk Market* ☎ *053/953040, 092/277561* ⊕ *www.capitoltourscambodia.com* ⊠ *From $35.*

EXPLORING

The few sights to see in and around town include some Angkor-era temple ruins and the Khmer Rouge "killing caves." The town is walkable, and strolling down to the river in the evening is a pleasant way to pass the time.

Phnom Banan. In the countryside 25 km (15 miles) south from the city, this 11th-century hilltop temple has five impressive towers and is sometimes referred to as "the mini Angkor Wat." Reaching the temple involves a hike up 350 or so steps. Tuk-tuks from Battambang charge $10–$15 for the round-trip. There is a mystical little cave round the side of the hill whose waters are supposed to induce visions. ⊠ *Banan Hill* ⊠ *$2.*

Phnom Sampeou. In addition to being the site of a temple, this hill, 10 km (7 miles) southwest of Battambang, was also used by the Khmer Rouge to execute prisoners in a group of killing caves. In one, which contains the skeletal remains of some of the victims, you can stand on the eerily dark floor and look up to a hole in the cave roof, with sunlight streaming through. The Khmer Rouge reportedly pushed their victims through that hole to their deaths on the rocks below. ⊠ *Hwy. 57.*

Psar Nath Market. Like most local markets, this is a great spot to buy fresh foods, and it's also known for gems and Battambang's famous fruit—lime-green oranges. Its vendors also sell everything from cheesy souvenirs to electronics imported from China. Some stalls have textiles, but most of these are imported. ⊠ *On the Sangker River* ☎ ☉ *Daily 7–5 (some stalls stay open later).*

Wat Ek Phnom. Long before the French arrived, Battambang was an important Khmer city, and among its many temples is this 11th-century Angkorian structure. Even though it was heavily looted, the temple still has a few fine stone carvings in excellent condition. In front of the ruins stands a newly built pagoda. It's 10 km (7 miles) north of the city and getting here via tuk-tuk or moto will cost around $10; negotiate a price before you leave. ⊠ *St. 1734* ⊠ *$2.*

8

WHERE TO EAT AND STAY

There's a good selection of restaurants in town, including some western cuisine. The places to eat here are all at the lower end of the price range. A Khmer food market down by the river is open in the late afternoon or early evening.

$ ✕ **Coconut Restaurant.** Well-presented, modern Khmer cuisine is lovingly
CAMBODIAN   prepared here by chef Lyly. Fronted by a garden, the restaurant, west of the Phsa Nat, its on the upscale side, but still has the feel of a local Cambodian restaurant, with warm and very attentive staff. Every dish is prepared to order, so be prepared for a wait while it cooks. The traditional amok (seafood curry) is one of the best in town, and the spring rolls are fresh and crispy. Coconut Restaurant also hosts super cooking classes ($10), either in the morning or afternoon—attendees get to go to the local market to source ingredients and then learn how to make four traditional Cambodian dishes. $ *Average main: $3* ⊠ *St. 111* ☏ *016/399339.*

$$ ⌂ **Battambang Resort.** A small paradise, this tranquil resort has a lush
RESORT   garden where you can relax in a hammock among exotic fruit trees
Fodor's Choice   and organically grown herbs, flowers, and vegetables, all used by its
★   restaurant to create healthy Asian and European dishes. **Pros:** friendly service; holistic concept; lovely pool; free use of bikes; free pickup and daily shuttle service to and from Battambang. **Cons:** a little out of the way; marriage venue nearby can be noisy; bring mosquito repellent. $ *Rooms from: $70* ⊠ *Wat Ko Village* ☏ *012/510100, 053/666–7001* ⊕ *www.battambangresort.com* ⤻ *10 rooms* ⟊ *Breakfast.*

$ ⌂ **Chez Sam.** This inn is very like a homestay, offering guests the oppor-
B&B/INN   tunity to get to know the goings-on of the local community through activities and tours guided by the gracious and knowledgeable host. **Pros:** an unique local experience; well located; tasty Khmer food. **Cons:** only three rooms; no shower or toilet in room; not all rooms have air-conditioning; 8 am breakfast, to allow for early start to tours. $ *Rooms from: $35* ⊠ *4 Groupe 1 Pong Preah Beit Tchan, Sangkat* ☏ *077/875911, 078/670357* ⊕ *samsguesthouse.wordpress.com* ⊟ *No credit cards* ⤻ *3 rooms* ⟊ *Breakfast.*

$$ ⌂ **La Villa.** This boutique hotel is in a beautifully restored 1930s colonial
HOTEL   house, with well-maintained, spacious rooms that have an old-world charm and quaint art-deco feel. **Pros:** beautiful architecture; lovely riverfront location; large, clean pool. **Cons:** not many facilities; service can lack attention to detail. $ *Rooms from: $75* ⊠ *185 Pom Romchek 5 Kom, Rattanak Commune* ☏ *017/411880, 053/730151* ⊕ *www.lavilla-battambang.net* ⤻ *3 rooms, 4 suites* ⟊ *Breakfast.*

SIEM REAP AND ANGKOR TEMPLE COMPLEX

The temples of Angkor, hailed as "the eighth wonder of the world" by some, constitute one of the world's great ancient sites and Southeast Asia's most impressive archaeological treasure. The massive structures, surrounded by tropical forest, are comparable to Central America's Mayan ruins—and far exceed them in size. Angkor Wat is the world's largest religious structure—so large that it's hard to describe

DID YOU KNOW?

The roots that creep over the ruins of Ta Prohm belong to either silk-cotton trees or thinner strangler fig trees. Strangler figs grow out of crevices in other trees, sometimes smothering their hosts over time.

its breadth to someone who hasn't seen it. And that's just one temple in a complex of hundreds.

Siem Reap was once a small, provincial town known only for the nearby Angkor ruins. Today it's a world-famous tourism hub critical to the Cambodian economy.

It's well worth spinning through the countryside around Siem Reap to get a feel for the way Cambodian farmers and fishermen live. Take a day to tour floating villages, some of the outlying temples, or Kulen Mountain, a sacred place for modern Cambodians, with tremendous views. Naturalists won't be sorry with a trip to see the birdlife at Prek Toal, near Tonle Sap, especially when birds are nesting (November or December). Local guesthouses and tour companies can arrange most trips.

SIEM REAP

315 km (195 miles) north of Phnom Penh.

Siem Reap, which means "Siam defeated," based on a 15th-century battle with Cambodia's neighbors to the west, has emerged as a modern, friendly, and elegantly low-key city with highly sophisticated shopping, dining, and nightlife options. After a long day at the Angkor Temple Complex, you'll be happy to spend your evening strolling along the Siem Reap River, and dining at an outdoor table on a back alley in the hip old French quarter or Alley West off the more boisterous Pub Street, which is closed to traffic in the evening.

The Old Market area is a big draw and the perfect place to shop for souvenirs; dig through the silk, wood, and silver ornaments and accessories and you may find your treasure. Many of the colonial buildings in the area were destroyed during the Khmer Rouge years, but many others have been restored and turned into world-class resorts and restaurants.

You could spend an entire afternoon in the Old Market area, wandering from shop to shop, café to café, gallery to gallery. It changes every month, with ever more delights in store. Long gone are the days when high-end souvenirs (the legal kind) came from Thailand. Today numerous shops offer high-quality Cambodian silks, Kampot pepper and other Cambodian spices, and herbal soaps and toiletries made from natural Cambodian products.

GETTING HERE AND AROUND

AIR TRAVEL   Angkor Air has five daily flights from Phnom Penh to Siem Reap costing about $100 each way and taking 40–45 minutes. Vietnam Airlines have five direct flights daily to and from Hanoi's Noibai Airport ($160 each way) and six daily flights direct to and from Ho Chi Minh City ($145 each way). There are also daily charter flights, which may offer a cheaper alternative.

Royal Khmer Airlines and Angkor Air fly between Phnom Penh and Siem Reap (one hour; from $65 and up one way). Siem Reap International Airport is 6 km (4 miles) northwest of town. The taxi fare to any hotel in Siem Reap is $5.

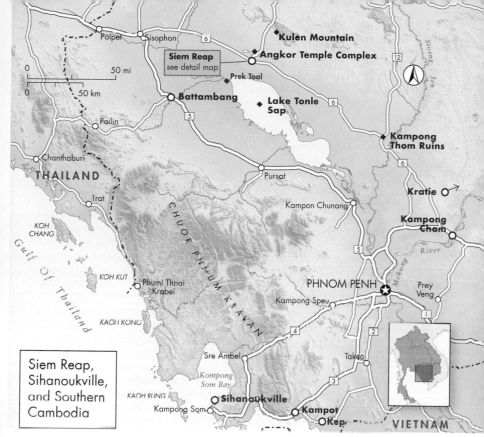

Siem Reap,
Sihanoukville,
and Southern
Cambodia

BOAT TRAVEL The road to Phnom Penh was upgraded several years ago, but some tourists still prefer the six-hour boat trip on the Tonle Sap. High-speed ferries, or "bullet boats," depart from Phnom Penh for Siem Reap daily.

A daily boat travels from Battambang to Siem Reap (5 to 10 hours; $20) on the Tonle Sap. ■**TIP→ In the dry season, the water level on the Tonle Sap is often low. Passengers may be required to switch boats, or boats might get stuck—a long ordeal.**

Boats arrive at the ferry port at Chong Khneas, 12 km (7½ miles) south of Siem Reap.

BUS TRAVEL Siem Reap is accessible by direct bus from Phnom Penh (five to six hours; $5 to $13) on all major lines.

Travel agencies can help you arrange all bus trips.

CAR TRAVEL The road to Siem Reap from Phnom Penh has greatly improved in recent years, and the trip by taxi takes four hours. However, you'll be putting your life in the hands of daredevil drivers with little care for the rules of the road or the function of the brake pedal. Take the bus instead.

MOTO AND
TUK-TUK
TRAVEL

Tuk-tuk and moto drivers have kept apace with the growing number of tourists visiting Siem Reap: they'll find you—you won't need to find them. They charge about $1 to $3 for a trip within town, but be sure to settle on the fare before setting off. There are no cruising taxis, but hotels can order one.

TOURS

FAMILY

Beyond Unique Escapes. Temple tours, village trips, cooking classes, and a lot, lot more are offered by this tour operator, and it also runs the local NGO Husk, which has a real and positive impact on local communities. ⊠ *St. 8, at corner Sivartha Blvd. and Pub St.* ☎ *077/562565, 063/969269* ⊕ *www.beyonduniqueescapes.com* ⊑ *From $25.*

IndochinEx. Bespoke ecotourism options are offered throughout Cambodia by this company whose partners are conservationists and expert explorers. Many of the employees here previously worked for oSmoSe and other conservation groups and this has become the preferred tour operator for all the established high-end hotels. A tour with IndochinEx will be a highlight of your trip to Siem Reap. ⊠ *Siem Reap* ☎ *092/650096* ⊕ *www.indochineex.com* ⊑ *From $65.*

FAMILY
Fodor'sChoice
★

oSmoSe Conservation Ecotourism Education. An agent of positive change in the area, oSmoSe, a nonprofit organization, has been fighting to conserve the unique biosphere of Tonle Sap and Prek Toal. By reeducating local villagers from poachers to protectors of the environment that sustains them and also lobbying against big commercial interests that have been involved in short-term exploitation of the ecosystem, they have successfully helped reharmonize many aspects of human-nature coexistence. On their exceptional tours you get to bird-watch at the bird sanctuary with an expert guide and also experience floating villages in a fascinating and respectful way. ⊠ *Sala Kamroeuk, close to Wat Damnak* ☎ *012/832812, 063/765506* ⊕ *www.osmosetonlesap. net* ⊑ *From $105.*

EXPLORING

Siem Reap is the base to use for exploring the temples at Angkor, but it has more to offer than that. It has its own great places to see, and there is something seductive about this city that makes visitors want to linger. You can wander around the contemporary Angkor National Museum, take a cooking class, visit a rural village, explore myriad art galleries, try a gourmet restaurant, or take a stroll down the central Pub Street. There's plenty to keep the temple-weary traveler occupied for two or three days, or even a week or more.

ANGKOR TEMPLE COMPLEX

Fodor'sChoice
★

Angkor Wat. *See the highlighted feature in this chapter.* ⊠ *6 km (4 miles) north of Siem Reap* ⊑ *$20 for one day; $40 for 3 consecutive days; $60 for a week* ☉ *Daily 5:30 am–6 pm.*

SIEM REAP

Fodor'sChoice
★

Angkor National Museum. This modern, interactive museum, which opened in 2008, gracefully guides you through the rise and fall of the Angkorian Empires, covering the religions, kings, and geopolitics that drove the Khmer to create the monumental cities whose ruins are highly visible in modern day Cambodia. With more than 1,300 artifacts on glossy display, complemented by multimedia installations, this museum experience helps demystify much of the material culture that visitors encounter at the archaeological parks and sites. The atmosphere is set in the impressive gallery of a thousand Buddhas, which plunges you into the serene spirituality that still dominates the region. Seven consequent galleries, set up chronologically, highlight the Funan and Chenia pre-Angkorian epochs, followed by the golden age of the Angkorian period led by the likes of King Soryavarman II, who built Angkor Wat. The final two galleries showcase stone inscriptions documenting some of the workings of the empires, and statues of Apsara, shedding light on the cult and fashions of these celestial dancers. The audio tour is excellent and well worth the extra $3. ⊠ *968, Vithei Charles de Gaulle, Khrum 6, Phoum Salakanseng, Khom Svaydangum* ☎ *063/966601* ⊕ *www.angkornationalmuseum.com* 🖾 *$12* ⊗ *Daily 8:30–6 (to 6:30 Oct.–Mar.).*

Cambodia Land Mine Museum. Be sure to visit this museum, established by Akira, a former child soldier who fought for the Khmer Rouge, the Vietnamese, and the Cambodian Army. Now he dedicates his life to removing the land mines he and thousands of others laid across Cambodia. His museum is a must-see, a sociopolitical eye-opener that portrays a different picture of Cambodia from the glorious temples and five-star hotels. Any tuk-tuk or taxi driver can find the museum. When in the Old Market area, visit the Akira Mine Action Gallery for more information on land mines and ways to help land-mine victims go to college. ■**TIP→** As it is a decent distance from Siem Reap, it's best to combine this with a visit to the Banteay Srey Temple complex. ⊹ *Off road to Angkor, 6 km (4 miles) south of Banteay Srey Temple, 25 km (15 miles) from Siem Reap* ☎ *015/674163* ⊕ *www.cambodialandminemuseum.org* 🖾 *$5* ⊗ *Daily 7:30–5:30.*

WHERE TO EAT

$$$$
INTERNATIONAL

✕ **Abacus.** Ideal for a romantic garden dinner or a fun, elegant night out with friends, Abacus offers an eclectic choice of French-international fusion cuisine. Through a weekly changing menu presented on a giant blackboard, chefs and co-owners Renaud and Pascal combine their creative talents and refined expertise to provide a high quality, welcome change from traditional restaurants or bland hotel fare. Regulars swear by the juicy Abacus burger, but there are always plenty of options to suit any taste or disposition. The restaurant also has a bar that welcomes guests for an aperitif or an after-dinner digestif. [$] *Average main: $17* ⊠ *Off Rd. 6* ⊹ *Take Rd. 6 toward the airport, pass Angkor Hotel, and turn right at ACLEDA Bank. After 100 meters turn left* ☎ *063/763660, 012/644286* ⊕ *cafeabacus.com* ⊗ *Closed June and 1 week in mid-Apr.* ⚎ *Reservations essential.*

$$$$
BISTRO FRENCH

✕ **Armand.** This is a chic little French bistro-bar that harks back to 1930s Paris, and it's set to become a hot spot in Siem Reap. It follows on from the success of the original Armand, a mainstay of Phnom Penh's dining scene, but here there are unique influences from all three partners. The manager is also a designer, and created a space inspired by Balthazars in New York and the sharp staff uniforms; another partner has a vineyard in France's Dordogne region, so the wine selection is excellent, and they

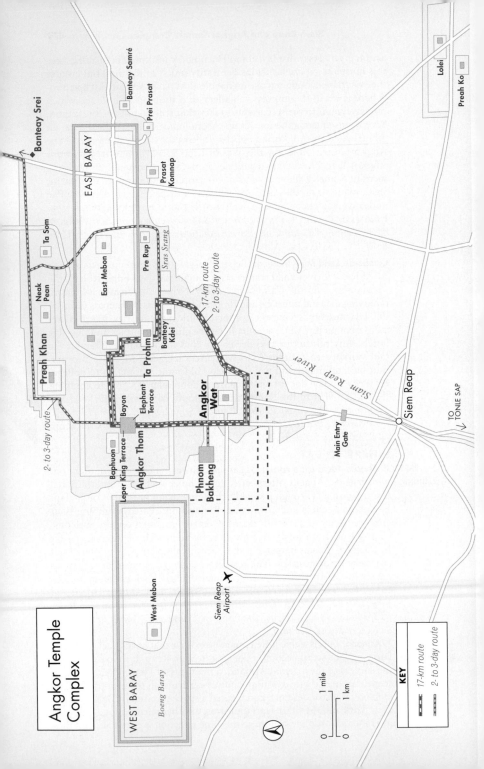

Angkor Temple Complex

KEY

- 17-km route
- 2- to 3-day route

Banteay Srei

EAST BARAY

Banteay Samré
Prei Prasat

Prasat Komnap

Lolei

Preah Ko

Ta Som

Neak Pean

East Mebon

Pre Rup

Sras Srang

17-km route

2- to 3-day route

Preah Khan

2- to 3-day route

Banteay Kdei

Ta Prohm

Baphuon

Bayon

Elephant Terrace

Leper King Terrace

Angkor Thom

Angkor Wat

Phnom Bakheng

Siam Reap River

Main Entry Gate

Siem Reap

TO TONLE SAP

Siem Reap Airport

WEST BARAY

West Mebon

Boeng Baray

1 mile

1 km

0
0

have the best house wine around. The stamp of Armand himself ensures that the place oozes charm and character. Come here for fine French cuisine and classic cocktails. $ *Average main: $18* ⊠ *586 Tep Vong St.* ☎ *095/684130* ⊘ *No lunch.*

$$$$
ECLECTIC
Fodor's Choice
★

✕ **Cuisine Wat Damnak.** One of the most unique restaurants in Siem Reap, Cuisine Wat Damnak offers a real journey for the taste buds with its five- or six-course set menus (the only options available). Beyond the apparent ambition for trendy sophistication in the indoor sala and romantic garden, the concept here is Cambodian food remodeled into creative modern dishes by French chef Joannes Riviere. Exclusively local, fresh, and seasonal ingredients are a top priority for Riviere, whose knowledge of the area allows him to source ingredients that are otherwise not easy to come by, such as shellfish unique to the Mekong and Tonle Sap lake, fresh lotus seeds, wild lily stems, and edible flowers. ■ TIP➜ If you're interested in learning more about Riviere's culinary philosophy and techniques, you can buy a copy of his cookbook here. $ *Average main: $24* ⊠ *Chocolate Rd., between Psa Dey Hoy market and Angkor High School, Sala Kamreuk Commune* ☎ *077/347762* ⊕ *www.cuisinewatdamnak.com* ⊘ *Closed Sun., Mon., and Apr. No lunch* ⚐ *Reservations essential.*

$$
ITALIAN

✕ **Il Forno.** Considered the best Italian restaurant in Siem Reap, Il Forno offers an enjoyable change from the Southeast Asian delights on offer at every turn. Just off Pub Street and near the Old Market, this "little corner of Italy" uses its Neapolitan wood-fire oven to make delicious pizza and calzone specialties. An authentic variety of pasta dishes, platters for one or for sharing, and *primi piatti* are also on offer, all made using quality imported ingredients, and accompanied by good regional wines. For desert try the devilishly good dragon-fruit-and-passion fruit panna cotta. The brick walls and aged-effect saffron walls are indeed reminiscent of a rustic Italian village, as is the hospitality that creates a warmly familial setting. $ *Average main: $10* ⊠ *Pari's Alley, 16 The-Lane, Old Market* ☎ *078/208174, 063/763380* ⊕ *www.ilfornorestaurantsiemreap.com.*

$
CAMBODIAN

✕ **Khmer Kitchen.** An established staple of Siem Reap dining, the expanded and very central Khmer Kitchen is basic—in cuisine and interior design—yet pleasantly authentic, serving tasty local dishes. Fresh spring rolls, Lo Lak beef curry, or baked pumpkin are recommended among a colorful variety of options. Cooking classes are available, if you'd like to take home the skills necessary to re-create some of the traditional dishes on offer. $ *Average main: $5* ⊠ *Mondul I, St. 9, Old Market* ☎ *063/964154, 012/763468* ⊕ *www.khmerkitchens. com* ▭ *No credit cards.*

$$
CAMBODIAN
FAMILY
Fodor's Choice
★

✕ **Mahob.** The name translates as "food," and if it's *mahob* you're after this is an excellent choice. Sothea, the owner, is a young, dynamic, and creative chef who cut his teeth and honed his talents working in Siem Reap's finest establishments and farther afield internationally. Here, he has created a Cambodian menu that appeals to the western palate but is not without an adventurous element. Try deep-fried frogs' legs coated with crispy rice flakes, or wok-fried local beef with tree red ants served with rice. If that's too much of a challenge, there's the duo amok soufflé

Continued on page 489

8

ANGKOR by Christina Knight

The scale of the ruins, the power of the encroaching jungle, and the beauty
of the architecture have made Angkor one of the world's most celebrated
ancient cities. This was the capital of the mighty Khmer empire (present-day Thailand, Laos, Vietnam, and Cambodia). The vast complex

contains more than 300 temples and monuments that four centuries of kings built to honor the gods they believed they would become after they died. It's not just the size of the structures that takes your breath away; it's the otherworldly setting and a pervading sense of mystery.

THE CITY OF ANGKOR

Silk-cotton tree roots growing over the ruins at Ta Prohm.

CONSTRUCTION

Angkor, which simply means "city," was founded in 839 AD when King Jayavarman II completed the first temple, Phnom Bakheng, using sandstone from the Kulen mountains, northeast of Angkor. Jayavarman II had established the empire in 802, uniting various principalities, securing independence from Java (in present-day Indonesia), and declaring himself the world emperor as well as a "god who is king," or *devaraja*.

Over the next 400 years, each successive Khmer emperor added to Angkor, erecting a *wat*, or temple, to worship either Shiva or Vishnu. The Khmer empire was Hindu except during the rule of Jayavarman VII (1181–1220), who was a Mahayana Buddhist. Theravada Buddhism became the dominant religion in Cambodia after the decline of the Khmer empire, in the 15th century.

Kings situated buildings according to principles of cosmology and numerology, so the center of the city shifted over the centuries. Only the wats, built with reddish-brown laterite, ochre brick, or gray sandstone, have survived; wooden structures perished long ago.

Historians estimate that the royal city had a population of 100,000 in the late 13th century; at that time, London's population was roughly 80,000. The royal city was ringed by a larger medieval city about 3,000 square km (1,150 square mile)—the world's largest pre-industrial settlement and more than twice the size of present-day Los Angeles, with an estimated population of 1 million. At its height, the Khmer empire covered about 1 million square km (400,000 square mile), stretching east from the Burmese border to southern Vietnam and north from Malaysia to Laos.

Archaeologists have only excavated the largest of the hundreds of temples that once dotted the royal city, and even fewer have been restored. The most impressive and best preserved temple, Angkor Wat, is also the world's largest religious monument; it covers approximately 2 square km (¾ square mile), including its moat.

Apsara bas-relief on a wall of Angkor Wat.

Angkor Wat.

DECLINE AND RENEWAL

In 1431, Thailand's Ayutthaya kingdom invaded and sacked Angkor. The following year, the declining Khmer empire moved its kingdom to Phnom Penh, 315 km (195 mile) south. Though a handful of foreign adventurers visited Angkor in the following centuries, it wasn't until 1861, when Frenchman and naturalist Henri Mouhot published a book about the site, that Angkor became famous. By this time, looting foreigners and the insistent forces of time and nature had taken a toll on the complex. Restoration efforts began in the early 20th century but were interrupted by the Cambodian Civil War in the 1960s and '70s; in 1992, UNESCO declared Angkor a World Heritage Site. Since that time the number of visitors has risen an average of 2 million annually. You won't have the place to yourself, but it's unlikely to feel crowded in comparison to famous European sites.

ANGKOR WAT

A monk looking at Angkor Wat across the moat.

The best-preserved temple has become shorthand for the entire complex: Angkor Wat, built by King Suryavarman II in the early 12th century. The king dedicated Angkor Wat to Vishnu (the preserver and protector), breaking with tradition—Khmer kings usually built their temples to honor Shiva, the god of destruction and rebirth, whose powers the kings considered more cosmically essential than Vishnu's.

It helps to think of the ancient city as a series of concentric protective layers: a 190-m- (623-ft-) wide moat surrounds an outer wall that's 1,024 by 802 m (3,359 by 2,630 ft) long—walking around the outside of the wall is a more than 2-mi stroll. A royal city and pal-ace once occupied the space inside the wall; you can still see traces of some streets, but the buildings did not survive. The temple itself sits on an elevated terrace that takes up about a tenth of the city.

APPROACHING THE TEMPLE

You'll reach the temple after crossing the moat, entering the western gateway (where you'll see a 10-foot, eight-armed Vishnu statue), and walking nearly a quarter of a mile along an unshaded causeway. Angkor Wat originally had nine towers (an auspicious number in Hindu mythology), though only five remain. These towers, which took 30 years to complete, are shaped like closed

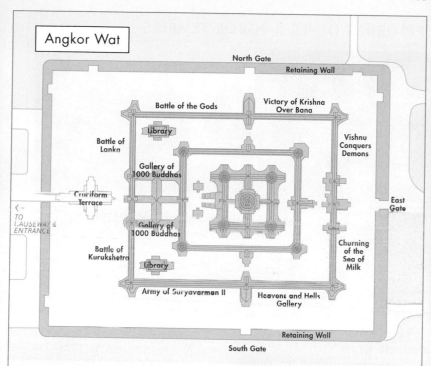

Angkor Wat

North Gate

Retaining Wall

Battle of the gods

Victory of Krishna Over Bana

Library

Battle of Lanka

Vishnu Conquers Demons

Gallery of 1000 Buddhas

Cruciform Terrace

← TO CAUSEWAY & ENTRANCE

East Gate

Gallery of 1000 Buddhas

Battle of Kurukshetra

Library

Churning of the Sea of Milk

Army of Suryavarman II

Heavens and Hells Gallery

Retaining Wall

South Gate

lotuses and form the center of the temple complex. Their ribbed appearance comes from rings of finials that also take the form of closed lotuses. These finials, along with statues of lions and multi-headed serpents called *nagas*, were believed to protect the temple from evil spirits.

Like the other major monuments at Angkor, the complex represents the Hindu universe. The central shrines symbolize Mt. Meru, mythical home of the Hindu gods, and the moats represent the seven oceans that surround Mt. Meru.

THE GALLERIES

Nearly 2,000 *Apsara*—celestial female dancers—are scattered in bas-relief on the outer entrances and columns of galleries. Inside the shaded galleries, 600 m (2,000 ft) of bas-reliefs tell

Bas-relief depicting a historical Khmer battle.

epic tales from the *Ramayana*, the *Churning of the Sea of Milk* (gods and demons join forces to find the immortality elixir), the punishments of the 32 hells, and the less-imaginative rewards of the 37 heavens.

86 <

EXPLORING OTHER ANGKOR TEMPLES

Banteay Srei temple complex.

ANGKOR THOM

King Jayavarman VII built the massive city known as Angkor Thom in 1181 and changed the state religion to Buddhism (although subsequent kings reverted to Hinduism). At the center of the city stands the 12th-century **Bayon**, a large, ornate state temple that rises into many towers (37 remain today), most of which are topped with giant, serene, smiling boddhisattva faces on four sides. These faces, the most photogenic and beatific in all of Angkor, resemble both the king and the boddhisattva of compassion—a Buddhist twist on the king-as-a-god tradition.

On the walls of Bayon's central sanctuary are 1½ km (1 mile) of marvelous bas-relief murals depicting historic sea battles scenes from daily life, and Hindu gods and mythical crea-

tures. You can pick out the Khmers in the reliefs because they are depicted with long earlobes; they frequently warred with the Cham, whose warriors wear headpieces that curl towards the jawline. Jayavarman VIII, a later king, added the Hindu iconography and destroyed some of his predecessor's Buddhist statuary.

Just to the north of the Bayon is the slightly older **Baphuon**, which King Udayadityavarman II built in the mid-11th century as part of a small settlement that predated Angkor Thom. The king built the temple on a hill without proper supports, so it collapsed during a 16th-century earthquake. In that same century, a magnificent reclining Buddha was added to the three-tiered temple pyramid, which was originally a Shiva sanctuary. The temple is undergoing reconstruction and is not open to the public; however, the exterior gate and elevated walkway are open.

King Jayavarman VII.

Once the foundation of the royal audience hall, the **Elephant Terrace** is adorned with carvings of *garudas* (birdlike creatures), lion-headed figures, and elephants tugging at strands of lotuses with their trunks.

Located at the north end of the Elephant Terrance, the **Terrace of the Leper King** area is named after a stone statue found here that now resides in the National Museum; a copy remains here. Precisely who the Leper King was and why he was so named remains uncertain, though several legends offer speculation. (One theory is that damage to the sculpture made the figure look leprous, leading people in later generations to believe the person depicted had been ill.) Today the terrace's two walls create a maze lined some seven layers high with gods, goddesses, and nagas.

TA PROHM

Jayavarman VII dedicated this large monastic complex to his mother. It once housed 2,700 monks and 615 royal dancers. Today the moss-covered ruins lie between tangles of silk-cotton and strangler fig trees whose gnarled offshoots drape window frames and grasp walls. This gorgeous, eerie spot gives you an idea of what the Angkor complex looked like when westerners first discovered it in the 19th century. Another famous mother—Angelina Jolie—shot scenes of *Lara Croft: Tomb Raider* here.

PHNOM BAKHENG

Sculptures of *devas* leading to Angkor Thom.

Two-storeyed pavilion at Preah Khan.

One of the oldest Angkor structures, dating from the 9th century, Bakheng temple was carved out of a rocky hilltop and occupied the center of the first royal city site. Phnom Bakheng is perhaps the most popular sunset destination, with views of the Tonle Sap Lake and the towers of Angkor Wat rising above the jungle. Climb a shaded trail or ride an elephant up the hill. You'll still have to climb steep stairs to reach the top of the temple.

PREAH KHAN

Dedicated to the Jayavarman VII's father, mossy Preah Khan was also a monastery. Its long, dim corridors are dramatically lit by openings where stones have fallen out. Preah Khan is the only Angkor site with an annex supported by rounded, not square, columns.

BANTEAY SREI

This restored 10th-century temple, whose name means "citadel of women," lies 38 km (24 mile) northeast of Siem Reap. Its scale is small (no stairs to climb), but its dark pink sandstone is celebrated for its intricate carvings of scenes from Hindu tales. The site is at least a 40-minute, somewhat-scenic drive from other Angkor sites; your driver will charge extra to take you here, but it's less crowded than other temples.

CLOSE UP

Planning Your Visit

TIMING

You can see most of the significant temples and monuments in a one-day sprint, although a three-day visit is recommended. If you have just one day, stick to a 17-km (11-mile) route that takes in the south gate of Angkor Thom, Bayon, Baphuon, the Elephant Terrace and the Terrace of the Leper King, and Ta Prohm, ending with a visit to Angkor Wat itself in time to catch the sunset. Leave the most time for the Bayon and Angkor Wat. If you have two or three days, cover ground at a more leisurely pace. You can also tack on additional sites such as Preah Khan, Neak Pean, Pre Rup (a good sunset spot), Phnom Bakheng, or farther-flung Banteay Srei. Another option is East Mebon, a 10th-century ruin in the East Baray, a former reservoir. The best way to experience Angkor is with a guide who can help you decode the bas-reliefs and architectural styles.

WHEN TO GO

Most people visit the east-facing temples of Bayon and Baphuon in the morning—the earlier you arrive, the better the light and the smaller the crowd. West-facing Angkor Wat gets the best light in the late afternoon, though these temples can also be stunning at sunrise. You can visit the woodland-surrounded Ta Prohm at any time, though photos will turn out best on cloudy days; the distant Banteay Srei is prettiest in late-afternoon light. If quiet is your priority, beat the crowds by visiting sunset spots in the morning and east-facing temples in the afternoon.

GETTING AROUND

The entrance to the complex is 4 km (2½ miles) north of Siem Reap; you'll need to arrange transportation to get here and around. Most independent travelers hire a car and driver ($35–$50 per day), moto (motorcycle) driver ($12–$18), or tuk-tuk ($20–$35, seats up to four). Renting bicycles ($3–$5) or electric bikes ($5–$8) is also an option. Tourists may not drive motorized vehicles in the park. If you hire a driver, he'll stick with you for the whole day, ferrying you between the sites.

ADMISSION

The Angkor complex is open from 5:30 am to 6 pm. Admission is $20 for one day, $40 for three consecutive days, and $60 for a week. You'll receive a ticket with your photo on it. Don't lose the ticket—you'll need it at each site and to access the restrooms. If you buy your ticket at 5 pm, you'll be admitted for the remaining open hour, in time to see the sunset. Your ticket will also count for the following day.

WHAT TO WEAR

Skimpy clothes violate the park's dress code. Shield yourself from the sun with light fabrics, and bring a wide brimmed hat. Note, however, that those wearing Vietnamese-style conical hats will be turned away since they cause offense. Drivers remain with the vehicle so you can leave items you don't want to carry.

ON THE GROUND

You'll find food and souvenir stalls inside the park near the temples; children also roam the sites selling trinkets and guidebooks. Consider breaking up the day by swinging back to Siem Reap for lunch or to your hotel for an afternoon rest. Make sure to drink plenty of water, which you can buy inside the park.

8

CLOSE UP

Hiring an Angkor Guide

A guide can greatly enrich your appreciation of Angkor's temples, which are full of details you might miss on your own. English-speaking guides can be hired through the tourism office on Pokambor Avenue, across from the Raffles Grand Hotel d'Angkor. But the best way to find a guide is through your hotel or guesthouse. Ask around. Most guides who work for tour companies (and the tourism office) are freelancers, and often when you book through a tour company, you'll pay a higher price. Find a young staffer at your hotel or guesthouse and tell him or her what you want—the type of tour, what you hope to learn from your guide, your particular interests in the temples.

Prices usually run around $45 a day, not including transportation, for a well-informed, English-speaking guide. Your guide will meet you at your hotel, along with a tuk-tuk or car driver, whom you'll need to pay separately ($12–$15 per day for a tuk-tuk; $25 for a car). Guides, who are almost always men, will typically cater to your interests and know how

to avoid crowds. You aren't expected to join your guide for lunch. Usually your driver will drop you and your guide at a temple and pick you up at another entrance, meaning you won't have to double back on yourself.

Hanuman Travel. If you feel more comfortable booking through a travel company, Hanuman Travel is an excellent choice. The expert company, which works throughout Cambodia and surrounding countries, has established a foundation to help eradicate poverty in Cambodia's hinterlands. Your tourist dollars will go toward wells, water filters, mosquito nets, and other amenities that can greatly improve a rural family's life. ⊠ 12 St. 310, Sangkat Tonle Bassac ☎ 023/218396, 023/218398 ⊕ www. hanuman.travel.

Sreang Teng. A knowledgeable, English-speaking local guide for the temple complex and other sights, Sreang Teng leads tours that seem to avoid the crowds. ⊠ Siem Reap ☎ 012/426764 ⊕ www. angkorsiemreaptourguide.com.

---

of lemongrass and coconut paste with chicken and river fish, or the fun option of cooking fish or meat exactly to your liking on hot stones. For dessert, the homemade ice creams are a great choice, with flavors ranging from rice milk to white Kampot pepper and lime. Set in an old Cambodian house, the restaurant also serves diners in the lovely front garden. $ *Average main: $8* ⊠ *137 Traing Village, off Charles de Gaulle Ave., Group 3* ☎ *063/966986, 017/550206* ⊕ *www.mahobkhmer.com.*

$ ✗ **Mie Cafe.** This top-notch restaurant reflects the upbeat, forward-
ASIAN thinking new generation of postdisaster Cambodia, represented here
Fodor's Choice by the determined and visionary young owner, Siv Pola. Although some
★ ingredients are imported, Pola makes fresh, local, seasonal ingredients a
priority. Try the popular spicy tuna tartare with mango or the wonderfully inventive Tonle Sap Fish, a carpaccio of snakehead fish fillet, marinated in fresh picked herbs, with a tempura poached egg. For dessert
the hot, creamy chocolate cake is a winner. Everything is prepared with
sensitivity, creativity, and great skill, right down to the home-mixed

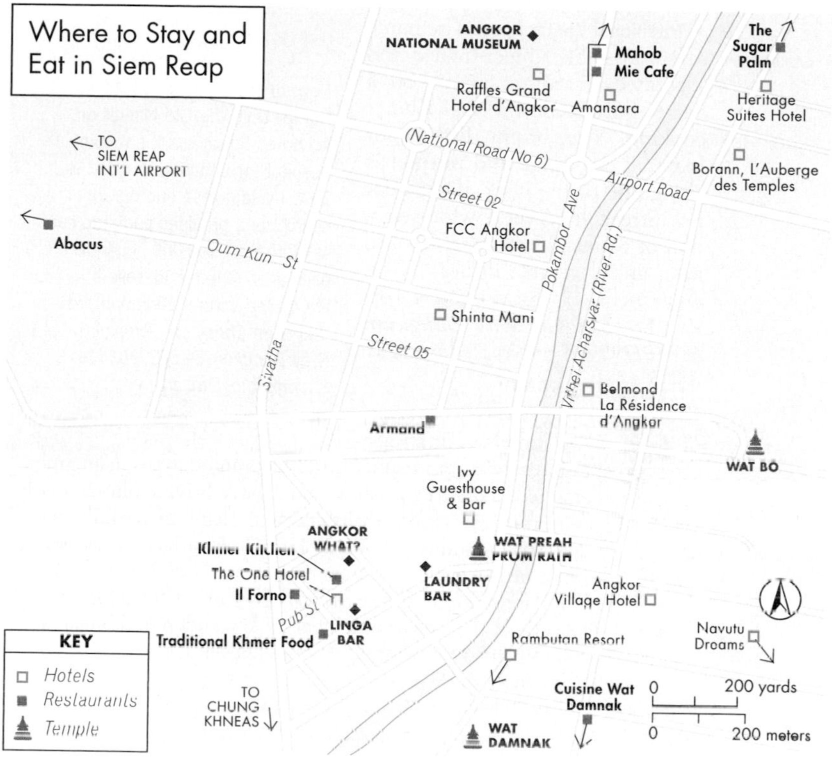
Where to Stay and Eat in Siem Reap
ANGKOR NATIONAL MUSEUM
Mahob
Mie Cafe
The Sugar Palm
Raffles Grand Hotel d'Angkor
Amansara
Heritage Suites Hotel
TO SIEM REAP INT'L AIRPORT
(National Road No 6)
Airport Road
Borann, L'Auberge des Temples
Street 02
Abacus
FCC Angkor Hotel
Oum Kun St
Pokambor Ave
Vithei Acharsvar (River Rd.)
Shinta Mani
Street 05
Sivatha
Belmond La Résidence d'Angkor
Armand
WAT BO
Ivy Guesthouse & Bar
ANGKOR WHAT?
Khmer Kitchen
WAT PREAH PRUM RATH
The One Hotel
LAUNDRY BAR
Il Forno
Angkor Village Hotel
Pub St
LINGA BAR
KEY
Hotels
Restaurants
Temple
Traditional Khmer Food
Rambutan Resort
Navutu Dreams
TO CHUNG KHNEAS
Cuisine Wat Damnak
0
200 yards
0
200 meters
WAT DAMNAK

8

herbal teas. The somewhat out-of-the-way location makes the open-air garden restaurant a sweet respite from noisier parts of the city, and the proudly low-budget Asian-chic style is a pleasing marriage of traditional and contemporary elements. [$] *Average main: $7* ✉ *0085 Phum Treng, Khum Slorgram* ☎ *012/791371, 069/999096* 🌐 *miocafe-siemreap.com* 🕓 *Closed Tues. and Oct.*

$ CAMBODIAN 🍴 **The Sugar Palm.** One of the best no-frills restaurants in Siem Reap, the Sugar Palm is infused with the owner's colorful enthusiasm for traditional Khmer cuisine learned from her mother and grandmother. After years in exile in New Zealand during the Khmer Rouge regime, Kethana returned to her homeland determined to create a familial place where diners could enjoy her favorite dishes, such as her uniquely soufflélike fish amok, which is made to order. As you wait, sample a flavorful variety of starters such as crispy shrimp cakes with black-pepper sauce or banana-blossom salad with chicken. The restaurant is on the second floor of a traditional-style timber house, and its food as well as its airy, modern-traditional atmosphere has drawn all manner of diners, including superstar chef Gordon Ramsay, who filmed a cooking show here. [$] *Average main: $7* ✉ *Taphul Rd.* ☎ *063/636–2060, 063/964838* 🌐 *www.thesugarpalm.com* 🕓 *Closed Sun.*

$ CAMBODIAN 🍴 **Traditional Khmer Food.** The name says it all—this Khmer-owned and -operated restaurant gives you a hearty introduction to real Khmer cooking. The bright little spot (painted in orange and purple) is along one of the back alleys near Pub Street. It serves a wide selection of Khmer soups, curries, and meat and vegetable dishes. [$] *Average main: $5* ✉ *Mondul 1, off Pub St., Sangkat Svay Dangkum* ☎ *019/999905* 💳 *No credit cards.*

GOOD DEEDS

Angkor Hospital for Children. Not far from the Old Market on Achamen Street sits the Angkor Hospital for Children, founded in 1999 by Japanese photographer Kenro Izu. It provides pediatric care to more than 100,000 children each year. Give blood, save a life. ✉ *Tep Vong (Achamean) Rd. and Oum Chhay St., Sangkat Svay Dangkum* ☎ *063/963409* 🌐 *angkorhospital.org.*

WHERE TO STAY

$$$$ RESORT Fodor's Choice ★ 🏨 **Amansara.** The jewel in the crown of Siem Reap hotels, Amansara offers exceptional service, atmosphere, and accommodations in an ambience of understated luxury. **Pros:** some suites have private plunge pool; rooftop open-air movies; impressive attention to detail by friendly management and staff; 10 minutes from Angkor. **Cons:** pricey; no in-room TV. [$] *Rooms from: $1770* ✉ *Road to Angkor, behind Tourism Dept.* ☎ *063/760333* 🌐 *www.amanresorts.com* 🛏 *24 suites* 🍽 *No meals.*

$$$ HOTEL 🏨 **Angkor Village Hotel.** This oasis of Khmer-style wooden buildings, lush gardens, and pools filled with lotus blossoms lies along a stone path a couple of blocks from the river in a green neighborhood. **Pros:** central location and easy access to tuk-tuks; spa with traditional therapies; the hotel organizes activities and trips. **Cons:** road can get congested during the rainy season; some rooms are looking a little worn. [$] *Rooms from: $150* ✉ *Wat Bo Rd.* ☎ *063/963361* 🌐 *www.angkorvillage.com* 🛏 *38 rooms* 🍽 *Breakfast.*

$$$$ RESORT FAMILY 🏨 **Belmond La Résidence d'Angkor.** Swathed in ancient Angkor style, this luxurious retreat, now part of the Belmond group, is within a walled compound with lovely gardens beside the river. **Pros:** attractive riverside location; family-friendly services; excellent restaurant; attentive service. **Cons:** some rooms have less than spectacular views; River Road rooms can get traffic noise. [$] *Rooms from: $400* ✉ *River Rd., Wat Bo* ☎ *063/963390, 800/237–1236 reservations* 🌐 *www.residencedangkor.com* 🛏 *54 rooms, 8 suites* 🍽 *Breakfast.*

$$ HOTEL 🏨 **Borann, l'Auberge des Temples.** The accommodations are attractive and the rates reliable at this tranquil, small hotel, a couple of blocks east of the river behind La Noria. **Pros:** large rooms; traditional style; terrace for every room. **Cons:** small pool; patchy Wi-Fi. [$] *Rooms from: $65* ✉ *Wat Bo St., north of N6, Wat Bo* ☎ *063/964242* 🌐 *www.borann.com* 🛏 *20 rooms* 🍽 *Breakfast.*

$$$ HOTEL 🏨 **FCC Angkor Hotel.** Next to the Royal Residence, the former French consulate has been turned into an inviting retreat along the river, removed from the noise of the city center. **Pros:** sleek contemporary design; riverside location; on-site spa. **Cons:** could do with a sprucing up; poor lighting in some rooms. [$] *Rooms from: $125* ✉ *Pokambor Ave.* ☎ *063/760280, 023/992284* 🌐 *www.fcccambodia.com* 🛏 *29 rooms, 2 suites* 🍽 *Breakfast.*

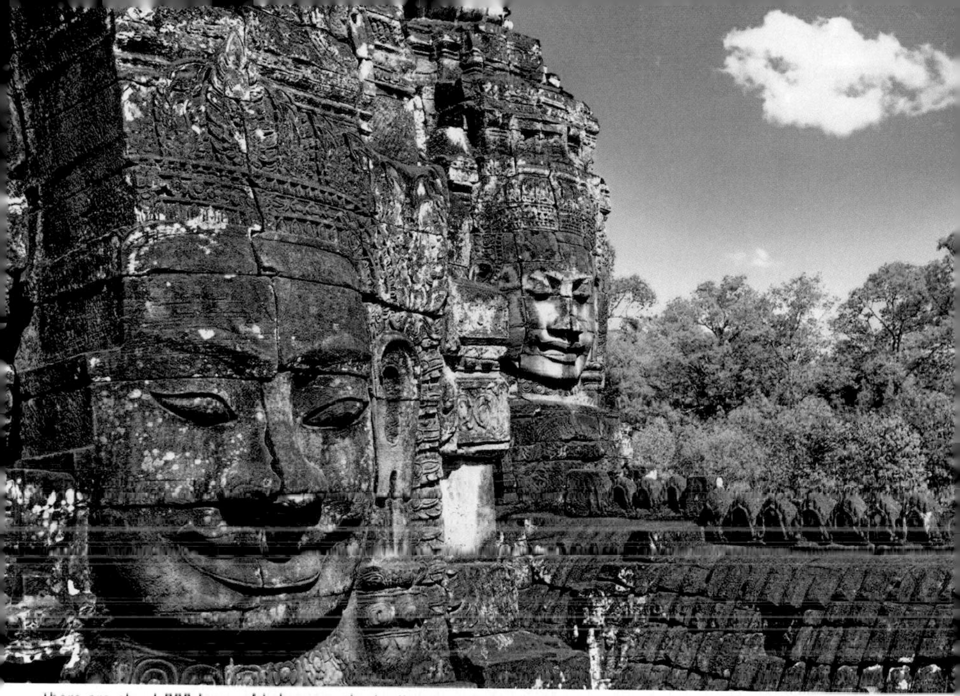

There are about 200 faces of Lokesvara, the bodhisattva of compassion, on Bayon's towers.

$$$ HOTEL Fodor's Choice ★ **Heritage Suites Hotel.** In a quiet neighborhood but still close to the town center, this wonderful little boutique hotel charms with its understated luxury and discrete attention to detail. **Pros:** warm, attentive staff; quiet, laid-back atmosphere; restaurant and bar are top drawer. **Cons:** hidden in Siem Reap's backstreets. *[$] Rooms from: $185 ✉ Wat Polanka Rd. ☎ 063/969100 🌐 www.heritagesuiteshotel.com 🛏 6 rooms, 20 suites 🍴 Breakfast.*

$ B&B/INN **Ivy Guesthouse & Bar.** As one of the best backpacker's options, the Ivy offers cheap accommodations a short walking distance to most central spots. **Pros:** central location; low prices; near all local nightlife; free Wi-Fi. **Cons:** rooms somewhat in need of an upgrade; breakfast not included; very basic. *[$] Rooms from: $8 ✉ Central Market St. and Shinta Mani St., Old Market ☎ 012/800860 cell phone 🌐 ivy-guesthouse.com 💳 No credit cards 🛏 20 rooms 🍴 No meals.*

$$$ RESORT **Navutu Dreams.** A slightly different Siem Reap experience is offered at this countryside bungalow resort, where the concept of well-being is promoted via resident yoga instructors, holistic practitioners, and healthy eating options. **Pros:** free yoga classes; free airport pickup and tuk-tuk shuttles to temples and town. **Cons:** about 5 to 10 minutes out of town. *[$] Rooms from: $155 ✉ Navutu Rd. ☎ 063/964864, 092/141694 🌐 navutudreams.com ⏲ Closed Sept. 🛏 26 rooms, 4 suites 🍴 Breakfast.*

$$$ HOTEL **The One Hotel.** There's only one suite here, but it's on the one street in town where you'd want to be and you'll have the undivided attention of the staff, including your own personal chef. **Pros:** prime location; unique experience. **Cons:** must be reserved months in advance (but last-minute deals sometimes available). *[$] Rooms from: $195 ✉ The Passage,*

Old Market ☎ *012/755311* 🌐 *www.theonehotelangkor.com* 🛏 *1 suite* 🍴 *Breakfast.*

$$$$ HOTEL 🏨 **Raffles Grand Hotel d'Angkor.** Built in 1932 and still featuring the cage elevator from that year in the lobby, this grande dame was restored and reopened after near destruction by occupying Khmer Rouge guerrillas. **Pros:** picturesque gardens; excellent restaurant; nicely designed and decorated. **Cons:** somewhat dependant on their name and former glory; more impersonal than smaller hotels; outside the center of Siem Reap. [$] *Rooms from: $300* ✉ *1 Vithei Charles de Gaulle, Khom Svaydangum* ☎ *063/963888* 🌐 *www.raffles.com/siem-reap* 🛏 *99 rooms, 18 suites, 2 villas* 🍴 *Breakfast.*

NIGHT FLIGHTS

Around sunset, the sky fills with thousands of large bats, which make their homes in the trees behind the Preah Ang Chek Preah Ang Chorm Shrine, near the gardens in front of the Raffles hotel.

$$ B&B/INN 🏨 **Rambutan Resort.** This gem of a getaway is one of the better boutique accommodations around, with rooms grouped around a stone-and-palm-enclosed pool. **Pros:** good prices; friendly staff; good value. **Cons:** tricky access; small swimming pool. [$] *Rooms from: $113* ✉ *Krom 10, Rambutan La., Wat Damnak* ☎ *012/654638* 🌐 *rambutanhotelsr.com* 🛏 *43 rooms* 🍴 *Breakfast.*

$$$ HOTEL Fodor's Choice ★ 🏨 **Shinta Mani.** Not only will you sleep and eat in luxurious style, your money will also help support projects bringing clean water, transportation, and jobs to underprivileged communities, via the Shinta Mani Foundation. **Pros:** Shinta Mani is a beacon in Siem Reap for the nonstop work it does to help and promote charitable causes; good location; great facilities. **Cons:** no elevator, which limits some accessibility. [$] *Rooms from: $200* ✉ *Oun Khum and 14th Sts., Old French Quarter* ☎ *063/761998* 🌐 *www.shintamani.com* 🛏 *61 rooms, 1 suite* 🍴 *Breakfast.*

$$$ RESORT Fodor's Choice ★ 🏨 **Sojourn Boutique Villas.** The layout of these villas, each with a pool or garden view, offers privacy and relaxation in lovingly maintained verdant grounds, and your stay will help the owners' ongoing support for underprivileged locals. **Pros:** poolside restaurant serves succulent Khmer specialties; extremely knowledgeable management; quality spa. **Cons:** a 10-minute tuk-tuk ride from town center; you either love or hate the 1980s-style swim-up pool bar. [$] *Rooms from: $200* ✉ *Treak Village Rd., Treak Village* ☎ *012/923437* 🌐 *www.sojournsiemreap.com* 🛏 *11 rooms* 🍴 *Breakfast.*

$$$$ RESORT 🏨 **Victoria Angkor Resort & Spa.** Just west of the Royal Gardens stands this sophisticated resort modeled on a strong colonial aesthetic. **Pros:** attentive service; friendly staff; top-quality breakfast buffet. **Cons:** a bit of a commercial feel; spa leaves much to be desired. [$] *Rooms from: $200* ✉ *National Hwy. 6 and Sivatha Rd., Khom Svaydangum* ☎ *063/760428* 🌐 *www.victoriahotels-asia.com* 🛏 *120 rooms, 9 suites* 🍴 *Breakfast.*

NIGHTLIFE AND PERFORMING ARTS

NIGHTLIFE

Most of Siem Reap's nightlife is concentrated around the Old Market, particularly on vibrant Pub Street, where some of the most popular spots are to be found. Just get a little lost, and you're sure to find a hangout that fits your style.

Angkor What? Graffiti-splattered Angkor What? was one of the first pumping dance clubs on Pub Street, in the old quarter, and it still lures in the cool young crowd nightly. Techno, trance, dance, and ambient sounds hypnotize the revelers and keep them going until the early hours, when there is the occasional fun dance-off with the bar opposite. You can also graffiti your personal philosophy on the walls. ⊠ *Pub St.* ☏ *012/490755.*

Asana. A grown-up playground strewn with hammocks, wooden bar stools, and tree-trunk tables, Asana is uniquely located in the one of the few remaining old, traditional Khmer houses in Siem Reap. The bar attracts a fun, artsy crowd and hosts live piano performances and other artistic events. Among a list of regular snacks and drinks, try the signature cocktail—tamarind sauce, made with rum, tamarind juice, Kaffir leaf, and lemony rice-paddy herbs. If you can't get enough of the drinks, they offer a cocktail class in the afternoon ($15). ⊠ *St. 7 and The Lane, Old French Quarter* ☏ *092/987801.*

Bar 543. Formerly known as "Under Construction," this bar is now well and truly constructed. True to the owners' aesthetic, it's a funky, airy, minimalist space where the action takes center stage. This place plays a bouncing mix of house, garage, and other uplifting beats, and when it gets busy you'll find it hard not to move to the grooves. It also serves some of the tastiest bar bites in town. ⊠ *Wat Bo Rd., Wat Bo.*

Charlie's. Word out on the street is "Finally! Charlie has opened his own bar." A big personality on Siem Reap's nightlife scene for many a year, Charlie has gone it alone, and his new bar, which opened in 2014, reflects his warm and quirky character—you'll feel right at home in this retro, American-style biker bar. ⊠ *Hospital St.* ☏ *012/181–4001* ⊕ *charliessiemreap.com.*

Laundry Bar. A favorite among visitors and expats yearning for a place to chill out, this bar is a little away from the madding crowds of Pub Street and features local and touring bands. When no live bands are playing, it's also popular for its creative cocktails and funky music playlists. ⊠ *St. 9 and Psah Chas Alley 1, Old Market* ☏ *016/962026.*

Linga Bar. Known for its inventive cocktails, gay-friendly Linga Bar is named after the archaic phallus that was broadly worshipped in Angkorian times. The bar, under the same ownership as The One Hotel, welcomes a mixed crowd of all ages and hosts regular drag shows and live DJ sets. It celebrated its 10-year anniversary in 2014, and also its move to new premises. ⊠ *The Passage, Old Market* ☎ *012/246912, 012/540548* ⊕ *lingabar.com.*

Fodor's Choice ★ **Miss Wong.** A favorite haunt of creative types, eclectic expats, and guests from exclusive resorts, this bar stands out with its sexy 1920s Shanghai-kitsch aesthetic—red walls, gold lanterns, and low lighting. Immersed in an era of glamorous decadence, guests are easily seduced into tasting cocktails made using local herbs, such as the apricot liqueur and Kaffir lime–infused gin martini. Dim sum and Asian-fusion finger food are also on the menu. ⊠ *The-Lane* ☎ *092/428332* ⊕ *www.misswong.net.*

Nest Angkor. For a change of scene head to this restaurant-bar located in a landscaped garden, where guests are invited to sip their designer cocktails lying on canopied loungers. ⊠ *Sivatha Blvd.* ☎ *063/966381* ⊕ *nestangkor.com.*

Picasso Tapas Bar. A real hub for foreign residents, the barrel-shape Picasso is a fun option for those who crave a few tasty Spanish tapas dishes with their drinks to keep them going late into the night. ⊠ *The Alley West, Old Market.*

Fodor's Choice ★ **The Yellow Submarine.** This off-the-wall, four-story gastropub is the owners' gushing tribute to the Beatles, whose memorabilia—and even personal objects such as toys, paintings, and family photos—decks practically every surface. Wacky cocktails such as the bubblegum martini are complemented by snacks like crunchy popcorn-crusted prawns. It's a real hit with the expat crowd. ■ TIP➔ Take in the sunset over Siem Reap from the lovely fourth-floor terrace. ⊠ *9A The Lane, Old Market* ☎ *088/665–5335* ⊕ *www.theyellow-sub.com.*

PERFORMING ARTS

The 1961. Get inspired! A really interesting initiative, The 1961 is a gallery-art-events-cowork space. People gather for the quality exhibitions, to enjoy cool drinks in the outdoor pavilion, or just to find a quiet little spot to catch up on some work and have a coffee. The 1961 has created quite a buzz in Siem Reap, and the management is at the forefront of most major events in town. The regular exhibitions feature local and international artists and aim to bring them closer to their audiences, showcasing classic to avant-garde, and visual to musical forms of art. ⊠ *211 Osaphear St., Upper West River Side* ☎ *015/378088* ⊕ *the1961.com.*

FAMILY **Fodor's Choice** ★ **Phare.** Cambodia's answer to the Cirque du Soleil is a must-see show. Previously only a traveling show, it has now found a permanent home in Siem Reap, in a cool, pink, high-top tent behind Angkor National Museum, although one of its troupes continues to take the show on the road internationally. The high-energy performances combine Cambodian storytelling traditions with circus arts, dance, acrobatics, and acting to captivate audiences every night. The Phare School is a charitable organization that has a positive impact on poor communities.

■**TIP→** Most seating is first come, first served, so try and get there early. ✉ *Comaille Rd., off Charles de Gaulle Ave.* ☎ *015/499480, 092/225320* ⊕ *www.pharecambodiancircus.org* ➦ *$35.*

SHOPPING

Angkor Night Market. Expanded to be more like multiple markets now, the original is still a fun, lively flea market where you can practice your bargaining skills and get lost in a maze that includes a food hall, massage stands, bars, and an enormous variety of clothes, accessories, souvenirs, food and cosmetic products, jewelry, and more. ✉ *Sivatha Blvd., Old Market* ⊕ *www.angkornightmarket.com.*

Artisans Angkor. With 38 workshops in Siem Reap, and more than 800 craftspeople employed around the country, Artisans Angkor offers a dazzling selection of Cambodian fine arts and crafts, accessories, and silverware from all over the country, and you can see skills such as woodworking, silk painting, and lacquering. It is refreshing that the movement toward the renewal and modernization of arts, crafts, and design is gathering momentum, with many of the high-grade products available in Siem Reap now manufactured locally. ✉ *Stung Thmey St.* ☎ *063/963330* ⊕ *www.artisansdangkor.com.*

Eric Raisina. Madagascar-born, French-raised fashion designer Eric Raisina has a couple of outlets in Siem Reap where he presents his impeccably stylish couture designs. The world-acclaimed designer uses stunning Khmer silks to create clothing and accessories that clearly stand a head above the rest. You'll find this outlet next to the Shinta Mani Hotel. ■**TIP→** You can also visit his atelier, at 75–81 Charles de Gaulle Avenue, by appointment only. ✉ *Cassia Gallery, Oum Khun St., Sangkat Svay Dangkum* ☎ *063/963207 atelier, for appointments, 063/963210 Cassia Gallery* ⊕ *www.ericraisina.com.*

Fodor's Choice ★ **Kandal Village.** This exclusive area near the center of town is a great place to find a range of upscale shops and cafés offering tasty bites to maintain your energy levels. Get eccentric artworks from the cool Trunkh or elegant luxury gifts from talented designer Louise Loubatieres. Clothing designer Sirivan Chak Dumas presents her collections at Sirivan, and you can pick up some exquisite handmade silks from the Takeo Province at Neary Khmer. If all this shopping makes you weary, treat yourself to a relaxing treatment at Frangipani Spa. ✉ *Hap Guan St.*

Mekong Quilts. Offering employment opportunities to disadvantaged women, Mekong Quilts sells beautiful handmade, durable quilts of all designs, colors, styles, and sizes. ✉ *5 Sivatha Blvd., Old Market* ☎ *063/964498* ⊕ *www.mekong-quilts.org.*

Psar Chaa Old Market. Perfect for last-minute shopping, you'll find just about everything here, from clothing to traditional woodcrafts, fabrics, and ceramic home-style items, kitschy souvenirs, attractive silverware, and all varieties of freshly cooked or packaged foods. ✉ *Market St. and Pokombor Ave.*

Senteurs d'Angkor. This store transforms spices and herbs used traditionally in Cambodia into delightful cosmetic or deli food products. Here you can find Kampot pepper, Rattanakiri coffee, soaps made with

8

lemongrass, turmeric, jasmine, or mango, and lots more. All the products make excellent gifts—especially for yourself. ✉ *Alley West, Old Market* ☎ *012/954815, 063/964801* ⊕ *www.senteursdangkor.com.*

Theam's House. This place specializes in unique lacquerware designs such as polychrome paintings and trademark colored elephants, as well as elegant traditional wood-carved Buddha statues and home style items. ✉ *25 Phum Veal, Kokchak Commune* ⊕ *www.theamshouse.com.*

AROUND SIEM REAP

TONLE SAP

10 km (6 miles) south of Siem Reap.

Covering 2,600 square km (1,000 square miles) in the dry season, Cambodia's vast Tonle Sap is the biggest freshwater lake in Southeast Asia. Its unique annual cycle of flood expansion and retreat dictates Cambodia's rice production and supplies of fish. During the rainy season the Mekong River backs into the Tonle Sap River, pushing waters into the lake, which quadruples in size. In the dry season, as the Mekong lowers, the Tonle Sap River reverses its direction, draining the lake. Boats make the river journey to the lake from Phnom Penh and Battambang, tying up at Chong Khneas, 12 km (7½ miles) south of Siem Reap. Two-hour tours of the lake, costing $15 to $20, set out from Chong Khneas, and you can tour the floating villages, with prices starting at $20.

Fodor's Choice
★
Prek Toal Biosphere Reserve. Between Chong Khneas and Battambang, this is mainland Southeast Asia's most important waterbird nesting site. It's a spectacular scene if you visit at the start of the dry season (November and December), when water remains high and thousands of rare birds begin to nest. Visits can be booked through **oSmoSe Conservation Ecotourism Education.** Day tours and overnight stays at the Prek Toal Research Station can be arranged. Prices vary. ✉ *Siem Reap.*

GETTING HERE AND AROUND

Boats make the river journey to the lake from Phnom Penh ($30) and Battambang ($20; usually during the wet season, May to October only), tying up at Chong Khneas, 12 km (7½ miles) south of Siem Reap.

Two-hour tours of the lake ($15) set out from Chong Khneas; arrange them at any travel agent in Siem Reap.

Transportation to and from the Tonle Sap can be arranged at any hotel or travel agent. Alternatively, ask any tuk-tuk or moto ($7 to $12).

KULEN MOUNTAIN

50 km (31 miles) north of Siem Reap.

King Jayavarman II established this mountain retreat 50 km (31 miles) northeast of Siem Reap in AD 802, the year regarded as the start of the Angkor dynasty. The area is strewn with the ruins of Khmer temples from that time, when the mountain was revered as holy, with a hallowed

Cambodia's Endangered Species

In an ironic contrast to the Khmer Rouge atrocities, at least some of Cambodia's wildlands and wildlife populations emerged from that period intact, and therefore the country has a far different scenario than that faced by its neighbors, where the rarest of species were expunged years ago.

The Prek Toal Biosphere Reserve is Southeast Asia's most important waterbird nesting site, home to several endangered species. Near Sre Ambel, in what was a Khmer Rouge hotbed, conservationists are working to save the Cambodian royal turtle, which was thought extinct until the early

2000s. In Kratie, some of the world's last Irrawaddy dolphins swim the Mekong in another area long held by the Khmer Rouge; and in Mondulkiri, conservationists report an increase in wildlife species in recent years.

The more tourists who express interest in Cambodia's natural environment, the better the outlook for these species and others. The jungles remain threatened by illegal logging (just visit Stung Treng and Ratanakkiri), and poaching is common. But if those in charge begin to see serious tourist dollars connected to conservation, there may be hope yet.

river and a waterfall. Admission to the area costs $20 and it is not included in the ticket price to the Angkor Temple Complex.

GETTING HERE AND AROUND

Tuk-tuks, motos, and local taxis can take you to Kulen Mountain; negotiate a price prior to departure, or ask your hotel to handle it (expect to pay around $20 for the trip). The journey should take no more than 50 minutes. Siem Reap tour companies also go here.

8

SIHANOUKVILLE AND SOUTHERN CAMBODIA

The beaches of Sihanoukville are quickly becoming a top Cambodian tourist destination (after Angkor, of course). Much of the country's stunning coastal area is currently under intense development, but some parts remain relatively undiscovered. A natural draw for those who tire of the crowds on neighboring Thai islands, Sihanoukville lies some 230 km (143 miles) southwest of Phnom Penh, a four-hour bus ride from the capital.

THE ROAD TO THE COAST

The four-hour bus journey from Phnom Penh to Sihanoukville along Highway 4 is an interesting one, winding through uplands, rice paddies, and orchards. Once you drive past Phnom Penh's Pochentong Airport and the prestigious Cambodia Golf & Country Club, and on through the area of Kompong Speu, the landscape turns rural, dotted with small villages where a major source of income seems to be the sale of firewood and charcoal. Somewhere around the entrance to Kirirom National Park all buses stop for refreshments at a roadside restaurant.

The halfway point of the journey lies at the top of the **Pich Nil mountain pass,** guarded by dozens of colorful spirit houses. These spirit houses were built for the legendary deity Yeah Mao, guardian of Sihanoukville and the coastal region. Legend has it that Yeah Mao was the wife of a village headman who worked in far-off Koh Kong, an island near today's border with Thailand. On a journey to visit him, Yeah Mao died when the boat transporting her sank in a storm—an all-too-believable story to anyone who has taken the boat from Sihanoukville to Koh Kong. Her spirit became the guardian of local villagers and fisherfolk.

At the small town of Chamcar Luang, a side road leads to the renowned smuggling port of Sre Ambel. The main highway threads along **Ream National Park,** with the Elephant Mountains as a backdrop. The national park is a highlight of Sihanoukville, with its mangroves, forests, waterfalls, and wildlife. The park is, unusually for Cambodia, well protected from the vagaries of modern development. The sprawling Angkor Beer brewery heralds the outskirts of Sihanoukville and the journey's end.

GETTING HERE AND AROUND

You can hire a private car and driver through your hotel or guesthouse for the trip to the coast from Phnom Penh. The price varies, but starts at approximately $50, and can be split with other passengers if you prefer. The drive (three to four hours) is often an alarmingly fast and dangerous ride along the well-maintained highway. However, it is common to see tourists who have rented motorcycles in Phnom Penh zipping past.

All major bus companies go to the coast, and Hunaman Travel and oSmoSe Conservation do tours.

SIHANOUKVILLE

230 km (143 miles) southwest of Phnom Penh.

A half a century ago, Cambodia's main port city, Sihanoukville, was a sleepy backwater called Kampong Som. Then a series of world-shattering events overtook it and gave rise to the busy industrial center and coastal resort now prominent on every tourist map.

The French laid the foundations of Kampong Som back in the mid-1950s, before they lost control of the Mekong Delta and its ports following their retreat after the French-Indochina War. The town was renamed Sihanoukville in honor of the then king. A decade later, Sihanoukville received a further boost when it became an important transit post for weapons destined for American forces fighting in the Vietnam War. In the mid-1970s Sihanoukville itself came under American attack and suffered heavy casualties after Khmer Rouge forces captured the SS *Mayaguez,* a United States container ship.

Today Sihanoukville presents a relatively peaceful face to the world as Cambodia's seaside playground. It has seven primary tourist beaches, all easily accessible from downtown by motorbike taxi or even a rented bicycle.

KHMER: A FEW KEY PHRASES

A knowledge of French may get you somewhere in francophone Cambodia, but these days it's far easier to find English speakers. The Cambodian language, Khmer, belongs to the Mon-Khmer family of languages, enriched by Indian Pali and Sanskrit vocabulary. It has many similarities to Thai and Lao, a reminder of their years as vassal lands in the Khmer Empire.

The following are some useful words and phrases:

Hello: joom reap soo-uh

Thank you: aw koun

Yes: bah (male speaker), jah (female speaker)

No: aw-te

Excuse me: som-toh

Where?: ai nah?

How much?: t'lay pohn mahn?

Never mind: mun ay dtay

Zero: sohn

One: muay

Two: bpee

Three: bay

Four: buon

Five: bpram

Six: bpram muay

Seven: bpram pull

Eight: bpram bay

Nine: bpram buon

Ten: dop

Eleven: dop muay

Hundred: muay roi

Thousand: muay poan

Food: m'hohp

Water: dteuk

Expensive: t'lay nah

Morning: bprek

Night: youp

Today: tngay nee

Tomorrow: tngay sa-ik

Yesterday: mus'el mun

Bus: laan ch'nual

Ferry: salang

Village: pum

Island: koh

River: tonle

Doctor: bpet

Hospital: moonty bpet

Bank: tia-nia-kia

Post Office: praisinee

Toilet: baan tawp tdeuk

GETTING HERE AND AROUND

Sihanoukville airport has undergone modernization over the past few years and it is set for more incoming and outgoing flights, but as of the end of 2014, only Angkor Air flies here from Siem Reap every day. Flights take one hour, with prices starting at $123.

Air-conditioned buses from Phnom Penh run several times daily ($6–$8), departing from the Central Market or the Hua Lian Station near Olympic Stadium. Four hours later, they arrive a couple of kilometers outside of Sihanoukville, and getting off the bus you're enthusiastically greeted by the local tuk-tuk and moto drivers who jostle for your custom. The farthest trip, to Otres, by tuk-tuk shouldn't cost more than $8, and going anywhere else shouldn't be more than $6 (there is a board with price suggestions at one end of the bus station). Prices for motos are half that of tuk-tuks and taxis will cost double, but don't expect them to have a meter. Buses from Bangkok (10 hours; from $25) and other towns on Thailand's eastern seaboard connect to Sihanoukville via Koh Kong.

You can hire a private car and driver through your hotel or guesthouse for the trip to the coast from Phnom Penh (three to four hours; starting at $50 excluding gas). ■TIP→ The highway to Sihanoukville is much improved and is now one of the better roads in Cambodia, but it is still hazardous to drive for anyone who is not familiar with roads in Cambodia. Buses are almost as quick and often safer.

Taxis make the trip to and from Sihanoukville and Phnom Penh. The charge is $10 per person for five people, but if you want to be a little less cramped you can pay $13 to have only three seated in the back, or try and get the coveted front seat.

EXPLORING

Sihanoukville is a beach town without a center. There is a market area with a surrounding business area that has all the banks and other basic facilities; however, the town's accommodations are spread out along the coast. There is a national park to visit that has mangroves and rivers, and is teeming with birdlife.

Fodor'sChoice
★

Koh Rong Samlem. The Sihanoukville coast is flanked by several islands, many of them untouristed and lightly populated by Khmer fishermen, and some are accessible by boat. **Koh Rong Samlem, Koh Tas,** and **Koh Russei** are popular day-trip destinations for snorkeling and picnicking, but local guides can arrange overnight stays in rustic bungalows if you'd like to linger for a few days. Koh Rong Samlem is about two-and-a-half hours by boat from the mainland, and there are some quiet and isolated beaches with a few basic bungalow options. The amenities vary depending where you go. ⚠ The jungle interior of the island is home to some of the deadliest snakes in Cambodia. They are more afraid of you, of course, but be aware. ⊠ *Sihanoukville.*

Ream National Park. Encompassing 210 square km (81 square miles) of coastal land 16 km (10 miles) north of Sihanoukville, this park includes mangrove forests, the Prek Tuk Sap estuary, two islands, isolated beaches, and offshore coral reefs. Macaques, pangolin (scaly anteaters), sun bears, and muntjac (barking deer) live in the forest. Tours can be booked from most hotels in town. ⊠ *Airport Rd.* ☎ *012/875096, 016/767686* 🖃 *Walking tour $6 for 2 hrs, $10 for 5 hrs, full-day boat trip $50* ☉ *Daily 7–5.*

Hawaii Beach. Where the foundations of Sihanoukville were dug in the early 1950s, this beach almost meets the promise of its name. Popular with the Phnom Penh crowd, it quickly gets packed on weekends, but is pleasantly quiet during the week. A huge bridge has just been built connecting the bordering headland with Snake Island (earmarked for a development project that has come to a shuddering halt), which is a bit of an eyesore. **Amenities:** food and drink; water sports. **Best for:** swimming. ⊠ *Southern end of Victory Beach.*

Independence Beach. Once a local favorite, there is little of this beach actually open to the public anymore. Also known as 7-Chann Beach, it is now only accessible at the northern end, but even this 500-meter strip (close to the towering Independence Hotel, after which the beach was named) makes for a nice little oasis away from the crowded Ochheuteal and Sokha beaches. Lining the beach is a row of restaurants and bar-cafés, where you can get tasty bites and cool cocktails. On the southern end is the new Holiday Palace Resort & Casino. **Amenities:** food and drink; toilets; parking (no fee). **Best for:** sunset; swimming. ⊠ *In front of Thnou St.*

Ochheuteal Beach. This is the busiest beach in the area, littered with loungers and umbrellas and its fair share of beggars and hawkers. The beach itself is a little narrow and not so clean but there are plenty of activities for the young at heart, as the bars close late every night and often throw beach parties. After dusk, roadside eateries open up on 23 Tola Street (one of the roads flanking the beach) selling barbecued seafood and meats. To the south of the beach is the once nice but now slightly run-down Queen Hill Resort, hiding among the trees on the hilly peninsula. **Amenities:** food and drink; toilets; water sports; parking (no fee). **Best for:** partiers; sunset; swimming. ⊠ *Ochheuteal St.*

FAMILY
Fodor's Choice
★
Otres Beach. This beach has managed to maintain the natural, peaceful vibe of a truly chilled-out beach vacation. Split into two parts, with a beautiful and empty 1½-km long (1-mile-long) creamy-brown fine-sand beach in between, it's usually lighted at night and has a paved side path. Otres I is the busier of the two areas, with some good bars and restaurants, as well as a scattering of accommodations. Otres II is developing quickly, and the road behind the beach is now full of little hotels and bungalow resorts, but even so it is still the more laid-back and peaceful of the two, and continues to be the best beach in the area. Aside from the variety of cheap, cheerful bungalow accommodations, there are some decent little resorts like Tamu, The Secret Garden, and Otres Beach Resort. **Amenities:** food and drink; parking (no fee); showers; toilets; water sports. **Best for:** solitude; sunsets; swimming; walking. ⊠ *Sihanoukville.*

Serendipity Beach. Neighboring Ochheuteal, this is a favorite with backpackers. Over the past few years a slew of bungalows, budget guesthouses, and earthy eateries have been added to the landscape, and the beach is now backed by one linear track of restaurants, bars, and cafés. Hawkers and beggars regularly patrol the walkway. There are constant rumors of large-scale development, but so far big resort development has stayed away. Boats for the islands, diving trips, and tours all leave from the pier to the right of the beach, and there is a constant rumble of Jet Skis, too close to the shore. After sunset fireworks herald the nighttime action. **Amenities:** food and drink; showers; toilets; water sports. **Best for:** partiers. ⊠ *Mithona St., north of Ochheuteal Beach.*

Sokha Beach. Some of the best swimming can be enjoyed here, at the site of Cambodia's first international-class beach resort, the Sokha Beach

Resort. Everyone has access to the beach and its beautiful singing sand—it squeaks underfoot—and good food can be had at the resort's beachside restaurants, like the Deck. **Amenities:** food and drink. **Best for:** sunset; swimming; walking. ⊠ *2 Thnou St.*

Victory Beach. Named after the Vietnamese victory over the Khmer Rouge regime in 1979, Victory Beach is separated from Hawaii Beach by an outcrop, on top of which sits the actual victory monument. The beach, which was a popular backpacker spot but now hosts a mid-range crowd, has a few average hotels and bungalows like the Queenco Casino Hotel. Its proximity to Sihanoukville's major port is a disadvantage, and the beaches to the north of the bluff, called Victory Hill, are far more picturesque and popular. **Amenities:** food and drink. **Best for:** sunset; swimming. ⊠ *In front of Krong St.*

WHERE TO EAT

The most inexpensive guesthouses, restaurants, and other tourist services are on Victory (Weather Station) Hill, Serendipity Beach, and Ochheuteal Beach. Some of the lodgings in these areas are quite attractive, although over the years these locations have become somewhat blighted by mass tourism.

$ ╳ **Cafe Sushi.** You can fish your own dinner right out of the Gulf of Siam on a trip arranged by this restaurant, then take a class to learn how to prepare it—or just choose whether to have it grilled or made into a tartare, sushi, nigiri, or tempura. By far the most authentic Japanese food in Sihanoukville, the menu is heavily reliant on the Japanese owner's whim and the fish caught that day. Bento boxes, *okonomiyaki*, and other delights are also on offer. $ *Average main: $7* ⊠ *25 Ekareach St., Sangkat 4, Khan Mittapheap* ☏ *012/940368* ▬ *No credit cards.*
JAPANESE
FUSION

$ ╳ **Chhne Meas Restaurant.** Dine on the edge of Victory Beach, next to the crashing waves, at this lovely indoor-outdoor Cambodian restaurant. All manner of fresh fish and seafood, from stir-fries to clay pots to barbecues and curries, is available. Locals eat at this little offbeat gem—which is always a good sign. As it is usually only frequented by locals, English is not really spoken, so go with the flow. $ *Average main: $6* ⊠ *Vithey Krong* ☏ *012/340060* ▬ *No credit cards.*
SEAFOOD

$$$ ╳ **The Deck.** In the Sokha Beach Resort, this outdoor beachfront restaurant is an idyllic dinner-and-drinks spot, from the dreamy sunset hour to late at night. The tapas menu is innovative and trendy, and Japanese dishes are authentic and refined. A wonderful selection of international wines and inventive cocktails make for a great accompaniment. $ *Average main: $12* ⊠ *Sokha Beach Resort, 2 Thnou St., Sokha Beach* ☏ *034/935999* ⊕ *www.sokhahotels.com/sihanoukville/ dining* ⊗ *No lunch.*
INTERNATIONAL

$ ╳ **Manoha.** Simple, unpretentious, Manoha serves French-Khmer cuisine with a sophisticated air, prepared by a Cambodian chef who utilizes the best of fresh local ingredients and the catch of the day. You'll get excellent value here, with delicate dishes like fish carpaccio and tartare, or fruitier options like the Bai Cha Manoha (prawns in a spicy sauce, with rice served in a pineapple). $ *Average main: $5* ⊠ *Serendipity Beach Rd.* ☏ *097/915–2814* ▬ *No credit cards.*
CAMBODIAN

$ 🍴 **Mushroom Point.** A bar-restaurant with a delightfully relaxed atmosphere, this place has the most offbeat architectural style on Otres beach—it looks like a miniscule village of mushroom-shape huts. It's a great place for a sunset aperitif with your toes in the sand, followed by a creamy Khmer curry or a large salad. Enjoy the laid-back hippie-chic vibe on this beautiful stretch of beach. [$] *Average main: $5* ✉ *Otres I Beach* ☎ *097/712–4635* 🕓 *No lunch.*

MODERN EUROPEAN

$ 🍴 **Sandan.** Operated by the M'Lop Tapang charity, this is a vocational training restaurant that consistently demonstrates just how good the training is—the service is attentive and the food exceptional. New and inventive Cambodian dishes are constantly being added and the specials change regularly. Try the fresh prawn ceviche or delightful *lort-cha* (Cambodian panfried noodles) and treat yourself to the grilled pork fillet stuffed with fresh-toasted coconut. The cocktails are pretty decent, too. [$] *Average main: $5* ✉ *2 Thnou St., Krong Preah* ☎ *034/452–4000* 🌐 *mloptapang.org/projects/sandan-restaurant.*

CAMBODIAN

Fodor's Choice ★

$ 🍴 **Starfish Bakery and Cafe.** Here you can try a shake, house-made yogurt, or a brownie, indulge in a massage, and learn about volunteering opportunities in Sihanoukville. The café has Wi-Fi and a handicrafts shop upstairs. It's not the easiest of places to find—hidden down a dirt road behind the Samudera Market in town—but it's well worth the trek. It's open from 7 am to 5 pm. Proceeds from this delightful little garden café go toward the Starfish Project, which supports individuals in need. [$] *Average main: $4* ✉ *On unmarked road off 7 Makara St.* ☎ *012/952011* 🌐 *www.starfishcambodia.org* 💳 *No credit cards.*

CAFÉ

WHERE TO STAY

$ 🏨 **Clearwater Guest House.** This small, modern lodging near Independence Beach offers a no-frills, but enjoyable stay. **Pros:** relaxed atmosphere; nice garden; friendly staff. **Cons:** can be difficult to find; five minutes away from beach; book in advance. [$] *Rooms from: $35* ✉ *Group 1, Village 1, off 19 Mithona St., Sangkat 3* ☎ *097/907–3765, 097/591–0765* 🌐 *www.clearwater-guesthouse.com* 🛏 *8 rooms* 🍽 *Breakfast.*

B&B/INN

8

$ 🏨 **Coolabah Hotel.** Aside from its pleasantly simple interiors, contemporary bathrooms, and sense of spaciousness, maybe the best feature of Coolabah is the lovely bistro, where the seafood platter is a highlight of a mainly French-inspired menu that also includes a good wine list. **Pros:** friendly staff; good eats; good value. **Cons:** can get noisy at night; nearest beach is not the best; not all rates include breakfast. [$] *Rooms from: $42* ✉ *14 Mithona St.* ☎ *017/678218* 🌐 *coolabah-hotel.com* 🛏 *30 rooms* 🍽 *Breakfast; No meals.*

HOTEL

$ 🏨 **Don Bosco Hotel School.** As the name suggests, this lodging doubles up as a school for trainees of the service industry, selected from a pool of local underprivileged young adults, but far from feeling like a guinea pig at a training facility, guests enjoy a high level of service and care. **Pros:** big swimming pool; shuttle services to town and beaches three times a day; excellent food. **Cons:** inconvenient location; part of a larger complex; somewhat impersonal. [$] *Rooms from: $35* ✉ *Group 13, Sangkat 4, Ou 5* ☎ *034/933765, 016/919834* 🌐 *www.donboscohotelschool.com* 🛏 *31 rooms* 🍽 *No meals.*

HOTEL
FAMILY

$$$ HOTEL **Independence Hotel.** First opened in 1963, with the interior designed by King Sihanouk himself, the Independence established itself as the premier destination of the era. **Pros:** wonderful mix of historic and modern design; great views; lush gardens. **Cons:** not necessarily family-friendly; slow service; overpriced (but look out for special offers). [$] *Rooms from: $105* ✉ *2 Thnou St., Sangkat 3, Khan Mittapheap* ☎ *034/934300/1/2/3* 🌐 *www.independencehotel.net* 🛏 *88 rooms, 25 suites* 🍴 *Breakfast.*

$$ B&B/INN Fodor's Choice ★ **Lazy Beach, Koh Rong.** Jump on the hotel's boat from Ochheuteal Beach at midday and two hours later marvel at this beautiful tropical hideout, made up of wooden bungalows stretched out along the powdery beige sand. **Pros:** peaceful getaway; pretty, natural setting; friendly management and staff. **Cons:** a two-hour boat ride; no electricity; not much to do (except relax). [$] *Rooms from: $60* ✉ *Koh Rong Saloem* ☎ *016/214211, 017/456536* 🌐 *lazybeachcambodia.com* 💳 *No credit cards* 🛏 *10 rooms* 🍴 *No meals.*

$ HOTEL **Orchidee Guesthouse.** This brick-and-stucco lodging is one of Sihanoukville's oldest and most consistently popular choices, just one block, or an easy five-minute walk, from the beach. **Pros:** great facilities for the price; nice pool; no-smoking rooms. **Cons:** away from the beach; hot water in the bathrooms not always a given; some areas could use an update. [$] *Rooms from: $18* ✉ *23 Tola St., Ochheuteal Beach* ☎ *012/380300, 034/933639* 🌐 *www.orchidee-guesthouse.com* 💳 *No credit cards* 🛏 *69 rooms* 🍴 *No meals.*

$ HOTEL **Small Hotel.** If you're looking for a clean budget hotel in Sihanoukville town that doesn't cater to bar girls and their clientele, this is it. **Pros:** small boutique style; family feel. **Cons:** far from the beach; not the largest rooms; breakfast not included in room price. [$] *Rooms from: $20* ✉ *Off Sopheakmongkol St., behind Caltex Station* ☎ *034/6306161* 🌐 *thesmallhotel.info* 💳 *No credit cards* 🛏 *11 rooms* 🍴 *No meals.*

$$$$ RESORT FAMILY **Sokha Beach Resort.** This is the top address in Sihanoukville—a huge first-class resort hotel with all the facilities required for a fun-filled beach holiday. **Pros:** great for families; private beach; nice location. **Cons:** not geared to romantic getaways; a bit short on the luxury status it claims. [$] *Rooms from: $175* ✉ *2 Thnou St.* ☎ *034/935999* 🌐 *www.sokhahotels.com* 🛏 *268 rooms, 20 suites, 79 villas* 🍴 *Breakfast.*

$$$$ RESORT Fodor's Choice ★ **Song Saa Private Island.** Barefoot luxury are the buzzwords most used to describe this multiple-award-winning resort, set on two small islands (*Song Saa* is Khmer for "sweet hearts") a 40-minute speedboat trip from Sihanoukville. **Pros:** created with sustainability in mind; surrounding waters are part of a marine park; exceptional and discreet staff; lots of activities included in the price. **Cons:** limited accommodations so book early; stepping off the speedboat at Port 1, Gate 1 (Sihanoukville's harbor) at the end of your stay. [$] *Rooms from: $2200* ✉ *Koh Ouen* ☎ *0236/860360, 0239/890009* 🌐 *songsaa.com* 🛏 *27 villas* 🍴 *All-inclusive.*

Jayavarman VII built Preah Khan in 1191 to commemorate the Khmers' victory over Cham invaders.

SPORTS AND THE OUTDOORS

Most hotels and guesthouses arrange boat trips, which include packed lunches, to the many offshore islands. Several companies offer diving and snorkeling; two of the most popular dive centers are EcoSea Dive and Scuba Nation.

EcoSea Dive. Eco-friendly instruction comes at very competitive prices, and they even have a resort of their own on Koh Rong Samloem. Dives start from $30. ✉ *Between Serendipity Beach and Golden Lions traffic circle* ☎ *034/934631, 012/654101* ⊕ *www.ecoseadive.com.*

Scuba Nation. This was Cambodia's first certified PADI dive center and is still probably the best around, taking trips out to good underwater sites. They offer all the courses, up to advanced levels, and have some fun options for children. Courses start at $35. ✉ *Mohachai Guesthouse, Serendipity Beach Rd.* ☎ *012/604680, 034/933700* ⊕ *www.divecambodia.com.*

KAMPOT

110 km (68 miles) east of Sihanoukville, 150 km (93 miles) south of Phnom Penh.

This attractive, if somewhat bland, riverside town at the foot of the Elephant Mountain range, not far from the sea, is known for its French colonial architectural remnants—and for salt and pepper. In the dry season, laborers can be seen along the highway to Kep, working long hours in the salt fields; pepper plantations are scattered around the province. Kampot is the departure point for trips to the seaside resort of Kep and Bokor Hill Station. The coastal road from Sihanoukville to Kampot is somewhat rough, but has spectacular views. Several limestone caves speckle the landscape from Kampot to Kep to the Vietnam border. Plan at least a morning or afternoon excursion to see the cave at Phnom Chhnork.

GETTING HERE AND AROUND

To get here, take a taxi or bus, or hire a car and driver through your hotel. The journey from Phnom Penh takes approximately four hours. A single bus ticket starts from $5 from Phnom Penh's Central Market. Prices for a taxi or a car with driver start at $35. Hotels are the best source for tour information in and around Kampot.

EXPLORING

Kampot has enough to keep the intrepid traveler busy for a couple of days. The town is sleepy and relaxed, with a wide river marking the center of the town's dining and lodging area. Kampot is the stepping-off point for nearby Kep, and it has rapids and a few caves to explore. Don't forget the world-renowned salt and pepper production. Bokor Hill Station remains the largest draw for visitors and is earmarked for a new spate of development.

Bokor Hill Station. In the early 20th century, the French built this station as a retreat from the heat and humidity of the coast. It is now a collection of ruins, but it's worth visiting for the spectacular sea views from its 3,000-foot heights. It's 35 km (22 miles) west of Kampot, and travel here is extremely rough in the rainy season. Hiring a motorbike ($5) for the day is a fun way to experience the local scenery on the way up and down. Development of the site is on the horizon. ⊠ *Kampot* ⊕ *phnombokor.com.*

Phnom Chhnork Caves. The limestone caves shelter a pre-Angkorian ruin, over which the stalagmites and stalactites are gradually growing. The less appealing cave of Phnom Sia (flashlight required) is more for the fun of exploring in the depths of a cave. The white elephant cave, or Cave of Sasear, has a shrine where worshippers pray to an elephant-shape limestone formation. Tuk-tuks from town cost $10 for the round-trip. ⊠ *On road from Kampot to Kep* ⊡ *$1.*

Phnom Voul Natural Pepper Plantation. Kampot's world-renowned aromatic pepper is sold all around the town and surrounding areas, but there's nothing quite like visiting where it's grown, sampling it right off the plant, and paying its producers in person for a certified 100% organic product. This is one of the most respectable producers, where you can buy white, red, or black pepper in half- or one-kilogram bags. It's not cheap, but it is top quality. ■TIP→ As most pepper plantations are in the countryside along dusty, rocky roads, it's best to arrange a taxi ride—tuk-tuks across this kind of terrain can be exhausting. ⊠ *Chom Ka 3 Village, Pong Tek Commune, Domnak Er district* ⊗ *Daily 8–5.*

WHERE TO EAT

$ ✕ **Cafe Espresso Kampot.** Caffeine lovers rejoice, for at Cafe Espresso
CAFÉ you are guaranteed to find the perfect, most elegantly presented cup of coffee. The news gets even better, as the coffee beans are locally grown, home roasted, and ground fresh for each order. The café, where you can

enjoy free Wi-Fi in a trendy, upbeat atmosphere, also serves fantastic breakfasts and brunches that include delights such as eggs Benedict and bagels. Vegetarians will also be pleased to find exciting options such as tofu or veggie burgers, falafel, crispy dumplings, and Mexican wraps. $ *Average main: $5* ⊠ *No. 17 down side street off Old Market St., across from 333 bakery* ☎ *092/388736* ⊕ *espressokampot.blogspot. gr* ⊗ *No dinner.*

$

CAFÉ

FAMILY

Fodor's Choice

★

✕ **Epic Arts Cafe.** Created as a positive, dynamic means of raising awareness and generating work opportunities for deaf or disabled people in the region, many of whom now work here, Epic Arts Cafe serves a good selection of tasty homemade breakfast dishes, including options like porridge, as well as lunch (try the BLT), dessert, and children's dishes, fresh fruit smoothies, and iced coffees brewed from local beans. $ *Average main: $3* ⊠ *1st May Rd., across from new Kampot Market, Kompong Kandal* ☎ *033/555–5201* ⊕ *www.epicarts.org.uk* ⊟ *No credit cards* ⊗ *No dinner.*

$

CAMBODIAN

✕ **La Java Bleu.** Fresh fish sourced daily from the local market and skillfully barbecued or cooked in other inventive styles is what distinguishes this popular restaurant, which is in a nicely renovated Chinese building near the river. The seafood-inspired menu, which does include some meat and chicken dishes, as well as a few vegetarian options, has French and Khmer influences. Try the grilled barracuda or the seafood platter with a good bottle of white from the restaurant's fine international wine selection. Breakfast or lunch omelets, salads, and sandwiches are available too. La Java Bleu is also a lovely place to stay for anyone looking for a boutique option in the heart of town. There are five rooms in Asian-chic style. $ *Average main: $7* ⊠ *27 Phoum Ouksophear Sangkat, French Quarter* ☎ *097/517–0023* ⊕ *www.lajavableue-kampot.com*

$$

PIZZA

✕ **Mea Culpa.** Set in the attractive garden of the Mea Culpa guesthouse, 50 meters from the riverside, this friendly restaurant offers a break from traditional cuisine (although there are well-prepared Khmer dishes on the menu as well) and serves what many consider to be the best pizza in the area, made with a thin, crispy crust in a wood-fire oven. There's also homemade bread, and a choice of tasty salads and starters. Mia Culpa is also a guesthouse and has six elegantly furnished rooms. $ *Average main: $8* ⊠ *44 Sovansokar (behind Governor's Mansion)* ☎ *012/504769* ⊕ *www.meaculpakampot.com.*

$

INTERNATIONAL

✕ **Rikitikitavi.** This cheery second-floor terrace restaurant has a youthful vibe, and serves European and American favorites such as burgers, bruschetta, and salads, but the cuisine also has a strong Khmer undercurrent. Try the creamy Saraman beef curry with peanuts, local herbs, and spices. Many ingredients are seasonal and locally sourced. Vegetarians be warned—your only option, albeit a very tasty one, is the non-Khmer vegetable burrito. $ *Average main: $7* ⊠ *Riverside Rd., next to post office* ☎ *012/235102, 012/274820* ⊕ *www.rikitikitavi-kampot.com.*

WHERE TO STAY

$

HOTEL

🖼 **Bokor Mountain Lodge.** Ideally set on the banks of Kampong Bay River in a restored colonial building, this centrally located boutique-style hotel offers a handful of clean, spacious, and affordable rooms. **Pros:** nice views; great restaurant; management knowledgeable about the area.

8

Cons: light sleepers may be irked by the noisy next-door pub; a little rough around the edges. [$] *Rooms from: $35* ✉ *Riverfront Rd.* ☎ *033/932314, 017/712062* 🌐 *www.bokorlodge.com* 🛏 *6 rooms* 🍴 *Breakfast.*

$ RESORT 🏨 **Ganesha Riverside Eco Resort.** Named after the Hindu elephant-headed deity who removes and creates obstacles, this little heaven for nature lovers offers a choice of budget, eco-friendly accommodations that are clean, spacious, and in a rustic local style. **Pros:** in the heart of nature; good service; yoga and meditation on offer. **Cons:** a little isolated ($4 tuk-tuk ride); not much to do here. [$] *Rooms from: $35* ✉ *Kampong Kreang* ☎ *092/724612* 🌐 *www.ganesharesort.com* 🛏 *8 rooms* 🍴 *Breakfast.*

$ B&B/INN 🏨 **Orchid Guesthouse.** This quiet but quaint little guesthouse on a neighborhood street offers bungalows and a patio in a pleasant garden setting. **Pros:** cheap; friendly staff; free Wi-Fi. **Cons:** away from the river; a little tacky; converted garage room is uncomfortable. [$] *Rooms from: $10* ✉ *Across from Acleda Bank and Blissful Guesthouse* ☎ *092/226996* ✎ *orchidguesthousekampot@yahoo.com* 💳 *No credit cards* 🛏 *34 rooms* 🍴 *No meals.*

KEP

25 km (16 miles) east of Kampot, 172 km (107 miles) south of Phnom Penh.

You'll never find another seaside getaway quite like Kep, with its narrow pebble-and-sand coastline bordered by the ghostly villa ruins of the Khmer Rouge era. What once was the coastal playground of Cambodia's elite and the international glitterati was destroyed in decades of war. Ever so slowly investors are refurbishing what's salvageable; most of the villas now being turned into resorts were bought for next to nothing in the early 1990s. When you arrive, tuk-tuk drivers and tour guides are sure to find you. Not much traffic comes through Kep, so the locals know the bus schedule. They're sure to offer you a tour of a nearby pepper plantation, which can be a rewarding experience but also a long, bumpy ride along dusty rural roads (a 4x4 or regular car is the best option). Kep grows some of the world's best pepper, which you can enjoy in its green, red, black and white phases in a multitude of traditional dishes—the crab with Kampot pepper is especially good.

The beach in town is small and a popular picnic spot for locals who come to relax at the water's edge. Offshore, beautiful **Rabbit Island** has attracted a lot of tourists over the last few years, and the unfortunate result is that it has become somewhat polluted. You can hire a boat to take you there for $7 to $10. If you are a true nature adventurer and choose to stay at one of the 30 or so bungalows here, be warned—there are snakes in the interior of the island and there is only sporadic electricity—and the nightly massing of bugs is not for the fainthearted; but, having said all this, the tropical paradise can inspire most to conquer their fears.

CLOSE UP

Cambodia's Early History

The earliest prehistoric site excavated in Cambodia is the cave of Laang Spean in the northwest. Archaeologists estimate that hunters and gatherers lived in the cave 7,000 years ago. Some 4,000 years ago this prehistoric people began to settle in permanent villages. The Bronze Age settlement of Samrong Sen, near Kampong Chhnang, indicates that 3,000 years ago people knew how to cast bronze axes, drums, and gongs for use in religious ceremonies; at the same time, they domesticated cattle, pigs, and water buffaloes. Rice and fish were then, as now, the staple diet. By 500 BC Ironworking had become widespread, rice production increased, and moats and embankments were being built to enclose their circular village settlements. It was at this stage that Indian traders and missionaries arrived—in a land then called Suvarnabhumi, or Golden Land.

Legend has it that in the 1st century AD the Indian Brahman Kaundinya arrived by ship in the Mekong Delta, where he met and married a local princess named Soma. The marriage led to the founding of the first kingdom on Cambodian soil. Archaeologists believe that the kingdom's capital was at Angkor Borei in Takeo Province.

In the 6th century the inland kingdom of Zhen La emerged. It comprised several small city-states in the Mekong River basin. A period of centralization followed, during which temples were built, cities enlarged, and land irrigated. Power later shifted to Siem Reap Province, where the history of the Khmer Empire started when a king of uncertain descent established the Devaraja line by becoming a "god-king." This royal line continues today.

8

GETTING HERE AND AROUND

To get here, take a taxi or bus, or hire a car and driver through your hotel. The journey from Phnom Penh takes approximately 3½ hours. A single bus ticket is $5 from Phnom Penh's Central Market. Hiring a taxi or a car with driver will cost at least $40.

WHERE TO EAT

A strip of simple cateries mainly run by local fishermen and their families can be found in the seafront Crab Market area. Here you can take your pick of these good-value local haunts, each serving tons of fresh seafood dishes—mainly finger lickin' crab—for around $6. Choices range from fresh salads and crunchy patties to succulent, spicy curries starring the famously flavorsome green, red, or black pepper from neighboring Kampot. Ideally, arrive around sunset to watch the fishermen returning with their catch, and to enjoy the mesmerizing colors play on the ocean before tucking into your dinner. Don't expect anything fancy from these basic restaurants; overall, hygiene standards are adhered to, and service is polite.

$ ✕ **Breezes.** In tiny Kep, where you can quickly tire of the Crab Market

SEAFOOD options or your hotel restaurant, this slightly out-of-the-way spot is a refreshing alternative, serving local seafood tapas style in a romantic seaside setting. The restaurant-lounge stands on a terrace in a pretty garden, where you can relax on loungers and enjoy the fresh sea breeze. Wi-Fi access makes this a great place to hang out for several hours. Try the fresh oysters, king prawns with a Kampot pepper sauce, or seafood wraps accompanied by a glass of chilled white wine. [$] *Average main: $8* ✉ *Rd. 33* ☎ *097/813–2642* ▭ *No credit cards.*

$$ INTERNATIONAL FAMILY 🍴 **Sailing Club.** A great way to combine seaside eating and fun, especially for families, the Knai Bang Chatt hotel's Sailing Club is open throughout the day and welcomes all for seafood barbecues, a popular Sunday brunch, and light meals as well as beach volleyball, sailing, Hobie Cat rentals, and kayaking. Linger on until the evening to sip a cocktail and take in the stunning sunset views. Those coming for a sunset dinner will be delighted by the range of delicious local and western dishes served at this revamped former fisherman's cottage. [$] *Average main: $10* ✉ *Phum Thmey, Sangkat Prey Thom* ☎ *036/210310* 🌐 *www.knaibangchatt.com* ⏲ *Closed Mon.*

WHERE TO STAY

$ B&B/INN 🏨 **Beach House.** Perched on a hillside overlooking the tree-lined coast, the Beach House offers picturesque perspectives of Kep, the sea, and a nice pool set in pretty gardens. **Pros:** enjoyable saltwater pool and Jacuzzi; centrally located; lovely ocean views. **Cons:** lower-floor room views obstructed by electrical wires; beach narrow and rocky in places; service can be sluggish. [$] *Rooms from: $35* ✉ *On beach road in central Kep, Kampot* ☎ *012/712750* 🌐 *www.thebeachhousekep.com* ▭ *No credit cards* 🛏 *16 rooms* 🍽 *No meals.*

$$$$ RESORT Fodor's Choice ★ 🏨 **Knai Bang Chatt.** In this scenic and luxurious resort you will experience the laissez-faire glamour of the Kep of the 1960s and 1970s, when it was a fashionable seaside escape for Cambodian royalty and the international elite. **Pros:** exclusive and luxurious; scenic beach location; old-fashioned elegance. **Cons:** a bit isolated; not the best beach in Cambodia. [$] *Rooms from: $200* ✉ *Phum Thmey, Sangkat Prey, Thom Khan, Kampot* ☎ *036/210310* 🌐 *www.knaibangchatt.com* 🛏 *18 rooms* 🍽 *No meals; Some meals.*

$$ RESORT 🏨 **Le Bout du Monde.** Meaning "the end of the world" in French, Le Bout du Monde is perched on the top of a steep hill near the national park, with beautifully landscaped gardens, far-reaching views, and eco-friendly credentials. **Pros:** ecological and social ethics; wonderfully scenic; enjoyable hiking trails nearby; truly tranquil ambience. **Cons:** in-room humidity can be challenging in wet season; mattresses are a little hard. [$] *Rooms from: $55* ✉ *Preah Thom* ☎ *097/5261846* 🌐 *www.leboutdumondekep.com* 🛏 *9 rooms* 🍽 *Breakfast.*

LAOS

WELCOME TO LAOS

TOP REASONS TO GO

★ **Natural Beauty:** It may not have the sheer variety of Thailand, but Laos is a beautiful country. Take a multiday trek or bike ride, or enjoy the fantastic mountain scenery from Luang Prabang to Vang Vieng. The far north from Luang Nam Tha to Phongsaly offers the best trekking and nature options.

★ **Archaeological Wonders:** The country's most unusual attraction is the Plain of Jars, which has 5-ton stone-and-clay jars of mysterious origin. Wat Phu, pre-Angkor Khmer ruins, is Laos's most recent UNESCO World Heritage Site.

★ **Buddhist Customs:** Observing or participating in morning alms in Luang Prabang is a magical experience; so, too, is sitting in a temple to chat with a novice monk, surrounded by the sounds of chanting and chiming bells.

★ **The Mekong:** The Mekong River is the lifeline of Laos. You can travel down the mighty tributary on a slow cruise, or stop at one of 4,000 islands for a chance to spot freshwater dolphins.

1 Vientiane and Nearby. Vientiane is a curiosity—more like a small market town than a national capital—but it has some fine temples, many French colonial buildings, and a riverside boulevard unmatched elsewhere in Laos. Vang Vieng, a short bus ride north, has beautiful mountains, caves, waterfalls, and a laid-back, rural vibe.

2 Luang Prabang and Northern Laos. Luang Prabang is the country's major tourist destination, thanks to its royal palace (now a museum), temples, French colonial architecture, and the villagelike ambience it retains and refines. Hill tribes, Buddhist rituals, and Lao textiles are also major draws of the country, as are trekking and river-rafting adventures.

3 **Southern Laos.** The far southern region sees fewer tourists than other parts, but Pakse is an interesting town and a convenient base from which to explore the fabulous Wat Phu and other ancient Khmer ruins. Fishing villages line the lower reaches of the Mekong River, a water wonderland with islands, countless waterfalls, and the rare Irrawaddy dolphin.

GETTING ORIENTED

Boxed in by China, Myanmar (Burma), Thailand, Cambodia, and Vietnam, Laos is geographically divided into three regions, each with its chief city: northern Laos and Luang Prabang, central Laos and Vientiane, southern Laos and Pakse. About 90% of Laos is mountainous, so once you leave Vientiane, Luang Prabang, and the southern lowlands you're in true off-the-beaten-track territory. Luang Prabang and Luang Nam Tha are the best bases for single or multiday trekking, biking, and river-rafting expeditions.

9

NEED TO KNOW

LAOS

Vientiane

AT A GLANCE

Capital: Vientiane

Population: 6,769,700

Currency: kip

Money: ATMs in cities; U.S. Dollar and Thai Bhat widely accepted; credit cards only in resort areas.

Language: Lao

Country Code: 856

Emergencies: Call local police

Driving: On the right

Electricity: 230v/50 cycle; plugs are either U.S. standard two- and three-prong or European standard with two round prongs. Power converter needed.

Time: 11 hours ahead of New York

Documents: Up to 30 days with valid passport; visa on arrival

Mobile Phones: GSM (900 and 1800 bands)

Major Mobile Companies: LaoTelecom, Unitel, Beeline, ETL Mobile

WEBSITES

National Tourism Authority of the Lao People's Democratic Republic.: ⊕ www.tourismlaos.org

Diethelm Travel: ⊕ www.visit-mekong.com/laos

Green Discovery Laos: ⊕ www.greendiscoverylaos.com

GETTING AROUND

✈ **Air Travel:** Luang Prabang International Airport is the busiest, followed by Wattay International Airport in Vientiane.

🚌 **Bus Travel:** A bus network covers almost the entire country. Though cheap, bus travel is slow and can be uncomfortable. VIP buses connect Vientiane, Luang Prabang, and Pakse.

🚗 **Car Travel:** Renting a car is not recommended, as driving conditions are extremely difficult

PLAN YOUR BUDGET

	HOTEL ROOM	MEAL	ATTRACTIONS
Low Budget	407,000 kip	40,700 kip	Night Market Luang Prabang, Free
Mid Budget	813,000 kip	81, 300 kip	Royal Palace, 32,500 kip
High Budget	1.4 million kip	162,000 kip	3-day Gibbon Experience, 2.5 million kip

WAYS TO SAVE

Go for carbs. Vietnamese pho noodles and baguette sandwich vendors are prolific and incredibly cheap eating options throughout Laos.

Know your *tuk-tuk* **or taxi fares.** Don't believe the "official" prices placard displayed by drivers. Don't get into a tuk-tuk or taxi before you've agreed on a fare, and negotiate in kip.

Hire a driver. A better alternative to renting a vehicle is to hire a car and driver for about $50 per day.

Pay for your visa in dollars. You can use dollars or Thai bhat freely in Laos but the price for a visa on arrival is about 30% more when paying with bhat.

PLAN YOUR TIME

Hassle Factor	High. There are no direct flights from the U.S. to Laos but it is easily accessed by flight through other points in SE Asia.
3 days	Experience the majesty of Luang Prabang, an entire city that has been declared a UNESCO World Heritage Site. Take a day trip up the Mekong River to see villages and explore cliff-side caves.
1 week	You have more time to spend in Luang Prabang and either take a Mekong River trip west to Huay Xai and do a 3-day gibbon eco-adventure or go north to hit Laos's northern-most province, Luang Nam Tha, to join a trek to visit forest-dwelling ethnic minorities.
2 weeks	Spend a full week in northern Laos in Luang Prabang and Luang Nam Tha and go west to Huay Xai. While up north, try to head to Phonsavan to reach The Plain of Jars. Then head back to Luang Prabang and go south on serene Route 13 to Vang Vieng and then Vientiane.

WHEN TO GO

High Season: November to March is the more comfortable time to tour Laos. Laos has a busy festival calendar and Vientiane and Luang Prabang, in particular, can get very crowded during the most important of these festivals.

Low Season: In the rainy season from June to October, road and air travel can be slower and days can get very hot and sticky. August and September see the most rain, but the country is greener and less crowded during the rains and prices are lower.

Value Season: In April and May you'll still have dry-season conditions, but lower hotel prices. The temperatures will creep up from the dry season to around the 70°F and 80°F mark, but not quite reach the rainy season's 100°F.

BIG EVENTS

April: Bun Pimai, or Lao New Year, is when all the important Buddha images get a cleaning with scented water.

May: During Bun Bang Fai, or The Rocket Festival, rockets are fired in the paddy fields to bring rain in time for the planting of the rice seedlings.

August: During the special rice ceremony of Bun Khao Padab Din, locals make offerings at temples to keep alive the memory of spirits who have no relatives.

October: Celebrate Bun Ok Pansa marking the end of Buddhist Lent with candlelight processions and boat races.

READ THIS

■ *The Coroner's Lunch,* Colin Cotterill. Paris-trained Dr.Paiboun becomes national coroner after the communist revolution.

■ *Flight Across the Mekong,* Jennifer Cook. A Canadian family trapped in Laos in 1975.

■ *The Ravens,* Christopher Robbins. American air con-trollers struggle during the CIA's secret war in Laos.

WATCH THIS

■ *Sabaidee Luang Pra-bang.* While visiting Laos, a Thai photographer falls in love with his tour guide.

■ *Chanthaly.* Horror film about a girl reconnecting with her dead mother.

■ *The Rocket.* Award-win-ning story of a determined young kid born in the mountains.

EAT THIS

■ *Larb*: meat salad with shallots, lime juice, chilies, and garlic

■ *Tam Mak Hu*: Lao ver-sion of green-papaya salad

■ *Orlam*: an eggplant-and-meat stew with bitter herbs

■ *Pho*: noodle soup, served for breakfast

■ *Grilled Seaweed*: sprin-kled with sesame seeds, with a spicy chili dip

■ *Catfish*: Prepared just about every way imaginable

Updated by Dave Stamboulis

Despite a limited infrastructure, Laos is a wonderful country to visit. Laotians are some of the friendliest, gentlest people in Southeast Asia—devoutly Buddhist and traditional in many ways. Laos has a rich culture and history, and though it's been a battleground many times in the past, this is a peaceful, stable country today. Fewer than 7 million people live in this landlocked nation whose countryside is dominated by often impenetrable forested mountains. Not yet inured to countless visiting foreigners, locals volunteer assistance and offer a genuine welcome.

Luang Prabang and its historic sites are the country's primary claim to fame and the reason most tourists visit, but as a destination Laos also excels with its abundant nature and the chance the small towns and villages here provide to escape normally overcrowded Southeast Asia. In many ways a visit to Laos is a placid throwback to what travel in Thailand was like two decades or so ago. Many parts of the country—among them 4,000 Islands in the Mekong, or Phongsaly, Muang Ngoi, and Luang Nam Tha in the north—offer a fabulous opportunity to unwind, relax, and get away from the stresses of big cities and got-to-see-everything travel. Most visitors to Laos enter via Vientiane, but even here the rhythm of life is calmer than in its regional counterparts. As you venture forth from the capital city, as nearly all visitors do and should, the vibe becomes mellower still.

PLANNING

WHEN TO GO

Laos has a tropical climate with two distinct seasons: the dry season, from November through May, and the rainy season, from June through October. The cooler portion of the dry season, from November through

February, is a comfortable time to tour Laos. By mid-March temperatures begin to soar. The country becomes baking hot, and because farmers burn their fields in spring, the air turns brown and hazy. In the rainy season, road and air travel can be slower and the days are often very hot and sticky; August and September see the most rain. On the upside, the country is greener and less crowded during the rains and prices are lower.

The yearly average temperature is about 82°F (28°C), rising to a maximum of 100°F (38°C) during April and May. In the mountainous areas around Luang Nam Tha, Phonsavan, and Phongsaly, however, temperatures can drop to 59°F (15°C) in winter and sometimes hit the freezing point at night.

Laos has a busy festival calendar and Vientiane and Luang Prabang, in particular, can get very crowded during the most important of these festivals, among them Lao New Year, in April, and Vientiane's That Luang Festival, in November. Book your hotel room well in advance during these periods.

PLANNING YOUR TIME

Given distances in Laos and its mountainous terrain, if you've only got a week to spend here, you'll have to choose between visiting the north or south. A popular strategy in the north would be to enter Laos in Huay Xai from Chiang Mai/Chiang Rai in Thailand, then take the two-day boat trip on the Mekong to Luang Prabang. If you are a mountain lover, you could skip the boat ride and take a minivan to Luang Nam Tha, and spend a couple of days here kayaking or trekking in the Nam Ha Reserve or visiting ethnic minority hill tribes. From here, it takes long day's journey to get to Luang Prabang, where you can relax in a colonial resort and enjoy the UNESCO World Heritage sites. Luang Prabang is more about the atmosphere than actual sights, so a few days can be enough for a quick visit. Afterward, take a bus south to Vang Vieng, or else a van to the Plain of Jars, and spend a few days in either of these spots, with Vang Vieng the best option for nature and scenery lovers, and the Plain of Jars of interest for history and archaeology buffs. From Vang Vieng, a few hours' drive by car will get you to Vientiane; from the Plain of Jars, you can fly. Spend your last night in Vientiane, which has all services and connections out of the country. If you opt for seeing the 4,000 Islands and southern Laos, it's best to head here from Ubon Ratchathani in Thailand, crossing over to Pakse (or else flying from Vientiane if you have been up north). Pakse isn't worth more than a day, so head down to Champasak for a day exploring Wat Phu and staying in the quiet river town or else across on Don Daeng Island. Then head to Don Khong, Don Khon, or Don Det for a few days, where you can investigate the Irrawaddy dolphins in the Mekong, check out the spectacular waterfalls, and enjoy the sleepy island life. It's worth it from here to make a side trip up to the Tad Fane waterfall and the coffee-growing region on the Bolaven Plateau. With all these side trips, you'll need at least four days here.

GETTING HERE AND AROUND
AIR TRAVEL
Most of Laos's mountainous terrain is impenetrable jungle, and road travel here is very slow; the only practical way to tour the country in less than a week is by plane. Bangkok Air has daily flights from Bangkok to Luang Prabang; Thai Air flies to Vientiane; and Lao Airlines runs frequent, slightly more expensive flights from Bangkok to Luang Prabang and Vientiane, as well as provincial cities including Pakse and Savannakhet. (⇨ *Air Travel in Travel Smart Thailand*).

■TIP➜ An inexpensive and convenient option to is to fly Air Asia Thai Smile, or Nok Air from Bangkok to either Ubon Ratchathani or Udon Thani and then cross the border by land, putting you in Vientiane or Pakse in less than an hour.

BOAT TRAVEL
Running virtually the entire length of the country, the Mekong River is a natural highway. Because all main cities lie along the Mekong, boats are an exotic yet practical means of travel. Mekong Cruises operates two luxury cruise routes, the Luang Say (⇨ *River Journey to Huay Xai*) and the Vat Phou (⇨ *Pakse*). Shompoo Cruise (⇨ *River Journey to Huay Xai*) offers a midrange alternative to the Luang Say cruise.

BUS TRAVEL
A network of bus services covers almost the entire country. Though cheap, bus travel is slow and not as comfortable as in Thailand. VIP buses, which connect Vientiane, Luang Prabang, and Pakse, are somewhat more comfortable—they have assigned seats and more legroom, and make fewer stops. Minivan service, common between cities, costs slightly more than the bus, but it's quicker and some companies pick up passengers at their hotels. ■TIP➜ Sleeper buses travel between Vientiane and Pakse, but beds are less than 6 feet long, so tall folks may want to buy both spots in what is essentially one shared small bed.

CAR TRAVEL
Although it's possible to enter Laos by car or motorbike and drive around on your own, this is not recommended, as driving conditions are difficult: nearly 90% of the country's 14,000 km (8,700 miles) of roads are unpaved; road signs are often indecipherable; and accidents will invariably be considered your fault. A better alternative is to hire a car and driver for about $50 per day.

SONGTHAEW AND TUK-TUK TRAVEL
Tuk-tuks and songthaews cruise the streets and are easy to flag down in most towns. Tuk-tuk drivers can be unscrupulous about fares, especially in Luang Prabang and Vientiane. ■TIP➜ Do not believe the "official" prices placard displayed by drivers in Vientiane. Don't get into a tuk-tuk before you've agreed on a fare and don't negotiate in dollars—get a quote in kip or baht. Expect to pay about 25% more than you would for a similar ride in Thailand.

BORDER CROSSINGS
In addition to the international airports in Vientiane, Luang Prabang, and Pakse, there are numerous land and river crossings into Laos. The busiest is the Friendship Bridge, between Laos and Thailand, which

spans the Mekong River 29 km (12 miles) east of Vientiane. Other border crossings from Thailand to Laos are: Chiang Khong to Huay Xai (by bridge across the Mekong River); Nakhon Phanom to Tha Kaek; Mukdahan to Savannakhet; and Chongmek to Vang Tao. There are also several new open crossings from the more remote Loei and Phrae provinces in northern Thailand. You can also enter Laos from Cambodia at Non Nok Khiene, and from Mohan, in China's Yunnan Province, at Boten. There are seven crossings between Laos and Vietnam, including Cau Treu to Nam Phao (from near Vinh, Vietnam, to Lak Xao in Laos), Nam Can to Nam Khan (Vinh to Phonsavan); and Lao Bao to Dansavan (on the Hue to Savannakhet route).

Border crossings are open daily from 8:30 to 5, except for the Friendship Bridge, which is open daily from 6 am to 10 pm.

> ## EXCHANGE RATE
>
> With an exchange rate of more than 8,100 Lao kip to the U.S. dollar, keeping track of what things cost can be difficult. Currency rates fluctuate daily, but below is a quick conversion chart, with kip figures rounded up or down as applicable.
>
> 8,100 kip = $1
>
> 41,000 kip = $5
>
> 81,000 kip = $10
>
> 162,000 kip = $20
>
> 410,000 kip = $50
>
> 820,000 kip = $100
>
> 1 million kip = $123

MONEY MATTERS

The currency is the Lao kip (LAK), which comes in relatively small notes (the largest denomination equals about $12). Most prices in this chapter are listed in kip, sometimes with the U.S. dollar equivalent for reference. The Thai baht is accepted in Vientiane, Luang Prabang, and border towns. It's best to carry most of your cash in dollars or baht and exchange relatively small amounts of kip as you travel. At this writing, the official exchange rate is approximately 250 kip to the Thai baht and a little more than 8,100 kip to one U.S. dollar.

There are ATMs throughout the country so changing money is not a big issue.

Credit cards are accepted in most hotels and some restaurants, but few shops. Banks in major tourist destinations will provide a cash advance on a MasterCard or Visa, typically for a 5% service charge. Western Union has branches in Vientiane and other major towns.

HEALTH AND SAFETY

■TIP➔ **Laos's health care is nowhere near as good as Thailand's. If you will be traveling extensively, consider buying international health insurance that covers evacuation to Thailand.**

Take the same health precautions in Laos that you would in Thailand (⇨ *Health in Travel Smart Thailand*). Pharmacies are stocked with Thai antibiotics and are often staffed with assistants who speak some English. Vientiane is malaria-free, but if you're visiting remote regions, consider taking prophylactics. HIV is widespread in border areas. Reliable Thai condoms are available in Laos.

Laos is fairly free of crime in tourist areas. Pickpocketing is rare, but you should still be careful in crowded areas. Never leave luggage unattended.

Penalties for drug possession are severe. Prostitution is illegal, and $500 fines can be levied against foreigners for having sexual relations with Lao citizens to whom they are not married (how this is enforced is unclear, but even public displays of affection may be interpreted as shady behavior).

■TIP➔ In the countryside, trekkers should watch out for unexploded ordnance left over from the Vietnam War, especially in Xieng Khuang (Plain of Jars) and Hua Phan provinces, and in southern Laos. Don't wander off well-traveled trails. Better yet, trek with a qualified guide. Do not photograph anything that may have military significance, such as airports or military installations.

PASSPORTS AND VISAS

You'll need a passport and a visa to enter Laos. Visas can be obtained on arrival at most entry points, but if you're taking the cross-border bus to Vientiane from Udon Thani or Nong Khai in Thailand, you'll need to get a visa in advance. You can do this at the Lao embassy in Bangkok *(Getting Here and Around in Vientiane)* or consulate in Khon Kaen in an hour or through an embassy or travel agency before you leave home. Tourist visas are good for 30 days, cost $35 for Americans, and can be paid for in U.S. dollars (if you are buying a visa at the Lao border or in a Lao embassy or consulate in Thailand, you can pay in baht, but you will be charged B1,500, which is much more than $35). You'll need to have two passport-size photos (one photo if buying at the border) with you. Bring photos from home, get them in Bangkok, or pay an extra 40 baht at the border for a photo. Occasionally immigration officials ask to see evidence of sufficient funds and a plane ticket out of the country. Showing them credit and ATM cards should be proof enough of funds.
■TIP➔ Regulations change without warning, so check with the Lao embassy in your home country before setting out.

Lao Embassy (Bangkok). ✉ *502/502/1–3 Soi Sahakarnpramoon, Pracha Uthit Rd., Wangthonglang, Bangkok* ☎ *02/539–6667.*

TOURS

Diethelm Travel. One of the oldest and most respected travel agencies offering package trips to Laos, Diethelm is a good source for travel information and tours in Laos. The agency's Taste of Laos tour focuses on the country's coffee industry. Multiday tours to Wat Phu take in other major attractions in southern Laos. ✉ *Kian Gwan II Building, 14/F, 140/1 Wireless Rd., Pathumwan* ☎ *02/660–7000* ⊕ *www. diethelmtravel.com* 💰 *From 925,000 kip ($114) per person for 2 travelers (higher rate for 1 person, lower for more than 2)* Ⓜ *BTS Ploenchit* ✉ *Thadeua Rd., Unit 10, Ban Phaxay, at That Khao Rd., Vientiane* ☎ *021/316393, 020/5556–6922* ⊕ *www.diethelmtravel.com.*

Green Discovery Laos. The top eco- and adventure-tour operator in Laos, Green Discovery offers a staggering array of adventure, eco, and cultural tours, from one day to one week, throughout the country. The company, which trains its guides well, is also the best source for local information. ✉ *54 Setthathirat Rd., Ban Xieng Ngeun, Nam Phou, Vientiane* ✛ *Next door to Kop Chai Deu* ☎ *021/223022* ⊕ *www.greendiscoverylaos.com* 💰 *From 1,000,000 kip ($123) per person for 2 travelers.*

National Tourism Authority of the Lao People's Democratic Republic. The official government tourist agency has offices in Vientiane and all other provinces in Laos. The staff provides some printed materials and tries to be helpful, but you are probably better off going to private travel agencies for more detailed information. ✉ *Box 3556 , Ave. Lane Xang, Vientiane* ✛ *East side of street near Dongpalane Rd.* ☎ *021/212248, 021/212251* ⊕ *www.tourismlaos.org* ☽ *Weekdays 9–noon and 1–4.*

RESTAURANTS

For a sleepy, off-the-beaten-path country, Laos has some excellent dining options. Choices in Luang Prabang and Vientiane are endless, among them high-end French restaurants; Japanese, Thai, Indian, and pizza places; and fantastic bakeries and coffee shops. In smaller locales, you might have to make do with sticky rice and grilled meats or fish, but most towns have at least one or two fancier places with decent menus. Lao food is similar to Thai, but not quite as spicy or varied. Vietnamese pho noodles are widely available, and the same goes for baguette sandwiches, which are a convenient option for bus trips.

Prices in the reviews are the average cost of a main course at dinner or, if dinner is not served, at lunch.

HOTELS

Luang Prabang has some of the most elegant resorts in the world. Vientiane has a classic colonial luxury hotel, a few boutique options, and several international-caliber business-style hotels. Upscale options have opened around Champasak in the south. Otherwise, fancy resorts in Laos are few and far between, though there are perfectly adequate facilities in Pakse and the Plain of Jars. New resorts are starting to spring up, but in Phongsaly, Muang Ngoi, 4,000 Islands, and other out-of-the-way places, amenities such as Wi-Fi connections and even basics like hot water may not be up to par.

Prices in the reviews are the lowest cost of a standard double room in high season.

WHAT IT COSTS			
$	**$$**	**$$$**	**$$$$**
Restaurants	under 81,000 kip	81,000– 122,000 kip	122,001– 162,000 kip	over 162,000 kip
Hotels	under 410,000 kip	410,000– 820,000 kip	820,001– 1,230,000 kip	over 1,230,000 kip

Restaurant prices are for a main course, excluding tax and tip. Hotel prices are for a standard double in high season, excluding service charge and tax.

VIENTIANE AND NEARBY

Vientiane is not only the capital of Laos but also the logical gateway to the country, as it's far more accessible to the outside world than Luang Prabang. The city sits along the Mekong River, with Thailand just across the water. A 20-minute ride by taxi or tuk-tuk brings you to the Friendship Bridge, which links Laos and Thailand. Crossing the bridge is a mere formality. On the Thai side of the bridge is the riverside frontier town of Nong Khai, which has direct rail services to Bangkok and a bus terminus serving the Thai capital and most cities in eastern Isan. Many tourists choose this route from Thailand into Laos, although Vientiane is easily and cheaply reached by air from Bangkok, Chiang Mai, and most Southeast Asian cities.

VIENTIANE

Laos's capital is a low-key, pleasant city thanks to its small size, relative lack of traffic, and navigable layout. The pace here is as slow as the Mekong River, which flows along the edge of town. Aside from the magnificent lotus-shape stupa Pha That Luang, there aren't too many must-sees, but the promenade along the Mekong and the many wats scattered about are great to explore by bicycle.

The abundance of ugly cement-block buildings in urgent need of paint gives Vientiane a superficially run-down appearance, but this only makes the remnants of elegant French colonial architecture stand out all the more. There are also dozens of temples—ornate, historic Buddhist structures that stand amid towering palms and flowering trees. First-time visitors often find Vientiane a drab, joyless city, but you only have to arrive during the weeklong That Luang Festival in November to be reminded that first impressions can be misleading.

GETTING HERE AND AROUND

AIR TRAVEL Vientiane's Wattay International Airport is about 4 km (2½ miles) from the city center. You can take a metered taxi from the airport into the city for 80,000 kip; get a taxi voucher from the kiosk in the arrivals hall. The ride to the city center takes about 15 minutes. Alternatively, if you don't have much luggage, walk out of the airport gate and take a tuk-tuk for 40,000 kip.

BUS TRAVEL The best way to get to Vientiane from Thailand via bus is to take one of the hourly buses from either Udon Thani (two hours; B80) or Nong Khai (one hour; B55). ■TIP→ These buses take you straight to Talat Sao, Vientiane's Morning Market, but you cannot board them unless you already have a Lao visa.

If you don't have an advance visa, you can take a bus from Udon Thani to Nong Khai, then a tuk-tuk to the border (from B30 to B50), cross the Friendship Bridge on a B20 shuttle bus, and take a taxi (B350), tuk-tuk (B150), or public bus (B20) from the Lao side of the border into Vientiane.

The Northern Bus Terminal for trips to and from northern Laos is 3 km (2 miles) northwest of the center. Buses bound for points in southern

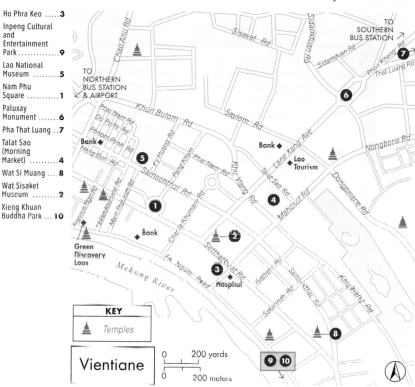

Laos leave from the Southern Bus Station, which is out on Highway 13. The Talat Sao (Morning Market) Bus Station handles local departures.

Although there's city bus service in Vientiane, schedules and routes are confusing for visitors, so it's best to stick to tuk-tuks and taxis. The city bus station is next to the Morning Market.

TAXI AND TUK-TUK TRAVEL You can cover Vientiane on foot, but tuk-tuks and jumbos, their larger brethren, are easy to flag down. Negotiate the price before setting off; you can expect to pay about 20,000 to 40,000 kip for a ride within the city if you are a firm negotiator. Taxis are available, but must be reserved, which you can do through your hotel or at the Morning Market. For day trips outside the city, ask your hotel or guesthouse to book a car with a driver.

SAFETY AND PRECAUTIONS

Vientiane is very safe, but beware of being fleeced by tuk-tuk drivers. Ask a local for correct fares.

TIMING

Most people stay in Vientiane a few days, time enough to tour That Luang and a few other monuments, soak up the sleepy ambience, and enjoy some creature comforts and a Beerlao on the Mekong before heading out into the wilds. If you throw in day trips to Nam Ngun or nearby national parks, you could make it a few more. Vientiane is also the place to take care of any business (onward visas, fax and computer connections, et cetera).

Etiquette and Behavior

Laotians are generally gentle and polite, and visitors should take their lead from them—avoiding any public display of anger or impolite behavior. Even showing affection in public is frowned on.

Laotians traditionally greet others by pressing their palms together in a sort of prayer gesture known as a *nop*; it is also acceptable for men to shake hands. If you attempt a nop, remember that it's basically reserved for social greetings; don't greet a hotel or restaurant employee this way. The general greeting is *sabai di* ("good health"), invariably said with a smile.

Avoid touching or embracing a Laotian, and keep in mind that the head has spiritual significance; even patting a child affectionately on the head could be misinterpreted. Feet are considered "unclean," so when you sit, make sure your feet are not pointing directly at anyone, and never use your foot to point in any situation. Shoes must be removed before you enter a temple or private home, as well as some restaurants and offices.

Shorts and sleeveless tops should not be worn in temple compounds. When visiting a temple, be careful not to touch anything of spiritual significance, such as altars, Buddha images, or spirit houses. Ask permission from anyone before taking a photograph of him or her.

EMERGENCIES
The new Alliance International Medical Centre Clinic, affiliated with the Wattana Hospital in Thailand, is the best medical center in Laos. Most expats and embassy personnel head here to attend to their health needs. ■TIP➔ For anything major, consider crossing the border to Thailand and going to Wattana Hospital in Nong Khai or Udon Thani.

ESSENTIALS
Air Contacts Lao Airlines. ✉ Wattay Airport, Hwy. 13 ☎ 021/212050 up to 54 for international flights, 021/212057, 021/212058 for domestic flights ⊕ www.laoairlines.com. **Thai Airways International.** ✉ M&N Building, ground fl., Souphanouvong Rd., Ban Kunta ✛ Just past Mercure Hotel on way to airport ☎ 021/222527 up to 29 in Vientiane ⊕ www.thaiair.com.

Banks Bank of Lao PDR. ✉ Yonnet Rd. ✛ Just north of Nam Phu Sq. ☎ 021/213300–01 ⊕ www.bol.gov.la. **Banque Pour le Commerce Exterieur Lao (BCEL).** ✉ 1 Pangkham St., Ban Xiengnheun ✛ 1 block south of Nam Phu Sq. ☎ 021/213200 ⊕ www.bcel.com.la.

Car-Rental Agency Avis. ✉ Setthathirat and Hengbounnoy Rds. ☎ 021/223867 ⊕ www.avrlaos.com.

Travel Agencies Diethelm Travel. ✉ Thadeua Rd., Unit 10, Ban Phaxay, at That Khao Rd. ☎ 021/316393 general inquiries, 020/5556–6922 ⊕ www.diethelmtravel.com. **Green Discovery Laos.** ✉ 54 Setthathirat Rd., Ban Xieng Ngeun, Nam Phou ✛ Next door to Kop Chai Deu ☎ 021/223022 ⊕ www.greendiscoverylaos.com. **Lao Top Travel.** ✉ 470 Unit 27 Phontong-Chommany, Chantabury ✛ Near Phontongchommany Market; best to take a tuk-tuk, as agency is hard to find ☎ 021/563058, 021/563057 ⊕ www.laotoptravel.com.

EXPLORING
TOP ATTRACTIONS

Ho Phra Keo. There's a good reason why Ho Phra Keo, one of the city's oldest and most impressive temples, has a name so similar to the wat in Bangkok's Grand Palace. The original Ho Phra Keo here was built by King Setthathirat in 1565 to house the Emerald Buddha, which he had taken from Chiang Mai in Thailand. The king installed the sacred statue first in Luang Prabang and then in Vientiane at Ho Phra Keo, but the Siamese army recaptured the Buddha in 1778 and it was installed in Bangkok. The present temple, restored in 1936, is a national museum. On display are Buddha sculptures of different styles, some wonderful chiseled images of Khmer deities, and a fine collection of stone inscriptions. The masterpiece of the museum is a 16th-century lacquered door carved with Hindu images. ⊠ *Setthathirat Rd. and Mahosot Rd.* ☎ *021/212621* ⊠ *5,000 kip* ☉ *Daily 8–noon and 1–4.*

THE RISE OF THE MOON CITY

Originally named Chanthaburi (City of the Moon), Vientiane was founded in the 16th century by King Setthathirat near a wide bend of the Mekong River, on the grounds of a Khmer fortress dating from the 9th to the 13th century. In 1828 the Siamese army from Bangkok razed the city. But the old part of Vientiane is still an attractive settlement, where museums, parks, and some ancient temples that survived the Siamese attack are all just a short distance from one another.

Fodor's Choice ★ **Pha That Luang.** The city's most sacred monument, this massive, 147-foot-high, gold-painted stupa is also the nation's most important cultural symbol, representing the unity of the Lao people. King Setthathirat had it built in 1566 to guard a relic of the Buddha's hair and to represent Mt. Meru, the holy mountain of Hindu mythology, the center and axis of the world. Surrounding the lotus-shape stupa are 30 pinnacles on the third level and a cloistered square on the ground with stone statues of the Buddha. Two brilliantly decorated temple halls, the survivors of four temples originally here, flank That Luang. On the avenue outside the west gate stands a bronze statue of King Setthathirat erected in the 1960s by a pious general. That Luang is the center of a major weeklong festival during November's full moon. The stupa is on the north end of town, a 10-minute songthaew ride from the city center. ⊠ *That Luang Rd.* ✢ *End of That Luang Rd., northeast of Patuxay Monument* ☎ *20/9521–0600* ⊠ *5,000 kip* ☉ *Daily 8–noon and 1:30–4.*

Talat Sao (*Morning Market*). To immerse yourself in Vientiane, visit this vast indoor bazaar that despite its name stays open all day. Shops within the bright and orderly space sell everything from handwoven fabrics and wooden Buddha figures to electric rice cookers and sneakers. Most vendors cater to locals, but there is plenty to interest travelers: fabric, handicrafts, intricate gold-and-silver work, jewelry, T-shirts, and bags and suitcases. Many products are imported from abroad. Fruits, confections, and noodle soups are sold at open-door stalls outside, where Vietnamese shoemakers also ply their trade. Near the main post office, the market is inside a large department store, Laos's first, and spills out into the surrounding area. ⊠ *Ave. Lane Xang and Khu Vieng St.* ☉ *Daily 7–6.*

9

Lao Festivals

Laos has many fascinating festivals, most of them steeped in Buddhism. Book hotels well in advance if you're planning on visiting during festival time, particularly in the big cities.

Bun Bang Fai: The Rocket Festival is held in the middle of May. Rockets are fired and prayers are said in the paddy fields to bring rain in time for the planting of the rice seedlings.

Bun Khao Padab Din: This special rice ceremony takes place in August; the exact date depends on the harvest schedule. People make offerings at temples to keep alive the memory of spirits who have no relatives.

Bun Khao Salak: This rice ceremony whose date also depends on the harvest schedule happens in September. For this one, people visit temples to make offerings for their ancestors. Boat races are held on the Mekong, especially in Luang Prabang and Khammuan Province.

Bun Ok Pansa: The day of the full moon in October marks the end of Buddhist Lent, and is celebrated with donations to local temples. Candlelight processions are held, and colorful floats are set adrift on the Mekong River. The following day, boat races are held in Vientiane, Savannakhet, and Pakse.

Bun Pimai: Lao New Year takes place from April 13 to 15. At this water festival similar to Thailand's Songkran,

all the important Buddha images are cleaned with scented water (and the public gets wet in the bargain). The festivities are particularly lively in Luang Prabang, where the holiday is celebrated for nearly a week.

Bun Visakhabucha (Buddha Day): On the day of the full moon in May, candlelight processions are held in temples to mark the birth, enlightenment, and death of the Buddha.

That Ing Hang Festival: This takes place in Savannakhet in December, and lasts several days on the grounds of the ancient Wat That Inhang, just outside the city. Events include sports contests, performances of traditional Lao music and dance, and a spectacular drumming competition.

That Luang Festival: This weeklong event in Vientiane in November ends with a grand fireworks display. Hundreds of monks gather to accept alms. The festival runs concurrently with an international trade fair showcasing the products of Laos and other countries of the Greater Mekong Subregion (GMS).

Wat Phu Festival: Also known as Makhabucha Day, this festival is held during the day of the first full moon in February at Wat Phu, near Champasak. Elephant races, buffalo fights, cockfights, and traditional Lao music-and-dance performances make for a very full schedule.

Xieng Khuan Buddha Park. The bizarre creation of an ecumenical monk, Luang Pa Bunleua Sulilat, who dreamed of a world religion embracing all faiths, this park is "peopled" by enormous Buddhist and Hindu sculptures spread across an attractive landscape of trees, shrubs, and flower gardens. Keep an eye out for the remarkable 165-foot-long sleeping Buddha. The park was laid out by the monk's followers in 1958 on a strip of land along the Mekong, opposite the Thai town of Nong

Thai invaders destroyed That Luang in 1828; it was restored in the 20th century.

Khai. Get there by taking public Bus 14 from the Talat Sao bus station. ✉ *Vientiane ✛ Thadeua Rd., Km 27–28, northeast of Thai-Lao Friendship Bridge* 🎟 *5,000 kip, 3,000 kip camera fee* ⏱ *Daily 7–6.*

WORTH NOTING

Inpeng Cultural and Entertainment Park. This large park near the river has waterslides, beer gardens, restaurants, and plenty of family fun, plus a model village of miniature Lao houses. Sculptures of Lao heroes dot the grounds, and there's a small zoo. Take a short stroll downriver to admire the sleek lines of the Friendship Bridge, and pop into one of the many restaurants lining the riverbank. Get here via public Bus 14 from the Talat Sao bus station. ✉ *Thadeua Rd. Km 14, Ban Dongphosy ✛ 14 km (9 miles) from Vientiane near Thai border* ☎ *020/5562–0191* 🎟 *5,000 kip, plus 30,000 kip to use pools* ⏱ *Daily 8–4.*

Lao National Museum. A two-story French colonial building houses this well-laid-out museum with interesting geological and historical displays. Exhibits touch on Laos's royal past, its colonial years, and its struggle for liberation. Other highlights include details about the country's 50 main ethnic groups, along with indigenous instruments that illustrate how they made music. ✉ *Samsenthai Rd., opposite Lao National Culture Hall* ☎ *021/212460* 🎟 *10,000 kip* ⏱ *Mon.–Sat. 8–noon and 1–4.*

Nam Phu Square (*Fountain Square*). The main square in Vientiane's tourist area, this used to reflect more emphatically the city's French colonial influence, reinforced further by the cadre of very Gallic restaurants along the perimeter. Unfortunately, a recent renovation saw Nam Phu's namesake central fountain incorporated into a fancy new restaurant, visually disrupting the plazalike feel. The fountain is lit up multicolor at night, and bands perform for a crowd dominated on most days by tourists and Lao youth hanging out. The square and surrounding streets still contain many eateries. ✉ *Nam Phu Fountain, Rue Pangkham.*

Patuxay Monument. An ersatz Arc de Triomphe, the monument is a prominent landmark, if minor attraction, between the city center and Pha That Luang. A disarmingly candid plaque describes Patuxay as a "monster of concrete." Harsh, if perhaps true, but if you have some time to kill during the day, you can scale its seven stories for a decent photo op. ✉ *Ave. Lang Xang* ✥ *2½ km (1½ miles) southeast of Pha That Luang* 🎫 *3,000 kip.*

Wat Si Muang. This wat that dates to 1563—its last major renovation was in 1956—guards the original city pillar, a revered foundation stone also from the 16th century. In a small park in front of the monastery stands a rare memorial to Laos's royal past: a large bronze statue of King Sisavang Vong. ✉ *Samsenthai Rd. at Setthathirat Rd.* ✥ *Near eastern end of Setthathirat Rd.* 🌐 *www.watsimuang.com* 🎫 *Free* 🕒 *Daily 7–5.*

Wat Sisaket Museum. A courtyard with 6,840 Buddha statues stops the show at this intriguing temple-monastery complex across from Ha Phra Keo. Built in 1818 by King Anu, the temple survived Vientiane's 1828 destruction by the Siamese army, and the monastery, still active, remains intact in its original form. The courtyard contains little niches and large platforms with Buddhas of all sizes. The impressive temple hall underwent some restoration in 1938, though it needs further repair. The intricately carved wooden ceiling and doors still impress, but time has taken its toll on the paintings that once covered the hall's walls. ✉ *Setthathirat Rd. at Ave. Lane Xang* ☎ *021/212622* 🎫 *5,000 kip* 🕒 *Daily 8–noon and 1–4.*

WHERE TO EAT

$$ ITALIAN Fodor's Choice ★

🍴 **Acqua.** This relative newcomer has raised the bar for fine dining in Vientiane. With chic mosaics and a cool bar downstairs and private VIP dining areas upstairs, Acqua is visually stunning, and the food keeps pace with the decor. Homemade potato gnocchi, risotto, and other Italian stalwarts grace the menu, along with imported oysters and Wagyu beef. There's a lunch buffet for 88,000 kip. The same owners also run the more affordable Ai Capone next door, a traditional pizzeria. [$] *Average main: kip98,000* ✉ *007/078 Rue Francois Ngin, Ban Mixay, Ban Mixay* ☎ *020/2811–7888, 020/5991–7888* 🌐 *www.acqua.la* 💳 *No credit cards.*

$ ECLECTIC

🍴 **Khop Chai Deu.** A popular downtown restaurant and bar inside a French colonial structure, this is an excellent stop for happy-hour cocktails or dinner. Lao, Asian, and international dishes are prepared, and there's a buffet. For a tasty introduction to traditional Lao cuisine, try the Lao Discovery, a set menu including *larb*, a semi-spicy salad; *tom yum*, a sour chili-and-lemongrass fish soup; *khao niaw*, Lao sticky rice; and a glass of *lao-lao* (rice whisky). Draft beer is on tap, musicians play nightly in the bar, and the kitchen is open until 11 pm. [$] *Average main: kip60,000* ✉ *54 Setthathirat Rd., near Nam Phu Sq.* ☎ *021/263829* 🌐 *www.inthira.com.*

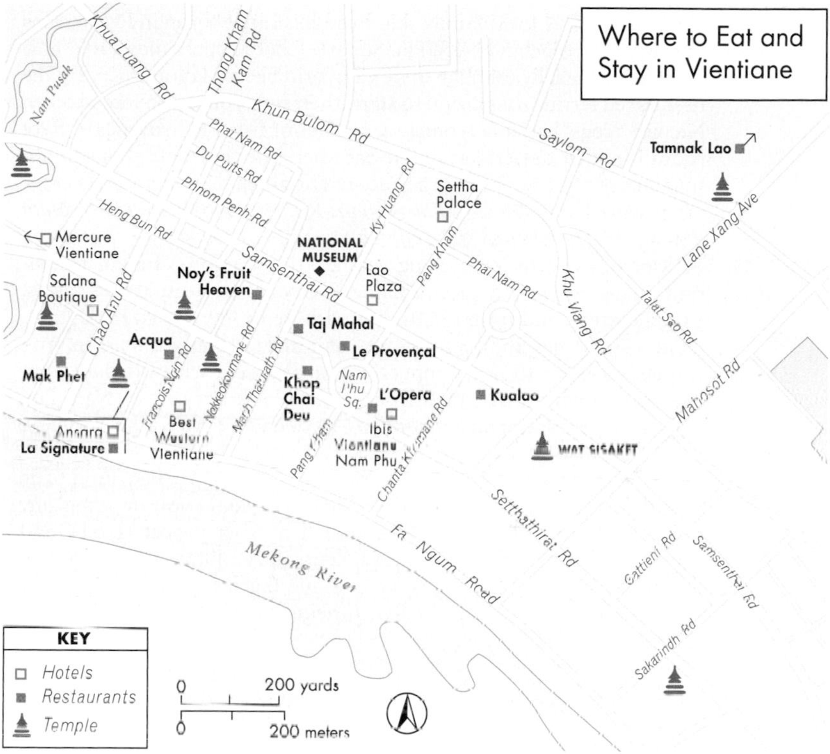

$$ 🍴 **Kualao.** The Lao cuisine at this restaurant inside a fading mansion is
LAO
among Vientiane's best. Favorites include *mok pa fork* (steamed fish wrapped in banana leaves and cooked with eggs, onions, and coconut milk), and *gaeng panaeng*, a thick red curry with chicken, pork, or beef. Servings are small, so most people order several entrées à la carte or from seven to nine dishes, plus dessert and coffee, off set menus. Photos and English descriptions facilitate the ordering process. There's Lao folk dancing nightly from 7 to 9. [$] *Average main: kip85,000* ✉ *134 Samsenthai Rd., 1 block southeast of Nam Phu Sq.* ☎ *021/214813* 🌐 *www.kualaorestaurant.com.*

$$$ 🍴 **La Signature.** The charming restaurant of the boutique Ansara Hotel
FRENCH
Fodor's Choice ★
serves authentic French cuisine in a romantic garden setting. Appetizers on the varied menu might include anything from fish carpaccio or a warm goat-cheese salad to the over-the-top combo of fried duck and duck foie gras. For your entrée you can go haute with rack of lamb or roast lobster, or casual with pizza or a croque monsieur. The daily chef's plates and the tasting menu are both worth checking out, and the wine selection is superb. [$] *Average main: kip150,000* ✉ *Ansara Hotel, Quai Fa Ngum, Ban Vat Cham Tha, Hom 5, Muang Chanthabury* ⊕ *100 meters up from river road on small side lane just past Wat Chan* ☎ *021/213514* 🌐 *www.ansarahotel.com.*

9

$$ FRENCH 🍴 **Le Provençal.** A local family that lived in France for many years runs this little bistro behind Nam Phu Square. Chef Daniel's menu is almost exclusively French, although there's a hybrid pizza à la française. Try the beef-based terrine *du maison* to start, then sink your teeth into chicken Niçoise, frogs' legs à la lyonnaise, or fillet of fish à la Provençale. Save room for such desserts as crème caramel and chocolate mousse. On sunny days you can sit on the terrace overlooking the square. [$] *Average main: kip100,000* ✉ *73/1 Pang Kham Rd.* ✣ *Northwest side of Nam Phu Sq.* ☎ *021/219685* ⏲ *No lunch Sun.*

$$$ ITALIAN 🍴 **L'Opera.** In a city embracing change, this longtime Italian restaurant reigns as a steady grande dame. L'Opera serves authentic pastas, baked entrées, and fresh salads, but with items like the Pizza de Laos, made with chilies and Lao sausage, isn't afraid to mix things up. You can get an espresso or a cappuccino, or choose a wine off the extensive list. Tables on the small front terrace look out on the Nam Phu Square action. [$] *Average main: kip150,000* ✉ *12 Nam Phu Fountain Sq.* ☎ *021/215099.*

$ LAO 🍴 **Mak Phet.** This nonprofit restaurant serves modern Lao food. The profits go toward providing street kids with education or some sort of training, and the very people helped by past proceeds staff and run the restaurant. The food is excellent, the employees well trained, happy, and motivated. Eating here is one big feel-good story. [$] *Average main: kip65,000* ✉ *78 Ban Inpeng Vat Chanh* ☎ *021/260587* 🌐 *www.tree-alliance.org.*

$ CAFÉ 🍴 **Noy's Fruit Heaven.** The family that runs this cute little café serves gourmet sandwiches, prepares various breakfasts, and can whip up just about any tropical fruit smoothie you can dream up. The sandwiches include imported feta, Camembert, or goat cheese melted onto fresh baguettes. The colorful place, which also sells local handicrafts, is a good spot to watch the world go by and meet other travelers. Noy's closes at 8 pm daily. [$] *Average main: kip30,000* ✉ *060 Hengbounnoy Rd.* ☎ *020/5539–6898* 💳 *No credit cards.*

$ INDIAN 🍴 **Taj Mahal.** A nondescript eatery tucked behind the Lao National Culture Hall, Taj Mahal serves Indian food at ridiculously cheap prices. Excellent tandoori naan bread, a good selection of dal and meat and fish curries, and other northern Indian favorites are among the many menu choices. [$] *Average main: kip30,000* ✉ *Setthathirat Rd.* ✣ *Off Nokkeokoumane Rd., behind Lao National Culture Hall* ☎ *020/5561–1003* 💳 *No credit cards.*

$ LAO Fodor's Choice ★ 🍴 **Tamnak Lao.** A wonderful place to experience Lao cuisine and culture, the latter in the form of classical dances performed nightly, this restaurant provides a blissful retreat from the downtown tourist frenzy. You can dine either in the teakwood interior space or outside in the garden. The specialty here is the cuisine of Luang Prabang. Many dishes, such as the *pla larb* (minced fish with herbs), are prepared with fish fresh from the Mekong River. Dinner service doesn't begin until 6. [$] *Average main: kip60,000* ✉ *100 Phonxay, 23 Singha Rd., Saysettha, just northeast of Patuxay Monument* ☎ *021/413562.*

CLOSE UP

Lao Cuisine

It may not be as famous as Thai food, but Lao cuisine is similar and often just as good, though usually less spicy. Chilies are used as a condiment, but Lao cuisine also makes good use of ginger, lemongrass, coconut, tamarind, crushed peanuts, and fish paste. Because so much of the country is wilderness, there's usually game, such as venison or wild boar, on the menu. Fresh river prawns and fish—including the famous, massive Mekong catfish, the world's largest freshwater fish—are also standard fare, along with chicken, vegetables, and sticky rice.

As in Isan, *larb* (meat salad with shallots, lime juice, chilies, garlic, and other spices) is a staple, as are sticky rice and *tam mak hu*, the Lao version of green-papaya salad. Grilled chicken, pork, and duck stalls can be found in every bus station and market in the country. Northern Laos, especially Luang Prabang, is noted for its distinctive cuisine: specialties include grilled Mekong seaweed, sprinkled with sesame seeds and served with a spicy chili dip; and *orlam*, an eggplant-and-meat stew with bitter herbs. Sticky rice, served in bamboo baskets, is the bread and butter of Laos. Locals eat it with their hands, squeezing it into a solid ball or log and dipping it in other dishes.

Throughout the country you'll find *pho*, a Vietnamese-style noodle soup, served for breakfast. Fresh baguettes, a throwback to the French colonial days, are also available everywhere, often made into sandwiches with meat pâté, vegetables, and chili sauce. Laotians wash it all down with extra-strong Lao coffee sweetened with condensed milk, or the ubiquitous Beerlao, a slightly sweet lager.

WHERE TO STAY

$$$ HOTEL Fodor's Choice ★ **Ansara Hotel.** A small boutique hotel on a quiet lane near the Mekong River, the Ansara is convenient to local attractions. **Pros:** extremely quiet; free laptops in rooms; free minibar replenished daily; excellent restaurant. **Cons:** expensive; a bit hard to find, lacks pool, spa, and similar amenities. [$] *Rooms from: kip1.1 million* ✉ *Quai Fa Ngum, Ban Vat Cham Tha, Hom 5, Muang Chanthabury* ✣ *100 meters up from river road on small side lane just past Wat Chan* ☎ *021/213514* 🌐 *www.ansarahotel.com* 🛏 *28 rooms* 🍴 *Breakfast.*

$$ HOTEL **Best Western Vientiane.** With a convenient location in the heart of town near the Mekong River, and comfort at competitive rates, this hotel is popular with business travelers. **Pros:** fitness center and Jacuzzi; quiet pool area; great location near river and restaurants. **Cons:** small pool; no views; rooms feel slightly worn. [$] *Rooms from: kip690,000* ✉ *2–12 Francois Ngin Rd., Ban Mixay* ☎ *021/216906 up to 09* 🌐 *www.bestwesternvientiane.com* 🛏 *44 rooms* 🍴 *Breakfast; No meals.*

$$ HOTEL **Ibis Vientiane Nam Phu.** This a good choice if you're after a trusted brand with clean and comfortable facilities. **Pros:** central Nam Phu Fountain location; blackout curtains on windows; trusted brand; clean and comfortable. **Cons:** no gym or pool; small rooms; breakfast not included. [$] *Rooms from: kip568,000* ✉ *Box 2359, Nam Phu Sq.* ☎ *021/262050* 🌐 *www.ibishotel.com* 🛏 *64 rooms* 🍴 *No meals.*

$$$$ HOTEL 🏨 **Lao Plaza Hotel.** Something of a local landmark, the Lao Plaza stands six stories tall in the center of town. **Pros:** large swimming pool and terrace; enormous beds; central location; three restaurants. **Cons:** way overpriced for what you get; on very busy street; constant hassle from tuk-tuk drivers outside. [$] *Rooms from: kip1.7 million* ✉ *Box 6708, 63 Samsenthai Rd.* ☎ *021/218800, 021/218801* 🌐 *www.laoplazahotel.com* 🛏 *142 rooms* 🍴 *Breakfast.*

$$$ HOTEL 🏨 **Mercure Vientiane.** A five-minute drive from the airport, this modern hotel with a sweeping art-nouveau facade has a pleasant location in front of Fa Ngum Park. **Pros:** tennis courts; full slate of amenities; good Internet discounts. **Cons:** out of town center; on very busy road; expensive. [$] *Rooms from: kip909,000* ✉ *Unit 10, Samsenthai Rd., at Setthathirat Rd.* ☎ *021/213570* 🌐 *www.accorhotels.com* 🛏 *172 rooms* 🍴 *No meals.*

$$$ HOTEL 🏨 **Salana Boutique Hotel.** Rooms with Lao textiles and decor, finely crafted wood floors, and modern amenities like flat-screen TVs and fast Wi-Fi make this boutique hotel on a quiet downtown street a splendid choice. **Pros:** in the heart of the city center; temple views from some rooms; chic, with fine wood floors and Lao decor. **Cons:** rooms are tiny; expensive for downtown. [$] *Rooms from: kip1.1 million* ✉ *Chao Anou Rd., 112 Ban Wat Chan* ☎ *021/254254* 🌐 *www.salanaboutique.com* 🛏 *42 rooms* 🍴 *Breakfast.*

$$$$ HOTEL Fodor's Choice ★ 🏨 **Settha Palace.** This landmark property has been through many changes: erected early in the French colonial period, it was converted into a hotel in the 1930s and expropriated by the communist government in the 1970s. **Pros:** elegant and private; gorgeous furnishings; beautiful pool garden; historical ambience. **Cons:** often fully booked; no elevator; only four standard rooms. [$] *Rooms from: kip1.8 million* ✉ *6 Pang Kham Rd.* ☎ *021/217581, 021/217582* 🌐 *www.setthapalace.com* 🛏 *29 rooms* 🍴 *Breakfast.*

NIGHTLIFE

The after-dark scene in Vientiane is very subdued, mostly confined to certain expensive hotels and a handful of bars and pubs along the Mekong River boulevard.

Bor Pen Yang. Vientiane's most popular bar, also a restaurant serving international cuisine, occupies a prime spot on the Mekong, with great views from the rooftop setting. On most nights the place is packed with locals and travelers—plus an assortment of ladyboys and bar girls—but the views, music, and camaraderie are good enough to prevent it from becoming seedy. Bor Pen Yang is open from 10 am to midnight. ✉ *Fah Ngum Quay, Ban Wat Chan* ☎ *021/264544 office, 020/787–3965.*

I-Beam. The vibe is intimate and elegant at the snazzy downstairs lounge of Le Silapa, a popular high-end French restaurant. There's a happy hour daily from 5 to 7, live music on several nights, and half-price ladies'-night wine specials on Wednesday. A welcome addition to Vientiane's minimal nightlife scene, the I-Beam serves tapas and has Vientiane's largest wine list. ✉ *88 Setthathirat Rd.* ✣ *In front of Wat Ong Teu* ☎ *021/254528, 020/5561–4092* 🌐 *www.facebook.com/ibeamvientiane.*

Jazzy Brick. Popular among foreign nongovernmental organization workers, this brick-and-wood-paneled club has a sophisticated vibe and a staggering 150-cocktail drink menu. You can sidle up to a stool at the downstairs bar, or head to the upstairs space, which is full of comfortable chairs and old TVs. True to its name, the bar occasionally hosts live jazz. Shorts and sleeveless tops are not allowed here. ⊠ *38 Setthathirat Rd., opposite Kop Chai Deu* ☎ *021/212489, 020/7785-7647.*

Lao Bowling Center. The bowling alley around the corner from Settha Palace serves food and drink to a rowdy mix of locals and expats. ⊠ *Khun Bulon Rd. and Rue Le Ky Huong* ☎ *021/218661, 021/223219.*

Traditional Lao Show. The Lane Xang Hotel presents traditional Lao dancing and music nightly from 7 to 9 at its restaurant. The performances are free, though you'll likely want to have dinner or at least drinks. ⊠ *Lane Xang Hotel, Rue Pangkham and Fa Ngum Rd.* ☎ *021/214100* ⊕ *www.lanexanghotel.com.la* 🎫 *Free.*

SHOPPING

Carol Cassidy Lao Textiles. American-born textile expert Carol Cassidy runs this beautiful weaving studio inside a renovated French colonial mansion. She and her team of local artisans, mostly women, create high-quality textiles and scarves, shawls, and wall hangings. ⊠ *84-86 Nok-keokoumane Rd,* ☎ *021/212123* ⊕ *www.laotextiles.com* ☉ *Closed Sun.*

Caruso Lao. For exquisite handwoven Lao silk and fine wood carvings, head to this riverside craft shop, one of the best in Laos. ⊠ *008 Fa Ngum Rd.* ✛ *A few blocks northwest of Don Chan Palace hotel* ☎ *021/223644* ⊕ *www.carusolao.com.*

Phaeng Mai Silk Gallery. This shop in Vientiane's old weaving district sells naturally dyed handwoven silk products. ⊠ *110 Ban Nongbuathong Tai* ☎ *021/217341* ⊕ *www.silk-phaengmai.laopdr.com* ☉ *Closed Sun.*

Saoban Crafts. A fair-trade business that works with traditional artisans to preserve and promote Lao village crafts and empower local women, this shop sells silk and cotton textiles, recycled bomb products, bags, jewelry, and other items. ⊠ *Chao Anou Rd., 97/1 Ban Watchan* ✛ *Near Wat Ong Teu* ☎ *020/5510-0034* ⊕ *www.saobancrafts.com.*

Talat Sao (*Morning Market*). With crafts, jewelry, T-shirts, and more, the morning market will satisfy most shoppers' needs. The adjacent indoor mall hosts many mobile phone sellers and electronics vendors. A visit to the morning market provides perspectives on modern Lao life and the lifestyles of young Laotians. ⊠ *Lane Xang Ave. at Khao Vieng St.*

NAM NGUM LAKE

90 km (56 miles) north of Vientiane.

Nam Ngum Lake. Forested mountains surround this island-dotted reservoir lake that's accessible by car from Vientiane. Floating restaurants here serve freshly caught lake fish, and there's a large hotel complex, the Dansavanh Nam Ngum Resort. Visitors with plenty of time to explore Laos's countryside may want to skip this trip—there are far better destinations—but those on tight schedules will enjoy the opportunity to experience rural Laos without having to venture too far from

Vientiane. Getting here by public transportation is time-consuming. A better option is to take a tour. Green Discovery Laos conducts excellent day trips, 2 million kip ($246) for two people, that include a boat ride on the lake and visits to markets, fishing villages, and salt-extraction cooperatives. ⊠ *Vientiane ✢ Hwy. 10 north from Vientiane.*

GETTING HERE AND AROUND

You can take a bus from Talat Sao Bus Station to the "Talat" bus stop, where songthaews (15,000 kip) continue on to Nam Ngum. The trip takes three hours. To really experience the area, though, consider taking a full-day Green Discovery Laos (⇨ *Tours, in Planning, above*) adventure tour, which includes a boat ride on the lake. Hiring a car and driver for the day will run about 500,000 kip ($62). If you're driving, take Highway 10 north from Vientiane to the Lao Zoo; from there, follow the road for the Dansavanh Resort.

TIMING

This trip is best done as a day tour, but if you have extra time, spend the night in one of the area's many lodges.

PHU KHAO KHOUAY

40 km (25 miles) northeast of Vientiane

Phu Khao Khouay National Protected Area. A dramatic area of sheer sandstone cliffs, river gorges, and abundant wildlife, this nature preserve also contains the Ang Nam Leuk reservoir, an artificial lake explorable by boat. The preserve's three rivers empty into the Mekong. Several simple restaurants and refreshment stands do business along the reservoir's banks. ⊠ *Vientiane ✢ Near Tha Bok village (before Pakxan on Hwy. 13)* ⊕ *www.trekkingcentrallaos.com* ✉ *Entry permit 50,000 kip, village fund 50,000 kip.*

GETTING HERE AND AROUND

The park is about three hours from Vientiane, via Highway 13 south to Tha Bok and then via a side road north from there. Green Discovery Laos (⇨ *Tours, in Planning, above*) runs reasonably priced one- to two-day treks and homestays; this is a good way to see the park, because hiring a car and driver is pricey. If coming on your own, buses run from Talat Sao to Tha Bok (25,000 kip); from there, songthaews go to Ban Hat Khai, where you can arrange treks.

TIMING

One day or an overnight trip is enough time to see the area.

PLAIN OF JARS

390 km (242 miles) northeast of Vientiane, 270 km (162 miles) southeast of Luang Prabang.

Plain of Jars. A major archaeological wonder, the Plain of Jars is one of the world's most tantalizing mysteries. The broad, mountain-ringed plain northeast of Vientiane is littered with hundreds of ancient stone and clay jars, some estimated to weigh 5 or 6 tons. The jars are said to be at least 2,000 years old, but no one knows who made them or why.

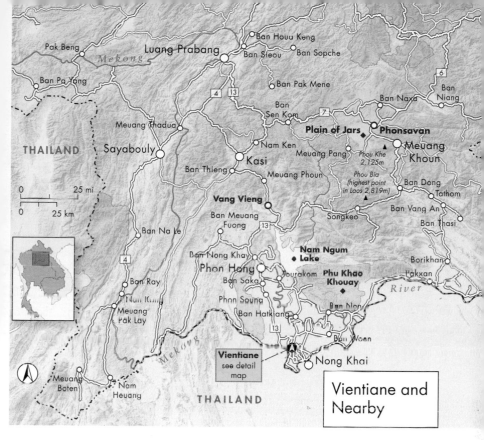

Vientiane and Nearby

They survived heavy bombing during the Vietnam War, and their sheer size has kept them out of the hands of antiquities hunters.

The jars are scattered over three main areas, but only the Ban Ang site is accessible and worth visiting. Here you can find some 300 jars dotting a windswept plateau about 12 km (7½ miles) from Phonsavan, the capital of Xieng Khuang Province. This is true Hmong territory: you pass Hmong villages on the way from Phonsavan to Ban Ang and on Highway 7, which leads east to the Vietnamese border at Nong Het. There's much of interest in this remote area along Highway 7, including hot mineral springs at Muang Kham. From Muang Kham, a road leads to Vieng Xay, which has more than 100 limestone caves, some of them used as hideouts by the revolutionary Pathet Lao during the war years. ⊠ *Phonsavan.*

UXO Visitor Center. Along with the adjoining Mines Advisory Group office, the center provides sobering insight into the horrifying realities of unexploded ordnance, much of which still litters the Plain of Jars area. The center has a small exhibition about the subject, and documentary films are shown each afternoon from 4:30 to 7:30. A visit here is a must for anyone exploring the region. ⊠ *Xaysana Rd. (Hwy. 7), Phonsavan* ⚕ *Across from Craters restaurant* ☎ *021/252004* ⊕ *www. maginternational.org/laos* ✉ *Free* ☉ *Weekdays 2–8, weekends 4–8.*

Who created the ancient jars on the Plain of Jars, and why, remains a mystery.

GETTING HERE AND AROUND

A long day's drive along Highway 7 from either Vang Vieng or Luang Prabang (about seven or eight hours), the vast plain is difficult to reach. Travel agencies in Vientiane and Luang Prabang, among them Diethelm Travel *(Laos Planner)*, offer tours. You'll fly into Xieng Khuang Airport in Phonsavan, which is 3 km (2 miles) outside town. Lao Airlines flies daily from Vientiane for about $100. There is also a paved road between Phonsavan and Pakxan, on the highway south of Vientiane. A trip on this road takes eight hours by bus. Most hotels and guesthouses in Phonsavan can arrange trips to the jar sites for 120,000 kip per person in a shared minivan; you can also take a taxi to the sites for about 250,000 kip.

The bus to Phonsavan from Luang Prabang costs 105,000 kip, and takes seven hours. From Vientiane the cost is 150,000 kip; the trip takes 10 hours or more.

SAFETY AND PRECAUTIONS

Stay on marked paths, and don't stray off into the countryside without a guide; the Plain of Jars area is still littered with unexploded ordnance.

TIMING

One day is enough to see the jar sites and visit some local villages. However, Phonsavan is a friendly place that doesn't see many tourists other than visitors to the jars, and it may be worthwhile to spend an extra day exploring the pretty surrounding countryside, hot springs, and local villages.

TOURS

Sousath Travel. This is the best tour operator in town. Run by the Maly Hotel family, it conducts many different trips around the area, from basic Plain of Jars tours to Luang Prabang boat trips. The day trips to the jars and local villages and overnight treks to visit Hmong villages are an excellent way to experience rural Laos. ✉ *Box 1105A, Xaysana Rd. (Hwy. 7), Phonsavan* ☎ *020/2294–6979* 🎫 *From 120,000 kip.*

WHERE TO EAT AND STAY

$ LAO 🍴 **Maly Restaurant.** In the hotel of the same name, the Maly serves Lao and western dishes that are surprisingly good given Phonsavan's remoteness. Staples include larb and decent curries. You can also try matsutake mushrooms. These pine mushrooms, widely grown in the area and usually available during the rainy season, are considered a delicacy. The restaurant is about a kilometer or two south of the main road, so take a tuk-tuk. [$] *Average main: kip50,000* ✉ *Maly Hotel, Muang Phouan Rd., east of Lao Mongol Hospital, Phonsavan* ☎ *061/312031* 🌐 *www.maly-hotel.com/resturant.html.*

$ INDIAN 🍴 **Nisha.** Here's a double surprise: some of the best food in Laos can be found in remote Phonsavan, and it's Indian to boot. Hole in the wall Nisha, presided over by its amiable owners from Tamil Nadu, serves fantastic Indian cuisine. An entire chicken tikka or tandoori costs only 28,000 kip, but the chicken *lessani*, marinated overnight in yogurt and spices, is the must-try dish. There's also a full vegetarian menu. The owners' family operates branches in Luang Prabang and Vang Vieng. [$] *Average main: kip40,000* ✉ *7th Rd., Ban Thai, eastern end of Phonsavan's main street (Hwy. 7), Phonsavan* ☎ *020/5569–8140* 💳 *No credit cards.*

$$ B&B/INN 🏨 **Auberge Plaine des Jarres.** These rustic cabins, set on a hill in a pine forest overlooking the surrounding area, feel more Wild West film than Southeast Asia. **Pros:** most scenic spot in town, romantic; fireplaces in rooms. **Cons:** far from town; no fans or air-conditioning; evening transportation is scarce. [$] *Rooms from: kip487,000* ✉ *Domaine de Phouphadeng, Phonsavan* ✣ *Across the road and up the hill from Phouviengkham Hotel* ☎ *020/235–3333, 030/517–0282* 🛏 *14 rooms* 🍴 *Breakfast.*

$ HOTEL FAMILY 🏨 **Maly Hotel.** With nice enough rooms to let, a good restaurant, and an excellent tour agency, the folks at Maly are jacks- and jills-of-all trades. **Pros:** excellent in-house tour agency; good restaurant ; discounts often available when hotel isn't full. **Cons:** deluxe rooms overpriced; a bit of a hike to center of town; not the best value for Phonsavan. [$] *Rooms from: kip284,000* ✉ *Muang Phouan Rd., Box 649A, Phonsavan* ✣ *East of Lao Mongol Hospital* ☎ *061/312031* 🌐 *www.maly-hotel.com* 🛏 *26 rooms* 🍴 *Breakfast.*

VANG VIENG

160 km (99 miles) north of Vientiane.

Fodor's Choice ★ Backpackers traveling between Vientiane and Luang Prabang on Highway 13 discovered the town of Vang Vieng in the mid-1990s. During the Vietnam War the United States maintained an airstrip in the town

The pretty village of Vang Vieng is surrounded by spectacular limestone cliffs.

center; there are rumors that the abandoned tarmac will someday field direct flights from Luang Prabang or elsewhere. Vang Vieng became famous for its rope-swing party bars along the river, attracting a huge backpacker crowd. In 2012, due to a huge number of deaths caused by drinking, drugs, and drowning, the Lao government closed the bars along the river. Today, Vang Vieng is starting to move slightly more upscale and trying to disassociate itself from the backpacker party scene.

GETTING HERE AND AROUND

BUS TRAVEL From Vientiane you can take a minibus (60,000 kip), which takes three to four hours to reach Vang Vieng.

VIP buses (105,000 kip) headed back to Vientiane from Luang Prabang stop here three times a day—the journey takes seven hours. Minivan rides to Vang Vieng can be arranged at travel agencies in both cities for about the same price as a VIP bus ticket.

A daily bus (110,000 kip) goes to Phonsavan (Plain of Jars), a six-hour ride.

SONGTHAEW Songthaews run from the bus station, 2 km (1 mile) north of town, to
TRAVEL all hotels for 15,000 kip per person. They can also be hired for excursions farther afield; prepare to bargain.

SAFETY AND PRECAUTIONS

Always double-check prices in Vang Vieng, as merchants are notorious for overcharging. Make sure to shop around and compare, as quotes for identical services may vary wildly.

The river can be fast flowing during rainy season. All but the strongest swimmers are advised to wear a life vest and take the necessary precautions when inner tubing or kayaking.

Do not under any circumstances accept offers for smoking marijuana or other drugs in Vang Vieng. Dealers are usually informants for the police, and visitors who are caught face paying a very large bribe or jail time.

TIMING

Vang Vieng itself is not all that pleasant, but the surrounding countryside merits investigation. One day to explore the caves and go farther afield, and one day to relax on the river should be plenty.

ESSENTIALS

Emergencies Provincial Hospital. ✉ *Ban Vieng Keo* ✛ *Across from Ban Sabai Guesthouse, along river* ☎ *023/511604.*

TOURS

Green Discovery Laos. Here's a unique way to travel from Vang Vieng to Vientiane: Starting downstream from Vang Vieng, you get in a kayak for the four-hour paddle to Vientiane, stopping for lunch and a 33-foot rock jump into the river. You're picked up riverside outside Vientiane in the afternoon, reunited with your luggage, and dropped off in town around 5 pm. In addition to the kayaking trip, you can also participate in a combination zip-lining and trekking option along the way. ✉ *Kangmuong St.* ☎ *023/511230* ⊕ *www.greendiscoverylaos.com* ⮞ *Kayaking trip 592,000 kip ($73) per person for 2 people, less for larger groups.*

EXPLORING

Vang Vieng. Some of the most attractive scenery and countryside in Laos, including the Nam Song River and a dramatic range of jagged limestone mountains, surrounds this convenient stopover between Vientiane and Luang Prabang. These days the town center is jam-packed with bars and backpacker hangouts, but you can escape the noise and the crowds by making for the river, which is lined with guesthouses and restaurants catering to both backpackers and those on a more flexible budget. The river is clean and good for swimming and kayaking, and the mountains beyond are riddled with caves and small, pleasant swimming holes. River trips and caving expeditions are organized by every guesthouse and hotel. Treks to the caves can be fairly arduous, and some are only accessible by motorbike. Less adventurous types can rent an inner tube for 55,000 kip and float down the river for a few hours. ✉ *Along Hwy. 13.*

WHERE TO EAT AND STAY

$

ECLECTIC

✕ **La Verandah Riverside.** Vang Vieng's cuisine leans toward the extremely bland, but this beautifully situated resort restaurant right on the river serves an impressive mix of Thai, Lao, French, and western dishes. The *penang* curry is aromatic and full of flavor, as is the spaghetti *pad kee mao* (drunken noodles, with basil and chili sauce). Coq au vin, ratatouille, and fresh organic salad are all on the French menu, which is complemented by a wine list that favors Gallic vintages. If you have room, for dessert there's homemade ice cream. $ *Average* *main: kip73,000* ✉ *Villa Nam Song Resort, Unit 9, Ban Viengkeo* ☎ *023/511637* 🌐 *www.villanamsong.com.*

$$ ECLECTIC 🍴 **Restaurant du Crabe d'Or.** Named for one of Vang Vieng's caves, this is probably the best restaurant in town. It's certainly the most expensive. The chefs prepare Lao, traditional Asian, and French cuisine, with the Laotian sampling menu the top draw. Salmon carpaccio and glazed duck breast are among the French dishes. Drink options include wines from an extensive list (heavy on French and Chilean vintages), and strong Lao coffee from the Bolaven Plateau. The indoor and outdoor dining areas command majestic views of the river and towering limestone cliffs. In addition to lunch and dinner, the Crabe d'Or lays out a swell buffet breakfast. [$] *Average main: kip95,000* ✉ *Riverside Boutique Resort, Ban Viengkeo* ☎ *023/511726* 🌐 *www.riversidevangvieng.com.*

$ B&B/INN 🏨 **Ban Sabai by Inthira.** Raised on stilts, the Ban Sabai's traditional Lao-style thatch-roof bungalows are among the most rustic accommodations in town. **Pros:** rustic bungalows; private decks with river views; charming restaurant on river; small pool. **Cons:** small rooms; often fully booked; rooms fairly basic for price. [$] *Rooms from: kip324,000* ✉ *Nam Song River Rd., Ban Savang* ✢ *On river just south of town center* ☎ *023/511088* 🌐 *www.inthira.com/hotel_about.php?hid=2* 🛏 *13 bungalows* 🍽 *Breakfast.*

$ RESORT 🏨 **Elephant Crossing Hotel.** Almost every room at this modern four-story hotel has a river view, a balcony, hardwood floors, and wooden trim constructed of recycled bits of old Lao houses. **Pros:** river views; free Wi-Fi; private balcony in each room. **Cons:** small rooms; fairly long walk to town center; often crowded with tour groups. [$] *Rooms from: kip410,000* ✉ *Ban Viengkeo (Namsong Riverside)* ☎ *023/511232, 020/560–2830* 🌐 *www.theelephantcrossinghotel.com* 🛏 *35 rooms* 🍽 *Breakfast.*

$$$ RESORT Fodor's Choice ★ 🏨 **Riverside Boutique Resort.** With the best riverside viewpoint in town, overlooking fabulous mountain scenery and an atmospheric wooden bridge, this upscale boutique hotel is blissfully, beautifully serene. **Pros:** best viewpoint in Vang Vieng; best swimming pool; quiet and away from the backpacking crowd; has Vang Vieng's most upscale restaurant. **Cons:** not all rooms have good river views; breakfast buffet a bit bland; expensive for the area. [$] *Rooms from: kip1.1 million* ✉ *Box 360, Ban Viengkeo* ☎ *023/511726, 023/511727* 🌐 *www.riversidevangvieng.com* 🛏 *34 rooms* 🍽 *Breakfast.*

$ B&B/INN 🏨 **Saysong Guest House.** This is one of the cheapest deals in town, with an unbeatable riverside location. **Pros:** excellent location in heart of town; river views from some rooms; super value. **Cons:** cheaper rooms dark and very basic; west-facing rooms get very hot in afternoon. [$] *Rooms from: kip243,000* ✉ *Ban Savang* ☎ *023/511130* ✉ *riverviewbungalows@hotmail.com* 🛏 *38 rooms* 🍽 *Breakfast.*

$$ RESORT 🏨 **Villa Nam Song.** The Mediterranean-style rooms at this hotel have wooden floors and ceilings, yellow concrete walls, and wooden beds, desks, and chairs. **Pros:** excellent location next to river; quiet; noted restaurant with great views. **Cons:** rooms a bit musty; not in town center; bathrooms looking worn; not the best value in town. [$] *Rooms from: kip650,000* ✉ *Unit 9, Ban Viengkeo* ☎ *023/511637* 🌐 *www.villanamsong.com* 🛏 *16 rooms* 🍽 *Breakfast.*

LUANG PRABANG AND NORTHERN LAOS

For all its popularity as a tourist destination, Luang Prabang remains one of the most isolated cities in Southeast Asia. Although a highway now runs north to the Chinese border, the hinterland of Luang Prabang is mostly off-the-beaten-track territory, a mountainous region of impenetrable forests and deep river valleys. Despite Luang Prabang's air links to the rest of the country and the outside world, the Mekong River is still a preferred travel route, with various cruise and ferry boats serving Luang Prabang, Pakbeng, and Huay Xai.

LUANG PRABANG

390 km (242 miles) north of Vientiane.

Luang Prabang is Laos's religious and artistic capital, and its combination of impressive natural surroundings, historic architecture, and friendly inhabitants make it one of the region's best stopovers. The abundance of ancient temples led UNESCO to declare Luang Prabang a World Heritage Site in 1995, and since then it's been bustling with construction and renovation activity.

But the charm of Luang Prabang is not exclusively architectural—just as appealing are the people, who seem to spend as much time on the streets as they do in their homes. Children play on the sidewalks while matrons gossip in the shade, young women in traditional dress zip past on motor scooters, and Buddhist monks in saffron robes stroll by with black umbrellas, which protect their shaven heads from the tropical sun. Some 36 temples are scattered around town, making Luang Prabang a fine place to explore on a rented bicycle or on foot. When you need a break from temple-hopping, there are plenty of appealing eateries and fashionable boutiques. Waking early one morning to watch the throngs of monks make their alms runs at dawn is highly recommended. Your hotel should be able to tell you what time to get up and suggest a good viewing spot.

■TIP→ Locals may approach you to buy food from them to serve to the monks, but this is not wise. The locals often give packs of unsuitable rice or other junk to turn a profit. Speak to someone at your lodging or a reputable agency in town about how best to donate to the monks.

GETTING HERE AND AROUND

AIR TRAVEL There are direct flights to Luang Prabang from Bangkok and Chiang Mai. Lao Airlines operates two flights daily from Bangkok and one from Chiang Mai, and Bangkok Airways flies twice daily from Bangkok. There is also service between Luang Prabang and Singapore, Hanoi, and, in Cambodia, Phnom Penh and Siem Reap. Lao Airlines also operates three flights a day between Vientiane and Luang Prabang.

Luang Prabang International Airport is 4 km (2½ miles) northeast of the city. The taxi ride to the city center costs 50,000 kip.

BIKE TRAVEL Biking is one of the best ways to visit all the interesting sights within Luang Prabang, and many hotels provide bicycles for guests. If yours

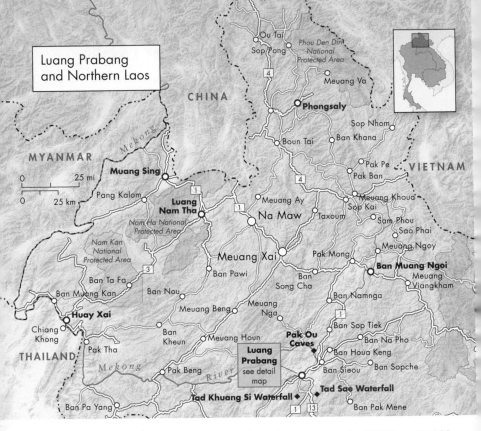

Luang Prabang
and Northern Laos

does not, you can rent one from shops in town for 20,000 to 30,000 kip per day.

BOAT AND FERRY TRAVEL Boats for hire can be found just about anywhere along the entire length of the road bordering the Mekong River; the main jetty is on the river side of Wat Xieng Thong.

BUS AND MINI-VAN TRAVEL Buses from Vientiane arrive four or five times daily; the trip to Luang Prabang takes between 9 and 11 hours. You have your choice of VIP (usually with air-conditioning and toilets aboard), express, and regular buses; prices range from 130,000 to 150,000 kip. You'll pay more if you buy your ticket from an agency in town, though it is convenient. There are also buses to Phonsavan (eight hours; 100,000 kip), Vang Vieng (seven hours; 105,000 kip), Oudomxay (four hours; 60,000 kip), and Luang Nam Tha (nine hours; 100,000 kip), among other places. There are two bus terminals in Luang Prabang, the Northern Bus Terminal, out near the airport, and the Ban Naluang Southern Bus Terminal, in the south of town, with services to respective destinations. ■TIP→ For about the same price as a bus, minivans make the trip to Luang Prabang and many other destinations far more comfortably and quickly, and service may include pickup from your hotel. There is a minivan station opposite the Southern Bus Terminal.

CAR TRAVEL Although you can drive from Vientiane to Luang Prabang, it takes from eight to nine hours to make the 365-km (240-mile) trip along the meandering, but paved, road up into the mountains.

TAXI, TUK-TUK, AND SONGTH-AEW TRAVEL Tuk-tuks and songthaews make up Luang Prabang's public transport system. They cruise all the streets and are easy to flag down, but the drivers are a pain to negotiate with and will attempt to charge extortionate prices. Plan on paying around 20,000 kip for a trip within the city. The few taxis in town must be booked through your hotel or guesthouse. ■TIP➜ There are now tramlike vehicles that cost only 5,000 kip. The locals use them and they are a great alternative to tuk-tuks, but they only run along fixed routes. If you'd like to use them, ask someone at your hotel for advice.

SAFETY AND PRECAUTIONS

For medical and police emergencies, use the services of your hotel or guesthouse. The higher-end resorts have a doctor on call from Luang Prabang Provincial Hospital. For serious emergencies, one needs to fly to Bangkok or Vientiane.

Luang Prabang is safe, but beware of unscrupulous tuk-tuk drivers.

TIMING

Unless you are a temple addict, three or four days in Luang Prabang is more than enough, although with the waterfalls and cave side trips, it's easy to pass more time here. If you have the extra time, try to get farther north, where there are fewer tourists and fantastic nature.

■TIP➜ Despite scores of guesthouses, finding accommodations here can be a challenge in the peak season and during holidays such as Lao New Year or Chinese New Year. When you visit the top attractions, be prepared for crowds of tourists.

TOURS

Shangri Lao. Have an old-fashioned luxury jungle adventure on one of Shangri Lao's all-inclusive tours. By elephant and horseback via an old explorer's trail, the company transports participants to fancy safari-style camp resorts on the Nam Khan River. ✉ *Sisavangvong Rd., Ban Xieng Lom* ⬦ *Across street and north 50 meters from Luang Prabang Bakery* ☎ *071/252417* ⊕ *www.shangri-lao.com* ✉ *$800 per person for 2 people.*

Fodor's Choice ★ **White Elephant Adventures.** By far Luang Prabang's best tour operator, White Elephant conducts single and multiday hiking, biking, and kayaking adventures led by well-trained local guides. The company's foreign-born owners are as enthusiastic about sharing their adopted country as they are about making sure each visitor's touring experience is authentic and fulfilling. They also strive to ensure that the impact of their journeys on the local people and the environment is low. A great source of local information, the organization is involved with literacy projects for rural Lao girls and other self-help initiatives. ✉ *44/3 Sisavangvong Rd.* ⬦ *Across street from Luang Prabang Bakery* ⊕ *www.white-elephant-adventures-laos.com* ✉ *From 400,000 kip ($50) per person.*

Green Discovery Laos, Lao Youth Travel, and **Diethelm Travel** *(Laos Planner)* have Luang Prabang branches.

9

A GOOD WALK (OR RIDE)

Touring the city's major sights takes a full day—maybe longer if you climb Phu Si Hill, which has particularly lovely views at sunset. The evening bazaar on Sisavangvong Road starts around 6. Though the distances between these attractions are walkable, you may not want to do this all on foot if it's really hot out. Rent a bike, or break this into a few shorter walks, and stay out of the sun during the heat of the day.

Start your tour of Luang Prabang at the **Tribal Market,** at the intersection of Sisavangvong Road and Setthathirat Road. From here, head northeast along Sisavangvong, stopping on the left at one of the city's most beautiful temples, **Wat Mai.** Magnificent wood carvings and golden murals decorate the main pillars and portico entrance to the temple. Continue down Sisavangvong to the compound of the **Royal Palace,** with its large bronze statue of King Sisavangvong. On leaving

the palace grounds by the main entrance, climb the staircase to **Phu Si Hill.** The climb is steep and takes about 15 minutes, but you'll be rewarded with an unforgettable view of Luang Prabang and the surrounding countryside.

Back in front of the Royal Palace, follow Sisavangvong toward the confluence of the Mekong and Nam Khan rivers, where you can find another fascinating Luang Prabang temple, **Wat Xieng Thong.** Leaving the compound on the Mekong River side, walk back to the city center along the romantic waterside road, which is fronted by several French colonial houses and Lao traditional homes. Passing the port area behind the Royal Palace, continue on to the intersection with Wat Phu Xay; turn left here to return to the Tribal Market. Every evening there's a local night market, stretching from the Tribal Market to the Royal Palace.

EXPLORING
TOP ATTRACTIONS

Fodor's Choice ★ **Night Market.** The night market is a hub of activity, full of colorful local souvenirs and cheap, delicious food, and a meeting place for locals and tourists. Starting in the late afternoon, Sisavangvong Road is closed to vehicles from the tourist office down to the Royal Palace, and a tented area is set up, thronged with vendors selling lanterns, patterned cushion covers, Lao coffee and tea, hand-stitched bags, and many other local crafts. Small side streets are lined with food stalls selling everything from fried chicken to Mekong seaweed and other treats at a fraction of the price you'll pay in a restaurant. It's worth strolling the market just for the atmosphere. ⊠ *Sisavangvong Rd., from Kitsarat Rd. to Royal Palace* ☾ *Daily 4:30–9.*

Phu Si Hill. Several shrines and temples and a golden stupa crown this forested hill, but the best reason to ascend its 328 steps is to enjoy the view from the summit: a panorama of Luang Prabang, the Nam Khan and Mekong rivers, and the surrounding mountains. It's a popular spot for watching the sunset (just be sure to bring insect repellent), but there are huge crowds, pickpockets, and the view from atop old Phu Si is probably better appreciated at sunrise, when you will have

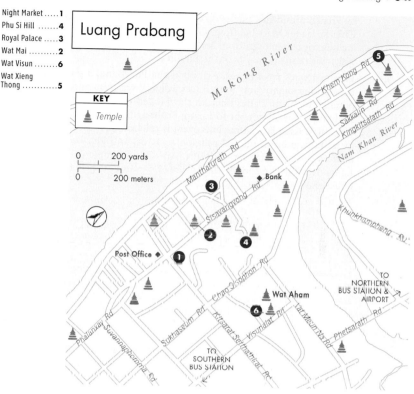

Luang Prabang

KEY

▲ *Temple*

0   200 yards

0   200 meters

it all to yourself. If you're not game for the steep climb up the staircase, try the more enjoyable hike up the trail on the "back" side of the hill. ✉ *Luang Prabang ⚐ Between Sisavangvong and Phousi Rds.* 🎫 *20,000 kip ⏱ Daily 6–6.*

Royal Palace. In a walled compound at the foot of Phu Si Hill stands this palace, the former home of the royal Savang family. Built at the beginning of the 20th century, the palace served as the royal residence until the Pathet Lao took over Laos in 1975 and exiled Crown Prince Savang Vatthana and his children to a remote region of the country (their fate has never been established). It still has the feel of a large family home—a maze of teak-floor rooms surprisingly modest in scale. The largest of them is the **Throne Room,** with its gilded furniture, colorful mosaic-covered walls, and display cases filled with rare Buddha images, royal regalia, and other priceless artifacts.

The walls of the **King's Reception Room** are decorated with scenes of traditional Lao life painted in 1930 by the French artist Alex de Fautereau. The **Queen's Reception Room** contains a collection of royal portraits by the Russian artist Ilya Glazunov. The room also has cabinets full of presents given to the royal couple by visiting heads of state; a model moon lander and a piece of moon rock from U.S. president Richard Nixon share shelf space with an exquisite Sèvres tea set presented by French president Charles de Gaulle and fine porcelain teacups from Chinese leader Mao Tse-tung. Other exhibits in this eclectic collection include friezes removed from local temples, Khmer drums, and elephant tusks with carved images of the Buddha.

The museum's most prized exhibit is the **Pha Bang,** a gold image of the Buddha slightly less than 3 feet tall and weighing more than 100 pounds. Its history goes back to the 1st century, when it was cast in Sri Lanka; it was brought to Luang Prabang from Cambodia in 1359 as a gift to King Fa Ngum. This event is celebrated as the introduction of Buddhism as an official religion to Laos, and Pha Bang is venerated as the protector of the faith. An ornate temple called Ho Pha Bang, near the entrance to the palace compound, is being restored to house the image.

Tucked away behind the palace is a crumbling wooden garage that houses the aging royal fleet of automobiles. You'll need about two hours to work through the Royal Palace's maze of rooms. ⊠ *Sisavangvong Rd., across from Phu Si Hill* ☎ *071/212470* 💲 *30,000 kip* ☉ *Wed.– Mon. 8:30–11 and 1:30–4.*

Wat Xieng Thong. Luang Prabang's most important and impressive temple complex is Wat Xieng Thong, a collection of ancient buildings near the tip of the peninsula where the Mekong and Nam Khan rivers meet. Erected in 1559 and 1560, the main temple is one of the few structures to have survived centuries of marauding Vietnamese, Chinese, and Siamese armies, and it's one of the region's best-preserved examples of Buddhist art and architecture. The intricate golden facades, colorful murals, sparkling glass mosaics, and low, sweeping roofs of the entire ensemble of buildings (which overlap to make complex patterns) all combine to create a feeling of harmony and peace.

The interior of the main temple has decorated wooden columns and a ceiling covered with wheels of dharma, representing the Buddha's teaching. The exterior is just as impressive thanks to mosaics of colored glass that were added at the beginning of the 20th century. Several small **chapels** at the sides of the main hall are also covered with mosaics and contain various images of the Buddha. The bronze 16th-century reclining Buddha in one chapel was displayed in the 1931 Paris Exhibition. The mosaic on the back wall of that chapel commemorates the 2,500th anniversary of the Buddha's birth with a depiction of Lao village life. The chapel near the compound's east gate, with a gilded facade, contains the royal family's funeral statuary and urns, including a 40-foot-long wooden boat that was used as a hearse. ⊠ *Sisaleumsak Rd. ✛ Between Suvannakhamvong Rd. and Sakkarin Rd., where Mekong and Nam Khan rivers meet* ☎ *071/212470* 💲 *20,000 kip* ☉ *Daily 6–6.*

WORTH NOTING

Wat Mai. This small but lovely temple next to the Royal Palace compound dates from 1796. Its four-tier roof is characteristic of Luang Prabang's religious architecture, but more impressive are the magnificent wood carvings and gold-leaf murals on the main pillars and portico entrance to the temple. These intricate panels depict the last life of the Buddha, as well as various Asian animals. During the Bun

The Prabang Buddha

But for a few simple facts, the Pha Bang Buddha image, the namesake of Luang Prabang, is shrouded in mystery. This much *is* known: the Prabang image is approximately 33 inches tall and weighs 110 pounds. Both hands of the Buddha are raised in double *abhaya mudra* position (the meaning of which has predictably ambiguous symbolic interpretations, including dispelling fear, teaching reason, and offering protection, benevolence, and peace). Historically, the Prabang Buddha has been a symbol of religious and political authority, including the legitimate right to rule the kingdom of Laos. Beyond that, there is much speculation.

It is believed that the image was cast in bronze in Ceylon (Sri Lanka) between the 1st and 9th century, although it has also been suggested that it is made primarily of gold, with silver and bronze alloys. Regardless of its composition, the double-raised palms indicate a later construction (14th century), and a possibly Khmer origin.

Nonetheless, in 1359 the Prabang was given to Fa Ngum, the son-in-law of the Khmer king at Angkor, and brought to Muang Swa, which was subsequently renamed Luang Prabang, the capital of the newly formed kingdom of Lang Xang. The Prabang Buddha became a symbol of the king's legitimacy and a means of promoting Theravada Buddhism throughout Laos.

In 1563 the Prabang image was relocated, along with the seat of power, to the new capital city of Vientiane. In 1778 Siamese invaders ransacked Vientiane and made off with both the Prabang and Emerald Buddhas. The Prabang was returned to Laos in 1782 after political and social unrest in Siam was attributed to the image. Similar circumstances surrounded the subsequent capture and release of the Prabang by the Siamese in 1827 and 1867.

Following its return to Laos, the Prabang was housed in Wat Wisunalat, Luang Prabang's oldest temple, and then at Wat Mai. In 1963, during the reign of Sisavang Vatthana, Laos's final monarch, construction began on Haw Pha Bang, a temple to house the Prabang on the grounds of the palace.

However, in 1975 the communist Pathet Lao rose to power, dissolved the monarchy, and installed a communist regime. The communist government, having little respect for any symbol of royalty *or* Buddhism, may have handed over the Prabang to Moscow in exchange for assistance from the Soviet Union. Other accounts of the image have it spirited away to Vientiane for safekeeping in a vault, where it may still reside today.

Regardless, there is a 33-inch-tall Buddha statue, real or replica, housed behind bars in an unassuming room beside the entrance to the Royal Palace Museum (until Haw Pha Bang is completed). On the third day of every Lao New Year (April 13–15), the image is ferried via chariot to Wat Mai, where it is cleansed with water by reverent Laotians.

As for its authenticity, a respectable and reliable source told me simply this: "People believe that it is real because the Prabang Buddha belongs in Luang Prabang."

—Trevor Ranges

COOKING CLASSES

Several Luang Prabang restaurants not only serve tasty Lao food, but also teach you how to cook it yourself. Classes cover Lao cuisine and its cultural influences, and the restaurants provide ingredients for recipes that students cook and then share as a meal. Daytime classes include a visit to a local food market to learn about the ingredients and how to select them; evening classes, which are shorter, lack this component. Class sizes are limited to a dozen or fewer students. The classes cost between 160,000 kip and 285,000 kip depending on the school and the length of the class. Tamarind Restaurant and Cooking School is by far—and deservedly—the most popular choice. Especially during high season, make reservations well ahead to ensure you get a space. Tamnak Lao, another good option, has been open since 1999. See Where to Eat for reviews of these restaurants and their contact information.

Pimai festival (Lao New Year), the Prabang sacred Buddha image is carried from the Royal Palace compound to Wat Mai for ritual cleansing ceremonies. ✉ *Sisavangvong Rd.* ✥ *Near Royal Palace Museum* 🎫 *10,000 kip* ⏲ *Daily 6–6.*

Wat Visun. The 16th-century Wat Visun and neighboring **Wat Aham** play a central role in Lao New Year celebrations, when ancestral masks, called *phu gneu gna gneu,* are taken from Wat Aham and displayed in public. Wat Visun was built in 1503, during the reign of King Visunalat, who had the temple named after himself. Within the compound is a large and unusual watermelon-shape stupa called **That Makmo** (literally Watermelon Stupa). The 100-foot-high mound is actually a royal tomb, where many small, precious Buddha statues were found when Chin Haw marauders destroyed the city in the late 19th century (these statues have since been moved to the Royal Palace). The temple hall was rebuilt in 1898 along the lines of the original wooden structure, and now houses an impressive collection of Buddha statues, stone inscriptions, and other Buddhist art. ✉ *Visunalat Rd., near Vat Muen Na Rd.* 🎫 *10,000 kip* ⏲ *Daily 6–6.*

WHERE TO EAT

$$ INTERNATIONAL

🍴 **Apsara Restaurant.** Occupying a lovely spot overlooking the Nam Khan River, Apsara serves western and Eastern cuisine, from baguette sandwiches for lunch to elegant set dinners starring dishes such as a whole Panin fish stuffed with lemongrass and served with tamarind dressing. The wine list isn't huge, but the selections complement the food perfectly. The quiet location makes this a good choice for a leisurely meal. In high season you may need a reservation. [$] *Average main: kip90,000* ✉ *Ban Wat Sene, Kingkitsarath St., Baan Wat Sene* ☎ *071/254670* 🌐 *www.theapsara.com* ✍ *Reservations essential.*

$ CAFÉ

🍴 **Joma Bakery Cafe.** Canadians run this inexpensive self-service restaurant, where an in-house bakery turns out delicious pastries, bagels, pizzas, and French bread. The homemade soups are excellent, as are the breakfast burritos and wraps, and you can pick up standard coffee and espresso drinks. A second Joma branch has a nice terrace over-looking the Nam Khan River; this is the original location. $ *Average main: kip30,000* ⊠ *Chao Fa Ngum Rd, Hua Xieng* ✤ *Near post office on Chao Fa Ngum* ☎ *071/252292* ⊕ *www.joma.biz* ▬ *No credit cards.*

$ ✕**Khaiphaen.** One of the SE Asian Tree Alliance's training restaurants
LAO for marginalized youths, Khaiphaen is following in the successful foot-steps of Makphet, its Vientiane relative. The menu at this relaxed place a block from the Mekong might include anything from a watermelon-and-goat-cheese salad to fusion Lao staples such as grilled buffalo steak with pickled daikon. With good food, artsy decor, and an inspiring mis-sion, it's hard to find fault with much here. $ *Average main: kip45,000* ⊠ *100 Sisavong Vatana Rd., Ban Wat Nong* ☎ *030/515–5221* ⊕ *www. khaiphaen-restaurant.org* ▬ *No credit cards.*

$ ✕**Kitchen by the Mekong.** The restaurant of the boutique hotel that occu-
LAO pies the former royal residence serves exquisite cuisine in a serene,
Fodor's Choice romantic setting. The Lao tasting menu, a good option, includes tama-
★ rind soup, orlam (spicy chicken stew), and *sai oua*, a homemade pork sausage, served with river weed and chili paste. Or else take on the signature pork-knuckle stew cooked in Lao beer. On the Mekong a block from the hotel entrance, this restaurant at the quiet end of the peninsula has so much going for it, from the creative French chef who presides over the kitchen to the reasonable prices compared to neighbor-ing eateries nowhere near as romantic or impressive. $ *Average main: kip80,000* ⊠ *Victoria Xiengthong Palace, Kounxoau Rd., Ban Phone-hueng* ✤ *Near Wat Xiengthong* ☎ *071/213200* ⊕ *www.victoriahotels. asia* ▬ *No credit cards.*

$ ✕**Le Café et Restaurant Ban Vat Sene.** Sidewalk seating and a retractable
FRENCH brown-striped awning contribute to the atmosphere of a traditional French café here. Freshly made quiche, baguettes, and *grandes tartines* (large slices of homemade bread with various toppings) are the menu highlights. The café, on the northern end of town, is a relaxing place for lunch or dinner or a cup of coffee and a pastry for breakfast. $ *Average main: kip50,000* ⊠ *Sakkarin Rd., Baan Wat Sene* ✤ *Across from Villa Santi Hotel* ☎ *071/252482* ⊕ *www.elephant-restau.com/cafebanvatsene* ⌦ *Reservations not accepted.*

$$$ ✕**L'Elephant Restaurant Français.** When you can't face another serving of
FRENCH rice or spicy sauces, it's time to amble over to this corner restaurant,
Fodor's Choice possibly Luang Prabang's finest. The menu is traditional French, with
★ a dash of Lao influence, especially when it comes to the ingredients. Consider, for example, the *chevreuil au poivre vert* (local venison in a pepper sauce). You can order from à la carte or three-course prix-fixe menus; the several daily specials usually include fish fresh from the Mekong. Seating is available in the bright, airy dining room or on the sidewalk, behind a barrier of plants. If you need relief from the heat, head to the air-conditioned section. $ *Average main: kip150,000* ⊠ *Ban Wat Nong, Box 812* ☎ *071/252482* ⊕ *www.elephant-restau.com* ⌦ *Reservations essential.*

$ ✕**Luang Prabang Bakery.** With a central location and the most enticing
CAFÉ atmosphere of several outdoor-seating restaurants in its part of town, the bakery is an ideal stop for people-watching and a cool drink or

9

coffee and pastries. You can also sample some of the nearly two dozen Laotian dishes, such as *jo mart len pak lae kout noi* (steamed fresh vegetables with a spicy grilled-tomato sauce) served here, or satisfy a craving for western food with a hamburger, a pizza, some pasta, or even a steak. $ *Average main: kip50,000* ⊠ *Sisavangvong Rd., Ban Chomkong* ✛ *North of Royal Palace Museum on right* ☎ *71/252499, 71/254844* ⊕ *luangprabang-bakery-guesthouse.com.*

$ ✕ **Restaurant les 3 Nagas.** River seaweed with spicy buffalo jam and

LAO steamed mushrooms in coconut mousse are just two of the local specialties served at this atmospheric restaurant. Spicy bamboo soup and grilled buffalo with coffee sauce are also prepared, and mango sticky rice with a pumpkin mousse is a typical dessert. Set menus are available from 200,000 kip, and you can order à la carte. Across the street from the 3 Nagas Luang Prabang hotel, the restaurant is under the same management; western cuisine is served on the hotel side. $ *Average main: kip80,000* ⊠ *Sakkarin Rd., Ban Wat Nong* ☎ *071/253888* ⊕ *www.3-nagas.com.*

$ ✕ **Rosella Fusion.** This humble restaurant under a tent awning overlook-

LAO ing the Nam Khan River churns out superb food. Dit, the chef, used to be the bartender at the nearby Amantaka and learned as well from his cousin, a Lao chef now in Perth. Despite the name this isn't really a fusion restaurant—Lao and western dishes are prepared but without overlapping influences. The food is fabulous, though, especially the *mok paa* fish steamed in banana leaf and served in a creamy dill sauce. Dit also concocts frozen margaritas and mojitos that rival any in town, and the prices are far lower than at comparable places. The food has no MSG and takes a while to prepare, so expect to wait, especially in high season. $ *Average main: kip45,000* ⊠ *Kingkitsarat Rd., Baan Wat Sene* ✛ *100 feet after Apsara on river side* ☎ *020/7777–5753* ▭ *No credit cards.*

$ ✕ **Tamarind Restaurant and Cooking School.** This riverside restaurant is *the*

LAO place to experience and understand Lao cuisine in Luang Prabang. You

Fodor's Choice may not see any locals here, but the well-crafted food is truly delicious

★ and the extremely well-trained staff members go out of their way to introduce local specialties and describe exactly what everything is. The various tasting menus feature five traditional types of *jeaow*, or dips, to be eaten with vegetables or sticky rice; there's also a five-bites selection that includes dried buffalo, sai oua (flavored local sausage), and other delicacies. The restaurant, which runs a popular cooking school worth checking out, is the only one in town these days that pretty much requires a reservation every night. $ *Average main: kip50,000* ⊠ *Kingkitsarath Rd., Baan Wat Sene* ✛ *Just before Apsara on Nam Khan River* ☎ *071/213128* ⊕ *www.tamarindlaos.com* ⚑ *Reservations essential.*

$ ✕ **Tamnak Lao.** The set menu is the way to go at this noted restaurant,

LAO cooking school, and (just for good measure) book exchange. Doing so allows you to sample a cross-section of dishes made in the country's various cooking styles. Alternatively, you can order à la carte from a lengthy menu that includes *kaipan,* a crispy dried Mekong River plant covered with sesame seeds (it's the local equivalent of chips and salsa), and a local favorite, orlam, an eggplant "casserole" that can

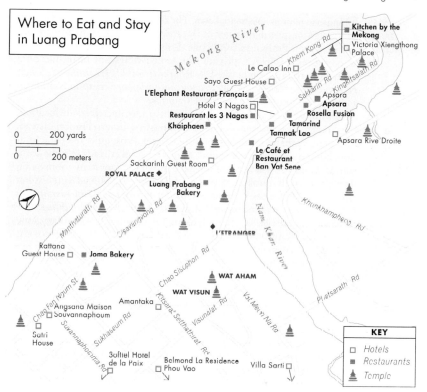

Where to Eat and Stay in Luang Prabang

Kitchen by the Mekong
Victoria Xiengthong Palace
Le Calao Inn □
Sayo Guest House □
L'Elephant Restaurant Français ■
Hotel 3 Nagas □
Restaurant les 3 Nagas ■
Khaiphaen ■
Apsara
Apsara
Rosella Fusion
Tamarind
Tamnak Lao
Apsara Rive Droite
Sackarinh Guest Room □
ROYAL PALACE ◆
Luang Prabang Bakery
Le Café et Restaurant Ban Vat Sene
L'ETRANGER
Rattana Guest House □ ■ Joma Bakery
WAT AHAM
WAT VISUN
Amantaka □
Angsana Maison Souvannaphoum
Satri House
Sofitel Hotel de la Paix
Belmond La Residence Phou Vao
Villa Sarti □

0 200 yards
0 200 meters

KEY

□ Hotels
■ Restaurants
▲ Temple

be compared to an exotic *gaeng kiew waan* (Thai green curry). Lao and western options are available for breakfast. $ *Average main: kip50,000 ⊠ Sakkarin Rd., Baan Wat Sene ✦ Across from Villa Santi Hotel ☎ 071/252525 restaurant, 071/212239 cooking school ⊕ www.tamnaklao.net ⊛ Reservations not accepted.*

WHERE TO STAY

New hotels are shooting up in Luang Prabang to accommodate the growing numbers of tourists. Many of the most attractive of them are in converted buildings dating from French colonial days, and several hotels are former royal properties.

$$$$ ⬚ **Amantaka.** The queen of resorts in Luang Prabang, this gorgeous and
RESORT tranquil oasis occupies an old French colonial building surrounded by leafy gardens and shaded verandas. **Pros:** perfectly situated and close to everything; spacious and private suites; excellent food served in the atmospheric restaurant; huge pool. **Cons:** extra 20% service charge; on the flight path into the LP airport, so jet noise when planes fly in; absurdly expensive. $ *Rooms from: kip7.7 million ⊠ 55/3 King-kitsarath Rd., Ban Thongchaleun, Box 1090 ☎ 071/860333 ⊕ www.amanresorts.com ⌲ 24 rooms* ¶○¶ *Some meals.*

9

$$$$ B&B/INN **Fodor's Choice** ★ 🏨 **Angsana Maison Souvannaphoum.** The former residence of Prince Souvannaphoum, prime minister in the 1960s, has been transformed into one of Luang Prabang's top hotels. **Pros:** spa; large claw-foot tubs in some rooms; exclusive, private feel. **Cons:** views not inspiring; on a fairly busy road; often booked. [$] *Rooms from: kip1.7 million* ✉ *Chao Fa Ngum Rd.* ☎ *071/254609* 🌐 *www.angsana.com/en/ap-laos-maison-souvannaphoum* 🛏 *24 rooms* 🍴 *Breakfast.*

$$ B&B/INN 🏨 **Apsara.** With its white facade and balustrades and riverside location, this French-style *maison* would be at home in southern France; instead, it's Luang Prabang's trendiest boutique hotel. **Pros:** quiet riverside location; beautifully furnished rooms; rain-style showerheads in some bathrooms. **Cons:** downstairs rooms have no views; standard rooms a bit dark; often fully booked. [$] *Rooms from: kip700,000* ✉ *Kingkitsarat Rd., Baan Wat Sene* ✥ *Between Tamarind and Rosella restaurants* ☎ *071/254670* 🌐 *www.theapsara.com* 🛏 *13 rooms* 🍴 *Breakfast.*

$$$$ B&B/INN 🏨 **Apsara Rive Droite.** For those looking for something even more glamorous and exclusive than the Apsara, this sister property across the Nam Khan River has a swimming pool, private verandas, and a free 24-hour shuttle-boat service to take guests across the river. **Pros:** luxurious isolation; quiet; nice swimming pool. **Cons:** across the river; little atmosphere in this neighborhood; only nine rooms, so often full. [$] *Rooms from: kip1.6 million* ✉ *Ban Phanluang* ✥ *Across Nam Khan River from Apsara* ☎ *071/254670 reservations, 071/213053* 🌐 *www.theapsara.com* 🛏 *9 rooms* 🍴 *Breakfast.*

$$$$ RESORT 🏨 **Belmond La Résidence Phou Vao Hotel.** Its prime position on Kite Hill gives this sumptuous hotel the best views in town. **Pros:** infinity pool; excellent restaurant; discounts for longer stays. **Cons:** garden rooms do not have great views; 20% service charge; not the best value. [$] *Rooms from: kip4.7 million* ✉ *Phu Vao Hill 3, Box 50* ☎ *071/212530 up to 33* 🌐 *www.belmond.com/la-residence-phou-vao-luang-prabang* 🛏 *34 rooms* 🍴 *Breakfast.*

$$$$ HOTEL **Fodor's Choice** ★ 🏨 **Hotel 3 Nagas.** This colonial mansion stands under official UNESCO World Heritage Site protection, thanks in no small measure to the efforts of the former owner to retain its weathered but handsome look. **Pros:** private patios; gorgeous garden; spacious bathrooms with claw-foot tubs; significant low-season discounts. **Cons:** often fully booked; poor lighting in rooms; 20% service charge. [$] *Rooms from: kip2 million* ✉ *Sakkarin Rd., Ban Wat Nong, Box 722* ☎ *071/253888* 🌐 *www.3-nagas.com* 🛏 *15 rooms* 🍴 *Breakfast.*

$$ B&B/INN 🏨 **Le Calao Inn.** Fronting the Mekong and just down the street from Wat Xieng Thong, this small hotel was resurrected from a ruined mansion built by a Portuguese merchant in 1904. **Pros:** quiet spot on the Mekong; upstairs rooms have private balconies with river views; atmospheric. **Cons:** almost always booked; interiors not as elegant as exterior; some rooms have unpleasant smell. [$] *Rooms from: kip650,000* ✉ *Khem Kong Rd.* ☎ *071/212100* 🌐 *www.calaohotel.com* 🛏 *6 rooms* 🍴 *Breakfast.*

$ HOTEL 🏨 **Rattana Guest House.** Family-run guesthouses are common in Luang Prabang, but this one stands out for making patrons feel right at home. **Pros:** spotlessly clean; new building with teak floors; firm mattresses.

Cons: bit of a walk to main dining and shopping area; smallish rooms in new wing; no views. [$] *Rooms from: kip125,000* ✉ *Koksack St., 3/2 Ban What That* ☎ *071/252255* 🌐 *www.rattanaguesthouse.com* 💳 *No credit cards* 🛏 *14 rooms* 🍴 *No meals.*

$ HOTEL 🏨 **Sackarinh Guest Room.** Spotless and super cheap, this place in the center of town is the ideal Luang Prabang guesthouse. **Pros:** ideal location; very clean; friendly staff. **Cons:** some rooms dark; low ceilings; often booked in high season. [$] *Rooms from: kip150,000* ✉ *Sisavangvong Rd., Ban Xieng Mouane* ✥ *Near Luang Prabang Bakery* ☎ *071/254512, 020/544–2001* 💳 *No credit cards* 🛏 *15 rooms* 🍴 *No meals.*

$$$$ HOTEL Fodor's Choice ★ 🏨 **Satri House.** This century-old property is one of Luang Prabang's best-kept secrets. **Pros:** beautiful colonial residence; quiet neighborhood but not far from night market; superior furnishings; shuttle service to town, free bicycles; furnished with antiques; plenty of charm. **Cons:** not all rooms have terraces. [$] *Rooms from: kip2.3 million* ✉ *057 Photisarath Rd., Ban Thatluang* ✥ *About 500 feet past Maison Souphannaboum on left* ☎ *071/253491* 🌐 *www.satrihouse.com* 🛏 *31 rooms* 🍴 *Breakfast.*

$$ B&B/INN 🏨 **Sayo Guest House.** A white colonial-style hotel with green shutters, the Sayo Guest House is chic yet unpretentious. **Pros:** serene riverside location; spacious, well-furnished rooms; some rooms have balconies. **Cons:** some rooms lack big windows; often full in high season; a walk from central area. [$] *Rooms from: kip490,000* ✉ *Khem Kong Rd., Ban Phone Meuang* ☎ *071/212484* 🌐 *www.sayoguesthouse.com/sayo-river* 🛏 *13 rooms* 🍴 *Breakfast.*

$$$$ HOTEL 🏨 **Sofitel Hotel de la Paix.** It doesn't get much more elegant than this in sleepy Laos. **Pros:** exquisite spa; exclusive retreat; quiet location; spacious rooms all with plunge pools or hot tubs in their own private gardens; historic buildings. **Cons:** a trek to the town center; very expensive for Luang Prabang; not many shops or restaurants nearby. [$] *Rooms from: kip3.2 million* ✉ *Ban Mano* ✥ *Off Manomai Rd. just past Lao Airlines office* ☎ *071/260777* 🌐 *www.hoteldelapaixlp.com* 🛏 *23 rooms* 🍴 *Breakfast.*

$$$$ HOTEL Fodor's Choice ★ 🏨 **Victoria Xiengthong Palace.** The final residence of Laos's royal family has been renovated into one of the town's most luxurious hostelries. **Pros:** fantastic location; extremely quiet; elegant room furnishings. **Cons:** tight spaces in some rooms; not all rooms have Mekong views or plunge pools; no swimming pool. [$] *Rooms from: kip1.9 million* ✉ *Kounxoau Rd., Ban Phonehueng* ✥ *Where Mekhong and Nam Khan rivers meet* ☎ *071/213200* 🌐 *www.victoriahotels.asia* 🛏 *26 rooms* 🍴 *Breakfast.*

$$$ B&B/INN 🏨 **Villa Santi.** A local princess's son-in-law converted this 19th-century royal residence in the heart of Luang Prabang into to a boutique hotel, and built a resort outside town. **Pros:** main property has central location; quiet side street; restaurant in pleasant garden; opulent Royal Suite rooms. **Cons:** tiny bathrooms; no balconies or views; overpriced. [$] *Rooms from: kip1 million* ✉ *Sakkarin Rd., Baan Wat Sene* ☎ *071/252157* 🌐 *www.villasantihotel.com* 🛏 *14 rooms, 6 suites* 🍴 *Breakfast.*

9

Samlors (three-wheeled bicycle carriages) are a leisurely way to get around Luang Prabang.

NIGHTLIFE AND PERFORMING ARTS

Luang Prabang's nightlife is limited—most places close by 11. On Sou-vannakhamphong Road, some bar-restaurants consisting of simple tables and chairs are located on the hill above the Mekong River. Over on Phu Si Hill are Lao Garden, a casual, open-air restaurant and bar, and the Hive Bar, where young backpackers congregate within a dimly lighted interior or around small outdoor "campfires" to mix, mingle, and share tales of the road. These two and L'etranger Books and Tea (⇨ see below) are near the corner of Phu Si and Phommathay streets.

Chez Matt. At this cozy, sophisticated wine bar, you can sample good wines and Champagne and some mean martinis. The prices are decent, jazz plays in the background, and the place is close enough to Nam Khan River restaurants you can slip in for a drink before or after dinner or while waiting for your table. ⊠ *Sisavang Vatthana Rd., Baan Wat Sene* ✛ *Across street from Icon Klub just off Nam Khan River* ☎ *020/7777–9497.*

Dao Fa. Luang Prabang's young nouveau riche strut their stuff at Dao Fa. The action doesn't heat up until after 10, and the party's over at midnight due to curfew, but for those who like thumping beats, this is the only real nightclub in town. Because it's out by the southern bus station, you won't see many foreign faces here. ⊠ *Rd. 13* ✛ *Across from National Stadium just near Southern bus terminal* ☎ *071/260789.*

Icon Klub. An engaging Hungarian named Lisa runs this hole-in-the-wall bohemian-style hangout. It's the perfect place to grab a well-mixed whisky sour or mojito and find out about life in Luang Prabang. Most tourists don't discover her tiny, eclectically decorated white house, but many expats drink here, and everyone knows everyone. It's easy to strike up a conversation, and Lisa runs theme nights with swing music and holds book discussions to keep things stimulating. ⊠ *Sisavang Vatthana Rd., Ban Xiengmouane 51/4* ✛ *Uphill from Saynamkhan Hotel between Nam Khan River and Sakkarin Rd., across from Chez Matt* ☎ *071/254905, 020/9930–0788* ⊕ *www.iconklub.com.*

L'etranger Books and Tea. From 7 am until 10 pm, patrons of this bookstore and hangout sip tea, coffee, and smoothies or nibble on snacks while reclining on comfortable and chic floor pillows. In the evening, the place fills up for DVD screenings. ⊠ *Ban Aphay, next to Hive Bar* ☎ *071/260248.*

Royal Ballet Theater Phralak-Phralam. Three times a week this troupe performs at the Royal Palace museum. The program includes a *bai-si* welcoming ceremony, local folk songs, classical dances enacting episodes from the Indian *Ramayana* epic, and outdoor presentations of the music and dances of Lao minorities. ⊠ *Royal Palace Museum, Sisavangvong Rd., across from Phu Si Hill* ☎ *071/253705* 🎫 *100,000 kip–150,000 kip* ☉ *Mon., Wed., Sat. at 6:30 pm.*

SPORTS AND THE OUTDOORS

Many of the tour operators in town offer interesting rafting and kayaking trips, plus cycling expeditions. Several shops rent bikes for about 20,000 kip a day.

SHOPPING

Luang Prabang has two principal markets where you can find handicrafts: the Dara Central Market, on Setthathirat Road, and the Tribal Market, on Sisavangvong Road. In the evening, most of Sisavangvong Road turns into an open bazaar, similar to Thailand's night markets. It's a pleasant place to stroll, bargain with hawkers, and stop for a simple meal and a beer at one of many roadside stalls.

Caruso Lao. The well-regarded Vientiane boutique noted for its fine wood carvings and high-end Lao silks has opened a Luang Prabang branch. All the products are handwoven and carved by master artisans. ⊠ *60 Sakkarin Rd., Baan Wat Sene* ✛ *Near Cafe Ban Vat Sene* ☎ *071/254574* ⊕ *www.carusolao.com.*

Pathana Boupha. An antiques and textile shop and museum, Pathana Boupha claims to produce the costumes and ornaments for Luang Prabang's Miss New Year pageant in (an apparently prestigious endeavor). A dizzying array of goods is on display, many not for sale. Shoppers *can*, however, purchase textiles produced by various Laotian ethnic groups. It is worth coming here just to check out the beautiful old building and antiques collection. ⊠ *26/2 Ban Visoun* ☎ *071/212262.*

Thitpheng Maniphone. Locally worked silver is cheap and very attractive. You can find a good selection at Thitpheng. ⊠ *48/2 Ban Wat That* ✛ *Around corner from Delilah restaurant, which is on Chao Fa Ngum* ☎ *071/212327.*

Tribal Market. Eclipsed by Luang Prabang's night market and these days less tribally oriented than its name might suggest, this covered market has piles of produce and household goods, including textiles and many Chinese-made items. ⊠ *Sisavangvong Rd. at Setthathirat Rd.* ☉ *Daily 7–5.*

Laos: Then and Now

EARLY SETTLERS
Prehistoric remains show that the river valleys and lowland areas of Laos were settled as far back as 40,000 years ago, first by hunters and gatherers and later by more developed communities. The mysterious Plain of Jars—a stretch of land littered with ancient stone and clay jars at least 2,000 years old—indicates the early presence of a sophisticated society skilled in the manufacture of bronze and iron implements and ceramics. Starting in the 3rd century BC, cultural and trading links were forged with Chinese and Indian civilizations.

Between the 4th and 8th century, farming communities along the Mekong River began to organize themselves into communities called "Muang"—a term still used in both Laos and neighboring Thailand. This network of Muang gave rise in the mid-14th century to the first Lao monarchy, given the fanciful name of Lan Xang, or the "Kingdom of a Million Elephants," for the large herds of the pachyderms that roamed the land.

COLONIZATION AND INDEPENDENCE
At the start of the 18th century, following fighting over the throne, the kingdom was partitioned into three realms: Luang Prabang, Vientiane, and Champasak. Throughout the latter part of the 18th century Laos was under the control of neighboring Siam. In the early 19th century Laos staged an uprising against the Siamese, but in 1828 an invading Siamese army under King Rama III sacked Vientiane and took firm control of most of Laos as a province of Siam. Siam maintained possession of Laos until the French established the Federation of French Indochina, which included Laos, Vietnam, and Cambodia, in 1893. In 1904 the Lao monarch Sisavang Vong set up court in Luang Prabang, but Laos remained part of French Indochina until 1949. For a brief period during World War II Laos was occupied by Japan, but reverted to French control at the end of the war. In 1953 the Lao PDR became an independent nation, which was confirmed by the passage of the Geneva Convention in 1954. The monarchy was finally dissolved in 1975, when the revolutionary group Pathet Lao, allied with North Vietnam's communist movement during the Vietnam War, seized power after a long guerrilla war.

THE VIETNAM WAR AND ITS AFTERMATH
During the Vietnam War the U.S. Air Force, in a vain attempt to disrupt the Ho Chi Minh Trail, dropped more tons of bombs on Laos than were dropped on Germany during World War II. Since the end of the Vietnam War the People's Democratic Party (formerly the Pathet Lao) has ruled the country, first on Marxist-Leninist lines and now on the basis of limited pro-market reforms. Overtures are being made to the outside, particularly to Thailand, Japan, and China, to assist in developing the country—not an easy task. The Friendship Bridge over the Mekong River connects Vientiane with Nong Khai in northeastern Thailand, making Laos more accessible to trade with neighboring countries. The Chinese have become a major player in Laos recently, financing dam and road projects, along with starting a massive construction boom in Vientiane.

GRADUAL GROWTH

Decentralization of the state-controlled economy began in 1986, resulting in a steady annual growth rate of around 6%. The country has continued to grow steadily: Vientiane, Luang Prabang, and Pakse have new airports; visitors from most countries can now get a visa on arrival, and those from some ASEAN (Association of South east Asian Nations) countries need no visa at all. New hotels are constantly opening. Nonetheless, infrastructure in the country remains primitive in comparison to the rest of the world. Laos has no railways; communications technology and electricity are common only in more densely populated areas (cell phones outnumber landlines five to one), and many of the country's airports and airstrips are paved. The road from the current capital, Vientiane, to Laos's ancient capital, Luang Prabang, has been paved and upgraded—though it still takes eight hours to make the serpentine, 320-km (190 mile) journey north, and many of the nation's roads are in poor condition or unpaved. The upgraded road running south from Vientiane can now accommodate tour buses going all the way to the Cambodian border. Other border crossings have also opened up, especially along the Vietnamese border.

A low standard of living (the GDP per capita of $3,000 is one of the world's lowest, and 22% of the population lives below the poverty line) and a rugged landscape that hampers transportation and communication have long made the countryside of Laos a sleepy backwater. But Luang Prabang, boosted by its status as a World Heritage Site, has become a busy and relatively prosperous tourist hub. Vientiane, despite its new hotels and restaurants, remains one of the world's sleepiest capital cities, but is getting set for some dramatic changes.

Despite their relative poverty, Lao people are frank, friendly, and outwardly cheerful people. Although Laos certainly has far to go economically, it is currently a member of the ASEAN trade group, has Normal Trade Relations status with the United States, and receives assistance from the European Union to help it acquire WTO membership. Growing investment in Laos and expanding numbers of tourists to both the main tourist centers and more remote areas should continue to benefit the people of Laos.

9

TAD KHUANG SI WATERFALL

29 km (18 miles) south of Luang Prabang.

This popular waterfall makes a pleasant half-day trip from Luang Prabang.

GETTING HERE AND AROUND

Tour operators in Luang Prabang offer day trips that combine Tad Khuang Si with a visit to a Khamu tribal village nearby for 55,000 kip. The drive, past rice farms and small Lao Lum tribal villages, is half the adventure. Taxi and tuk-tuk drivers in Luang Prabang all want to take you to the falls, quoting around 150,000 kip round-trip, but unless you have your own group, a tour is a better deal.

EXPLORING

Tad Khuang Si Waterfall. A series of cascades surrounded by lush foliage, this attraction is popular with Lao residents and foreigners. Many visitors merely view the falls from the lower pool, where picnic tables and food vendors invite lingering, but a steep path through the forest leads to pools above the falls that are perfect for a swim. Two nearby diversions most groups include on a waterfall outing are a **rescue center** that rehabilitates bears saved from poachers, and a recently opened **butterfly park** (closed on Tuesday). The best time to visit the area is between November and April, after the rainy season. Watch your footing around the falls. ⊠ *Luang Prabang* 🖃 *30,000 kip.*

TAD SAE WATERFALL

15 km (9 miles) east of Luang Prabang.

This dramatic cascade makes a worthy side trip from Luang Prabang, with opportunities for zip-lining, swimming, and more.

GETTING HERE AND AROUND

From Luang Prabang you can hire a tuk-tuk for about 150,000 kip for a return journey, but you are best to let a travel agency arrange a trip by boat. Adventure-tour agencies like White Elephant *(see Tour Information in Luang Prabang)* and Green Discovery *(see Laos Planner)* also organize kayaking day trips to the falls.

EXPLORING

Tad Sae Waterfall. Most scenically reached by boat, this waterfall is best visited during the rainy season, when the rivers are high and their combined waters form a thundering cascade. The waterfall has multilevel limestone formations divided into three steps with big pools beneath them—don't forget your bathing suit. Old waterwheels and new ziplines add an adventure component, and elephant riding also takes place. There is a small, simple resort nearby. You can get here by road, but it's delightful to arrive here by boat. Be careful on the slippery paths around the falls. ⊠ *Luang Prabang* ✛ *Southeast of Luang Prabang, accessed by road from Ban Aen village* 🖃 *15,000 kip.*

PAK OU CAVES

25 km (16 miles) up the Mekong from Luang Prabang.

While the caves themselves leave some visitors underwhelmed, the scenery en route is pleasant and the area is worth spending a couple of hours exploring.

GETTING HERE AND AROUND

It takes 1½ hours to get to Pak Ou by boat from Luang Prabang. Many agencies in town organize tours for 90,000 kip per person, not including admission to the caves. Tours leave Luang Prabang around 8 am and include visits to waterside villages for a look at the rich variety of local handicrafts, a nip of lao-lao, and perhaps a bowl of noodles. You can also take a tuk-tuk to the village of Pak Ou, and then a quick boat ride across the Mekong, but few people use this option, as it is less scenic and pricier than taking a tour.

EXPLORING

Pak Ou Caves. In high limestone cliffs above the Mekong River, at the point where it meets the Nam Ou River from northern Laos, lie two sacred caves filled with thousands of Buddha statues dating from the 16th century. The lower cave, **Tham Thing,** is accessible from the river by a stairway and has enough daylight to allow you to find your way around. The stairway continues to the upper cave, **Tham Phum,** for which you need a flashlight. The admission charge of 20,000 kip includes a flashlight and a guide. Many visitors are not impressed by the caves or the tourist hordes but find that the scenery along the way makes the trip worth the effort. Ideally, it's best to visit the caves as part of a cruise tour to or from Huay Xai.

The town of Pak Ou, across the river from the caves and accessible by ferry, has several passable restaurants. It is possible to get to the cave by tuk-tuk from town, but then you'd miss the scenery. ✉ *Luang Prabang* ✛ *At confluence of Nam Ou and Mekong rivers* 🎫 *30,000 kip.*

9

BAN MUANG NGOI

150 km (93 miles) northeast of Luang Prabang.

This picturesque village sits on the eastern side of the Nam Ou River, which descends from Phongsaly Province in the north to meet the Mekong River opposite the famous Pak Ou Caves.

GETTING HERE AND AROUND

The journey here is an adventure in itself: a minivan takes you from Luang Prabang's Northern Bus Terminal to a pier at Nong Khiaw (four hours; 45,000 kip), where boats (25,000 kip) continue on a one-hour trip upstream to the village. Boats leave Nong Khiaw at 11 am and 2 pm, and return from Muang Ngoi at 9:30 am daily, which means that you need to charter your own boat or go on a tour if you don't want to spend the night. Just about any travel agent in Luang Prabang can arrange a guide or a tour. When the water is high enough, you can continue upriver from Muang Ngoi to Muang Khoua.

TIMING

Two or three days will give you a chance to go for some hikes or boat trips and just relax in one of Laos's more tranquil spots.

EXPLORING

Ban Muang Ngoi. The village, populated by Lao Lum and surrounded by unusual limestone peaks, has become a popular traveler hangout, with friendly locals, gorgeous scenery, and plenty of treks and river-touring options. All-day electricity has only recently arrived in Muang Ngoi, but Wi-Fi is now available and several fancy restaurants line its one street. With these upgrades the village looks poised to roll into the future, but accommodations remain pretty basic and may lack amenities travelers desire. ✉ *Ban Muang Ngoi.*

WHERE TO STAY

$ B&B/INN 🏨 **Ning Ning Guesthouse.** Of Ban Muang Ngoi's many simple guesthouses, this is probably the best. **Pros:** good mosquito netting; riverside restaurant; quiet. **Cons:** bungalows lack river views; expensive for Muang Ngoi; crowded in high season. [$] *Rooms from: kip162,000* ✉ *Ban Muang Ngoi* ✣ *Near boat landing* ☎ *020/2388–0122* ✎ *ningning_guesthouse@hotmail.com* ▭ *No credit cards* 🛏 *10 bungalows* 🍴 *Breakfast.*

LUANG NAM THA

319 km (198 miles) north of Luang Prabang.

The capital of Laos's northernmost province is the headquarters of the groundbreaking Nam Ha Ecotourism. Nam Tha town itself isn't very exciting, but give yourself a couple of days to do an ecotour or trek, kayak, bicycle, or explore the sights along the Nam Tha River and the Nam Ha Protected Area.

GETTING HERE AND AROUND

Luang Nam Tha is tiny, and can be navigated on foot, although many places rent mountain bikes (from 10,000 kip to 25,000 kip per day) for exploring the surrounding countryside.

AIR TRAVEL Lao Airlines flies from Vientiane to Luang Nam Tha on Monday, Wednesday, and Friday for $100. Tuk-tuks run from the airport and bus station into town for about 30,000 kip.

BOAT TRAVEL Longtail boats can be arranged for the two-day trip on the Nam Tha River, running all the way down to Pak Tha, where the Nam Tha meets the Mekong, and on to Huay Xai. The same trip can also be done in reverse, although it makes more sense to go downriver. A boat costs about 1.8 million kip (about $220), and can take four to six passengers. Unless you speak Lao, it's best to make arrangements through the Boat Landing *(see Where to Eat and Stay, below)* or Forest Retreat *(see below)*. Note that the boats can only travel the Nam Tha during times of high water, basically from July to October.

BUS TRAVEL The Luang Nam Tha bus station is 10 km (6 miles) out of town, past the airport. Buses go to Oudomxay three times a day (four hours; 40,000 kip); to Luang Prabang and Vientiane each morning (8 and 19 hours;

90,000 kip and 200,000 kip, respectively); and to Muang Sing every hour and a half (two hours; 25,000 kip).

SAFETY AND PRECAUTIONS

Be careful of snakes if trekking in the area, and know that leeches (harmless but very annoying) come out during the rainy season.

VISITOR AND TOUR INFORMATION

Visitor and Tour Information Forest Retreat Laos. ⊠ *Main St.* ⌖ *Next to Minority Restaurant* ☎ *020/5556–0007* ⊕ *www.forestretreatlaos.com.*

EXPLORING

Nam Ha Ecotourism. This ecotourism program, a model for Southeast Asia, actively encourages the involvement of local communities in the development and management of tourism policies. You can join a two- or three-day trek through the Nam Ha Protected Area, which provides some excellent opportunities for communing with nature, having outdoor adventures, and visiting ethnic minorities (Khamu, Akha, Lunten, and Yao tribes live in the dense forest). The Boat Landing Guesthouse, Forest Retreat Laos, and Green Discovery Laos (all in Luang Nam Tha) conduct or arrange tours. ⊠ *Luang Nam Tha.*

WHERE TO EAT AND STAY

$ ✕ **The Bamboo Lounge.** A husband-and-wife team from New Zealand
INTERNATIONAL opened this happening eatery that serves outstanding wood-fired piz-
Fodor's Choice zas, freshly baked bread, hummus, pesto, pasta, and other western
★ dishes you can enjoy with a real espresso or cappuccino. The restaurant, which opens at 7 am, is affiliated with Forest Retreat Laos, a trekking agency across the street that works with local people to create and promote sustainable tourism in the Nam Ha Protected Area. $ *Average main: kip57,000* ☐ *The Green Building, Main St,* ☎ *020/5568–0031* ⊕ *bambooloungelaos.com* ▬ *No credit cards* ⌖ *Reservations not accepted.*

$ ✕ **Luang Nam Tha Night Market.** Local families mix with tourists under
LAO the night-market sky to sample grilled meats and fish served alongside papaya salad, noodle dishes, and other local specialties. Ignore the pesky ladies selling trinkets and head straight for the food stalls, where for 30,000 kip you can score an entire chicken, dip it in hot sauce along with a fingerful of sticky rice, and wash down the ensemble with a cold beer Lao. Luang Nam Tha isn't known for its restaurants, which makes the market an all the more convivial and convenient place to dine out. $ *Average main: kip30,000* ⊠ *Nam Tha Rd.* ⌖ *Downtown next to Bank of Commerce, across street from Zuela Guesthouse* ⌂ *Reservations not accepted* ▬ *No credit cards.*

$ ☷ **Boat Landing Guesthouse.** The timber-and-bamboo bungalows at this
B&B/INN eco-friendly place are comfortably furnished in rattan. **Pros:** open-air restaurant with traditional food; great source of local information; bicycles available; close to airport. **Cons:** not convenient to town and restaurants; expensive for Luang Nam Tha. $ *Rooms from: kip382,000* ⊠ *Box 28, Ban Kone* ☎ *086/312398* ⊕ *www.theboatlanding.laopdr. com* ⇆ *11 rooms* ❍❘ *Breakfast.*

9

Most Lao men, like Thai men, join the *sangha* (monastic community) at least temporarily.

MUANG SING

60 km (37 miles) north of Luang Nam Tha.

The appeal of Muang Sing lies in what is out of town. Unless you're coming here to trek and visit the hill tribes, the town isn't worth more than a day.

GETTING HERE AND AROUND

The only way in and out of Muang Sing is by bus from Luang Nam Tha. There are five to six departures each day; the two-hour journey costs 25,000 kip.

EXPLORING

Muang Sing. In the late 19th century this mountain-ringed town on the Sing Mountain River was the seat of a Tai Lue prince, Chao Fa Silino. Muang Sing lost its regional prominence, however, when French colonial forces occupied the town and established a garrison here. These days, it's known for its morning market, which draws throngs of traditional ethnic hill tribes. Shoppers from among the 20 different tribes living in the area, and even traders from China, visit the market to buy locally produced goods and handicrafts. The market is open daily throughout the day, but it is best to go from 6 to 8 before the minority groups return to their villages. ⊠ *Muang Sing.*

RIVER JOURNEY TO HUAY XAI

297 km (184 miles) up the Mekong from Luang Prabang.

The 300-km (186-mile) trip along the Mekong River between Luang Prabang and Huay Xai is a leisurely journey on one of the world's most famous stretches of river. Your boat drifts along the meandering Mekong past a constantly changing primeval scene of towering cliffs, huge mud flats and sandbanks, rocky islands, and riverbanks smothered in thick jungle, the riverscape occasionally interrupted by swaths of cultivated land, mulberry trees, bananas, and tiny garlic fields. There are no roads, just forest paths linking dusty settlements where the boats tie up for refreshment stops.

There are several ways to make this journey: by regular "slow" boat, which holds about 50 passengers; by speedboat (not recommended), which seats about four; or on the midrange Shompoo Cruise boat or the luxury *Luang Say* boat of Mekong Cruises. All these trips can be arranged in Luang Prabang.

The only village of note is a halfway station, **Pakbeng**, which has many guesthouses and restaurants along its one main street and seems to exist solely to serve the boat passengers who arrive each night. Once you arrive in Huay Xai (which has little of interest in itself other than the Gibbon Experience), a good way to enter Thailand is to cross the river on the bridge to Chiang Khong and then take a bus to Chiang Rai, 60 km (37 miles) inland.

GETTING HERE AND AROUND

BOAT TRAVEL You can journey from Luang Prabang to Huay Xai on regular "slow" boat, a speedboat, or a cruise liner.

The slow boat trip is a 12- to 14-hour journey over two days. Taking the slow boat allows you to soak in local color, but you will be sitting on uncomfortable wooden seats for the privilege. The night is spent in Pakbeng, in basic guesthouses whose owners come to greet the boats and corral guests. The fare is 220,000 kip per person; slow boats depart daily from a recently constructed pier 7 km (4½ miles) outside Luang Prabang.

Speedboats make the journey between Luang Prabang and Huay Xai in six hours. ■TIP➔ Speedboats may be fun for the first hour, but they are not safe, and become extremely uncomfortable after the novelty wears off. The seats are hard, the engine noise is deafening (earplugs are advised), and the wind and spray can be chilling. If you're determined to take one, bring a warm, waterproof windbreaker, and make sure the boat driver provides you with a life jacket and crash helmet with a visor. Speedboats cost 340,000 kip per person, and leave daily from a pier on the outskirts of Huay Xai.

SAFETY AND PRECAUTIONS
Speedboats are uncomfortable and unsafe.

ESSENTIALS
Guesthouse staffers in Huay Xai can answer most questions travelers have.

EXPLORING

The Gibbon Experience. Popular and unique, this experience combines a visit to the Bokeo Nature Reserve with jungle trekking, sleeping in canopy-level tree houses, traveling among the trees by zip-lines, and watching gibbons and other wildlife. Profits benefit gibbon rehabilitation and sustainable conservation projects. Be prepared to rough it a bit. Groups are small, so book the experience well ahead. ✉ *Th. Saykhong, Huay Xai* ☎ *084/212021* 🌐 *gibbonexperience.org* 🎫 *2.5 million kip ($310) for 3-day all-inclusive package.*

Luang Say Lodge & Cruises. The *Luang Say* luxury boat travels between Luang Prabang and Huay Xai along the Mekong River. Much more comfortable than the regular boats and speedboats that make this journey, the *Luang Say* is also far more expensive. English- and French-speaking guides accompany the voyages. Two-day, one-night and three-day, two night options are available, with meals and visits to a few sights included in the rates. Overnight stays are at the attractive Luang Say Lodge in Pakbeng. ✉ *50/4 Sakkarin Rd., Luang Prabang* ☎ *071/252553,* 🌐 *www.luangsay.com* 🎫 *4.3 million kip ($531) all-inclusive Oct.–Apr.; 3.5 million kip ($425) May–Sept. (prices sometimes lower, depending on number of travelers)* ☞ *Oct.–Apr. cruises 3 times a week in each direction, May–Sept. 2 times; no cruises in June.*

Shompoo Cruise. Providing a much-needed alternative to expensive cruises and the uncomfortable and crowded slow boats plying the Mekong River between Luang Prabang and Huay Xai, this new company operates affordable two-day journeys. Costs in high season range from $145, not including accommodations in Pakbeng, to $205 with higher-end lodgings. The boats travel with a maximum of 40 people, but will sail with as few as 10. Stops along the way include a local Khmu village and the Pak Ou Caves. ✉ *18/02 Ounkham Rd., Bat Wat Nong, Luang Prabang* ☎ *071/213189* 🌐 *www.shompoocruise.com* 🎫 *From $145 in high season.*

WHERE TO EAT AND STAY

$ LAO 🍴 **Daauw Home.** Inside a thatched hillside bungalow overlooking Huay Xai's main street, Daauw Home is run by an nongovernmental organization that helps local women and ethnic minorities empower themselves. Cooking over an open fire, the chefs prepare amazing *gai baan* grilled chicken and fish dishes that diners enjoy with "mojitlao" cocktails. There are knockout sunset views, and a bonfire keeps things warm when it's chilly. Hmong women's handicrafts are for sale. [$] *Average main: kip73,000* ✉ *Wat Jom Kao Manilat, Huay Xai* ☎ *030/904–1296* ✍ *Reservations not accepted* 💳 *No credit cards.*

$ LAO 🍴 **Riverside Houayxay.** Anchoring a prime spot along the Mekong, this restaurant has an enormous menu of Thai and Lao dishes. In the evening, try the *dath* barbecue, or perhaps curried crab or steamed fish with lemon. Popular with tour groups, the open-air eatery sits right above the river and offers ample vistas. Western breakfasts are served. [$] *Average main: kip60,000* ✉ *168 Centre Rd., Huay Xai* ☎ *084/211064, 020/5420–2222* 💳 *No credit cards* ✍ *Reservations not accepted.*

$ HOTEL 🏨 **Riverside Houayxay.** About a third of the wood-floor rooms in this mid-town hotel have superb Mekong River views. **Pros:** centrally located;

CLOSE UP

Religion in Laos

The overwhelming majority of Laotians are Buddhists, yet as in neighboring Thailand, spirit worship is widespread, blending easily with temple traditions and rituals. A common belief holds that supernatural spirits called *phi* have power over individual and community life.

Laotians believe that each person has 32 *khwan*, or individual spirits, which must be appeased and kept "bound" to the body. If one of the khwan leaves the body, sickness can result, and then a ceremony must be performed to reattach the errant spirit. In this ritual, which is known as *bai-si*, white threads are tied to the wrist of the ailing person in order to fasten the spirits. Apart from the khwan, there are countless other spirits inhabiting the home, gardens, orchards, fields, forests, mountains, rivers, and even individual rocks and trees.

Luang Prabang has a team of ancestral guardian spirits, the Pu Nyeu Na Nyeu, who are lodged in a special temple, Wat Aham. In the south, the fierce guardian spirits of Wat Phu are appeased every year with the sacrifice of a buffalo to guarantee an abundance of rain during the rice-growing season.

Despite the common belief in a spirit world, more than 90% of Laotians are officially Theravada Buddhists, a conservative nontheistic form of Buddhism said to be derived directly from the words of the Buddha. Buddhism arrived in Laos in the 3rd century BC by way of Ashoka, an Indian emperor who helped spread the religion. A later form of Buddhism, Mahayana, which arose in the 1st century AD, is also practiced in Laos,

particularly in the cities. It differs from Theravada in that followers venerate the bodhisattvas. This northern school of Buddhism spread from India to Nepal, China, Korea, and Japan, and is practiced by Vietnamese and Chinese alike in all the bigger towns of Laos. The Chinese in Laos also follow Taoism and Confucianism.

Buddhism in Laos is so interlaced with daily life that you have a good chance of witnessing its practices and rituals firsthand—from the early-morning sight of women giving alms to monks on their rounds through the neighborhood to the evening routine of monks gathering for their temple recitations. If you visit temples on Buddhist holy days, which coincide with the new moon, you'll likely hear monks chanting texts of the Buddha's teachings.

Christianity is followed by a small minority of mostly French-educated, elite Laotians, although the faith also has adherents among hill tribe converts in areas that have been visited by foreign missionaries. Missionary activity has been curbed in recent years, however, as the Lao government forbids the dissemination of foreign religious materials.

Islam is practiced by a handful of Arab and Indian businesspeople in Vientiane. There are also some Muslims from Yunnan, China, called Chin Haw, in the northern part of Laos. More recently, a very small number of Cham refugees from Pol Pot's Cambodia (1975–79) took refuge in Vientiane, where they have established a mosque.

9

Mekong views from some rooms; good restaurant with memorable views. **Cons:** expensive for Huay Xai; river-facing rooms get very hot in the afternoon; often packed with noisy tour groups. [$] *Rooms from: kip205,000* ✉ *168 Centre Rd., Huay Xai* ☎ *084/211064,* ✉ *riverside_huayxai_laos_@hotmail.com* 💳 *No credit cards* 🛏 *38 rooms* 🍴 *No meals.*

PHONGSALY

425 km (264 miles) north of Luang Prabang.

If you're looking for off-the-beaten-track adventure, head for the provincial capital Phongsaly, in the far north of Laos. It's a hill station and market town nearly 5,000 feet above sea level in the country's most spectacular mountain range, Phu Fa. Trekking through this land of forest-covered mountains and rushing rivers may be as close as you'll ever get to the thrill of exploring virgin territory.

GETTING HERE AND AROUND

Buses from Oudomxay make the nine-hour run to Phongsaly (80,000 kip) daily at 8 am, with the journey taking slightly less time each year as the road receives upgrades. In town, tuk-tuks can take you wherever you need to go for 10,000 kip.

SAFETY AND PRECAUTIONS

Always trek with a local guide. The terrain is mountainous jungle, and it's easy to get lost. It is also close to the Chinese border, which is not always clearly marked. English is not widely spoken here.

TIMING

The only reason to come to Phongsaly is to go trekking, experience one of Laos's most untouched spots, and enjoy the cool weather and fabulous scenery. Plan on spending a minimum of three days to experience Phongsaly. If you're pressed for time, skip this area, as the journey is a difficult one.

TOURS

The Phongsaly Provincial Tourism office runs a good ecotourism program providing treks and homestays in hill tribe areas with English-speaking guides.

ESSENTIALS

Visitor and Tour Information Phongsaly Tourism Office. ✉ *Phongsaly* ✥ *Downhill from morning market* ☎ *020/5428–4600.*

EXPLORING

Tribal Museum. For a break from trekking, drop by this museum whose exhibits provide a glimpse into the lives and culture of the area's 25 different ethnic groups. The tribal costume display is delightfully kaleidoscopic. ✉ *Phongsaly* ✥ *Next to Agricultural Bank, near post office* ☎ *020/5657–6050* 🎟 *5,000 kip* ⏲ *Weekdays 8:30–11:30 and 1:30–4:30.*

WHERE TO EAT AND STAY

OUDOMXAY

$
LAO
Fodor's Choice
★
✕**Souphailin's Restaurant.** Despite its humble appearance, this small thatch-roof eatery serves the best food in Oudomxay, and is itself a reason to slip into this otherwise colorless town. The owner, Mrs. Souphailin, specializes in northern Lao cuisine. It's well worth the effort to come in early and preorder any of the first 15 dishes on the menu, all authentic local specialties that require several hours of prep time. Try the delicious *mok het khao*, white mushrooms cooked in a banana leaf, or the *kaeng naw som sai sin gai*, bamboo soup with chicken. ⓢ *Average main: kip40,000* ⊠ *Ban Vieng Hai, Rd. 13 Nua, Oudomxay* ✛ *Across from Bank of Lao building, a few steps up side road* ☎*081/211147, 020/5606-2474* ▭ *No credit cards* ⚞ *Reservations not accepted.*

$
HOTEL
🖾 **Litthavixay Guesthouse.** Rooms here are simple but clean, with comfortable beds, hot showers, TVs, air-conditioning, and fans—all luxuries in this neck of the woods. Pros: centrally located, best Wi-Fi in town; owners can speak English and assist tourists. Cons: noisy street outside; west-facing rooms get quite hot in the afternoon. ⓢ *Rooms from: kip73,000* ⊠ *Na Wan Noi, Rd. 13 Nua, Oudomxay* ✛ *400 meters north of northern bus station on right* ☎ *081/212175* ▭ No credit cards ⤳ *18 rooms* ⦿*No meals.*

PHONGSALY

$
B&B/INN
🖾 **Ban Homsawan.** A superb value near Phongsaly's tourist office, this cozy guesthouse has eight immaculately clean rooms. Pros: welcoming, family feel; good Wi-Fi; reliable hot water supply. Cons: basic accommodations; popularity makes booking difficult in high season. ⓢ *Rooms from: kip81,000* ⊠ *Phongsaly* ✛ *Below Phongsaly Tourist office down road on left* ☎*020/2239-5018, 020/2299-9924* ▭ No credit cards ⤳ *8 rooms* ⦿*No meals.*

$
HOTEL
🖾 **Phou Fa.** In the old Chinese consulate near the roundabout and governor's house, the Phou Fa is overpriced for what you get but arguably the best choice in remote Phongsaly, where the pickings are slim. Pros: good amenities for Phongsaly; decent selection of rooms; great views. Cons: up a hill and a bit of a walk from town; overpriced for what you get; not overly tourist-friendly; little English spoken. ⓢ *Rooms from: kip205,000* ⊠ *Old Chinese Consulate* ☎ *088/210031* ▭ *No credit cards* ⤳ *28 rooms* ⦿*Breakfast.*

SOUTHERN LAOS

In some ways, Laos is really two countries: the south and north are as different as two sides of a coin. The mountainous north was for centuries virtually isolated from the more accessible south, where lowlands, the broad Mekong valley, and high plateaus were easier to traverse and settle. The south does have its mountains, however: notably the Annamite range, called Phu Luang, home of the aboriginal Mon-Khmer ethnic groups who lived here long before Lao farmers and traders arrived from northern Laos and China. The Lao were followed by French colonists, who built the cities of Pakxan, Tha Kaek, Savannakhet, and Pakse. Although the French influence is still tangible, the

CLOSE UP

Lao: A Few Key Phrases

The official language is Lao, part of the extensive Thai family of languages of Southeast Asia spoken from Vietnam in the east to India in the west. Spoken Lao is very similar to the northern Thai language, as well as local dialects in the Shan states in Myanmar and Sipsongbanna in China. Lao is tonal, meaning a word can have several meanings according to the tone in which it's spoken.

Here are a few common and useful words:

Hello: sabai di (pronounced *sa-bye dee*)

Thank you: khop chai deu (pronounced *cop jai der*; use khop cheu neu in northern Laos)

Yes: heu (pronounced like deux) *or* thia

No: bor

Where?: iu sai (pronounced *you sai*)?

How much?: to dai (pronounced *tao dai*)?

Zero: sun (pronounced *soon*)

One: neung

Two: song

Three: sam

Four: si

Five: ha

Six: hok

Seven: tiet (pronounced *jee-yet*)

Eight: pet

Nine: kao

Ten: sip

Twenty: sao (rhymes with cow; different from Thai "yee sip")

Hundred: neung loi

Thousand: neung phan

To have fun: muan

To eat: kin khao (pronounced *kin cow*)

To drink: kin nam

Water: nam

Rice: khao

Expensive: peng

Bus: lot me (pronounced *lot may*)

House: ban

Road: thanon

Village: ban

Island: don

River: mae nam (pronounced *may nam*)

Doctor: maw

Hospital: hong mo (pronounced *hong maw*)

Post Office: paisani

Hotel: hong hem

Toilet: hong nam

southern Lao cling tenaciously to their old traditions, making the south a fascinating destination.

Pakse is the regional capital, and has an international airport with daily flights to Vientiane, as well as to Phnom Penh and Siem Reap in neighboring Cambodia. There's also overnight bus service to Pakse from Vientiane, plus good local service in the area.

Southern Laos

HIGHWAY 13 SOUTH ALONG THE MEKONG

Highway 13 out of Vientiane penetrates as far as the deep south of Laos and the Cambodian border, a distance of 835 km (518 miles). It's paved all the way. The section between Vientiane and Pakse is not noted for sightseeing opportunities, but if you have time you can stop to savor the slow-paced, timeless river life here.

GETTING HERE AND AROUND

AIR TRAVEL Lao Airlines flies from Vientiane to Savannakhet several times daily for 850,000 kip ($82).

BUS TRAVEL Local bus service connects all the towns on Highway 13, from Vientiane or Pakse. VIP buses traveling the Vientiane–Pakse route do not stop in the small towns; they will stop in Savannakhet and Tha Kaek, but they'll charge you the full fare to Vientiane or Pakse, and you'll arrive in the middle of the night. Local buses depart hourly until midday for Savannakhet, Tha Kaek, Pakxan, and all other destinations along the Mekong from Pakse's Northern Bus Station (about five hours to Savannakhet; 45,000 kip) and from Vientiane's Southern Bus Station.

SAFETY AND PRECAUTIONS

Safety isn't an issue here, but take the usual precautions with your money and belongings.

The Bolaven Plateau's volcanic soil is ideal for farming.

TIMING
This area is only for those with extra time. There are some ecotourism and trekking projects that have sprung up in Tha Kaek and Savannakhet, but one would need an extra three to five days to cover this area. Most visitors bypass it for the sights farther south.

ESSENTIALS
Visitor and Tour Information Provincial Tourist Office. ✉ *Si Muang Rd. 9W, near downtown plaza, Savannakhet* ☎ *041/212755.*

EXPLORING
Pakxan and Nearby. A Mekong River port and former French colonial outpost, this town 150 km (93 miles) south of Vientiane is now the center of the Lao Christian community. About 43 km (26 miles) south of Pakxan, Highway 13 crosses the Nam Kading River, for which the National Biodiversity Conservation Area Nam Kading, a protected forest, is named. About 90 km (56 miles) south of Pakxan, Highway 13 meets Highway 8, which leads via Lak Sao to Nam Pho on the Vietnamese border. (If you want to get to the Plain of Jars from Pakxan, a good paved road winds north from here to Phonsavan, an eight-hour bus ride away.) ✚ *Hwy. 13.*

Tha Kaek. Parts of the ancient city wall in this port in Khammuan Province are still intact. Stunning countryside and karst (limestone caverns and sinkholes) surround Tha Kaek, and the area contains dramatic limestone caves, most notably **Tham Khong Lor.** More than 6½ km (4 miles) long, this cave is so large that the Nam Hin Bun River runs through it. Thailand's provincial capital of Nakhon Phanom sits across the Mekong River from

Tha Kaek. Ferries connect the two cities. ✛ *Hwy. 13, 350 km (217 miles) south of Vientiane; 125 km (78 miles) north of Savannakhet.*

SAVANNAKHET

470 km (290 miles) south of Vientiane.

A former French colonial provincial center, the riverside town of Savannakhet is today the urban hub of a vast rice-growing plain. It's distinguished by some fine examples of French colonial architecture. There are some options for eco-trekking north of Savannakhet in Tha Kaek at the fantastic Khong Lor Cave, but given the distances and slow transport down here, this will take a lot of extra time. Most visitors bypass it for the more interesting options farther south.

GETTING HERE AND AROUND

Lao Airlines flies from Vientiane to Savannakhet several times daily for 850,000 kip ($82). From Pakse, buses depart hourly until midday for Savannakhet from the northern bus station (five hours; 45,000 kip). VIP buses (115,000 kip) from Vientiane's southern bus terminal to Savannakhet depart daily at 8:30 pm and arrive about seven hours later. A songthaew in town will cost around 20,000 kip to most any point.

The Thai town of Mukdahan lies just across the Mekong River and is accessible by ferry or by crossing the second of three bridges connecting Thailand and Laos. The bridge, one of several established to create an East–West Economic Corridor connecting the Vietnamese port of Da Nang with Laos, Thailand, and Myanmar (Burma), also greatly facilitates tourist travel between Thailand and Laos. Eight to twelve buses shuttle passengers the 10 miles in either direction; buses depart daily from 7 am to 5:30 pm, stopping briefly at the border, where passengers must pay a fee of 10 Thai baht.

TIMING

The city itself is worth a daylong visit, tops.

EXPLORING

Dinosaur Museum. One of Savannakhet's curiosities is this dinosaur museum that displays fossils discovered in the area. ✉ *Kanthabuli Rd. and Chaimeuang Rd.* ☎ *041/212.597* 💲 *5,000 kip* ☼ *Weekdays 8–noon and 1–4.*

PAKSE

205 km (127 miles) south of Savannakhet, 675 km (420 miles) south of Vientiane.

Pakse is a former French colonial stronghold, linked now with neighboring Thailand by a bridge 40 km (25 miles) away. It plays a central role in an ambitious regional plan to create an "Emerald Triangle"—a trade and tourism community grouping Laos, Thailand, and Cambodia. The city has few attractions, but is the starting point for tours to the Khmer ruins at Wat Phu, the 4,000 Islands, and the Bolaven Plateau, which straddles the southern provinces of Saravan, Sekon, Attapeu, and Champasak. The volcanic soil of the plateau makes the vast region ideal for agriculture: it's the source of much of the country's prized coffee, tea, and spices. Despite its beauty and central role in the Lao economy, the plateau has minimal tourist infrastructure, and is very much off-the-beaten-track territory.

GETTING HERE AND AROUND

AIR TRAVEL   There are several Lao Airlines flights each day from Vientiane to Pakse, sometimes routed via Savannakhet; the flight takes an hour and costs about 1.2 million kip ($150) one way. Lao Airlines flights from Siem Reap, Cambodia, arrive every Wednesday, Friday, and Sunday. The price of a one-way ticket is similar. A tuk-tuk from Pakse International Airport, which is 4 km (2 miles) northwest of the city center, costs from 30,000 kip to 40,000 kip.

BOAT TRAVEL   **Vat Phou Cruises.** A luxurious double-decker houseboat, the *Vat Phou*, plies the southern length of the Mekong between Pakse and Si Phan Don. The all-inclusive cruises, which last three days and two nights, stop at Champasak, Vat Phou, Don Khong Island, a small village containing the temple of Oum Muong, and the waterfall at Phapheng, near Laos's border with Cambodia. The cruise guide speaks English, French, and Thai. ⊠ *Mekong Cruises (tour operator), 108 Th. 11, Ban Wat Luang* ☎ *031/251446* ⊕ *www.vatphou.com* ✉ *From 6 million kip ($739) all-inclusive Oct.–Apr., 4.5 million kip ($549) May–Sept.* ☞ *Oct.–Apr., Tues., Thurs., and Sat.; May–Sept., Tues. and Sat.; no cruises in June.*

BUS TRAVEL   Pakse is the transportation hub for all destinations in the south. By 2016, all bus stations in Pakse are slated to be moved out of town near the airport. Comfortable VIP bed buses make the overnight, 11-hour journey to and from Vientiane (200,000 kip from Vientiane, including transfer to bus station, 170,000 kip from Pakse to Vientiane). Buses leave Vientiane nightly at 8 or 8:30 pm and arrive in Pakse at 6:30 am; the times are the same from Pakse to Vientiane. Pakse's central bus station, a short walk east of the VIP terminal, has hourly departures to Savannakhet (five hours; 50,000 kip) and other points north. If you're headed to Si Phan Don, it's more convenient to take a minibus, which will pick you up at your hotel for 65,000 kip; all guesthouses sell tickets.

For international departures, you can get direct buses to Ubon in Thailand from Pakse as well as to Siem Reap and Phnom Penh in Cambodia.

CAR TRAVEL   Any travel agent in town can arrange car rental with a driver.

TAXI, TUK-TUK,   Tuk-tuks around town cost 10,000 kip (although you will be hard-
AND SONGTH-   pressed to get this price as a tourist). Songthaews to Champasak (one
AEW TRAVEL   hour; 30,000 kip) leave from the Dao Heuang market.

TIMING

There's little in the way of sights here—this is more a place to book tickets, go to the bank, and deal with any kind of communications or business before moving on to Champasak, Tad Fane, or the 4,000 Islands. Unless you are using Pakse as a base for visiting Champasak or elsewhere as a day tour, one night should be enough. Because Pakse has decent hotels, restaurants, and cafés, some visitors end up spending a little more time.

TOURS

Pakse Travel. This company arranges ecotours to Champasak, Si Phan Don, and farther afield, conducted by trained guides and with excellent transportation options. Day tours to the Bolaven Plateau, homestays on Don Daeng and in ethnic villages, tea-and-coffee plantation tours are just some of the offerings. ✉ *Box 108 Thaluang, Hwy. 13* ✥ *Next to Phi Dao Hotel downtown* ☎ *020/227–7277, 020/773–4567* ✉ *paksetravel@yahoo.com, pakse-travel@etllao.com* ☞ *Prices vary depending on number of travelers.*

ESSENTIALS

Visitor and Tour Information **Champasak Provincial Tourism.** ✉ *Th. 11, Ban Thasalakam* ✥ *Near BCEL bank* ☎ *031/212021, 020/5676–4144* 🌐 *www.champasaktourism.com.*

EXPLORING

Historical Heritage Museum. Pakse's history museum displays stonework from the famous Wat Phu in Champasak, handicrafts from the Bolaven Plateau ethnic groups, and locally made musical instruments. ✉ *Hwy. 13, 1 km (½ mile) before Dao Heung Market turnoff* ☎ *020/5527–1733* 🎫 *10,000 kip* 🕒 *Daily 8–11:30 and 1:30–4.*

WHERE TO EAT AND STAY

$ INDIAN 🍴 **Jasmin.** A Pakse mainstay, this restaurant serves vegetarian and nonvegetarian Indian and Malay food, including excellent dosas and curries. Western-style breakfasts are prepared starting at 6:30 am—perfect for the early-morning minivan crowd heading to the 4,000 Islands. The kind owner, Mr. Haja Maideen, also can arrange bus tickets and other travel services. [$] *Average main: kip25,000* ✉ *385 Banthaluang, Rd. 13, across from Phi Dao Hotel* ☎ *031/251002* 💳 *No credit cards.*

$ ASIAN FUSION 🍴 **Le Panorama.** The sixth-floor restaurant at the Pakse Hotel not only has the best view in town, but it also has the best food. Start with a sunset cocktail on the romantic rooftop terrace, and then move on to a romantic candlelight dinner. The *gai vat phou* (chicken breast stuffed with crabmeat) is divine, and the delicious pizzas are the most authentic in all southern Laos. [$] *Average main: kip50,000* ✉ *Pakse Hotel, Th. 5, Ban Wat Luang* ☎ *031/212131, 031/252993* 🌐 *www.hotelpakse.com* 💳 *No credit cards* 🕒 *No lunch.*

$$ HOTEL 🏨 **Champasak Grand Hotel.** Pakse's fanciest digs, this recently built hotel has a splendid riverbank location next to the Japanese-Lao Friendship Bridge. **Pros:** fantastic Mekong views; close to airport; nice swimming pool. **Cons:** a bit far from downtown; next to noisy and busy road; not all rooms have Mekong views (though they cost the same). [$] *Rooms from: kip487,000* ✉ *Lao Nippon Bridge Riverside* ☎ *031/255–1110 up to 18* 🌐 *www.champasakgrand.com* 🛏 *215 rooms* 🍽 *Breakfast.*

$ HOTEL 🏨 **Champasak Palace.** Though once the residence of a local prince, this hotel on the bank of the Seddon River is impressive if hardly palatial. **Pros:** beautiful terrace over the river; huge beds; new bar overlooking the garden. **Cons:** not central; dirty walls in some rooms; better value to be had elsewhere. [$] *Rooms from: kip244,000* ✉ *Box 178, Rd. 13,*

Ban Prabaht, near roundabout to airport ☎ 031/212263, 031/212779 ⊕ www.champasakpalacehotel.com ⥢ 114 rooms ⊠ Breakfast.

$ ⊡ **Pakse Hotel.** The knowledgeable management and staff at this well-
HOTEL maintained, centrally located hotel provide comfort and service up to international standards. **Pros:** great central location; clean; comfortable rooms with plenty of light; attentive staff. **Cons:** small elevator; standard rooms don't have views; busy with tour groups. $ *Rooms from: kip252,000 ⊠ Th. 5, Ban Wat Luang ☎ 031/212131, 031/252993 ⊕ www.paksehotel.com ⥢ 63 rooms ⊠ Breakfast.*

CHAMPASAK

40 km (25 miles) south of Pakse.

In the early 18th century the kingdom of Laos was partitioned into three realms: Luang Prabang, Vientiane, and Champasak. During the 18th and 19th centuries this small village on the west bank of the Mekong River was the royal center of a wide area of what is today Thailand and Cambodia. The area's most unique lodging option, with a Robinson Crusoe feel, is La Folie on Don Daeng, an island near Champasak that remains largely untouched by tourism and is an excellent base for visiting Wat Phu and Champasak. The River Resort, just north of Champasak, is upscale and romantic.

GETTING HERE AND AROUND

Songthaews travel here from the Dao Heuang Market in Pakse three times each morning (one hour; 20,000 kip). Minibuses can be arranged through guesthouses and travel agencies in Pakse for 60,000 kip. While most tour agency minibuses take the road toward the 4,000 Islands and drop you off at the Ban Muang boat pier on the east bank of the Mekong—Don Daeng Island is accessed from here—a new road down the west side cuts out the need for a boat ride across if coming via local songthaew. A car with a driver can be hired from all tour agencies in Pakse for about 500,000 kip. Tuk-tuks run to Wat Phu from Champasak for 10,000 kip per person.

■ **TIP→** These days the best way to get to Champasak from Pakse is by the new road; the ferry crossing gets far less use now, and you may find yourself stuck waiting for a boat.

If you do take a boat, the correct price for crossing is 10,000 kip, but the boatman will likely try to extract more.

SAFETY AND PRECAUTIONS

This is a safe town, but take the sensible precautions with your belongings.

TIMING

One day should be enough time to tour the ruins.

EXPLORING

Don Daeng Island. In the middle of the Mekong opposite Wat Phu, this island is a fantastic escape. Nine km (5½ miles) long, Dong Daeng has gorgeous views of the river and the surrounding countryside. An eco-tourism program and a long sandy beach have made it popular with visitors to Wat Phu as an alternative to staying in Pakse or Champasak. Bicycles can be rented on the island, and the Provincial Tourist Office in Pakse can arrange homestays. There's also a charming upscale hotel, La Folie Lodge. ⊠ *Champasak.*

Fodor's Choice
★

Wat Phu. This temple sits grandly on heights above the Mekong River, about 8 km (5 miles) south of Champasak, looking back on a centuries-old history that won it UNESCO recognition as a World Heritage Site. Wat Phu predates Cambodia's Angkor Wat—Wat Phu's hilltop site was chosen by Khmer Hindus in the 6th century AD, probably because of a nearby spring of freshwater. Construction of the wat continued into the 13th century, at which point it finally became a Buddhist temple. Much of the original Hindu sculpture remains unchanged, however, including representations on the temple's lintels of the Hindu gods Vishnu, Shiva, and Kala. The staircase is particularly beautiful, its protective *nagas* (mystical serpents) decorated with plumeria, the national flower of Laos. Many of the temple's treasures, including pre-Angkor–era inscriptions, are preserved in an archaeology museum that is part of the complex. An impressive festival takes place at the temple each January. ⊠ *Rd. 14, 8 km (5 miles) south of town* ☎ *030/956–5325* ⊕ *www.vatphou-champassak. com/en* ✆ *50,000 kip; 40,000 kip 6 am–8 am and 4:30–6, with no museum entry* ⊘ *Daily 8–6.*

WHERE TO EAT AND STAY

$
ECLECTIC
Fodor's Choice
★

✕ **The River Resort Restaurant.** The international team in the kitchen of the River Resort's elegant restaurant prepares fine Asian and western dishes—the best food you will find in all southern Laos—with equal skill and panache. Highly recommended is the local Mekong fish, which can either be grilled and served with tamarind sauce and lime, or steamed in a banana leaf Lao style. The grilled asparagus starter is another sure-fire bet. The wines here are well chosen, and the prices are extremely reasonable for a resort of this caliber. $ *Average main: kip80,000* ⊠ *Ban Phaphinnoy, Rd. 14A* ✛ *North of Champasak town, about 1 km (½ mile) north of boat-pier turnoff* ☎ *020/5685–0198* ⊕ *theriverresortlaos.com.*

$$$$
B&B/INN
Fodor's Choice
★

🛏 **La Folie Lodge.** For a luxury Robinson Crusoe experience, nothing surpasses La Folie. **Pros:** stunning views; unique escapist experience; authentic local hospitality; off-season discounts up to 40%. **Cons:** no other dining options nearby; very expensive; most staffers do not speak English. $ *Rooms from: kip1.46 million* ⊠ *Don Daeng, Pathoumphone* ✛ *Opposite Champasak in middle of Mekong* ☎ *030/534–7603* ⊕ *www. lafolie-laos.com* ✎ *24 rooms* ⦿ *Breakfast.*

$$$
RESORT
Fodor's Choice
★

🛏 **The River Resort.** This gorgeous riverfront boutique resort is the perfect spot to start or end a southern Laos excursion. **Pros:** stunning Mekong River location; riverside swimming pool; free bicycles for guests. **Cons:** outside town; no facilities near resort; not convenient to Wat Phu. $ *Rooms from: kip975,000* ⊠ *Ban Phaphinnoy, Rd. 14A* ✛ *North of Champasak town, about 1 km (½ mile) north of boat-pier turnoff* ☎ *020/5685–0198* ⊕ *theriverresortlaos.com* ✎ *28 rooms* ⦿ *Breakfast.*

The Irrawaddy Dolphin

CLOSE UP

The freshwater Irrawaddy dolphin, known as *pla ka* in Lao, is one of the world's most endangered species; according to a 2008 study, fewer than 50 now remain in the Mekong. The Irrawaddy has mythical origins. According to Lao and Khmer legend, a beautiful maiden, in despair over being forced to marry a snake, attempted suicide by jumping into the Mekong. But the gods intervened, saving her life by transforming her into a dolphin.

Lao people do not traditionally hunt the dolphins, but the Irrawaddy have been casualties of overfishing, getting tangled in nets. New dams in the Mekong have altered their ecosystem, further threatening their survival.

Catching a glimpse of these majestic animals—which look more like orcas than dolphins—can be a thrilling experience. The least obtrusive way to visit the Irrawaddy is in a kayak or other nonmotorized boat. If you go by motorboat and do spot dolphins, ask your driver to cut the engine when you're still 100 yards or so away. You can then paddle closer to the animals without disturbing them. Do not try to swim with the dolphins, and—of course—don't throw any trash into the water.

SI PHAN DON AND THE 4,000 ISLANDS

80 km (50 miles) south of Champasak, 120 km (74 miles) south of Pakse.

If you've made it as far south as Champasak, then a visit to the Si Phan Don area—celebrated for its 4,000 Mekong River islands and freshwater dolphins—is a must. *Don* means island, and two in this area are especially worth checking out: Don Khon (and its connected counterpart, Don Det) and the similarly named Don Khong. The Khone Phapheng Falls, on the mainland near Don Khon, are a highlight, and visiting them can be combined with seeing the freshwater Irrawaddy dolphins. You'll find many boat operators happy to escort you. Don Det, connected to Don Khon by a bridge, attracts the backpacker crowd. Don Khong has scenic rice fields and more upscale lodging choices and is far more peaceful than Don Khon, but is not as interesting or attractive. Most lodging options on Don Khon, Det, and Khong are fairly standard, but this is changing as progress comes to the islands.

GETTING HERE AND AROUND

Any travel agency in Pakse can help you make arrangements for getting to and from the islands. If going to Don Khong, consider taking a boat onward to Don Khon rather than taking the road. A boat usually makes the island hop (40,000 kip) every morning at 8:30.

From Pakse you can take a minibus, arranged at any travel agency or guesthouse, to the boat crossing at either Hai Sai Khun (for Don Khong) or Nakasang (for Don Khon) with tickets for the small boat crossing to the islands included. The journey takes from two to three hours and costs between 60,000 and 70,000 kip depending which island you go

9

to. A bridge completed in late 2014 connects Don Khong Island and Highway 13 on the Mekong's eastern bank, but the bridge is in the southern part of the island, so most minibuses still drop passengers at the boat pier farther north.

Boat crossings from the mainland to Don Khon (from Nakasang) cost 250,000 kip and take 15 minutes; to Don Khong (from Hat Sai Khun) it's a five-minute trip and costs 15,000 kip.

SAFETY AND PRECAUTIONS

Take care when kayaking on the Mekong. The water may appear still, but the currents are stronger than they seem, and eddies can suck you in. It's best to go with a guide. The name Liphi Falls means "spirit trap," and there's a lot of superstition surrounding them. It is considered offensive to swim here, so do refrain. Also, the rapids are strong, and there have been a number of tourist deaths in years past.

TIMING

The major sights can be seen in one day, but it would be a shame to not budget a few more days to relax and enjoy the local pace of life.

EXPLORING

Don Khon Island. You can hike or bicycle to the beautiful Liphi waterfall on the island of Don Khon, though an even more stunning one, **Khone Phapheng**, is just east of Don Khon on the mainland. Day-trip tours that include visits to the Irrawaddy dolphins and the mainland's Phapheng fall set out from Don Khon. Also on Don Khon, and the connected Don Det, are the remains of a French-built railway. ⊠ *Don Khon Island* 🎫 *Liphi waterfall 35,000 kip.*

Don Khong Island. The largest island in the area, Don Khong is inhabited by a community of fisherfolk living in small villages amid ancient Buddhist temples. The best way to explore is by bicycle—this a pretty big place. Far less visited than Don Det/Don Khon, it's also a great spot to chill out along the river. A new bridge across the Mekong now connects Don Khong to the mainland, but minibuses still use the boat pier for travelers to cross. The bridge has yet to spoil the quiet pace of the island, which has beautiful rice fields in the middle. ⊠ *Don Khong Island.*

Irrawaddy dolphins. Downstream from Don Khon, at the border between Laos and Cambodia, freshwater Irrawaddy dolphins frolic in a protected area of the Mekong. Boat trips to view the dolphins set off from Tha Sanam Beach, south of Liphi Falls. Even better, head out to see the dolphins by kayak. All the guesthouses in town can arrange trips. ⊹ *Boats depart from southern tip of Don Khon Island* 🎫 *70,000 kip per person, minimum of 3 people.*

WHERE TO EAT AND STAY

$ ✕ **Seng Ahloune Restaurant.** This rickety restaurant on wooden planks
LAO just above the Mekong may not look like much, but its cooks consistently deliver tasty and authentic Lao food. The setting is intimate and romantic, though the place can get busy with tour groups staying at the family's decent guesthouse. Don't confuse this restaurant west of Don Khon's railway bridge with the family's second restaurant and hotel,

Seng Ahloune 2, which is east of the bridge and doesn't face the river. $ *Average main: kip50,000* ✉ *Don Khon Island* ✛ *Just west of bridge connecting Don Khon with Don Det* ☎ *031/260934, 020/5583–1399* ▭ *No credit cards.*

$
HOTEL
🏠 **Pon Arena Hotel.** The rooms with a Mekong view are the way to go at this inviting riverside property—they're enormous and have terraces overlooking Si Phan Don. All the rooms, though, are modern and well-equipped with flat-screen TVs, safes, minibars, and other amenities. **Pros:** right on the river; large Mekong-view rooms with fabulous vistas; beautiful riverside pool; owner speaks fluent English. **Cons:** expensive for Don Khong; standard and deluxe rooms lack views; Mekong-view rooms cost twice as much as standard ones; often crowded with tour groups. $ *Rooms from: kip365,000* ✉ *Ban Kang Khong, Don Khong Island* ✛ *To right of boat pier on Don Khong* ☎ *031/515018 reservations, 020/2227–0037 manager's cell* ⊕ *www.ponarenahotel.com* ⟳ *35 rooms* ⋈ *Breakfast.*

$$
B&B/INN
🏠 **Sala Done Khone.** The accommodations at this charming resort come in three flavors: French colonial–style rooms, adobe-style "green" rooms set in a garden, and atmospheric "raftels" floating on the Mekong. **Pros:** beautiful riverside location; most upmarket hotel on the island; some raftels have sunroofs. **Cons:** rooms book up quickly in high season; mosquitoes prevalent at sunset; expensive for Don Khon. $ *Rooms from: kip487,000* ✉ *Don Khon Island* ✛ *Just east of boat drop-off in Don Khon* ☎ *031/260940* ⊕ *www.salalaoboutique.com* ⟳ *30 rooms (17 colonial wing, 5 adobe rooms, 8 raftels)* ⋈ *Breakfast.*

TAD FANE

38 km (24 miles) east of Pakse.

Tad Fane is Laos's most impressive waterfall, pounding down through magnificent jungle foliage for almost 400 feet.

GETTING HERE AND AROUND

Buses and songthaews run from the Pakse bus station several times each morning. The trip up to Tad Fane and the Bolaven Plateau town of Paksong takes an hour and costs 40,000 kip.

SAFETY AND PRECAUTIONS

The trails around the falls are slippery and can be dangerous, especially during the rainy season (when the leeches come out). Proceed with caution and take a guide if you feel unsure about getting around on your own.

TIMING

Take one day for the falls and possibly another day to do some hiking in the park or explore the area around Paksong.

Tad Fane. The waterfall is set on the border of the Dong Hua Sao National Park and up in the cool air of the Bolaven Plateau, Laos's premiere coffee-growing region. There's good hiking here, and the cool temperatures are a relief from the heat and humidity down on the Mekong. The area is accessible as a day trip from Pakse, though there is a somewhat run-down and overpriced resort at the base of the falls

9

should you care to stay. Aside from the easy stroll out to the viewing platform above the main falls, you can also take a guided walk down to the base of the falls, or venture onto one of the roundabout trails going up above the falls. These trails take in some minor falls and some fun swimming holes. Farther afield, the beautiful **Tat Yuang falls** can be reached in about an hour via a trail from Tad Fane, or from a turnout at Km 40 on the main road. Inquire at the resort about guides and trail information. ⊠ *Tad Fane.*

MYANMAR

WELCOME TO MYANMAR

TOP REASONS TO GO

★ **Explore Pagodas:** Slip off your shoes and stare slack-jawed at Bagan's staggering spread of 2,000-plus 11th- to 13th-century pagodas.

★ **Sweat It Out:** Spicy curries, fiery relishes, and piquant salads help you beat the heat.

★ **Travel Back in Time:** The turn-of-the-century colonial buildings that line Yangon's Strand Road stand just as they did during British rule.

★ **Get in Early:** Yangon may be changing rapidly but much of Myanmar is still blissfully undeveloped. Go now!

★ **Know Kindness:** Burmese locals will welcome you warmly; some might even invite you into their homes.

1 **Yangon (Rangoon).** The onetime capital of British Burma, Japanese Burma, and the country formerly and often still known as Burma, this is the country's biggest, most bustling city.

2 **Bagan.** Along the sides of a dusty stretch of road, more than 2,000 11th- and 12th-century pagodas are waiting to be explored. Even with the surge in tourists, you can still find yourself alone among the stupas.

3 **Inle Lake.** Get a close insight into everyday life as you explore this picturesque lake by boat, stopping at daily markets, floating gardens, and golden pagodas.

4 **Mandalay and Nearby.** The dusty roads here belie Mandalay's gems—the former royal palace, home to the last king of Burma, Mandalay Hill, and nearby hill station Pyin-U Lwin.

GETTING ORIENTED

Myanmar (Burma) is Southeast Asia's second-largest country (after Indonesia)—roughly the size of Texas. It's bordered to the southeast by Thailand, the northeast by Laos and China, and the west by India and Bangladesh. Roughly a third of the country's perimeter is gorgeous coastline along the Bay of Bengal and Andaman Sea, a whopping 1,200 miles. Compared with neighboring Thailand, Myanmar's coastline is undeveloped. A number of mountain ranges cut through Myanmar, running from the Himalayas north to south. The country has three rivers that are divided by the mountain ranges, and of them, the 1,348-mile Irrawaddy is the longest.

10

NEED TO KNOW

MYANMAR

Nay Pyi Taw ★

AT A GLANCE

Capital: Yangon

Population: 53,000,000

Currency: Kyat

Money: ATMs are becoming more common; they dispense kyat, so you'll still need to bring USD. Credit cards are accepted in some locations but cash is much more widely used.

Language: Burmese

Country Code: 95

Emergencies: Fire: 191; Ambulance: 192; Police: 199

Driving: Left

Electricity: 230v/50 cycles; electrical plugs have two flat prongs, two round prongs, or three flat prongs forming a triangle

Time: 11 hours ahead of New York

Documents: 28-day visa valid for 3 months from date of issue

Mobile Phones: GSM (900)

Major Mobile Companies: MPT, Telenor, Ooredoo (as of June 24, you will need to purchase a local SIM card).

GETTING AROUND

✈ **Air Travel:** International flights are serviced by Yangon Airport and Mandalay airport.

🚌 **Bus Travel:** The bus network is extensive. Many roads are rough, but this is the cheapest way to get around. Quality varies—there are "luxury" buses that run Mandalay–Yangon, and then there's the rest.

🚗 **Car Travel:** A car and driver can be hired for less money than you'd think. You can also try your luck with taxi drivers, who may be eager for a much larger fare.

🚃 **Train Travel:** Train travel is a delightful way to see the countryside. A number of routes originate in Yangon and Mandalay.

PLAN YOUR BUDGET

	HOTEL ROOM	MEAL	ATTRACTIONS
Low Budget	K48,000	K5,800	Bike rental in Bagan, K3,000
Mid Budget	K176,000	K11,700	Shwedagon Pagoda, K7,800
High Budget	K292,500	K19,500	Bagan admission, K14,600

WAYS TO SAVE

Eat on the street. In Yangon, street food abounds, from sweet banana cake to chili-topped tofu, all available for a pittance.

Book early through an agent. Demand outweighs supply, and there are few good midrange hotel options. Book with a travel agent to get the best price.

Stay on the ground. Flying is the fastest way around the country, but buses and trains are far cheaper and offer a much more authentic experience.

Go people-watching. In bustling Yangon, one of the best free activities is people-watching, especially before and after school when local kids will be excited to see you.

PLAN YOUR TIME

Hassle Factor	Medium. There are direct flights from Bangkok, Singapore, Hong Kong, Doha, Guangzhou, and Seoul, some of which can be reached by direct flight from the U.S.
3 days	Soak up the atmosphere in Yangon (Rangoon), the country's vibrant capital city. Shwedagon Pagoda, Myanmar's holiest sight, is a must-see; go at night when it's cooler and beautifully lit up.
1 week	Start in capital Yangon before flying to Bagan, home to 2,000 ancient stupas and pagodas. Spend a day or two ogling them before flying to Inle Lake and experiencing village life.

WHEN TO GO

High Season: Mid-October to February sees temperatures in the mid-90sF (mid-30sC) in October, down to the mid-80sF (around 26C) in February. Hotels fill up quickly and rates will be highest. Domestic flights book up quickly.

Low Season: From late May to late September, monsoons leave the country drenched, particularly in the western Rakhine State, and dirt roads become impassible mud. This is the least expensive time to go. Around Pyay and Mandalay, you should be able to sightsee without getting soaked.

Value Season: It's always hot and humid in Myanmar, but March to May are the hottest. Temperatures in Yangon can easily top 100°F (38°C), and it can be hotter still in Bagan and Mandalay. Still, because it's dry, hotel rates are not at their lowest, especially those with pools.

BIG EVENTS

April: A new year's celebration, Thingyan sees hoses, buckets, and water balloons being used to soak anyone in sight.

Usually November: During Tazaungdaing (Festival of Lights), a robe-weaving competition is held at Shwedagon Pagoda. Floating lanterns are set off around the country.

Usually October: During 18-day Phaung Daw U Festival, four Buddha images are placed on a replica of a royal barge and floated around Inle Lake.

December/January: At the Ananda Temple in Bagan, a thousand monks offer scriptures for three days and then line up to offer alms.

READ THIS

- **The Glass Palace,** Amitav Ghosh. Love, loss, death, and birth over 100 years, starting in 1885.

- **Burmese Days,** George Orwell. In 1920s Burma, British expats debate the ethics of letting a local into their club.

- **The River of Lost Footsteps,** Thant Myint-U. Burmese history and the story of the author's grandfather, who in the 1960s became UN Secretary-General.

WATCH THIS

- **The Lady.** A biopic about the life of Aung San Suu Kyi.

- **Beyond Rangoon.** American Laura Bowman, visiting then-Burma in 1988, gets caught up in an antigovernment uprising.

- **The Purple Plain.** Gregory Peck is a depressed pilot serving in Myanmar at the end of WWII.

EAT THIS

- **Shwe gye**: Semi-sweet banana cake.

- **Dosa**: Sweet or savory are made with rice flour.

- **Buthi kyaw**: Battered, deep-fried chunks of gourd.

- **Mohinga**: Rice vermicelli in a fish broth.

- **Laphet thoke**: Pickled tea leaves, peanuts, sesame seeds, garlic, and tomato.

- **Falooda**: A sweet drink made from rose syrup, tapioca pearls, vermicelli, jelly, and milk/ice cream.

IRRAWADDY RIVER CRUISES

A cruise on the Irrawaddy river is a unique way to experience Myanmar. Beyond visiting land sights, cruises provide for an up-close look at the riverside villages that depend on the water for their livelihood.

Not to be confused with the less expensive Irrawaddy River ferries, cruises range in length from two-day/one-night to more than three weeks. The cruises can be classed as either upmarket or very upmarket. There's no single departure point for Irrawaddy River cruises; most leave from Mandalay or Yangon, but others start in Bagan and even Bangkok (on land). All cruises include stops in Bagan and Mandalay (the shorter cruises run back and forth between the two).

ESSENTIALS

Meals and drinks are included in the cruise price but snacks are not. You'll be able to pick these up in Yangon or at the more populated port towns. Anything ordered on the ship not included in the meal plan must be paid for in cash. You will definitely need to bring your own sunblock. You should arrive in your cruise's departure city one day before your ship is set to sail, even if your cruise doesn't depart until the following evening. Included in many cruises' pricing is one night in the departure city, but be sure to confirm with your individual operator.

Most of the boats that ply the Irrawaddy are bi-level; some are cruise ships while others are colonial steam-ship style. Each ship has between 5 and 30 cabins, accommodating 10 to 60 people. The cruise lines stop in different places, but all cover Bagan and Mandalay. Unless otherwise indicated, all prices listed are per person for a double cabin during high season.

Abercrombie and Kent. Abercrombie and Kent is best known for its luxury excursions, and its 10-night, 11-day Myanmar & the Irrawaddy cruise (from $5,295) ensures guests' every whim is catered to. The tour starts and ends in Yangon. In between, travelers visit Inle Lake and Mandalay by land and cruise the Irrawaddy for four nights on A&K's luxurious, all-balcony-suite *Sanctuary Ananda*. Day 7, between Mandalay and Bagan, is spent almost entirely on the water. ✉ *1411 Opus Pl., Downers Grove* ☎ *888/611–4711 weekdays 8 am–7 pm, Sat. 9 am–1 pm CST* ⊕ *www.abercrombiekent.com.*

Amara River Cruise. Amara's two boutique boats, the *Amara I* and *II*, are built of strong, gleaming teak and have just seven and five rooms, respectively. Because the boats are so small, the service is extremely personalized and the entire boat can be chartered if a party so wishes. Amara offers three-night, four-day Mandalay–Bagan and Bagan–Mandalay cruises (from $1,024) ,and eight-day, seven-night Mandalay–Bhamo and Bhamo–Mandalay (from $2,386). Bhamo is a town in Myanmar's northernmost state, Kachin, and is 40 miles from the border of Yunnan province, China. Visited by few tourists, it offers a real look at how Burmese villagers live along the river. ✉ *6 Tayza Rd., Yangon (Rangoon)* ☎ *01/652191* ⊕ *www.amaragroup.net.*

Belmond Road to Mandalay. In a nod to Rudyard Kipling, the massive ship run by the Belmond group (formerly the Orient Express) is called the *Road to Mandalay*. This vessel can accommodate up to 82 guests and is equipped with a swimming pool and a well-being and fitness area, including a spa. Tours are 2, 3, 4, 7, and 11 nights long. The shorter cruises sail between Bagan and Mandalay, the longer cruises are at a more leisurely pace. ✉ *441 Lexington Ave., New York* ☎ *800/524–2420* ⊕ *www.belmond.com.*

Pandaw River Expeditions in Asia. Singaporean-owned Pandaw has 12 Irrawaddy River cruises. While you can take an overnight cruise between Mandalay and Pagan (from $371), Pandaw's longest cruise is a whopping 20 nights on the water, starting in Yangon and ending in Mandalay (from $7,056). It makes many stops in rural Myanmar, to tiny villages along the river, and to Katha, made famous by Orwell. Pandaw has a 10% discount for those who book early. Twelve custom-built colonial steamship-style boats make up the fleet, all hand-finished in brass and teak by traditional craftsmen. The Pandaw Charity is the cruise operator's nonprofit arm, based in the United Kingdom. and working mostly in Myanmar supporting education and health care. A portion of the cruises' annual profits is donated to the charities. ☎ *208/326–5620 U.K. office,*

10

280/067013 *Australia office,* 800/729–2651 *U.S. office* ⊕ *www.pandaw.com.*

Paukan Cruises by Ayravata Cruise Company. Paukan's fleet of three comprises a lovingly restored 1947 Scottish-built steamship and three newer vessels: the 2007, which looks much like the 1947 outfit, a sleek, teak 2012 model and a modern hotel-style one built in 2014. Paukan is one of a few operators who have short cruises; there's a one-night trip from Mandalay to Bagan and a two-night trip that runs both the Bagan–Mandalay and Mandalay–Bagan routes (both from $780). One of the most popular tours is the four-night Royal Myanmar (from $1,860), which starts in Bagan and ends in Mandalay following stops at Yandabo (a pot-making village, where the peace treaty for the First Anglo-Burmese war was signed; we know how that ended), Monywa (caves with hundreds of Buddha statues), Ava (teak monastery and 88½-foot watchtower), and Amarapura (penultimate capital city). Paukan also offers 5-, 6-, 7-, and 10-night cruises. ⊠ *25 38th St., Yangon (Rangoon)* ☎ *01/380877* ⊕ *www.ayravatacruises.com.*

Viking River Cruises. Viking hosts a 15-day Myanmar Explorer trip that starts with two nights in Bangkok before flying to Yangon, then on to Inle Lake, and then to Mandalay, where passengers board an eight-day Irrawaddy River cruise. Guests will see Ohn Ne Choung, a traditional riverside farming and fishing community, Bagan, then the Salé Monasteries. The terra-cotta pottery town of Yandabo is visited, as is Monywa, where Mohnyin Thambuddhei Paya is a massive Buddhist temple originally built in 1303 containing 500,000 images of the Buddha. The tour ends with a flight back to Bangkok and a stay overnight there. ⊠ *Yangon (Rangoon)* ☎ *800/706–1483 in California* ⊕ *www.vikingrivercruises.com.*

Updated by
Lara Dunston
and Sophie
Friedman

Myanmar (Burma) is simply amazing. This country of 55 million is rapidly emerging from more than 50 years of military dictatorship, blossoming into as worthy a stop as its popular neighbors. The people are more than friendly; they're thrilled to have tourists after being closed off to the West for so long. And it's safe; you won't constantly need to feel for your purse or hold your jewelry tightly.

Myanmar is a country straddling two worlds—Wi-Fi has arrived, but just 10% of the population has a mobile phone. There are pristine 12th-century pagodas and beautiful beaux arts buildings, though how long they'll be preserved remains to be seen, which makes now the time to go. A note about this guide: it is impossible to go to Myanmar and not indirectly give money to the government; the airlines and many of the better hotels are connected to the government. We encourage travelers to do their best to support independent businesses.

PLANNING

10

WHEN TO GO
PEAK SEASON: MID-OCTOBER TO FEBRUARY
The Burmese call this the cold season, but you'll still find yourself plenty toasty, with temperatures in the hotter areas hovering in the mid-90s (mid-30s) in October, down to the mid-80s (around 26°C) in February. Hotels fill up quickly and rates will be at their highest. Airline prices won't skyrocket but planes are quite small and book up quickly.

OFF-SEASON: LATE MAY TO LATE SEPTEMBER
Southwestern monsoons, particularly from July to September, leave the country drenched, particularly in the western Rakhine State. The problem is not so much the rain itself as the aftermath, when dirt roads become impassable fields of mud. This is certainly the least expensive and most beautiful time to go. Around Pyay and Mandalay, you should be able to sightsee without getting soaked.

SHOULDER SEASON: MARCH TO MAY

It's always hot and humid in Myanmar, but these are the months during which you'll roast if not careful. Temperatures in Yangon can easily top 100°F (38°F), with temperatures going even higher in Bagan and Mandalay. Still, because it's dry, hotel rates are not at their lowest, especially those with pools.

GETTING HERE AND AROUND

Foreigners can cross into Myanmar from Thailand's three overland border crossings and can now travel freely through most of Myanmar, something that was previously restricted. As of this writing the following border points are open with Thailand (Thai border towns are in parentheses): Myawaddy (Mae Sot), Tachileik (Mae Sai), and Kawthaung (Ranong). The entry fee is $10, valid for a one-week stay in Myanmar. If you wish to stay the full month, a tourist visa will have to be arranged in advance.

There are direct flights to Yangon from a growing number of cities, including Bangkok, Singapore, Hong Kong, Doha, Guangzhou, and Seoul. Air Asia, Thai Airways, Myanmar Airways International, Nok Air, and Korean Airlines are just a few that run regular flights. Mandalay can be reached from Bangkok (Air Asia and Thai Air) and Kunming (China Eastern Airlines). Myanmar has some half-dozen domestic airlines, including KBZ, Air Mandalay, Asian Wings Airways, and Yangon Airways, which run to all major tourist destinations and beyond.

There are two methods of boat travel in Myanmar—luxury riverboat cruises, and regular ferries. The latter is further divided into two categories—slow, and what is called express but is still fairly slow. Ferries run Yangon to Mandalay and back, with stops in Bagan and Pyay. A ticket on the Mandalay–Bagan express ferry will cost you $45 and the Bagan-Mandalay journey $35. *For more information on cruise lines, see Irrawaddy River Cruise spotlight.*

Myanmar has an extensive bus network and although many roads are pretty rough, this is the cheapest way to get around. The quality of buses varies—there are the "luxury" buses that run the Mandalay–Yangon route, and then there's the rest. Because so many roads are in poor condition, trips take longer than advertised; the drive from Yangon to Bagan should be around 10 hours and the fare no more than K80,000. When possible, opt for the air-conditioned buses (pack something in which to wrap yourself) and sit in the front next to a window, where it's least bumpy.

A car and driver can be very costly. If you're staying at an upscale hotel, do not try to arrange one with the concierge or you will end up overpaying. As well as tour companies, you can also try your luck with taxi drivers, who may be eager for a much larger fare.

Motos (motorcycle taxis), tuk-tuks or trishaws (three-wheeled cabs), and cyclos (pedal-powered trishaws) are popular forms of transportation in cities and towns across Myanmar except in Yangon, where motorcycles are illegal. Hiring a bicycle is easy, but those wishing to hire their own moto or scooter will have a tougher time.

ESSENTIALS

It's not acceptable for women to wear short shorts on the street and a *longyi* (traditional sarong) or long skirt is needed when entering pagodas and temples. Visitors are also required to remove shoes and socks. There's no need to hike up your skirt or sarong while you're walking around the temples; it's okay if it drags a bit on the ground.

Business-card customs here are the same as elsewhere in Asia. If you plan on doing business in Myanmar, have cards printed up with English on one side, Burmese on the other. Business cards are exchanged with two hands.

Be respectful of language difficulties. Although English is widely spoken, try and speak slowly and enunciate when talking to locals, especially over the phone.

Everyone needs a visa to enter Myanmar. For most nationalities, a 28-day single-entry tourist visa is easily available online for $50 from the Ministry of Immigration and Population website (⊕ *evisa.moip.gov.mm*). Allow three days to process, although it can take as little as a few hours. It is not extendable and entry is only allowed at Yangon, Nay Pyi Taw, and Mandalay International Airports. Technically, you can get a visa on arrival, but this is highly unreliable and airlines may not let you board without a visa in your passport. You'll need a passport that's valid for six months from the date of your arrival in Myanmar.

Crossing the Tachileik/Mae Sai border into Thailand if you entered Myanmar by air is now simple. Note that you only get a two-week visa when entering Thailand by land. Crossing *from* Mae Sai into Myanmar at the Tachileik checkpoint will cost you $10 and three passport photos, valid for two weeks, and you can exit at any border.

While a visit to Myanmar used to mean taking in a huge wad of U.S. dollars, there are now ATMs throughout the country that accept Visa and MasterCard, which visitors can use to withdraw the local currency, kyat. A fee of K5,000 ($4) is charged for each transaction; K300,000 ($233) can be withdrawn up to three times per day. Visitors should still bring U.S. dollars in denominations of $20 or less ($1, $5, and $10 are preferable), as long as they are crisp and not damaged. In Yangon and Mandalay, it's possible to exchange euros, Chinese yuan, and Thai baht into local currency. Coins exist but are rarely given as change. Banknotes range from 50 pyas (cents) up to K10,000. *An important note: Prices in Myanmar are rising rapidly; those given were correct at the time of writing. We list prices in U.S. dollars where they are exclusively used.*

Myanmar is very hot for much of the year, and it's essential to stay hydrated and protect your skin. We recommend using bottled water, even for brushing your teeth. Sunscreen is only available at supermarkets, but bring your own if you have fair skin.

Malaria is a problem in rural Myanmar. Be vigilant about bug spray, which is available in supermarkets, and sleep with the windows closed or inside a mosquito net.

10

The state of health care in Myanmar is very poor and HIV/AIDS is an issue; avoid needles at local hospitals. Poor food-hygiene practices of street vendors poses your biggest sickness risk in the country, so note the food handling of vendors before ordering.

Myanmar is extremely safe. Crime, especially against foreigners, is severely punished. Even petty crime, such as pickpocketing, is rare. Visitors do not need to be concerned about wearing backpacks or carrying open-top tote bags or purses. The Burmese, many of whom are devout Buddhists, are markedly friendly; however, you may be "robbed" by paying too much for a taxi or jade at the markets.

RESTAURANTS

Given Myanmar's many different ethnic groups and regions, as well as the historical influences of neighboring Thailand, India, and China, the food of the country is fascinating—particularly for those happy to eat on the streets, in the markets, or at local eateries. Recent contact with the West and the influx of tourists—many not willing to gamble on the food safety of the street vendors—means that western tastes are catered to wherever tourists travel, such as Yangon, Bagan, Inle Lake, and Mandalay. If you tire of local food, it's easy to find pastas, pizzas, burgers, and the like in these destinations.

Prices in the reviews are the average cost of a main course at dinner or, if dinner is not served, at lunch.

HOTELS

Because demand far outweighs supply, hotels in Myanmar are significantly more expensive than in neighboring Thailand. Yangon has the biggest concentration of upscale accommodations—some tip the scale at $500 a night—including two classic colonial luxury hotels and a handful of international business hotels. Places in Yangon catering to foreigners almost always have 24-hour electricity and most have some degree of Wi-Fi. Mandalay has a few luxury big-box hotels, including western chains, and several options considered midrange by Myanmar standards. Brief electricity blackouts are common, but the more upscale hotels have generators that start automatically during power failures. At many smaller hotels they may wait to see how long the outage lasts before starting up their generator.

Prices in the reviews are the lowest cost of a standard double room in high season.

WHAT IT COSTS IN BURMESE K AND USD			
$	$$	$$$	$$$$
RESTAURANTS under K1,500	K1,500–2,500	K2,500–4,000	Over K4,000
HOTELS under $80	$80–$180	$180–$300	over $300

Restaurant prices are for a main course, excluding tax and tip. Hotel prices are for a standard double in high season, excluding service charge and tax.

TOURS

Myanmar is perfectly friendly to independent travelers, and there's enough infrastructure for tourists that you'll get where you want to go, one way or another. That said, a trip to Myanmar during peak season requires serious advance research and planning. The agencies listed here cater to those wishing to join a guided tour, or have a tour arranged.

Exotic Myanmar Travels and Tours. This agency is particularly helpful when it comes to arranging plane, train, and bus tickets. ✉ *#225, 15th fl., Olympic Tower, Aung Kyaw St.* ☎ *09/392778* ⊕ *www.exoticmyanmartravel.com.*

Kengtung Trekking Guide - Sai Sam Tip. Local guide Sai Sam Tip leads treks to ethnic villages and elsewhere. ✉ *Yangon (Rangoon)* ☎ *09/4100–6263* ✐ *saisamtip3@gmail.com.*

Myanmar Travel and Tours. MTT is the government-run agency you need to see if you want permits for traveling to restricted areas. If you plan to cross from Tachileik into Mae Sai, Thailand, you'll need a permit. MTT runs its own tours and manages state owned hotels. ✉ *118 Mahabandoola Garden St., Yangon (Rangoon)* ☎ *095/371286, 095/378376.*

One Stop Travel and Tours. This highly rated agency organizes a variety of cultural tours, as well as hotels, plane tickets, and everything in between. ✉ *160/3C Kyuntaw St., Yangon (Rangoon)* ☎ *01/523486* ⊕ *www.onestop-myanmar.com.*

Shan Yoma Travel and Tours. Established in 1996, this company organizes multiday itineraries, river cruises, bike tours, diving and more ✉ *124-126 50th St., Yangon (Rangoon)* ☎ *01/295510, 01/299389, 01/204152* ⊕ *www.exploremyanmar.com.*

Sun Far Travels and Tours. This reliable ticketing agency can also help with visas and arranging tours. ✉ *27-31 38th St., Yangon (Rangoon)* ☎ *01/380211* ⊕ *www.sunfartravels.com.*

Fodor's Choice ★ Tour Mandalay. This family-owned business is by far the best tour and travel company in Myanmar, for everything from day trips to complete trip itineraries and planning. ✉ *#02/03, 2nd fl., Pearl Condominium A, Kaba Aye Pagoda Rd.* ☎ *09/5154–0475* ⊕ *www.tourmandalay.travel.*

VISITOR INFORMATION

Myanmar Tourism Promotion Board. The Myanmar Tourism Promotion Board is state owned. We recommend using local, privately owned tour agencies—it's worth shopping around. ✉ *Diamond Condo A, 497 Pyay Rd., Room 904, Yangon (Rangoon)* ☎ *01/242828.*

10

YANGON (RANGOON)

The capital until 2006, Yangon (Rangoon) is Myanmar's largest city and its commercial center. It is truly developing, and full of juxtapositions: new high-rises abut traditional Southeast Asian shophouses while down the street from a frozen yogurt bar, a sidewalk dentist goes to work. Yangon's rich collection of colonial architecture is one of its biggest draws; The Strand and its surrounding side streets look today much as they did at the turn of the century, when Yangon—then Rangoon— was under British rule. Yangon's most iconic sight is unquestionably

Admission to the Shwedagon Pagoda is free for locals and many come by night to pay their respects.

the enormous gilded Shwedagon Pagoda, but what makes it worth visiting beyond that is the rich, vibrant life that spills out of people's homes and onto the streets. Colorful and chaotic, Yangon is a feast for the senses. Grinning uniformed schoolchildren and preadolescent monks vie for sidewalk space as vendors hawk fried goods and longyi-wearing businessmen go off to work. On a street of Indian-run paint shops sits the country's only synagogue, a 19th-century relic; blocks away rise the steeples of St. Mary's Cathedral, another reminder of the city's colonial past.

GETTING HERE AND AROUND

AIR TRAVEL Most international flights arrive at Yangon, including a number of direct flights; however, airlines are increasingly flying into Mandalay. China Southern Airlines and Myanmar Airways International fly from Guangzhou; Nok Air, Air Asia, and Thai International Airways fly from Bangkok; Korean Airlines flies from Seoul; and Malaysia Airlines flies from Kuala Lumpur. From Cambodia, Bangkok Airways and Air Asia offer connecting flights via Bangkok to Yangon, although changing in Bangkok to Nok Air is more affordable.

Yangon's airport, 30–40 minutes north of the city center, has domestic and international terminals less than 700 feet apart. The airport is easy to navigate, and customs is a breeze. A taxi downtown will run you K7,000, less if you bargain. Be aware that the porters are not airport volunteers and expect to be paid for their services; they will grab your bags unless you say otherwise. About K1,250, or $1, per bag should suffice.

BOAT TRAVEL Ferries leave from Yangon's jetty, just off Strand Road, running north and making stops in Mandalay, Bagan, and Pyay. There's also an overnight ferry to Pathein ($40 per cabin) and ferries to Dallah (10 minutes; K4,000), just across the Rangoon River. All tickets can be purchased from the Inland Water Transport (☏ 095/380–764) office on Strand Road, just across from the jetty.

BUS TRAVEL Most tourists stick to cabs and cyclo rickshaws or get around on foot, but Yangon also has an extensive bus system. Don't try and navigate the bus system, but rather consider it an adventure and hop aboard. Tickets are K100. Regional buses leave from the Highway Bus Center; route maps and tickets are available from ⊕ *myanmarbusticket.com.*

CAR TRAVEL A car and driver can be hired through any travel agency and can cost up to $60–$80 a day, but a hired vehicle is not necessary in Yangon, because the major sights are relatively close to one another.

TAXI AND Cabs and cyclos are abundant in Yangon. Neither are metered; a taxi
CYCLO TRAVEL ride within downtown should not run you more than K2,500 and a cyclo ride will cost less, while a ride to Inya Lake can cost up to K4,500. Taxis and cyclos can both be hired for touring, and in fact touring by cyclo is much more interesting than doing so in a car. Agree with the driver on a fare before you take off.

ESSENTIALS

Yangon's airport has several ATMs that accept international cards, and services have become much more reliable in recent years; however, always arrive with some crisp, recent U.S. dollar bills just in case, so you can get from the airport to the hotel. Exchange rates around town at markets and banks are pretty good, but always check before making a transaction.

Airport Information Yangon International Airport. ✉ *Yangon (Rangoon)* ☏ *095/162712.*

Bus Contacts The Highway Bus Center (Aung Mingalar Bus Terminal). ✉ *Just southwest of airport, off Pyay Rd.* ☏ *No phone.*

Visitor and Tour Information Tourist Information Office (Ministry of Hotels and Tourism). ✉ *77-91 Sule Pagoda Rd.* ☏ *095/252859.*

10

EXPLORING YANGON

Yangon is not difficult to navigate on foot, as most of downtown is laid out on a grid and the area where tourists explore is quite compact. Addresses are easily recognizable, and it's simple to ask for directions. The area of Yangon that's the easiest to navigate is that which surrounds the Bogyoke Market, from Bogyoke Aung San Road south to The Strand, and from Aung Yadana Street east to May Yu Road. Be careful walking around at night. Crime is not the issue—Myanmar is extremely safe—but many streets have large holes in the sidewalks and no street lamps.

The farther-flung areas can be reached without hassle by taxi or rickshaw. A fast-paced traveler could cover the best of Yangon in two days.

Monks stroll the grounds at the Myanmar's most sacred site, the Shwedagon Pagoda.

TOP ATTRACTIONS

FAMILY

Fodor's Choice
★

Shwedagon Pagoda. This 325-foot-tall gilded pagoda is Yangon's top tourist attraction and, at 2,500 years old, the world's oldest pagoda. It is simply stunning. Admission is free for locals, and you'll see families, kids, groups of teenagers, and solo visitors milling around the pagoda all day, every day—praying, meditating, and just hanging out. The space is massive and never feels crowded. Women need a longyi (traditional sarong) or knee-length skirt to enter the pagoda, and all visitors are required to remove their shoes in the parking lot. During Yangon's hot days the pagoda glistens in the sun—it can be truly sweltering, and the floor can burn your bare feet. A better option is to come after the sun's gone down, when the Shwedagon is beautifully illuminated. There is an elevator for those who do not wish to climb up. ⊠ *Ar Za Nir St.* ⊕ *www. shwedagonpagoda.com* ⊠ *K8,000* ⊙ *Daily 4 am–10 pm.*

Strand Road and Southern Yangon. This meandering walk through southern Yangon gives a good overview of the city's streets, leading you to the Strand Hotel on Yangon's southernmost boulevard, adjacent to the river. Your first stop is **Saint Mary's Cathedral** (Bogyoke Aung San Road and Bo Aung Kyaw Street), a Dutch-designed Gothic Revival structure dating back to 1899. The cathedral survived a 1930 earthquake and the World War II bombings, although its original stained-glass windows were shattered and have been replaced. There's a small swing set in the cathedral's yard. Backtracking a bit, walk south and west toward **Musmeah Yeshua Synagogue** (85 26th Street, near Maha Bandoola Road), Burma's only remaining synagogue. Constructed in 1896, it's small but well maintained, with beautiful, simple stained-glass windows. Today

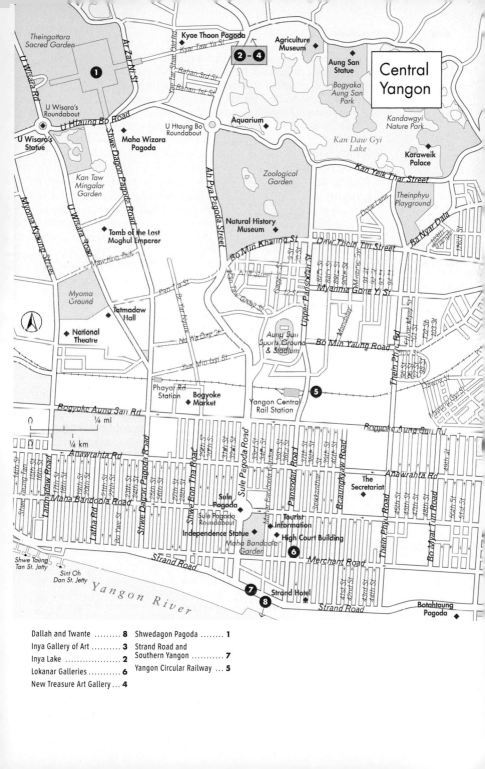

Central Yangon

Theingottara Sacred Garden

Kyae Thoon Pagoda

2 – 4

Agriculture Museum

Aung San Statue

Bogyoka Aung San Park

Kandawgyi Nature Park

1

Kyar Taw Ya St.

Tat-Tar Street Otht Rd.

Bahan 3rd St.

Bahan 1st St.

Ar Zar Ni St.

U Wisara Rd

U Htaung Bo Road

U Htaung Bo Roundabout

Aquarium

Kan Daw Gyi Lake

Kan Yeik Thar Street

Karaweik Palace

U Wisara's Roundabout

U Wisara's Statue

Maha Wizara Pagoda

Shwe Dagon Pagoda Road

Dote Lane

Theinphyu Playground

Ba Nyar Dala

126th St.

Kan Taw Mingalar Garden

Myoma Kyaung Street

U Wisara Road

Ah Pya Pagoda Street

Zoological Garden

Tomb of the Last Moghul Emperor

Maw Kon Path

Natural History Museum

Bo Min Khaing St.

Daw Thein Tin Street

Myanma Gone Yi St.

Thein Phyu Rd

A Pya Street

Pan Ta St.

Ganges St.

Kan Zin Gway St.

Upper Pansodan St.

Myaing St.

Mandalay

122nd St.

123rd St.

Myoma Ground

Tatmadaw Hall

Bo Yar Street

Na War Day St.

Yan Min Gyi St.

Aung San Sports Ground & Stadium

Bo Min Yaung Road

National Theatre

Phayar Rd Station

Bogyoke Market

Yangon Central Rail Station

5

Bogyoke Aung San Rd

Dawe St.

Myoma St.

Anawrahta Rd

Anawrahta Rd.

The Secretariat

Bogyoke Aung San Rd.

¼ mi

¼ km

Maha Bandoola Road

Shwe Eon Tha Road

Shwe Dagon Pagoda Road

Sule Pagoda Road

Maha Bandoola Garden St.

Pansodan Road

Sorkanthar St.

Braungkyaw Road

Thein Phyu Road

Sint Aung Tan

Tanthada Rd

Latha Rd

Shwe Bon Yee St.

15th St. 16th St. 18th St. 19th St. 20th St. 23rd St. 24th St. 46th St.

27th St. 28th St. 29th St. 30th St. 31st St. 33rd St. 34th St. 35th St. 36th St.

37th St. 38th St. 39th St.

44th St. 45th St. 46th St.

47th St. 48th St. 49th St.

Sule Pagoda

Sule Pagoda Roundabout

Independence Statue

Maha Bandoola Garden

Tourist Information

High Court Building

6

Merchant Road

Strand Road

Shwe Taung Tan St. Jetty

Sint Oh Dan St. Jetty

Yangon River

7

8

Strand Hotel

Strand Road

Botahtaung Pagoda

its congregation contains just a few families. The street on which the synagogue sits is lined with Indian-run paint shops, and the shophouses are painted in gorgeous, eye-popping colors such as robin's egg blue, violet, and dark orange. From the synagogue, walk east and south to the **Strand Hotel** (92 Strand Road at 38th Street), which opened in 1901 and was frequented by Rudyard Kipling. Steep yourself in the hotel's rich history by enjoying traditional afternoon tea; both the classic English and a Burmese version are available. ⊠ *Bogyoke Aung San Rd. and Bo Aung Kyaw St.*

Yangon Circular Railway. There's no better bang for your buck in Yangon than a ride on the city's circle line. The three-hour tour covers 46 km (29 miles) and 39 stations on a railway loop that connects tiny towns and the suburbs with downtown Yangon. You'll see urban Yangon followed by shantytowns, grazing cows, ponds, barefoot giggling kids, and lots of greenery. The journey starts from the grand Yangon Central Station, whose style combines colonial and traditional Burmese architectural elements and is itself a sight. The train is the great unifier, with vegetable sellers, monks, kids, and commuters all hanging tight. Trains leave from Yangon Central platforms 4 and 7, one going clockwise and the other counterclockwise; the kindly ticket seller will personally guide you to the proper platform. Tickets are available at the station master's office at platform 7. You may be asked to show your passport to purchase tickets. ⊠ *Yangon Central Station, Pansodan St. and Kun Can Rd.* ⊠ *K1,000* ☉ *Daily 4 am–10 pm.*

WORTH NOTING

Dallah and Twante. Just across the river from Yangon is the small village of Dallah, reached by ferry from the city's jetty. It's a 10-minute ride where you'll stand among vendors selling fruit, fried snacks, knick-knacks, and fresh-rolled cheroots and cigarettes. Make a quick stop at the pagoda in Dallah before moving on to Twante (40-minute drive; go via cab, moto, or pickup truck). Once there, hop a trishaw or a horse and buggy for a visit to the Shwesandaw Pagoda, a miniaturized version of the Shwedagon, and to the local pottery sheds. From Yangon, you can also go to Twante directly on the two-hour ferry. Tickets for both ferries are K1,200 each and can be purchased at Pandosan Street Jetty, from which the boat leaves (across from Strand Hotel). ⊠ *Yangon (Rangoon).*

Inya Gallery of Art. Yangon native and self-taught artist Aung Myint opened this gallery in 1989. Aung was the first Burmese artist to win an ASEAN Art Award, and his work is in the permanent collections of the National Art Museum of Singapore and National Art Gallery of Malaysia, among others. Inya Gallery of Art showcases Aung's work as well as that of artists who work with similar themes. Most of the paintings are colorful, though Aung does have a series of black and whites. ⊠ *50B Inya Rd.* ☎ *095/524818* ⊕ *inyaartgallery.tripod.com.*

FAMILY **Inya Lake.** The British created this artificial lake in 1883, and it's said to look much the same today as it did then. About 10 km (6 miles) north of downtown, the area surrounding the lake is home to the Yangon Sailing Club (established in 1924) and expensive homes belonging to Aung San Suu Kyi and the U.S. ambassador. You can circle the lake on foot in about two hours, and many of the paths are well shaded. Adjacent to the lake and next to Yangon University is the 37-acre Inya Park, enormously popular with young couples who come to canoodle, watch movies on their laptops, and gaze at the lake. There are small snack and drink shops near the parking lot and benches dotted all over. On the western side of the lake is Mya Kyuan Thar, a peninsula with a kids' playground and an amusement park. ✉ *Intersection of Inya Rd. and Pyay Rd.*

Lokanat Galleries. The motto of this gallery, which opened in 1971 and claims to be Myanmar's longest-running gallery, is "Truth, Beauty, Love." The nonprofit NGO is dedicated to promoting local artists, and represents 21 of them. It hosts exhibitions every few months and also works with embassies and other NGOs to put on shows and fairs. ✉ *62 Pansodan St.* ☎ *095/382269* 🌐 *www.lokanatgalleries.com.*

New Treasure Art Gallery. Halfway between the Shwedagon Pagoda and Inya Lake is this gallery, which is owned in part by Min Wae Aung, Burma's best-selling artist, most well known for his highly detailed paintings of Buddhist monks. New Treasure's goal is to showcase the work of young Burmese artists, but Min Wae Aung also has a collection of 20th-century work from which today's artists draw much inspiration. Walk directly north and you'll reach the southern tip of Inya Lake; walk directly south and you can enter People's Park from the northern gate. ✉ *84A Thanlwin St.* ☎ *095/526776.*

WHERE TO EAT

Yangon has a vibrant culinary scene, with everything from street-food stalls and boisterous teahouses to French fine dining and an array of restaurants representing the diverse cuisines of the country, from Shan to Rakhine, Burmese to Kachin.

$ BURMESE 🍴 **999 Shan Noodle Shop.** This pint-size, cheap-and-cheerful noodle eatery is equally popular with locals and tourists. The friendly proprietors speak English well, and the picture menu has English descriptions. The noodles are those of the Shan ethnic group, and noodles are served in soups or smothered in scrumptious toppings such as creamy tofu. Rounding out the menu are sautéed vegetables, fried tofu, and pork skin. The owners can prepare plain and mild noodle dishes if you're not one for spice. Inexpensive local beer is available, too. [$] *Average main: K1000* ✉ *130B 34th St. near Anawrahta Rd.* 💳 *No credit cards* 🕒 *Open until 7 pm* ✥ *C5.*

$$ BURMESE 🍴 **Aung Mingalar.** You'll see few tourists at this cheap, cheerful, and unpretentious family-owned eatery, which gets packed with local office workers during the day, students in the late afternoon, and local residents and expats in the early evening. While there's a long menu of dishes from across Myanmar, unlike other Shan eateries, the specialty is Shan noodles, so order the heavenly warm tofu chicken noodle (K1,500). The fried tofu is also delicious, and if you're with a few friends it's hard to go past the big plate of fried pork dumplings (18 for K3,500). [$] *Average main: K1500* ✉ *Corner Nawady St. and Bo Yar Nyunt St.* 💳 *No credit cards* ✥ *B4.*

CUISINE OF MYANMAR

Thanks to centuries of trade, occupation, and migration, the cuisine of Myanmar has influenced, and been influenced by, its neighbors India, China, Laos, and Thailand, well before they were so demarcated by national borders. Steamed rice is always served along with some half-dozen small dishes, generally curry, vegetables, and fish. Chicken and fish are quite popular, as Buddhists avoid beef and Muslims pork, although you'll be able to order all four at any restaurant that's neither vegetarian nor halal. **Freshwater fish** and shrimp are served salted, fried, dried, fermented, and made into a paste. One of the most popular cuisines is that of the Shan states, distinguished by its many salads. One of the most popular is a Shan dish called *laphet*, made with pickled tea leaves, fried broad beans, peanuts and garlic, green chilies, tomato, and preserved ginger and tossed with peanut oil, fish sauce, and lime; it's tart, sharp, and refreshing.

The farther north you go toward the border, the more **Chinese cuisine** you'll see. In the areas that cater particularly to tourists, such as Bagan, restaurants serve a smattering of Chinese, Indian, Thai, and Burmese dishes. Mandalay has lots of Chinese and Indian restaurants, and it's here that you'll find some of the best Indian street food, including hot-off-the-grill chapatis and buttery naan.

In general, Burmese food is not very spicy, but those who like it hot can certainly ask for extra chilies. **Curries** are enormously popular in Myanmar, eaten with white rice.

Burmese curries tend to be oilier than their Indian and Thai cousins.

As in its neighboring countries, eating is a communal experience here; everyone will have rice, and then can serve themselves from the array of small plates on the table. At some Burmese restaurants, it's buffet, and the waitstaff will keep refilling your bowls until you're stuffed.

You'll see **street snack** vendors all over Yangon, with rows of them lining the sidewalk on both sides of Bogyoke Aung San Road near Bogyoke Market and the Shangri-La. The most common snacks include:

Shwe gye: This semisweet banana cake, sold in neatly sliced hunks, gets its distinct flavor from semolina and coconut milk. You'll be thinking about it long after you leave Yangon.

Dosa: The southern Indian snack is known in Burmese as *toshay* and also referred to as *khout mote* (literally, "folded snack") and *mont pyar thalet.* The crepes are made with rice flour and come in sweet (shredded coconut and palm sugar syrup, sometimes red bean) and savory (tomatoes, chickpeas, cabbage, and sometimes chili).

Buthi kyaw: Battered, deep-fried chunks of gourd are far from healthy but taste delicious dipped in the accompanying sauce (slightly sour and a little spicy).

Mohinga: Eaten nationwide, this popular breakfast dish is rice vermicelli in a fish broth made from fresh fish, onions, garlic, lemongrass, banana tree stem, and a dash of ginger.

$$$$ JAPANESE 🍴 **Kohaku Japanese.** Arguably Yangon's, if not Myanmar's, finest Japanese restaurant, Kohaku is a favorite with affluent Burmese, business travelers, and tourists looking for a change from local food, and is therefore full most nights, so call ahead. Everything's fresh, especially the sushi (the fish is flown in daily), and the hamachi nigiri sushi is sublime. Best values are the generous all-you-can-eat buffet menus: the Japanese À La Carte Buffet (US$38; Monday to Thursday) and Kohaku Deluxe Buffet (US$42; Friday to Sunday). [$] *Average main: K30988* ✉ *Chatrium Hotel, 40 Natmauk Rd., Tamwe Township* ☎ *01/544500* 🌐 *www.chatrium.com* 💳 *No credit cards* ✥ *C1.*

$$$ BURMESE FAMILY 🍴 **Min Lane Seafood.** Pull up a chair near one of the fans here and order an avocado shake to enjoy while you peruse the menu. Once you're finished, order another; you'll need something to cool your mouth down after a bite of the rice noodles in a fiery broth. Once your sinuses have been cleared, move on to the delectable grilled seafood; there's crab, oysters, prawns, squid, and shellfish to choose from, and all come to the table expertly charred. [$] *Average main: K3000* ✉ *Pyay Rd. at Parami Rd.* 💳 *No credit cards* ✥ *C1.*

$ INDIAN 🍴 **Nilar Biryani.** Eating at this busy spot that's always packed with locals is a delicious, inexpensive affair. The menu is tiny, with just three types of biryani—chicken, mutton, and vegetable (which sells out the fastest). Be sure to order your meal with pickles. Service is fast and efficient; this is the place to grab a lassi and eat quickly before returning to sightseeing. Nilar Biryani is always crowded. If you can't get a table, head just down the street to the equally good **New Delhi** (Anawratha Road between Shwe Bontha and 28th Street), where the menu is longer and includes plenty of vegetarian dishes. Don't miss the potato chapati, daal, and very spicy curries. [$] *Average main: K1300* ✉ *216 Anawratha Rd.* 💳 *No credit cards* ✥ *C4.*

$$$$ BURMESE Fodor's Choice ★ 🍴 **Rangoon Tea House.** This casual, light-filled restaurant would be at home in Sydney or Singapore, and yet it somehow feels distinctly Yangon. Set on the first floor of a beautifully restored white colonial building, it can nevertheless be tricky to find, located above an electrical appliance store; look for the doorway and stairs on the right of the building. Once inside you'll find a lovely whitewashed space with wooden floorboards and whooshing ceiling fans, and the most delicious food you'll find in Myanmar. Expect anything from traditional samosas (K2,500) and tea leaf salad (K2,000) to modern pan-Asian favorites such as pork belly bao (K3,000). Open for breakfast, lunch, and dinner, you can order a full meal or simply pop in for tea or cocktails (K4,000). Try the Mandalay rum sour or Dragon martini. [$] *Average main: K4000* ✉ *1st fl., 77-79 Pansodan Rd., Lower-Middle Block, Kyauktada Township* ☎ *01/122–4534* 💳 *No credit cards* ✥ *C5.*

$$$$ BURMESE 🍴 **Shan Yoe Yar.** The food of the Shan State is the "it" cuisine in Yangon, and this two-story restaurant in a refurbished teakwood house claims to be the first Shan fine-dining restaurant in Myanmar. Specializing in the cuisines of the Shan ethnic minorities, the highlight is the lovely, light food of the Intha people of Inle Lake. Don't miss *sa kone,* a traditional beef salad and the fried fish with tamarind sauce. Upstairs has more

atmosphere than the modernized downstairs space with the annoying television; however, service is slower. $ *Average main: K5000* ⊠ *169 War Tan St., Lanmadaw Township* ☎ *01/ 221524* ▭ *No credit cards* ✛ *A4.*

WHERE TO STAY

Hotel rooms are in high demand across Myanmar and prices reflect that. Yangon has some of the country's best and most expensive hotels, but there are still a few midrange options to be had.

$$$$
RESORT
🏨 **Belmond Governor's Residence.** It's a trip back in time at this 1920s colonial-style mansion located on a quiet backstreet in the Embassy Quarter. **Pros:** quiet and serene; lovely pool; superb service; free Wi-Fi. **Cons:** not within walking distance of downtown; taxis are often slow to arrive. $ *Rooms from: US$370* ⊠ *35 Taw Win Rd.* ☎ *951/229860* ⊕ *www.belmond.com/governors-residence-yangon* ▭ *No credit cards* ⤴ *470 rooms* ⦙⦙ *Breakfast* ✛ *A2.*

$
HOTEL
🏨 **Best Western Chinatown Hotel.** Aimed squarely at business travelers, this new midrange hotel is a gleaming tower and a terrific option for tourists as well, with some of the best-value lodgings in Yangon. **Pros:** great value; huge rooms; excellent location for sightseeing, eating, and shopping. **Cons:** surprisingly slow Wi-Fi. $ *Rooms from: US$80* ⊠ *127-137 Anawratha Rd., corner of Lanmadaw St., Latha Township* ☎ *01/251080* ⊕ *www.bestwestern.com* ⤴ *91 rooms* ⦙⦙ *Breakfast* ▭ *No credit cards* ✛ *A5.*

$$
HOTEL
🏨 **Chatrium Hotel Royal Lake.** Overlooking Kandawgyi Lake, with glimpses of gleaming Shwedagon Pagoda in the distance, the luxurious Chatrium maybe a business hotel, but it's a fantastic choice for the beginning or end of a countrywide Myanmar trip. **Pros:** superb restaurants; lavish breakfast; enormous swimming pool. **Cons:** can be a 30-minute ride to the city center at peak times. $ *Rooms from: US$170* ⊠ *40 Natmauk Rd., Tamwe Township* ☎ *01/544500* ⊕ *www.chatrium. com* ⤴ *303 rooms* ⦙⦙ *Breakfast* ✛ *D1.*

$
HOTEL
🏨 **East Hotel.** This boutique hotel offers an especially good value and is well located for those wishing to sample a bevy of local street snacks. **Pros:** central location; free (but slow) Wi-Fi; free bottled water. **Cons:** beaded curtains instead of bathroom doors; some rooms have plumbing problems and others are dim. $ *Rooms from: US$55* ⊠ *234-240 Sule Pagoda Rd.* ☎ *959/7313–5311* ▭ *No credit cards* ⤴ *48 rooms* ⦙⦙ *Breakfast* ✛ *C4.*

$$
B&B/INN
FAMILY
🏨 **Hotel Alamanda.** Quiet and quaint, this six-room former colonial home is just out of the city center, between Inya Lake and the Shwedagon Pagoda. **Pros:** delicious French-style breakfasts; tucked away in the quiet, residential Embassy District. **Cons:** you'll need a ride to go downtown; some guests find the owners aloof. $ *Rooms from: US$110* ⊠ *60B Shwe Taung Kyar Rd.* ☎ *951/534513* ⊕ *hotel-alamanda.com* ▭ *No credit cards* ⤴ *6 rooms* ⦙⦙ *Breakfast* ✛ *C1.*

$$
HOTEL
🏨 **The Loft.** Located in the increasingly fashionable neighborhood of Dagon Township, on the edge of downtown Yangon, this stylish boutique hotel—the city's first—is well located for sightseeing as much as sampling the local eating and drinking scene. **Pros:** fantastic amenities,

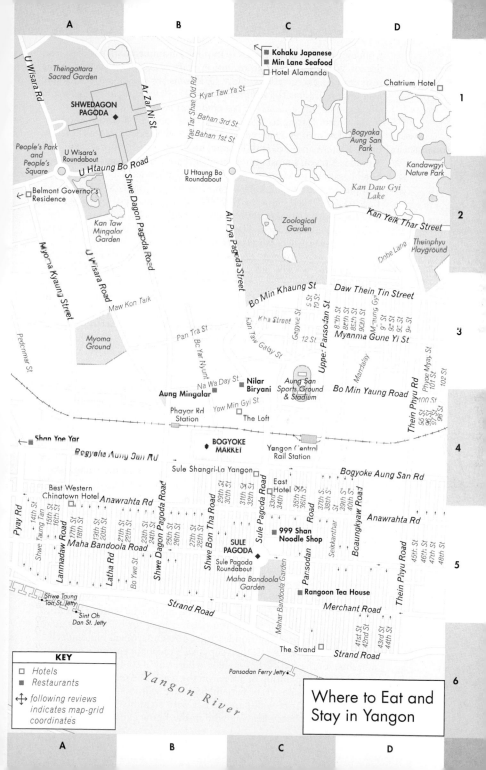

A   **B**   **C**   **D**

U Wisara Rd

Theingottara
Sacred Garden

Ar Zar Ni St

Kyar Taw Ya St

■ Kohaku Japanese
■ Min Lane Seafood
□ Hotel Alamanda

Chatrium Hotel □

1

**SHWEDAGON
PAGODA** ◆

Yae Tar Shae Old Rd

Bahan 3rd St

Bahan 1st St

Bogyaka
Aung San
Park

People's Park
and
People's
Square

U Wisara's
Roundabout

U Htaung Bo Road

U Htaung Bo
Roundabout

Kandawgyi
Nature Park

← □ Belmont Governor's
Residence

Shwe Dagon Pagoda Road

Kan Daw Gyi
Lake

Kan Yeik Thar Street

2

Kan Taw
Mingalar
Garden

Ah Pya Pagoda Street

Zoological
Garden

Dobe Lane

Theinphyu
Playground

Myoma Kyaung Street

U Wisara Road

Maw Kon Taik

Bo Min Khaung St

5 St

19 St

Daw Thein Tin Street

8th St

8th St

85th St

90th St

Maung Gyi

9 - St

9: St

9: St

9: St

3

Pedennar St

Myoma
Ground

Pan Tra St

Bc Yar Nyunt

Kan Taw Gaby St

Kha Street

Gabye St

12 St

Upper Pansodan St

Myanma Gone Yi St

Marrabay

Thein Phyu Rd

Phyoe Myai St

101 St

102 St

100 St

Na Wa Day St

■ Nilar
Biryani

Aung Mingalar ■

Aung San
Sports Ground
& Stadium

Bo Min Yaung Road

56 St

96 St

97 St

98 St

99 St

Phayar Rd
Station

Yaw Min Gyi St

□ The Loft

← Shan Yoe Yar

Bogyoke Aung San Rd

◆ **BOGYOKE
MARKET**

Yangon Central
Rail Station

Bogyoke Aung San Rd

4

Best Western
Chinatown Hotel

Pyay Rd

14th St

Shwe Taung Tan

15th St

16th St

17th St

18th St

Anawrahta Rd

Sule Shangri-La Yangon □

29th St

30th St

31st St

32nd St

33rd St

East
Hotel □
34th St

35th St

36th St

37th St.

38th St

39th St

40th St

Anawrahta Rd

Lanmadaw Road

19th St

20th St

21st St

22th St

Maha Bandoola Road

Latha Rd

23th St

24th St

Shwe Dagon Pagoda Road

25th St

26th St

27th St

28th St

Bo Ywe St

Shwe Bon Tha Road

**SULE
PAGODA**

Sule Pagoda Road

Sule Pagoda
Roundabout

■ **999 Shan
Noodle Shop**

Pansodan

Seikkanthar

Bcaungkyaw Road

Thein Phyu Road

45th St

46th St

47th St

48th St

5

Shwe Taung
Tan St. Jetty

Sint Oh
Dan St. Jetty

◆

Strand Road

Maha
Bandoola Garden

Mahar Bandoola Garden

■ **Rangoon Tea House**

Merchant Road

41st St

42nd St

43rd St

44th St

Strand Road

The Strand □

Strand Road

6

Pansodan Ferry Jetty ◄

Yangon River

KEY

□ Hotels
■ Restaurants
✥ following reviews
indicates map-grid
coordinates

Where to Eat and
Stay in Yangon

A   **B**   **C**   **D**

from espresso coffee machines to minibars crammed with goodies; free, decent Wi-Fi. **Cons:** while reception staff is excellent, service in the restaurant is excruciatingly slow. [$] *Rooms from: US$140* ✉ *33 Yaw Min Gyi St., Dagon Township* ☎ *01/372299* 🌐 *www.theloftyangon.com* 🛏 *32 rooms* 🍴 *Breakfast* 💳 *No credit cards* ✥ *C4.*

$$$ HOTEL Fodor's Choice ★ 🏨 **The Strand.** Dating to 1901, when it was built by a British entrepreneur, and soon after acquired by the legendary Sarkies brothers hoteliers of the Eastern and Oriental (Penang) and Raffles (Singapore) fame, The Strand is Yangon's most atmospheric lodging. **Pros:** attentive staff; best hotel breakfast in Myanmar; 24-hour butler service. **Cons:** on-site restaurants expensive; smoking allowed in bar; no pool. [$] *Rooms from: US$195* ✉ *92 The Strand Rd.* ☎ *01/243377* 🌐 *www.hotelthestrand.com* 🛏 *31 rooms* 🍴 *Breakfast* 💳 *No credit cards* ✥ *C6.*

$$$ HOTEL Fodor's Choice ★ 🏨 **Sule Shangri-La Yangon.** There is no better luxurious base than the iconic former Traders Hotel, which Shangri-La took over in 2014 after a two-year refurbishment. **Pros:** free, strong Wi-Fi; right downtown. **Cons:** rooms are small and a bit dated; if you've stayed in many Shangri-La hotels, this one will not feel up to international standards. [$] *Rooms from: US$220* ✉ *223 Sule Pagoda Rd.* ☎ *01/242828* 🌐 *www.shangri-la.com/yangon/suleshangrila* 🛏 *242 rooms, 237 suites* 🍴 *Breakfast* ✥ *C4.*

NIGHTLIFE AND PERFORMING ARTS

NIGHTLIFE

Yangon has Myanmar's best nightlife by far. Expect anything from colonial-inspired bars with potted palms and British-style pubs with dart boards to elegant wine bars with jazz sound tracks and dimly lit speakeasies doing heady cocktails.

19th Street, Chinatown. For a whole barbecued fish and a draft beer, 19th street in Yangon's Chinatown is unbeatable. There are restaurants along both sides of the street, with little outdoor grills and plastic tables and chairs set up, the stools often occupied by locals in their undershirts and pajama bottoms. ✉ *19th St. near Maha Bandula.*

FAMILY Fodor's Choice ★ **50th Street.** 50th Street is a proper pub, one that's been honing its craft since it opened in 1997. Today, the bi-level bar remains enormously popular with expats, foreign tourists, and a few middle-class Burmese. The extensive menu includes a selection of pizzas; portions are hearty, the better to be washed down with a good selection of beers, wines by the glass, and decent cocktails. ✉ *9-13 50th St.* ☎ *95/139–7060* 🌐 *50thstreetyangon.com.*

The Blind Tiger. This hot bar, started by an arty Yangon expat and a Bangkok-based art curator, is a speakeasy in the true sense of the word. There are no signs out front. You need to look for the security guard lingering out front of this nondescript corner apartment building, chatting to the local residents, then slip inside the main entrance and make a beeline for the end of the corridor, where you'll come to a closed door and a street-art painting of a tiger on the wall. The security guy should follow, but if he doesn't, be patient. Someone will soon open the door to this dimly lit, scarlet-wall-papered bar with an atmospheric jazz sound track that is probably heaving with in-the-know expats. The cocktails are great and the tapas-style sharing plates are delicious. ⊠ *Unit 111 Condominium, Corner of Nawaday St. and Alain Pyar Pagoda Rd., Dagon Township* ☎ *01/388488* ⊕ *blindtiger-yangon.com.*

Sapphire Bar & Lounge. The Shwedagon Pagoda is at its most gorgeous at night and, from Alfa Hotel's rooftop bar, you can see it clearly in the distance, a gilded piece of history shining bright. It's a simple bar where people gather for a drink or two and quiet conversation. A local saung harpist places plays nightly from 7 to 9. Because the rooftop is open to the elements, the bar is closed during Myanmar's rainy season, roughly June to September. ⊠ *Alfa Hotel, 41 Nawaday St.* ☎ *095/137–7964* ⊙ *Daily 3 pm–3 am.*

Strand Bar. When the Strand Hotel opened in 1901, its swanky bar was the place to see and be seen. Today, Yangon is a very different place and the bar is still pretty, if pretty staid, except on Friday night, when it comes alive with expats who giddily pack in for two-for-one happy hour, which runs 5 to 10 pm. ⊠ *Strand Hotel, 92 Strand Rd.* ☎ *095/124-33/7* ⊕ *www.lhw.com/hotel/The-Strand-Yangon-Yangon-Myanmar.*

PERFORMING ARTS

FAMILY **New Zero Art Space.** This nonprofit works to promote young Myanmar artists and to bring together artists and the community at large. New Zero hosts regular exhibitions, seminars, and workshops on art and film. Friday to Sunday from 4 to 6 pm there are free art classes (donations accepted) for children and adults. The space also has a small library with books and films about Myanmar's art scene. When it has the funds, New Zero also runs an artist-in-residence program to encourage Burmese artists to meet those from abroad. ⊠ *202 Ahlan Pya Phyar Rd., Dagon Township* ☎ *095/7312–9520* ⊕ *www.newzeroartspace. com.mm* ⊙ *Tues.–Sun. 9:30–5.*

Pansodan Gallery. Vibrant paintings by local artists pack the walls at this gallery, which opened in 2008 and has frequently rotating exhibitions. The gallery is more than just a place where art hangs and is sold; it's a gathering place for Burmese artists both established and rising, as well as Yangon's expats and tourists. On Tuesday nights from 7:30 pm, Pansodan hosts a weekly gathering, with snacks, drinks, and usually one or two people playing guitar. The event is free, but donations are welcome. ⊠ *286 Pansodan St., 1st fl.* ☎ *095/130846* ⊕ *pansodan. blogspot.com* ⊙ *Daily 10–6.*

SHOPPING

Yangon is a shopper's delight with an abundance of beautiful handicrafts—many, such as traditional lacquerware, dating back to the medieval Pagan empire of Bagan—and wonderful textiles handwoven by hill tribe minorities from around the country.

Bogyoke Market. This market, which opened in 1926, is enormous, well-organized, and—despite sweltering temperatures outside—not an oven. Come here on your first day in Yangon to peruse the offerings, and pick up a longyi (sarong) for temple visits. Shops here sell stone and wood carvings; jade, silver, and gold jewelry; lacquerware; paintings by local artists; and a smattering of cosmetics and toiletries. The finest and most authentic hill tribe handicrafts can be found upstairs in the main front building Yoyamay (shop #20) and nearby Myanmar Folk Art (#24), where you'll find vintage, antique, and new textiles produced by weavers in the Chin, Kayin, and Kayah States. ⊠ *27th St. and Bogyoke Aung San Rd.*

FAMILY   **City Mart.** This citywide chain of small supermarkets offers the best selection of edible souvenirs. Among the many options in the grocery section of the store are the makings for pickled tea-leaf salad (leaves and fried beans), which is served across the country, and all manner of candy ranging from ginger chews to chocolates. You'll also find local teas, beers, and spirits. The Chinatown branch is particularly handy. ⊠ *Corner of Phonegyi and Maharbandoola Rds.*

Fodor'sChoice   **Pomelo.** Pomelo supports nonprofits in Myanmar that work with disadvantaged groups, including families in poverty, those with HIV, the
★   mentally and physically disabled, and the homeless. The goods at this fair-trade boutique are made by those with whom the NGOs work, and the results are fantastic. Sein Na Garr Glass Factory, for example, makes its beautiful vases with recycled glass bought from Yangon's garbage collectors. Lovely beaded jewelry comes from the children at Hlaing Thar Yar Disability Centre. Action for Public works with women and children with HIV, and the sweet stuffed animals and chic wallets and ornaments that dot Pomelo were expertly sewn by them. This is one of Yangon's loveliest shops and a great place to pick up meaningful souvenirs. ⊠ *89 Thein Pyu Rd., 2nd fl.* ⊕ *www.pomeloyangon.com.*

BAGAN

Bagan is 622 km (386 miles) north of Yangon.

Between the 9th and 13th centuries, Bagan (née Pagan) was the capital of the Kingdom of Pagan, once a tiny settlement that became one of Southeast Asia's greatest empires. The 11th through mid-13th centuries were the height of the Kingdom of Pagan's prosperity, and it was during those 250 years that the then-10,000 stupas, temples, and pagodas were built. Today, just 2,000 remain, but their expanse is staggering. The stupas dot the sides of the long road that runs through Bagan, and the awe-inspiring larger temples are clustered across from Tharabar (née Tharbha) Gate, the only surviving section of Bagan's city wall.

GETTING HERE AND AROUND

Connecting the three main areas of Bagan—Old Bagan, New Bagan, and Nyaung Shrine-U—is the Bagan-Nyaung-U Road. On the side streets off the main road are a smattering of hotels and restaurants. It's possible to traverse Bagan on foot, and some tourists do, but it's a long walk from New Bagan up to Nyaung-U. A better and much more common option is hiring a bicycle and riding along Bagan-Nyaung-U Road, off the sides of which are plenty of stupas. Bicycles will cost between K9,000 a day; K4,700 half day; and K2,500 per hour. Other available forms of transportation include hired cars (including taxis) or horse carts. Your hotel can arrange for both.

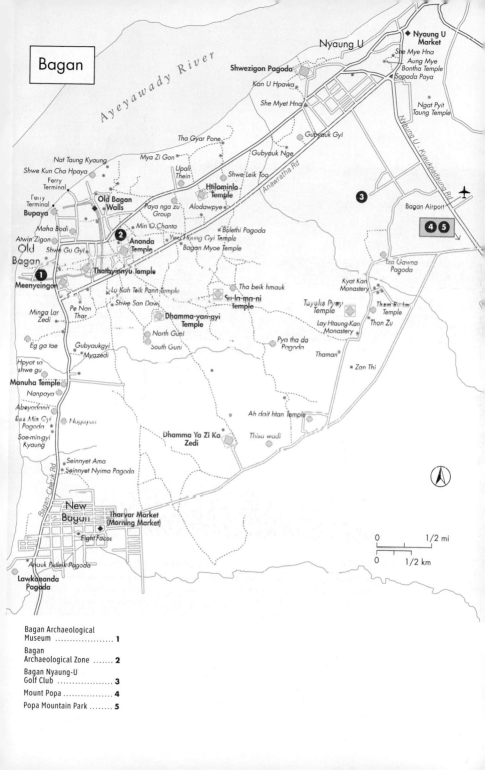

Bagan

Ayeyawady River

Nyaung U

◆ Nyaung U Market
She Mye Hna
Aung Mye
Bontha Temple
Sapada Paya

Shwezigon Pagoda

Kan U Hpaw

Ngat Pyit Taung Temple

She Myet Hna

Gubyauk Gyi

Tha Gyar Pone

Gubyauk Nge

Mya Zi Gon

Nat Taung Kyaung

Bagan Airport

Shwe Kun Cha Hpaya

Upali Thein

Shwe Leik Too

Ferry Terminal

Htilominlo Temple

Anawratha Rd

3

Ferry Terminal

Old Bagan Walls

Paya nga zu Group

Alodawpye

Nyaung U Kyaukpadaung Rd

Bupaya

Min O Chanta

4 **5**

Maha Bodi

Bulethi Pagoda

Atwin Zigon

Ananda Temple

Nyaung Gyi Temple

Iza Gawna Pagoda

2

Shwe Gu Gyi

Bagan Myoe Temple

Old Bagan

1

Thatbyinnyu Temple

Tha beik hmauk

Kyat Kan Monastery

Meenyeingon

Lo Kah Teik Pann Temple

Su-la-ma-ni Temple

Tuyohi Pyay Temple

Tham Bin In Temple

Minga Lar Zedi

Shwe San Daw

Dhamma-yan-gyi Temple

Lay Htaung-Kan Monastery

Thon Zu

Pe Nan Thar

Eg ga tae

Gubyaukgyi Myazedi

North Guni

South Guni

Pya tha da Pagoda

Hpyat sa shwe gu

Thaman

Zan Thi

Manuha Temple

Nanpaya

Abeyadana

Ah dait htan Temple

Daa Min Gyi Pagoda

Nagayon

Dhamma Ya Zi Ka Zedi

Thisa wadi

Soe-min-gyi Kyaung

Seinnyet Ama

Seinnyet Nyima Pagoda

New Bagan

Tharyar Market (Morning Market)

Eight Faces

Anauk Pellek Pagoda

Lawkananda Pagoda

Bagan-Chauk Rd

0   1/2 mi

0   1/2 km

Myanmar's growing tourism industry is centered on Bagan's collection of 11th- and 12th-century temples and stupas.

AIR TRAVEL   Bagan's airport is in Nyaung-U, a 15-minute drive from the city. There are some half a dozen flights per day on domestic Burmese airlines. None can be booked online, although Air Mandalay is the easiest to deal with. Have your hotel or a travel agent book air tickets for you or, if you're starting in Yangon, go directly to the airline's office. The flight from Yangon is 70 minutes and costs around $130; flights from Mandalay and Heho (Inle Lake) are shorter and cheaper. Airport taxis cost K11,700.

BOAT TRAVEL   Taking a ferry from Yangon or Mandalay to Bagan is time-consuming, but a unique experience you certainly won't get flying. From Mandalay, the Malikha Express (⊕ *www.malikha-rivercruises.com*) costs $42, departs at 8 am, and should arrive at 6 pm, though it's been reported that journeys can take more than 12 hours.

BUS TRAVEL   Buses leave Yangon regularly, taking around 10 hours. Ask your hotel or an agent to book a ticket for you. Give yourself plenty of time to get your bearings, as the Yangon bus station is large and confusing. Tickets start at around K25,000 and range up to K80,000 for luxury services such as those offered by JJ Express, with just three (leather-bound, low reclining) seats across the width of the bus. Bring earplugs and something warm to wear. Arrange to have your hotel collect you from the bus depot, as taxis will not be plentiful.

CAR TRAVEL   It's a long drive from Yangon to Bagan; you can hire a car and driver through a tour agency or, if you fancy trying your luck, ask a cab driver. The drive from Mandalay to Bagan takes about five hours without stops and costs around $150.

TRAIN TRAVEL There's an overnight train from Yangon to Bagan, departing Yangon Central Railway Station at 4 pm and scheduled to arrive in Bagan at 9:30 am; tickets are $30 for an upper-class seat and $50 for a sleeper. The trains are often delayed so don't have any plans hinging on your timely arrival. A helpful resource is ⊕ *www.go-myanmar.com/by-train*.

TRAVEL AGENCIES AND TOURS

Balloons over Bagan. Eastern Safaris' hot-air-balloon flights over the temples of Bagan and the Irrawaddy River offer unparalleled views and a truly unique experience. The British-made balloons are flown by U.K.-certified pilots, and passenger safety is the number one priority; balloons won't fly in winds exceeding 15 mph. Rides last 45 minutes to an hour and are followed by a light Champagne breakfast. The balloons go wherever the wind takes them, so which pagodas you'll see and where you'll end up landing are a surprise even to the pilots. Travel agents can usually get a significant discount on the rack rate. Price includes a hotel transfer. ⊠ *Sedona Hotel, Bagan Thiripyitsaya Sanctuary Resort, Old Bagan., Yangon (Rangoon)* ☎ *061/60058* ⊕ *easternsafaris.com/balloonsoverbagan_home.html* ⊠ *From $320.*

Ever Sky Information Service. As well as providing information, this company runs a transport service between Bagan and Inle Lake. ⊠ *Intersection of restaurant row and Thiripyitsaya 5, Nyaung-U* ☎ *061/60895.*

Min Thu Travel Service. Two friendly and professional local brothers run this business offering a horse-cart service (K10,000 per hour) and car-and-driver rental (K25,000 for half a day; K10,000 for airport pickup/drop-off; K40,000 to Mount Popa). ☎ *09/4314–9273* ⊕ *www.minthubaganhorsecart.com* ⊠ *From K10,000.*

Myanmar Travels and Tours. Those wishing to cross the Tachileik/Mae Sai border into Thailand will need to organize permits with state-owned Myanmar Travels and Tours. As of this writing, you should allow yourself at least two weeks for permit processing. Those crossing from Mae Sai into Myanmar at the Tachileik checkpoint do not need a permit from MTT. ⊠ *Bagan-Nyaung-U Rd. at Thiri Marlar St., Nyaung-U* ☎ *061/65040 government-run.*

Su Yadanar Wai. This very knowledgeable, local female guide offers a range of tours around Bagan. ☎ *094/0250–1371* ⊠ *suyadanawai@gmail.com.*

Sun Far Travels & Tours. This excellent travel agency can organize everything from domestic flights to river cruises, as well as bus and train tickets. ⊠ *Main Rd., West of Nyaung-U Market, next to CB Bank, Nyaung-U* ☎ *09/204–2001, 09/204–2991* ⊠ *kothannaingoo@gmail.com* ⊕ *www.sunfartravels.com.*

EXPLORING

Visitors flock to Bagan for its staggering spread of 11th- to 13th-century pagodas, and the area where most are concentrated is often explored by bicycle, although the heat can take its toll. A taxi or private car is more comfortable and, while romantic, a horse and cart is best for a short trip, not an all-day outing.

10

TOP ATTRACTIONS

Bagan Archaeological Zone. Some 2,200 11th- to 13th-century ruins dot Bagan, an enormous amount but a mere fraction of the more than 10,000 that once stood. The temples, pagodas, and stupas are simply astonishing. Some are very large and have been renovated, while others are tiny and stand in disrepair among rambling grasses and brambles. The expanse of the ruins is staggering; from the side of a long, dusty dirt road they pop up, completely abandoned and yours for taking. Each and every stupa, temple, and pagoda is truly breathtaking, but visitors will find the liveliest is **Ananda Temple,** which has beautiful frescoes and houses four 31-foot-tall Buddha statues. Its location at the end of restaurant row means it gets busiest around lunch. ⊠ *Old Bagan* 🖻 *$20, paid at airport on arrival.*

WORTH NOTING

Bagan Archaeological Museum. Complement the stupa ogling with a visit to this museum, which is a short walk from Ananda Temple and Old Bagan's restaurant row. It's been woefully neglected and is a mess, but there are roughly 850 objects on display here, all pieces of Bagan's rich history. There are excellent wood carvings of the Buddha, intricate bronze pieces, and even ancient coiffures used at the time by the chicest of women. It's interesting to see the frescoes here and then compare them to the real ones inside the temples. ⊠ *Bagan-Nyaung-U Rd., near Ananda Temple, Old Bagan* 🖻 *061/60048* 🖻 *$5; kyat sometimes accepted* 🕙 *Daily 9–4:30.*

Mount Popa. If you've got an extra day in Bagan and have tired of the temples, this is an easy half-day trip. Fifty miles southeast of Bagan, the extinct volcano of Mount Popa, known as Popa Taung Kalat, rises to 2,418 feet, on the flank of Taung Ma-gyi (the "Mother Mountain"), an extinct volcano which is almost 4,980 feet high. It's a 777-step barefoot climb all the way to the top; along the stairwell are souvenir sellers and, at the top of Mount Popa, a complex of pagodas, monasteries, shrines, and stupas, collectively known as Popa Taung Kalat Temple. Beware of monkeys who can turn nasty if they sense you've got treats and whose droppings are everywhere; wet wipes are a must. A taxi (four passengers) from Bagan will run you around K45,000, and you can stop on your way at a palm sugar plantation and distillery. Nearby Popa Mountain Resort is lovely and offers great views. ⊠ *Off Byat Ta Pan Sat Rd., Kyauk Paduang Township.*

SPORTS AND THE OUTDOORS

Bagan Nyaung-U Golf Club. This 18-hole (72-par) course may not be celebrity designed or have hosted PGA tournaments, but it's got something with which no other course in the world can compete—a smattering of Bagan's pagodas dotted around the green. ⊠ *2, Nyaung-U, Mandalay Division, Nyaung-U* 🖻 *061/60035* ⊕ *www.bagangolfresort. net/golfclub.html* 🖻 *$40/$70 for 9/18 holes includes clubs and caddy* 🕙 *Daily 6–6.*

Popa Mountain Park. If you fancy more exercise than stepping your way to the top of Mount Popa and intend to take to the trails around Taung Ma-gyi, the "Mother Mountain," allow an additional full day (or leave at dawn) and bring your hiking shoes. There are a variety of hiking trails, some leading to the rim of the volcano crater and others to waterfalls. The word *popa* comes from the Sanskrit word for flower, and as you're hiking up, you'll see how lush it is, and how the vegetation changes with the altitude. This is a good hike on which to follow a guide; your driver should be able to find you one or you can ask at Popa Mountain Resort. From there to the crater can take up to five hours. ✉ *Off Byat Ta Pan Sat Rd., Kyauk Paduang Township.*

WHERE TO EAT

Bagan has a good selection of restaurants across Old and New Bagan and Nyaung-U, so if your first choice is full, there's another option not far away. Among the cheerful Burmese, Indian, and Thai places are a handful of tasty, inexpensive Myanmar family-style restaurants.

$$$$ INDIAN 🍴 **Aroma 2.** This is one of the better spots along this happening strip of restaurants, where you're likely to bump into friends you've made earlier in the day during temple hopping. These places are geared to tourists and so prices are inflated, but the "no good, no pay" offer at this Indian restaurant is hard to resist. Curries are tasty but mild, so definitely ask for more spice if you like a kick. All the breads are worth a try, especially the hot, fluffy naan. Aroma 2 gets packed so it's best to have your hotel make reservations. [$] *Average main: K5000* ✉ *Yarkinnthar Hotel Rd., Nyaung-U* ☎ *09/204–2630* 💳 *No credit cards.*

$$$ VEGETARIAN FAMILY 🍴 **Be Kind to Animals the Moon.** A charming little restaurant, Be Kind to Animals the Moon is constantly packed with ravenous temple-goers. The menu offers traditional Burmese dishes like a refreshing tea leaf salad alongside gussied-up backpacker staples. Dip papadums into a chutney and cool down with refreshing shakes or the restaurant's top-notch lime, ginger, and honey juice. [$] *Average main: K4000* ✉ *Off Bagan-Nyaung-U Rd., between Tharabar Gate and Ananda Temple, Old Bagan* ☎ *061/60481* 💳 *No credit cards.*

$$$ INDIAN 🍴 **Black Rose.** On New Bagan's restaurant row, Black Rose serves up Burmese, Thai, Indian, and Chinese food to tourists staying in the nearby hotels. Most dishes are quite mild, so tell your waiter if you like your food on the spicy side. The chicken curry is excellent. The restaurant owners, a husband-and-wife duo, speak English well and are on hand, but service is extremely slow. Order a drink to start and sip slowly while you wait for your food. [$] *Average main: K3500* ✉ *Khayea Pin St. (main road), just south of Thiri Marlar, New Bagan* 💳 *No credit cards.*

$$$ BURMESE 🍴 **Golden Myanmar 2.** Of the cluster of restaurants just north of Ananda Temple, Golden Myanmar 1 and 2, owned by the same family, are the most popular with local drivers and guides, and offer the most authentic Burmese food. Sit down, smile expectantly, and dishes will begin appearing on your table faster than you can wash the grime from your face. Mutton, pork, and an array of chicken curries, fried fish, sautéed vegetables, Burmese salads (pickled tea leaf), and rice will leave you stuffed, but then dessert comes out—short, squat bananas and sweet little tamarind candies. The friendly staff will keep refilling your plates unless you say otherwise. The buffet is K3,000 per person,

excluding drinks. $\boxed{\text{\$}}$ *Average main: K4000* $\boxtimes$ *Off Bagan-Nyaung-U Rd. near Ananda Temple, Old Bagan* $\equiv$ *No credit cards.*

$$$$ ✕**Green Elephant.** If you want to try a wide variety of Burmese food
BURMESE   and aren't ready to dive into street stalls, Green Elephant is a safe bet. It's popular with tour groups, but don't let that put you off: service is friendly and efficient, and the food, though certainly not mind-blowing, is toothsome and comes from a clean kitchen. Indeed, it was her own food allergies that drove Cherie Aung-Khin to open Green Elephant. Because Aung-Khin previously lived in Thailand, Thai and Chinese dishes are available as well, but we recommend the Burmese dishes, especially the tea leaf salad, eggplant salad, and fish curry. Prices for fairly standard Burmese dishes here are much higher than what you'll pay elsewhere, but this is a safe, clean place to sit down to eat. $\boxed{\text{\$}}$ *Average main: K8500* $\boxtimes$ *Main Road (Kayay St) near 2nd St, New Bagan* ☎ *061/65365* ⊕ *www.greenelephant-restaurants.com/* $\equiv$ *No credit cards.*

WHERE TO STAY

Visitors can choose from hotels in Old Bagan, closest to the big temples, New Bagan, which has more restaurants and budget accommodations, and Nyaung-U, which is more residential and has plenty of restaurants but is a 2-mile cycle from most of the temples.

$$ 🏨**Bagan Lodge.** After a hot, dusty day of temple hopping, this resort's
RESORT   pool and surrounding sun loungers will welcome you with open arms.
FAMILY   **Pros:** free Wi-Fi; generous buffet breakfast; free airport transfer. **Cons:** very few restaurants within walking distance; too far from town to walk back at night, so you'll need to take a taxi or moto. $\boxed{\text{\$}}$ *Rooms from: US$165* $\boxtimes$ *Myat Lay Rd., New Bagan* ☎ *061/65456* ⊕ *www.bagan-lodge.com/* ↩ *82 rooms, 5 suites* ⦿|*Breakfast.*

$$$ 🏨**Blue Bird.** Owned by a charming French-Burmese couple, and recently
HOTEL   renovated, this lovely 24-room boutique hotel packs in a motley crew
FAMILY   of travelers. **Pros:** free Wi-Fi; pool is just the right temperature; owners on hand to help. **Cons:** extremely thin walls; outside noise; dependence on the hotel's cab service. $\boxed{\text{\$}}$ *Rooms from: US$190* $\boxtimes$ *10 Naratheinkha, New Bagan* ☎ *61/65051* ⊕ *www.bluebirdbagan.com* $\equiv$ *No credit cards* ↩ *24 rooms* ⦿|*Breakfast.*

$$$ 🏨**The Hotel at Tharabar Gate.** Long been *the* place to stay in Bagan
RESORT   because it's a stone's throw from Ananda Temple and plenty of restaurants, this hotel demonstrates a common trend in Bagan—when demand for accommodations far outweighs supply. **Pros:** walking distance to restaurants and temples; partially shaded pool. **Cons:** rooms and bathrooms need refurbishment; food, other than breakfast, can be hit or miss. $\boxed{\text{\$}}$ *Rooms from: US$245* $\boxtimes$ *Near Tharabar Gate, Old Bagan* ☎ *61/60037* ⊕ *www.tharabargate.com* $\equiv$ *No credit cards* ↩ *80 rooms, 4 suites* ⦿|*Breakfast.*

$ 🏨**Ostello Bello Bagan.** This is a fairly good option for New Bagan (where
B&B/INN   accommodations are priciest and book up quickly), with sun-filled twin, double, and triple rooms that are more like guesthouse rooms than those of your typical hostel. **Pros:** free Wi-Fi; air-conditioning and hot water; ample breakfast. **Cons:** rooms near the terrace can be noisy; a private

room here can be nearly as expensive as a budget hotel. [$] *Rooms from: US$97* ✉ *Thiri Sandar, Kayay St., next to AGD Bank ATM, New Bagan* ☎ *061/6569* 🛏 *27 rooms* 🍴 *Breakfast* 💳 *No credit cards.*

$$ RESORT FAMILY 🏨 **Thazin Garden Hotel.** Between the dreamy pool surrounded by flowers and the guest bungalows, each with its own veranda, you may just find yourself lazing here all day. **Pros:** stupa on the grounds; spacious rooms; lovely gardens. **Cons:** service can be lackluster; thin walls. [$] *Rooms from: US$160* ✉ *Thazin Rd., New Bagan* ☎ *02/153–7898* 🌐 *www.thazingarden.com* 🛏 *60 rooms* 🍴 *Breakfast* 💳 *No credit cards.*

NIGHTLIFE AND PERFORMING ARTS

There's no art scene to speak of in Bagan, and no real bar scene either, but all restaurants serve local beer and a few can put together mixed drinks.

Shwe Ya Su. This is a simple, unpretentious Burmese restaurant that also serves local draft beer and can concoct simple mixed drinks like rum and coke (no gin and tonics, though). Locals tuck into a bevy of dishes and watch soccer on a big screen indoors while tourists, exhausted from cycling all day, lounge in outdoor seating, surrounded by trees wrapped in strings of twinkling lights. The young servers are eager to please and the whole place has a lovely, laid-back vibe. ✉ *Yarkinnthar Hotel Rd., near Aroma 2, Nyaung-U* 🕒 *Daily 7 am–10:30 pm.*

Weather Spoon's Bagan Restaurant and Bar. A popular backpacker joint beloved for good burgers and free Wi-Fi, Weather Spoon's also serves strong rum cocktails and is always buzzing. It's a great spot to meet other travelers. They stop serving at 10 pm. ✉ *Yarkinthar St., Nyaung-U* ☎ *0943/092640.*

SHOPPING

Lacquerware is the big to-buy in Bagan; it's best purchased from workshops in the Myinkaba area, half a mile south of Thiripyitsaya Sanctuary Resort, where the artists will show you how it's made and where the quality is higher. From the street vendors outside the temples, cute pottery pieces make good souvenirs. Be sure to compare prices and bargain for a discount of around 10%.

Bagan House. This upmarket workshop accepts credit cards (plus 5% surcharge) if you spend more than $100. Bagan House sells a huge array of products fit for a [Burmese] king or queen, from chic coasters to lamps. ✉ *9 Jasmin Rd., 1 block south of Thiri Marlar St., Nyaung-U* ☎ *061/65133.*

Golden Cuckoo. The owners here have a workshop where visitors can see the lacquerware being made alongside a slew of vases, bowls, cups, and jewelry for sale. The family-run shop has been open since 1975, and the owner speaks English. ✉ *Bagan-Chauk Rd., behind Manuha Temple, Myinkaba* ☎ *061/65156.*

Jasmine Family Lacquerware Workshop. This small, family-run business makes everything on-site and then sells its wares both directly to customers and to larger lacquerware shops. Prices here are at least 20% cheaper than the more tourist-focused workshops, and the family themselves are quite lovely. Expect to pay around $25 for a 14-layer vase (the more layers, the higher the quality). ⊠ *Just off main road, near Manuha Temple and Yaung Chi Oo Guest House, Myinkaba* ⊕ *jasminelacquer.notlong.com.*

Mani-Sithu Market. Locals do their produce shopping at this market, where the array of colorful fruits, vegetables, and flowers is simply gorgeous. This is also a fantastic one-stop spot to shop for gifts and souvenirs, with countless stalls selling beautiful handicrafts, lacquerware, and textiles, including longyis. The market runs 6 am to 5 pm, but is at its most lively before noon. ⊠ *Anawrahta Rd. at Bagan-Nyaung-U Rd., Nyaung-U* ☉ *Closed Sun.*

Shwe War Thein Handicrafts Shop. You'll find all manner of trinkets at this shop. Peruse faux antiques, wood carvings, carved stone pieces, wind chimes, and leogryph figurines as well as puppets and assorted jewelry. ⊠ *Off Bagan-Nyaung-U Rd., just east of Tharabar Gate, Old Bagan* ☎ *061/67032.*

INLE LAKE

Tranquil Inle Lake is where visitors come to decompress after hot, dusty tours through the rest of the country's must-see spots. Myanmar's second-largest lake, Inle is best accessed from Nyaung Shwe Township in Myanmar's Shan State, which borders China to the north, Laos to the east, and Thailand to the south. Most of the people living on and around the lake are the Intha people. They are self-sufficient farmers and fishermen practicing a unique form of paddling their boats called leg rowing. The gateway village to the lake, Nyaung Shwe, is where visitors arrive after the drive from the airport at Heho, and it has evolved to cater to tourists and makes a good place to kick back for a few days. Once out on the lake, however, you're witness to a very different way of life, with locals elegantly gliding their long, narrow boats between stilt-house villages, stopping at Buddhist temples, tending their floating gardens, and visiting the markets where members of other ethnic groups come down from their mountain villages to sell their wares.

GETTING HERE AND AROUND

AIR TRAVEL   The airport closest to Inle Lake is Heho, about an hour drive from the lake's jetty. There are half a dozen flights per day on domestic Myanmar airlines. The flight from Yangon is 75 minutes and starts at around $110; flights from Mandalay and Bagan are cheaper and shorter. Even though you'll have arrived on a domestic flight, you will still have your passport checked on arrival in Heho. Once you exit the airport, you'll see a slew of vans waiting to fill up with passengers; if the van isn't full, you'll pay a minimum of K25,000. If your driver can fill every seat, you're likely to pay around K20,000. Just outside the town of Nyaung Shwe where the jetty is, you'll have your passport checked again and pay a K12,500 entrance fee for seven days. Keep your ticket on you at all times—you will be required to buy a new one if randomly checked and found without it.

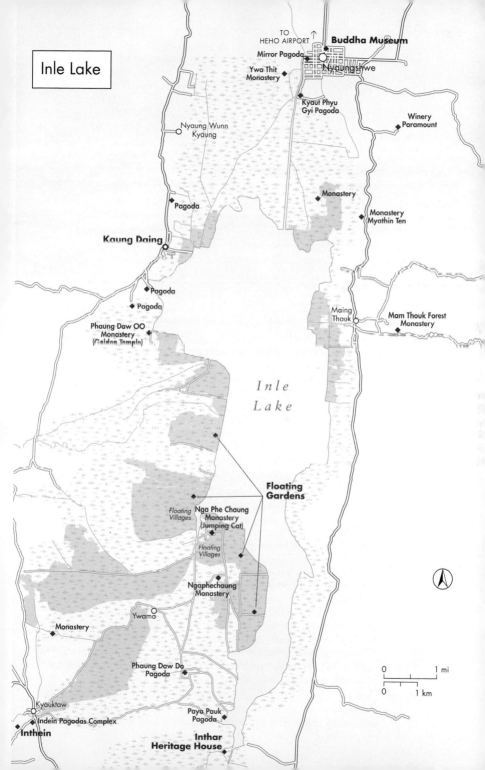

Inle Lake

TO
HEHO AIRPORT
Buddha Museum

Mirror Pagoda

Nyaungshwe

Ywa Thit
Monastery

Kyaut Phyu
Gyi Pagoda

Winery
Paramount

Nyaung Wunn
Kyaung

Monastery

Monastery
Myathin Ten

Pagoda

Kaung Daing

Pagoda

Pagoda

Maing
Thauk

Mam Thouk Forest
Monastery

Phaung Daw OO
Monastery
(Golden Temple)

*Inle
Lake*

**Floating
Gardens**

*Floating
Villages*

**Nga Phe Chaung
Monastery
(Jumping Cat)**

*Floating
Villages*

Ngaphechaung
Monastery

Ywama

Monastery

Phaung Daw Do
Pagoda

Kyauktaw

Indein Pagodas Complex

Inthein

Paya Pauk
Pagoda

**Inthar
Heritage House**

0   1 mi

0   1 km

Most of the villagers living on Inle Lake are self-sufficient farmers.

BOAT TRAVEL Unless you're staying on land, once you arrive at Inle Lake's jetty in Nyaung Shwe you'll need to board a boat to your hotel. These are long wooden canoes with seats like lawn chairs and run by inboard motors. These men (always men) stand on one leg and wrap the other around a paddle, using it to move the boat. Expect to pay around K15,000 for this trip alone. A standard half day of touring costs K15,000 and a full day K20,000–K30,000, depending on the distance.

BUS TRAVEL Buses leave Yangon daily between 4 and 5 pm and arrive in Nyaung Shwe around 5 am. Tickets cost K13,000. From here you'll have to get a ride to Nyuang Shwe. These are two separate towns; Nyaung Shwe surrounds the lake's jetty, while Shwe Nyaung is about 12 kilometers (7½ miles) north. There will be a few cars and a bus or two waiting to ferry passengers to Nyaung Shwe, but if you're traveling in a large group or you have heavy luggage, you should arrange with your guesthouse ahead of time to have someone come meet you at the bus station. A taxi will cost around K6,500; the bus will cost around K1,600. From Mandalay, the 10-hour overnight bus costs K16,000. From Bagan, there's the Bagan Minn Thar Express, a daily bus that departs at 7:30 am, arrives at 5:30 pm, and costs K13,000. Make sure you get off at Nyaung Shwe. Theoretically, tickets can be purchased on the bus, but it's easier to have your hotel help you book in advance, especially in peak season. Buses depart from a variety of locations; have your hotel or guesthouse confirm departure location.

CAR TRAVEL Two types of hired cars and drivers can be had. The first is either through a travel agent or through your hotel. The second is a standard taxi; many cab drivers are happy to make a long journey in exchange for much more than they'd make in a day of staying in town. With a cabbie, you can negotiate—not so with the hotel or agency. The drive from Mandalay or Bagan to Inle Lake takes a bit over eight hours; going with a cab driver, you should pay around $180.

MOTO TRAVEL From Heho Airport, it is possible to take a moto to the jetty in Nyaung Shwe. Not for the faint of heart, it's a drive that takes an hour in a car along a bumpy dirt road. One person can fit on a moto. Expect to pay around K15,000.

TRAIN TRAVEL Trains run from Mandalay and Yangon to Thazi, 11 km (7 miles) from Inle Lake's jetty in Nyaung Shwe. The train from Yangon (K31,000 upper class) runs five times a day. You will then have to take a bus from Thazi to Shwe Nyaung (frequent, K7,000, six hours). There's another train from Yangon that has sleeper cars; it departs at 3 pm, gets you to Thazi just after 3 am, and leaves you with three hours to connect to the 6 am train bound for Shwen Yaung. Another option is the 6 am train from Yangon that gets to Thazi at 7 pm; you can stay overnight in Thazi and then take the aforementioned 6 am train. The train from Mandalay also connects in Thazi. As with the Nyaung Shwe bus stop, there will be cars and a pickup truck or two waiting outside. To make things easier, reserve transport with your hotel or guesthouse ahead of time.

ESSENTIALS

Inle Lake has a dozen or so floating restaurants, but if you want to pick something up before you board the boat to your hotel, Nyaung Shwe is the best place to do it. Likewise, this is where you'll find the bank where you can exchange money; your hotel will accept USD but you'll need small kyat bills if you wish to buy souvenirs.

Bank Contacts KBZ Bank, ⊠ *30 Lanmadaw St., Nyaung Shwe* ☎ *081/209894.*

Visitor and Tour Information WIN Travel Services. ⊠ *Yonegyi Rd., Kanthar Quarter, Nyaung Shwe* ☎ *081/209920* ✉ *wintravel9@gmail.com.*

EXPLORING INLE LAKE

The number one activity at Inle Lake is cruising the water. Most visitors spend a day or two crisscrossing the lake in narrow wooden canoes powered by inboard motors, visiting different villages and taking in the scenery. It takes almost an hour to get to the southern end of the lake. If you're staying on land, you can explore the village of Nyaung Shwe, which has a backpacker vibe and which can be easily traversed on foot or by bike.

TOP ATTRACTIONS

Fodor's Choice **Boating.** Although the inboard motors make boat trips around Inle Lake
★ loud (we recommend earplugs), they're still languid and, more importantly, the reason visitors come here in the first place. Inle is Myanmar's second largest lake, 44.9 square miles at an altitude of 2,900 feet. Boats leave from the jetty in the village of Nyaung Shwe, where you'll be dropped off after the trip in from the airport; the ride from the airport is an hour, and it takes almost an hour to get to the southern end of the lake. Lining the narrow road where the airport vans leave you off are a handful of tiny travel agencies through which you can arrange boat

10

trips, bicycle hire, and airport drop-off service. Expect to pay around K25,000 for a full-day boat tour and K19,000 for half a day. The only way to get to hotels on the lake is by boat; depending on how far south you are, expect to pay up to K63,000, though the price will drop significantly if you're using the same boatman for touring. ⊠ *Inle Lake.*

Inthar Heritage House. This beautiful wooden house, on stilts in the middle of Inle Lake, was completed in 2008 but appears older, thanks to reclaimed wood from which 80% of it is built. It's a wonderfully multiuse space. Downstairs is a cat sanctuary, where pampered Burmese felines lounge about lazily. The cats are the result of a two-year breeding program, an effort to reintroduce them to their native Myanmar. Upstairs from the cats is a re-creation of a traditional bedroom with impressive dark wooden period furniture. Then there's the hotel and catering school, and the art gallery, which hosts quarterly exhibitions of local artists' work, and then Inthar Restaurant, which is excellent—mostly Chinese dishes, with coffee, tea, shakes, and desserts—and a lovely, peaceful space. The restaurant's vegetables come from the house's own organic farm; cooking classes are also offered. ⊠ *Inpawkhon Village* ☎ *95/251232* ⊕ *inleheritage.org.*

Inthein. Spending an hour or two meandering around this village, which is on land and reached by a narrow canal, is a nice way to break up monotonous, albeit pretty, Inle Lake cruising. The stupas start just behind the village proper with **Nyaung Ohak**, where a grouping of them stands in disrepair, surrounded by jungle. Keep going up the hill until you reach **Shwe Inn Thein Paya**; on the way up the stairs, you'll see vendors selling souvenirs, so bring some cash with you. The climb is worth it; you'll find a slew of 17th- and 18th-century stupas—some are crumbling, but others have been lovingly renovated, so there's a nice contrast. ⊠ *Inthein Village.*

WORTH NOTING

Buddha Museum. The Shan ethnic group has its own unique culture but, because this is a government-run museum, you'll find no symbols of it here. Instead, eye Buddha images before turning your attention to the building itself, a teak-and-brick mansion that was once home to Sao Shwe Thaike; he was the 33rd and last Shan king and the first president of independent Burma, from 1948 to 1962, until the junta coup d'état. ⊠ *Museum Rd. (Haw St.) near Myawady Rd.* ☷ *K2,500* ⊙ *Wed.–Sun. 10–4.*

Floating Gardens. A far cry from the vegetable farms of the west, these floating gardens are a testament to the ingenuity of Inle Lake's villagers. The floating gardens are just north of Nampan (the southern end of the lake), and here Intha farmers grow a cornucopia of colorful produce using wooden trellises that rely on floating mats for support. Vegetables and flowers stand tall and strong on the trellises, which are lovingly tended by farmers floating by in their long wooden canoes. ⊠ *Nampan Village.*

Kaung Daing. Five miles from Nyaung Shwe is this sleepy village inhabited by the Intha ethnic group, who live around Inle Lake. Shan tofu is made here using not soybeans, but yellow split peas. Kaung Daing's big

Rice-noodle fish soup Mohinga is considered Myanmar's national dish and is commonly eaten for breakfast.

draw is its hot springs; there's a swimming pool and private bathhouses for men and women, and the water supply all comes from natural springs. It's a 45-minute bike ride here from Nyaung Shwe, one that runs over a bridge, along a dirt road, and through marshes, eventually depositing you at the hot springs for a well-deserved soak. A boat here will take 30 minutes (K3,000–K3,500 each way), and a moto will do the round-trip for K5,000–K5,500. ✉ *Kaung Daing Village.*

WHERE TO EAT

If you're staying at a hotel on the lake, you'll be eating breakfast and dinner there. Lunch can be enjoyed at one of the restaurants on the lake, which, like the hotels, stand on stilts. If you're staying in or spending time in Nyaung Shwe, there are a dozen or so eateries, including the food stalls at Mingala Market.

$ BURMESE 🍴 **Food Stalls at Mingalar Market.** Open for breakfast and lunch only, the food stalls at this colorful market are an experience for the senses. Everything is handmade and the sellers take pride in what they're offering. Featured dishes include Shan tofu salad, noodle soup, and enormous round rice crackers that will be devoured by those who've had a bit too much spice. Just across from the market are a few other food stalls where you'll find inexpensive plates of tea leaf salad and spicy noodle soup. [$] *Average main: K1000* ✉ *Yone Gyi Rd. near Mong Li Chuang, Nyaung Shwe* ✣ *Walk from Viewpoint in direction of Paradise Hotel; market is about three-fourths of way there, on left-hand side of main road* 💳 *No credit cards.*

$$$ EUROPEAN 🍴 **Inle Pancake Kingdom.** Inle Lake is unlikely to be your first stop in Myanmar, and so by this time a break from Burmese food is likely a top priority. Pancake Kingdom is a classic backpacker restaurant, with friendly service, inexpensive sweet and savory pancakes (really somewhere between crepes and American-style pancakes), Wi-Fi, and computers. Proximity to the docks, indoor and outdoor seating, and a general laid-back and quiet atmosphere make this popular with tourists looking for a little western flavor. [$] *Average main: K3000* ✉ *Just south of Yone Gyi Rd., near Phaung Daw Seiq Rd., Nyaung Shwe* ☎ *081/29288* 💳 *No credit cards.*

$$$ BURMESE 🍴 **Lotus Restaurant.** This diminutive, family-run space fills up quickly, and with good reason. Salads, which utilize pickled tea leaves, coriander, bits of chili, and other assorted delicious odds and ends, have great texture and go down nicely alongside the restaurant's curries. Round out the meal with a refreshing fruit plate and a chat with the friendly owner. [$] *Average main: K4000* ✉ *Museum Rd. (Haw St.) and Myawady St., Nyaung Shwe* ✥ *Close to Paradise Hotel* 💳 *No credit cards.*

$$$$ ECLECTIC 🍴 **Red Mountain Estate Vineyards.** There are nine varieties here, and the wine-making process is overseen by a Frenchman who joined the winery in 2002. Tours are basic but give a good overview of Red Mountain's production process. Both wine and food are quite average, but the K3,000 wine tasting paired with lovely views of the fields and cool breezes makes for a very pleasant afternoon. Note that service is molasses slow, so budget at least an hour. The vineyard can be reached by bike in about 20 minutes, and it's an easy ride save for the very last uphill stretch. [$] *Average main: K5000* ✉ *Taung Chay Village Group* ☎ *081/209366* 🌐 *www.redmountain-estate.com* 💳 *No credit cards.*

WHERE TO STAY

There are hotels on the lake and then there are those in Nyaung Shwe, the village surrounding the lake's jetty. The lake hotels are arguably better positioned for touring, but the hotels in Nyaung Shwe offer easy access to restaurants and services.

$$ HOTEL 🏨 **Golden Island Cottages.** This immersive hotel experience on one of Myanmar's largest lakes will have you living like a local in a simple over-water cottage built on stilts—even the welcoming public spaces and on-site restaurant serving local cuisine are suspended over the water. **Pros:** connection to community (it's run as a co-op); reasonably priced; tasty food at in-house restaurants; warm service. **Cons:** noisy boat motors; Thale-U outpost is far from town. [$] *Rooms from: US$100* ✉ *Thale-U Village* ☎ *081/209390 Nampan, 081/209389 Thale-U* 🌐 *www.gichotelgroup.com* 💳 *No credit cards* 🛏 *52 rooms (Nampan), 25 rooms (Thale-U)* 🍽 *Breakfast.*

$$ HOTEL 🏨 **Hotel Amazing Nyaung Shwe.** In the village of Nyaung Shwe, a 15-minute walk to the Inle Lake jetty, this hotel is ideally positioned for those who want to stretch their sea and land legs. **Pros:** plenty to see in the immediate area; very helpful staff. **Cons:** so popular it's hard to get a room; noise at ground level can be a problem. [$] *Rooms from: US$140* ✉ *Mong Li Chuang near Myawady Rd., Nyaung Shwe* ☎ *081/209477* 🌐 *www.hotelamazingnyaungshwe.com* 💳 *No credit cards* 🛏 *13 rooms, 3 suites* 🍽 *Breakfast.*

$$$ RESORT Fodor's Choice ★ 🏨 **Inle Lake View Resort.** On land overlooking Inle Lake (rather than on stilts floating on the lake), this boutique hotel is spread across 24 acres of lush grounds. **Pros:** quiet; great service; good-value spa. **Cons:** hotel is remote, so you either need to get a ride into town or eat here; weak Wi-Fi signal. [$] *Rooms from: US$225* ✉ *Kaung Daing Village* ☎ *081/23656* 🌐 *www.inlelakeview.com* 🛏 *20 rooms, 20 suites* 🍴 *Breakfast* 💳 *No credit cards.*

$$ RESORT 🏨 **Inle Princess Resort.** The quaint bungalows that make up this hotel are removed from the main lake to give you a quieter, more peaceful experience; rather than using noisy outboard motors to dock, boat drivers row. **Pros:** free Wi-Fi; a bang-up breakfast spread. **Cons:** a/c weak; so popular you need to book far in advance or find a well connected travel agent. [$] *Rooms from: US$180* ✉ *Magyizin Village* ☎ *081/209055* 📧 *inleprincess@gmail.com* 🌐 *www.inle-princess.com* 💳 *No credit cards* 🛏 *45 suites* 🍴 *Breakfast.*

$$ B&B/INN 🏨 **Paramount Inle Resort.** Though by no means budget, this is one of the less expensive hotels on the lake proper. **Pros:** warm service; prime lake location; huge breakfasts. **Cons:** poor Wi-Fi signal outside the lobby; lake facing rooms are loud; bathrooms need updating. [$] *Rooms from: US$100* ✉ *Nga Phe Chaung Village, Nga Phe Chaung Village* ☎ *094/936–0855* 🌐 *www.paramountinleresort.com* 💳 *No credit cards* 🛏 *16 rooms, 12 suites* 🍴 *Breakfast.*

$$ RESORT Fodor's Choice ★ 🏨 **ViewPoint Lodge.** This eco-friendly, Swiss-managed property on one of Myanmar's largest lakes lives up to its name: from your over-water bungalow, prepare to be entranced by longboats putting by, barefoot monks walking onshore, and water buffalo being driven over an ancient bridge. **Pros:** beautiful rooms; warm service; delicious food; scenic surroundings; easy walk to village of Nyaung Shwe. **Cons:** not all rooms have balconies; noise from the boats carries into the rooms; touch-and-go Wi-Fi. [$] *Rooms from: US$100* ✉ *Near Talk Nan Bridge and jetty* ☎ *081/209062* 🌐 *inleviewpoint.com* 💳 *No credit cards* 🛏 *24 rooms* 🍴 *Breakfast*

NIGHTLIFE AND PERFORMING ARTS

If you're staying on the lake, there are no bars to speak of, though your hotel restaurant will definitely serve wine, beer, and liquor. In Nyaung Shwe, not every restaurant serves alcohol, but many do, and here you'll find visitors and some locals enjoying a drink.

FAMILY **Aung Puppet Show.** Within a pocket-size theater, local puppeteer Aung (who is also a cab driver) puts on a nightly half-hour show in which he showcases his skills. It's cute and very entertaining, a nice evening activity in a place where there aren't any. Aung knows exactly what he's doing and his marionettes have the audience in constant giggles. On the premises is a puppet shop with marionettes and other souvenirs. Reservations are essential for the show. ✉ *Opposite Nanda Wunn Hotel, 80 Yone Gyi Rd.* 🎟 *K3,000* 🕒 *Daily, 7 and 8:30 pm.*

FAMILY **Min Min's.** This sweet little eatery doubles as a western-style watering hole, with good cocktails. It's a family affair, with Min Min and his wife running things and their daughter Soe Soe acting as a runner. Visitors tuck into heaping plates of pasta with homemade pesto washed down

10

with proper piña coladas, made with plenty of rum and fresh lime. Nearly 10,000 miles from Havana, Min Min's mojitos are spot on, a most welcome refreshment after a hot day of touring. Min Min's also offers tour services, though we caution you not to sign up for any treks after your second mojito. ⊠ *Yone Gyi Rd. near Kyaung Taw Anouk Rd., Nyaung Shwe* ⊕ *www.min-mins.com.*

SHOPPING

Shopping at Inle Lake is limited to the workshops, which nicely showcase traditional handicrafts but are truly shops for tourists, and the markets, which are interesting and a good spot to purchase fresh produce.

Mingala Market. Mornings see this market packed with locals doing their shopping. What's on offer can be divided into three categories—groceries (fresh fish, produce), home goods (fishing supplies, bowls, the occasional knife), and handicrafts, which are sold at a few stalls. The market isn't too chaotic except every five days, when Inle's regular rotating market sets up shop here. Your hotel will be able to tell you when this is. ⊠ *Yone Gyi Rd. near Mong Li Chuang, Nyaung Shwe.*

Ywama. This is where to come if you're keen to purchase souvenirs. Ywama was the first of Inle Lake's many small villages to get a big tourism push and, as such, its waterways are more packed than the others. Ywama is still charming and has retained its authenticity—certainly families still live here and you'll see giggling kids running around—but there are also lots of tchotchke peddlers. Every five days, a floating market is held, when even more hawkers convene on Ywama. Thrown into the mix are a handful of farmers who continue selling vegetables to locals. ⊠ *Inle Lake.*

MANDALAY AND NEARBY

Myanmar's second-largest city and its last royal capital, Mandalay is home to the rebuilt Mandalay Palace; the original, destroyed during WWII, was home to then-Burma's last monarchy. Downtown Mandalay is heavy on the concrete and urban sprawl; unlike Yangon, it looks nothing like it did when it was part British Burma. Mandalay is laid out on a grid, and from 35th Street north to the citadel walls can be easily traversed on foot or by bicycle. Mandalay offers a sharp contrast to Yangon and is interesting taken from both a historical and an urban-planning point of view. A further juxtaposition to the big, dusty city is its nearby hill station Pyin U Lwin (née Maymo). Here is where Upper Burma's strongest colonial legacy lies, in the form of manicured gardens, horse-drawn carriages, and homes straight out of the English countryside.

GETTING HERE AND AROUND

Tourists' Mandalay has two distinct sections—Mandalay Hill and the palace entrance and downtown Mandalay. Although it is possible to walk between the two, a far easier way to go from the palace downtown to the restaurants is by bike, pickup truck, or cab; coming back from downtown, you'll also have the option of a moto. Bikes can be hired from your hotel for around K4,000 per hour.

AIR TRAVEL   Half a dozen domestic flights land in Mandalay every day. The trip from Yangon takes one hour 25 minutes and starts at around $150; the trips from Bagan and Heho (Inle Lake) are about half the time and less expensive. Air Asia and Thai Airways both fly in from Bangkok and China Eastern flies in from Kunming. Mandalay's airport is almost an hour from the city. Expect to pay at least K10,000; K6,000 if you're sharing.

BOAT TRAVEL   Boats arrive to and depart from the area around Gawein Jetty at 35th Street. The Malikha express ferry is the most popular, running between Mandalay to Bagan. Boats depart at 7 am, arriving in Bagan at 3:30 pm; tickets are $45 and a western breakfast, with lots of toast, is served on board. The ferry schedule is issued a month in advance. There are many more boats, varying in price, quality, frequency, and duration, but you can expect to pay $15–$45 for a 10–14 hour trip. For a good schedule and information see ⊕ *www.myanmarrivercruises.com.*

BUS TRAVEL   There are half a dozen buses a day leaving Yangon for Mandalay and a couple from Bagan. Bus schedules can change, so have your hotel or guesthouse book tickets for you. Almost all buses from Yangon run overnight, leaving around 6 pm (9–10 hours, from K15,000). The trip from Bagan (K12,500) takes eight hours. Just outside the bus station you'll find a sea of taxis; bargain, and you should be able to get a cab to your hotel for around K5,000.

CAR TRAVEL   From Bagan or Inle Lake to Mandalay, expect to spend from around $180 and eight hours in the car. Within Mandalay, pickups trucks will drive between downtown and Mandalay Hill and the palace for around K5,000. A car out to Pyin-U Lwin will cost around K30,000 to K35,000, or K7,000 for a shared taxi.

TAXI, MOTO, AND CYCLO TRAVEL   Motos and cyclos are easy to find in Mandalay and trips within the city center shouldn't cost more than K2,000. Taxis are a bit harder to come by, but when you find them don't pay more than K6,000 within downtown and K7,500 out to Mandalay Hill.

TRAIN TRAVEL   Trains from Yangon to Mandalay run over old British-built railway tracks. The fastest trains depart from Yangon Central at 6 am, 3 pm, and 5 pm, arriving at 8:30 pm, 6:30 am, and 9:15 am, respectively. Prices are $50 (sleeper), $25 (upper-class seat), and $22 (first-class seat). Trains from Bagan leave Mandalay at 7 am and arrive at 2:30 pm ($10, $7, $4 for upper-class, first-class, and ordinary seats, respectively). Trains from Inle Lake to Mandalay leave from Shwen Yaung (11 km [7 miles] from the jetty) to Thazi, where you switch to a Mandalay-bound train. Note that prices are listed in dollars online, and can be paid in dollars if booked online but must be paid for in kyat at railway ticketing offices. A good source of information on train travel is ⊕ *www. go-myanmar.com/by-train.*

10

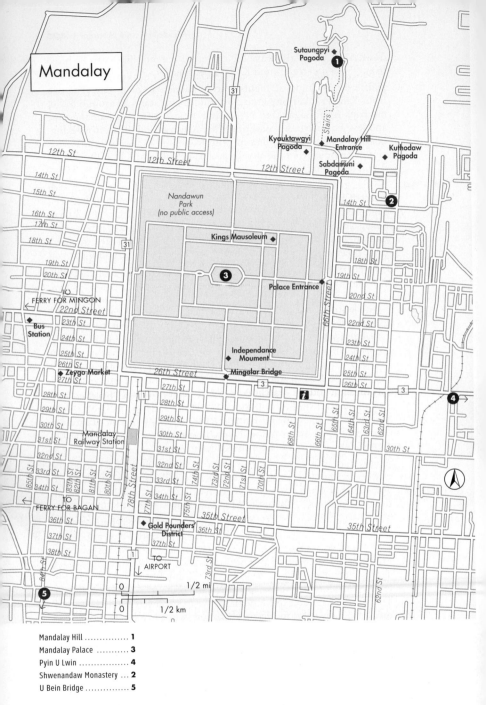

Mandalay

- 12th St
- 14th St
- 15th St
- 16th St
- 17th St
- 18th St
- 19th St
- 20th St
- NO FERRY FOR MINGON
- 22nd Street
- 23th St
- Bus Station
- 24th St
- 25th St
- 26th St
- 27th St
- Zeyga Market
- 28th St
- 29th St
- 30th St
- Mandalay Railway Station
- 31st St
- 32nd St
- 33rd St
- 34th St
- TO FERRY FOR BAGAN
- 36th St
- 37th St
- 38th St

- 12th Street
- 12th Street
- 14th St
- Nandawun Park (no public access)
- Kings Mausoleum
- **3**
- Palace Entrance
- Independance Moument
- 26th Street
- Mingalar Bridge
- 27th St
- 28th St
- 29th St
- 30th St
- 31st St
- 32nd St
- 33rd St
- 34th St
- 35th Street
- Gold Pounders District
- 36th St
- 37th St
- TO AIRPORT

- Sutaungpyi Pagoda **1**
- Kyauktawgyi Pagoda
- Mandalay Hill Entrance
- Kuthodaw Pagoda
- Sabdamuni Pagoda
- Stairs
- **2**
- 18th St
- 19th St
- 20nd St
- 22nd St
- 23th St
- 24th St
- 25th St
- 26th St
- **3** (route 3)
- **i**
- 68th St
- 66th St
- 65th St
- 64th St
- 63rd St
- 62nd St
- **4**
- 30th St
- 74th St
- 73rd St
- 72nd St
- 71st St
- 70th St
- 30th St
- 35th Street
- 69th St
- **5**
- 1/2 mi
- 0
- 1/2 km

ESSENTIALS

CB Bank. ✉ E-1,2,3 78th St. between 27th and 28th Sts. ☎ 02/69901.

VISITOR
AND TOUR
INFORMATION

Inland Water Transport Office. Tickets for the ferries are sold here. ✉ *35th St. at water.*

Sun Far Travels and Tours. This branch of the well-established travel and tour company can help with tours, hotel reservations, and air tickets. ✉ *SY Bldg., 30th St. between 77th and 78th Sts., across from railway station* ☎ *02/69712* ⊕ *www.sunfartravels.com* ⊙ *Weekdays 9–5; weekends and public holidays 9–noon.*

EXPLORING MANDALAY

TOP ATTRACTIONS

Mandalay Palace. The last royal palace of the ultimate Burmese monarchy, Kings Mindon and Thebaw's onetime residence was built between 1857 and 1859 in accordance with the Buddha's prophecy that, in the year 2400 (1857 in the Gregorian calendar), a "great city" would be built at the bottom of Mandalay Hill. The east facing palace is inside a walled fort whose four 1¼-mile walls form a perfect square. Part of the palace was transported by elephant from then-kingdom Amarapura. When the palace was later looted by invading British troops, many artifacts were swiped, and some can now be seen at London's Victoria and Albert Museum. During WWII, the Japanese took over the palace and, when bombs hit the city, it was almost entirely destroyed, with only the mint and one watchtower (which can be climbed today) surviving the attack. The structure that now stands was built in 1989 and is a faithful re-creation of the original. The palace itself is an important sight, but what's even more interesting is the village inside the citadel walls, where locals go about their daily business within spitting distance of what were once Burma's most hallowed halls. ✉ *East Moat at 19th St.* 🎫 *K10,000 combination ticket with the Shwenandaw Monastery.*

OFF THE
BEATEN
PATH

Pyin U Lwin. Pyin U Lwin is 67½ km (42 miles) from Mandalay and, at an elevation of 3,500 feet, feels much cooler than the stifling town. After capturing Mandalay during the Third Anglo-Burmese War, the British set upon Pyin U Lwin (then known as Maymo or May Town) and made it their hill station, and it remained as such until the end of British rule in 1948. The town is still quite charming and is best enjoyed by bicycle or perched in a colonial-style horse-drawn carriage. Start off in the town center where you'll see the **Purcell Clock Tower** (1936) and redbrick **All Saints' Church** (1912). Mandalay is a desert compared with Pyin U Lwin, so soak up the green at the 435-acre **National Kandawgyi Gardens,** which were built in 1915 and in which can be found nearly 500 plant species. There's a lovely lake, a butterfly museum, an orchid garden, an aviary, and a swimming pool. The best place to see Pyin U Lwin's old colonial buildings is along roads **Circular and Forest,** which you can cycle or bump along in your horse cart. Buildings run the style gamut from Tudor to plantation, and both the Candacraig Hotel (once the British Club) and the former Croxton Hotel are worth an ogle. A private car to Pyin U Lwin should cost K30,000–K35,000; a shared taxi,

10

Mandalay Palace, in Myanmar's last royal capital, one of the gems that reward exploration of Mandalay's dusty streets.

which leaves from downtown Mandalay (27th and 83rd Streets) should cost K7,000 per person; the trip takes two hours. A more scenic, albeit bumpy, trip can be made by train, which leaves around 4 am and arrives just before 8 am; tickets are K5,000 for ordinary, K10,000 for first class, and K12,000 for upper class. ⊠ *Mandalay* ✉ *K6,500 adult, K2,500 kids under 12, K1,250 camera (not strictly enforced)* ⊙ *Daily 7 am–6 pm.*

Fodor'sChoice
★ **U Bein Bridge.** The world's longest teak bridge runs three-quarters of a mile over Taungthaman Lake in Amarapura, Burma's former capital and now part of Mandalay. More than 1,000 teak poles make up the bridge, each scavenged from the former royal palace by then-mayor U Bein. During dry season (November to April) the lake is quite shallow but, during summer, it nearly doubles in height, with water reaching up to just below the bridge's planks. Around sunrise is the best time to come, when a stream of monks and villagers, some on bike, cross back and forth. Most visitors are dropped off at the western end and then walk across; at the eastern end is a small village where you can munch on hot, fresh chapatis and sip very sweet tea. If you're staying near Mandalay Hill and heading to the bridge for sunrise, book a cab the night before; it will run you around K18,000. ⊠ *Amarapura.*

WORTH NOTING

Mandalay Hill. The city's name is derived from this hill, which, at nearly 800 feet, can seem a lot more like a mountain when you're schlepping up it on a 100-degree day. For those unable to make the climb, there's an elevator as well as a road to an escalator that leads up to the gilded Sutaungpyei Pagoda at the top of the hill. Burmese Buddhists have been coming here for nearly two centuries, paying their respects, and you'll still see monks here, mostly sweet teenage boys who are eager to chat with visitors and practice their (already quite good) English. On the way up, you'll see a giant standing Buddha, his right hand pointing to the city. Legend has it that when the Buddha visited Mandalay Hill, he prophesied that in the year 2400 (Buddhist calendar), a "great city" would be founded at the bottom of the hill. In the Gregorian calendar, that year is 1857, exactly when King Mindon decreed that Mandalay would be Burma's new capital. Sunset over Mandalay is best viewed from the top of the hill, and the climb can take 40 minutes, so give yourself plenty of time. Bring wet wipes to clean off your feet. ⊠ *Mandalay Hill* ⊠ *K1,000 camera fee.*

Shwenandaw Monastery. King Mindon built this intricately carved structure in the mid-19th century as his apartment and then died there in 1878. His son Thebaw believed his father's ghost was still in the building, refused to live there, and had it taken down and moved outside the citadel walls and turned into a monastery. In doing so, he unknowingly saved it from pillaging by the British (1885) and certain ruin during the WWII Japanese invasion. At its inception, the building was more regal than it is today because gold plating and the exterior glass mosaics are now gone, but the interior remains in quite good shape. ⊠ *62nd St. near 14th St., next to university* ⊠ *K10,000 combination ticket with Mandalay Palace.*

WHERE TO EAT

There's some excellent Indian food in Mandalay, along with the Myanmar buffets available countrywide. Restaurants on the whole are inexpensive and offer good value for money.

$$

BURMESE

✕ **84th and 23rd Streets Restaurants.** A handful of Shan restaurants have set up shop around this intersection. Both **Golden Shan** and **Lashio Lay** offer sizeable buffet spreads of standard Myanmar dishes like chicken curry and assorted sautéed greens, served with big helpings of white rice. Teashop **Karaweik** does excellent Shan noodles and sweet naan straight from the tandoor, best enjoyed alongside a cup of tea. $ *Average main: K2500* ⊠ *84th St. near 23rd St.* ▭ *No credit cards.*

$$$

VEGETARIAN
FAMILY

✕ **Marie Min.** Burmese, Indian, and western dishes pack the vegetarian menu at this Sri Lankan family place. The all-day breakfast, with dishes like muesli and pancakes, are big with backpackers staying nearby, but most come here for lunch and dinner, snagging coveted seats on the upper-level balcony. The menu includes dal and curries (the pumpkin is the best), guacamole and eggplant dip, and tart, fresh tomato salad. Wash it all down with lassis or chocolate–peanut butter milk shakes. Service is friendly but there have been reports of bill discrepancies; check yours carefully. $ *Average main: K3000* ⊠ *27th St. between 74th and 75th Sts.* ▭ *No credit cards* ☉ *Closed May–Aug.*

$

CAFÉ
FAMILY

✕ **Nylon Ice Cream Bar.** The ice cream here is not the best you'll ever have, but you won't be able to find cold scoops anywhere else in Mandalay. The atmosphere is really the big draw, with locals and foreigners coming by all day to hang out at the sidewalk tables and people-watch while sipping beer and shakes. The short flavor list includes chocolate,

10

strawberry, vanilla, and durian, of which the durian is the best. Eco-warriors, beware: unless you specifically ask for a bowl or glass, scoops come served in little Styrofoam containers. $ *Average main: K1000* ⊠ *83rd St. between 25th and 26th Sts.* = *No credit cards.*

$$$
BAKERY
FAMILY
Fodor'sChoice
★

✕ **Simplicity Organic Food and Bakery.** Enormously charming and truly unique in Mandalay, this pint-size, family-run café is near Mandalay's jetty, an area otherwise devoid of much in the way of dining. The sweet owner and his son speak English well and are passionate and knowledgeable about organic food, the environment, and the use of MSG. There are delicious Chinese-style pastries, some ice cream and, like manna from heaven, proper coffee, available in several variations including iced and even cappuccinos. On the savory side are traditional Shan noodles, which the locals eat for breakfast, house-made dumplings, and simple stir-fry dishes like chicken with rice and vegetables. 35th Street runs the length of downtown Mandalay, so be sure to indicate to whomever is driving you that you want to be near the jetty. $ *Average main: K3000* ⊠ *35th St. between 91st and 92nd Sts., near jetty* = *No credit cards.*

WHERE TO STAY

Mandalay's more expensive hotels are near Mandalay Palace, but within the city are a few budget options that offer easier access to restaurants.

$
HOTEL

▦ **Ayarwaddy River View Hotel.** Set right along the river, this hotel offers a nice alternative to the luxury behemoths and boxy city hotels. **Pros:** river views; friendly and efficient service; free happy-hour drinks. **Cons:** some rooms can be loud; no dining options in the immediate area. $ *Rooms from: US$70* ⊠ *Strand Rd. between 22nd and 23rd Sts., Strand Rd. becomes Myo Pat Rd. and 22nd becomes Pinya* ☎ *02/72373* ⊕ *www.ayarwaddyriverview-hotel.com* = *No credit cards* ⤳ *56 rooms* ⦿l *No meals.*

$
HOTEL

▦ **Emerald Land Inn.** Though it looks a bit tired, this budget hotel (by Myanmar standards) with its neatly tended gardens and swimming pool offers respite from downtown Mandalay. **Pros:** decent value for money; attentive staff; plentiful hot water. **Cons:** far from most everything; road-facing rooms are noisy; power outages. $ *Rooms from: US$70* ⊠ *9 14th St., near 87th St.* ☎ *02/39471* = *No credit cards* ⤳ *38 rooms* ⦿l *Breakfast.*

$
HOTEL

▦ **Mandalay City Hotel.** Swimming pools at budget hotels are far and few between, and Mandalay City delivers on that front. **Pros:** pool; downtown location; free Wi-Fi. **Cons:** loud rooms; no elevators; some rooms are small. $ *Rooms from: US$56* ⊠ *26th St. between 82nd and 83rd Sts.* ☎ *02/61700* ⊕ *www.mandalaycityhotel.com* = *No credit cards* ⤳ *67 rooms* ⦿l *Breakfast.*

$$$
RESORT
FAMILY
Fodor'sChoice
★

▦ **Mandalay Hill Resort.** A stone's throw from Mandalay Hill and a short jaunt to the royal palace, this Thai-owned big-box hotel offers easy access to Mandalay's main sites. **Pros:** very close to Mandalay Hill and royal palace; great pool; lovely grounds. **Cons:** a cab ride from downtown; two tiny elevators are extremely slow. $ *Rooms from: US$200* ⊠ *9, 416/B Kwin, 10th St., near foot of Mandalay Hill* ☎ *02/35638* ⊕ *www.mandalayhillresorthotel.com* ⤳ *192 rooms, 14 suites* ⦿l *Breakfast.*

$$$$ RESORT **Rupar Mandalar Resort.** Idyllic and full of local flavor, this resort is a ways from downtown but is a real oasis. **Pros:** lovely rooms, staff, and pool. **Cons:** far from the city; breakfast buffet has limited choice. [$] *Rooms from: US$300* ✉ *Corner of 53rd and 30th Sts.* ☎ *02/61555* 🌐 *www.ruparmandalar.com* 💳 *No credit cards* 🛏 *10 rooms, 5 suites* 🍴 *Breakfast.*

NIGHTLIFE AND PERFORMING ARTS

To say that nightlife in Mandalay is nonexistent would be a stretch; it's more that there's little divide between restaurants and bars. Almost all eateries serve beer, and you'll see locals sitting around enjoying drinks as the next table over has a full meal. Of all the big cities in Myanmar, however, Mandalay has the most active theater scene, made up of the famous Moustache Brothers, a marionette theater, and a dance troupe.

FAMILY **Mandalay Marionettes.** Mu Mu Naing and Naing Yee Mar founded this theater in 1986 and, in 2000, performed in France, the Netherlands, and the United States. The team also works with NGOs to put on puppet shows that aim at improving AIDS awareness. The expert manipulators here use colorful marionettes to tell classic Burmese tales, including love stories and one about a flying alchemist. Read the program so you understand more about what you're watching. The hour-long show starts nightly from 8:30 pm. ✉ *66th St. between 26th and 27th Sts.* ☎ *02/34446* 🎟 *K1,000.*

FAMILY **Mintha Theater.** Accompanied by eight musicians, seven talented dancers kitted out in bright costumes perform classical Burmese routines. Twelve dances are on the rotating program, which changes nightly and highlights Myanmar's variety of traditional dances. The lively, colorful show runs an hour and kids who can sit for that long will certainly be entertained. The performance starts at 8:30 pm. ✉ *27th St. between 66th and 65th Sts.* ☎ *09/680–3607* 🌐 *www.minthatheater.com* 🎟 *K8,000.*

Moustache Brothers. For this comedic trio, two brothers (Par Par Lay and Lu Maw) and a cousin (Lu Zaw), an Independence Day gig at Aung San Suu Kyi's compound in 1996 turned serious. Par Par and Lu Maw were arrested for their political satire and jokes and served seven years in prison. Brother Lu Maw kept the show going until their release, but later in 2007, group leader Par Par Lay served a month in prison. Though he passed away in 2013, the Moustache Brothers still perform as a duo to this day. Expect a mix of music, dance, satire, and screwball comedy. ✉ *39th St. between 80th and 81st Sts.* 🎟 *K12,500.*

10

SHOPPING

Shopping areas in Mandalay are a bit spread out, so hiring a taxi would be most convenient way to visit the stores we recommend. Mandalay is known for its handicrafts, especially puppets. These can be purchased at Moustache Brothers and Mandalay Marionettes *(Nightlife and Performing Arts)*. If you've got a ride and fancy some more shopping, there are rows of stone carvers' workshops west of Mahamuni Temple where slabs of stone are chipped, carved, and polished into Buddhas of varying sizes and into more manageable souvenirs like marble elephants. If your time is limited in Mandalay, the easiest place to buy souvenirs is at Mandalay Hill, where there are vendors on the lower-level steps.

Gold Pounders' District. Local worshippers will often put gold leaf onto images of the Buddha, and this is where the bits are made, each pounded between heavy blocks by muscular craftsmen. At **Golden Rose** (36th Street between 78th and 79th Streets) and **King Galon** (36th Street between 77th and 78th Streets), you can observe the craftsmen as the English-speaking staff explain the production process. The information is not a sales pitch, but the most popular thing to buy here is sheets of gold leaf (10 for K2,500). ⊠ *36th St. from 77th to 79th Sts.*

Jade Market. A warren of worktables, this jam-packed market is filled with jade traders inspecting uncut pieces and then having them cut, shaped, and polished to their specifications. The trading floor could give Wall Street a run for its money, with buyers and sellers bent over tables, intently discussing business. Outside, on the eastern side of the market, the cutting and polishing continues. If you do want to buy jade, it's best to come here with a reputable guide. ⊠ *South of 38th St., near 87th St.* ≊ *$1, not always enforced.*

Soe Moe. For impressive embroidered tapestries, bronze sculptures, and carved wood and stone pieces, visit Soe Moe, where the staff can arrange for your purchases to be shipped to Yangon. ⊠ *36th St. between 77th and 78th Sts.*

Sunflower. In the same building as vegetarian restaurant Marie Min, Sunflower sells attractive bronze and wood carvings. ⊠ *27th St. between 75th and 74th Sts.*

Zegyo Market. Mandalay's oldest market dates back to King Mindon (father of Thebaw, the last king of Burma). The original structure has been replaced by a Chinese-style mall, but the hive of activity outside is more interesting than the household goods sold within. A wide array of produce is available here, neatly grouped in colorful piles, and locals come out in full force to do their marketing. Dried shrimp and fish paste make good, nonperishable souvenirs. ⊠ *84th St. at 26th St.*

UNDERSTANDING THAILAND

**INTRODUCTION TO
THAI ARCHITECTURE**

VOCABULARY

MENU GUIDE

INTRODUCTION TO THAI ARCHITECTURE

Though real architecture buffs are few and far between, you'd be hard-pressed to find a visitor to Thailand who doesn't spend at least a little time staring in slack-jawed amazement at the country's glittering wats and ornate palaces—and the elegant sculptures of the mythical beasts that protect them. As befits this spiritual nation, most of the fanfare is saved for religious structures, but you can find plenty to admire in the much simpler lines of the traditional houses of the Central Plains and northern Thailand.

Wats

Wat is the Thai name for what can range from a simple ordination hall for monks and nuns to a huge sprawling complex comprising libraries, bell towers, and meditation rooms. Usually the focal point for a community, it's not unusual for a wat to also be the grounds for village fêtes and festivals. Although most wats you come across symbolize some aspect of Thai-style Theravada Buddhism, examples of other architectural styles are relatively easy to find: Khmer ruins dot the Isan countryside to the east, while northern Thailand showcases many Burmese-style temples.

Wats are erected as acts of merit—allowing the donor to improve his karma and perhaps be reborn as a higher being—or in memory of great events. You can tell much about a wat's origin by its name. A wat *luang* (royal wat), for example, was constructed or restored by royals and may have the words *rat, raja,* or *racha* in its name (e.g., Ratburana or Rajapradit). The word *phra* may indicate that a wat contains an image of the Buddha. Wats that contain an important relic of the Buddha have the words *maha* (great) and *that* (relic) in their names. Thailand's nine major wat mahathats are in Chiang Rai, Chai Nat, Sukhothai, Phisanulk, Ayutthaya, Bangkok, Yasothon, Phetchaburi, and Nakhon Si Thammarat.

Thai wats, especially in the later periods, were seldom planned as entire units, so they often appear disjointed and crowded. To appreciate a wat's beauty you often have to look at its individual buildings.

Perhaps the most recognizable feature of a wat, and certainly a useful landmark when hunting them down, is the towering conelike *chedi*. Originally used to hold relics of the Buddha (hair, bones, or even nails), chedis can now be built by anyone with enough cash to house their ashes. At the base of the chedi you can find three platforms representing hell, earth, and heaven, while the 33 Buddhist heavens are symbolized at the top of the tallest spire by a number of rings.

The main buildings of a wat are the *bot*, which contains a Buddha image and functions as congregation and ordination hall for the monks, and the *viharn*, which serves a similar function, but will hold the most important Buddha image. Standard bot and viharn roofs will feature three steeply curved levels featuring red, gold, and green tiles; the outer walls range from highly decorated to simply whitewashed.

Other noticeable features include the *mondop, prang,* and *ho trai.* Usually square with a pyramid-shape roof, the mondop is reminiscent of Indian temple architecture and serves as a kind of storeroom for holy artifacts, books, and ceremonial objects. The prang is a tall tower similar to the chedi, which came to Thailand by way of the Khmer empire and is used to store images of the Buddha. Easily identifiable by its stilts or raised platform, the ho trai is a library for holy scriptures.

Roofs, which are covered in glazed clay tiles or wooden shakes, generally consist of three overlapping sections, with the lower roof set at gentle slopes, increasing to a topmost roof with a pitch of 60 degrees. Eave brackets in the form of a *naga* (snakes believed to control the irrigation waters of rice fields) with its head at the bottom often support the lower edges of the roofs. Along the eaves of many roofs are a row of small brass bells with clappers attached to thin brass pieces shaped like Bodhi tree leaves.

During the early Ayutthaya period (1350–1767), wat interiors were illuminated by the light passing through vertical slits in the walls (wider, more elaborate windows would have compromised the strength of the walls and, thus, the integrity of the structure). In the Bangkok period (1767–1932), the slits were replaced by proper windows set below wide lintels that supported the upper portions of the brick walls. There are usually five, seven, or nine windows on a side in accordance with the Thai preference for odd numbers. The entrance doors are in the end wall facing the Buddha image; narrower doors may flank the entrance door.

Principal building materials have varied with the ages. Khmer and Lopburi architects built in stone and laterite; Sukhothai and Lanna builders worked with laterite and brick. Ayutthaya and Bangkok architects opted for brick cemented by mortar and covered with one or more coats of stucco (made of lime, sand, and, often, rice husks). In early construction, walls were often several feet thick; as binding materials and construction techniques improved they became thinner.

The mid-13th century saw an enormous wave of men entering the monkhood as the Kingdom of Sukhothai adopted Hinayana Buddhism as its official religion. Consequently there was a need for bigger monasteries. Due to the lack of quality stone and brick available, wood became the building material of choice, marking a shift away from the exclusively stone structures of the Khmer period.

Sculpture

The Thai image of the Buddha usually features markedly long ears weighed down by heavy earrings in reference to his royal background, and is cast in bronze and covered in gold leaf by followers. He is typically depicted seated or standing; less common images are reclining Buddhas, acknowledging impending death, and walking Buddhas, which were favored during the Sukhothai period (13th to 15th century). Statues from the Lanna period of the 13th to 15th century and the present Ratanakosin era feature eyes fashioned from colored gems or enamel, while the Lopburi period of the 10th to 13th century favored metal.

A collection of 32 Pali *lakshanas,* descriptions used to identify future incarnations of the Buddha, popularly serve as a kind of blueprint for reproductions. The lakshanas include reference to wedge-shape heels, long fingers, and toes of equal length, legs like an antelope, arms long enough that he could touch either knee without bending, skin so smooth that dust wouldn't adhere to it, a body as thick as a banyan tree, long eyelashes like those of a cow, 40 teeth, a hairy white mole between his eyebrows, deep blue eyes, and an *ushnisha* (protuberance) atop his head—either a turban, a topknot, or a bump on his skull.

Palaces

Although King Bhumibol currently uses Chitlada Palace when in Bangkok, the Chakri Dynasty monarchs who preceded him used the showpiece Grand Palace as their official residence. Shots of the palace with its gleaming spires floodlighted up at night fill every postcard stand, and it's arguably Bangkok's single most important tourist attraction.

Built in 1782 when King Rama I chose Bangkok as Siam's new capital, the Grand Palace is the only remaining example of early Ratanakosin architecture—Rama II and III chose not to initiate any large-scale construction projects in the face of economic hardship. A primarily functional collection of buildings, the compound contains the Royal Thai Decorations and Coin Pavilion, the Museum of Fine Art, and the Weapons Museum.

Also worth checking out while in the capital is what is believed to be the world's largest golden teak-wood building. The three-story Vimanmek Palace was moved from Chonburi in the east to Bangkok's Dusit Palace, and contains jewelry and gifts given as presents from around the world.

Rama IV led the revival of palace construction in the second half of the 19th century, overseeing the building of several royal getaways. Perhaps the most impressive of these is Phra Nakhon Khiri in the southern town of Phetchaburi. Known locally as Khao Wang, the palace sits atop a mountain with wonderful panoramic views. Sharing its mountain home are various wat, halls, and thousands of macaque monkeys. Klai Kangwon in nearby Hua Hin is still used as a seaside getaway for the royal family and as a base when they visit southern provinces. Built in 1926 by Rama VI, the two-story concrete palace's name translates as Far From Worries and was built in the style of European châteaux.

Houses

Look around many Thai towns and you can see that this is a swiftly modernizing country: whitewashed apartment blocks, everything-under-one-roof shopping malls, and glass-fronted fast-food outlets are testaments to a growing economy and general rush to get ahead (as well as to the disappearance of Thailand's forests, which once provided cheap and sturdy building materials). However, peer a little closer and you will find Thailand's heritage staring right back at you.

Traditional Thai houses are usually very simple and essentially boil down to three basic components: stilts, a deck, and a sloping roof. Heavy, annual monsoon rains all over the country necessitate that living quarters be raised on stilts to escape flooding; in the dry season the space under the house is typically used as storage for farming equipment or other machinery. The deck of the house is essentially the living room—it's where you can find families eating, cooking, and just plain relaxing.

As with wats, it's often the roofs of houses that are the most interesting. Lanna-style (northern Thailand) roofs, usually thatched or tiled, are thought to have evolved from the Thai people's roots in southern China, where steeply pitched roofs would have been needed to combat heavy snows. Although there's no real chance of a snowball fight in Thailand, the gradient and overhang allows for quick runoff of the rains and welcome shade from the sun.

These basics are fairly uniform throughout the country, with a few small adjustments to accommodate different climates. For example, roofs are steepest in areas with more intense weather patterns, like the Central Plains, and northern Thai houses have smaller windows to conserve heat better.

VOCABULARY

Thai has several distinct forms for different social levels. The most common one is the street language, which is used in everyday situations. If you want to be polite, add "khrup" (men) or "kah" (women) to the end of your sentence. For the word "I," men should use "phom" and women should use "deeshan."

Note that the "h" is silent when combined with most other consonants (th, ph, kh, etc.). Double vowels indicate long vowel sounds (uu=oo, as in food), except for "aa," which is pronounced "ah."

ENGLISH	THAI

BASICS

Hello/goodbye	Sa-wa-dee-khrup/kah.
How are you?	Sa-bai-dee-mai khrup/kah.
I'm fine.	Sa-bai-dee khrup/kah.
I'm very well.	Dee-mark khrup/kah.
I'm so so.	Sa-bai sa-bai.
What's your name?	Khun-chue-ar-rai khrup/kah?
My name is Joe.	Phom-chue Joe khrup.
My name is Alice.	Deeshan chue Alice kah.
It's nice to meet you.	Yin-dee-tee dai ruu jak khun khrup kah.
Excuse me.	Khor thod khrup/kah.
I'm sorry	Phom sia jai khrup (M)/Deeshan sia chy kah (F).
It's okay/It doesn't matter.	Mai pen rai khrup/kah.
Yes.	Chai khrup/kah
No.	Mai chai khrup/kah
Please.	Karoona
Thank you.	Khop-khun-khrup/kah.
You're welcome.	Mai pen rai khrup/kah.

GETTING AROUND

How do I get to . . .	Phom/chan ja pai . . . (name of the place) . . . dai yang-ngai khrup/kah?
. . . the train station?	sa-ta-nee rod-fai
. . . the post office?	pai-sa-nee
. . . the tourist office?	sam-nak-ngan tong-teow
. . . the hospital?	rong-pha-ya-barn
Does this bus go to?	Rod-khan-nee bpai-nai khrup/ka?

ENGLISH	THAI
Where is . . .	Yoo tee-nai khrup/ka?
. . . the bathroom?	hong nam
. . . the subway?	sa-ta-nee rot-fai-tai-din
. . . he bank?	ta-na-kahn
. . . the hotel?	rong ram
. . . the store?	Rarn
. . . the market?	Talaat
Left	Sai
Right	Kwah
Straight ahead	trong-pai
Is it far?	Klai mai khrup/kah?

USEFUL PHRASES

Do you speak English?	Khun pood pa-sa ung-grid dai mai khrup/kah?
I don't speak Thai.	Phom/chan pood pa-sa Thai mai dai khrup/kah.
I don't understand.	Phom/chan mai cao jai khrup/kah.
I don't know.	Phom/chan mai roo khrup/kah.
I'm American/British.	Phom/chan pen American/Ung-grid khrup/kah.
I'm sick.	Phom/chan mai sa-bai khrup/kah.
Please call a doctor.	Choo-ay re-ak mor doo-ay khrup/kah.
Do you have any rooms?	Khun-mee hawng-mai khrup/kah?
How much does it cost?	Tao rai khrup/kah?
Too expensive.	pa-eng gern-pai
It's beautiful.	soo-ay.
When?	Muah-rai khrup/kah?
Where?	Tee-nai khrup/kah?
Help!	Choo-ay doo-ay!
Stop!	Yoot!

NUMBERS

1	nueng
2	song

ENGLISH	THAI
3	sam
4	see
5	hah
6	hok
7	jet
8	bpaet
9	gao
10	sib
11	sib-et
12	sib-song
13	sib-sam
14	sib-see
15	sib-hah
16	sib-hok
17	sib-jet
18	sib-bpaet
19	sib-gao
20	yee-sib
21	yee-sib-et
30	sam-sib
40	see-sib
50	hah-sib
60	hok-sib
70	jet-sib
80	bpaet-sib
90	gao-sib
100	nueng-roy
101	nueng-roy-nung
200	Song-roy

ENGLISH	THAI

DAYS AND TIME

Today	wannee
Tomorrow	proong nee
Yesterday	Muah-waan-nee
Morning	thawn-chao
Afternoon	thawn bai
Night	thorn muet
What time is it?	gee-mong-laew khrup/kah?
It's 2	song mong.
It's 4	see mong.
It's 2:30	song mong sarm-sip na-tee.
It's 2:45	song mong see-sip hah na-tee.
Monday	wan-jun
Tuesday	wan-ung-kan
Wednesday	wan-poot
Thursday	wan-phra-roo-hud
Friday	wan-sook
Saturday	an-sao
Sunday	an-ar-teet
January	ok-ka-ra-kom
February	oom-pha-parn
March	ee-na-kom
April	ay-sar-yon
May	rus-sa-pa-kom
June	e-tu-na-yon
July	a-rak-ga-da-kom
August	ing-ha-kom
September	un-ya-yon
October	hu-la-kom
November	rus-sa-ji-ga-yon
December	an-wa-kom

MENU GUIDE

The first term you should file away is "aroi," which means delicious. You'll no doubt use that one again and again, whether you're dining at food stalls or upscale restaurants. When someone asks "Aroi mai?" that's your cue to practice your Thai—most likely your answer will be a resounding "aroi mak" (It's very delicious).

Another useful word is "Kaw," which simply means "Could I have ...?" However, the most important phrase to remember may be "Gin ped dai mai?" or "Can you eat spicy food?" Answer this one wrong and you might have a five-alarm fire in your mouth. You can answer with a basic "dai" (can), "mai dai" (cannot), or "dai nit noi" (a little). Most restaurants will tone down dishes for foreigners, but if you're visiting a food stall or if you're nervous, you can ask your server "Ped mai?" ("Is it spicy?") or specify that you would like your food "mai ped" (not spicy), "ped nit noi khrup/kah" (a little spicy), or if you have very resilient taste buds, "ped ped" (very spicy). Don't be surprised if the latter request is met with some laughter—and if all Thai eyes are on you when you take your first bite. Remember, water won't put out the fire; you'll need to eat something sweet or oily, or drink beer or milk.

ENGLISH	THAI
food	a-harn
breakfast	a-harn chao
lunch	a-harn klang wan
dinner	a-harn yen
eat here	gin tee nee khrup/kah
take away	kaw glub baan khrup/kah
The check, please.	Check bin khrup/kah
More, please.	Kaw eek noi khrup/kah
Another please.	Kaw eek an khrup/kah
A table for two, please.	Kaw toh song tee khrup/kah
vegetarian	gin jay
spicy	ped
Is it spicy?	Ped mai?
not spicy	mai ped
a little spicy	ped nit noi khrup/kah
very spicy	ped ped
steamed	nueng
stir-fried	pad

ENGLISH	THAI
stir-fried with ginger	pad king
stir-fried hot and spicy	pad ped
grilled (use phao instead when referring to seafood)	ping
deep-fried	tawd
boiled	thom

BASIC INGREDIENTS

rice	khao
steamed rice	khao suay
fried rice	khao pad
sticky rice	khao niao
rice with curry sauce	khao gaeng
rice porridge (usually for breakfast)	joke
noodles	kuay theow
egg noodles	ba mee
egg	kai
vegetables	pak
meat	nua
pork	moo
chicken	gai
roast duck	bped
beef	nua (same as meat)
fish	pla
prawns	gung
squid	pla muek
crab	bpu
vegetarian	jay
galanga (herb)	ka
ginger	king
lemongrass	ta krai

ENGLISH	THAI
garlic	kratiam
fish sauce	nam pla
soy sauce	see-ew
chili paste (spicy dips usually accompanied by various vegetables)	nam prik
satay sauce (peanut base sauce made of crushed peanuts, coconut milk, chili, and curry)	satay

BEVERAGES

ice	nam kang
iced coffee	ga-fare-yen
coffee with milk	ga-fare sai noom
whisky	wis-gee
tea	nam charr
plain water	nam plao
soda water	nam soda
a sweet drink brewed from lemongrass	nam takrai
vodka	what gaa
gin	gin

APPETIZERS

spring rolls	por pia tawd
panfried rice noodles	mee krob
spicy raw papaya salad	som tam
spicy beef salad	yum nua

MEAT AND SEAFOOD

chicken fried with cashew nuts	gai pad med mamuang himmapan
spicy chicken with basil	gai ka-prao
grilled chicken	gai yang
curry soup	gaeng ga-ree
green curry soup	gaeng keow wan

ENGLISH	THAI
mild yellow curry soup	gaeng massaman
red curry soup	gaeng ped
hot and sour curry	kaeng som
minced meat with chilies and lime juice	larb
spicy salad	yum
panfried rice noodles	pad tai
"soup made with coconut cream, chicken, lemongrass, and chilies"	tom ka gai
lemongrass soup with shrimp and mushrooms	tom yum kung

FRUIT

banana	gluay
tamarind	ma karm
papaya	ma la gore
mango	ma muang
coconut	ma prao
mangosteen	mung kood
mandarin orange	som
pomegranate	tub tim

DESSERTS

dessert	ka nom
mango with sticky rice	kao niao ma muang
grilled bananas	gluay bping
coconut pudding	ka nom krog
rice based dessert cooked in coconut milk	kao larm
spicy raw papaya salad	som tam
spicy beef salad	yum nua

TRAVEL SMART
THAILAND

GETTING HERE AND AROUND

Thailand is a long country, stretching some 1,100 miles north to south. Bangkok is a major Asian travel hub, so you'll likely begin your trip by flying into the capital. Relatively affordable flights are available from Bangkok to every major city in the country, and if you're strapped for time, flying is a great way to get around. But train travel, where available, can be an enjoyable sightseeing experience if you're not in a rush, and Thailand also has a comprehensive bus system.

▎AIR TRAVEL

Bangkok is 17 hours from San Francisco, 18 hours from Seattle and Vancouver, 20 hours from Chicago, 22 hours from New York, and 10 hours from Sydney. Adjust accordingly for long stopovers and connections, especially if you're using more than one carrier. Be sure to check your itinerary carefully if you are transferring in Bangkok—most low-cost carriers and domestic flights now operate out of Don Muang airport, while Suvarnabhumi Airport remains the international hub. On popular tourist routes during peak holiday times, domestic flights in Thailand are often fully booked. Make sure you have reservations, and make them well in advance of your travel date. Be sure to reconfirm your return flight when you arrive in Thailand.

Airline Security Issues Transportation Security Administration. ⊕ www.tsa.gov.

AIRPORTS

Bangkok remains Thailand's gateway to the world. The look of that gateway changed several years ago with the opening of the new international Suvarnabhumi (pronounced *soo-wanna-poom*) Airport, 30 km (18 miles) southeast of town. The new airport quickly exceeded capacity, however, and Don Muang is back in service: almost all budget airlines and domestic flights now operate out of

Don Muang. Shuttle service is available between the two airports. Neither airport is close to the city, but both offer shuttle links and/or bus and taxi service throughout Bangkok. The smoothest ride to Suvarnabhumi is the BTS Skytrain, which now links the international airport with key areas in the city. Chiang Mai International Airport, which lies on the edge of that town, has a large new terminal to handle the recent sharp increases in national and regional air traffic. Taxi service to most hotels costs about B120 (about $4).

Perhaps Thailand's third-busiest airport (especially in high season) is the one at Phuket, a major link to the southern beaches region, particularly the islands of the Andaman Coast.

Bangkok Airways owns and runs the airports in Sukhothai, Trat, and Koh Samui. They have the only flights to these destinations, which can be expensive in high season. You also have to use the airport transport options they offer unless your hotel picks you up.

Airport Information Airports of Thailand. ⊕ www.airportthai.co.th. **Don Muang Airport.** ⊕ www.donmuangairportonline.com. **Suvarnabhumi Airport.** ⊕ www.suvarnabhumiairport.com.

GROUND TRANSPORTATION

At Suvarnabhumi, free shuttle buses run from the airport to a public bus stand, where you can catch a bus into the city. Many public buses stop near Don Muang; there's also a train stop across the highway from the airport, accessible by footbridge.

Meter taxis run between both airports and town and charge a B50 airport fee on top of the meter charge. Be sure to find the public taxis. (Touts are notorious for approaching travelers in the airport and offering rides at rates that far exceed the norm.) In December 2014, new automatic queue-card kiosks were opened outside gates 4 and 7 on the first floor; these are aimed at reducing the wait time for a taxi and smoothing the process. Taxis in town will often try to set a high flat fee to take you to the airport, though this is technically illegal. If you do talk a taxi driver into charging by the meter, expect a long, scenic trip to the airport.

Suvarnabhumi Airport offers several types of limousines for hire, 24 hours a day—visit the limo counter on Level 2 in the baggage claim hall.

If possible, plan your flights to arrive and depart outside of rush hours. A trip to Suvarnabhumi from the main hotel strip along Sukhumvit Road can take as little as 25 minutes if traffic is moving, but hours during traffic jams—the same goes for the Khao San Road area.

■ TIP→ It helps to have a hotel brochure or an address in Thai for the driver. Also, stop at one of the ATMs in the arrival hall and get some baht before leaving the airport so you can pay your taxi driver.

INTERNATIONAL FLIGHTS

Bangkok is one of Asia's—and the world's—largest air hubs, with flights to most corners of the globe and service from nearly all of the world's major carriers, plus dozens of minor carriers. Most flights from the United States stop in Hong Kong, Tokyo, China, Singapore, or Taipei on the way to Bangkok.

Delta and Japan Airlines (JAL) are both major carriers with hubs in the United States and offer daily flights between the United States and Thailand. JAL is one of the best options, with a flight time of 17 hours from Dallas including a stopover at Tokyo's Narita airport. East Coast travelers could also consider using American Airlines via Tokyo; Cathay Pacific via Hong Kong; or Air China via Beijing. From the West Coast, Thai Airways has connections from Los Angeles. Cathay Pacific often has good fares from San Francisco as well. Often the best prices can be found on sites such as Kayak (⊕ *www.kayak.com*) or Vayama (⊕ *www.vayama.com*).

■ TIP→ Some of the world's top-rated airlines for service—such as Cathay Pacific, Qatar, and Singapore—fly between the United States and Bangkok. These airlines (and Asian airlines in general) often have more comfortable seats, better food selections (still without extra charge), and more entertainment options than do most U.S.-based carriers. Many Asian airlines also allow you to change your bookings for free (or for a nominal charge) if done a week in advance. Lastly, tickets purchased from these carriers are generally no more expensive than those offered by U.S. carriers. And the extra creature comforts these airlines provide can leave you a little less frazzled when you reach your destination, ensuring that you don't spend half your vacation recovering from the trip over.

For years, Bangkok Airways offered the only direct flights between Bangkok and Siem Reap, Cambodia (home of Angkor Wat), with exorbitant prices. A cheaper alternative exists now: Cambodia Angkor Air. The airline flies throughout the region, as do several budget airlines, making short country-hopping excursions far more feasible than before.

Chiang Mai, Thailand's second-biggest city, is slowly becoming an important regional destination, and direct flights between here and Hong Kong, Singapore, Tokyo, Taipei, various points in China, Luang Prabang in Laos, and other Asian destinations may be available. However, these routes seem to change with the wind, so check before your trip. As Myanmar opens up, more travelers are adding that country to their regional itineraries. Several carriers—Thai, Bangkok Airways, Myanmar Airways International—offer regular nonstop flights between Bangkok and Yangon, as do budget carriers AirAsia and Nok.

In March 2015, the UN International Civil Aviation Organization reported "significant safety concerns" with Thailand's air safety practices. This caused some countries to block flights from Thailand, and as of this writing, Thai aviation authorities feared more flights to and from other countries might be affected. It's wise to check the latest safety reports on Thailand and its carriers before booking.

Airline Contacts American Airlines.
🖷 *800/433-7300* ⊕ *www.aa.com.* **Air China.**
🖷 *800/882-8122* ⊕ *www.airchina.us.* **Asiana Airlines.** 🖷 *800/227-4262* ⊕ *us.flyasiana. com.* **British Airways.** 🖷 *800/247-9297* ⊕ *www.britishairways.com.* **Cathay Pacific.** 🖷 *800/233-2742* ⊕ *www.cathaypacific. com.* **China Airlines.** 🖷 *800/227-5118* ⊕ *www.china-airlines.com.* **Delta Airlines.** 🖷 *888/750-3284 for U.S. reservations, 800/241-4141 for international reservations* ⊕ *www.delta.com.* **EVA Air.** 🖷 *800/695-1188* ⊕ *www.evaair.com.* **Japan Airlines.** 🖷 *800/525 3663* ⊕ *www.jal.com.* **Korean Air.** 🖷 *800/438-5000* ⊕ *www.koreanair. com.* **Lao Airlines.** 🖷 *21/513250 in Laos* ⊕ *www.laoairlines.com.* **Malaysia Airlines.** 🖷 *800/552-9264* ⊕ *www.malaysiaairlines.com.* **Qatar Airways.** 🖷 *877/777-2827* ⊕ *www. qatarairways.com.* **Royal Khmer Airlines.** 🖷 *855/2399-4888* ⊕ *www.royalkhmerairlines. com.* **Singapore Airlines.** 🖷 *800/742-3333* ⊕ *www.singaporeair.com.* **Thai Airways.** 🖷 *800/426-5204* ⊕ *www.thaiairwaysusa.com.* **United Airlines.** 🖷 *800/864-8331 for U.S. reservations, 800/864-8331* ⊕ *www.united.com.*

AIR TRAVEL WITHIN THAILAND

Thai Airways has by far the largest network of any airline in Thailand, and connects all major and many minor destinations across the country. Bangkok Airways, which bills itself as a luxury boutique airline with comfy seats and good food, covers many routes and is the only airline to service Koh Samui, Trat, and Sukhothai. Both Thai and Bangkok Airways fly a mix of larger jet aircraft and smaller turbo-props. In past years, buying tickets on the Thai Airways website was an act reserved for masochists, but it was easy (and cheaper) to go to a travel agent to get Thai Airways tickets. The websites of other Thai airlines generally work well for online bookings.

Budget airlines now cover Thailand's skies and have dramatically lowered the cost of travel. Best known are Nok Air (a subsidiary of Thai Airways), Thai AirAsia, and Orient Thai (parent company of the now-defunct One-Two-Go, which was grounded temporarily by the Thai government following a fatal crash in Phuket).

With budget carriers, you'll save the most by booking online and as far in advance as you can. There's a small fee for booking over the phone, and you may not get an English-speaking operator. The airlines keep their prices low by charging extra for services like food—or not offering it at all. They charge less for flights at odd hours (often late in the day), and change their schedules based on the availability of cheap landing and takeoff times. AirAsia, generally the cheapest of the budget carriers, seems to change its flight times and routes every couple of months.

■**TIP**➜ Delays are more common the later in the day you're flying, so if you need to make an international connection, morning flights are a safer bet.

Regional Carriers AirAsia. 🖷 *2/515-9999 in Thailand* ⊕ *www.airasia.com.* **Bangkok Airways.** 🖷 *2/270-6699 in Thailand* ⊕ *www. bangkokair.com.* **JetStar Asia.** 🖷 *649/99702, 866/397-8170* ⊕ *www.jetstar.com.* **Myanmar Airways International.** 🖷 *12/55260 in Myanmar* ⊕ *maiair.com/.* **Nok Air.** 🖷 *290/09955* ⊕ *www.nokair.com.* **Orient Thai Airlines.** 🖷 *2/2294-1001* ⊕ *flyorientthai.com/ en/home/.* **Silk Airlines.** 🖷 *053/904985 in Thailand* ⊕ *www.silkair.com.* **Thai Airways.** 🖷 *02/288-7000 in Thailand* ⊕ *www. thaiairways.com.* **Tiger Airways.** 🖷 *315/76434* ⊕ *www.tigerair.com/sg/en.*

▌ BUS TRAVEL

Thai buses are cheap and faster than trains, and reach every corner of the country. There are usually two to three buses a day on most routes and several daily (or even hourly) buses on popular routes between major towns. Most buses leave in the morning, with a few other runs spaced out in the afternoon and evening. Buses leave in the evening for long overnight trips. Overnight buses are very popular with Thais, and they're a more efficient use of time, but they do crash with disturbing regularity and many expats avoid them.

■ TIP→ Avoid taking private bus company trips from the Khao San Road area. The buses are not as comfortable as public buses, they take longer, and they usually try to trap you at an affiliated hotel once you reach your destination. This is particularly the case for cross-border travel into Cambodia. There have also been many reports of rip-offs, scams, and luggage thefts on these buses over the years.

There are, generally speaking, three classes of bus service: cheap, no-frills locals on short routes that stop at every road crossing and for anyone who waves them down; second and first-class buses on specific routes that have air-conditioning, toilets (sometimes), and loud chop-socky movies (too often); and VIP buses that provide nonstop service between major bus stations and have comfortable seats, drinks, snacks, air-conditioning, and movies (often starring Steven Seagal or Jean-Claude Van Damme). If you're setting out on a long bus journey, it's worth inquiring about the onboard entertainment—14 hours on a bus with continuous karaoke VCDs blasting out old pop hits can be torturous. Air-conditioned buses are usually so cold that you'll want an extra sweater. On local buses, space at the back soon fills up with all kinds of oversize luggage, so it's best to sit toward the middle or the front.

Bangkok has three main bus stations, serving routes to the north (Mo Chit), south (Southern Terminal), and east (Ekamai). Chiang Mai has one major terminal. All have telephone information lines, but the operators rarely speak English. It's best to buy tickets at the bus station, where the bigger bus companies have ticket windows. Thais usually just head to the station an hour before they'd like to leave; you may want to go a day early to be sure you get a ticket if your plans aren't flexible—especially if you hope to get VIP tickets. Travel agents can sometimes get tickets for you, but often the fee is more than half the cost of the ticket. All fares are paid in cash.

Many small towns don't have formal bus terminals, but rather a spot along a main road where buses stop. Information concerning schedules can be obtained from TAT offices and the bus stations.

■ CAR TRAVEL

Car travel in Thailand has its ups and downs. Major thoroughfares tend to be congested, but the limited number of roads and the straightforward layout of cities combine to make navigation relatively easy. The exception, of course, is Bangkok. Don't even think about negotiating that tangled mass of traffic-clogged streets. Hire a driver instead.

Cars are available for rent in Bangkok and in major tourist destinations. However, even outside Bangkok the additional cost of hiring a driver is a small price to pay for peace of mind. If a foreigner is involved in an automobile accident, he or she not the Thai—is likely to be judged at fault, no matter who hit whom.

That said, car rental can be the most pleasant, affordable way to tour the country's rural areas.

If you do decide to rent a car, know that traffic laws are routinely disregarded. Bigger vehicles have the unspoken right-of-way, motorcyclists seem to think they are invincible, and bicyclists often don't look around them. Few Thai drivers go anywhere anymore without a cell phone stuck to one ear. ■ TIP→ Drive very carefully, as those around you generally won't.

Police checkpoints are common, especially near international borders and in the restive south. You must stop for them, but will most likely be waved through.

Rental-company rates in Thailand begin at about $40 a day for a jeep or $50 for an economy car with unlimited mileage.

It's better to make your car-rental reservations when you arrive in Thailand, as you can usually secure a discount.

Jeeps and other vehicles are widely available for rent from private owners in tourist spots—particularly beach areas—and prices generally begin at about $25 a day. But be wary of the renter and any contract you sign (which might be in Thai). Often these vehicles come with no insurance that covers you, so you are liable for any damage incurred.

You must have an International Driving Permit (IDP) to drive or rent a car in Thailand. IDP's are not difficult to obtain, and having one in your wallet may save you from unwanted headaches if you do have to deal with local authorities. Check the AAA website for more info as well as for IDPs ($15) themselves.

GASOLINE
As of this writing, a liter of gasoline costs B33, just over $1. Many gas stations stay open 24 hours and have clean toilet facilities and minimarts. As you get farther away from developed areas, roadside stalls sell gasoline from bottles or tanks.

PARKING
You can park on most streets; no-parking areas are marked either with red-and-white bars on the curb or with circular blue signs with a red "don't" stroke through the middle. The less urban the area, the more likely locals will double- and triple-park to be as close as possible to their destination. Thai traffic police do "boot" cars and motorcycles that are improperly parked, though only when they feel like it. The ticketing officer usually leaves a sheet of paper with a contact number to call; once you call, he returns, you pay your fine (often subject to negotiation), and he removes the boot.

In cities the larger hotels, restaurants, and department stores have garages or parking lots. Rates vary, but count on B10 or more an hour. If you purchase something, parking is often free, but you must have your ticket validated.

ROAD CONDITIONS
Thai highways and town roads are generally quite good. Byways and rural roads range from good to indescribably bad. In rainy season expect rural dirt roads to be impassable bogs.

■TIP→ Leafy twigs and branches lying on a road are not decorations but warnings that something is amiss ahead. Slow down and proceed with caution.

Thai traffic signs will be familiar to all international drivers, though most roads are marked in Thai. Fortunately, larger roads, highways, and tourist attractions often have English signs, too. Signs aren't always clear, so you may find yourself asking for directions quite often—or just consult your smartphone and GPS.

If you have a choice, don't drive at night. Motorists out after dark often drive like maniacs, and may be drunk. Likewise, if you have a choice, avoid driving during key holidays such as Songkran. The Bangkok newspapers keep tallies of road deaths during each big holiday, and the numbers are enough to frighten anyone off the highway. When you are driving anywhere in the country, at all times beware of oxcarts, cows, dogs, small children, and people on bikes suddenly joining the traffic fray.

ROADSIDE EMERGENCIES
Should you run into any problems, you can contact the Tourist Police at their hotline, 1155.

RULES OF THE ROAD
As in the United Kingdom, drive on the left side of the road, even if the locals don't. Speed limits are 60 kph (37 mph) in cities, 90 kph (56 mph) outside, and 130 kph (81 mph) on expressways, not that anyone pays much heed. If you're caught breaking traffic laws, you officially have to report to the police station to pay a large fine. In reality, an on-the-spot fine of B100 or B200 can usually be paid. Never presume to have the right of way in Thailand, and always expect the other driver to do exactly what you think they should not.

MOTORCYCLE TRAVEL

Many people rent small motorcycles to get around the countryside or the islands. ■TIP→ A Thai city is not the place to learn how to drive a motorcycle. Phuket in particular is unforgiving to novices—don't think of driving one around there unless you are experienced. Motorcycles skid easily on wet or gravel roads. On Koh Samui a sign posts the year's count of foreigners who never made it home from their vacations because of such accidents. In the past people often did not bother to wear a helmet in the evening, but government crackdowns have made it common practice to drive as safely at night as during the day. Shoes, a shirt, and long pants will also offer some protection in wrecks, which are common. When driving a motorbike, make sure your vehicle has a rectangular sticker showing up-to-date insurance and registration. The sticker should be pasted somewhere toward the front of the bike, with the Buddhist year in big, bold numbers. You can rent smaller 100cc to 125cc motorcycles for only a few dollars a day. Dirt bikes and bigger road bikes, 250cc and above, start at about $25 per day.

Two-wheeled vacations are a growing segment of Thai tourism, especially in the north. With Thailand's crazy traffic, this is not a good option for first-time tourists to the area. That said, Golden Triangle Rider has a fantastic website (⊕ *www. gt-rider.com*) on biking in the area, with information on rentals and routes.

TAXI TRAVEL

Most Thai taxis now have meters installed, and these are the ones tourists should take. (However, the drivers of Chiang Mai's small fleet of "meter" taxis often demand flat fees instead. Bargain.) Taxis waiting at hotels are more likely to demand a high flat fare than those flagged down on the street. ■TIP→ Never enter any taxi until the price has been established or the driver agrees to use the meter. Most taxi drivers do not speak English, but all understand the finger count. One finger means B10, two is for B20, and so on. Whenever possible, ask at your hotel front desk what the approximate fare should be. If you flag down a meter taxi and the driver refuses to use the meter, you can try to negotiate a better fare or simply get another taxi. If you negotiate too much, he will simply take you on a long route to jack the meter price up.

TRAIN TRAVEL

Trains are a great way to get around Thailand. Though they're a bit slower and generally more expensive than buses, they're more comfortable and safer. They go to (or close to) most major tourist destinations, and many go through areas where major roads don't venture. The State Railway of Thailand has four lines, all of which terminate in Bangkok. Hualamphong is Bangkok's main terminal; you can book tickets for any route in the country there. (Chiang Mai's station is another major hub, where you can also buy tickets for any route.)

TRAIN ROUTES

The Northern Line connects Bangkok with Chiang Mai, passing through Ayutthaya, Phitsanulok, and Sukhothai. The Northeastern Line travels up to Nong Khai, on the Laotian border (across from Vientiane), and has a branch that goes east to Ubon Ratchathani. The Southern Line goes all the way south through Surat Thani (get off here for Koh Samui) to the Malaysian border and on to Kuala Lumpur and Singapore, a journey that takes 37 hours. The Eastern Line splits and goes to both Pattaya and Aranyaprathet on the Cambodian border. A short line also connects Bangkok with Nam Tok to the west, passing through Kanchanaburi and the bridge over the River Kwai along the way. (There's no train to Phuket; you have to go to the Phun Phin station, about 14 km [9 miles] from Surat Thani and change to a bus.) ■TIP→ The Southern Line has been attacked in insurgency-related violence. Check the security situation before booking a trip to the south.

TICKETS AND RAIL PASSES

The State Railway of Thailand offers two types of rail passes. Both are valid for 20 days of unlimited travel on all trains in either second or third class. The cheaper of the two does not include supplementary charges such as air-conditioning and berths. Ask at Bangkok's Hualamphong Station for up-to-date prices and purchasing; if the train is your primary mode of transportation, it may be worth it. If you don't plan to cover many miles by train, individual tickets are probably the way to go.

Even if you purchase a rail pass, you're not guaranteed seats on any particular train; you'll need to book these ahead of time through a travel agent or by visiting the advance booking office of the nearest train station. Seat reservations are required on some trains and are strongly advised on long-distance routes, especially if you want a sleeper on the Bangkok to Chiang Mai trip. Bangkok to Chiang Mai and other popular routes need to be booked several days in advance, especially during the popular tourist season between November and January, as well as during the Thai New Year in April. Tickets for shorter, less frequented routes can be bought a day in advance or, sometimes, right at the station before departure. Most travel agencies have information on train schedules, and many will book seats for you for a small fee, saving you a trip to the station.

The State Railway of Thailand's rather basic website has timetables, routes, available seats, and other information, but no way to book tickets. The British-based website Seat 61 also has lots of helpful information about train travel in Thailand. Train schedules in English are available from travel agents and from major railway stations.

CLASSES OF SERVICE

Local trains are generally pretty slow and can get crowded, but you'll never be lonely! On some local trains there's a choice between second and third class.

Most long-distance trains offer second- or third-class tickets, and some overnight trains to the north (Chiang Mai) and to the south offer first-class sleeping cabins. First-class sleepers have nice individual rooms for two to four people, but they are increasingly rare. If you have the chance, splurging on a first-class overnight cabin can be a unique, almost romantic experience. You'd be hard-pressed to find a first-class sleeper cabin this cheap anywhere else in the world (B1,453 for a Bangkok to Chiang Mai ticket).

Second-class cars have comfy padded bench seats or sleeper bunks with sheets and curtains. Tickets are about half the price of first-class (B881, Bangkok to Chiang Mai), and since the couchettes are quite comfortable, most westerners choose these. Second class is generally air-conditioned, but on overnight journeys you have a choice of air-conditioning or fan-cooled cars. The air-conditioning tends to be freezing (bring a sweater and socks) and leave you dehydrated. Sleeping next to an open train window can leave you deaf and covered in soot. It's your choice. Third-class cars have hard benches and no air-conditioning and are not recommended for overnight trips but they are wildly cheap.

Meals are served at your seat in first and second classes.

Information Chiang Mai Railway Station. ⌨ ⊕ www.thairailways.com/train-station. chiangmai.html. **Hualamphong Railway Station.** ☎ 1690 railway call center, ⊕ www. thairailways.com/train-station.bangkok. html. **Seat 61.** ⊕ seat61.com/Thailand.htm. **The State of the Railways of Thailand.** ⊕ www.railway.co.th/checktime/checktime. asp?lenguage=Eng.

▌ TUK-TUK TRAVEL

So-called because of their flatulent sound, these three-wheel cabs can be slightly less expensive than taxis, and are, because of their maneuverability, sometimes a more rapid form of travel through congested traffic. All tuk-tuk operators drive as if chased by hellhounds. Tuk-tuks are not very comfortable, require hard bargaining skills, are noisy, are very polluting, are very difficult to see out of if you are more than 4 feet tall, and subject you to the polluted air they create—so they're best used for short journeys, if at all. They are fun to take once, mildly amusing the second time, and fully unpleasant by the third.

If a tuk-tuk driver rolls up and offers to drive you to the other side of Bangkok for B20, think twice before accepting, because you will definitely be getting more than you bargained for. By dragging you along to his friend's gem store, tailor's shop, or handicraft showroom, he'll usually get a petrol voucher as commission. He'll tell you that all you need to do to help him put rice on his family's table is take a five-minute look around. Sometimes that's accurate, but sometimes you'll find it difficult to leave without buying something. It can be fun at times to go along with it all and watch everybody play out their little roles, but other times you really just want a ride to your chosen destination. Either way you end up paying for it.

ESSENTIALS

■ ACCOMMODATIONS

Nearly every town offers accommodation. In smaller towns hotels may be fairly simple, but they will usually be clean and inexpensive. In major cities or resort areas there are hotels to fit all price categories. The least-expensive places may have a fan rather than air-conditioning. Breakfast is sometimes included in the room rate at hotels and guesthouses.

During the peak tourist season hotels are often fully booked and rates are at their highest. During holidays, such as between December 30 and January 2, Chinese New Year (in January or February, depending on the year), and Songkran (the Thai New Year in April), rates climb even higher, and reservations are difficult to obtain on short notice. Weekday rates at some resorts are often lower, and virtually all hotels will discount their rooms if they are not fully booked. You often can get a deal by booking mid- to upper-range hotel rooms through Thai travel agents. They get a deeply discounted rate, part of which they then pass on to you.

Don't be reticent about asking for a special rate. Though it may feel awkward to haggle, because western hotel prices aren't negotiable, this practice is perfectly normal in Thailand. Often it will get you nothing, but occasionally it can save you up to 50% if you catch a manager in the right mood with a bunch of empty rooms. Give it a whirl. The worst they can say is "no."

The lodgings we list are the cream of the crop in each price category. When pricing accommodations, always ask what's included and what costs extra. Hotels have private bath unless otherwise noted.

APARTMENT AND HOUSE RENTALS

It is possible to rent apartments or houses for longer stays in most places in Thailand. Bangkok, Chiang Mai, Phuket, and Pattaya in particular have large expat and long-term tourist communities. Also, many hotels and guesthouses are willing to offer greatly reduced rates for long-term guests. Agents are available in all big cities, and are used to helping foreigners. Often they will be the only way to find an affordable place quickly in a city like Bangkok. The *Bangkok Post*, *Chiang Mai CityLife* magazine, *Chiang Mai Mail*, *Phuket Gazette*, and *Pattaya Mail* are all good places to begin looking for agents or places for rent.

GUESTHOUSES

Though the "guesthouse" label is tacked onto accommodations of all sizes and prices, guesthouses are generally smaller, cheaper, and more casual than hotels. They are often family-run, with small restaurants. The least-expensive rooms often have shared baths, and linens may not be included. At the other end of the spectrum, $35 will get you a room with all the amenities—air-conditioning, cable TV, en suite bathrooms, even Internet access—in just about every corner of the country.

■ TIP➔ **Even if you're traveling on a strict budget, make sure your room has window screens or a mosquito net.**

HOTELS

Thai luxury hotels are among the best in the world. Service is generally superb—polite and efficient—and most of the staff speak English. At the other end of the scale, budget lodgings are simple and basic—a room with little more than a bed. Expect any room costing more than the equivalent of $35 a night to come with hot water, air-conditioning, and a TV. Southeast Asian hotels traditionally have two twin beds. Make sure to ask for one big bed if that is your preference, though this is often two twins pushed together.

Many hotels have restaurants and offer room service throughout most of the day and night. Many will also be happy to make travel arrangements for you—for which they receive commissions. Use hotel safe-deposit boxes if they are offered.

■ COMMUNICATIONS

INTERNET

Most hotels and guesthouses now offer Wi-Fi connections. Some are free, others are not, and many can be very slow. This is, however, slowly starting to improve, and reliable Wi-Fi connections are becoming more common. Many hotels also have business centers that provide Internet access. Thais also love to do their digital work at hip coffee shops, just as the rest of the world does. Expect to pay western prices for that mocha latte.

Outside of large hotels and business centers, the electrical supply can be temperamental. Surging and dipping power supplies are normal, and power outages are not unheard-of.

Even many the smallest towns have Internet shops, although they are becoming less popular as more people have smartphones. Most restaurants and cafés offer Wi-Fi (with purchase). Shops used to dealing with foreigners often will allow you to connect a laptop. Typical Internet prices in tourist areas range from about B20 to B60 per hour, sometimes more in coffee shops. Larger hotels and resorts can charge a lot more, so make sure to ask in advance. Then again, many high-end resorts now offer free Wi-Fi, too.

Contacts Cybercafes. ⊕ *www.cybercafes.com.*

PHONES

The country code for Thailand is 66. When dialing a Thailand number from abroad, drop the initial 0 from the local area code.

To call Cambodia from overseas, dial the country code (855) and then the area code, omitting the first 0. The code for Phnom Penh is 023; for Siem Reap it's 063. Unfortunately, Cambodia's international lines are sometimes jammed; booking and requesting information through websites is consequently the best option. Almost all Internet shops offer overseas calling, which runs up to 50¢ a minute, depending on the location. Skype and other Internet calling options are often the easiest, cheapest methods for international calls—especially if you're in a place with free Wi-Fi.

To call Laos from overseas, dial the country code (856) and then the area code, omitting the first 0. The outgoing international code is 00, but IDD phones are rare. In cities, Wi-Fi is becoming more readily available and so, too, is the option of Skype.

To call Myanmar from overseas, dial the country code (95), and then the area code, omitting the first 0. The country is just starting to catch up, and communications are changing rapidly since the government lowered the price of a SIM card from $1,000-plus to just a few dollars. More and more Myanmar businesses now have websites, email addresses, and mobile-phone numbers. People are using Skype, too.

CALLING WITHIN THAILAND

There are numerous phone companies and cell-phone operators throughout the country. Pay phones are still widely available, and they generally work, though long-distance calls can only be made on phones that accept both B1 and B5 coins. But fewer people are using pay phones as most people now have smartphones.

CALLING OUTSIDE THAILAND

The country code for the United States is 1.

To make overseas calls, you can use either your hotel switchboard—Chiang Mai and Bangkok have direct dialing—or the overseas telephone facilities at the central post office and telecommunications building. You'll find one in all towns. But by far, it's easiest now to use Skype or another online service.

MOBILE PHONES AND SMARTPHONES

Mobile phone plans vary widely, and some in the United States offer free roaming throughout Thailand. Check with your service provider before leaving the United States. Otherwise, the roaming charges can be deadly. Many travelers use their cell phones to send and receive text messages, a cheap way to stay in touch.

Alternatively, if you have an unlocked mobile phone, you can buy a SIM card (the chip that keeps your phone number and account) in Thailand. These are often offered for free on arrival at Thai airports. Pop the SIM card into your phone, and have a local number while visiting. Then buy phone cards (available at all minimarts) in B100 to B500 denominations and pay for calls as you go, generally B3 to B10 a minute depending on the time of day and number you are calling. International calls will run about B5 to B40 a minute.

Another option is to buy a used phone at any cell-phone shop, which are ubiquitous (all malls in Thailand have them). You can usually find a used but reliable phone for $20 to $40.

Contacts Cellular Abroad. ☎ 800/287–5072 ⊕ www.cellularabroad.com. **Mobal.** ☎ 888/888–9162 ⊕ www.mobal.com. **Planet Fone.** ☎ 888/988–4777 ⊕ www.planetfone.com.

▐ CUSTOMS AND DUTIES

THAILAND

Most people pass through customs at Suvarnabhumi without even so much as a glance from a customs officer. Officers worry more about people smuggling opium across borders than they do about an extra bottle of wine or your new camera. That said, if you're bringing any exorbitantly expensive foreign-made equipment from home, such as cameras or video gear, it's wise to carry the original receipt with you or register it with U.S. Customs before you leave (Form 4457). Otherwise, you may end up paying duty on your return.

One liter of wine or liquor, 200 cigarettes or 250 grams of smoking tobacco, and all personal effects may be brought into Thailand duty-free. Visitors may bring in and leave with any amount of foreign currency; you cannot leave with more than B50,000 without obtaining a permit. Narcotics, pornographic materials, protected wild animals and wild animal parts, and firearms are strictly prohibited.

Some tourists dream of Thailand as a tropical paradise floating on a cloud of marijuana smoke—not so. Narcotics are strictly illegal, and jail terms for the transporting or possession of even the smallest amounts are extremely harsh.

If you purchase any Buddha images (originals or reproductions), artifacts, or true antiques and want to take them home, you need to get a certificate from the Fine Arts Department. Taking unregistered or unauthorized antiques out of the country is a major offense to the culture conscious Thais. If you get a particularly good reproduction of an antique, get a letter or certificate from the seller saying it is a reproduction, or risk losing it on your way out of the country. Art or antiques requiring export permits must be taken to one of the museums listed here at least a week before the departure date. You will have to fill out an application and provide two photographs—front and side views—of the object as well as a photocopy of your passport information page.

Antiques Permits Chiang Mai National Museum. ☎ 053/221308. **National Museum–Bangkok.** ☎ 02/224-1333.

CAMBODIA AND LAOS

You are allowed to bring 200 cigarettes or the equivalent in cigars or tobacco and one bottle of liquor into Cambodia. You are not allowed to bring in or take out local currency, nor are you allowed to remove Angkor antiquities (even though, sadly, they can be found for sale in shops across Thailand). The export of other antiques or religious objects requires a permit. Contact your embassy for assistance in obtaining one before laying out money on an expensive purchase.

Tourists are allowed to bring up to one liter of spirits and two liters of wine into Laos, as well as 200 cigarettes, 50 cigars, or 250 grams of tobacco. Bringing in or

LOCAL DO'S AND TABOOS

THE KING AND THE ROYAL FAMILY

King Bhumibol Adulyadej has ruled Thailand for more than 60 years, and is revered by his people. Any insult against him is an insult against the national religion and patrimony. Lighthearted remarks or comparisons to any other person living or dead are also taboo. These cautions extend to comments about anyone in the Royal Family. If you don't have something nice to say about the king or his relatives, don't say anything at all—it's an offense punishable by jail time.

GOOD MANNERS

Thais aim to live with a "cool heart" or *jai yen*—free from emotional extremes. Since being in a hurry shows an obvious lack of calm, they don't rush and aren't always punctual. Try to leave space in your itinerary for this relaxed attitude, since something will invariably happen to slow your progress.

Always remove your shoes when you enter a home. Do not step over a seated person's legs. Don't point your feet at anyone; keep them on the floor, and take care not to show the soles of your feet (as the lowest part of the body, they are seen by Buddhists as the least holy). Never touch a person's head, even a child's (the head is the most sacred part of the body in Buddhist cultures), and avoid touching a monk if you're a woman.

When possible do not give or receive anything with your left hand; use your right hand and support it lightly at the elbow with your left hand to show greater respect. Don't be touchy-feely in public. Speak softly and politely—a calm demeanor always accomplishes more than a hot-headed attitude. Displays of anger, raised voices, or even very direct speech are considered bad form.

Thais don't like anything done in twos, a number associated with death. Hence, you should buy three mangoes, not two; stairways have odd numbers of stairs; and people rarely want to have their photo taken if there are only two people.

Thais are devout Buddhists, and it's important for visitors to respect the religion. You might see scantily clad tourists visiting ancient temples—don't follow suit. Cover your arms and legs (no shorts or tank tops) and be respectful.

OUT ON THE TOWN

Many Thais drink and smoke, but smoking is banned in many public buildings (including restaurants and bars). While you might spot a few drunken Thais stumbling about on a Saturday night, public drunkenness is not any more welcome here than it would be at home. Backpackers who flock to Thailand for cheap beer and beach parties rarely leave a favorable impression on the locals.

DOING BUSINESS

Thais are polite and formal in their business doings, employing the same sense of propriety as in everyday life. In professional settings, it is always best to address people with the courtesy title, *khun* (for males and females). As anywhere, greet a business associate with a Buddhist *wai* (hands clasped, head bowed.)

Business cards are hugely popular in Southeast Asia and it's a good idea to have some on hand. You can have them made quickly and cheaply in Thailand if necessary.

taking out local currency is prohibited, as is the export of antiques and religious artifacts without a permit.

Note that the dissemination of foreign religious and political materials is forbidden, and you should refrain from bringing such materials into the country.

MYANMAR (BURMA)

Visitors to Myanmar are allowed to bring two bottles of liquor, 400 cigarettes, 100 cigars, 250 grams of tobacco and half a liter of perfume per person.

Thailand Contacts Thai Customs Department. ☎ 2/667-6000 ⊕ www.customs. go.th/wps/wcm/connect/custen/home/ homewelcome.

U.S. Information U.S. Customs and Border Protection. ⊕ www.cbp.gov.

▌ EATING OUT

Thai food is eaten with a fork and spoon; the spoon held in the right hand and the fork is used like a plow to push food into the spoon. Chopsticks are used only for Chinese food, such as noodle dishes. After you have finished eating, place your fork and spoon on the plate at the 5:25 position; otherwise the server will assume you would like another helping.

If you want to catch a waiter's attention, use the all-purpose polite word, *krup* if you are a man and *ka* if you are a woman. Beckoning with a hand and fingers pointed upward is considered rude; point your fingers downward instead.

MEALS AND MEALTIMES

Thai cuisine's distinctive flavor comes particularly from the use of fresh Thai basil, lemongrass, tamarind, lime, and citrus leaves. And though some Thai food is fiery hot from garlic and chilies, an equal number of dishes serve the spices on the side, so that you can adjust the incendiary level. Thais use *nam pla,* a fish sauce, instead of salt.

Restaurant hours vary, but Thais eat at all times of day, and in cities you will find eateries open through the night. In Thailand breakfast outside the hotel often means noodle soup or curry on the street (or banana pancakes in backpacker areas). Street vendors also sell coffee, although die-hard caffeine addicts may not get enough of a fix; Thai coffee isn't simply coffee, but a combination of ground beans with nuts and spices. If you're desperate, look for a western-style espresso machine or a Chinese coffee shop.

The lunch hour is long—roughly 11:30 to 2—in smaller towns and rural areas, a holdover from when Thailand was primarily a country of rice farmers and everyone napped during the hottest hours of the day.

Unless otherwise noted, the restaurants listed *in this guide* are open daily for lunch and dinner.

PAYING

Expect to pay for most meals in cash. Larger hotels and fancy restaurants in metropolitan areas accept some major credit cards, but they will often charge an extra 2% to 4% for the convenience. If you are at the restaurant of the hotel where you are staying, you can generally just add the bill to your room and leave a cash tip if you desire. Street vendors and small, local restaurants only accept cash. *(see Tipping, below.)*

RESERVATIONS AND DRESS

Generally, reservations are not necessary at Thai restaurants, and even then are only accepted at the most expensive and popular ones.

Because Thailand has a hot climate, jackets and ties are rarely worn at dinner except in expensive hotel restaurants. Attire tends to fit the setting: people dress casually at simple restaurants and in small towns, but the Bangkok and Chiang Mai elite love dressing to the hilt for a posh night on the town. We mention dress only when men are required to wear a jacket or tie.

WINES, BEER, AND SPIRITS

Singha, Tiger, and Heineken are at the top end of Thailand's beer market, while Chang, Leo, and a host of other brands fight it out for the budget drinkers. It's also becoming more common to find imports such as Guinness, Corona, Budweiser, and the ever-popular Beerlao lining the shelves of cosmopolitan bars.

If you want to drink like the hip locals, don't bother with beer. Grab a bottle of whisky (Chivas Regal, Johnnie Walker, or the very affordable 100 Pipers) to mix with soda.

Rice whisky, which tastes sweet and has a whopping 35% alcohol content, is another favorite throughout Thailand. It tastes and mixes more like rum than whisky. Mekong and Sam Song are by far the most popular rice whiskies, but you will also see labels such as Kwangthong, Hong Thong, Hong Ngoen, Hong Yok, and Hong Tho. Thais mix their rice whisky with soda water, though it goes great with Coke, too.

Many Thais are just beginning to develop a taste for wine, and the foreign tipples on offer are expensive and generally mediocre. Thirty years ago the king first brought up the idea of growing grapes for wine and fruit through his Royal Projects Foundation. Now both fruit- and grape-based wines are made in various places up-country. Their quality generally does not match international offerings (they tend to taste better if you don't think of them as wines, as such), but some are quite pleasant. International markets often carry them, and they can occasionally be found on the menus of larger restaurants.

■ ELECTRICITY

The electrical current in Thailand is 220 volts, 50 cycles alternating current (AC); wall outlets take either two flat prongs, like outlets in the United States, or Continental-type plugs, with two round prongs, or sometimes both. Plug adapters are cheap and can be found without

great difficulty in tourist areas and electrical shops. Outlets outside expensive international hotels are rarely grounded, so use caution when plugging in delicate electronic equipment like laptops.

In Cambodia, Laos, and Myanmar the electrical current is 220 volts AC, 50 Hz. In Laos, outside Vientiane and Luang Prabang, electricity is spotty, and even in Luang Prabang there are frequent late-afternoon outages in hot weather. In Myanmar, locals joke that Yangon (Rangoon) is so advanced, the city has power six times a day. Actually, many cities throughout the region suffer power outages as development and demand exceed supply.

Consider making a small investment in a universal adapter, which has several types of plugs in one lightweight, compact unit. Most laptops and mobile-phone chargers are dual voltage (i.e., they operate equally well on 110 and 220 volts), so require only an adapter. These days the same is true of small appliances such as hair dryers. Always check labels and manufacturer instructions to be sure. Don't use 110-volt outlets marked "For shavers only" for high-wattage appliances such as hair dryers.

Contacts Walkabout Travel Gear. ⊕ *www.walkabouttravelgear.com.*

■ EMERGENCIES

Thais are generally quite helpful, so you should get assistance from locals if you need it. The Tourist Police will help you in case of a robbery or rip-off. The Tourist Police hotline is *1155.*

Many hotels can refer you to an English-speaking doctor. Major cities in Thailand have some of Southeast Asia's best hospitals, and the country is quickly becoming a "medical holiday" destination (i.e., a cost-effective place to have plastic surgery, dental work). However, if you are still wary about treating serious health problems in Thailand, you can fly cheaply to Singapore for the best medical care in the region.

Most nations maintain diplomatic relations with Thailand and have embassies in Bangkok; a few have consulates also in Chiang Mai.

In Bangkok U.S. Embassy. ⊠ *95 Wireless Rd.* ☎ *2/205–4000* ⊕ *www.bangkok.usembassy.gov/.*

In Chiang Mai U.S. Consulate. ⊠ *387 Wichaynond Rd.* ☎ *053/107700* ⊕ *www. chiangmai.usconsulate.gov/.*

In Phnom Penh, Cambodia U.S. Embassy. ⊠ *No. 1 St. 96, behind Wat Phnom* ☎ *023/728000* ⊕ *cambodia.usembassy.gov/.*

In Vientiane, Laos U.S. Embassy. ⊠ *Thadeua Rd KM9, Ban Somvang Tai, Hatsayfong District* ☎ *21/487000* ⊕ *www.laos.usembassy.gov/.*

In Yangon, Myanmar U.S. Embassy Rangoon. ⊠ *110 University Ave., Kamayut Township, Yangon (Rangoon)* ☎ *1/500547* ⊕ *burma.usembassy.gov.*

General Emergency Contacts Police. ☎ *191.* **Tourist Police.** ☎ *1155.*

∎ HEALTH

The most common vacation sickness in Thailand is traveler's diarrhea. You can take some solace in knowing that it is also the most common affliction of the locals. It generally comes from eating contaminated food, be it fruit, veggies, unclean water, or badly prepared or stored foods—really anything. It can also be triggered by a change in diet. Avoid ice unless you know it comes from clean water, uncooked or undercooked foods (particularly seafood, sometimes served raw in salads), and unpasteurized dairy products. ∎TIP→ **Drink only bottled water or water that has been boiled for at least 20 minutes, even when brushing your teeth.** The water served in pitchers at small restaurants or in hotel rooms is generally safe, as it is either boiled or from a larger bottle of purified water, though if you have any suspicions about its origins, it's best to go with your gut feeling.

The best way to treat "Bangkok belly" is to wait for it to pass. Take Pepto-Bismol to help ease your discomfort and if you must travel, take Imodium (known generically as loperamide), which will immobilize your lower gut and everything in it. It doesn't cure the problem, but simply postpones it until a more convenient time. Note that if you have a serious stomach sickness, taking Imodium can occasionally intensify the problem, leading to a debilitating fever and sickness. If at any time you get a high fever with stomach sickness, find a doctor.

If you have frequent, watery diarrhea for more than two days, see a doctor for diagnosis and treatment. Days of sickness can leave you seriously dehydrated and weak in the tropics.

In any case, drink plenty of purified water or tea—chamomile, lemongrass, and ginger are good choices. In severe cases, rehydrate yourself with a salt-sugar solution (½ teaspoon salt and 4 tablespoons sugar per quart of water) or rehydration salts, available at any pharmacy.

SHOTS AND MEDICATIONS
∎TIP→ **No vaccinations are required to enter Thailand, but we strongly recommend the hepatitis A vaccination as well as typhoid; and you should make sure your tetanus and polio vaccinations are up-to-date, as well as measles, mumps, and rubella.**

Malaria and dengue fever are also possible (though remote) risks as you move out of the main tourist areas. There is much debate about whether travelers headed to Thailand should take malarial prophylactics. Though many western doctors recommend that you take antimalarials, many health-care workers in Thailand believe they can do more harm than good: they can have side effects, they are not 100% effective, they can mask the symptoms of the disease if you do contract it, and they can make treatment more complicated. Consult your physician, see what medications your insurance will cover, and do what makes you feel most comfortable.

There are no prophylactics available for dengue fever. The best way to prevent mosquito-borne illness is to protect yourself against mosquitoes as much as possible *(Specific Issues in Thailand, below)*. According to the U.S. government's National Centers for Disease Control (CDC) there's also a risk of hepatitis B, rabies, and Japanese encephalitis in rural areas of Thailand, as well as drug-resistant malaria near the Myanmar border and in parts of Cambodia. In most urban or easily accessible areas you need not worry. However, if you plan to visit remote regions or stay for more than six weeks, check with the CDC's International Travelers Hotline.

Health Warnings National Centers for Disease Control & Prevention (CDC). 📠 *800/232-4636 International travelers' health line* ⊕ *www.cdc.gov/travel.* **World Health Organization (WHO).** ⊕ *www.who.int/en.*

SPECIFIC ISSUES IN THAILAND

The avian flu crisis that ripped through Southeast Asia at the start of the 21st century had a devastating impact on Thailand. Poultry farmers went out of business, tourists stayed away, and each week brought news of a new species found to be infected (including isolated cases of humans contracting the virus). At this writing, the worry has died down as human cases continue to be exceedingly rare. That doesn't mean it won't flare up again, but note that all cases have occurred in rural areas outside the tourist track, and most infected people dealt with large numbers of dead birds.

Malaria and dengue fever, though more common than bird flu, are still fairly rare in well-traveled areas. Malarial mosquitoes generally fly from dusk to dawn, while dengue carriers do the opposite; both are most numerous during the rainy season, as they breed in stagnant water.

The best policy is to avoid being bitten. To that end, wear light-color clothing and some form of insect repellent (preferably containing DEET) on any exposed skin when out and about in the mornings and evenings, especially during the rainy season. Make sure that hotel rooms have air-conditioning, mosquito nets over the bed, good screens over windows, or some combination thereof. You can also use a bug spray (available everywhere) in your room before heading out to dinner, and return to a bug-free room. ■TIP➔ The ubiquitous bottles of menthol-scented Siang Pure Oil both ward off mosquitoes and stop the incessant itching of bites.

Dengue fever tends to appear with a sudden high fever, sweating, headache, joint and muscle pain (where it got the name "breakbone fever"), and nausea. A rash of red spots on the chest or legs is a telltale sign. Malaria offers a raft of symptoms, including fever, chills, headache, sweating, diarrhea, and abdominal pain. A key sign is the recurrent nature of the symptoms, coming in waves every day or two.

Find a doctor immediately if you think you may have either disease. In Thailand, the test for both is quick and accurate and the doctors are much more accustomed to treating these diseases than are doctors in the United States. Left untreated, both diseases can quickly become serious, possibly fatal. Even when properly treated, dengue has a long recovery period, leaving the victim debilitated for weeks, sometimes months.

Reliable condoms in a variety of brands and styles are available at most 7-Elevens, supermarkets, and minimarts, usually near the checkout counter. ■TIP➔ Be aware that a high percentage of sex workers in Thailand are HIV positive, and unprotected sex is extremely risky.

Do not fly within 24 hours of scuba diving, as you may risk decompression sickness, which is caused by tiny bubbles forming in the body if you move from deep water (higher pressure) to the surface (lower pressure) too quickly. The water pressure while diving causes nitrogen in the air you are breathing to dissolve in your blood. Quickly encountering low pressure (whether from surfacing rapidly, flying at altitude, or even driving over mountain passes) can cause sickness if your body has not had time to off-gas the nitrogen.

OVER-THE-COUNTER REMEDIES

Thailand has nearly every drug known to the western world, and many that aren't. All are readily available at pharmacies throughout the country. They are also often cheaper than in the United States, and many drugs don't require the prescriptions and doctor visits needed at home. Be wary, however, of fake medications. It's best to visit larger, well-established pharmacies that locals vouch for.

▌ HOURS OF OPERATION

Thai business hours generally follow the 9 to 5 model, though the smaller the business, the more eclectic the hours. Nearly all businesses either close or slow to a halt during lunch hour—don't expect to accomplish anything important at this time. Many tourist businesses in the north and on the beaches and islands in the south often shut down outside the main tourist seasons of November through January and June through August.

Thai and foreign banks are open weekdays 8:30 to 3:30 (sometimes longer), except for public holidays. Most commercial concerns in Bangkok operate on a five-day week and are open 8 to 5. Government offices are generally open weekdays 8:30 to 4:30, with a noon to 1 lunch break. Generally speaking, avoid visiting any sort of office during the Thai lunch hour—or bring a book to pass the time.

Gas stations in Thailand are usually open at least 8 to 8 daily; many, particularly those on the highways, are open 24 hours a day. Twenty-four-hour minimart-style gas stations are growing in popularity. Many also have fast-food restaurants and convenience stores.

Each museum keeps its own hours and may select a different day of the week to close (though it's usually Monday); it's best to call before visiting.

Temples are generally open to visitors from 7 or 8 in the morning to 5 or 6 pm, but in truth they don't really have set hours. If a compound has gates, they open at dawn to allow the monks to do their rounds. Outside of major tourist sights like Wat Po in Bangkok, few temples appear to have fixed closing times.

Most pharmacies are open daily 9 to 9. You'll find a few 24-hour pharmacies in tourist areas.

Most small stores are open daily 8 to 8, whereas department and chain stores are usually open from 10 until 10.

HOLIDAYS

Thailand: New Year's Day (January 1); Chinese New Year (January 28, 2017); Makha Bhucha Day (on the full moon of the third lunar month); Chakri Day (April 6); Songkran (mid-April); Labor Day (May 1); Coronation Day (May 5); Ploughing Day (May 9); Visakha Bucha (May, on the full moon of the sixth lunar month); Buddhist Lent day (July); Queen's Birthday (August 12); Chulalongkorn Memorial Day (October 23); King's Birthday (December 5); Constitution Day (December 10). Government offices, banks, commercial concerns, and department stores are usually closed on these days, but smaller shops stay open.

Cambodia: New Year's Day (January 1); Victory Day (January 7); Meak Bochea Day (February); International Women's Day (March 8); Cambodian New Year (mid-April, depending on the lunar cycle); Labor Day (May 1); Visak Bochea (the Buddha's Birthday, early May); King Sihamoni's birthday (May 13–15); Visaka Bochea (May 19); Royal Ploughing Ceremony (May); International Children's Day (June 1); Queen Mother's birthday (June 18); Pchum Ben (September); Constitution Day (September 24); Anniversary of Paris Peace Agreement (October 23); Coronation Day (October 29); Sihanouk's birthday (October 31); Independence Day (November 9); Water Festival (November); Human Rights Day (December 10).

Laos: New Year's Day (January 1); Pathet Lao Day (January 6); Army Day (late January); International Women Day (March 8); Day of the People's Party (March 22); Lao New Year (Water Festival, April 13–15); Labor Day (May 1); Buddha Day (May 2); Children's Day (June 1); Lao Issara (August 13); Day of Liberation (October 12); National Day (December 2).

Myanmar: Independence Day (January 4); Union Day (February 12); Peasants' Day (March 2); Full Moon of Tabaung (March); Armed Forces Day (March 27); Thingyan (April); Burmese New Year (April); Labor Day (May 1); Buddha's Birthday (May 25); Martyr's Day (July 19); Buddhist Lent (July); Thadingyut, End of Lent (October); Full Moon of Thauzangmone (November); National Day (December 8); Christmas Day (December 25).

LANGUAGE

Thai is the country's national language. It has five tones, which makes it confusing to most foreigners. Thankfully, Thais tend to be patient with people trying to speak their language, and will often guess what you are trying to say, even if it's badly mispronounced. In polite conversation, a male speaker will use the word "krup" to end a sentence or to acknowledge what someone has said. Female speakers use "ka." It's easy to speak a few words, such as "sawahdee krup" or "sawahdee ka" (good day) and "khop khun krup" or "khop khun ka" (thank you).

With the exception of taxi drivers, Thais working with travelers in the resort and tourist areas of Thailand generally speak sufficient English to permit basic communication. If you find yourself truly unable to communicate something important to a Thai, he or she will often start grabbing people from the street at random to see if they speak English to help you out.

MAIL

Thailand's mail service is generally reliable and efficient. It is a good idea—and cheap—to send all packages registered mail. Major hotels provide basic postal services.

If something must get to its destination quickly, send it via FedEx, UPS, or DHL, which have branches in the major tourist centers. "Overnight" shipping time from Thailand to the United States via these international carriers is actually at least two working days. Expect to pay at least B800 to B1,000 for an "overnight" letter. Major offices of the Thailand Post also offer overseas express mail service (EMS), though it usually takes longer than an international carrier and costs nearly as much.

Letter, packet, and parcel rates through the Thailand Post are low—B30 for a letter to the United States, B25 for a letter to Europe. Allow at least 10 days for your mail to arrive. A sea, air, and land service (SAL) is available for less urgent mail at a much cheaper rate. Note it can take up to three months for packages to reach their destination by this method. Bangkok's central general post office on Charoen Krung (New Road) is open weekdays 8 to 8, weekends and public holidays 8 to 1. Up-country post offices close at 4:30 pm.

Post offices in major towns are often quite crowded. Never go to a post office during lunch hour unless you bring a book and a mountain of patience.

If you need to receive mail in Bangkok, have it sent to you "poste restante" at the following address: Poste Restante, General Post Office, Bangkok, Thailand. There's a small charge for each piece collected. Thais write their last name first, so be sure to have your last name written in capital letters and underlined.

SHIPPING PACKAGES

Parcels are easy to send from Thailand via Thai Post. Rates vary according to weight, destination, and shipping style (air or surface). Expect to pay between B700 and B1,100 for a kilo package shipped by sea, which will take up to three months to arrive in the United States and another additional B300 to B350 per additional kilo. Most shops catering to tourists will offer to pack and ship your purchases anywhere in the world, usually at very reasonable rates. If you want to ship a larger piece, most furniture and antiques stores can help with freight shipping.

Although thousands of travelers have had no problems with the Thai Post, there has been at least one major incident of postal larceny in Chiang Mai, so if you're shipping something precious, consider paying the extra money to send it by an international courier like DHL, Federal Express, or UPS.

Express Services DHL Worldwide. ⊠ *Chidlom BTS station, Room No. E1-1, Ploenchit Rd., Lumphini, Bangkok ✛ Exit to Grand Hyatt Erawan Hotel* ☎ *02/650–3550.* **Federal Express.** ⊠ *8th fl., Green Tower, Rama IV, Bangkok* ☎ *2/229–8900 Bangkok hotline.* **UPS.** ⊠ *16/1 Sukhumvit Soi 44/1, Bangkok* ☎ *272/89000.*

▋ MONEY

It's possible to live and travel quite inexpensively if you do as Thais do—eat in small, neighborhood restaurants, use buses, and stay at non-air-conditioned hotels. Traveling this way, two people could easily get by on $50 a day or less. Once you start enjoying a little luxury, prices can jump as much as you let them. Imported items are heavily taxed.

Resort areas and Bangkok are much pricier than other parts of the country.

Prices here are given for adults. Substantially reduced fees are almost always available for children, students, and senior citizens.

ATMS AND BANKS

Your own bank will probably charge a fee for using ATMs abroad, as will the foreign bank you use. Nevertheless, you'll usually get a better rate of exchange at an ATM than you will at a currency-exchange office or even when changing money in a bank.

■TIP→ **PIN numbers with more than four digits are not recognized at ATMs in many countries. If yours has five or more, remember to change it before you leave.**

Even smaller towns have ATMs. Most accept foreign bank cards; all pay in baht. As of this writing, most Thai ATMs charge extra B150 ($5) fee per transaction, plus your home bank may well add extra fees for using a foreign bank and/or converting foreign currency. Do contact your bank and ask about this before leaving to avoid any nasty billing surprises. Some Thai ATMs take Cirrus, some take Plus, some take both.

CREDIT CARDS

It's a good idea to inform your credit-card company and the bank that issues your ATM card before you travel, especially if you don't travel internationally very often. Otherwise, the credit-card company might put a hold on your card owing to unusual activity—not a good thing halfway through your trip. Record all your credit-card numbers—as well as the phone numbers to call if your cards are lost or stolen—in a safe place, so you're prepared should something go wrong. Both MasterCard and Visa have general numbers you can call (collect if you're abroad) if your card is lost, but you're better off calling the number of your issuing bank, since MasterCard and Visa usually just transfer you to your bank; your bank's number is usually printed on your card.

If you plan to use your credit card for cash advances, you'll need to apply for a PIN at least two weeks before your trip. Although it's usually cheaper (and safer) to use a credit card abroad for large purchases (so you can cancel payments or be reimbursed if there's a problem), note that some credit-card companies *and* the banks that issue them add substantial percentages to all foreign transactions, whether they're in a foreign currency or not. Check on these fees before leaving home, so there won't be any surprises when you get the bill.

■TIP→ Before you charge something at shops, restaurants or hotels that cater to tourists, ask the merchant whether he or she plans to do a dynamic currency conversion (DCC). In such a transaction the credit-card processor (shop, restaurant, or hotel, not Visa or MasterCard) converts the currency and charges you in dollars. In most cases you'll pay the merchant a 3% fee for this service in addition to any credit-card company and issuing-bank foreign-transaction surcharges.

Dynamic currency conversion programs are becoming increasingly widespread. Merchants who participate in them are supposed to ask whether you want to be charged in dollars or the local currency, but they don't always do so. And even if they do offer you a choice, they may well avoid mentioning the additional surcharges. The good news is that you *do* have a choice. And if this practice really gets your goat, you can avoid it entirely thanks to American Express; with its cards, DCC simply isn't an option.

Credit cards are almost always accepted at upper-end hotels, resorts, boutique stores, and shopping malls, and that list is slowly expanding. Expect to pay a 2% to 4% service charge. It is often illegal, but that's what everyone does.

Reporting Lost Cards American Express. ☎ 800/528-4800 ⊕ www.americanexpress. com. **Diners Club.** ☎ 800/2-DINERS, ⊕ www. dinersclub.com. **MasterCard.** ☎ 800/307-7309 in U.S., 800/11-887-0663 Thailand ⊕ www. mastercard.com. **Visa.** ☎ 800/847-2911 in U.S., 800/11-535-0660 Thailand ⊕ www.visa.com.

WORST-CASE SCENARIO

Your money and credit cards have just been stolen. These days, this shouldn't ruin your vacation. First, report the theft of the credit cards, then replace get any traveler's checks you were carrying.

Overseas Citizens Services. The U.S. State Department's Overseas Citizens Services can wire money to any U.S. consulate or embassy abroad for a fee. Just have someone back home wire money or send a money order or cashier's check to the state department, which will then disburse the funds. ☎ 888/407-4747.

Western Union. Western Union sends money almost anywhere. Have someone back home order a transfer online, over the phone, or at one of the company's offices. ☎ 800/325-6000 ⊕ www.westernunion.com.

CURRENCY AND EXCHANGE

The basic unit of currency is the baht. There are 100 satang to one baht. Baht come in six different bills, each a different color: B10, brown; B20, green; B50, blue; B100, red; B500, purple; and B1,000, beige. Coins in use are 25 satang, 50 satang, B1, B2, B5, and B10. The B10 coin has a gold-color center surrounded by silver.

Major hotels will convert traveler's checks and major currencies into baht, though exchange rates are better at banks and authorized money changers. The rate tends to be better in any larger city than up-country, and is better in Thailand than in the United States.

At this writing, B35 = US$1.

CURRENCY CONVERSION
Oanda.com. Oanda.com allows you to print out a handy table with the current day's conversion rates. ⊕ www.oanda.com.

XE.com. XE.com is a good currency conversion website. ⊕ www.xe.com.

■TIP→ Even if a currency-exchange booth has a sign promising no commission, rest assured that there's some kind of huge, hidden fee. (Oh, that's right. The sign didn't say no fee.) And as for rates, you're almost always better off getting foreign currency at an ATM or exchanging money at a bank.

PACKING

Light cotton or other natural-fiber clothing is appropriate for Thailand; drip-dry is an especially good idea, because the tropical sun and high humidity encourage frequent changes of clothing. Avoid delicate fabrics, because you may have difficulty getting them laundered. A sweater is welcome on cool evenings or in overly air-conditioned restaurants, buses, and trains.

The paths leading to temples can be rough, so bring a sturdy pair of walking shoes. Slip-ons are preferable to lace-up shoes, as they must be removed before you enter shrines and temples.

Bring a hat and UV-protection sunglasses and use them. The tropical sun is powerful, and its effects long-lasting and painful.

Thailand has a huge range of clothing options at good prices, though it may be difficult to find the right sizes if you're not petite.

PASSPORTS AND VISAS

U.S. citizens arriving by air need only a valid passport, not a prearranged visa, to visit Thailand for less than 30 days. Technically, travelers need an outgoing ticket and "adequate finances" for the duration of their Thailand stay to receive a 30-day stamp upon entry, though authorities in Bangkok rarely check your finances. They do occasionally ask to see an outbound ticket. Scrutiny is inconsistent; authorities periodically crack down on long-term tourists who try to hang out in Thailand indefinitely by making monthly "visa runs" across international borders.

■TIP→ Tourists who arrive in Thailand by land from a neighboring country are now granted only a 14-day visa. As of this writing, tourists are not allowed to spend more than 90 days of any six-month period in Thailand, and immigration officials sometimes opt to count days and stamps in your passport.

If for whatever reason you are traveling to Thailand on a one-way ticket, airline officials might ask you to sign a waiver before allowing you to board, relieving them of responsibility should you be turned away at immigration.

If you want to stay longer than one month, you can apply for a 60-day tourist visa through a Royal Thai embassy. The embassy in Washington, D.C., charges about $40 for this visa, and you'll need to show them a round-trip ticket and a current bank statement to prove you can afford the trip. Be sure to apply for the correct number of entries; for example, if you're going to Laos for a few days in the middle of your stay, you'll need to apply for two Thailand entries.

Tourist visas can also be extended one month at a time once you're in Thailand. You must apply in person at a Thai immigration office; expect the process to take a day. Your application will be granted at the discretion of the immigration office where you apply.

If you overstay your visa by a day or two, you'll have to pay a B500 fine for each day overstayed when you leave the country. Recently, immigration officials have reportedly started jailing foreigners who overstay by more than six weeks. And, since the military junta took control in 2014, who knows what will happen with visa requirements and services in the future.

U.S. Passport Information
U.S. Department of State. ☎ *877/487–2778* ⊕ *travel.state.gov/passport.*

Visa Extensions Bangkok Immigration.
✉ *Soi Suan Phlu, S. Sathorn Rd., Bangkok*
☏ *02/141–9889.* **Chiang Mai Immigration.** ✉ *71 Moo 3 Sanambin Rd., Chiang Mai* ☏ *053/277510.* **Royal Thai Embassy in Washington, D.C.** ☏ *202/944–3600* ⊕ *www.thaiembdc.org.*

▮ RESTROOMS

Western-style facilities are usually available, although you still may find squat toilets in older buildings. For the uninitiated, squat toilets can be something of a puzzle. You will doubtless find a method that works best for you, but here's a general guide: squat down with feet on either side of the basin and use one hand to keep your clothes out of the way and the other for balance or, if you're really good, holding your newspaper. The Thai version of a bidet is either a hose or a big tank of water with a bowl. If you've had the foresight to bring tissues with you, throw the used paper into the basket alongside the basin. Finally, pour bowls of water into the toilet to flush it—and after thoroughly washing your hands, give yourself a pat on the back. Except at plusher hotels and restaurants, plumbing in most buildings is archaic, so resist the temptation to flush your paper unless you want to be remembered as the foreigner who ruined the toilet.

▮ SAFETY

You should not travel in the four southern provinces closest to the Malaysian border: Yala, Pattani, Songkhla, and Narathiwat. A low-grade and seemingly endless insurgency there, which began in 2004, has led to the deaths of more than 6,000, with more than 10,000 injured. Although the insurgents originally targeted government institutions and officials, they have also bombed tourist centers, shopping malls, restaurants, trains, and the airport at Hat Yai. Fear permeates both Buddhist and Muslim communities in these southern

provinces; often locals have no idea who is attacking or why. Witnesses to drive-bys and bombings are afraid to speak. Residents avoid driving at night, shops close early, and southern towns turn eerily quiet by sundown.

In spring 2010 political demonstrations in Bangkok resulted in the worst outbreaks of violence in decades. Demonstrations continued through May 2014, when the military seized control in a coup. At this writing, the political situation remains tenuous and the military remains in control, though day-to-day life in Thailand is generally not affected. Stay informed about local developments as best you can, and determine whether the possible dangers make you too uneasy to travel or stay in Thailand. The *Bangkok Post* (⊕ *www.bangkokpost.com*) and the *Nation* (⊕ *www.nationmultimedia.com*) are the best sources of local news.

Thailand is generally a safe country, and millions of foreigners visit each year without incident. That said, every year a few tourists are attacked or raped and murdered, generally either in Bangkok or in the southern beaches regions. Be careful at night, particularly in poorly lighted areas or on lonely beaches. Follow other normal precautions: watch your valuables in crowded areas and lock your hotel rooms securely. Thai crooks generally try to relieve you of cash through crimes of convenience or negligence, not violence.

Credit-card scams—from stealing your card to swiping it several times when you use it at stores—are a frequent problem. Don't leave your wallet behind when you go trekking, and make sure you keep an eye on the card when you give it to a salesperson.

▮ TIP→ A great little invention is the metal doorknob cup that can be found at Thai hardware shops. It covers your doorknob and locks it in place with a padlock, keeping anyone from using a spare key or even twisting the knob to get into your room. A good B300 investment, it's usable anywhere.

Guesthouses also offer commission for customers brought in by drivers, so be wary of anyone telling you that the place where you booked a room has burned down overnight or is suddenly full. Smile and be courteous, but be firm about where you want to go. If the driver doesn't immediately take you where you want to go, get out and get another taxi.

Watch out for scams while shopping. Bait and switch is common, as is trying to pass off reproductions as authentic antiques. True antiques and artifact vendors will gladly help you finish the necessary government paperwork to take your purchase home. Keep in mind that authentic Thai or other Southeast Asian antiques in Thailand are usually stunningly expensive. Thais, Chinese, Malaysians, and Singaporeans are all fanatical collectors themselves, and pay as much as any western buyer. If you think you're getting a super deal on a Thai antique, think twice.

Thailand offers many adventurous ways to spend your days, few of which include the safety provisions demanded in western countries. Motorcycle wrecks are a common way to cut a vacation tragically short.

Thailand's most famous danger comes from the ocean. The Asian tsunami hit the Andaman coast in December 2004 and killed more than 5,300 people in Thailand. Reports from the areas hit show that many people could have been saved if they had known how to recognize the signs of an impending tsunami, or if an evacuation plan had been in place. Tsunamis are rare and very unpredictable. It's highly unlikely you'll experience one, but it pays to be prepared. If you plan to stay in a beach resort, ask if they have a tsunami plan in place, and ask what it is. If you feel an earthquake, leave any waterside area. ■TIP➜ **Pay attention to the ocean: if you see all of the water race off the beach, evacuate immediately and head for high ground.** A tsunami could be

only minutes away. Remember, a tsunami is a series of waves that could go on for hours. Do not assume it is over after the first wave.

■TIP➜ **Thai beaches almost never have lifeguards, but that doesn't mean they don't have undertows or other dangers.**

FEMALE TRAVELERS

Foreign women in Thailand get quite a few stares, and Thai women as often as Thai men will be eager to chat and become your friend. Although there's no doubt that attitudes are changing, traditional Thai women dress and act modestly, so loud or overly confident behavior from a foreign woman can be a shock to both men and women alike. It's also worth noting that Thai men often see foreign women as something exotic. If you're being subjected to unwelcome attention, be firm, but try to stay calm—"losing face" is a big concern among Thai men, and embarrassing them (even if it's deserved) can have ugly repercussions.

General Information U.S. Department of State. ⊕ *www.travel.state.gov.*

Safety Transportation Security Administration (*TSA*). ⊕ *www.tsa.gov.*

▌ TAXES

A 7% (and sometimes more) value-added tax (V.A.T.) is built into the price of all goods and services, including restaurant meals. You can reclaim some of this tax on souvenirs and other high-price items purchased at stores that are part of the V.A.T. refund program at the airport upon leaving the country. You cannot claim the V.A.T. refund when leaving Thailand by land at a border crossing. Shops that offer this refund will have a sign displayed; ask shopkeepers to fill out the necessary forms and make sure you keep your receipts. You'll have to fill out additional forms at the airport.

V.A.T. refund guidelines are particular. The goods must be purchased from stores displaying the "V.A.T. Refund for

Tourists" sign. Purchases at each shop you visit must total more than B2,000 before they can fill out the necessary forms. The total amount claimed for refund upon leaving the country cannot be less than B5,000. You must depart the country from an international airport, where you finish claiming your refund at the V.A.T. Refund Counter—allow an extra hour at the airport for this process. You cannot claim V.A.T. refunds for gemstones.

For refunds less than B30,000 you can receive the money in cash at the airport, or have it wired to a bank account or to a credit card for a B100 fee. Refunds over B30,000 are paid either to a bank account or credit card for a B100 fee.

■ VISITOR INFO

ONLINE TRAVEL TOOLS
ALL ABOUT THAILAND
Sites worth checking out are: ⊕ *www.discoverythailand.com* and ⊕ *www.sawadee.com.*

Visitor Information Tourism Authority of Thailand (TAT). ☎ *1672 Thailand contact center, 323/461-9814 in Los Angeles, 212/432-0433 in New York* ⊕ *www. tourismthailand.org.*

■ TIME

Thailand is 7 hours ahead of Greenwich Mean Time. It's 12 hours ahead of New York, 15 hours ahead of Los Angeles, 7 hours ahead of London, and 3 hours behind Sydney.

Time Zones Timeanddate.com. ⊕ *www. timeanddate.com/worldclock.*

■ TIPPING

Tipping is not a local custom, but it is expected of foreigners, especially at larger hotels and restaurants and for taxi rides. If you feel the service has been less than stellar, you are under no obligation to leave a tip, especially with crabby cabbies.

In Thailand tips are generally given for good service, except when a price has been negotiated in advance. If you hire a private driver for an excursion, do tip him. With metered taxis in Bangkok, however, the custom is to round the fare up to the nearest B5. Hotel porters expect at least a B20 tip, and hotel staff who have given good personal service are usually tipped. A 10% tip is appreciated at a restaurant when no service charge has been added to the bill.

INDEX

684 <

PHOTO CREDITS

Front cover: Pongphan Ruengchai / Alamy [Description: Tropical beach, Kho Poda in Krabi, Thailand.] Back cover, from left to right: Dudarev Mikhail / Shutterstock; Olives Jean-Michel/Shutterstock; Andy Lim/Shutterstock. Spine: Chaloemphan / Shutterstock. 1, Michael Yamashita I Aurora Press. 2, Eddy Galeotti / Shutterstock. 5. José Fuste Raga/age fotostock. Chapter 1: Experience Thailand: 10-11, Ingolf Pompe 17 / Alamy. 20 (left), iNNOCENt/Shutterstock. 20 (center), Christine Gonsalves/Shutterstock. 20 (top right), John Hemmings/Shutterstock. 20 (bottom right), Punyafamily I Dreamstime.com. 21 (top left), sippakorn/Shutterstock. 21 (center), Frank van den Bergh/iStockphoto. 21 (right), Bartlomiej K. Kwieciszewski/Shutterstock. 21 (bottom left), siambizkit/Shutterstock. 34, Muellek/Shutterstock. 35, North Wind Picture Archives/Alamy. 36 (left), Alvaro Leiva/age fotostock. 36 (top right), Thomas Cockrem/Alamy. 36 (bottom right), Genevieve Dietrich/Shutterstock. 37 (left), Juha Sompinmäki/Shutterstock. 37 (top right), Thomas Cockrem/Alamy. 37 (bottom right), Bryan Busovicki/Shutterstock. 38 (left), Mary Evans Picture Library/Alamy. 38 (top right), Content Mine International/Alamy. 38 (bottom right), Public domain. 39 (left), Sam DCruz/Shutterstock. 39 (top right), Newscom. 39 (bottom right), Ivan Vdovin/age fotostock. 40 (left and top right), Thor Jorgen Udvang/Shutterstock. 40 (bottom right), AFP/Getty Images/Newscom. Chapter 2: Bangkok: 41, Angelo Cavalli/age fotostock. 42, Marco Simoni/age fotostock. 43 (top), Steve Silver/age fotostock. 43 (bottom), Peter Hooree/Alamy. 44, jaume/Shutterstock. 56-57, Chris L. Jones/ Photolibrary.com. 58 (top), Gina Smith/Shutterstock. 58 (bottom left), PCL/Alamy. 58 (bottom right), John Hemmings/Shutterstock. 60, Andy Lim/Shutterstock. 61 (top left), do_ok/Shutterstock. 61 (center left), Heinrich Damm. 61 (bottom left), Steve Vidler/eStockphoto. 61 (right), Plotnikoff/Shutterstock. 62 (top), P. Narayan/age fotostock. 62 (bottom), Dave Stamboulis. 63, Wayne Planz/Shutterstock. 79, Travel Pix Collection/age fotostock. 80 (top), Juha Sompinmäki/Shutterstock. 80 (bottom), SuperStock/age fotostock. 81 (top), BlueMoon Stock/Alamy. 81 (2nd from top), John Lander/Alamy. 81 (3rd from top), kd2/Shutterstock. 81 (bottom), Mireille Vautier/Alamy. 82 (top), David Kay/Shutterstock. 82 (center), ARCO/I Schulz/age fotostock. 82 (bottom), jamalludin/Shutterstock. 89, Songchai W/Shutterstock. 119, Luca Invernizzi Tettoni/Tips Italia/ photolibrary.com. Chapter 3: Around Bangkok: 131, Jon Arnold Images / Alamy. 132, Steve Raymer/age fotostock. 133, Jeremy Horner / Alamy. 134, Olympus/Shutterstock. 141, Juriah Mosin/Shutterstock. 142 (top right), Ian Trower/Alamy. 142 (top left), Andy Lim/Shutterstock. 142 (bottom left), Elena Elisseeva/Shutterstock. 142 (bottom right), Robert Fried/Alamy. 143 (top), Juriah Mosin/Shutterstock. 143 (bottom), Chris Howey/Shutterstock. 144 (top), Asia/Alamy. 144 (bottom), Ronald Sumners/Shutterstock. 145, dbimages/Alamy. 163, Tourism Authority of Thailand. Chapter 4: The Gulf Coast Beaches: 169, travelstock44 / Alamy. 171, Craig Lovell/Alamy. 172, Ozerov Alexander/Shutterstock. 184-85, José Fuste Raga/age fotostock. 187 (left), Gonzalo Azumendi/age fotostock. 187 (right), LOOK Die Bildagentur der Fotografen GmbH/Alamy. 189 (left), Gavriel Jecan/age fotostock. 189 (right) and 197, Dave Stamboulis. 212, GUIZIOU Franck/age fotostock. 224, aragami12345s/Shutterstock. 228, Ozerov Alexander/Shutterstock. Chapter 5: Phuket and the Andaman Coast: 231, Efired/Shutterstock. 232, Phaitoon Sutunyawatchai/Shutterstock. 233 (top), Ozerov Alexander/Shutterstock. 233 (bottom), Banana Republic images/Shutterstock. 234, Chie Ushio. 235 (top), Dave Stamboulis. 235 (bottom), William Berry/Shutterstock. 236, Stephane Bidouze/Shutterstock. 267, Dave Stamboulis. 275, Pichugin Dmitry/Shutterstock. 294, Andy Lim/Shutterstock. Chapter 6: Chang Mai: 301, Gonzalo Azumendi/age fotostock. 302), Blanscape/Shutterstock. 303 (top), stoykovic/Shutterstock. 303 (bottom), Brukenkam/Shutterstock. 304, 501room/Shutterstock. 312, Valery Shanin/Shutterstock. 315, Muellek/Shutterstock. 317, Jean Du Boisberranger / Hemis.fr /Aurora Photos. 342-43, Dave Stamboulis. 344 (top and 2nd from top), wikipedia.org. 344 (3rd from top), mediacolor's/Alamy. 344 (4th from top), Dave Stamboulis. 344 (bottom), Hemis/Alamy. 345 (top), Dave Stamboulis. 345 (center), Bryan Busovicki/Shutterstock. 345 (bottom), David Bleeker Photography.com/Alamy. 352, TC, fodors.com member. Chapter 7: Northern Thailand: 357, Gonzalo Azumendi/age fotostock. 358, MERVYN REES / Alamy. 360, Dave Stamboulis / Alamy. 361(top), kentoh/Shutterstock. 361 (bottom), Andrea Skjold/Shutterstock. 362, Vitaly Maksimchuk/Shutterstock. 374, David South / Alamy. 394, Raffaele Meucci/age fotostock. 395, Stuart Pearce/age fotostock. 396 (top and bottom), SuperStock/age fotostock. 397 (top), John Arnold Images Ltd/Alamy. 397 (bottom), KLJ Photographic Ltd/iStockphoto. 398 (top), SuperStock/age fotostock. 398 (bottom), Anders Ryman/Alamy. 399 (top), Val Duncan/Kenebec Images/Alamy. 399 (bottom), Simon Podgorsek/iStockphoto. 400, Robert Fried/Alamy. 414, Luciano Mortula/Shutterstock. 416, Juha Sompinmäki/Shutterstock. 417 (top), Chie Ushio. 417 (center), Khoo Si Lin/Shutterstock. 417 (bottom), N. Frey Photography/Shutterstock. 418, Idealink Photography/Alamy. 419, Pipopthai I Dreamstime.com. 420 (top), David Halbakken/Alamy. 420 (bottom), SteveSPF/Shutterstock. 421 (left), javarman/Shutterstock. 421 (top right), qingqing/Shutterstock. 421 (bottom right), Michele Falzone/Alamy. 422 (left), J Marshall - Tribaleye Images/Alamy. 422 (top right), Julien Gron-

NOTES

NOTES

ABOUT OUR WRITERS

Karen Coates reports on food, environment, health, and human rights for publications around the world. She is a senior fellow at the Schuster Institute for Investigative Journalism at Brandeis University. Her latest books are *This Way More Better: Stories and Photos from Asia's Back Roads and Eternal Harvest: The Legacy of American Bombs in Laos*, both published by ThingsAsian Press in 2013. Karen updated our Experience Thailand chapter.

Lara Dunston is a travel and food writer who has experienced over 70 countries and written for many publications including *The Guardian, National Geographic Traveller, Travel+Leisure Asia,* and *AFAR*. She updated the Chiang Mai, Northern Thailand, and Myanmar Chapters.

Sophie Friedman is a transplanted New Yorker living in Shanghai. She has previously worked at *Time Out New York* and the Huffington Post and is a contributor to *Condé Nast Traveler, South China Morning Post, The Wall Street Journal,* and CNN. She contributed to the Myanmar chapter.

Dave Stamboulis is a well-worn road veteran who has bicycled more than 25,000 miles around the world. The Society of American Travel Writers awarded his book about this adventure, *Odysseus' Last Stand: The Chronicles of a Bicycle Nomad,* the silver medal for travel book of the year in 2006. Born in Greece and raised in the United States, Dave has called Thailand home for over 8 years now. His photographs and articles have appeared in publications, books, and elsewhere throughout the globe. For this edition, he kept busy running back and forth between Laos and Bangkok, as well as taking photos.

Simon Stewart has lived in Thailand since 2003 and works as a freelance writer and university lecturer. He writes about traveling and cycle touring in Southeast Asia. This year he updated the Gulf Coast Beaches and Around Bangkok chapters.

Adrian Vrettos grew up in the United Kingdom, where he studied archaeology and anthropology. After a few years of working in London the call of the road was too strong for him so he packed a bag and set off to explore the four corners of the world, becoming a travel writer for various international publications and websites. Now based in Athens, Greece, he fills his time with website production, avid travel, reflexology, and writing. He updated the Cambodia chapter.